Keep Watching the Skies!

Volume II

The author (right) with one of the icons of his childhood, the original Robby the Robot, on the set of "Gremlins."

Keep Watching the Skies!

American Science Fiction Movies of the Fifties

VOLUME II
1958–1962

by

Bill Warren

Research Associate
Bill Thomas

Jefferson & London : McFarland
1986

Cover illustration by Cathy Hill, interior drawings by Marc
   Schirmeister.

Frontispiece photo of the author and Robby the Robot
   courtesy of Joe Dante and Bill Malone.

Photographs on pages 50, 79, 87, 94, 114, 156, 157, 167,
   192, 223, 265, 270, 305, 326, 343, 346, 370, 398, 414,
   436, 451, 466, 470, 494, 523, 539, 575, 584, 607, 671,
   674, 688, and 708 are courtesy of Forrest J Ackerman,
   2495 Glendower, Hollywood, California 90027.

Photographs on pages 28, 72, 139, 258, 318, 481, and 529
   are from the collection of the author.

Library of Congress Cataloguing-in-Publication Data
(Revised for Volume II)

Warren, Bill, 1943–
   Keep watching the skies!

   Bibliography: v. 2, p. 725
   Includes index.
   1. Science fiction films–United States–History and
criticism. I. Title.
PN1995.9.S26W37   1982   791.43′09′0915   81-19324

ISBN 0-89950-032-3 (v. 1)   ISBN 0-89950-170-2 (v. 2)
ISBN 0-89950-191-5 (set)
(acid-free natural paper) ∞

Manufactured in the United States of America

McFarland & Company, Inc., Publishers,
   Box 611, Jefferson, North Carolina 28640.

This book is dedicated to George Pal,
Nigel (Tom) Kneale and Jack Arnold.
And, peculiarly enough, to Bronson Caverns.

Acknowledgments

There are many people who deserve thanks for their help on this book, but there are several who need thanks most particularly and prominently.

Joe Dante took time out from working on what must have been a fiendishly difficult film to make, *Gremlins*, to read the entire manuscript of this book—when it was even longer than it is now. His annotations, criticisms and suggestions were deeply appreciated. Joe knows more about these films than anyone I have ever met, and if he wasn't directing movies, he'd probably have beaten me to publication with a book like this.

Scot Holton gave me access to dozens of these films and was unfailingly warm and friendly, even when delays in returning them caused him problems elsewhere.

Michael Hayes annotated and added to the lists of credits; his contributions were surprising at times, and always appreciated; I cannot say enough about his help.

Jim Ashbacher risked the incredible in his efforts to help this book, and the absolute least I can do to repay him is to say that if you are in the vicinity of his bookstore at 707 Pacific Avenue in Santa Cruz, California, go buy everything in sight.

During what was unquestionably the worst week of his entire life, John Landis took time to see to it that I received important research materials. John is a good person, and he has more friends than he knows.

Miller Drake and Eric Hoffman gave me access to many hard-to-find films, and were always available for encouragement and advice.

Forrest J Ackerman provided research materials and the majority of the stills that grace this volume. Forry is and always will be the Pied Piper for people like myself; he's a father figure, an elf and a good friend. He's had more books—including Volume 1 of this set—dedicated to him than anyone else I know of, and deserves it.

Dons Glut and Willis also provided information, encouragement and advice. And if it hadn't been that Don G. chose *not* to do a book on the SF films of the 1970s, I would never have done this one.

Greg Shoemaker gave much-needed help in the area of Japanese SF movies, and through Greg, Horacio Higuchi was also of significant assistance.

After the manuscript of this book was delivered, I met the dedicated Tom Weaver for the first time, and somewhat abashedly admitted I quoted from his *Fangoria* and *Fantastic Films* articles extensively, saying I hoped he didn't mind. Far from it—he was delighted, he said. So Tom Weaver deserves very special thanks.

Mark McGee gave not only advice and suggestions throughout the entire project, but at one point, gave me several hours of his time, providing a tape full of information he had gleaned in his own research. Any references in the text to what "Mark McGee said" and similar phrases refer to this question-and-answer session.

The contributions of these people have been very great; for a variety of reasons, I cannot always specify just how these people helped me. I have been given great encouragement by the many favorable reviews volume 1 of this book received, particularly those by writers I deeply admire myself, including Harlan Ellison, Philip Strick, Ed Bryant and others. And friends have always been willing to put up with tardiness from me, and have listened to me talk about these films endlessly. Friends like Allan Rothstein, Mike Shupp, R.J. Robertson, Ron Hale, Charlie (Buzz) Letts, Cathy Hill, Paula Ann Anthony, Jean-Marc Lofficier, Laurie Reinecke Welden, Bill Welden, Elizabeth Fox, Mark Kausler, Vanessa Schnatmeier, Ron Borst, Bob Greenberg, Jim Shapiro and many others have helped me in ways they are probably not even aware of themselves.

But above all, there are two who must be thanked again and again. In fact, without these two, not only would there not be this book, but there probably wouldn't even be *me*. Bill Thomas, the person listed as "Research Associate" on the title page, at first even refused to take a percentage of the profits from this book. He has researched, he has proofread, indexed, and worn his eyes out reading the manuscript through at least twice. His quiet, unassuming presence and steadfast friendship throughout this entire project made it possible. I would not have wanted to do it with anyone else, and we will be heard from again.

And, of course, my wife Beverly. As with most writers, there have been periods when I was earning little or nothing as a writer. Beverly has always had a job, not always one she liked. But she has supported me throughout all my ups and downs and ins and outs; she has encouraged me to go to movies, buy books and comics, to spend *her* money on things *I* wanted. She treats me better than I deserve, and I love her more than I can tell.

Table of Contents

The Illustrations

First, a word of thanks for the artist, Marc Schirmeister, who did the chapter illustrations out of friendship. He's one of the most distinctive and best cartoonists to come out of science fiction fandom, and I urge all interested parties to contact him at his home, 1555 Vista Lane, Pasadena CA 91103.

1958: Disgusted, The Blob, The Colossus of New York and a Fiend Without a Face leave a double bill of "Plan 9 from Outer Space" and "Attack of the 50 Foot Woman." Note: The Gordon is a Hollywood theater that for years had private Saturday morning screenings regularly attended by many who were of assistance to this book, including Bob Greenberg (who often organized them), Mark McGee, R.J. Robertson, Joe Dante, John Landis and others. It is now refurbished as the Showcase. Hail and farewell, Saturday mornings at the Gordon.

1959: Lizards eat bugs, something the title character from *Return of the Fly* has just discovered, as he's being pursued by Gigantis the Fire Monster, the Giant Behemoth, a dimetrodon from *Journey to the Center of the Earth*, the Giant Gila Monster, and even a treacherous Alligator Person (*The Alligator People* was the cofeature with *Return of the Fly*.)

1960: Apparently tired of being merely fed, Audrey, Jr. (of *The Little Shop of Horrors*, of course) here uses The Time Machine itself to pursue a Morlock. A case of the biter being bit.

1961: Konga and Gorgo's mama try to bring down the flying flivver of The Absent Minded Professor. Little Gorgo himself stands by to help.

1962: Mothra and the tiny twins take care of The Three Stooges (in costume for meeting Hercules).

Cathy Hill's Cover: Clockwise from top center: a Morlock, the Brain from Planet Arous, the Time Machine, the bat-rat-spider from *The Angry Red Planet*, the Seaview from *Voyage to the Bottom of the Sea*, an increasingly-disillusioned SF movie fan, the Albatross from *Master of the World* and the Colossus of New York. Cathy, a friend and fine illustrator, can be contacted at 374 N. Grove St., Sierra Madre, CA 91024. She's a treasure.

A Note on
Quotations in the Text

Certain reviewers, commentators and authors are quoted from extensively in the following pages; to avoid repeating each of the titles or sources over and over in each entry, I have used shorthand methods of referring to them.

During the period covered by this book, the *Monthly Film Bulletin*, a publication of the British Film Institute, used a rough rating system: *I* meant an above-average film for its class; *II* meant an average film for its class; *III* meant a below-average film for its class. I sometimes refer to "a rating of I" (or II, or III) when quoting the *Monthly Film Bulletin*; it is this rating to which I am referring when doing that. If I say "the highest" or "lowest" rating, I am referring to their I or III designations, respectively.

Don Willis has, to date, done three books on science fiction, fantasy and horror films. The designation (I) after his name refers to his earlier book, *Horror and Science Fiction Films: A Checklist* (Scarecrow, 1972); the designation (II) after his name refers to *Horror and Science Fiction Films II* (Scarecrow, 1982).

Alan Frank (*SF*) refers to *The Science Fiction and Fantasy Film Handbook* (Barnes & Noble, 1982), by Alan Frank, and Alan Frank (*Horror*) refers to *The Horror Film Handbook* (Barnes & Noble, 1982) by Alan Frank.

Psychotronic refers to *The Psychotronic Encyclopedia of Film* (Ballantine, 1983); most entries were by Michael Weldon.

If Jack Moffitt is quoted without a source being cited, the source is always the movie trade publication, *Hollywood Reporter*.

A citation to John Baxter refers to his ground-breaking *Science Fiction in the Cinema* (1970).

Note: the above are all highly recommended.

Parish and Pitts refers to *The Great Science Fiction Pictures* (Scarecrow, 1977) by James Robert Parish and Michael R. Pitts.

Preface

I covered most of what I have to say on the subject of science fiction films of the 1950s in the preface to Volume 1 (*Keep Watching the Skies! American Science Fiction Movies of the Fifties. 1950–1957*). The story of the period covered by this volume is sadder, as things in decline always are. The genre underwent two cycles in the 1950s, that of 1951–54, spurred as it was by novelty and 3D, and the renaissance that got underway in mid-1956; the SF film form underwent a change, and was actually dying out by 1960, although the number of titles produced in that and the next two years doesn't look like it. What was happening in the period beginning roughly in late 1959 on through the 60s was that the 1950s-type SF film was being supplanted by another kind of movie: the horror film.

The famous "Shock Theatre" package of movies was released to television in 1957. This contained some Columbia thrillers of the Boris Karloff mad-doctor variety, but the important films were the great (and not so great) Universal horror movies of the 1930s and 40s, which had never been shown on television—they'd remained popular enough to allow frequent theatrical reissues. They proved to be a smash sensation on television all across the country, and horror movies were revived as a genre.

At first, in the minds of filmmakers, there wasn't really a difference between the SF movies that were still popular in theatres, and the old-type horror movies that were wowing much the same audience on television. But there are differences, in the approach more than the content, so there are several SF movies included in this book that bridge the gap between SF and horror movies: those that included horror content, and featured a science fiction (rationalistic) approach.

As mentioned in several entries in Volume 1, there was an attitude that assumed that audiences wouldn't sit still for traditional horror concepts (vampires, werewolves) unless they were treated as science fiction: explained scientifically, not as supernatural fantasy. Even Hammer's precedent-setting *Horror of Dracula* (1958) played it safe; though Dracula was pretty much a traditional vampire in the movie, Dr. Van Helsing carefully explained that some elements of the vampire myth (such as the ability to turn into a bat) were folklore. This may have been a budgetary decision on Hammer's part (but probably wasn't; the vampire in their sequel, *Brides of Dracula*, turned readily into a bat); it was probably because they didn't think "modern" audiences would swallow the same old malarkey. *Return of Dracula* had a vampire with all the old abilities, but the film was basically made in the flat, gray, quasi-documentary look of many 1950s SF films.

But, if the old malarkey was given a new look, audiences were ready to swallow it. Blood and sex were added to the old formulas, a brightly-colored style was employed, and immediately Hammer and other studios trotted out all the hoary clichés: mummies, zombies, the Phantom of the Opera, Jekyll and Hyde and so forth. This revival of horror fantasy films was one of the main causes of the decline of the 1950s-style science fiction films.

But audiences weren't just turning *to* horror and fantasies, they were turning *away* from SF films. Of course, the two genres could and still do co-exist and overlap, but the 1950s-type SF film was swiftly fading. The content went first. Radiation, for instance, does not play a large part in most of the films covered in this book. It is sometimes invoked, like a charm, to dress up a film or to lend a feeling of credibility, but there are very few monsters of the 1958–1962 period which are created or powered by radiation.

When a movie genre is discovered (or rediscovered), it's usually by the relatively daring. Most people in Hollywood are cautious; everyone wants to be first to be second—let the other guy take the risks, and when proved profitable, rush in and exploit the hell out of it. This was done with 1950s-type SF movies.

The usual films that break new ground, set new precedents, are medium-budget pictures, usually made by talented filmmakers who have seen a trend coming before anyone else, or who are daring enough to try something on the off-chance that it might make money. George Pal, Robert Wise and Howard Hawks pointed the way in the early 1950s; later, Don Siegel, Jack Arnold and Hammer Films made movies that caught the public fancy.

I do not mean to suggest for a moment that these people (and one company) were not out for money; they most certainly were, and sometimes it wasn't their choice to make the film. But they had talent and vision, and tried things that others imitated.

The usual precedent-setting films (at all times) are rarely expensive major studio productions, *or* the cheapest of the cheap—in both cases, the profit margin is too slim to take chances. But once the middle-budget films make a mint in a new area, in come the bigger-budgeted movies and the cheapie fast-buck operators. The gap between the highest-budgeted and lowest-budgeted SF film of the first half of the 1950s is much less than that between the highest and lowest of the last part of the period.

The vitality is drained; genre audiences are not very interested in the bland, play-it-safe, big studio films, and repelled by the wretched cheapies. The big-budget studio films were made by people who knew only how to make films in the studio manner; they knew there was a traditional family audience out there, the one that had always supported the more expensive studio pictures, and so they tailored their SF films to that audience. There were even a few SF films—*On the Beach*, for instance—that were not even regarded as being science fiction. Fox, the leading practitioner in this field, didn't seem to quite realize that the SF audience was a different kind of audience. They tapped it once, almost accidentally, with *The Fly*; it was given a high-B budget, advertised like an A (but still had a standard double bill, like a minor movie), but was entrusted to Kurt Neumann, a director who had made several medium-budget SF films already.

The concerns of SF films were diluted by bigger money; star-laden pictures had to appeal to everyone to make a profit, and so were of less interest to the thrill-seeking kids who had been the biggest audience. These kids wanted to see Vincent Price in the Edgar Allan Poe thrillers, not in *Master of the World*.

These kids were even more mistreated by the greedy schlockmeisters, who didn't care at all about the quality of their films. These cynical, talentless hacks realized that if they could deliver films that merely resembled the right kind of stuff, they would make their money back. Double bills like *Frankenstein's Daughter/Missile to the Moon*, *The Incredible Petrified World/Teenage Zombies* and *Invasion of the Star Creatures/The Brain That Wouldn't Die* represent film-making at its rock-bottom worst. They soon turned off the teenagers who, laughing though they may have been, formed the biggest audience for SF movies. They couldn't even *laugh* at boring disasters like these.

The men who made these films aren't evil; they probably have children (even grandchildren) and are active in civic affairs. But they were fastbuck operators who saw a chance for quick money, and took it. That's not admirable, really, but it isn't a crime. But in time, this attitude smashed the SF movie market flat. The films continued to be made and released, but by rote; the vitality had gone. As bad a movie as *The Mole People* is, it looks like a master-piece beside the likes of *Reptilicus*.

By 1962, the usual 50s-type SF film had fairly well vanished. There were several foreign SF pictures given an American release, and some that had been filmed earlier finally crept to market. But there were none made by or starring the icons of the 50s: Richard Carlson, Jack Arnold, Kenneth Tobey. Even Roger Corman had given them up, and Herman Cohen was on his way to other material. The 1950s SF movie was moribund. And that's why I chose that as the final year for this survey.

Oddly enough, one element of the Real World that some have thought spurred the SF movies of the 1950s instead probably had a dampening effect (after a brief impetus). When artificial satellites and spaceships were still in the realm of imagination, movies could do anything and be anything; space was a weird, mysterious realm. But soon enough, when there were people whose profession was spaceship pilot (we called them astronauts), filmed SF contracted rather than expanded. (At the time I was even asked, now that there were space satellites, how could there be any more science fiction at all?) In 1958, just after the space boom started, there were 16 English-language films that dealt in some way with space travel; in 1962, there were three.

At some point, I must confront a question that may occur to the idly curious who happen upon a book of this size on such a narrow subject as science fiction films released over only a dozen years. This is the most extensive survey of such a limited focus undertaken in the history of film scholarship—and I should know, as I make my living generally as a film scholar.

First and most important among the reasons is, to me at least, that SF movies of this period are, as a group, my favorite kind of movies. As noted in the preface to Volume 1, they were deeply important to me as a child. They provided me with escape and entertainment when I needed both the most. But though such affection for a particular genre of films (or any other form of story-telling) can be rationalized, in a real sense it cannot be explained, at least by the person holding the affection. A fellow I know quotes an old cliché, something like "the heart has reasons that reason cannot know." One cannot really explain or even justify one's fondness for something like this any more than one can explain a preference for a particular color. Such inclinations, obsessions and loves are a sum total of all we have been becoming all our lives; they are a part of our innermost selves. True love, of anything at all, including people, is never arrived at intellectually—it cannot be. My fondness for these films is emotional, not intellectual, although (as can be seen from the book itself, I hope) I can explain my liking for a particular film.

There are other reasons for doing a book of this length. I believe that each and every film* should be examined in detail by someone who loves them. This, if for no other reason than to satisfy simple curiosity; I'm a collector and insatiably curious myself, and there are others like that.

We can analyze why and how a given film worked; we can go into details behind the making, and explain links it has with other such movies; we can talk about the individuals who made these films. We can, in short, give histories of them, and analyses of them. But those of us who love these films are generally not those to connect the films into the social Gestalt out of which they spring— that remains for others to do. Books like this one will provide the research tools for future cinema sociologists, who will be coming. Those people will have their own obsessions and drives, and here they can connect with mine and, it is to be hoped, find a way *into* 1950s SF films.

But it's also futile to explain why this book is so large, why I have spent over four years of my life on it (and in a sense, my entire life). For those who do not understand, as was once said, no explanation is possible; for those who do understand, no explanation is necessary. By the sheer number of books on SF movies, rivaling if not surpassing the number of volumes on musicals and Westerns, by the love that moviemakers of today have for 1950s SF movies, even the rotten ones, by their constant revival on television, it's clear that I am not alone in loving these crass, unlovable films.

On the Size of This Book

Bill Thomas and I would like to admit to an error. The reason we divided the period of the 1950s into 1950–1957 and 1958–1962 had nothing whatever to do with any thematic split occuring at that time. The reason was much more simple, and seemed logical: there were approximately as many films made in both periods. We had to divide the book somewhere, and did so on the basis of numbers. It was just to try to make the volumes equal in size.

But we were wrong. Although the numbers of the films were very similar on either side of that split, the overall importance of them most certainly was not. While the period covered in Volume 1 does have more of the films generally thought of as classics, the period covered by Volume 2 has far more standard SF films altogether. That is, Volume 1 is diluted with Jungle Jim movies, Bowery Boys comedies, Abbott & Costello Meet movies, and so forth—films with SF content, but ones about which it is not necessary to say very much regarding how they fit into the overall 1950s science-fiction movie scheme. Unfortunately for length, Volume 2 includes many more films about which a good deal needed to be said. Furthermore, the films in the second grouping are far more accessible than the older ones; for this book I watched a much greater percentage of the movies than I was able to for Volume 1. The miracle of videotape helped greatly; I was able to watch the *majority* of films in Volume 2 and to make notes on them. This makes each entry more complete and fresh—and the whole book longer. (It also improves the credits for those who are addicted to such things.)

Perhaps B Westerns and porno films don't need quite this intensive treatment. B Westerns are more like each other than any other genre of films, but don't get me wrong: I like them, too. But each Hopalong Cassidy film is more like every other Hoppy film than each Roger Corman SF film is like other Corman SF films.

The Astounding She-Monster

This boring, dismal little picture takes place almost entirely in one poor mountain cabin set, and in some well-traveled woods nearby. It really is astonishingly bad, but was graced with an appealing, sexy ad campaign, featuring the slinky alien woman of the title peering with one eye from between her upraised hands. The woman in the film isn't as sexy, though she looks quite healthy, and in fact, is pretty foolish most of the time.

The first part of the film has a portentous, doom-laden (and quite unprofessional) narration, explaining why the She-Monster was sent to us in the first place. It proposes a strange Big Bang theory, about how the explosion of a planet almost upset the cosmic balance, and how the inhabitants of a planet around Antares have concluded that we here on Earth are about to repeat this terrible catastrophe.

Which, of course, raises a few pointless but interesting questions. Every now and then in SF films, following the lead of *The Day the Earth Stood Still,* an alien visitor shows up to tell us we'd better quit whatever it is we are doing, or face obliteration. So maybe we should wonder if we are, out of all the (presumably) billions of inhabited planets, the only one that is messing around irresponsibily with atomic radiation and/or space travel. Or perhaps these do-gooder aliens are sending scads of flying saucers, rockets and meteor craft around to all these other sites of potential atomic catastrophe.

In *The Astounding She-Monster*, a meteorlike craft is sent "hurtling through space" toward Earth.

Here on Earth, in Los Angeles, socialite Margaret Chaffee (Marilyn Harvey) is heading out for a hard day of whatever it is that socialites do. The narrator, who seems to hate socialites, keeps asking rhetorical questions, giving hints addressed to Margaret that she's heading into disaster. This "Inner Sanctum" style of narration rarely adds anything to a film, and in a movie like this, which has so little to offer in the first place, it simply serves to slow the snail-like pace, generating a maddening frustration in those who are paying attention.

"There's the gate, Margaret!" whispers the narrator. "Beyond it lies the most fantastic experience of your life!" That experience, however, isn't the abduction that takes place just outside Margaret's estate—a car pulls in front of hers, two men jump out, grab her, put her in their car and drive off. After all, the narrator says, being kidnapped could be almost considered normal for a socialite. No, what she's heading into is nothing less than a "rendezvous with fate." As it turns out, Margaret does absolutely nothing for the rest of the film, and seems totally unaltered by the ensuing events.

We next see geologist Dick Cutler (Robert Clarke) in the Angeles National Forest near Los Angeles. He sees a "meteor" (unconvincingly represented by a fuzzy ball of light) pass over some nearby trees and crash in the woods beyond. "It's night," says the narrator superfluously, and here is "the ever-present innocent bystander and his canine friend." (The dog with Clarke could almost have a sign hung around its neck: future victim.) Dick watches the meteor fall as the narrator says, "our visitor from beyond the imagination. Evil unto evil." That, by the way, is a lie—never trust narrators. The alien visitor, we learn at the end, is benign.

We then see the alien woman (Shirley Kilpatrick) striding along a forest road, frightening stock-footage animals (a coyote, a deer, a snake). She picks up a rubber snake and throws it aside. As an alien, she's pretty mild stuff, clad in a skintight Spandex jump suit and shiny shoes. There's a medallion around her neck, and her eyebrows take off at 45° angles from her nose. She's wearing dark lipstick, her blonde hair is tied back and, apart from a peculiar vertical blurring on the film whenever she's by herself (perhaps indicating radiation), she looks totally human. She is also supposed to appear naked, but the sparkly Spandex makes her look like Esther Williams as Annette Kellerman.

In the first day of filming, the She-Monster bent over to kill one of the characters and ripped the suit in the back; there wasn't time in the four-day shooting schedule, said Mark McGee, to repair it, so in all subsequent scenes, the She-Monster makes exits and entrances facing the camera. Of course, this means she is walking *backward* much of the time, but aliens are weird.

Eventually, the kidnappers and Margaret pass through the same part of the woods. Brad (Ewing Brown), a jerk clad in a loud sports jacket, is the driver; he swerves to miss a "naked dame" beside the road, disabling the car. The brains of the gang, Nat Burdell (Western actor Kenne Duncan), insists that all of them head off into the woods, instead of flagging down another car. And so they leave the car and walk away, "as apart from one another as the stars from the Earth," the philosophical narrator tells us.

While Dick is talking to his dog about its eating habits, he doesn't know that the bad guys are creeping up on him. First Nat attempts to talk Dick out of his Jeep, but learning it has no lights, he is trying to figure out some other plan of escape when his little party troops in.

The film borrows a relationship from John Huston's *Key Largo* (as many other low-budget crime films do), but only shows that in the hands of a director like Ronnie Ashcroft, what was solid, moving melodrama before, is here time-wasting boredom. Nat's girlfriend is Esther (Jeanne Tatum), and he gets mad at her. "Ya lousy drunk!" he shouts. She draws herself up haughtily. "I prefer to be referred to as an alcoholic," which idea is introduced solely to set up a pointless, time-consuming scene later. The main question raised is why Esther is along at all; no one seems to like her, and it's not likely that she'd be used as a chaperone.

While everyone hangs around the mountain cabin, pretty soon the alien woman shows up and looks in the window. Brad takes time off from carving his initials in Dick's table to go out and see what's up. After several long scenes of him wandering around in the woods, when he does find her, she's impervious to bullets and her touch kills him. Shortly, she also kills the dog. She is apparently supposed to be glowing in the dark, but it's hard to tell.

Brad's body is brought back, and Dick examines the parallel lines on his neck (which look like bandages). The dead man exhibits "all the symptoms of radium poisoning," he expertly points out. "She glows," he adds, "like radium."

The radio, which always tells them just what they need to hear when they switch it on, now says that the authorities are closing in on the Angeles Forest region, seeking the kidnappers. Nat is more anxious than ever to get away. "It's obvious that she's coated in a thin protective metal of some kind," muses Dick. "I wonder what it is?" (Later, he knows for certain, without getting any further information.) They conclude it might be possible to burn it off her, so they all go outside and chase her around with torches.

The alien kills Esther, but as she's about to lunge at Nat, he cleverly leaps aside and she plunges down a hill. The three survivors assume she's dead. They go back to the cabin.

Driving off in the Jeep, hang the lack of headlights, they soon encounter the alien again, and this time Nat gets it: she grabs his ass, and he expires. Dick and the socialite go back to the cabin again, and the alien shows up there, leaping through a window she previously broke (and facing the camera). They leave the cabin, and she follows them, this time encountering a stock-footage bear. There's a brief close-up of the alien grappling with a rug. Back to the cabin.

Now Dick realizes something important. "I got an idea, it may work," he says breathlessly. "In order for her to give off alpha and gamma rays, which are the basis for her radium poisoning, she's got to have a considerable portion of radium in her physical construction." From that, he jumps to: "We know that there's radium metal in the film that protects her, obviously combined with other metals of course." (Which means she's made of radium and wearing radium clothes.) So he quickly mixes up a batch of aqua regia, and leaves the cabin looking for the alien.

But aha, she's in his bedroom. Margaret screams, Dick returns and douses the alien with the acid which, we are told, eats through the metal sheath. (She looks unchanged.) The alien screams and falls decorously to the floor (facing the camera), then vanishes in a long, slow lap dissolve, leaving behind a locket.

"Why did she leave it?" asks Margaret, crazily implying that the alien could somehow choose which parts of her would not dissolve. "In her own fiendish way," says Dick, "she wanted to have the last laugh." Out of curiosity, he opens the locket and finds a document within, written in English.

"To the people of Earth: you have been under our close surveillance for a number of decades. We now feel your civilization has progressed far enough to make you eligible for membership in the council of planets. This council, for your information, is a universal governing body dedicated to the advancement of planetary progress. It's an agency which Earth seriously needs in this period of crisis and chaos in which it now finds itself. Many of our member planets have faced the same disturbing problems which confront Earth today. We feel that a meeting with the heads of these planets would definitely benefit Earth in the solution of its own global difficulties. If you would like a meeting so arranged, relate your wishes to the bearer of this message and she will return to us with word of your decision." Oops, blew that one, didn't we. There follows some stupid moralizing by Dick.

This ending is just a rabbit out of a hat, and has no relation to the previous story. Granted, the alien woman harms no one except that rubber snake until Brad shoots at her, but leaping through windows, striking menacing poses, and chasing people around when she certainly must be aware that they know her touch can kill, wouldn't seem to be the actions of a friendly, intelligent emissary.

This ham-fisted attempt at irony is just cheap cynicism. It adds nothing to the film, and instead only brings into sharper relief all the rottenness of the picture, especially the hypocrisy of the filmmakers, which makes this movie seem far more distasteful than movies of the earlier 50s, including *Phantom from Space*, which is otherwise similar. At least that film was moderately positive rather than cheaply ironic.

The low budget would have damaged even a better script. The black-and-white photography by William C. Thompson is flat and dimensionless; there are virtually no close-ups, and in fact, almost every shot is from clear across the set. There are no intercuts of objects, no suspense-generating shots of door-knobs turning, feet approaching, etc., which surely must have made the uncredited editor's job (the film was cut in Ashcroft's living room) both very simple and very frustrating. The one "suspenseful" shot of a door opening is from across the room, which drains it of any possible value.

The cutting is, therefore, very simple: inside shot, outside shot, this person, that person, all medium shots. This makes the film seem as if it is happening at a distance; there's certainly nothing in the writing, direction or performances to engage our attention.

The only moderately capable actors in the film are Robert Clarke and Kenne Duncan. Clarke turned up in several other science fiction films; in fact, he made *The Hideous Sun Demon* because he realized that if something as poor as *Astounding She-Monster* could get released, he could do the same with something he made himself. Clarke is not a good actor, but he is at least professional. Here, he's helpless; there's no character at all, just The Hero, and without close-ups, he looks like he's being seen through the wrong end of a telescope. Kenne Duncan, often a villain in Westerns, looks rather frantic most of the time, as if he can't understand what he's doing in these surroundings. He tries his best, but he's no Bogart. He's not even Gerald Mohr.

The writing is not only ghastly, at times it is barely literate. The radio says that "a truck service who has just come down the Angeles Crest road" reported on the kidnappers. What's a truck service? Sometimes, the dialogue is flat and "realistic," other times it has all the overwritten pomposity of the narration: "this creature lurking in the darkness outside," someone mutters, as the alien lays siege to the cabin.

Don Willis (I) called it "one of those that have to be seen to be believed, they're so bad." Actually that's not true; no one has to see this film; there's not even any laughter to be had.

Psychotronic called it "wonderful ultra-cheap junk," but it's wonderful only in that sense of amused contempt. Alan Frank (*SF*) was more accurate: "Dimly scripted, dimly photographed, and dimly directed, only the [title character] herself is minimally brighter than the movie."

The *Motion Picture Herald* vastly overpraised it by calling it "fair," saying "it should be welcomed by those patrons who dote on the far-from-conventional behavior of mere earthlings when confronted by visitors from outer space." The *Herald* added, "The over-all effect is one of satisfying melodrama." This attitude, that science fiction movie buffs would be satisfied with any kind of crud as long as it was indeed science fiction took a very long time to die in Hollywood, and, as far as television is concerned, it isn't dead yet. Fortunately, the attitude is moribund among makers of SF films. George Lucas, Steven Spielberg, Ridley Scott and others actually respect the genre and those who like it.

In England, the film was known as *The Mysterious Invader*, and was seen for what it was. The *Monthly Film Bulletin* gave the film its lowest rating, saying, "The feminine monster shimmers and wobbles and oscillates on each of her many sinister appearances—but, unfortunately, the rest of the picture behaves accordingly, and it is only the absence of the monster that allows the image to remain static. The film is a feeble and ridiculous contribution to the science fiction library, weakly scripted and poorly acted."

It is indeed; it's one of the worst science fiction films ever made.

Attack of the 50 Foot Woman

Some people consider this to be one of the great inadvertent comedies of the 1950s. Director Joe Dante says that it is "perfect." In 1982, it was shown in Los Angeles with the sound off while an improvisational comedy troupe ad-libbed dialogue for the film, although it is impossible to imagine how they could come up with deliberately-funny dialogue that was funnier than the real thing in the film. While I consider both *Cat-Women of the Moon* and *The Giant Claw* funnier and more consistently stupid than *Attack of the 50 Foot Woman*, Dante does have a point. The film's own screwy logic is relentless, there are several scenes which couldn't have been more outrageous if they had been designed to be, and the special effects are jaw-droppingly awful.

But in other ways, the film is too *good* to be perfectly bad. While the movie is truly terrible, the acting of William Hudson, Allison Hayes, Ken Terrell and Yvette Vickers is above average for a cheap SF film, and occasionally, Nathan Juran's direction rises above the pedestrian. (Here, as with *Brain from Planet Arous*, Juran billed himself as "Nathan Hertz," reserving his real name for more prestigious features.) Except for scenes involving the two giants featured in the picture, the film has a smooth pace; certainly not fast, but at least endurable. For the most part, the dialogue is only bad, not campy, and the simple story line doesn't include any major elements so preposterous as to be hilarious.

Clearly, the film was designed as a distaff follow-up to *The Amazing Colossal Man* (which itself was just the reverse of *The Incredible Shrinking Man*), and in fact was called "The Astounding Giant Woman" while in production. In 1958, however, there seemed to be a small trend toward titles with "Attack" and "War" in them; this was cobbled with *War of the Satellites*, while *Attack of the Puppet People* was released with *War of the Colossal Beast*.

The most glorious aspect of the film, not uncommon as SF films ran out of steam, was the advertising, which showed a woman far larger than 50 feet (probably well over 200), straddling a freeway and angrily plucking up cars. My associate Bill Thomas points out that this wonderfully sensationalistic ad promises a Brobdignagian crotch-shot not delivered in the film. The copy for the ad hyphenated the word "mountainous" after the "t," leading to (a) a gynecological and (b) a scatological reference, probably not intended.

But sex was certainly part of the appeal of this film. In their interesting *Playboy* article, "The Horror of It All," Hollis Alpert and Charles Beaumont point out that *Attack of the 50 Foot Woman* "makes possible a literal return to the womb." And others have referred to the film as "Attack of the 50 Foot Wet Dream." Certainly, the film did feature two of the low-budget actresses most capable of delivering a raw sensuality, Allison Hayes and Yvette Vickers. I myself learned that open-mouth kissing *existed* from watching Vickers clamp down on William Hudson. The plot hinges on a man who is unquestionably cheating on his wife; he has that slut Honey Parker stashed in a hotel downtown, where he spends a great deal of his time, including some nights. *Attack of the 50 Foot Woman* is one of the few SF movies of the 50s in which sexual activity plays an active part in the story; it's a randy little movie in its own way. This probably derives from having a woman as the monster, who, once she's a giant, goes after her philandering husband out of simple jealousy. In fact, the last line, delivered over the corpses of giant Allison and squashed Hudson is, "She finally got Harry all to herself."

The film opens with a cynical TV commentator announcing that sightings around the world have poured in, describing a fiery object in the sky. He traces the path of the object from the reports over a globe ("Auckland," he says, pointing at Africa, then "New Zealand," pointing at that island), concluding that it should be over the California desert right about now. And so, of course, it is. Nancy Archer (Hayes) is roaring along Route 66 somewhere near Baker, when a big quasi-transparent sphere drifts down out of the sky and stops in the road in front of her.

A giant, also transparent, promptly emerges and reaches for Nancy, who leaps out of the car shrieking "Harry!" and runs off down the road. (As Jack Moffitt pointed out, the giant spaceman "must be a fugitive from medieval France since, on his chest, he wears a shield bearing the fleur-de-lis. On his back there is an Assyrian bull, indicating he may have had his cleaning, pressing and mending done in Babylon.") In this scene, we first get a look at the awkward and phony giant hand later reused frequently. When it is the giant spaceman's hand, as here, it is very hairy—maybe that's why Nancy was screaming—when it is later used as Nancy's hand, it is hairless.

In any event, Nancy outruns the giant, and screams to the local sheriff (George Douglas) that a huge satellite landed and a giant chased her. Since Nancy is only recently out of a mental institution, the sheriff is disinclined to at least follow up on her story. ("She pays most of the taxes around here," he says.) But the giant is gone, though Nancy's car is still there.

She tells the sheriff and the deputy she thinks the giant was after her diamond—the Star of India, no less—but the sheriff implies that she saw a mere bum, and mistook him for a giant. As she drives off in a snit, the sheriff admits to feeling some pity for her, no doubt because of her philandering husband, Handsome Harry Archer (William Hudson).

While Nancy was hightailing it toward town, we were shown a little scene in the small town's bar, where Handsome Harry and Honey Parker (Yvette Vickers) are openly fooling around. We learn that he and Nancy had been separated, and only recently got back together. Nancy had seen Harry flirting with Honey, and roared out into the desert. We also learn that Nancy is a drunk, madly in love with Harry, and has fifty million bucks. We also learn Honey wants Harry to murder Nancy. This scene is, if nothing else, fully expository.

Nancy goes home, where she's met by her loyal butler Jess (Ken Terrell), as well as Harry, who hates the butler and is loathed by Jess in return. (Jess is given to lurking in doorways, Joe Dante points out, as an all-purpose cutaway.)

Poor Nancy; she knows Harry is absolutely no good at all, but she loves him anyway. (We never know why.) She tells him about the satellite* but, of course, he doesn't believe her either. Harry puts her to bed and runs back to Honey, who is dancing with comic-relief deputy Charlie (Frank Chase).

Harry tells Honey he figures he can have Nancy put back in the booby hatch and thereby get all her millions without murder being necessary.

The next day, kindly Dr. Cushing (Roy Gordon) tells both Nancy and Harry that she should lay off the booze and get plenty of rest. Like everyone else, the doctor doesn't believe she saw a giant get out of a satellite. After he leaves,

---

*In Trumpet, Tom Reamy pointed out no one ever calls the spaceship anything other than a satellite; the movie was made right after Sputnik, and satellites were on everyone's mind; writer Mark Hanna apparently thought that "satellite" simply meant a spherical spaceship. It doesn't.

George Douglas and (barely visible) Ken Terrell react in terror to the highly realistic hand of the giant spaceman in the inimitable Attack of the 50 Foot Woman (1958).

there's an angry little scene between Nancy and Harry. "Does he think I'm crazy too?" Nancy asks, taking a drink.

"No one thinks you're—crazy," Harry says, his little pause telling volumes. She says that she knows where he was the night before, and Harry indignantly leaves, tossing her the Star of India, which he'd dangled in front of Honey the night before.

Nancy's alone in the room, and the television starts talking about her and her satellite-spotting activities. "From Calabasas, home of the Archers' palatial 'home away from home' comes a report that Mrs. Archer has been seeing not only a sociable satellite, but its inhabitant as well, a thirty-foot giant." The announcer (Dale Tate) goes on in this vein for a while, and then begins addressing Nancy herself, teasing her about her marital problems with Handsome Harry. "Come, come, now, Mrs. Archer... A man can ignore *one* million dollars—but fifty!—that's too much to ask, even from the man in the Moon!" Nancy tosses a bottle through the tube, as well she might. Poor Nancy, not only will no one believe she saw the big spaceman, but now even her TV set has turned on her.

Nancy grabs the butler's gun, and Harry, and they drive out into the desert (actually, rather arable-looking land) to search for her damned satellite. After driving around a while, they do indeed spot it, and here comes the giant again. Harry fires a couple of shots, jumps in the car and takes off, leaving Nancy to the mercy of the giant. This time, she doesn't outrun it.

Back at the house, Harry immediately starts packing (Why? Does he think the giant has his address?), has a fight with loyal Jess, and runs off to Honey.

Tom Reamy questions just why Harry is trying to make a run for it, and does indicate Jess is properly suspicious of a known-to-be-rotten husband who drives into the desert with his wife and a gun and returns with neither.

Harry tries to get Honey to leave with him *fast* — "I've no time for questions and answers now" — but deputy Charlie, this time serious, shows up and stops them; Jess has reported Nancy's disappearance. Charlie and Harry hang around the sheriff's office and play gin, until someone says Nancy's turned up back at home, on top of the pool house.

Everyone thinks this is remarkable, for her to be on such a high, inaccessible building; when the sheriff later climbs up onto the pool house, he needs Charlie's help. However, the top of the pool house is only about three feet above the ground.

Nancy seems to be all right, except for a few scratches, and is put in bed upstairs. Somehow, Dr. Cushing knows she's been exposed to radiation, even though he can't detect any. He has a nurse prepare an injection, and Honey overhears him saying an overdose would be fatal. So as she and Harry leave, she suggests he go back and give beleaguered Nancy an overdose.

He creeps into her room armed with the hypodermic needle, but the nurse comes in behind him and switches on the light just as he has reached Nancy's bedside. Egad! There is that giant hand! Behind him, the nurse screams, "Dr. Cushing! Dr. Cushing! Something's happened to Mrs. Archer!" You bet.

She has somehow grown to 50 feet in height without (a) needing a bigger room or even a bigger bed, or (b) smashing through the floor into the room below. For most of the rest of the picture, she stays (offscreen) in that room, in that bed. This is perhaps the most amazing thing in the picture; as Joe Dante has said, the film seems to be written as if she has a disease like leprosy, not that she has suddenly grown to 50 feet in height.

Apparently the growth was a side effect of the scratches she received when the giant plucked away the Star of India; it's not likely he intended for her to get that big. It's also clear that the giant brought her back home and put her on the pool house roof, for huge footprints are found leading away from — but not up to — the pool house. Maybe Harry was right to flee; the giant clearly had their address.

Dr. Cushing and Von Loeb (Otto Waldis), a specialist he calls in, mutter knowingly about reasons for the giantism. "If only it were filaria! We'd have something to go on!" (Elephantiasis, an enlargement and thickening of tissues, not abnormal growth, is caused by filarial worms.) Von Loeb is learnedly distressed. "There's not even a streptococcal infection to incite the inflammation of the lymph channels!" He also points out that "giantism can result from an overactive forward lobe in the pituitary fossa," so Cushing feels surgery is indicated. (This indicates the extent of Hanna's research into medical causes of giantism.) The more philosophical Von Loeb credits it all to "the supersonic age we live in." What?

Jess and the sheriff go out into the desert, and soon find the satellite, which seems always to be around when you need it, except when Nancy tried to show it to the sheriff. Entering it, they find it has six-foot doorways and eight-foot ceilings. There are several diamonds suspended in clear globes, presumably a part of the propulsion system. The giant shows up, so they back out of the satellite and try to drive away, but the giant picks up their car (it becomes much older when it is off the ground), and drops it again. The sheriff flings a grenade at the giant; it makes the big guy wince. He gets into his satellite and flies away, never to be seen again.

Meanwhile, Harry and Honey are hugging again, and the two doctors chain up the hapless Nancy while discussing where to begin the operation. (She is perhaps still growing, though this is not made clear; in the script, at least, she has also turned bright green.) Jess and the sheriff, shaken by their ordeal and tuckered out by the long walk back from the desert, meet the two doctors musing on unhappy Nancy.

Unhappy Nancy herself has now awakened, and immediately gets out of bed, smashing through the roof. She's demurely clad in what the script terms bedsheets, but which in the film look like a dark bathing suit. She wanders off for town, looking for that two-timing Handsome Harry.

She peers into the hotel, then rips the top off the bar. Honey is killed when she dives screaming under a table. Nancy picks up Harry, now a stuffed doll, and begins to leave – going where? and why? – when the sheriff shoots at some high tension lines Nancy is conveniently near. Sparks jump out and hit her; she glows a moment, and collapses. Tom Reamy has the most interesting last words: "And thus ends the saga of Handsome Harry Archer, the most inept fortune hunter since Daffy Duck."

Mark McGee said that Bernard Woolner asked Jacques Marquette to budget the picture, which he did, at around $65,000. (Woolner told Tom Weaver the budget was $88,000.) Woolner was disturbed that Allied Artists would consider that absurdly low, so they simply added $10,000 to the cost, but made it for $65,000. After the film was completed, they still had that extra $10,000, and thought about beefing it up in certain areas. But Woolner said that it wouldn't make a nickel more if they did, so they refrained. The sad thing is that they were probably right.

The actual attack of the 50 foot woman is a long time in coming. The film is mainly a marital melodrama about a rich drunken wife, slavishly in love with a rotten, two-timing husband. Instead of the wronged wife finally getting a gun, and shooting her rival and husband dead, she turns into a giant and crushes them both. That would seem to be a significant change, but the plot works the same either way.

Nathan Juran was an art director turned director. He began as a director in 1952 with a desultory Boris Karloff gothic called *The Black Castle*, and for most of the 50s, worked primarily on second features and leading Bs for Universal-International and Allied Artists. He began directing science fiction films primarily because they were in the budget category he usually found himself rather than because he had any special affinity for them. He also directed Westerns, such as *Gunsmoke* and *Law and Order* (both 1953), some crime films including *The Crooked Web* (1955) and the not-bad *Highway Dragnet* (1954). He also did some costume adventures, including the entertaining *The Golden Blade* (1953) and the highly profitable *The Seventh Voyage of Sinbad* (1958). His biggest film was *First Men IN the Moon* (1964), which like *Sinbad* and Juran's *20 Million Miles to Earth*, was produced by Charles H. Schneer and had effects by Ray Harryhausen. Juran also made *East of Sudan* (1965) and *Land Raiders* (1970) for Schneer. One lesser film was *Hellcats of the Navy* (1957), notable solely because it is the only movie that starred Ronald Reagan and his wife Nancy.

On at least two films, *50 Foot Woman* and *Brain from Planet Arous*, Juran used the last name of Hertz. I suspect this was because his other two films of the year, *Seventh Voyage* and *Good Day for a Hanging*, were far more prestigious. *Brain* and *Woman* very much have the air of having been made back to back; Jacques Marquette served in a production capacity on both and photographed them; they have some of the same visual ideas, and both had short shooting schedules. I didn't detect any overlapping sets or locations, however. In both films, we see several scenes taken from inside a car roaring along a back road; there are shots in which a central character is abruptly grabbed on the shoulder by a harmless friend (this happens twice to the same person in *50 Foot Woman*), and, most distinctively, in both films leading characters gaze at the camera through clear containers of water, for a crazily distorted effect. In *50 Foot Woman*, both George Douglas and Ken Terrell do this as they creep through the "satellite."

Attack of the 50 Foot Woman was made in a hurry on a low budget. Several scenes run on at great length with no cuts, and as in the barroom scene, it is painfully obvious that all the scenes in one location were shot sequentially. Honey and Harry are always sitting in the same booth in the same positions, for instance.

Still, Juran does manage to vary things somewhat, by using one or two visually-interesting (if silly) shots, as when Honey dives under the table at the climax. The camera is under the table already, and Vickers crawls into close-up in an admirably panicked fashion, screaming into the camera as the giant Nancy reaches into the bar.

Mostly, the film is flat and visually uninteresting. The sets are bland, with little distinction between them. The exteriors, mostly in town, around Nancy's house and out in the desert, are shot without any visual interest. The film looks washed-out and lifeless.

There is some life, however, in the playing, and even though the film is basically worse, this in some senses lifts it above Juran's larger-budgeted but worse directed *Deadly Mantis*. Furthermore, *50 Foot Woman* is far more fun.

William Hudson turned up in several science fiction films during this period, including *The Amazing Colossal Man*, *The Man Who Turned to Stone* and *Moon Pilot*. The last film for which I have information on Hudson was *The Reluctant Astronaut* (1967), in which he had a small part. He appeared in films as early as 1944's *Weird Woman*, and turned up in several major pictures, though never in important parts, including *Mr. Roberts* (1955), *Darby's Rangers* (1958), *The Great Impostor* (1961) and *The Oscar* (1966). He had a larger role in *The She Creature* (1957). He was a smooth actor, and was well-cast as Handsome Harry Archer; he had slightly dissipated features, but was still good-looking enough to make his being able to capture women as different as Nancy and Honey plausible. Hudson always gave good value, but was just one of those dozens of lesser actors who survive in Hollywood any way they know how. Of course, even a much finer actor than Hudson would have been as ineffectual as he is when confronted by scenes such as the one in which he dashes back from the desert and inexplicably begins packing, or when later, he creeps into Nancy's room to give her a fatal injection only to find she's grown a lot. Hudson comes through the film unscathed — as an actor, at least. He died in 1974.

Of the minor actors, Frank Chase as Charlie is required to play the role broadly and in the corniest possible fashion; Charlie is a typical hick deputy, the kind of jerk who loses his glasses on his forehead. He's supposed to do big broad takes, but actually Chase is a good enough actor that he makes these takes look as uncomfortable for him to do as they are for us to watch. That is, he can't quite bring them off — and we can see why. He's better than the material, though that isn't saying much.

As Jess the butler, Ken Terrell brings a kind of sad dignity to his role, a dignity that never leaves him even when he's tumbling around the set in a surprisingly vigorous fight with Hudson, or when he's shoving the sheriff's car out of a rut.

Yvette Vickers is hot stuff. I know of few other actresses who look so — well, *dirtily* sexy. She's anything but smouldering, and instead embodies a sleazy, hot-to-trot little slut perfectly. I know that I had never seen anything like her by 1958. Her peculiar, heart-shaped face with its massive brow and sharp nose makes her look like a brainy weasel, and her lush figure and sloppy hair (in *50 Foot Woman*, at least) are those of a barely-reformed whore. She gives Hudson calculated and lively French kisses repeatedly, which was quite against the Production Code but served the intended purpose of making her look as randy as a rabbit. She was actually a good actress, but because of her physical equipment, was again and again cast in the role of a small-town slut.

According to Calvin Beck's *Scream Queens*, Vickers got her start as the "White Rain" girl in a series of TV commercials for White Rain Shampoo in the early 1950s. She appeared in films from 1957, with *Short Cut to Hell*, directed by James Cagney, to *Hud* (1963). And in virtually all of her films, including *Attack of the Giant Leeches*, *Reform School Girl* (1958) and *I, Mobster* (1959), she played that same scheming little tramp. Occasionally she had somewhat better parts, but despite that and her obvious talent, doesn't seem to have been in any feature films from 1963 to 1971. Director Curtis Harrington, himself an expert in fantasy films, featured scenes from *50 Foot Woman* in his *Ruby* of 1977; Vickers appeared in Harrington's *What's the Matter with Helen* (1971) and his TV movie, *The Dead Don't Die* (1975). He's only doing what many of us would do for Vickers, if we could: giving employment to a good, distinctive actress.

Allison Hayes is the main reason most people recall *Attack of the 50 Foot Woman*, and not solely because she *is* the 50 Foot Woman, though her stunning figure looks awfully good on a giant. Hayes was a beautiful, sloe-eyed actress, something like a second-string Jane Russell; she was also genuinely sexy in a lush, almost exotic fashion. She began as a professional pianist with symphony orchestras, but began winning beauty contests and decided on a career as an actress. She turned up in small roles in several Universal films in 1954, including *Sign of the Pagan* and *The Purple Mask*, and later starred in *Gunslinger* (1956) for Roger Corman. In 1957, she began the series of cheap horror films which garnered her most of her fans: *The Unearthly*, *The Disembodied*, *The Undead*, and *Zombies of Mora Tau* (all 1957); she also appeared in *The Hypnotic Eye* (1959), and had a small part in *The Crawling Hand* (1963). In most of these, there was an excuse to get Hayes into a low-cut, tight-fitting garment, which she filled beautifully. In a sense, it's pointless to talk about her acting, as few recall her for that; she was Sultry Sex embodied. But the fact is that she was a good actress, and generated some sympathy for herself even in *50 Foot Woman*, in which her character is crazily erratic. (She also managed to look attractive in a pair of toreador pants that look as if they were cut from an awning.)

Hayes ceased acting in films after the mid-60s. During the 1970s, actor Barry Brown sought her out, as he did many of the lesser-known actors in science fiction and horror films. She fell ill around this time, and while in the hospital, died in 1977 of complications following surgery. Brown himself followed a year later.

The special effects in *Attack of the 50 Foot Woman* are among the worst ever done in a film of even this low budget. This would not ordinarily be disastrous, except that there are many effects. The "satellite" itself looks like a slightly transparent ping-pong ball, and maneuvers as if inertia wasn't a consideration. The alien that emerges is also slightly transparent; when he appears, the background becomes much darker, and he looks so pale he might have been dipped in flour. The alien is played by a gentleman (see below) of late middle age, who looks like a tired studio security guard. He's certainly not much of an actor, lumbering through his scenes with a dour, sour expression, showing emotion only when he's reaching for the diamond, and when the grenade goes off. His costuming, as mentioned earlier, is best described as quaint, and makes him look like a eunuch from late Roman times, or perhaps a minor guard at a Babylonian palace — anything other than a man from outer space. I suppose his being bald was to suggest an alien origin. He never looks like anything other than an effect.

In Tom Weaver's interview with Marquette in *Fangoria* #39, the filmmaker claimed that the transparency of the giants was deliberate, an "iridescent" quality that pleased him. Weaver himself spotted the giant as being played by Mike Ross, who also played the bartender in the film.

The interior of the spaceship, with everything scaled for normal human size, compounds the air of zany unreality, but the film never takes on the feeling of a dream, because the primary romantic-conflict story is so pedestrian. But dream-logic is the only way that the spaceman and his cramped "satellite" can be explained.

When Nancy Archer gets to her full size, which never is consistent, and is rarely 50 feet, things aren't any better. Hayes has been directed to walk in a dreamy slow motion, sometimes being overcranked. This was to give her a feeling of mass and ponderousness, but only makes it seem as if everything is happening underwater. The pace of the film is smooth but never swift, and Hayes' meandering giant woman slows it down even more.

The combination of giant effect scenes and live action is haphazard at best. In one scene, screaming townspeople back slowly into the scene, staring over the camera toward the audience's right; the 50 Foot Woman then enters from the *left*, 90° away from where everyone was staring in terror.

That giant hand is used from time to time to indicate the enormous sizes of Nancy and the spaceman (who is only a mere 30 feet; everything is bigger on Earth?), but it is so stiff, unarticulated and rubbery, that the hand adds to the air of dizzy unreality of the film.

Ronald Stein's music is as ponderous as the film; instead of a driving action theme when the 50 Foot Woman finally does attack, he uses a slow, thudding rhythm. It's as if everyone conspired to create a sense of dreamy, retarded motion.

Actually, of course, no one was concerned with making a good movie; they just wanted to make money. Certainly writer Mark Hanna didn't care, or didn't know how to care. He didn't bother to wonder about possible differences between satellites and spaceships, but then no one else connected with the film did, either. Hanna's gaps in logic don't hurt the film; it's already a battered corpse, and thereby immune to mere logic flaws.

Perhaps not surprisingly, Hanna also wrote *The Amazing Colossal Man* with Bert I. Gordon, director of that film. While *Colossal Man* is no masterpiece of screencraft, the script is much better than *50 Foot Woman*. Hanna's two other fantastic films were cowritten with Charles B. Griffith, and one of those, *Not of This Earth*, is a decent script all around, but with some gaps in logic. The other script was apparently rewritten by Hanna after Griffith completed it: *The*

Undead was written in, of all things, blank verse, and was a take-off on the "Bridey Murphy" reincarnation fad. The resulting film is a bizarre farrago with some life and Allison Hayes.

Variety's "Whit" said that the film "shapes up as a minor offering for the scifi trade, where demands aren't too great," and noted that Nathan Juran's "direction is routine, up against considerable corny dialogue in Mark Hanna's screenplay."

The *Monthly Film Bulletin* gave the film its lowest rating, referring to it as a "feeble tale," and adding that "the trick photography is weaker than the novelettish plot, while the standard of acting is weaker than either."

Jack Moffitt saw the film for the crazy absurdity it is, even though it was a "cheaply made and perfunctorily contrived exploitation picture." He then relates the story of the film in sardonic terms, pointing out some of the logical flaws, such as having Nancy's medicine downstairs while she's in bed upstairs, "which necessitates an inconvenient gallop upstairs with a loaded syringe whenever the lady of the establishment requires medication."

Even the easy-to-please *Motion Picture Exhibitor* found little to like in the film. "Rather slow in pace, this science fiction thriller is for the most part ineffective. Acting, direction and effects offer little, and many things are left unexplained."

Picturegoer found it "gloriously batty nonsense" with "a couple of deft performances ... it doesn't deserve."

In *Fantastic Films* #25, Leonard Pinth Mandell (possibly Paul Mandell) calls *50 Foot Woman* "a delightful romp through [the] nether region of the absurd." Alan Frank (*Horror*) described it as "quite dotty in concept and execution" which makes it "a hugely entertaining minor genre entry."

Attack of the 50 Foot Woman did make money. So much so that in the early 1960s, the Woolner Brothers announced a sequel to the movie, this time to be done in color, CinemaScope and with a large budget. This got as far as the scripting stages, but not beyond. (A Hollywood bookstore had a copy of the sequel script for years, for sale at a very high price.) Later, in the mid-70s, a film to be called "Fifty Foot Woman" was announced by a minor Hollywood independent company but this, too, never reached the screen.

Attack of the 50 Foot Woman could have been the camp classic some find it if it hadn't been ponderous and flat. There are delightful moments throughout, and it does have Allison Hayes and Yvette Vickers, virtues indeed. Although it is funny from time to time, and the total lack of logic makes it appealing in a surrealistic fashion, the movie has too many conventional defects to rise to the daffy heights of *Cat-Women of the Moon*, although it is probably the best contender for such honors of the films in this volume.

Attack of the Puppet People

As usual for Bert I. Gordon in the 1950s, his *Attack of the Puppet People* deals with problems of size. He mimicked *The Incredible Shrinking Man*, going in the opposite direction, with *The Amazing Colossal Man*, his most profitable film of the period, and sought to mine the same vein again. That is, he wanted to copy the success of *Shrinking Man* on its own terms.

Filmed as "The Fantastic Puppet People," Gordon's adventure in miniaturization at least has the benefit of a slightly different story line, but suffers from his lackluster direction, a foolish scientific gimmick, and mostly inept acting. The special effects are variable, but are rarely better than mediocre. Why Gordon is reputed in some quarters to be a master of special effects can only be explained by his persistence in using them; he's not good at effects.

Attack of the Puppet People is structured as a mystery, but as the gimmick is revealed in the title, instead of being intriguing, the long delay in showing us the puppet people themselves becomes tedious. Gordon's ponderous direction doesn't help things.

John Hoyt plays Mr. Franz, once a famous European puppeteer now reduced to running a very small doll-making company. Bob Westley (John Agar) comes to work for Franz as a combination salesman and coworker, and is soon attracted to Sally (June Kenney), Franz's new secretary. Where the old one went is part of that mystery mentioned above.

When Franz learns that Bob is going to leave him to marry Sally, Bob too disappears. Sally has paid no attention to various omens—on a date at the Rosecrans Drive-In, she and Bob watched *The Amazing Colossal Man*, in particular the scene in which Glen Langan gloats that "I'm not growing, you're shrinking." Also, Sally told Bob that Franz had the unusual habit of talking to his dolls. And the local mail carrier has disappeared—we are shown a mailbag hanging on Franz's door, hardly a place of concealment.

There's a cabinet full of small cylinders with people inside which Sally happens on—actually carefully cut-out full-length photos of the shrunken people—and Sally runs to tell a cop that Franz has been turning people into dolls. The cop doesn't blink, and even accepts the idea; he returns with her to the studio, where Franz demonstrates that the miniature people are really just photos of his favorite people. He drops a match into one cylinder, and the photo of Bob curls up and burns. He also shows us a suitcase full of plastic tubes containing miniature John Agars, a disquieting sight.

After the policeman leaves, Franz overpowers Sally too, and she wakes up on a tabletop. When she sees the gigantic telephone beside her, she screams in horror. We soon see that lonely old Franz keeps these people around to fend off loneliness. He was in love with a woman who left him, and so now when anyone threatens to leave his life, he shrinks them and puts them into his cabinet. (It could not be made clear why he has shrunken a couple of teenagers, a Marine in full dress uniform, the mailman and others. Surely he couldn't have felt a deep personal attachment to all these strangers?)

He occasionally takes out a few of the puppet people, frees them from their cylinders—where a gas keeps them immobile between "shows"—and allows them to sport around on the tabletop. He feeds them, gives them a little champagne, and teenager Laurie (Marlene Willis) even sings one of the quasi-rock 'n' roll songs that had begun to turn up in these pictures. This one, "You're My Living Doll," crudely recapitulates the theme of the film, with lyrics like "Don't deceive me, never leave me, stay with me forever, my living doll."

Although some of the people seem content with their lot—"I kinda like it," says Cheap Floozie Georgia (Laurie Mitchell, the Queen of Outer Space)—the rest are anxious to escape. In the best sequence in the picture, Bob, the Marine (Scott Peters) and teenaged Stan (Ken Miller) try to make their way to the shrinking machine, which can be run in reverse. To the accompaniment of a record on the phonograph, they separately clamber up to a doorknob, the tabletop, and the controls of the machine, but Franz's return spoils everything, and they hurry back to the desk where the others wait.

Big-hearted Franz decides that his puppet people could perform in a real (if private) puppet show, and, packing them in a suitcase, goes to a deserted theatre where he forces Bob and Sally to participate in a puppet show of "Dr. Jekyll and Mr. Hyde." The life-size (to them) puppet of Jekyll changes to Hyde, and frightens Sally, so Bob demolishes it, tangling himself in the strings momentarily. This upsets Franz, but his attention is suddenly distracted, so Bob and Sally flee the theatre. Although large back-projected animals, including a dog and a rat, menace them, they manage to reach Franz's laboratory and restore themselves to full size.

In the meantime, a little girl (Susan Gordon, daughter of the director) has told police sergeant Patterson that Franz showed her some little people (we never saw this scene), so poor Franz's goose is cooked from several directions.

As Bob and Sally indignantly leave — perhaps another emotion might have been more appropriate — Franz is left dejectedly sitting in his doll-making room, saying over and over, "Don't leave me, please don't leave me. I'll be alone." This bid at pathos is almost as awkward as everything else in the film, but thanks to John Hoyt, comes close to working.

Gordon told an interviewer in *Famous Monsters of Filmland* #14 that the title was changed to make the film more salable; he regarded the movie as "a tongue-in-cheek production aimed at teenagers, with light and humorous elements included to offset some of its more terrifying aspects." But since the film is neither humorous nor terrifying, it's unclear as to which elements were which; the tongue-in-cheek approach is totally invisible.

Jack Moffitt said, "It seems fair to apply the same critical standards to the acting that one would apply to a class play. By that standard, 'everybody does just fine.'" Actually, Moffitt was wrong; Hoyt is considerably better than that, and June Kenney is much worse.

This is one of the few films in which John Hoyt played a weak character. Franz is a frightened man, fearful of being left alone; this may be crude motivation, but it is real motivation. Hoyt manages to make the character seem more real than his studio-bound surroundings. The strangely pathetic Franz is not only one of Hoyt's most unusual parts in a science fiction film (in *When Worlds Collide*, he was a tyrannical businessman; in *The Lost Continent*, he was a sympathetic but self-reliant Russian), he is also one of the most unusual mad scientists. Generally, mad scientists are working to prove some wild-eyed theory or other, and lose track of the consequences on the way to the goals. Franz isn't interested in long-term goals; he just wants friends he can control, like puppets. This theme is muddled in the film, but is more interesting by far than the usual driving force in Bert I. Gordon's films: here comes the monster.

Hoyt has no real opportunities as an actor in the film, except for his sad little final scene; there are no set pieces in which he can bring the character to life, but he is an actor of some ability, and is far better than others would be in the part.

Unfortunately, in their scenes together, veteran supporting player Michael Mark (it was his little girl that Boris Karloff drowned in *Frankenstein*) shows why he was never anything other than a background figure. He's a former puppeteer himself, but is just an actor reading lines; Hoyt manages to rise above the material, even if only briefly. Despite the limitations, Hoyt gives what is the best performance in a Bert I. Gordon film of the period. (Although Glen Langan is not at all bad in *The Amazing Colossal Man*, at least while he's sane.)

I comment on John Agar elsewhere; he's not good here, but he's in there slugging. The rest of the cast is quite ordinary, except for June Kenney, who's below that. Ken Miller appeared in several films for American International, usually in a kind of sub-Nick Adams part, as he somewhat resembled Adams.

The special effects are as crude as the story line. When we first see Hoyt's workbench, it's clearly designed to be used as a setting for later puppet people antics. The props are very simplified, and there are few of them. The scale is also off in some of the props; for instance, the paint can is too small in relation to the telephone.

Most scenes are accomplished either by very rigid split-screen shots, always from the same angles and always with strong vertical or horizontal lines on the sets for the splits, or by rear-screen projection. There is one use of a matte, in which Hoyt reaches into the scene to prod tiny Agar, but it's not convincing.

Some contemporary critics were easily fooled. "In one amazing triumph of special-effects photography," said Dick Williams in the Los Angeles *Mirror-News*, "a luscious doll-size beauty takes a bath in a coffee tin!" Actually, it was merely a fake coffee can large enough for an ordinary woman to bathe in it. No special effects were involved at all.

One of the few interesting special effects scenes involves a shrunken cat climbing out of a match box, to the amazement of Susan Gordon. Bert Gordon photographed the cat from a high, distant angle, so that the illusion of a tiny cat is not at all bad. But then he spoils it by running the film in reverse, so that the cat *backs* into the match box.

The explanation offered for the shrinking process shows that Gordon felt it was the least important aspect of the story. He wanted shrunken people and wasn't concerned as to how he got them. "A very simple principle, really," says Hoyt. He points out to his victims that a slide projector can make an image of any size, and he has merely applied that principle to living people. It is "only necessary to change them to energy first," clearly child's play for this man, who has worked his entire life as a puppeteer. He subjects whatever he wants to shrink to high-frequency vibrations, breaking them down at their "resonant frequency," then refocuses them at a smaller size. This is such balderdash that the film is nearer to fantasy than science fiction.

Except for Jack Moffitt, who didn't like the film, most contemporary critics were surprisingly kind to *Attack of the Puppet People*. "Powr" in *Daily Variety* claimed that Gordon was "a master of special effects," and that in this film, the effects "are as ingenious and intriguing as ever." In general, he found the film to be "satisfactory." He did add that "the story lacks punch because there is no real point to it, so the ending ... is inconclusive and somewhat flat."

Dick Williams, in addition to being dazzled by a giant coffee can, also thought the movie was "ingenious." In the *Los Angeles Times*, Charles Stinson thought it was "rather well-done minor-key science fiction." The story, Stinson said, was "commendably free from sleazy sensationalism and technical carelessness." He also said that "George Worthing Yates' script—which is not without a certain humor—is several cuts above average in this genre."

The *Monthly Film Bulletin*, reviewing the film under its British title, *Six Inches Tall*, said that "The wild absurdity of the script ... keeps the story amusing and intriguing," but also added that "some ruthless cutting and a brisker pace would have helped the film."

Attack of the Puppet People is a lethargic, drab and inconclusive little picture. John Hoyt's performance and one or two scenes make it more watchable than most of Bert Gordon's films, but it is also lacking in excitement and real interest.

The Blob

Much more than the film itself, the title of this movie is very famous, even notorious, and during the 1960s, *The Blob* was used in stand-up comics' routines as a synonym for a terrible film. It's also famous as "the first film of Steve McQueen," but he'd appeared in three films before this; *Somebody Up There Likes Me* (1956) was his screen debut. In 1972, *Son of Blob* (also known as *Beware the Blob*) appeared, and the arrival of this sequel so long after the first film, plus the fact that the sequel was a comedy, only brought *The Blob* itself further notoriety as a terrible movie.

Actually, it's a decent enough little film. The monster couldn't be more simply conceived, and there are near-successful tries at characterization throughout. There's a feeling that the filmmakers were almost slumming, that they knew their abilities were above this story about a shapeless mass from outer space that eats people. And they probably were correct. The script by Theodore Simonson and Kate Phillips (from a story by Irvin H. Millgate), is solidly structured, with decent dialogue and relatively rounded characterizations. Director Irvin S. Yeaworth, Jr. is somewhat plodding, not helped by the slow-paced editing of Alfred Hillman, and the film never builds up a head of steam. But it is a promising attempt, and has a commendably un–Hollywood air about it. *The Blob* could actually have been a classic, if the production values had been better and if the pacing was faster. As it is, it's still a distinctly above-average monster movie.

The story opens as Steve (McQueen) and Jane (Aneta Corseaut; in all reference sources, including official Paramount credits, she's listed as "Judy," but it's "Jane" in the film) are necking in his car in lovers' lane near a large town. Steve is clearly attracted to her as more than a mere date, but she's suspicious of his intentions as he keeps lapsing into standard come-on lines, of which he's uncomfortably aware. Just after Jane talks about shooting stars, a meteor flashes overhead. As it came down nearby, they leave to find it.

An old man (Olin Howlin) finds the meteor, which looks like a small model of the moon, complete with craters. He prods it with a stick and it falls into several neat sections, revealing a mass of transparent, viscous material: a blob. He raises this stuff on his stick—the goo resembles model airplane cement—and it slithers *up* onto his hand. As The Blob begins to turn pink from the flesh and blood it is ingesting, the old man shrieks and runs, coming out of the woods near Steve's passing car.

The two young people take the old man to a doctor (Steven Chase) Steve knows, and the doctor immediately recognizes the strange creature as something beyond his experience. Steve and Jane go outside, where they encounter some teenagers who are annoyed at Steve for having rocketed by them on the highway.

These kids challenge Steve to a drag race, and he complies—except that the race must be in reverse. As the two cars shoot backwards down the street, officer Dave (Earl Rowe) catches Steve and gives him a strange little lecture, establishing the cop as stern but fair, and as someone who knows Steve well. (The drag race is the only extraneous material in the film.)

Steve promised the doctor that he would try to find the old man's relatives, and he and the other teenagers go out to the old man's place, where they find the remains of the meteor and, in the shack, a puppy which Jane takes with her.

Meanwhile, the doctor notices that the blanket he's thrown over the old man is being shifted around by something underneath it, something that does not behave like an arm. (This is a surprisingly chilling shot.) He tells his nurse that the old man has a "parasite on his arm" which is "assimilating his flesh at fantastic speed."

The nurse enters the examining room, but the old man is entirely gone, and The Blob, now about the mass of a human being and looking like a big blood clot, is pulsating in a corner. As the doctor edgily advises her from the doorway, the nurse throws acid on it, but The Blob only turns yellowish for a moment, then comes after her. She screams and falls, knocking over a light.

The doctor grabs a shotgun and watches the doorway into the examining room; soon The Blob heaves itself into view, larger still and almost glowing. The doctor fires at it, but the surface merely wrinkles then returns to normal. The doctor locks himself in his office.

Steve returns, but no one answers the doorbell; he catches a glimpse of the doctor, completely covered by The Blob, flailing at the venetian blinds at his window, then the doctor collapses out of sight.

Steve and Jane rush to the police station to report what he saw to Dave, who at first is prepared to believe him, but is made skeptical by the anger of officer Jim, who dislikes teenagers (we later learn that one "smacked into his wife on the turnpike").

Although there is no trace of the doctor at his office, and there is evidence of a struggle, the housekeeper convinces Dave that the doctor has gone to a medical convention; everyone tends to believe that Steve staged the whole thing.

Elsewhere, The Blob rolls along, gobbling up a man working under a car and again, this is someone who is expected to be out of town.

The fathers of Steve and Jane (hers is the high school principal) arrive at the police station and cart their apparently errant children home, her father insisting that Jane never see Steve again. But later, avoiding her obnoxious little brother Danny (Keith Almoney), she sneaks out and meets him.

The two of them go to the local theatre where their friends are watching a double bill of horror movies, and Steve manages to convince them to go around town and try to warn people against The Blob. Some dialogue we (over)hear at this point indicates that The Blob has wiped out the patrons of a bar, but the kids can't convince anyone of the danger. Some drunken louts at a party scoff at them, and a bartender mentions someone coming over from another bar with a story about a monster, but he doesn't believe them either.

Jane spots the old man's runaway puppy in front of the supermarket owned by Steve's father, and the door is found unlocked. The two go in, prowling around the darkened aisles, until they run into The Blob, now very much larger. It pursues them to the back of the store, where they take refuge in a large meat locker. They shiver in cold and fear as they see The Blob start to ooze in around the doorjamb. But it unexpectedly retreats, and they make their getaway.

One of the teenagers tries to tell Jim about what's going on, but he doesn't believe him. So the kids set off all the alarms in town and blow car horns (we see an old man trying vainly to decide between his civil defense and his volunteer fireman's helmet). Everyone comes down to the store, and simply because Steve seems honest and genuinely frightened, Dave finally believes him that something is up.

By this time, The Blob has arrived at the movie theatre. It oozes through a heating vent into the projection booth and devours the projectionist. When the film runs out, the kids in the audience are at first annoyed, but this turns to terror when The Blob comes squirting out of the projection booth into the auditorium. Everyone flees in panic as the monster heads through town (not seen).

Jane grabs her kid brother, who is overly-cutely dressed in Dr. Denton pajamas and a cowboy hat and pistol, snapping caps off at The Blob, and with Steve, they dash into a nearby diner.

Blork. The Blob plops down on top of the diner, totally enveloping it, then starts oozing in around all the windows. Steve and the other people in the diner dash down to the basement for refuge. A phone has been left off the hook upstairs, so by shouting, Steve can make himself heard through The Blob (which is translucent; "Home Baking" can be read through the monster's gelatinous mass).

Jim is chosen to shoot down a high-tension line over the diner, which falls on The Blob but doesn't do it any harm, although the electricity does start a fire in the diner, which someone points out to Dave, suggesting it be put out. The sardonic response is, "Any suggestions how?"

Inside the diner, the owner (Vince Barbi) uses a CO_2 fire extinguisher to put out the fire, and Steve notices that The Blob, which has begun to ooze down the stairs, recoils from the cold fog of the extinguisher. He remembers that it didn't come into the meat locker after him and Jane, and shouts to those outside that they should get all the CO_2 extinguishers in town and freeze the thing solid.

Jane's father rises to the occasion, smashing the window of the high school to get at the extinguishers there, and before long, The Blob is chilled enough to withdraw from the diner, and those inside escape. The last shot in the film is of The Blob being parachuted into the Arctic, and the words "The End" reform into an ambiguous "?" (which would be repeated in the next two films produced by Jack H. Harris, 4D Man and Dinosaurus).

The Blob was filmed for a reported $240,000 in Valley Forge, Pennsylvania (the real cost was probably lower), and was financed locally; it was later sold to Paramount at a substantial profit. Furthermore, after a time the rights to the film reverted to producer Harris, who has reissued it several times to even greater profits.

The film was not only made far from Hollywood, it is also rather un–Hollywood in its approach at times. If the picture had been made by Roger Corman or Sam Katzman, it probably would have gained some values, such as a swifter pace and better acting overall, but it would have lost all the features that make the film distinctive and interesting. The small town settings, although unusually lit by Hollywood cinematography standards, add a sense that Hollywood would have been hard-pressed to duplicate. The unpolished actors also seem somehow more real than would a cast of Hollywood regulars.

As Charles Stinson said in the Los Angeles Times, the script by Simonson and Phillips "is intelligent; perhaps, paradoxically, a trifle too much so." The movie is far better written than most Hollywood monster movies, certainly of this period; care is taken to give adequate motivation for all characters, and vignettes of characterization are provided from time to time. As Stinson said, "the horror story ... is at many junctures submerged in a network of personal cameo portraits." This is so unusual for a mere monster movie that it's astonishing more reviewers at the time didn't notice. The only other contemporary critic who seemed to be aware of the unusual approach was Paul V. Beckley in the *New York Herald Tribune*, who actually *overpraised* the film: "A minor classic in its field," he said. "One of the best pseudo-scientific films to come along in recent years ... it is made with a stress on naturalism of behavior by the human beings."

In the opening scene, things get off at once to an unusual start as Steve is trying awkwardly to simultaneously put the make on Jane and convince her that he really feels genuine affection for her. It may not be their first date, but he has never taken her up to this lovers' lane before. They are mutually ill at ease, but attracted to one another. This is, in fact, the sort of scene writers create when they are trying to depict the early stages in a romance that will lead to marriage. It's not outstanding dialogue, but it is easy and natural, and McQueen is very good in these scenes, as in fact he is throughout the film.

Later, when they visit the doctor, he immediately thinks that they struck the old man with their car, establishing early the idea of mistrust of teenagers, and when the cop gives Steve his lecture, the idea is reinforced, as is the notion that Steve is a cut above the other local kids.

The doctor's approach to The Blob is also realistic; he immediately recognizes it as something very dangerous, and might even have found a way to stop it at once if it hadn't been so rapacious.

When we first see the police station, one of the cops is playing chess over the radio with a cop in another town. There's an attempt to generate some sympathy for the teen-hating Jim by giving him a good reason to dislike teenagers (in a Hollywood film, no reason would have been thought necessary), and to make him a war hero. There is hostility between Jim and the local teens; they've already played a prank on him the same night, but it's obviously a case of each side misjudging the other. In short, he's not a bad guy; there are, in fact, no bad guys in *The Blob* at all.

Further touches of characterization continue: for instance, the two men chatting in the garage (just before The Blob gets one) are old friends, but it is also clear that one is the employer of the other. Making Jane's father the high school principal is a little obvious and cheap, especially in this film which doesn't otherwise stoop to simpleminded ideas of this nature.

There's an interesting but superfluous scene right after Jane sneaks out to meet Steve, when they are on the track of The Blob. The dialogue is especially good here (Steve longs for yesterday; "good old yesterday," he says bitterly), and the writers are clearly trying to depict the development of their relationship. However, at this point it's unnecessary; we aren't as interested in the rest of their lives together as we are in stopping the man-eating monster.

Even in the climax, there's a further attempt at giving us believable characters: when Dave decides to shoot down the power line, he has Jim do it, partly because Jim is the best man for the job, and partly to allow Jim to make amends for his hostility to the kids earlier in the evening (the film takes place in one night, in not much more time than it takes to watch it). Jim's a little surprised, but clearly grateful.

In short, throughout, these two writers have tried to write a decent, craftsmanlike script. And on the level of their work, the film is not only basically a success, it is distinctive and admirable. I know nothing about them, except that the script for *4D Man* cowritten by Simonson was equally inventive.

However, the film is diminished by Irvin S. Yeaworth, Jr.'s earnest, intelligent but plodding direction. Almost every scene runs a little too long; except for McQueen, people don't move quickly, and an air of amateurishness hangs over the picture. Yeaworth seems to be picking his way, trying out ideas without having a clear notion as to their effects. He gives equal weight to the backwards drag race as to scenes of The Blob devouring people. The sequence in which the doctor paws at the venetian blinds before Steve's horrified eyes has almost no impact at all; although it is nicely conceived, Yeaworth doesn't have a clear idea how to build tension, how to deliver horror.

The sequence that works best is primarily satisfactory as black comedy, which surfaces again and again in the film. When The Blob nonchalantly rolls up the incline behind the car—we're observing it from under the car—and eats the mechanic, the contrast between his jovial dialogue and the approaching doom is amusing. Also, the scene in the projection booth, in which we hear nothing but the sounds of the movie and of the projectors has a certain impact, and there are tiny elements of tension in the scene in the supermarket. But by and large, The Blob is not a suspenseful film.

The directness and simplicity of the monster gave it fame at the time, not the terror or suspense in the movie. Those elements, and one other: the title song, "The Blob." This was one of the earliest hits for Burt Bacharach and Mack David, and was recorded by several different groups; it made a modest showing on the charts. (The best-selling version was that heard behind the opening credits, by "The Five Blobs"; actually, by redubbing, singer Bernie Knee did all the voices.) It's an amusing song, almost an instrumental. "Oh, beware of The Blob, it creeps, and leaps, and glides and slides across the floor, right through the door, and all around the walls, a splotch, a blotch, be careful of The Blob." That's all the lyrics there are. The fact that it's a light novelty song heard over the film's interestingly-designed credits (the title appears at the *end* of the pulsating credits, even after the director's name), led many to assume that The Blob is a parody of horror films.

Many have also assumed that "The Blob" was written by Bacharach and his most frequent collaborator, Hal David (Mack's brother), but though they worked together before this, and had two hits ("Magic Moments" and "The Story of My Life"), "The Blob" was written by Bacharach and *Mack* David. They worked together for about a year, and Bacharach reteamed with Hal in the 1960s.

Though it is done with some wit and sophistication, the story is quite serious. Apparently the idea was to make a film with a simple, direct story line, and a simple, direct monster; filming it in color made it distinctive and more salable. Furthermore, the production company apparently hired Steve McQueen on the basis of his *acting* ability, certainly an unusual idea at the time. The Blob has the feeling of intelligent people making a film in a disreputable genre, trying to do something they could be proud of. They don't seem to have realized that films like this almost never dealt with characters, but with stereotypes. There's hackneyed material in The Blob, to be sure, but the writers' attempt to characterize people does raise the film above the level of the usual teenagers-versus-monsters story.

The Blob itself has no personality at all; it is merely a mass of unexplained protoplasm driven to ingest living creatures, and does so in a very simple fashion: it merely absorbs them into the tissues of its own body. There's a grisly touch in having The Blob transparent when it first appears, but later turning red as it gobbles up blood and flesh. I suspect its devouring clothing, shoes, etc., was more for the sake of the plot (no clues) than out of logic, but otherwise the rolling menace is conceived with a clean logic. Not only is it shapeless, it doesn't seem to have a bodily structure at all. It can seep through grilles, around several windows at once, and out all the apertures of a projection booth without any damage. It merely reforms beyond the barrier. That's basic. Even the method of destroying (or halting) The Blob is simple. It is just frozen into one big blobsicle and dropped at the North Pole where, presumably, it won't thaw out. (A chunk is brought back to warmth in *Son of Blob*.) It would have been cold in that meteor in space, too.

The Blob eats people and gets bigger and tries to eat more people. That's *monster* reduced to its most irreducible. It's probably this almost elegant simplicity that made the film noticeable on its first release.

The special effects that bring The Blob to life are inventive. Barton Sloane created some sort of slippery compound for The Blob, one that rolled around on objects without sticking to them—The Blob looks as slick as a plastic footstool—and it's also one that seems to last a while. Some movie fan claims to have The Blob itself in a sealed container; it tends to evaporate.

Most of the scenes with The Blob were cleverly done with photos of the required location. They are carefully matched to the set and real objects. We'll see a shot, as in the doctor's office, of the examining room through a doorway; there's a cut back to the doctor, and when we return to the doorway, everything but The Blob is a photograph. The color balancing is usually excellent, and on a first viewing, many of the illusions are highly persuasive.

However, it doesn't work with the diner, when a tendril of The Blob twines around an all-too-obviously photographic counter stool. Other times, Sloane uses simple but effective miniatures, as in the projection booth exterior, but once he disastrously uses a painting, when The Blob engulfs the diner. There are some rotoscoped animation effects, as when The Blob is hit with acid and when electricity crackles over it. These are up to the standards of similar Hollywood effects at the time. For a film that cost as little as did *The Blob*, the effects are very good. That they are variable is too bad, but the unevenness doesn't really detract from things overall.

Ralph Carmichael's music for *The Blob* is as intelligent and low-key as the rest of the film; it is similar to James Bernard's scoring for the Hammer Films that were just beginning to become popular, in that the scary scenes receive emphatic treatment while the rest is understated. It's not a memorable score, except for the comic, haunting title song, but it is effective and efficient.

This was the first film produced by Jack H. Harris; *The Blob* made a handsome profit even before release, so Harris was able to film *4D Man* soon thereafter. *Dinosaurus* was actually made in conjunction with a studio, Universal. However, the rights to at least the first two eventually reverted to Harris, and he released them again and again. For some time, his Los Angeles-based distribution company was known for releasing odd little films under several different titles (Claude Chabrol's *Les Biches* became *The Heterosexual*), and for buying or paying for the completion of very low budget films by first-time filmmakers, movies like *Equinox* (1970), John Landis' *Schlock* (1971, retitled *The Banana Monster*), and John Carpenter and Dan O'Bannon's *Dark Star* (1974). Harris has long been known for very sharp business practices, but has never been accused of anything worse than opportunism. People who had followed his career through these small-budget productions were surprised when he turned up as an executive on the expensive *Eyes of Laura Mars* (1978).

Steve McQueen and Olin Howlin seem to be the only actors of the principal cast who ever worked very much in Hollywood movies. Aneta Corseaut (who later spelled her first name more conventionally as "Anita") played the love interest for Andy Griffith on "The Andy Griffith Show," and had a small part in *Good Neighbor Sam* (1964). In *The Blob*, she's a conventional

50s teenager, always wearing a dress and usually a little sweater. Her performance is adequate.

Olin Howlin was a busy character actor in Hollywood, working in films at least as early as *Janice Meredith* in 1924. He used "Howland" as his last name until the early 40s, then switched to "Howlin" for the rest of his long career. Howlin rarely had large roles, and was instead just one of the dozens upon dozens of expert character actors who played sheriffs, hicks, minor villains, desk clerks, deckhands and so forth in Hollywood films. His two very small claims to SF immortality are, first, his showy little bit in *Them!*, in which he plays a drunken derelict the heroes question; he keeps singing "Make me sergeant in charge of the booze" until he lets slip some useful information; and, second, the old man who is the first victim in this film. He was also an undertaker in *The Return of Dr. X* (1939), notable as the film in which Humphrey Bogart played a vampire. *The Blob* seems to have been Howlin's last film; he died in 1959.

Other than McQueen, the rest of the cast ranges from high school level performances, to fully competent. Earl Rowe is somewhat stiff and amateurish as the main cop, but he's not unpleasant, and is quite likable on his own terms. Role names are available for very few of the other actors, so some of the smaller effective bits can't be praised by name, but the actor playing officer Jim is quite good. On the other hand, Keith (or Kieth) Almoney, as Jane's kid brother, is one of the most unpleasant child actors of all time.

Among these minor actors, there are several who have appeared in other films, including Vincent Barbi, John Benson, Steven Chase, Robert Fields, James Bonnet, Anthony Franke, and Pamela Curran (who was also in *Mutiny in Outer Space* in 1965). Writer Doug Crepeau says Godfrey Cambridge was an extra in this; he also appeared in *Son of Blob*.

Steve McQueen was billed here as Steven McQueen, for which several conflicting reasons have been given. According to Leslie Halliwell's *Filmgoer's Companion*, he was using that as his professional name, but he's billed as just plain Steve in *Somebody Up There Likes Me*. I have also heard that it was because this was his first starring role, but he wasn't being paid much, so he wanted all the credit space he could get.

His loose, honest style of playing fit the role perfectly, and is unusual though useful for this kind of film. He's not in the Actors School mode; he was simply too original for that. As is often true of stars, his range as an actor was limited, but people remembered him, and within his limits, he was usually excellent. It's often said that his TV series, "Wanted Dead or Alive," which was already on the air when *The Blob* opened, made McQueen a star, but that's not true: he made himself a star. His performance in *The Blob* is a star performance, written for and played by a star. You remember him as much as the monster itself, almost unheard of for a cheap science fiction film. It's no wonder that he immediately became known around the world.

He soon was one of the biggest stars of the 1960s, although probably only *The Great Escape* (1963) and *Bullitt* (1969) can be counted as genuine smash hits. But he also appeared in popular films such as *Love with the Proper Stranger* (1963), *The Cincinnati Kid* (1966), *The Thomas Crown Affair* (1968), *The Reivers* (1969) and *The Getaway* (1972). Oddly, after that point, his career disintegrated; he was still personally popular, but he made few films. He took several years in getting a film version of Ibsen's *An Enemy of the People* (1977) made; when it was finished, it received very little distribution.

In his last few years of life, McQueen attempted to make a comeback. *Tom*

Horn (1980) was an interesting reversal of the usual McQueen loner-as-hero character, but it was diffuse and ill-timed; Westerns were not popular. His last movie, *The Hunter* (1980), was also an oddball variation on his usual character, partly played for laughs, and featured one of his most likable performances. McQueen died of cancer in 1980, surely made more painful by his death being so public, as he was reclusive and publicity-hating in real life. He was one of the first main stars of the 60s to die, and although his passing didn't engender such powerful emotions as other deaths, such as that of John Lennon, it made all of us who grew up watching McQueen's career aware of mortality in a special way. He seemed above death in most of his films; after 1963, he died in only two of his movies. He was a distinctive screen presence, and he is missed.

For years, the movies that the crowd at the local theatre in the film are watching remained mysteries to horror and SF fans. They are *Daughter of Horror* and *The Vampire and the Robot* with Bela Lugosi. Inside the theatre on the screen, we see some preposterously overatmospheric scenes of a forest and laughing faces. Most assumed for years that these films were fictitious, and that the odd poster for *Daughter of Horror* that's briefly glimpsed in the theatre foyer was created for *The Blob*. After all, the poster for *Vampire and the Robot* is simply one for *Forbidden Planet* with another title pasted over it.

But oddly enough, *Daughter of Horror* at least is a real movie, and the sequence on the screen is actually from it. The movie is also called *Dementia*, and was written and directed by character actor Bruno Ve Sota. The 1953 film is sometimes credited to John Parker, but Ve Sota is its one true auteur, and it was his bid for movie immortality. Unfortunately, it's pretentious, impenetrable, boring and ludicrous; it's all style and no content. For more on Ve Sota as an actor, see *Attack of the Giant Leeches*; for further notes on him as a director, see the entry on *The Brain Eaters*.

As for the other film, *Vampire and the Robot*, it is likely to be a real film as well. (After all, why make up *one* fake title?) In 1952, Bela Lugosi went to London to appear in a film that has had several alternate titles, first being released as *Old Mother Riley Meets the Vampire*. It was eventually released in the United States in 1967 as *My Son, the Vampire*. In the movie, Lugosi plays a criminal who calls himself The Vampire, and does have a robot hanging around the hideout. As this movie has had so many different titles, it is far from inconceivable that it had regional U.S. release as *The Vampire and the Robot*.

The Blob was greeted with some amazingly contemptuous reviews, but I suspect this was more a matter of timing than any horrible quality of the film itself. Most major reviewers had only just begun to be aware that there was a horror movie boom on, and because of its blunt directness, *The Blob* was often singled out for special scorn.

In *Saturday Review* for instance, Arthur Knight was incensed. "Not so much horror as horrid," he said. "The real horror is that these pictures, with their bestialities, their sadism, their lust for blood and their primitive level of conception and execution should find their greatest acceptance among the youth." Knight conveniently overlooks the fact that this was equally true of the horror movies of *any* period, including those of his own youth. Horror films always have and always will "find their greatest acceptance among the young," as much for their imagination as their brutality. And each generation finds its own level of acceptable brutality, always outraging the next older generation.

The unnamed reviewer in *Cue* was equally harsh. "The sickening cycle of horror films (I think we may fairly well call them horrible as well) continues with the gruesome exhibit ... called *The Blob*... One person in every ten, according to statisticians, is emotionally disturbed. The percentage of children so affected is increasing, and it is not unlikely that these film horrors—growing week by week and battening on the pennies of thrill-hungry kids—are doing their fair share to promote this unhappy condition." When kids get out of hand, adults always look for convenient scapegoats, and always find these in activities adults don't indulge in: horror movies, comic books, video games. It's interesting that adults never do go after the kind of entertainment that appeals to *them*: boxing, crime shows on TV (well, some do attack these, but not by and large).

Other critics were a shade more sane, even if no more favorable. Although the *Monthly Film Bulletin* (which gave the film an average rating) thought that the "special effects are splendidly contrived," but the film became too un-believable, and "fails to maintain its early promise as an eerie exercise in Science Fiction hokum."

Harrison's Reports felt the color made it notable, but that otherwise "it is a routine program picture of its type.... Much that happens is so illogical that the whole never takes on even a semblance of reality." (I suspect this is an instance of "it's impossible and can't happen" being mistaken for "illogic.")

Howard Thompson of the *New York Times* was a sucker for thrillers, and often mentioned how he "shot through the roof" in some scary scene, but even he didn't care for *The Blob*. He thought it was "woodenly presented," even though it had a plot that "would have been enough to scare the quills off a porcupine." Thompson felt the picture "talks itself to death," but did note some virtues. "The camera very snugly frames the small town background," and he praised the projection room scene, but thought that "the acting is pretty terrible in itself."

More recent critics are also harsh on the film. Don Willis (I) said "McQueen gives maybe his most interesting performance; The Blob does some cute tricks; but it's all very lackadaisical and flat." In *Horrors from Screen to Scream*, Ed Naha (who gets the method of blob-immobilization wrong) said that it was "a pretty amusing relic of the fad-infested fifties." In *Future Tense*, John Brosnan had this to say: "About the most interesting thing in *The Blob* was Steve McQueen masquerading as a typical movie teenager, but his natural screen presence and his age (he was then 26) worked against him, as did the script, ... the special effects, ... the title song ... and so on." I certainly take exception with this: McQueen's age is never specified, he's not a typical anything, and could be in his 20s; the other "defects" are, as I see them, the primary *virtues* of the film. In *The Science Fiction Encyclopedia* Brosnan incredibly says *Son of Blob* was *superior* to the original, whereas it is faddish, limp and confused. In *Castle of Frankenstein* #7, Joe Dante didn't care for it: "This SF-horror comes out as slightly flat imitation of both *Rebel Without a Cause* and *The Creeping Unknown*.... Ridiculous ending." At least *Psychotronic* considered it an "ingenious teen science-fiction classic."

Overall, *The Blob* is not a classic, but it is respectable and intelligent, certainly worthy of more praise than it has generally received.

Blood of the Vampire

During the transition period from low-budget science fiction films to low-budget horror films, there were several movies in which the two genres mingled. *Blood of the Vampire* is one of these, and a rare British entry in the blended genres. It's a shade better than some of its class, but the lumpy direction, muddled plot and slow pace make it look much worse now than it did when it was new.

Almost inevitably, the story opens in Transylvania, the year, 1874. A little legend on the screen explains that vampires must be buried with a stake through their hearts, and sure enough, we see the body of Dr. Callistratus (Sir Donald Wolfit) impaled with a metal stake driven into his body by a huge executioner (Milton Reid) wielding a giant mallet. As the blood of the vampire wells up, the credits begin.

Later, hunchbacked, deformed and mute Carl (Victor Maddern) lurches into a bustling inn and approaches a drunken doctor. The two go to an old building where the doctor places a throbbing heart in Callistratus's damaged chest — apparently many doctors are capable of bringing the dead back to life — after which Carl kills the doctor. A bat flies over.

In 1878, in Carlstadt, Dr. John Pierre (Vincent Ball) is sentenced to death for his part in a death resulting from blood transfusions, which he performed to try to save a life. However, he is instead taken by a coachman — Carl — to a huge prison for criminally insane convicts, perched like Dracula's castle on a hill, where we learn the prison governor is the revived Callistratus.

He tries to force Pierre to help him. Callistratus is suffering from a rare blood disease, the result of the heart transplant, and he has been draining prisoners of their blood to prolong his life as he seeks a cure for his malady. (Jimmy Sangster's script ignores an important question: if his death and resurrection are what caused Callistratus to need blood like a supernatural vampire, why was he buried with a stake through his heart in the first place? Excellent foresight?) Pierre, being a Good Doctor, balks at this, especially when a drained prisoner dies. "You murdered this man!" he shouts at the aloof Callistratus.

"And you ruined an important experiment," Callistratus retorts, "which is infinitely worse." So it's clear we're back on the old mad scientist path.

Eventually, Pierre's loyal fiancée Madeleine (the beautiful Barbara Shelley) enters the prison, passing herself off as a chambermaid. Callistratus immediately takes a passionate interest in her, but this will prove to be his undoing: some time before, Carl had fallen in love with a portrait of her. Unlike the Hunchback of Notre Dame, Carl doesn't even need to be given water by Madeleine; her beauty alone is enough to entrap him.

Things become confusing near the climax. Pierre and an evil guard fight, and the guard falls onto a sword which has somehow become embedded in a coffin lid, skewering him in traditional vampire fashion. Carl strangles a prison official who is trying to rape Madeleine. Callistratus takes Madeleine downstairs to his laboratory, where he (unaccountably) keeps a body frozen in a big block of phony-looking ice. He also has an artificial heart beating nearby. We learn he had actually been in a state of suspended animation when he was staked at the beginning of the picture, and that his revival created a condition in which "one group of cells in my body is destroying the other."

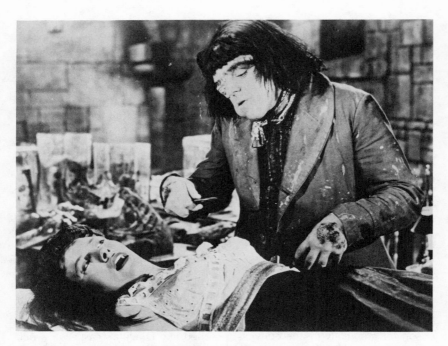

Barbara Shelley being menaced by Victor Maddern as Carl – not noted for his cleanliness – in the colorful but unconvincing Blood of the Vampire (1958). He appears to be about to stab himself.

Kurt (William Devlin), a prisoner befriended by Pierre and who was apparently torn apart by Callistratus' vicious guard dogs, is wheeled in; he's been reduced to a torso with one arm and a head. Pierre and Madeleine are chained to a wall. Carl confronts Callistratus, seeking to save Madeleine, but Callistratus shoots him. Kurt grabs Callistratus, who staggers across the room most unconvincingly until Pierre can reach him. He frees himself and Madeleine, and they make their getaway, pursued by Callistratus, and by Carl, who was only wounded. Madeleine and Pierre are outside the main gates and Callistratus is within the walls when Carl, shot again and dying, sets free the dogs, which tear Callistratus apart. All this happens in less than 10 minutes.

This climax is, clearly, very busy and neatly ties up all loose ends, but it is as contrived and unbelievable as the rest of the picture.

Jimmy Sangster's scripts for *Curse of Frankenstein* and *Horror of Dracula* had established Hammer Films as a company producing fast-paced, vivid shockers that were popular the world over. Sangster's contract with Hammer was apparently not exclusive, for this film was produced by Artistes Alliance Ltd., a short-lived British company. They saw the handwriting on the wall; *Blood of the Vampire* must have been written before *Horror of Dracula* was released.

The intent was to create a film as much like Hammer as possible, but either their instructions to the filmmakers, or Sangster and director Henry Cass let them down. The script is busy, but endlessly contrived with too many "colorful" characters, a ludicrous henchman, and stereotyped heroes and villains. It's a jumble of science fiction–horror themes: revival of the dead, scientific vampirism, suspended animation, mad scientist stuff. But none of these imbue the film with any interest; the story lurches from point to point, without the kind of intelligent enthusiasm that infused the best – and sometimes the worst – Hammer films. This is horror by the book, circa 1958, and it's pretty drab.

No one theme is dwelled on long enough, graphically enough, or with enough emphasis to become frightening or shocking. A rat calmly wanders through a scene with Pierre and Kurt. There are sadistic guards (who occasionally mutter in a dubbed-in gibberish that is quite mystifying), a smidgen of torture, some bloodletting, Carl's ugly face (that changes from scene to scene), a suggestion of rape, vicious dogs. It's as if Sangster had a checklist of horrific elements for inclusion, and just kept adding more until the list was exhausted.

Cass' direction is, at best, pedestrian, but he probably had very little time to do anything. His other films released in the United States, however, such as *The Hand* (1961), are just as uninspired, so it's probably as much a function of the director as it is of low budget and short schedule. Cass later left films altogether to work in the Moral Re-Armament movement.

Sir Donald Wolfit was primarily a stage actor in Britain. Most of his film performances were hammy, albeit generally enjoyably so, but he was never one of the glorious, Barrymoresque hams. His best film role was probably in *Room at the Top* (1959), but he was also good in *Lawrence of Arabia* (1962) and *Becket* (1964). His other films of most interest to readers of this book, *Svengali* (1954), *Satellite in the Sky*, and *Hands of Orlac* (1960) were not laurels in his crown. His autobiography, *First Interval*, appeared in 1954, and a biography, *The Knight Has Been Unruly*, by Ronald Harwood was published in 1971. He was best known for his touring Shakespearean company, and he was the basis of the character played by Albert Finney in *The Dresser* (1983).

In *Blood of the Vampire*, Wolfit is handicapped by being made up to resemble Bela Lugosi, which he otherwise does not. A widow's peak was added to his hairline, and something was done to his nose and upper lip. The result is an artificial, theatrical makeup which didn't increase the believability of Callistratus as a character. Wolfit appears to be suffering in the film, and brings no conviction nor much of his hammy joy in acting to the part. He seems to be doing it strictly for the money. Critics at the time tended to accuse Wolfit of overacting here, but looking at the picture today, it's hard to see how they reached that conclusion, unless it was the makeup and the role itself. If anything, Wolfit rather underplays the part of Callistratus, which was probably the wrong decision.

The film does have some virtues. The art direction by John Elphick is imaginative, and makes the picture look more expensive than it was. Several sets seem positively cavernous, but this probably was due more to judicious use of lenses on the part of cinematographer Geoffrey Seaholme. Other than this, Seaholme's photography isn't very good, being overlit and lacking in atmospheric stylization. He shows a certain flair for textures, but otherwise there is no mood to his work.

The cast members other than Wolfit do their jobs adequately, but little is called for. Characters pop up, deliver their lines, and are quickly disposed of. As Jack Moffitt said, the superintendent of prisons (Bryan Coleman) isn't allowed ample footage to get a good reason to ravish Shelley. "He simply says, 'My deah, we've met before!' and proceeds to throw her on the bed." Other than the leads, no character in this overpopulated film has ample footage for anything.

Victor Maddern is trapped in the role of one of the most ill-conceived characters of the 50s. Carl seems to be at once a restating of the Hunchback of Notre Dame and characters of the type once often played by Dwight Frye. Presumably, Callistratus keeps him around solely because he's so malleable; with his deformed, twisted hands, he couldn't be of much use in the surgery. After the murder of the drunken doctor in the opening scenes, until the climax, Maddern has almost nothing to do except stand around and look ugly. His sacrifice at the end is intended to generate sympathy, but it fails; this is not really the actor's fault. Denied a voice, given almost nothing to do physically, and hidden within an ugly, phony makeup, Maddern gets our sympathy as an actor, though not as a character.

Although the film was popular and still has its adherents, *Blood of the Vampire* was not greeted with much enthusiasm by critics, although most thought it somewhat above average. The *Motion Picture Herald*'s C.S.A. rated it "good," although he clearly was not fond of horror films. Charles Stinson, one of the few who named it science fiction, said in the *Los Angeles Times*, "It is gratifying to be able to turn in an on-the-whole good report on *Blood of the Vampire*.... [It] is intelligently scripted and well acted by a group of British performers." Even the hard-to-please Jack Moffitt said that "it rates more serious audience attention than most of the contemporary rash of domestic horror films. Direction by Henry Cass is brisk enough to keep yawning from being contagious to the audience." But "Rich" in *Variety* said that it was a "routine horror film, indifferently acted and written." Alan Frank (*Horror*) thought that "for its time, the movie was suitably horrific, despite a total lack of style in direction."

Despite its handsome art direction, *Blood of the Vampire* is notable today mainly for its bogus qualities: it is a fake Hammer film, about a scientific vampire, with an imitation Bela Lugosi.

The Brain Eaters

This is a dull little movie about furry parasites from the center of the Earth. It was never intended to be more than the bottom half of a double bill, and is largely forgettable—except that it is one of the most notorious examples of alleged plagiarism in science fiction film history, about which more later.

Just outside a small Illinois town, Glenn (Alan Frost) and Elaine (Jody Fair) discover a mysterious metallic cone; the scene dissolves to a shot of the U.S. Capitol dome, which almost matches the shot of the cone. Senator Powers (Jack Hill) goes to Illinois to investigate the cone, which everyone thinks is from outer space. A series of scientific tests are conducted, and we are informed that the "39.7 ratio test is negative." At one point, someone fires a shot into the opening on the cone—apparently forgetting that this might be considered a hostile act by whatever is in the cone—and the bullet comes ricocheting back to the opening.

The researchers go into town where they talk to the mayor, and we know something strange is up because the camera angles suddenly go all slanty. And the mayor's back is pulsing.

All of a sudden, he jumps up and Dr. Kettering (Ed Nelson), a researcher, swats the mayor's back, which makes him splay out. They discover an ugly furry thing on the mayor's shoulders, which had drilled into his head with two little antennae, and was controlling his actions.

They realize that the furry creature must be from the cone, or rather from a larger, unfound one, as they have deduced the one they were experimenting on was just a fuel section. Parasites need things to live on, such as the mayor, so Kettering, his assistant Alice (Joanna Lee), the senator and others try to find out who is being possessed by the parasites, and where the main cone is.

Messages can't get into or out of the little town, because communications are controlled by the people being ridden by the parasites. We see the little creatures in glowing glass spheres being carried around by their slaves.

Eventually, the main ship is located, and Kettering enters it to discover an old man (Leonard Nimoy), who is apparently helping the parasites with their conquest of the Earth. It all has something to do with the Carboniferous age, and Kettering realizes to his surprise that the parasites come from inside the Earth, rather than from outer space. It is never mentioned what they would have down there to live on, parasites though they are.

By this time, Alice is possessed, and there is an odd fight outside the telegraph office. It's all in one long master shot, but there is plenty of action. Possessed cops climb up the scaffolding around the cone to shoot at people on the ground, but this also makes them targets, and *they* are shot.

Inside the cone, the old man is revealed to be Professor Cole, who once was a prominent educator. "Now," he says solemnly, "I hold a position of a much higher order." And he serves the parasites willingly, without needing to be possessed. He sees their coming to the surface of the Earth as the dawning of a new age. "Our social order is pure, innocent," he says, and hopes to "free men from strife and turmoil."

Kettering leaves Cole to his maunderings, and rigs a wire from high tension lines to the cone. However, at the last minute the possessed Alice appears at the door of the cone to talk Kettering into joining the parasites. He runs over and argues with her, but the electricity kills both of them and all the creatures.

The film was produced by actor Ed Nelson (here billed as Edwin), at the time one of Roger Corman's "repertory company." He later broke away from this sort of thing by appearing in the TV series "Peyton Place," and since then is often seen on television. He makes an adequate hero, even giving himself a tragic death, but the production values are low as the film is so cheap, and it's heavy going.

Bruno Ve Sota directed *The Brain Eaters*; for comments on Ve Sota as an actor, see the entry on *Attack of the Giant Leeches*. He previously directed *Dementia* (1953), also called *Daughter of Horror*, a turgid, impenetrable psychological mystery, best known as the film playing at the movie theatre in *The Blob*. He later directed the excruciating *Invasion of the Star Creatures*, so I suppose this makes *The Brain Eaters* his best film as a director. It is not as terrible as the other two, and he tries hard to bring off a visual style — very hard.

Throughout, Ve Sota uses extreme camera angles (his cinematographer was Larry Raimond), often tilting the camera during scenes involving the parasites. There's a parasite's-eye-view shot, as it creeps along the floor and up the bed toward its sleeping victim, similar to shots in *Cult of the Cobra* (1955). Ve Sota attempts to develop an atmosphere suitable to a horror film. Occasionally we see shadows of parasite-ridden victims cast on walls, and he usually tries to let us know subtly that someone in a scene is carrying a parasite: the camera often prowls around behind someone slowly to reveal a pulsating lump on the back.

But he's defeated by his own pretensions—he can't tell a story coherently—and by the low budget. All the atmosphere in the world won't help an inept story and poor acting.

The script of *The Brain Eaters* was by Gordon Urquhart, who must have been quite naive. Readers of science fiction will probably have recognized the central idea already as that of Robert A. Heinlein's scary *The Puppet Masters* (1951). That novel was set slightly in the future, and the creatures that possessed people were sluglike aliens from Titan. The storyline differed, but the idea of parasites riding on human shoulders and controlling their actions is clearly from Heinlein's novel.

This wasn't lost on Heinlein, and he sued. He charged that *The Puppet Masters* had been "copied, imitated and appropriated," and lodged the suit against American International, Corinthian Productions (the company that produced the film), Roger Corman (who apparently was the unbilled executive producer) and scenarist Gordon Urquhart. (From a 13 January 1960 *Variety* clipping.) Heinlein told me in 1961 that the lawsuit never reached the point of a trial, as the defendants settled out of court. Supposedly, they agreed never to show the film again, but it did turn up on television later. (Heinlein's novel would make a splendid film itself.)

According to Mark McGee, Bruno Ve Sota was contacted by Corman, who was unaware of the connection with *The Puppet Masters*. Ve Sota read the book, but told Barry Brown that it didn't seem enough like his film to worry about. Clearly he was mistaken.

The parasites looked like horned tribbles, and have variously been described as "hamburgers equipped with tiny handlebars" (Jack Moffitt) and "bunny slippers" (actor Larry Vincent, in his persona as TV horror host "Seymour"). They are not very convincing or frightening as menaces, and the logic in having them be parasites from a region where there is nothing on which to be parasitic destroys any logic.

According to Mark McGee, Ed Nelson himself made the Brain Eaters. They were little windup-motor-powered orange ladybug toys often seen in stores during the late 1950s. McGee said Nelson cut up a fur coat and fastened sections to the ladybugs, then added pipe cleaners for the antennae. He had Bruno Ve Sota come to his house for a demonstration. Out in the garage, Nelson switched out the light and he started up the ladybug monsters; he shined a flashlight on the floor, and here came the thingies crawling along the ground. Ve Sota thought they looked good in that light, but when they got them into the picture, they looked like hell. The little beasties wouldn't move on grass, nor would they perform elsewhere as they should.

Except for Nelson, the cast is pretty drab. Alan Frost, Jody Fair and Jack Hill (later a director) make almost no impression. Joanna Lee is also inadequate, which might explain why she later gave up acting in favor of being a busy producer of TV movies. At that, she was quite good; among her credits are *Babe* (1975), *Mary Jane Harper Cried Last Night* (1977), *Like Normal People* and *Mirror, Mirror* (both 1979). As an actress, she said in the 24 May, 1979, *TV Guide*, "all I seemed to get were films like *The Brain Eaters* or *Plan 9 from Outer Space*," so while recuperating from an automobile accident, she turned to writing, and eventually worked her way up to deserved prominence in the restricted field of TV movies.

The actor playing elderly Professor Cole, the bearded spokesman for the parasites, was Leonard Nimoy, who later had no reason to even consider accepting roles in films of this nature.

The Brain Eaters had an especially large number of working titles, including "The Keepers," "Keepers of the Earth," "Attack of the Blood-Leeches" and "Battle of the Brain Eaters." The title finally chosen is misleading: they don't eat brains.

The reviews were mostly negative. Jack Moffitt dismissed it as "a routine science fiction job," but did give it some points for having the menaces come from inside the Earth rather than from outer space (a fact most reviewers got wrong). "Powr" in *Daily Variety* thought that "within [its] drawbacks, it is competently done." But the *Monthly Film Bulletin* critic disliked it, calling it a "crude and murky production" that was "all extravagant fiction and no science." He concluded that "the presentation remains as dull as the story is familiar, while the trick work and special effects are exceptionally tame."

Alan Frank (*SF*) thought it just "more of the usual 'B' picture nonsense, only worse," but *Psychotronic* felt it "a good, imaginative low-budget science-fiction movie."

The Brain from Planet Arous

In doing research for this film, I was startled to find that several reviews called the plot "conventional." Though the film is conventionally made, the premise is truly bizarre, anything but "conventional." The idea is too grandiose for the budget level, and it's silly throughout, but at least it's imaginative and unusual. The film also required a better actor for a leading man; though he tries, John Agar is not up to the requirements of the role.

Agar plays Steve March, a nuclear research scientist working somewhere in the Southwest with his partner Dan (Robert Fuller), who is first seen reading a science fiction magazine. Behind the credits, we see a light descend on a mesa, followed by a small explosion. After the credits, Steve and Dan discuss the intermittent radiation coming from Mystery Mountain, the mesa.

After Steve briefly meets with his fiancée Sally Fallon (Joyce Meadows), whose father John (Thomas Browne Henry) suggests that they not go, Steve and Dan take a Jeep out into the desert to investigate the radiation coming from Mystery Mountain. The trip is shown in some detail to emphasize the isolation of the mountain, which must give it its name. But they wind up at the usual location for low-budget SF movies: Bronson Caverns.

They explore the cave for a while, but the radiation suddenly increases, a huge floating brain with glowing eyes appears, kills Dan, and knocks out Steve.

A week later, Sally and John are expressing worry about Steve when he suddenly returns from the mountain, seemingly none the worse, with a slightly unlikely story that Dan has gone to Las Vegas. Steve is acting a little different, Sally notices. "I don't know what you mean, 'different,'" Steve complains. "I'm still the same old lovable character I always was." This line is followed by a close-up of Agar looking sinister, calculated to make the audience suspicious — at least those who were too slow to catch on to what happened in the cave.

Steve suddenly doubles up in pain. A moment later, he is smothering Sally with passionate kisses, which is a big surprise to her (once again, passion and scientific interests don't go together), and eventually this frightens her. Steve is jumped by a white German shepherd, George (Agar is doubled by a stunt man here), and he calms down, then leaves. "What happened to him out there?" Sally asks in fear.

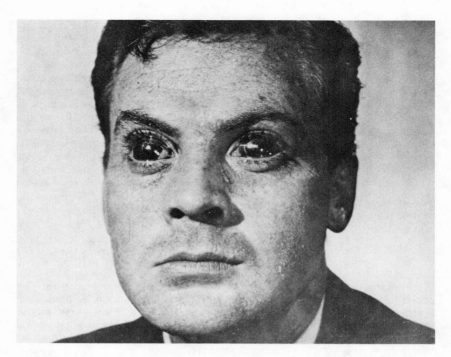

John Agar in enormous contact lenses painfully worn by the actor to indicate that he is in the mental thrall of The Brain from Planet Arous (1958). Alas, photos of the brain itself are scarce, and we must make do with this uncomfortable photo.

At his lab, Steve collapses into a chain in pain, and in poor superimposition, the alien brain leaves his body where it has been, and hovers in the room. He (and it is undoubtedly male) reveals his plans to the angry, frightened Steve in a rich and fruity baritone. The brain explains that he is from the planet Arous, and is named Gor. He needs Steve because his fame as a nuclear scientist will allow Gor, controlling Steve's body and actions, to take over the world more quickly. It is "strangely"excited by Sally, and may put that excitement to the test. "For as long as I wish to be," Gor says, "I am you." He then chuckles evilly, revealing at least something of a sense of humor, which puts him on a different level than most alien invaders, by and large a humorless group. (The brain's voices are done by Dale Tate.)

Sally and her father are still troubled by Steve's strange behavior, especially when he angrily tells them (at his lab) there's nothing wrong, while staring through a water jug (like a similar shot in *Attack of the 50 Foot Woman*). Sally and John go out to Mystery Mountain themselves.

Retracing Steve's steps, they find Dan's charred body in the cave. And another brain from planet Arous. This one is Vol, an interplanetary policeman, here in search of criminal Gor. "He voided that human," says Vol, referring to Dan. Vol asks the help of Sally and John in capturing Gor, warning that Gor/Steve must never know Vol is here. He tells them about the possession-ability of Gor. The two immediately agree to his plans, which seems a mite precipitous to me. I would not be immediately inclined to trust an enormous, floating brain found in a cave over the body of a dead friend.

Meanwhile, Gor is hovering around Steve's room, gloating about his plans to demonstrate his powers at an upcoming atomic test. "So, Friday the savages are going to play with their new toy," he says. "Gor will be there," and then he chuckles again. Illogically, he explains his points of vulnerability to Steve, who sits still while Gor outlines his plans of conquest. "When I am occupying your body, or in my present transitory form [he's transparent], I am without substance and indestructible." He also offers the only explanation in the film as to why the inhabitants of Arous are large disembodied brains: Arous is "a world where intelligence is all," he says, bragging about "the power of pure intellect."

Back at John and Sally's home, Vol shows up, and George shows signs of springing at the big brain. "Good dog, good dog," appeases Vol. He tells Sally and John that he has to force Gor out of Steve's body to vanquish him, or kill Steve while Gor still inhabits him. Vol, too, needs an earthly host, one that can be around Gor/Steve without the criminal brain being suspicious, so Sally suggests George, and Vol enters the canine container.

Over at Steve's place, Gor tells him that he is eventually going to have his way with Sally. "She gives me a very strange, a very new elation" purrs the brain, as Steve throws something at it. But Gor's in his transitional state, and the missile passes through the chuckling alien, which then repossesses Steve.

En route to the Fallon home, Gor/Steve pauses to watch a passing plane (a poor model). He stares at it with eyes that become huge and silvery, and the plane explodes as Gor/Steve laughs. After a nicely edgy scene with John, Gor/Steve offers Sally the world, and then comes on even stronger. "I'm going to introduce my new discovery," he tells her. "It will make the atomic bomb look like a firecracker." (Often in SF films of this period, a new power is mentioned that will make the atomic bomb look like a firecracker, sometimes a *wet* firecracker. It made me long for a power that would make a firecracker look like an atomic bomb.) He then makes a little speech about power, how it is what everyone, including him, wants, although he wants other things as well. "I want you, Sally," he says firmly, "and what I want, I take."

Hearing the reports of the plane crash, Sally urges Gor/Steve to go and see if there's anything they can do, but there isn't. Bodies are being hauled away, bodies that were charred like Dan's. Gor/Steve is beginning to let things slip, to exhibit alien attitudes even while pretending to be human. He says that the power that brought down the plane "could be the beginning of the end," and openly speculates that the force was "a power from outside this world"; the plane crash was just "to demonstrate its power over the Earth." No one seems suspicious when Steve adds that if a creature from another planet did have such power, it "could rule the whole world." (As Gor's plans are more grandiose— ruling the Earth is just a stepping-stone to bigger things— perhaps he didn't feel he was giving all that much away.)

Later, when Steve is gone, Vol tells the Fallons that Gor is vulnerable in his true state, to which he must return every 24 hours to assimilate oxygen. A sharp blow to the area that, in human brains, is known as the Fissure of Rolando, could kill Gor.

Back at Steve's place— the film shifts often between the two main locations— the sheriff turns up to ask him a few questions about Dan's death, and Gor/Steve's evil grin makes the sheriff suspicious. Too suspicious. Gor/Steve calmly tells the elderly lawman, "I killed Dan, and I killed those people in the plane. And now I'm going to kill you." And, with those silvery eyes, he does.

Elsewhere, the government concludes that the plane crash must be the result of an alien invasion, which seems a shade hasty. There's more talk by Gor/Steve about power, this time focusing on wealth and fame, as he tears leaves off a branch, apparently to demonstrate his ruthlessness.

At the military base, Gor/Steve finally reveals his plans, and to demonstrate his power, creates an explosion even more powerful than the atomic bomb's by just staring out the window through venetian blinds. He then insists on meeting with representatives of all the world's governments, on pain of losing their capitals, and laughs again as everyone rushes out of the room.

Vol reminds Sally of Gor's weakness, and she marks the Fissure of Rolando on the picture of a brain in a medical book as "Gor's Achilles Heel." Then we return to the military base, where in a highly superfluous scene, a general tells everyone again what Gor/Steve did the day before. To once again prove his power, Gor/Steve detonates another (model of an) airplane, then announces his master plan.

He wants all industrial and nuclear facilities to create an interplanetary invasion force, designed to conquer Arous, making Gor the master of the universe. Everyone seems reluctantly to agree to this, and Gor/Steve returns home. (No one follows him; no one wonders how nuclear scientist Steve suddenly got all this power.)

In the meantime, Sally has placed the page from the medical text under Steve's pipe rack, although the possibility that Gor might notice it first hasn't occurred to her. She couldn't have been certain that only Steve would see it, for in the last few scenes around the lab, Gor/Steve has taken to smoking a pipe. (Also near the pipe rack are a few science fiction magazines.)

She hides in the lab as Steve returns home, flops onto the couch, and Gor emerges. This time, instead of a mere superimposition, it's the real thing: a three-foot brain hanging there, five feet off the ground, played by an amazing balloon. The brain even has a dangling spinal cord.

Steve catches sight of the page from the book, while Gor praises himself, and just beyond the pipe rack, a convenient axe. Things happen fast: Sally bumps into the body of the dead sheriff and screams, Gor whisks across the lab at her, Steve grabs the axe, and starts hacking away at Gor. And whambo, the Brain from Planet Arous is scrambled.

There remains one of the more peculiar wrap-ups of SF film history. George, still inhabited by Vol, peers in the window and sees that Arousian justice has been served; Vol slips out and flies away. Now himself again, Steve asks Sally how she knew about Gor's weakness. George has come into the house, and Sally tells Steve there was another brain from planet Arous, and asks Vol to emerge. Nothing happens. "You and your imagination," chuckles Steve indulgently — this man who has just spent the past several days inhabited by an evil alien brain, which lies dead in the same room. Clinch and fadeout.

Apart from this bizarre madness involving flying alien brains, there's nothing very special about The Brain from Planet Arous; it's an ordinary little SF movie. It is, of course, more preposterous than some, as well as better made and more entertaining than others on its budget level. Despite being limited to three sets, it's fast-paced, inventively staged and has a good deal of incident in the course of its plot. Nathan Juran (here working as Nathan

Hertz) was not an outstanding director for any kind of film, but he was above average and knew how to keep a plot percolating.

Juran is hampered by the low budget; he is allowed few camera setups, and must duplicate some in the interest of economy. For instance, when Steve and Dan, and later the Fallons, go to Mystery Mountain, the exact same camera setups are used for each group; the two sets of scenes were shot at the same time. Although this was to save money, it has an interesting dramatic effect: both groups go through the same adventures up to the encounters with the two brains, at which point the story takes a different turn. In this way, it's suggested that the same fate might overtake Sally and her father, which generates a little suspense.

The staging of the actors throughout does overcome some of the budget limitations. Although this film may have been even cheaper than *Attack of the 50 Foot Woman* (it seems to have been made back-to-back with that Juran-directed film), the maneuvering of the actors around the set is as interesting, if not as fluid, as in films by Roger Corman. Except for a few silly horror close-ups of the brains' glowering eyes, and of Agar laughing with those big contact lenses in his eyes (both sets of eye shots are deliberately out of focus), there are very few close-ups in the film. The exteriors are largely confined to the area around the Fallons' house, Bronson Caverns and environs, and the scene of the airplane crash.

Ray Buffum's screenplay is a confusing mixture of the banal and the inventive. His other genre films were *Island of Lost Women* and *Teenage Monster*, the double bill with *The Brain from Planet Arous*, both of which were highly unimaginative. Here, the basic idea is oddball, but all Buffum can do with his body-snatching brains is to make one a standard world-conquering villain, complete with tyrant's chuckle. The good brain has scarcely any personality, and apart from suggesting the Fissure of Rolando as a point of vulnerability, plays little part in the story. As a matter of fact, once Gor is in his solid state, it's hard to imagine that a vigorously wielded axe wouldn't have sliced and diced him, no matter where he was struck.

Buffum's plotting raises questions: Why does Gor hide in the cave? What was the pulsing radiation for? Did Gor choose Mystery Mountain because of its name? At the end, all those military and political types should conclude that Steve is the villain; was he executed after the movie ended? After all, defending oneself by saying a giant flying brain was living inside you isn't likely to induce much belief, even with the dead brain as proof.

At least Buffum was trying to write dialogue that was more than the minimum necessary to get through the film. In the cave, Dan says "suddenly it's as cool as a well-digger's foot," a variation on a phrase that couldn't have been used in any movie made in 1957. Buffum tries to have quiet-shock dialogue, as in the scene in which Gor/Steve calmly and confidently tells the sheriff he's going to kill him; it's an attempt at a scene with a sting in its tail.

Buffum fails to generate a sense of towering alien intellect in the dialogue he gives Gor and Vol. Gor's grandiloquent pronouncements merely sound pompous and arrogant, not filled with evil power, though the writer does manage to give Gor a sense of humor. He cannot suggest a blend of alien and human motivations in the dialogue Steve has while Gor is inhabiting him; it just sounds like Steve with delusions of grandeur. Gor in his own body uses different language than when he is in control of Steve. All the gab over power is supposed to justify Gor's intentions, but it makes him seem insane, which perhaps was the idea.

As far as Vol goes, he is given the silliest line in the film. When he materializes in the Fallons' house, he immediately calms the dog down with "Good dog, good dog." Leaving aside any puzzlement as to whether Vol's speech is telepathic (he doesn't seem to have a mouth), this wacky attempt at humanizing the alien brain, showing he's kind to animals, fails utterly. It only makes your jaw drop.

In science fiction movies, the idea is usually that too much intelligence is bad for you, leading to dehumanization and cruelty. At the same time, it's typical that when one of these soulless geniuses gets control of a human being's body, the pleasures of the flesh tempt them mightily. What gives *The Brain from Planet Arous* a slightly more sophisticated feeling is that Gor is the *exception* to this among Arousians. Judging from Vol, most brains back there on Arous, wherever that might be, are decent, law-abiding sorts, full of good-will and niceness. Gor is a bodiless, heartless superintellect – but he's a criminal. I don't think Ray Buffum was trying to make a point here, but the idea that if evolution does eventually turn us all into flying brains, we'll still retain our humanity, is refreshing.

I've praised the film, in a way, for its novelty, but it may not be that original. Hal Clement's novel *Needle* (1950) is about an alien cop in pursuit of an alien criminal, hiding out on Earth. In this interesting juvenile, the aliens were both intelligent creatures formed of filterable viruses, in essence, benign parasites. They both could enter the body of a host organism, and work with it. Both criminal and pursuer find it necessary to inhabit local bodies to carry out their goals. There are a few major similarities to *The Brain from Planet Arous*. While I am not accusing Ray Buffum of plagiarizing Clement's novel (his first), the fact that SF magazines are displayed several times in the movie does raise the possibility that someone knew of Clement's work.

Among the other films written by Ray Buffum were *Girls in the Night* (1953, Jack Arnold's first feature), *The Black Dakotas* (1954) and *Teenage Crime Wave* (1955), which he cowrote. *Who Wrote the Movie?* also credits Buffum with *Playgirl* (1954) and *So This Is Paris* (1955), but other sources do not agree. Writers like Buffum wrote SF movies because that was where the money was, not because of any special affinity for the material.

The photography by Jacques Marquette (who also produced) is ordinary, although there is one interesting shot in Bronson Caverns. The repeated shots of Agar leering and laughing with those hideous contact lenses are almost all out of focus, undoubtedly for dramatic impact, but they just look out of place and curious.

Although it is greatly overused as a location, it's fun to see Bronson Caverns in all these films. The cave, a former quarry, has one long tunnel and three branches, like a trident, and lends itself to many different angles. Being a part of Griffith Park, it is highly accessible to anyone,* and so eventually winds up laden with litter. In *Brain*, Robert Fuller says "It's probably full of beer cans." And it is.

The score by Walter Greene is rather modern for a cheap film, with some

---

*Including you. In Hollywood, drive north (toward the hills) on Canyon from the intersection with Franklin Avenue. Just keep going, until the street (now in Griffith Park) stops altogether. A dirt road leads up the east side of the little canyon you're now in; walk up that dirt road until it ends – not far – and you will be facing Bronson Caverns.

invention and imagination. It doesn't deserve an album, but its main themes would be nice to have.

Most of the acting in the film is adequate, but not better. Meadows, Henry and Fuller all do what is expected of them, and don't bump into the furniture. Meadows played leads in a few other minor films in the 60s, then slipped into supporting parts. Henry, a fixture of these pictures, could have walked through a role like this, but as always, he gives it his all. He was a limited actor, generally playing his parts with a puzzled and worried frown; it was usually what was needed. Fuller is breezy and mild in his few scenes; he soon became (and remained) something of a television star, with regular roles in "Wagon Train," "Laramie" and "Emergency."

John Agar is out of his depth. As Steve-sans-Gor, he plays in his usual flat, slightly likable fashion; the character was pretty much the same he had in his other SF films: the genial, intelligent scientist who is at heart an ordinary Joe. When Gor takes over and he is supposedly suffused with a masterful power, Agar just can't deliver. For one thing, he just doesn't have the face for it; Agar's round, smooth countenance, with his clownish smile and round cheeks, just can't convey villainy, and his laugh is anything but sinister.

Agar is making a genuine effort at acting. He comes closest to seeming like a powerful, evil genius in the scene with the sheriff, but can't do anything in the scenes with the military leaders. He's a decent person, good-natured, likable and friendly; he's just not an actor.

The poor guy suffered for the film, though. In *Cinemacabre* #4, he told about wearing the big contact lenses: "They were extremely painful. To get the effect, they painted silver on the lenses and every time I'd blink my eyes, why some of that silver would come loose, you know, and it was like having sand in your eyes. It just hurt like heck." In some of the publicity photos taken of Agar wearing the lenses, tears are running down his cheeks. In *Fangoria* #39, Jacques Marquette told Tom Weaver the lenses could only be worn 15 minutes at a time.

The brain needed more money to work. The prop is silly-looking, with big, glowing eyes mounted on the front, and a very flat bottom; it pulsed, according to Marquette. The prop has little mass, and hung from (impressively-invisible) wires, Marquette told Weaver. Mark McGee quoted Agar as saying the actor was offered a percentage of the film if he would defer his salary, but when he saw the prop (McGee believes it was a balloon), he wished them luck and took the salary. I'm not sure how a flying brain could look anything but silly, in fact. Even the ghastly little monsters in *Fiend Without a Face* look preposterous, until they start squirting goo.

It's too bad that some slight variation between Gor and Vol wasn't indicated, but the same prop is used for both.

There are a few curious shots of Agar slumped in a chair at the right of the screen; the brain was clearly intended to be seen at the left, but I presume the budget was too low to insert the planned shots of the brain. These scenes look off-balance, and you keep waiting for the brain to turn up.

The shots of the brain in superimposition are insultingly bad; although the picture is hardly a classic, it deserved better effects work.

One curious question, left unanswered, is just how the name of the planet Arous is pronounced. When Gor first speaks, he pronounces "Arous" as a homonym of "Eros," but Vol calls it "arras."

One of the stranger side effects of the film—perhaps the only one—was that it somehow gave Stephen King the inspiration for his first published novel

Carrie, or so he told an interviewer. Clips from the film were included in 1982's loathesome *It Came from Hollywood*.

The reviews of *Brain from Planet Arous* were fair. *Motion Picture Herald* thought the movie was "not so imaginative," that Buffum's script was "standard," and that the "greatest appeal is to the action houses." The *Motion Picture Exhibitor* felt that while it was "wildly unbelievable," some "interesting special effects are achieved. It is a superior film in every respect to its companion feature in the package, *Teenage Monster*."

"Neal" in *Weekly Variety* thought the movie was "better than average" and that "there's good suspense worked into the familiar ... screenplay."

James Powers of the *Hollywood Reporter* noted that teenagers judged SF films as being either "cool" or "stupid," and that *Arous* "seems to be in the 'cool' category," as "within its modest limits [it is] intelligently and resourcefully produced.... It plays well and interestingly. The dialogue is sensible, the characters never extreme, and the film tricks are capably done. The direction is crisp and clear and the acting carries conviction."

However, the unnamed reviewer at the *Los Angeles Times* considered the film to be "pure hash from the cutting-room floor." Margaret Harford of the Los Angeles *Mirror-News* had an odd comment: "The trick effects are good and there's enough suspense to keep science-fiction clubbers satisfied. But please, don't renew my membership."

I concur most with the *Monthly Film Bulletin*; it gave the film an average rating, and called it "a far-fetched science fiction thriller in the low budget class, well paced and energetic, but disappointingly conventional in format."

Parish and Pitts called the film "undernourished" but said it had one interesting aspect: at the climax the two brains battle it out. This does not happen at all.

"Dr. Cyclops," reviewing the videotape release in *Fangoria*, called it "a rusty old clunker [but] a videocassette that trash fans will not want to miss." Alan Frank (*SF*) described it as "energetic hokum with poor special effects," while *Psychotronic* enthused about it as "the ultimate John Agar film! A hugely enjoyable invasion-attempt story."

The film was made for a certain market, the mostly-teenager crowd that were these movies' biggest market by this period. They probably wouldn't have been interested in a story about aliens that didn't involve (at least) an attempt at conquering the world. It's pointless to speculate on the film that, given more money and a better script, *The Brain from Planet Arous* might have been. It's a cheap little shocker, reasonably effective despite lapses into ludicrousness.

The Colossus of New York

There are those who find this William Alland production for Paramount an unsung classic, but I find it a dry and ponderous story, bearing resemblances to both *Frankenstein* and *The Golem*. The film is crippled by its adherence to a monster-movie formula, by its low budget, and by its lack of imagination. Eugene Lourié directed it from a script by Thelma Schnee. John F. Warren's photography is good, John Goodman's art direction is occasionally very imaginative, and the score by Van Cleave, which is a composition for one piano, is unusually interesting, although not really appropriate.

The Colossus of New York was prepared as half of a double bill with *The Space Children*, a livelier movie, but they don't seem to have played as a "shock package" anywhere; the movies were used as general support for other Paramount films. They were both produced by William Alland, and both stories center around children, presumably because that's who the films were made for. (Actually, teenagers were the biggest fans of SF movies.) However, in the case of *The Colossus of New York*, the involvement of the child is minimal and forced.

Dr. Jeremy Spensser (Ross Martin) has just returned from Stockholm where he won the "International Peace Prize," and as he runs out into the street to rescue a toy plane for his son Billy (Charles Herbert), he is struck by a truck and killed. His father, Dr. William Spensser (Otto Kruger), also a brilliant scientist, determines that Jeremy's genius must not die. The body in the coffin has bandages around the head, a broad hint as to what William is up to.

He wants Jeremy to accomplish the goals of geniuses, as he sees them: the first level is merely selfish; at the second level, the genius devotes himself to the needs of his family and community; and at the third, best, level, the genius works to help all mankind, which was the level Jeremy reached. His work must not be allowed to die, decides William.

He calls his other son Henry (John Baragrey), heretofore overlooked, down into the basement laboratory, where William reveals he has kept Jeremy's brain alive.

William's brilliance is in the field of surgery, and Henry's is in the area of automation and robotics. He insists that Henry, who has always been jealous of Jeremy's superior intellect and greater happiness, build a robotlike body to house Jeremy's brain so that Jeremy can continue to benefit mankind. At least, that is William's ostensible purpose; actually, of course his pride is at stake: he was immensely proud of Jeremy, and William's ego will not let his son die in peace.

The result is an eight-foot cloaked thing resembling a robot (and often called one, in writings on SF films), with an expressionless face that somewhat resembles Ross Martin. It takes a year of work to build the Colossus (played by Ed Wolff), and during that time Jeremy's widow Anne (Mala Powers) has become friendly with Professor John Corrington (Robert Hutton), who is also working on the project, which is being kept secret from Anne and Billy. Neither know that Jeremy's brain is alive, much less that it is housed in a huge metallic body.

The Colossus catches sight of itself one night, and shrieks electronically. This wakes Anne, and for some reason—female intuition?—it reminds her of Jeremy's voice. (When quiescent, the Colossus goes "uvvuvvuvv.")

During the year of work on the Colossus, it (or he?) develops precognitive powers, predicting the collision of the *Andrea Doria* and the *Stockholm*. He also loses almost all human compassion, which Carrington predicted.

When William objects to a new line of research, the Colossus uses his glowing eyes to hypnotize him, and goes outdoors into the garden (his footsteps make clump-clump sounds even on the grass), where he meets and befriends Billy; fatherly love remains. The Colossus tells the absurdly naive child that he is a giant (and Billy calls him Mr. Giant). He even brings the boy a plane like the one Jeremy was chasing when he was killed. "Are you a good giant or a bad giant?" Billy asks—the lines seem to have been written for a child much younger than Herbert—and the Colossus responds, "I try to be good, but it isn't easy."

Mala Powers hoisted by Ed Wolff costumed for his title role as The Colossus of New York (1958), the robot in a cloak; if you look very closely between Wolff's feet, you can see where the cord powering his glowing eyes has been retouched out.

When the Colossus returns to the lab, he's furious with William, who had let him believe that both Anne and Billy were killed. He smashes the controls that can switch him off at long distance (William and Henry prudently put the on-off switch on the Colossus himself in a position he couldn't reach), and begins running the show. He's jealous of Henry, who has been courting Anne (who isn't interested); Henry wants out of things.

The Colossus forces William to make arrangements to meet Henry with enough money to get away, but after walking along the bottom of the East River (and going clump-clump again), the Colossus climbs some riverside stairs (used most famously in Hitchcock's *Vertigo*) and surprises Henry, killing him with totally unexplained rays from those glowing eyes.

Back at the lab, the Colossus smashes a project designed to grow ice-resistant vegetation, and thus increase harvest periods. Why try to save the lame? the Colossus asks, announcing his intention to rid the world of humanitarians.

Darling Billy, who spreads word that a giant is hanging around the estate, says, "I love Mr. Giant. He's keen.... He wants me to call him Daddy."

Finally, while William, Anne and Billy are visiting the United Nations, the Colossus decides to act on his goal of wiping out humanitarians. He arrives at the U.N., smashing through a huge sheet of glass. He stands in front of the swords-into-plowshares inscription, and uses his eye rays to wipe out a dozen or so people. He suddenly plucks up Billy, for Jeremy's mind in the robot's body has suddenly realized that "without a soul there's nothing but monstrousness," and tells the boy where to reach the switch that will turn him off, because "I don't think I can stop myself." The boy does, and the Colossus collapses. As everyone walks off, tears trickle from his dimming eyes.

The Colossus of New York is just a variation on a combination of old themes; it echoes *Frankenstein* in its emphasis on bringing a giant to life, *Donovan's Brain* in preserving a brain which loses its humanity for lack of a body, and *The Golem* in being destroyed by a child.

According to Paul Mandell in *Fantastic Films* #17, Eugene Lourié made the film while waiting the go-ahead on *The Giant Behemoth*. The idea behind *Colossus* intrigued Lourié, but the final script didn't please him and he wanted out of the project, but as it took only eight days of shooting, he went ahead. He told Mandell that "I remember very little of the actual shooting as I remember very little of the scarlet fever I had when I was eight years old."

The other features Lourié directed all involved giant monsters smashing up cities. He directed several TV series episodes during the 1950s, but it is primarily as an art director that Lourié has made his fame; occasionally, his designs are superb. He worked with Jean Renoir on *Rules of the Game* (1938), and in the United States, first continued his association with Renoir, and went on to work on a surprising variety of films, ranging from *Confessions of an Opium Eater* (1962) through *Burnt Offerings* (1976) to *An Enemy of the People* (1977). Unlike some other famous designers, Lourié has never sought to impose his own style on the material, but instead provides the best possible imagery for the film in question. I don't think there's any other great designer who has a more eclectic range of films: two for Sam Fuller, *Shock Corridor* (1963) and *The Naked Kiss* (1964), big-budget films like *The Battle of the Bulge* (1965) and *The Royal Hunt of the Sun* (1969) mingle with low-budget offerings like *A Crack in the World* (1965, for which Lourié also did the effects) and *Bikini Paradise* (1967). As Leon Barsacq said in *Caligari's Cabinet and Other Grand Illusions*, Lourié has had "a singular career which has often veered from the sublime to the ridiculous and back again," but will be remembered for his work on eight films for Jean Renoir, including that great French director's finest movies.

In an interview with Al Taylor and David Everitt in *Fantastic Films* #25, the late actor Ross Martin commented on Lourié as a director: "Mr. Lourié was a little tentative; he didn't jump in with both feet. He was very gentle with the actors, an extremely kind, extremely thoughtful kind of director. He wasn't crisp or aggressive about telling us what he wanted and where he wanted us to go. It was more of a search, more European in style, I would guess, than it was American. And he was under the kind of pressure that you get in television. We were on a very short shooting schedule. Mr. Alland wanted the picture done in something like three or four weeks." (Actually, two weeks, but Martin was on the film as an actor a relatively short time.)

The designs for *The Colossus of New York* are credited to John Goodman and Hal Pereira, although Pereira's credit was almost certainly only contractural, as he was the head of Paramount's art department. Set decoration was by Sam Comer and Grace Gregory. The most interesting (and most used) set in the film is the basement laboratory, which has a lot of visual interest, especially in the scene in which Jeremy's brain is floating in a tank. Fine wires run from the brain all over the room, in a bizarre and interesting pattern; it looks as if the brain is the literal nerve center of the room.

On the other hand, the design of the Colossus itself, while visually arresting, is cumbersome and illogical. The face and hands were the work of Charles Gemora, the rest was designed by Ralph Jester. There is no justification for housing the brain in any kind of mobile body, and to place it in one that is so similar to the human form seems psychologically counterproductive, as it would only remind Jeremy of everything he's now missing.

The Colossus is carefully draped in a heavy cloak, which makes it look more massive and photogenic, but you pause to wonder why a robot (or a thing like a robot) needs clothes at all. The face is interesting: it's expressionless, but the open mouth works slightly. The grilles under the eyes are all too clearly designed for Ed Wolff to see through. When the Colossus walks about, he tends to move (understandably) very stiffly; the jerky, robotlike motion is aided by what seems to have been the removal of occasional frames when the film was printed. Wolff was not very mobile in the cumbersome suit. According to the article/interview by Taylor and Everitt, Wolff was 7' 4" and began in films as early as 1925, as one of the mob in *Phantom of the Opera* chasing Lon Chaney. Wolff accidentally disarrayed the Phantom makeup, but Chaney wasn't annoyed, and allowed Wolff to watch him reapply it. Wolff was often used down through the years when a huge stunt man was required, as in the 1936 *Flash Gordon*, a serial in which Wolff played "The Gocko." In *Return of the Fly*, Wolff played the fly-headed man.

The Colossus costume weighed 160 pounds and was eight feet tall (on Wolff). It was made of burlap, plastic, rubber and chicken wire. "To get in or out of the costume," said Taylor and Everitt, "was a 40-minute affair and during those times when the robot [sic] wasn't needed on the set, Wolff could only rest by reclining on a specially-built rack. Taking up space inside the outfit along with Wolff were the batteries, cables, air tanks and oxygen tubes that moved the mechanical parts and kept the big man breathing."

To keep the Colossus acting more or less like Jeremy, Ross Martin worked with Wolff. He told Taylor and Everitt, "we rehearsed with me delivering the [Colossus'] lines into a microphone just off stage with Mr. Wolff moving about as though he were delivering the lines. We were trying to get as much of the feel of the young doctor who had been killed into the actions of the robot [sic] as we could. On occasion, I'd step into the set and act the scene out as the robot, without the costume. Then Mr. Wolff, who had observed my actions, would step in and do the scene following what I had done. After the rehearsal, I would try to integrate my dialogue to his movements.... We missed cues on several occasions but didn't really have the time to go back and get it perfectly right."

Thelma Schnee's script has poor dialogue and several peculiar ideas. The dialogue for Billy is especially bad, and makes Charles Herbert, never a good child actor, seem retarded. Everyone else speaks in florid, stilted language, more suited to a 40s pulp short story than to a 50s SF movie.

The Colossus' suddenly-developed eye rays go unexplained, but no one in the story seems surprised by them. They were probably added because, after Gort in *The Day the Earth Stood Still*, as well as lesser films like *Target Earth*, movie and comic book robots often had ray-emitting eyes. The Colossus is virtually a robot, and the suit was cumbersome enough to prevent swift movement, so a means of killing people at a distance had to be devised; hence the rays. It's too bad that at least a quick justification for them wasn't written into the script.

Some have objected to the scenes in which the Colossus crosses the East River (or is it the Hudson?) by simply walking along the bottom, but I found it an intriguing idea. Because the shot of it emerging from the river is footage run in reverse, it emerges from the river completely dry, but that's understandable. The suit was hard enough to move in dry; that giant cloak soaking wet would have been so heavy Wolff probably wouldn't have been able to move at all.

The relationship with the boy goes nowhere, and certainly has none of the intended poignancy. The robot clumps out of the bushes, talks to Billy, and clumps back in. There isn't any real payoff for this; *any* kid could have turned the machine off at the end; the action does not arise from any father-son relationship.

The idea that a brain divorced from a body would lose compassion is simply lifted from *Donovan's Brain*, but it's questionable. Is it our heavy animal bodies that give us human compassion? Aren't we capable of feeling emotional ties when we aren't dragging around 150 pounds or so of meat? If that's the case, quadriplegics would all be soulless, selfish and arrogant, and they don't seem to be.

Nathan Van Cleave's piano score for the film is expressive and moody, and an odd choice for such an unventuresome picture. It becomes repetitious at times, especially near the climax with the Colossus lumbering back and forth from house to Manhattan, but it's imaginative and intelligent, two qualities not otherwise applicable to the film. It is inadequate for the big action climax, however.

Otto Kruger seemed to feel he was above his material, and gives an unfeeling performance. He doesn't quite walk through the picture, but he certainly doesn't seem involved. Everyone else is either adequate, like Robert Hutton, stiff like John Baragrey, or inadequate, like Charles Herbert. Ross Martin puts more into his few minutes on screen than the other performers do with the whole picture to work in.

Reviews were as tame as the film. Given the lowest rating by the *Monthly Film Bulletin*, the movie rated a terse dismissal: "There is nothing colossal about this colossus." The writer praised the "electronic" music, but judged the film "tame and unexciting." On the other hand, another British review journal, *Picturegoer* (quoted by Alan Frank), was more impressed. "A neat, brisk plot and skilful dialogue manage to pilot through this fanciful nonsense with some deadpan conviction."

Variety's "Gilb" said it was an "okay horror meller for the moppet trade," but decided that adults would find it "pretty hokey fare," and added that the "story, direction and performances are just about as mechanical as the monster." The *Motion Picture Exhibitor* said "there is little that is new in this science fiction meller, which features another mechanical monster with an urge to destroy."

Jack Moffitt found something to praise: "It is not as good as the best science fiction pictures," he said, "but it is far better than most of the quickies being turned out in this category," but summed up by saying the film was "adequate."

Seen today, *The Colossus of New York* seems somewhat frustrating. It has some interesting designs, a workable amalgam of borrowed ideas, and an unusual central figure, but the film itself is routine and flat.

The Cosmic Monster

The Strange World of Planet X was the original title of this minor and mostly-forgotten British film, the same as that of the novel by actress René Ray on which it was based. It was reviewed in *Film Daily* as *The Crawling Terror* (perhaps a mistake on the reviewer's part), and the ads called it *Cosmic Monsters*. However, the title in the United States on screen definitely is *The Cosmic Monster*. It has to be, as one of the last lines in the film is "*Man* is the cosmic monster." This reversal, making *us* into the monster of the title, is one of the most interesting aspects of the film, usually regarded as dull and pedestrian.

My memory of it differs a little. I saw it on a double bill with its standard co-feature, *The Crawling Eye* (also made by Eros, also starring Forrest Tucker), and at the time, both seemed impressive to me. Both Richard North and I immediately recognized the films as imitations of the two Quatermass films, which we'd enjoyed tremendously. However, we both also realized that *The Cosmic Monster* and *The Crawling Eye* were lesser creations, cheap rather than economical, and not as well-thought-out as the Quatermass duo. Still, the two seemed above average for the period and quite satisfactory. Although I've seen *The Crawling Eye* several times since that night, I have not seen *The Cosmic Monster* again, yet I still remember certain scenes from it with an uncomfortable vividness.

Most of the early scenes in the laboratory are gone from my memory, along with much of the material with the alien "Smith" (Martin Benson). But I do have recollections of a little girl walking through a dark and sinister forest which, just outside her range of vision, crawls with ravenous giant insects. I recall her seeming like a little spot of light moving through a dank, ominous tangle of vegetation, with these unspeakable horrors adding a sinister aura of menace. In my memory, it's as if Shirley Temple was Little Red Riding Hood in a Doré forest full of particularly awful wolves.

I also recall silhouettes of giant centipedes—a particular phobia of mine—crawling up a window, and some kind of nasty creature devouring parts of a person's face; the heroine becomes entangled in a giant spider web.

I mention these memories because I want to emphasize the great power these films had, even the least of them, when they tried to be vivid. There was, by those in the audience, a willing, even grateful suspension of disbelief. We *wanted* these films to be memorable, and partly because they occasionally did achieve a riveting image, but mostly because of that desire by us for something exciting and full of wonder, memories became powerfully etched in our minds. For those of us who grew up in the 1950s, this kind of engraved, astonishing imagery usually came from science fiction films. I know someone who was so overwhelmed by *The Creature from the Black Lagoon* that, in his memory, it was not just in 3-D, but vivid Technicolor. Like all memories, these can become distorted with time; there's little doubt that *The Cosmic Monster* isn't as effective as I recall. Too many people whose opinions I respect denigrate the film; in a way, I hope I never do see it again. The movie whose fragments remain lodged in my memory matters too much for me to want it displaced by reality.

In watching these films again, we are not attempting to relive our childhoods—few really would want to do that—we are trying to recapture the uncritical, receptive reactions we had at that age. And often, even the worst of these films can accomplish that.

In a laboratory in the English countryside, Dr. Laird (Alec Mango) conducts experiments in metallurgy, trying to find if powerful magnetic fields can change the basic qualities of metals. He's assisted by American Gil Graham (Forrest Tucker). When Laird's computer assistant is killed during an experiment, he is replaced by French Michele Dupont (Gaby André), and a romance begins to bloom between her and Gil.

Strange events and disappearances occur in the vicinity, and one evening Gil and Michele meet the enigmatic Mr. Smith, who has been hanging around for a while.

In the meantime, little Jane (Susan Redway) has been befriended by a wandering tramp, who sleeps in the woods surrounding Laird's laboratory. Later, the tramp turns up with strange burns on his face, and a desire to strangle women. And then there's those marauding giant insects.

Smith reveals to Gil and Michele that Laird's experiments with supermagnetism have punched a hole in the ionosphere, permitting cosmic rays to pour down on an area 80 miles across. The result: mutated insects and psychotic tramps. (Actually, the ionosphere does not shield us from cosmic rays.)

Gil and Michele try to persuade Laird to give up his experiments but, perhaps affected by the cosmic rays himself, he has gone insane and barricades himself in the laboratory.

Meanwhile, Jane's teacher (Catherine Lancaster) barricades herself in the schoolhouse, besieged by more giant insects which bang on the walls and crawl over the windows. Jane herself has found an enormous egg in the woods. (Note: the latter action may occur earlier in the film; the available synopses are none too complete.)

Smith has friends in a spaceship, who blow up Laird's laboratory, putting an end to the menace. Gil and Michele ask Smith if it will ever be possible for mankind to join the community of worlds Smith represents. He seems dubious; to the aliens, Earth is a mysterious place, "the strange world of Planet X," full of beings whose motives and thought processes are impossible for the aliens to understand. To them, he says, "Man is the cosmic monster."

Forrest Tucker made three of these low-budget SF films back to back in England, and fared better with *The Abominable Snowman* and *The Crawling Eye* than with *The Cosmic Monster*. His big bluff heartiness is out of place in the role of a thoughtful scientist, and he's never really been an effective romantic lead—he looks like he'd rather playfully wrestle with a girl than seduce her.

Alec Mango, playing Laird the mad scientist here, also appeared in *Captain Horatio Hornblower* (1951), *The Seventh Voyage of Sinbad*, *3 Worlds of Gulliver* (1960), *Freud* (1962) and *Frankenstein Created Woman* (1967), among many other films.

Gaby André makes an attractive heroine, but is not a particularly good actress; she soon returned to Europe, and her credits in American-released films are few; among them, *East of Kilimanjaro* (1957), *Goliath and the Dragon* (1960) and *Pussycat Pussycat I Love You* (1970).

Martin Benson as the enigmatic alien Mr. Smith is the best thing about *The Cosmic Monster*. His smooth performance and faintly unusual looks made him an ideal choice for the part. He's a frequent supporting player in major films, occasionally turning up in SF thrillers. Among his other films: *Exodus* (1960), *3 Worlds of Gulliver*, *Gorgo*, *Night Creatures* (1962), *Cleopatra* (1963), *Goldfinger* (1964, as gangster Mr. Solo, left in a car crushed for scrap), *A Shot in the Dark* (1964), *Battle Beneath the Earth* (1967, as the main villain), and *The Omen* (1976).

I know almost nothing about Gilbert Gunn, the director of *The Cosmic Monster*. I've been able to identify only *Girls at Sea* (1958) and *Operation Bullshine* (1959) of other films he directed. He directs *The Cosmic Monster* to be appropriately laden with shadows, eerie shapes and some suspense, but it's also stodgy and slow.

The film was based on a British television serial that was apparently quite popular, and that serial was based on the novel *The Strange World of Planet X* by René Ray, published in 1957. (Her novel may be an adaptation of the teleplay.) Even the thorough *Science Fiction Encyclopedia* — which called the book "a routine SF novel about the fourth dimension" — was unable to discover anything about René Ray, except that she had written another fantasy earlier, *Wraxton Marne* (1946). John Clute, who wrote the very short entry on Ray, was unaware that she was a reasonably well-known British actress, born in 1912, on stage from childhood. According to *The Filmgoer's Companion*, she "often played downtrodden waifs," and appeared in *The Passing of the Third Floor Back* (1935), *The Rat* (1938), *The Return of the Frog* (1939), *If Winter Comes* (1947) and many other films. It's a little odd that no room was found for her in the cast of *The Cosmic Monster*.

As I recall them, the special effects in the film are elementary, with only a couple of big-bug props, and those briefly seen. For the most part, the insects are routinely rendered by means of macrophotography of real bugs, usually placed in the scene with live actors by means of rear-screen projection or elementary mattes. Except for the scene with the devoured face, there was little interaction between the actors and the bugs.

The film has some fairly good design, particularly of the giant egg little Jane finds, but it has an aura of cheapness: things done hastily for effect and for as little money as possible. There's little style to the film.

Reviews were not favorable. In *Variety*, "Rich" called it a "gloomy little item" which was "not ingenious enough or sufficiently 'horrific' to add up to anything but a naive [and] singularly uninspired pot-boiler.... [The monsters] look rather daft and add up to fairly tepid entertainment.... Robert Sharples' music has an efficiently eerie note [but] Joe Ambor's camera work is not sufficiently distinguished to hide the phoniness of the studio-made insects, designed to provide thrill which is more revolting than hair-raising."

The *Motion Picture Herald* thought the film only "fair." Giving it a II rating, the *Monthly Film Bulletin* found some worth in the film. "This piece of British science fiction is resourcefully directed, and only some badly handled process work lets the film down. The giant ants, spiders, worms, etc. are all too obviously stock micro-cinematographic material; and the spectacle of the cast running in terror from them is a trifle absurd. Only a most unpleasant shot of an ant feeding off a human face makes the film unsuitable for younger audiences."

Parents thought the film "Good of Kind," and *Film Daily* was actually quite impressed, calling it "a neat little science fiction chiller, more scientifically plausible than many. With plenty of action, suspense and properly terrifying shots of giant insects, [it] should be pleasing to all who favor this type of film."

The scant recent commentary is on the negative side: *Castle of Frankenstein* #8 called it "dull and boring," Alan Frank (*SF*) thought it a "naive 'B' feature replete with abysmal process photography," and Don Willis (I) dismissed it as "poor."

It's a little unusual that *The Cosmic Monster* hasn't popped up again somewhere. With a slight but burgeoning interest in SF movies of the 1950s in general, and British films *and* giant insect films in particular, it should surface someday. I believe this is the *only* giant insect 1950s British SF film, so why hasn't someone rediscovered it? Perhaps it really is just as mediocre as the reviews indicate, but I have my memories.

The Crawling Eye

Nigel Kneale made a strong impact on British science fiction films; when his own teleplays didn't serve as the source of scripts, *imitations* of Kneale were sometimes filmed. In December, 1956, a six-part serial by Peter Key, "The Trollenberg Terror," was broadcast on Britain's ATV channel. If the film that resulted, which had the same title in Britain but was *The Crawling Eye* in the United States, is any indication, while the teleplay was imitation Kneale, writer Key misunderstood much of what made Kneale's work effective and believable. He got the scientific mystery aspect down fairly pat, and also tried to have a sense of an ongoing story of which we are seeing just the climax. But whereas Kneale's tendencies toward gruesomeness were solidly motivated in his well-crafted plots, Key seems to have been gratuitously violent here and there.

In *Starburst* #16, writer Tise Vahimagi says, "'The Trollenberg Terror' premiered with 'The Mind of Ann Pilgrim'.... Quentin Lawrence was at the helm ... as producer-director, with Sarah Lawson, Rosemary Miller and Laurence Payne heading the cast.... [It] told of an alien influence affecting various people at an Austrian resort located at the foot of the towering Trollenberg mountain. The aliens weren't 'revealed' — if that is actually the word for it — until the fourth episode, entitled 'The Power of the Ixodes.'" In translating from TV to movies, *The Crawling Eye* retained Quentin Lawrence as director and Laurence Payne in the cast, but lost "Ixodes," the comic-book name for the aliens, which in the film are called nothing at all. Not even aliens, and certainly not crawling eyes.

The film opens with mountain climbers suffering a mysterious accident: one of three men falls but is caught by his rope. When his friends haul him up, they discover to their horror that his head is gone.

After this teaser, we meet Sarah and Anne Pilgrim (Jennifer Jayne and Janet Munro), a mentalist sister act traveling by train. Anne is drawn by some strange compulsion to stop at a small hotel at the base of the Trollenberg, a towering Alpine peak.

We meet American Alan Brooks (Forrest Tucker), also on the train and acting mysterious, which catches the attention of reporter Philip Truscott (Laurence Payne). It turns out that Alan's behavior is innocent; he's come to

This frame blow-up from The Crawling Eye (1958) shows one of Les Bowie's aliens, resembling a cantaloupe with an unpleasantly realistic eye, attacking the inn. The little girl's ball, foreground, has just rolled into the room.

meet with Professor Crevett (Warren Mitchell), head of an observatory on the Trollenberg and an old colleague of Alan's.

When they meet, he points out a stationary cloud on the side of the Trollenberg. "A freak of nature?" suggests Alan. "A *radioactive* freak of nature?" retorts Crevett. (As it often is, radioactivity is used here as a mysterious and alien force. It has nothing to do with the plot otherwise; there isn't even the usual suggestion that the aliens want our planet because they have made their own radioactive. Presumably, here the aliens simply *like* radioactivity, the way they like clouds.)

We soon learn that this isn't the first time that Alan and Crevett have encountered very similar phenomena. Some time before, in the Andes, they detected an unmoving, radioactive cloud, and soon there were mysterious deaths and strange mental compulsions involving a clairvoyant, later murdered.

Alan had reported the strange events in the Andes to the authorities, but too late; when they investigated, the cloud was gone. Alan looked like a fool, so he's cautious about plunging into the same thing again.

With TV cameras stationed (for no clear reason) on top of the observatory, they watch two climbers, geologist Dewhurst (Stuart Saunders), and guide Brett (Andrew Faulds), as they ascend the Trollenberg to a way-station cabin.

That night, as Anne (who has genuine ESP powers) and Sarah are performing their act in the hotel, Anne suddenly goes into a trance. She's been holding a snow-filled paperweight with a mountain hut within, and this somehow puts her in touch with Brett and Dewhurst in their real hut up on the

Trollenberg. She describes some activity, but the point of view of her description is from somewhere *above* the hut on the mountain.

We then see what she's describing: Brett leaves the hut, puzzled at the icy fog outside. Dewhurst sees something horrible, screams and slams the door. And then turns in horror at something *inside* the hut. (This odd ability of the aliens to enter the hut is unexplained.)

Alan and others head up the mountain at once, to discover the inside of the cabin, including Dewhurst's headless body, covered in icy crystals. Meanwhile, wild-eyed Brett kills a member of the search party, and returns to the hotel, still acting and talking strangely.

When Anne enters, he grabs a knife and tries to kill her. After he's subdued, he's found to be dead. The body is locked away, but gets up and comes after Anne again. Subdued once more, Brett dissolves into a skeleton.

Alan recalls that the man who killed the clairvoyant in the Andes had been dead 24 hours.

Apparently realizing their human proxy didn't accomplish the end of wiping out the threat to their plan of conquest, the aliens themselves, wrapped in their portable cloud, begin coming down the mountain.

Alerted by Alan, the villagers hurry up to the observatory via a cable car. A small child is missing; we see her playing in the hotel lobby. The door bursts open, so that we get our first view of the hideous alien invader: it is an octopus-like creature, a huge, globular head resembling a cantaloupe, with a single very active eye directly in front. Slender, fluted tentacles emerge from under the head. The tentacles grasp at the child, but Alan rushes in, chops a tentacle in two, grabs the little girl and rushes out. The monster screams.

Alan is in the last trip up the cable car, which the aliens try to halt by pumping their frigid fog into the shed housing the winch. It frosts over and almost stops, but our heroes manage to reach the observatory.

Earlier, after he was taken over by the aliens, Brett complained of being very hot, so when bartender Hans (Colin Douglas), who had fled in his car when the aliens started down the mountain, turns up at the observatory and says "It iss zo *hot* in here," we know he's been had. Sure enough, he almost kills Anne, although this would seem pointless now – after all, the aliens have revealed themselves.

The aliens crawl up to the observatory and lay it under siege (they have no visible weapons, tools, etc.), until Alan rather belatedly realizes that if the aliens like cold, they probably *don't* like heat. A squadron of fighters is called, and they drop incendiary bombs on the aliens, still attacking the insulated observatory. The end.

The Crawling Eye keeps threatening to be better than it is, but for once, good direction and acting are dragged down by an illogical script, so that the film only barely rises above the routine. The various fantastical ideas it presents are never integrated, and there are no real attempts to do so. Why are psychics in contact with the aliens? How do the aliens know they are? What threat does this constitute for the would-be invaders? *Are* they invaders from another world? Why do they occasionally decapitate human victims? Why did they pick a mountain peak in populous Europe? Why does Brett turn into a skeleton? In short, what in the heck is going on, and why?

There isn't any attempt to even ask these questions in the film, much less answer them. *The Crawling Eye* may be imitation Kneale, but in a Quatermass film, *all* loose ends are tied up neatly, and all fanciful elements are carefully related to one another. Here, the head-hunting aspect is simply ghoulish, but it might have been suggested to be allied to an effort by the aliens to find out how some human beings can tune in on them. Kneale would have, perhaps, made this mind reading an atavistic trait from when the aliens visited us in the distant past. He certainly would have made the people who brushed minds with the aliens terrified at the sheer unearthliness of the alien minds. Instead, Jimmy Sangster, who scripted the film, merely trots these ideas out one after another, apparently hoping that the sheer number of them will somehow make a whole, like separate vegetables make a salad. He probably was using only the ideas that Key presented him, so the error may lie in the original TV script.

As it is, we don't know why the creatures are here, except that they seem mean. At one point, Crevett says, "There are many galaxies besides ours. Now, who knows what is happening millions of miles out in space? Perhaps the world these creatures inhabit is coming to an end, perhaps they need to find somewhere else to live." And perhaps not, Professor Crevett. There are other possible explanations, after all, but none are offered; none are needed. These are squidgy, nasty, murderous aliens, radioactive and ugly as sin: they *must* be evil.

However, all this being said, it must also be admitted that *The Crawling Eye* is very well made for its budget, and achieves certain nervous excitement here and there. The dialogue and visual elements integrate well, especially in sequences in the main room at the hotel, where there may have been a little more time for rehearsals. Where the footage allows it, the editing is good; the scene in which Brett, now an alien-controlled zombie, returns to the hotel is quite well done, and some business with spilled matches has a sharp if minor impact. The editor was Henry Richardson, who never rose above middle-grade pictures, but some of those are worth noting: *A Study in Terror* (1966), Ray Harryhausen's *The Valley of Gwangi* (1969), *The Revolutionary* (1970).

The photography by coproducer Monty Berman is efficient and atmospheric at times, although other sequences, notably those in the observatory, are uninteresting. Berman often photographed the films he coproduced, including *No Place Like Homicide* (1961), *Jack the Ripper* (1959) and *Mania* (1960). Among his other films as coproducer are *Home Is the Hero* (1959), *The Hellfire Club* (1961) and *Blood of the Vampire*. Almost always partnered with Robert S. Baker, Berman has also been active in television. His work there and his films are about on the same level of quality, but because of the generally dismal level of television, Berman-Baker material stands out slightly. Among the series that Berman was associated with are "The Saint," "The Baron," "The Champions" and "My Partner the Ghost."

There is no reason to have two heroes, Forrest Tucker and Laurence Payne who, in particular, has little to do. Almost all heroics and deductions are by Tucker's character, but Payne (left over from the TV play) still hangs around cluttering up the plot. Furthermore, there's no reason to have Tucker's mission be mysterious, with a suddenly-revealed gun in his valise, and so forth.

Partly no doubt because of the film's being taken from a six-part serial, it is crammed with incident, however unconnected the story elements might be. *The Crawling Eye* is not a boring film. There's ESP, decapitations, mysterious clouds, radioactivity, the walking dead, hideous aliens, jet planes and fiery explosions. It is all presented by the director as serious stuff, and it is primarily a movie for adults rather than children.

The acting is not bad. Forrest Tucker seems to play the film in a troubled, nervous state, as if he wasn't sure what he was doing there. He does try to contribute, though—he's not walking through the picture. When Dewhurst's headless body is seen, Tucker claps his hands over his eyes and turns aside. Although his acting is somewhat one-note, it's mostly the right note.

Tucker is at his best in rough, manly parts, the big-mouthed, booming side-kick of the hero, or the principal thug. He's a reasonably talented actor in this area, especially when he's allowed to play it in a comic tone, and has had a long career. He began as early as 1940 in *The Westerner;* his career was interrupted, presumably by war service, and he then came back as second leads in major films and leads in lesser films. Tucker mostly appeared in Westerns; his rugged appearance and tough-guy physique make him suitable for such parts.

Along the way, he was in a few unusual films, as in *Trouble in the Glen* (1953), *The Night They Raided Minsky's* (1968) and, notably, *Auntie Mame* (1958), where he was Beauregard Pickett Burnside, Mame's affable Southern-fried husband. He made three low-budget British SF films (each adapted from a TV serial) in the late 50s, *The Crawling Eye,* *The Cosmic Monster* and, the best one, *The Abominable Snowman of the Himalayas,* which also featured the best Tucker performance of the three. He also starred in several TV series, including "Crunch and Des," "Dusty's Trail," "The Ghost Chasers" and "The Rebels," as well as most famously, "F Troop."

Laurence Payne is forgettable as the reporter, a role that was undoubtedly more significant in the TV serial. Payne continued to act until 1972. Leslie Halliwell says that Payne's career began as early as 1945, and that he is primarily a stage actor. Among his other films are *Train of Events* (1949), *Ben-Hur* (1957), *Barabbas* (1961), *The Singer Not the Song* (1961), *The Tell-Tale Heart* (1962) and *Vampire Circus* (1972).

The best performance in *The Crawling Eye* is by Janet Munro as the troubled Anne. She is convincingly confused and frightened, and she makes her ESP powers believable, even though the part is meaningless. She is also charming and attractive in herself, no doubt the reasons she was hired soon by Walt Disney, to appear in three of his bigger productions of the era, *Third Man on the Mountain* (1959), *The Swiss Family Robinson* (1960) and *Darby O'Gill and the Little People* (1959), in which she is especially winning. She was also in *The Day the Earth Caught Fire,* and there's more on her there. She was no relation to current star Caroline Munro.

Jennifer Jayne, as the Pilgrim sister without the ESP talent, has a thankless role; she mostly just stands there looking worried. She was also in *Hysteria* (1964), *Dr. Terror's House of Horrors* (1965), *They Came from Beyond Space* (1967) and *The Medusa Touch* (1978), but had starring roles only in low-budget films.

The special effects in *The Crawling Eye* were by the remarkably inventive Les Bowie, often termed the father of British special effects, although there are others who might equally deserve the honor, such as Percy Day or even American Ned Mann. Bowie had a long career in British special effects, primarily on low-budget films, and did the effects for most of the famous Hammer pictures. He was often called on to destroy Dracula, paint mattes of castles on mountaintops, *revive* Dracula, and so forth. Bowie was primarily an artist, as he worked so much with mattes, but he was also expert in all aspects of effects. Many people in the industry have high praise for Bowie's ability. Derek Meddings, Roy Field, even Stanley Kubrick have praised Bowie. He was working on *Dracula* when he died in January, 1979, and posthumously shared the Oscar for the effects in *Superman.*

There is excellent commentary on Bowie and his career in John Brosnan's

Movie Magic, and in issues 28 and 29 of *Starlog*. The latter issue contains an inadequate filmography on Bowie, mentioning some of his fantastic films. This is probably only a partial list: *The Creeping Unknown*, *X the Unknown*, *Enemy from Space*, most of the Hammer Frankenstein films and all of their Draculas except the first, *The Mummy* (1959), *The Curse of the Werewolf* (1961), *The Day the Earth Caught Fire*, *Jason and the Argonauts*, *Kiss of the Vampire* (both 1963), *First Men IN the Moon*, *Dr. Strangelove* (both 1964), *She*, *The Face of Fu Manchu* (both 1965), *Plague of the Zombies*, *The Reptile*, *Fahrenheit 451* (all 1966), *The Mummy's Shroud*, *Five Million Years to Earth* (both 1967), *2001: A Space Odyssey* (1968), *Moon Zero Two* (1969), *Vampire Circus*, *Golden Voyage of Sinbad* (1973), *To the Devil, a Daughter* (1976), *Sinbad and the Eye of the Tiger*, *Star Wars* (both 1977), *Superman* (1978) and *Dracula* (1979).

About *The Crawling Eye*, Bowie told John Brosnan that "I squirm when I see it on TV now and I squirmed when I filmed it." Although Bowie was referring to one shot in particular, the effects in general are not up to his standards. The ambition of the script was far beyond the ability of anyone to produce adequate effects on the budget the film had.

As with some other films and their monsters, the attempt at making the aliens as ghoulish and hideous as possible backfires. When they appear, they inevitably get laughter from contemporary audiences. Although as usual, Bowie's monsters can look disturbingly lifelike in close-ups, the basic unimaginative design and slimy, gloppy look the creatures have make them preposterous instead of menacing. They crawl without any legs, and shriek madly without mouths while waving their thin tentacles, which only produces a comical effect.

There is an admirable attempt at blending live action and miniatures, when an alien lurking on top of the observatory grabs Laurence Payne when he runs out to fling a Molotov cocktail. The long shot of the doll in the alien tentacles almost works. There is a nice try at realism in having the miniature of the observatory with its attacking aliens in the same shot as one of the bombing planes (also in miniature).

But despite the efforts of Les Bowie and his crew, the creatures are so unbelievable in design that the purpose of the film would probably have been better served by keeping them offscreen altogether.

What Bowie himself squirmed about was the cloud on the Trollenberg. "There was one shot of a cloud on a mountain that was really terrible," Bowie told Brosnan. "I did it in a mad hurry at the time. We did the cloud effect with a piece of cotton wool [which we stuck] on a photograph of a mountain with a nail and then filmed it. And they used that photograph again and again during the film.... Every time a character looked out of a window they'd cut to this mountain and we'd have stuck the cotton wool in a new position. Awful!" Actually, it isn't anywhere near as bad as that, and Bowie did manage some interesting shots involving the cloud, although not with the cotton. As the cloud descends into the village, there is a long shot of a miniature town as the cloud pours over it, which works rather well. The scene of the powered winch freezing up from the touch of the cloud is surprisingly effective.

Although Richard W. Nason in the *New York Times* felt that the film "does nothing to advance the copious genre of science fiction," in general reviews of the picture were favorable and, in some cases, close to raves. Paul V. Beckley in the New York *Herald-Tribune*, for instance, thought that the movie was "not the best of its breed but more than satisfactory for most of its length.... It shows real skill in quick development of a sense of threat and mystery and manages to hold this in suspense while concentrating on character and atmosphere.... *The Crawling Eye* has its moments of terror and has been deftly filmed and nicely edited."

Cue magazine loved it. It is "a first-rate hair-raiser – jammed-with-suspense package of sci-fi excitement that comes just about as close to reality as anyone might wish.... The production is excellent, the photography beautiful (is *that* the word?), and the cast tops. If you enjoy movie shock, try this one for whammo."

The *Monthly Film Bulletin* gave this film only an average rating, but seemed to like it better in the commentary. "Several sequences in this Alpine science fiction production are genuinely alarming, although much more could have been made of the dramatic moments. The film gives the impression of having been shot and edited in a great hurry and the characteristic addiction to close-ups of such details as severed heads and melting flesh is more in evidence than in most science fiction pieces. More accomplished direction might have resulted in a film as effective as the Quatermass series."

"Rich" in *Variety*: *The Crawling Eye* "is a likely candidate for big b.o. honors in the science-fiction pic realm.... The tension of this well-made and gripping thriller comes not so much from seeing the creature in the final stages ... but from the eeriness of the atmosphere and doubt about when the cloud will strike.... Jimmy Sangster's taut screenplay extracts the most from the situations and is helped by strong, resourceful acting.... This is a better-than-most horror film which, despite its extravagant play upon the imagination, retains a chilling air of plausibility.

Picturegoer thought it "uproarious nonsense with plenty of get-up-and-go." Alan Frank (*SF*), source of the previous quote, himself called it an "efficient low-budget science fiction thriller spoiled by unimpressive special effects, slack direction and hurried exposition." Frank also adds a surprising bit of trivia: walking corpse Andrew Faulds later became a member of Parliament.

Joe Dante in *Castle of Frankenstein* #8 called it "suspenseful" and a "rather well-made adventure." *Psychotronic* referred to it as "popular and scary."

The Crawling Eye is a decent enough film, above average for this kind of thing; it shifts from stodginess, as in the early observatory scenes, to eerie, suspenseful scare scenes. The entire business with Brett is satisfactorily creepy and charged with tension, helped by Andrew Faulds' good performance and by the earlier establishing of Brett as a person who might act like this even if he wasn't a zombie. Considerable imagination and intelligence are on view throughout, and despite the many unexplained elements, Sangster's screenplay is well-structured. But the haste of the production, the peculiar illogic of the story, and the inadequacy of the monsters themselves severely damage what could have been a superior low-budget film.

Curse of the Faceless Man

"A lot of thinking went into *Curse of the Faceless Man*," said Jack Moffitt, "and very little of it was any good." That describes the situation rather well; the story is hopeless. Moffitt's review, in fact, consisted entirely of a summary of the plot, as follows:

"The story concerns a group of modern Neapolitan scientists who discover that the volcanic eruption of Vesuvius, 2000 years ago, was due to an Etruscan curse. The curse was pronounced by a gladiator who was in love with the daughter of a Pompeiian senator. Before uttering the curse and setting off the fireworks, the gladiator was careful to have his whole malediction inscribed on a medallion.

"Pressing deeper for information about the ancients, the modern researchers discover that, in those far off days, it was the custom for men to give jewelry to women. Having set off Vesuvius, the gladiator, who may have been a bit punch drunk from his bouts in the arena, soon realizes that if he is to enjoy the society of the senator's daughter, he must rescue her from the red hot lava he has set in motion. But first, he must provide her with some token of his esteem, so he drops into an Egyptian temple to steal some jewels for his beloved. Here some radioactive embalming fluid gets spilled on him. This converts him into living stone for 2000 years.

"Dug up in our confusing times, the living stone gladiator discovers that, through an impressive coincidence, the sweetheart of the very scientist who is working on him is the reincarnation of the senator's daughter from back in Pompeii. Thinking the volcano still is erupting, he insists on carrying the pretty lady (Elaine Edwards) into the Bay of Naples, where she is in grave danger of drowning. She is saved through the wonders of chemistry. Radioactive Egyptian embalming fluid, when combined with salt water, dissolves living stone.

"So Miss Edwards is saved by her scientist (Richard Anderson) who has been saying all along, 'This is entirely unlike life as we know it.' He will find few to disagree with him."

When I first heard of *Curse of the Faceless Man* and that it was written by Jerome Bixby, I expected much more than I got. I was surprised that this and its companion feature, *It! The Terror from Beyond Space*, were written by Bixby, a real science fiction writer, instead of some standard Hollywood hack. Actually, overall Bixby was little more than that himself. Certainly, the bizarre fantasy/science fiction story line of *Curse of the Faceless Man* doesn't require any special knowledge in the field of science fiction. In fact, Bixby told interviewer Dennis Fischer (*Enterprise Incidents*, summer 1983) that he didn't even come up with the story line of *Faceless Man* himself. He was assigned the story by the production company. Perhaps naively he envisioned a big-budget film and wrote the script accordingly, but director Edward L. Cahn quickly rewrote it for a budget of about $100,000. For more on Bixby, see the entry on *It! The Terror from Beyond Space*.

Curse of the Faceless Man is a sluggish slumgullion of fantasy and science fictional ideas. The curse of the Etruscan gladiator, one Quintillus Aurelius, is treated as being just as real as the Egyptian embalming fluid and radioactivity that turn Quintillus into a stone man. Yet later, there is a struggle to explain how this literally faceless man can see with no eyes. The best the script can come up with is that "Quintillus may have some sort of inner vision." Forgetting that "inner vision" usually means insight, why would the writer feel it necessary to rationalize sight in a film in which curses work? Because the film is ostensibly science fiction, and the business with the curse starting Vesuvius erupting is just to match the title. The rest of the film is science fiction because that's what audiences of 1958 were buying.

But just in case fantasy was also on the upswing, the currently hot topic of reincarnation, from the Bridey Murphy business, was dropped into the film. While the Faceless Man is being shipped to Naples, Tina Enright (Edwards) is having dreams about him, and begins doing a very interesting painting of Quintillus' cinder- and ash-encrusted form bound by heavy chains. Throughout the film, there is a telepathic rapport between Tina and the Faceless Man, and that she is a reincarnation of Lucilla Helena, the senator's daughter, is made very clear.

The movie has elements of a mystery, too. After Quintillus is unearthed and being shipped into Naples to the Pompeii Museum, he suddenly comes to life and kills Tony the Truck Driver, then collapses back into inactivity, leaving quite a puzzle for the scientists. After various short bursts of activity, he returns to his original position as a museum exhibit, and the scientists remain puzzled for a time as to just who is banging up the Pompeii Museum. Why he returns to the exact same position (or nearly so—a change in his position later is an important clue) is inexplicable.

Jack Moffitt was slightly wrong. The embalming fluid wasn't radioactive, it was the soil into which Quintillus fell, soaked in embalming fluid, during the eruption. His activity is explained by saying that when the X-ray machine is used on him, it gives him renewed energy. There's no explanation offered as to why he strangled Tony the Truck Driver, though.

The X-rays are as much a desultory gimmick as the radiation. A Faceless Man was needed, and an explanation for him was needed, too. When I first saw this film, long after it was made and after I had begun working on this book, I felt pleased for most of its length that I wouldn't have to discuss it, since it was clearly just a fantasy, hence outside the scope of selection. But suddenly someone mentioned radioactivity; that made it "science fiction" and so it had to be included.

The movie was directed by Edward L. Cahn, who worked from 1931 to 1962; he died in 1963 at the age of 64. He was a minor figure in Hollywood, dismissed by Halliwell in *The Filmgoer's Companion* as "American director of second features." Although there is a filmography on Cahn in the back of *Kings of the Bs*, there is no mention of him in the text.

His first major film was in 1932, *Law and Order*, which is a highly regarded Western starring Walter Huston and Harry Carey. But by 1937, Cahn had slipped from directing for Universal and RKO to poverty row's Mascot. Through the 40s, he directed for PRC and Eagle-Lion, as well as doing a couple of minor MGM films.

By the mid-50s, he had lost what vitality he may have had as a director in his early days, spending the rest of his career directing second features and exploitation movies of all genres. His first SF/horror movie was *Creature with the Atom Brain* in 1955, and he then did *The She Creature* (1956), *Voodoo Woman*, *Zombies of Mora Tau*, *Invasion of the Saucer Men*, *It! The Terror from Beyond Space*, *Invisible Invaders* and *The Four Skulls of Jonathan Drake* (1959), his last such film of the period. The remainder of his career was busily spent on crime films (*Inside the Mafia*, *The Boy Who Caught a Crook*, etc.), Westerns (*Gunfighters of Abilene*, *Frontier Uprising*, *Gun Fight*), and miscellaneous melodramas (*The Music Box Kid*, *You Have to Run Fast*, *The Clown and the Kid*). Among his last films was a peculiar version of *Beauty and the Beast*, in which not only was the beast a werewolf, but the title was the only real connection to the fairy tale.

Cahn managed to create a sense of mood and had a hint of style in some of his films, especially when the story allowed for Gothic visual elements, as in *The She Creature* and *It! The Terror from Beyond Space*. But ordinarily, the budgets were so low and the shooting schedule so rushed that Cahn merely did the least he could to get by. His staging is generally unimaginative, even dull, and (because of the low budget haste), scenes tend to go on at some length.

Curse of the Faceless Man often looks as if it had no director at all; the actors seem lost (Richard Anderson appears to be acutely suffering most of the time), and the camerawork is perfunctory. In one take, Anderson flubs a line but the schedule was apparently so tight that there was no opportunity for retakes—unless, of course, this was the *best* take available.

The script is loaded with clunker lines, such as "What we believe is not important. What is important is what we can prove." Lines like that exist solely to be disproven. "Shock is like a heavy door in the mind," someone says. "Sometimes it can be opened with the same key that caused it to close," which presents a peculiar image of someone using a key to shove a door shut.

There's little or no characterization in the script, but it does at least try for a continued emphasis on blindness throughout, not that it really results in anything meaningful. Not only does the Faceless Man have no eyes, but during the eruption of Vesuvius, he had been on his way to take his lady love to the Cove of the Blind Fisherman.

When my sweetly sentimental wife Beverly saw the film as a child, she was moved to tears by the poignancy of the ending. It was rare in the 1950s (though not rare earlier) for the monster to be destroyed—and to have become a monster in the first place—by an excess of love. Quintillus' grand passion for that departed Roman beauty caused the volcano to erupt, and his desire to give her a gem to wear over her heart led to his own entombment. When he revives, all he can think of is to carry his beloved to a place of safety, so he grabs her (highly convenient) reincarnation and lurches off to the Cove of the Blind Fisherman, finally completing the action interrupted 2000 years before. With a modestly respectable irony, all this passion results in Quintillus' own destruction as he dissolves (mostly dry-ice fog effects) in the waters of the Mediterranean.

Charles Gemora built the suit for the Faceless Man, and apparently both he and Bob Bryant play Quintillus in different scenes. Gemora really made an effort to make the Faceless Man look like one of the cinder- and ash-encrusted bodies found in the ruins of Pompeii, and while this is effective in long shots, in closer shots he looks more like he was made out of flannel. There's also a plaster Faceless Man, used in the shots in which Quintillus is in a quiescent mode.

The actors are usually of little importance in films of this nature, built around a gimmick and not much else. Here, most of them act as if they know it. As Inspector Rinaldi Jan Arvan is the only performer who shows any liveliness, and he overdoes it.

At the time, some of the critics liked the ending almost as much as my wife did. In the *Motion Picture Herald*, Floyd Stone said that "There is in the primeval surge of the blind, grappling relic of historic tragedy, a certain poignance." Although this ending does manage to be almost touching, the concept of the destruction of Pompeii, one of the greatest and most spectacular tragedies in world history, serving only as a backdrop for the corny romance between a Roman senator's daughter and an Etruscan gladiator seems awfully cheap.

Reviews were not entirely unfavorable. The *Monthly Film Bulletin* said "this unpretentious film holds attention by straightforward presentation of its story. Its relation of character to surroundings is clearcut and uncomplicated, and it avoids overplaying of the sensational material. Quintillus is reminiscent of a

Golem designed by Henry Moore, and makes a charming addition to the catalogue of the screen's abnormalities. The acting is adequate, the photography pleasant, and the editing is by Grant Whytock, once a close collaborator of Rex Ingram." Although I think the film inferior to this opinion, at least it makes sense.

But Floyd Stone's comments in his lengthy *Motion Picture Herald* review are puzzling. He said that *Curse of the Faceless Man* entered the field of horror "with boldness and clarity," and that it "has a script which stays logically in line in developing its fantastic thesis." He said, "suspense is tangible." Actually, seen today, the film is rather boring, with occasional well-photographed scenes in which Quintillus does very little — it being difficult for writer and director to present him simultaneously as a menace and a figure of sympathy.

Several reviews especially mentioned the narration, done by Morris Ankrum, but it has very little effect. It constantly describes scenes as we see them, imparts motivation to Quintillus when it's not necessary, and in general sounds peculiarly like a documentary. But the narrator reads the lines expertly.

The Curse of the Faceless Man is primarily a pedestrian, preposterous film that does manage to work up a little interest by the end, but it's too late and not enough to save the picture.

Earth vs. the Spider

While one hesitates to use the word "good" in relation to any Bert I. Gordon film, it's safe to say that *Earth vs. the Spider* is one of his least terrible, second only to *The Amazing Colossal Man* in providing entertainment of the kind Gordon intended. *Earth vs. the Spider* is so simply conceived that it verges on elegance, in the mathematical sense of the word, but is still silly and shoddy.

A note on the title: the film was shot as "The Spider," but was changed to *Earth vs. the Spider* on release, which is the title all prints bear. However, *The Fly* became a big hit in the same year; American International, never one to miss an opportunity to trade on the popularity of another film, reverted to the original title for all advertising. Most reference sources call it "The Spider," but they are wrong. Wrong, do you hear, wrong.

Almost everything in the film relates directly to the spider menace, giving it a strong narrative thrust; the climax is well-conceived for suspense; there are few of the scenes one usually expects in a giant-bug movie. In hands other than Bert Gordon's, *Earth vs. the Spider* might have turned out well enough to be regarded as one of the best of the big-bug movies.

But Gordon did direct it; he also wrote the original story and, as usual, did the inept special effects. On the title page of the script, the writing credit reads "Screenplay Laslo [sic] Gorog; Additional Dialogue George Worthing Yates; Story Bert I. Gordon." It's typical of Gordon to have hired George Worthing Yates to *dialogue* his film; Yates' worst feature as a writer is his dialogue. The finished film credits Laszlo Gorog and Yates as cowriters, perhaps as a result of arbitration; judging by the number of rewritten pages, most of the script was written by Gorog, who also wrote the inept *The Mole People*. Yates wrote or cowrote *Them!*, *It Came from Beneath the Sea*, *The Conquest of Space*, *Earth vs. the Flying Saucers*, *The Flame Barrier*, *Frankenstein 1970*, *Space Master X-7*, *War of the Colossal Beast* and *Tormented*. Three of his films were for Bert I. Gordon; six were released in 1958. For more on Yates, see *Them!* in Volume 1.

Earth vs. the Spider gets off to a quick start as a man driving on a lonely road unexpectedly collides with a cable stretched across the road. At school the next day, his teenage daughter Carol (June Kenny) and her boyfriend Mike (Gene Persson) discuss the nonappearance of her father. Mike annoys Carol by alluding to her father's heavy drinking (an odd and extraneous element), but they soon make up.

In the science class conducted by Mr. Kingman (Ed Kemmer), he demonstrates some features of electricity—the class chants "anode" and "cathode" in unison—which will stand him in good stead later. The scene is in a high school, but the simplistic science is best suited for a grade school; however, Gordon and his writers aimed the film directly at teenagers, so they had to have a high school and an explanation of the means ultimately used to kill the big bug.

Carol and Mike borrow a pal's car and go in search of her father, quickly finding the cable across the road and his wrecked, empty truck. They go directly to a nearby cave—Bronson Caverns, of course—which has numerous warnings: "Danger! No Trespassing! Do Not Enter!" Mike says he "never believed those stories about the cave," and despite Carol's further warning that "people have gone in there and never come out," he leads her directly in. There is one final warning: he finds her father's hat, torn and bloody, but says nothing.

Either these kids are very brave or very stupid—if I'd found that stuff I'd have gone back for the sheriff—but in the long run, it doesn't matter. The plot had to start. Inside the cave, partly a set and partly slides taken in Carlsbad Caverns (into which the actors are unconvincingly inserted), a stalactite almost falls on them, but they persevere. They find skeletons, but still push on.

They fall into a huge spider web, strongly resembling a cargo net. They hear a hideous scream and, sure enough, there's a giant spider. (Of course, the kind of spider used in the film, a South American "tarantula" by the look of it, doesn't weave webs of this nature; of course, they also don't get to be the size of a bank.) The kids beat a hasty retreat as the spider screams in frustration.

They tell Mr. Kingman that the sheriff didn't believe their story of a giant spider. Kingman is impressed with the sample of giant spider web they've brought, and calls the scoffing sheriff (Gene Roth). "Naturally," Kingman says, "I didn't call you up to get you to investigate abnormal insect life." (Yes, this science teacher always calls the arachnid an "insect.") He reminds the sheriff that Carol's father is still missing, so the sheriff agrees to check out the cave.

A group of searchers, including Carol, Mike, Kingman, the sheriff, some deputies and, amusingly, an exterminator, arrive at the cave. The writers carefully scripted the incidents in the cave for quick irony: Kingman remarks on the lack of the usual animal life, and a bat flies by (the sheriff shoots it); he tells the sheriff that spiders devour their prey by encasing them in silk, then sucking all the fluid parts out, and at once the dried body of Carol's father is found. Mike tells Kingman the web is in the next chamber, and Kingman warns the sheriff about walking into the chamber. The sheriff laughs, and immediately almost falls into the web.

The pest-control man is summoned with his DDT sprayer as the sheriff's men stupidly entangle themselves in the web. The spider rushes out, is sprayed, kills one of the deputies, and falls over itself, its hairy legs in the air.

As they head back to town, Carol is upset that she dropped her father's gift for her, a locket, in the cave. Mike promises to help her look for it.

The sheriff proposes boarding up the cave, but Kingman says that if he does, he'd better put a big door in the boards so people can come look at the spider. He says he has a better idea himself (it turns out to be a worse one). "You know what we eggheads are like, sheriff. We want to know why this, how come that? What about the other? It's a matter of scientific interest to find out what made that creature tick." Yes, all you scientists out there, adopt this as your creed: "How come that?"

Kingman raises some intersting questions which are dropped at once: how come the spider got so big, and what about other cave spiders? "There might be more giant spiders coming into the world," he tells the sheriff, who really didn't want to hear that. "They may even be hatching from their eggs in some remote spot right now."

Kingman takes the spider into town. Scenes of how he did this would have been interesting, but since it seems to be impossible, Gordon didn't show us this. The next time we see the spider, it has been put on display in the high school gymnasium. Why there? Why not a better-protected site? Because this movie is for teenagers. (The town is "isolated" so no reporters have arrived.)

Carol contacts Mike at the movie theatre where he works for his father (allowing Gordon to get in a self-reference: Mike says "My dad just got in a new picture and I haven't even seen it yet. Something about Puppet People. Sounds pretty wild.") He agrees to help her look in the cave for the locket, and they head out there while the town goes to rack and ruin behind them. (They seem to be gone a very long time, but the events in the story also seem to take place entirely in one day, despite the story line sometimes indicating otherwise.)

A school dance is coming up, so some teenagers who form a rock group want to rehearse in the gym. The kids give out with the lamest, least authentic teenage gab since Andy Hardy. "We got to get in," says one; "the dance is tomorrow night. The cats'll have a blast if we don't swing solid." (The dialoguer apparently didn't know that "blast" meant a *good* time, and felt that teenagers in 1958 talked like 1952 jazz musicians.) "Maybe [the janitor will] open the pad," suggests one. "Oh," responds another, "not with Mr. Eight Legs still in there."

Hugo the janitor (Hank Patterson) comes in; he doesn't want to let the kids in with the spider. "Kingman didn't mean *us*," one kid explains, "He meant Squares. We're the coolest zoologists in town." So Hugo lets them in.

They promptly play a limp rock number, and a class enters to dance. The vibrations of the music and dance revive the spider, perhaps the first monster (but not the last) to be energized by rock 'n' roll. Everyone flees, and Hugo is killed while trying to tell Kingman the spider is loose.

There follow several scenes of the spider roaming through town, including some from the spider's point of view, as someone stands frozen in its path, screaming like mad, while the spider advances on them. Gordon had one, count them, one, slender giant spider leg built, which doesn't remotely match the thick, hairy legs of the real back-projected spider. He frequently employs the leg in a vain attempt to convince us that the actors are on the set with the real spider.

The "long-distance" lines are conveniently down, and apparently no one has a radio, so someone is sent on a motorcycle to fetch help, but he turns up dead later, killed by the spider. In the meantime, things calm down slightly, signified by a heart-tugging after-the-disaster scene: "Exterior, street, medium long shot. Camera pans left showing overturned car with Just Married sign on it [for poignancy]. Then to dead body in street [for tragedy] and deserted houses to little baby in middle of street, crying [for sentimentality]."

The spider is still at large, however, and Kingman rushes to his own home in time to ram his car (unconvincingly) into the spider, thus saving his wife and baby from being poked by the giant spider leg prop. Apparently finding people en masse more trouble than they're worth, the spider heads back for his cave.

Meanwhile, Carol and Mike have found the locket, but lose their way and wander around aimlessly in the peculiarly well-lit caverns.

The spider is seen entering the cave, so the sheriff, Kingman and others dynamite the entrance shut. Then they realize that they have trapped the spider inside with Mike and Carol, who by now are aware that the spider has returned and have found the sealed entrance.

Someone expresses worry that even if the kids can hide from the spider, they'll soon run out of air. Which, in view of the vast extent of the caverns, seems highly unlikely. Much activity ensues as they prepare to blast a new hole into the cave.

A hole is opened in the top of the cave just as the spider locates Carol and Mike. In the meantime, Kingman has decided to kill the spider, and so gets the proper equipment (anode, cathode) to set up a powerful electrical arc. As Mike nears the hole into the cave, he takes one of the electrodes from Kingman, who holds the other, and a big spark, like lightning, is thrown through the spider, now climbing the wall to get at them. The spider loses its grip and falls to the floor of the cave, impaled on several stalagmites for good measure.

Nothing in his other films leads one to suspect that Gordon is ever trying for logical reactions, clarity and simplicity, but despite its many failings, that's what we get in *Earth vs. the Spider*.

At no time does anyone seem to regard the giant spider with anything like awe; to Kingman, it's an interesting phenomenon; to the sheriff, it's a menace in his town; to the kids, it's a joke. In general, the spider is just a big menace, like an especially large bear; the fact that it is a creepy-crawly, ugly bug is beside the point. This is a peculiarly realistic reaction; even in real life, people who have a horror of spiders often don't react to tarantulas with the same shudders they feel for smaller spiders, and I speak from personal experience. If a giant spider did turn up, people would be briefly fascinated, then relegate it to the realm of large curious creatures. The spider here is menacing because it is a gigantic carnivore, not because it is a gigantic spider.

The story is simply conceived and, in a sense, doesn't deal much with the spider itself, although everything is structured around it. Every plot detail is generated by the spider and its actions, but there's no speculation as to where it came from. Though both heroes, Mike and Kingman, are paired off with women, there are no romance scenes at all, perhaps unique for a Bert I. Gordon film.

The spider eats Carol's father while he's bringing her a gift; while looking for him, Carol loses the gift; she and Mike return to the cave to find the gift, and are trapped in the cave by people trying to isolate the spider. All motivations hinge on the first death we see.

This shows classic dramatic unity, even following the suggestions of Edgar Allan Poe as to how to plot a short story. While the film is generally mediocre, this singleness of purpose and the connection of all actions to the spider make the film especially coherent. If the same overall structure had been used in a script with good dialogue and characterizations—this film *has* no characters—it might have been a classic of its kind.

But due to Bert I. Gordon's ineptitude, scenes are flat and dull. There's no flow to the action from scene to scene, no actions begun in one shot and finished in another. The settings are also dull—a studio back lot, rather than any of the many small communities in the Los Angeles area. And they're familiar—Bronson Caverns again. The acting, too, is dull, but the performers had nothing to work with.

There's no straining after effect, so the dialogue isn't laughable; it's just hollow, the least wordage necessary to get a scene over with. There's no imagination, no life, except in the weirdly inaccurate "teenage" talk; everything else seems trite.

The simplicity of the film leaves many things unanswered. What has the spider been eating all this time? Why didn't it kill anyone on the road before? Or did it? Why hasn't anyone seen it before? Where did it come from? The film had no responsibility to answer all these questions, but some suggestions (other than mysterious rumors about the cave) might have been possible.

The special effects are the usual for Gordon. For exterior scenes involving the (real) spider, it forever either appears from or vanishes behind a building, and the matte line is heavy and obvious. Sometimes the spider appears in the foreground in what is called a "burn-in" matte (basically a superimposition with an especially dense image to be supered). At those times, the lighter-colored parts of the spider, such as its leg joints, become transparent.

The spider's size varies drastically. In the cave, it's one size; it's smaller in the gym, but vastly larger in the streets, where it towers over a three-story building. When it returns to the cave, it's only about twelve feet wide, including the spread of its legs.

The spider screams a lot, sounding much like an angry ape. Most people know spiders don't make any noises (that we can hear), so this is a silly idea in the first place, and becomes sillier the more the spider screams.

Mark McGee reports that "Bert thought he was doing a swell job on these pictures. He thought that for the money he really brought in a good show, and was proud of the fact that he filmed that cavern sequence in a studio rather than actually going to Carlsbad Caverns." McGee added that Gordon thought he fooled people into believing he'd taken actors to Carlsbad, but the slides shot there never look like anything else; the actors look no more like they are really in Carlsbad than they are in scenes with a giant spider.

The reviews of the film in some cases were among the best Bert I. Gordon ever received. Jack Moffitt called it "a better-than-average film shocker," saying that Gordon "has given this tale of a gigantic man-eating spider more careful production than is usual in the case of low-budget horror pictures and the special effects (including some ingenious split screen work) [are] first rate."

"Powe" in *Variety* called it a "good exploitationer ... characterized by well done special effects [and] a reasonably credible plot.... [It] will be a good feature for the exploitation market." Scenes in the caves "are particularly interesting and well done. Acting and direction are routine in the bridge sequences not directly involving the spider.... Jack Marta's photography is capable, Ronald Sinclair's editing is a plus factor, and Albert Glasser's music is good."

Even the usually critical *Monthly Film Bulletin* gave the movie a II. "The success of any routine, low-budget 'monster' thriller with no other aspirations, lies almost entirely with the trick work, which here is variable; acting and general production values are adequately imaginative and frightening."

More recently, however, *Earth vs. the Spider* has not fared as well with reviewers. Don Willis (I) was uncharacteristically lenient, however, saying it had "a few shocks; otherwise the usual giant-spider antics." Joe Dante in *Castle of Frankenstein* #9 called it a "stupefying teen-slanted monster film with obvious, inept technical effects. Giant spider unleashed in small town menaces teenagers. Is it a diabolical plot by adults to rid town of teenagers? No. It's a diabolical plot by producer-director Bert Gordon to make money on smallest possible investment."

This was Bert I. Gordon's last black-and-white giant monster thriller, and the third for him in 1958 (counting *Puppet People*). In its uncluttered, direct plot, he'd actually found a way to make his films a shade more palatable than previously. *Earth vs. the Spider* is a bad movie, but it's a bad movie with a major good idea, but Gordon didn't learn from it. He decided to try new directions in the next few years, with *The Boy and the Pirates* and *The Magic Sword* fairy tales, and his one ghost movie, *Tormented*. He dabbled in some other areas, such as crime films (*Picture Mommy Dead*) and even soft-core pornography (*How to Succeed with Sex*). He learned nothing from the simple clarity of *Earth vs. the Spider*.

But there was no reason he should. The movie was one of the last of a dying breed; the giant-bug movie had fallen on hard times because, as usual, greed became the dominant factor in the creation of the films. When that was merely a very important measure, but not the only driving force, the films weren't bad. But greed took over; worse, the people who became so greedy had no interest in making a good film, only a profitable one. Repetition set in. Although giant spiders are a time-honored film tradition, it was *Tarantula* that begat *Earth vs. the Spider*; Gordon's film even seems to have been shot on the same exterior sets. The giant bug that laid the golden eggs was chopped to pieces. The chief culprit was Bert I. Gordon. Of his 15 fantasy, SF and/or horror movies, *ten* dealt with oversized creatures, and eight of those were made by 1958.

Fiend Without a Face

This mostly lively pseudo–American thriller is one of the most ghoulish, gory pictures of the 50s; I presume it got away with the ghastly effects of the climax because the creatures expiring in welters of blood weren't human *or* animal. They were evil disembodied brains.

There doesn't seem to have been much logic expended in deciding just what the monsters should look like. The decision was apparently made to just go with something disgusting, and that is what they got. However, thanks to excellent, imaginative stop-motion animation, the monsters have distinct personalities (as a group), and are, for all their nefarious activities, rather appealing in a bizarre way.

Although not bad overall, the film has a very conventional plot structure, with the addition of these incredible brains, and there's some uninteresting stuff until the fiends make their appearance. The acting is mediocre, the dialogue is perfunctory. There's also a scientific blunder at the climax: the control room of an atomic pile is blown up to shut down the pile. That would hardly do the trick.

Nonetheless, director Arthur Crabtree at least tries to build suspense in unconventional ways, and strives to keep the action going even when nothing is really happening. Sound technicians Peter Davies and Terence Poulton contribute some of the most repulsive sound effects in movie history, and the fine stop-motion animation at the climax alone would make *Fiend Without a Face* distinct and memorable.

The film opens outside an American air base in Winthrop, Manitoba. An uneasy sentry hears strange slurping sounds, then a scream, and rushes to find a man's dead body, a look of horror frozen on the face. Then the credits roll.

The Colonel (Stanley Maxted) in charge of the base knows that, because of the tension that already exists between the local Canadians and the air base over the experiments in atomic-powered radar, many will assume that the radiation was somehow responsible for the man's death. His right-hand man, Major Jeff Cummings (Marshall Thompson), is unable to persuade Barbara Griselle (Kim Parker), the man's surviving relative, to allow an autopsy. During the funeral, U.S. planes flying overhead disrupt the proceedings.

At a farm near the base, a farmer (R. Meadows White) and his wife (Lala Lloyd) are attacked by some invisible creature. We see the straw in the barn stirring, and then each of them in turn contorts in horror and tries to get an unseen something off their necks. They too die to that moist slurping sound.

This time there is an autopsy, and in addition to the already-familiar expression of horror frozen on the victims' faces, the doctor announces something truly macabre: the brains and spinal cords have been sucked out of the bodies like eggs, through two holes in the neck. They are dealing with a "mental vampire," someone says.

Jeff returns to visit Barbara, catching her coming out of the shower, to try to persuade her again to allow an autopsy, and gets into a fistfight with Constable Gibbons (Robert MacKenzie), her boyfriend. While at her house, he notices some books by R.E. Walgate, including *The Principles of Thought Control*, *The Energy of Thought*, as well as one on "Sibonetics." Jeff is impressed; even if Walgate's publisher can't spell cybernetics, Walgate is a famous and respected scientist-philosopher. Barbara tells Jeff Walgate lives nearby.

The mayor of the town (James Dyrenforth) is the next victim, and we see a little more of how these creatures operate. The camera follows an invisible form crawling along the porch, knocking over a couple of bottles. The unseen shape squeegees through some spilled water, then cuts a hole in the screen door (all this in stop-motion animation). Inside the house, it rumples the rug, making those horrible juicy noises. The mayor hears the sounds, pauses on the stairway, and the creature springs at him. (The camera follows its flight, even though it's invisible.) The mayor dies as did the others, with an expression of shock as his brain and spinal cord are sucked out.

Jeff goes to see if Professor Walgate (Kynaston Reeves) might have some ideas about the mystery, and discovers Barbara there—she works for Walgate. When Jeff asks Walgate if a supernatural force might be at work, the elderly professor gets overexcited and Jeff leaves.

Meanwhile, a posse is organized in town to try to run down the constable's suspected fiendish GI. They spread out through the quiet woods, the constable pairing off with a friend, but the two are soon separated. The friend runs through the woods, calling for Gibbons, but there's no answer. At a town council meeting shortly thereafter, horrifying moaning sounds are heard, and Gibbons staggers into the meeting room. I suppose his brains have only been partially sucked, leaving him a mindless vegetable.

For no very clear reason, Jeff goes to the cemetery and enters a mausoleum, where he finds a pipe—and someone locks him in. Later Barbara and Captain Chester (Terence Kilburn), Jeff's buddy, rescue him. Jeff recognizes the pipe as Walgate's, and goes to confront the old man.

Under pressure, the aging scientist admits that he is the cause of the horrible deaths. He tells them a strange tale, and we see it in flashback. He wanted to learn how to move objects with his thoughts, and so struggled mightily to send out a thought. (I know that this is confusing, but this really is how the film explains things.) At this point in his story, Walgate hears the slurping, gurgling sounds of a fiend, and passes out.

Meanwhile, back at the radar base, all the control rods for the atomic pile have been smashed, and it's starting to run wild. More rods are called for from the Hanford atomic plant near the Columbia River.

Most of the town officials and major military figures gather (for no good reason) at Walgate's house to hear his strange tale, and the flashbacks begin again.

In his lab, secret even from Barbara, he'd continued his experimentation on thought materialization. One night, lightning struck Walgate's equipment, giving his brain a tremendous shock, almost to the point of electrocution. "My thought was freed," Walgate tells his listeners, "free to turn the pages of a book," and we see the pages of a book turning. Eventually, with practice Walgate found he could use his thoughts to move other objects around.

But he needed a more consistent, smoother flow of power, and so devised a way to tap the atomic energy from the U.S. radar base. This made him "able to detach my thoughts and allow them to work on their own." (It's at this juncture that the plot really comes unhinged.)

Walgate goes on. "I began to devise a being into which the thought, once released, could enter and preserve itself for all humanity. I envisaged something akin to the human brain, with life and mobility, but without the limitations of man's body." This is also a little odd. Fiends seem to have even more limitations; they can't walk, for one thing, but can only crawl laboriously, although they are great jumpers.

"I succeeded," says Walgate, "but like thought itself, it was invisible." He returns to his lab later, and finds it in a shambles. "I had created a fiend," Walgate says. From the noises in the lab, he knows that there are now more than one (where'd the others come from?), and that they are intelligent. *His* creation is a "fiend," he says in terror, "that needs to prey on the intellect to survive and multiply." In what is surely a misreading of a line, Walgate says the fiends live "in the brains and nerve centers removed from these dead people." He must have meant *"on the brains,"* etc. Otherwise we have the baffling idea that the fiends have no bodies other than those brains and spinal cords they suck out of their victims — but what did they use for bodies before?

In any event, by now there are fiends galore. As if to prove this, one of the windows in the room smashes, the gobbling sound is heard, and Sergeant Kasper (Michael Balfour) is killed by a fiend.

The group realizes that the house is under siege by the fiends (who were eavesdropping?), now crawling around in the garden. The group quickly boards up the windows. The fiends' invisibility, someone says, is "a question of the amount of atomic radiation that's available" — and there's a cut to a dial at the lab showing the power climbing. What about the broken rods?

A worker tries to radio for help, but an invisible fiend gets him. The power surge makes the fiend that's operating the atomic plant controls flicker into visibility. It's just as Walgate said. The fiends really do look like well-rounded human brains, including spinal column attached (with bones). They have bundles of feelers (ganglia?) under their "chins," and two antennae atop the heads. And as the title says, no faces at all.

Back at Walgate's house, the people inside see the fiends in the yard becoming visible, and there are a lot of them, brains crawling around on the ground, inching up and down trees (their spinal cord "tails" propel them like inchworms), resting in branches like bleached birds' nests.

The three military men begin firing at the fiends, which die in a ghastly spurting of blood and with more disgusting sounds. (Helpful note if you are ever combatting fiends without faces: if they bleed black, it is a fatal wound; if they only bleed gray, they've merely been grazed, and can still getcha.) Walgate says that the fiends will go on increasing in power unless the atomic plant can be shut down, so Jeff says he will go blow up the control room.

After Jeff leaves, Walgate sneaks out of the house to draw the fiends away from Jeff. The fiends swarm all over Walgate, apparently sucking his brains from every part of his body, and Jeff does make his getaway.

There follows reasonably suspenseful intercutting. The fiends steal a hammer, and also use their spinal-cord tails to pull the boards off the windows, then start zipping in through the holes.

Jeff drives frantically to the explosive storage shed, shoots a fiend that is sneaking up on him, and heads on to the atomic pile. (Another helpful note on fiend fighting: they generally crawl along beeping electronically, but when they sight on an object, their little antennae point at the target and the beeping increases. In the next moment, the fiend leaps. So watch it.)

Meanwhile, back at the house, the Captain and the Colonel are shooting the fiends, which splutter and spray blood all over the place.

In the control room, Jeff sets the dynamite and lights the fuse, shooting but only wounding a nearby fiend (gray blood). As Jeff flees, the wounded fiend heroically drags itself to the blazing fuse, and with a little puff of breath (from where?), it *almost* blows the fuse out, but collapses in death as the fuse burns down.

More fiends fly in the window and are shot. One gets on Barbara, but is pulled off in time. Another jumps on her just as the atomic pile control room blows up. The fiend goes limp and drops dead. Outside, all the other fiends drop dead too, falling out of trees like autumn leaves. We now see that, in fact, there were *hundreds* of the curious creatures. After they die, for no other reason than sheer disgustingness, they dissolve into putrescent puddles of slime.

Jeff rushes back to Barbara, in time for the fadeout clinch.

Amelia Reynolds Long's short story, "The Thought Monster," appeared in an old issue of the pulp magazine, *Weird Tales*. Forrest J Ackerman was the agent for Long. He suggested the story to Richard Gordon and sold him the property.

Herbert J. Leder was an American working at this time mostly in Europe. In 1963, he coproduced, wrote and directed a suspense thriller, *9 Miles to Noon*, filmed on location in Athens. In 1967, a double bill of films written, produced and directed by Leder were released, *The Frozen Dead* and *It!*, a bizarre little film about the revival of the Golem, made entertaining and above-average by its lead actor, Roddy McDowall. Leder also produced, directed and wrote *The Candy Man* (1969), a highly derivative kidnapping story starring George Sanders, filmed in Mexico City. He began in television, on a variety of shows, including "The Red Skelton Show" and "Captain Video." He created the soap opera "The Doctors." For eleven years, he was a popular instructor in media arts at Jersey City State College. He died August 14, 1983.

Leder's script for *Fiend Without a Face* is the least interesting aspect of the picture. There are no clever ideas, no good dialogue, very little characterization. It's just a blueprint to get from the beginning to the end of the film. As mentioned, Leder also had freakish ideas about thoughts, which partly originated in the short story. Leder did nothing to improve on Long's ideas, and a great deal to make them more confusing.

"Having a thought" is only a figure of speech, but Leder makes it into something literal, a discrete *entity*. Walgate sends out a thought, and it takes on its own life, presumably with thoughts of its own, which may explain the rapid proliferation of fiends.

To literally embody these "thoughts" as crawling, evil brains is quite a leap of imagination, but a monster was needed. The fiends are a menace while invisible, because they are so voracious and invisible. Once they are visible, they are vulnerable—"at least they're mortal!" Marshall Thompson exclaims—in fact, almost absurdly so. One or two bullets and they're finished, in spluttering puddles of blood. Their biggest weapon is that there are so many of them, and they are in fact apparently multiplying as we watch, although the reproductive habits of faceless fiends don't bear much thought.

In short, what Leder brought to the film was its conventional elements and these wild ideas about thoughts. There are at least two completely extraneous scenes, in a movie that even before the credits starts with an attack by the monsters. Almost everything is neatly tied together: the heroine's relative was an early victim, she works for the man who started the whole thing, the hero's atomic-powered radiation project is necessary for the fiends, too.

So why does Jeff get into a fight with the constable? Undoubtedly to add running time, and to bring in a spot of action. But it seems forced, contrived, and a waste of time. Likewise, he could have found Walgate's pipe in any suspicious place, or something else could have directed him toward the old man, of whom he is already suspicious. Why do we have the long, pointless and out-of-character scene in the mausoleum? Probably because cemeteries are Officially Scary Places, and more running time was needed. It certainly adds nothing to the film; it's not remotely scary, or even interesting. It's out of character for Walgate to lock Jeff in the tomb. It seems like a sequence added solely for the trailers.

There are two major virtues to *Fiend Without a Face*: the special effects, and the direction by Arthur Crabtree. Crabtree had been a cinematographer (one of his films was *The Remarkable Mr. Kipps*, 1941) before turning to direction. Most of his films were for Gainsborough, noted for its glossy production values and costume melodramas. His titles include *Madonna of the Seven Moons* (1944), *Caravan* (1946), *Lilli Marlene* (1950) and *West of Suez* (1957), as well as most notoriously, *Horrors of the Black Museum*, which may have been his last film.

Fiend Without a Face was filmed efficiently on a low budget—the sets seem positively flimsy—and undoubtedly very rapidly. But Crabtree generates suspense in several sequences. When the constable disappears in the woods, Crabtree follows the friend as he shouts Gibbons' name again and again, interspersing shots of the desperate searcher with shots of black, brooding pine trees. There is no sound at all except the wind and the man's voice; it's as if the forest is cooperating with the monsters. It's a surprisingly eerie scene for a film of this nature.

Crabtree does frequently try to evoke a feeling that all this is taking place in Canada's North Woods; a few second-unit location scenes help very much, as do the accurate accents of most of the cast.

Another reasonably good scene involves the attack on the mayor; with the cooperation of his British special effects unit and the outstanding, if repulsive, sound effects, Crabtree evokes a feeling of genuinely monstrous presence.

Crabtree also attempts a few stabs at characterization. Deputy Mayor Melville (Launce Maraschal) is treated as a petty tyrant who degenerates into total cowardice as the fiends launch their attack on Walgate's house. In Leder's script, second male lead Chester was the usual womanizing military second banana, but Crabtree treats this with the contempt it deserves.

For the most part, however, the film is colorless; it moves at a good pace, but never comes to life except in the attacks by the fiends (the reason it was made), and in the outrageous climax, which owes much more to the effects crew than to Crabtree or Leder.

The only notable thing about the acting is that the mostly British cast does manage American/Canadian accents quite well. Kynaston Reeves, Walgate, was a veteran British character actor, who died in 1971 at 88. Here, however, he doesn't seem to have cared at all about what he was doing. In scenes in which he is supposed to be undergoing an almost total emotional collapse, he merely looks mildly worried. The role has little depth as written, but Reeves didn't attempt to add any of his own.

Marshall Thompson is just the stalwart hero; there was nothing that could be done with the part, but he's adequate. For more on Thompson, see the entry on *First Man into Space*.

The most memorable aspect of *Fiend Without a Face* are those outstanding special effects. In *Fangoria* #46, producer John Croydon wrote about the effects, unconvincingly claiming that an early form of motion-control photography was used in the scenes which are clearly stop-motion animation. According to Croydon, the brains were maneuvered by wires attached to computer-directed Selsen motors, but they certainly look like stop-motion in the film. At least I can mention the names of the talented men who brought the fiends to life: the director was Baron Florenz Von Nordhoff, who won a Silver Bear at the Berlin Film Festival (1960) for his short *The Purple Line*. The animation itself was done in Munich by German special effects artist K.L. Ruppel. Peter Neilson apparently headed the British crew.

There are real exuberance and attention to detail shown in the startling effects that mark the climax of the picture. The fiends are treated inventively, with wit, and even given a kind of characterization, at least enough to generate a bizarre, cockamamie pathos for these crawling brains. (As they also eat brains, a fair motto for faceless fiends might be "you eat what you are.") Although faceless, and hence eyeless, the fiends clearly peer at people from time to time. In the big battle, one lands on a couch and cocks its "head" at Kim Parker, just before using its spinal-cord tail to launch itself at her. The motion makes it look rather like a quizzical but hideous puppy dog.

When they crawl, the fiends make a little coiling flip with their inch-worming tails, almost a flourish. Their antennae quiver constantly, and when they spot a potential meal source, the antennae straighten out and point at the victim with an electronic tremolo.

I suspect the noble gesture by a dying fiend, in trying to blow out the fuse and save all of fiendkind, was the invention of Ruppel and Nordhoff. Everything the fiends do that show characterization and inventiveness is in the stop-motion scenes. When they try to break into the room, one first grabs a hammer with its feelers, and when that proves unhelpful, turns around and uses its feelers and tail to pull the boards open. They do have high intelligence: it is shown in their actions.

Ruppel and Von Nordhoff show their own intelligence and inventiveness again and again: there's a shot of the floor, someone walks by, and immediately a fiend drops into the shot and begins crawling away. There's no cut, the man walking by and the stop-motion figure are on the same set. This was done to emphasize the reality of the fiends by placing them in the same shot as a live human being. And it works.

There are other attempts to blend live action and animation effects, and I confess my knowledge of the field is too limited to say how these were done, but it looks like the actors were on a process screen, with animated fiends in the foreground, leaping at the actors. This is done in the scene in which Marshall Thompson gets the dynamite, and when the fiends gang up on Kynaston Reeves. The only reason I doubt this was rear-screen projection was that the image was so clear and lacking in grain; the contrast also was excellent.

Reviews of the film at the time were less than enthusiastic. The *Monthly Film Bulletin* gave the film an average rating, and said "For the most part this is tepidly macabre. What may give the film a special interest for devotees of the genre is the final scene in which the creatures, hitherto invisible, appear.... The trick photography is the best [in] a long time and the monsters have been devised with a certain amount of originality."

Jack Moffitt didn't care for the picture. "The more preposterous a horror film is, the more the audience seems to enjoy laughing at it. Those who seek such pleasures should have plenty of fun at *Fiend Without a Face*, a wildly gory fantasy imported from England.... [At the climax the] brains become visible and fly through the air like winged hamburgers.... By this time [the heroes], like the authors, have been through too much to distinguish between a brain and a thought."

Weekly *Variety* also noted the horrific effects of the film: "It oozes and gurgles with Grand Guignol blood and crunching bones, easily one of the goriest horror pictures in the current cycle. Story, direction and acting are primitive."

Parents Magazine philosophized about the movie: "If wishes ever do become horses no one could seriously object, especially beggars who may ride them. But in this fantastic opus, thought ... becomes a disgusting mass of brain." The unnamed reviewer also said that "the film mixes international relations and science fiction irresponsibly," although the fact that the film takes place in Canada merely seemed a way of explaining the British accents of some of the cast. *Parents'* reviewer reached a conclusion few could disagree with: the movie was "horror compounded."

In *Castle of Frankenstein* #9, Joe Dante said, "German-made special fx of this British sf-thriller are so effective it's regrettable that rest of film is so routine.... [A] wonderfully nightmarish ending."

Psychotronic: "This film ... might seem pretty ordinary for a while, but stick with it.... The scenes of these partially animated creatures choking their screaming victims with their [spinal] cords while sucking their brains out are the most nightmarish and shocking you'll ever see. Real breathtaking stuff!"

Even Don Willis (II) liked the ending, saying that when the fiends become visible, "they're a *real* treat—brain-spine wriggling and writhing and ... splattering ... all over walls, rugs and couches."

It's a shame that no other company ever turned to Ruppel and Von Nordhoff for similar effects; they remain an unknown team—even experts in the field of special effects, such as Jim Danforth, confess to total ignorance about them. But this one film shows that they are imaginative, amusing and highly inventive. Without their effects, *Fiend Without a Face* would merely be a rather ordinary science fiction horror film with odd monsters; with their effects, it has one of the most entertaining and repulsive final reels of any SF film, anytime.

The Flame Barrier

This minor little picture primarily consists of jungle thrills and a romantic triangle; the science fiction elements don't come in until the last few minutes, and are conventional. The plot line doesn't make much sense, as there are some unexplained elements. It's a hastily-made second feature, being released with the much better *Return of Dracula*. It was designed to capitalize on interest in satellites.

An undated clip from *Daily Variety* said that "'The Flame Barrier,' an original story by Sam X. Abarbanel, has been acquired by Gramercy Pictures. The indie company headed by Jules Levy, Arthur Gardner and Arnold Laven, has signed George Worthing Yates to screenplay 'Flame.'" When the film was released, Yates was credited with the story, and Abarbanel's name was not included in the credits. I suspect his story line was jettisoned, with Yates fashioning a new one around the title.

In the opening narration (apparently written by coscenarist Pat Fielder), the "flame barrier" of the title is defined: "Approximately five hundred miles above our Earth lies a protective barrier—sometimes called 'The Flame Barrier.' Above that barrier which protects our planet from the unknown rays of outer space lies the unexplored. Scientists say that beyond our sphere a perfect vacuum exists; poets say there is eternal night; dreamers say there is life." There is no flame barrier in reality.

Carol Dahlmann (Kathleen Crowley) arrives in Campeche, in Mexico's Yucatán peninsula. She's looking for her husband who disappeared into the nearby jungles in search of a satellite most thought burned on reentry. Dahlmann, seen only as a corpse in the film, is apparently a Howard Hughes–type multimillionaire, who pursues an interest in science as a hobby. His will prevents his wife from inheriting until Dahlmann is proved dead, and she's arrived to find evidence.

She approaches the Hollister brothers, oil geologists, standard types: younger Matt (Robert Brown), dissolute but charming drunkard and womanizer, fairly well forced out of the business, and Dave (Arthur Franz), stern, cold expert on jungles and exploration. He's been burned by a love affair in his past and is arrogant and tyrannical in his aloof treatment of Carol.

Carol agrees to pay Dave 10 percent of the estate if Dahlmann proves to be dead, and $7,000 if he's alive. She tells him about the purpose of Dahlmann's expedition: he felt the satellite would prove there was life in outer space.

As usual in such films, when the expedition (one Jeep) prepares to depart, Carol arrives attired in all the wrong kind of clothes, and hauls along several suitcases. Dave sternly orders her to reduce her luggage to one suitcase, and warns her that she'd be better off dressed in pants rather than her skirt. Matt hides some tequila in the Jeep, and later fills a canteen with it.

As they head toward the jungle, they meet some natives—conveniently, Dave speaks the language of all Indians they meet—who are fleeing because "something deep in the jungle has made the gods angry ... the animals die for no reason."

They push on, finding a deserted village splashed with blood. Nearby, they find Waumi (Rodd Redwing), a Noble Savage, virtually crucified. They cut him down, and he and Tispe (Kaz Oran; called "Koko" in the script and perhaps the film, "Tispe" is the name in the *Filmfacts* credit list and in one line in the script) and a third Indian (Larry Duran) agree to act as their guides. They press onward, eventually having to abandon the Jeep. There are fewer jungle thrills than usual, and much less stock footage. At one point Carol is menaced by a snake, but it's quickly dispatched by Dave.

The romance settles itself conventionally: Dave thaws and he and Carol fall in love; Matt is sexually interested and superficially charming, but is clearly a Loser. Haven't we been here before?

Further in the jungle, they find a charred human skeleton with a metal necklace melted and fused. About this time, they begin hearing strange, unearthly screams, which go without adequate explanation. They also find a burned Indian (Bernie Gozier), who can only gasp out the name of the local fire god before dying. After his death, his body turns into a charred skeleton.

The little expedition, now consisting of the three white people and Waumi (who fought with Tispe), see a field with a large charred streak across it, presumably where the satellite landed. Not far away, they find Dahlmann's deserted camp, which has a laboratory powered by electricity from a convenient solar generator, and a noisy chimpanzee tied to a stake. One line says the chimp has been in the satellite.

The recording left by Dahlmann is unintelligible due to a loud electrical interference on the tape. A deafening humming is heard from offscreen. The group goes to a nearby cave (exterior: Bronson Caverns; interior: cheap set) where they find the satellite. The description given in the script was not followed exactly in the film, partly to good effect: "On an outcropping of rock against one wall is a most incredible sight. The large globe of an Earth satellite has been placed on this shelf, as if by human hands. But the form of it has altered. The skin, which was once apparently metallic, appears living, scaled and porous, like a reptile skin." In the film, it's still just a metal sphere; it's unclear what this skinlike appearance of the satellite itself was supposed to signify, which may explain why this aspect was eliminated. "And pouring out from it, in every direction, like a cancerous growth, is a peculiar jelly-like form of life, spreading in every direction in wild profusion. But most terrifying of all, encased in this slime—this translucent, almost transparent cellular growth, is the body of HOWARD DAHLMANN, perfectly preserved, hanging suspended, and quite lifeless. The whole makes a giant living pulsing mass of quivering malignant terror. [Whew!] And in the center of the satellite itself, where the escape hatch has been, is an opening, now filled with the growth, which appears as an immense eye, staring outward [not in the finished film]. The light which emanates from it pulses in the way a heart beat pulses—strong, then faint, then strong again." The chimp runs toward the mass of jelly, and suddenly disintegrates. There is a flame barrier around the Thing.

Back at the camp, Dave uses Dahlmann's notes and discovers that the Thing doubles in size on a periodic cycle, which they eventually deduce is about two hours. The "magnetic" field around it grows in geometric proportion

Opposite: At the climax of The Flame Barrier (1958), Robert Brown (left) and Arthur Franz confront the strange space thingy enveloping a satellite and a corpse. The space substance looks more like cellophane than protoplasm and the "metallic streaks" on the wall look like decorations. This cave scene was not shot in Bronson Caverns.

to the mass—the field grows faster than the Thing—and soon it will engulf the world, or something.

Back in the cave, Dave notices very convenient metallic streaks on the wall behind the Thing: one leads to where he's standing, the other goes up the back of the cave. Intending to electrocute the monster, they bring the solar battery into the cave and hook a wire from one terminal to the nearby streak. Matt will have to climb above the monster to fasten the other terminal to the streak there. But the field begins growing sooner than they expected, and to force Dave to throw the switch, Matt deliberately drops into the field and disintegrates. Dave throws the switch, and kills the monster.

As Carol and Dave prepare to return to civilization, Dahlmann's tape recorder starts up to provide a kind of afterword: "The nations of the world must exert great caution. We are pioneers again into a new frontier—but the terrors we may find cannot be measured by the known... It is the unknown that holds the key to the strange phenomena beyond."

Speaking of unknown, just what is going on in *The Flame Barrier*? The satellite was found by Dahlmann, who took it to the cave but was caught in the growth when it burst out of the satellite—after it was in the cave. Which leaves several things unexplained: how did the chimp survive in the satellite with the monster? Why does the native turn up burned? Why does he turn into a charred skeleton after death? Why did the animals flee? Why is that blood-splashed village deserted? What is the monster? There's nothing in the script to indicate that the monster from the satellite is mobile and, in fact, the story depends on its remaining in one place—so what was all that fiery activity elsewhere? It's almost as if there's *another* fire monster active elsewhere, and our heroes just never run across it.

The explanation is that the script was written and filmed in a great hurry—it was shot in late December, 1957, and ready for release by early April, 1958—and no one bothered to make all the parts match. It was just a jungle-movie imitation of the Quatermass films. Of the several Gramercy fantasies of this period, including *Monster That Challenged the World*, *The Vampire* and *Return of Dracula*, *The Flame Barrier* is definitely the least interesting.

It's really a jungle adventure with the usual characters that populate such films. There are fewer encounters with animals, and no hostile natives, but those were left out for budgetary reasons.

The title is a giveaway, but has no rational explanation. (The title may have varied in different parts of the country; Joe Dante swears it was *Beyond the Flame Barrier* when he saw it and some seem to recall it as *It Fell from the Flame Barrier*.) The Flame Barrier is really the combination of speed and angle of reentry of a spacecraft at which it begins to heat up from friction, all the way to the burning point if things aren't done right. There's no actual "barrier" in space of course. By some associative response, the monster that comes from the flame barrier is itself hot, with a flame barrier of its own. In the film, this is described both as a magnetic and an electrical field. There's a rigid if expanding line of demarcation: at *this* point, things catch fire.

Both Kathleen Crowley and Arthur Franz were better actors than this kind of film deserved. I've commented on Franz elsewhere, but I should point out that this was his busiest period for this kind of film, with *Back from the Dead*, *The Flame Barrier*, *Monster on the Campus* and *The Atomic Submarine* all made within a few months. Franz worked primarily in television during and after this period, including on many of the SF and fantasy series, such as "Science Fiction Theatre," "Men into Space," "One Step Beyond," "Voyage to the Bottom of the

Sea," "Tarzan," "The Invaders" and "The Six Million Dollar Man." He was a regular in the short-lived series "World of the Giants" and appeared in an episode of "Land of the Giants." Joe Dante informs us Franz was regularly cast in films directed by Edward Dmytryk.

Kathleen Crowley is an attractive actress who found her most promising roles as a supporting player. She was the female lead in several B movies of the 1950s, including *The Female Jungle* (1956), *Target Earth*, *Westward Ho the Wagons* (1957) and *Curse of the Undead* (1959), but later had good parts in *Downhill Racer* (1969) and *The Lawyer* (1970).

Reviews reflected the film. James M. Jerauld in the *Motion Picture Herald* thought the film "good" but added that its main appeal would be to "the youngsters." *Film Daily* observed that "the production obviously is of modest budget. Some of the special effects are worthy of mention, adding some small amount of pictorial excitement to an otherwise drab scenario.... Performances are adequate."

Giving the film a surprisingly favorable II, the *Monthly Film Bulletin* seemingly contradicted itself in the commentary: "The amateurishness of the science fiction elements ... deprives the [horror scenes] of any terror. The quarrels of the small search party provide the film's better moments, but the studio jungle clearings are wearisomely like each other and unlike Mexico."

The Flame Barrier is just another cheap little science fiction movie, with scant science fiction and fewer adequate explanations than most.

The Fly

A certifiable hit, *The Fly* is also famous. It was an elaborate, moderately expensive ($325,000) production from 20th Century–Fox that was wildly popular in 1958. It was almost *The Exorcist* of its day, with lines waiting to get in, the eager audience primed for the horrifying scenes. It must have made indelible impressions on most of those who saw it. For years afterward, I was able to get a shriek out of my younger sister Judy by whispering "helllp meeee" in a shrill little voice. Once on "Mork and Mindy," Robin Williams picked up some bit of crud, muttered "hellllp meeee" and tossed it aside as the audience laughed – they got the joke.

Reviews at the time were mostly very favorable, and the movie was profitable enough to spawn two sequels, both of which were much inferior to the first. But in recent years, some writers have dismissed the film as absurd claptrap. Admitting it had some "few unforgettable scenes," Don Willis (I) tersely termed it "poorly acted and directed." In *Future Tense*, John Brosnan said *The Fly* had "an unusually absurd story," and complained about technical drawbacks he sees in the film (while getting a crucial plot point wrong). In Peter Nicholls' *The Science Fiction Encyclopedia*, Brosnan complains further: "An absurd film, its ludicrous excesses are amusing." In *Science Fiction Movies*, Philip Strick says that "the movie was never as good as it should have been." In *Horror and Fantasy in the Movies*, Tom Hutchinson says that although *The Fly* has "now become a kind of cult film," it is actually "high camp, pitched at its seemingly most ludicrous."

The Fly is indeed based on an absurd premise, if one should be so foolish as to take the central idea on its face value, but it isn't intended to be a chiller centered on logic. The horror is almost entirely emotional in basis, not intellectual; it's the kind of picture that is genuinely quite terrifying the first time through, but can suffer greatly on calm reflection and, particularly, over-familiarity gained from repeat viewings. In 1958, however, *The Fly* was one of the most effective, even grueling, science fiction horror films ever made.

The story by George Langelaan first appeared in the United States in *Playboy*, June, 1957, hardly as unlikely a source as some might think: the magazine has consistently printed good science fiction and horror stories down through the years. The story won a prize as the most popular piece of short fiction in *Playboy* that year; it was reprinted in Judith Merrill's Best-SF-of-the-Year anthology, and occasionally turns up in other anthologies.

The script was by James Clavell who, of course, has become internationally famous for other sorts of fiction altogether. *The Fly* was apparently his first-produced script; his others are of varying quality, but *The Fly* is astute and intelligent. Clavell follows Langelaan's very canny structure, but does not employ the writer's almost flippant tone. The ending is changed (in the story, the wife commits suicide), although the struggle to give the film an upbeat tone is apparent.

Clavell arrived from England in 1953; Halliwell's *Filmgoer's Companion* reveals that Clavell was born in Australia, the son of Sir Richard Clavell. He has frequently directed the films he writes, as early as *Walk Like a Dragon* in 1960. *633 Squadron* (1964) and *The Satan Bug* (1965), both directed by others, were adapted by Clavell from novels, and were expensively-produced programmers with clichéd characters and unmemorable dialogue. His best film as director/writer/producer is probably *To Sir with Love* (1967), a schmaltzy and unrealistic film in which by being Very Good, Sidney Poitier reforms a classroom of British juvenile delinquents. Some favor Clavell's later *The Last Valley* (1971), which is ambitious enough, but it's also pretentious, awkward and boring. When he turned his talents more frequently to fiction, he fared much better, and has written several critically-applauded best-sellers, most notably *Tai-Pan* and *Shogun*.

20th Century–Fox distributed a couple of low-budget Regalscope science fiction films directed by Kurt Neumann, *She-Devil* and *Kronos*, which were made for Fox's subsidiary, Regal Pictures. Buddy Adler, a Fox executive, had noted the grosses on these pictures (backed by Fox head Spyros Skouras), and decided that such a film could be made directly for Fox, using much of the same quick, efficient production techniques employed by Regal. Naturally, as it would be for the parent studio, the film would have to be somewhat classier. Special effects would be kept at a minimum—there are almost no effects at all in *The Fly*—so that money could be spent more wisely in other areas of production. I presume Langelaan's story was chosen because it was vivid, allowed a monster and an unmasking, and had already achieved a certain amount of fame.

Kurt Neumann's wise production techniques kept the costs down on *Kronos* and *She-Devil*, so it seemed reasonable to hire him to direct *The Fly*, and his cinematographer, Karl Struss, to photograph it. Furthermore, Kurt Neumann was fond of science fiction himself; he always wanted to do another significant film in the genre, after his *Rocketship X-M*. His talents were not up to his intentions, however; he was an unimaginative and pedestrian director, but the basic seriousness of his approach, even with unpromising material, deserves more credit than he is generally given.

Everyone was determined to make *The Fly* a film to be proud of, and they also realized that with a story as preposterous as this, a very straightforward approach was demanded. Neumann was probably incapable of any other approach, and does in fact show little imagination in the film. The shot from the fly's perspective (in multiple images) of the screaming Patricia Owens was probably Karl Struss' idea.

One odd note: the original story, being French, was set in France. This is probably the reason the film is set in Canada—you get people with French names who talk pure United Statesian. But it's a peculiar fidelity to the source.

The story begins with the discovery that Hélène Delambre (Owens) has murdered her brilliant scientist husband André (Al Hedison) by crushing his head and arm in a mighty metal press in a factory owned by André and his staid brother François (Vincent Price). Hélène refuses to tell François or Inspector Charas (Herbert Marshall) why she did it, and feigns insanity. However, she becomes genuinely upset when a mere fly buzzes through the room. François eventually learns from Hélène's young son Philippe (Charles Herbert) that she is especially interested in a certain fly with a white head and leg, which escaped, so François tells her that he has that fly captive. She assumes he knows the awful truth, so she agrees to tell the entire story to François and Charas and we see it in flashback.

André reveals to Hélène that he's working on a matter transmitter, a device capable of disintegrating matter in one chamber, transmitting it like a television picture to another chamber, and reintegrating it. André sees this device as a potentially great boon for mankind, in fact the most exciting thing since the invention of the wheel.

He's wealthy, and finances his own private research in the basement of their home. He has a few setbacks. The first time he demonstrates the machine to Hélène, the lettering on an ashtray comes out reversed, which means the entire atomic structure of the ashtray has been reversed. He tinkers further with the machine, and tries transmitting their cat, Dandelo, but the cat doesn't reintegrate at all, it's turned into a "stream of cat atoms" wandering through the universe. But finally, a guinea pig is transmitted with success.

Hélène later comes down to the lab, but the door is locked, and André passes a note under it to her, revealing something has gone wrong and he can't talk. He allows her to enter. André has a cloth draped over his head, and one hand thrust into his lab coat pocket. He insists (via typewriter) that she try to find a certain fly for him, one with a peculiar head and foreleg. It is a matter of life and death—if they can't find the fly, he'll have to kill himself.

After a frantic search of the house by Hélène, Philippe and their puzzled housekeeper (Kathleen Freeman), the fly is seen but not caught, so Hélène, back in the lab, insists that André try transmitting himself again, assuming that something similar to the accident with the ashtray has befallen her husband.

He transmits himself again, and Hélène eagerly pulls the cloth off his head. To her horror, she discovers that her beloved André has the head of a gigantic housefly, as well as the foreleg. When he transmitted himself, he admits, a fly was in the chamber with him, and their atoms became scrambled, trading their heads and left "arms."

André feels his mind becoming more and more like that of a fly, and insists that Hélène help him crush his insect parts in the metal press, with contact set at zero: the upper plate touching the bottom plate. This will squash his alien parts to such a degree that their insect nature will be undetectable. She sadly agrees. André smashes his equipment and burns his notes, and they carry out his plan.

Back in the present, François reluctantly reveals that not only does he not have the fly, he has never seen the fly, and does not believe her story. Hélène is about to be hauled off to the booby hatch when François discovers the fly with André's head and arm caught in a spider web in the garden. He shows it to Charas, and they watch in horror as the spider descends on the horrified fly-man (screaming "hellllp meeee"). Charas smashes both spider and victim with a rock. They realize that, of course, Hélène's story was true. Sometime later, Philippe, Hélène and François talk about the great explorer that André was, and how he made just one little mistake.

As several writers point out, the story of The Fly is riddled with improbabilities, although in fairness, some are easily rationalized by using the same logic the story does. Some have wondered why the fly ends up with a fly-sized André head and arm, and André with a man-sized fly head and leg. This is not a story of surgical transplants, it is a story of, as the ads said, "atoms gone wild." The atomic patterns for the various heads and arms were switched, not the actual limbs themselves. This might explain why, at first, André has his own mind, even with the head of a fly, and the fly thinks flyish thoughts, even with André's head. It would take time for the separate patterns that make up the respective minds to accommodate themselves to the new brains they now occupy so that André would, as he does, gradually slip into fly behavior, and the fly itself would slowly develop a human mind.

Others have complained that the matter transmitter fouls up in different ways every time it makes a mistake. Once it reverses the atoms of the ashtray, another time the cat vanishes altogether, and finally it scrambles the atomic patterns of a man and a fly. I find this complaint trivial; a machine of unfathomable complexity like the matter transmitter would certainly have more than one failure mode. Does your TV set always go wrong the same way?

There's no point in dealing with the concept of a matter transmitter strictly on the basis of scientific logic; given today's technology, or even our foreseeable future, matter transmitters are highly unlikely if not impossible. But that's not the point; they make sense, in the same way that even less likely devices as time machines make sense: they work by analogy, not scientific logic. Even if impossible, the right kind of analogies make sense to most people, like sympathetic magic does, and thereby are perfectly good devices for fiction.

We know that, however unlikely it may seem to many, pictures are transmitted through the air and "reintegrated" on our TV screens. All the machine in The Fly does is to apply this same idea to physical objects; most moviegoers wouldn't care if it was impossible.

In the film, the explanation of the machine is careful, logical and lucid. Although rather gaudy, the machinery doesn't look totally silly, and the results — obtained by a bright light and a simple jump cut — seem reasonable.

The family in The Fly is presented as carefully as the central gimmick. This is a standard happy-young-couple family, with one kid and lots of money. Daddy may be a scientific genius, but he's also a loving father, actively sexually interested in his wife (unusual in science fiction films), handsome and an altogether decent sort. André's eccentricities don't annoy Hélène; she finds them endearing. This family may be stereotyped, but it's a different kind of stereotyping than we are used to in science fiction films; the Delambres seem almost like a situation-comedy family, so this makes the horror even stronger: you don't expect Ward Cleaver to end up with the head of a fly.

There's an extra humanizing touch as well: brother François is the central character in the frame story, and he's in love with Hélène himself.

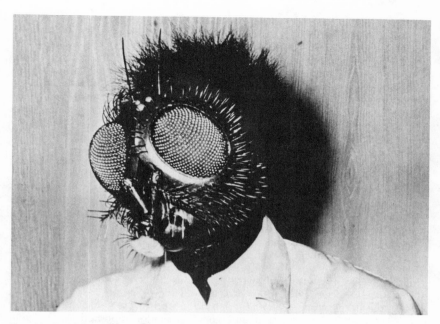

Ben Nye's trial makeup for The Fly (1958); for the film, these faceted eyes were replaced with larger ones that had an oil-like sheen.

The Fly does not work on scientific logic; by the introduction of this family, it works on *emotional* logic, and it does that very effectively. I first saw the film in a huge theatre in San Francisco, and despite some laughter here and there, the audience was responding as if directed: shrieking and jumping in the scary scenes—and *The Fly* has several riveting, memorable images—and calm and attentive during the long, precise buildup to the big unmasking scene. The audience had no difficulty swallowing the idea, and were clearly impressed, if not overwhelmed, by the movie.

Clavell's script and Struss' photography are the main assets of the film. While at times the dialogue tends toward the galumphingly ironic ("the sacredness of life" as a tenet of André's life is trotted out again and again) and the truly tired ("You're a strange man," Hélène says to her obsessed husband), the structure is impeccable. The three-act format, borrowed from the story, eases us into the strange events, creating a sense of movie-normalcy long before anything fantastic actually turns up.

Yet there is already plenty of foreshadowing: the bizarre opening scene, in which an old guard (Torben Meyer) discovers Hélène with André's body, has allusions to the vanquished cat Dandelo, and in the original script, a fly was to be bothering the old man. In the script, François says André couldn't even hurt a fly.

Of course, the business of the recovery of André's body from the press is incredibly grisly for the time; there's lots of blood, and when the press is raised, the torso sticks gummily to the top for a moment. This movie *means business*.

When Hélène begins her tale, however, it's all sweetness and sunlight; how could something so horrible come from a family so happy? The mystery elements keep the audience interested in what's happening, and Hélène's panic when a nurse swats at a fly. When she starts talking, we're certainly prepared.

In her story, there's still more careful buildup, but the nature of the structure means the mystery elements are put aside. We share Hélène's wonder at André's miracle machine, and his annoyance when it doesn't work quite right. Finally, when Hélène sees André with the hood, the movie has become almost compelling. (It seems unlikely that very many guessed what was under that hood; this is one of the few movies with an unmasking scene in which the revealed face is a genuine surprise, maybe even a shock. Most thought his eyes were going to be in the wrong place.)

Despite Neumann's efforts along these lines, his direction is just not good enough to make us *really* care about André and Hélène as people, but the story is almost compelling. Patricia Owens and Al (later David) Hedison are attractive, and there is actually some effort at characterization. The script suggested more ideas in this area for the performers than the actors and Neumann deliver. Nonetheless, it does follow one good rule for developing sympathetic characters: have them like *each other*, and we'll like them more; and André and Hélène are clearly in love.

When André begins wearing the hood, it is slightly surprising. Despite the gruesome opening, the rhythm of the story doesn't demand something horrible at this point, and we are slightly off-balance, which is good. Hélène's growing horror, the notes slipped under the lab door, and André's shrouded form all lend a new air of mystery and emergency. Clavell's approach is intelligent enough to allow some comedy after the horror cranks up again (Freeman's owl-eyed "flies, madame?" as she's ordered to search for the insects gets laughs, as intended), but Neumann's direction is awkward here. The flailing around for the fly remains urgent, but also tends toward the comic, and it takes a bit for the film to recover its equilibrium.

The buildup to the unmasking scene, which the audience is now both dreading and anticipating, is extremely well done, the best sequence in any of Neumann's films that I've seen. Struss' low-key lighting in all the fly-man scenes, unlike the sunny openness of the early parts of the film, maintains an eerie mood, and the mixture of moving camera, zoom shot and swift cut to a horrifying close-up of the fly head are timed with great precision. It carries an impact even on repeated viewings. However, we thereafter see far too much of the fly-headed man, and the shocking face becomes familiar rather than frightening, which pushes it toward the comic.

Clavell sought to depict the conflicts in André's disintegrating mind, the war between his fly- and man-natures, by having the fly arm literally battle for supremacy with the human arm. However, this, too, heads toward the comic, and makes you wonder what side the head is on. (Also, seen after similar battles between Peter Sellers' mechanical and human arms in *Dr. Strangelove*, even perfectly directed scenes of this nature would likely be funny.)

However, after the scenes of André smashing the lab, and after the fly-man (and his sex-happy fly hand) stop pawing the unconscious Hélène—she fainted, not surprisingly—the picture achieves a macabre poignancy. André's final instructions to Hélène are scrawled on a blackboard in the lab; the last thing he writes is "I love you" in a shaky scrawl. Because we accepted their love before this, it remains acceptable now, and the movie becomes somewhat touching. This mood continues right up until the press starts descending. André's hand clutches at Hélène, in an attempt to create some suspense, and audiences jumped around excitedly, but they knew she wasn't squashed with her husband.

After the return to the framing story, the wrap-up is protracted. When François lounges in the garden beside the spider web, failing to hear the screams of the tiny man-fly, the timing is off; he sits there too long. We can hear the high-pitched shrieks, why can't he?

He returns soon, with Charas, and in one of the screen's most bizarre mixtures of the genuinely horrifying and the ludicrous, the picture achieves its climax. We see the fly with André's head and arm — his head looks aged, with white hair, and his mouth seems toothless — and we see close-ups of a hideous spider as it descends on the little monster. Charas crashes the rock down, but a beat too late; we know the spider got to the shrieking thing.

Spiders are innately horrifying for most people, and the man-fly's terror and helplessness combine with this spider-loathing to produce an image so surrealistic as to be indelible. But it's simultaneously funny, because it is so unlikely. (Price says he and Herbert Marshall couldn't look at each other during the filming of their reaction shots to this scene: they kept bursting into laughter.)

A fly is about as trivial an insect as there is which is why Langelaan used one in his story. The film would not have worked as well with any other insect; a crawling one would have been too easy to find.

The script contains some ideas I do not believe are in the film; the best one is poignant. When Hélène is trying to convince François to kill the fly she thinks he has (and therefore, thinks he's seen that it has André's head): "What else could it do but go to someone it loves, to me or [Philippe] or you?" But some ideas should have been omitted, and were. Following Langelaan's lead, Clavell had long shots of the white-headed fly (before the unmasking scene) accompanied by high-pitched insane laughter. This certainly would have been met with enthusiastic echoes of laughter from the audience. The scene of the head-crushing is far more shocking in the script, but there's only one shot of the fly in the web.

Kurt Neumann was probably at his best in this film, perhaps because this was one of his most important movies; as it turned out, it was also one of his last. He came from Germany to the United States in the same wave that brought over Billy Wilder and other famous talents. Neumann started directing in his middle 20s, working steadily from the 1930s until the late 1950s, when he died. (Halliwell gives his death date as 1958, but films directed by Neumann were released well into 1959.)

Most of his output was B movies, although his first couple of years at Universal were spent on lower-case A films, like The Big Cage, The Secret of the Blue Room, and The Affair of Susan, which garnered him some favorable reviews. Through the remainder of the 30s, he worked on minor films for major studios, including Paramount, MGM and RKO. In 1946–47, he directed three Tarzan films: Tarzan and the Amazons, Tarzan and the Leopard Woman and Tarzan and the Huntress; he returned to the Burroughs character in 1953, with Tarzan and the She-Devil.

He formed a good working relationship with cinematographer Karl Struss, who shot many of Neumann's films, including The Fly. After it, Neumann made four more films and died relatively young. Although his output was mostly in other areas, he will probably be remembered best for his four science fiction films.

He was a one-two-three, by-the-book director, with almost no visual flair, an inept handling of actors, and only that dogged sincerity as a virtue. He fluffs major scenes in *The Fly*; for instance, when poor André jerks his fly hand out of his lab coat, the shot is well-photographed and a good idea in that it is both shocking and deepens the mystery, but Neumann's staging is off: Hedison telegraphs the action, we stay on it too long, and it doesn't have the needed impact. Also, when Patricia Owens is floundering about the house with a butterfly net, her wild swings are overchoreographed, and quite unbelievable. Neumann gets highly variable performances from his cast; he can't rouse Herbert Marshall from somnambulism, and is unable to keep Vincent Price interested and in check at the same time. He must have spent most of his time on Hedison and Owens; though their performances are somewhat wooden, they are also serious and intelligent, within the bounds of the script.

Neumann brings off the unmasking scene with a certain panache, and it definitely worked on audiences in 1958; as unlikely as it may seem (with 20–20 hindsight), they were simply not expecting a fly head at all. But the scenes following are overstated and show a fatal lack of imagination. Neumann is incapable of making us feel sorry for André at the same time that we regard him as a figure of horror; the director and Hedison alternate clumsily from one approach to the other.

In a way, Neumann's simple literalness is the right approach for most of the film, and he maintains a very brisk pace (as he almost always did). He wanted to give us a sense of normalcy and impending mystery; with the help of Clavell's script, he does. It's when the film takes on its outré aspects, with some of the scenes in the lab that Neumann's failings are most apparent.

He seems to have been responsible for the silly idea in the scene in which Dandelo the cat disappears. Clavell's script simply called for the cat to vanish; in the film, we hear a frightened, forlorn meowing from all parts of the room. What was going on? Maybe Dandelo's "stream of cat atoms" caused metal in the room to resonate? It made the audience laugh.

The unmasking scene works, the aftermath doesn't; but it's mostly the material, not the direction, that keeps things on an even keel. With Clavell's careful script, Neumann does manage to bring off the explanation of the matter transmitter with clarity and precision; though this would seem to be a simply-explained idea, the two later sequels, *Return of the Fly* (discussed in this volume) and *Curse of the Fly* (1965), garbled the details, especially the third film. Neumann was unimaginative, but he was working with simple, sensational material, and despite his failings, did the job better than many directors would have.

Patricia Owens was beautiful in a down-home fashion, and was a good choice physically for the role. But she was a new actress Fox was trying to build up; she's honest and sincere, but the minor complexities of the role of Hélène are beyond her. Neumann probably didn't help her much. Hélène is intelligent as well as loving and frightened; Owens manages to capture the latter two qualities, but never seems to be very smart. Alone among the major cast members, Owens actually was Canadian. She was in films as early as 1943 (she's older than she looks, being born in 1925); she came to the United States for *Sayonara* (1957), in which she played Marlon Brando's abandoned fiancée. She also had a good role in *No Down Payment* (1957). After her Fox contract ran out, she began appearing in films for lesser studios; the last film I have information on for her is *The Destructors* in 1968; she presumably retired. Generally, her performances were better than the one she gives in *The Fly*.

Al Hedison soon changed his name to David, and for a brief time gave signs of becoming a leading man, but he arrived on screen with his almost-pretty face just at a time when the star system had entered its terminal phase. Hedison is certainly handsome enough to have been a star in Hollywood of old, but he's only a mediocre actor; he has a certain almost oily slickness, but also usually seems tentative. He soon faded into television.

His first series, "Five Fingers," was a one-season flop, but he appeared for years in the series "Voyage to the Bottom of the Sea," itself based on a 20th Century–Fox science fiction movie. Hedison played Commander Lee Crane in this colorful but basically rotten series that ran on ABC for four years. He never developed a personal style to go with his handsome face; I believe his most recent appearance in a feature film was in the Roger Moore movie *ffolkes* (1980).

Herbert Marshall was only adequate as Inspector Charas. His days of glory had long since passed, from his high point in the early 30s, when he was splendidly urbane and witty in Ernst Lubitsch's wonderful *Trouble in Paradise* (1932). Through the 30s and 40s, Marshall was intelligent, British and cultured in a variety of pictures. He appeared with Garbo in *The Painted Veil* (1934), with Katharine Hepburn in *A Woman Rebels* (1936), was excellent as a British Nazi in Hitchcock's *Foreign Correspondent* (1940), splendidly battled Bette Davis in *The Letter* (1940) and *The Little Foxes* (1941), and played Somerset Maugham in both *The Moon and Sixpence* (1942) and *The Razor's Edge* (1946). By the 1950s, however, his genteel style had worn thin, and films had changed; he appeared primarily in minor pictures, including the SF films *Gog* and *Riders to the Stars*. He was the smiling host of a syndicated TV anthology series. His last film was *The Third Day* in 1965; he died in 1966. Marshall had little to do as Charas in *The Fly*, probably completing his scenes in less than a week. He relied lightly on his own charm for the role, which is superfluous anyway.

An actor for whom *The Fly* was very significant was Vincent Price, as it firmly established his earlier tentative identification with horror movies. In fact, so strongly is Price identified with *The Fly* that most people believe that he played the title role.

Price is an amazingly variable actor; he can sometimes be absolutely out-standing, as in *Theatre of Blood* (1973), the two *Dr. Phibes* films, *Laura* (1944), *Masque of the Red Death* (1964), *House on Haunted Hill* (otherwise a poor film), *Champagne for Caesar*, *The Baron of Arizona* (both 1950) and a few others. His sensual features, highly expressive eyebrows and rich voice are excellent actor's tools, and he can use them to great effect when he's cast well, and doesn't go over the top, which he often does. He's so hammy as to be somewhere between embarrassing and delightful (though the delight springs from an appreciation of excess) in pictures like *House of Wax* (1953), *The Mad Magician* (1954), *The Ten Commandments* (1956), *Pit and the Pendulum* (1964, his ripest, funniest "straight" performance), and *Madhouse* (1974). Even when he's over the mark, Price is still entertaining. This, incidentally, is not at all *poor* acting, but acting in a mode that is unfamiliar to most audiences today: the bravura, theatrical style of actors like John Barrymore. Some of Price's most interesting performances have been those where he uses both precise, "modern" acting and flamboyant "overacting," such as in *Master of the World*, most of the Poe films, and *War-Gods of the Deep*. Price seems to be enjoying himself in these parts, making them fun to watch.

But occasionally Vincent Price has been very badly miscast. He played Boss Tweed in *Up in Central Park* (1948); Tweed was coarse, fat, and direct, and the role called for that approach; Price is sophisticated, slender and evasive. In *The Last Man on Earth* (1964), Price was required to play something on the order of an Ordinary Guy, which he most emphatically is not. In *Scream and Scream Again* (1970), his mad scientist was just too mild for Price. And the same is true of François Delambre in *The Fly* and *Return of the Fly*.

When Price is miscast, he sometimes almost walks through the role, or flails around trying to find the character. In *The Fly*, he's lost; this quiet, troubled man is just not a role Price should have been asked to play. There's not even a smidgen of excess for him to bounce off. He overacts without the conviction he brings to more flamboyant parts; he's incapable here of registering sorrow, and instead relies on a pained, troubled look through most of the film. Price, who is himself a witty man, is definitely at his best in roles where he can exhibit a sense of humor, either through the character directly or around the edges, doing a mild send-up. François Delambre is a totally humorless part, and the only scene in which Price seems comfortable is a brief one in which he listens to the prattling of Charles Herbert as they descend a flight of stairs.

Since 1958, Price has appeared in around 30 films in the horror genre; along with Boris Karloff and Bela Lugosi, he is probably the only actor the average person would name as a star of horror movies.

The special effects in *The Fly* are few and simple. Most are on-set effects, such as the neon-beribboned computer, or minor camera tricks like the jump cuts for the transmission-reintegration. The business with the human-headed fly is more complex, involving what seems to be a miniature fly and spider, with Hedison matted into the fly body. The effects works well, mostly because of the realistic and ugly spider head.

The main "effect" in *The Fly* is the fly-head mask that Hedison (and not a stunt man) wears, which was created by Fox makeup chief Ben Nye and technical expert Dick Smith. (Smith is not the famous makeup artist. Presumably he is the same technician who built the giant ants for *Them!*; I suspect he was hired because of his association with insects, by some kind of typically Hollywood associative reflex. This Dick Smith also worked on *The Alligator People*.)

In their informative book on makeup, *Making a Monster*, Al Taylor and Sue Roy described the creation of the fly-head mask in great detail. The true proportions of a fly head were discarded — a fly's head is much larger in proportion to its body than a man's head is to his body — although they were followed in the sequel. In this film, the head had to be capable of being covered by that cloth.

A rubber sheath was fitted over Hedison's head, with other details of the mask being added to the sheath once it was in place. The mobile proboscis was attached to a wooden plug which Hedison held in his mouth and wiggled for a properly disgusting look. The eyes were a last-minute decision. The first eyes were beaded domes (seen in the photo here), but after a test film was shot, these were discarded in favor of the golden, iridescent domes finally used. Although the head doesn't resemble a fly at all, it does look properly insectile, and is one of Nye's best extravagant makeups.

The fly hand is less successful; it looks just like what it is: a claw-shaped glove, and doesn't look like the foot of any fly that ever lived, nor does it look particularly insectoid. It does look menacing, however, and that's what was required.

The Fly was made for less than $400,000, which even in those days was inexpensive, and quickly grossed at least $3,000,000, making it one of the most profitable horror movies of the time. No wonder two sequels followed, even though in those days moviemakers didn't rush into sequels with quite the greedy abandon they show today.

The reviews of *The Fly* were generally very favorable. *Film Daily* called it "a memorable experience for the horror movie-goer" (and like it or not, that's certainly true). Jack Moffitt said, "if the science fiction fans know the difference between dramatic skill and mere 'shilling shockers,' it should be a gold mine.... An A horror picture deals with the believable reactions monsters might have on convincingly imagined human beings. By this standard, *The Fly* is as fine an A picture as the best.... Hedison and Miss Owens constantly keep the story real (and therefore doubly shocking) by emphasizing their emotional desperation instead of the mechanical gimmicks."

Howard Thompson in the *New York Times* felt that the movie "happens to be one of the better, more restrained entries of the 'shock' school.... A quiet, uncluttered and even unpretentious picture, building up almost unbearable tension by simple suggestion."

Paul V. Beckley in the New York *Herald-Tribune* thought *The Fly* was "one of the more gruesome films in this genre.... Both the gory and the bizarre details are made extraordinarily explicit."

Jesse Zunser in *Cue* thought it was "crammed with a kind of eerie compulsion that turns the film into a celluloid screaming terror." Noting its "unconventionally unhappy ending," "Powe" in Weekly *Variety* said that it was a "high-budget, beautifully and expensively mounted exploitation picture," and that "one strong factor of the picture is its unusual believability." *Parents* thought it "excellent of kind," and *Playboy* cautioned "you'll have nightmares."

Monthly Film Bulletin gave the film an average rating. "The early sequences of this film have great mystery and tension, and the situation is ingeniously built up. But the film soon becomes as nauseating as its bare outline suggests; even the moments which in healthier pictures might provoke a laugh through sheer absurdity offer little relief. The horror is set among scenes of dogged respectability, matched by empty but determinedly genteel performances."

Writers on SF and horror films more recently have not liked the film as well as reviewers did in 1958. In *Focus on the Science Fiction Film*, Richard Hodgens considered the film "morally repugnant." In *Horror in the Cinema* Ivan Butler seems to be overreacting: "This is probably the most ludicrous, and certainly one of the most revolting science-horror films ever perpetrated."

On the other hand, Alan G. Frank in *Horror Movies* liked the film; in another book (*Horror*), he described it as "genuinely horrifying." In his pioneering *An Illustrated History of the Horror Film*, Carlos Clarens liked it with reservations: "*The Fly* stands out from the ordinary run of horror movies in nearly creating an authentic science-fiction monster and botching the job with an unscientific – and illogical – story-idea.... The film collapses under the weight of many [unanswered] questions."

Psychotronic, bless its heart, called it "a brilliant, sick, absurd hit ... unforgettable." And it is, too. It is not a masterpiece; it is not especially well-acted, Neumann's direction is unimaginative. But it's fast-paced, care was taken with the script, the film approached its material with seriousness, and it has several sequences of truly impressive horror. *The Fly* is a memorable film.*

---

*A violent remake, possibly to be directed by David Cronenberg, has been announced.

Frankenstein 1970

If this unimaginative movie didn't feature Boris Karloff himself as the last Baron Frankenstein, it would not warrant lengthy commentary—but Karloff *is* in it, and because of his immense importance to the genre, the film needs to be discussed. It's an attempt to blend atomic-age horrors with Gothic chills, but the former are so slight as to be almost nonexistent, and the latter are intermittent and mostly fake. The script has some disturbing if faint hints of sexual deviation which director Howard W. Koch thankfully does not exploit, but he does emphasize ghoulishness out of place in the relatively polite surroundings of the story. The Monster itself this time is curiously ill-conceived: it's just a big man wrapped in bandages with a large bandage-enclosed shell over his head, like an upturned wastepaper basket. The Monster is menacing solely because of his size, and that isn't enough.

The script was titled "Frankenstein 1960," which would have placed it only two years in the future from when it was released. That makes more sense than the "1970" tag on the finished feature, as there's nothing remotely futuristic about the movie. Of course, it takes place almost entirely inside Baron Victor Frankenstein's castle with a few scenes in nearby locations. Even the atomic stuff is kept offscreen; after Karloff's eagerly-awaited atomic reactor arrives, his laboratory doesn't change.

The film gets off to an interesting and by now well-known start. A girl (Jana Lund), dressed in period clothing, runs in terror down a deserted country lane. Behind her lurches a pursuing thing in the shape of a man, whom we see only from the shoulders down. The scene builds to a nice climax as the thing, with twisted, clawed fingers, walking as if one knee is permanently bent, pursues the girl into a rippling, fog-shrouded lake, where it begins to drown her as the music reaches a crescendo.

But it's a cheat (though the trickery can be fun). We hear a voice call "cut" and discover we've been watching a television crew shoot a documentary on the 230th anniversary of Frankenstein (treated as a historically-real person). The TV director is Douglas Row (Donald Barry), his publicist is Mike Shaw (Tom Duggan), the star is Carolyn Hayes (Lund), continuity is Judy Stevens (Charlotte Austin), Row's ex-wife, and cinematographer is Morgan Haley (John Dennis). They're all staying at the nearby castle of Baron Victor Von Frankenstein (Karloff).

Back at the castle, Frankenstein complains to his friend and business manager Wilhelm Gottfried (Rudolph Anders) about the tragedies in his life that have made it necessary for him to allow these vulgar Americans into his castle. Frankenstein is disfigured: an eye drawn down with a scar, his thick, potatolike nose also scarred, his body twisted and deformed. (Karloff's own unfortunate crippling, which steadily worsened from 1945 on, is used as part of the plot here, both ingeniously and distastefully.)

Although for some reason the Nazis are never named, we learn that Frankenstein defied them, so they mercilessly tortured him, leading to his present physical state. Though they never touched his surgeon's hands, they left him less than a man. (Presumably a veiled reference to castration.) Furthermore, Frankenstein has fallen on hard financial times, and Gottfried's been forced to sell off many of the Frankenstein family treasures.

The troupe returns, and Row asks Frankenstein to appear in the film. The

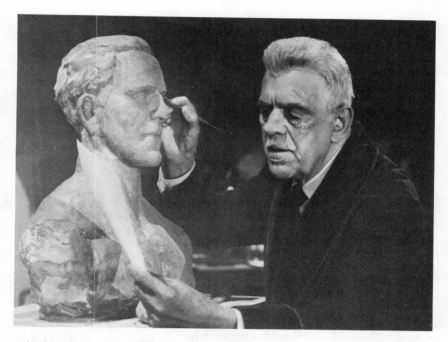

In his last Frankenstein film, Boris Karloff switched roles to Dr. Frankenstein, but in a peculiar type of logic, attempted to make the monster look like — Boris Karloff. Here he's trying to sculpt a bust of himself as a young man. From Frankenstein 1970 (1958).

disgusted Baron is cool to the idea, until Carolyn shows an interest in him. He responds in an unpleasantly suave manner, then laughing madly, lurches off to play his organ. His pipe organ.

The next scene is another cheat. Frankenstein, in his family crypt, talks about his ancestor who created the Monster, Richard Freiherr Von Frankenstein. The Baron says Richard "had to learn how *flesh* was made. He had to discover the art of transplanting vital organs from human beings into his creature and knitting them together [Karloff places his hands together, the fingers curling upward] until they had all the attributes of God-inspired birth [forefinger stabs heavenward]. 'Course, I must admit that perhaps he was not too scrupulous about where he got his raw materials." Karloff's hammy delivery of these lines is disturbing: a smooth, elegant actor of the old school, unlike many of his contemporaries he almost never overplayed a scene, but *Frankenstein 1970* is riddled with scenes of Karloff as a ham.

All this material is *another* scene being filmed by Row and his troupe; this is especially irritating, because we're fooled twice.

Later, Carolyn gives a nice scarf to Shuter (Norbert Schiller), the Baron's devoted butler. This scene comes out of nowhere, but certainly leads somewhere — for that is the only reason it's in the film. We have previously seen Shuter only as a hovering presence, and before this Carolyn took no notice of him. The scarf has two plot functions: it makes the Baron uncomfortably aware that even a servant might be more attractive than he is, and inasmuch as

Shuter's brain ends up in the Monster's body, at the climax it gives the Monster reason not to kill Carolyn.

Later, Frankenstein sends everyone to bed, and goes down into the crypt alone. Twisting a carved cherub's head causes the top of a sarcophagus to slide aside. He descends a staircase into his laboratory and switches on the lights, revealing a modern Scientific Laboratory. We can tell it is scientific because it has plenty of gauges, dials, switches, etc. There's a circular, bull's-eye-like shape, six feet high, on one wall, the only unusual feature of the room.

Except for a sculpted bust. The Baron lurches over to the bust, and makes a minute adjustment in the clay, checking a photo to be sure. The photo is of Boris Karloff himself as a younger man – it appears to date from around 1945 – and the bust is clearly supposed to duplicate the Baron's younger face. But oddly enough, the bust has only a passing resemblance to Karloff, especially unfortunate for purposes of the plot.

The Baron is obviously Up To Something, as he puts on his various surgical gear and washes up. The also checks his intercom: he has all the rooms in his house bugged (why?), and can listen in from the lab. Everyone is engaged in relatively dull pursuits, so he goes back to Monster-creating activities.

The bull's-eye arrangement opens, and a gurney with a bandaged form slides awkwardly out. The head of the wrapped figure is a naked skull. Frankenstein begins dictating his actions like an autopsy surgeon into a tape recorder. This was a good idea; not only does it allow for exposition which otherwise would have been awkward, but all kinds of ghoulish words can be dropped in. Best of all, it is thoroughly authentic: a scientist doing this kind of work in reality probably would use just such a device.

Cleaning up, Shuter pulls his scarf off the cherub where he draped it, which opens the sarcophagus. Curious, he descends, to find the Baron leaning over the Monster's inactive body. "Shuter!" the Baron exclaims in surprise, then changes his tone. "Ah, my poor Shuter," he says sorrowfully, "why did it have to be you?"

Shuter stammeringly asks what's going on. "A miracle, Shuter," Frankenstein says in an ominous tone. "Come here." He uses his surgical scissors to hypnotize Shuter, promising the frightened butler that he will live forever. We next see Shuter unconscious on an operating table as Frankenstein removes his heart – seen in close-up – and installs it in the Monster's chest.

The next day, after making apologies for Shuter's "departure," Frankenstein returns to the lab and works on his newly-delivered reactor. He finishes installing Shuter's brain in the Monster, now complete except for the eyes. He gets a pair from the refrigerator – we see them in another close-up – but drops the jar. He disgustedly tosses the eyes away.

After some byplay among various characters – Frankenstein wears Shuter's scarf as he plays his organ, Row tries to get into Carolyn's room, Gottfried lectures Frankenstein again – the next night, Frankenstein uses the atomic reactor to bring the Monster back to life in a most unspectacular manner. This does cause the lights in the house to dim, however, which the guests notice. Frankenstein tries out a few commands on the blind Monster, which obeys lethargically.

Judy has sent Mike away several times, and thinking it's him at her door again, opens it to discover the Monster, eeek. Downstairs, Frankenstein chastises the Monster; he'd wanted it to kill Row (whom he despises), not "this poor girl." He tosses Judy's remains into a disposal, which makes the noises of a toilet as it grinds her up.

Later, the Monster finds cameraman Haley alone in the crypt, after some nonsuspense involving Carolyn almost being grabbed by the Monster. It kills Haley, but Frankenstein sighs that the dead man had the wrong blood type. The eyes are useless.

Summoned by Row, the police poke around the crypt, led by the extremely non-German Inspector Raab (Irwin Berke). They unknowingly almost open the sarcophagus, but Frankenstein covers up. They leave.

Gottfried confronts Frankenstein yet again over the Baron's mysterious activities and changed outlook. Promising to finally reveal the truth, Frankenstein takes Gottfried to the crypt, opens the sarcophagus, and the Monster emerges. We see Gottfried's eyes in extreme close-up; there's a slow matching dissolve and we see them, still in close-up, in the Monster's eye sockets, peering out through the holes in the bandages. (This is the most imaginative shot in the film.)

Frankenstein hypnotizes Mike into revealing that Row is off seeing the police. At the police station, everyone finally puts evidence together and realizes that Frankenstein must be behind the disappearances.

Back at the castle, the Baron has the hypnotized Mike lure Carolyn downstairs, where the Monster grabs her and takes her to the Baron, just as the police—shown driving for miles and miles—arrive at the castle with Row. Over the intercom, the Baron orders Shuter (by name) to bring the girl to him. Carolyn, realizing who is carrying her, asks Shuter not to harm her, but doesn't rudely bring up the scarf. The Monster sets her down, goes into the lab, and smashes a few things as the Baron stands frozen in horror. The lab is suddenly enveloped in steam, and there's a fadeout on the least exciting climax of a Frankenstein film. Even *Frankenstein's Daughter* is livelier.

People in radiation gear are seen poking around the lab; the Baron's body lies in the background, the Monster, slightly blackened, in the foreground. They open the bandages around the Monster's face to reveal a younger Karloff. This is done in the manner of a surprise revelation, but it is certainly not that.

Frankenstein 1970 is filmed in a clear, uncomplicated style, entirely the wrong approach. There seems to be a basic misunderstanding of what an audience wants from a Frankenstein film. Working from a story by producers Aubrey Schenck and Charles A. Moses, writers Richard Landau and George Worthing Yates seem to have felt that a soap opera with interludes in a laboratory was just what everyone was dying to see. The classic Frankenstein movies had become popular on television, and the year before, both *Curse of Frankenstein* and *I Was a Teenage Frankenstein* had been popular. Apart from whatever qualities those films had, they at least gave audiences the expected material: a scientist piecing together a Monster from fragments of corpses, a Monster with a hideous face, a sensational climax.

Oddly, *Frankenstein 1970* opens with a scene indicating that the people who made it, including director Koch and cinematographer Carl E. Guthrie, knew what was needed: a Gothic approach. But the story that follows leads me to suspect that they thought they would "turn the tables" on the audience, perhaps feeling that the traditional Gothicism of the opening (which was added to the opening and dream sequences of *Daughter of Dr. Jekyll* for that terrible film's television showings) was hackneyed. Hackneyed it may have been, but it's still the most effective scene in the movie: it's scary and to the point, highly atmospheric, with the foggy lake surrounded by gnarled trees, photographed in an old-fashioned, Germanic manner.

The rest of the film is visually flat and dull. Koch and his crew seem to be trying to film it in the flat, gray style of 1950s SF films, yet at heart the film is a Gothic horror film. A blend of the two approaches is possible, but this film didn't find the right combination.

For instance, the laboratory would be appropriate to a film like *The Fly*: hard edges, high technology, and so forth. But though the plot line here is science fiction, the Frankenstein idea is basically a ghoulish fairy tale, and should be treated that way. It's intriguing when a man creates a living being out of flashing lightning and rolling thunder; when, as here, he rolls the undone body into an atomic oven and merely bakes it into life like a cake, it's humdrum and uninteresting.

The basic wrongness of the approach is embodied in the Monster. It's not frightening, lacks personality, shows no attitude toward its creator, and except at the climax, does nothing the creator doesn't want it to. Although there are interesting reverberations in having Boris Karloff recreate the Monster he once famously played and to give it his own face (which we knew it had all along anyway), there's no plot connection, no real payoff. He seems to be giving the Monster his own face out of a kind of arrogant nostalgia, which might have seemed wistful and maybe touching if the revelation at the end had been the surprise the filmmakers seemed to think it was. But the constant visual referrals to that bust make it reasonably clear what the Baron was up to, so the Monster having Karloff's face surprises few. The way the film is presented, it would have been surprising if it *didn't* have his face. It's an odd, melodramatic idea, but is badly handled.

There's muddled logic in the Monster's characterization (or lack of it). At no time does Frankenstein suggest that the brain transplant didn't go well; in short, the Monster has Shuter's brain—but not his personality. It acts like a Monster, not like a butler, only because it *is* a Monster. Monsters act in a Monstery fashion. This simply does not match with Frankenstein's apparent goals, and turns the entire film into rote Monster-making. Was he trying to create a mindless automaton with his own face? Didn't he notice or care that Shuter acted strange? Did he have him hypnotized all the time? This is the kind of writing engaged in by people who have contempt or little understanding for their subject, and an uncaring attitude toward the intended audiences.

Random ugly shocks are tossed in. We see those realistic eyeballs in close-ups several times, and there's a close-up of a heart being massaged. However there's no blood at all. This gives the impression that the people who made the film realized that standards had changed, and organs, previously avoided in U.S. Frankenstein films, could be exhibited—but that they still felt squeamish about blood itself. It makes for a strangely anatomical feel to these scenes, as if they are part of a lecture on body parts.

There is a minor note of sexual frustration in the Baron's characterization. He refers to himself as less than a man in his first scene; later, he makes a pass at Carolyn, and exhibits jealousy when she gives that damned scarf to Shuter. Finally, he has the Monster grab her—but at this point, we have absolutely no idea what he wants her for. The Monster is working fine, and the police are on their way—you'd think the Baron's mind would be on other things than sex. But the script doesn't give a hint as to his intentions. The climax has to have the heroine in danger, so it does.

There's an attempt to give the Baron a kind of tragic grandeur, with his torture at the hands of the Nazis, and to make him a thorough villain at the same time; this is a good idea, but the film seems more ambiguous and divided than complex, and Karloff's hammy performance damages this idea.

The film lacks a sense of humor about itself. Reviewer Jack Moffitt suggested it would have been better as a comedy along the lines of *The Cat and the Canary*, with the real Monster getting mixed up with the movie Monster, and refusing to take direction. Certainly the underpopulated plot suggests this approach, but the only jokes are very, very lame ones delivered by Tom Duggan. The famous Frankenstein pair directed by James Whale were witty and even comic at times; the Hammer Frankenstein films often took a sardonic and amusing approach to the character of the Baron. But *Frankenstein 1970* is straight-faced and pompous.

It has a few good touches here and there. When the Monster revives, this is shown by means of the needles of an electroencephalograph. There are a few good shots, as when Karloff finally gets the Monster upright and begins talking to it, framed in the bull's-eye of the reactor door behind him. But these moments are more than offset by failed scenes, such as the climax. The Monster stands in a cloud of steam, waving its arms; the Baron simply collapses. This is such a terrible idea it's amazing it was filmed.

Karloff overacts in many scenes, but he has a few brilliant moments, the old fire and sardonic menace shining clean. When Shuter enters the lab, Karloff is at first sorrowful, then immediately realizes he can put the butler to use. His delivery here, and the photography of Karloff, are outstanding, rich with amused power and menace. Later, when he notices Lund wearing the scarf, Karloff's reaction is chilling yet polite, and makes us aware how inadequate is the material he's working with. If it's hard for those of us who adore Karloff to watch him in these scenes, it must have been that much harder for him to play them.

Donald "Red" Barry was primarily a Western villain, although he'd occasionally been a hero in B Westerns, mostly in the 1940s. A limited actor who gained notice as Red Ryder (hence the nickname) in a series of B Westerns for Republic, he had an agreeably aggressive style that fit well into the mold of heroes or villains. After he left Republic, he almost immediately declined to supporting roles, though he did direct himself in one movie, *Jesse James' Women* (1954). He worked steadily in films and television, almost always in supporting roles, until his death by suicide in 1980.

He's lousy in *Frankenstein 1970*'s early scenes. He broadly plays the director, making him even more painful than was intended; there's not only nothing there to like, there's nothing that's interesting, either. Barry is more at home in the scenes toward the end, where he takes charge of things.

Jana Lund was a pretty young actress somewhat resembling Sandra Dee. She made only a few films, *Loving You* (1957), *Hot Car Girl* (1958) and *Married Too Young* (1962) among them. She's vivacious and has a strangely intelligent charm (especially considering the bubblehead she's playing here), but isn't much of an actress.

On the other hand, Charlotte Austin is very good as Judy, creating a rounded character — sad, bitter, yet self-aware — amidst these unpromising surroundings. (According to Joe Dante, "these characters appear with some regularity in Howard W. Koch's films.") She seems to have had a contract with Fox in the early 1950s, but her roles in films like *Belles on Their Toes* (1952), *Desirée* (1954) and *Daddy Long Legs* (1955) were small. She had larger parts in *Rainbow Round My Shoulder* (1952), *The Man Who Turned to Stone* and *The Bride and the Beast* (1958), but neither those films nor her performances were notable. Her performance in *Frankenstein 1970* is uneven, but well above average, so good that it's too bad this seems to have been her last film.

Tom Duggan was a Los Angeles radio and TV personality who appeared in a few films during this period. A weak, unconvincing actor, when he's hypnotized he seems about the same as when he's not. A detriment to the film, he's topped (if that's the word) by Irwin Berke, another L.A. radio and TV personality, playing the police inspector. Duggan seems like an inadequate actor; Berke isn't an actor at all.

The story is raggedly organized; it takes some time for us to learn that Frankenstein is even building a Monster, although there are allusions to fears that he's doing something or other. When the Monster business gets started, the only way the writers can find for Victor to carry out his plans is to use the hoary, hackneyed device of hypnotism. At least the film improves on the script, in which he hypnotizes three people with a coin. But the idea shouldn't have been used at all.

Victor isn't just a mad scientist, he's a stupid one. Instead of robbing graves for the organs and other parts necessary to revive the Monster, as any self-respecting Frankenstein would do, he's been openly buying things from the local mortician or charnel house or whatever, then begins knocking off people in his own castle. He acts as if no one would notice that people vanish, but then he doesn't seem to have had much in mind for the Monster, either.

"Powr" in *Variety* was reasonably impressed, though confused: "With Frankenstein and his heirs and assigns now in the public domain, it must be somewhat confusing to the horror addict who tries to figure out who done what and to whom.... [*Frankenstein 1970*] puts the Baron and his family in Germany, although the last previous picture on the Monster-maker had him in Switzerland (...*The Revenge of Frankenstein*) on his way to England.... [The new film] is a competently made production that will do well in its class.... Karloff ... does a careful, convincing job with his role, which is competently written."

The *Monthly Film Bulletin* was harsh, giving the film a III rating. "There is nothing in this latest addition to the Frankenstein saga to suggest the traditional Monster created on the screen a quarter of a century ago. Despite the title, there is no sign of this story being set in the future, and the whole inept effort is a slight on the horrific name of Frankenstein."

Don Willis (I) thought it "dismal," and in *Castle of Frankenstein* #9, Joe Dante considered it "generally mediocre mad doctor stuff with a good opening and ending, but otherwise routine."

Denis Gifford, in *Karloff* (1973), found the business of the Baron giving the Monster his own face "a clever plot payoff," but did note that "Karloff was not happy with the production."

Peter Underwood, in his book *Karloff* (1972), described the film as "an ill-conceived attempt in CinemaScope to mix the Frankenstein Monster with hypnotism and atomic steam." Later discussing *Frankenstein 1970* with *Voodoo Island*, a fantasy horror film Karloff made for the same company, Underwood said "neither film had much cinematic quality or opportunity for expressing acting ability."

In his fine *Boris Karloff and His Films* (1974), Paul M. Jensen describes the picture as "an interesting failure that tries to be an affectionate salute to the old style, but instead hovers too close to imitation and cliché." He considered Baron Frankenstein here to be "interesting only because of Karloff, who gives a richly articulated performance." Jensen points out that the film betrays itself by its lack of imagination and ghoulishness. He rightly says that although discovering the Monster has Karloff's youthful face "might inspire intriguingly Pirandellian thoughts about Frankenstein's 'creating' Karloff, or Karloff's 'creating' the Monster, or even Karloff's 'creating' Karloff, but unfortunately they would be pointless, because the fact that the Baron made the Monster in his own image is included only as a gimmick, with no effect on the plot or situations."

In *The Frankenstein Legend* (1973), Don Glut described the film as a "shoddy production," and noted that "Karloff himself seemed to express a contempt for the role he was playing."

As a director, Howard W. Koch rarely rose above the mediocre. He was busy in the late 1950s, with *Untamed Youth, Bop Girl, Jungle Heat* and *The Girl in Black Stockings* all being released in 1957, and *Fort Bowie, Violent Road, Frankenstein 1970* and *Andy Hardy Comes Home* out in 1958. He also found time to produce *The Black Sleep, The Pharaoh's Curse* and *Voodoo Island* during this period.

As a producer, Koch has proved to be more able. (He's also one of the better presidents the Motion Picture Academy has had.) During the 1960s, he was closely associated with Frank Sinatra, and served as executive producer on the string of "Rat Pack" movies Sinatra made, including the noncanonical *The Manchurian Candidate.* After his association with Sinatra, with mixed results Koch produced several films based on Neil Simon plays, ranging from a high of *The Odd Couple* (1968) to a low of *Last of the Red Hot Lovers* (1972). He returned temporarily to directing with *Badge 373* (1973), an efficient, violent melodrama with a brilliant performance by Robert Duvall.

Frankenstein 1970 is a film of lost opportunities. It's the only Frankenstein film so far to link the Monster to atomic energy, but even clichés of radiation aren't used: no one tracks the Monster with Geiger counters, it doesn't leave radioactive burns on its victims, it doesn't even glow in the dark. For the only time in his long career, Boris Karloff plays a Frankenstein—but is not allowed to bring his full talent to bear on the role. It's an underwritten part that Karloff was directed (or allowed) to overplay. The Monster is a pathetic, unfrightening thing, just a piece of machinery with no motivations and no personality. The movie seems to have been made with some affection, but unfortunately a complete lack of understanding as to the requirements of this kind of film dooms it to less than mediocrity.

Frankenstein's Daughter

"Oliver, you're a strange boy," someone says to the Dr. Frankenstein of this dreadful film. The sentiment certainly cannot be argued with; Oliver Frank (Donald Murphy) is a mad scientist and a sex fiend as well.

Oliver is using the name Frank so no one will know his father was the famous monster-maker. He is working with elderly scientist Carter Morton (Felix Locher) in developing an important new drug, which will be "a boon to mankind." It is designed to wipe out "all cells and organisms negative to man" but it does have an unfortunate side effect. It temporarily turns people into monsters.

Oliver has been testing the drug secretly on Morton's teenaged niece Trudy (Susan Knight), and she occasionally turns into a bucktoothed fiend, prowling the Los Angeles streets and scaring people. She's ugly enough, with big gray teeth, shaggy brows and staring eyes (the makeup is highly variable). But she

Harry Wilson as the probably-female monster in the awesomely tacky Frankenstein's Daughter (1958). Not-bad makeup by Harry Thomas, who didn't know the monster was supposed to be female. Realizing this at the last moment, he slapped lipstick on Harry.

doesn't really do much other than lurk in the shadows in her bathrobe. Once, she trips over some garbage cans and some cops shoot at her.

But Oliver has bigger things in mind. With the help of his own reluctant assistant Elsu (Wolfe Barzell), he has been constructing a monster in a hidden room, trying to do things right that his father did wrong. He wants to use the drug to make his monster all-powerful. Elsu brings in the bodies, and Oliver sews them together. It seems that he intends to make a female monster, in line with the title. However, this is very confusing. It's never clear if the monster is entirely a female – it certainly doesn't look like a woman – or has the body of a man and the head of a woman. It is notably ugly by anybody's standards, male or female.

"I need a brain, I need a brain," mutters Oliver, getting no argument from me. Local girl Suzie Lawler (Sally Todd) is jealous of Trudy, who is pretty when she's not a monster, and who has handsome boyfriend Johnny (John Ashley). Suzie thinks Trudy's after glory because Trudy steals her thunder. Oliver plans to steal her brain. Oliver takes Suzie out on a date, but she rejects him up on Mulholland Drive, so he runs over her with his car, and *voila*, the needed brain. A female brain, too. He assumes the woman's brain will take orders from him because women are conditioned to obey men. Not only is this sexism, but it shows a poor memory: Suzie didn't obey him when her brain was in her head, so what makes Oliver think she will obey him when it's elsewhere is a mystery.

The monster (Harry Wilson) comes to life, and shambles off to the Associated Storage Company on behalf of Oliver – he was being obedient – where it kills someone by squashing him with a door. In the next scene, the door has healed, but the man is still dead. The monster shambles back to Oliver to be revitalized.

Nothing happens for quite a while, other than a barbecue and some other teenage hijinks.

Later, Oliver decides to have his way with Trudy, who has no memory of being an occasional monster. Neither does Oliver, for he proclaims, "You've always treated me as a monster, Trudy. Now you're going to be one." He hopes to make her into a monster like the one in the closet, but Johnny hits Oliver in the face with a beaker of acid. The monster shambles out of the closet, gazing in confusion at Oliver, who is writhing in pain and holding his smoking face. The monster blunders into a Bunsen burner which sets it, and later the whole house, afire. Johnny and Trudy escape. As they watch the house go up in flames, Trudy shudders. "Oh, Johnny, it was gruesome."

Frankenstein's Daughter is one of the worst films ever made. The direction by Richard Cunha is dismal, with no imagination or inventiveness discernible. The movie is ponderous, slow, repetitious, meandering. It was made on an extremely short schedule with almost no money, and H.E. Barrie's script is absolutely terrible, but Cunha does nothing to improve things, and much to make everything worse.

Cunha photographed *Bloodlust* (made 1959, released 1961) and *The Silent Witness* (1962), and directed *Girl in Room 13* (1961), which starred Brian Donlevy. After 1962, the *American Film Institute Catalog* lists no further credits for Cunha, who went into commercials and industrial films. (See also *Giant from the Unknown, Missile to the Moon* and *She Demons*.)

Judging from the interview with him in *Fangoria* #31, Cunha sounds genial enough. He told interviewer Tom Weaver that the films he made for Astor release were each brought in for $65,000 or less. "Our shooting schedules were always six days," he told Weaver. The exteriors for *Frankenstein's Daughter* were shot at producer Marc Frederic's home, the interiors on a set.

They got laboratory props in a cheap, efficient manner. "We [found] a character [who] was furnishing these [props] to the studios and we took what the studio wouldn't take.... We'd say, 'We can't afford your real prices, so give us the junk from your back yard.' He'd say, 'Okay, if you guys clean 'em up, make 'em look pretty good, you can have 'em.' So we'd do it, and returned them to him in twice better shape than he gave them to us."

The makeup man on the picture was busy Harry Thomas, who did the variable makeup on Sandra Knight and the odd, melted-face makeup on the quasi-female monster. The makeup is unusual because of the short schedule; no one seems to have told Thomas the monster was supposed to be female, and his work was not what they wanted. "We had no preparation time," Cunha said in *Fangoria*," and the monster was designed on the set on the first day of shooting. And I nearly *died*. We said, 'No, that's not *quite* what we need, but by God we can't do anything about it.' And we pushed the guy on the set and started shooting. The show must go on."

H.E. Barrie also cowrote *Girl in Room 13*. The plot of that film seems as awkward and coincidence-filled as *Frankenstein's Daughter*. Barrie's script for the horror movie is so weak that we never know if the monster is male, female, or a mixture—or why that would make any difference. Tossing in another monster of the Jekyll-Hyde type may have been the idea of the distributor or the producers, but it's silly anyway, making no logical sense. Why experiment on Trudy? Why not on Oliver's assistant? Why try it out anyway? It only calls police attention to the neighborhood.

Harry Thomas' makeup is not badly executed; the preposterous face on Sandra Knight is professional, but is such a silly design, with big shaggy eyebrows and tombstone teeth, that it always produces more laughter than horror. Thomas almost always worked in these terrible low-budget films, and frequently did better-than-average work. The Frankenstein monster here is little more than a rubber mask, and is well-executed. But it certainly doesn't look like a woman. The hastily added lipstick doesn't help this plug-ugly.

The monster was Harry Wilson who, Tom Weaver said, "had been Wallace Beery's stand-in for 25 years, and had dubbed himself 'The Ugliest Man in Pictures." George Barrows, who also has an acting job in the film, doubled for Wilson in the fire scene.

Frankenstein's Daughter was greeted by the few who reviewed it with the contempt it deserved. Howard Thompson in the *New York Times* said "it's a toss-up whether [*Frankenstein's Daughter* or its cofeature] *Missile to the Moon* is the cheaper, duller piece of claptrap. Both are horror entries, being simply horrible bores." Paul V. Beckley in the New York *Herald-Tribune* felt that "*Frankenstein's Daughter* is a little better [than *Missile to the Moon*], although much more confusing." The Los Angeles *Examiner* called the film "a dismal clinker" and a "farrago."

The *Monthly Film Bulletin* gave the film its lowest rating, saying "Due, possibly, as devotees will surely point out, to Oliver's use of the wrong apparatus, the monsters only frighten facially; indeed, the whole creative process, interrupted by teenage barbecues and jam sessions, is now a most perfunctory matter. The conception throughout is naive and crude, while the almost incredibly weak performance by Felix Locher as an elderly, well-meaning scientist adds an unintentionally humorous note."

Castle of Frankenstein #9 rightly termed it a "ridiculous grade-D horror film; funny in wrong places." Don Willis (I) thought it "even below par for Astor." In *The Frankenstein Legend*, Don Glut called *Frankenstein's Daughter* "Astor Pictures' contribution to the list of worst horror films of all time." Even bad-film-loving *Psychotronic* felt it was "incredibly shoddy."

The final (or first, in a sense) insult was the truly horrible advertising art, among the worst of all time, matched only by the atrocious ads for its cofeature *Missile to the Moon*, and for *From Hell It Came*.

The only reason for the existence of this movie is that *Frankenstein* was both popular and in the public domain. *Frankenstein's Daughter* was just another cheap, cynical effort to capitalize on this renewed popularity; it is certainly one of the worst Frankenstein films ever made.

From the Earth to the Moon

Having author Jules Verne in the cast didn't save this from being a dismal, wrongheaded and boring movie, one of the last gasps of RKO as a production company. Headed by Benedict Bogeaus, Waverly Films entered into a distribution deal with RKO General to deliver two films, *From the Earth to the Moon* and *Enchanted Island*, but when RKO stopped distributing films, Bogeaus sought to sell the films elsewhere. He was initially prevented from doing so, and apparently RKO and not Bogeaus made the deal that resulted in Warner Bros. handling U.S. distribution of both films. (There was a 1961 lawsuit over this matter.)

In the case of *From the Earth to the Moon*, at least, no one should have bothered to release it at all. It's a talky, attenuated movie, full of anachronistic ideas and attitudes. It is not, it hardly seems necessary to say, faithful to Jules Verne's 1865 novel, but that's of little consequence, for if the novel had been filmed as written it would have been even more dated than the movie is. But the script devised by Robert Blees and James Leicester isn't an improvement.

Just after the Civil War, Victor Barbicane (Joseph Cotten) and Stuyvesant Nicholls (George Sanders) are rivals. Nicholls hates Barbicane because he feels that if Barbicane had used his knowledge properly, the South would have won the Civil War.

Barbicane announces that he has produced an ultimate weapon which he terms "Power X" (a fluid which looks like ginger ale), that can fire a shell through almost any obstacle. Nicholls' specialty being metallurgy, he produces a sheet of metal he describes as impenetrable, but Barbicane's little brass cannon, powered by Power X and firing a shell full of the stuff, not only demolishes Nicholls' armor plate, but blows up a distant mountain. (In other words, the hero is a creator of offensive weapons, and the "villain" a manufacturer of defensive armor.)

Barbicane announces he is going to fire a shell at the Moon, which is assumed to be a lifeless body, but a letter from President Grant (Morris Ankrum) asks Barbicane to call things off. Grant is afraid the shell will fall back onto the Earth. So instead Barbicane proposes firing a *manned* shell at the Moon, and raises $50 million to this end. Nicholls insists he be allowed to go along with Barbicane and his assistant Ben Sharpe (Don Dubbins).

After the shell is launched, Barbicane's daughter Virginia (Debra Paget, here a blonde), is discovered aboard the craft; she stowed away to be near Ben, whom she loves.

After plenty of talk and an elegant dinner aboard the spaceship prepared, of course, by Virginia—if she hadn't stowed away, would they have eaten canned beans?—Nicholls, who feels Barbicane is violating God's laws, sabotages the shell, and it splits into two separate compartments.

One, containing Ben and Virginia, orbits the Moon, while the other, with Nicholls and Barbicane, lands on it. They fire off a shell to show they have arrived intact. (There are no scenes on the surface of the Moon.)

Back on Earth, a man who has been hanging around all the time is revealed to be Jules Verne himself (Carl Esmond), and presumably he rushes back to France to write a novel based on this adventure.

The lovers are left in orbit.

The script for *From the Earth to the Moon* is hopelessly talky, and the talk isn't any good. John Cutts in *Films and Filming* said "how they go on. Squawk, squawk, squawk. Jabber, jabber, jabber. They literally talk themselves and the film to death." The dialogue is full of clunker lines, but their pomposity keeps them from being funny. "I deal almost exclusively with the incredible," says Barbicane (whose name sounds like an ointment). Nicholls wants to disgrace or destroy Barbicane because he is "incontestably the most wicked man on the face of the Earth [who] inspires a morbid desire to slaughter millions, nay *tens* of millions." And aboard the craft, Nicholls exults, "Feel it! Feel the weight of the finger of God!" All this awful language seems to be the result of an over-earnest attempt to make the dialogue sound genuinely of the 19th century, but instead it's stilted and cumbersome.

The script development is clumsy as well. It takes most of the picture to even get our heroes off the ground,* and then finds nothing for them to do except argue while on their way to the Moon. The President prevents Barbicane from firing off his explosive Moon shell because if it fell back to Earth it might be construed an act of war. But why does this idea even come up? Why doesn't Barbicane proceed directly to the idea of shooting himself (and a handpicked crew of one) to the Moon? Perhaps it was just to add running time, perhaps it was misplaced fidelity to the novel, perhaps it was to indicate a kind of progression of thinking — but it's just time-wasting boredom in the movie. It's about a 19th century trip to the Moon, so they should simply have gotten on with it.

When the movie was made, most readily accepted Barbicane as the hero, and his warmongering ideas as justified. He even proposes a very 1950s-type balance of power among the world's great nations: if each of them had Power X, none would dare launch an attack on the others. His serene belief in the superiority of technology and the virtues of high explosives are typical of both Jules Verne's attitudes and of the 50s. Contrasted with him is Nicholls and his fears that such power is ungodly, and could become terribly ill-used by unscrupulous men. Today, despite the inflamed language of the fanatic that is given to Nicholls by the writers, he seems to be slightly more correct than Barbicane, but mostly they both seem like dangerous fools.

It's odd that with a role model such as *20,000 Leagues Under the Sea* of only a few years before, this film should have gone so wrong. Didn't anyone connected with *From the Earth to the Moon* even *see* the Disney picture? It managed to be adventuresome and exciting while being convincingly a period piece; *From the Earth to the Moon* is ponderous and dull, with no feeling of the period and no sense of wonder.

In a brief interview with Los Angeles *Mirror-News* entertainment editor Dick Williams, Joseph Cotten said the film had been made in a tongue-in-cheek style, but that isn't discernible in the film itself, which seems serious, even glum. Byron Haskin, who directed, wasn't much at humor, for the most part. This is his worst science fiction film. All the others, including *War of the*

---

*Verne didn't do better. The projectile is launched at the end of the 1865 De la Terre à la Lune; no space action occurred until the 1870 sequel, Autour de la Lune. Today the books are generally published in one volume.

Worlds, Robinson Crusoe on Mars and *The Power*, have a much faster pace; *From the Earth to the Moon* just shambles along at the same unvarying, uninteresting tempo.

The photography is also no better than mediocre. Edwin DuPar seems to choose the least interesting angle in scene after scene, but he was working with a Mexican crew — the film was shot in Mexico, oddly enough — and so language problems may have hampered him from getting the results he wanted. Perhaps not, though; he had been a special effects man at Warner Bros. for several years in the 30s and 40s, and had turned to photography only in 1950 or shortly before. Most of his films were medium-budget A pictures, none notable for their camerawork. Among his titles as effects man: *Castle on the Hudson, They Drive by Night* (both 1940), *Cloak and Dagger* (1946), *Task Force* (1949). As cinematographer: *Springfield Rifle* (1952), *The Eddie Cantor Story* (1953), *The Lone Ranger* (1956). This may have been DuPar's last film; a little-known story of Christ, *The Redeemer*, was released in the United States in 1965, with photography by DuPar, but it was filmed in Spain in 1957.

20,000 Leagues Under the Sea yanked atomic power back into the science fiction of the 19th century. Verne's propulsion system for the submarine in the novel was left vague, and it's unlikely that he ever heard of splitting the atom to gain energy. But once the Disney film raised that idea, other movies on Verne seem to have been forced into using it. The golden, effervescent "Power X" in *From the Earth to the Moon* is clearly meant to represent atomic power, but not only is this false to Verne, it's damaging to the simple idea of setting a science fiction story in the past. It's as if 19th-century science fiction isn't interesting enough unless it is also prophetic, specifically of atomic power, as if that was the most important discovery, ever. This endows Verne and other writers with phony insight, while their actual ideas were sufficiently interesting already. It's another example of the self-centered myopia of the 50s: our concerns are the world's concerns, both into the future (*The Time Machine*) and into the past. This happens again and again in science fiction created or adapted by the unimaginative: confidently pretending to know that future concerns will mirror present concerns might be regarded as satire, but it's really just lame prediction.

From the Earth to the Moon not only is bad prediction, it shows bad research as well, and the failure of research results in the film's script overlooking good story material. When Barbicane proposes firing that explosive shell at the Moon, the only concern he hears is about it falling back to Earth. But in the mid-19th century, some people suspected that the Moon might be inhabited. An outcry on these grounds would have been interesting, but probably the writers never thought of that, perhaps because such a concern would have sounded foolish in the late 50s.

On Earth, the set design is pedestrian and clichéd; it looks like that for a Western. The occasional attempts at being epic misfire; the budget didn't allow it. Cotten addresses a huge throng — but all we see is the actor standing in front of a curtain. When the story takes us aboard the lunar missile, the set design changes abruptly. It doesn't look like an attempt at 19th-century design anymore, though it's hard to tell what it is supposed to look like; perhaps a 1930s SF magazine cover. There are glowing spirals, an illuminated sphere and other gimcrackery, including an exposed gyroscope. Again, with the example of *Leagues* and *Around the World in 80 Days*, it seems strange that this aspect of the film would misfire so badly. The design was by Hal Wilson Cox, and while it's clear he had little money to work with, surely he could have designed a spacecraft that looked more like it belonged in the 19th century, and less like the inside of a jukebox.

There is no scientific accuracy, so I should not complain about its absence. But even in Verne's time, one of the main complaints lodged against his novel was that the space travelers were fired out of an enormous cannon. The shock of such impact would have reduced them to jelly instantly, and Verne should have known that. The craft still is shot out of a cannon in the film. For protection, the cast rides in some whirling tubes; but Paget is found hiding in a closet, not a whirling tube. With the reality of impending space travel so obvious by 1958 — the real trip from the Earth to the Moon was only 11 years in the future — a little more accuracy would have been in line.

When they are about to orbit the Moon, Sanders worries about the ship burning up from friction, but as they are in airless space, this seems a misplaced concern. Cotten says he has some inertia gas which will protect them, but it is never explained what that might be.

Under the direction of Lee Zavitz, who certainly should have known better, the special effects are dismal, probably again a function of budget. The model of the ship is supported by a rod running up through the base. The intention was to hide this rod in the flames and smoke shooting out the rear of the rocket/shell, but they fail to hide the support, which gives the ship something of the appearance of a flaming lollipop. (In its original aspect ratio of 1.85X1, this rod may have been hidden by the frame line.) If the ship had been mounted upside down, which would have looked the same to the camera, the problem of the smoke rising past it — which it does — would have been eliminated. And something surely could have been done about the constantly blue sky background which appears in all the shots of the spaceship in flight.

The film was so cheap it couldn't afford any scenes on the surface of the Moon, and when we see the Moon out the ship's big windows (which, incidentally, are not visible on the model), it is an especially poor painting of a *backlit* moon. In this film our solar system has two suns.

Zavitz has been around a while, but apparently most of his effects are of the mechanical, on-set nature. Among his other films: *Destination Moon, Around the World in 80 Days, On the Beach, The Alamo* (1960), *Captain Sindbad* (1963), *The Train* (1964), *Castle Keep* (1969). *From the Earth to the Moon* probably has the least satisfactory effects of Zavitz's career.

George Sanders gives a wooden, uncaring performance, as he often did in this period, although he was fine in *Village of the Damned* a few years later. Debra Paget provides little interest or animation, and Don Dubbins is just a standard love-interest type. Morris Ankrum is miscast as Grant; it would take more than a beard to make him look like the President.

On the other hand, Joseph Cotten is, as almost always, very good especially considering that his character is badly conceived and wildly inconsistent. Cotten is strong, forceful and convincingly intelligent — and there doesn't seem to be any tongue-in-cheek quality to his performance.

The music by Louis Forbes is trite and unimaginative; when Cotten opens a letter from President Grant, we hear the opening chords of "The Battle Hymn of the Republic." Some music by Louis and Bebe Barron for *Forbidden Planet* was appropriated for the scenes aboard the Moon ship.

It's difficult to understand now, other than making a buck, just what was the intention of the makers of *From the Earth to the Moon*. It seems like a film that had a larger-planned budget than it finally was allowed. There's a feeling of cost-cutting here and there, and the whole movie has a hangdog air. In Dick

Williams' column, he said that the film "has received almost no advance mention to date." Part of that was no doubt due to the problems RKO was having at the time, but I also suspect that no one was very proud of the film. Williams said the special effects work "employed a crew of 45 men for months at the Churubusco studio" near Mexico City. But there's no evidence of this care in the film. The effects are simple and cheap, not to mention totally ineffective. At any rate, the film was badly received by critics, and presumably was not very profitable; it soon went to television.

In the New York *Herald-Tribune*, Paul V. Beckley seems to have liked it more than most, saying that there are "a number of spectacular effects," but he also does complain about the film's "juvenile interpretation" and its "peculiarly unfortunate dialogue.... One wonders if the writers had their tongues in cheek." Hello, Joseph Cotten.

Even unimaginative, pedestrian Bosley Crowther in the *New York Times* expressed disapproval. "Pretty much of a dud," he said, adding that it was "extremely remote." Arrogantly, he concluded "what could have been outrageous and highly amusing is merely mixed-up science fiction decked out in fancy costumes," as if science fiction could not be outrageous and highly amusing, or perhaps as if it *had* to be outrageous to *be* amusing.

Jack Moffitt also noted the confusion of intent. "The hero is a munitions magnate, the chief 'merchant of death' in an international explosives cartel, who bemoans the fact that peace is bad for business. Its villain is a manufacturer of protective armor plate, a humanitarian and a God-fearing individual who, in the course of narrative gyrations, gets identified as a 'bigot.'" Moffitt termed the film "neither very good science nor very good fiction," and said that it was a "tediously dialogued and jumble-plotted affair."

In the *Los Angeles Times*, Charles Stinson said, "Unfortunately, Robert Blees and James Leicester's script is so intolerably gabby, as gassily pseudo-philosophical (could Jules Verne have been this bad?) and as leisurely as a mid-Victorian novel." He especially complained about the direction and about Debra Paget, whom he termed "an actress of the frailest, most insecure resources."

John Cutts in *Films and Filming* called it "a dull dog of a picture" and said that it was "completely devoid of any sort of imaginative spark." Alan Frank (*SF*) described it as "dreary" with "dull dialogue and even duller direction."

Some sources say that the later film variously called *Those Fantastic Flying Fools* (1967) and *Blastoff* was a remake of *From the Earth to the Moon*; indeed, while it was in production, it was called "Jules Verne's Rocket to the Moon," but that film—no better than this one—was an original story with only the idea of 19th-century types being mixed up with a moon craft remaining from Verne's story.

From the Earth to the Moon is almost totally forgotten today, a just and fitting fate.

Giant from the Unknown

This odd and lesser film was the first feature directed by the ineffable Richard Cunha, who went on to *She Demons*, *Frankenstein's Daughter* and *Missile to the Moon*. The title, *Giant from the Unknown*, and the advertising

that went with it, cheated; the principal ad lines were "the creeping terror that arose from the depths of the unknown!" and "IT Came From Another World!" The ad art, actually Astor's best, showed a shaggy giant awkwardly clutching a young lady whose hands are flung wide. All of this implies some kind of hairy monster from outer space; what the film delivers is a giant Spanish conquistador, awakened from a 500-year sleep with a bad temper.

Really not a bad variation on the usual sort of thing one finds in these cheap little pictures, if it had kept one of its several working titles—"Giant from Devil's Crag," "The Diablo Giant" or "Giant from Diablo Pass"—perhaps the film wouldn't have annoyed youngsters as much as it did.

Archaeologist Dr. Cleveland (Morris Ankrum, hooray) and his daughter Janet (Sally Fraser) are in the California mountain town of Pine Ridge, searching for Spanish artifacts. Local townspeople, including the sheriff (Bob Steele), warn them that animals have recently been mysteriously killed.

Another scientist, Wayne Brooks (Ed Kemmer), meets Cleveland and Janet—of course, the Scientist's Beautiful Daughter and the Handsome Researcher are soon in love—because he has a peculiar theory. Wayne recently found a lizard which had been imprisoned in rock for centuries but which, when removed from the rock, returned to life. (Legends of frogs found alive under these circumstances were widespread for centuries.) He knows that Cleveland is searching for the remains of a specific Spaniard, a vicious giant called Vargas, who vanished in the area 500 years before. Wayne suspects that Vargas himself underwent the same suspended animation process.

As if in confirmation, they find some armor and weaponry that could only have belonged to a man far larger than the average. That night, a fierce electrical storm strikes, and lo and behold, from the ground near the camp, Vargas (Buddy Baer) himself emerges, returned to life. He collects his armor and helmet, plus a gigantic battle axe, and goes about doing nasty things.

Wayne sees Vargas, but no one believes his story, and when the giant kills a village girl (Joline Brand), Wayne is suspected. Then Vargas abducts Janet and heads for high ground, followed by a posse including Wayne, who battles with the giant in an old mill. Vargas loses his balance and falls to his death, without ever seeing what became of Spanish California.

If you've been paying attention, and there's no reason why you should, you'll note that the townspeople are alarmed by the mysterious killings of animals when the scientists first arrive—before Vargas revives, so presumably whatever was killing those animals just kept on doing it. The reason for this strange glitch in the plot is probably that the film was written and shot in such a great haste that no one had the time to notice (or adjust) "minor" plot elements like that.

Fangoria, the entertaining magazine devoted to lurid horror films, has a harmless and charming fondness for cruddy older pictures as well, and runs interviews (by devoted fans) of the damnedest people, including Richard Cunha.

In issue #31, the most devoted fan, Tom Weaver, reported on his chat with the director. Weaver tells us Cunha was born in Hawaii and "received his film training in the newsreel and motion picture units of the U.S. Air Corps during

Opposite: In a peculiar behind-the-scenes shot, famed makeup artist Jack P. Pierce buries Buddy Baer in what looks like wood chips for Baer's resurrection as Giant from the Unknown (1958).

World War II. He made his first step into the civilian film business by making industrial films and commercials, and then moved on to shoot, write and direct such early TV shows as 'The Adventures of Marshal O'Dell' and 'Captain Bob Steele and the Border Patrol' for Toby Anguish Productions."

When Anguish left show biz, Cunha and Arthur A. Jacobs (not, as some believe, Arthur P. Jacobs) bought the studio and began producing television commercials. They decided to venture into Real Movies when Ralph Brooke, a friend of theirs, "finally convinced us that it'd be kind of fun to [make a feature,] and maybe we could make a dollar-and-a-quarter out of it," Cunha told Weaver.

Jacobs added that "we were all sitting in the office one day," himself, Cunha, Brooke and Frank Taussig, "and we wondered 'What kind of picture do we want to make?' And then we said, 'Well, we should make a monster movie.' Then, 'What kind of monster?' "

This kind of let's-do-the-show-right-here filmmaking must have been exhilarating and entertaining. It rarely resulted in good movies—though even that could happen—because the people involved weren't thinking about the quality of the product, merely in finishing a film, any kind of film. In fact, as Jacobs told Weaver, the budget for *Giant from the Unknown* was $55,000 (incredibly low). It was only 60 days from the moment they decided to make the movie until they had the answer print.

When you are working that quickly and that cheaply, the best you can really hope for is a film that people won't walk out on. Some despair over these movies, feeling *if only* this, or *if only* that, they could have been so much better. Being closer to the problems, the filmmakers knew that the movie could have been a whole lot *worse*. After all, they were dealing with a whole raft of *if onlys* that armchair filmmakers, watching the finished product, never have to concern themselves with.

When you have only two months to bring a film from concept to print, and only six days for shooting, you don't have enough time to concern yourselves with quality—just completion. I suppose it could be argued that these people should not have made movies at all, but that's naive as well as begging the question. Though these pictures don't deserve praise, instead of complaining that they could have been much better, as I've said before, we really should be grateful that they aren't any worse than they are.

Jacobs and Cunha used various dodges to lower the cost of their film. It was nonunion (though made with union personnel), as paying union scale would have jacked the price up. They planned to shoot it at Southern California mountain resorts near Big Bear, but told all workers that they were going to shoot on the beach at Paradise Cove. (Hadn't any of the crew read the script?) When everyone was aboard the bus, Cunha and Jacobs told Weaver, they headed in the opposite direction, toward the mountains, which "gave us a two-day start on all the unions before they really did find out where we were hidden off in the mountains—and, by God, they found us!"

Cunha and Jacobs told Weaver other amusing stories, such as the day in which Cunha managed to shoot 20 usable minutes of film, or the fact that they had to reshoot an entire climactic fight when they found the camera shutter was stuck. Most low-budget filmmakers have stories of this nature to tell, and rarely do their stories touch on the finished picture. They chat about funny incidents, actors who were hard to deal with, how they managed to save a buck or two by some kind of crazy scheme, how some foul-up set them back—because the fun for these people lay in *making* the pictures. (Sometimes you will hear one of these quickie directors blow hot air about how good their film was, despite it all, but that generally sounds apologetic.)

Giant from the Unknown had one surprising feature, makeup by Jack P. Pierce, discussed more thoroughly in the entry on Teenage Monster. The cranky old genius of makeup had only a few hours to make Buddy Baer look like he'd been encased in stone for centuries, and though the result is nothing much, Pierce probably did a better job than other makeup men might have. He gave Baer a large, ugly scar across the forehead, but mostly the makeup is simply pasty gray with Baer's own coarse features emphasized.

Enormous, good-natured Buddy Baer was the brother of former heavy-weight boxing champ Max Baer. He was rarely hired for his acting ability, though he was a better actor than Max. Buddy was around 6'6", but his propor-tions made him seem even larger. He appeared with Max in Africa Screams (1949), battling their way through that below-par Abbott and Costello vehicle, and turned up occasionally in other 1950s films, including Abbott and Costello's Jack and the Beanstalk (as the giant of course), The Big Sky (both 1952) and Dream Wife (1953). Giant from the Unknown was his first film in a while, and Buddy was selected after several other big guys, apparently including Lock Martin, were interviewed. Baer also appeared in The Magic Fountain, Snow White and the Three Stooges (both 1961) and Ride Beyond Vengeance (1966), the last film for Baer I have a record of.

His most famous movie role was as the gentle giant in Quo Vadis (1951), who wrestled a bull to save a young Christian woman in the Roman arena. Baer's own quiet sweetness was effectively used, and many remember his big scene more vividly than other elements of the star-studded spectacle.

Giant from the Unknown received the kind of reviews it deserved: luke-warm to poor. The Monthly Film Bulletin was especially severe, giving the film its lowest rating. "The giant Conquistador, once resurrected, runs true to form and after the heroine. Unhappily, though, his long period of hibernation appears to have left him more sluggish than ferocious, and Buddy Baer's impersonation has little to offer beyond sheer physique." Bet you wouldn't say that to his face.

Walter Greene in the Hollywood Reporter didn't like it, thinking it "plods along with boresome dialogue" and that it showed "no imagination [in its] basic familiar situations.... Direction and cast [are] adequate for this minor-league entry, which was mainly filmed outdoors."

Castle of Frankenstein #10 regarded Giant from the Unknown somewhat less than illuminatingly as "cinematic mockery," but even Don Willis (I) thought it was "not as bad as some of Astor's pictures, but then again, nothing is as bad as some of Astor's pictures."

While I don't think anyone could regard Giant from the Unknown as a "promising" feature debut for director Richard Cunha (at last report, running the Video Depot in Oceanside, California), it wasn't as bad as his later three SF pictures. It's pointless to speculate on what happened, because the slightly higher quality of Giant from the Unknown probably has as much to do with mere chance as with skill.

Half Human

As have several other pictures of this era, *Half Human* seems to have vanished. It is not available for rental from any company that I know of, it is not listed in the *TV Feature Film Source Book*, it has not become available on videotape, and no one I know owns a print. It's almost as if it never existed; it vanished so thoroughly it leaves nothing behind but a few scattered reviews, some stills and posters, and memories. I have never seen it, so I don't even have the memories, but I would like to see it.

According to *Filmfacts* and *Monthly Film Bulletin*, the plot of *Half Human* is as follows: Japanese university students, climbing in the "Alps" of northern Japan, discover a giant, hairy creature living on one of the highest peaks. Believing the creature may be the missing link, a group of anthropologists organizes a search party.

One of the students, Iijima (Akira Takarada), follows the creature, dubbed "The Snowman," and coincidentally discovers a lost village inhabited by primitive mountain people.

In the meantime, a circus manager who is also looking for The Snowman finds the creature's cave, where the Snowman's son (a little Snowkid) is hiding. As an attempt is made to capture the Snowman, the young one is killed, which enrages his heretofore gentle father. He tosses a truck and some men over a cliff, and demolishes the lost village, killing all the inhabitants except one mountain girl (Akemi Negishi), who flees.

The Snowman attacks the anthropologists' camp and kidnaps one of the students, but drops her when he spots the mountain girl. He chases her, but within a cave, they both tumble into a volcano crater to their deaths.

The anthropologists take the dead body of the young Snowman back to the university for scientific study. The dead creature is only one generation removed from being human, we're told.

The original Japanese title of the film was *Jujin Yukiotoko*, and it was released in its home country in 1955. It has become common to think that Japanese monster films released during this period always had many scenes shot in the United States to insert into the films for release here, but to the best of my knowledge, this was done only with *Godzilla*, *Varan the Unbelievable* and *Half Human*. The other films were simply the Japanese versions, sometimes shortened and reedited. They were dubbed into English and released pretty much as they were made. Some confusion arises at times because later Japanese monster movies often starred American actors, but their scenes were in the original Japanese versions.

According to film researcher Mark McGee, "All the American scenes [for *Half Human*] were shot in two rooms. [The actors] were just talking about this Snowman, and [John Carradine] would then tell the story; [in fact] the entire picture was narrated by Carradine. There was *no* dialogue dubbed into the Japanese mouths. They would just ... speak Japanese, and Carradine['s voice was heard] over, telling you what they were saying."

There was cooperation between Toho, the Japanese production company, and Distributors Corporation of America (DCA), the U.S. distributors, indicated by the fact that Toho sent over the costume for the young Snowman, so that Carradine, Morris Ankrum and other actors were filmed examining it. However, this seems to have been to no avail; no one was fooled. Reportedly, the American scenes stand out from the Japanese sequences, and it looks just like what it is: a foreign movie with added American scenes.

The Snowman suit is elaborate, although all American stills are so heavily retouched it's hard to make out just what the monster might look like in the film itself. The special-effects blending of a monster that is only about 12 feet high with normal-sized actors is peculiar for a Japanese film, in which the monsters are usually enormous.

There is a quaint still from *Half Human*, showing both the daddy monster and his son, who is riding on a bear. This shot alone would make me itchingly anxious to see the movie: a baby monster riding a *bear*? While Daddy watches? Incredible.

John Carradine began to turn up in science fiction films in this period. He claims to have been in more films than any other living actor, which may be true, although there certainly were bit players and supporting actors (such as James Flavin) whose appearances far outnumber those of Carradine. Nonetheless, of featured players, Carradine probably has appeared in more science fiction and horror movies than anyone else. He certainly has appeared in more *bad* movies than any other actor who is capable of giving good performances.

Carradine occasionally downplays the number of horror films he has appeared in, but that surely is a futile effort now. In recent years especially he so frequently appears in this kind of movie that it sometimes seems he's a good luck charm for the genre. By simple longevity alone, he is worthy of considerable respect.

The following is a *partial* list of John Carradine's horror and SF movie appearances: *The Invisible Man* (1933), *The Black Cat* (1934), *Bride of Frankenstein* (1935), *Hound of the Baskervilles* (1939), *Whispering Ghosts* (1942), *Revenge of the Zombies*, *Captive Wild Women* (both 1943), *The Mummy's Ghost*, *Bluebeard*, *The Invisible Man's Revenge*, *Voodoo Man*, *Return of the Ape Man* (all 1944), *House of Frankenstein*, *House of Dracula* (both 1945), and *Face of Marble* (1946). From 1950 through 1953, Carradine seems to have made no films at all, but he resumed in 1954. *The Black Sleep*, *Half Human*, *The Unearthly*, *The Cosmic Man*, *Curse of the Stone Hand* (1959), *The Incredible Petrified World*, *Invisible Invaders*, *Sex Kittens Go to College*, *Tarzan the Magnificent* (1960), *Wizard of Mars* (1964), *House of the Black Death* (1965), *Munster Go Home* (1966), *Dr. Terror's Gallery of Horrors*, *Hillbillys in a Haunted House*, *Autopsia de una Fantasma* (all 1967), *Pacto Diabólico*, *La Señora Muerte*, *Las Vampiras*, *Blood of Dracula's Castle* (all 1968), *Blood of the Iron Maiden*, *The Astro-Zombies*, *Daughter of the Mind* (all 1969), *Crowhaven Farm*, *Horror of the Blood Monsters* (both 1970), *Bigfoot*, *Five Bloody Graves*, *Blood of Ghastly Horror* (all 1971), *Moonchild*, *Everything You Always Wanted to Know about Sex but Were Afraid to Ask*, *Legacy of Blood* (all 1972), *The Night Strangler*, *Silent Night Bloody Night*, *Superchick*, *Terror in the Wax Museum*, *Hex* (European prints only), *The Cat Creature* (all 1973), *A Journey into the Beyond*, *Mary Mary Bloody Mary*, *Stowaway to the Moon* (all 1975), *Death at Love House*, *The Killer Inside Me*, *Satan's Cheerleaders* (all 1976), *Crash!*, *The White Buffalo*, *Shock Waves* (all 1977), *The Bees*, *Vampire Hookers* (both 1978), *Monstroid*, *Dr. Dracula*, *Nocturna* (all 1979), *The Boogey Man* (1980), *The Monster Club*, *The Howling*, *Frankenstein Island*, *The Nesting*, *Demon Rage*, *Klynham Summer* (all 1981), *House of the Long Shadows*, *Evil in the Night* (both 1983) and *The Ice Pirates* (1984). He did a voice for *The Secret of NIMH* (1982).

No one should claim that Carradine was very good in all these films, and some people claim that he was never any good, which is shortsighted. At his best, he has a kind of seedy grandeur and a sly, wry wit that are highly entertaining. He's not used now because he is a great actor, but even at his worst he has an old-school dignity that somehow brings a touch of something approaching nobility to even the sleaziest of these pictures. His hands and feet are now severely crippled by arthritis, making it difficult for him to walk or even pick things up. But he perseveres, going from big to little films, from continent to continent, always working. He is one of the last surviving figures of the old, bravura school of acting, the Booth-Barrymore tradition. I enjoy him in these films, and when he is finally gone, I shall miss him terribly, and will drink a toast to the person who really is the Grand Old Man of horror movies.

Half Human seems to owe much of its inspiration to *King Kong*. Special effects director Eiji Tsuburaya was always enamored of the 1933 classic, and this film seems to be his effort at emulating it. We have a big ape-man in a remote region of the world, a lost primitive tribe and some attempt at pathos. There is also a relationship between the ape-man and not one, but two, attractive women, although here the relationship is more murderous than winsome.

From reading reviews of the period, and discussing the picture with those who have been privileged to see it, *Half Human* seems to have been well-photographed, but slow-paced and a bit silly. The consensus is that while the American-filmed scenes damage the film or add nothing to it, the original picture was not very impressive, although likable.

The *Monthly Film Bulletin* gave the film an average rating, and said "Like *Godzilla*, this Japanese horror film has been adapted by severe cutting and the interpolation of scenes in which a group of American scientists discuss at great length aspects of the monster's behavior. Even before the continuity was so arbitrarily dealt with, however, the plot must have been too stereotyped and slow-moving to be really exciting. The monster, though unconvincing, is a most sympathetic creature; and even in his most murderous moments quite fails to inspire any horror."

Paul V. Beckley in the New York *Herald-Tribune* said "the development is generally slow and the outcome disappointing."

Half Human was released on a double bill with *Monster from Green Hell*, and boasted some exceptionally exciting advertising. "14 Tons of Frozen Fury that Moves Like Man!" screamed the ads, surely overestimating the weight of the Snowman. "Half Man, Half Beast But ALL MONSTER!" And the canniest boast of all: "Actually filmed in Asia." The implication that this was about the *Abominable* Snowman, which everyone knew lived in Asia, was quite clever.

How to Make a Monster

The title and advertising for *How to Make a Monster* were prepared before the script was written, and both are cheats. The imaginative, preposterous poster shows only the eyes and mouth (all three ringed in hair) of some fang-faced monster; one of the eyes is huge and bulging, not unlike that of the Teenage Frankenstein, and a knife protrudes from the eyeball. (Either the monster is very large or the knife is very small, but never mind.) And of course, the title promises something like a Frankenstein story.

But what's delivered is a tame murder melodrama, with a mad makeup artist substituting for a mad scientist. As horror, it fails to deliver, and it is only marginally science fiction, but still enough to qualify for this book.

American International made the film, and it is set at the American International studio lot. The company did own a small lot near Paramount briefly during this period, but this film wasn't made there; it also implies that the company has been there for years.

Pete Drummond (Robert H. Harris) is the resident makeup artist at the studio, immensely proud of his monsters, in which he specializes. His assistant Rivero (Paul Brinegar) has been with Pete for 25 years, and is obsequious and subservient to Pete, who continually dominates the weak Rivero.

Although two of Pete's creations, the Teenage Werewolf and the Teenage Frankenstein, are being featured in AIP's latest film, "Werewolf Meets Frankenstein," Pete is informed by new studio heads, Nixon (Eddie Marr) and Clayton (Paul Maxwell) that monsters are on the way out, and that the services of Pete will no longer be required. (Apparently Pete isn't necessary for straight makeup.)

Pete is outraged. He feels his monsters are art, and he hates the idea of losing his job. He cannot convince either executive that he is right, that monsters will soon be back. "That's the way the footage cuts," he is callously told. So Pete decides to have his revenge. "I am going to stop these men from destroying us," he tells Rivero. "You know those fools think that a monster is just put together with glue, hair, putty, foam rubber. They don't realize that a monster even on the screen is human and must be infused with a spirit by his creator."

He begins mixing up a special batch of foundation cream. "If they knew how many long hours I experimented with different chemical agents," he mutters. He reminds Rivero of a time he put Novocain in the cream and hypnotized an actor playing a caveman (which seems irresponsible). Despite Rivero's fear that doing the same to the actors playing the Teenage Werewolf (Gary Clarke) and Teenage Frankenstein (Gary Conway) is dangerous, Pete declares that they are fighting for their lives.

"This," he says, dipping a stick into his boiling makeup, "enters the pores and paralyzes the will. It will have the same effect chemically as a surgical prefrontal lobotomy. It blocks the nerve synapses. It makes the subject passive, obedient to my will." (The script is by "Kenneth Langtry," actually Aben Kandel and producer Herman Cohen; like several others by these two, it has elements of domination by a wise if crazy older man over a naive youth.)

After telling Werewolf actor Larry that his career is washed up because he's played a monster, Pete applies the makeup for the day's shooting, then gives him an order which we don't hear.

Later, we see Nixon watching the dailies of the monster picture alone in a studio projection room. The Teenage Werewolf, unaccountably in the same room with him, stands up abruptly and kills the new executive.

Naturally, the police (including reliable old Morris Ankrum) are puzzled, and there follow several scenes of pointless interrogation and discussion of the idea of back-East businessmen like Nixon and Clayton taking over a Hollywood studio.

Later, an ambitious studio guard (Dennis Cross) hints to Pete that he knows that Pete was responsible for the crime because of the time he left the lot. Of course, in real life the cops would have checked that detail at once, but this is very far from real life. So Pete immediately disguises himself as a caveman and catches the guard on his rounds, bashing in his head with a club.

Later, he hypnotizes Tony, the Frankenstein actor, with the makeup cream and soon Clayton is murdered in his garage by the actor. (Judging from this scene, the cream not only paralyzes the actors' wills, it makes them take on the strength of the monsters.)

However, this time, someone saw the fleeing killer, and under the nails of the victim, the police find traces of makeup cream. Instead of this clue leading them directly to Pete, the cops fool around a while as Pete lures Larry and Tony over to his house.

At this point, the film changes from black and white to color. At the house, where Pete has examples of his handiwork on display, he cracks up completely, murders cowardly Rivero, who had been mercilessly grilled by the cops, and broadly hints to Tony and Larry that he wants to add their heads to his collection—literally. A candle is knocked over, "which immediately causes a conflagration that can roughly be compared to the Chicago fire," said Jack Moffitt; "it is a discriminating accident that barbeques the bad people and spares the good people." (Rare in a Cohen film, in which generally everyone buys it.)

The fire also burns the faces off some of the displayed makeups, revealing skulls. Larry and Tony escape, as Moffitt said, and Pete perishes.

Herbert Strock has told several interviewers about that fire. Effects man Charles Duncan decided to rehearse the gas jets for the scene where Pete's place goes up in flames, and things suddenly got out of hand. Although the fire department was standing by, Strock insisted that the cameraman just start shooting what he could with one camera while Strock himself grabbed another. Mark McGee reports that Herman Cohen denies this story, but Strock told not only McGee, but also interviewers Tom Weaver and John Brunas in *Fangoria* #33 the same story. The actors do look uncomfortable in the scene, and some of the masks in the background, not intended to actually be burned, got badly scorched.

In fact, one of the more depressing aspects of *How to Make a Monster* is the callous destruction of the monster masks at the climax. While they are not classics of makeup, they were part of Hollywood history. Among those we see are The She Creature, an alien from *Invasion of the Saucermen*, the Venusian from *It Conquered the World*, the puppet Hyde from *Attack of the Puppet People*, and the mask made for insert scenes in *The Cat Girl*. Although the masks we actually see burning were apparently constructed for *How to Make a Monster*, some of the others were damaged or totally destroyed during the fire scene, according to the late Paul Blaisdell, the man who made them. I visited Blaisdell in the late 1960s, and indeed the big face of the Venusian, which he had over his fireplace, showed signs of severe fire damage.

The film has several ironies, mostly accidental. The central idea of the story line, that AIP is giving up horror movies for musicals, wasn't intended to reflect reality. The studio undoubtedly felt that although the science fiction cycle was declining slightly, AIP would keep making that kind of movie. However, not long thereafter, the studio did almost totally abandon the kind of science fiction and horror films it had been making in favor of the Edgar Allan Poe period films, as well as the Beach Party movies, a series of teenage musicals.

Furthermore, Pete tells Larry that he's typed as a teenage monster and will never be able to get a decent part again. The actor who did play the title role in *I Was a Teenage Werewolf* was not available for *How to Make a Monster*. Michael Landon graduated from the part into TV's long-running "Bonanza," which made him a television star, apparently forever. Far from being typed by playing a monster, in many interviews he says he still feels that it was the Teenage Werewolf which brought him to the attention of the public and producers.

On the other hand, the Teenage Werewolf in *this* film, Gary Clarke, was never able to make much success as an actor. He appeared in the terrible *12 to the Moon*, and later in *Wild Wild Winter* and *Passion Street, U.S.A.* (both 1966). In the 1960–61 TV season, Clarke was a regular on "Michael Shayne," and worked for two seasons on "The Virginian." But it wasn't for want of trying that Clarke failed to make the grade, and it certainly wasn't because he played the Teenage Werewolf.

The greatest irony was in showing East Coast nonmovie types taking over the management of American International Pictures. At the time, and for many years to come, AIP was managed by its founders, Samuel Z. Arkoff and James H. Nicholson, who were not from the East Coast, and who considered themselves thorough Hollywood types. There still is much controversy about studios being taken over by "outsiders" from back East, but undoubtedly AIP felt itself immune to such problems.

However, in the 1980s, AIP *was* taken over by "outsiders" who soon changed the name to Filmways and forced Samuel Z. Arkoff out of the company he helped found. (He soon began Arkoff International Pictures; he claimed that the initials also spelled AIP was a coincidence. Sure, Sam.) This time, there was no mad makeup artist hanging around the "studio" to send actors in to rip out the throats of wrong-thinking studio execs, but Filmways released a slate of notoriously unprofitable films, and *it* was taken over by Orion.

Herbert L. Strock directed, as he had *I Was a Teenage Frankenstein*. He's much smoother by this time, without the start-and-stop problems that marred *Gog*. Although it's not a good film, *How to Make a Monster* is probably the best movie credited to Strock. Certainly, it is better than *The Crawling Hand* (1963), his last released fantastic film. His two later films, *Monstroid* (1978) and *Witches' Brew* (1979), both of which he codirected, were, respectively, not released theatrically at all, and released only to cable television.

The script by Kandel and Cohen is insufferably talky, and keeps metaphorically opening doors no one goes through (the business with the studio takeover seems to have come from some other movie). But Strock keeps things moving reasonably well, and it's not boring.

The script has one bright idea: a crazy makeup artist. And nothing else. It presents a view of Hollywood as odd as anything ever depicted, lying between the Hollywood imagined by moviegoers, and that imagined by Hollywood itself. (The real Hollywood just isn't shown in movies.) The studio lot is crawling with people in all kinds of costumes—frogmen, sailors, Indians, etc.—as if AIP was producing a vast number of movies, each requiring elaborate costumes.

The barest idea of what a director does is sketched in at the beginning of the picture, in which a director tells the Teenage Werewolf and the Teenage Frankenstein how to play the scene. "This is the big scene of the picture," the director (Thomas Browne Henry) says. "The audience is waiting for this where, finally, werewolf meets Frankenstein." (Although this epic battle was promised in the advertising, all we see is two actors in a quick clinch.) The function of a director is apparently to act out the scene for the actors, and to tell them to "watch your chalk lines and listen to the directions carefully." (Later, we hear a choreographer tell his chorus line "just do the steps I taught you and watch the tempo." Life can be so simple.)

It's interesting that the ghastly musical number in the film, "You've Got to Have Ee-oo" is presented as the new direction for AIP. The kind of musicals they did make not long after this hardly resembled this stage-bound, imitation

MGM number, and instead usually took place outdoors on the beach. John Ashley, here playing himself, did turn up in a few of those pictures but not as the star. In fact, in a further odd irony, he became a star of cheap horror movies himself.

The plot demands that the cops act like idiots. No one suspects Pete until a sufficient number of people have been killed. Of course, the plot also demands that *Pete* act like an idiot. Why would he use the actors as murder instruments? Why does he disguise himself as a caveman? Does he think that if someone sees these monsters, the witness will simply assume it is a *real* caveman, werewolf or Frankenstein monster?

As Pete, Richard H. Harris gives a better performance than the film deserves, although it is broad. He really tries to build a character out of the bits and pieces provided by the script, but he's laboring in a vacuum. No one could really care if the performance was good. Harris continued to act through the 60s and 70s, often in television; he died in the early 1980s.

Paul Brinegar, as Pete's slightly moronic assistant looks uncomfortable in the part. He more often appeared in Westerns, usually with a beard, and gave far more effective performances in his several TV series. He was Jim Kelly for two years on "The Life and Legend of Wyatt Earp," and played Jelly Hoskins in "Lancer" from 1969 to 70. His best-known part was as the cook "Wishbone" on "Rawhide," playing the part for the entire run of the show, 1959–1966.

Among the other actors are Morris Ankrum and Thomas Browne Henry. This time, neither is playing a military man, as they often did in science fiction films, but both lend their reliable presence to the picture, which needs such help.

Reviews were perhaps a bit more favorable than the film deserved. Although "the horror effects are rather mild," *Daily Variety* said, "the script has some sharp dialog and occasionally pungent Hollywood talk." The reviewer said "it appears headed for a healthy [box-office] response." *Harrison's Reports* felt the picture "on the whole is less horrific than the usual run of horror films but it has effective suspense values."

The *Monthly Film Bulletin* said that the interest lay in depicting the young men playing the monsters as "ordinary" and "agreeable," and it "ranks as a collectors' curiosity even if its vengeance theme is developed on lines more akin to murder melodrama than genuine horror." Don Willis (I) said that it was "slightly different; more-than-slightly bad." In *Castle of Frankenstein* #10, Joe Dante called the film a "near plotless showcase for previous AIP monster makeups" with an "atrocious musical sequence ... cheap, lowest-grade shock stuff."

How to Make a Monster is indeed primarily interesting for its premise and for the accidental ironies it reflects. Although it is not as badly made as most films produced by Herman Cohen, there's little in the film of interest to other than completists in this field.

I Married a Monster from Outer Space

Though it suffers from a sensationalistic title, some clichéd "emotionless" aliens and a routine story line, the development of the story, some touches of characterization, the direction by Gene Fowler, Jr. and photography by

Haskell Boggs make *I Married a Monster from Outer Space* an interesting, smooth and scary science fiction–horror thriller.

In *Fangoria* #28, Fowler was interviewed by David Everitt on both this film and *I Was a Teenage Werewolf*, which he also directed. According to Fowler, *I Married a Monster from Outer Space* (hereafter abbreviated under its working title, *IMAMFOS*) came about because he was impressed by the grosses on the werewolf picture. Fowler and Louis Vittes wrote the script of *IMAMFOS*, a title chosen because it was exploitable, but they "tried to make the best movie we could with this ridiculous title.... One of the things I've always found is that you've got to accept the premise, regardless of how ridiculous it is. If you accept the thing as very realistic and very honest, then you can come up with very honest performances and make a fairly honest picture out of it." He lived up to his intent, too.

IMAMFOS was shot in eight days on a budget of $175,000, remarkably quick and low for a film made by Paramount. It was shot mostly on standing sets at the Paramount lot which helps give it a polished look denied to other quick films on this budget level. (Some have claimed the forest set used in this film was built for *Visit to a Small Planet*, but that film wasn't shot for at least another year.)

On his way to be married, Bill Farrell (Tom Tryon) is stopped by a ruse, and when he gets out of his car to investigate, a black cloud engulfs him. Later, he does arrive at the wedding, but it's clear to the audience that this Bill is an impostor, the monster from outer space of the title. On their wedding night, Bill stands on a balcony during a lightning storm, and a flash reveals his alien features beneath Tryon's handsome face. (This is genuinely eerie and disturbing.) He then returns to the bedroom to, as was said in those days, claim his wife.

A year passes, and Bill's wife Marge (Gloria Talbott) has become increasingly suspicious, even frightened, of her strangely unfeeling husband. We soon learn that many other men in town, including Bill's friend Sam (Alan Dexter), have also been taken over by the aliens. In his interesting commentary on the film in *Cult Movies*, Danny Peary points out that "we are not limited to the point of view of a single character," as we were in the somewhat similar *Invasion of the Body Snatchers*. Although we do follow Gloria as she learns increasingly frightening things about Bill, we are also shown other events happening in town.

The aliens have an aversion to alcohol, and although several of the impostors occasionally gather in a bar run by Grady (Maxie Rosenbloom), they never touch their drinks. The alien Sam is administered oxygen after a boating mishap, and it kills him. Bill kills first a cat, and later a puppy Marge buys for him: animals can detect aliens. This is often true in other aliens-among-us films, but there's a payoff at the climax.

One night, Marge follows Bill as he leaves the house. He goes into the woods, stops dead, and black smoke issues from him, forming itself into an alien figure. She rushes up to the figure of Bill, still standing there, and it topples over stiffly. A beetle scurries across Bill's immobile face, even across his open eyes.

Marge tries to contact someone outside town, but the telephone operator (a *female* impostor, the only one we see) tells her all lines are busy. The male telegrapher discards her message. Even Police Chief Collins (John Eldredge), Marge's godfather, is an impostor. The town has been sealed off by the aliens.

Bill reveals all to Marge. His race is from the Andromeda Nebula, where a

Charles Gemora's crude but imaginative costume for the aliens in I Married a Monster from Outer Space (1958); the suits must not have been designed to last long; note the retouched left armpit.

solar explosion destroyed all the females of his race, and they have come to Earth in order to mate with women and ensure the survival of their species. But so far it hasn't worked out. When it does, however, the children will take after their fathers.

Marge goes to Dr. Wayne (Ken Lynch), who previously assured her there was nothing wrong with her that would prevent her becoming pregnant, and explains things to him. He believes her, and realizes there is a sure way to tell alien men from human men: those who have become fathers recently are true human beings.

The true human men form a posse and head out to where Marge saw the monster and the spaceship she saw him enter. One man brings along his German shepherds. There is a pitched battle between the human beings and the aliens, which have a kind of self-sealing skin, so that bullets don't affect them. Their ray guns evaporate human beings. The dogs leap at the aliens and rip loose the peculiar tubes that run from the aliens' faces to their chests. This kills them, and they dissolve into puddles.

Inside the ship, the posse finds the kidnapped original men, dangling in the air over little machines transmitting the forms and memories to the impostor duplicates. When the wires from the machines to the human beings are torn loose, the surviving impostors all over town dissolve into a repulsive tapioca-like goo.

The fake Bill meets this fate, and the real Bill and Marge are reunited.

Louis Vittes is listed as the original writer of *IMAMFOS*, and I have no doubt that he is the principal author, but the story was cowritten by Gene Fowler, Jr. Originally, the picture was to be called *IMAMFOS* in fact, but Paramount apparently opted to use all the words the initials stood for. There was very little alteration from the original script (available in the Paramount Collection in the library of the Academy of Motion Picture Arts and Sciences) to the finished film. A scene in which the false Bill hits the deck when a football is thrown at him—the alien thinking it's a bomb—was wisely eliminated. The film was released four months after it was shot.

IMAMFOS is frequently compared to *Invasion of the Body Snatchers* in terms of plot, and undoubtedly that's the film that inspired Vittes and Fowler to write their story (adapting the title from 1949's *I Married a Communist?*). But the essential theme is somewhat different. In *Body Snatchers*, the pods make duplicates of Earth people with their own memories and personalities; in essence, the pod duplicates are the people themselves, with their emotions removed. The aliens in *IMAMFOS* remain aliens at all times, merely masquerading as human beings. And, of course, the human beings are still alive elsewhere.

This is a much less sophisticated concept, though probably more logical. It is less believable, however, because of the trappings of the film, and because of the dream-logic of the earlier film: we've had nightmares in which everyone around us simply stops caring. *IMAMFOS* is more clearly a low-budget picture, done with care and imagination, but rooted in a movie-reality, unlike *Body Snatchers*, which tried hard to make the reality in the film at least approach that of the audience. It was a more expensive picture, far more important to Allied Artists than *IMAMFOS* was to Paramount. That the later picture is as good as it is, is a tribute to the craftsmen who made it.

The basis of the script is sensationalistic. Alien monsters from space invade Earth to mate with human women!* The aliens are ugly, superscientific, use ray guns and can be spotted by faithful animals. The most clichéd aspect of the film is that they are basically unemotional and ruthless, caring little for the people whose lives they disrupt, and even less for those they kill. One can easily imagine this same story line being used by Sam Katzman, Roger Corman or other producers of the period, but they would have treated the material very

*This idea doesn't turn up as often in SF films as detractors of the genre believe. It's the motivation of The Mysterians, and there was a film called Mars Needs Women!; the distaff side was seen in Devil Girl from Mars, but usually aliens merely want to take over, not impregnate our women. The result, when they do want to, can be seen in Village of the Damned.

differently. Louis Vittes' script is a model of economy and intelligence; he deals with the preposterous happenings of the story with sympathy and responsibility. Despite the story, the script is, in fact, one of the best-developed and most logical of the 1950s. Gene Fowler, Jr. developed it about as well as possible, considering the budgetary limitations.

Without being blatant in any way — of course, he couldn't be — Vittes makes it clear that the impostor Bill and Marge are having sex, which, after a year of marriage, would seem likely. We see Marge writing a letter to her mother, complaining about Bill; it "has been a horrible year," she writes, telling her mother that Bill "isn't the man I fell in love with — he's almost a stranger." If she and Bill had not been having sex, there would have been phrases indicating this, perhaps a line about "he hasn't really been a husband to me." The absence of those lines is telling — as is the fact that Marge destroys the letter rather than sending it. Vittes wants to establish uncertainty on Marge's part — she's not sure she's right about Bill — which in itself goes a long way to convince us of the effectiveness of the alien disguises.

There's no doubt these guys are *really* alien, too. When Bill (the real one) is stopped in the woods by a fake body in the road, after which the body disappears, we see a glowing, glistening alien touch him. Later, after the ceremony, Marge and Bill's car passes through the same section of the woods, and we again see the alien.

The fake Bill drives for a while without lights, until another car almost hits his, which rouses Marge. The aliens aren't superpowerful, but they are superhuman in some ways. And these scenes near the beginning establish both that idea and a base for Marge's later more serious doubts.

Still, the phony Bill develops human habits, including smoking. So good are the alien disguises that the Sam impostor has to reveal his alien face to Bill in order to be accepted as a fellow invader. The disguised aliens are deftly treated in several scenes. Even in a film which offers relatively few plot surprises, it's startling to learn that Chief Collins is an alien. When Marge visits him, he exhibits just the right blend of incredulity and belief: "I wouldn't risk a nickel on your temper or your cooking," he tells Marge, "but I'd risk my pension on your sanity." This kind of avuncular approach, plus his being willing *almost* to believe Marge's story help prevent us from suspecting he's an impostor until, a moment later, he reveals himself to us as an alien.

As in *It Came from Outer Space*, the aliens are individuals with different attitudes, but all bent on conquest. The fake Sam actually likes human beings, we learn in one of their tavern conversations, while another despises them, finds them disgusting. The Bill impostor has found that wearing human bodies has brought "other things" with it, and he is almost falling in love with Marge. There's never any thought that he might betray his own people, but he is becoming fond of this woman he has spent a year with as her husband. He's still an alien, but he feels sympathy, and receives ours in return.

The idea that animals are aware of the impostors' alienness is a cliché, but it pays off at the climax, when dogs attack the aliens on their own initiative, and one dog dies protecting the Earth from invaders. (I don't recall any serious film in which animals *like* the fantastic characters until *E.T.*)

The aliens are not all-powerful, or they would have swooped down and conquered the world by force. They are impervious to bullets, but this is rationalized in some good special-effects close-ups of alien torsos as bullets strike them: the holes simply vanish in a little fwooping sound. They are strong — the fake Bill knocks a door off its hinges — but not outrageously so, as they don't toss the posse around like beach balls at the end. They have limited telepathic abilities; when Bill notices someone hanging around the house, with an effort he summons two alien cops to dispose of the intruder. In short, both in personalities and powers, there has been an effort to make these aliens a believable menace, with their own, understandable motivations. They aren't just monsters from outer space, despite the title.

Gene Fowler, Jr. directed only a few films before returning to film editing. *I Was a Teenage Werewolf* had a poor script, but Fowler's direction was good and made the film much better than its title indicates. *Gang War* (1958) was a confused, confusing and tedious picture, apparently made even more rapidly than *IMAMFOS*, and shows little of the ability Fowler sometimes indicated elsewhere. Other than his two science fiction–horror films, Fowler's most notable movie was *Showdown at Boot Hill* (1958), an intelligent if talky Western, with good performances and an effective small-town atmosphere. *Here Come the Jets* and *The Rebel Set* (both 1959) are unknown quantities to me, but *The Oregon Trail* (1959) is a bad, uninteresting Western made primarily to celebrate the Oregon Centennial.

When Fowler was involved in his material, he was a notably good director; his best film probably is *I Married a Monster from Outer Space*. It is carefully done in all respects. The sets, mostly standing sets on the Paramount lot, are textured, looking lived-in and believable, except for the overlit and drab tavern.

Mark McGee was astounded by the "gall" shown in one scene. The characters were approaching the spaceship, which is surrounded by bushes to cut down on the need for constructing anything; they go inside, and Fowler cuts to a reverse angle, and you are actually seeing the *boards* that form the back of the spaceship wall, the side of "flats" never shown in movies. "Now that was nerve," McGee said admiringly.

Fowler uses lots of camera movement throughout, which when it is handled as it is here, generates unease and tension. At one point, he employs a meaningless but intriguing hidden cut on the couple's honeymoon night. Bill and Marge look out a window; there's a trick dissolve using a lightning flash, hiding the fact that there's a dissolve at all, and we are seeing the same scene hours later. Fowler had been an editor for Fritz Lang, who used tricks like this from time to time, as Danny Peary points out in *Cult Movies*.

Fowler told David Everitt, "Fritz was more or less my mentor. He was very strong on horror and suspense. I learned a lot from him and put it in [my movies], in the building of suspense, the building of horror, the juxtaposition of shots and how to put them together, rather than just throwing everything in. He taught me the use of the crane—that guy was a genius on that. He taught me not to use the equipment as toys and [to] use them as tools. And the structuring of scenes, how you get shock values, that kind of thing, even though I never copied him slavishly because I had my own ideas on how to do that."

Some of the editing employs matched cuts. In one scene, lamps on two different sets overlap during a dissolve. And once irony is underlined neatly by a well-timed cut. We see the two alien cops cold-bloodedly kill the snooper, and the scene cuts inside the house, where Bill and Marge are talking. "It's a nice idea anyway," he says somewhat disconsolately. "What is?" Marge asks, having just learned that her husband is an alien. "Making guests feel comfortable," he replies. Maybe Bill regards himself as a guest, but clearly the attitude of the two alien cops is more like that of an arrogant, superior species toward unimportant animals—and alien Bill knows it.

There's a splendid scene which begins in Maxie Rosenbloom's bar. A prostitute has had no luck in the bar—she's been trying to pick up disguised aliens—and goes outside. Across the street, she sees a lone figure in a hooded jacket. The prostitute forlornly adjusts her stockings, sashays over to the figure, and addresses him coquettishly. She can't get his attention, so she swats him on the arm lightly. His head turns toward her (and away from the camera), and she reacts to a horrifying sight, then starts to run. The figure disintegrates her with a ray gun, and turns back to the window. We see its face reflected in the glass as it looks in at a display of baby dolls, for a faint touch of ironic poignancy. The scene is not frightening, but it is moody and effective as melodrama. And it does indicate something disquieting: in this town, even aliens not disguised as men feel free to walk about.

The acting is generally competent, although Tom Tryon is weak as Bill real and Bill false. He's stiff and expressionless, and the role called for someone who was neither. He doesn't give a bad performance, but it does not come up to the demands of the script.

However, Gloria Talbott is excellent as Marge. She's convincing throughout, and considering the circumstances, that's a major accomplishment. In *Cinefantastique* (vol. 3, no. 2), David J. Hogan said Talbott "performs more than capably as a most unconventional heroine." Danny Peary felt that "she was a terrific heroine for science fiction and horror films because she projected a rare combination of strength and vulnerability." She is both convincingly frightened, and still believable when she decides to act against the aliens.

The other actors are all capable, although there are no stand-out performances other than Talbott's. Nor should there be; believability is best served when all the acting is on the same level of competence.

The special effects are credited to John P. Fulton, but were probably executed by members of the Paramount effects department. They do bear the Fulton mark of quality however, being some of the better effects produced for a low-budget picture. When a real human being is captured by an alien, a thick black smoke rolls over the body, then rolls back offscreen, and the body is gone. This is simple and impressive, and as it is used early in the film, establishes the aliens' intent quickly. When seen in their alien forms, the invaders both shimmer and glow; they look greasy. The best-known effect is the brief show-through of the true alien face when lightning strikes nearby or when an alien concentrates hard. The beams and vanishing effects are simple rotoscoping, but serve their purpose well.

The aliens themselves are unusual but believable. Part of their strange quality is due to what seems to have been a mistake on the part of Charles Gemora, who is credited with makeup and who almost certainly designed and built the alien costumes (and quite possibly plays one of them). In the script, Vittes described the aliens as wearing breathing masks similar to scuba gear, with tubes running from their mouths to the chest of the suit they were wearing, hooking to breathing apparatus. However, in the film, the aliens are only wearing pants, and the tubes are part of their faces, connecting their nasal region to the chest. This is odd but acceptable physiology, and does create a genuinely alien and legitimately frightening appearance. The long, tentacular fingers are also a nice touch, as is the stocky appearance of the creatures, and their huge eyes with light pupils and black "whites."

What failings of logic the film has are very minor. We never know if the aliens put on artificial human bodies, or if the minds and shapes of the real people being held captive in the ship are somehow being transmitted to the aliens who otherwise look like themselves. There's evidence for both ideas. When Marge follows the false Bill into the woods, she sees the body separate from the alien inhabiting it, which oozes out in the form of smoke and coalesces into an invader's form. On the other hand, we do see the people suspended above small crackling electronic devices, and lightning does disrupt the alien disguises, as if they are electronic in nature.

Although Fowler's direction is intelligent and artful, it is also somehow slow. He was interested in creating an atmosphere of tense menace, and that almost precludes much action, which tends to be cathartic. The younger monster fans, who were the most numerous by 1958, probably became restive during IMAMFOS, and no doubt preferred the cofeature, The Blob.

Furthermore, the standard monsters-from-space trappings interfere with intelligent development of the story. There's no particular reason that the aliens should have been low on emotions, a tenet of the group. (Individuals vary, as noted before.) In fact, if they had been in a state of permanent grief over the loss of their own women, a major degree of poignancy for this loss—which Fowler and Vittes do try for in some scenes—would have been added to the picture. The business of the aliens taking over the entire town and preventing Marge from leaving is too familiar and too pat.

There's the odd bit of the telephone operator. She is female, and she is an alien, yet we are told in no uncertain terms that all the alien women are dead. Therefore this must be a male alien, and the first intergalactic transvestite in films. Eat your heart out, Dr. Frank N. Furter.

The ending of the picture is exciting and horrifying in a way that very few 50s SF movies are: it's extravagantly disgusting. The battle between the posse and the aliens is well-staged and exciting, and builds to an effective climax. The scenes of the fake human beings dissolving into piles of disgusting ooze shocked viewers in 1958. The most horrifying ones are Bill and Chief Norris—they are the aliens we have come to know the best, and even though we're intellectually aware that they are not really human beings, they are still characters we know. When Norris slumps across his table and in a very swift dissolve turns into piles of runny goo, it's horror at its most immediate. (The goo was Jell-o mixed up by Fowler's wife.)

I Married a Monster from Outer Space was greeted with some critical favor. The Monthly Film Bulletin said, "This generally well-acted and -staged ... thriller, though novelettish in its personal story, has an intriguing situation and some effective, if rather sparse, trick camerawork.... The overall treatment, though polished, is a bit short on action and excitement." Variety's "Whit" called it "imaginative" and noted that it had "been given class production." He said that Fowler's direction "latches onto mounting suspense as action moves to a climax." Jack Moffitt surprisingly began his review with reference to the sixth chapter of Genesis in the Bible, the passage about giants having intercourse with the daughters of men. He considered the movie "fairly interesting and intelligent" and thought that Fowler's direction was "well paced and first rate."

The film has been discussed frequently in recent years. Don Willis (I) regarded IMAMFOS rather sourly as "another picture that supposedly isn't as bad as its title that isn't—quite." On the other hand, in Science Fiction Movies, John Baxter said rather grandly that it was "a work of more than usual brilliance" and suggested that it was "dark [and] smoothly shot" enough to be an episode of "The Outer Limits" TV series, but it's actually less ponderously pseudointellectual than any episode of that greatly overrated series, and is better than any except Harlan Ellison's "Demon with a Glass Hand."

In *Future Tense*, John Brosnan felt that "Fowler's film represented female [fears]—the ultimate feminist nightmare that lurking behind the handsome façade of one's husband is a foul monster whose only interest is the exploitation of the female body." In a similar vein, David Hogan in *Cinefantastique* thought that the picture was almost a feminist tract. "Fowler and ... Vittes consistently emphasize the weak and even subservient position of women." While part of this is true—and it's certain Marge would have been more likely to be believed if she were male—it's actually a direct consequence of the plot, and doesn't really represent an early feminist manifesto. Vittes and Fowler were merely using the situation as it would have prevailed in real life, not seeking to make any real points. After all, no one believes Bennell in *Invasion of the Body Snatchers* or Putnam in *It Came from Outer Space*, and both were male. Furthermore, in *IMAMFOS*, why doesn't Marge turn to the one group she can be absolutely certain are not aliens: the *wives* of the suspected men?

In a follow-up to Hogan's well-intentioned but inaccurate approach to *IMAMFOS* as an early feminist film, Alan G. Hill wrote a letter to *Cinefantastique* which was published in vol. 3, no. 3. He pointed out that the aliens were "individuals with differing viewpoints.... The strength of the film is just this: it transforms the commonplace invasion theme into a mature treatment of the clash of mutually alien cultures." Although this is also an overstatement, it is certainly more accurate than Hogan's approach. While some of the aliens, particularly the duplicate Bill, are treated with some sympathy, they are also murderous and thoughtless. Surely under the circumstances, it wasn't wrong for the human men to try to kill the invaders. Hill does suggest otherwise: "only an insensitive viewer can watch the destruction of the aliens and not feel a sense of regret." Maybe, but I recalled the murdered prostitute and snooper, and I thought the aliens got what was coming to them.

Danny Peary's reasonable summation of the film in his highly variable book *Cult Movies* is nearer the point. "Only in the last few years," he said, "have horror and science fiction fans come to realize that the outrageous title is totally unsuited for what is basically an intelligent, atmospheric, subtly made sci-fi thriller."

Alan Frank (*SF*) is clearly fond of the film: "one of the most enjoyable titles in the genre. The film itself is well acted and directed, although the monster ... is more risible than credible." *Psychotronic* called it "an over-looked, well-made science fiction hit."

I Married a Monster from Outer Space has a painful title, and a plot that is too conventional for its own good. But writer Louis Vittes and director Gene Fowler, Jr., working with a very good female lead, excellent production values for the budget level, and much intelligence, imagination and insight, have produced a film that stands the test of time. It can be watched by today's audiences with great pleasure and appreciation.

Invisible Avenger

This film may not belong in this book, but information on it is so scant that it is quite impossible to tell. The plot line includes invisibility, but it may be magical or mystical in nature, or possibly even faked; however, it may be ESP-powered invisibility, which would qualify it for inclusion. Final determination will have to be made when and if a print of this almost unknown film surfaces. Until then, as always, I would rather err on the side of inclusion than exclusion.

Its obscurity is somewhat surprising, considering that it was codirected by renowned cinematographer James Wong Howe, and it is the only feature film after the early 40s to be about the famous pulp detective character "The Shadow." (Although as this book was being completed, a new film about Lamont Cranston was announced.)

When dixieland musician Tony Alcalde (Steve Dano) is murdered in New Orleans, his friend, crime fighter Lamont Cranston (Richard Derr), to whom Tony was talking on the phone when he was killed, comes to New Orleans to investigate. Accompanying him is Oriental mystic Jogendra (Mark Daniels), who has taught Cranston the ability to make himself invisible.

By probing the French Quarter, Cranston learns Tony was aiding the exiled president of Santa Cruz, Pablo Ramirez (Dan Mullin) and his daughter Felicia (Jeanne Neher), in hiding from Pablo's evil twin brother Victor (also Mullin), out to assassinate Pablo. Victor has exiled Pablo and seized dictatorial power in the Latin American country (perhaps an island, plot sources aren't clear).

When he is tricked into believing Victor has been executed, Pablo comes out into the open and addresses a group of followers. Victor's men kidnap him and Felicia, and rush them to a waiting yacht, which is to take them to Santa Cruz for execution. But Cranston and Jogendra make themselves invisible, slip aboard the yacht, and conquer the bad guys. The way is paved for Pablo to return to power.

Various credits for *Invisible Avenger* feature two people for several positions; as usual, this indicates that the film is episodes of a TV series edited together to make a feature film. And so it is: the movie is made of episodes of an unsold series about The Shadow.

It is completely unclear as to whether Lamont Cranston is ever actually referred to as The Shadow in the film, much less whether he turns up in his usual cloak with twin .45s blazing, but it's unlikely, even with the indication of the film's reissue title, *Bourbon Street Shadows*. Maxwell Grant's famous character was undoubtedly considered dated by the late 50s, and it was too early to consider such characters as nostalgia. So why was it made at all?

There are no reviews for this film that I have been able to discover. The quality is not likely to be high, but I cannot judge it on any level, and can only note that it does exist. Or did.

It! The Terror from Beyond Space

Although a low-budget film, this has an unusually good idea, and is well-made for its budget level, resulting in an above-average exploitation thriller. It's not outstanding on any level, and is routinely developed with performances that are rarely better than adequate, but in a period of declining quality in SF movies, this film does deserve some credit for a job well done.

The plot is *very* simple. Set in 1964, it begins with a press conference in which a military officer explains to a throng of reporters that the second spaceship to Mars is now returning with a terrible story. There was only one survivor from the first expedition, Col. Ed Carruthers, and he is being brought back under arrest for the murder of his crew. This causes a sensation.

Aboard the second spaceship, just before it launches itself from Mars, we are treated to a quick inventory of personnel (each seen briefly as a count-down check routine is followed); during this, someone notices that a hatch was left open. As it is closed, we see a shot of monstrous feet entering the compartment.

The ship takes off, and once in space the commander of the ship, Col. James Van Heusen* (Kim Spalding) quickly confronts Ed (Marshall Thompson), the man under arrest, with grisly evidence. Ed has been claiming some mysterious monster on Mars, not himself, killed his fellow crewmen. Van Heusen maintains correct military respect for a fellow officer, but angrily points out that while ten men could survive a month on the supplies in the disabled first rocket, one man could survive a year. To prove his point, he shows Ed something he found on Mars: a human skull with a bullet hole in it. "Only one kind of monster uses bullets," Van Heusen says cruelly. Ed is shaken.

Ed later talks to Ann (Shawn Smith), a geologist/archaeologist on the expedition, and apparently Van Heusen's fiancée. In a grim little monologue, more effective for being understated, Ed tells how he and his crewmen were caught in a sandstorm on Mars, and while heading back to the ship in their Jeeps, something running along beside them, hidden by the blowing sand, plucked each of the men out of the Jeep. The others fired into the opaque air around them, which must be how the bullet struck the skull. When Ed got back to the ship, he was alone; he waited for the others to show up, but no one ever did.

Soon, the stowaway begins making its presence known. Kienholz (Thom Carney), a biologist, is grabbed by the offscreen monster, and we see its arms waving in shadow as it attacks the man. (Later, it's reported there are no punctures, which seems unlikely especially after this windmill-shredding job.) The only one to hear the scream, quickly cut off, is Ed. Were his senses more attuned by his year of Martian isolation?

Ed raises a fuss; he's sure something has happened. No one else seems especially concerned as Ed uses the intercom to call around the ship. We see shots of intercoms in unused parts of the ship calling Kienholz's name. Ed rouses the ship and an unenthusiastic search is mounted, although why no one believes him is a little unclear. During the search, the monster grabs Gino Finelli (Richard Hervey), but this is seen by no one (but us).

Now that Gino is gone, which upsets his brother Bob (Richard Benedict), the crew begin to realize that something serious and strange is going on.

While Van Heusen and Bob are standing near a ventilation grille, puzzled, Kienholz's body drops into view behind them. He's pasty-faced and dead. (The script called for him to appear shriveled and crushed, but this was apparently beyond the scope of the makeup department.)

Purdue (Robert Bice) spots Gino in the ventilation shaft; he is pale and has black rings around his eyes, but he's still alive. Despite Gino's feeble protests, Purdue crawls in after him, and the monster grabs at Purdue from beyond Gino.

Purdue scrambles out without Gino; the grille is hastily replaced. Ed and Van Heusen hook a series of grenades over the grille, arranged to explode if it is removed, then everyone beats a hasty retreat from the compartment.

*Presumably a reference to famous songwriter Jimmy Van Heusen; he wrote the melodies for "All the Way," "Moonlight Becomes You" and, perhaps significantly for this film, "Swingin' on a Star," among many others.

While they wait elsewhere, Royce (Dabbs Greer) pointlessly suggests that the monster may be a survivor of a once-high civilization on Mars that has slipped back into savagery. It's obscure as to why this is more likely than it being a member of a race rising for the first time from savagery.

When the monster finally emerges from the shaft, there is an explosion which not only doesn't blow a hole in the side of the ship (a possibility no one seems to have considered), but which doesn't injure the Martian.

Van Heusen, Ed and some of the others go back to the chamber where the grenades exploded, and open the door to the room cautiously, but (as in *The Thing from Another World*), the monster's right there so they try to shut it again. No dice. It batters open the door, easily bending the metal, and makes a grab at the men who manage to get up the ladder. They drop gas grenades down at it, but these have no more effect than the explosions. The monster does manage to scratch Van Heusen's foot.

Later, Mary (Ann Doran) reveals that all "edible" fluid was absorbed from Kienholz's body—blood, water, bone marrow, everything—without any punctures. This would seem to be the Martian way of life, someone suggests. As Mars is such a dry world it would be difficult for living creatures to find moisture. The monster's poisonous scratch has made Van Heusen ill; it isn't serious yet, but there's nothing on the ship to combat it. The infection produces symptoms similar to anemia, so they need to get blood.

During all this, the specter of a romantic triangle, between Ed, Ann and Van Heusen rears its pointy little head, and although it's obvious now that Ed was telling the simple truth about what happened on Mars, Van Heusen still resents him.

Ed and Calder (Paul Langton) don space suits and walk "down" the outside of the ship to reenter below the area where the monster is apparently lounging around. They rig powerful electrical connections to the ladder, but these don't faze the Martian when it comes down to investigate, for despite their stealth, the monster catches them.

It attacks Calder, smashing his faceplate and breaking his leg. He manages to get into an inaccessible area between two large machines, and holds the monster off with an acetylene torch.

Ed returns to the upper portion of the ship, but soon he and Bob have to go back after blood.

While they are gone, apparently wild-eyed from his infection, Van Heusen unshields the main reactor while the monster is wandering around aimlessly in the reactor room. It's exposed to the full fury of the reactor, but this doesn't hurt it either. It smashes its way out.

Ed and Bob try to get back to the upper level with the blood, so Bob, out of revenge and to enable Ed to get away, confronts the monster, but it grabs him and, in shadow, breaks his back.

While everyone huddles in the control room at the upper portion of the ship, Van Heusen finally realizes that Ann has now fallen in love with Ed. He's bitter but resigned.

While Calder reports on the activities of the monster via his suit radio from his shelter, the others try to figure out some way to kill the damned thing. The monster finally decides to get at the only food supply it's aware of, all those juicy people in the control room, and starts battering its way up through the central shaft's series of hatches.

Suddenly Ed notices from gauges beside him that there has been greater oxygen consumption than there should be, given the number of people aboard, and realizes that the monster breathes too. (This would seem to be obvious.) He immediately has everyone get into space suits, and as the monster crashes its way through the last hatch, he heads for the control panel near the hatch to open the inner and outer air-lock doors simultaneously. This would mean his death, but Van Heusen gets there first; he opens the doors, and the monster does kill him.

All the air is sucked out of the ship, and the monster slowly dies. The story ends on a note of fatalism: we can't go back to Mars, for "another name for Mars is *Death!*"

The script of *It! The Terror from Beyond Space* was by Jerome Bixby, a sometime science fiction writer. It is, in fact, the first produced SF film after *Project Moonbase* to be written by a practicing science fiction writer.

Actually, while his output is large, little is actually science fiction; he only wrote it for about ten years. His best-known story was "It's a *Good* Life" (1953), about a child with incredible powers who holds a town in thrall. It was dramatized on "Twilight Zone" and was also redone by Joe Dante for *Twilight Zone: The Movie* (1983).

Bixby edited *Planet Stories* (1950–51), putting more emphasis on intelligent mood pieces than on space opera. He later was assistant to H.L. Gold on *Galaxy*, but in 1955, decided he wanted to try his hand at films, and so moved to Los Angeles. Bixby wrote about 300 science fiction stories, which would seem by today's standards to be a phenomenal output, but overall he wrote over 1300 different stories of all kinds under 50 different pseudonyms. Some of his best SF and fantasy short stories were included in two books, *Space by the Tale* and *Devil's Scrapbook* (both 1964).

Although competent enough by the standards of the 50s, and occasionally showing some wit and imagination, Bixby cannot be considered a major figure in the field; in fact, virtually the only story he is known for is "It's a *Good* Life." In *Enterprise Incidents* (summer 1983 special), Bixby told interviewer Dennis Fischer that he himself was also fond of his short stories "Trace," "Angels in the Jets" and "Small War." Fischer himself also cites "The Holes Around Mars" as a particularly good Bixby story.

Virtually no major writers of SF or fantasy have written produced films. There are some few exceptions, notably Ray Bradbury and Richard Matheson (who is as much a screenwriter as a fiction writer), but by and large, SF writers who have done screenplays have either written primarily other types of films (Leigh Brackett wrote mostly Westerns and mysteries, but did cowrite *The Empire Strikes Back*; Harlan Ellison's only produced film to date is *The Oscar*, which he disowns), or movies quite unlike their published fiction (J.G. Ballard wrote the original story for *When Dinosaurs Ruled the Earth*).

Bixby turned to films because that's where the money was, but he's written or cowritten only four movies. He got assignments probably because he was willing to turn out the kind of pulpy stories that other SF writers of the time would have disdained. His work as a film writer is as mixed as that of any other writer of films on this budget level. His first, *The Lost Missile*, had some interest but not for the script. *Curse of the Faceless Man* was heavily rewritten and the resulting film is mediocre. *It! The Terror from Beyond Space*, however, is well above average and would have been even better if Bixby's original script had been followed more closely. Bixby later cowrote the original story of *Fantastic Voyage*, which isn't very good, but did do the script of "Mirror, Mirror," one of the very best episodes of "Star Trek."

It seems likely that Bixby's script for *It!* underwent some of the same tampering he told Fischer doomed *Faceless Man*. The copy of the script I have is dated November 11, 1957, and seems to be first draft. In this draft, Bixby is scrupulously careful to be logical and scientifically reasonable throughout. His structure is awkward: the entire story is in flashback. However, his script is more ambitious and intelligent than the film that resulted.

Certain changes were obviously for budgetary reasons (he describes special effects scenes better not attempted on a low budget), but others were simply foolish. For instance, early in his draft, Bixby introduces the idea that oxygen consumption aboard the ship is greatly and mysteriously increased. At this point, no one knows the monster is aboard. One character even mentions that since the consumption is so high, they are in danger of not reaching Earth. If this idea had been retained, there would have been even more urgency in the need to destroy the Martian. But in the finished film, this idea is dropped. Instead Our Hero has the traditional (and dumb) last-minute inspiration upon suddenly noticing there's increased oxygen use, and insists on removing all the air from the ship.

To be sure, the idea of releasing all the air is still a last-minute idea in Bixby's first draft, but the characters have already toyed with the idea of asphyxiating the monster. Someone even suggests donning their suits and going outside until it smothers, but someone else points out that the air supply in the suits is good for only a few hours. Of course, the solution that's used would seem to present the same problem—where are they going to get the air to fill the ship again?

One inventive aspect of the script, retained in the film, is that the weapons used by the Earthmen are simply .45 automatic pistols, not ray guns or any other fancy-shmancy Flash Gordonesque hardware; it's only 1964, after all. Of course, the guns don't hurt the monster, but it's still a nice touch.

Bixby concentrates on logic throughout this draft, and even tries to emphasize a certain degree of characterization, clichéd though it is. His draft is not a perfect script, but it would have been better than the script that was used.

"I wrote it in terms of an 'A' picture with somewhat grander production values," Bixby told Fischer. "In all, I thought they did a pretty credible job. The set design and the cinematography [were] good.... [Cinematographer Kenneth Peach] had a lot of imagination and good lighting. The special effects, unfortunately, were not convincing. You can't have a person stick a Roman candle into a bazooka and have it be believable. There were also problems in the final confrontation." Bixby admitted that *The Thing from Another World*, a film he greatly admires, was one of the key inspirations for his story, which is essentially the same as that of the Howard Hawks film, with the monster and all his potential victims aboard a spaceship instead of trapped in an Arctic research base.

Apparently, Bixby thought that reusing the word "death" over and over would create a sense of foreboding, but it just sounds comically morbid. At the beginning, Ed says that Mars was "alive with something we came to know only as Death." When Calder is trapped by the monster, he reports its position: there it is, he says, "big as Death." And the last words in the film: "Another name for Mars is Death." Well maybe, but that monster seemed pretty lively for a while.

Both Bixby's original and the final script err in revealing to the audience that there really is a monster aboard the ship. The film would have worked better if we simply had not seen the feet in that early scene. No one seeing the film thought there would *not* be a monster—the title is more than a hint that there is one—but to withhold it, giving only clues that it's there, would have built a kind of entertaining if bogus suspense.

Edward L. Cahn directed *It! The Terror from Beyond Space*. This veteran low-budget filmmaker was generally mediocre and unimaginative, but his work here, though it is staid and not venturesome, does show some flashes of intelligence and imagination; he's trying to make his movie scary. For more on Cahn, see the entry on *Curse of the Faceless Man*, which was the cofeature with *It!*

Cahn did occasionally give hints that he was capable of better things, when he was working with Gothic-like material, but even on a film such as *Four Skulls of Jonathan Drake*, which would demand that treatment, Cahn can't deliver.

Roger Corman, working at the same time, with much the same kind of material, showed much more imagination and invention, even with tighter schedules, less money and fewer opportunities for retakes. The major difference between them, however, probably wasn't in talent; Corman was a young man, and Cahn was not.

The actors don't seem to have had much guidance. They're mostly on their own. With pros like Marshall Thompson, Ann Doran, Dabbs Greer and Paul Langton, this doesn't present a problem. Even Shawn Smith is acceptable as the heroine, who doesn't have much to do. But Kim Spalding is weak as the other male lead, and no one has made an attempt to hide his ineptitude.

It's a conventional film; there's little camera movement and, typically for Cahn, the camera often seems too far from the actors, making the action seem remote. Aboard a spaceship, there should have been a feeling of claustrophobia. Cahn and Peach do occasionally try for this feeling, with objects crowding in from the sides and in front of the frame, but this is only used below decks and only when the monster is at large. There's some attempt at creating a suspenseful atmosphere by means of shadows, but this is inconsistent. And the film has long dull spots here and there.

The movie is still above average for a film of this nature, and has an original (if derivative) idea. However, not all agree. In both *The Science Fiction Encyclopedia* and his own book *Future Tense*, John Brosnan suggests that the story line is somewhat similar to the "Black Destroyer" portion of A.E. Van Vogt's novel/story collection *Voyage of the Space Beagle*. It is similar, but I feel that Bixby's admission that he was inspired by *The Thing from Another World* is factual.

The monster suit in the film was designed by Paul Blaisdell, but may have been constructed by someone else. It has most of the virtues and flaws of Blaisdell's work: an interesting basic concept, a silly face, and a generally cumbersome look. Richard Matheson told Joe Dante that when Bixby saw the suit, he rewrote the script to keep the monster in the shadows most of the time.

Bixby told Dennis Fischer, "In the script, I emphasized that the creature was quick, frighteningly quick in its movements. This is one thing I wanted very much, and instead they stuck Ray Corrigan [into the suit; he] had been playing gorillas for twenty years, and he immediately bent over and scratched his armpit. And that was the way the creature was portrayed, as lumbering and slow, except [that] they wanted two scenes where he acted very quickly."

Ray "Crash" Corrigan was a stunt man and cowboy actor who indeed often played gorillas in films. Aside from his activities as a gorilla and as one of the Three Mesquiteers, Corrigan is perhaps best known for one of the most extravagantly brave lines in the history of movies. In the screwy serial *Undersea*

Kingdom (1936), he's strapped to the front of a futuristic tank. The driver (Lon Chaney, Jr.) threatens to ram the doors of a fortress with Corrigan still strapped there. "Go ahead and *ram!*" Corrigan snarls. No wonder he was called "Crash."

He's not up to that delirious height here. In fact, of course, he has no lines at all. He mostly lumbers around the ship rather arthritically, looking ponderous and apelike. Just as Bixby told Fischer, his script calls for the monster to be agile and graceful, but in his ill-fitting monster suit, Corrigan is about as agile and graceful as a cigar store wooden Indian. Here was an opportunity for a genuinely unusual monster, but Corrigan and/or Cahn opted for a standard, rather Frankensteinian monster with the habits of Dracula.

Corrigan was hampered by the suit, which was designed for a man of different porportions; Corrigan apparently had a potbelly by this time (he died in 1976), and the monster looks awkward. Its face is strange; it has a permanent, squinty snarl frozen on it, which makes it look rather silly, and its tongue always seems to be protruding because that's where Corrigan's chin fit into the mask. The suit does have some interesting aspects, in its armor-plated look and the thick but wicked-looking talons.

There actually are special effects in *It! The Terror*, although they are mostly limited to the same shot of the spaceship flying by vertically from bottom to top of the screen. I suppose the reason we rarely saw ships appear in the distance and shoot toward the camera was because those setups demanded a higher standard of realism. As it is, the effects here are elementary but occasionally ambitious. There are several scenes of space-suit-clad actors walking down the outside of the ship, with a star field in the background. One of these is an extreme long shot, pretty brave for a low-budget effects team (not credited in the print I saw), although one does wonder why a spaceship has rectangular windows.

The music by Paul Sawtell and Bert Shefter is mostly above average for a film of this nature, although the dull "weeeooooweeeooooweeeoooo" that we hear every time the ship is shown in space becomes mighty wearisome after even one hearing.

Reviews of the time were moderate, and many reviewers commented that the monster resembled the Creature from the Black Lagoon. "Ron" in *Variety* said that "it's old stuff, with only a slight twist." Jack Moffitt, who was usually a better judge of such stuff, considered it "a rousing science-fiction film." The *Monthly Film Bulletin* also generously thought it "effectively staged and, if not in the front rank of science fiction, [it] provides an acceptable addition to the gallery of monsters."

Don Willis (I) allowed as to how there "are a few tense moments in the latter half"; in (II) he added that it was "silly/tense SF-suspense," which is poetic and not inaccurate. Alan Frank (*SF*) described it as a "briskly directed horror piece." Parish and Pitts said, "The low-keyed production demonstrates how a director can produce an entertaining film on a small budget."

While admitting that the film is a little above average, John Brosnan (like many other writers) calls into question the possibility that *Alien* (1978) owes a great deal to *It! The Terror from Beyond Space*, as well as suggesting that the *older* film had elements in common with the previously-mentioned A.E. Van Vogt story.

As a matter of fact, Van Vogt threatened suit against 20th Century–Fox concerning *Alien* specifically referring to the habit of that monster of laying eggs in its victims' bodies. There was an out-of-court settlement in that case.

Dennis Fischer asked Jerome Bixby about *Alien*. "You have to understand that I have to be careful in answering that one," Bixby said. "There certainly were conspicuous similarities. The creature on the spaceship sneaking people off into the ventilation systems, between the hulls, in air ducts. Invincible. Busts through every defense they could erect. Killing the crew members one by one and at the end snuffed by suffocation." Fischer himself summed up Bixby's comments: "He felt that *It!* very probably seeded *Alien* screenwriter Dan O'Bannon's mind, but was noncommital. [Bixby] admitted that many of these similarities would be likely given the basic situation of a monster aboard a spaceship." Quoting Bixby again, about *Alien*: "I loved it! I saw it twice! I liked it best for its visual impact, which was remarkable."

My own opinion: while there are undeniable story similarities, particularly regarding the encounter with the monsters in the air conditioning systems of the spaceships in both films, the treatment is different. In *Alien*, the emphasis is on when-is-it-gonna-getcha, while in *It!* the emphasis is on how-do-we-get-rid-of-it. In short, *Alien* is primarily a horror and suspense film, while *It!* is a problem film with some tension in its tail.

Ron Shusett and Dan O'Bannon, who wrote the original story of *Alien*, have never denied that they saw *It! The Terror from Beyond Space*, as far as I know, but there are dozens of other stories, several in the old E.C. comics, about monsters and other menaces aboard spaceships. *Alien* is not an original idea, but it is also not a stolen one, any more than *It!* was stolen from *The Thing from Another World*. After all, Bixby told Fischer "I wanted ... the same sort of ... isolation situation, a small group of people faced with something that was overwhelming them, ripping them [up] one by one... I thought a spaceship would be the perfect place and the perfect setting."

It! The Terror from Beyond Space is a fairly tidy little picture. It presents a problem, raises possibilities as to how to solve it, and finally solves it in an irritating burst of inspiration. No one would ever mistake this film for a classic, but it was adequate entertainment, and much above average for the level of SF films of its period.

The Lost Missile

This cut-rate disaster film is efficient, making good use of little-seen stock footage and utilizing its low budget to the fullest. Let down by mediocre special effects—the idea is too ambitious for the money—the story also tends toward the repetitious, but for a short, unpretentious film, it's not bad. And for the period, the ending was a surprise.

It may also be the only U.S.-Canadian coproduction made in the period covered by this book; this may explain why Ottawa is one of the locations wiped out by the menace of the title.

It isn't a deliberate menace; it's an unmanned craft from outer space. How it got here and what its purpose is goes completely unexplained in the film; for once, that's something of a strength. The unexplained nature of the craft makes it more mysterious and ominous.

A rocket-shaped craft traveling almost 5,000 miles per hour appears on American radar screens in northern Alaska. The craft does not appear to be from any Earth nation, and moves in a very low orbit—five miles up—on a path that will soon bring it over New York City.

None of this would be particularly threatening, except that for reasons insufficiently explained in the film, the object has a temperature of one million degrees (Fahrenheit, I presume), destroying everything on the ground in a swath beneath it.

Meanwhile, American nuclear scientist Dr. David Loring (Robert Loggia) is putting the finishing touches on the minihydrogen bomb warhead of the Jove missile, and preparing for his impending marriage to his assistant Joan Woods (Ellen Parker).

Around the world, various defense mechanisms are brought into play; no one knows for sure what the missile will do next, and everyone wants to be ready. Eventually, we learn that a Soviet missile had struck this one while it was passing in space, deflecting it onto its present course.

David and fellow scientist Joe (Phillip Pine) learn that it will pass over New York in 63 minutes. David convinces the commanding military officer at the nuclear base that if the new Jove missile can be armed in time, it probably can demolish the lost missile.

The scenes of the activity involving David are intercut with sequences showing the onrushing missile and the destruction it causes. A radar station in Alaska transmits a wirephoto of the missile just before the station is destroyed by the missile's heat.

Ottawa and Manhattan are both in the missile's path, and we see scenes of people in the latter city hiding in bomb shelters, fleeing in panic and jamming streets in their terror. This stock footage seems to be partly from disaster drills conducted in New York, and partly from civil defense training films.

Ottawa is indeed wiped out, with only melted stumps of buildings remaining as the missile roars by.

Back in New Jersey, David and Joan rush to the Jove site with the warhead in a lead box in their Jeep. They are waylaid by juvenile delinquents who steal the Jeep and the warhead. David pursues in another car, finds the Jeep with the warhead exposed and some of the hoods dead of radiation poisoning.

The missile will reach New York in 14 minutes, so David takes a desperate and fatal step: he simply picks up the warhead, tosses it into the Jeep, and roars on to the launch site. He is a walking dead man. He manages to install the warhead and the Jove is launched in the nick of time (i.e., in time to save Manhattan, the Bronx and Staten Island, too—forget about upstate New York). The 7,000 mph Jove meets the alien craft and destroys it 140 miles from New York. Joan is left crying for David.

The origin of The Lost Missile is confused. In Daily Variety, 18 June 1957, a small piece read: "Film rights to Lost Missile, novel by John McPartland, has [sic] been acquired by indie producer-director William Berke for August shooting. McPartland will also screenplay." On the film itself, however, Lester William Berke (son of William Berke) is credited with the story, and McPartland with the coauthorship (with Jerome Bixby) of the script. There's no mention of a novel.

William Berke began the project as producer. He'd been around Hollywood many years, directing low-budget exploitation films, sometimes for himself as producer, sometimes for others, such as Sam Katzman. (Berke occasionally used the name William Lester.) Berke directed the features Dick Tracy (1945) and Zamba the Gorilla (1949); for Katzman, he helmed Jungle Jim (1948) and others in the series, including Fury of the Congo. He produced and directed The Jungle. When The Lost Missile was partway through production, Berke died.

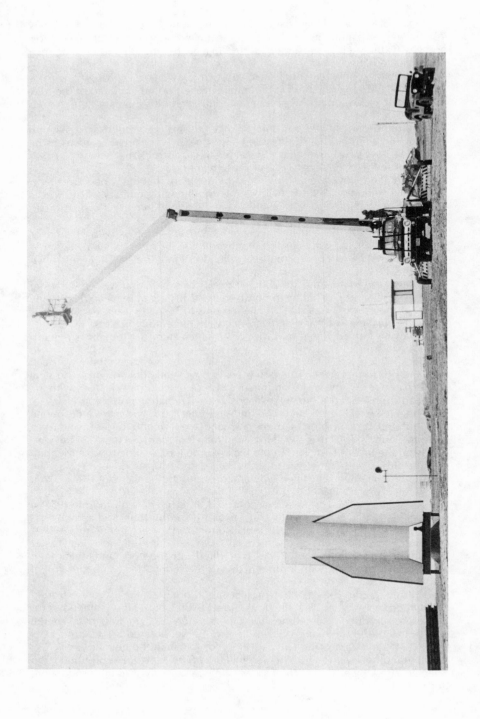

Low-budget films are more dependent on a strong producer than films on higher budget levels; a director is usually second in power to the producer on such films. Berke's son Lester was directing the film, so Berke's longtime production associate Lee Gordon took over producer's chores, and she brought the film in.

The film actually couldn't have been shooting much more than a week; a great deal of it is stock footage which, although ingeniously used, certainly doesn't require any more shooting time.

The special effects are elementary; virtually everything is done through simple paintings. Not matte paintings, but paintings photographed by the camera with no live-action parts of the screen: one before the missile passes by (roar), one afterwards, showing the smouldering ruins of radar base, forest or city.

The film is brisk and efficient; the sets are minimal, but not unimaginative, and the direction is well above average for a picture of this nature. It builds up quite a head of tension by the climax, but this is partly dissipated by the reliance on stock footage (cleverly-used though it is), and by the inadequate special effects. The script wisely focuses on the actions of David and the sacrifice involved in his saving Manhattan; it couldn't show us screaming thousands going up in flames as the blazing missile sweeps by overhead, so the story centers around the tragedy of one brave man. This is intelligent use of your limitations.

Several reviews singled out Robert Loggia for praise. This solid but under-rated actor has had a busy career since *The Lost Missile*; his films are relatively few, and include *The Greatest Story Ever Told* (1965), *Che!* (1969), *Revenge of the Pink Panther* (1978), *Scarface* (1983, in which he was especially good), and *Prizzi's Honor* (1985), but he is quite active on television. Some still fondly remember him for the title role in the 1966–67 TV series, "T.H.E. Cat."

Phillip Pine was also mentioned favorably by some reviews. Pine really is one of the actors about whom the trite phrase is true: everyone knows his face, but no one knows his name. He appeared in some other genre films, including *Phantom from 10,000 Leagues*, *Brainstorm* (1965) and *Project X* (1967), but he'd been busy in films since the late 1940s. He was a regular in the short-lived "Blue Knight" TV series. Pine is frequently a guest star in almost every kind of TV show other than situation comedies.

Jack Moffitt, who always applauded initiative in low-budget films, was especially pleased, considering the film "exciting.... As in every good suspense story, one feels the ticking of a clock through every minute of *The Lost Missile*.... A large part of the film is stock shots, but these are so well-integrated with the dramatic footage by editor Edward Sutherland as to constitute a minor masterpiece of documentation. Location photography in Canada and New York's subways by Kenneth Peach expertly matches the prevailing newsreel style."

"Powe" in *Variety* was less enthused. "Routine science fiction, highlighted by some fair special effects and well-used stock.... [Though it is] tightly made and should be a satisfactory entry ... there is plenty left unexplained.... Best points of the production ... are the results of research on stock footage by Berke and his producer Lee Gordon.... The actors are less happily served by the screenplay ... not always too clear on sequence, [going] overboard heavily

Opposite: Even cheap films sometimes have sizable props built; this bottom section of a rocket was constructed for The Lost Missile (1958).

for melodrama. Dialog tends to be oratorical, particularly in high-echelon scenes involving civilian and military officials."

In *Enterprise Incidents* (summer, 1983), Dennis Fischer talked with Jerome Bixby about his science fiction screenplays. Bixby said, "John [McPartland] and I wrote a not very good picture called *The Lost Missile*. Unfortunately, on the first day of shooting, the producer, Bill Berke, had a coronary and died, so his son took over and directed and made an earnest effort, but the picture did not turn out well. John and I did no treatment, we simply decided on a story line, and he decided on which scenes he would be more comfortable writing and which scenes I would be more comfortable writing, mainly the technical stuff, and we did the whole thing in a week and a half." Perhaps McPartland only sold Berke the promise of a novel. For more on Bixby, and more quotes from Fischer's interesting interview, see the entries on *It! The Terror from Beyond Space* and *Curse of the Faceless Man*.

The *Monthly Film Bulletin* gave *The Lost Missile* a II rating. "This science fiction thriller has its weaknesses—the trick work is not very impressive and is rather repetitive—but at least it marks a definite departure from the standard formula."

And that it does. The basic idea is, so far, unique in films: an alien artifact which has no evil programming of its own is accidentally turned into an instrument of destruction. I'm surprised that this idea hasn't been used again; it's a useful variation on the bomb-defusing formula—a machine which must be turned off on a time schedule. To have the machine be from outer space is unusual and interesting. *The Lost Missile* is cheap, but it is also novel, tense and well-made.

Missile Monsters

It's too bad that when Republic decided to turn a couple of old serials into features they didn't choose better source material than *Flying Disc Man from Mars*, which was shortened into *Missile Monsters*, or *Zombies of the Stratosphere*, which became *Satan's Satellites*. Those two serials are not among Republic's best, particularly *Flying Disc Man*.

As the vogue for serials waned and production costs rose, Republic began mining their older serials more and more for stock footage, so that many of their later serials had relatively few new action or special effects scenes. Costuming for the actors in the new footage was chosen to match that from the older serials. This explains why the Martian in *Flying Disc Man/Missile Monsters* is garbed exactly as Roy Barcroft was in *The Purple Monster Strikes*. (In fact, *Flying Disc Man* is presented as a sequel to the earlier serial, although the connections—other than the stock footage itself—are slight.)

Presumably, Republic chose these two serials because (a) they were science fiction, and the studio wanted to cash in on the vogue for such features, and (b) they were among the most recent of their SF serials, thereby ensuring a less dated look. Of course, there's a flaw in that latter reason: so much of both serials was stock footage the costuming had to match that the films still did look dated.

Outfitting the films with highly misleading titles (no monsters or missiles in *Missile Monsters*, no satellites or satans in *Satan's Satellites*), and a reasonably clever if campy ad campaign fooled almost no one, I presume. However, some reviewers seemed to think that the films were made when they were released — but in a style designed to resemble the serials. The techniques were dated and the action scenes repetitious and dull; the stories were incredibly primitive by the standards of 1958. By that point, few were prepared to accept invading aliens that looked exactly like human beings (except for wearing tights). Furthermore, the two films were quite similar to each other: Martian comes to Earth and makes a deal with a renegade Earth scientist, who provides the Martian assistance in his effort to destroy the Earth. They are combatted by Earth's hero, who saves the day.

Republic would have been better off to turn into features one (or two) of their other science fiction serials, such as *Radar Men from the Moon* or *The Purple Monster Strikes*. But the decision to make these into features was probably hasty, without much planning. They cost little to prepare, they came and went swiftly, and so probably made satisfactory profits for Republic, their only real consideration.

In *Missile Monsters*, aviator Ken Fowler (Walter Reed) is hired by eccentric scientist Dr. Bryant (James Craven) to shoot down an unusual aircraft that has been hovering over Bryant's aircraft factory. The downed plane is found by Bryant, and its occupant is revealed as Mota (Gregory Gay), a Martian bent on taking over the Earth.

Mota promises to give Bryant atomic secrets enabling him to build super-planes and atomic bombs, and Bryant agrees to aid in the conquest of the Earth. There follows a seemingly endless series of encounters between Kent Fowler and the henchmen of Bryant and Mota, Drake (Harry Lauter) and Ryan (Richard Irving). The henchmen are supposed to gather certain materials for use in the conquest, and Kent keeps thwarting them. However, they finally do get enough stuff together to make several bat planes of Martian design.

Mota and Bryant begin their campaign of nationwide bombings designed to terrorize the government into submission, and Kent and his chums battle just as hard at stopping them.

(Note: the bat planes—all the same model—have the World War II Japanese "Rising Sun" emblem on their tails, because stock footage of the bat planes came from the wartime serial *G-Men vs. the Black Dragon*, which featured Japanese villains.)

Kent finally traces the villainy to Bryant, and he and his girlfriend Helen (Lois Collier) head for the volcano headquarters of the would-be Martian conqueror and his interplanetary traitor pal. In a fierce fight an atom bomb is knocked into the crater, starting an eruption. Kent and Lois escape in one of the atom-powered bat planes, but Mota, Bryant and the gang are killed by molten lava.

Some reviewers spotted the film for what it was; giving it a rating of III, the *Monthly Film Bulletin* said it was "a stripped-down and patched-up juvenile serial, best regarded as a blueprint for the later and rather better *Satan's Satellites*."

Allen M. Widem in the *Motion Picture Herald* thought *Missile Monsters* "fair," and added, "The script is routine and the acting less from [sic] inspired. Accolades, if any, go to special effects."

The *Los Angeles Times* considered *Missile Monsters* "even cruder" than *Satan's Satellites*, adding "the acting ... is unbelievably amateurish.... The script ... and the direction ... have that ragged sketchy quality—all standard form, no content—of the old-time Saturday afternoon 15-part kiddy serials."

Parish and Pitts said, "The Golden Age of Republic serials had long since passed and with the pressing competition of television, the studio made [*Flying Disc Man from Mars*] on a shoestring. It employed a good deal of stock footage from such previous Republic serials as *The Purple Monster Strikes, King of the Mounties* (1942), *G-Men vs. the Black Dragon, Secret Service in Darkest Africa* (1943) and *King of the Rocket Men* (1949).... Cheapness in production diminished any entertainment value this ... might have had for its action-oriented audiences."

Perhaps the best indication of the level of thinking involved in *Missile Monsters* is the name of the villain, Mota. Spell it backwards.

Missile to the Moon

In the late 1950s, Astor Pictures developed an unenviable but justified reputation for releasing the very worst science fiction and horror films. This reputation rests on such firm foundations as *Missile to the Moon*, one of the most woebegone, uncaring science fiction movies of all time. It is, incredibly, a loose remake of *Cat-Women of the Moon*, but effortlessly manages to be even worse, as it substitutes a jaded incompetence for that film's innocent naiveté. *Missile to the Moon* is not only one of the most boring, preposterous movies ever made, it is one of the most cynically motivated: just take the bucks and run. It isn't even up to the level of *Richard Cunha's* other films.

The bare bones of the *Cat-Women* screen story by Jack Rabin and Al Zimbalist have been fleshed out, if that's the term, by writers H.E. Barrie and Vincent Fotre for *Missile to the Moon*, mostly with chunks from juvenile delinquent films of the period, and H. Rider Haggard's *She*.

The military tells missile expert Dirk Green (Michael Whalen) that money is being diverted from his space research back to the government, that his planned trip to the Moon – the rocket stands ready outside the office window – will just have to be called off. Missile research is for the government only, not private individuals. Green's associate Steve Dayton (Richard Travis) agrees with his partner, that space exploration is a good thing, but plans to go along with the government.

Green has other ideas. A sheriff tells him that two escaped convicts are in the vicinity. (Some sources say they are reform school escapees, but although they are young, they are definitely said to be from a prison.) Green and the sheriff investigate around the rocket, and, going into the craft alone, Green discovers the two young men, Gary (Tommy Cook) and Lon (Gary Clarke), holed up within. Without saying anything he locks the hatch and leaves. He tells the sheriff they weren't in there, and the sheriff leaves.

Green tells the teenage crooks that they have a choice: they can go to the Moon or to the sheriff. Their decision is made easy by the fact that flying the rocket is not at all difficult. Preparations are made for takeoff. Steve and his fiancée June (Cathy Downs) reach the rocket just before launching, and as the door shuts behind them, Steve grabs oxygen masks.

It isn't long before Green discovers the two stowaways, and more or less makes them welcome. Nothing further is said about his intense desire to get to the Moon.

En route, Gary, the less savory of the two crooks, makes a pass at June when the two of them are alone. However, Green intercedes and they have a brief fistfight.

Just then, the rocket passes through a "meteorite field" and in the process of dodging the hurtling boulders, the ship lurches and something falls on Green's head. Just before dying, he gives Steve a medallion and asks "my Lido" to forgive him. Exit Dirk Green.

Once on the Moon, everyone dons space suits and leaves the ship. They are briefly menaced by walking Rock Men, and duck into a cave for safety. They find a stick, and light it. Gary arrogantly wanders off alone, but screams a moment later. The group is captured by mysterious cloaked figures who knock them out with gas.

They awaken in a vaguely Greek-styled "palace" filled with attractive women. The leader, called the Lido (K.T. Stevens) is dressed in a gown and wears an elaborate headdress; she is blind. "I bid you welcome to Orlanda," she says. Because of the medallion around Steve's neck, everyone assumes he is Dirk Green, returned at last from the Earth.

Steve plays along with this, even though "Green" seems to be engaged to predatory Alpha (Nina Bara). He eventually learns that Green was the sole survivor of a spaceship full of Moon men sent to Earth a generation ago to find out if it could be conquered. Green was returning with the rocket in an effort to rescue the surviving women. The oxygen and food are running out and the need to escape grows daily. (The idea that taking these women to Earth might be a good, humanitarian idea is never raised; all the Earth people want to do is leave them to rot on the Moon.)

Meanwhile, Gary is making time with Moon girl Lambda (Laurie Mitchell, demoted from Queen of Outer Space), and June is fretting about Steve's seeming engagement to Alpha. Lon is also befriended by Moon girl Zeema (Marjorie Hellen), who wonderingly asks him if there are Rock Creatures on Earth. (In the original film, the equivalent character tells her Earthman that she wants to go to Earth so she can visit the beach and have a Coke. Not the same thing as worrying about Rock Creatures.)

There follows a great deal of palace-intrigue plotting. Alpha wants Steve, and also to be the *only* Lido. She releases a Dark Creature (a giant spider) which kills Lambda. After placing Steve under hypnotic control, she kills the Lido and proclaims herself the *new* Lido. "Tell the others to prepare for a wedding," she says as her first royal proclamation, "which will follow an event—an event in the Extermination Chamber." Under her control, Steve wanders around glassy-eyed in Moon robes, ignoring his friends.

June is taken off to the Extermination Chamber and chained to a cross while the others watch a bunch of Moon women do an endless ceremonial dance. Zeema gives Lon and Gary the keys to the space suit locker, so they get the equipment and rescue June from a giant spider, which they kill.

Meanwhile, back at the palace, by using her own whammy power, Zeema manages to free Steve from Alpha's spell. Alpha tries to force Zeema to gas our escaping heroes, but instead Zeema uses a bomb that "releases" all the atmosphere from this land beneath the Moon's surface. (Subselenian? Sublunarian?) As she dies, along with everyone else in her civilization, Zeema whispers, "Lon, now I can join you forever."

While the escaping air howls like a hurricane and pillars tumble neatly around her, Alpha tries to put a long-distance whammy on the fleeing Steve, and almost succeeds. He turns back and heads for the cave, but the ghost of the Lido appears and stabs Alpha right between her breasts. She expires.

Out on the Lunar surface, Gary shows up carrying bags of diamonds. The Rock Creatures—who blow up real good when hit with little bombs—come at him; inexplicably, he backs right out into the sunlight. There's a little smoke, and he drops, screaming, presumably fried by the sunlight's intensity.

As the three survivors head for home, June asks Steve is he thought Alpha was prettier than she.

As perhaps can be told from this plot synopsis, the *Monthly Film Bulletin* was correct in saying the film "becomes progressively sillier as it proceeds." It starts out as a bizarrely-motivated, crude rocket ship melodrama, and heads straight into a lost-civilization melodrama. In *Cat-Women*, the only intrigue was that the Moon women had the heroine under their control. Here, we have a blind leader, a childhood betrothal, suggested conquest of the Earth, a scheming princess, a palace revolution, and the toppling of an empire.

Wondering to whom the film was supposed to appeal is pointless. Surely the filmmakers just didn't care about good reviews, good opinion, or anything else except money. They knew that the title, the cofeature (*Frankenstein's Daughter*) and a wretched but flamboyant ad would draw in the necessary crowds.

Surely no one cared about the dialogue. It isn't merely lumpy; it's *all* lumps. When they arrive on the Moon, Gary tells Steve he wants a piece of hardware. What? Steve asks. "You know," says Gary, "the hardware—the gat—the gun." Did crooks ever call guns gats? If so, they weren't doing so by the late 1950s. The Lido refers to our little band of stalwarts as "intruders from an unknown origin." As Gary wanders off with Lambda, he smirks, "I used to think those scientists who wanted to reach the Moon were kooky." There's a brief and pointless grasp at a different language for the Moon women: "The sun comes around every 17 nimbos," someone says.

There is neither scientific accuracy nor interest in it. Just after takeoff, Green tells the convicts that they don't want to wear space suits. "We're sealed, not under pressure." Down below, Steve saves himself and June in the oxygen-free environment by donning face masks. On the Moon, no one considers that the surface is airless; in fact, they hear sounds *more* acutely, instead of not at all. "Your hearing is more sensitive through your receiving set," Steve says, to explain Gary's hearing a Rock Creature sneaking up behind them. No one wonders why there is a stick in the cave, when there are no trees or bushes anywhere around. When Zeema battles Alpha, she uses a bomb that "releases" all the atmosphere—but what kept it in?

The special effects consist almost entirely of stock footage of real rockets, mostly V-2s. Once again, the takeoff scene from *Rocketship X-M* is used. When they land on the Moon, a takeoff of a V-2 is run backwards, which not only means the rocket sucks up its exhaust, but that a blockhouse floats around on the Moon's surface, awaiting the rocket's arrival. On the Moon, the heroes walk past a cardboard replica of the rocket's tail.

The giant spider puppet is familiar-looking, and rather well-articulated. It was built for use in Universal's *Tarantula*, and was heavily used in advertising for that film. At the end, the puppet was apparently burned, but here it is again, although shaved. It marionettes along on its tippy-toes as it heads for its prey.

The first appearance of a Rock Creature is better than one might expect. Just after our little group walks past an innocent-looking outcropping of rock, it stirs, pebbles fall away, and a Rock Creature stands up. It's a little surprising, because the suit really does look like part of the surface around it. But once the Rock Creatures start lurching around, they look silly. In *Fangoria* #31, director

Richard Cunha told interviewer Tom Weaver about the Rock Creatures. "They were made of sponge rubber that was cast. Harold Banks made those for us. He was the very creative man who made the Fiberglas outfits for *Giant from the Unknown*.... If you'll remember we had one scene where we had to bury them into the rock and then plaster 'em in there for them to break out. And, you know, it took a while for the plaster to dry with them in there! They'd be yelling, 'Get us out of here, get us out of here.' So ... that was very, very difficult for them ... but they were all good guys. We laughed over a beer about it later." The film was shot at Red Rock Canyon near Mojave in the heat of summer, which gives *Missile to the Moon* its only slight edge on *Cat-Women of the Moon*: there are real exteriors.

But as far as the Rock Creatures go, although they are an odd concept, they do raise more questions than they answer: what are they doing stuck to outcroppings of rock? What do they want from the Earthlings?

Then, the motivation of almost everyone is screwy. Why do the convicts hide in the rocket, surely a place that would be searched? Why does Green force them to be his crew? Why does June accompany Steve to the rocket to investigate Green's strange activities? Why doesn't someone do something about Gary's crude pass at June? What does Alpha see in Steve? Why did the Lido pretend like she believed Steve? What has four pairs of pants, lives in Philadelphia, and it never rains but it pours?

Director Richard Cunha shows not a trace of talent. Scenes are overlit, there's no imagination displayed in staging or the use of the camera. Everything is plodding and dull. No one could have made anything coherent out of the wretched script, but Cunha doesn't even try. It's first-take time, do it and print it, never mind if it looks or sounds uninteresting.

The acting in *Missile to the Moon* is variable; it ranges from mediocre to wretched. Those faring the best include Cathy Downs, Tommy Cook and Michael Whalen. Richard Travis and Gary Clarke seem to have phoned their roles in, but the worst-acting prize goes to Nina Bara as Alpha. She apparently looked on this as her Big Opportunity, and gives it her all, which is far too much.

The Moon Women are played by a group of young women referred to as the "International Beauty Contest Winners," but I suspect the contest is bogus. It's hard to believe in a contest which pits contestants from Yugoslavia and Germany against entrants from Minnesota and New Hampshire. This is another lift from *Cat-Women*, which introduced "The Hollywood Cover Girls."

It's odd how often the same phrase regarding this film recurs: however bad *Cat-Women of the Moon* may have been, this one is far worse.

In *Fangoria*, Cunha told Weaver that the idea to remake *Cat-Women* was Astor's. "They thought, well, shucks, it'd be a good idea to redo the movie, they could get a little bit of sex in and have some pretty girls wandering through the scenes. And it *was* patterned after *their* movie."

He also told Weaver that even he was disappointed in the picture; there wasn't enough money. "The money was so meager ... that it was just impossible to create the proper atmosphere for a spaceship—although I think, on the money we did have, the interior of the spaceship worked well. It included many pieces of grip equipment, as I recall, and we used a big dimmer bank for some of the controls on the missile."

He also added some illuminating comments on how to film a very low-budget film: "You *don't* run over on these [cheap films]—you shoot the opening scenes and you shoot the end scenes, and then fill in the picture in between. And so if you run out of days, *somehow* they'll dissolve between what you missed and the next scene in there."

Paul V. Beckley in the New York *Herald-Tribune* felt that "None of *Missile* is very rewarding and is so clumsily and unimaginatively done that the lack of conviction is staggering." The Los Angeles *Herald Examiner* called it "torpid twaddle." I can only concur.

Monster from Green Hell

This offspring of *Them!* is in all ways generations removed from the original. There's no mystery, the big bugs are kept off in the distant jungle, and our heroes never seem to be in much danger. It's one of the worst of the giant insect films, and the fact that the climax is filmed in a kind of bizarre pseudo-color doesn't make it better.

In fact, *Monster from Green Hell* is only barely about monsters at all. Scientists Brady (Jim Davis) and Morgan (Robert E. Griffin) send up a test rocket with monkeys, spider crabs, wasps and a guinea pig, but the rocket goes astray and crashes in Africa. Humanitarian Dr. Lorentz (Vladimir Sokoloff), a Schweitzer clone working in Africa, hears terrible tales of huge monsters off in a remote section of the jungle that the natives call Green Hell.

Brady and Morgan learn of this, and head for Africa. After an arduous trek through the jungles—apparently no one thought of using aircraft—they arrive at Lorentz's camp, but he is already dead, killed by one of the monsters which, we are informed, are probably big wasps.

Together with Lorentz's beautiful daughter Lorna (Barbara Turner), Brady, Morgan and their native guide Mahri (a wildly miscast Eduardo Ciannelli) head into the jungle. After another long trek, they encounter the wasps, take refuge in a cave (Bronson Caverns) and accidentally seal themselves in.

After another arduous—and boring—series of scenes in the cave, our heroes reach the surface in time to see a convenient volcano erupt and bury the swarming giant wasps. "Nature has a way of correcting its own mistakes," says Brady, who made the mistake in the first place, rather than Nature.

By this time, in late 1958, science fiction and monster movies were being made by rote. Producer Al Zimbalist doesn't seem to have cared about anything except exploitation. He put in the minimal effort required to even create a movie. He probably made back his money, but *Monster from Green Hell* is sleazy, tiresome and forgettable.

When Irving Block and his partners, Jack Rabin and Louis DeWitt, first talked to Zimbalist about the movie, he revealed he was going to use extensive footage from the 1939 film, *Stanley and Livingstone*. Block pointed out that the lead actors in the safari scenes in that film, Spencer Tracy and Walter Brennan, were wearing costumes from the 19th century, including pith helmets draped with scarves. Zimbalist said that would present no problem, and in that sense, there was no problem: Jim Davis wore a pith helmet draped with a scarf. (Also, as Davis was almost exclusively a Western and crime film actor, never identified with science fiction films, I suspect the reason he was hired was because he at least faintly resembled the young Spencer Tracy.)

This use of stock footage forced the plot to be as archaic as the costumes. All modern equipment had to be ignored. Our heroes have to *walk* to a distant

Jim Davis looks more amused than frightened as he's menaced by the giant-head prop of the Monster from Green Hell (1958). Seeing glories like this giant head always leads me to wonder where they are today.

location, simply because that's how Spencer Tracy found Livingstone. Most of the movie is devoted to these traditional safari adventures: battles with unfriendly natives, thirst, and simply slogging along over hill and dale. The monsters lurch in at odd moments, but create no sense of menace, and seem dissociated from the action.

The screenplay by Endre Bohen and Louis Vittes (who was capable of better things, such as *I Married a Monster from Outer Space*) is talky, meandering and derivative, even when the movie isn't featuring scenes from *Stanley and*

Livingstone. The dialogue is hopeless, the characterization is nonexistent. "The sun beat down as though it hated us," says Jim Davis in his endless narration. He tells the heroine (futilely, of course) that she shouldn't go into Green Hell with them to find the big bugs. "It isn't the kind of thing for a girl." When they find a village wiped out by water buffalo stampeded by the giant wasps, a survivor tells them, "A stampeding herd of water buffalo is not stopped by an arrow—or a word."

In a story in which the monsters are wiped out by a *deus ex machina*, to point out that while Davis is narrating the film in first person, we are also shown many scenes which he couldn't have known about, seems a trivial complaint.

The monsters are depicted in two methods, one rather surprising for such a cheap picture. The less expensive method was a huge head of one of the monsters, which occasionally pokes out of bush while a claw snakes out and grabs a hapless native; the head and claw seem totally unrelated. The head certainly doesn't look much like a wasp, but it is archetypically an insect: it has mandibles, a hard shell, and compound eyes (which move back and forth). Beside the mandibles are some pronglike objects, which is where the producer apparently thought wasps had their stings, instead of in the ends of their abdomens. Some sources claim that Paul Blaisdell designed the wasp heads, but he is not credited on screen.

The other method of bringing the monsters to life was stop-motion animation, but this was also done in a budget-conscious manner. In Bob Skotak's *Fantascene #2*, Gene Warren said, "I did the wasps in *Monster from Green Hell*. Those were pretty crude puppets. They were all wire and stuck together with pins and spit—no armatured figures ... at all. There were a lot of them because they were simple castings with very simple dressings on them [apparently just the wings and legs]. There was only one that was fairly sophisticated, [but] even that was just wire. In the scene at night the giant snake [which fights a wasp] had just one plain copper wire in it.... I really fought with that, especially the snake ... trying to make it follow through properly.... That film was done very, very cheap. I don't think I put more than three weeks total animation into it."

From what's on screen, the estimate of three weeks seems very high. The battle with the snake, which is very much underexposed, is brief and undramatic. There are some scenes of the animated wasps (which can't fly but do buzz like chain saws) appearing at the edge of some rear-projected scenes of fleeing wildlife, a repeated shot of a wasp meandering through some shubbery, and a couple of shots of several wasps at once. That's about all the animation the film has. It's okay for what it is, within its limitations, but the low budget and lack of imagination in filming the wasp scenes reduces believability to zero. The fact that the monsters look and act much more like beetles than wasps doesn't help. Wasps are skinny, even elegant little beasts; these are thick-bodied, clumsy and undramatic. They don't even sting people.

Mark McGee said that at the end of the film, when the wasps are covered by lava, a more elaborate setup and climax were envisioned and even shot. They had originally built a big cavern with wasps all over it; they were going to be puppet wasps, rather than animated ones, but it was a fairly elaborate scene. Two cameras, shooting in slow motion (overcranked), filmed the scene of phony lava pouring down over the wasps. One of the effects crew thought it wasn't steamy-looking enough, and started tossing in chunks of dry ice. When the film came back from the lab, one of the cameras had been so fogged by the dry-ice clouds that it picked up nothing usable. The other one wasn't foggy, but the impulsive effects man's hands were right in the middle of the frame, tossing in the dry ice. None of the footage was usable, and there was no opportunity for retakes, so previously-shot footage of the wasps, clumsily superimposed with scenes of lava, were used for the climax – which had to be explained to us, because the action is unclear.

The scale of the wasps changes. Quoting again from *Fantascene*, Irving Block said that because the writers envisaged wasps about the size of terriers (which would be interesting) while the producers wanted wasps the size of elephants, "the scale keeps changing. Sometimes they look as big as a house, other times they look the size of a cow – it depends on where they are sticking their heads out."

At the climax, the film sort of turns to color, to use some color shots of erupting volcanoes. It's a confusing welter of disconnected images: volcanoes (in color), wasps, and our heroes observing from a ridge. The footage shot for the film is not in color at all, but is tinted a hot pink. There was no new animation footage shot of the wasps being wiped out, for reasons already explained.

The actors look as bored as the audience was, except for Vladimir Sokoloff and Eduardo Ciannelli, who always performed to the best of their abilities. Barbara Turner doesn't seem to have been an actor at all. Oddly, there is no hint of a romance between her character and Jim Davis', unless merely the juxtaposition of two relatively young leads is supposed to generate romance in the minds of the viewers, like an optical illusion.

Davis is definitely out of place, both in the archaic safari suit and in a film of this nature. He looks embarrassed and bored, and was probably all too glad when the film was finished. He was long a laborer in the Hollywood vineyards, usually in Westerns. Solid, believable and likable, he finally achieved stardom on TV's "Dallas" before his untimely death.

There are a couple of unusual elements in *Monster from Green Hell*, other than the use of stop motion. Ernst Fegte's production design for the lab scene at the beginning is eccentric: the sloping windowed walls with a view of a distant butte add visual interest the picture strongly needs. There is also a strange little demonstration of mutations apparently caused by cosmic radiation: brown guinea pigs turn white, alligators go into trances, and the offspring of spider crabs are twice as large as their parents. This effort at scientific verisimilitude is more puzzling than anything else, and doesn't explain why the wasps got big, and not the monkeys, spider crabs or the guinea pig, all of which were in the lost rocket.

Albert Glasser's title music is quite effective and far better than a picture like this deserves. It's driving, with a kind of African subrhythm that hints of things to come. The rest of the score is unimaginative and forgettable.

In the *Los Angeles Times*, Charles Stinson said that *Monster from Green Hell*, like its cofeature *Half Human*, was "distinguished for neither much cinematic merit nor atrocity…. Louis Vittes and Endre Bohen's script, while not too badly encumbered with obvious clichés, is nevertheless very unimaginative with dialogue that is flat and prone at times to talkiness. A more fundamental weakness is the fact that the picture can never decide whether it's going to be a science fiction tale or a safari story…. Kenneth Crane's direction lags and all possibility of physical suspense fades away." (Crane also directed the U.S. scenes for *Half Human*.)

Paul V. Beckley in the *Herald-Tribune* said that it "has almost nothing to recommend it," and *Monthly Film Bulletin*, giving it the lowest rating, called it "cheaply produced and absurd." Don Willis (I) thought it "dully, shoddily-made sf," and Parish and Pitts thought it "a very limp entry."

Monster from Green Hell is a boring, insignificant film; it has a couple of brief imaginative touches, but is recommended only to those who are determined to be completists in this field—and for them, there's nothing I could say that would discourage them anyway. There may be those who would want to follow the career of Al Zimbalist, who produced the film. After all, he was also responsible for *Robot Monster, Cat-Women of the Moon* and *Valley of the Dragons.*

Monster on the Campus

This variation on the Jekyll-Hyde theme is the least interesting of Jack Arnold's science fiction films. It had a short shooting schedule and a weak script, and Arnold always maintains that he did the film primarily as a favor to Joseph Gershenson. In *Cinefantastique*, Arnold told interviewer Bill Kelley that "Joe Gershenson was head of music at Universal. He was a wonderful man, and he wanted like mad to produce. The only thing they'd let him have was this film, and they asked me to direct it. Because I liked him, I did it. It's not my favorite."

And so wonder. David Duncan's script is more-than-usually preposterous, with weak motivation and several silly scenes. Arnold didn't like the script, and told the bosses at Universal. "They insisted that I go ahead," he told Kelley, "and since I was a contract director, I could either turn the script down and be put on suspension, or do it, and because of my relationship with Gershenson, I decided to do it."

In another interview, with Mark McGee in *Photon*, Arnold said that he was his own worst critic. "I didn't really hate it," he said, "but I didn't think it was up to the other films I had done." McGee, who likes the film, could get little else out of Arnold, who tended to respond to questions on *Monster on the Campus* with monosyllables.

In the movie, Arthur Franz plays (quite well) Dr. Donald Blake, a researcher and professor at a California university. He receives the preserved body of a coelacanth for his paleontological research (typically, the script madly scrambles paleontology and anthropology). When a friendly dog laps up some water mixed with blood dripping from the coelacanth, it temporarily turns into a wolf-dog. Later, Blake himself is "bitten" by the dead fish when its teeth close on his hand. We don't see what happens next, but an ape-man on campus frightens an amorous nurse to death.

Later still, a dragonfly feeds on the coelacanth, and it becomes a giant, prehistoric dragonfly.

Some blood from the fish finds its way into Blake's ever-present pipe; when he smokes it, he reverts again to the caveman and kills a guard. Finally realizing that there is a connection between all this rampant atavism, Blake locks himself in a mountain cabin and deliberately injects himself with the serum from the coelacanth blood. He becomes an ape-man again, almost killing his own fiancée (Joanna Moore). He does kill a forest ranger (Richard Cutting), and so when the police arrive at the cabin for no clear reason, he transforms himself into the ape-man in front of them so that they shoot him dead. As he turns back

The man in this Neanderthal man suit by Universal's makeup department probably isn't Arthur Franz, who played the leading character, but whoever it is seems too small for it. This is not one of Universal's triumphs of makeup art. Joanna Moore takes it easy. From Monster on the Campus (1958).

into Blake, his dying words are that he has found the courage to die like a man.

The film features several unfortunate, silly situations. The one most often cited is how the blood gets into Blake's pipe: the giant dragonfly lands on the coelacanth body, and when he and a student (Troy Donahue, before the days of greatness) are unable to capture it, he stabs it with a knife that goes right through the insect's body into the dead fish. Later, while Blake is examining the still-impaled bug, blood drips from the knife blade into the bowl of his pipe, miraculously in precisely the right spot to receive it. Blake lights the pipe again later—the sodden tobacco still manages to ignite—and although he notices that the tobacco tastes funny, he keeps on smoking until the transformation takes place.

Monster on the Campus is almost a catalog of ways this transforming blood can get into places it shouldn't: a dog laps it up, a bug eats some, a man *smokes* some. This inventiveness is interesting in a cockeyed way, but the script shows little imagination other than this.

But there are other foolish elements in this film besides the notorious blood-in-the-pipe sequence. At the scene of the first killing, the police find clearly nonhuman fingerprints, which lets Blake off the hook; otherwise he would be (as he should) their only suspect. These fingerprints keep turning up again and again in the dialogue until they become hilarious. We are told that they aren't on file locally, so they've been sent along to the FBI and the department of motor vehicles. When those institutions also fail to turn up the identity of the prints, we are told that the police are "fingerprinting the football squad." Now granted, football players are stereotypically apish jocks, but it still seems a bit much to assume that they really *are* apes. Even though the fingerprints and handprints (and later, footprints) are unquestionably not human, nobody even mentions an escaped ape.

The hero is a fairly standard professorial type, not really different from heroes in other SF and monster movies of the time. He's engaged to the boss' daughter, and that's all we know about their relationship, other than that she's inclined to jump to conclusions (which usually puts her way ahead of everyone else in the picture). When the nurse's car is discovered outside Blake's home, fiancée Madeline immediately assumes there was some hanky-panky; she even seems to suspect that Blake might be the Monster on the Campus, but when she sees a photo Blake took of himself while a monster (by means of a camera and trip wires), all she can do is remark that the beast is wearing Blake's clothes. At *this* point, she does not jump to conclusions.

Some like the ending, in which Blake sets himself up to be killed, but it's morally and logically muddled. Blake is *accidentally* transformed into an ape-man with ape-man desires and behavior. Surely Blake would not be held responsible for the crimes, or even if he was, institutionalization would seem to be a logical solution. Yet he decides he's as guilty as hell, but even when all evidence is pointing at him as the guilty party, no one else believes he's the killer. So he turns himself into the beast right in front of them. And the cops obligingly shoot him. Blake has committed suicide at one remove, not unlike André in *The Fly*. Even his guilt would seem capable of being assuaged, but apparently Blake is not willing to try. So, in a cowardly way (hardly brave), he arranges his own death. He doesn't "die like a man," he takes the easy way out; if he was brave, and a dedicated researcher, he would have allowed himself to be locked up *before* demonstrating that he turns into an ape-man. This isn't self-sacrifice—he's not turning into the monster willy-nilly, like Jekyll, it *always* takes a dose of coelacanth blood—it's just a particularly stupid suicide.

David Duncan's script keeps coming up to and backing away from the evidence. No one seems to be able to make that last jump in intuition about where the ape-man is coming from, which has the effect of making everyone seem rather like idiots. For instance, even when Blake and the student see the big dragonfly, and Blake mentions having seen a dragonfly around the coelacanth earlier—and all this *after* the dog turned primitive—neither Blake nor the student consider that the little and big dragonflies are the same insect.

The scene in which what's really going on dawns on Blake is badly written.

Director Arnold and actor Franz try to make it work, but it's a lost cause. First Blake says that someone must be turning into an ape-man, and insists the second transformation was deliberate. He ignores the obvious facts, that only *he* had access to the coelacanth, and that he has twice awakened after blackouts to discover his clothes torn and that something terrible happened to someone nearby while he was blacked out. No, his eyes have to fall on his injured hand, then he has to notice that the aroma of the coelacanth serum and the strange smell he noted in his pipe are one and the same before the Dreaded Truth makes itself known to him. Well, he is a scientist and scientists are not supposed to leap to conclusions, but this one seems to have to be battered to the ground with evidence before he will consider the possibility that's been obvious all along. If this had been written differently, with Blake fighting the obvious idea while knowing it must be true, it would have had some strength, and might have tied in with his foolish suicide at the climax, but instead Duncan wrote it so that Blake *just doesn't get it*.

Bizarrely, the film is structured as a mystery. First, the film, like Blake, doesn't seem to "know" that Blake is the ape-man. Secondly, the ape-man is kept off the screen most of the time. This does allow for lots of red herrings as the police grimly continue their investigation, but it also eats up a lot of running time that would have been better used in showing us something else.

Monster on the Campus (filmed as "Monster in the Night") was apparently an idea concocted by others than the men who wrote, produced and directed it. Left to his own devices, David Duncan has written several interesting science fiction novels, including *Dark Dominion* (1954), *Beyond Eden* (1955) and *Occam's Razor* (1957). They're all well-written and of more than usual intelligence, with clever ideas behind them. (In *Occam's Razor*, a key element is the surface tension in soap film, which leads to an infinite series of parallel worlds.) I have the feeling that he was told to write a story about a man who occasionally turns into an ape-man, and that *Monster on the Campus* was hastily written. It doesn't give much evidence of careful thought, and simply latches onto a once-trendy idea about coelacanths, even bringing in radiation.

Coelacanths were thought to have been extinct for 70 million years, until one was dredged up off the coast of South Africa in 1938. Though huge rewards were offered and major searches were mounted, no more of these strange, semiarmored fish with limblike fins were found for 14 years, when one was caught a thousand miles from the original spot. It turned out that fishermen in the region of the Comoro Islands between Madagascar and Tanzania had caught them from time to time for generations; they were even sold in fish markets.

Duncan pegged his screenplay on the survival of this relic of the Devonian Age. Supposedly, Blake's coelacanth was preserved using gamma rays to kill bacteria, and this radiation altered the coelacanth blood (which would certainly seem to be dead) so that it reverted whatever ingested it back into a primitive form.

But this makes no sense, even in a science fiction context. What sets the time span of regression? Why do the minds of the individuals involved also revert? Why do they change back again later? But of course, these are meaningless questions; Duncan was required to come up with a plausible gimmick for reversing evolution, and at least to the satisfaction of the Universal top brass, he did just that. It's basically sympathetic magic. A low-budget quickly-made monster movie doesn't require anything else. His script for *The Time Machine* was much better.

However, the idea does require some internal logic, and this film is weak in that department. The first and second times Blake turns into an ape-man, we see his hair. It is long, straight and black. When he changes at the end and we see the makeup in detail, the monster has short, curly and light-colored hair. And the hands look different with each transformation. At the end, the face is very strange, it doesn't look like any ape-man I've seen. He doesn't even have a nose, but two vertical slits somewhere between his mouth and his eyes. It's a monster, really, not an ape-man.

The film can easily be compared with *Altered States* (1980), which has several strong resemblances to *Monster on the Campus* (which itself resembles *The Neanderthal Man*). These resemblances are probably coincidental, as it's hard to imagine Paddy Chayefsky bothering to see the Jack Arnold film. But there are some parallels: a researcher on a college campus is transformed into an ape-man, and in an extended sequence, does battle with a campus security officer. Of course, in the newer film, the ape-man actually looked like a primitive man: small, agile, hairy and active. When Arthur Franz transforms, he becomes *larger*. Instead of trying to get the hell away from whatever it is that's bothering him, in an environment that it must find totally alien, the Franz ape-man keeps attacking people.

The makeup is actually a full-head mask, probably worn by a stunt man such as Ed Parker or Regis Parton rather than Franz himself. There is one brief transformation scene. The makeup is unconvincing, with tiny shell-like teeth and a built-in scowl.

The other main props are the coelacanth corpse and the giant dragonfly; neither is any more convincing than the ape-man himself. The dead fish doesn't particularly resemble a coelacanth, although photos of the rare real fish did exist. The dragonfly is massive and lumpy, apparently sculpted by whoever built the bug in *The Deadly Mantis*. It certainly does not have the slender, needlelike form of a real dragonfly (which are strictly predators, not carrion-eaters at all).

Jack Arnold tries to develop the film as best he can, but he's trapped in a concept that must have bored him. In his other SF films, he deals with *intelligence*, not brute force; even the Creature from the Black Lagoon is as smart as the men who are out to capture him. Also, in his other SF pictures, Arnold usually finds striking images; in *Monster on the Campus*, he's hampered by trivial locations and drab sets. There are no arresting images in the film at all. The best he can come up with is a swift glance the ape-man gives a mirror before smashing it, and one shot of a woman dangling from a tree by her hair. Arnold is clearly out of his element here, and it's no wonder he disdains the film.

Arthur Franz is surprisingly good as Blake. He is a careful, understated actor who has rarely worked in the last ten years or so. His gentle, sensitive features often resulted in leads in lesser films, including several science fiction and fantasy films, such as *Abbott and Costello Meet the Invisible Man* (as the Invisible Man), *Flight to Mars*, *The Flame Barrier*, *The Atomic Submarine* and *Back from the Dead* (1957). His best role in films was in *The Sniper* (1952), a Stanley Kramer production in which Franz was effectively cast against type as the psychotic killer of the title.

Joanna Moore is beautiful, and little else is required of her. It would have taken a better actress than Moore was at this time to make sense of a role that requires the performer to keep coming up with outlandish explanations for Franz's apparent culpability. She was a major starlet for Universal during this period, and appeared in Orson Welles' *Touch of Evil* (1955), as well as *Slim Carter* (1957), *Appointment with a Shadow*, *Flood Tide* (both 1958) and *The Last Angry Man* (1959). With that film, she began to free-lance, and appeared to moderately good effect in a wide range of roles in the 1960s, including *Walk on the Wild Side* (1962, as a whore), *Follow That Dream* (1962, opposite Elvis Presley), *The Man from Galveston* (1963, as an accused murderess), *Son of Flubber* (1963, as a femme fatale), *Countdown* (1968, as the female lead), and *Never a Dull Moment* (1968), with Dick Van Dyke and Edward G. Robinson. Apart from a role in *The Hindenburg* (1975), she seems to have retired from acting. Although her performance in *Monster on the Campus* is not bad, she's not likely to be recalled by any except diehard monster movie fans for her role here. In fact, Joanna Moore probably will best be known as the former wife of Ryan O'Neal and the mother of Tatum O'Neal.

Troy Donahue was also being given a star buildup at this time, but didn't reach the pinnacle of his fame, such as it was, until he left Universal, which was featuring him in supporting roles in *The Voice in the Mirror* and *Live Fast, Die Young* (both 1958 — in fact, Donahue was in seven Universal films in 1958). In 1959, he moved to Warner Bros., which immediately starred him in *A Summer Place*. He had several starring roles at Warner Bros. at this time, but soon became a laughingstock; with his sullen, immobile baby face, he was clearly not much of an actor. After *My Blood Runs Cold* (1965), in which he failed to convince as a psychotic killer, his career virtually came to a halt, and when he appears now, it is usually in small supporting roles. (In *The Godfather Part II*, he played Merle Johnson, which is Donahue's own real name.) He is as vapid and dull in his *Monster on the Campus* scenes as he is in his other films.

The film features several reliable supporting players, including the ubiquitous Whit Bissell as a traditionally skeptical doctor. But no one ever watched *Monster on the Campus* for the acting, although if they did, they would probably be pleasantly surprised by Arthur Franz.

The film was released as the bottom half of a double bill with the more colorful *Blood of the Vampire*, and did not receive many reviews. Both *Daily Variety* and Jack Moffitt liked the film. "Whit" in *Variety* said that Universal had come up "with a pretty fair shocker in this expertly produced story of retrogression." Moffitt was especially fond of it. "By emphasizing the human rather than the monstrous side of this modern 'Dr. Jekyll' story," Moffitt said, "Franz gives gentlemanly and scholastic values few boogey tales possess."

The *Monthly Film Bulletin* termed it "a depressing variation on the Jekyll-and-Hyde theme, tailored for the teenage horror market and marking a further decline in Jack Arnold's melancholy and at one time thoughtful talent." Even John Baxter, Arnold's staunchest supporter, said "the film is lamentably feeble."

The trouble is that it's routine, unimaginative and foolish. A decent performance by Arthur Franz and a few good nighttime scenes don't save this from being Jack Arnold's worst science fiction film.

Night of the Blood Beast

If it weren't for its talky, derivative script and pathetic monster, *Night of the Blood Beast* might be widely regarded as one of the better low-budget SF thrillers of the period. It's well-acted by a small cast, tightly edited and efficiently directed by Bernard Kowalski. Though just a little cheapie, there are several good things about it, and one element of the story line is unique in films up to 1958. One of the men in the cast essentially becomes pregnant. In one of the great, sick shocks of American International Pictures, we even see the embryos pulsing away in his chest.

But unfortunately, the very low budget of the film and the muddled premise of the script, as well as the defects mentioned above, make *Night of the Blood Beast* into just another minor SF-horror movie.

As the story opens, Major John Corcoran (Michael Emmet) is flying into space. The cheap, tacky rocket interior is anything but convincing, and Emmet is wearing the kind of high-altitude suit sold in military surplus stores and through the back pages of *Famous Monsters of Filmland*. The rocket gets into trouble, and comes back too fast.

From a tracking station, Dave Randall (Ed Nelson) and photographer Donna Bixby (Georgianna Carter) head to the crash site. Donna notices that the rocket is covered with a kind of mud; there's also a hole in the ship. Dave reaches inside, but Johnny is dead. As they turn away momentarily, part of the mud slides off.

The rest of the group arrives: Dr. Julie Benson (Angela Greene), engaged to Corcoran, Steve Dunlap (John Baer) and Dr. Alex Wyman (Tyler McVey). Wyman notices a boomerang-shaped mark on Johnny's arm, "not a lesion," he says, "more like something had been forced through the tissues under high pressure."

Back at the station, they cannot reach Cape Canaveral by radio. While Wyman and Julie examine Johnny's body, Dave investigates a noise he hears outside. There's some eerie music on the soundtrack and a restless point-of-view shot from bushes, implying something is watching Dave. Sure enough, it suddenly rushes at him, and he shoots at it. Everyone comes out at the gun-shots; Dave is dazed. "It was big," he says, "like a bear."

More noises, from inside this time, and they all rush back to find a broken window and a leatherlike fragment of flesh caught on the glass.

Johnny's body seems strange. He has no heartbeat, but there's also no rigor mortis, and he actually has blood pressure. (He could not have blood pressure without circulation; that's what it is.) Examining a sample of Johnny's blood on a slide, Julie sees that in addition to the normal blood cells, there's also a number of amorphous, amoebalike cells busily devouring the normal ones. (We are shown this a couple of times in adequate cartoon animation.)

All the machinery and electricity at the base cease working; Dave suggests they are caught in a magnetic force field, as all watches stop, too. He suspects the rocket capsule may be the cause; other rockets have returned with magnetic anomalies.

That night, Dave and Steve awake, roused by a noise they can't identify. In the lab, where Dr. Wyman was working, they find his body slung over a beam. "Half his head's gone," one chokes, an observation not confirmed by the shadow of Wyman's head on a wall. The women enter. After noting that Johnny's body is gone from the examining table, they turn to watch what the men are doing. Johnny (in mysterioso lighting) stands up behind them.

After requisite eeeeeeks from the women, the others rush to Johnny's side and help him to a table. Naturally, he is disconcerted when they tell him he's been dead for a while. He says he wasn't dead, but in a "hypometabolistic state, a type of suspended animation brought on by a contraction of the mesentery blood vessels in the pressure change of landing."

The others are nonplused. "That sounds like Dr. Wyman," one suggests, not like astronaut Johnny. But Corcoran is puzzled too, although he thinks that Wyman "may be a part of me now." Saying this startles him, and he begs for help. But he adds, "I'm not afraid. It didn't come here to destroy." He collapses while the others ponder his words. This is the first they've heard of any "it" at all.

Johnny's blood is now normal. He suggests they examine him by means of a fluoroscope, still working because it has "a radium cathode tube." To the shock of the cast as well as a goodly portion of the audience, nine pulsating little embryos are found within his chest cavity. Julie realizes that they were the amorphous cells she saw only shortly before. Okay, I'll buy that. But why only nine? Did they eat the others?

Everyone is upset and wants to destroy the weird embryos. "You can't destroy them," Johnny says.

"Why not?" one of the others asks.

"That's why not," Johnny says, inclining his head toward the door. And the Blood Beast bursts in, gesturing wildly, creating a commotion. Everyone dashes around vigorously but aimlessly, until someone waves a lantern at the monster, which flees as suddenly as it came.

Realizing it killed Wyman, everyone is in favor of killing it. "Why are we so quick to destroy?" Johnny asks desperately. "You don't understand, it didn't come in malice... It had to come back to me, to nourish its young." He cannot, however, explain why it killed Dr. Wyman.

Armed with Very pistols, Dave, Steve and Donna return to the capsule, thinking the alien may have gone there too. Leaving Donna by a bridge while they poke around the ship, the men glance up when she calls to them. The monster rushes out from under the bridge, grabs her, and heads for the hills. Steve and Dave pursue; the Blood Beast abruptly abandons Donna and leaps athletically into some bushes.

Meanwhile, back at the lab, Johnny is concerned that his being dead for a while and reviving pregnant may have caused a change in Julie's feelings for him.

After the others return, they talk about the alien's intentions, while Johnny pleads on behalf of interplanetary understanding. They decide to go to the cave where Johnny knows it hides. Dave and Steve promise Johnny they won't harm it until they find out what it is up to, but also prudently arm themselves with Very pistols, guns, knives, and jars of gasoline. They take the "girls" with them; as Dave says, it's "better than leaving them unprotected." (No one seems much in need of protection, except Donna; maybe they're feeling abashed.)

They arrive at the cave, Bronson Caverns of course. When Johnny realizes that they intend to destroy the creature without hearing it out, he grabs a knife and dashes into the cave. The monster now talks in Wyman's voice. "By assimilation, a form of photosynthesis," it "explains," "I've been able to incorporate Dr. Wyman's functional processes."

The Blood Beast leaves the cave with Johnny, and tries to make its case to the others. The alien, and others like it, come from another planet which was destroyed by the "ultimate power," which we too are about to discover. They tried to use it wisely, but greed, hatred and prejudice led to their destruction, though some escaped. For centuries they have been circling Earth, unable to enter the atmosphere; when Johnny's ship passed through them (all this sounds odd, doesn't it?), they took advantage of the chance to come to Earth. Now they want to "unite our intellects in one body"; the young within Johnny will be

In this scene from Night of the Blood Beast (1958), alien Ross Sturlin grapples with Michael Emmet at one of the entrances to Bronson Caverns. Compare this with the scene from Teenage Caveman on page 192.

born in an hour, it says, thought it doesn't mention what the birth process might do to Johnny.

Suddenly Johnny realizes what the alien is really up to (an understanding not vouchsafed the audience): "You're sacrificing our civilization for the resurrection of your own!" he shouts. "What you propose is dominance, not salvation." Actually, it didn't sound like either.

The Blood Beast realizes the jig is up, and grabs Johnny, who begs the others to kill him along with the monster. When they are reluctant to do so, Johnny stabs himself in the stomach.

The others immediately use the Very pistols and gasoline to immolate the creature. As it sinks into the blaze, the alien says "You're not ready, but we'll still save you. In your quest for self-destruction, you'll send up more satellites, and we'll be there. We'll come again!" It is impossible to determine if this is a threat or a promise.

Producer Gene Corman came up with the story of *Night of the Blood Beast*. He turned the scripting chores over to young Martin Varno (son of actor Roland Varno, who appeared in *The Blue Angel* [1930], *Gunga Din* [1939], *To Be or Not to Be* [1942] and *Return of the Vampire* [1943], among many other films). Martin, a client of Forrest J Ackerman, wrote the script in record time, under the title "Creature from Galaxy 27." Gene Corman and his brother Roger, executive producer, kept demanding further changes in the script. Eventually Varno, who was paid little enough in the first place, requested more money for the changes. The Cormans refused, and Ackerman took the matter to the Writers' Guild of America. The WGA demanded that the Cormans pay the extra money, but they obstinately held out until after the deadline was up before complying. Both Cormans were on the WGA blacklist for some months (and Roger Corman is on it as this is written) before they finally paid Varno, according to Ackerman's records.

At the premiere of the film, according to Mark McGee, Martin Varno told friends that he wished he had enough money to buy the negative and burn it. But a comparison of Varno's script with the finished film leads one to wonder why Varno disliked it so. Except for the shoddy monster, the finished film accurately reflects the script. Of course, there were the usual changes: dialogue was tightened and some explanations went out the window.

This was Varno's only produced screenplay. He later did some makeup under the name Martin Vernaux, creating Cameron Mitchell's scarred face in *Nightmare in Wax* (1969), for instance, but seemingly has now fallen away from movies altogether.

The Cormans were unsure about the title, and so conducted a survey of high school students in Southern California; they expressed a preference for *Night of the Blood Beast* over "Creature from Galaxy 27." There's nothing in the film, of course, to support the title it has; the monster kills only one person, and we never really know why it did that. The ad line used, "No Woman Was Safe As Long As This Head-Hunting THING Roamed The Land!" is as improperly applied to the film as the ad art, showing a clawed hand clutching a human head in its oversized fingers.

The plot line of the movie is clearly derived from *The Thing from Another World* and *The Creeping Unknown*, with faint overtones of *The Day the Earth Stood Still*. From the Quatermass film comes the mysterious survival of the astronaut, and his suddenly gaining the knowledge of a dead man. From *The Thing* comes the isolated group battling an alien; the sequence in which the monster bursts in on them is directly taken from a scene in *The Thing*. From

The Day the Earth Stood Still comes the more or less benign motives of the alien, as well as the shutdown of electrical equipment and watches.

Some of these elements are not well-integrated into the movie. The alien kills Wyman and devours part of his brain presumably in order to gain knowledge and to learn our language. However, there's no explanation for *Johnny's* gaining knowledge like this. This was probably to indicate the link between Johnny and the alien, but sometimes Johnny knows where the creature is and what it's up to, and at other times, has no idea what's going on. Certainly his sudden reversal at the end, believing the alien's motives are selfish, comes out of left field; before he'd always said the creature was here for good purposes. The scene implies the only reason Johnny turns against the alien is because it made him pregnant.

The major confusion in the picture centers on the alien's motives. It's possible director Bernard Kowalski and Varno wanted the story to be ambiguous: was the monster good or evil? But the way the film develops, the monster is more erratic than ambiguous. At least the movie does try for something different regarding aliens. Creatures from another world to which we would be less closely related than we are to, say, moss, would easily have inexplicable motivations. I doubt that's what Varno and Kowalski were after—they were probably simply reaching for a lady-or-the-tiger ending—but at least that overtone can be fairly read into the picture.

Kowalski does very well by the uneven script. The staging of the action throughout is imaginative and to the point. For instance, while Johnny is apparently dead, his body is frequently seen in the background of shots dealing with other story elements, not only emphasizing his immobility and seeming death, but adding a constant feeling of apprehension and suspense, and reminding us that *he* is what the story is about. We keep expecting him to open his eyes and sit up in one of these shots (and that's the way the script handled his revival), but instead he lies there inert.

The script is too talky, but Kowalski tries to overcome this by having the talk fast-paced, and by using more camera angles and a greater mixture of styles of shots (close-ups, long shots, etc.) than would ordinarily be expected in a movie of this budget. At the climax, when Johnny has dashed off to join the alien, Kowalski goes into a virtual paroxysm of varied shots: we see the group from high on the cliffs opposite the cave, from ground level behind them, in individual shots, including close-ups, medium shots and long shots, as well as a few tableaux seen from *inside* the cave. Kowalski is clearly trying everything he can pictorially to overcome the wordiness of these scenes, and while this does little to heighten suspense, it gives an expansive feeling to the scene, making it seem more Important. The payoff is drab—Johnny stabs himself and collapses, then the monster is roasted.

In addition to frequent changes of locale and much physical movement in most scenes, Kowalski brings off a couple of showy "busses" that made the audience I first saw it with, much to their surprise, jump. They weren't expecting this in a cheap little monster picture. When the alien first bursts into the room, the camera is already panning toward the door. The other good "bus" is when the alien grabs Donna. We see this from behind Steve and Dave, and we already get a glimpse of the monster advancing on her before the camera cuts to a close shot of it grabbing her.

This slight anticipation is what makes "busses" work; we *must* have an almost subliminal awareness that there's going to be an abrupt appearance of something. In *Cat People* (1942), in the scene that gives "busses" their name, the bus is visible on screen slightly before its noise is heard; what we're reacting to is our almost unconscious awareness of the arriving bus coupled with the sound it makes. Kowalski has clearly done his homework, and his "busses" work.

Occasionally, Kowalski reaches too far for effect. When Ed Nelson arrives at the capsule, he sprays the interior with a fire extinguisher; the camera's point of view is from *within* the capsule, so he fogs up the lens, a pointless flourish that calls attention to itself. When Johnny first revives, he's lit from beneath. The same thing happens when he confronts the alien in the cave. There's no reason for this, and it looks tacky.

On the other hand, though many scenes have little or no visual interest, there will be one or two elements that pay off, such as a ghoulish shot of Wyman's body draped in a sheet. Where the cloth covers his head, it's absolutely drenched in blood, making us queasily aware of what must lie beneath the cloth. This is all the more effective because otherwise the film is remarkably free of violence and gore, especially considering the extravagant promise of the title.

The performances are remarkably consistent for a low-budget film; no one stands out. Michael Emmet, also in Kowalski's *Attack of the Giant Leeches*, is colorless as the revived astronaut, but he's physically right; it's hard to imagine how a pregnant walking corpse should react anyway.

Angela Greene is adequate as the scientist whose fiancé suffers a fate stranger than death. She'd been around since 1944, and occasionally starred in lesser films such as *Jungle Jim in the Forbidden Land*. She was working in supporting roles as late as the mid-70s, when she appeared in *Day of the Locust* and *Futureworld*.

John Baer is a utility minor lead; based on the evidence of *Night of the Blood Beast*, he's a better actor than the size of his usual roles indicates. He had a fairly good part in *The Mississippi Gambler* (1953), but smaller ones in *We're No Angels* (1955), *Fear No More* (1961) and *The Chapman Report* (1963).

Tyler McVey, the ill-fated Wyman, was a seasoned Hollywood character actor who seemed as if he'd been around a lot longer than only the early 50s. His first film may have been *The Day the Earth Stood Still*, but he was busy all through the 50s/60s, and 70s in many films, big and small, including *From Here to Eternity* (1953), *Day of Triumph* and *Francis Joins the WACS* (both 1954), *Attack of the Giant Leeches*, *The Best Man* (1964), *The Resurrection of Zachary Wheeler* (1971) and many others. He was also active on television.

Gene Corman was ill-advised to use the monster suit he did. It's cumbersome, with a kind of beak, two big glassy eyes, and hands with wicked claws. It wasn't built for this movie, but for *Teenage Caveman*, where it was a radiation suit worn by a man *mistaken* for a monster. Though the suit is ugly, it is highly recognizable; inasmuch as the same audience went to *Teenage Caveman* and *Night of the Blood Beast*, to reuse such a shoddy and recognizable suit shows either an overconcern for saving money, a contempt for the audience, or both. Ross Sturlin played the Blood Beast, and is impressively vigorous at times. It's too bad the suit wasn't better.

"Ron" in *Variety* considered *Blood Beast* "a suspenseful picture that is the better half of a new American International package. Sold with *She Gods of Shark Reef*, pic lends itself to exploitation.... Although the screenplay does fall into expected pitfalls, it is strong enough to sustain interest all the way."

Walter Greene in the *Hollywood Reporter* was less impressed. "Production has been given adequate mounting in a restricted interior set and several location areas for chases. Director Bernard L. Kowalski took every advantage to generate suspense, even though it is formula."

The *Monthly Film Bulletin* gave the film its lowest rating. "A routine science fiction thriller, despite the picturesque title. There are one or two original ideas ... but the monster itself is a commonplace thing and the staging very modest."

By this time, even as early as 1958, this type of quickie SF movie had begun to wear out its welcome. Even films in which the director tried to invest talent and energy were gradually dismissed. This is perfectly understandable; the differences between pictures like *Night of the Blood Beast* and the same year's *War of the Colossal Beast* are unimportant to the main mass of moviegoers. The differences are not even noticeable unless the films are analyzed carefully—but this does not mean the differences are *unimportant*. Films like these have strong if subliminal impact on viewers; it's from them that, as children, we begin to learn the differences between good and bad moviemaking. I firmly believe that almost every film ever made deserves this kind of analysis, except probably for most in the minor series. Furthermore, to those of us who steep ourselves in genre, the differences are matters of great importance, leading to lively arguments, striking to the uninitiated by their apparent lack of point. But we who love these films, love fiercely.

Night of the Blood Beast is hardly an unsung classic, nor even much above average for this sort of trash; however, Kowalski's efforts at improving the quickie he was assigned to should not go unnoticed. The slight promise he showed here did not really pay off in his later films (see the entry on *Attack of the Giant Leeches*), but he still exhibited an effort to make, if not gold out of dross, at least a higher quality dross.

Plan 9 from Outer Space

There are some movies that by now have been written on so frequently that it seems unlikely anyone will find something new to say about them. Perhaps we should call for a moratorium on *Psycho, Citizen Kane, 2001*—and *Plan 9 from Outer Space*. This is undoubtedly the only film that has been written on extensively because it is atrocious. In a poll conducted by Harry and Michael Medved for their contemptible *Golden Turkey Awards, Plan 9* won easily as Worst Film of All Time. (However, in the earlier *Fifty Worst Films of All Time*, cowritten by Harry Medved, *Plan 9* isn't even in the running.)

It's been written on in almost all the currently-published magazines on fantasy and horror films; Danny Peary has some surprising things to say about it in *Cult Movies*; the film frequently appears at revival theatres and on TV around the country; it is available for purchase on videotape. When the film was first released, however, it received almost no attention; it's only been since the late 70s that it has become everyone's favorite terrible film. In the face of all this attention, there really isn't much more that can be said about it. When I commented on *Cat-Women of the Moon* in Volume 1, I was exploring virgin territory; in talking about *Plan 9*, which I must do, to maintain the metaphor, I'm covering territory that has been tamed, plowed, and covered with condominiums.

Plan 9 from Outer Space was directed, written and (essentially) produced by Edward D. Wood, Jr., the transvestite (but not homosexual, he pointed out repeatedly in his *Glen or Glenda?*) ex-Marine who was devoted to making films but who lacked the ability to do anything better than the terrible films he created.

And "created" is the right word. Ed Wood had a vision; blurred, grotesque and cross-eyed, but a vision nonetheless. By all accounts, he was an intelligent, friendly man, devoted to his work and secure in his image of himself as a great director. And he was distinctive. As bad as Ed Wood's films are, it's not likely that, once having seen one, anyone would ever mistake one of his films for the work of anyone else.

Bela Lugosi was near the end of his life in 1956, and had recently recovered, at great physical cost, from his addiction to morphine. He was wasted, emaciated and elderly, but still entertained hopes of someday making a comeback in films. Lugosi must have blinded himself to the kind of films that he had been making for 15 years, probably living a life of great self-deception. How could he otherwise have thought that Ed Wood might be his savior? He had already been in *Glen or Glenda?* and *Bride of the Monster* under Wood's direction; once Lugosi saw those films, surely he couldn't have dreamed that Wood was capable of creating a film that would bring Lugosi back into the position of fame he had once enjoyed.

But he was still determined to work, and undoubtedly needed even the little money Wood was able to pay him. In the late summer of 1956, Lugosi began work on a film that was to be titled "The Vampire's Tomb." Lugosi and some others, including Tor Johnson and his son Carl, went to a Spanish cemetery in the San Fernando Valley with Wood to shoot some scenes before the cemetery was moved. A few other scenes were shot of Lugosi coming and going from Tor Johnson's house, dressed as a mourning old man and, later, in his Dracula outfit. It's a bit of a puzzle to imagine how Lugosi could have appeared in one film both as the old man in a slouch hat and as a lurking vampire, but the footage of him in *Plan 9* shows him in both costumes. In all, there is probably only about five minutes of footage of Lugosi in *Plan 9 from Outer Space*, and it was all intended for "The Vampire's Tomb." We see Lugosi among other mourners at a funeral, we see him leaving Johnson's house; in these scenes, he's dressed as the Old Man. Later, dressed as a vampire, he rushes out of some woods, spreads his vampire cape, and rushes back into the woods; there are three different takes of this scene, but most people seeing *Plan 9* assume it is the same footage again and again. Finally, still dressed as a vampire, he skulks back into the house.

And then, in August 1956, Lugosi died peacefully in bed. Wood was left without a star and only a few minutes of footage. Some time later, he wrote a script called "Grave Robbers from Outer Space," designed to incorporate the footage of Lugosi. Before release, the film was retitled *Plan 9 from Outer Space*, a title peculiarly much less exploitable than the shooting title.

Plan 9 opens with a Los Angeles television celebrity, the broad, campy Criswell (his head is strangely asymmetrical) who was known for his outrageously unlikely predictions. "Greetings, my friends," Criswell says in his mellifluous voice. "We are all interested in the future, for that is where you and I are going to spend the rest of our lives." (This is also how he opened his TV show.) "Future events, such as these, will affect you in the future!" he says, somewhat redundantly. "And now, for the first time, we are bringing to you the *full story* of what happened on that fateful day. We are giving you *all the evidence* based only on the secret testimony of the miserable souls who survived this terrifying ordeal." He warms to the topic. "The incidents—the

Maila Nurmi, Vampira herself, on the famous set from Plan 9 from Outer Space (1958); note the burlap draped over boxes at the left, representing the grassy waves of a cemetery. This photo was originally the property of Edward D. Wood, Jr., himself.

places—my friends, we cannot keep this a secret any longer. Let us punish the guilty; let us reward the innocent. My friends, can your heart stand the shocking facts about—*GRAVE ROBBERS FROM OUTER SPACE?!!*" After a lead-in like that, it seems downright perverse for the film to be called *Plan 9 from Outer Space.*

An old man (Lugosi) mourns his dead wife and goes home, leaving behind two gravediggers. The dead wife (Vampira), looking for some reason just like a vampire, scares the two gravediggers to death.

By now, we have already been introduced to our hero, pilot Jeff Trent (Gregory Walcott), who has been frightened by a passing flying saucer.

Elsewhere, the old man still mourns the loss of his wife. "The sky to which he had once looked," narrates Criswell, "was now only a covering for *her* dead body." The old man wanders sadly offscreen and is promptly hit by a truck.

Inspector Clay (Tor Johnson) joins some other cops in a graveyard; the dead gravediggers had been spotted when the old man was laid to rest in his teensy-tiny tomb. (During his funeral, we see Vampira watching from some dead bushes, and we hear an electronic beeping on the soundtrack.) Clay says he's going to poke around the graveyard; someone warns him to be careful.

Mona McKinnon being carried off by Tor Johnson on the set of Plan 9 from Outer Space (1958). The great realism is somewhat spoiled by the lamp at the lower right.

"I'm a big boy now, Johnny!" Clay laughs jovially. This can hardly be denied. Johnson seems around 6'4" and must weigh at least 300 pounds.

Soon enough, Clay is also killed by Vampira and the old man, now back from his tomb. (It's at this point that a double for Lugosi—chiropractor Tom Mason—begins to be used. He walks around with his cape over his face at all times; rather than disguising the fact that he's not Lugosi, this calls attention to it.) Over Clay's body, Lieutenant Harper (Duke Moore) pronounces the most famous line from the film: "Inspector Clay is dead—murdered—and someone's responsible!"

The film becomes more incoherent as it progresses, with the introduction of Jeff's wife Paula (Mona McKinnon); they live near the graveyard. Also, we soon meet Col. Tom Edwards (Tom Keene), a military man who is upset by a brief, pointless battle with some flying saucers. The saucers not long ago wiped out a small town (plan 8, perhaps?); "A small town, I'll admit," says Edwards, "but nevertheless a town of people."

We also meet Eros (Dudley Manlove) and Tanna (Joanna Lee), aliens who are intent on either conquering the world, or making Earthlings realize that any second now our irresponsibilities will destroy the universe (which Wood thinks is synonymous with the solar system). It is they who are controlling the walking corpses, now including Clay, and it is they *then* get permission from the Ruler (John Breckinridge) to revive the corpses. It is unclear as to whether this odd progression of events is because of Machiavellian scheming by Eros, or because of Wood's bad writing and/or editing.

After a lot of aimless activity, including occasional passes over the Trents' house and the graveyard by flying saucers (which also fly over Hollywood, taking care to pass the headquarters of ABC, CBS and NBC), an attempt at grabbing Paula by the zombie Lugosi double, who is later turned into a skeleton by Eros when things don't work out, and a successful kidnapping of Paula by Clay, Jeff, Edwards and Harper finally confront Eros and Tanna in their spaceship.

Eros, who is waspishly effeminate, is thrown into a series of snits by the Earthmen. "I? A fiend?" he cries indignantly. "I am a soldier of our planet. I a fiend? We did not come as enemies. We came only with friendly intentions, to talk, to ask your aid." (After his having killed several people and revived some corpses, his claim rings a little false.) "All of you of Earth are idiots!" he shouts, which doesn't win him the support of the Earthmen.

Eros explains impatiently that Earthlings are on the verge of creating the Solaronite, a bomb that can ignite the very sunlight. "There is no such thing," says the colonel.

Eros loftily responds, with fractured grammar: "Perhaps to you, but we have known of it for centuries. Your scientists will stumble upon it as they did all the others [*sic?*], and the juvenile minds you possess will not comprehend its strength until it is too late." Jeff says that Solaronite will only make the United States stronger, which really sets Eros off (not without some justification): "You see! You see!" he shrieks. "Your stupid minds! Stupid! Stupid!"

Apparently all the business with the walking corpses was just to get Earthlings to believe that the benign outer-space visitors actually exist, although why this couldn't have been accomplished with a simple meeting rather than grave-robbing is never explained. "We had to use drastic means to get to you," says Eros. "But you left us no other alternative. When you have the Solaronite, you have nothing, and so does the universe." He then goes into a lengthy metaphorical explanation, likening sunlight to gasoline, but to no avail.

Now the Earthmen think he's crazy as well as a liar. And when he strikes Tanna, explaining that "in my land women are for advancing the race, not for fighting man's battle," the jig is really up for him.

Or is it? Out the window, the Earthmen see Clay standing there holding Paula as a threat, but two cops overpower him, so those in the ship jump Eros. Shots are fired, things in the control room burst into flame, and the Earthmen flee the spaceship. It takes off, and while Tanna still struggles to revive Eros, it explodes over Hollywood.

We return to Criswell, still sitting at his desk. "My friends, you have seen this incident, based on sworn testimony. Can *you* prove it didn't happen? Perhaps, on your way home, someone will pass you in the dark, and you will never know it, for they will be from outer space!" He goes on for a moment, and suddenly concludes, "God help us in the future!" Criswell wrote his own narration, but it is easily on a par with Wood's dialogue. Criswell, who became, sadly, apparently somewhat senile in his later years, died in 1982, not long after making a personal appearance at a Hollywood theatre showing three of Wood's films.

Is *Plan 9 from Outer Space* the worst movie ever made? Who can say? I haven't seen every contender, but apart from minor porno films (another area Wood worked), it may be the cheapest-looking professional movie ever filmed in English. The flying saucers are paper plates, decorated with pointy things to be sure, but still paper plates, hanging on strings. (They actually don't look any worse than spaceships in some other more expensive films, such as *Attack of the 50 Foot Woman*.) The cemetery is merely a small area of soundstage covered with a hairy drop cloth, and dotted here and there with studio trees and cardboard tombstones, often knocked about by winds of the saucers' passage, or the careless foot of an actor. Nonetheless, as Joe Dante points out, it *is* a soundstage; the film is more professional looking than *Glen or Glenda?*, but looks just as cheap. The patio furniture on the Trents' patio also turns up in their bedroom. The "airplane" consists of a doorway, two chairs, and two anonymous-looking stanchions, indicating the presence of controls; the doorway is covered by a shower curtain. One could go on at some length in this manner (and many have), detailing the cheapness of the picture, and indeed, its impoverished look is integral to its overall impact.

But what really makes *Plan 9 from Outer Space* distinctive is the dialogue and direction of Edward D. Wood, Jr. The acting is bad, but except for being wildly variable, not much worse than in other cheap films. No, it's Wood and Wood alone who gives *Plan 9* its weird charm and all of its fame.

It's hard to know where to start quoting from that film, or for that matter, where to stop. Randy Simon and Harold Benjamin, the authors of the rare but indispensible pamphlet, *Edward D. Wood, Jr. A Man and His Films*, delight in quoting from Wood again and again, dividing up quotes into "Woodese" (general quotes from Wood, sort of mushed into blank verse) and "The Wisdom of Wood," with sections on "Wood on Womanhood," "Wood on the State of Life," "Wood on Knowledge," and a catchall, "Wood at Large."

Jeff says, "I saw a flying saucer." "Saucer?" asks Paula, "You mean the kind from up there?" "Yeah," he replies, "or its counterpart." Later, she tells him, "The saucers are up there and the cemetery is out there but I'll be locked up in there." The actress was supposed to indicate the various theres with her chin or something, but doesn't, and the line has a dadaesque quality.

"Looks like a bobcat tore into them," says Harper, indicating the dead gravediggers, who had died of fright. (Note: the footage of the gravediggers also may have been filmed for "The Vampire's Tomb.")

"It flew right over us," says Paula, "only a few feet up!" "Maybe it was indigestion," Danny the copilot suggests.

"There's got to be a reason for their visits," muses the colonel after the saucers he's been shooting at depart. "Visits!" exclaims a captain. "That would indicate visitors!"

When, aboard a space station, Eros tells the Ruler that he now intends to use Plan 9, the Ruler considers this. "Ah, yes. Plan 9 deals with the resurrection of the dead. Long distant [sic] electrodes shot into the pineal and pituitary glands of recent dead." In the hallway outside, Eros chats with Tanna. "You know, it's an interesting thing when you consider the Earth people who can think are so frightened by those who cannot, the dead."

And on and on and on. *Plan 9* does deserve its fame, and should be suffered through at least once by anyone who is interested in movie history.

As pointed out in *Edward D. Wood, Jr.: A Man and His Films* (don't you wish *you* had a copy?), most of the cast of *Plan 9* consists of friends of Ed Wood, or people who were simply available cheap. Tom Keene, Colonel Edwards, was a minor cowboy actor. Duke Moore, who played Lieutenant Harper, appeared only in Ed Wood films, but in several of those. He is perhaps at his peak in *Plan 9*, playing a cop who is so used to having a gun in his hand that he forgets it's there. He scratches his neck with the barrel of the pistol several times, and in one memorable scene, scratches his neck, tips his hat *and* points with the gun, all in the same take.

Lyle Talbot is in briefly as an officer who lectures Keene. He's been an active performer since 1932, starring in good and bad B movies, including *The 13th Guest* (1932), *A Shriek in the Night* (1933), *The Devil's Cargo* (1948), *Target, Sea of China* (1954), and many, many others. He played character roles in major films, was in at least three serials, *Trader Tom of the China Seas*, *Batman and Robin* (1949) and *Atom Man vs. Superman* (1950, as Luthor), and costarred simultaneously in two long-running TV series, "The Adventures of Ozzie and Harriet" and "The Bob Cummings Show." It was, in fact, while he was in both series that he shot his scenes for *Plan 9 from Outer Space*, which were filmed on a one-room set; it probably took him all of an afternoon. He was also in *Glen or Glenda?* for Wood. Among his other genre films were *The Dragon Murder Case*, *Return of the Terror* (both 1934), *Strange Impersonation* (1945), *Hurricane Island*, *Fury of the Congo* (both 1950), *Jungle Manhunt*, *Mesa of Lost Women* (as narrator), *Untamed Women*, *Jalopy*, the serial/series *Commando Cody* (1953) and *Tobor the Great*. Talbot was never out of demand as a character actor for *good* movies, so God only knows why he chose to appear in some of the cheapest movies of all times. Maybe he liked to work. Maybe he liked Ed Wood.

Dudley Manlove, the memorably frustrated and petulant Eros, was primarily a radio actor; according to Simon and Benjamin, he was "the voice of Lux Soap. Manlove has numerous film and television credits, mostly from the 50s and before. His only film appearance after ... *Plan 9* was in a 1965 [*sic*] winner called *Creation of the Humanoids*." A check of a reference source listing thousands of films from the early 30s to the present doesn't show any other credits for Manlove at all. It really isn't surprising, however. His rich, fruity voice was suited for the radio styles of the 30s and 40s, but not thereafter and, as an actor, he's truly terrible.

Hero Gregory Walcott appeared in many major films, though usually in a supporting role. He was in films as early as *Above and Beyond* (1952), and also appeared in *Battle Cry*, *Mister Roberts* (both 1955), *The Outsider* (1962), *Joe Kidd* (1972, and at least three other Clint Eastwood films), *The Last American Hero* (1973), *The Gemini Man* (TV, 1976), and *Norma Rae* (1979), among many others. In 1967, Walcott produced and starred in a little-known film, *Bill Wallace of China*, playing the title role, a real-life missionary doctor in China. He also costarred in the 1961–62 series "87th Precinct."

Perhaps the most noticeable actor in the film was big Tor Johnson, often described as being hideously fat. Actually, although Johnson was unquestionably fat (he weighed anywhere from 300 to 400 pounds, sources differ), much of that girth was muscle. He had earned a living for years as a wrestler, billing himself as "The Super-Swedish Angel." (The "Swedish Angel" himself was a rival wrestler, disfigured by acromegaly.)

Tor achieved what little fame he had from his handful of science fiction and horror films, which include Wood's *Bride of the Monster*, *The Black Sleep*, *Plan 9*, *The Unearthly* and *The Beast of Yucca Flats*. Johnson was also in Wood's

Night of the Ghouls, which was unreleased for years; it finally emerged on videotape in 1984. Tor also appeared in many mainstream movies, including *Kid Millions* (1936), *The Man on the Flying Trapeze* (1935, as a wrestler), *Shadow of the Thin Man* (1941), *The Ghost Catchers* (1944), *The Canterville Ghost* (1944, as the fierce knight who causes Charles Laughton to flee), *Houdini* (1953) and *Carousel* (1956), among many other films. He also turned up on Groucho Marx's "You Bet Your Life" as a contestant; his roaring grimace sent Groucho scurrying for cover.

Tor was not an actor, partly because of his heavy Swedish accent; he was simply a living prop, because of his size. *Plan 9* may, in fact, be the only film in which Tor actually has something like dialogue, rather than grunts and groans. (He was dubbed in *The Canterville Ghost*.) His accent and peculiar ideas about delivery, obvious in *Plan 9*, may indicate why Johnson never worked as a real actor. According to Johnny Legend in *Fangoria* #22, Tor was a good-natured fellow who was distantly related to onetime heavyweight boxing champ Ingemar Johansson. Legend called Tor "sweet, gentle and quite unassuming, considering his formidable presence," with "a wry, understated wit."

Legend also related a remarkable story about Tor and Bela Lugosi, which doesn't speak at all well of Johnson's temper or judgment. While on a promotional tour for *The Black Sleep* with Lugosi, Johnson became so weary of Lugosi's "constant whining," as Lugosi was in the depths of depression, that Johnson angrily dangled Lugosi out a hotel room window, several stories above the street. Legend quotes Johnson as saying, "Is this what you want, you miserable Hunkie?"

Tor Johnson died May, 1971.

The old man's dead wife was played by Vampira, which is how actress Maila Nurmi began billing herself in the early 1950s. She got her start as a spooky type by appearing in Mike Todd's very short-lived Broadway production of 1943, "Spook Scandals." She was, according to her article in *Fangoria* #30, brought to Hollywood by Howard Hawks, but nothing came of this. She appeared at a major masquerade ball dressed as the vampiric woman from Charles Addams' *New Yorker* cartoons, and won first prize. Later, she was approached by KABC-TV in Los Angeles to host a series of horror movies, the low-budget Monogram, PRC and other poverty-row efforts from the 30s and 40s. This began in 1954, and she soon acquired a tremendous local reputation in Los Angeles for her Mae Westian/Charles Addamsish put-downs of the movies she hosted. The show began in May, and was off the air by December; Vampira claims she was blackballed, which is entirely possible. She was known for her friendships with James Dean and other of the more eccentric young people in Hollywood, but remained mostly a shadowy figure for years. She turned up in a scant few fantasy films, including Wood's *Night of the Ghouls*, as well as *Sex Kittens Go to College* and *The Magic Sword* (1962). She occasionally worked in other films as well, such as *The Big Operator* and *The Beat Generation* (both 1959), but mostly got by as a "Hollywood character." She was born in Finland in 1921, and contrary to her image, is a blonde.

As for Wood himself, he was born in Poughkeepsie, New York, in 1921, and had a lifelong interest in theatre and the movies. He served in the Marines during World War II, and was injured during the assaults of Tarawa and Guam. He had moved to Los Angeles by 1948, and tried several times to make a success at writing plays. He toyed with the idea of movies in the early 50s, and in 1952, produced his first feature, *Glen or Glenda?*, one of the most freakish films of all time; it dealt with transvestites, and Wood played the leading role (under a pseudonym). He persevered in his filmmaking efforts, despite no discernible talent as a director. As Simon and Benjamin accurately put it, "Ed Wood approached filmmaking with boundless enthusiasm and optimism.... Unfortunately, [he] did not have the talent to wear all the hats. Having no training in direction and no inborn feel for it, he produced static scenes, heavy with dialogue and lacking any real use of the visual medium (try listening to a Wood soundtrack without the picture; little is lost). His scripts, in fact, actually read far better than the finished films turned out."

Almost until the time of his death in 1978, Wood kept returning to films. His other titles as director-writer are *Jail Bait* (1954), *Bride of the Monster*, *The Sinister Urge* (1961), and a few pornographic films, including *Take It Out in Trade* (1971) and *Necromania* (1972). He also shot a few shorts, including *The Final Curtain* (1957), and two undated shorts, *The Sun Also Sets* and *The Cross-roads Avenger*. He wrote several films directed by others, including *The Bride and the Beast* (1958), *The Shotgun Wedding* (1963), *Orgy of the Dead* (1965) and *The Violent Years* (1956). In the 70s, he had little opportunity to make films, and so wrote many quick pornographic novels, which often centered on transvestism. He also wrote political campaign literature at this time, according to Simon and Benjamin, including material for Mayor Sam Yorty of Los Angeles. His last few years were not happy; he was "fighting alcoholism," as Simon and Benjamin said, and had been evicted from his small apartment not long before he died, December 10, 1978.

And as they also point out, there's a major difference between Edward D. Wood, Jr. and his detractors. Despite the scorn and contempt his films have received, despite the laughter they engender—there's one thing that no one can ever take away from him. He *made* those movies, and he made them his way. Like his films or not, Ed Wood was a true *auteur*.

The cheapness of *Plan 9* is fascinating in itself, and writers about the film never fail to point out that night and day alternate from shot to shot, because Wood didn't have the money to have his day-for-night shots printed dark enough to look like night. Out of the window of Eros' spaceship, we can see blue skies and fleecy clouds, no matter what time of day it is out the door of the spaceship.

The cemetery set included a miniscule crypt from which far too many people emerge, but there's no particular reason for the crypt even being there, though Wood carefully has its presence explained in dialogue.

Wood's fussiness over some details, such as the electronic beeping we hear whenever any of the radio-controlled zombies are present, is especially puzzling when a total lack of care is apparent in so many other details, including plotting: Clay shoots at the Ghoul Man and Ghoul Woman (as they are called in the credits), despite their having made no menacing moves whatever.

The space station headquarters of the Ruler consists primarily of curtained walls, a table, a desk chair and a few scattered objects. The spaceship itself has more wooden tables, a cardboard box under one of them, a 16mm projector, and the same desk chair. However, in a nod to the primacy of established imagery, there's also a Jacob's ladder sending little lightning bolts crackling up its V-shaped wires, and sliding doors. (Science fiction = sliding doors.)

When *Plan 9* was released, not surprisingly it received little critical attention. Allen M. Widem in *Motion Picture Herald* called the film "poor" and its script "rather routine," also saying it was for audiences "not particularly concerned with logic." Not surprisingly (or unjustly), the *Monthly Film Bulletin* gave the film their lowest rating, saying, "A routine idea, crudely written, directed and acted, provides just about the weakest SF-cum-horror thriller to come out of Hollywood in years."

In more recent years, however, it seems as if almost everyone has something to say about *Plan 9 from Outer Space*. It is now the most famous terrible movie ever made. J. Hoberman said in the *Village Voice* that while the film may not be the worst movie, "it's a delightful exercise in desultory special effects, off-the-wall dialogue, and low-budget *mishigas*." He added that "Not only does [Wood] deploy a cape-shrouded stand-in a full head taller than [Lugosi], but he employs nonexistent points of view ... and reuses the same stock footage with impunity.... Many of the tackier details of Wood's mise-en-scène are lost on [television], but his astonishing, Gertrude Stein–like dialogue remains intact: 'That's the most fantastic story I've ever heard!' 'And every word is true, too!' 'That's the fantastic part of it!'"

In *Famous Monsters of Filmland*, then 13-year-old Joe Dante said, "There is a distinct possibility it [is] the cheapest film ever made. The entire cast was awful.... The scene where Tor Johnson rose from the grave was the only good five seconds in the whole film." Later, in *Castle of Frankenstein*, an aged Dante said, "From the hammy intro by Criswell to the hammy afterword by Criswell, this grade Z 1956 home movie masquerading as a theatrical film is an unalloyed delight, raising rank amateurishness to the level of high comic art."

Leonard Maltin's *TV Movies* (1981–82 edition) dismissed it as "wacked-out sci fi that isn't much of anything," but by the 83–84 edition, Maltin had more to say. "The one, the only, the legendary movie widely believed to be the worst ever made.... Mesmerizing in its awfulness."

In *Science Fiction Movies*, Philip Strick says, "the film gives the appearance of having been slung together by drugged mortuary attendants." After disposing of *Plan 9* in Volume 1 of his book as "really bad," Don Willis had more to say about it in Volume 2. "Near-legendary filmic atrocity is too-well-known-and-loved by now to need any further introduction. Suffice it to say that with a little larger budget, *Plan 9* could have been another *Cosmic Man* – and no one would remember *it* now, either." *Psychotronic* said, "The merits of this incredible film have not been exaggerated ... it's the most entertaining bad [film] you'll find.... [W]orth watching 9 times." Reviewing the videotape for *Fangoria*, "Dr. Cyclops" called it "Wood's most consistently and unintentionally funny movie.... No respectable video collection would be complete without it."

The most unusual commentary to date on *Plan 9 from Outer Space* is by Danny Peary in *Cult Movies*. "It's so bad that it borders on the ludicrous.... To think that such an inept, *berserk* picture exists truly boggles the mind." After this conventional beginning, Peary discusses the various shortcomings of the film, and concludes in an interesting vein. "*Plan 9* is a delirious movie," Peary says, "but perhaps we are missing the point. Could it be that putting up a crazy façade is the only way that Wood can get away with making a *subversive* movie?" Peary suggests that in Eros' outrageous speech at the end, Wood is really attacking the American political and military establishment. "Eros," says Peary, is for peace.... The fact that these aliens believe in God is further proof that Eros is Wood's spokesman ... and Jeff and Edwards, whom we mistakenly accept as heroes, turn out to be brutish jerks who rely on the fist and the gun. Don't let the fact that Eros is a maniac throw you off – at rare moments, he is as sound a visionary as is Preacher Casey in *The Grapes of Wrath*.... *Plan 9*, dreadful as it is, is something far more significant, and therefore better, than 'The Worse Film of All Time' could possible be."

All that is interesting, but does overlook that aliens in 50s SF movies were *frequently* here to stop us from continuing in warfare. This idea began with *The Day the Earth Stood Still* and was echoed again and again through the decade. Wood wasn't being cautionary, he was being imitative.

Plan 9 from Outer Space is an anomaly: a film revered today for its amazing badness, and for the crack-brained visions of its enthusiastic director. Wood was talentless, but relentless. It's almost as if he didn't know or care that he had no talent; the movies themselves may not have mattered to him at all. As with some great directors, perhaps the only thing that mattered to Ed Wood was *making* movies, not *having made* movies.

Now that almost all great directors have been thoroughly analyzed in print, zonked-out eccentrics are having their day, and Ed Wood is the zonkiest of all. He lies somewhere in the twilight zone between idiocy and inspiration, between genius and hopelessness. He was inspired all right, but by goals and desires incomprehensible to us mere mortals. *Plan 9 from Outer Space*, the most watchable of his films, is testimony to Wood's guilelessness—he can't even make a cheap bad movie right, but he makes it his own way.

Perhaps the best final word on Wood and his goals is at the very end of *Plan 9*, where a title reads:

THE END
Made in Hollywood, U.S.A.

Queen of Outer Space

This flashily-titled film has some oddities in the credits. The original story is credited to Ben Hecht, the script is by Charles Beaumont, and a leading role (though *not* the title character) is played by hyperglamorous Zsa Zsa Gabor, Miss Hungary of 1936. This strange salad of famous names doesn't result in a good film, although *Queen of Outer Space* does have some interest.

In 1985, hot young rocket captain Patterson (Eric Fleming) and his crew, Turner (Patrick Waltz) and Cruze (Dave Willock) reluctantly take brainy scientist Professor Konrad (Paul Birch) by spaceship to the wheel-shaped space station he helped design. However, en route, they see a red ray shooting out of the depths of space, aimed at the space station. The ray caroms off the spinning station with a crashing sound, but finally focuses and blasts the wheel to bits. Then the ray strikes Patterson's ship and sends it shooting off course at high speed (stock footage from *World Without End*), causing the four men aboard to black out.

The ship crashes onto a snowy mountain, apparently on an unknown planet. When the men revive, the professor points out that since gravity is so similar to Earth's, the air is probably breathable, so they set out in search of food, eventually encountering a garish jungle. Konrad reveals his suspicion that they are on Venus. Patterson sputters, "You don't just accidentally land on a planet 26 million miles away!" Konrad replies, "It would appear that all things are possible in space."

Electronic signals "passing overhead" reveal that Venus must be inhabited, and after a night's sleep, this is confirmed: they are captured by a bevy of gorgeous, scantily-clad and heavily-armed women.

Speaking a language unknown to the Earthmen, the women warriors force our little band of heroes to accompany them to the capitol of Venus, played by the stock shot of a city from an Arabian Nights movie.

The Earthmen are ushered into a council chamber and are confronted by Yllana (Laurie Mitchell), the shapely Queen of Venus herself, who wears a filigreed silver mask, as do her four advisors. She begins questioning the men in English ("we have monitored your electronic waves for years"), and haughtily reveals that she assumes everyone on Earth is warlike. She refuses to allow them to leave, and orders them imprisoned, but we get the idea she's attracted to Patterson. The Earthmen are pretty excited themselves. Indicating a Venusian beauty, one leers, "How'd you like to drag that to the high school prom?"

In a nearby laboratory, famous Venusian scientist Taleeah (Zsa Zsa Gabor) questions her assistant about the Earthmen captives, and we learn that Taleeah is opposed to Yllana's dictatorial rule, and that she believes the Earthmen's claims that they come in peace.

As the Earthmen fret in captivity, Patterson and Konrad explain to the other two that they think the ray that destroyed the space station and brought them to Venus may have originated on this planet, apparently populated by women. Cruze is disbelieving. "Oh, come off it! How could a bunch of women invent a gizmo like that? And even if they invented it, how could they *aim* it? You know how women drivers are!"

Taleeah visits the prisoners, and she too is attracted to Patterson. She offers to help the Earthmen, and tells them the sad story of Venus. Ten years before, they were involved in a fierce war with the planet Mordo, and although eventually Mordo was completely destroyed, most cities on Venus were obliterated. Masked peasant girl Yllana led a revolt against the male rulers of Venus, and because the men did not take the threat seriously, her uprising was successful. Yllana spared only those men she needed — scientists, mathematicians — and banished them to a small satellite that circles Venus.

When guards come to take Patterson to Yllana, the other three men urge him to use his masculine charm to gain the masked queen's confidence, and to trick her into freeing them. Fortunately, the guards do not now understand English (some did before), and when he is escorted into Yllana's presence, Patterson puts this plan into practice.

Back in the prison cell, Konrad muses, "there is a certain irony in the fact that our lives — and perhaps the lives of everyone on Earth — depend upon Captain Patterson's sex appeal."

Yllana is instantly seductive when she and Patterson are alone, and plies him with wine. She is still urging him to reveal the true nature of his trip to Venus, adding that "even a queen can be lonely, Captain." But when Patterson attempts to seduce her, she becomes furious — especially when he asks her to remove her mask. "Did you promise your men you'd sweep me off my feet — use your male magnetism to win freedom for all of you? ... I know you and your men are seething inwardly, consumed with frustration because you are the prisoners and not the masters of what you call the weaker sex."

Her grand plan is to establish the perfect order and crush the forces that stand in her way, apparently starting with the four men from Earth. To convince him to cooperate, she shows him on television a scene on the prison satellite, where a man is being tortured, then a scene of the control room for the terrible Beta Disintegrator, the source of the ray that destroyed the space station, and which can also destroy the Earth just as easily.

Patterson accuses Yllana. "You're denying man's love, substituting hatred and a passion for this monstrous power you possess.... You're not only a queen, you're a woman too. And a woman needs a man's love!" With that timeless phrase, he whips off Yllana's mask.

He reveals a pasty, rotten-looking mass of sores. This disfigurement is what caused Yllana's passionate desire to destroy men: her face was obliterated by radiation burns. "*Men* did this to me! Men and their wars!" She sardonically tries to kiss Patterson, who turns away in horror from the hideous face, so he is taken back to the prison room.

Taleeah's associates secretly free the Earthmen and take them to her laboratory, where she reveals that Yllana intends to destroy the Earth in two days, so they must hurry. She wants to overthrow Yllana because "ve haff no life here vitout lahff and shildren."

Taleeah, Patterson and the others—Cruze and Turner have also acquired Venusian girlfriends—escape from the queen's palace and hide in the woods. A giant spider unsuccessfully attacks Turner in a cave. When recapture seems imminent, Taleeah pretends to the searching women warriors that she and her assistants have captured the Earthmen, and everyone returns to the palace.

After a great deal of intrigue, including Taleeah briefly masquerading as Yllana, the evil queen again gets the upper hand and prepares to disintegrate the Earth. However, the rebel Venusian women rise up and overthrow the queen's guards. The Beta Disintegrator does not fire, but instead explodes, killing Yllana.

Now with Taleeah in charge, men can again be welcome on Venus. Patterson radios Earth and is told he and his party will have to remain on Venus until a rescue operation can be mounted. What with all the Earthmen matched up—Konrad is last seen surrounded by several beauties—no one is objecting.

Queen of Outer Space was written to be a spoof of the childish space operas that had become prevalent on television during the 1950s. There aren't very many examples of this kind of thing in movies, at least with a science fiction setting, except for a few stray titles such as *Flight to Mars, Cat-Women of the Moon* and *Fire Maidens of Outer Space*. These space operas usually featured a granite-jawed hero and his wisecracking crew, with a sage scientist in tow, who land on another planet to discover a bad situation among the English-speaking natives. There's usually some intrigue and romance, a monster or two, and a fight. At the end, everything is wrapped up nicely. Oddly enough, the best space movie of the 50s, *Forbidden Planet*, was also an example of this subgenre, as is "Star Trek."

These stories owe little to science fiction itself, and are simply space-oriented examples of an older breed of adventure fiction, the Lost Civilization story. Indeed, other than some minor trappings such as a spaceship, ray guns and disintegrator beams, there's very little in *Queen of Outer Space* that distinguishes it from these tired old romances. The same kind of palace intrigue, slightly bizarre situation (here, women in control), and escapes and recaptures occur in all these stories. The basic storyline of *Queen of Outer Space* has been set in the past as well as the future.

Ben Hecht is credited with the original storyline, which must have made some eyes pop in 1958. Hecht was one of the preeminent film writers of his time, having written or cowritten films such as *Nothing Sacred* (1937), *Wuthering Heights, Gone with the Wind* (both 1939), *Spellbound* (1945) and *Notorious* (1946). He wrote or cowrote the original stories (usually plays) for such classic films as *The Front Page* (several versions) and *Twentieth Century* (1934).

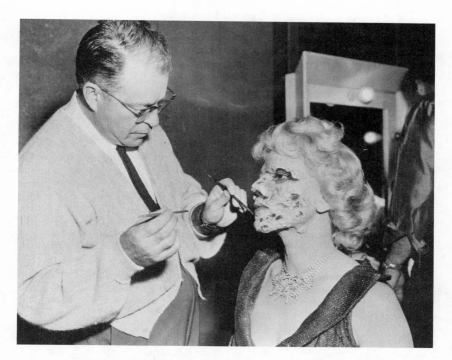

Makeup artist Emile La Vigne applies the radiation-burn makeup to Laurie Mitchell for her role as the Queen of Outer Space (1958); La Vigne's makeups are generally better than this pasty mess.

Of course, Hecht also slummed from time to time, and some of his films, such as *The Goldwyn Follies* (1937), *The Miracle of the Bells* (1948) and *Circus World* (1964) were anything but distinguished.

By the early 50s, Hecht's movie scripts were fewer and farther between. Edward Bernds, who directed *Queen*, told interviewer Tom Weaver in *Fantastic Films* #37, that Hecht's contribution was a ten-page outline, a satire on women ineptly in charge of another planet. In *The Five Lives of Ben Hecht*, Doug Fetherling dismissed Hecht's contribution altogether. "At least once, in a 1958 schlocker entitled *Queen of Outer Space*, [Hecht] was given a credit by contract when he had in fact contributed nothing to the film."

According to Bernds, "Walter Wanger thought that his wife, Joan Bennett, might be having an affair with her agent, so he shot the agent in the crotch.... Wanger was out in a year or so. He needed a job, but the big studios ... didn't want to give him a break. The president of Allied Artists finally did hire him ... and Walter Wanger came to AA as a producer. He brought with him a ten-page outline by Ben Hecht called 'Queen of the Universe.' I don't know how Ben Schwalb came to produce the picture instead of Wanger, but that's what happened."

This seems accurate. As early as 1951 (*New York Times*, July 15) Wanger announced that he was about to produce "Queen of the Universe" from a story by Ben Hecht, a "speculation on life on the planet Venus when the world is being properly run by women."

The only author credited for the final script is Charles Beaumont. In the notes on *Abbott and Costello Go to Mars* in Volume 1, I related a story, which may or may not be true, that Beaumont tried to submit a story about Abbott and Costello in space, but found it taken from him by someone else. It's possible that much of the story Beaumont devised for Abbott and Costello became the basis of *Queen of Outer Space*. It's true there are similarities: both pictures take their heroes to Venus, both deal with planets populated entirely by women, in both the queens fall for one of the Earthmen, and in both there are a series of escapes and recaptures.

The best evidence that the film was written as a spoof — which has been denied by Bernds, see below — is that Beaumont's other fantasy writing is sophisticated; it seems highly unlikely that he would expect a plot as silly as *Queen's* to be taken seriously.* But, Bernds told Tom Weaver, "The screenplay was pretty much an original ... a straight science-fiction melodrama [and] it wasn't very good." Bernds decided "that it would have a better chance if we lightened it up, you might say — spoofed it — and we did.... I wish that we had done more [rewriting]. I think the light parts of it worked, but the melodrama parts were — a little heavy for my taste."

The only really obvious clue in the film that it is all a big yok is in the end credits, where the cast is individually identified in little groups: The Leaders, The Lovers, The Lovelorn, The Professor, The Wicked Queen and Her Posse. For most audiences, who were no doubt unaware that it was a joke, those little categories must have come as a surprise.

When stripped of exaggeration and comic elements, the plot of a parody should be a good example of the kind of thing it is parodying. The plot of *Queen of Outer Space* may be that, but it is also not very interesting. It follows traditional lines too closely.

Edwards Bernds also directed *World Without End*, a movie with a plot somewhat similar to *Queen of Outer Space*. He did both films in almost precisely the same mode and tone, with no comic exaggeration in *Queen*. He had done comedy often enough before, mostly slapstick, starting his career as director with at least five in Columbia's "Blondie" series; he also did the little-known *Gasoline Alley* and *Corky of Gasoline Alley* (both 1951). He directed the first Three Stooges feature *Gold Raiders* (1951), and returned to them for *The Three Stooges in Orbit* and *The Three Stooges Meet Hercules*; he also directed many shorts starring the Stooges. He directed several Bowery Boys films in the mid-50s. His other science fiction films include *Space Master X-7* and *Return of the Fly*.

All this experience with low- and middlebrow comedy doesn't seem to have affected Bernds' directorial approach to *Queen*. He apparently relied on the absurdities of the script to carry the humor, and simply employed his usual flat, uninteresting style. He is slightly better than Edward L. Cahn, though I

*Nor, according to his friend William F. Nolan, did he. In a letter dated 20 April 1984, Nolan told me, "I recall visiting Chuck [Beaumont] at the studio while he was writing [the film] and he was amused by the fact that Bernds was taking his script as a 'serious' screenplay. He, Chuck, thought it was ridiculous, but was 'writing it straight to please the studio people'.... Hecht got basic story credit but I don't think Chuck worked from any Hecht material.... And it had nothing to do with Abbott and Costello Go to Mars. (Yes, the story you tell is true — about the mimeo of his being filmed; at least that was what Chuck told me.)"

doubt that anyone seeing two unidentified films by each of them would quickly pick out who directed which film.

In short, based on their respective careers, I would make a sound guess that Charles Beaumont wrote Queen of Outer Space as a spoof, despite Bernds' claims that he, and not Beaumont, added the satiric elements.

Reviewers of the time generally spotted Queen as a parody, and seemed relieved. They didn't have to try to treat the film seriously, which would have presented some problems. But Queen isn't all that much different from other films that were intended to be taken straight, and audiences who didn't realize it was a spoof should be forgiven. There are no exaggerations, to speak of, the hero is not too military, the professor is not too scientific. The film would have been more successful if it had been a screwy lampoon like the Airplane movies of the early 1980s. You have to overdo spoofs for audiences even to recognize them as such. Sophistication and subtlety, even as lamely done as those aspects are in Queen, are invisible to most moviegoers.

As a movie, Queen of Outer Space isn't very good. It is slow, tame and uninteresting. The middle third is clotted with palace intrigue, visits and revisits with the queen, and skulking around corridors. Nothing much happens until the meaningless escape; even the climax is botched. The picture is pretty tough going for today's audiences, even when they are aware that it was all meant as a joke.

It's also cheap. Much of the hardware and the costumes were from Forbidden Planet, including several of the dresses the leggy Venusian women wear. This was so apparent to audiences in 1958, that when I first saw the film at a hot, uncomfortable theatre in Florence, Oregon, there were catcalls concerning the props. The sets, credited to David Milton, are badly designed, and in the case of the jungle scenes, very poorly executed without even a hint of conviction. The film is in color and CinemaScope, but they don't add anything here. The awful disintegrator set, said Bernds, was supposed to be a joke, but it's no worse than the "straight" sets.

The special effects are limp and familiar. Several scenes are lifted from World Without End, but they weren't good there, either. The ship never looks like anything other than a model, and most of the shots of it are from World Without End. Even the shot of the giant spider jumping is from that picture.

Even by 1958 standards, Queen of Outer Space is wildly sexist, although that was part of the joke. The Earthmen are amazed that women could design and build a world-destroying ray machine—but we later learn that it was probably designed by captive men. When the queen tries to blow up the Earth, she does something wrong and blows herself up instead. All the women on Venus, except the queen, miss the men and want them back. The revolt couldn't happen until men helped. Sexual jealousy fuels intrigue. It's doubtful that Queen of Outer Space could ever serve as anything but a horrible example.

The cast is mostly dull. Although Eric Fleming achieved some fame later as Gil Favor in the TV series "Rawhide," where he was fine, he's lost in Queen of Outer Space, playing the entire film in the same tight-lipped, gimlet-eyed fashion, making the line about survival depending on his sex appeal even stranger than was intended. Paul Birch looks confused most of the time, and Dave Willock and Patrick Waltz deliver standard Comic Sidekick and Horny Sidekick material in standard fashion.

Even though she's masked for almost all her scenes, as the Queen of Venus Laurie Mitchell is better than most of the rest of the cast. She seems evil and imperious, as well as bitter and forlorn when required. It's not an outstanding performance, but it's energetic and better than you'd have any reason to expect.

On the other hand, Zsa Zsa Gabor is exactly what you'd expect. The film was advertised to emphasize her fame as a glamour girl, and anyone who still thinks *she* was the Queen of Outer Space should be forgiven the error. Zsa Zsa was one of the last of the old-line glamour queens, and her fame has almost always rested on that most unusual of foundations: she's famous because she's famous. She is certainly not much of an actress; the only time she was required to deliver a real performance was in *Moulin Rouge* (1952), and she was still basically being Zsa Zsa. But I don't resent her. She's intelligent and has a sense of humor about herself. All she's required to do in *Queen of Outer Space* is to be there and deliver her lines. Nobody should complain. Not even about her being the only Venusian scientist with a thick Hungarian accent.

Reviews at the time were fairly kind to the film. The *Monthly Film Bulletin* said that "the stylised settings, costume and effects are pleasantly shot in shiny space-colour. Otherwise, this is an amiable, if rather tame burlesque of science fiction formulae." "Powe" in *Variety* said "Ben Schwalb's production is a good-natured attempt to put some honest sex into science fiction and as such it is an attractive production." (Powe didn't recognize the film as a parody.) Charles Stinson in the *Los Angeles Times* did catch it, even saying "it is not science fiction" but rather "an elaborate parody of science fiction and, as such, it is quite good, indeed."

Jack Moffitt also thought it an "amiable burlesque of science fiction" and complimented producer Ben Schwalb on creating "a show that the lowbrows will drool over and the highbrows will chuckle over."

The film must have looked good by contrast in 1958—it did to me, for one—because more recent commentators have given it short shrift. Parish and Pitts said the film "should have been funny but it was too silly and too pathetically dull." Neither Ed Naha, in *The Science Fictionary*, nor Don Willis (I) realized the film was a parody. Neither John Brosnan (*Future Tense*) nor Philip Strick (*Science Fiction Movies*) even mentions it.

In *Cinefantastique* (old series, #5), Tom Reamy said that "Charles Beaumont has written a tongue-in-cheek spoof of filmed space opera; the only trouble is the director didn't recognize it for what it was and has turned out exactly what Beaumont was spoofing. But for the obvious comic dialogue, which the director could not fail to interpret correctly, Beaumont's absurd situations have been transposed to the screen with deadly seriousness.... [When the mask is removed] Beaumont fails us. He gets original—or reasonably so. The mask wasn't hiding the queen's incredible beauty but her incredible ugliness.... Even though most of Beaumont's satire has been buried in the very drivel it was spoofing, the film manages to be entertaining. It has been fairly handsomely mounted without anything spectacular being done. Zsa Zsa is about the only one to portray her role as Beaumont intended but, then, even in a serious role, she seems to be pulling somebody's leg."

Queen of Outer Space does deserve some points for trying to make fun of a subgenre of science fiction, but it just didn't have the resources. The script was too subtle and the direction and cast were too flat and pedestrian. It's a curiosity today, but little more.

The Revenge of Frankenstein

In the 1930s, the first sequel to Universal's popular *Frankenstein* was the even better *Bride of Frankenstein*, which continued the adventures of both Dr. Frankenstein and his creation. By the third film, *Son of Frankenstein* (1939), however, it's clear that the Monster is the central character. It was obvious that the public confused the Monster with the creator (a confusion that predated the Universal films), and so as the Monster was both the best known and most vivid character, he not only became Frankenstein, but the central character in the remainder of the Universal series.

However, when in 1957, Hammer Films' *Curse of Frankenstein* became a worldwide hit, the public was clearly responding much more to Dr. Frankenstein, as played by Peter Cushing, than to the Monster, which was not only a relatively minor character in the film, but not very interesting. Thus, when a sequel was planned, unlike Universal, Hammer continued to use Baron Victor Frankenstein as the central character. Peter Cushing played the baron through six of the seven Frankenstein films Hammer made.

This allowed for somewhat more variety in the plots than Universal's formula did, although the Hammer films usually consisted of Frankenstein doggedly trying to perfect a new creation, only to have outside forces foul him up once again. Cushing is always superb in the part, although the variable intents of the scripts have him veering from being basically decent (as, ironically enough, in *The Evil of Frankenstein* [1964]) to outright villainous (as in *Frankenstein Must Be Destroyed* [1970]). Nonetheless, Cushing is able to maintain an equilibrium in the role; he is always clearly playing the same character that he did in the first film. His Frankenstein is no tortured, guilt-ridden weakling, unsure of his intent (as Colin Clive could be considered to have been); Cushing's Frankenstein is an elegant, graceful aesthete, a nobleman who, like others of his period, has the time, money and inclination to devote himself to scientific pursuits. As David Pirie points out in *A Heritage of Horror*, Frankenstein is a true dandy. He hums to himself in his laboratory, he reclines rather than sits, and he seems to be stylishly conscious of his clothes, although he doesn't mind smearing them with a little blood at times.

Cushing's Frankenstein has little use for outsiders. He also has little use for fame. He's intent on his goals, and as he is also cruel, ruthless and self-obsessed, he commonly tramples over the lives of those around him. He's a juggernaut. He has no compunctions about committing mayhem and mutilation (as here, in *Revenge of Frankenstein*), or murder (in several films) to achieve his goals. His sensuality, very much a part of *Curse of Frankenstein*, was soon leached out of him, leaving a gaunt, obsessed scientist. Never simply a *mad* scientist, distinctions like sanity and insanity simply don't matter to Cushing's Frankenstein.

The Revenge of Frankenstein begins precisely where *Curse* ended, with Victor on his way to the guillotine. He is rescued (offscreen) by Karl (Oscar Quitak), a deformed man referred to in available credits as "The Dwarf," although he's of average height.

Frankenstein sets up practice under the name "Dr. Stein" in Carlsbruck where, three years later, he's earnestly sought by romantically-inclined women as a possible husband for their daughters, and where he has come under scrutiny by the local medical board, as he's very popular yet refuses to join the board. He's also resident physician at a local poor clinic where he occasionally removes limbs from patients, though sometimes the limbs do not seem to require amputation. We know what he's doing with those removed limbs.

Dr. Kleve (Francis Matthews), a young local doctor, recognizes Dr. Stein as Frankenstein, and on threat of exposure blackmails him into making Kleve his partner. Even though by this Kleve would certainly seem to be potentially less than trustworthy, Frankenstein immediately shows him around the lab, located in a dingy part of town.

Here, he's got equipment similar to that used in *Curse* with some new refinements; when he brings his creations to life, for instance, he doesn't have to immerse them in a tank. But he does have other uses for tanks; in one, he has a disembodied tattooed arm (previously heavily established, and it turns up again later), and in another, a pair of eyeballs attached to a frame, hovering in the tank. Both are connected to a primitive artificial "brain" of tubing and wires; when Frankenstein waves a Bunsen burner at the hand, it twitches in fear; the eyeballs move around the tank to follow the flame. This gruesome scene is the best-remembered element of *The Revenge of Frankenstein*. It's so extravagant in its attempt at being horrifying that it becomes comic; the staring eyeballs would be hideously funny on their own.

Frankenstein has constructed a new body mostly out of the parts he's removed from the poor patients, and has promised it to deformed, twisted Karl, who occasionally stands around staring into the foggy case where the body hangs upright.

Karl has a chance encounter with Margaret Konrad (Eunice Gayson), a young woman of good family who arrives at the poor clinic to help out. He is immediately smitten, simply because she's kind to him. (Deformed characters in horror films often form these instant crushes on the leading lady.)

Soon enough, Karl's brain is transferred to the new body in a smooth operation, with a minor setback when the electrified body begins thrashing about and gives Frankenstein a good jolt when he grabs it.

Telling the new Karl (Michael Gwynn) not to make any sudden movements until he's satisfactorily healed, Frankenstein and Kleve strap him into a bed in a secluded attic room. However, a cynical patient (Richard Wordsworth) who sweeps up around the hospital tips off Margaret to this fact and she visits the new Karl without, of course, realizing they've met before.

Meanwhile back at the lab, Frankenstein tends to Otto, a chimpanzee with the transplanted brain of an orangutan, feeding him meat. He developed this un-chimp-like diet after the brain transplant; in fact, says Frankenstein, "Otto cannibalized his wife." He's serenely confident Karl will not go the way of Otto.

Frankenstein has also assembled *another* body out of filched spare parts, and this time (significantly) the creature looks exactly like Frankenstein himself.

Karl is freed from his bed by Margaret, and immediately returns to the laboratory to destroy his old body, for Frankenstein unwisely has told him of plans to exhibit the new and old bodies together. Karl is tired of being stared at. He encounters a drunken janitor, and in a poorly-motivated fight, the janitor clubs Karl over his tender head. This, understandably, rouses him to anger, and he kills the janitor. In an incredible scene, he stands gazing at Otto the oranganzee eating meat, then gazes down at the body of the janitor—and literally begins to *drool*. But he comes to his senses and rushes out.

He later encounters Margaret, who offers to help him. When alone again, Karl discovers to his horror that his old deformities are returning: his right leg has become stiff, his right hand has twisted upward into a useless claw, and his right eye is slowly shutting. And he's turning monstrous in behavior. He grabs a young girl and kills her; there's a slight hint that he also eats her, but in American prints at least, this is vague and inconclusive. He is pursued by police.

Frankenstein is at a fancy society party when Karl spies him through the window, bursts into the room, and collapses, crying out, "Frankenstein, help me!" before he dies.

This certainly exposes "Dr. Stein" to the local folks, but he tries to brazen it out before the medical council. He might have gotten away with it, too, but back in his hometown, the coffin of "Dr. Frankenstein" has been opened, and the body of a priest is found within (he was murdered by Karl at the beginning of the film).

Frankenstein returns to the poor clinic, but with the help of the sweeper, the patients have figured out just what Dr. Stein has been doing to them. He almost makes it out of the ward by force of personality alone, but they leap on him and beat him almost to death.

Kleve recovers the dying man, and takes him to the lab, where Frankenstein manages to mutter, "You know what to do."

Soon, in London, "Dr. Franck," with a mustache, monocle and tattooed arm, sets up practice. In the neatest trick in all the Hammer series, Frankenstein has become his own monster.

However, Hammer ignored this interesting development in later films; in fact, there seems to be nothing really connecting *Revenge* with *Evil of Frankenstein*, next in the series.

In some ways, *The Revenge of Frankenstein* is a peculiar film. There isn't much in the line of menace; Frankenstein himself isn't endangering anyone, other than his swiping of limbs, and he's not in any danger himself, until the end. After the transplant, Karl seems fairly placid, with occasional moments of anger. The business of cannibalism seems extraneous, added only to make an already extravagantly horrible movie more horrifying. The movie also doesn't have a plot, so much as it is an incident in the life of Dr. Frankenstein. Events don't progress to a climax that arises from earlier actions. Except toward the end, actions have no consequences, and some characters seem lacking in motivation, just doing what's necessary to keep the film moving. Kleve seems to have no function in the story at all, except to provide someone for Frankenstein to explain things to, and to make the brain-switch at the end. He doesn't even have a romance with Margaret, which is surprising considering the randy nature of many Hammer second leads. The unnamed patient played by Wordsworth simply seems to be a troublemaker; there's no good reason for him to tell Margaret about the strange patient in the upstairs room, nor for him to spill the beans to the other patients. Margaret herself seems to be in the film only because a woman was considered necessary in films of this nature; she doesn't have a relationship with anyone else in the story, except Karl, slightly, and her motivation for arriving to work at the hospital is insubstantial.

The Revenge of Frankenstein is a rather tame adventure in the life of the monster-builder, with occasional nuggets of gruesomeness. What interest the film does have—and it *is* interesting throughout—is simply in what's going to happen next. Events may not really connect, but something is generally happening, even if it's only Peter Cushing puttering around in the lab. It's a talky film, but not slow-moving.

Compared to *Curse*, it's more adult and responsible, which along with its much-improved production values, makes *Revenge* slightly the better film. It doesn't have the strange structure of *Curse*, in which the Monster is assembled *twice*; the monster in *Revenge* is much more interesting (if less horrifying). However, the film also lacks *Curse's* cheeky nature. *Curse* might be described as a smart-aleck adolescent horror film, while *Revenge* is more staid and adult. Both have their virtues, neither is outstanding. (The best in the series is, in American prints anyway, *Frankenstein Must Be Destroyed*, which is fast-paced, brutal, funny and touching, with Cushing's best performance as the baron.)

The film gives evidence of rewriting before production—there's a credit to Hurford Janes for additional dialogue—as well as indications of cutting and restructuring afterward.

For example, near the end, when Karl attacks the young woman he already has blood on his mouth, but we never saw how it got there. Later, there's an odd scene in which he stares at Margaret from a distance, but doesn't approach her. He seems less maniacal and distorted in this shot than he did just a few moments before, so perhaps this scene was originally intended to precede the murder of the young woman.

Rewriting is indicated in the scene in which the janitor attacks Karl. There's no reason for this, although the janitor's drunkenness was established earlier. Why he would suddenly (and gleefully) attack a stranger isn't clear. Nor is much of the action of the patient played by Richard Wordsworth, who isn't even the voice of sanity in the film (incredibly, that seems to be Kleve); he's just a sarcastic, grimy troublemaker.

The production values are very good; even though it wasn't much more expensive than the American International films of the same period, it looks more costly, simply because Hammer had a better art department and access to genuine older buildings, as at the time, the studio was housed in an older manor house, Bray.

The main factor that distinguished Hammer films from their American counterparts was that no matter how gory and exploitative they got, Hammer films did not play down to their audiences. They were cheap, yes, and every bit as money-hungry, but the films were better crafted, better written, and better designed than their American rivals. Hammer films were made for adults.

They were also far, far better acted. I've always assumed the British tradition of repertory theatre helped in this regard, but whatever the cause, Hammer films are among the best-acted horror and SF films ever made, as a group, and often featured outstanding performers. In the opening scene of *Revenge*, for instance, there are two comic grave robbers; one is Hammer regular Michael Ripper, almost the Hammer equivalent of Universal's Dwight Frye; the other is Lionel Jeffries.

While Jeffries' role is small, with hindsight it's easy to see why he would soon become one of Britain's most popular character actors. From 1960, when he appeared in *The Trials of Oscar Wilde* and *Two-Way Stretch*, Jeffries was much in demand; he appeared notably in *The Notorious Landlady* (1962), *The Wrong Arm of the Law* (1963), *The First Men IN the Moon* (1964), *The Secret of My Success* (1965), *Camelot* (1967, as King Pellinore), *Chitty Chitty Bang Bang* (1968), and many more. In 1971, he turned to writing and directing. Although all his films as director are interesting, his best is still his first, *The Railway Children*, although *The Amazing Mr. Blunden* (1972) is also fine. Jeffries still turns up as an actor occasionally, as in *Royal Flash* (1975).

Michael Gwynn is good as the new Karl, but the script seems deliberately to have left his character undeveloped, presumably so that the two actors playing the same role wouldn't have an uphill battle to seem to be the same person in two bodies. Gwynn is effective as Karl's deformities and fear gradually make themselves felt, but he's not one of the classic Frankenstein monsters. Gwynn was also good in *Village of the Damned*, and later turned up in *The Deadly Bees* (1967) and *Scars of Dracula* (1970). He had the starring role in *Question 7* (1961), and also appeared in *Dunkirk* (1958), *Jason and the Argonauts* and *Cleopatra* (both 1963). He was a good actor in general, but also lacked real distinction.

Eunice Gayson is gorgeous, but the character of Margaret is peculiarly conceived; she isn't even menaced, and seems puzzled at what's going on. Under the circumstances, it would have taken a far more vivid actress to make her presence felt. Gayson was in films as early as 1954, with *Dance Little Lady*, and was in both *Dr. No* (1962) and *From Russia with Love* (1963) as Sylvia Trench, a young woman James Bond had no time to romance. According to Steve Rubin's *The James Bond Films*, director Terence Young was a friend of Gayson's, and intended for her Sylvia to be a recurring character in the series, but *Russia* was her last Bond film—and apparently her last film of any sort.

Francis Matthews' role as Kleve is almost as desultory as Gayson's, and Matthews is too mild an actor to make much of an impression. His part is simply that of Lab Assistant, required to listen while Cushing tells him what he's going to do next. Matthews was in *Bhowani Junction* (1956) and *Corridors of Blood* (1963), and reappeared in Hammer's *Dracula—Prince of Darkness* and *Rasputin the Mad Monk* (both 1966), among several other films in the 1960s. In the 1967 British TV series, "Captain Scarlet and the Mysterons," he was the voice of Captain Scarlet.

But the central character, and most important and finest actor in the film is, of course, Peter Cushing. He plays Victor Frankenstein with delicacy, insight, humor, and Frankenstein's own precision. When Kleve first confronts him, Frankenstein is very carefully *dissecting* a roast chicken, which he then daintily eats with his fingers. Cushing's aloof absorption in this, and the care with which he slices the bird, are riveting; it's hard to listen to the dialogue.

The dialogue is above average for a Hammer film, and Cushing makes it vivid. "I swore I would have my revenge," Frankenstein tells Kleve. "They will *never* be rid of me." His icy delivery makes the line ring with conviction. Later he stands staring at the still brainless creature in its beautiful chamber: "He isn't born yet. But this time he is perfect. Except for a few scars, he's perfect." And you can feel the artist's love of his creation in the words.

He still hums a little tune occasionally, and still shows a waspish anger when things don't go right. Cushing seems fully at home in this part. He is the ultimate Dr. Frankenstein of the movies; not at all the character Mary Shelley created, he is still the most convincing of men. As David Pirie says about the character, "Frankenstein's complex and ambiguous character becomes a host for two distinct opposing forces, the one of generosity, self-sacrifice and exploration, the other of greed, cruelty and blasphemy." Cushing embodies all the facets and contradictions; while in more mundane parts, Cushing is some-times too carefully controlled, as Frankenstein this control translates into the scientist's mania, and his performance, even in shoddy films, borders on per-fection.

Terence Fisher's direction is uneven. On the one hand, it is clear and lucid, but on the other, he is ham-fisted about certain elements, such as the thudding establishment of that damned tattooed arm. When we see it for the first time (on its rightful owner), Fisher dwells on the arm so long we know for sure that we are going to see it again. And again. Fisher deals with the horror elements so literally, without any sense of excitement, that they often seem more silly than frightening. Even in 1958, we were past the point of considering such sights as a brain plopped into a beaker as being the height of horror. The most horrifying thing in *Revenge* is Gwynn's shuddering fear that his body is returning to its former crippled state.

Still, Fisher does manage some very effective shocks. After the janitor bashes Karl with a stool, we know he's going to come up angry, but Gwynn's sudden whipping around and his frozen grimace are unexpected and fairly shocking. At the end, when Karl bursts into the party, at first we suspect he might do something dreadful, and there's a nice uneasy anticipation. But thanks to Gwynn's miming and Fisher's staging, the scene becomes touching.

Cinematographer Jack Asher worked often for Hammer, photographing most of their earliest and best films, but his output was variable. He tended to overlight things, creating an air of unreality; he occasionally uses low-key lighting effectively, but by and large, his work on some of the Hammer films is undistinguished. On the other hand, in some, such as *Horror of Dracula* (1958), *The Mummy* (1959) and *Brides of Dracula* (1960), he's much better.

As was usually the case with Hammer, *Revenge* was disliked by the *Monthly Film Bulletin*, which gave the film its lowest rating. The reviewer commented on the film's "failure" due to its "contrived plot and a notable lack of pace and imagination.... Cushing's stylish and diffident performance serves only to underline the farcical effects of a crude and pedestrian handling of the little legitimate horror left."

"Powe" in weekly *Variety* thought it a "high grade horror film," but Jack Moffitt felt it was "a disjointed tale," and wondered why it was given the "rich and physically accurate period production" it has. He correctly points out that the script "lacks one of the basic essentials for a good horror tale – an anxiety for the characters being menaced."

Joe Dante, in *Castle of Frankenstein* #24, appreciated the film, feeling it benefited from "superior screenplay, better production and first-rate performances.... Jimmy Sangster's script endows the Baron with far more wit and eccentricity than was displayed in the original.... [T]his stacks up as Hammer's most intelligent Frankenstein film to date." Alan Frank (*Horror*) thought it had "excellent performances, first rate production values and Gothic atmosphere. But the script veers near to parody." Don Willis (I) thought it was an "offbeat little horror drama [that] is probably Hammer's best Frankenstein," and in (II) thought it had an "essentially pointless script" but a "cute ending."

In a way, it's not surprising that *The Revenge of Frankenstein* prompted this almost schizophrenic reaction in critics; the film is more than a little divided itself. On the one hand, the makers of the movie seem to have tried hard to come up with a legitimate variation on the Frankenstein theme, to give it an adult, responsible approach, but also to have scenes of gruesome horror. However, they neglected to provide a strong storyline. As a result, while interesting and graced by Cushing's fine performance, *Revenge* is a mixed bag of horrors. While it is neither as good as its supporters claim nor as bad as its detractors would have it, there's still plenty of evidence in the film to support both views.

Satan's Satellites

Usually judged better than its companion feature, *Missile Monsters*, this is another cut-down serial, *Zombies of the Stratosphere* (1952). The films have almost identical plots, the main difference being that in *Satan's Satellites*, the hero flies by means of a rocket pack attached to his back (a device that turned up in several Republic serials of this period), while in *Missile Monsters* he more conventionally uses an airplane. Other than that, the mixture is much the same, although *Satan's Satellites* is more vigorous and slightly less repetitious.

In both films, the actual cliff-hanger is not shown. At the end of a serial chapter, the hero was traditionally shown in a highly dangerous and presumably fatal situation. The beginning of the next episode would show how he got out of it. (Sometimes this involved outrageous cheats: for instance, we might see the hero fall off a perpendicular cliff, but the next week, the cliff had turned into a relatively shallow slope, and he would roll to a halt.) In *Satan's Satellites*, what we see are essentially chapter beginnings, so the heroes are continually getting out of peculiarly suspenseful situations.

Larry Martin (Judd Holdren) of the Interplanetary Patrol—apparently confined to Earth—spots a space rocket coming to land on Earth. The rocket is met by a truck driven by Earthly henchmen of the arriving Martian, Marex (Lane Bradford). Marex departs in the truck with the henchmen, while his own ship, manned by Narab (Leonard Nimoy, no less) and Elah (Robert Garabedian), takes off again. When Larry arrives in his Rocketman flying suit, both vehicles are gone.

Marex and the lead bad Earth guy call on scientist Dr. Harding (Stanley Waxman). Marex is here on Earth to plant a hydrogen bomb so that our planet will be knocked out of its orbit. The Martians will then move Mars into Earth's orbit, so they can have an improved climate. (This may be the only science fiction film in which a desire for sunny skies is the motivation of the evil aliens.)

Marex threatens to reveal to the American government that Harding is an atomic spy, and so forces the scientist's assistance in assembling the hydrogen bomb. (But why didn't Marex bring a bomb with him? Couldn't he get the parts on Mars? He gets them rather easily on Earth.)

As in *Missile Monsters*, once we learn of the alien's plan, most of the rest of the film consists of thwarted attempts by the bad guys to get their hands on needed parts, although they gradually do acquire everything they need.

Larry has a couple of partners: heroine Sue (Aline Towne), who has even less to do than women generally had in serials, and cohero Bob Wilson (Wilson Wood), whose purpose is to (a) hand Larry his flying suit, (b) hold Larry's jacket when he has to jump into water, as he frequently does, and (c) occasionally get Larry out of danger.

Through most of the film, there is one rescue or one narrow escape after another. For instance, Bob chases after Larry, hooked to a train, in a speedy little tank, and jumps from the tank to the moving train to effect the rescue. In his Rocketman suit, Larry lands on top of a truck, which brushes him off when it passes beneath a tree. There's a motorboat chase or two, climaxed by one craft plunging over a dam spillway. If nothing else, serials are anthologies of great stunts.

At one point, the bad guys get control of a big, steely robot, shaped rather like an old-fashioned hot-water heater with flexible arms and legs. Originally built for *Undersea Kingdom* (1936), it was revised for *The Mysterious Dr. Satan* (1940), and also turns up in the 1953 TV series-cum-serial, *Commando Cody, Sky Marshal of the Universe*. The robot was apparently always played (or inhabited) by the appropriately-named Tom Steele. In the full serial *Zombies of the Stratosphere*, the robot is used to rob a bank (in stock footage), but the robbery is only discussed in *Satan's Satellites*.

The heroes then get custody of the robot; while it is lounging around their office, the bad guys gain radio control of it, and it almost brains Larry with an axe. (It has powerful-looking claws, so an axe seems superfluous, but bad guys are sadists.) Larry and Bob easily overcome the robot.

Larry has long since discovered the cave that is the hideout of Marex and his playmates. What he has not discovered, however, is that an innocent pool of water in the cave (which has a suspicious-looking ladder descending into it) leads via a water-filled passage to another part of the cave where the real work is being done. Republic seemed inordinately proud of this underwater passage, and seemingly dozens of scenes are set there. Apparently all of Leonard Nimoy's little journeys through this passage are included from the serial. He gets wet more often in this serial than the entire cast of *The Poseidon Adventure*.

Larry has an inconclusive fight with Narab (really shot underwater) while trying to discover the secret of that underwater/underground passage, but returns to headquarters instead of pursuing Narab.

One other thing about serials: as in comic books, villains often feel that they must try to kill the hero in worrisomely complicated ways. They don't just shoot the jerk and get it over with, they have to lay elaborate death traps. In this case, the human henchmen sneak into the headquarters of the Interplanetary Patrol and repair the broken robot. Then, heh heh, Marex can use it to kill Larry and stop his confounded interference with Martian plans to get a suntan.

But Bob and Larry spot the robot when it gets up again. After a scuffle, they push it into a big bank of dials, levers, etc., and shout at Sue to "throw the main switch." She does, and in a big cloud of sparks, the robot bites the dust.

They return to the cave, where Narab sets underwater explosives. While Larry descends into the pool, Bob has a gunfight with some stray henchmen, but Larry manages to return just before the bomb can kill him.

In the next ten minutes, as he moves uranium in big cans from the known to the unknown side of the cave, Narab/Nimoy gets wet again and again and again.

Back to speedboats, as a superfluous henchman is killed following a big chase over the bay.

Larry has his own rocket ship, and he and his pilot try to follow the Martian rocket — which has been busy shuttling supplies from a secret island to the cave — but the Martians use a ray gun to fire a shell (yes) at Larry's rocket. It's a gas bomb, and, thinking fast, Larry uses a fire extinguisher to put out the gas.

Finally, the big showdown arrives. Bob and Larry chase the remaining human henchmen with the robot — the heroes have fixed it — and coldbloodedly shove the bad guys over a cliff to their deaths.

Meanwhile, in the secret cave, Dr. Harding gets cold feet and tells Marex not to set off the bomb. The Martian refuses, and kills Harding. When Bob and Larry come into the cave, the Martians use gas bombs to make their getaway. The idea of Martians fleeing in a sedan seems incongruous, but that's what happens here. Then they take off in their rocket.

Larry flies after them in his rocket and shoots down the Martian craft. Narab is the only survivor, and manages to gasp out the secret of the bomb's location before dying.

Larry zooms away in his Rocketman suit, enters the cave, climbs down into the water, makes his way to the secret entrance of the hidden half of the cave, climbs up into the secret cave, finds the bomb, and switches it off before it can explode.

Whew.

Allen M. Widem of the *Motion Picture Herald* seemed somewhat better disposed to *Satan's Satellites* than to *Missile Monsters*, and didn't seem to notice both were from serials. "Special effects are something to write home about – the world police fly realistically through space, apparently without the aid of such man-made contrivances as airplanes. The kids in the audiences will probably scream with delight." However, he judged it only "fair."

The *Monthly Film Bulletin* enjoyed the movie, rating it II. "This pocket serial has an unusually cracking pace and much spectacular action. The comic strip content is disarmingly artless, the continuity understandably erratic, and the hero's ability to fly at jet speed over mountains, thanks to his built-in-rocket-take-off unit, makes for extreme narrative mobility."

You can note such interesting sidelights as that the film is a sequel to *The Purple Monster Strikes*, or the fact that hero and villain alike almost always wear hats through their vigorous fistfights (the hats helped disguise the stunt men). Also, Rocketman's controls are arresting in their simplicity: beneath his bullet-shaped helmet, on his leather jacket, he wears a metal plate with three dials. They read ON OFF, FAST SLOW and UP DOWN. Even as a kid, I always wondered why, in the middle of a fight, the villains didn't suddenly flip the controls to ON DOWN FAST, and laugh in fiendish delight as Rocketman burrowed his way toward China.

She Demons

Astor turned out the worst science fiction/horror movies of the late 50s; never has less care or thought gone into a production company's films. All their releases, including *Giant from the Unknown*, *Missile to the Moon* and *Frankenstein's Daughter* are nearly unwatchable; all were directed by Richard Cunha. His *She Demons* is no better than the others, and in some ways, even worse. This one cost only $65,000, and looks cheaper.

This plot is simple but strenuously overworked. Spoiled heiress Jerrie Turner (Irish McCalla) and Fred Maklin (Tod Griffin) are among those shipwrecked on an uncharted volcanic island (improbably located near Florida). Fred has been searching for an island populated by animal people; there have been reports of women with beautiful bodies but hideous faces, and he's trying to learn if this has anything to do with the 30 women who disappeared from a nearby island.

On this island, which they learn is used as a practice bombing area, they find human footprints bearing marks of claws, and soon one of the crewmen is killed by a shapely woman with a hideous face. Later, the three remaining survivors, Jerrie, Fred and Sammy (Victor Sen Yung), see a flock of wildly dancing "She Demons" (the Diana Nellis Dancers) being herded around by some thugs dressed in SS uniforms, led by slobby Egore (Gene Roth).

Our heroes follow the group to a cave where Egore tortures one of the dancers. They eventually (and stupidly) follow him through a steel door into a laboratory, where Jerrie is captured by Egore who tells her that she's a prisoner of the German Reich, and that Herr Osler (Rudolph Anders) will be delighted to add her to his group of experimental subjects.

Fred jumps out and fights Egore as Jerrie and Sammy flee. Egore is grabbed by a group of caged She Demons and clawed to death. The She Demons escape, but Jerrie and her friends are captured by Osler's troops.

Osler tells them that he's one of the most wanted of all war criminals. During World War II, he'd been a Nazi scientist, experimenting on scar tissue replacement. On this island, he'd found a way to generate great amounts of electricity using lava, and powering his ray devices from this source, he'd continued his experiments. The research was aimed mainly at restoring the beauty of his wife Mona (Leni Tana), who was disfigured by a laboratory accident.

He's been drawing what he calls "Character X" from the captive women; this determines personal appearance, and seems to be genetic in nature. He infuses his wife with new Character X, but the restoration isn't permanent. He also adds Character X from animals to the drained woman, which turns her into a She Demon. After a while, her own face returns, but she retains the mind of an animal. Sometimes this sci-fi stuff becomes delirious.

Despite his ostensible loyalty to his wife, Osler makes a play for Jerrie, who rejects him; Mona sees this. Jerrie escapes into the jungle, where Mona meets her and gives her the keys to Fred and Sammy's cage, and tells her where a boat is hidden. Somehow by all this, Mona plans to regain her husband's love.

However, after Jerrie frees Fred and Sammy, all three are recaptured, and Osler decides to turn Jerrie into a She Demon. Mona tries to stop him just as the bombing practice runs start. Osler has never worried about the bombs before, but this time they start up the volcano, and he's engulfed in lava. Fred, Sammy and Jerrie flee on Mona's boat, and watch as the island goes up in smoke and flames. Fred and Jerrie, no longer a spoiled brat, find love.

There's nothing noteworthy about *She Demons*. The plot line is clichéd; it's only fodder for theatres, and no one involved could possibly have cared very much about it.

The story is an unimaginative blend of several traditional exploitation film themes: Nazi scientists continuing their work after the war, a mad scientist holed up on an island; the creation of monsters by making people into animals; the restoration of the destroyed features of a loved one. This latter theme dates at least as far back as *The Corpse Vanishes* (1942) and *Voodoo Man* (1944), both of which starred Bela Lugosi. In the 1960s, we were treated to such variations on this theme as *The Brain That Wouldn't Die*, *Face of Terror*, *Awful Dr. Orlof* (all 1962), *Monstrosity*, *Atom Age Vampire* (both 1963), *Corruption* (1968) and *The Blood Rose* (1970). The only good film with this theme was *Horror Chamber of Dr. Faustus*.

The "scientific" aspects of the plot are there just to keep things going, and to deliver the monsters of the title. The idea of "Character X" is not only preposterous, but rather dull. The idea of women monsters clearly preceded the restoration-of-disfigurement theme, and the latter was added only to explain the former, and the story is really about using animal traits to create monsters. (The film was so cheap, however, that they couldn't even afford any mean-looking animals in cages to show the source of the animal Character X; all we see are a few sad-looking pigeons.)

The makeup, credited to Carlie Taylor, is god-awful. It's not remotely convincing, nor do any of the She Demons look particularly animalistic; they are just lumpy with fangs. And Mona's famous disfigurement is never even seen. Urged to escape at the climax, she says, "Would you go if you looked like— this?" whipping off her bandages. All we see are her eyes.

There are no optical effects in the picture, but the mechanical effects of the destruction of the island are slightly more elaborate than you'd expect from such a rock-bottom picture. Some of the final destruction, however, is managed with the usual stock footage from the usual source: *One Million B.C.* The part that wasn't, however, was done with, surprisingly, sawdust—"sawdust mixed with a mudpack thing, as I recall," director Cunha told interviewer Tom Weaver in *Fangoria* #31. "We built a great big tank above [the set] and just filled it, and then I think they pumped steam through it to get the smoke and stuff out of it. We had a good time with that."

The script by Cunha and coauthor H.E. Barrie is dreadful, but does have a stab at character development in having heroine Jerrie change from a spoiled brat to a decent person. Furthermore, the storyline actually gives more for the heroine to do than the hero, who spends much of his time in a cage.

There are some outrageous lines in the script: as Egore whips the She Demons, he calls one a "Schweinhund," and later, during his battle with the hero, actually sneers, "that was your fatal mistake, American swine." The hero makes a request of Osler, and concludes, "—if there's any sense of decency left in that worm-ridden body of yours," which doesn't seem well-chosen for cooperation.

Weaver noted that *She Demons* contains more humor than most Cunha films. The director responded, "I was trying to get even with the world ... and just having a good time. These were really tongue-in-cheek films and we enjoyed doing them a great deal and had as much fun as possible.... So [the lines] were put in there purposely and I have to take all the credit for that."

Though some of Cunha's lines may be jokes, his direction is poor and the script is talky. There are long scenes of people wandering through the jungle to pad out the running time.

The acting is mostly terrible. Irish McCalla, famed for her TV portrayal of "Sheena, Queen of the Jungle" was exotically gorgeous (one of the few exotic blondes in films), but not much of an actress. As the head villain, Rudolph Anders reminds one of a hammy Aubrey Morris. Hero Tod Griffin is totally forgettable, but his sidekick is amusingly played by Victor Sen Yung, far too good an actor for this film. Head henchman was Gene Roth, a serviceable Nazi swine, who also turned up as sheriffs, seamen and other working-class types. Roth wasn't really much of an actor, but he had presence and a great, scowly Lee J. Cobb-Fred Clarke face. For more on Roth, see the entry on *Attack of the Giant Leeches*.

The film was not greeted with raves. Margaret Harford in the Los Angeles *Mirror-News*, termed it a "potboiler." The *Monthly Film Bulletin* gave the film its lowest rating, saying "the direction does nothing to enhance the lurid values of this impossible horror film.... The plot consists of a weary succession of convenient clichés, and the cast walk through their parts with noticeable lack of enthusiasm."

Today, *She Demons* is as unwatchable as the other Astor efforts. Though *Psychotronic* terms it, a bit ambiguously, "a true wonder," Leonard Maltin's *TV Movies* calls it a "dull cheapie" and Don Willis (I) is right in calling it "abominable."

The Space Children

This serious, well-intentioned film was the last 1950s-type SF film from Jack Arnold, the director who had done a lot to establish the genre. Unlike most of his other SF films, *The Space Children* has A Message, and is notably lacking in suspense because it's unthinkable for a film that presents children in this light to kill them off, or to make them menaces. The film is gentle and is compromised by this very gentleness. However, it's not a bad film, despite a misleading and even silly title, and as Arnold's farewell to the genre, it's worthwhile and respectable. It contains elements that would lead John Brosnan (*Future Tense*) to describe it as a "dull and pretentious children's film," but is also good enough that John Baxter (*Science Fiction in the Cinema*) is not wrong in describing it as "restrained and thoughtful." Brosnan's point, however, is well-taken: it was designed to appeal to the children many studios had concluded were the only profitable audience for this kind of film. It was originally scheduled to be released as a double bill with *Colossus of New York*, which also prominently featured a child.

The story is set on an isolated area of the California coast, about halfway between Los Angeles and San Francisco. A military base in the area is developing the Thunderer, a powerful missile with a hydrogen-bomb warhead, what would today be called an intercontinental ballistic missile.

The civilian scientists and workers on the missile project live in a nearby cluster of mobile homes and temporary housing. Dave Brewster (Adam Williams), his wife Anne (Peggy Webber), and their sons Ken (Johnny Crawford) and slightly older Bud (Michel Ray) are new arrivals at the settlement. They soon fit in, the boys finding friends among the other children, including Eadie (Sandy Descher) and older Tim (John Washbrook).

But while the family is driving to their new home, the car begins behaving strangely, and suddenly the boys—but not the adults—become aware of a mysterious presence. They are unable to tell anything about it.

Later, the kids talk among themselves about the Thunderer, by which they are sort of routinely impressed. But while playing on the beach one day, they see a strange beam of light stab down out of the sky, and watch as a small glowing object slides down the light (which some writers have called a "rainbow," although it isn't) to the ground.

They investigate, and discover a small, glowing blob of extraterrestrial protoplasm; it's a knotted oval resembling a brain. Although we never hear this thing's voice, it contacts the children, and they hide it in a seashore cave.

From this point on, the children set about sabotaging the rocket. Dave is introduced to the Thing, but he and the children don't agree on its goals. The Thing gives the children the power to stop trucks, open locks, and so forth. When Tim is chased by his angry, drunken father (Russell Johnson), the Thing protects him by killing the man. When the Thunderer is about to be launched, it explodes, and Dave, who has been mentally prevented from telling any other scientists about the Thing, leads a group of them to the cave where the children have hidden it.

The Thing, which has (unaccountably) been growing steadily throughout

Probably based on Vandenberg Air Force Base, established in 1958 to test ICBMs, later to launch spy satellites. — Bill Thomas

the film, slowly slides out behind the children, who are lined up to protect it. It returns to the sky, and there's the distinct suggestion that it has given the world a second chance. All over the world, other children have done the same thing.

After finishing *Monster on the Campus* at Universal, Jack Arnold followed his frequent producer William Alland to Paramount for *The Space Children*. Arnold seems to have cared more about the film than he had any other SF project since, perhaps, *It Came from Outer Space* (although *The Incredible Shrinking Man* remains his best film in the genre).

The story by Tom Filer or Tom Hanford is very different from the finished film. (Sources differ as to the correct name, although Filer is more likely; he wrote the slightly similar *Beast with 1,000,000 Eyes*.) Titled "The Egg," in some ways Filer's original idea is more interesting than *The Space Children*. The main elements they have in common are the setting, the idea of an alien presence contacting children, and a peaceful motive on behalf of the "invader." Here's the official Paramount brief synopsis: "Kathy, a young victim of polio, sees an object fall from the sky during a freak storm, and gets a mysterious message to protect the thing—a giant egg—for a period of ten hours. Against the wishes of her parents and neighbors, she frantically looks after the ominous ... object that grows to monstrous size and sends out vibrations that seem to threaten the very Earth. Authorities try to destroy it, until the egg absorbs the girl. It then mysteriously disappears. Now healed of her lameness, Kathy is left behind to assure her parents that it has all been a mistake. 'They' had not intended to land on the Earth."

Among other elements: as the egg lands, Kathy sees a cloud take on the shape of a huge bird. Kathy's dog is involved, and is engulfed by the egg; it can be seen through the egg. At the climax, the cloud appears again, and seems to talk to the egg. At the end, the egg hatches, but we were not to see what was within, although the people in the film were to see something beautiful.

"The Egg" would clearly present problems to any filmmaker. The story is slight for a full-length film, and most audiences would find the overtones of mysticism pretty silly. The sentimental business of the dog and a little crippled girl is a depressing cliché. But the story does have a virtue missing from *The Space Children*: it deals with the unknowability of alien motivations. Did the egg come to Earth to hatch? Was curing Kathy a side effect or a goal? Were the cloud and egg adult and infant? Unanswered questions about aliens which have a logic behind their potential answers are too often ignored in science fiction films, which tend to depict aliens as being just like us, only maybe funny-looking. But you are more closely related to penicillin than you would be to *any* creature from another world. Of American filmmakers, only Steven Spielberg, in *Close Encounters of the Third Kind* and *E.T.* has even come close to realizing that this mysteriousness can be an effective part of SF storytelling.

For the most part, in *The Space Children*, the potential for lyrical mystery is replaced by a thudding literalness. The globular Thing that replaces the weird egg looks like many another alien creature. As *Parents Magazine* said in its review of the film, "It's time a new gimmick to replace the revolting mass of brain-like tissue were used to represent materialized spirit." (An interesting idea only very faintly hinted at in the film is that the Thing might actually be an angel from Heaven.)

William Alland brought "The Egg" to the attention of Paramount, and then he and writer Bernard Schoenfeld presented a proposal to the studio as to how the raw material of the story could be altered into an effective film. To quote from this proposal, "Our film will retain the outstanding virtue of the original story: the unique method of handling the situation of a visit of Intelligence from Outer Space; the extra-terrestrial Intelligence ... *appealing to and employing the innocence of children*.... As the original story is conceived at present, it is highly lyrical and possesses only as much suspense and drama as a story of such limited scope could have.... From a symbolic point of view, the forces of Good—i.e., innocence and Intelligence, must be in conflict with the forces of Evil—man bent on destroying himself in total atomic war.... If an Alien Intelligence patrolling a Universe too huge to muster larger inter-terrestial [*sic*] policing on every planet, an Intelligence further incapable of absolute violence, were to undertake the prevention of [atomic war on Earth]—what better way for that Intelligence to assure control than *through the innocent minds of children?*" I suspect other ways, equally as effective, could be found, such as taking over the minds of military and political leaders.

Most of the suggestions in the proposal by Alland and Schoenfeld were followed in the finished film, including all suggested changes in the plot line. It seems clear that Alland may have had a more personal involvement in this film than he did in others. In various interviews, Jack Arnold has cited it as one of his films he likes the most.

Arnold, Alland and Schoenfeld tried hard to create an atmosphere of normalcy and reality in the film. The principal married couple, Dave and Anne, are depicted as not being any better than they should be. She's tired and tends to bicker from time to time; when strange things start happening, she's not swayed by the children's lack of fear, but is instead frightened and bossy. There's a good effort made to establish her unease. Peggy Webber, playing Anne, is plain and housewifely looking, rather than the slick beauties who populate similar films.

Although the husband is presented more conventionally, Adam Williams is an unconventional choice. He has thick, crudely sensuous features, and usually played unsympathetic characters or outright villains. His most noticeable role is as one of James Mason's two henchmen in *North by Northwest* (1959). But he was capable of projecting a kind of resolute sympathy, and he is quite good as the boys' understanding father. Williams had major parts in *Without Warning* (1952), *The Big Heat* (1953) and *Fear Strikes Out* (1957), but by the late 60s, his roles had declined in frequency and importance.

Michel Ray was a British child actor who made his first major appearance in *The Divided Heart* (1954). He was quickly brought to the United States, where he appeared in *The Brave One* (1956), a film made famous by winning an Oscar for blacklisted writer Dalton Trumbo, working under a pseudonym. Ray was also in *The Tin Star* (1957) and *Flood Tide* (1958), but seems to have retired from screen acting until 1962, when he played one of the two homosexual camp followers who attach themselves to Peter O'Toole in *Lawrence of Arabia*. The *American Film Institute Catalog* doesn't list any other 1960s appearances for him, and Leslie Halliwell does not include an entry on Ray in his *Filmgoer's Companion*, nor does Ephraim Katz in *The Film Encyclopedia*. Ray simply vanished.

He was an unusual child actor, in that for a boy, he was beautiful. His delicate, sensitive features and large, liquid eyes gave him a poetic and faintly haunted appearance, but he was also masculine and not pouty. He was a good choice as the leader of the children, and plays his role with understanding apparently beyond his years. He is the least "actory" of any of the space children.

Most of the other children are fairly standard Hollywood acting kids: they overplay their parts without meaning to, and seem unreal. Only Johnny Crawford and Sandy Descher seem to belong to the reality of the film. Crawford is probably best known as the son of TV's "The Rifleman," and Descher as the little girl found in the desert in *Them!*

The children's dialogue is not well-written. It is the usual movie-false language given to kids by adults who don't understand them at all well, but some of their actions are more believable than in other films of the period. For instance, before they come under the sway of the Thing, they are impressed by the destructive power of the rocket on which their fathers are working. One child, acting as a focus for its powers, forces a truck off the road, and smiles with satisfaction as the incredulous drivers realize the only person around was that kid on a bike.

Furthermore, the very core of the film, that children would want to protect their friend from adults who refuse to understand, is true to childhood. They fall into groups too conventionally—John Washbrook is too old, and is always on the verge of telling the adults—but the central idea that they must protect this wonderful Thing from adults who would destroy it is convincing and believable. Spielberg did much the same in *E.T.*, although few would have considered the lost little botanist a threat.

Arnold treats the sparse landscape of this film, a long, treeless shoreline and the expanse of the ocean, much as he did the desert in several of his earlier films. He wanted to find uncluttered landscapes where the interactions between people and the mysteries/menaces can stand out in sharper relief. He told Mark and Susan Turner McGee in *Photon* that he felt no special fondness for the desert, and later said to Bill Kelley (*Cinefantastique*, vol. 4, #2) that he "tried to use the beaches and the ocean [in *The Space Children*] the way I used the desert in *It Came from Outer Space.*" That is, for the bleakness, isolation, and lack of background clutter. In the *Cinefantastique* interview, and an interview I conducted with him myself, Arnold said that he always tried to establish the atmosphere at the outset of the film, and bleak landscapes had an instant atmosphere appropriate to the eerie stories he was trying to tell.

There's only one human "villain," played by Russell Johnson, a veteran of several SF films, including *It Came from Outer Space*, *This Island Earth* and *Attack of the Crab Monsters*. He plays a hard-drinking, brutal thug of a father, who when he finally chases Washbrook into the Thing's cave, gives every indication of being about to bash the kid's head in. The Thing kills him. The scene exists solely to indicate that the alien visitor means business, and is capable of killing to accomplish its goals and to protect its youthful helpers. Unfortunately, because the Johnson character is so clearly a bad guy and because no one else is, there's no feeling of threat at any other time.

Even the various military and scientific leaders at the base are not villains, in keeping with the proposal by Alland ("None are villains"). Some have praised the film for showing the usual gulf that exists between parents and children, but it is far more successful in showing that among these nonvillains, there's an unspoken fear: they always know what they are doing at the base, and what that means. As the proposal said, "Those living at this missile-launching project have become more and more afraid that the Enemy will launch the intercontinental ballistic missile before we are ready to retaliate."

Some of these fears are not really depicted, but there really is a melancholy sense of malaise, a feeling that everything is somewhat futile. The missile isn't for protection, it's for further destruction. It is to Arnold's great credit that he manages to infuse this idea into the film.

But the adult/children conflict is a consequence of the story, not the subject of it. The movie is not an allegory about adult/children relationships. It does have its allegorical aspects, mainly religious in tone: "Except ye be as little children, ye cannot enter the Kingdom of Heaven." Only the innocent can truly see goodness for what it is; the cynicism of adults prevents them from seeing this possibly literal heavenly messenger for the emissary of peace that it is. If the film is allegorical about anything else, it is more directed at youthful outlook versus hardening-of-the-imaginative arteries.

The music by Van Cleave is melodramatic and oppressive. A lighter, more delicate score would have been far more appropriate. The music continually gets between the audience and the film, instead of enhancing the responses the director wanted them to feel.

The Thing in the cave is a mistake; we shouldn't have seen it at all. It's too grotesque and too conventional to be interesting. According to *Famous Fantastic Films* #1, it wasn't easy to build. "The creature ... was constructed by Ivyl Burks, head of the [Paramount Prop Department]. It was made from a plastic material, a gelatinous mass that was tough but still able to transmit light. More than $3300 worth of neon lights were implanted within its core, which was then covered with strips of lucite and lemurith. The whole thing was welded together with acids. [At its largest] it weighed more than 1000 pounds and measure five feet wide, ten feet long, and five feet, six inches high. Also, the creature [pulsated], responding to an elaborate system of air pressure, controlled by a myriad of solenoids and needle valves and manifolds."

The film was greeted with a certain amount of respect. Giving it an average rating, the *Monthly Film Bulletin* said, "This moral tale achieves some success as an essay in science fiction for children and, apart from the frightening precocity of one of the child actors, it is convincingly presented." Jack Moffitt termed it "a distinguished little picture" that "adds the new element of tenderness to science fiction films." He praised the child actors, saying that they "manage while exercising horrific powers to be gently appealing at all times." "Gilb" in *Variety* said "basically, this is a crack, suspense thriller for the Saturday matinee trade [though] it's only too obvious that the mesmerized youngsters will succeed in foiling" the rocket launch.

John Baxter's praise for Jack Arnold on this film comes, as usual for Baxter, from slightly the wrong direction. "Ostensibly made for children," he says, "the film is so bleakly unsympathetic in its study of adults that it must have widened inestimably the gulf between the generations." Apart from the fact that this vastly overestimates the impact of the film, the adults in the movie are presented *sympathetically*. He adds that the film "contains the best of Arnold's mature work."

But as the talented director was working from a script distinctly inferior to some of his earlier films, the film can never quite reach their heights. It's always a little too slick, too conventional, too predictable; there's not enough suspense, there's too much talk (and some of that is comical). Some scenes are very good, and the whole film has an air of sincerity and conviction that is especially admirable coming during the downturn in quality of SF films, but it is not Arnold's best film by a long way.

Space Master X-7

This modest but somewhat sensationalistic little film would have more reasonably been titled "Invasion of the Blood Rust," but undoubtedly the title that was used (referring to a space satellite) was chosen because space travel had recently developed a sizzling topicality. Blood fungi were out, space satellites were in. I would not be at all surprised to learn that the working title was something more lurid. (In *Fantastic Films* #38, in fact, director Edward Bernds told interviewer Tom Weaver that the original title was "*Doomsday* something-or-other.")

It's a particularly difficult film to evaluate today, inasmuch as it does not seem to be in release to television, nor has it ever been reissued. And it certainly hasn't yet turned up on videotape. I have not seen it since 1958, and as a result, my memories are quite hazy.

The satellite Space Master X-7 returns from space carrying samples of a fungus it found there, and scientist Dr. Charles Pommer (Paul Frees) begins examining the spores in his New Mexico laboratory. His former wife, Laura Greeling (Lyn Thomas), shows up to argue with him about child custody. During the argument, they scuffle and Pommer's head is cut; the blood falls on the spores, as Laura storms out.

The fungus seems to really like the blood. It expands tremendously, bursts out of the container, and attacks Pommer who manages to warn security chief John Hand (Bill Williams) by phone before the fungus devours him.

When Hand and his partner Joe Rattigan (Robert Ellis) arrive on the scene, they find the lab covered thickly with big sheets of the fungus, which Pommer had named "Blood Rust." They destroy what they find with flamethrowers, and at first think the menace of Blood Rust was short-lived, but when they play back the recording on which Pommer was making his notes, they discover that a woman—whose identity is unknown to them—had visited the lab, and may be carrying spores of the fungus which Pommer felt covers the planet Mars, giving it its red color. She may be a "Typhoid Mary" of Blood Rust, which could destroy the world as Pommer felt it had destroyed Mars.

They begin a nationwide search for the woman, who is unaware of any of this, making plans to return to her home in Hawaii. When she learns of the efforts to find her, she becomes convinced that she's wanted for Pommer's murder, and so does not reveal herself.

On her way to Los Angeles to catch the plane, the Blood Rust bursts out of her luggage, kills the train's baggage man and permeates the baggage car. In Los Angeles, the frightened Laura hides out in a small hotel.

Eventually, after much documentary-style attempts at tracing her, Rattigan boards the same Honolulu–bound plane. He eventually finds her among the passengers, but by this time, out of her purse, Blood Rust has spread enough to begin to cover the plane. The plane returns to Los Angeles and makes an emergency crash landing at the airport. (The landing is stock newsreel footage and, of course the Blood Rust is not visible on the plane.)

The passengers are removed and decontaminated in the nick of time, and the plane is burned, destroying the last of the Blood Rust. I guess that's a good idea, but it also means the first extraterrestrial organism ever discovered is wiped out.

The reviews were moderate. Jack Moffitt thought it "a better than average

second feature.... A neat plot gimmick has the girl believe she's wanted for the scientist's murder.... The picture plays well with an audience and is better than many films of this calibre."

"Powe" at *Variety* concurred: "a competent science fiction tale with horror touches [that] runs out of story before it runs out of film, but for the lower half of a double bill, it is passable." *Motion Picture Exhibitor*'s unnamed reviewer felt that "performances are adequate, and direction manages to sustain interest. While the story contains little that is new, science fiction addicts should find it to their liking. It is a satisfactory addition to the program."

In *Fantastic Films* #38, Tom Weaver said, "What the film may have lacked in the way of marquee namebait it compensated for with a dogged documentary-style approach, on-location RegalScope photography and a riveting climactic scare scene." Alan Frank (*SF*) thought it a "brisk, if styleless mixture of suspense and science fiction."

Monthly Film Bulletin gave it a II, and said, "If one excludes the fairly absurd science fiction trimmings, the film follows the pattern of many location thrillers of the late 1940s. On this level, it is quite gripping in an elementary way, with some lively location shooting in railway stations, aerodromes and city streets. The fungus itself is rather insipid, resembling large quantities of omelette mixture."

Actually, Blood Rust was sheets of rubber. Liquid latex was whipped up slightly at Don Post's studios, and simply spilled in big puddles over a cement floor. It was peeled up, painted, and tossed over the sets in big sheets to play Blood Rust.

The film seems to be equally inspired by the "location thrillers" alluded to by the *Monthly Film Bulletin*, and by the Quatermass films from England. It's low-key and realistic, and attempts to deal with one specific menace that isn't even conscious, much less intelligent. It's a natural-disaster film, with the disaster being an alien fungus. Many real locations were used, all over Los Angeles, adding to the verisimilitude of the film. It's competent enough, and its total absence from TV is puzzling.

It's more interesting, overall, because of those who worked on it than for the film itself. Thomas Browne Henry, who has a small role, is that familiar stern, hook-nosed gentleman who often played generals when Morris Ankrum was busy elsewhere. Bill Williams was famous with kids at the time for being "Kit Carson" on television. Paul Frees, the doomed scientist, narrated the film and is, in fact, one of the most famous voice artists in Hollywood.

But the single oddest person among the cast is none other than Moe Howard of the Three Stooges. (His son-in-law, Norman Maurer, also worked on the film.) Director Edward Bernds had helmed many of the Stooges' shorts, and he and Howard were friends. The Columbia contract with the Stooges had just run out, and Howard was out of work after 25 years of banging various brothers and Larry Fine over the head. Bernds gave Howard the small part of a cab driver in the film, trying to describe the fugitive Laura; both Jack Moffitt and "Powe" singled him out for favorable mention.

George Worthing Yates wrote several SF films, and cowrote *Space Master X-7* with Daniel Mainwaring who scripted *Invasion of the Body Snatchers* (1956).

Opposite: Bill Williams, left, and Robert Ellis confront the menace of Blood Rust in this scene from Space Master X-7 (1958); the Blood Rust was created by tossing buckets of liquid latex over a cement floor. When hardened, it was painted appropriately and draped over sets.

Teenage Caveman

This absurdly-titled film is distinguished by a certain seriousness of purpose and a relatively intelligent approach to some of the rituals of the primitive tribe the title character belongs to; it also has an ending that surprised 1958 audiences. However, overall, it's one of director Roger Corman's most feeble efforts, with a heavy air of cheapness and an overabundance of stock footage.

The primitive tribe lives in a barren, rocky area. They are bound by the stern laws of the Symbol Maker (Leslie Bradley) and his comrades. The Law they follow outlines everything they must do, and is very serious about the one thing they must never do: go to the land beyond the river, where there is dirt that eats men. The danger across the river, says the Symbol Maker, is "called by a name – The God That Gives Death With Its Touch."

The son of the Symbol Maker, known in the credits only as the Boy (Robert Vaughn), is filled with curiosity about what lies over the next hill, and feels that there must be knowledge somewhere that he could apply to the betterment of the conditions of the tribe. He continually asks questions but gets few answers. The Boy feels that there is "food beyond the river, food beyond the burning plain." He tells someone that "the Law is old but age is not always truth," the standard complaint of youth.

Three men guard the Great Gifts of Man; Fire, the Thing That Turns (a wheel, never put to use), and Breaking Things (pottery). They use their ritual magic to try to attract prey; there's a moderately interesting scene of the tribesmen on a hunt, with much shaking of rattles and many tracking shots. Unfortunately, the hunt culminates with the tribe killing the phoniest-looking bear in cinema history.

The Boy leads a group of other young men of the tribe on a hunt for more game, heading into the Forbidden Area across the river. They see the usual lizard fight from *One Million B.C.*, and a big monitor lizard from the same film clambers over a rock. One of the youths, disingenuously called the Fair-Haired Boy (Beach Dickerson) is devoured by the "dirt that eats men," quicksand, and except for our hero, all the other young men head back to the caves. (Almost all of the film is shot in and near Bronson Caverns and other areas of Griffith Park.)

The Boy goes on alone, and sees a variety of monsters, mostly more stock footage from *One Million B.C.*, but also a few shots from *Unknown Island*. There is a brontosaurus, a tyrannosauroid with a snake in its mouth (unused footage from *One Million B.C.*, according to *One Million B.C.* expert Don Glut), *very* large armadillos, Gila monsters, and a baby alligator with a rubber fin on its back.

Finally, he sees (but we see only a shadow) a mysterious, man-shaped monster; this is too much even for his inquiring mind, and he flees back toward his tribe. He's helped along his way by being pursued by wild dogs. Before he gets home, he takes time to invent the bow and arrow, and kills a stuffed deer.

He's met by his father, who takes him back to the tribe, but though the other people demand the Boy's death for breaking the Law, his father's respected position as Symbol Maker persuades the tribe to reduce the punishment to exile, until the Boy becomes a man.

A young woman of the tribe, called the Maiden (Darrah Marshall), falls in love with the Boy and goes to live with him in his cave. After a time, he is forgiven and is initiated into the tribe in a long ritual.

His bride is coveted by the villain of the piece, named the Villain (Frank De Kova) in the credits, who is solidly on the side of tradition, fear and superstition. When a dying stranger arrives from the desert, and collapses, the Boy is once again filled with a desire to see what lies across the river. He heads out into the wilderness to kill the creature he saw before, the God That Gives Death With Its Touch.

The Villain rouses the wrath of the tribe, who march off to find the Boy and destroy him for his heresy, but by the time they catch up with him, he has again encountered (and killed?) the monster, which turns out to be a very old man in a radiation-proof suit, who carries a book with him.

We learn at this point that the story is set not in the past, but in the future, after the world has been destroyed by atomic war. The old man, now dead, narrates the tag. He tells them (through the book they can't read?) that after the war, there were horrible mutations of man (shots of the She-Creature and of the mutant from *The Day the World Ended*), and the old beasts (dinosaurs) were revived. His radiation suit kept him alive many years longer than his normal span of years, but the suit itself was radioactive, and he did kill with a touch.

Instead of The End, it's The Beginning again.

Partly because of novelty, its setting and surprise ending, *Teenage Caveman* has some appeal, but it is also slow-paced and uninteresting. Furthermore, the same gimmick had been used before in comic books and science fiction short stories; it bore a resemblance to *Captive Women*, a movie of a few years before. According to Joe Dante, Corman based the film (without securing the rights) on Stephen Vincent Benét's often-anthologized 1937 novella, "By the Waters of Babylon."

Corman was not displeased with the film.* "Aside from its horrible title," Corman told Naha, "*Teenage Caveman* was a pretty good film. We shot it under the title *Prehistoric World*, and I almost died when I saw it emerge with AIP's new title." He told di Franco's interviewer that it played under the *Teenage Caveman* title "in only one or two theatres before the title went back to *Prehistoric World*." In fact, although some of the posters for the film had the words "Prehistoric World" pasted over the words "Teenage Caveman," the film did play almost everywhere under the title Corman disliked. (It was called *Out of the Darkness* in England.)

Corman's initial interest in the idea was the ending, plus the varous aspects of ritual, and those are the strongest elements of the film. "You follow a prehistoric tribe with very strange customs and unusual culture and a very complicated religion," he told Naha, "you follow [a young man growing up in that tribe] in his initiation into the religion and the mysteries.... The picture ends with him looking at the book, with the implication that civilization will now start once more."

---

*His interviews tend to sound very much alike, so I've interspersed quotes from both Ed Naha's The Films of Roger Corman: Brilliance on a Budget, and The Movie World of Roger Corman, edited by J. Philip di Franco. Although both of these books on Corman are inadequate and rather redundant, they are both must-haves for the true Cormanphile. But if a choice must be made, it should be for the Naha book, despite quotes from many people who worked for Corman that enliven di Franco's book, which is much harder to locate and cheaply produced. Which is, considering the subject matter, appropriate.

Corman told both interviewers that he was unhappy with the prop deer that Vaughn had to "kill" with his little bow and arrow. "I told [the prop man] I didn't want this stiff deer, and he told me it was this stuffed deer or no deer. So we shot the scene with Vaughn carrying this petrified animal through the woods." He added in the other interview, "At the sneak preview the picture was really playing well—I mean the people liked the film. Then that shot came on, and the people laughed as they saw the ridiculous deer. It was the only thing I later cut out of the picture." It must have been much later, because the shot with the deer exists in all prints of the film that I've seen.

Corman told di Franco's interviewer that "if the picture suffered, it was for the same reasons as *Viking Women* [another Corman film of the period]: we were trying to do too much in ten days, with a budget under $100,000, and the shallowness of the production showed." He told Naha, "It was a very successful film, but I've always thought of it as a [missed] opportunity. With a few more days and a little bit more money, we could have made a genuinely good film instead of a pretty good one."

In the di Franco book, actor/propman/general factotum Beach Dickerson told the interviewer about his involvement in the film. After his death in the quicksand bog shot at the Los Angeles Arboretum, he thought he was through as an actor. But Corman wasn't one for wasting talent. "We moved to Bronson Canyon in Hollywood," Dickerson said, and I'm sitting in this wagon, and [Corman] says, 'What are you doing *here*?' I say, 'Well, they're having my funeral.' He says, 'Who the hell will recognize you? Get over here immediately.'" And Dickerson wound up playing a tom-tom at his own funeral.

But Corman wasn't through with him yet. When the Man from the Burning Plains rides in on his spavined old horse, in a bearskin and heavy beard, it's Dickerson again. He's no stunt man, but Corman insisted he could fall off a horse as well as anyone. He dies again, saying "Peace" as he expires; Dickerson was pleased to have two death scenes in one film.

But Corman had further use for him. Dickerson is also the awful bear that lumbers down a hill near the beginning of the film. He was just getting into the ferocity of his part when, "I hear this low voice say 'kill the bear!' and thirty people jump on me and beat the hell out of me." So he ended up with three death scenes in one film.

Teenage Caveman was written by R. (Robert) Wright Campbell. *Man of a Thousand Faces* (1957), his script cowritten with Ivan Goff and Ben Roberts, was nominated for an Academy Award. In the same year, Campbell also wrote the scripts for two slightly offbeat Westerns with Fred MacMurray, *Quantez* and *Gun for a Coward*. But he'd already worked with Corman, and after 1958, wrote almost exclusively for the producer-director. For Corman, Campbell wrote or cowrote *Five Guns West* (1955), *Machine Gun Kelly* (1958), *Dementia 13*, *The Young Racers* (both 1963), *The Masque of the Red Death* and *The Secret Invasion* (both 1964). His script for Richard Rush's *Hell's Angels on Wheels* (1967) was considerably above average for a biker film, and helped to establish Rush's reputation. Campbell also contributed to the script for *Captain Nemo and the Underwater City* (1970), originally scheduled for Corman.

Campbell wasn't as idiosyncratic or novel as Corman's other most inter-

Opposite: Stalwart Teenage Caveman (1958) Robert Vaughn is a picture of mild nervousness as he confronts the God That Gives Death With Its Touch (a man in a radiation suit)—in Roger Corman's stilted but earnest SF epic. The suit is the same one used in Night of the Blood Beast; see page 150.

esting writer, Charles B. Griffith, but he wrote intelligently and with some skill. Though the dialogue in *Teenage Caveman* is ponderous and pompous, it shows care. Campbell tries to embody the traditional adult/youth conflict into the fabric of the story, though that is clichéd.

The Big Surprise ending, wherein it's revealed that all this has taken place in the future, rather than the past, has something of a feeling of having been tacked on during rewrites, but it wasn't. Near the end, the Things of the Gods are shown to Vaughn, and they are indeed puzzling artifacts, but there should have been further hints that this isn't the past.

The lack of names is an error; even the most primitive tribespeople have names, sometimes several for different aspects of their lives. Campbell doesn't seem to have done anthropological research, but relied instead on logic.

The movie doesn't pretend to offer solutions; it's just a simple warning, something a little odd to find embedded in a cheap exploitation picture, but it was just that kind of thing that set Corman's pictures apart from (if not always above) the kind of movie turned out by his contemporaries. *Teenage Caveman* may not actually be *better* than, say, *The Flame Barrier* (of the same year), but it is more intelligent, and actually has a point of view as well as something to say.

Many people have assumed that *Teenage Caveman* was Robert Vaughn's first film, but he had already appeared in *The Ten Commandments* (1956) in several bit parts, *Hell's Crossroads* and *No Time to Be Young* (both 1957) before *Teenage Caveman*, and perhaps was in others as well.

He was entirely unsuited for the part of the Boy, and turns in what is undoubtedly his worst acting job in films. He was at a loss, the part was beneath him. A less gifted actor could have played the role much better. Vaughn is an intelligent man, and as with some other intelligent actors, such as Dustin Hoffman, Alan Arkin and Martin Sheen, his intelligence sometimes comes between him and a performance: he visibly *thinks* his way through it, rather than becoming the character; the thought shows more than the performance.

Shortly after this film, he began to be noticed for his cold-eyed, tight-lipped and upper-crust villainy in a variety of films, but it was his playing Napoleon Solo in the TV series "The Man from U.N.C.L.E." that clinched his fame. (He recently revived the role in a TV movie.) Since U.N.C.L.E., he has provided good support in a wide range of roles, although he is by far at his best when being a ruthless, intelligent villain, as in *Bullitt* (1968), *S.O.B.* (1980) and the unfortunate *Superman III* (1983). However, he was also fine in an uncharacteristic part in *The Mind of Mr. Soames* (1969) and had fun sending up his *Magnificent Seven* role in *Battle Beyond the Stars* (1980). He was the voice of the supercomputer in *Demon Seed* (1977), seemed out of place in *Starship Invasions* (1977), had a brief role as a dying senator in the little-seen *Virus* (1980), and played a ruthless politico in *Hangar 18* (1980).

Vaughn is one of the few actors in Hollywood to have received a Ph.D. (in political science); his doctoral thesis, a study of the Hollywood Blacklist, was published as *Only Victims*. He's still very active as an actor both on television and films. He's a reliable supporting player, but it's unlikely that his range will ever be expanded much; he's just too believable as a coldhearted, ambitious intellect.

Darrah Marshall is unacceptable as the Boy's bride, but Leslie Bradley and Frank De Kova are professional if hammy in the other two leading roles. Veteran cinematographer Floyd Crosby can add little to the quality of the movie; when you're shooting outdoors for ten days (probably less), you take what you get.

"Powr" in *Variety* found some merit to the film, saying it was "somewhat surprisingly a plea for international cooperation in terms of the dangers of atomic radiation.... [In] theatrical terms, it doesn't always sustain, but the 'message' is handled with restraint and good taste." He also felt that the "action in the story isn't always strong enough to keep the excitement keyed very high," and while the screenplay "tends to get a little heavily symbolic at times [at least] its symbols are fresh and thoughtful and the ending is provocative."

Jack Moffitt didn't really review the film; he commented on the young audience with which he saw it and its cofeature *How to Make a Monster* at a local theatre, but did say "Robert Vaughn, as the principal teenaged caveman, plays his part with a fixed skeptical expression which indicates that he doubts everything he sees. This can well be possible. He lives in a region where the principal game is taxidermist's deer."

John Baxter felt the film was a "clever Z picture given some ingenious twists by Roger Corman," which seems to ignore the contribution of R. Wright Campbell. "Cleverly contrived," Baxter goes on, "Corman's world is odd enough to be subtly wrong despite its similarities to prehistoric film worlds we know.... *Teenage Caveman* is a good example of Corman's genius." However, one of the problems with *Teenage Caveman* is precisely that it *does* look like every other prehistoric picture we've seen; any subtle differences are equally attributable to the cheapness of the production as to hints that it's set in the future. I don't deny the possibility that such hints are there, but they are mild and meaningless.

Psychotronic said that "in an interview Vaughn called it 'one of the worst films of all time.' He probably said that before starring in *Starship Invasions*." Alan Frank (*SF*) seems to be talking about some other film: "engaging low budget youth-oriented picture with dreadful special effects but a definite naive charm."

Teenage Caveman seems to be one of Roger Corman's most perfunctory films: get the shot and get going to the next. In some of the other films of the period he does try for some stylization, but with this quickly-shot, cheap outdoor film, the direction apparently consisted of simply telling everyone when to start and to stop acting. It is more notable as a film *produced* by Roger Corman, than one directed by him.

Teenage Monster

Undoubtedly filmed in a great hurry, this dull, silly film was known as *Meteor Monster* while shooting, and is shown on television under that title, which is more appropriate anyway, as the monster is not a teenager. This film is a true "B movie" in that it was made to support the bottom half of a double bill, with the much better *Brain from Planet Arous*.

The storyline of *Teenage Monster* is peculiar, considering the title; "teenage" in a movie title had come to promise black leather jackets, quarrels with parents, rock music and ducktailed hairdos. *This* is a Western. Undoubtedly retitled to cash in on this market, but clearly without caring whether or not teenagers would even like the damned thing, "Meteor Monster" became *Teenage Monster*.

In the Old West, a fireball shoots out of the sky and strikes the miner husband (Jim McCullough) and son Charles (Stephen Parker) of Ruth Cannon (Anne Gwynne). The husband dies, but the son seems to recover. Over the years as the boy grows, however, he becomes hairy, ugly and stupid, occasionally killing sheep and cattle. Seven years later (after the fireball? sources aren't clear), Ruth's perseverence in working the mine pays off; she strikes pay dirt.

Moving into town with Charles (now Gilbert Perkins), whom she always keeps hidden, Ruth is befriended by Sheriff Bob (Stuart Wade). Ambitious waitress Kathy (Gloria Castillo) eventually learns of Charles' existence, and blackmails Ruth with threats of disclosure of the horrible son.

Kathy gradually wins Charles' trust, and has him kill a few people for her out of revenge. "Oh, Charlie," sighs Ruth, "you've been bad again, haven't you?" Eventually, Kathy goes too far; while they're out in the countryside, she tries to induce Charlie to kill his own mother, but he refuses and kills Kathy instead. Sheriff Bob, just arriving, shoots poor Charlie who cries "Mama!" and falls off a convenient cliff, allowing Sheriff Bob to get both Mama and her gold.

As Don Willis (I) said, the film is an "indescribable mixture of horror and pathos," and neither element works.

Charlie isn't really a monster, teenage or meteor, he's just a "huge hairy imbecile" (as "Neal" in Variety put it), a brute with the mind of a child. It's somewhat unclear as to why Ruth keeps Charlie hidden; he's a burden on her, and seems capable of being institutionalized. But then, who can explain mother love?

There's no logic in Charlie's plight. The stock-footage meteor that strikes down father and son goes without any discussion whatsoever. Something from outer space can do all kinds of strange things, and cheesy writers like Ray Buffum felt that meteors were the equivalent of a magic wand. You need a big hairy brute, so a meteor comes by, and hey presto, there's your big hairy brute.

The film is pedestrian, a boring, tepid, unimaginative piece of junk. Clearly, no one connected with the picture thought of it as anything other than a product. Producer-director Jacques Marquette, better known as a cinematographer, exhibits here the lowest kind of cynical nonconcern with his material and for the audience. Asked about the movie years later by Mark McGee, Marquette could barely remember the film. He told the admirable Tom Weaver a good deal about it in Fangoria #39; the budget, for instance, was $57,000.

Joe Dante adds, "you might mention this is probably the most depressing horror film of the 50s; it's like 'Revenge of the Retard.' The monster is uncomfortably imbecilic and handicapped, and moans and wails throughout in a most clinical and unpleasant manner. Also, it's one of the comparatively few horror–Westerns, two genres that are seldom mixed, and no wonder." To the best of my knowledge, there are no good Western horror films, although there have been several attempts this way, including Curse of the Undead, Billy the Kid vs. Dracula and Jesse James Meets Frankenstein's Daughter.

Probably the only aspect of any interest about Teenage Monster is the presence of Anne Gwynne in the cast. She was an ingenue at Universal pictures during the 1950s, apparently their substitute for Evelyn Ankers as horror heroine, although their careers overlapped; both were in Weird Woman (1944), for instance. Among the horror and thriller films Gwynne appeared in during that period were Black Friday, the serial Flash Gordon Conquers the Universe (both 1940), The Black Cat (1941), The Strange Case of Dr. Rx (1942), Murder in the Blue Room (1944) and House of Frankenstein (1945). Indications are that when Universal became Universal-International and tried to upgrade their image, Gwynne's contract was dropped, as her last Universal film was in

1945. She also appeared in the peculiar *Charlie McCarthy, Detective* (1949), *The Ghost Goes Wild* and *Dick Tracy Meets Gruesome* (both 1947). *Teenage Monster* was her first film in many years, and she didn't appear again until *Adam at 6 A.M.* in 1970. She doesn't seem to have made anything since.

In the 1940s, Gwynne was a pretty redhead, but although she aged reasonably gracefully, her limited acting ability makes her no more interesting than any other moderately attractive actress. She was typical of those who were made stars (for their looks) by profit-minded studios, and who suffered when studios began retrenching in the 1950s. And who often found themselves in films of this nature by the late 50s.

The other cast members of *Teenage Monster* are typical featured players in low-budget films: young starlets, like Gloria Castillo, attempting to make their mark, and all-purpose supporting players, like Stuart Wade, who are taking one of the few chances they get at starring in a film. Castillo also appeared in *Night of the Hunter, The Vanishing American* (both 1955), *Reform School Girl* (1957) and *You've Got to Be Smart* (1967). Wade had small parts in a variety of films, mostly for Universal, including *Tarantula, Tammy Tell Me True* (1961), *Lonely Are the Brave* (1962) and *The Brass Bottle* (1964). He was the star of Roger Corman's *Monster from the Ocean Floor*.

Gilbert Perkins plays Charlie as an adult. The performer is clearly no teenager, but a man near his fifties, covered with shaggy hair. Gilbert Perkins is the same as Gil Perkins, a character actor and stunt man whose career stretches at least from 1933 to 1977. Perkins appeared in a variety of films during that period, including *King Kong, Captains Courageous* (1937), *Father of the Bride* (1950), *Abbott and Costello Meet Dr. Jekyll and Mr. Hyde, Spartacus* (1960), *Valley of the Dragons, Batman* (1966) and *Sourdough* (1977), in which he played the leading role. Whatever Perkins' abilities as an actor might be under more favorable circumstances, his performance in *Teenage Monster* didn't garner him any laurels. Charlie the Hairy Imbecile, the 50-year-old teenager, is just a shaggy menace speaking in baby-talk.

The makeup was by the great Jack Pierce, here in his declining years. The makeup on Charlie is elementary: mounds of fake hair, including a beard, and slight makeup on the parts of the face that are visible. Pierce was one of the true giants in the field of makeup, not only for execution, but for the unforgettable qualities of his design. He was the resident makeup artist at Universal during the golden years of horror films; he invented the most famous Frankenstein makeup of all, that which originated with Boris Karloff. Pierce also designed and executed Karloff's *Mummy* makeup, Henry Hull's in *The WereWolf of London* (1935) and Lon Chaney, Jr.'s in *The Wolfman* (1941). After about 1944 however, Pierce was free-lancing, perhaps because he was, according to some sources, an acerbic, cantankerous, self-styled genius. Bud Westmore took over Universal's makeup department, and Pierce never again had a job as studio department head. His last full-scale makeup of record was for the 1963 *Beauty and the Beast*, in which he, somewhat sadly, recreated the Lon Chaney, Jr. Wolfman makeup. He also did work on other minor SF films of this period, including *Giant from the Unknown* and *Beyond the Time Barrier*.

Jacques Marquette, who produced and directed *Teenage Monster*, made other SF and fantasy films during this period, including *Brain from Planet Arous* and *Attack of the 50 Foot Woman*. He was executive producer and cinematographer on *Flight of the Lost Balloon* (1961), which seems to have been his last film as anything other than cinematographer. In that capacity, he worked on *Creature from the Haunted Sea, Varan the Unbelievable, Trauma* (1962), *The*

Strangler (1964) and *Arizona Raiders* (1965). At that time, Marquette's career took a considerable jump in prestige, and he filmed *The Wicked Dreams of Paula Schultz* (1968), *Fuzz* (1972) and *Burnt Offerings* (1976), among others. He is far better as a cinematographer than he ever was as a producer or director. He took over direction of *Teenage Monster* when the scheduled director bowed out at the last minute.

Understandably, reviews of *Teenage Monster* were hardly favorable. After suggesting the idea had some potential, Charles Stinson in the *Los Angeles Times* said "but the idea was demolished by sleazy production, absurd casting ... and an utterly darling script." "Neal" in *Variety* said, "This is a silly bit of nonsense.... Majority of the players way overact under [Marquette's direction]." James Powers in *Hollywood Reporter* said the film was "weaker" than its cofeature, and pointed out "that the monster is more pitiful than horrible; [another flaw] is that he never seems a teenager.... It would have given the picture strength if the youthful and undeveloped character of the monster had been established better." Or at all.

Teenage Monster was filmed on standing Western sets and at the ever-popular Bronson Caverns in Griffith Park. If the shooting schedule was more than five days, something must have gone wrong. When this film was first released, there probably was some annoyance when audiences realized it was just a Western, but that annoyance couldn't have lasted long: this is the kind of movie that turns the brains of audiences into cottage cheese. Who could have cared anything about it at all?

Terror from the Year 5,000

This modest film is somewhat interesting for an imaginative premise, and is the first American feature film I know of to depict a time machine. Scientific time travel via machine turned up in some serials, notably *Brick Bradford* (1947), and there was accidental time travel in *World Without End*. (The public was familiar with time travel from the comic strip "Alley Oop.") Furthermore, the story is scaled to the limitations of the budget. Knowing his limitations made producer-writer-director Robert J. Gurney, Jr. a little unusual for the period; Roger Corman's ambitions, for instance, sometimes far outstripped his budget's ability to deliver. Finally, *Terror from the Year 5,000* is certainly different in featuring a four-eyed cat and hypnotic fingernails.

According to Forrest J Ackerman, the film was derived very loosely from "Bottle Baby," a short story by Henry Slesar; by the time it reached the screen, it underwent so many changes that the story was almost unrecognizable. Slesar received no screen credit (and, says Ackerman, very little money); Gurney takes sole writing credit.

On an island in Florida, Professor Howard Erling (Frederic Downs) and his assistant Victor (John Stratton) materialize a strange statue in a chamber in their laboratory; they don't notice a face briefly appear in negative over the statue. Impatient, rich Victor is financing the project; "You know I wouldn't walk out," he tells the older professor, "and you know why." (But we don't; vaulting ambition, apparently.)

Erling sends the statue to former student Robert Hedges (Ward Costello), now an archaeologist living in New York. The odd statuette intrigues Hedges, and acting on a suggestion from Erling, he subjects it to a carbon-14 dating process, and gets a date 3,000 years in the future. Although this is sheer fantasy — even if the object really was from the future, the test couldn't give such results — it's still a striking idea.

Robert also discovers the statue is highly radioactive, so dumps it in a bucket of water. He fears Erling may have flipped out and is trying to murder him with radioactivity, so he leaves for Spooner Beach, Florida, to confront Erling directly.

He and the professor's daughter Claire (Joyce Holden) have a meet-cute scene after a mild car chase, and Hedges learns that she sent the statue on her father's behalf. Erling had some problems, she says. Robert goes with her to the island laboratory, where Victor, who is engaged to Claire, is immediately hostile to him. Victor sees Hedges as a rival for both the professor's attentions and Claire's affections.

Victor sneaks off into the swamps with something in a suitcase, and Robert follows him. Meanwhile, handyman Angelo (Fred Herrick) is spying on Claire as she swims. He leaves, and Robert and Claire talk about the experiments. He learns that the mysterious machine in the laboratory is a time machine, which they have been using to *trade* for objects from the future. The first activity of the explorers of any new region, Hedges is told, is barter, trade. To demonstrate, they send a Phi Beta Kappa key forward in time, and it is swapped for a medallion with more Greek writing, which says "Save us."

Against Erling's wishes, Victor runs the equipment himself alone, and an arm reaches out of the chamber at him. Victor is injured in the struggle, and the arm returns to the future. Later, Victor tries to kill Robert as he starts to dive for the object Victor threw into the water earlier. After a fight, Hedges subdues Victor, who proves to have radiation burns where the arm grabbed him.

While Bob, Claire and Erling go to a movie (*I Was a Teenage Frankenstein* — AIP never missed an opportunity for self-promotion), Victor escapes from the hospital and returns to the island where he fires up the machine. This time, he gets a living woman from the future, who strides out of the machine like a clockwork doll, arms swinging stiffly. She's dressed in skin-clinging black tights, and is obscured by white dots added optically to the film. She screams with her mouth closed and pounces on Victor.

Bob dives into the lake and recovers the object Victor tossed in: a suitcase containing a dead, four-eyed cat. Bob immediately recognizes it as an atomic mutation (not bad for an archaeologist).

The Future Woman is now hiding in the forest on the island, and follows a nurse (Salome Jens) who arrives alone, apparently to tend Victor. She speaks to the nurse in Greek (the Phi Beta Kappa key led future people to expect everyone in our time to speak Greek) but switches to English when she realizes her error. The nurse flees, but the Future Woman chases and kills her. She then uses a device she (must have) brought from the future to steal the nurse's face (leaving the dead woman's features a ghastly blank), and alters her own radiation-distorted face to duplicate that of the dead nurse. The Future Woman (now played by Jens) then goes on to the house, where she introduces herself as the nurse.

Recovering from his attack at the hands of the Future Woman, Victor is easy prey for her, and she hypnotizes him by wiggling her glittering fingernails. She tells him that by the year 5000, because of atomic radiation every fifth child was born a mutant like herself. These mutants were put into special isolated colonies, and it's one of these colonies that the time-trading machine has contacted. They need undamaged genes, so she's planning to take Victor back with her.

Later, the glittering high heels she still wears lead Bob and the professor to decide she's not all she claims to be, so they decide to search the island. While they do, the Future Woman puts back on her glittering tights (glitter seems to be a dominant design feature in clothing and cosmetics of the year 5000) and takes Victor to the laboratory. She tells Claire, who is more or less standing around, that "our history clearly records how the women of the twentieth century stood idly by while the atmosphere was contaminated." She begins preparing to take Victor into the future with her.

Bob and Erling by now have discovered the real nurse's dead body, and race back to the laboratory. There's a brief fight, the time machine is short-circuited, and both Victor and the Future Woman are killed. Bob wants to ride to the rescue of the desperate inhabitants of the 51st century, and immediately start sending them useful items, but the professor wisely tells him that the way to change the future is to change the present.

Terror from the Year 5,000 (known a bit obscurely as *Cage of Doom* in England) is somewhat lackluster, with variable acting and sets. But it doesn't bite off more than it can chew, and sticks to its storyline throughout. At least for the storylines of SF films of the period, it is not particularly clichéd. Having the professor's beautiful daughter already engaged to his nefarious lab assistant was old hat during the 1930s, but by 1958, that kind of plotting hadn't been seen in a while, making it seem almost fresh. The business of Claire and Bob meeting because of a car chase was also a so-old-it's-new-again idea, as is setting the whole story on an island, but it does have the desirable effect of isolating the menace and keeping the number of characters down.

There's too much rambling back and forth from the house to the spot where Victor tossed the dead cat into the drink; they go out there at least three times, and Angelo is killed by the Future Woman nearby.

It's unclear as to why the Future Woman doesn't grab Victor the minute she pops out of the machine and flee back to her own time with him—after all, he's right where she wants him. Thankfully, however, the business with the nurse seems logical. Apart from being radioactive, the Future Woman has no particular powers, and needs a disguise to get back to Victor. However, the main plot hole is left wide open; there isn't even an effort to hide it. Namely, why don't the future people immediately explain their desperate plight?

There are occasionally imaginative, if not outright exotic, touches, such as the carbon-14 dating of the statue, the misunderstanding over Greek, and the gimmick of hypnotic fingernails. There's too much glitzy glitter, with the costume, shoes *and* fingernails of the Future Woman all sparkling (what, no eye shadow?). The interesting device of obscuring her with expanding and contracting animated white spots may have been done in an effort to hide the mediocre makeup, but it's still visually unusual and hints at her radioactivity.

Bob, the professor and Victor represent three different aspects of scientific ambition: Bob is acting primarily on simply scientific curiosity, the professor has become enmeshed in his research, and Victor is a wild-eyed zealot. This is not uncommon, but it is also not a real cliché.

The Future Woman herself is a novelty. First of all, why a woman? To mate with a man of our time? If so, why does she try to take Victor back with her? When she first appears, why does she walk with stiff arms and legs? Later, she's lithe as a gibbon as she scampers through the forest. When she's first seen, the Future Woman is small and wiry; when she takes over as the nurse, she's large and broad-shouldered. Clearly, the first person playing the Future Woman wasn't Salome Jens, but after she takes over the nurse, only Jens plays her.

Salome Jens' name does not appear in any advertising or official credit listings for the film; I don't know why. For several years, I heard that she was in the film; film expert Ted Zaske once got a free drink from the actress when he mentioned the film to her. But *Terror from the Year 5,000* is not listed in any of Salome Jens' filmographies. Leslie Halliwell seems to think he's listed all of her films in his *Filmgoer's Companion*, and does not mention this one. So when I saw it again for this book, I was stunned to see her simply listed in the cast at the beginning, right between John Stratton and Fred Herrick. And, of course, she's recognizable.

Jens has made relatively few films. Her official "debut" was in *Angel Baby* (1961) in the title role. Her other credits include *The Fool Killer* (1965), *Seconds* (1966), *Me, Natalie* (1969) and *Savages* (1972). She has a very odd intensity which films never seem to know how to exploit properly; furthermore, I suspect she may not be very interested in making any films other than those which attract her particular attention. Except for *Me, Natalie*, all of her films (including *Terror from the Year 5,000* are quirky and distinctive. Those words could also be used to describe Jens as a performer. She's often excellent, but sometimes strained and artificial.

Joyce Holden starred in a few films in the early 1950s, including *Girls in the Night* (1953), *Murder Without Tears* (1953) and *Private Eyes* (1953) with the Bowery Boys. Her best film is undoubtedly the bizarre and funny *You Never Can Tell* (1951). Her part in *Terror from the Year 5,000* was her first role of any size since 1953, and despite the completely clichéd nature of the part—the professor's beautiful daughter—Holden is quite good in it.

In what seems to be his film debut, Ward Costello is adequate as the hero. He also appeared in *The Gallant Hours* (1960), *MacArthur* (1977) and *Return from Witch Mountain* (1978).

I doubt that the John Stratton who appeared in such British films as *The Cruel Sea* (1952), *The Third Key* (1956) and *Strangler's Web* (1965) is the same person as the John Stratton in this film. However, the John Stratton in *It Takes a Thief* (1961) is probably the same one. In any event, despite the peculiarities of the role, he's acceptable as Victor.

On the other hand, Frederic Downs is inadequate as the professor, and has little to do. He also appeared in *Experiment in Terror* (1962), *I Love My Wife* (1970) and *1776* (1972), among other films.

The most notable debut on *Terror from the Year 5,000* wasn't that of an actor, it was editor Dede Allen, who eventually became one of the very few stars of that profession, cutting major films including *The Hustler* (1961), *America America* (1963), *Bonnie and Clyde* (1967), *Rachel, Rachel* (1968), *Alice's Restaurant* (1969), *Little Big Man* (1970), *Slaughterhouse-Five* (1972), *Serpico* (1973), *Dog Day Afternoon* (1973) and others. She has been a special favorite of directors Sidney Lumet and Arthur Penn. There's little in the editing of *Terror from the Year 5,000* that gives hints of her fame to come, but at least she keeps the action moving; despite a script that tends to wander, the film never becomes confusing.

The photography is well-above average for a film of this nature; given what must have been a very brief shooting schedule, cinematographer Arthur Florman provides an occasional imaginative angle, and maintains a consistent crisp look.

The sets by Beatrice Gurney and William Hoffman are above average as well; the lab has a nicely jury-rigged look, except for a trite Jacob's ladder zapping away in the background.

"Whit" at *Variety* found the film lacking in coherence. "Overall unfoldment is so clothed in confusion ... that it's a weakie for even the small exploitation field." He added that "players are hard put to make any sense of their characters." The *Monthly Film Bulletin* gave the film its lowest rating, and said "The woman from the future is an unimaginative creation and whatever horrific possibilities she has are soon expended.... [She's] a sad little creature in a tight set of black woolies. The film is crudely photographed, with no noticeable interest in continuity and little attempt at convincing settings."

On the other hand, Walter Greene at *Hollywood Reporter* found the movie to be "highly imaginative" and considered it "pretty fantastic, but fairly interesting because of the far-fetched novelty." The reviewer for the *Beverly Hills Citizen* viewed the events as "fairly interesting and, for fantasy, not too ridiculous." The players were "very good, especially the irradiated leading lady in what looks to be spangled tights."

Psychotronic finds it "a favorite '50s cheapie," and Don Willis (I) thought it was "fairly pleasant for a while until the plot bogs down."

Terror from the Year 5,000 is only adequate in terms of production; a few of the actors do fairly good work; there's a hangdog air to the whole movie. Most audiences probably found it of little interest, but I don't think it deserves to be completely overlooked. It has some imagination in its conception and enterprise in its execution. It is not a good film, but I am not sorry it was made.

War of the Colossal Beast

The choice of a title for this sequel to *The Amazing Colossal Man* is a bit peculiar; nothing in the advertising indicated it was a sequel. (In England, it was known even more obscurely as *The Terror Strikes*.) It was called "The Return of the Colossal Man" while shooting. You'd think that once American International cofinanced a sequel to the earlier picture, they would at least try to get those who had liked the first one into the theatre — the audience, presumably, at which any sequel is aimed. Perhaps the word "colossal" would be enough to tip off Glenn Manning fans that this was another adventure of the Colossal Man? But that's doubtful too. For whatever reason, AIP was hiding the fact that it was a sequel.

Even a fan as slavishly devoted to discovering all I could about these movies as I was, was not expecting a sequel. I entered the Port Theatre in North Bend well after *War of the Colossal Beast* had begun, and to my surprise, saw scenes from *The Amazing Colossal Man*. Even by 1958, I had begun to suspect American International might be guilty of almost any duplicity, including retitling a film they had released only the year before and passing it off as something new, so I rushed out to the candy counter to complain indignantly. To my great shock, I was told that the film was "a sequel or something" to the earlier picture. Almost numb, and greatly disappointed, I returned to watch the picture.

I was disappointed because, good or bad, I wanted each and every science fiction movie to be a separate entity; I was not fond of sequels, feeling the film expended on them could have been better used in filming an altogether new story. Furthermore, I didn't think the original films generally warranted sequels anyway, certainly in this case.

Incidentally, *War of the Colossal Beast* was released with *Attack of the Puppet People*, making it noteworthy (or something), because it was the only Bert I. Gordon double feature. At least they were thematically linked, with one film being about a giant man, and the other about miniaturized people.

For those who came in late: in *The Amazing Colossal Man*, a plutonium explosion causes Col. Glenn Manning (Glenn Langan) to rapidly grow to the height of 60 feet. But the rapid growth also causes Manning to lose his mind; he becomes a menace, and the Army shoots him off Hoover Dam.

As with several other Gordon pictures, *War of the Colossal Beast* opens very well, with an exciting scene of a frightened boy in Mexico racing away in a truck from some huge, unseen pursuer. When the truck itself vanishes, the report is carried on a Los Angeles telecast (in cheap little pictures, newscasters always make fun of strange events, which rarely occurs in real life). It's seen by Joyce Manning (Sally Fraser), still convinced that her brother Glenn survived his fall off Hoover Dam.

Joyce immediately goes to Mexico, because she thinks that the disappearance of the truck—one in a series—may be due to her brother still being alive and grabbing food where he can get it. Despite the unmotivated skepticism of Major Baird (Roger Pace), an American Army officer somehow assigned to the case, Joyce does persuade all concerned to examine the spot where the truck was last seen and, sure enough, there are the tracks of (as someone says) "a man, a very big man."

Soon, Baird and Joyce locate big Glenn (Dean Parkin), who is hiding out in the mountains and is indeed snatching what food he can from passing trucks, usually taking the trucks, too. He's horribly scarred, with an eye gone and his lips on the right side of his face turned into teeth. (I'm being sarcastic, but when he grimaces, you can see other teeth beneath those painstakingly painted on his face). His mind is still addled and his disposition is even worse than when we last saw him, so a truckload of doped bread is left where he can find it. It works almost immediately; he passes out, and (offscreen) is returned to Los Angeles.

Freakishly, at this point Bert I. Gordon drags in a spot of heavy political satire. In a series of shots of men at desks talking on the phone (with occasional Washington, D.C. scenes backprojected behind them), first a congressman says that a 60-foot Army officer doesn't fall into their jurisdiction, and passes the matter over to the Department of Medical Research, which in turn passes it on to the Department of Health and Welfare, who in turn passes the question of Glenn back to Congress. The same congressman now decides that since Glenn was an Army officer when he was caught in the radioactive blast, it's a matter for the Pentagon. Which returns it all to Baird, still sitting around the Los Angeles airport with, presumably, a plane full of Colossal Man.

Poor Glenn ends up tied to a huge pallet in a hangar, where he remembers in flashback how all his trouble started. (It was at this point I walked in, baffled.) After the flashbacks, Glenn escapes from the hangar and wanders around the airport briefly in wildly mismatching shots, until he is captured again and returned to the hangar.

Joyce desperately projects slides of Glenn's past where he can see them—"Remember your bicycle, Glenn? It was red and had a light on it"—but there's no glimmer of recognition. Plans are being made to ship Glenn to an un-inhabited island, but Joyce considers this horribly inhuman. All things

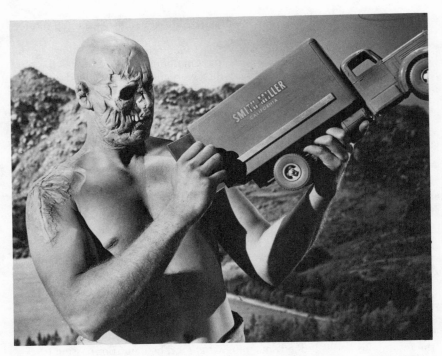

As giant Glenn Manning, Dean Parkin examines a truck for little loaves of bread. The surprisingly effective makeup is by Jack H. Young; the film, not surprisingly ineffective, is by Bert I. Gordon. War of the Colossal Beast (1958).

considered, however, it seems like a practical, humane solution to the problem of housing a 60-foot lunatic.

Glenn isn't entirely crazy, though. He pretends to be asleep, then when no one is looking, dashes away (offscreen) from the hangar.

He's next seen in Griffith Park near the observatory, where he raises a bus-load of kids over his head and roars at the searchlights being aimed at him from below. Joyce persuades him to put the bus down, he mutters her name, and wanders off. Apparently feeling the only way out is suicide, he grabs some power lines, and the film briefly switches to a garish color process. Glenn glows several vivid hues and then *vanishes* altogether, neatly solving the problem of colossal corpse disposal.

Bert I. Gordon just is not a good writer, director, or special effects technician, although there are signs in some of his films that he thinks he's doing a good job in all departments. But he is inept, even when he cares, and when he doesn't care, as in *War of the Colossal Beast*, the results are dismal indeed.

The script is so perfunctory, with so few thrills, that it plays as if Gordon was given the money for a sequel, and then almost literally walked away. The Colossal Man is off the screen for most of the picture, and during his brief appearances, he's generally either tied up, or standing in one place, behind something. Gordon couldn't think of anything for him to do—which may be a good thing, because it's depressing to contemplate what the special effects might have been like if the Colossal Man actually *did* do something.

Gordon's effects are no good because he always uses the cheapest, quickest methods of combining images. In these giant-man films (including *The Cyclops*), he seems to have filmed his oversize players on black backdrops, or behind black objects, gesturing, walking a little. Gordon then combined this with the other footage, of people reacting to the terrible sight. While this works after a fashion, it almost always results in the giant man looking pale and washed-out, when he isn't actually transparent.

In *Colossal Beast*, all sense of realism in scale completely vanishes. When Glenn first appears, he seems much larger than 60 feet. Later, when chasing the bread truck, his size remains consistent, but when the chloral hydrate overwhelms him, he seems to shrink several yards. In the hangar, his size is consistent, but outside, he shifts in size from shot to shot. When he's at Griffith Park, he's standing behind the observatory, and reaches forward to almost touch Joyce. That reach covers a distance of at least 200 feet, but he doesn't come around the observatory for this.

If the size of the big star is all wrong, it's nothing compared to Gordon's ideas about geography. He proposes that once Glenn fell off Hoover Dam, he would drift down the Colorado River into Mexico. While it is true that the river does trace that path, there are *many* small dams along it, the river passes through populated areas, and it is never very deep. Certainly someone would have noticed a 60-foot giant with a hideously disfigured face drifting by, even if he didn't get stuck behind a dam.

Once he's in Los Angeles, Glenn is housed at the L.A. airport, from which he vanishes to reappear at the Griffith Park Observatory. This means he passed through Inglewood, Los Angeles and Hollywood, through some of the most densely-populated regions of Southern California, without anyone noticing. It's difficult to ascertain if Gordon thought the audience (most of whom, of course, would not know how far the airport is from the observatory) wouldn't realize this small blunder, or if the director himself was unaware how preposterous this is.

In a sense, all the foregoing is nit-picking, and some of the same complaints can be lodged against much better films, such as *King Kong*. But *War of the Colossal Beast* is a terrible film in almost every other way as well.

The opening scene, with the terrified boy driving madly away, has a certain excitement, helped by Albert Glasser's score (mostly a reprise of themes for the earlier film). At the climax, there's an interesting very long view of Glenn standing near the observatory that is oddly believable.

But Gordon's plot, scripted by George Worthing Yates, is hopeless; it has no story. There is no hint of a love interest between Joyce and Baird; we never know or care about any of the characters, including Glenn (unlike the first film, in which Glenn Langan did a reasonably good job; in a couple of scenes, he made us feel the Colossal Man's anger and frustration). It merely lumbers from incident to incident, with little excitement, to a preordained conclusion. No one seems to have cared much about anything other than exposing enough footage to release as a film. And even at that, a certain amount of footage is from the first film.

Gordon draws out each scene endlessly. At one point, after finding Glenn's footprints, everyone climbs into a Jeep to drive back to town, and we see them get in, watch as they back up, pull away, and disappear over a hill.

Even as a sequel, the film doesn't work.* It was established in the first film

---

*Bert I. Gordon isn't the only person who can make embarrassing blunders. In my notes

that a way had been found to halt Glenn's growth, and that this in time would destroy his deteriorating mind. Furthermore, a means was found to shrink him again. But except for the fact that Glenn is not growing, all this is disregarded in *Colossal Beast*.

Maybe the biggest cheat of all is the ending, in which (in the color footage missing from TV and 16mm prints) Glenn vanishes while electrocuting himself. I'm not sure what Bert Gordon thought the reaction of his audiences would be, but even the Saturday matinee audience with which I saw the film hissed at this monstrous cop-out.

Few films have been as desultory as *War of the Colossal Beast*, so perhaps it's not surprising that the acting is fairly desultory itself. Sally Fraser plays Glenn's sister presumably because Cathy Downs wasn't available (or refused) to repeat her role as Glenn's fiancée from the first film — in which, incidentally, we were told that Glenn had no living relatives. Fraser was a mildly attractive minor actress whose best performance and role in a science fiction film was in *It Conquered the World*. She also appeared in *Earth vs. the Spider* and *Giant from the Unknown*, starred in *Dangerous Charter* (released 1962), had a secondary role in *It's a Dog's Life* (1955) and a small part in *North by Northwest* (1959).

Roger Pace is completely colorless and uninteresting as the military man who tries to help Joyce. The only other film I'm aware of him appearing in was *It Should Happen to You* (1954), although he has undoubtedly appeared in small parts in other pictures.

Unless Dean Parkin played the title role in Bert Gordon's *The Cyclops*, as some sources have claimed, this is his only screen appearance of record. Unlike Glenn Langan in the earlier film, here Parkin's Glenn Manning is just a monster.

The makeup by Jack H. Young is, all things considered, surprisingly good, but seems designed to be seen only in stills. The exposed bones and teeth are painted on Parkin's skin, and with every movement, the truth of their nature is revealed.

Of the few people who bothered to review the film, only Jack Moffitt found anything likable about it, calling it "a pretty fair low budget boogie tale.... In spite of the hoke, Dean Parkin creates a few moments of pathos as the monster." "Powr" at *Daily Variety* felt otherwise: " ... invention seems to have been largely exhausted in the first picture and this later version will have to ride to whatever success it enjoys on [the reputation of] that picture.... Word of mouth will not be enthusiastic."

The *Monthly Film Bulletin* had a nice summation: "The trick photography of these Further Adventures of the Amazing Colossal Man is ludicrously unconvincing, and in any case, the idea has lost its pristine impact. The dialogue strikes an oddly hieratic note, the charm school heroine reacts to every plot development with a winsome smile, while the rest of the players apparently prefer not to react at all."

Don Willis (I) thought that while the film was "pretty dumb" it was "not as bad as some Gordons." Parish and Pitts said, "the low-grade production values, synonymous with Gordon's output, are not even forgivable." Alan Frank

on The Amazing Colossal Man in Volume 1, I said "[William] Hudson turns up in the sequel in a completely different part, which makes for peculiar flashbacks." He's not in War of the Colossal Beast, *except in flashbacks. I was wrong. I apologize. He is a costar of* Attack of the 50 Foot Woman, *however.*

(*Horror*) found it "fairly mediocre with variable special effects and poor acting." On the other hand, *Psychotronic* enthused that it was "funnier than the original!"

Heaven help us all if bad-movie aficionados ever discover Bert I. Gordon.

War of the Satellites

Roger Corman's entry in the space race is one of his most confusing, poorly-structured films, but it has some interesting performances and is smoothly made for an eight-day picture. It was fast in all departments. On October 4, 1957, the Soviet Union launched Sputnik I, the first Earth satellite; eight months later, almost to the day, *War of the Satellites* was reviewed by *Variety*. But some have claimed it was even faster.

In an interview with Ed Naha for his book on Roger Corman, the producer-director said that just after the satellite was launched, Jack Rabin came to him with an idea for "a movie to cash in on the satellite craze." Rabin assured Corman he could do the special effects if the picture could be shot at once. Corman contacted Allied Artists and said he could have a satellite picture in movie theatres in two months' time. "It was one of the fastest movies ever made," Corman told Naha. "The script was written in less than two weeks. Six weeks after that, the film was being shown coast to coast."

In *Fantascene* #2, Jack Rabin said that *War of the Satellites* was entirely conceived and filmed in an eight-week period of time. The publicity and play-dates were all lined up before the film was even made, and it became a big commercial success when it was completed and released.

While the film certainly looks like it was shot and released quickly, unless Rabin and Irving Block, who came up with the story together, contacted Corman as late as February, 1958, there's some confusion. Sputnik was launched in October, 1957; *War of the Satellites* was not in theatres before May, 1958. That's a six-month gap, not eight weeks. However, the time scale makes more sense if Rabin and Block got their brainstorm after the first successful launching of an *American* satellite, Explorer I, on January 31, 1958. This ties in quite nicely with the eight-week start-to-release period.

War of the Satellites was not the only film of 1958 to deal with artificial satellites. *Spy in the Sky*, a nicely exploitative title, dealt with decoding a series of satellite beeps. In *Attack of the 50 Foot Woman* (cofeature with *War of the Satellites*), the giant alien's spacecraft is always referred to as a "satellite" apparently in order to be topical. *The Flame Barrier*, reviewed the same week as *War of the Satellites*, dealt with a downed satellite, exploited in the advertising art but not in the title. *Satan's Satellites* was hastily reedited from a serial and rushed into release so fast that it may have beat *War of the Satellites* to some screens; the plot has nothing to do with satellites. The artificial moons figured in the summer release, *Space Master X-7*. The Corman–produced *Night of the Blood Beast* began with the return of a manned satellite.

The storyline of *War of the Satellites* — the title is meaningless, incidentally — is muddled and, at times, almost impenetrable. As the film begins, the U.N. has been having a hard time with its satellites*: ten of them have been de-

*The writers of the story, Block and Rabin, and scripter Lawrence Louis Goldman, don't

stroyed when they try to pass through what seems to be a barrier in space, dubbed the Sigma Barrier.

Pol Van Ponder (Richard Devon), chief of U.N. rocket operations, is dismayed but not defeated by the explosion of the tenth satellite. He intends to launch another, this time carrying human beings. But other representatives at the U.N. vow to oppose him.

Meanwhile, out in the desert someplace, another pair of teenagers is (are?) necking. "I'm getting warmer every second, ring-a-ding-ding," says the boy, obviously overdosed on Sinatra. "A shooting stah!" she cries, anything to get his attentions off her. "It can't be Sputnik," he says; it's "not listed in *TV Guide*." There's a big boom, and on investigating, they find a cylinder sticking in the ground like an arrow. Writing appears in Latin on the cylinder, and it is taken to the United Nations Security Council (housed in a surprisingly small room). The material of the cylinder defies analysis, and the message appears only when one thinks of it. Stop thinking, and it goes blank again.

The message is a warning from "the masters of the spiral nebula Ganna." It says, "Know, Earthlings, that we look with disfavor upon your persistent efforts to depart from your own planet and infest other areas of the universe.... Knowing that Earthlings are equipped with rudimentary reflex-type intelligence, we are taking this means of conveying our command that all such efforts to expand and depart from the infected planet Earth shall from this moment be stopped." (But they weren't letting us out before.)

Van Ponder believes the message is a hoax, but others don't. Now he has all the support he needs for his manned satellite. The Security Council doesn't take kindly to mankind being treated as a germ plague—and a stupid plague at that. They want to break the quarantine. Akad (Michael Fox), clearly from an Unfriendly Power, is still opposed to Van Ponder's plans, even when he has three rockets almost ready to go.

While Van Ponder is driving rapidly back from the U.N., a glow stabs down from space and strikes his car; he is apparently killed in the wreck. But he's still alive, though Strangely Emotionless (when possessed by alien forces, why don't people become *more* emotional?), and when alone, he quickly splits in two. (He will do this several more times; there's rarely a good reason for it.)

Dave Boyer (Dick Miller), our Young Hero, asks Van Ponder if the scientist can let fellow worker Sybil Carrington (Susan Cabot) down easily; she's started to fall in love with Van Ponder, but he's clearly not in love with her—although Dave apparently is. They're interrupted by the breathless arrival of Sybil herself, and all three listen to reports of simultaneous disasters happening all over the world. (Van Ponder has informed the annoyed aliens that the Earthlings are not heeding their warning.)

At another U.N. meeting, Dave arrives to present Van Ponder's prepared total capitulation to the aliens, but instead ringingly declares that for "pure, naked survival" humanity must fight the alien threat. "If we give in now, let down our defenses, give this alien planet full control over our actions and our lives ... will they decide to take even that mess of pottage from us?" He speeds

seem to understand that an orbit is an elliptical path around another object in space, and that a satellite is an object that follows such an orbit. They seem to feel that an orbit is any path taken by any object in space (which is, however, literally true), and that satellites and spaceships are the same thing. As the climax of the film has the "satellite" passing at the speed of light through Andromeda, it is certainly a spaceship and not a satellite, and has a very impressive propulsion system.

through a declaration of war and concludes, "We must proceed with Project Sigma at all costs!" The only delegate who does not cheer him is Akad, who's practically a dupe of the aliens himself.

The alien Van Ponder's ace has been trumped, and for the time being he has little choice but to go along with the last-minute preparations to launch the three rockets. While helping John Campo (Jerry Barclay), Van Ponder unthinkingly allows his hand to dangle in front of an acetylene torch. John spots this in horror and dashes out for help. Exasperated at this accident, Van Ponder rubs his charred hand with his good one, and restores the burned skin to normal. When John returns with a doctor, the hand is fine, and the flabbergasted John is told that his reactions are the equivalent of buck fever, and he's grounded.

Van Ponder splits again, duplicating everything but the clipboard he's carrying, and each goes off to an important appointment. Only this time Dave sees him, and he's upset when, just before the rocket launch, Sybil is switched from Dave's rocket to Van Ponder's. John is also sent up after all. "See you aboard," Van Ponder tells him in a chilly tone.

The rockets rendezvous in space. Each spits out a section of satellite, and the sections all come together to form a spherical satellite with three small "outrigger" balls, attached by tangential framework. Everything goes smoothly, and when the artificial gravity (a must in low-budget films) is turned on, people start moving around. Even though he has become reluctant to do so, Van Ponder kills John with a touch, passing off the fatality as a result of the launch.

The supersatellite is now in "an orbit far beyond the Moon." The theory is that if they can go fast enough, they will crash through the Sigma Barrier. As Van Ponder is in charge of this, we expect failure.

Dave confronts Sybil and Van Ponder with the fact that he saw the scientist split in two, but not surprisingly, Sybil doesn't believe him. Van Ponder icily warns Dave that "astroplanetary law" gives him supreme command of the satellite, so Dave had just better watch his step.

John is buried in space, and afterward, Dave tells the doctor (Eric Sinclair) that John was murdered by Van Ponder. He demonstrates something eerie about Van Ponder's face: using a photo of the scientist and a hand mirror, he shows the doctor that Van Ponder's face is exactly symmetrical. Now the doctor is curious, and forces a sudden examination on Van Ponder, who mentally creates a momentary diversion by causing some dials to run wild. He leaves for a moment, ducks into a room, and wills a beating heart into his chest. He passes Sybil and, as he now has a heart, is instantly attracted to her. Van Ponder allows the doctor to listen to his brand-new heart, then tries to kill the doctor with a touch (why did he bother to invent a heart?); this fails, so he strangles the doctor.

Sybil encounters Van Ponder tossing the doctor's body out of the ship while, under Van Ponder's orders, Dave is being arrested. Van Ponder tries to persuade Sybil of his love, and Dave escapes from the guards. Now desperate, Van splits again (we never do see him reassemble) right in front of Sybil, and the duplicate leaves to do battle while the other chases Sybil, apparently bent on rape.

Elsewhere, the astrogator and other crew are still heading the satellite directly for the Sigma Barrier, operating under Plan B on Van Ponder's orders. This, Dave knows, is sure death.

Dave tries to get the duplicate Van to reverse the orders, and shoots at him when Van Ponder advances on him. To the villain's surprise, he bleeds—having a heart has given him *several* weaknesses (love, inability to kill with touch, blood in veins). After a struggle, in which the duplicate Van Ponder proves to be stronger than a human being, Dave shoots him again and kills him, which also kills the original, saving Sybil in the nick of time.

Dave quickly grabs a mike and shouts, "Activate Plan A!" which is all that's necessary to save the day. The satellite roars on toward the invisible barrier, blinking positive to negative, and smashes through it, heading out into the starry heavens. Space now belongs to mankind.

Corman says the script by Lawrence Louis Goldman was written in two weeks, but it doesn't play as if it took anywhere near that long. It is illogical and very poorly structured, until the three-way climax. The aliens don't take over Van Ponder until some way into the film; Dave doesn't declare his interest in Sybil until after that; the aliens can destroy our crops and buildings, but apparently cannot touch the rockets. The endless duplication of Van Ponder leads nowhere, and plays a part only in the Corsican Brothers–inspired climax. The aliens never give any clear reason for hating us—we are just an infection. They don't even use the standard movie alien complaint, that we are warlike and would probably blow up the universe. There's too much running back and forth through corridors, and the idea that only Van Ponder and Dave would know that Plan A was the sole safe solution seems unlikely. In fact, any film in which everything is put right by someone merely executing Plan A would seem to be wanting in believability.

But War of the Satellites has its merits, too. It is efficient and economical, without looking tacky. In Fangoria #23, Dick Miller told an interviewer that "we had two of the best lounge chairs money could buy to take off for the Moon in. The type where you hit the sides and the chair slides down into a [reclining] position.... For the hallways on the spaceship ... we had four arches, that's all they were. The entire set was arches. You could set them close together to make a short hall or set them farther apart and make a long hall. At the end of the hall was a flat—you made a turn. So on our spaceship you always ran down to the end of the hall and made a turn. That was the entire ship." It is not ineffective, and art director Daniel Haller made varied enough use of the arches and halls that the ship seems expansive, if confusing and repetitious (not unlike the film itself).

The special effects by Jack Rabin, Irving Block and Louis DeWitt were especially good for a low-budget film made in a great rush. The scenes in which the satellite arrives in space and assembles itself feature good model work, if a rather simplistic idea of satellite assembly. This one just snaps together as if all parts were magnetized, and no one even has to don a space suit. There's a good matte painting, probably by Block, early in the film when the three rockets are established. The same effects would not be acceptable in an expensive film, but there have been movies that cost a lot more than War of the Satellites that had much less believable effects. Block, Rabin and DeWitt were usually way ahead of others working on their budget level, but they were especially effective here.

The music by Walter Greene is also very good for a film of this nature, especially behind the titles, which also feature the effective graphics common to Corman's Allied Artists pictures of this period. The music is never overdone, and always supports the images. The single weak element is that in every one of the repetitious shots of the satellite rotating past the camera, the same electronic wail is heard. This eventually becomes comic.

Despite being miscast as a dashing young hero, Dick Miller is quite good. He seems tense and involved throughout, and plays the part seriously, with intelligence and skill. He feels he was physically unsuited for the role, and perhaps he was, but he's more than acceptable. It's not one of his best screen performances, however; he's much more comfortable when he can be a crabby smartmouth, at which few actors are better.

Susan Cabot has little to do other than look beautiful, but she does seem intelligent, unlike other actresses in similar parts. She seems so bright, in fact, that it's surprising she doesn't find a way to defeat the evil Van Ponder herself. She is a notably good actress.

It was common (but not invariable) for Corman to cast especially good performers in his films, so even when the rest of the movie was no better than those being turned out by his contemporaries, the performances carried an air of conviction. It's a shame that, unlike performers in later Corman films, those in most of his low-budget SF and horror films never broke out of them and became stars on their own. Several, including Dick Miller and Susan Cabot, certainly were good enough to.

As the alien and human Pol Van Ponder, Richard Devon, another Corman regular, provided intelligence and menace when required. His sinister looks helped, but he also had an Oil-Can Harry slickness that worked to his advantage in roles like this. He's somewhat helpless when the script bizarrely calls for him to grow a heart and the ability to love. The idea of an alien menace backing a woman into a corner and declaring his love for her is, shall we say, outré. It doesn't come off here, and audiences laughed.

The remainder of the cast includes several Corman regulars, such as Bruno Ve Sota and Beach Dickerson — and Corman himself, as a ground controller. All turn in standard, reliable performances for a picture like this.

Corman has told several interviewers (including Ed Naha) that the film was budgeted for ten days, but was brought in at eight. Again, as with his other genre film of 1958, *Teenage Caveman*, Corman wasn't able to bring much in the line of style to the film. His brisk efficiency is better demonstrated here than in *Teenage Caveman*, however, and no matter how tangled and confusing the movie gets, on a first viewing, *War of the Satellites* is not boring. Because of the low budget and that it takes place on a few sets, it is rather talky, but things constantly seem on the verge of happening, and you have a feeling of anticipation throughout. It doesn't deliver, and the big climax is a big fizzle: a flash of light, some photos of starry skies, and that's it. Even the fight with the two Van Ponders is muffed.

"Whit" in *Variety* considered it a "lesser entry for the exploitation market," finding the film "so contrived and confusing it misses fire completely. [The] over-talky script by Lawrence Louis Goldman [leaves] audiences unenlightened through most of film's rambling unfoldment."

On the other hand, Jack Moffitt, always more fond of SF efforts than "Whit," and always on the lookout for a diamond in the rough, was easier on the film. "A topical [story] and some very good miniature work by [the effects team] give this Roger Corman film a chance to cash in on the exploitation angles." He also said that "Dick Miller and Susan Cabot have very pleasant screen personalities and, when given a chance, nice acting abilities." The plot, however, did bother him.

The *Monthly Film Bulletin* gave the film an average rating. "Reasonably diverting science fantasy, unduly cluttered with international problems and the inevitable brainy beauty in the spaceship. The production is generally makeshift, but the trick effects work, the atmosphere is occasionally eerie, and Richard Devon supplies a nice, gaunt presence as the unearthly rocket scientist."

Don Willis (I) thought *War of the Satellites* was "one of Corman's worst," but he's anything but sympathetic to the director in the first place. Even *Psychotronic* called it "one of Corman's dullest," while Alan Frank (*SF*) had a contrary opinion: "The movie, though showing in its special effects the speed of its making, is fast-moving and efficiently made."

Life magazine did an article on science fiction monsters in early 1958, and mentioned that *War of the Satellites* would contain "the ultimate in scientific monsters," a bodiless alien made of pure energy. There's not a hint of this in the movie, but advertising for the film certainly capitalized on the *Life* quote.

War of the Satellites is essentially just another mediocre space movie made to cash in on a fad, but some good model work, decent performances and smooth, quick direction keep it watchable throughout. At least the first time through.

Keep Watching   1959   *the Skies!*

The Alligator People

With the *Return of the Fly* arrived this curious film, which apparently was developed backward from the title; it's rarely seen today. Although almost never on television, rarely shown at science fiction conventions, and, in fact, generally unknown, it isn't as bad as its almost total obscurity indicates. In fact, until the climax, when an altogether unsuitable makeup is revealed, despite some problems the film is above average for a programmer horror-SF film. The script is partly responsible, but intelligent direction by Roy Del Ruth and good camerawork by Karl Struss make major contributions.

The film has an unusual framework, perhaps inspired by "The Search for Bridey Murphy"; the plot has overtones of *Rebecca*. Psychiatrist McGregor (Douglas Kennedy) calls in associate Lorimer (Bruce Bennett) because McGregor's competent, cheerful nurse Jane (Beverly Garland) has a mental block: she can't remember what happened during one year of her life, some time ago. Jane willingly undergoes hypnotherapy, with questions by McGregor and Jane's responses recorded on tape, and we see in flashback what she recalls.

Jane has just married Paul Webster (Richard Crane), and they're on a train heading for their honeymoon. It's been a whirlwind courtship, and Jane is so in love with Paul that she finds it difficult to believe his claims that he had been in a terrible plane crash a short time before; he shows no signs of injury. They open congratulatory telegrams, but one makes Paul go white and immediately ask the porter when the next stop is so he can make a phone call.

The train makes a momentary mail stop, and Paul gets off; the train leaves without him, as Jane frantically calls to him from their car. (She doesn't pull the emergency cord.) She tells the psychiatrists of her difficulties in tracking Paul down, although we don't see any of this activity; he told her nothing of his background. (This difficulty is contrived; he has no reason to hide his background, as we later learn. It's only an element to make things more mysterious.) She does eventually track him through school records to Bayou Landing, La Fourche Parish, Louisiana. There's no one at the train station, and she waits for someone who might take her to the address she has. There's also a box of radioactive material waiting, and she sits on it.

Soon, unshaven, dirty but good-natured Mannon (Lon Chaney, Jr.) arrives; being a nurse, Jane doesn't blanch at the fact that Mannon's right hand has been replaced by a hook. He loads up the radioactive material, and takes it and Jane into the swampland. She learns very little about her destination, the mansion called The Cypresses, where Mannon works. As they pass a few alligators, she does learn that Mannon has a passionate hatred of the big reptiles. One bit off his hand some years before.

He deposits her on the veranda of a honeysuckle-and-magnolia-drenched mansion, where she's greeted frostily by Mrs. Henry Hawthorne (Frieda Inescort), who seems to have wandered in from one of Tennessee Williams' lesser plays. Mrs. Hawthorne immediately urges Jane to leave, telling her she's never heard of any Paul Webster. But a servant tells Mrs. Hawthorne there's no train until tomorrow, so she immediately becomes the genteel hostess (though still with a touch of ice), and offers Jane a room upstairs.

That evening, Jane hears gunfire outside, where Mannon is taking potshots at gators with his pistol. Hawthorne servant Toby (Vince Townsend, Jr.) tries to stop Mannon, who's drunk and shouting his litany: "Dirty stinking nasty slimy gators!" Toby says he doesn't like them either, but shooting at them doesn't do any good. "I ain't never gonna stop shootin' gators," Mannon declares. "No, never, Yah hah hah hah!" Bang bang.

Lou Ann (Ruby Goodwin), another servant, tells Jane she should leave The Cypresses at once. "This is a trouble house," she tells her. "Real deep big trouble." But this only makes Jane more curious.

The curiosity of the audience is aroused as well. We suddenly meet Dr. Mark Sinclair (George Macready) in a sophisticated laboratory somewhere in the house; he has an alligator strapped to a surgical table.

After Dr. Sinclair and his helpers struggle with someone in a hooded terry-cloth robe — we are prevented from seeing the face by a flat silvery shield in the shape of a toilet seat — he meets with Mrs. Hawthorne. Their conversation is one of those so necessary to these films, but which are so hard to make convincing: we have to be fed a little information (here, that Sinclair's experiments are not turning out well, and he has to resort to radioactive materials), without being told too much (just what the experiments are). This sort of scene is hard to believe because they wouldn't talk so elliptically in real life. But then, this isn't real life, this is a movie called The Alligator People — which, you'd think, would tend to give a clue as to the nature of the experiments in the first place.

Jane hears a piano from downstairs later that night, and slips out the previously-locked door; the piano is being played by a shadowy figure we recognize as Paul, with various facial disfigurements. Jane recognizes him too, but can't see what's wrong. He flees outside, leaving a trail of muddy footprints, even though it hasn't been raining. (This is a clue to something apparently written out of the script; there's no further hint as to why Paul was in the mud.) Paul stops Mrs. Hawthorne's car, and urges her to get Jane to leave; we see his face clearly — his skin looks like alligator hide.

The next day, Dr. Sinclair returns from somewhere or other, driving an amphibious vehicle right out of the swamp and up onto the land. (It was handy, I suppose; it's never seen again.) He, too, tries to get Jane to leave.

Jane finally has a confrontation with Mrs. Hawthorne, telling her that she must be doing terrible things to Paul. This causes Mrs. Hawthorne to unbend enough to admit something almost surprising: she's Paul's mother.

Later that evening, Paul enters the house again and immediately encounters Jane. She tries to get him to stay and talk, but he flees back outside into the rain; Jane follows. She staggers along through the swamp, literally tripping over alligators, and is almost bitten by a poisonous snake before being rescued by Mannon.

He takes her to his shack, wraps her in a blanket, and slobberingly tries to kiss her. She struggles, so he knocks her to the bed, then begins to get some ideas about rape. However, Paul bursts into the cabin, beats the crap out of Mannon, and dashes back into the rain. Mannon calls him "alligator man" and shouts that he'll kill Paul just "like any four-legged gator."

Paul insists to Sinclair that he try the next step in the experiments by the following night. He wants to become human again and be a husband to Jane. Sinclair reluctantly agrees to this.

Later, we see Sinclair trying out his giant X-ray machine on an alligator, shooting a foggy ray at the strapped-down gator's head. Then he explains to Jane what's going on, beginning by pointing out that "higher life forms" are governed by the mind and nerve impulses, while in lower forms, "life processes are governed by chemical substances." All this is a preamble to telling her that

Beverly Garland struggles photogenically with Boyd Stockman in the suit by Ben Nye and Dick Smith (not the current makeup maestro); you may be forgiven if you find this more than a little silly. From The Alligator People (1959).

he'd observed reptiles regenerate missing limbs, so he tried to do the same in human beings, by using serum extracted from alligators. He'd wanted to save mangled people like Paul, and restore them to a useful life. (He probably didn't try it on convenient Mannon, with his missing hand, because the guy was just too disgusting.) Sinclair was financed by Mrs. Hawthorne, so that Paul was an early patient. And the whole thing has worked fine, for a while.

They're interrupted by one of Sinclair's brawny staff workers, who takes them to a cell-like room; alligator-skinned patient #6 is struggling with the workers, making incoherent noises. Sinclair turns on a sunlamp, and the man begins to quiet down. He can't be helped now, Sinclair says; "I'm afraid the brain tissues have been affected."

The sunlamp quiets them, he says, because reptiles are made lethargic and relaxed in sunlight, being cold-blooded. The patients are "turning into [long pause] alligators!" exclaims Jane. "In effect you could say that," Sinclair concedes.

That night, Sinclair tries the big experiment on Paul, who strips to the waist—he's alligatory on his hands and face, very slightly elsewhere—and reclines on the operating table. The ray machine, combining gamma and X rays (powered by the radioactive substances that arrived when Jane did) is aimed at Paul's head, and turned on.

Everything has to be timed precisely, but it all goes to hell in a handbasket when Mannon, intent on having his revenge on Paul, bursts in. He knocks out

Sinclair, causing sparkly little short circuits everywhere, and extending the exposure on Paul far beyond what it should be.

Mannon staggers into the X-ray room and gazes through the smoke: boo! Paul has been turned into an alligator man for sure: his skin is scaly everywhere, and his head has become that of an alligator. This alligator man (now played by Boyd Stockman) leaps to his feet, and Mannon swings at him with his hook hand, catching it on a wire and electrocuting himself. Pauligator lurches into the other room where, understandably enough, his mother faints and his wife screams at what Paul has become. He dashes outside into the cypress forest.

Jane follows him—the lab and house exploding behind her, conveniently killing everyone who might corroborate her story—and watches in horror as he briefly wrestles with a real alligator. Followed by Jane, Paul staggers on further into the swamp, and for a moment catches a glimpse of his reflection in a pond. There's a quicksand bog nearby, and Paul ends up in it. It's unclear if this is an accident or suicide, but he doesn't struggle as he quickly sinks out of sight.

We return to Dr. McGregor's office, where he's discussing Jane's case with Lorimer. They are hesitant to tell Jane this terrible tale which her memory has blotted out, and decide that it would only ruin her life. She's made a satisfactory, if amnesiac, adjustment; she's well and healthy. They decide to leave her that way, and never to tell her the story of the alligator people.

Associated Producers, an independent company working for 20th Century–Fox, needed a cofeature for *Return of the Fly*. It's easy to imagine people sitting around trying out different movie ideas (using the plot of *The Fly* as a basic form), and finally happening on *The Alligator People* as a title. It's clear that there's no real impetus to the plot beyond that, and so a story was concocted—and that's the word—to give us alligator people.

While not a film that we can be grateful for being as good as it is, *The Alligator People* is nonetheless acceptable for being no worse than it is. It could have been wretched, but it's somewhat above average for a minor SF-horror effort of the period. The artificial premise is approached cautiously, an effort has been made, mostly through the use of the flashback, to create something a shade different, and everyone connected with the picture attempted to turn in intelligent work.

However, it's handicapped. Instead of being exciting, the story is mostly depressing. There are no villains; Mannon is just an obnoxious drunk, not evil and scheming. Dr. Sinclair is a dedicated scientist who might actually be on the right track. For all we will ever know, his treatment could have been exactly right if Mannon hadn't interfered. Mrs. Hawthorne is trying to spare the feelings of her son and the woman he loves. Paul is terrified of what he is becoming, but is still courageous and loving. Jane is merely trying to find out what is happening and, later, to deal with a bizarre situation.

Everything goes smash in the last reel; all these honest, dedicated scientists, loving mothers, loyal servants, hopeful experimental subjects, all are blown to smithereens because a lout got drunk. Even if the film was a lot better, it would still be morbid and unhappy.

Another major drawback is that alligator people aren't inherently menacing. Alligators aren't monsters; they're just big, slow canivores that usually can be avoided. An alligator man might be ugly and a monster by definition, but he isn't inherently a menace. At the climax, it's just *The Fly* all over again, except that Paul isn't even suffering from the war between his human and animal natures; he's just a victim. He doesn't even kill Mannon.

But more importantly, he looks silly. The suit and head are mediocre and not frightening. When Paul sinks without struggling into the quicksand, the last shot of the expressionless alligator head disappearing beneath the muck is funny.

The script by Orville H. Hampton, from a story by Hampton and Charles O'Neal, gets us from the beginning to the end painlessly. Things slow down for a while as characters enter and leave the mansion. This is, however, the kind of story where generally things have to mark time until the end of the picture. So after Jane gets to The Cypresses, there really isn't much that can happen – other than reconciliations and tale-telling – until the end, when everything has to be wrapped up. But it's still one of Hampton's least offensive scripts.

Hampton wrote several other mildly eccentric fantasy films, including *The Snake Woman*, *Jack the Giant Killer* (1962) and *Beauty and the Beast* (1963), in which the Beast was a werewolf. His most important credit was as the writer of the hackneyed but well-intentioned *One Potato, Two Potato* (1964). He also wrote as Owen Harris. See *The Underwater City* entry for more on Hampton.

The coauthor of the original story, Charles O'Neal, has at least one surprise in his credits: he wrote Val Lewton's fine *The Seventh Victim* (1943). The quality of his other scripts, including *Missing Juror* (1944), *Montana* (1950) and *Johnny Trouble* (1957) indicate that Lewton probably heavily rewrote O'Neal's script.

Veteran director Roy Del Ruth does his best with a limited budget and cast. Del Ruth had a long career which began in the late 1920s, with the first version of *The Desert Song*. He also directed the first versions of *Three Faces East* (1930) and *The Maltese Falcon* (1931), and did several neat little melodramas for Warner Bros., starring James Cagney (*Blonde Crazy*, *Taxi*, *Winner Take All*, *Lady Killer*), Edward G. Robinson (*Little Giant*), Leslie Howard (*Captured*) and Bette Davis (*Bureau of Missing Persons*). Later, he smoothly switched to musicals, such as *Kid Millions* (1934) with Eddie Cantor, *Folies Bergère* (1935) with Maurice Chevalier, *Broadway Melody of 1936* (1935) with Jack Benny, *Thanks a Million* (1935) with Dick Powell, *Born to Dance* (1936) with Eleanor Powell and James Stewart, a couple of Sonja Henie films, Bing Crosby's *The Star Maker*, and Alice Faye's *Tail Spin* (both 1939).

But by the early 40s, with few exceptions, Del Ruth had been switched to minor melodramas for major studios, or major melodramas for minor studios. He did do *Topper Returns* in 1941, but the next year did B-movie *Maisie Gets Her Man*. In 1943, he helmed the big-budget musical, *DuBarry Was a Lady*, but the year after that could fare no better than *Barbary Coast Gent*. He didn't work in films for three years, returning for the newly-formed Allied Artists (out of Monogram). In the early 50s, his fortunes improved with *The West Point Story* (1950) with Cagney, and *On Moonlight Bay* (1951). He directed *Phantom of the Rue Morgue* (1954), but directed no features until *The Alligator People*, his last movie. He died in 1961.

Del Ruth tries to keep things smooth and atmospheric, but *The Alligator People* tends to be talky and static, and he can't seem to generate much energy. He works reasonably well with the awkward CinemaScope frame, and doesn't misuse close-ups. There are some scenes with good pacing, such as Garland's two pursuits of Crane through the swamps, and the scene with Chaney in the shack has a little tension. The script does get into mysterious but insignificant things fairly swiftly, although we don't see our first alligator person until the film is almost half over. In short, Del Ruth was a competent professional, but can't generate excitement that is missing from the material.

The cast is above average for the genre. Beverly Garland was no stranger to this kind of film, having already appeared in *Curucu, Beast of the Amazon* (1956), *It Conquered the World* and *Not of This Earth*. Talented actress though she is, she's simply too tough and too intelligent to portray a fainthearted, negligee-clad heroine. Instead, as usual with Garland, she's the boss of her scenes; even the script sometimes allows this. When she encounters her husband in the old house, she immediately takes out after him, gamely stumbling over real alligators. At the end, when most women would collapse on seeing their husband has turned into an alligator-headed freak, Garland gives one lusty scream, and again sets out in pursuit through the swamps. In a character sense, the least believable parts of the film are those requiring her to act like a traditional horror movie heroine.

George Macready moved easily from playing villains in major films to troubled older leads in supporting fare. His hard, scarred face lent him mostly to villainous parts, and he was sometimes at a loss to project sympathy, usually settling for a kind of frowning weariness, which he alternates here with over-playing scenes of scientific worry. His films probably of most interest to readers of this book include *I Love a Mystery* (1944), *Soul of a Monster* (1945), *The Monster and the Ape* (1945), *Down to Earth* (1947), *Alias Nick Beal* (1949), *Tarzan's Peril* (1950), *The Golden Blade* (1953), *Seven Days in May* (1964), *The Human Duplicators* (1965), *Dead Ringer* (1964), *Night Gallery, Daughter of the Mind* (both 1969 TV movies), and *The Return of Count Yorga* (1971), produced by his son. However, Macready also played in a wide variety of other films, ranging from *The Black Arrow* (1948) to *Paths of Glory* (1957), probably his best role. He died in 1973.

As the unfortunate Paul, Richard Crane is competent enough for the level of the film. He never seems tortured enough, but also is thankfully free from maudlin self-pity. Crane was one of several male ingenues who became minor stars during the latter years of World War II, when many of the bigger stars in his category were absent in the service. He came to prominence in *Happy Land* (1943), but had relatively few other leading roles in major films. He was the star of the syndicated TV series, "Rocky Jones, Space Ranger" in the early 1950s. Several of these episodes were edited together to make a few "movies" that have played only on television. Among his other films were *Angel on the Amazon* (1948), *Mysterious Island* (serial, 1952), *The Neanderthal Man*, *The Devil's Partner* (1958), *House of the Damned* (1963), and *Surf Party* (1964). He died in 1969.

The Southern-as-a-mint-julep mother was rather overplayed by Frieda Inescort, a frequent supporting player from the mid-30s on. She appeared with Bela Lugosi in 1943's *Return of the Vampire*, and in many A-budget films, including *Mary of Scotland* (1936), *The Letter* (1940), and *A Place in the Sun* (1951).

The two psychiatrists were given star billing in the film, but are relatively unimportant. It's possible though not likely that the film was originally completed without the flashback structure at all; nothing in the film as we see it demands this. Bruce Bennett, as one of the psychiatrists, is flat and unconvincing in *The Alligator People*. For more on Bennett, see the entry on *The Cosmic Man*.

Douglas Kennedy, the other psychiatrist, also has an unimportant role, but does have the burden of asking Garland stilted questions in order to prompt her into telling the plot. Kennedy was limited, but could project a certain intensity in melodramatic parts. For more on Kennedy, see the entry on *The Amazing Transparent Man*.

Apart from Garland, the best performance in the film is Lon Chaney's, which is somewhat unusual for him at this point in his career, but he was well-cast as Mannon. Totally out of his depth in roles requiring subtlety and reticence, Chaney always came into his own when playing larger-than-life louts. He's outrageously hammy in some scenes in *The Alligator People*, but it is in keeping with the character he plays. He relishes his comic big scene, when he's shooting at the gators, and has a good time hating them in the pickup trip from the depot to The Cypresses, running over a gator with great glee. The role of Mannon really seems crammed into the picture, just a device to keep the plot bubbling, but Chaney is great fun in the part.

Karl Struss' photography is very good; he always knows where to place the lights in shadowy scenes for maximum effect, and throughout makes the sets (apparently left over from other productions) seem real and solid. His great reputation is fully deserved. During the 1920s, 30s and 40s, he worked on important films, including *Ben Hur* (1926), *Sunrise* (1927), D.W. Griffith's *Abraham Lincoln* (1930), *Island of Lost Souls* (1933), *Dr. Jekyll and Mr. Hyde* (1932), several for Mae West, Chaplin's *The Great Dictator* (1940) and *Limelight* (1952), and one for Orson Welles, *Journey into Fear* (1942). After the late 40s, however, the always somewhat eccentric Struss worked primarily with director Kurt Neumann. It seems likely that Struss simply did the pictures he chose to, and didn't mind that they were low-budget exploitation pictures.

The makeup effects are credited to Ben Nye and Dick Smith (not the current makeup master). The makeups are fairly simple; the alligator people have thick appliances on the forehead, cheeks and necks, with the forehead piece built up to resemble heavy brow ridges. Crane wears alligatory gloves too, but they oddly lack claws. One other actor, Bill Bradley, is also seen in alligator-man makeup. At the end, when Paul goes mostly gator, it's via an elaborately sculpted but only slightly articulated alligator head. (It actually resembles a crocodile more than an alligator, but let that pass.) This is simply not believable. This lack of believability is emphasized when Paul has to gaze into a pond to discover that he indeed has the head of an alligator; couldn't he see that long snout sticking out in front of his eyes? In fact, the head is so far from believability as to become comic, deadly to a horror film. It brings the last few minutes of the film crashing down in ruins; despite the efforts of the talented people involved, the film becomes a fiasco.

The American movie trade publications liked it. Jack Moffitt thought it "a better than average horror film, based on a remote but accurate scientific gimmick," and added that the screenplay and direction "keep the yarn from being as hokey as it sounds" and that the flashbacks "carry considerable suspense." In *Variety*, "Glen" thought it was a "good program horror film" which was "logically developed" with "good characterizations." The script provided "plausible explanations for the implausible and injects warmth and humor at points making the horror more horrible," although it "lags in the middle stretch."

Alan Frank (*Horror*) found it "predictable enough" but "good of its 'B' movie type."

The critic at the *Monthly Film Bulletin* was much less generous, leaning heavily on *Variety* and *Reporter* reviews. "After the mystery has been intriguingly unravelled against a suitably grim background ... its atmosphere deteriorates and melodrama ... takes over." The *Bulletin* gave the film its lowest rating.

Actually, *The Alligator People* is a decently-crafted and intelligently-made program SF-horror film, sadly let down by misconceived makeup and perfunctory ideas.

The Angry Red Planet

The strange appearance of the Martian scenes in *The Angry Red Planet* baffled me when I first saw the film. I couldn't understand what the point was in tinting red all the scenes set on the Martian surface, and photographing them in a process which made the blacks generally print as light-colored areas. People emerging from a shadowy doorway look as if they are stepping out of a pale pink solid. This process, plus the occasional use of very cartoony-looking drawings of Martian plants, cities and landscapes certainly give *The Angry Red Planet* a distinctive look, but it's not an interesting look; it's just different.

When I learned that the intent was to make the live-action scenes look like cartoons (to "hide" the cartoony look of the scenery), I was even more puzzled. To this day I see no advantage in doing it. Supposedly, it was so that expensive matte paintings or even more expensive miniatures could be dispensed with, and simple line drawings could be used for sets and backgrounds, as all would be on the same level of reality. But a live-action film in which all the characters, props and effects look like cartoons seems perverse.

Even if it had worked perfectly, however, it would have not made the film anything other than the tepid bore it is. There are a few mildly interesting ideas in the script by Sid Pink and Ib Melchior, but not enough to offset the film's essential dreariness.

The story opens as the first expedition to Mars is returning. Of the four who went, only two were returning, Dr. Iris Ryan (Nora Hayden), and an unidentified figure covered in green-black goo. Melchior and Pink intended for the identity of the second survivor to be a mystery. However, it's patently obvious the survivor must be the romantic lead, pilot Tom O'Banion (Gerald Mohr). As Eugene Archer said in the *New York Times*, "any observer who cannot guess which two came back alive should have a fine time at the film." Clearly, neither Brooklynesque Chief Warrant Officer Sam Jacobs (Jack Kruschen) nor wise old scientist Professor Theodore Gettell (Les Tremayne) could come back at the expense of True Love.

Under sodium pentothal in the hospital, Iris tells the strange story of their trip to Mars. The voyage there is uneventful, except for the usual glowing red meteorite (here it's also radioactive), and the landing is accomplished without mishap. However, not long after their arrival, Iris sees a strange, three-eyed face peering in the window. She screams, and we return to the present, only to hear her start telling the story again so we can go back to those flashbacks.

One of the doctors tending her points out that we are seeing only Iris' memories and not necessarily what really happened. Some people who have written about *The Angry Red Planet* have made much of this idea, but in the film, there's nothing whatsoever to indicate that we are seeing anything other than the movie's reality. At the end, there's even a tape recording of a Martian voice which confirms everything Iris has said, so this hint is merely misdirection and, perhaps, an effort to explain away the "dreamlike" look of the Martian landscape.

Back on Mars, they leave the ship to "explore" (at no time does there seem to be any rationale for their wanderings hither and yon). Sam tries out his trusty ray gun, which for some reason crystallizes things; novelty, I presume. He also falls in love with it, a tradition for comic, sexually-starved and ill-fated second bananas. (Sid Melton became enamored of a parachute in *Lost Continent*, and he came to a sad end.) He has use for it, too, as very shortly Iris blunders into a carnivorous plant, which tries to make a meal of her. Considering the scarcity of Martian animal life, the plant was probably pretty hungry. Fortunately, Sam uses his freeze gun on the thick-leaved plant, and Iris is saved.

The next day, all four again go exploring, and leave the liver-leaved forest (invisible in long shots of the ship). They spot some spiny "trees" nearby; when Tom and Iris go to investigate, they discover the trees are the legs of a tall, spindly creature, usually called the Bat-Rat-Spider, because it has features of all three animals (as well as claws like a crab). It stands on tall, slender spider legs, supporting a furry body with a long, ratlike tail; the face, which has huge eyes suitable for a nocturnal animal, is also ratlike, but it has a bat's huge ears. It's a monster-movie monster; it's difficult to imagine how evolution could have produced such a preposterous beast. However, the damned thing is almost endearing.

It toddles over Iris and Tom, heading for the professor; he hides in a cleft of rock, which the Bat-Rat-Spider squeezes together like a nutcracker. There's a great deal of shouting by all the Earth people, some shrieks by the Bat-Rat-Spider, and much confusion until Sam aims his trusty gun (which he calls Cleopatra) at its face, causing the pupils of its eyes to disappear. Shrieking, the monster dashes away over a nearby horizon. "Some playmate!" Sam cries. "King Kong's big brother!" He's a card.

The brave little band presses on and discovers a gigantic sea, which would be (but is not) plainly visible to astronomers on Earth. They return to the ship and, because of the encounters with the alien creatures, decide to leave. But some mysterious force prevents the ship from taking off. The professor said earlier that he felt there was a hidden controlling force on Mars which is running things and creating a feeling of dread and quiet. Based on no evidence whatsoever, he proposed a community mind.

Since they can't leave—which in view of what we learn is the Martians' intent, seems odd—they decide to cross the sea. They take their rubber life raft, unusual equipment for an expedition to a desert planet, and set out across the sea. They see the (cartoon) spires of a futuristic city on the far side, but a giant amoeba bubbles to the surface of the sea and chases them back to their ship.

The monster, which trundles over the land behind them like a biological tank, is described by all as an amoeba, but it looks more like a colossal Portuguese man-o'-war, a colony creature found in most of the oceans of the Earth. It also has a rotating eye resembling a demented gun turret, a feature that always gets the laughs it deserves.

Just like The Blob, the amoeba glops itself down onto the rocket, preventing takeoff (as if they could anyway). It also eats Sam, and wounds Tom's arm as he tries to rescue the beloved ship's clown. The three rig the electrical system into shocking the creature until it lets go. The Martian, which had peeked over a rock at them when they first left the sea, now speaks to them over their radio, and Iris records the message.

She looks outside, and sees the Martian's face again, so she screams and blacks out. The ship takes off; it manages to return to Earth, but somewhere along the line loses the professor. He just vanishes.

This graceful/awkward, almost surrealistic Bat-Rat-Spider Martian monster is the element most people remember with something like fondness from the lethargic Angry Red Planet (1959).

Back on Earth, no one seems quite ready to believe her story, although there's no good reason they shouldn't. Things look all up for Tom, hidden in that slimy mass of Martian amoeba, until Iris suddenly remembers that electricity chased away the big one. They try it (offscreen) on the mass sort of consuming Tom, which rescues him. Presumably he's a bit thinner.

They all listen to the recording of the Martian voice.

"Men of Earth! We of the planet Mars give you this warning! Listen carefully—and remember! We have known your planet, Earth, since the first creature crawled out of the primeval slime of your seas to become Man. For millenia, we have followed your progress. For centuries, we have watched you, listened to your radio signals, and learned your speech and culture. And now, you have invaded our home, technological adults but spiritual and emotional infants. We kept you here, deciding your fate. Had the lower forms of our planet destroyed you, we would not have interfered. But you survived! Your civilization has not progressed beyond destruction, war and violence against yourselves and others [what others?]. Do as you will to your own and your planet, but remember this warning. Do not return to Mars! You will be permitted to leave for this sole purpose: carry the warning to Earth. *Do not come here.* We can and will destroy you, all life on your planet, if you do not heed us. You have seen us, been permitted to glimpse our world. Go now—warn mankind not to return unbidden. When we consider 'Man' mature, the planet Mars will call her sister Earth."

The film's original title was "Invasion of Mars," reflecting an interesting viewpoint. There had been many stories of aliens invading Earth; this time, we were the invaders, or so was the original intent. Unfortunately, ultimately it was just like any other planetary exploration film, and the "invasion" aspects remained hidden until the Martian message, which of course seems arrogant, pompous and threatening to no good end. The explorers were always attacked first, and only defended themselves. If we had seen them behave in destructive, ill-considered ways, the we're-the-invaders idea would have had some impact. As it is, it's not even an undertone.

The film was produced by Sidney Pink and Norman Maurer. Pink had dabbled briefly in film production in the early 50s, when he formed a partnership with Arch Oboler to make *Bwana Devil*, the film that began the 3-D craze of the period. He went back into film distribution after that, apparently burned by legal complications, but Maurer's development of a new process for films spurred his enthusiasm to get back into filmmaking.

Special effects technician Robert F. Skotak apparently has a fondness for *Angry Red Planet*, as he has written two long articles on the film, the first for *Fantascene #1*, the second for *Fantastic Films*. In them, he overpraises the picture, but also gives extensive information on its production history. Most of my commentary on the background of the movie comes from Skotak's articles. (The article in *Fantascene* covers all of Melchior's SF films, and was cowritten with Bob Scott.)

Norman Maurer was a graphic artist who had worked a long time in comic books; although a fine comic book artist, he was more concerned with layouts and design than with actual drawing. As he was the son-in-law of Moe Howard of the Three Stooges, Maurer was instrumental in getting 3-D comic books launched with a Stooges comic in that process. Maurer's method for printing comics in the anaglyph process was by far the best. For films, he had developed a lens-and-printing technique which he called Artiscope. Redubbed Cinemagic, it was the technique used for the Martian landscape scenes in *The Angry Red Planet*. It was also used, more in line with what Maurer wanted, in *The Three Stooges in Orbit*, also covered in this book.

The intent was to make live action look like line drawings, so that the drawings by comics artist Alex Toth, used for the cityscape and much of the vegetation, would look just as real as the live-action footage. Pink told Skotak, "The idea was to make the backgrounds as cartoon illustrations. We could then project whatever we wanted behind the actors and Cinemagic would blend them right into these backgrounds." The footage was shot in black and white; after etching the negative with acid to remove some of the darker areas, it was printed onto a positive of the same scene, resulting in the bizarre, burned-out image that was used. A similar effect can be obtained through a process called "solarization," which can be seen in the alien landscapes in *2001*.

Cinemagic involved four separate printings involving a special lens, which rumor has it was damaged when one of the producers petulantly threw it against a wall. Furthermore, for the process to work properly, the actors had to wear dead-white makeup. Unfortunately, after all this work, the basic idea was doomed from the start.

After all, who really wants to watch a movie in which the effects as well as the people look like cartoons, but aren't? Even if the film hadn't been plodding, unimaginative and underproduced, the Cinemagic effects would have been wildly out of place in a movie which is otherwise conventionally filmed.

Other than the perplexing Cinemagic scenes, the most memorable aspects of *The Angry Red Planet* are the wild monsters, all based on drawings by

Norman Maurer. The Bat-Rat-Spider, which I would love to own, was a very lightweight marionette, and always looks like one. The puppet was made from lightweight resin, and covered in latex rubber and monkey fur. It was built on a scale of 5/16" to one foot, and the lightness of the model, according to Skotak, caused the special effects director "knotty physics problems in working out the delicate weight-to-support ratios." He must have done something wrong, because the monster seems barely to touch the surface of Mars, skittering around as if a mild breeze would waft it over a hilltop.

According to Mark McGee, model-builder Howard Weeks "was working on that thing when [Sidney] Pink came up behind him and, as producers are often compelled to do, made some remark about how that wasn't what he had in mind at all. [Weeks] threw it in the trash can and said, 'Well, what *did* you have in mind?' Of course, it eventually wound up fished out because ... *he had nothing* in mind."

The amoeba was cast in "Ken-plastic" (polyvinyl chloride), and was about three feet long. It was, says Skotak, "attached to an underwater track along with a cluster of air hoses which were used to achieve bubbling and churning effects. The breathing and tentacles were rigged to operate hydraulically, but only the breathing function ever worked properly." A misreading of the script ("two ... nuclei almost like eyes ... which revolve constantly") resulted in gun-turret eyes which rotate madly while the amoeba is in motion.

Mark McGee told me how Maurer and other workers mixed up a batch of Jell-o and fingerpaint to make the goo for the arms and for the scene in which the amoeba is visibly covering the window of the spaceship. They also placed their model ship in a pile of Jell-o and heated it on a hot plate. It melted while they filmed it; when this was printed in reverse, the slimy mass engulfed the ship.

The plant that tries to eat Nora Hayden was made out of styrofoam with rubbery tentacles, operated from behind. The Martian was a simple suit worn by midget actor Billy Curtis. In the script, there's a scene, probably the only one intended to be an exaggerated memory by the heroine, in which the Martian appears in giant form, towering over the ship; although there's a still like this, the scene does not appear in the film.

For the scene in which they try to paddle across the Martian ocean in their rubber life raft, the actors were sitting on the bottom of the tank, going nowhere. This is just what it looks like, too; there's no hint that the raft is buoying them up.

As to the disappearing Professor mystery (on the return trip), there are two stories as to what happened. In the script, the Professor died and Iris buried him in space. According to Mark McGee, the scene was removed because the sound effect involved sounded like a toilet flushing. This would seem to be easily remedied. On the other hand, there was an article in a Portland news-paper,* in which actor Les Tremayne said the audience burst into laughter at the pompous solemnity of the scene. "I went to the preview," Tremayne said, "and that was a horrible mistake. I about died of embarrassment at the raucous laughter when this great moment came on. I'm thankful it was clipped by the producers—but they never did reshoot anything. Now I'm getting fan mail asking where I disappeared to!" Then again, both stories might be true. The article begins by saying Tremayne was "still flushed with embarrassment...."

*During this period, I scrupulously clipped and saved articles and reviews of SF movies, but didn't date the clippings or indicate their sources. Give me a break; I was a kid.

Initially, *Red Planet* was distributed by the company that financed it, Sino Productions, but this was only in its first Los Angeles engagements. It was quickly picked up by American International, the company that seemed destined to release it, and the film seems to have done good business across the country. It had an especially sensational ad campaign.

Reviews were mixed. The *Motion Picture Herald* was very favorable, and referred to Cinemagic as a "well-conceived optical effect," finding the film itself to be a "thrilling adventure." However, the *Monthly Film Bulletin* gave it their lowest rating, and called it "A juvenile piece of science-fiction, distinguished by the tameness of its 'Cinemagic' technical effects, the unpleasantness of its subject matter, and the basic inconsistency which postulates the existence side-by-side of a "higher civilisation' and such amiable fauna as the Bat-Rat-Spider. The Martian landscape is a risible collection of cardboard cut-outs, photographed in a kind of infra-red light against which the human figures blur like ink on blotting-paper."

"Powe" in weekly *Variety* called it an "ordinary sci-fi horror item," and said that the movie "has little to recommend it," adding that the story was "routine." Of Cinemagic, Powe said, "While it may take considerable ingenuity to produce this effect, the result isn't really worth it."

Charles Stinson in the *Los Angeles Times* didn't care for Cinemagic either, calling it a "technique of waterily blurring the screen for a weird, unearthly effect." The script he found "simply embarrassing. Prosaically talky, insipidly, maladroitly 'humorous,' unbelievably stilted. Many in the audience finished the final 10 minutes of gripping drama in near-hysterics." He also demonstrated how far Cinemagic fell short of its intended effect: "the potentially clever blurring process is rendered useless by producer Pink's use of cheap, clearly unreal backdrops"—the same "backdrops" that were intended to blend seamlessly with the live action. Stinson concluded his scathing review, "The Martians send us home with a warning that they're losing patience with our moral infantilism and will wipe us out some day if we don't improve. A few more films like this and that day might be sooner than we think."

Jack Moffitt was slightly more favorable, but only by comparison. He called the prologue "Long, dull and seemingly endless," and considered the epilogue "involved and badly dialogued." He judged the film "primarily for the scream and clutch type of filmgoer," although there are damned few scare scenes.

Eugene Archer in the *New York Times* said that audiences would "discover that the planet looks like a cardboard illustration from Flash Gordon and is inhabited by carnivorous plants, a giant amoeba and a species resembling a three-eyed green ant."

In fact, all commentary on *The Angry Red Planet* I found was unfavorable, except for the *Motion Picture Herald*. More recently, Bob Skotak said, "No one will argue that *The Angry Red Planet* is a great, monumental work of cinematic art. But it doesn't deserve to be quickly dismissed and forgotten either, for its ingenuity and imagination dollar for dollar far outclasses many bigger, more celebrated films." While this may possibly be true regarding the special effects—the film certainly has plenty of them—it is not true for its dramatic values.

Les Tremayne has been better, and so has Gerald Mohr; Jack Kruschen has never been worse. As for Nora Hayden, she doesn't really seem to be an actress, so judging her as one would be unfair; she's gorgeous, and has an appealing personality, but is so limited as a performer it's not surprising that I can find only two other film credits for her, *Alaska Passage* (1959) and *Operation Camel* (1960).

Gerald Mohr had small roles in films as early as 1939, although most sources cite a 1941 serial as his first screen appearance. He rose quickly from bit parts in B films to starring roles in them; he played the eponymous character in the "Lone Wolf" series in the late 40s. He also appeared in *The Monster and the Girl* (1941), *The Catman of Paris* (1946), *Invasion U.S.A.*, and *Terror in the Haunted House* (1958). His last film was *Funny Girl*, released in 1968, the year Mohr died.

Les Tremayne is still busy as an actor, but has worked lately primarily as a voice only, for cartoons and commercials; this is how he began, in the heyday of radio. For seven years, he was "The First Nighter" on radio. Among his television series was the early soap opera, "One Man's Family" (itself a carry-over from radio), as well as "The Adventures of Ellery Queen" (1958–59), in which he played Inspector Queen, father to George Nader's Ellery. More recently, he played "Mentor" on the live-action Saturday morning series of "Shazam"; Tremayne was the adviser to Billy Batson, who could turn himself into Captain Marvel. An actor as busy and versatile as Tremayne automatically shows up in science fiction films again and again; he was notable as the tight-lipped general in *War of the Worlds*, but hammy in *The Slime People* (1963). Tremayne also appeared in *The Monster of Piedras Blancas*, *It Grows on Trees* (1952), *The Monolith Monsters*, and *Creature of Destruction* (1967). He narrated *Forbidden Planet*. He is a solid, reliable character actor, but can do little to improve *Angry Red Planet*.

The year after his appearance here, Jack Kruschen appeared in Billy Wilder's *The Apartment*, and received an Oscar nomination for Best Supporting Actor. Kruschen is generally a fine supporting player, at his best in comedies, and also appeared in a few other SF and fantasy films, including *Abbott and Costello Go to Mars*, *Carolina Cannonball*, *War of the Worlds*, *Satan's Cheerleaders* (1977) and *The Time Machine* (TV movie, 1978). He also appeared as a regular in two TV series, "Hong Kong" (1960–61) and "Busting Loose" (1977). He's absolutely awful in *Angry Red Planet*, aggressively "comic" and relentlessly cute, but to be fair to Kruschen, the role seems to require such overplaying.

Ib Nelchior's first association with science fiction was scripting two episodes of the 1959 TV series, "Men into Space." He has written several science fiction films, none as good as some of the ideas they contain. Melchior's talents seem to lie in devising story ideas, but not in writing dialogue or directing. He also wrote *Journey to the Seventh Planet*, *Reptilicus*, and the overrated *Robinson Crusoe on Mars* (1964). He cowrote *Planet of the Vampires* (1965), wrote the original story for *Death Race 2000* (1975), wrote a 1964 episode of "The Outer Limits," and wrote and directed *The Time Travelers* (1964). His non–SF scripts include *Live Fast, Die Young* (1958), *When Hell Broke Loose* (1958) and *Ambush Bay* (1966).

The Angry Red Planet was photographed by veteran cameraman Stanley Cortez (brother of actor Ricardo Cortez). In a long career, he photographed many notable films, but, oddly enough, it seems that for the most part, all his best films are black and white, while the color films he shot (solo) are lesser films. Among his titles: *The Black Cat* (1941), *The Magnificent Ambersons* (1942), *Flesh and Fantasy* (1943), *The Secret Beyond the Door* (1948), *Riders to the Stars*, *Night of the Hunter* (1955), *The Three Faces of Eve* (1957), *Dinosaurus*, *Shock Corridor* (1963), *The Naked Kiss* (1964), *The Ghost in the Invisible Bikini* (1966) and *Blue* (1968). He shot parts of *Chinatown* (1974) and *Damien Omen II* (1978). That's an odd mixture.

The Angry Red Planet is a tedious, boring and talky movie, with mismatched performances—all the lead actors seem to be playing in different films—and preposterous (though fun) monsters. The music score by Paul Dunlap is dreadful, occasionally gonging away in an attempt at being "celestial," usually slowing the slow pace even further. We get tired of Cinemagic, tired of the control room, tired of the characters, and tired of such small bizarre touches as a scene in which Sam is making fun of monster-oriented science fiction—which, of course, is just what The Angry Red Planet itself is.

Beast from Haunted Cave

The ads shrieked, "See screaming young girls sucked into a labyrinth of horror by a blood-starved ghoul from hell!" The film itself fails to live up to this slogan by rising above it. This dark little film is from Roger Corman's Filmgroup, and was shot in the Black Hills of South Dakota at the same time as the non–SF Filmgroup picture, Ski Troop Attack. The films had overlapping casts and crew, and physically resemble one another. The cheap film and processing used causes the dark shapes in the film to have a kind of nimbus around them. In a way, this adds a little to the film, a grim tale of bank robbers, snow, and a mysterious and unidentifiable monster.

In terms of movie history, the most significant aspect of the film is that it's the first directed by Monte Hellman, a talented if peculiar director who has made fewer films than his reputation would indicate. According to Roger Corman (in several interviews), Hellman has a deep interest in film as an art form, and his later movies attest to that. They are distinctive and serious, with strong control of place and character, although the storylines ramble at times and occasionally, as in China 9, Liberty 37, the point of the whole enterprise seems blurry. But Hellman has a real talent, although in Beast from Haunted Cave, it's still too early to see much of it.

The film has several virtues and, in fact, despite its basically familiar plot and low budget, comes very near at times to rising well above the mechanics of the monster-versus-crooks storyline. Several Filmgroup movies in this period are well-written, with better direction and acting than anyone had a right to expect, yet are still doomed to being cinematic trivia because of the limiting plots and genres. Like Roger Corman himself, they are just too intelligent for their own good. But, like him, they occasionally justify their existence just by the application of this intelligence to limited plots.

Charles B. Griffith, one of the most eccentric yet talented writers for Corman's group, wrote Beast from Haunted Cave, probably, as he usually did, in a matter of days. He was clearly told by producer Gene Corman the title, the locale and the number of characters. I suspect that Griffith provided almost everything else. Beach Dickerson has been quoted as saying this film has the same plot as Roger Corman's Naked Paradise and Creature from the Haunted Sea which, to a degree, is true. For more on Griffith, see the notes on Little Shop of Horrors.

Wealthy Alex (Frank Wolff), his alcoholic girlfriend Gypsy (Sheila Carol) and his two thugs, serious Marty (Richard Sinatra) and clownish Byron (Wally Campo), arrive in the snowbound town of Deadwood, South Dakota, intent on robbery. First they hang around town, making themselves known, and hire ski instructor Gill (Michael Forest), to take them on a cross-country skiing excursion to Gill's isolated cabin.

Marty is constantly trying to pick up women, but he's scared off Gill's sister, and transfers his attentions to barmaid Natalie.

We learn that Alex's plan is to explode a bomb in a nearby mine to divert everyone's attention away from town so he and his gang can rob the bank of some gold. Then, at Gill's cabin, they'll wait for a prearranged plane.

To Alex's annoyance, Gypsy makes a mild play for Gill, as Marty and Natalie go to the mine for some fooling around, and so he can set the bomb. They neck rather sweetly, until Marty excuses himself and goes farther back into the mine tunnel to plant the bomb. He notices a cobweb-covered egglike mass, but ignores it and returns to Natalie. As they kiss again, a spindly leg and more cobwebs edge into the shot; Natalie screams and Marty flees, returning to town without her. When Alex learns Marty took Natalie with him, he slugs him; Marty tells Alex that Natalie is dead.

The explosion and robbery go (offscreen) as Alex planned, and they set out on the cross-country trip with the unsuspecting Gill. Unknown to everyone, the monster from the mine (occasionally seen at the edge of the frame) is following them. It is after Marty, who seems almost telepathically aware of it. The first night out, he alone hears a kind of wailing roar, and searches for its source. He hears a moan, and looks up into the fork of a tree where he sees Natalie's body, cloaked in cobwebs. As he stares in horror at her pale face, she suddenly opens her eyes. He shoots her. The monster makes a grab for him but he dodges it and returns to camp.

Inexplicably, he doesn't tell anyone about what happened, except that it was horrible. "What I saw," he tells Alex, "you wouldn't believe."

They arrive at Gill's well-appointed cabin, which is tended by Small Dove, an Indian woman. In absolutely wretched and insulting "comedy relief," goony Byron dashes out of the cabin, expecting to be scalped. However, eventually he and Small Dove fall in love or something; at least they are inseparable, though why she would want to put up with such a scuzzy dullard is a mystery.

As they wait uneasily for the plane, Gypsy impulsively kisses Gill, which causes a sudden burst of violence. Later, she tells him that she was "an underpaid model in a wholesale house" (i.e., a whore in a whorehouse) when she met Alex. She liked the way he knocked her around, so she went with him, but she's beginning to get some pride back now. Gill has become aware (from the radio) that Alex and his group are those who robbed the bank, and Gypsy tells him that Alex will kill him when the plane arrives. She's decided to throw her lot in with Gill, however, and will help him if she can. The only question she has is "What happens when you get bored?" The relationships between everyone in this film are a little unexpected here and there.

As a matter of fact, Alex plans to kill not only Gill but Marty and Small Dove when the plane arrives.

While tensions build in the cabin, the monster grabs Small Dove and Byron hits it with a hatchet, but it escapes with its captive. While Gill and Gypsy flee on their own in the confusion, Byron heads after the monster, followed by Marty and, reluctantly, Alex. Marty in particular has a strange affinity/fear for the monster: "It's the most personal thing that's ever happened to me," he says.

Meanwhile, Gill and Gypsy are caught in a snowstorm and have to take refuge. "I know of a haunted cave not far from here," he tells her. Soon, everyone is converging on that cave.

Already there, Byron finds Small Dove stuck to the wall by the monster's cobwebs; while he's trying to free her, the monster grabs him too, and pins him to the wall. It sucks blood from both of them, in a scene similar to one in *Attack of the Giant Leeches*, also produced by Gene Corman.

Gill and Gypsy enter the cave and the monster chases them. She runs outside, encountering Alex and telling him several quick lies: "He forced me [to go with him]; he's in there without a gun." Alex dashes into the cave, but is killed by the monster. Marty shoots the strange, flimsy creature with a flare pistol after it wounds him and, as Marty dies, the beast goes up in flames. Gill and Gypsy are reunited.

By late 1959, the market for low-budget SF films had dwindled; the golden-egg goose had been strangled by increasing competition from the bigger studios, the inroads made on the market by imports, and growing disinterest of the public. Some variation had to be found just to keep the films going, and setting monster against crooks out in the snow seemed to provide that kind of novelty. *Beast from Haunted Cave* is certainly a cheap picture, but the setting is unusual, and though the monster does the usual things, it's one of the oddest-looking beasts in movies.

There are interesting touches throughout *Beast*, some from the direction, some from the script, and some from unexpectedly good acting on the part of almost everyone.

Marty is not the usual kind of thug; when he tries to pick up women, as Tom Reamy said in *Trumpet #2*, "his attentions are not vulgar and crude as you would expect from a gunman, but gentle and somewhat shy." He becomes obsessed with a kind of link between him and the monster, possibly because his cowardice caused Natalie to be captured by the monster, forcing him later to kill her himself. As he says, it's the most personal thing that has ever happened to him.

Although he does approach women in almost an innocently boyish manner, he doesn't really seem to connect with them. It's the *monster* with whom he has the personal relationship; it seems like some kind of avenging angel, pursuing him for his guilt in abandoning Natalie to the beast. (Joe Dante thinks this may relate to the myth of *Sisyphus*, which Hellman says provides the basis for most of his films.) It even shows him her web-covered body, his guilt made flesh. It is Marty, the second-string crook, rather than ostensible hero Gill, who eventually does kill the monster at the end and, in so doing, dies. He expiates his guilt for Natalie in a spectacular cloud of fire.

While fulfilling the requirements of a film called *Beast from Haunted Cave* (i.e., one, a beast, two, a haunted cave), writer Griffith and director Hellman clearly have other things on their minds. Within this modest little picture, they took a stab at the nature of guilt. This is done around the edges of the film, almost subliminally, and it's only an attempt, but that this kind of thing was even tried in a low-budget monster movie is a credit to those concerned.

There are other elements of decent characterization here and there. Gypsy and Alex call each other Charles, like something from a Howard Hawks picture, and she's drawn to him not despite his physical brutality, but partly *because* of it. This is only hinted at in the movie, so it's impossible to tell if this is masochism or another attempt at dealing with the ways people have of handling guilt. It's clear that Gypsy was a whore when she met Alex, and perhaps her allowing him to knock her around is a way of ridding herself of guilt for having been a prostitute.

Gypsy is the sort of moll who gets dragged around by cheap hoods in all kinds of these films, from the highest to the lowest; as with several other movies of this period, she seems to owe much of her origin to the role played by Claire Trevor in *Key Largo*. There's nothing much novel to the character, except that Sheila Carol makes her seem more alive than most, and gives stronger hints of a past. Unlike most molls who fall in love with a good guy (the old "why couldn't I have met you years ago" routine), at the end Gypsy still gives slight hints of not being entirely reformed. She still has some doubts about Gill, as in her line about how to fend off boredom, and she lies to Alex when it really wasn't necessary. Gypsy is a good-time girl who may regret her good times, but is used to them now. She's prepared a two-way path, depending on whoever walks out of the cave alive, Alex or Gill. Sheila Carol is very good in the role, and it is a shame that *Beast from Haunted Cave* seems to be her only movie of any consequence. (According to Don Willis [I], the Sheila Noonan who stars in *The Incredible Petrified World* is Sheila Carol.)

Wally Campo's Byron seems to have wandered in from some other film. Most of *Beast from Haunted Cave* is so low-key, direct and uncomplicated as to border at times on being semi-documentary; the photography is grimly realistic, and the performances are not showy, even when they are especially good. But Campo's painfully unfunny clowning seems to belong to one of the Griffith/Corman comedies, like *Creature from the Haunted Sea*. He's embarrassing here, and director Hellman hasn't any idea how to sell this humor; he just watches it, like the rest of us.

Marty and Gill are faintly linked; at one point, Marty is making a play for Gill's sister, which implies something of a connection. Later, in the cabin, Alex, Gypsy and Byron compare their lives to Gill's; only Marty doesn't join in this game. If Marty hadn't gotten involved with The Wrong Crowd, his life might have been more like Gill's. This, also, is a little unusual; when such contrasts are made in most films of this nature, it's between the head bad guy and the head good guy.

Richard Sinatra (son of orchestra leader Ray, cousin of Frank) is very good as the relatively complex Marty. He seems primarily like a nice, shy boy but does give indications that he's capable of greater violence. He, too, is knocked around a bit by Alex, but unlike Gypsy, doesn't enjoy it. He's along for the money, afraid to strike back. Sinatra later appeared in several films made by his famous cousin, including *Ocean's 11* (1960), *Robin and the 7 Hoods* (1964) and the dreadful *None but the Brave* (1965). Based on the evidence of his performance here, as with Sheila Carol, it's too bad Richard Sinatra hasn't worked more in films in prominent roles.

Frank Wolff's Alex is stereotyped in characterization, although his background as something of a dilettante crook is a little out of the ordinary. A fireworks manufacturer who is a part-time robber is not what you usually find in films like this. Generally, Alex would be a big-time gangster on the lam. Wolff is good in the role, the first of many villainous characters he would play, sometimes in major films.

Soon after *Haunted Cave*, he went to Italy, and became a major bad-guy character actor in the spaghetti Westerns of the late 1960s. Among his other films were Corman's *Atlas* (1961), *America America* (1963), *The Four Days of Naples* (1963), *Judith* (1966), *God Forgives—I Don't*, *Once upon a Time in the West* (both 1969) and *When Women Lost Their Tails* (1971), which may have been his last film, as he died in 1971. He had the leading role in *The Lickerish Quartet* (1970).

Many major actors are cited as having gotten their starts in Roger Corman–produced and/or directed films; Frank Wolff has almost never been mentioned in this regard, and that's unjust. He's fine as Alex in *Haunted Cave*, and his later performances were also usually well above average.

Michael Forest is inadequate as Gill, but that's partly not his fault. This may have been his first film, and the role is distinctly undeveloped, so it's not surprising that Forest does little with it. He's mostly just what would today be called a hunk, standing around looking heroic, all he has a chance to do.

Forest went on to play the title role in *Atlas*, and appeared in a wide variety of films, including *A House Is Not a Home* (1964), *The Glory Guys* (1965), *Deathwatch* (1966) and *The Loves and Times of Scaramouche* (1976). Forest steadily improved as an actor, and found better opportunities when not playing leads.

Monte Hellman was born in 1932, and studied film at UCLA. Roger Corman soon gave him a job after that, and for a while it looked as though Hellman might rise up in the ranks of directors like other Corman alumni, such as Francis Coppola and Martin Scorsese. But Hellman seems destined to remain on the outer fringes of moviemaking, never really achieving a success. In 1961, he directed the precredit sequence for *Creature from the Haunted Sea*, and was one of several people who directed parts of *The Terror*. With his friend Jack Nicholson, Hellman made *Back Door to Hell* and *Flight to Fury* in the Philippines in 1964, directing both and cowriting the second. The next year, with Nicholson and a small crew, he made two interesting if overrated Westerns, *The Shooting* and *Ride in the Whirlwind*, of quite different quality.

In 1971, Hellman was given his first chance at a major studio picture, *Two Lane Blacktop*. Warren Oates, who was in *The Shooting*, gives an outstanding performance, but the film itself did not live up to its overpublicized advance word. As Danny Peary says in his *Cult Movies*, the film was more like a European art film than like the popular *Easy Rider* of the time. However, despite the stillborn performance of James Taylor, *Two-Lane Blacktop* may eventually prove more memorable than *Easy Rider*. It failed at the box office, and Hellman didn't get another chance to direct for several years.

In 1974, he made *Cockfighter* for Roger Corman's New World Pictures, but once again the film that resulted—again with a fine performance by Warren Oates—didn't match its expectations. It's a bizarre, fascinating movie about a man obsessed with winning a cockfighting competition, but its approach is cerebral and cool, and its violent subject matter made it of little interest to most audiences. Corman cut it slightly and reissued it at various times as *Born to Kill*, *Gamblin' Man* and *Wild Drifter*, but it never found its audience.

Since then, Hellman has completed only *China 9, Liberty 37* (1980), an odd, out-of-step-with-the-times little Western with a meandering plot and mostly uninteresting characters. It has been seen almost entirely on television in the United States, a fate it doesn't really deserve, although it is not anywhere near as good as Hellman's best films.

He's popped up in odd places from time to time, as assistant editor on *Bus Riley's Back in Town* (1965), editor on Roger Corman's *The Wild Angels* (1966) and Corman's obscure *Target: Harry*, also known as *How to Make It* (1969). Hellman began as editor on *A Time for Killing* (1967), but left not long after Corman was replaced as director. Hellman was coeditor of Sam Peckinpah's *The Killer Elite* (1975), and began *Shatter*, aka *Call Him Mr. Shatter* (1976) as director, but was replaced after less than two weeks of shooting. He's considered something of an additional director on *Avalanche Express* (1979); director Mark Robson died before he could edit the film, so Hellman shot some additional footage and cut the movie. It isn't much of a credit to either Robson or Hellman, but it did get finished.

The monster in *Beast from Haunted Cave* was constructed out of aluminum and Christmastime spun glass ("Angel hair") by actor Chris Robinson, who also "wore" the lightweight structure like a costume. The monster is not described in the film, and although it is occasionally referred to as a spider in the few mentions of the picture that have turned up through the years, it doesn't look like a spider.

In fact, it doesn't look like much of anything: it's just a rounded shape with a harder understructure, including long teeth, visible through all the spun glass. It has both spindly legs and tentacles, and sucks blood out of its victims. It is at once one of the most biazarre-looking and yet most credible low-budget monsters. It moves in a jerky, floppy manner, but still is convincingly alive. The only times it seems phony is when it is poorly superimposed on the footage shot outdoors in South Dakota; at these times, it is transparent.

In *Famous Monsters of Filmland* #8, Robinson described the building of the beast, which he called "Humphrass," and which was seven feet tall with eleven-foot arms. He based the design on that of an insect he discovered in a book on unusual animals, the wingless hanging fly. "To one plywood base, I added a thin aluminum stripping to create the skeletal form. I then covered the skeleton over with chicken wire. After that I wrapped it in sheets and muslin, sort of like I was making a mummy. I had to waterproof the body because in this case it was going to be exposed to snow, so I soaked it with several coats of vinyl paint.

"The head was fashioned out of quarter-inch aluminum wire, with steel wire wrapped around that and then once again muslin, forming a sort of shroud.... More aluminum wire went into the construction of his jaws and teeth, and I topped the whole concept off with ... putty and patches of crepe hair."

Robinson completed Humphrass by adding spun glass to give it an appropriately cobwebby appearance. While, in a sense, the beast is not realistic, it is eerie and unusual, and it's too bad that this more imaginative type of monster-making wasn't used again. Compared, for instance, to the poor and almost indecipherable wasp mask in the film's cofeature, *The Wasp Woman*, the monster from *Haunted Cave* is an impressive creation, and an experiment that was well worth the effort.

Robinson himself went on to play juvenile support in major films like *Birdman of Alcatraz* (1962), *Darker than Amber* (1970) and *The Hawaiians* (1970), and occasionally starred in lower-budgeted films such as *Shoot Out at Big Sag* (1962), *The Cycle Savages* (1969), *Revenge Is My Destiny* (1971) and the horror film *Stanley* (1972). He is often seen on stage in Los Angeles, giving solid performances. He's genuinely fond of horror and science fiction films.

Being the bottom half of a double bill of inexpensive pictures more or less tossed out onto the marketplace by Allied Artists, *Beast from Haunted Cave* received very little critical notice other than in the trade publications.

"Gen" in *Daily Variety* said, "Gene Corman has provided *Beast from Haunted Cave* with a good cast and some very interesting locales; if there's still a market for horror pix, it should do fairly well." He was not impressed by the horror content, however: "We've grown inured to monsters and hardly blink when this one guzzles its customary quota of blood." He reserved most of his praise for the five leads, and especially for Charles B. Griffith's screenplay, which he thought was "an honest piece of work for the most part, considering the exigencies of this sort of film: e.g., the monster is caused to menace illogically from widely separated points." Which is true; one could also ask how a newborn monster of any sort, even one without any explanation (Marty suggests it was buried for centuries before being uncovered by miners) could locate "haunted cave" so easily.

Allen M. Widem in the *Motion Picture Herald* referred to the film's "semi-documentary" style, and thought that it was "sometimes taut." James Powers in *Hollywood Reporter* thought that Hellman's direction was "competent," but that the movie was otherwise "run-of-the-mill."

The *Monthly Film Bulletin* was, in this period, usually astute about low-budget SF and horror thrillers—always excepting those from England itself—but missed the boat on *Haunted Cave*: "Though substantially dissimilar to most monster pieces, particularly in its effective snowscapes, this rather crude and drab terror piece has few positive virtues. For much of the time, the creature is a tenuous, wispy affair, but in the later stages, when revealed in all its blood-sucking glory, it turns out to be sadly reminiscent of its many predecessors. With uneven acting and direction, the package rates as a very minor addition to the cycle."

More recent reviewers have found more virtues in the film. In *Trumpet*, Tom Reamy said, "*Beast from Haunted Cave* ... manages to hold its own. As a matter of fact, the subject is old and tired. Without the monster the whole thing would hardly be worth a second glance. As it stands, its only salvation from ignominy is the dialogue, good acting and a highly imaginative creature."

In *Castle of Frankenstein* #7, Bhob Stewart said, "Despite [a] 'C' budget, script and most of [the] shocks are good. At times excellent."

Don Willis (I) didn't care for the film: "Sheila Carol's classy, self-confident performance acts very agreeably against the generally dismal tone of the proceedings. The movie is mainly a showcase for her talent and style, but there are a few shudders."

The film, in fact, has one great shudder scene, the shot of Natalie, encased in the webbing, opening her eyes. Our first glimpse of her has a peculiar impact; it's so unexpected that you have a hard time adjusting to what you are seeing. And the image is *beautiful*. About the time you recognize it as a corpse caught in the branches, the "corpse" opens her eyes. It's an imaginative, almost poetic moment, at once both conventional and unusual, like the film itself.

As with so many of these films, I am not really attempting to make a claim for *Beast from Haunted Cave* as a classic, but am endeavoring to point out that even as the SF cycle waned, even within such essentially formula pictures as these, occasionally writers, directors and actors rose above the restrictions of the genre, and made interesting, imaginative films.

The Cosmic Man

This minor, low-budget cousin to *The Day the Earth Stood Still* evades me; I missed it when it was first released, never caught it in its many TV showings of the 1960s and early 70s, and it's not available on videotape. Perhaps because it was an independent production distributed by Allied Artists, it doesn't seem to be currently available for TV showings. Although I am curious about it, I don't feel I'm missing much for not having seen it.

Futura Pictures produced the film, directed by Herbert Greene from a screenplay by Arthur C. Pierce. (For commentary on Pierce, see the entry on

Invasion of the Animal People.) The film was shot quickly, primarily on a hotel lobby set, and in Bronson Canyon (though the Caverns themselves weren't used). It couldn't have taken more than ten shooting days altogether, and the resulting film is not well thought of.

After a U.F.O. is tracked at 50 miles per second (180,000 miles per hour, we're soon informed), someone discovers a strange object in Rock Canyon, in the hills near an air base and also near the Pacific Institute of Technology, good ol' PIT. Dr. Karl Sorenson (Bruce Bennett) of Pacific Tech and Colonel Mathews (Paul Langton) of the military both arrive at Rock Canyon. They antagonize one another immediately, partly because Sorenson is clearly not pro-military. "There are two kinds of power,"* he tells Mathews. "Constructive and destructive. You say knowledge of the workings of this object would be a great military power. In my opinion, that's the wrong thinking."

They are arguing about a large sphere, ten feet in diameter. According to the script: "In the clear air near the base of the sheer cliff rests the huge ball-shaped object. It is suspended, motionless and noiseless, six feet above the ground. There are no seams or openings of any kind in evidence on the surface of the sphere. The thing appears to be a solid metal mass." Perhaps it is metal, "but more like glass," suggests Sorenson. It resembles an immense ping-pong ball.

Could there be anything alive in the sphere? Mathews wonders. "Not as we know it," Sorenson says in the time-honored phrase from too many low-budget SF movies. At this point, Kathy Grant (Angela Greene) arrives, the proprietress of the nearby Grant's Lodge; with her is her young son Ken (Scotty Morrow), confined to a wheelchair. Perhaps because he is crippled, the boy has come to idolize scientists the way normal kids his age (that's the tone) usually love base-ball players or other athletes. He's overjoyed to meet Sorenson, whom until now he worshiped from afar.

Immediately, both Mathews and Sorenson show attraction for the young widow, but inasmuch as she feels a certain antipathy to the military — her husband died in Korea — and because Sorenson shows interest in Ken as well as Kathy, we have little doubt as to who will win her eventually. Also, Sorenson has been making a plea for interplanetary understanding.

Mathews grouses to his superior, General Knowland (Herbert Lytton), about Sorenson's interference, but Knowland sets him straight. In the first place, Knowland says, "Karl Sorenson holds the rank of Major General in the reserves. In the second place, if it hadn't been for Karl Sorenson, we might never have had the A-bomb. How would you feel if you were a man responsible for a weapon like that?" Writer Pierce seems to be saying that military men should find Sorenson okay because he's really one of them (a mere civilian couldn't be okay) and because he invented the A-bomb, but then again, inventing the A-bomb takes a lot out of a guy, so give him a little slack when he's testy.

Back at his lab, Karl chats with his assistant, Dr. Richie (Walter Maslow), proposing one of the oddest ideas about gravity I've encountered. Sorenson says that maybe gravity isn't a force that *pulls* us down, it might be one that *pushes* us down. This fails to explain a great deal, but never mind, it's a theory designed to intrigue 12-year-olds, the audience for whom the film was intended. He proposes a force (or particle?) called the "anti-graviton," keeping that sphere six feet above ground out in Rock Canyon. Dr. Richie is dazzled.

*Quotes are from the script; lines in the film may vary.

Meanwhile, in Rock Canyon, some soldiers on guard are disturbed by strange sounds, but can't really see anything. The sergeant (Lyn Osborn) scoffs at their fears, but when he arrives back at the Lodge, he hears strange sounds, too.

While in the Lodge, Mathews flirts with Kathy, we learn the sad, tragic truth about Ken: "The little darling," Kathy chokes, "will never get to do any [of the things he wants to]." Mathews understands. "How long?" he asks delicately. (When children are dying in movies, the word "death" is rarely used. On the other hand, "How long till the kid croaks?" would indicate a certain insensitivity.)

"Six months—a year maybe," replies the sad mother. "The doctors don't really know."

When Mathews is called away, a few moving objects frighten Kathy—no one (gasp!) is near them! She shines a bright light into that area, and for the first time we see the astonishing Cosmic Man (John Carradine). "In the scene," says the script, "is a partially visible form of something, human in shape, yet not human. It is a negative image of a man-like creature."

Pierce's theory is that the Cosmic Man is made of something like anti-matter. As Karl says later, the C.M. is "a solid mass and yet not a solid, a creature made of matter but more like anti-matter, emitting rays instead of reflecting them." He's also probably sky-blue pink. Carradine plays the C.M. in a skintight white costume, with a cape and skullcap, although he's shown in double-exposed negative. I presume this was supposed to be eerie and unusual, but most reviewers (and probably most audiences) spotted it for what it was: a cheap method of doing a spooky effect. Mostly he's seen in a slouch hat, overcoat and dark glasses.

Seeing this apparition, Kathy quite naturally screams, bringing everyone on the run, but also sending C.M. tiptoeing away. (Just why everyone constantly converges on the Lodge, especially the Cosmic Man, is probably explained by Kismet.)

That night in the nearby town, eerie things happen—burglar alarms go off, dogs bark, etc.—and a scantily-clad coed sees the Cosmic Man peeking in at her, an interstellar Peeping Tom. Actually, C.M. is on his way to Karl's lab, apparently just to poke around. Invisible, in a hall he passes some fluids and chemicals, set to boiling by his passage. (Eerie enough, but preposterous: why doesn't human blood boil in the veins when he passes?)

C.M. spots a flaw in the equation Karl and Richie have been working on, and in the interests of interplanetary goodwill, fixes it up. We later learn he also erases all the memory tapes of the nearby computer, which no one regards as a major setback.

Karl was ready for him, however, and later shows Richie a kind of image of the Cosmic Man on an electronic device he left around his lab on the off-chance that an alien visitor would happen by. He tries to tell Mathews that C.M. visited the lab, but because of professional and personal jealousy, Mathews merely sneers. While Karl and Mathews head up to Rock Canyon to see if they can move the sphere, Kathy has a visitor.

The stranger, clad in overcoat, hat and dark glasses, doesn't give his name (but we know who he is), talks in a stilted fashion, knows things about Kathy he couldn't, and says he needs a room. "I would like complete privacy," the gaunt stranger says, "I am much in need of rest." By now, Kathy is used to peculiar people traipsing through the Lodge, and assumes that the stranger is another scientist up there to poke around the sphere. He goes off to his room.

John Carradine in all his glory as The Cosmic Man (1959); lucky you, through the miracle of negative printing, you can see him just as he appears (or almost appears) in the movie.

At Rock Canyon, to Mathews' annoyance, a big truck cannot move the sphere. Oxyaluminum torches can't cut a hole in it. Karl and Mathews discover that the sphere turns sunlight into electricity, and deafeningly discover that it turns electricity into sound. Leaving Mathews to mess around with the sphere, Karl goes back to the Lodge and (again) chats with Richie and Ken about the sphere and whatnot.

"... and suppose this phantom atom," Karl says, "contains particles of a mass of M minus, vibrating along an axis X, under a force of KX toward the origin." Karl is clearly a scientist and talks calculus like a native, but I don't have any idea what he's saying; I suspect that Arthur C. Pierce didn't, either. Dazzle 'em with jargon.

Pretending they have forgotten the speed of light, Karl and Richie patronize Ken, sitting in on the conversation. Ken also knows all about the Cosmic Man — his mother overheard a conversation on the subject earlier.

Karl points out that the Cosmic Man operates only at night, which is "part of the answer" (but what was the question?). "In daylight, he is obviously partially visible, at night totally invisible." He feels he can probably disable the sphere with magnetism, but isn't sure if he wants to do that.

Knowland plans to ring the sphere with bright lights and dazzle the Cosmic Man into visibility, forcing him to give up at gunpoint. Sorenson points out that guns may not pose C.M. a threat, but Knowland doesn't change his mind.

It disturbs Karl to learn eminent scientist Dr. Steinholtz will arrive because he, too, could figure out how to disable the Cosmic Man via magnetism, but

Karl lets it slide for the time being. He has more pressing matters. He gives Ken a six-inch reflector telescope, which understandably pleases the star-loving kid.

Ken suggests that a "space chamber" could be built for the Cosmic Man, in which the alien's atmospheric conditions could be duplicated on the Earth's surface, enabling us to converse with him. This suggestion impresses Karl and, we learn later, C.M. himself, who sees it as a means by which many different alien races could visit Earth.

While the military types begin acting somewhat disgruntled about the attention being paid little Ken and his telescope, the Cosmic Man makes a semiappearance. In a notably foggy speech, he tries to tell everyone that he has come in the interests of peace, understanding and brotherhood. He wants the Earth to shape up before we make contact with other peoples, but unlike Klaatu in The Day the Earth Stood Still, doesn't say we'll be reduced to a burned-out cinder if we aren't good.

The night before, the Cosmic Man destroyed valuable equipment, and though no one was harmed, all think that this behavior indicates a threat to humanity. So Knowland tries to prevent C.M. from leaving the room, having his soldiers shoot at him, but the alien simply walks away.

Everyone assumes he's headed back for the sphere—C.M. has just said he has to leave Earth by dawn—and they go there to wait for him. Karl and Richie want to sabotage what they correctly assume are Steinholtz's attempts to disable the sphere magnetically. Karl bids a fond farewell to Kathy, and takes off after the others.

After everyone leaves, voices coming from Ken's bedroom awake Kathy in the wee hours of the morning. She discovers the boy playing chess with the mysterious stranger, who tells her, "the boy has given me much pleasure and a needed diversion from my work." Kathy, who must not be too bright, doesn't recognize the stranger as the Cosmic Man, and isn't particularly disturbed when he leaves.

But later the stranger returns and, in a scene designed to make us worry about Ken, approaches the boy's bed. Karl returns, and Kathy mentions the stranger. Karl's bright, and immediately realizes that the Stranger and the Cosmic Man are one and the same. (Is that a surprise? Could it be?) They rush to the stranger's room and discover makeup, the hat, and other discarded garments. Ken is gone.

Karl heads back to the sphere just as the Cosmic Man arrives, carrying Ken. C.M. warns them not to come closer, but assures them that no harm will come to the boy. There's some byplay with the lights and the big magnets Steinholtz has set up, but Knowland complies with C.M.'s demands that the lights be disconnected. C.M. puts the boy down and approaches the ship, but Steinholtz treacherously turns the lights on again.

The beams from the searchlights disable the Cosmic Man. Ken suddenly can walk (and, by implication, is cured of his fatal disease), apparently made whole simply by being carried by C.M. He rushes to where the alien has collapsed, wounded by the searchlights, and just as the sun comes up, says goodbye to him. The script says both Cosmic Man and his sphere vanish.

However, the Monthly Film Bulletin says, "the Cosmic Man gets away safely"; the Hollywood Reporter says, "for a moment he is clobbered by a sun arc. But soon he is off into the firmament." On the other hand, like the script, the official Allied Artists synopsis and FilmFacts say the Cosmic Man and the sphere vanish. I don't know what happens, and no one I've talked to recalls.

The borrowings from other sources are painfully obvious in The Cosmic

Man. The main source is *The Day the Earth Stood Still*; there's a benign space visitor who runs afoul of the military, but who is understood and accepted by scientists (and solves an equation for the main one); the alien befriends a small boy; he is killed (or not) as he heads for his ship; his mission, to tell us that we should be nice and unwarlike, and then we'll be admitted into the fraternity of the planets. Even Pierce's suggested behind-the-credits scene is similar: a view of our solar system from the perspective of a ship heading for Earth. The other main borrowing is from *The Invisible Man*: the invisible character arrives at an inn while clad in clothes and other apparel to hide his invisibility, and seeks quiet lodgings.

Virtually nothing about the film has originality. The spaceship is spherical instead of looking like a flying saucer, as in *Earth Stood Still*, but otherwise is similar. It can't be affected by machines or cutting tools, and remains in place.

The only added idea is curing the boy, so sentimental and contrived as to be almost repellent, quite the opposite of the intended effect. When unimaginative writers want to make a questionable character look thoroughly benign, they show him/her being friendly with some representative of innocence: a child, a puppy dog, a blind person, whose "purity" allows them to see through the aspect that frightens others. We never see the alien, monster, whatever, being befriended by say, an axe murderer, prostitute or lawman— people whose innocence is *not* obvious. The military is opposed to this type of alien and, usually, science is in favor of whatever is going on. Just once, I wish someone would make a film in which the benign alien was befriended by the military and opposed by some scientist, jealous of his lowered status. (In the inventive, imaginative *Strange Invaders* [1983], a tribute to the 50s SF films, this is *almost* what happens.)

Bruce Bennett began his acting career under the name Herman Brix, and played Tarzan in a film produced by Edgar Rice Burroughs, which in various forms is called *Tarzan and the Green Goddess*, *The New Adventures of Tarzan*, and other titles. This was also made as a serial, and in the 1930s, Brix appeared in several other serials, including *Shadow of Chinatown* (1937), *Hawk of the Wilderness* and *The Lone Ranger* (both 1938). He ceased acting briefly, took some acting courses, and returned to the screen in 1940 as Bruce Bennett. He was in both *Before I Hang* and *The Man with Nine Lives* (both 1940) with Boris Karloff, lower-case A films. Bennett graduated to real A films, appearing in a variety of them during the 1940s, including *Sahara* (1943), *Mildred Pierce* (1946) and *Dark Passage* (1947). His most important movie, one of the best ever made, was John Huston's *Treasure of the Sierra Madre* in 1948; he was the miner who tried to convince the three leads to allow him to share their claim.

Bennett always had an air of calm, dignified reserve, and rarely seemed able to work up convincing anger or excitement. Never an outstanding actor, his natural dignity was occasionally used to good effect. In the 1950s, he continued to appear in top-budgeted films, but his roles became smaller. He was in *Angels in the Outfield* (1951), *Strategic Air Command* (1955), *Love Me Tender* (1956) and *The Bottom of the Bottle* (1956). Bennett was active in television in the 1950s—he appeared in several episodes of "Science Fiction Theater"—but movie roles became fewer. After *The Cosmic Man* and *The Alligator People*, Bennett appeared in two films in 1961, which seem to be a high and low point of his career: *The Outsider* and the title role in *Fiend of Dope Island*.

Bennett made no further films until 1972's little-shown *Deadhead Miles*, a peculiar road movie starring Alan Arkin. Although Bennett's role in the picture is very small, it's also very memorable. A disabled truck sits by the road in a small, deserted town; Paul Benedict waits for Arkin to return with help. Bruce Bennett suddenly appears, dressed in an all-black Western suit and a Stetson, and offers to fix the truck. His own big rig, also all black, idles nearby; even though the motor is obviously running, Bennett's truck is soundless. We hear only the wind among the old buildings. Bennett reaches inside the disabled truck's motor and at once it's fixed. He bids Benedict farewell, and drives off in his eerily silent truck. We learn he's a ghost who wanders the highways, assisting disabled truckers. Even in this brief scene, Bennett's air of gentle, American dignity comes through strongly.

Bennett was a peculiar choice for the role of Karl Sorenson; at least he wasn't another scientist in the by now weary Richard Carlson mode, although Pierce wrote the part that way. Without having seen the film, I can easily imagine that the strengths Bennett would bring to the role would be unusual for a film of this type.

Except for *Deadhead Miles*, Bennett retired from films after 1961, and made a good living in real estate.

I discuss John Carradine in the entry on *Half Human*.

Reviews were not kind to *The Cosmic Man*. The *Monthly Film Bulletin* called it "naive, indifferently mounted stuff with interminable sci-fi jargon, a sticky crippled child motif, and an unexciting space man occasionally projected in negative, but mostly looking exactly like John Carradine in pebble glasses." They gave the film a rating of III.

After calling it "a dull science fictioner," "Powe" in *Variety* said that although it was apparently "designed to be a thoughtful science fiction thriller ... thought, in drama, is no substitute for action, and certainly not when the thoughts are banal as they are in this one. Word of mouth is likely to be deadly."

Although something can be said for the makers of *The Cosmic Man* apparently having the desire to make something a little different from the usual story of invaders, their lack of skill apparently made the film dull, and the lack of originality made it too familiar.

First Man into Space

This film was deceptively titled, but the deception was clever and exploitatively opportunistic. The film went into production shortly after Sputnik was launched (October 4, 1957), and the idea that people might actually go into space was suddenly on everyone's mind. Wyott Ordung's original story was called "Satellite of Blood," which was exploitative itself (satellite had become a favorite buzzword), but too ghoulish for use at the time.

The advertising for the film emphasized the realistic aspects of the story, with charts and diagrams showing how high a plane would have to travel in order to be considered actually in space. The tone of the publicity was sober and rational. Many people, including my schoolteacher aunt Irma Pajari, went to the film under the impression that they were going to see a realistic treatment of early space travel, not unlike *Breaking the Sound Barrier*. This caused a good deal of trauma for certain viewers.

Because what they got was a thriller about a blood-drinking monster from outer space. It's not as lurid as the other science fiction film made by the same company, *Fiend Without a Face*, but it was certainly more gruesome than *Breaking the Sound Barrier*. The elaborate monster suit wasn't even shown in the ads, possibly a first for a film of this nature. It isn't a *bad* thriller, but it isn't a sober semidocumentary on space travel. Now it is seriously dated, almost archaic.

The film begins in a realistic, if melodramatic, vein. Lt. Dan Prescott (Bill Edwards), a daring and devil-may-care test pilot, full of The Right Stuff, is flying the test plane, the Y-12, while being directed from ground control by his more conservative older brother, Commander Charles Ernest "Chuck" Prescott (Marshall Thompson). In defiance of Chuck's orders, Dan gets more than 100 miles high before he has to come back down.

By the time Chuck arrives at the landing site, Dan has beat it into town for some hanky-panky with his girlfriend, Tia Francesca (Marla Landi), herself a scientist—which means little in this film. Chuck catches up with him at Tia's, and sends his hot-tempered hotshot brother packing; Chuck scolds Tia for keeping Dan up late, or something.

Later, Dan is launched in the Y-13, obviously an advanced model (although the plane we see is actually an earlier design). When ordered to come back down, as he's getting too high, Dan replies, "No sir, I'm going straight up. First man into space!" And he fires the emergency booster, taking him higher than 250 miles. A ground technician says, "He'll either hit the Moon or orbit the Earth the rest of his life."

Neither happens. Dan's plane can't be turned, however, as there's not enough atmosphere for the plane's controls to react on. As the Y-13 enters a mysterious cloud, Dan ejects.

When his escape capsule is found, it's encased in a mysterious, cratery-looking substance, but Dan's body can't be found. Chuck and Tia, now beginning to become attracted to one another, commiserate over Dan's death.

The strange coating on the capsule defies analysis. Although it can be cut, X rays will not pass through it, nor will infrared rays. While experiments on the substance continue, mysterious killings in the area begin to occur, and a shadowy, grunting figure breaks into a blood bank, killing a nurse.

The local New Mexico police inspector, Chief Wilson (Bill Nagy), meets with Chuck at the wreckage of the blood bank, where it looks as though blood was "scooped up."

The monster kills a truck driver and steals the truck.

The head scientist on the project, Dr. Paul Von Essen (Carl Jaffe), determines that the strange coating was meteorite dust that hadn't previously passed through the atmosphere. The meteor dust coated the ship, keeping it from being damaged, while other parts of the ship, not coated, have been destroyed by the hazards of outer space. The dust provides a kind of "cosmic protection," says Von Essen. "Assume that there is life in outer space," he says, making an unwarranted assumption, "it would have to create a protective coating to survive those destructive forces up there."

Chuck has discovered another property of the coating. He shows Von Essen that the substance doesn't feel dangerous, but when he wraps a sheet of it around his hand, and swipes at a sheet of foam rubber, the rubber is deeply sliced by apparently intangible projections from the coating's surface. (However improbable, this is an effectively chilling scene.) Furthermore, this leaves micalike flakes in its wake, similar to those found on recently-killed cattle and at the blood bank.

The monster kills a couple of cops when they stop a car it's driving. By now, Chuck knows the monster must be Dan. (Things like this didn't happen to

Chuck Yeager.) The coating saved Dan from death in outer space, but altered his metabolism; apparently, the only way he can get oxygen is to drink blood. "It's incredible," Chuck says to Tia, "to think of your brother as a blood-drinking mon—" he breaks off.

Dan smashes into the room where Chuck and Tia are talking, and as he flees, Chuck realizes that Dan, though his mind is malfunctioning, is probably searching for Von Essen. Using loudspeakers placed throughout the laboratory complex, Von Essen lures Dan toward the high-altitude chamber. Chuck follows, and Dan takes swings at him every now and then.

Dan enters the chamber, but his hands are now too clumsy to work the controls, so Chuck goes in too, wearing an oxygen mask. As air is drained from the chamber, Dan's mind recovers enough to talk. (You'd think oxygen should be pumped *into* the chamber.) "Everything seems strange and dark," Dan moans. "I've been groping my way through a maze of fear and doubt." He was searching for Von Essen, and was unaware he was killing people. "Sorry things had to happen this way," he says weakly, "but I just had to be the first man into space." He dies.

Tia catches up with Chuck, who's sadly walking out of the space laboratory, as a narrator says, "The conquest of new worlds always makes demands of human life, and there will always be men who will accept the risks." Even though this suggests that being turned into a blood-drinking monster is an acceptable risk, at least it is a positive expression of "the outward urge," making it a slightly uncommon message for one of these films.

Although set in New Mexico, *First Man into Space* was filmed entirely in England. It's convincingly American, unless you are looking for flaws; you'll find them if you try. A shore patrolman who arrives at Tia's apartment with Chuck is dressed entirely wrong and is clearly dubbed. New Mexico is presented as being heavily forested, and the University of Albuquerque is covered with trees and looks like an Ivy League college. Alvarado is pronounced *alva-RAID-o* (rather than *alva-RAH-doe*). The New Mexico police chief is dressed in fedora and heavy tweed overcoat, like a New York police inspector. A Mexican farmer sounds like an Italian. A Mexican consul speaks Spanish with a heavy French accent.

But all these mistakes are certainly less serious than similar blunders Hollywood has always made when setting films in foreign countries. I mention them only for the record.

As a science fiction film, *First Man into Space* is a peculiar mixture of the conservative and the flamboyant. It opens with a reasonably realistic sequence of airplane testing, going not much beyond what was known and accepted at the time as scientific truth. There's little that's novel or surprising until the plane runs into that meteor dust.

Until that point, I suspect that those who went to this expecting a tame exploration of possible space travel were satisfied, if bored.

However, once the plane encounters the meteor dust, the story suddenly becomes a horror thriller, with that lumbering monster intent on ingesting blood. The two halves of the story have little to do with one another.

I suspect this strange bifurcation is a result of the production company hedging its bets. They probably assumed that it wouldn't be financially feasible to produce a simple, realistic film about the first man into space. George Pal they're not, and this certainly isn't *Destination Moon*. They must have decided that having a monster in the film would generate word-of-mouth among the youngsters to whom such things appealed; and calling it what they did, with the realistic opening, would attract "cross-over" customers that "Satellite of Blood" never could.

Although the film's story is strangely split in this manner, the film itself is more of a piece. Writers John C. Cooper and Lance Z. Hargraves, and director Robert Day tried to pull things together. Although the makeup and costume are definitely Scary Stuff, by and large the horror aspects are treated as a mystery rather than as conventional, terror scenes.

Except for the first major sequence, the raid on the hospital blood bank, featuring groping shadows and mysterious noises, the attacks by monster Dan are filmed as straightforwardly as everything else. Although the film has a horror-movie plot, Day and the writers keep pulling back from the horror-movie trappings. They do indulge in them at the climax, when Dan bursts into the space lab and stomps off toward the high-altitude chamber. Some tension and fear are developed here, in a conventional though not ineffective monster-on-the-loose style.

But mostly, the film is a SF mystery more than a SF horror film. As a mystery, it's certainly minor; there's no question that the blood-drinking monster is Dan, but the director at least tries to keep us entertained while we're waiting for the big revelation.

The photography by Geoffrey Faithfull is low-key and undramatic, in the flat gray style common to SF movies and crime films of the 50s. Despite the horror-movie aspects, First Man into Space generally looks like a semi-documentary SF film. This unsensationalistic approach to the photography and direction has led some people to overestimate the picture. It seems rational and believable. Indeed, this way of presenting the film does make the more outlandish parts of the story more believable than they would have been if it was all sensationalistic.

The film has some significant virtues, but they are not in the storyline. In his few scenes as Dan before monsterizing (I suspect another actor played Dan afterward), Bill Edwards is fairly good, and the scenes of him gazing ecstatically out his window at thousands of stars as he enters space itself communicate the driving attitude of an explorer with more effectiveness than you might expect in a picture of this nature. Edwards continued to act, but most of his other roles were much smaller. He was in both The Mouse That Roared and its sequel, Mouse on the Moon (1963), The War Lover (1962), The Bedford Incident (1965), and Chaplin's A Countess from Hong Kong (1967). (He should not be confused with the American actor of the same name, whose career does not seem to extend beyond 1951.)

This careful, rational approach of the film is reflected in Marshall Thompson's serious performance. He does manage often to seem like a big brother, fussily concerned about Dan's recklessness. Thompson also makes Chuck's initial hostility toward Tia believable, as well as his later thawing.

When he was younger, Thompson had an eager, boyish style that didn't age well. From the mid-40s until 1951, he was under contract to MGM, and appeared in many major films, usually in the male ingenue role. After that, however, he free-lanced, and his roles decreased in importance. His youthfulness was not replaced by a feeling of maturity, just a kind of worried seriousness. Still, he's a better actor than usually appears in films of this nature.

Among his other fantastic films were Cult of the Cobra (1955), It! The Terror from Beyond Space, Fiend Without a Face, Around the World Under the Sea (1966), and the TV movie, Cruise into Terror (1978). He had small roles in The Turning Point (1977), The Formula (1981) and White Dog (1983). He's probably best known for his numerous TV appearances. He costarred in at least four series, "Men into Space" (1959–60), "Angel" (1960–61), the syndicated SF series, "World of Giants" (1961), and the modest hit, "Daktari" (1966–69), which was based on the 1965 movie, *Clarence the Cross-Eyed Lion*, also costarring Thompson. He was a frequent guest star on "Science Fiction Theater."

In *First Man*, Thompson is slightly strained—he almost never seems to stop scowling in worry—but perfectly believable as the slightly hard-nosed Commander. (To today's viewers, an odd aspect of the film is that the branch of the service involved is the Navy.*)

Marla Landi isn't believable as the female lead; she is more acceptable while screaming than when acting like a scientist. Her switch from favoring the younger brother to the older is a traditional one in such films, and nothing more should be made of it than that. She was also in *Across the Bridge* (1957), *Dublin Nightmare* (1958), Hammer's *The Hound of the Baskervilles* (1959), *Pirates of Blood River* (1962) and *The Murder Game* (1966). She's beautiful, with an interesting, crooked smile and a slightly exotic air.

Robert Day directed, somewhat ploddingly. He is to the point at all times, but in its emphasis on realism rather than shocks, the film is slightly lifeless. He's straightforward and sober, but cannot seem to generate much excitement. He also has the actor playing Dan after the accident move in a downright silly manner: arms upraised and feet widespread, as if his pants are full of mud.

Day directed a couple of lesser Boris Karloff films, *The Haunted Strangler* (1958) and *Corridors of Blood* (1960), both for Richard Gordon, the executive producer in charge of *First Man*. Day's career has an odd three-way split: horror films, comedies, including *The Green Man* (1956), *Bobbikins* (1959), *Two-Way Stretch* (1960, perhaps his best film), *Call Me Genius* (1961), and *Operation Snatch* (1962); and adventure melodramas, including Hammer's *She* (1965), and a batch of Tarzan films, ranging from a high of *Tarzan the Magnificent* (1960), through *Tarzan's Three Challenges* (1963), *Tarzan and the Valley of Gold* (1966), *Tarzan and the Great River* (1967), to a low of *Tarzan and the Jungle Boy* (1968), which essentially finished off the series.

Day's work as a director is competent and workmanlike, without ever being inspired or original. His best films are probably due as much to the scripts (on which he sometimes collaborated) as to his direction. While he never made an outstanding film, he also has remarkably few truly bad ones, with *Bobbikins* the worst. His horror films are not very frightening, but they are careful and rational, while his jungle films are similarly conservative. Day's efforts at being realistic about the fanciful script for *First Man* extend to shooting nighttime scenes actually at night, with the actors having foggy breath and all.

The special effects are fair. The same model is used for the Y-12 and Y-13, and looks realistic enough for a cheap picture, although also like it is made of

---

The Navy was first to propose a satellite (in 1945!). The Army and Navy cooperated on Project Orbiter starting in 1954. Concurrently, the Navy started Project Vanguard in 1955, but had troubles with its launch vehicle. The Army got the go-ahead after Sputnik II was launched November 1957, and the Navy's Vanguard I blew up on the launchpad in December 1957. Werner von Braun and his Army team launched Explorer I, January 1958. That year NASA was created from the National Advisory Committee for Aeronautics (NACA), which had been formed in 1915; NASA consolidated the U.S. space programs. Otherwise Army-Navy rivalry might have continued. (The Air Force also had its own space program.) — Bill Thomas.

plastic. There's an interesting shot, overused, of the rocket plane spiraling down at the camera, a perspective notable for its novelty.

The monster suit is both interesting and preposterous. The mask worn by Edwards or his double is very good. Although the mouth never moves, the eye is disturbingly real, and seems to have an expression of anguish. However, the *design* of the monster suit is ridiculous: the suit-makers were stuck with having the story-required coating cover both Dan's head and his pressure suit, but I doubt that it called for them to make the coating look like the surface of the Moon, down to miniature craters.

Some, such as Parish and Pitts, have accused the film of being an imitation of *The Creeping Unknown*, and there may be some justification. In both films, a ship returns with the occupant having undergone a mysterious change that requires the murder of innocent bystanders. But the central idea, of someone going into space and returning as a monster, is basic pulp sci-fi material, and although it's not terribly common in films (usually turning up in grotesque low-budget efforts, like *The Incredible Melting Man* and *Xtro*), I suspect that too much can be made of the similarities between *Creeping Unknown* and *First Man*. I suspect that it was Nigel Kneale's realistic treatment, rather than his storyline, that was being aped in *First Man*.

Reviewers were moderately kind to *First Man into Space*. The *Monthly Film Bulletin* gave the film its rare above-average rating, announcing it "competently made ... with one eye on the American market." The reviewer also said, "The makeup is uncommonly skilful and survives some strongly lit closeups with no loss of conviction. The dialogue and an eerie climax are quite compelling, and although the film is still far from having achieved Ray Bradbury quality, it represents a move in the right direction."

Jack Moffitt was bored with the emphasis on scientific verisimilitude in the first part of the film, so that "it is a great relief when the good old-fashioned hokum sets in and the audience [i.e. Jack Moffitt] knows what is being talked about." "Powe" at *Variety* considered the film "a good entry in the exploitation class. It has excitement and some genuine horror. It is generally well-made and suffers only from a tendency to get cosmic in philosophy as well as geography."

James D. Ivers at the *Motion Picture Herald*: "This effort is reasonably well done. Lacking marquee names, exploitation will have to be of the horror variety.... Implausibilities in the story are compensated for by generally excellent performances, tight direction, and interesting technical details, which with the title, give the picture a very exploitable topicality." However, he termed the film only "fair."

More contemporary writers, no longer impressed by mere competence, have sometimes been less friendly. In *Future Tense*, John Brosnan considered it "an inferior film with a script of crippling banality," which is rather harsh. Parish and Pitts called it "badly dated."

In *Castle of Frankenstein* #9, Joe Dante described it as "already dated, but quite competently made ... despite familiar ideas." *Psychotronic* called it "Another scary hit from [Amalgamated.] Somebody there knew how to deliver uneasy shocks."

There is always a problem in evaluating older films. Judging them by the standards of their time is probably a fair approach: the films were made for audiences of their time. Exploitation pictures are never intended as works of art for the ages. That the best ones do achieve that status is a testament to the abilities of their creators as well as, often, to the timelessness of their themes. Those that fail to pass the test of time should not be condemned for that, but neither should they be recommended to contemporary audiences without sufficient cautionary words.

First Man into Space did look exceptional at the time. Sensible, sober and realistic, albeit with a monster, it was better than the other films released then. However, it is indeed dated, and the lumbering monster now looks more foolish than it did when the film was new. In short, the film still has historical significance, but contemporary audiences are likely to find it unsatisfactory.

4D Man

Certain concepts are obviously more amenable to fantasy treatment than to science fiction. There are ideas that are trivial, used only as jokes or gags in movies in which the emphasis is on another idea. An idea that's both trivial and almost always treated as a fantasy is the ability to walk through walls. It turns up as a side element in films involving ghosts, angels, and other supernatural beings.

The only films I know of which involve this ability as the central element are two based on the same novel (*Le Passe-Muraille*) by Marcel Ayme, *Mr. Peek-a-Boo* (French, 1951) and *The Man Who Walked Through the Wall* (West German, 1959), in which the ability of the hero is not really explained at all, and *4D Man*, the only science fiction treatment of the theme yet filmed.*

Although it's inexpensive and has limited ambitions, *4D Man* is an intelligent, responsible treatment of the idea, somewhat compromised by giving the hero vampiric tendencies. It's not sensationalistic, and has the feeling of a story made by adults for adults, certainly unusual in SF films by 1959.

The main difficulties with the film are the low budget and that vampiric theme that may possibly have been the impetus for the storyline. When the 4D Man touches anyone, he absorbs their "life energy," causing them to die at once of old age while his own youth is replenished.† This particular method of killing people hadn't been used in films before, but although this gives the plot some of its momentum in the latter half, it's too bad that the 4D Man had to turn into just another monster on the rampage. The film is too smart and too well-written to have to rely on this kind of sensationalism; fortunately, it is good enough that it largely overcomes this flaw.

4D Man was produced by Jack H. Harris and Irwin S. Yeaworth, Jr. at the same Pennsylvania film studios where they made *The Blob* the year before. *4D Man* continues the strengths of the earlier film, expands on them and dodges some of the weaknesses. There's real characterization, interesting motivations, a few surprising plot twists and imagination shown throughout. Although by no means could the film be considered a classic 50s SF film on a par with *Forbidden Planet, Incredible Shrinking Man, Invasion of the Body Snatchers*, et al., it certainly ranks with such "second-string classics" as *I Married a Monster from Outer Space, The Monster That Challenged the World* and *The Space Children*.

Incidentally, these films are united in that SF film buffs generally appreciate them, but they tend to be disregarded by general movie fans. That's their loss.

*The proposed film based on Marvel Comics' "The X-Men" will feature a character, Kitty Pride, who can walk through walls, but she's just one of a team. Superman can also walk through walls, but when he's done, there's no wall left.

†Not uncommon in SF-horror fiction, this is rare in films but something similar turns up again in the bizarre Lifeforce (1985).

Research physicist Tony Nelson (James Congdon) loses his job at a research facility, so he joins his staid older brother Scott (Robert Lansing), working for egocentric Dr. Theodore W. Carson (Edgar Stehli) at Carson's facility, the Fairview Research Center.

Scott is both pleased and dismayed to see his enthusiastic younger brother, whom he put through college, as Tony is something of a scientific gadfly.

Scott has just developed an impenetrable metal for Carson, who only finances research, but takes credit for the developments of the scientists in his employ. In fact, soon after Tony's arrival, Carson calls a press conference to announce the new metal, which he names "Cargonite." (Why not "Carsonite"?) Scott ruefully leaves the room, to the mild exasperation of his assistant Linda (Lee Meriwether).

Tony shows Scott the phenomenon which has fired his enthusiasm: a pencil partway through a block of metal. Not piercing the metal, but passing *through* it—the atoms of the pencil and the metal are mingled. While Tony was experimenting with amplification of brain waves, the pencil passed partway through the metal. He's convinced that he *willed* this to happen, by creating a speeded-up process of fusion. He amplified atomic fields, but his device affected him, not the instruments.

Scott gets Tony a job at Fairview, but warns him not to try anything fancy at the lab. Scott's mild, plodding nature is partly his own fault; he's convinced himself that Tony is more brilliant, more worthy—and when Linda and Tony clearly begin falling in love, Scott does nothing about it, until it's too late.

Scott has a rival at the lab, Roy Parker (Robert Strauss), who's much less brilliant than Scott, but unprincipled and ambitious.

Pressures pile up on Scott, and his recurring headaches finally send him to see Dr. Brian Schwartz (Dean Newman), who suspects that Scott's experiments with atomic radiation have amplified his brain waves, causing his headaches.

Fearing the worst about Tony and Linda, he visits her to propose, but she tells him it's too late—she's now in love with Tony.

Determined to beat or equal Tony at something, the unhappy Scott returns to the laboratory and takes Tony's mental-power amplification equipment and notes to a lab bench. For hours, he strains with a piece of metal doweling, trying to force it through a steel block—and finally, shockingly, it happens: the doweling *and* Scott's hand plunge into the block. For a moment, stunned, he stares at what's happened. When he tries to withdraw his hand, he can't. His fingers start to turn blue from the cutoff circulation, as he hears someone coming. It's Parker. Scott hides under the table as Parker enters, finds Tony's notes providentially spread out before him, takes them and leaves.

Scott leaps back to the table and with great effort manages to withdraw his hand from the block. Some time later, he calls Tony; at the lab, Tony is briefly angry when he sees that Scott has been messing around with his stuff, but then Scott, in a daze of discovery, shows Tony that he can pass his hand at will through the steel block with no resistance at all. Then Tony notices something very important (but fails to notice the missing notes): "The amplifier isn't working. You did that by yourself."

Elsewhere, Parker works out a deal with Carson: Carson will finance Parker's "newly-found" research, and not ask any questions as to where or how Parker managed to stumble onto this line of research.

As the brothers drive home, Scott aks Tony not to tell anyone about this ability just yet. "Maybe I just like the power of being able to do something

Robert Lansing makes a splashy entrance in this scene from 4D Man (1959) near the climax. The effects are not especially good, but Lansing's vibrant performance lends credibility to this unfortunately-overlooked film.

nobody else can do." He's lived in the shadow of other people for years; now he has a real distinction.

As Scott meanders through the quiet streets alone, he tries out the new power. He reaches into a mailbox (in a stunningly-good effects shot, the best in the film), extracts a letter, sniffs the perfume on it bemusedly, then drops it back into the mailbox through the slot. (Old habits die hard.) He reaches through windows along the street, taking an apple, toying with some jewelry—and then sees, across the street, a bank...

He wakes up in bed. The radio announces that $50,000 was stolen from a bank vault that's still locked. Scott staggers to the mirror and stares in shock: he looks like a man of 70. (Though restrained, the makeup is not very good.) He races to Dr. Schwartz's house, seeking help. Schwartz at first doesn't recognize him, and then realizes with horror who it is. Scott demonstrates his power, plunging his hand into a wall of the house, and then in desperation clutches at the doctor's shoulders, forgetting he is in his "4D" state.

His hands pass through Schwartz's shoulders, and he staggers in pain, falls to the floor, and in an instant withers and dies of old age. Filled with guilt and terror, Scott flees.

At the laboratory later, Linda and Tony discuss the strange old man who was found dead in Schwartz's home, dressed in his clothes. When Scott enters, he's his normal age: he has sucked the youth from the doctor and restored his own.

He and Tony talk about the speeded-up process of fusion: Scott has "compressed the energy of years into a moment." Linda says, "that's like the fourth dimension." (Or 4D, from 3D, for third dimension.)

For a time, Scott does not use his power, but from the many pressures on him, his mind is starting to go. He hides Tony's equipment within a reactor, and then visits Carson.

The old man is sitting alone in his plush home study when Scott nonchalantly strolls through the closed door. Carson didn't see this—but he does see Scott walk through a chair. Scott doesn't want anything that Carson offers him, he's sardonically bent on revenge. (Lansing is excellent in this scene.) He forces the old man outside, and uses his 4D youth-sucking power—we see Carson's hand wither.

When Tony is later questioned by the police, the bank is mentioned—as is the fact that a thousand dollar bill was found embedded in the bank vault. He realizes the thief was Scott.

At Linda's, we see Scott standing over her like a vampire while she sleeps. She awakes just as he bends down to kiss her, and she rushes downstairs, opening the front door to flee, only to find Scott standing there. There's no follow-up to this scene at all, suggesting that material was cut.

From this point, 4D Man becomes more conventional. Scott picks up a B-girl (Chic James) at a bar, and, partly accidentally, drains her youth. Offscreen, he kills four more people in the same manner. By now, because of the strain of guilt and other pressures, Scott is insane.

Tony tells the police what's going on, that by using his 4D power, Scott is committing the murders. The police corner Scott during a rainstorm, but he easily escapes. "A man in the fourth dimension is indestructible," says Tony.

There's a cut to the indestructible 4D man, huddled in a bush, protected by newspapers, again apparently in his 70s. When a little girl (Patty Duke, in fact) tries to befriend him, without recognizing him, Scott is overcome by shame and horror, but uses his power on her, too. (Offscreen. Which raises a question that has perplexed viewers of this film: Did she suddenly grow up and die of old age, or turn into an old little girl, or what?)

Working with the police, Tony decides the only way to stop Scott is to become a 4D man himself, and goes to the lab to try to find a way. Parker, always one to grab glory, reveals this plan to the reporters and Scott hears of it.

He arrives at Fairview, killing Parker offscreen outside the lab, then walks through an electrified fence, looking for Tony. He knows that Tony can't do the 4D trick without his equipment, so he's worried it's been found inside the reactor.

Scott enters the reactor room (through the wall), where everyone is waiting for him. He leans into the furnace and discovers that the equipment is still there, but Tony turns the reactor on, which drives Scott out. Everyone but Linda flees the reactor control room, realizing that Scott may be unstoppable.

He angrily enters the control room in his 4D state, and asks Linda that if he promises to stop killing, will she come with him? He wants to kiss her, but can't come out of his 4D state: it will make him vulnerable. His insanity while being confronted with this dilemma, plus his overwhelming sense of guilt, reduce him to tears. He finally reverts to solidity, and eagerly kisses Linda—and as he does so, she shoots him.

He's not especially surprised by this as he staggers out of the control room.

It's not clear whether his wound is fatal, but he shouts that nothing can hurt him. He can walk through anything, even a solid wall of Cargonite, the super-dense metal he himself devised. He lunges forward into the Cargonite wall, and sinks slowly into it. He turns back for a last look at Linda, leaving only his hand protruding at last. It goes limp (indicating death), just as it falls into the wall.

As usual with Harris-produced films of the period, "The End" turns into a question mark.

As with *The Blob*, it seems almost perverse to complain that a low-budget SF movie spends too much time on characterization, but that is a flaw in *4D Man*. Based on an idea by Jack H. Harris, the script by Theodore Simonson and Cy Chermak works carefully to establish and develop the growing love triangle between Scott, Linda and Tony. There are semilyrical scenes in a schoolyard, and much frowning and stares from Lansing as he sees the attraction grow between his brother and the woman he loves. This is commendable, but it also has the effect of delaying the real material of the film, so that things are slow for the first half.

Still, it's good, honest work, and even if the situation is clichéd, at least it's unusually well-developed for a film of this nature. Most often in a triangle situation, it's the younger, more reckless of the two central characters who ends up in trouble, dead, behind bars, as a monster, etc. The staid, older friend/brother usually sets things right, and the heroine chooses stability over glamor.

But in *4D Man*, things just don't work out that way for poor Scott, making the film a shade more true to life than the formula. He's *too* staid, even cowardly; his fate with Linda is sealed, although neither knows it, when he walks out of Carson's press conference. Her faith in him is weakened, and he no longer seems desirable, especially with the arrival of Tony, who's closer to her age. Scott has moved from possible husband to older brother, and he doesn't know it at once.

Scott's fate was self-ordained. He loves his brother, but he also fears him; they're both brilliant scientists, but Tony's is a more daring brilliance. Scott is the safe plodder, insecure and working with self-fulfilling prophecies based on that insecurity. If Tony had not arrived, he might actually have married Linda, but it wouldn't have been a good marriage for her—or him. His convictions about his unworthiness would have surfaced. For her, something would always have been lacking, and that something is what Tony has.

Scott has lived with these self-fulfilling prophecies all his life, but when he becomes the 4D Man, even his worst fears for himself are exceeded. For a brief moment, he's something very special, a man who can walk through walls; possibilities are open to him, but he isn't sure what to do with them. His bank robbery is a prank (he simply hides all the money, not spending any), but it does point in the unpleasant direction that Scott's insecurities may lead him. He has a lot of resentment built up, and now he has the power to expiate it.

But in a horrifying and almost cosmic sense of rightness, even Scott's new distinction turns out to be a drawback; it ages him, and makes him a killer. He can't win for losing. Even though he has a new power, the new power is destroying him.

The final irony is that he is given a way out of this instant aging: he can steal youth from others. There's a subtle parallel with both Parker and Carson here: Scott gains the power by trying to steal Tony's ideas, just as Parker tries to get power by stealing from Tony. Scott can maintain his youth only by draining it from others, just as Carson maintains his power in the world by leeching on the ideas of younger men. Parker and Scott are thieves, Carson and Scott are vampires.

This richness of characterization is confined almost entirely to Scott, and a great deal of it is due to Lansing's fine performance. The various parallels are in the script, however, one of the best-written for a low-budget SF film. When a script is as astute and intelligent as this one is, with such a novel gimmick, it's a shame that it has to be compromised by the more or less standard horror escapades toward the end. Still, it is a rare SF movie that permits a detailed discussion of the motivation of the main character, and Simonson and Chermak certainly deserve credit for trying to turn out an adult film.

The only other credit for Theodore Simonson I know of is as cowriter of the script for *The Blob*. Cy Chermak has no other feature credits I have been able to discover, but he's active in television; he produced "The Night Stalker" TV series, for instance.

The dialogue is intelligent without being flashy, having few real jokes, although there are some ironic comments. The closest thing to an actual joke is also irony, when Carson asks Scott, who has already discovered his power, if he has anything new up his sleeve.

Scott Nelson is one of the most tortured man-into-monsters of any period, although his feelings of guilt are fully justified. His first killing is accidental, and of the others we see, only those of Carson and Parker are deliberate murder, and those guys more or less had it coming. But it is in Scott's nature to be a weakling. When he is confronted with the your-life-or-mine decision, he agonizes, suffers, feels (safe) pangs of guilt, and then takes the life, even that of a child. Confronted with the same decision, Tony probably would have lived out his life as a sudden old man, experimented with animals, anything other than kill people for his own rejuvenation. Scott probably decides he has no choice, and has gone insane from frustration, guilt and longing. His paranoia precludes suicide.

Despite occasional tendencies to slip into overplaying, Lansing's performance is excellent. He seems to have understood the character and plays him with sympathy and insight. Lansing's strange combination of slender face and beetling brows gives him an intense, brooding look, and he knows how to marshal his physical attributes for the camera: he knows what he really looks like. It's surprising to find a performance of complexity, ability and strength in a low-budget science fiction film, where we were usually offered only bland, colorless actors. Lansing gives the role everything he has, and it's a vivid screen debut.

His speech at the end is too flamboyant, and he's perhaps a little too crazily sure of himself in his final confrontation with Carson, but those are small defects in his overall work. His growing sense of wonder and fun, and finally a touch of boredom (there must be something else I can do) as he wanders through the quiet city streets playing with apples and diamonds through shop windows is expertly played. He makes us care about this hapless, selfish schmo of a 4D Man, and we never quite realize what a loser Scott is, unless we reflect on the film later, and Lansing's performance makes us want to do this.

He didn't have another role in films of any note until 1963, when he played a major character in *A Gathering of Eagles*. He's never achieved movie stardom, with titles like *An Eye for an Eye* (1966), *Namu the Killer Whale* (1966), which also starred Lee Meriwether, *It Takes All Kinds* (1969) and *Bittersweet Love* (1976) as his major starring films. He's also appeared in several TV movies, including *Killer by Night*, *The Astronaut* (both 1972), *Crime Club* (1975), *Widow* (1976) and *The Deadly Triangle* (1977). His major television stardom was brief; he wasn't made a star, really, by the "87th Precinct" and "Man Who Never Was" series, in which he was the leading player, but his role in the 1964–65 season of "Twelve O'Clock High" was a favorite of fans of the show, and when he was killed at the beginning of the next season, there was quite an outcry. However, Lansing or his agent failed to capitalize on this, and he soon returned to the ranks of familiar though not famous faces. He was a supporting regular on the TV series "Automan."

In 1977, he made two inexpensive horror films, one with a science fiction basis: *Empire of the Ants*. This is a typically dreadful Bert I. Gordon film with only the most tenuous relationship to the H.G. Wells story from which it derives its title. As the hero, however, Lansing was fine. I have not seen the other film, *Scalpel*, also known as *False Face*, but its restoring-the-loved-one's-face plot is hackneyed and the film does not sound promising. He starred in a not-bad giant crab film, *Island Claws*, shown on TV in 1984.

The trouble with Lansing is definitely not a lack of ability, but that he does not have a clearly definable screen personality, or rather that which he has isn't distinct enough to make him sought by producers. He's essentially interchangeable with many other actors, many of whom are not as talented as he is.

As Linda, Lee Meriwether doesn't have much to do. She's not a bad actress, and plays her role with intelligence, but it's an underwritten part, and stereotyped as well. Meriwether does as well with the role as could be expected, but there's not much room for characterization or insight.

Meriwether's career has been similar to Lansing's, although she luckily ended up in a hit TV series, "Barnaby Jones," in which she played Buddy Ebsen's daughter-in-law. She was also in the unimaginative TV series "The Time Tunnel" (1966–67), and in the 1971, short-lived "New Andy Griffith Show." Her other films include *Batman* (1966), in which she played the Catwoman, *Angel in My Pocket* (1968) with Griffith, and *The Legend of Lylah Clare* (1969). What with the success of "Barnaby Jones," Meriwether's movie appearances were confined to a few made for television: *Having Babies II* (1977), *Cruise into Terror* (1978) and *True Grit* (1978).

James Congdon is far too broad and intense as Tony. Don Willis (II) dismisses the entire cast of *4D Man* other than Lansing with "the other actors can hardly walk into a room, let alone through a wall." This is hardly accurate; in fact, everyone except Congdon is acceptable. It's not a technically inept performance; at least he is clearly an *actor*, unlike supporting players in many other SF films of the period. But he's way over the top, unrestrained by himself or director Yeaworth. He's hammy, perhaps highlighted by a scene in which he's so eager to show Scott his pencil-through-a-slab thingy that he trips and falls, but springs back to his feet. Why bother? Congdon seems determined to grab the role by the scruff of the neck, and energetically subdue it. He appeared in few other films; the only others I know of were *The Group* (1966), *The Left-Handed Gun* (1958) and *When Worlds Collide*, where he was one of the two young lovers who are allowed to escape the end of the world by the sacrifice of a noble scientist. He was too broad then as well.

As Parker, Robert Strauss plays one of the few intelligent, relatively normal characters of his career. Parker is a conniving cheat, but he's neither a Damon Runyonesque con man, nor a slovenly pig, Strauss' normal screen personae. Strauss is more than acceptable in the role, nastily oily and opportunistic.

He began in films with good parts in three Dean Martin-Jerry Lewis films,

Jumping Jacks, Sailor Beware (both 1952) and *Money from Home* (1953), but it was his flamboyant role as "Animal" in *Stalag 17* that gave Strauss what fame he achieved. Strauss was nominated for an Oscar as Best Supporting Actor. Although he lost (to Frank Sinatra), it established Strauss as a major character player, at least for the next few years. *The Atomic Kid* was probably made before fame from *Stalag 17* lifted Strauss out of such low-class epics, as his next few films were all major: *The Bridges at Toko-Ri, The Man with the Golden Arm, The Seven Year Itch* (all 1955) and *Attack* (1956).

After that, his fortunes fell. During the 1960s he appeared in lesser films, including *Dondi, The Last Time I Saw Archie* (both 1961), *The Thrill of It All* (1963, a rare bigger-budgeted film), and *Fort Utah* (1967). For whatever reason, probably simply his crude-brute character going out of style, Strauss faded out with notably poor films, such as *Movie Star American Style or; LSD I Hate You* (1966) and *Dagmar's Hot Pants Inc.* (1971). He died in 1975.

Edgar Stehli, modestly effective in the underwritten role of Carson, was a very busy character actor on radio, television and in the movies from the late 40s through the early 70s. Among his other films were *Boomerang* (1947), *Executive Suite* (1954), *The Brothers Karamazov* (1958), *Atlantis the Lost Continent, A Pocketful of Miracles* (1961) and *Loving* (1970).

Yeaworth was not a bad director, and here showed considerable improvement over his work in *The Blob*. He has a tendency to be too fussy for the subject matter, and too conventional overall. He, or his writers, had several good ideas in *4D Man*, and it's surprising he only made one further theatrical film, the religious-oriented *Way Out* (1967). He keeps things clear and uncluttered, with a minimum of fancy camera angles (mounting the camera on a children's merry-go-round is as artsy as he gets). He subtly likens Scott to a vampire, without the word ever being used in the film; in one imaginative scene, he cuts to Scott already standing over Linda's bed, in a vampirish pose. Lansing is eerily lit, and leans forward menacingly.

There's also an oddly-conceived but effective set of matching shots. On the night that Scott comes to propose to Linda, she opens the door and finds him standing in a slouch; as the door opens, he raises his head and looks at her. Later, when she flees after he appears in her room, she runs downstairs and opens the door—and there's Scott again, in the same pose, even raising his head the same way. I suppose the intent was to both surprise us and reassure us that he meant Linda no harm, but we also are left wondering how he got there so fast.

The editing is especially imaginative, and I suspect that editor William B. Murphy, or the director or writers, had been influenced by television and by French films. The film jumps forward quickly; the standard connecting material —showing us characters going places, reactions to impulses, etc.—is either very terse or omitted altogether.

The entire business of walking through walls is almost fantasy. It doesn't really make much sense; if Scott can make himself transparent to a solid wall, why doesn't he simply sink into the ground as well? Nonetheless, the idea is worked out in a science fictional context in *4D Man*, involving radiation once again, as it was Scott's work with radioactive substances that strengthened his brain waves. He walks quickly through thin walls, more slowly through denser walls, and when he passes through an electric fence, we can briefly see his darker skeleton against the incandescent electrical discharge. Some thought was given to the concept.

The special effects by Barton Sloane (another repeat from *The Blob*) are certainly imaginative, but unfortunately the execution is often not up to the level of Sloane's imagination. When Scott visits the doctor and plunges his hand into the wall to demonstrate his power, Sloane is careful to put Lansing's shadow on the wall (vanishing where his hand passes into the wall and the shadow), which subliminally adds verisimilitude to the scene. However, belief is damaged because there's a strong matte line all around Lansing's figure. He was apparently shot against a black backing rather than a blue one, and, judging from the raggedness of the image, it's possible that the mattes were hand-painted, rather than photographically generated. Matte lines intrude on many of the scenes in the film, which has the unfortunate effect of drawing the attention of a viewer to the effects.

The best-achieved effect in the film is brief, but in its modest way, dazzling. Scott reaches through the front of a mailbox and withdraws a letter (we see his cuff pass through a white card on the front of the box), which he then, being human, replaces in the box in the normal fashion. One of the chief means by which great believability is achieved in this scene is by careful control of lighting.

Occasionally, other means than mattes were employed. When Scott demonstrates to Tony how his hand passes through the steel block, a cartoon of Lansing's hand is used. When he reaches through the windows on the street, a thin, bright blue light is projected down on Lansing's hand and sleeve, indicating the glass of the window.

Whenever Scott pulls a 4D stunt, a musical trilling is heard on the soundtrack. Though tired, this device is used wittily a couple of times. Scott flees past us, and we hear the trilling and a scream; he's gone 4D *out of our view*, and has killed someone.

Ralph Carmichael's jazz score has been cursed by some, praised by others. I find it moderately effective myself, and for a science fiction film, a score of this nature is different. One does get tired of hearing pseudo–Herrmann, pseudo–Tiomkin and pseudo–Korngold. Carmichael also did the scores for *The Blob*, *The Restless Ones* (1965), *Three Weeks of Love* (1965), *For Pete's Sake* (1966) and *The Cross and the Switchblade* (1970), but overall, the music for *4D Man* may be his best movie score, although sometimes it seems to work against the action on the screen.

The sets are simple but generally okay, although a great deal of blue paint was used. "Powe" in *Variety* noted that the screening print was "very blue, and this was partly the fault of the lighting and partly that of the art director, who had an unusual number of settings with that dead, dark color for background."

As was true of *The Blob*, *4D Man* gives indications of having been made by people unfamiliar with this genre, but who approached the subject with taste and intelligence. Reviews of this time tend to agree with this viewpoint.

Jack Moffitt said that the film "has the advantage of a sound screenplay ... and better than average direction.... It will interest all those who appreciate science-fiction as a form of literature. But the very soundness of its motivation and the quality of its acting may be a disadvantage when playing it before indiscriminate teenage fans who want the chills and shivers to start within the first five minutes." He said that Lansing "does a much better job than is usual in this sort of picture," praised the "truly ingenious special effects," but concluded (with some justification) that the "inconclusive finish of the picture is not quite up to the rest of it."

"Powe" in *Variety* felt that "it is not offensively gruesome and has a fairly interesting gimmick." Mystifyingly, he also said "this general theme has been the focus of several other films" without naming them. He added that "the mechanical aspects of it are given some novelty in Harris' production and [it] occasionally achieves some genuine excitement."

The *Monthly Film Bulletin* gave the film an average rating, and said that "some of the background argument is fascinating, and considerably closer to genuine science fiction than is usual in this sort of film. But the slow buildup is stretched still further by the painstaking development of the triangle situation." The commentary concluded that "The special effects are adequately managed but the routine [later part of the film] is a disappointing end to a more ambitious beginning. All the same, science fiction enthusiasts should find much of it interesting."

Don Willis (II) was harsher: "The first half ... is a loss although Robert Lansing is effective.... In the latter half, Lansing goes on a sometimes impressive, Invisible Man–like super-power trip.... [T]he final shot of his hand sticking out of the wall has a kind of perverse bravura to it."

Psychotronic called it "a science fiction hit.... The special effects are great." Alan Frank (*SF*) said, "rather too much of an emphasis on a hackneyed romance tends to hold up the proceedings but the film moves briskly enough, the idea is well used and the special effects effective."

Although Warren Publications (and I'm definitely no relation) claimed that they never accepted outside advertising, it's hard to know what else to call what appears on page 55 and the back cover of *Famous Monsters of Filmland* #6. There's a photo of Jack H. Harris and the following text:

"The Producer of *The Blob* Will Give Away ONE MILLION DOLLARS to the first living person who actually performs in real life the feats ascribed to the 4D Man in the widescreen color picture by the same name.

"Jack H. Harris, the dynamic producer of *The Blob* now amazes the world with his announcement of ONE MILLION DOLLAR CASH AWARD to the person who successfully performs the feats attributed to the 4D MAN.

"Universal-International, the studio that gave you *The Invisible Man* and *The Incredible Shrinking Man*, now joins with Jack H. Harris to bring you the WideScreen of 4D MAN, lavishly produced in color by DeLuxe. In this exciting story you will watch a man cross the threshold into the Fourth Dimension; you will watch him perform feats that may seem totally unbelievable—but: what the 4D MAN does can be done!

"Find out from your local theater manager when he will be playing 4D Man. He will also give you information on how YOU can qualify to win the ONE MILLION DOLLAR CASH award!

"Remember—your admission ticket to see 4D MAN could be worth ONE MILLION DOLLARS.

"Coming soon to your local theater 4D MAN."

I don't think Harris' million dollars was ever at stake; furthermore, if someone could do what Scott Nelson does, he wouldn't *need* Harris' mere million bucks.

Rights to *4D Man* reverted to Harris after a while, and by the mid-60s, he was distributing it and *The Blob* on a double bill. By that time, *4D Man* had undergone a title change to *Master of Terror* for its previous reissue on a double bill with an Argentine film retitled *Master of Horror*. In England, *4D Man* was called *The Evil Force*. It still plays on U.S. television with the Universal-International logo under the title *4D Man*.

Although *4D Man* cannot be considered an unsung classic, it is a decent, well-written and well-acted thriller, intelligent and imaginative. It shows that good work could still be done on low budgets in the field of science fiction films, even as late as 1959.

The Giant Behemoth

Despite a good performance by Gene Evans and a no-nonsense but atmospheric approach, this is a perfunctory monster-on-the-loose film of little distinction. Not badly done, although the budget was too low, the only real problem with the film is there's nothing new about it at all. In fact, it is essentially a remake of *Beast from 20,000 Fathoms* and, like that, was directed by Eugene Lourié, who also wrote it with the uncredited Daniel Hyatt. The monster shakes up London rather than New York, but many of the elements are almost identical, including the structure and the monster itself.

While American marine biologist Steve Karnes (Evans) is in London giving a lecture on the dangers of radioactive waste (one of the earliest comments on this problem in movies), he meets Prof. James Bickford (André Morell), a sympathetic nuclear physicist. In countering the arguments of another scientist, who claims (not incorrectly) that radiation from atomic fallout per person is at this point less than that produced by a radium-dial watch, Steve replies that radioactivity is concentrated in greater and greater amounts further up the food chain. He suggests that something very large that lives in the sea will soon be powerfully radioactive, perhaps even mutated.

In apparent response, a fisherman in Cornwall is found covered with strange burns; before he dies, he mutters the word "behemoth," a Biblical monster, now believed to have been a hippopotamus.

Steve learns of the death of the fisherman, thousands of dead fish washing ashore, as well as reported sightings of a sea monster, before he leaves England, and postpones his return trip. He and Bickford go down to Cornwall where the fiancé of the dead man's daughter was also burned by a strange, glowing object found among the dead fish. (This is about the only SF movie to suggest that radioactive things do not automatically glow, however.) Other fishermen declare that they saw a white glow, like a sunken cloud, moving beneath the water.

Steve and Bickford examine some of the dead fish, discovering that they were killed by radiation. Steve now knows that there is some large radioactive animal at sea, but is curious why its path isn't traceable. (This idea is never followed up.)

A ship is beached with the surviving crew and passengers suffering from radiation. Soon, on a farm, a farmer and his dog encounter the monster (seen for the first time), which beams radiation at them, then destroys the farm. Steve and Bickford examine photos taken on the site, and see that one contains a footprint of the monster.

They take the photo to paleontologist Dr. Sampson (Jack MacGowran), who immediately recognizes it as that of a (fictitious) "paleosaurus," a gigantic, carnivorous prehistoric animal — presumably a dinosaur but never called that — which Sampson is longing to see. "I have always hoped this day would come,"* he tells them. "From my childhood, I've expected it. I've known these creatures

*Quotes from script; dialogue in film may differ.

were still alive—somewhere. But no proof, no form of proof." And he launches into a rhapsodic description of the paleosaurus, linking it with reports of sea serpents. "The giant teeth, the head carried high; what could that be but the graceful neck of paleosaurus?" This monster, which in the film somewhat resembles a brachiosaurus with a different head, has gills as well as lungs, and also is electric, like an electric eel. This, Steve says, explains the glow, and how it can cut people down with radioactivity: it projects the radioactivity with its electrical charge. (This, incidentally, is preposterous though inventive.)

When Steve tells Sampson that the monster is probably dying of its own radiation, the paleontologist says that that explains its activities: it's heading for the Thames to die in fresh water, a habit of paleosaurs. (He seems to know a great deal about them.) London is its target.

An admiral warned about the approach of the Behemoth feels that radar and sonar will handily spot it. However, the Behemoth somehow eludes this net of early warning systems, and sinks a ferryboat in the heart of London. (But not before it kills its only friend, Dr. Sampson.) People flee in panic, there's much activity on the part of the army, and so forth. Steve and Bickford point out that blowing up the Behemoth is out of the question, for that would rain radioactive chunks of monster all over the city, rendering parts uninhabitable for many years. (It seems to be *very* radioactive.) The creature can be killed if its internal radioactivity is increased, so a radium-tipped torpedo is prepared.

The black and shiny Behemoth comes ashore in London, blunders into power lines, causes gasoline tanks to explode, and chases people, occasionally firing off its radioactive electricity. (This is signified by concentric circles spreading out from the head, making the monster seem to have the Evil Eye.)

Eventually the creature returns to the Thames, where Steve and his submarine crew fire the radioactive torpedo into it, and the monster dies. Steve returns ashore, and he and Bickford hear a radio report of thousands of dead fish washing ashore in America.

Fantastic Films #15 published Paul Mandell's typically ineptly-written but fact-filled article on the making of *The Giant Behemoth*. Eugene Lourié was originally scheduled to direct *The Black Scorpion*, but he had a falling-out with one of the backers of the picture, and so was approached by producer David Diamond to direct *The Giant Behemoth*. The original story of the project (perhaps a complete script) was written by Robert Abel and Allan Adler, and dealt with an invisible but glowing monster, but no one seemed satisfied with that idea.

Lourié told Mandell that "the only element specified was that there was something electrically charged and dangerous—a kind of strange radioactive substance floating on the water.... I started to work, trying to invent visual means to translate the dangers of radiation. But the basic concept did not sit well with the distributors." They wanted something you could *see*, and felt a prehistoric monster was just the ticket. So, using *Beast from 20,000 Fathoms* as a model, he and Daniel Hyatt quickly wrote a script which, Lourié told both Mark McGee and Mandell, he expected to be able to change later. But the script was shot basically as written, making it an ipso facto remake.

Ray Harryhausen animated *Beast*, but was now partnered with Charles H. Schneer, and perhaps it was he who recommended Willis O'Brien and Pete Peterson to Diamond. Lourié told Mandell he felt sure that O'Brien and Peterson, who had done *The Black Scorpion*, could do all the effects. However, Diamond himself contracted with Jack Rabin and his associates (Irving Block and Louis DeWitt) to do the effects. As a result, O'Brien and Peterson were sub-

contracted by Rabin and paid out of the paltry $20,000 special effects budget.

Rabin and his crew did most of the live-action effects. Willis O'Brien and Phil Kellison (who built some of the miniatures destroyed by the Behemoth) built a wire-controlled model head of the creature for the scene in which it sinks the ferry. Because of time and budget restrictions, the scene had to be shot in one day. However, an overzealous effects worker (Irving Block, says McGee; Rabin isn't telling) fiddled vigorously with the model's controls, and broke them. As a result, the ship had to be sunk by an intricately-detailed but immobile Behemoth head. The same head was used in a few other shots.

The budget didn't allow the construction of a model gasoline storage tank for the scene in which one had to explode, so Irving Block hastily stacked some empty 35mm film cans, doused them in gasoline, set it afire and photographed the blaze. This was superimposed over a real gas tank, which looked okay, but gave the tank peculiar striations. Phil Kellison told Paul Mandell, "it annoyed the hell out of me because I didn't get a chance to build the miniature, but I had to admire Blocky's chutzpah for doing something like that."

The Behemoth lacks any real distinction. Looking like an average prehistoric monster, it's memorable primarily for the life Pete Peterson was able to instill into it in some scenes. (And for the fact that the mold seams on the model are visible.) At this time OBie was over 70, and Peterson was suffering from multiple sclerosis, making it very painful to stand. The table for the animation scenes was built low enough that Peterson could work on it sitting down, but he was still in considerable pain.

Instead of the six months or so that OBie and Peterson were allowed for *The Black Scorpion*, they had only six to eight *weeks* for *The Giant Behemoth*. As a result, some of their work is hasty and incomplete, but occasionally the monster seems awesome and menacing. Unfortunately, much of their good work was subverted by the speeded-up schedule. For instance, more scenes of destruction were required but were too expensive, so some of the already-filmed scenes were used again—and again. Shots of the Behemoth were optically enlarged, flopped, run in negative, and so forth. One shot of a car being crushed under the monster's foot is used *three* times.

Reviews were remarkably favorable, and many people today regard *The Giant Behemoth* as one of the best of the giant-monster films. The film was reviewed twice in weekly *Variety*, once (18 March 1959) under its American title, once (4 November 1959) under the British title, *Behemoth the Sea Monster*. "Ron," who wrote the earlier review, was pleased, calling the film "alluringly horrifying" and potentially "exploitable, marketable and profitable.... Director Lourié has successfully piled one chill on another, a proposition that the cast goes along with.... Filmed in England, the benefits of seldom-seen settings are a decided bonus as effectively caught by photographer Ken Hodges."

The later *Variety* review, done from London by "Rich," praised the sincerity and effectiveness of the actors, who "do their thesping stints with as much serious intent as if they were all in the line for Oscars," but otherwise considered it "a modestly made, routine science-fiction yarn" which was suitable as

Opposite: The Giant Behemoth (1959) stalks the streets of London as residents flee in panic, though in small numbers. This inexpensive film featured fairly good stop-motion animation by Willis O'Brien and Pete Peterson, although the model was unimaginative. Inset: The Giant Behemoth rears its graceful if slightly crude head over London; the model has an unfinished look, and is unimaginative in design.

little more "than a useful dualer.... Apart from the first moment when an agonized victim is struck down by the unknown creature, there's not much horror and precious few thrills in this pic.... Behemoth looks the sort of cute working model that, reduced to about a foot, would be a wow with children at Christmas."

Jack Moffitt enjoyed the film, calling it "an intelligently made monster picture ... skillfully written and directed by Eugene Lourié [who] builds up excellent suspense.... Mob scenes of panic lend bigness to the production and are extremely well done.... It would be a mistake to classify this with the current rash of quickie horror movies." (But that is how the film was promoted.)

Even the usual grumpy *Monthly Film Bulletin* gave the film no worse than a rating of II. "This is considerably better than many recent essays in monster science-fiction, both in its suspense and staging; but the story, though put over as convincingly as possible, remains stuck at routine outsize-paleontology level."

In *Castle of Frankenstein* #9, Joe Dante thought it was "probably the best film yet made from this [giant monster on the loose] formula, with some good suspense and solid script which overcome uneven Willis O'Brien special effects."

Alan Frank (*Horror*) described it as a "competent fifties monster-on-the-loose movie with good special effects," and *Psychotronic* felt it was the "scariest monster-on-the-loose movie ever made... Even though the animation was rushed, the results are fine." On the other hand, Don Willis (I) dismissed it as "resolutely routine."

The film is not badly made, except for the inadequate effects budget, but it simply progresses from one expected event to another. The low-key black-and-white photography is good throughout, and both Gene Evans and André Morell are intelligent performers. (There is no love interest at all.) If, in fact, this were the only giant-dinosaur-trashing-city film, it would be better-regarded than it is, but it was done better both before and later; the two others made by Lourié himself are better than this.

The crowd scenes look cramped, not helped by Allied Artists' double-printing many of the action scenes for television release. The "rhedosaurus" in *Beast* was more lifelike, and had a far more expressive head and face, though exaggerated. The Behemoth may actually resemble a real lizardy animal more than other such monsters, but this realism also makes it less interesting.

Our heroes are never in any danger from the creature—except for the underwater scenes, they are, in fact, never *near* it. The one other character we get to know at all well is wiped out so quickly there's no suspense. (Jack Mac-Gowran, doing a reprise of the Cecil Kellaway role in *Beast*; MacGowran later appeared in *The Exorcist*.)

This is one of those films you sit through with moderate interest but no real enthusiasm. Under the restrictive circumstances surrounding the production of the film, it's a wonder, really, that *The Giant Behemoth* was not a lot worse. As it is, it's primarily a sad reminder about how ill-used Willis O'Brien was. Though his career has only three highlights, *The Lost World*, *King Kong* and *Mighty Joe Young*, they are eloquent testimony to his genuine brilliance. *The Giant Behemoth* is merely a coda to his career.

The Giant Gila Monster

Made in Texas, this has the air of a monster movie filmed by people who only had heard rumors of monster movies before, but had never seen one. Some of the common elements are there—necking teenagers killed by a marauding beast, for instace—but sometimes they are shuffled into new combinations. The hero is strangely conceived: he's a good family boy who drives a hot rod, cares for his crippled kid sister, and writes bland songs (three of which he performs in the course of the film).

As for the menace itself, as the title states, it's just an overgrown Gila monster. These are sluggish, gaudy lizards that live in the deserts of the Southwestern United States and Mexico. Aside from the fact that they have very attractive orange-and-black skins, the main characteristic of the Gila monster and its near relative, the beaded lizard, is that they are the world's only poisonous lizards. However, this is never alluded to at all in the movie. Gila monsters, though carnivorous, are not especially aggressive, and not an exciting beast to have as a giant menace. It would seem that any lizard, or any carnivorous desert animal would have sufficed. It was probably "monster" in the name alone that attracted producer Ken Curtis (Festus of "Gunsmoke") to the idea of using one of these creatures as a giant menace.

The story is as sluggish as a Gila monster. The beast appears occasionally, but no one knows it's out there for a long while—although a colorful lizard the size of a school bus (or larger, the size is variable) would be easily spotted from the air. We see the creature's foot almost immediately in the film, as it attacks two teenagers who are in a car. A good deal of time is exhausted in the film as the sheriff (Fred Graham, in a low-key, satisfactory performance) drives around the countryside investigating the couple's disappearance .

The Sheriff—given no other name—is friendly with Chace Winstead (Don Sullivan), the head of a peace-loving local hot-rod gang. They have long, pointless conversations about the missing couple. We learn that Chace's father died on an oil rig owned by the father of the missing boy, that Chace is the sole support of his crippled little sister and his mother, that he writes songs, and that he has a batch of nitroglycerin stored in a shed.

Scenes of the Gila monster creeping around rather good miniature canyons and gullies alternate with scenes of the Sheriff talking and talking to Chace. A painfully quaint Local Character, Mr. Harris (Shug Fisher) turns up from time to time, given overly-colorful dialogue like "Give me a snort of that there sody pop."

Chace helps stranded Steamroller Smith (Ken Knox) who saw the Gila monster while he was drunk. After sleeping off his drunk, Steamroller awakes to hear Chace banging away on a Fender and singing one of his own songs (which were written by Sullivan): "My baby she rocks and rolls whenever she walks and strolls" is a typical line. Steamroller gives Chace his business card: whoopee, he's a disc jockey working for KILT—the Houston radio station owned by Gordon McLendon, who was one of the executive producers of the film. Giant Gila monsters can sometimes lead to decent young men becoming singing idols. More on McLendon in the entry on *The Killer Shrews*.

Chace's girlfriend Lisa (Lisa Simone) is French for no clear reason, other than that the actress was, and she's as Goody Twoshoes as Chace himself: she helped buy braces for Chace's little sister Missy (Janice Stone). There's a sticky "heartwarming" scene in which dear little Missy struggles to walk for Chace, and he is given a chance to sing another song. Though Chace is ostensibly a rock 'n' roll idol in the making, he accompanies himself on one of the least rock-oriented instruments, a ukelele. This song, which people recall as "Let the Children Laugh," is actually called "The Mushroom Song," and has some of the strangest lyrics I can recall, bordering on the surrealistic: "There was a mushroom, sad little mushroom, There was a meadow, ready to cry. There was a sparrow, gray little sparrow, There was an eagle, silent and high." The chorus, which has no relationship to the lyric: "And the Lord said 'Let the children laugh,' the Lord said 'Let the children laugh,'" (repeat twice). There is another verse, but let us be merciful to Don Sullivan, wherever he may be.

More people, including Chace's employer, are killed by the Gila monster. It derails a train, and finally its presence is known. There's a big barn dance just down the road a piece, and the Gila monster comes snooping around there, knocking a hole in the side of the building and scaring the hell out of everybody.

It conveniently meanders out onto a field, and the big lizard is bearing down on Missy, who for some reason is in the field by herself. Chace loads his precious hot rod full of nitroglycerin—remember?—and drives it full tilt at the lizard. He leaps out at the last moment. Kablooey, no more giant Gila monster.

After *Them!* and *Tarantula*, the quality of giant-beast-on-the-loose films declined sharply; *The Giant Gila Monster* is simply another tepid entry in this genre, although not as stereotyped in story. The gigantism of the lead beast is not explained as being due to radiation; in fact, in a sense no explanation at all is offered. The doom-laden opening narration merely declares "how large the dreaded Gila monster grows, no man can say." Later, the Sheriff cites big bones found in Tanganyika, and a 130 pound ten-month-old baby as somehow supportive of the theory of a giant Gila monster. He adds that the salts and minerals in the river delta country where the giant lizard originated probably caused it to grow so large.

"Explanations" like this are obviously not intended as real explanations at all. They are merely the required narrative material to make the picture remotely plausible.

The Giant Gila Monster was first budgeted at $300,000, but completed for merely $138,000, and it shows. Except for the miniatures and the close angles on the lizard intended to make it look gigantic, there are virtually no special effects in the entire picture. There are no rear-screen projections, no mattes, no split screens; as a result, the monster never appears in the same shot with a human being at all, which makes it a very remote menace. The miniature highway it crosses once, a railroad trestle and the miniature barn are the only man-made objects it appears with, except for a toy hot rod, but these aren't enough to create even a thin illusion of reality.

The size of the creature varies, as well. It crawls across a two-lane highway, and seems about twice as long as the highway is wide, making it around 50 feet in length. Outside the barn, it seems much larger; under the trestle, it seems much smaller. But as that is typical of even good giant monster movies as far back as *King Kong*, it hardly seems fair to complain about relative scale in this case; I'm just remarking on it.

The lamebrained script by Jay Simms (whose name is spelled "Sims" in the credits) is poorly constructed, with lumbering and unnecessary stretches of very talky exposition that has nothing to do with the monster. The characterization is by the numbers, with a folksy, humorless sheriff, an arrogant rich man, wisecracking teenagers, and a noble hero. The film lurches from scene to scene, always unclear about the points it's trying to make. Why is there so much talk about the vanished pair of teenagers? Probably because Simms saw that kind of thing in other movies about teenagers, and felt it needed to be added. But then why does he add a crippled little kid, hot rods and a singing hero?

The songs by Don Sullivan are colorless, confusing, and uninteresting. Perhaps the most unbelievable thing about the picture—including the giant lizard—is when the teenage crowd goes wild for one of Sullivan's songs at the big barn dance. Sullivan is personable as an actor, but his character Chace is so impossibly good and right at all times that he becomes saccharin and boring.

Jack Marshall's music is unfortunate. It is full of slow, heavy rhythms, to emphasize the menace of the slithering beast, but instead produces only boredom. His son Frank went on to bigger things, incidentally; in a varied career, he produced *Raiders of the Lost Ark* and *Poltergeist*, among other things.

Other people involved in *The Giant Gila Monster* worked elsewhere too. Audrey Blasdel, script girl, became Columbia Pictures television division's head set decorator. Audrey Granville, music associate, was supervising music editor for David O. Selznick. Camera operator George Nogle worked with director Ray Kellogg on some of Kellogg's more prestigious films, where Kellogg was 2nd unit director, such as *Cheyenne Autumn* (1964). This information courtesy of Michael Hayes the indefatigable.

The photography by Wilfrid M. Cline is one of the best aspects of the picture. It's bleak, but that's the nature of the countryside. The crisp, natural realism of the camerawork is attractive, but overall adds nothing to the picture.

Films like *The Giant Gila Monster*, a small-time production with a cast of unknowns, were reviewed only infrequently, and then mostly by daily newspapers, which routinely review most movies. Charles Stinson at the *Los Angeles Times* was a conscientious critic, even noting that he had spotted Don Sullivan as an actor before. He avoided criticizing the films too severely—*Monster* was reviewed in tandem with its cofeature, *The Killer Shrews*; his harshest judgment was "They're not very much, I'm afraid." He did note that in *Monster*, "the special effects are superior to the story and most of the acting." Weekly *Variety*'s "Bark" said that the "story is mild, but as an 'audience reaction' feature, [it] has appeal for the science fiction situations." The *Monthly Film Bulletin* gave the film its lowest rating, and said that it was "a particularly trite variation on a routine theme." Don Willis (I) said that it "turns sappily sentimental at the worst times." So what would have been the *best* times to turn sappily sentimental?

The Giant Gila Monster was released on a double bill with *The Killer Shrews*, also made in Texas by the same company. Despite the problems with *Shrews*, its fast pace, inexorable if silly logic, and some good shocks made *The Giant Gila Monster* look even more pedestrian and boring than it really is. Which is plenty.

Gigantis the Fire Monster

Aside from entertaining scenes of destruction, as Gigantis/Godzilla and his opponent Angilas/Angurus romp around elaborate miniature sets of Osaka,

Gigantis the Fire Monster is the least of the Godzilla films. It wasn't until the 1960s that Godzilla became the true King of the Giant Monsters, with what seemed to be an unending series of amusingly awesome films in which the Big G evolved from a dangerous villain to Protector of the Earth. These films show an antic, even sophisticated slapstick humor—Godzilla doing a little jig for joy in *Monster Zero* (1970), Titanosaurus tucking his hands behind his back and bouncing from one foot to the other on Godzilla's grave, Godzilla's son Minya blowing smoke rings, etc.—making them occasionally delightful and almost always entertaining. What Godzilla lost in terror, he made up for in a silly, endearing personality. (In 1984, he returned to menace status in the elaborate *Godzilla 1985*.)

However, back here in the 50s, Godzilla was still a lumbering menace. Also, after the first film, a thoroughly dead one. At the end of *Godzilla, King of the Monsters*, the "oxygen destroyer" dissolved Godzilla right down to a skeleton, making, in the wake of the film's worldwide success, his mandatory revival impossible. The solution was anything but ingenious; without any explanation, *another* Godzilla turned up. (A narrator in *Gigantis* suggests that radiation might have played a part in the new Godzilla's appearance, but it's passed over in the film.)

Gojira No Gyakushyu (Godzilla's Counterattack) features two monsters for the price of one, but is in every way a lesser production than the first, though the destruction scenes are somewhat more spectacular, despite being fewer in number. Strung around set pieces, the storyline is lumpy: Godzilla is found, Godzilla smashes Osaka and opponent, Godzilla flees, Godzilla is buried. There's none of the awe of the first, amazement at the devastation a prehistoric monster wreaks on Tokyo's buildings. Things in the second are more perfunctory, and the film has a quickie air to it, though it's not impossible it was more expensive. It just looks cheaper, and is definitely less interesting.

In 1957, the American rights to *Gojira No Gyakushyu* were purchased by AB–PT Pictures Corporation, a company owned by American Broadcasting and Paramount Theatres. That same year, through Republic, the company released *Beginning of the End* and *The Unearthly*, but those don't appear to have done well enough to keep AB–PT in business.

They did commission a script by Ib Melchior and Ed Watson for "The Vocano Monsters" (dated 7 May 1957). This was to have been an American redo of *Gojira No Gyakushyu*, with extensive new American footage, using only the monster stuff from the Japanese original (cf. *Varan the Unbelievable*).

Judging from a reading of the script, Melchior and Watson were instructed to omit all scenes of the new Godzilla's blazing atomic breath; furthermore, they were allowed to write in some *new* action scenes for Godzilla. Presumably, as with *Half Human*, the monster suit was to be shipped to the United States for this new footage. For historical interest, here is the planned plot of "The Volcano Monsters."

After a volcanic eruption on a Japanese island, a joint Japanese–U.S. geological/paleontological team discovers the bodies of two gigantic dinosaurs preserved inside a limestone cavern uncovered by the volcano. The two dinosaurs, an ankylosaurus and a female Tyrannosaurus rex, are put on a U.S. aircraft carrier for a trip to the United States.

On the way, someone discovers the two creatures are in suspended animation, but no decisions are made. A storm comes up, the sleeping tyrannosaur breaks loose and falls into the sea. The carrier continues on to San Francisco.

There, the tyrannosaur surfaces just as the ankylosaur, still fastened to the

Angilus (or Angurus) biting the hand that fed Toho for years; although called Gigantis the Fire Monster (U.S. release 1959), we know that the big bruiser on the right (played by Haruo Nakajima) is really Godzilla, King of the Monsters. This is an unusually clear shot for one of these things.

aircraft carrier's deck, revives. It breaks free and scrambles ashore, and the two fight all over San Francisco, amid rocket fire and flames. Because of the presence of so many Oriental buildings in the monster footage, the writers were careful to include a scene in which the battling giants trash Chinatown.

The tyrannosaur kills the ankylosaur, as well as most of the main cast except the Hero and Heroine, and leaves town, heading north. The rest of the action in the proposed script is virtually identical to that in the actual film.

Although the script by Melchior and Watson has many flaws, it's still superior to that written for the actual film by Takeo Murata and Shigeaki Hidaka, from a story by Shigero Kayama. In the American prints, *Gigantis the Fire Monster* (acquired by Warner Bros. when AB–PT collapsed) opens with stock footage of atomic explosions, various rockets taking off (including a mysterious shot of an unidentified rocket ship from some SF movie or serial), while the narrator, who sounds like Marvin Miller, tells us that these "giant mechanical monsters" are opening the heavens to us though the Earth still harbors "darker and more sinister secrets." Except for this footage and that, for some reason, all shots of Godzilla's/Gigantis' dorsal plates lighting up are cut, the film seems to be exactly the same in the United States and Japan.

The film is narrated throughout, supposedly by Shoichi Tsukoka, pilot for a cannery whose job it is to spot shoals of fish for the fishing fleet. Tsukoka is played by Hiroshi Koizumi, a busy Toho contract player who later appeared in *Mothra, Godzilla vs. the Thing* and *Ghidrah the Three-Headed Monster,* among other films, but the narrator is an American actor who speaks with a strong but intelligible Japanese accent.

Shoichi's pal Koji Kobayashi (Minoru Chiaki, about whom more later), a carefree joker type, common to Japanese films, has been forced to land near desolate Iwato island. Shoichi is directed there by radio operator Hidemi Yamaji (Setsuko Wakayama), his girlfriend and daughter of the fishing and cannery company president (Yuko Kasama).

Shoichi lands his seaplane safely; he and Kobayashi are stunned to see a battle between two giant dinosaurs, who grapple then fall into the sea. The two pilots contact authorities at once. Dr. Tadokoro (Maso Shimizu, in an ill-fitting white wig) has them pick over photos of dinosaurs—as in *Beast from 20,000 Fathoms*, which this film strongly resembles—until they come to a photo of "angilasaurus" (presumably ankylosaurus), which Tadokoro describes as "killer of the living," one of the "original plundering murderers" of the prehistoric world. The other monster, whom *we* recognize as Godzilla, is identified as a Gigantis.

Reading from an authoritative-looking paleontological text, Tadokoro tells them, "somewhere, although it is not know when, these creatures may come alive after years of hibernation due to radioactive fallout." Describing the "angilasaurus," more familiarly called "Angurus" (by his friends?), Tadokoro reads "he has brains in several parts of his body, including head, abdomen and chest. He is a member of the Angurus family of fire monsters and can wipe out the human race." He soberly closes the book. "These boys are both Gigantis and Angurus," he informs the stunned assembly.

He's flown in Dr. Yamane (Takashi Shimura, briefly reprising his role from *Godzilla*), who is familiar with the Gigantis type. Yamane tells them that Gigantis cannot be destroyed, and shows them a bizarre little film to prove how dangerous this monster is. The film includes a brief stop-motion shot of a pair of battling brontosauruses, a live-action dimetrodon, and a shot of the droopy-looking dinosaurs from *Unknown Island* (1948). The little film concludes with some scenes of the destruction and devastation of Tokyo from *Godzilla* (the "history of life" scene was not in the original Japanese prints, being added in the United States). That monster, Yamane says, was killed by the oxygen destroyer, whose inventor also died, and the secret of his invention went with him.

These monsters were born out of fire, they breathed fire, fire was part of their organic makeup. The monsters are attracted and infuriated by light, Yamane says, surely strange behavior for fire monsters. The monsters went underground and hibernated.

After a good deal more stock footage—the film seems to be about 40 percent stock—which traces the progress of the unseen Gigantis on his way to Osaka, quaking in fear about his approach, there's an all-clear signal. Gigantis will bypass Osaka. Everyone is relieved and all go to nightclubs where they dance, while a woman sings. But it's only a lull before the storm. Soon a voice on a loudspeaker—the film is rife with loudspeakers—warns them that Gigantis is heading for Osaka after all. "Please remain calm!" the voice cries as the crowd flees in panic.

Since light attracts and angers this fire monster, the city is put under black-out conditions (more stock footage). Gigantis surfaces in the harbor, and planes fly around at sea, dropping flares in a temporarily-successful attempt to lure him away.

However, while a truckload of convicts leaves Osaka, they overcome their guards, grab a gasoline truck and try to flee. There's a long chase through city streets before the truck crashes into an oil refinery and sets it ablaze.

Gigantis sees the fire and heads for the city. Angurus, about whom everyone seems to have forgotten, was swimming past Osaka and spotted the blaze, too. He comes ashore, and the two monsters fight all over town, knocking down many buildings and raising a lot of dust.

In these scenes, unlike other Japanese giant monster films, the fights are played in normal motion, perhaps even a little speeded up. This makes the clashes extremely lively, but also results in their looking like nothing other than what they are: men in monster suits wrestling amid miniature buildings. Also, in some of the close-ups, the monsters, tossing their heads challengingly, are played by elaborate hand puppets.

These fights are occasionally attractively photographed, with a vast cityscape between the camera and the struggling titans. Clouds of dust are kicked up, and they usually fight against a spectacular backdrop of flames. Gigantis only rarely uses his flaming breath.

During this epic struggle, more convicts flee (rather stupidly) into a vast subway for shelter, but Gigantis and Angurus topple into a riverbed, breaking open the subway; a flood of water pours in. In a very effective shot, the fleeing convicts are overwhelmed by the onrushing flood.

The two monsters battle their way to the dramatic Osaka Castle, jouncing against it, and causing stop-motion cracks to appear in the old building before they finally topple it.

Eventually, Gigantis gets the upper hand and kills Angurus by biting him in the neck; blood spurts forth. Gigantis sprays his atomic breath over his rival in a coup de grace. Gigantis leaves.

The city is now but "a smoking cemetery with charred memories," narrating Shoichi tells us. The fishery sends Kobayashi to Hokkaido for awhile, and despite the disaster, everyone goes back to work.

The monster plot stops dead. Gigantis isn't even mentioned for some time as the cannery plot continues at length. Eventually Hidemi and Shoichi join Kobayashi in Hokkaido, and they have a party with the two pilots' former squadron and commander. Feeling jolly, they all sing "we won't get home in the morning" to the tune of "the bear came over the mountain" until they are informed that Gigantis has sunk one of the fishing trawlers.

Worldwide panic sets in, which seems excessive, and there are mass evacuations (more stock footage). Shoichi finally spots Gigantis swimming along amid icebergs, and the fleet, raised to destroy the monster, heads that way.

Shoichi sees Kobayashi's plane winging toward his, and cries "what a sight for sore eyes!" The two locate Gigantis in a deep canyon on an icy island. There are some interesting aerial shots of an immobile statuette of the monster in the realistic miniature set, but the most impressive shot in this sequence is of Haruo Nakajima in the Godzilla suit, standing in a vast canyon as Kobayashi's plane flies by him at shoulder level. The monster has a sense of scale and menace in this scene (though he's much smaller than he was back in Osaka; maybe cold shrinks godzilloids), and it is handsomely photographed by Eiji Tsuburaya's effects team. Until this point, except for the battle in the city, the film was lifeless and Gigantis seemed a distant menace, but the climax is visually impressive and the monster seems more real.

Inexplicably, Kobayashi shouts, "So help me!" and dives his plane toward Gigantis, who fries it with his fiery breath. The plane crashes into a cliff above the monster, and sends a cascade of ice down into the canyon around Gigantis' feet. (Another handsome scene.)

By his friend's sacrifice, Shoichi has seen the way to conquer Gigantis: bury him alive in an avalanche of ice and rock. He and other pilots try this, but, rolling his eyes, Gigantis climbs out of the pile of rock and ice. However, the means is now clear, and Sabre jets, one piloted by Shoichi, increase the tempo and strength of the bombardment, finally burying the monster completely in what looks like piles of ice cubes. But don't worry. Eight years later, Gigantis—back to being called Godzilla—burst out of his icy prison in *King Kong vs. Godzilla*, and never went back.

Gigantis the Fire Monster looks depressingly cheap. The vast amount of stock footage, the minimal and heavily reused sets for the live-action scenes, and the relatively few shots of the monster, indicate it was made in a great hurry on a low budget. Special effects director Eiji Tsuburaya did his usual fine job—within the limits of the type of effects he was doing—and his sequences are, by a long margin, the most visually-impressive material in the film. The only serious failings on Tsuburaya's part were the too-fast fight scenes between the monsters, and the cascade of ice which buries Gigantis at the end. The miniature head of Gigantis doesn't really match that on the suit worn by Nakajima, but that's a minor failing; the miniatures are quite animalistic in their movements.

However, the rest of the film is one of Toho's least impressive efforts. I presume the peculiar choice of a fishery as a backdrop was because of available stock footage. It lacks any relationship to the monsters, and to return to it after Osaka is flattened by Gigantis and his playmate seems very trivial. The photography is uninteresting, the human relationships contrived and intrusive, and in general, the acting is dull, though it's hard to tell sometimes, because of the dubbing.

Which is a story in itself. In the romantic-triangle subplot which clutters up the film, Kobayashi (secretly in love with Hidemi) refuses to tell her the name of his own true love, and says no woman will win him. "All men are like fish in a woman's net," she tells him smilingly. "She's got you there," says Shoichi, and all laugh. At another point, when Hidemi praises Shoichi, he brushes aside her compliments with "Ah, banana oil!"

Kobayashi was played by Minoru Chiaki, a fine comic actor who can do straight drama. He's one of the favorite performers of Akira Kurosawa. He appeared in *Seven Samurai* (1954, as the samurai woodchopper), *I Live in Fear* (1955, as one of the sons), *Throne of Blood* (1957, as "Banquo"), *The Lower Depths* (1957, as the ex-samurai), and *Sanjuro* (1962). His two most prominent roles for Kurosawa are as the priest who rescues the baby in *Rashomon* (1950) and as one of the two cowardly rascals in *The Hidden Fortress* (1958), making Chiaki the inspiration for C-3PO in the "Star Wars" series. He also wrote an introduction for Donald Richie's excellent *Films of Kurosawa*. Chiaki is somewhat out of place in *Gigantis the Fire Monster*, but no more so than Takashi Shimura, who appeared in almost all the films directed by Kurosawa until the late 1960s.

Gigantis was rushed onto the U.S. market by Warner Bros., who showed what they thought of it by double-billing it with *Teenagers from Outer Space*. It received scant reviews.

Samuel D. Berns in the *Motion Picture Herald* called it "good," describing *Gigantis* as "another exploitable Japanese film, designed to attract seekers of action and thrills proffered by gigantic, indestructible monsters of ancient vintage."

"Powe" in *Variety* was less pleased, calling it "mediocre." He said, "it is an inept and tedious attempt at an exploitation film of the science fantasy variety. The Japanese have made some good ones of this type, but *Gigantis* is not one of them."

An odd note on the score for the film; it is credited to the estimable Masaru Sato, but there's some indication the score on the U.S. prints was "library music." The title theme, for instance, is the title music from *Kronos*.

Despite *Variety's* expectations, audiences generally enjoyed the film very much; they didn't take it seriously, so phrases like "banana oil" only added to the entertainment value. Though this film is far below Toho's standards, and though *Teenagers from Outer Space* is pretty bad, together they made a very entertaining double bill.

The H-Man

This is a highly colorful and grisly Japanese thriller seemingly made in imitation of *The Blob*, but since it was made in the same year that the American film was released, similarities are probably due more to coincidence than imitation. The blob monster in this one is a radioactively mutated human being, and his story involves a good deal of police-versus-gangster action. As with other Japanese science fiction films, the involvement of gangsters seems more to satisfy local needs than to make the films more exportable.

In Tokyo, a young man steals a huge quantity of narcotics, and on a rainy night, literally vanishes, leaving behind only his clothing. His girlfriend Chikako Arai (Yumi Shirakawa) is approached by Chief Investigator Tominaga (Akihiko Hirata), but she knows nothing of what befell the missing man.

Later, one of his criminal associates calls in Chikako, and when he departs, she sees him encounter something like a green shadow, then collapse and wilt, leaving nothing but his clothes in the rain. She reports this to the police, but they don't believe her.

However, scientist Masada (Kenji Sahara) does, for he has an incredible theory. He knows that a fishing boat encountered a drifting craft which had passed through fallout from a hydrogen bomb. The men on the ship reported a gelatinous green mass before they fell silent. Masada believes one crewman touched the stuff and was transformed into an H-Man. He believes the missing men have been melted to death by the creature who was once the crewman, now a liquid H-Man, who must dissolve others in order to live.

Masada demonstrates his theory by turning a normal frog into an H-frog; the gelatinous mass dissolves another frog in a macabre, disturbing scene.

Once the threat has been identified as a liquid man, there's an obvious way to destroy him: evaporation. But first you have to find him.

The mob of dope dealers comes into the action again. They use the sewers of Tokyo as a rendezvous point, which also happens to be where the H-Man lives. A liquid creature can move around damp places readily, which is why most of the deaths occur in the rain. The H-Man also seems to be able to form himself into a vaguely human-shaped mass (of a lovely shade of blue), but in that state, he doesn't seem to be able to do much of anything. (Note: my memory seems to insist that aboard the trawler we saw several H-People in human shape, but synopses are confusing on this.)

The gang chief kidnaps Chikako and takes her to the sewer, whereupon he

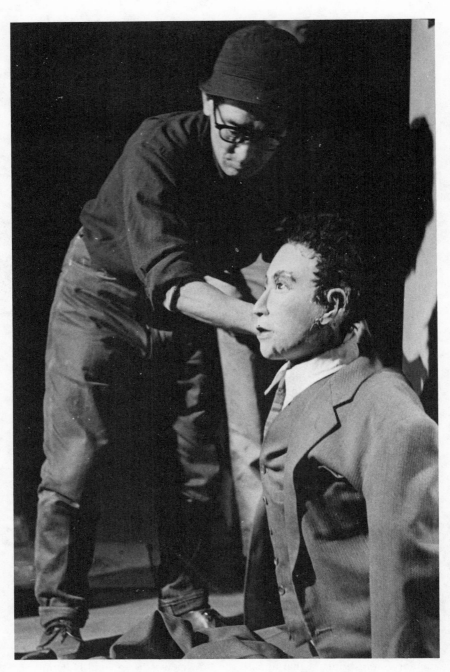

Special effects director Eiji Tsuburaya adjusts one of the man-shaped balloons used to depict a person melting, from The H-Man (U.S. release 1959).

270 **1959**

is killed by the H-Man. The police and scientists enter, and soon destroy the H-Man with flame throwers. There are some interesting scenes of the H-Man flowing along vertical walls before being turned to steam.

The H-Man is not usually highly regarded even by aficionados of Japanese monster pictures, perhaps because not even one building is flattened. But it's far creepier than most such films, well-produced on interesting locations, with vivid color and a tour of Tokyo's seamier neighborhoods and nightclubs. Furthermore, there's a very peculiar atmosphere to the monster side of the story, with a human being turned into liquid, then devouring other normal people. It is presented in a matter-of-fact fashion, as if in the long run we are all fated to become H-People.

There are several horrifying scenes in the picture which scared and delighted American children, its largest and most enthusiastic audience here. (My cousin Robert Street was nearly frightened into catatonia by the film, which for years he thought of as the scariest thing he ever saw.) Blue goo cascades down over hapless victims, who then collapse in upon themselves in a most disquieting and horrifyingly comic fashion. For these shots, special effects director Eiji Tsuburaya used inflated, clothed rubber dummies of the actors, from which he slowly bled the air to shrivel up the victims.

One of the high (or low, depending) points of the film is the scene in which that frog is turned into an H-frog. First, this also has that matter-of-fact air, as if this liquefaction process is a normal by-product of nuclear radiation, one with which we should already be familiar. Secondly, despite their carnivorous voraciousness, frogs are charming little creatures. For them to be so horribly treated is somehow more shocking and disturbing than similar scenes of people. We're accustomed to seeing mere human beings toasted, melted, devoured, etc., but dissolving a couple of bulgy-eyed frogs is a new and not pleasant experience.

The climax is highly colorful and exciting, taking place as it does in dank sewers, with flames squirting down the tunnels and the desperate H-Man slithering along the wall. It's certainly novel, which makes the fact that this film is so rarely shown something of a mystery.

According to John Brosnan in *Movie Magic*, effects expert Eiji Tsuburaya and his assistants created the mobile jelly from a special chemical compound. (Talk about vague...) In front of the camera, they forced it under pressure through the cracks and under doors in various sets. The wall-climbing sequences were equally simple: the sets were simply built on their sides, and the stuff poured down them.

"Ron" in *Daily Variety* was pleased with the film, calling it "well made and seemingly more thoughtful than [Toho's] two other U.S. summer releases (Metro's *The Mysterians* and Warner Bros.' *Gigantis*) and Columbia should be able to exploit good bookings with [this] widescreen, color production.... While recollective science-fiction addicts may pooh-pooh the idea of an Oriental copy [of *The Blob*], they should be pleased indeed with the quality of the replica.... Its one effect—namely, the disintegration of the human body—is skillfully and terrifyingly adept.... Yumi Shirakawa, as a delightful-looking night-club entertainer, is excellent, as are Kenji Sahara ... and Akihiko Hirata.... The Takeshi Kimura screenplay ... is effective, and Inoshiro Honda's direction takes full advantage of the story [which is a] technically excellent production."

The *Monthly Film Bulletin* gave it a II, saying *The H-Man* "has all the usual faults and virtues of Japanese SF-cum-horror fiction. The story is imitative and undisciplined, spending far too much time on an erratic police vs. racketeers sub-plot which is vague and gets nowhere; characterisation is virtually non-existent.... But for special effects, trick photography and spectacular staging, the Japanese again beat their Hollywood counterparts at their own game: the fantasy element of vanishing bodies and mobile liquid is brilliantly done."

Jack Moffitt felt that "it is said that the Japanese can imitate anything, but, when one recalls such native masterpieces as *Rashomon* and *Gate of Hell*, one wishes this knack of parroting American hokum could be held in check."

Joe Pihodna in the New York *Herald-Tribune* got into the spirit of things: "A good-natured poke at atom-bomb [*sic*] tests... The picture is plainly making a case against the use of nuclear bombs. At the same time, there is a great deal of lively entertainment in the story involving the police, dope smugglers, scientists, and some very pretty Japanese girls.... [Final] scenes are spectacular."

As for *new* blob monster movies, Larry Cohen's *The Stuff* (1985) was about blob-like food that eats you, and was entertaining enough, but I doubt it had the impact on younger kids that *The H-Man* had in 1959.

Have Rocket, Will Travel

In 1958, after 190 shorts and 28 years on screen, the Three Stooges seemed destined for the scrap heap. Their contract with Columbia expired, and the studio was no more interested in continuing to make two-reel shorts than any other studio in town. Furthermore, the Stooges were old men.

The group on screen had originally been Moe Howard, Jerry (Curly) Howard and Larry Fine. When Curly was felled by a stroke in the mid-40s, he was replaced by the third Howard brother, Shemp, who'd had a career as a supporting player on his own. Curly died without recovering, and later Shemp died, too. Moe wanted to call a halt to the Three Stooges at that point, but Columbia insisted he live up to the contract, so Joe Besser was recruited as a new Stooge. But the end of the short subject trail came in 1957; their last few are dismal, even by Three Stooges standards, and they disbanded.

Moe appeared in one film, *Space Master X-7*, as director Edward Bernds was an old friend, and perhaps would have continued to work as a bit player with the occasional comedy scene.

But television came to the rescue of the Three Stooges. In 1958, Columbia sold the entire package of Stooge shorts for a profit of $12 million. Of which the Stooges got not a penny. However, as the well-researched *The Three Stooges Scrapbook* points out, despite some complaints by parents, the popularity of the Stooges was renewed, and obvious to all. (The *Scrapbook*, incidentally, has excellent research on the Stooges; it has serious errors elsewhere.)

Columbia was anxious to cash in on the renewed popularity, so the studio made a deal with the Stooges' longtime manager Harry Romm to quickly make a low-budget ($127,000) feature to capitalize on the TV fame. The *Scrapbook* reveals the sad facts of the Stooges' financial participation: "For their efforts, the Stooges received $30,000 and had to split one-half of producer-agent Harry Romm's 50% of the net profits derived from the film's distribution."

Have Rocket, Will Travel was released on a double bill with *The Legend of Tom Dooley*, a Civil War Western itself designed to cash in on a popular phenomenon, the Kingston Trio's folk song "Tom Dooley." Unfortunately, neither film was any good, but the pair did well financially.

Much more than their later films, *Have Rocket, Will Travel* resembles nothing more than an extended Stooges short. It was shot swiftly on available locations; special effects were either minimal or bad, and the film itself is an unpleasant mixture of slapstick and sentimentality. There's even a song.

Joe Besser was passed over in favor of new Stooge Joe De Rita, chosen for no better reason than that he was the right height, and somewhat resembled the long-gone (and superior) Curly Howard. He was even called "Curley Joe" in hopes of making the small children who were always the Stooges' biggest fans think that he might actually *be* Curly Howard. Unfortunately, De Rita was a minimally talented comedian who never threw himself into things with the insane abandon of Curly Howard, who with his squeals, nyuk-nyuk-nyuks, shoulder spins and general frantic activity, was the busy center of the Stooges in the 30s and 40s (though Moe was always top dog). Adults often find Curly funny, but even kids didn't care for Curley Joe.

But he was the official third Stooge for the remainder of the group's life as performers, and outlived both Moe and Larry. He is still alive as I write, though inactive as a performer. (Coincidentally, he lives near Joe Besser.)

In *Have Rocket, Will Travel*, the Stooges play handymen at a missile plant run by J.P. Morse (Jerome Cowan). They go through their usual routines: Larry and Curley Joe's stupidity results in Moe getting banged in the head with something, and he belts them in retaliation. This goes on for a while until they decide to help beautiful scientist Dr. Ingrid Naarveg (Anna-Lisa), trying to develop a proper fuel for interplanetary flight.

She's been kind to the smitten "boys" (Moe was 63, Larry was 47, Curley Joe was 49), so they decide to help her out. They toss all kinds of chemicals into their would-be rocket fuel, and in the manner of such films, it turns out to be exactly the right stuff, so to speak. The rocket takes off with the Stooges aboard.

After some of the usual weightless gags, in which instead of suddenly weighing nothing, objects fall up, seemingly having negative weight, the rocket lands on Venus.

A flame-breathing giant spider scorches their pants, and they meet a talking unicorn. It takes them to the main city of Venus, where they encounter a mad computer. The trio are shrunken to doll size, put in a cage, and later restored to normal. The computer creates robot duplicates of the Stooges, and the trio have some hectic moments before they manage to return to Earth. On their return, they are greeted as heroes, but turn their welcoming ceremony into a shambles.

The film was pounced on eagerly by audiences curious about the Stooges in what was falsely billed as their first full-length feature. (They made the little-known *Gold Raiders* in 1951, and had walk-on and guest spots in several 1930s features.) Most people were disappointed; the "touching" scenes with the unicorn were embarrassing, the comedy was repetitious and familiar, and like the Stooges themselves, the film was lethargic. Nonetheless, the film did well enough that Columbia decided to delve further into Stooge fever.

Columbia wanted a sequel. After so many years of low pay, the Stooges demanded quite reasonably that Romm give them $50,000 and a larger share of the profits of their next film. He refused, and with Columbia's blessing, made *Stop, Look and Laugh*, a feature composed of clips of old Stooge material and some new introductory scenes with ventriloquist Paul Winchell, also popular then.

The Stooges sued on the basis that Columbia had no right to make a feature in this manner without consulting them; an out-of-court settlement was reached, and Romm was fired by the Stooges.

Norman Maurer, an enterprising comic book artist and publisher, was also Moe Howard's son-in-law. He entered the picture at this point, and together with the Stooges (presumably only Howard and Fine), formed Normandy Productions. For a much better share of the wealth, the Stooges and Maurer embarked on a multipicture contract with Columbia, which kept them busy until Moe, Larry and Curley Joe were almost ready to retire and the bloom was off the Stooges' rose.

In their shorts, the Stooges were purveyors of slapstick: banging each other around, flinging pies and falling into vats of plaster. When they moved into features, someone made the idiot decision that they should try to help True Love whenever it springs up, as if such romance was of interest to anyone. Though it remained an element in all their later pictures, it was dealt with as perfunctorily as possible, except in *Snow White and the Three Stooges* (1961), made for another studio. The Stooges were perhaps the least "touching" comedy team in the history of films, with the possible exception of the Ritz Brothers, so bringing in sentimentality was a truly stupid idea. But then again, the Stooges aren't a brilliant idea...

Director David Lowell Rich was a Columbia B-feature regular at this time, having already helmed *No Time to Be Young* (1957) and *Senior Prom* (1958), among other films. He later went to Universal, where he made competent but highly uninspired studio features including *Rosie* (1967), *Eye of the Cat* (1969), and the wondrous *Airport '79 Concorde*. He's especially active in TV movies, averaging more than two a year. (If Rich and John Llewellyn Moxey retire, TV movies may cease.) Among his TV films are some genre pieces, including *The Horror at 37,000 Feet* and *Satan's School for Girls* (both 1973). He's the equivalent of a busy B-movie director of the old days; there's certainly no apparent Richian style.

Have Rocket, Will Travel is obviously not a film for reviewers. Technically, it's about as good as a low-budget studio-made film usually is, but it's still a Three Stooges film, and if you don't like the Three Stooges—there's no reason why you should—you won't like the movie. Even people who do like the Stooges, some of whom are actually normal, intelligent people, don't care for this film. On television, *Have Rocket, Will Travel* has long since been eclipsed by the later Stooges features; the first two from Columbia that followed, *The Three Stooges Meet Hercules* and *...In Orbit* are often shown. They're much better than this try at establishing them as feature comedians.

The Hideous Sun Demon

"The rest of us can only hope that his life was not wasted," says one of the characters at the end of *The Hideous Sun Demon*, after the Tragic Protagonist has taken a header off an oil tank. Many in the audience felt that their time had been wasted with the movie, of course, and no wonder. *The Hideous Sun Demon*, known in Britain obscurely if grotesquely as *Blood on His Lips*, is a dreary, boring and erratic variation on "Dr. Jekyll and Mr. Hyde." In this film, instead of turning into a monster with the rising of the full Moon, like a self-respecting werewolf, our hero becomes a monster as the result of sunlight. He doesn't turn tan, he becomes what *TV Guide* has immortalized as "a scaly lizard-like creature." It's hard to determine what the transformation does to his

Robert Clarke (left) in his swell Sun Demon mask menaces Nan Peterson in this posed shot for The Hideous Sun Demon (1959). The mask has an interesting design and was well-executed by Richard Cassarino; the same cannot be said for Clarke's direction of the film.

mind. Sometimes, when he's scaly and monstrous—the mask/makeup is quite good—he clearly has a normal human mind; at other times, the sunlight makes him a homicidal maniac even when he looks perfectly normal. No one seems to have given this element much thought, but then no one seems to have given anything about this picture much thought. It's just a reverse werewolf movie.

Even the title has caused some confusion. A local Los Angeles theatre used to run three SF-horror movies every weekend, and their phone message proclaimed the film as "High Dee-yuss the Sun Demon." That might have been better.

The picture hasn't attracted the campy cult following that has given other cheap monster movies, such as *Cat-Women of the Moon* and *Plan 9 from Outer Space*, new leases on life. Like *Teenagers from Outer Space*, no one seems yet to have discovered *The Hideous Sun Demon*. It should only remain obscure, but it won't. More on this later.

Tom Weaver's amusing interview with director-star Robert Clarke was printed in *Fangoria* #34, and from that interview, as well as from Mark McGee, comes much of the following information. (Weaver is a treasure, and should do a book of his own.) "For *The Astounding She Monster*," Weaver said, "Clarke was promised 5% of the film's profits in addition to his salary. He didn't think anything would come of this percentage, but then found that it eventually brought him a sizeable sum of money." Clarke told Mark McGee further that since *She Monster* was unquestionably awful and yet profitable, he decided to make a monster movie of his own.

He came up with the idea on his own, and cowrote the script with a friend, Phil Hiner. The production crew was drawn from a film class at the University of Southern California; one, Robin Kirkman, even invested in it, and brought in E.S. Seeley, who rewrote. Clarke told Weaver, "We shot on weekends. We'd have a spot picked for our shooting that weekend, we rented our camera, lighting and sound equipment on a Friday afternoon and we actually got two days of shooting for one day's rental. We thought that was pretty clever. We shot 12 consecutive weekends" because Clarke was still working as an actor in other people's productions, and because his crew had to go back to school. The overall cost of the film was under $50,000; the film looks awkward and amateurish at times, but it also looks more expensive than that.

Clarke did all the Sun Demon stunts himself. Richard Cassarino built the mask and face of the Sun Demon at a low cost. The torso costume was built on a skin diver's wet suit, which meant that Clarke sweated mightily during production, causing perspiration to run down his body, and he ended up looking like the Sun Demon had just wet his pants.

Three cinematographers are credited because three cinematographers did the work. John Morrill shot at least half, Stan Follis "worked with us throughout the picture as assistant cameraman *and* did some first unit work," Clarke told Weaver, but Vilis Lapenieks' work was the best.

Unfortunately for Clarke, 18 months after Pacific International began distributing *The Hideous Sun Demon*, the firm went bankrupt and he lost his profits on the picture. He sold television rights, and later all rights. "I took such a terrible bath with the bankruptcy on both *The Sun Demon* and *[Beyond] the Time Barrier* that I just felt there was no way to make another one and come out with anything."

The patchwork method of making the film explains the peculiar unevenness of the photography. It must explain why there's such a huge discrepancy between the script and the finished film; the script isn't good, but it's far more ambitious than the released movie, and transitional material probably wasn't shot at all.

As it is, the film is almost schematic. Clarke plays Dr. Gilbert McKenna, atomic radiation researcher, accidentally exposed to radiation. He's rushed to a hospital to recover while we are *told* about (not shown) the accident. (There's a peculiar emphasis on a toy train that lugs about the isotopes Gil was working with.) We're also told that Gil drinks heavily, and we see him flirting with nurses. This seems to be the results of actual efforts at characterization, and does tie in with later behavior.

While sitting in the sun as part of his recuperation, Gil suddenly feels peculiar. A nearby old lady patient screams, and he dashes into his room, where we get only the briefest glimpse of his reptilian face before he smashes the mirror. (This is one of the two effective scenes in the movie.)

We soon learn that the isotopes caused a kind of reverse evolution, but on their own, they weren't enough to bring about a transformation; they needed a catalyst, and that is ordinary sunlight. Of course, no one bothers to explain why he changes back, nor does anyone point out that much radiation from the sun comes right through solid objects most of the time—including the Earth itself—so he would be constantly exposed to some kinds of solar radiation. But that's not important; what is, is that sunlight turns Gil into a lizard man.

His fiancée Ann (Patricia Manning) is upset, and Gil is depressed and fatalistic. His freakish transformation burned the scientific curiosity right out of Gil McKenna, and he goes home and hides from the world.

Almost immediately, however, he goes to a nearby nightclub where he's attracted to singer Trudy (Nan Peterson). Later at home, he moodily contemplates suicide, but the sound of children playing outside dissuades him.

Bitter Gil goes back to the bar where Trudy is now singing (with Marilyn King's dubbed-in voice) "Strange Pursuit," written by Marilyn King. She sings the entire song, which may be explained by the fact that "Strange Pursuit" was one of the working titles of *The Hideous Sun Demon*, but more by the fact that Marilyn King is Robert Clarke's sister-in-law (yes, he's a member of the King Family). Although the song is monotonous, it does expand the film's length.

While defending Trudy from George, apparently her lover, Gil gets into a fight and leaves with her. They frolic on the beach at night, and, between cuts, have sex. He wakes up in the morning still at the beach, realizes that the sun is up and he might turn into a monster at any moment, and flees back home.

Sure enough, by the time he gets there, he's the Sun Demon. There's a grotesque scene in which he grabs a rat and squeezes it gorily to death, growling and snarling all the while. This isn't in the script, and was improvised on location.

Ann arrives, and prowls through the house in a sequence designed to be highly suspenseful, but it's cut badly and clearly comes too early in the film for the heroine to be in real danger. In the only other good scene in the film (than the mirror shot earlier), she opens a basement closet to discover frightened, tortured Gil, huddled on the floor. The impact of the scene is damaged by the closet light being on before she "turns" it on.

At Ann's urging Gil sees another scientist, and discovers that while a cure might be possible, shorter and shorter doses of sunlight will be required to turn him into the Sun Demon, and that it will take longer for him to turn back.

But Gil is by now (unaccountably) obsessed with Trudy, and so goes back to the bar where she performs. She's miffed at his abandoning her on the beach, so her pals beat him up and take him back to her place. By now, of course, it is daytime.

George forces Gil out into the sunlight, and he turns maniacal and kills George. (He does not become the Sun Demon at once; there are no transformation scenes, in fact.) Trudy is upset.

Still a monster, Gil rushes home; a dog chases him, and he kills it. Somehow the police manage to identify Gil, and come in search of him for killing George.

By the time the police arrive, he has turned back into Gil. Ann tries to stave them off, but Gil jumps in his car and roars off, right over one cop, whose cap poignantly spins to a halt in the street, signifying death.

A manhunt is launched, far out of proportion to Gil's crime. The murder of George was in self-defense, and the death of the cop was accidental. But the entire police force of Los Angeles is engaged in tracking him down.

For some reason, not shown, Gil abandons his car and hides out near some oil wells, where a little girl finds and befriends him. But she spills the beans to her mother and Gil's on the lam again. He turns back into the Sun Demon— this time without a shirt, so we can see that his torso has gone all scaly—and climbs an oil tank. He tosses one cop off before another shoots him, and Gil plunges to his death. He seemed a particularly easy monster to kill.

The Hideous Sun Demon is a depressing film on several levels. The basic idea, of a man turning into a monster because of sunlight, is an okay cheap science fiction movie monster idea, and one that had not been used before (or since). Clarke was also working to his utmost in the movie—he told Bob Skotak in *Famous Monsters of Filmland* that "I acted the part out as if I wouldn't let *anything* get in my way." But the editing is slow-paced, and the peculiar mixture of visual styles is jarring. There is very little original music in the film; most of it comes from "library" (prerecorded) music, and sounds painfully familiar. Also, the sound recording is flat, hollow and tinny, among the worst ever done for a professionally-released film.

Occasionally there are scenes that look as though they were shot with a view to making the film look gloomy, moody and shadowy—real *film noir* stylization, which does match the plot and the emphasis on sexual obsession. When Gil is beaten by George and his friends, it's to a strange jazz theme, which also ties in with the *film noir* pretensions. But most of the rest of the picture is shot in the usual science fiction flat gray style; because of the jumbled production schedule, the picture jumps from the atmospheric material to true-crime "realistic" photography within the same sequence.

The only other film that Nan Peterson appeared in, according to my sources, was *The Shotgun Wedding* (1963). Patricia Manning fared only slightly better; she was in *Rebel Angel* (1962) and *A House Is Not a Home* (1964) as one of the whores, along with Raquel Welch.

I have been unable to find any other credits for screenwriter E.S. Seeley, Jr., or for Richard Cassarino, who built the suit, and worked as art director and production assistant; he also plays a cop. Nor do I have any further credits for cinematographer Stan Follis. John Morrill, one of the other cameramen, worked as gaffer on the 1967 documentary, *The Really Big Family*, and photographed *Brothers* (1977). That documentary was photographed by Vilis Lapenieks, who also shot *Magic Spectacles*, *Capture That Capsule* (1961), *Eegah*, *Night Tide* (1963) and *Queen of Blood* (1966), then took a jump to bigger projects with films like *If It's Tuesday This Must Be Belgium* (1969), *Cisco Pike* (1971), *Newman's Law* (1974) and *Capone* (1975).

Thomas Boutross was credited as editor and codirector; he soon changed his first name to Tom, and worked as a production assistant on *Yellowstone Cubs* and *The Right Hand of the Devil* (both 1963), then returned to editing on a variety of films including *Rat Fink* (1965) and *A Man Called Dagger* (1968).

Costar Patrick Whyte had been under contract to MGM in the early 1950s, where he appeared in films such as *Soldiers Three* (1951), *Plymouth Adventure*

(1952) and *Young Bess* (1953). He was also in *The Man Who Knew Too Much* (1956) and *The Saint Valentine's Day Massacre* (1967), among others. He'd begun in films as early as 1947, and worked at least until the early 70s.

Robert Clarke certainly gives his all in the acting department; it is almost certainly his most energetic performance, but he's also pretty hammy at times. He was never an outstanding actor; his face is somewhat expressionless and rather too bland for character parts. He's not quite handsome enough for leads in A films, but has appeared in them. Over the years, he's turned up in several fantasy and horror movies, including *The Body Snatcher* (1945), *Bedlam* (1946), *Dick Tracy Meets Gruesome* (1947), *The Man from Planet X, Captive Women, The Astounding She-Monster, The Incredible Petrified World* and *Terror of the Bloodhunters* (1962). His last film to date seems to have been *Zebra in the Kitchen* (1965). Along the way, he also played Robin Hood in the desultory *Tales of Robin Hood* (1951), comprised of episodes of an unsold TV series.

The budget didn't allow any transformation scenes at all. Whenever Clarke turns into the Sun Demon, it's offscreen, or between cuts. The suit itself is elaborate and well-done; Clarke probably knew that stills can often help sell a monster movie, at least when the monster is worth looking at.

Alas, despite Clarke's feverish histrionics, no one has ever wept for the Sun Demon when he plummets stiffly off the oil tank. Even the children *in* the film don't react.

The film received few reviews. The *Monthly Film Bulletin* gave it its lowest rating, saying, "Until the monster-hunt on top of a gasometer in the last reel, this ... has an air of shabby economy, and rarely excites or entertains. Wordy dialogue, poor acting, uneven photography and sub-standard sound all add to the disadvantage of a hopelessly illogical plot."

More contemporary reviews tend to dismiss the film curtly. "Terrible film," said Joe Dante in *Castle of Frankenstein*. Don Willis (I) called it "ludicrous" but allowed as to how there might be "one or two nice camera angles." *Psychotronic* shows great tolerance for boredom in calling it "a great laughable hit."

The Sun Demon refuses to be ignored, however. There was, to begin with, an unauthorized sequel. Don Glut, an indefatigable maker of backyard monster movies, discovered that Bob Burns had one of Clarke's original Sun Demon masks. (There seems to have been more than one.) So in 1965, Glut made a little black-and-white short, *Wrath of the Sun Demon*, in which Burns, presumably playing Gil McKenna, suddenly turns into the lizard man, menaces a couple of people, and is thrown off a cliff. The film was made under the auspices of USC, where Glut was a student at the time. Others appearing in the 3½-minute film were John Schuyler and Cathy Burns.

Secondly, there is a remake/updating in the works, probably in release before this book is published. Hadi John Salem and Gregory Steven Brown purchased the rights to the film from Wade Williams. They have shot *Hideous Sun Demon: The Special Edition*, a redubbing of the film intended to be comic. According to an article on the project by David J. Hogan in *Cinefantastique* (Dec.–Jan. 1983/84), the 1959 footage will be redubbed from a "wholly new screenplay by Mark and Allen Estrin. The Robert Clarke character becomes hapless Ishmael Pivnik, whose formula for an oral suntan lotion is a rousing success except for a nasty side effect: monsterdom.

"Robert Clarke's son Cameron will fill in for his dad in new footage, and other cast members include Nicolas Guest (as Pivnik's voice) and Jennifer Richards.

"Although former documentarist Stephen La Rocque directed some dialogue and a few bridging scenes, he was ... replaced by Craig Mitchell, an early advisor and writer of some of the film's witty barbs.

"'We wanted our film to be upbeat and cool,' said co-producer Gregory Brown. 'Stephen [La Rocque] brought in too much Woody Allen angst. It was just a clash of direction and philosophy.'

"To make sure the old and new footage match, director of photography used shooting notes from the technically successful *Dead Men Don't Wear Plaid*."

The two producers wanted to produce a low-budget film quickly, then took a leaf from Woody Allen's book; Allen once redubbed a Japanese spy thriller as *What's Up Tiger Lily?* The result was reasonably popular, so they decided to use "a really bad American horror film. It's a very vivid genre, and an especially bad example would lend itself to all sorts of comic alterations." Stupefyingly, the producers "don't think we're exploiting Clarke's movie. We're not mocking it, but walking arm in arm with it. We extended our hand, but our hand happened to have a buzzer in it."

It's hard to imagine how treating any film in this manner, even one as poor as *The Hideous Sun Demon*, could ever be considered anything other than contempt-laden mockery.

Horrors of the Black Museum

The inclusion of this film in a book on science fiction movies will probably surprise some readers, but although its SF elements are somewhat minor and relegated to the last reel, it is legitimately, even classically science fiction. The most notorious aspect of *Horrors of the Black Museum* is its gruesomeness, which for the period is unprecedented and quite astonishing. It is a literally sadistic film, with sadism directed at the audience as well as the killer's victims. But it made a bundle for American International; they cofinanced the next few films produced by Herman Cohen, who made this one.

The film opens with one of the most ghastly murders in movie history, apparently to show it means business. A young London woman receives a pair of binoculars in the mail. Peering through them, she adjusts the focus. The camera cuts to her roommate, who hears a "chung" sound; she looks back at the first woman, who is standing there with her hands over her eyes, silently mouthing the words "my eyes, my eyes" as blood runs down between her fingers. The camera pans to the floor to find the binoculars—which have long steel spikes, covered with blood, protruding from the eyepieces. Springs drove the spikes into the woman's brain, right through her eyes.

Two more hideous murders take place (offscreen). When crime writer Edmund Bancroft (Michael Gough), autographing copies of his latest book, *Terror in the Dark*, learns about these gruesome deaths, he goes into shock. Later he angrily confronts Scotland Yard about their inability to solve the crimes; he calls them incompetents.

Initially, director Arthur Crabtree attempts to have us see Bancroft as a sympathetic character, albeit a little sinister, but then Bancroft takes his young assistant Rick (Graham Curnow) downstairs into his private museum of crime. Here he keeps weapons (or replicas of them) that were used in famous murders, a "Black Museum" much like the one of the same name at Scotland

Yard. We begin to realize that Bancroft's interest in death isn't exactly healthy.

Bancroft is slightly crippled. His girlfriend Joan (June Cunningham), a shapely stripper, is contemptuous of him and of his impotence. She's vulgar, blowsy and cheap, which makes one wonder how he became involved with her in the first place. No answer is offered.

She says she wants to find a real man, "a man I can do things with, things I can't do with you." She immediately follows this with "I haven't danced in months," but there's no doubt what she really meant.

That night, she flops back in her high-topped bed, looks up and shrieks. A blue-faced fiend (who is clearly Rick, although it's also clear we're not supposed to recognize him) has rigged a portable guillotine over the head of her bed. The blade drops and decapitates the shrieking Joan. The blue-faced fiend grabs the equipment and dashes out the door.

Back at Bancroft's, we learn that Rick does not know he's the killer, that he is being hypnotically dominated by the misogynistic Bancroft, who is using famous murder weapons from the past to kill new victims. He is, in fact, committing the murders (through Rick) in order to have something to write about, one of the most cold-blooded motives in murder history.

Bancroft, who seeks out old items which look like exhibits in the real Black Museum, visits a favorite supplier, antique dealer Aggie (Beatrice Varley). She's figured out that Bancroft is using the old weapons for new crimes, and threatens blackmail, but this exhibits poor timing. Bancroft is holding a pair of big black ice tongs, and thwack! end of Aggie, as the tongs slam into her throat.

All this time, Scotland Yard Superintendent Graham (Geoffrey Keen) has been drawing closer and closer to Bancroft, who persists in his taunts.

Bancroft's physician (Gerald Andersen) realizes what his illustrious patient is up to, and threatens to tell all to the authorities, so Bancroft electrocutes him slowly with some unexplained equipment in his basement museum. Then he and Rick—now aware that Bancroft is the killer, but still cooperating—dangle the body in a handy acid vat and reduce it to a mounted skeleton.

Rick is dubious about all this, saying his girlfriend Angela (Shirley Ann Field) has been suggesting his relationship with Bancroft is unhealthy. He brings her to Bancroft's home, but the writer catches them kissing and is furious.

"No woman can hold her tongue!" Bancroft rages. "They're a suspicious, unreliable breed!" He decides to once again give Rick "the gift of true obedience" in order to eliminate Angela. Then he says magnanimously, "someday all this will be yours," indicating the gruesome museum.

What he uses to give this "gift" of true obedience qualifies *Horrors of the Black Museum* for this book. It is nothing less than the serum Dr. Jekyll invented. The serum, says Bancroft, "makes reality out of myth" and he uses it on Rick. "[You] must never put any trust in a woman," says Bancroft to the drugged Rick, and sends him out on his date with Angela at a local funfair (amusement park).

Rick still seems somewhat out of it as he and Angela wander through the park. Unlike Jekyll's serum, this one takes some time to take effect; perhaps that's due to the extra brain-dominating ingredient. But it does work. As they are traveling through the Tunnel of Love, Rick is suddenly revealed as the blue-faced fiend, and he stabs Angela to death with an antique Circassian dagger Bancroft gave him for just this purpose.

Rick dashes madly through the park, including through the inevitable hall of mirrors, finally climbing a Ferris wheel. Superintendent Graham and

Bancroft both arrive at the park at this point. The maddened Rick spots his master on the ground below, so Bancroft urges Graham to shoot him (because Rick might spill the beans). But Rick leaps from the Ferris wheel, burying the dagger in Bancroft's chest as he dies. What would have happened if he'd missed?

In my remarks on *I Was a Teenage Frankenstein* (Vol. 1), I referred to the "domination of a young man by an older, wiser—and crazy—one" that turns up in several of the films produced by Herman Cohen and written or cowritten by Aben Kandel; Cohen and Kandel wrote this one. *Horrors of the Black Museum* has probably the most vivid, undiluted example of this theme in any of Cohen's films. There's no real reason that Rick is associated with Bancroft other than enslavement, and here the older man actually uses the younger as a murder weapon, to kill a (sexual?) rival.

In interviews, such as in *Fangoria* #18, Cohen maintains that the focus on teenagers in his films was a box office–motivated decision, and that the rebelliousness of teenagers plays a large part in his stories. "Let's face it," Cohen told interviewer David Everitt, "having been a teenager once myself, teenagers are always rebels against adults or authority, whether it be parents or teachers. That was my theory in making the adult the culprit. The teenager is really being suppressed or controlled by the adults."

There's an inherent contradiction here, in that if teenagers are rebels *against* authority, why do most of Cohen's films that center on teenagers show them being enslaved to an especially exploitative adult? To engender teenage wrath against the "culprit"? At the end, when the teenagers rebel against this domineering adult figure, they *die*. Mark McGee has suggested that Cohen was grafting what he thought of as a good teenage-oriented plot onto the standard mad scientist plot of the 1940s. That may be true, but the elements of domination don't originate in either subgenre. (There have been some mad scientist films, such as *The Mad Ghoul*, in which an innocent is forced to do the villain's biddings, but that isn't usual.)

Whatever the explanation, unpleasant family relationships, doomed romantic connections, and male-male domination do turn up frequently in Cohen films. Except for his rare comedies, such as *The Headless Ghost* (1959, the cofeature with *Horrors of the Black Museum*) and *Sophie's Place* (1970), Cohen's stories all end in deep tragedy, with either everyone concerned dead, guilty and innocent, or all relationships destroyed. There's a distinctly unpleasant tone to his pictures; although they are usually glossily produced and cast with entertaining and/or capable actors, Cohen's movies are uniquely sleazy.

Michael Gough starred in several more films for Cohen. He was the lead in *Konga, Black Zoo* (1963), and appeared in *Berserk* (1967) and *Trog* (1970). These films helped to establish Gough as a sometimes-horror actor, not quite as identified with the genre as his contemporaries Christopher Lee and Peter Cushing. Among his other horror thrillers are *Horror of Dracula* (1958), *Phantom of the Opera* (1962), *Dr. Terror's House of Horrors* (1965), *They Came from Beyond Space* (1967), *Crucible of Horror/Velvet House* (1972) and *Horror Hospital* (1973). He even made a nonspeaking guest appearance in *Legend of Hell House* (1972) as a corpse, and was in the SF-oriented thriller *The Boys from Brazil* (1978), albeit in a small part.

Gough is an odd case. In many of his horror movies, he's hammy, gleefully flamboyant. He seems to belong to the old bravura school of acting, a latter-day Barrymore or Lugosi; he outrageously overplays at times, especially in

Konga and Black Zoo, but has shown relative restraint in others, like Dr. Terror's House of Horrors. He seems to enjoy the opportunity he feels is offered by horror thrillers, of sending them up with "bad acting." He lets himself run riot in the pictures, and while one can't applaud his taste, his energy is often amusing.

On the other hand, in "straight" films, Gough is capable of subtle, expressive acting; he's almost another person. He began in films in 1946 and quickly rose to supporting player status. He has never starred in a film other than a horror movie, but is a dependable character lead. Among his straight films are The Man in the White Suit, Rob Roy the Highland Rogue (1953), Richard III (1955), The Go-Between (1970), Galileo (1975) and others. He appeared in an interesting if stilted TV "inquiry" into the life of Vincent van Gogh, playing both himself and van Gogh. It was probably his finest performance: careful, modulated and sincere. A far cry from his broad slumming performances in horror movies.

Graham Curnow, who played Rick, has, as far as I can determine, no other film credits at all. His peculiarly domed head makes him an odd choice for a leading man anyway, and he is stiff and unconvincing. As "Hyde," he has a fixed expression of rage.

June Cunningham, who loses her head to Rick, had notable roles in a few other films, including The Smallest Show on Earth (1957) and The Small World of Sammy Lee (1963). Shirley Ann Field, Rick's girlfriend, soon became a reliable British leading lady, and appeared in important roles in major movies, including Man in the Moon, The Entertainer (1961), Peeping Tom (1960), Saturday Night and Sunday Morning (1960), These Are the Damned (1963) and Alfie (1966). Her lone American-filmed movie was Kings of the Sun (1963). She appeared in few if any films between the late 1960s and The Wind and the Lion (1975). She's adequate as the ingenue in Horrors of the Black Museum, but like almost all female characters in Cohen films, she's virtually ignored except to be murdered.

Geoffrey Keen, the police superintendent, has been a major British character actor, termed "incisive" by Leslie Halliwell, from at least The Fallen Idol (1948) to Moonraker (1979).

Horrors of the Black Museum was photographed by Desmond Dickinson, once one of Britain's leading cameramen, having filmed, among others, Hamlet (1948), The Rocking Horse Winner (1949), The Browning Version (1951) and Importance of Being Earnest (1952). But in the late 50s, his star fell, and he turned to exploitation films, shooting Konga, A Study in Terror (1965), Berserk, Trog and Sophie's Place for Herman Cohen. Among his other fantastic films are Horror Hotel (1962), Hands of Orlac (1963), Beast in the Cellar and Whoever Slew Auntie Roo? (both 1971). He was working quickly and to a budget in Black Museum, and so didn't have many opportunities for creativity, but he did manage some interesting shots.

For commentary on director Arthur Crabtree, see the entry on Fiend Without a Face.

The storyline of Horrors of the Black Museum is, as Don Willis (I) says, "utter nonsense." It shows contempt for the audience, and is poorly written and constructed as well. Cohen developed the idea around the real Black Museum, the famous museum of Scotland Yard. He was not given access to it, so Cohen instead used the cumbersome, pointless device of a writer inventing his own Black Museum. (Cohen claims the various murder weapons used in the picture are based on real ones in the Black Museum.) But then Cohen and Kandel didn't bother to give the writer any real motivation for his crimes. He's just crazy and wants to write sensational books, so he kills people sensational-istically. How he ever decided to do this isn't even touched on; the writers needed a villain and a Black Museum, so they simply put the two together without any regard to logic or psychological validity. *I Was a Teenage Werewolf* had better motivation for everyone concerned.

Everything goes Bancroft's way until the end, and even that would have turned out all right if he'd just stayed home. No reason is really given for Bancroft's arrival at the funfair, except that's where the climax is supposed to take place. That's truly cheap, shoddy plotting.

But then the film is distinctive for its cheap, shoddy plotting. The Jekyll-Hyde serum is brought in with no prior hints that it exists, except in the shots of Curnow as Hyde in the guillotine scene. It may have even been added as an afterthought. Certainly Bancroft gives no other hints of being a scientific genius. The serum is just tossed in to explain how Bancroft can dominate Rick.

Agatha Christie might have done interesting things with a killer who commits murders solely in order to have something to write about; in one of her mysteries, someone is murdered totally at random as a means of *rehearsing* the killing of the intended victim. That's cold-blooded too, but not as chilly as Bancroft's motivation.

Director Arthur Crabtree and editor Geoffrey Muller do keep things bubbling, however, as silly as things are. The movie is gaudy, colorful and vicious, and despite its complete absurdity, is moderately entertaining.

Horrors of the Black Museum was released during William Castle's heyday. His gimmick for *Macabre* (a life insurance policy, payable if you died of fright while watching the film) was widely imitated, while Castle himself came up with different gimmicks for his later pictures. For *Horrors of the Black Museum*, American-International shot a 13-minute prologue in Hollywood. In it, hypnotist Emile Franchel tried to get everyone in the proper mood by sug-gestion, which allowed the film to be advertised as being in "Hypno-Vista." Jack Moffitt described the effect of the sequence: "Show opens with a 13-minute spiel on hypnotism by Dr. Emile Franchel. The doc gets the jump on his audiences—at least the younger ones—right off by telling them that only idiots and fools can't be hypnotized. Thereafter at the previews, the kids hastened to prove their mental health by yawning when the doc told them to, forcing their hands apart at his bidding, shivering when he suggested a blue light was cold, and mopping when he said a red light was blistering. Such handy exercises to convince yourself you are not an idiot are certainly worth the price of admis-sion and while all this is but remotely related to the story that follows, it does supply a sort of exploitation gimmick an exhibitor can use to promote word-of-mouth interest in his offering."

This prologue does not seem to have been included in the prints currently shown on television, which are derived from the British negative, even to having the Anglo-Amalgamated emblem at the beginning rather than that of American-International. The prologue was not shown in Britain.

The emphasis on gore in the picture was even more unusual for the period than the hypnotism prologue (a similar gimmick was used the following year for *The Hypnotic Eye*). While there isn't much blood to be seen in the film, and that which was visible was of distinctly the wrong hue, the sadistic means of murder were genuinely shocking. Eye injuries are especially disturbing to audiences, and *Black Museum* opens with one of the most spectacular. The brain-piercing needles mounted in binoculars "had been used by a jilted stable boy on an ex-girlfriend in the late 30s," according to the article on Cohen in

Fangoria. But whether they came out of the imagination of Herman Cohen and Aben Kandel or were actually used in real life is of little importance. The writers at least reused the sadistic idea, which should have been left alone. It's a nightmarish, deeply disturbing image, not "scary" but unpleasantly shocking.

The other murders in the film aren't as brutal, but this eye-stabbing opens the picture and sets the tone.

The film was reviewed twice in *Variety*, once in April by "Glen," who said that it "vends horror in its most nauseating form for the sake of slaking a thirst for gore. So long as this is commercially profitable, such pictures will be made but thoughtful tradesters wonder to what expedients producers will resort when the public is sated with the current extremes." Which was an interesting question, and has been gruesomely answered in the last several years, in which almost no form of physical injury has gone undepicted. Films like *Horrors of the Black Museum* were the first trickle under the door before the flood smashed its way through.

The other *Variety* review appeared in May, and was by "Rich" from London. He was even harsher. "Unpleasant and ridiculous.... Producers have relied on sensationalism without subtlety or characterization, situation or dialog. As a result, this rather distasteful item is likely to gather more misplaced laughs than shudders among discriminating audiences."

Joe Pihodna in the New York *Herald-Tribune* enjoyed the film. He thought it "has a way of making its points as a spine-chiller.... Michael Gough has a field day as the loony writer. He has the opportunity to be urbane and patronizing with the police and hysterical with his assistant. This range is about all an actor can hope for."

Richard W. Nason in the *New York Times* thought the film had "more significance as a promotional stunt than as a motion picture.... The attraction ... makes an embarrassing mockery of ... advance billing. In virtually every category of craftsmanship, this picture bears evidence of only an ounce of thought for every pound of CinemaScope footage.... [The script is a] gauche tale ... whose dialogue shows a convenient disregard for motivation and dramatic technique. The acting and directing seem designed more for quick production than for entertainment effects.... The film's main impact is wrung from the suggestion of sharp objects penetrating human flesh."

And in the *Monthly Film Bulletin*, the reviewer expressed disdain as well as distaste (but still gave it a II rating): "For all its contemporary setting, the plot of this lurid melodrama relies almost entirely on hackneyed Gothic paraphernalia. It makes the merest nod towards medical jargon, never attempts to penetrate Bancroft's obsession, and gains any persuasion it may have from the Eastman Colour-and-CinemaScope trappings rather than from Michael Gough's conventional portrait of menace. At any rate, and given their brutalising intention, the scriptwriters have judged rightly in allowing their monster at least the appearance of a man."

The basic idea is not dissimilar to films made at Universal in the early 50s, such as *The Black Castle*, but in those, there is not only the compensation of period settings, but heroes as well as villains. *Horrors of the Black Museum* presents only morbid, twisted villainy.

Even David Pirie, in *A Heritage of Horror*, who defends the film to a degree, takes issue with its tone. "The plot might deserve detailed consideration as a serious treatment on violence if it were not executed quite so titillatingly. Crabtree's direction is unashamedly blatant, lingering over the prosecution of each crime with the maximum enjoyment and making the most out of every sexual innuendo. His approach makes it impossible to take the film seriously and the overall effect is finally innocuous like a Grand Guignol review sketch. Most of the more fanciful murders are clearly used only as a means of conveying sexual suggestion." Although I do not consider the film innocuous, and I suspect that Herman Cohen is more responsible for the tone than Arthur Crabtree, this isn't a bad analysis of why the film actually carries very little impact today.

Invisible Invaders

This cheesy little exploitation picture at least has the virtue of being heavily laden with ideas, but ideas alone aren't enough, and it has many drawbacks. I once "deduced" that any SF movie starring John Agar was likely to be bad; likewise, any starring Robert Hutton or John Carradine was questionable. So any movie that starred *all three* seemed a serious risk. I wasn't far wrong. All three actors are in *Invisible Invaders*, and it is a bad movie. It is slightly below average for the time, and the average was way down.

The central gimmick of the picture, of our own dead turning on us, in a science fictional context (the invisibility idea is relatively minor), turned up in several other films: *Plan 9 from Outer Space*, *Night of the Living Dead* (1968), *The Alien Dead* (1980) and *The Day It Came to Earth* (1977) are among those that used the idea. Also, there have been several imitations of *Night of the Living Dead*, generally Italian in origin, that feature the same basic idea.

The story opens as Dr. Karol Noyman (John Carradine) is blown to pieces in his laboratory. Dr. Penner (Philip Tonge) resigns from the atomic energy commission, or its equivalent, because no one listens to his pleas to ban nuclear tests. He feels that radioactive particles have been blown into space.

At Noyman's funeral, we briefly see legs of an alien, which vanish, and then two parallel grooves in the dirt as it shuffles its invisible way to eavesdrop on the funeral; it also invisibly pushes some bushes aside. Later, after everyone is gone, we see these *same* shots again, not even filtered to look like night (*Invisible Invaders* relies so heavily on stock footage that it generates its own). Then the flowers on Noyman's grave are pushed aside.

That night, Penner is aroused by a knock on his door. He discovers Noyman standing there, looking spooky. "This is the corpse of an Earthman who was known as Karol Noyman," says the body. "I'm from another planet outside your galaxy." The corpse says that he is one of a mass of invaders who have had a base on the Moon for 20,000 years, but have ignored Earth until now because of our "slow scientific development." But now we have space travel, so they have come here to stop us, approaching Penner because they see him as a voice for peace.

The alien in control of Noyman's body confides that they are invisible because they have "long ago ... learned to control the molecular structure of our bodies." He gives Penner a piece of invisible mineral (apparently they can control molecular structure of any old thing) as evidence, adding "we cannot be defeated. We have never been defeated." Unless Earth gives in at once, the invader promises that they will take over the bodies of the dead of our planet in 24 hours, and conquer the world. The leaders of the world's countries must surrender at once or be destroyed.

Penner at once tells his assistant, Dr. John LaMont (Robert Hutton), who is highly skeptical, afraid to side with Penner as he thinks it may endanger his career, even though he's engaged to Penner's daughter Phyllis (Jean Byron). Penner enlists his cooperation by pointing out that "in 24 hours you may not be alive to enjoy that precious career of yours."

Penner tells the world of the threat, and within a very short time (it must be less than 24 hours), there are headlines such as "Little Man Who Wasn't There Here from Space," and "This Time It's INVISIBLE Saucers from Space!" One wiseacre even runs a big blank on the front page, captioned "First photo of an invisible invader."

Penner hopes he is insane. He wants the sun to shine on the world of the living, not "where only the Dead walk the Earth." There's some awkward stalling as he, John and Phyllis go back to Noyman's grave in a desperate attempt to address the invaders. We again see the same shot of invisible feet leaving parallel grooves—these invaders must be lead-footed—and Carradine's voice is heard granting us one more warning.

After a plane crash outside Syracuse, New York, the pilot's body is inhabited by an invisible invader, goes to a hockey game and kills one of the announcers, then makes a dread announcement and warning. Later, there's more stock footage of a car wreck (from Thunder Road), and another walking corpse goes to a sports stadium and makes the same announcement. (The invaders have an affinity for sports?)

Then there's a great flurry of stock shots as the invaders smash things all over the world—fires, quakes, buildings collapsing, dams bursting. We see the same few walking dead men—always men, always white, always well-dressed—meandering stiffly around Griffith Park near Bronson Caverns. This is superimposed over the stock-footage disasters.

Penner, Phyllis and John are joined by Major Bruce Jay (John Agar), a no-nonsense military type, tough as nails—you can tell by his butch haircut—who escorts them 27 miles outside the city. (Twenty-seven other scientists are given the same treatment elsewhere, offscreen.) As they roar toward their destination in a Jeep, a farmer (Hal Torey) stops them, training his gun on our heroes. But he's distracted by an invisible invader fumbling around in some nearby bushes, and Jay shoots the farmer dead. After our heroes leave, the farmer, now possessed, irony of ironies, by the very invisible invader who caused his death, gets up and shambles after them.

Our brave little band takes refuge in a bunker built in a cave system (Bronson Caverns, of course), and begin discussing ways to rid the Earth of the invisible invaders and their walking-corpse vehicles.

For the first time, we hear that the invaders are not only invisible and inclined to shamble around in possessed stiffs, but they are radioactive. The corpses are powered by "cyclic pulsations of radiation."

After an initial clash, Jay and Phyllis are mutually attracted, which annoys jealous, slightly cowardly John. Of course, the only reason Phyllis is there at all is to take notes and make coffee.

More stock sabotage occurs, and someone points out that the invaders aren't using their horrendous weapons of superscience (whatever they might be) in our atmosphere, because of a molecular weakness that undoubtedly affects their bodies. Hence, their only weapons are (a) they are invisible and (b) they can inhabit corpses. Our scientific team assumes that the invaders enter the bodies through the pores, so they decide to make an acrylic spray to seal a body, thus trapping the invader inside and giving them one to study.

After working all night, they devise their spray, which looks coincidentally

just like a CO_2 fire extinguisher. But, as Jay aims it at the first invisible invader/corpse happening by on its way to report to its nearby spaceship, the spray doesn't work. The alien escapes from the body, and is tracked by a Geiger counter.

So they dig a pit and fill it full of liquid acrylic, then attract the attention of that same farmer (now possessed), and he tumbles into the acrylic. The result resembles the title character from *Curse of the Faceless Man*, but at least they have their invisible invader.

They put it in a sealed room, and eventually the invader manages to leave the body, but it is trapped in the room. It still speaks with Carradine's voice. There are some minor tricks with a wire-controlled chair and microphone.

Optical equipment is no help seeing the alien. The narrator (heard throughout) tells us that our heroes have been working for days, and that if they don't solve the problem by midnight, the "human race on Earth would cease to exist." There's no clue as to why they've decided on this deadline; surely the aliens' 24-hour period is long up, but they didn't give any new deadline.

John, who is brave and spineless alternately as the script requires, suggests surrendering to the invaders, but his companions staunchly refuse. Partly because of this, and partly because of the interest Jay has been showing in Phyllis (for her diligent coffee-making and note-taking), the major and the scientist get into a lively fight. (Agar takes some genuine rough tumbles.) John flings a bottle of acid at Jay, hitting the air conditioner and causing it to emit an ultrasonic screech, which disables the invader.

Everyone immediately forgives John. "Major," he says, "I want to apologize." Bighearted Jay replies, "It's okay, forget it." The fight has accomplished its plot purpose: they have found the Big Secret, high-pitched sound waves will kill the invaders and make them visible as well.

Thus, another key discovery is made by accident; scientific knowledge is not good enough. At least in the other 50s SF film featuring sound waves as a weapon against invaders, *Target Earth*, the discovery was made after trial and error. In *Not of This Earth*, Mr. Johnson is bothered by any loud noise.

They quickly make riflelike sound generators, which produce vibrating concentric circles. When one of these jerry-rigged gadgets is aimed at the sealed room, where the invader still lives (he was only injured earlier), it reveals the invader as a glowing humanoid shape, and kills him. (It's indistinct, but there are hints of an actual alien costume.)

They immediately go out to take care of the invisible invaders in the vicinity. One of the walking corpses is packing a rod, which seems a bit unfair, all things considered, and also raises the question of why *all* of them aren't armed.

While John and Jay are walking around in what looks like radiation armor, aiming the sound waves at invisible invaders, Penner broadcasts the good news to what must have been a severely underpopulated world. The story ends with a "truly *United* Nations."

This cheap little picture, which couldn't possibly have had a shooting schedule longer than two weeks (and was probably shot in one), was produced

Opposite: Inhabited by Invisible Invaders (1959), hordes of the well-dressed dead walk the Earth. In a way, it's ludicrous that these reanimated corpses are all outfitted in suits and ties, but then again, that's the way most men are buried. But where are the walking-dead women?

by Robert E. Kent, who'd been working around Hollywood at least since 1940, when he did some writing on the film *Flowing Gold*. He later provided the original story for *Dick Tracy Meets Gruesome* (1947), but soon became a producer of low-budget films. He was associated with *Fort Ti* (1953), *Rock Around the Clock* (1956), *The Four Skulls of Jonathan Drake* (1959), *Jack the Giant Killer* (1962), *Diary of a Madman, Beauty and the Beast* (both 1963), *Twice Told Tales* (1964), and *The Christine Jorgensen Story* (1970), among many others. Kent worked quickly and to a budget, but the films made by his independent production company in the 60s were above average for their budget level. While movies like *Twice Told Tales* probably couldn't be considered good, they are still relatively lavish, and weren't embarrassing to audiences or crew.

Mark McGee says that *Invisible Invaders* was one of the films director Edward L. Cahn tried to shoot as rapidly as possible, going from one setup to another very swiftly. McGee quotes Agar as saying that Cahn was actually trying to impress the cast with his speed, but it was probably more *de-* than *im*pressive. The film certainly gives every evidence of having been made in great haste.

The snake-eating-its-own-tail quality of using its own footage for stock shots is dispiriting, and the very cheap and shoddy effects only match the overall tone of the film. There's no way this could ever have been a good movie, but just a little more time and some actual *caring* about the finished product on the part of the director probably would have made it more palatable. But by this time, no one cared about SF movies made on this budget level. They were just a product to get on the screen as soon as possible.

The idea of doing *invisible* invaders is so sleazily, brassily cheap as almost to be amusing: invisible invaders in an invisible spaceship is as cheap as you can get. Of course, they really aren't invisible most of the time: they're wandering around in those corpses. There are only one or two shots involving wire effects, in which objects are manipulated by offscreen effects men to suggest an invisible presence, and no optical-invisible effects at all, such as the walking suits of clothes that turned up in Universal's Invisible Man series. No, here, the invisible invaders are done as cheaply as possible.

No one seems very concerned about the walking corpses, they're just a menace. The idea that these are our very own friends and neighbors, come back from the grave to kill us, is mentioned briefly by the farmer who is shortly one of the inhabited stiffs himself. This idea, so eerily forceful in *Night of the Living Dead*, could have been played up; writer Samuel Newman was clearly aware of the idea. But to acknowledge this might have raised issues everyone was anxious to avoid; it might have made the movie scary.

The dull, flat look of the picture, once deliberately chosen for SF films to make them more believable, was now done totally by rote. Everything is overlit, and there aren't enough close-ups. Editor Grant Whytock does what he can, but he just wasn't given any footage worth playing with.

The actors try, but Agar is given a completely stock character, the granite-jawed military man; as always, he tries his best, and is actually not bad in some scenes, but he's generally inadequate.

Once a promising contract player at Warner Bros., Robert Hutton had fallen on somewhat hard times. His first major role had been in *Hollywood Canteen* (1944), as the young soldier around whom the story revolves. He was cast in leading roles in *Janie* (1944) and its 1946 sequel, *Live and Learn* (1947), *Always Together*, and *Wallflower* (both 1948). When the studios were shedding themselves of minor players following the advent of TV and the loss of studio-owned theatres, Hutton left Warner Bros., and his films were increasingly less important. He occasionally turned up in major films, such as one of the "ugly stepbrothers" in *Cinderfella* (1960), but most of his films were very minor.

Hutton was once a mildly pleasant male ingenue, with a slightly Jimmy Stewart–like earnest callowness, but he did not age well. Eventually Hutton reduced his acting to a few mannerisms, such as tucking his chin into his chest and gazing slightly up at the camera or costar; it's no wonder his career petered out in minor pictures. He suffered from the same calamity that afflicted so many other actors of his generation: the war was over, the big stars came back, and he just wasn't good enough.

Among his other fantastic films—and Hutton eventually became a regular in them—were *The Man Without a Body*, *The Colossus of New York*, *The Slime People* (1963, which he directed), *They Came from Beyond Space*, *The Vulture*, *You Only Live Twice* (all 1967), *Torture Garden* (1968), *Cry of the Banshee*, *Trog* (both 1970) and *Tales from the Crypt* (1972). After living in England for ten years, Hutton returned to the states in the early 1970s, but has done little or no acting. He wrote a script while in England that was produced, but the film got very little distribution here under either its original British title of *Persecution* (1974) or its American title *The Terror of Sheba*, even though it starred Lana Turner.

This may have been the last film of Philip Tonge, who died in 1959 before the film was released. He'd been a supporting player at least since the mid-40s. I have a credit for a Philip Tonge in 1934, but nothing after that until 1947. He was a character lead in *Miracle on 34th Street* (1947), *Hans Christian Andersen* (1952), *House of Wax* (1953), *Pardners* (1956) and *Witness for the Prosecution* (1957). He really gives it his all in *Invisible Invaders*; he may have been slumming, but he was too professional an actor to perform as if he was in something beneath contempt. If it was indeed his last movie, his performance is not an unfitting finale, although the movie itself was unworthy of him.

Jean Byron was one of the usual type of attractive minor leading ladies who usually turned up in low-budget movies. She probably led a completely ordinary life, occasionally acting in films of this nature because it pleased her to be a star, even in small films. She worked a great deal on television in the 1950s. She appeared in *Voodoo Tiger* (1952), *Magnetic Monster* and *Jungle Moon Men* (1953), and turned up later in much smaller parts in *Wall of Noise* (1963) and *Flareup* (1969). She's adequate in her role, but this typical ingenue part wasn't taxing. She was required to look frightened, romantic and intelligent, and she does this capably enough.

For comments on John Carradine, see the entry on *Half Human*.

Invisible Invaders was a typical cheap SF movie of the late 50s, very slightly more imaginative than most, but perfunctorily made. Reviews reflected this. "Gilb" in *Variety* said that it "offers little interest to adult audiences, but the Saturday matinee trade should find it interesting escapist fare.... Technical aspects of the picture reflect the low budget."

Jack Moffitt: "This celluloid equivalent of a literary 'penny dreadful' deals with an invasion of invisible spacemen in an invisible space ship from the Moon. It is a pretty sure way of holding down production costs, but for long stretches of time, it leaves Samuel Newman's script with no visible means of support."

After quoting without credit this opening paragraph by Moffitt, the *Monthly Film Bulletin* concluded, "this is an ineptly written variation on a hackneyed theme, naive as propaganda and, despite a hectic finale, tepid as entertainment." The "propaganda" is presumably the faint touches of one-worldism that creep in at the end.

Invisibility can be one of the most entertaining and spectacular effects for movies, but when it is done, as here, just with wires, it looks cheap. *Invisible Invaders* doesn't use the idea at all well, and the title was for exploitation come-ons only. It is a third-rate film.

Island of Lost Women

Competently made but drab, this film seems divided against itself. It sets up a quasi–science fiction situation—atomic scientist isolates self on island with three gorgeous daughters—then continually backs away from any SF elements. It's hard to imagine for whom the film was made. It's not sexy, despite the three young women; except for a stock-footage shark fight, there's no action; until the last ten minutes, it lacks suspense. It's not a story, it's just a situation thoroughly but unrewardingly discussed during the picture. (Such as it is, the plot line resembles *Forbidden Planet*, but I suspect that's mere chance. This is not another version of *The Tempest*.)

Flying over the South Pacific, Joe Walker (John Smith) and reporter Mark Bradley (Jeff Richards) receive a radio message from an island they've spotted: "Do not land here. You will meet certain destruction." However, their plane is out of commission, and they are forced to land. Wouldn't you know it?

To their surprise, the two handsome young men are met by an annoyed scientist (Alan Napier), who tells them to call him Dr. Paul, and his three daughters, improbably named Venus (Venetia Stevenson), Mercuria (June Blair) and Urana (Diane Jergens). Dr. Paul orders them to leave at once, but Joe points out that the plane needs repair.

Eventually, they learn that Dr. Paul is really Dr. Paul Lujan, a famous nuclear scientist who disappeared some time before. He tells them he left civilization because he expects it to blow itself up (with inventions he helped devise) sooner or later, and wants to spare his daughters. Perversely, he is still working with an atomic pile and a solar furnace in an effort to refine uranium as a power source.

Ever the reporter, Mark becomes excited and wants to radio out a story, but Lujan says his transmitter doesn't work (contradicted by the radio message warning them not to land), so after the plane is fixed, Joe and Mark make plans to take off. However, Mark will not promise Lujan to keep the scientist's where-abouts a secret, so Lujan uses a Luger he has turned into "a condensed flame-thrower" to destroy the plane.

The girls aren't unhappy about this turn of events. They've been waiting for years to meet young men. Venus and Mark begin to fall in love, and Mercuria is attracted to Joe. Urana, who's still a giddy teenager, thinks *she* falls in love with Mark, but we know how silly teenagers can be. (Or such is the tone of the film.)

Eventually, Mark tricks Lujan into saying he'll kill them if they try to leave, and makes sure the women overhear it. This, of course, convinces them to side with their new boyfriends against good old dad.

A plane searching for Mark and Joe nears the island, and Lujan uses some unmentioned (and truly science fictional) device to shake the plane, so that it turns back. The machine is not shown, but its effect on the plane is clear.

Venus goes for a swim, and is saved from a shark attack by Mark. We see several different kinds of shark, all supposed to be the same fish, and Mark struggles with a small dead shark.

Feeling rejected, Urana assists her father in capturing Joe so that Lujan can thereby force Mark into sending Venus and Mercuria back to the cave, and into ceasing work on their boat. However, Urana accidentally sets off the flame pistol, starting a fire clearly about to burn down the cave and fry the imprisoned Joe. However, Lujan has a change of heart and rescues the pilot.

Damaged in the fire, the atomic pile is heading toward an explosion (rather than the more realistic meltdown). Everyone runs off to a nearby sand dune and hides it as all of Lujan's life work (and the girls' combs and undies and everything) goes up in an atomic explosion.

The cast is unharmed. Lujan feels dejected but philosophical, and the women look forward to their first adult experience of civilization as rescue planes wing their way toward them from Australia.

Island of Lost Women was an independent production by Alan Ladd's Jaguar company for Warner Bros. distribution. Ladd made several films under the Jaguar banner, but none of them were profitable or memorable. (While in charge of Fox, Alan Ladd, Jr., oversaw *Star Wars*, and later formed his own production company, which released through Warner Bros. Their best film was *The Right Stuff*.)

It isn't so much bad as lacking in interest. Frank Tuttle (whose last film this was) directs smoothly but with no involvement. His great years were far behind him. He began in 1929, and directed several major pictures, including *Roman Scandals* (1933) and *The Glass Key* (1935). Most of his pictures were lower-berth As or more respectable Bs. His most famous was undoubtedly also his best, the grim, gripping *This Gun for Hire* (1942), which made a star of Alan Ladd. The actor seems to have been a decent, responsible person who, when he was able, returned the favor by giving Tuttle several directorial jobs, including this one.

The script, by Ray Buffum from a story by Prescott Chaplain, is naively sexist, although the writers probably thought they were creating stronger and more self-reliant female characters than the norm for 1959. Nonetheless, although Lujan has clearly educated his daughters well, it's still the Man who does all the really important stuff — researching, warning planes away, fishing — while the women cook, sew and gather eggs. Furthermore, when Mark and Venus have the required getting-to-know-you chat, she wants to visit civilization so she can go shopping and look at men. She's not interested in baseball.

The characterizations are nil. Lujan is described as a scientist who helped Einstein discover atomic power. (Virtually every scientist in SF movies of the 1950s helped Einstein discover atomic power, or so it seems at times.) There's not much more to him than that: a stern papa, a genius. At least, he's not a mad scientist, and Napier (best known as Batman's butler Alfred from the TV series) is a decent enough actor that Lujan actually almost comes to life in a scene or two.

The two young men are virtually interchangeable, except that one is brunette and square-jawed, and the other is blonde and square-jawed. As usual in trivial movies, characterization is linked to their hair color: the brunette is serious; the blonde tends to flippancy. (However, aside from a reference to "One touch of Venus" after Mark returns from his talk with her, the best Joe can come up with is, "Oh man, I'm bushed.")

Of the women, characterization is expended only on Venus and Urana;

Mercuria isn't even mercurial. Venus is intelligent and attractive; Urana is girlish, impulsive and attractive; Mercuria is merely attractive. Venetia Stevenson, who plays Venus, later became a film production executive; the other two made a couple more films as actresses, and gave it up.

Though minimal, there are science fictional elements. That flamethrower pistol seems fantastic, as does the means of preventing the second plane from landing. On the other hand, the business with the atomic pile seems thoroughly researched and sounds perfectly plausible, except for the explosion.

The film has innocence, although it's not unsophisticated. The two young men never evince any sexual interest in the women, nor do the women become overtly physically attracted to the men. Everyone is extremely polite, though quietly flirtatious. For a movie with such a steamy title, *Island of Lost Women* is remarkably sedate and passionless.

Reviews were as perfunctory as the film. Vincent Canby (who soon went on to bigger things) in the *Motion Picture Herald* called it "naively plotted" but no worse than "fair."

"Whit" in *Variety* thought it was well-made enough "to provide okay entertainment for the program trade.... [It] is leisurely but to the point, and [Tuttle] gets satisfactory if standard performances from [his] cast."

Jack Moffitt found it "a fairly pleasant combination of sex and escapism that should get back its low cost. The escapism includes a complete escape from logic that should please those who do not go to the theatre to think."

Island of Lost Women is a film so nebulous that it seems to vanish as you watch it; it's one of the last gasps of the true B movie.

Journey to the Center of the Earth

I presume this gaudy Christmas present from 20th Century–Fox to America made a lot of money, because the company released a similar film each year for the next several, including *The Lost World* (1960), *Voyage to the Bottom of the Sea* (1961) and *Five Weeks in a Balloon* (1962). However much the studio regarded the later films as follow-ups to *Journey to the Center of the Earth*, it's doubtful that audiences noticed resemblances; *Journey* is a good movie, the other three are not.

It was produced and cowritten by Charles Brackett, a man of wit and sophistication, as well as motives that embraced quality as well as box-office returns. The three follow-ups were all produced by Irwin Allen who, on the basis of all available evidence, never seems to have had anything on his mind other than cheap sensationalism. It's the difference between a man of taste and a vulgar promoter. Whatever the problems with *Journey*, it gave audiences more than just thrills and spectacle; it was a film that could be *listened* to as well as watched. It is partly a spoof of itself, a novelty in this period.

Fox executives were probably befuddled by the varying responses to the pictures. They probably thought the films were very similar. After all, the three later films aped the structure of *Journey*, and provided spectacle as well. There was an expedition to strange realms: to a lost world of dinosaurs, to the bottom of the sea, over Africa in a balloon. There was an older, wiser man, played by an authenticated character-actor star: Claude Rains, Walter Pidgeon, Sir Cedric

Hardwicke; a lead for the teenage crowd: Jill St. John, Frankie Avalon, Fabian; an "amusing" character: Richard Haydn, Peter Lorre, Peter Lorre. But without the guiding hand as well as the astutely-presented charm of Charles Brackett, it just wasn't the same thing. *Journey* can be watched today with great pleasure, but the other three are depressing and boring.

I went to see *Journey to the Center of the Earth* with great anticipation and a little trepidation. I thought myself sophisticated — I was, after all, 16. I had learned that films which received rave reviews weren't always good, and that those that cost the most weren't always the best. I enjoyed James Mason and usually Pat Boone; the layout in *Life* on the film looked promising but somewhat unconvincing. I had recently read a translation of Jules Verne's 1864 novel, *Voyage au Centre de la Terre*, and feared that the novel might be mangled by Hollywood. A woman had been added, which seemed unnecessary to me. So I entered the Egyptian Theatre in Coos Bay both excited and slightly nervous. I left delighted.

In recent years, the reputation of *Journey to the Center of the Earth* has fallen; it is rarely revived at science fiction conventions, books on SF movies give it short shrift, and to a degree it has been forgotten. (It was shown widely on American cable services in early 1984, however.) I think the reason for its relative obscurity is that its delights are best appreciated on one viewing. The overall buoyancy of the film deflates when it is watched again and again. There's a certain plodding quality to the picture, perhaps inherent in the plot, and some elements seem overly farcical. The mismatch between the constructed sets and the few scenes actually shot underground in Carlsbad Caverns becomes apparent on repeated viewings. The wry quality of the humor has aged to archness here and there, and the stylized performances sometimes seem frivolous.

But it is still basically a good movie with an admirable approach to the material, a good script, some above-average special effects, a superlative score by Bernard Herrmann, and an interesting story (which, nonetheless, muffs the most important scene — the moment they reach the center of the Earth is not emphasized).

In 19th-century Scotland, professor of geology Oliver Lindenbrook (James Mason) is knighted, and subsequently toasted in song by his affectionate students, including Alec McEwen (Pat Boone). The students present Oliver with a hideous inkwell, and Alec gives him an interesting lump of lava.

Later, Alex arrives at Oliver's home to woo Oliver's niece Jenny (Diane Baker) by singing Robert Burns' "My Love Is Like a Red, Red Rose." (Boone sings it perfectly well.) Meanwhile, Oliver has become intrigued by the lump of lava, for it contains a rock found only in Iceland, while the lava itself is of Mediterranean origin. He tries to melt the lava, but there's an explosion and the Icelandic rock is revealed to be a plumb bob. Inscribed on it is a message from a famous Swedish explorer, Arne Saknussem. (Atlantis is mentioned here, as an "early phase" of Saknussem's career.)

Oliver is afire with curiosity — how did the plumb bob get into the lava? — and writes to well-known Swedish geologist Goetaborg for a translation. Though Goetaborg does not reply, he learns that the message gives directions for finding a passage within an Icelandic volcano that will lead the intrepid to nothing less than the center of the Earth. "I did it," Saknussem's message concludes.

Oliver later learns that, throwing ethics to the winds, Goetaborg has set out for Iceland himself. Taking Alec, Oliver heads for Iceland too, but finds that

Goetaborg has purchased all the available equipment. There's some milling around in Iceland, and after a wild carriage ride, Alec and Oliver end up in an eiderdown storage bin. (Writers Walter Reisch and Charles Brackett inventively use authentic Icelandic details.) There's a mildly amusing bit involving a duck, before they are freed from the bin by big Icelander Hans (Peter Ronson), who owns the duck, Gertrude.

Oliver and Alec hire Hans to assist them, and back at their hotel discover in Goetaborg's room all the purchased equipment—as well as the dead body of Goetaborg. We learn there is a *third* rival expedition, that of the villainous Count Saknussem (Thayer David), a descendant of Arne Saknussem, who considers the interior of the Earth his property and who is determined to claim it, by murder or any other means. The only problem for Saknussem is that Oliver now has the only set of directions.

Also turning up is Carla Goetaborg (Arlene Dahl), widow of the treacherous professor. She refuses to allow Oliver access to any of the equipment unless he takes her on the expedition as an equal partner. Oliver's propriety is outraged. "But madame," he cries, "think of the inconvenience—the lack of privacy!" Nonetheless, Carla has her way, and together with Hans and Gertrude, they all set out for the volcano that leads the way to the center of the Earth.

On one particular day only, an alignment of sunlight and shadows between a pierced peak and the sun causes a beam to fall directly on the only one of many volcanic vents that leads to the center of the Earth.

Soon, looking underequipped, Oliver, Alec, Carla, Hans and his duck are strolling downward, illuminated by portable lights, and unaware they are followed by the sinister Count Saknussem and his groom (Robert Adler).

Not long after they start, their passage disturbs a gigantic spherical boulder which rolls menacingly downward at our heroes, who manage to dodge it in the nick of time. (This sequence was echoed later in *Raiders of the Lost Ark*.)

The boulder knocks a hole in a cave wall, and they discover a chamber with warm running water and giant crystals. All pause to refresh themselves, but Alec becomes separated. In the meantime, a wall of the chamber bursts and water gushes in, almost drowning the others. Alec wanders alone through twisted rock formations and drifts of salt, while the others sadly presume he fell to his death in a phosphorescent pool.

Alec happens upon the body of Saknussem's groom. Saknussem arrogantly assumes that Alec will take the dead man's place, but Alec tosses salt in the count's face. Saknussem shoots at the young man. Elsewhere, Oliver uses a fanciful little gadget that sorts true directional sound out of the welter of echoes of the gunshot, and leads the group to Saknussem and Alec.

They capture the aloof count, and decide to execute him, but no one is capable of this cold-blooded act, so they reluctantly take Saknussem with them. Months go by (without a clue as to where they are getting food), as they pass through many strange areas—cold blue regions, windy orange ones, and so forth. They find luminous algae when their lamps finally fail. At the same time they also find a forest of giant mushrooms, which provide food to replace the salted beef they had been living on. Our heroes don't see the huge eye of a monster reptile peering in a hole at them.

The next morning, Oliver finds Saknussem standing at the shore of a vast underground sea, with a stone sky. Saknussem hasn't slept. "I don't sleep," he says. "I hate those little slices of death." He's already named the body of water the Saknussem Ocean. Suddenly, giant prehistoric dimetrodons attack our group, but Hans manages to kill one of them. The other giant beasts (played by iguanas with realistic fins attached) attack the fallen one and devour it.

The party makes a raft of giant mushroom stalks and pushes onward across the sea, right through a terrifying storm. They also pass through the center of the Earth, and all metal is jerked away by magnetic forces. Almost submerged in a whirlpool, they are tossed off the raft, but wash ashore near one another.

Saknussem kills and eats Gertrude, while the rest of the party discover the sunken continent of Atlantis. They also find Arne Saknussem's skeleton, pointing toward a distant shaft. They assume the shaft must once have led to the surface, but in recent years, an earthquake has blocked it with a huge stone.

When Hans discovers what has happened to his beloved duck, he confronts Saknussem, but a tremor tosses the arrogant "ruler of the center of the Earth" into a pit, killing him.

The others discover that a huge dish-shaped altar stone in the ruins of Atlantis is made mostly of serpentine, a mineral form of asbestos. After planting some hastily-improvised blasting powder in the passage-blocking stone, they run for the serpentine altar.

A huge "chameleon" snares Oliver with its prehensile tongue (an odd shot: we see this happen from *inside* the big lizard's mouth). In a surprisingly gory scene, Alec rescues him by stabbing the monster's tongue. They dive into the altar stone just as the explosives go off, but though this demolishes the blockade, it also causes an upheaval of lava, which engulfs the now bright red, angry chameleon.

Safely on the heat-resistant altar stone, the little group is churned by the lava up the shaft; they shoot upwards at a tremendous rate, riding the altar stone like an elevator. They are shot out of a volcano in Sicily, landing safely in the sea, except for Alec, who lands naked in a tree. He uses a sheep to shield himself from some surprised nuns.

Back in Edinburgh, Oliver and Carla as well as Alec and Jenny (seen occasionally throughout in cutaways) look like they're headed for marriage, while Hans is headed for Iceland. Oliver says that he cannot prove they actually made a journey to the center of the Earth, but claims that "the spirit of man cannot be stopped."

Once the science fiction film boom got underway in the mid-50s and *20,000 Leagues Under the Sea* and *Around the World in 80 Days* were big hits, Jules Verne was fair game for producers. An unusual story like *Journey to the Center of the Earth* was very attractive. It had been filmed in France in 1909 by Segundo de Chomon, a rival to Georges Méliès, but no one approached the idea since then. The 1951 *Unknown World*, about a drill machine that took people to a land beneath the ground was advertised as "a journey to the center of the Earth," but only its setting related to Verne's novel.

In 1956, Eugene Lourié was scheduled to make the film in Italy as an independent production, and later in the same year, it was announced that Stanley Rubin was scheduled to produce it for RKO. Still later that year, Columbia announced it as a follow-up to their planned *Mysterious Island*, which itself wasn't filmed until 1961. Bryan Foy was announced as producer of the Columbia project. The rights to the Verne title were owned by Joseph M. Schenck, whose company coproduced the film with 20th Century–Fox in 1958. These various projected versions were dutifully reported in *Daily Variety*, *Hollywood Reporter* and other movie trade magazines, but as there was no mention of budgets or scripts, I presume the projects were only tentative.

The appeal of Verne's novels was obvious, at least in box office terms. He was famous, of course; in fact, in the 1950s probably the only science fiction writers most Americans had heard of were Jules Verne and H.G. Wells and, to a much lesser degree, Ray Bradbury. *Journey to the Center of the Earth* is one of Verne's most spectacular books, and needed relatively few alterations to film it. The villainous Saknussem and Carla Goetaborg were added and Gertrude the duck was also new to the film. The professor became Scottish rather than German. Otherwise, the story progressed much as in the novel. Oddly, however, two of the most visually-interesting concepts were deleted: in the novel, they saw a giant man driving a herd of mastodons in a jungle, and prehistoric monsters battled around the raft as it rode across the underground sea.

As early as 1925, plays by Charles Brackett were being turned into films. By the early 30s, he'd come to Hollywood, and in 1938, Brackett collaborated on the first of several scripts with the acerbic, sarcastic Billy Wilder. They wrote some of the most interesting films of the period, including Lubitsch's *Bluebeard's Eighth Wife* (1938), *What a Life* (1939), *Midnight* (1939), *Hold Back the Dawn* and *Arise My Love* (both 1941). Their most famous collaborations, prior to Wilder's becoming a director himself, were *Ball of Fire* (1941) for Howard Hawks, and *Ninotchka* (1939), again for Lubitsch. Then in 1942, Wilder became a director with *The Major and the Minor*, and Brackett continued as his co-writer and coproducer for the next eight years: *Five Graves to Cairo* (1943), *Double Indemnity* (1944), *The Lost Weekend* (1945), *The Emperor Waltz* (1948), *A Foreign Affair* (1948) and *Sunset Boulevard* (1950), one of the best movies anyone has ever made.

Occasionally on his own as producer, as early as 1944's marvelous *The Uninvited*, Brackett showed taste. Among the other films he worked on as producer-writer were *To Each His Own* (1946), *Miss Tatlock's Millions* (1948) and *The Mating Season* (1951). After dissolving his partnership with Wilder, in 1952 Brackett moved to 20th Century–Fox, where he remained until his retirement in the early 1960s.

He occasionally produced and cowrote his films there, including *The Model and the Marriage Broker* (1952), *Niagara*, *Titanic* (both 1953), and *The Girl in the Red Velvet Swing* (1955). As producer only, he helmed a variety of films, mostly standard medium-A studio projects, but the list does include *The King and I* (1956), *Blue Denim* (1959), *10 North Frederick* (1958), *The Remarkable Mr. Pennypacker* (1959) and his last film, *State Fair* (1962). Brackett died in 1969.

Brackett's films generally give the impression of a man writing somewhat beneath his abilities for a cut-and-dried audience, making relatively adult films that offered few surprises or innovations. The tone of *Journey to the Center of the Earth* is similar to that of *Around the World in 80 Days*, the most famous Verne adaptation up until that time (and maybe ever). Perhaps Brackett was amused by the idea of 19th-century explorers hiking off to the Earth's core. He had not often worked as a writer in this period; perhaps the approach to the project brought out something in him, appealed to him on a new level.

Walter Reisch, the coauthor of the film, had worked often previously with Brackett, on *Ninotchka*, *The Mating Season*, *Niagara*, *Titanic* and, later, *Mr. Pennypacker*. I suspect the light tone of *Journey* is due more to Brackett than to Reisch, but whoever is responsible, the movie is amusing in an *80 Days* fashion (and is better than that film), while being remarkably well-constructed, if somewhat low on excitement at times. The dialogue is mostly above average, especially that given to James Mason and Thayer David, both of whom are excellent.

The film baffled some reviewers; they didn't know if it was a spoof or a straight adventure, as if the distinction needed to be made. The approach is that of a jolly adventure for the entire family: danger, but never too much danger—the film is only briefly scary—and with jokes and amusing situations. Some of the jokes are probably over the heads of children or of no importance to them, but others are primarily for kids, such as much of the business with Gertrude.

The movie is slow in getting to the actual journey but that probably was seen as necessary by the studio to ease people into a "fantastic" situation. Fox had shown the same reticence (or care) the year before with *The Fly*. But during the preliminaries, the story still has nice touches of mystery.

Brackett and Reisch were amused by Oliver Lindenbrook's stuffy, pompous character, but he's not really modeled on *80 Days'* Phileas Fogg. Oliver is as tactless as Fogg—at one point he says (the authors being ironic), "For once we must dispense with tact"—but he's less self-involved, more human. Mason plays Oliver with a twinkle in his eye, as if Lindenbrook himself knows he's occasionally being impossible. The romance between Carla and Oliver is inevitable.

Thayer David is a thoroughly rotten villain, never clownish. He's so arrogant he's not even blithe about it—he's imperious. It's not at all surprising he considers himself the ruler of the interior of the Earth. Even eating Gertrude the duck is so thoroughly in character for the count that it's not surprising. (What is surprising is that he actually does it. The duck does not turn up later, unscathed. This bothered children at the time—the film tricked them by not tricking them. It was a convention of such films to let us think such a dear animal would not be killed, but here Gertrude goes to duck heaven. Many kids felt betrayed.)

The rest of the cast is mostly along for the ride, including Pat Boone, who doesn't stay in character—he doesn't even attempt a Scottish accent—but he's completely harmless and even appealing in a great-big-little-boy way. He sings well, and he doesn't bump into things, occasionally entering into the spirit exuberantly. But he's not believable.

The film isn't really about the characters, anyway. It's about the story, the sets, the special effects and the music. It is a moderately high-budget spectacle for the family.

Art direction is credited to Lyle R. Wheeler, Franz Bachelin and Herman A. Blumenthal; set decorators were Walter M. Scott and Joseph Kish. I suspect that Wheeler can be discounted as a creative force in the film, as he was head of the Fox art department and was routinely credited on all their movies. Whoever was responsible, the sets are variable. The "real world" sets at the beginning, especially Lindenbrook's home and the low-ceilinged Icelandic hotel, are excellent: they are not only physically beautiful, they have an aura of authenticity. However, once the journey is actually begun, the sets begin to seem unreal. The scenes actually shot in Carlsbad Caverns simply don't match the studio's plaster rocks and carefully-planned pathways and trails. Much of the film looks like an amusement-park ride, an appearance greatly enhanced by the bright, even lighting in most scenes. Occasionally, there are sets that show real imagination, such as the twisting vinelike rocks in the salt cave where Boone meets Thayer David, or the big crystalline grotto where our heroes bathe. The occasional brief montages of travel show a few sets which are more interesting then those dwelled on, but they may have been real cavern scenes, or sets that wouldn't sustain being seen longer.

As a result, there's an aura of fantasy to the underground scenes, as if the cast is traipsing through fairyland; this feeling, which may have been intentional, is increased by their not needing much gear or food. They rarely suffer.

The special effects were under the direction of L.B. Abbott, James B. Gordon and Emil Kosa, Jr., and like the sets, are variable. Some of the miniatures, such as the altar stone carrying the survivors up through the volcanic chimney, are difficult to accept even when one squints. The great success of the fin-backed iguanas, convincing dimetrodons, is offset by the misuse of the wrong, immobile lizard for a "chameleon." The impulse to feature one more menace at the penultimate moment should have been avoided.

The matte paintings of the volcano crater and, later, the stone sky over the underground sea are acceptable, and the miniature of the city of Atlantis is reasonably well done, but the lava that covers up the "chameleon" looks like what it probably was: red-dyed oatmeal.

Aside from the story, the one element that probably contributes the most to the overall success of the film is the great score by Bernard Herrmann. He was one of the greatest composers in movie history, and was often allied with fantasy films, as early as *The Ghost and Mrs. Muir* (1947) until the last film released with a score attributed to him, *It's Alive 2* (1978).

Herrmann's score for *Journey to the Center of the Earth* deserves a virtual thesaurus of adjectives: resonant, sonorous, eerie, deep, evocative, otherworldly, menacing, rich. For the liner notes for the album which features a suite from the film, Herrmann wrote: "I decided to evoke the mood and feeling of inner Earth by using only instruments played in low registers. Eliminating all strings, I utilized an orchestra of woodwinds and brass, with a large percussion section and many harps. But the truly unique feature of this score is the inclusion of five organs, one large Cathedral and four electronic. These organs were used in many adroit ways to suggest ascent and descent, as well as the mystery of Atlantis. For the scene involving the dangerous serpent [sic], I resurrected an obsolete medieval instrument called a serpent, which has been dropped from contemporary orchestras." Herrmann was not noted for modesty.

The score is thunderous and majestic, and while some have complained about its repetitiveness, I find it to be one of his most impressive scores for a fantasy film.

Henry Levin directed the movie, but his contribution does not seem significant. He rarely rose above the level of standard studio director, and occasionally sank beneath it. He was at Columbia from 1944 to 1949, where he began with *Cry of the Werewolf* and ended with *Jolson Sings Again*. He worked at Fox until 1959. Among his other titles are *Night Editor* (1946), *The Man from Colorado* (1948), *Mr. Scoutmaster* (1953, one of Clifton Webb's most sentimental vehicles), *Bernadine* (1957), and parts of *The Wonderful World of the Brothers Grimm* (1962). In the rest of the 60s and 70s, he worked mostly on comic thrillers, such as the Matt Helm film *Murderer's Row* (1967).

The film was a major holiday release, so it received many reviews, but though mostly favorable, they were mixed. The worst U.S. notice probably came from Bosley Crowther in the *New York Times*: "It's really not very striking make-believe, when all is said and done.... They certainly could have got someone who would not be as blasé as [Mason], this veteran of *20,000 Leagues Under the Sea*." Crowther concluded, "even those horrible giant lizards are grotesque without being good. Their only service is to frighten little children who should be the best customers for this foolish film." Children loved those horrible giant lizards.

In *Hollywood Reporter*, Jack Harrison, unlike Crowther, noticed that the film was partly tongue in cheek. "Juveniles of all ages and all lands will be fascinated and thrilled, their elders and caretakers will be entertained and amused.... Many of the titillations bear a sharp resemblance to those in the classic cliffhangers. The novelty here is that the ridiculous is exaggerated and the entire proceedings spoofed in a tongue-in-cheek, mock-serious manner that will provide an amusing fillip for the mature and not offend the kiddies.... Producer Brackett has given us an entertaining takeoff on science-adventure films, which will be even more fun for those who like the stuff straight."

"Holl" in *Daily Variety* was puzzled by this approach: "There are times when it is difficult to determine whether the filmmakers are kidding or playing it straight.... If one is willing to accept the film as one big spoof, it can turn out to be a fairly amusing entry."

John P. Case in *Films in Review* regarded it as "Good, clean, gaudy fun without a brain or message in its pretty little head, which should be enough for anyone.... A great spoof of special-effects fantasies and 'science-fiction' weirdies.... [It] builds to a fine, farcical ending that endows the principal players with the physical invulnerability of Donald Duck."

Paul V. Beckley in the New York *Herald-Tribune* thought "its main success is as a children's film, one of the best to come along in some time.... It is not intended for the sophisticate.... The overall tone of the picture is one of persistent good nature."

British reviewers reacted similarly. Quoted in *The Films of James Mason*, the *Sunday Express* thought it "a super glossy, unintentionally [*sic*] hilarious version of a Jules Verne adventure story.... A very odd film indeed; almost a collector's piece." The London *Times* enjoyed it: "The story retains its interest throughout the two hours and a bit it takes to run. Mr. James Mason manages, at one and the same time, to have his tongue in his cheek and to keep it in its proper place, to parody the role, yet to play it straight." (That is perfectly accurate.) Dilys Powell in the Sunday *Times* thought it was "hilarious science fiction, full of straight-faced extravagances.... I haven't enjoyed nonsense of this sort so much for years."

As some American reviewers did, the British occasionally missed the point: "Preposterous," said the *Daily Herald*, "but not quite the way its makers intended.... Studded with unintentional laughs." The *Evening News* concurred: "Laughs of the unrewarding kind.... You laugh at, but not with the characters.... A lot of deliberate unintentional fun." (Whatever that might mean.)

James Mason himself, quoted in the same book, thought the film had a "good script ... so I guess it must have been actors and director who so let down the English critics."

Don Willis (I) thought it "fun," *Psychotronic* regarded it as "effective," and Alan Frank (*SF*) described it as "an enjoyable lighthearted adventure which the cast, writers and director properly refuse to take seriously." However, in *Future Tense*, John Brosnan thought it only "moderate," and John Baxter didn't even mention it.

In addition to the 1909 silent French film, the novel was filmed again in 1977 as a Spanish production with Kenneth More (in the James Mason role) the only actor known to Westerners. The film, with many scenes shot in claustrophobic caves, was released in the United States as *Where Time Began*. It is clumsy and pedestrian, with inadequate though ambitious special effects. We see giant turtles, sea monsters, a giant ape and a herd of dinosaurs, none convincing. There is also the pointless and puzzling addition of a man from the future who, in disguise, first gives the professor the book that will lead him to the center of the Earth. It's a second-rate, boring movie.

There was also a Mexican film in 1964, *Aventuro al Center al Tierre*, but whether it was actually based on Verne's novel, or simply borrowed the theme, is unknown to me. According to Walt Lee's *Reference Guide to Fantastic Films*, there were several monsters, including a cyclops and a dinosaur.

A TV series loosely derived from the Fox film was shown on ABC 1967–69; it is poorly animated and not worth watching. *The Goonies*, 1985's hit summer movie, has a plot structure surprisingly similar to *Journey*, but this may be coincidence.

Despite its occasional gaucheries and a tendency to stroll where it should gallop, *Journey to the Center of the Earth* is one of the best SF movies of the declining 1950s. It isn't so much *of* its era as just *in* it. It's the kind of film that could easily have been produced, even on this scale, if the 50s SF boom had never existed. Perhaps it's this aura of being aloof from the period that has caused some 1950s SF film buffs to disregard it. For the average filmgoer, however, it is a decent, entertaining movie.

The Killer Shrews

For a bad film, *The Killer Shrews* is surprisingly good. The movie had a very low budget (allegedly $123,000), was shot on a quick schedule with inadequate monsters, and suffers from clichéd characters. However, there are pleasant compensations for those willing to sit through a physically unattractive film with a very bad sound track.

Although writer Jay Simms conceived the leading role tritely, director Ray Kellogg and actor James Best made him more unusual: a brisk, testy Southerner.

The giant shrew menace in the script is logically conceived and, in fact, logic informs much of the film with a kind of intelligence not usually found in these movies. At the climax, for instance, our hero and his friends make their getaway by crawling along under upturned metal tubs. While this looks absurd, and many have found it laughable, it plays by the movie's established rules: the shrews are big, vicious carnivores, but not especially strong. They're vulnerable to gunfire, but there are several hundred of the damned things (or so we're told). The location is an isolated island; there's nothing for protection—even the adobe walls of the house are penetrated by the scrabbling shrews. And these big metal tubs have been there all along. Instead of the hero suddenly finding that the shrews are vulnerable to something unexpected, simple protection against their poisoned fangs and claws is employed.

It is a bit disconcerting to see the hero of a monster movie make his getaway duckwalking inside a giant can, but *it makes sense*. It plays fair with us—and has an added bonus: it's an escape anyone might have thought of. The scientists in the film are stymied—unwordly dreamers who are virtually waiting to be the shrews' dinner. Our hero is just a skipper of a small boat, but he sees the tubs for what they are, or can be: protection.

The film opens with a doom-laden narration: "Those who hunt by night will tell you that the wildest and most vicious of all animals is the tiny shrew. The shrew feeds only by the dark of the Moon. He must eat his own body weight every few hours, or starve. And the shrew devours everything, bones, flesh, marrow—everything." So far, so good—and not too inaccurate. But then, "In March, first in Alaska and then invading steadily southward, there were reports of a new species, the giant Killer Shrew!" The credits follow, but what does not follow is any hint in the story to Alaska or the roaming bands of Killer Shrews. It is, in fact, very clearly established in the story that the shrews are confined to one island, presumably in the South, and that as they cannot swim and do indeed need to eat their own weight every few hours, after the finale they will soon all be dead of starvation. I suppose the narration was to make us all feel threatened by giant shrews.

I was prepared to be highly critical of *The Killer Shrews*. I had closely observed the little animals (about the size of a dime), and had read as much about them, the smallest mammal, as I could find. To my amazement, the film did not violate anything I knew about shrews except, of course, their size (and shape). In the movie, the shrews are played by what appear to be greyhounds in fur coats, the worst aspect of the film. But even the plot premise which enlarges the shrews isn't altogether unreasonable.

Even more to my surprise, the film played fair in all departments. The script is pretty bad, but the acting is generally good, and unlike many low-budget films, *The Killer Shrews* doesn't try anything it can't really do. It delivers several sudden shocks, and director Ray Kellogg handles suspense scenes remarkably well.

Thorne Sherman (James Best) and his black pal Rook (J.H. "Judge" DuPree) sail in Thorne's small cabin cruiser to the island inhabited solely by Dr. Milo Craigis (Baruch Lumet; writer Simms is fond of this name: in his *Creation of the Humanoids*, Don Megowan plays a "Kenneth Cragis"), his beautiful daughter Ann (Ingrid Goude), and Craigis' two assistants, surly Jerry Farrell (Ken Curtis) and dedicated Dr. Radford Baines (Gordon McLendon). Craigis wants Sherman to leave the supplies he's brought, then depart, taking the reluctant Ann with him. But Thorne can't leave—a hurricane is coming up, and he's curious about Farrell's obvious hostility and even more obvious rifle.

Craigis invites Thorne in for drinks, while Rook stays on the boat, anchored offshore. Thorne's curiosity is further aroused: there's a general air of tension, and the house seems almost barricaded. Craigis is a chatty type, and delights in telling Sherman that he and the others—his daughter is a zoologist—have been trying to find a way of combatting overpopulation, which Craigis feels is coming in the future.

Craigis has been trying to "isolate and identify the inherited factor in each gene" (accurate prediction). He's been working with shrews, tiny animals with high metabolisms and therefore short life spans, in an effort to create smaller animals with lower metabolisms and thereby longer life spans. He hopes to be able to apply this latter research to human beings. (An interesting sidelight is that Craigis is anything but mad; he's not even *wrong*; the experiment doesn't go haywire, the experimental animals merely escape.)

Dr. Baines comes in with a shrew, so we can actually see one of the little devils. It's 28 months old, the equivalent of 128 years for a human being. "How big do they get?" asks Thorne innocently. Craigis pauses, then says, "That's an adult." It's an inch or so long.

Craigis happily describes the nasty wonders of shrews—they eat bones to get the marrow, leaving only teeth, horns and hooves. (The latter may be a mistake on the part of writer Simms, or might be an early clue—other than the naked title—that there are great big shrews at large. After all, in the ordinary course of events, the prey of shrews would hardly be likely to have horns or hooves.)

Thorne overhears Ann chastising Farrell for having left open a cage door; she adds angrily that this happened because Farrell drinks too much. Shortly thereafter, Farrell finds Ann talking to Thorne, and becomes jealous. Farrell and Ann were engaged, but she declares that that ended the night before. We later learn that this dark hint does not refer to attempted rape, the usual secret in such scenes, but rather to Farrell's abandoning Ann the previous night when they fled the giant shrews. (But, of course, someone did rescue her.)

Scenes of Rook coming ashore are intercut with Thorne chatting with the inhabitants of the house. Rook is pursued by the long-legged, shaggy shrews; he takes refuge in a tree, but as he's rather fat, he falls over and is devoured (behind a bush) by the big shrews.

I suspect film editor Aaron Stell may have gotten the order of some scenes wrong. In the next sequence, Ann pulls a gun on Thorne to prevent him from opening the fence gate after dark, then tells him the island's dread but simple secret. Yet in a scene that follows this, she chides him for not showing curiosity about the island. Ann says shrews are "the most horrible animals on the face of the Earth." In an effort to slow the shrews' metabolism, they first enlarged the beasties while keeping their metabolism the same. And then Farrell accidentally released some mated pairs of the big shrews. The result is that "there are two or three hundred giant shrews out there, monsters weighing between 50 and 100 pounds." They tried to kill the nasty things, but failed to get all of them. Actually, these monsters have a built-in self-destruct system: they are so voracious that they will soon kill off all available prey, then turn on each other. ("This species does not swim," says Craigis.) In a matter of days, overpopulation will be acted out on the island, and all the shrews will be dead. Of course, there is some prey they haven't got to yet—the people.

Because of the increasing storm winds, the lights go out, and candles have to be used. While the people spend time talking to each other or themselves (Farrell tries to convince himself that it's better for him than Ann to leave with Thorne), the shrews dig their way into the barn and kill the frightened horse penned there.

Thorne asks Craigis why he hasn't called in the authorities to combat the menace. Craigis less than illuminatingly says, "Any unusual experiment can produce unusual results."

Thorne takes charge, and has them stand watch in shifts. He points out that the walls of the building are adobe. In the rainstorm, the walls will soften and the shrews can dig their way in.

And one does, but through a window rather than the wall. Craigis' employee Mario (Alfredo DeSoto) awakens Thorne to tell him that a shrew is in the basement. "I hear him *singin'* down *there*," he says. (The shrews make a high-pitched, interrupted chattering.)

In a tense sequence, Thorne and Mario enter the basement. A shrew is hiding under the stairs, and Thorne is unable to prevent it from biting Mario. Thorne kills the animal, but Mario also abruptly dies. Thorne exclaims that the corpse does not resemble the small shrew he was shown. "That's a monster!" Craigis is abashed. "In controlling the size factor," he says sheepishly, "we seem to have crossed some of the other characteristics."

Craigis discovers that Mario was killed by a powerful poison they had previously put out to kill the escaped shrews. It didn't work. Instead, the

In the logical if outrageous climax of **The Killer Shrews** (1959), the surviving cast waddle to safety inside big metal vats, with the giant shrews (here played by a hand-puppet construction) trying to get them under the edges.

shrews assimilated the poison and it "remained in the salivary glands," Baines exclaims excitedly. This, he thinks, is "wonderful." (Shrews actually are mildly poisonous.) They cannot afford to be even scratched by a killer shrew.

Offscreen, Thorne tosses the dead shrew over the fence. When other shrews don't rush out to get it, he and Farrell take a chance on getting to the boat. However, Farrell turns his gun on Thorne, and the two have a fight. Thorne overcomes Farrell. They find Rook's remains, and see that the boat has survived the first half of the hurricane (the island is now in the eye of the storm). On the way back to the house, shrews begin pursuing them; Farrell makes it back first, and locks the door in Thorne's face. Thorne manages to climb the wall, however, and they continue their fight, but it doesn't last long.

In the house, Ann opens the door to the kitchen and begins to enter, but a shrew (which we saw burrowing into the house earlier) bursts out and attacks them. They kill it, but not before it bites Baines, who at once sits down at a typewriter and records his symptoms of approaching death before finally expiring.

More shrews dig their way through the weakened walls, and the four survivors barricade themselves in the fenced patio area. Despite Thorne's warning that the rising storm winds are likely to blow him off, Farrell climbs on the roof, armed with a rifle.

Under Thorne's direction, Craigis and his daughter assist him in welding four large metal buckets together, intending to use this contraption as a tank, walking beneath it to the water.

Despite the shrews snapping at them under the edges of the tubs, the three manage to do this. Farrell leaps from the roof and tries to run to the shore, but he's overtaken and devoured by the shrews. The other three swim to Thorne's boat.

Ray Kellogg, who directed *The Killer Shrews*, was in special effects at 20th Century–Fox in the late forties through the mid-fifties; among the films he worked on in that capacity were *The Day the Earth Stood Still*, *Inferno*, *Titanic* (both 1953), *Hell and High Water* and *Prince Valiant* (both 1954). He directed *Killer Shrews* and *The Giant Gila Monster* in Texas, then returned to Hollywood and a new job as second-unit director. Among the films he worked on as 2nd AD were *Cleopatra* (1963), *Batman* (1966), *Hombre* (1967) and *Tora! Tora! Tora!* (1970). He was assistant director to John Ford on *Cheyenne Autumn* (1964) and codirected the infamous *The Green Berets* (1968) with John Wayne. (I am assuming that the Ray Kellogg who was an actor during this period is another person.)

As a director of actors, Kellogg is nothing much. He can't really get a performance out of Ingrid Goude, and Ken Curtis plays his role on only two notes: sullen and frightened/sullen. Kellogg is much more inventive with the suspense scenes. He peppers the film with gruesome, ominous shots of the shrews (here, big hand puppets) struggling to get through the fence, or peeping in with shiny black eyes through cracks in the wall. When the first one gets into the house, Kellogg shows it to us only in brief cuts illuminated by flashes of lightning. (They aren't brief enough, though, and the very canine look of the "stunt shrews" is a serious weakness.) The scene in the basement, though like the entire film, burdened with far too much music, is brief and to the point: we see the men, we see the shrew—but *they* don't. Their spatial relationship is always clear.

The scenes of the shrews busily digging their way into the barn is followed by a matching shot some time later: no shrews, and the horse is now silent. The various pursuit scenes in the forest (such as it is) are also terse and swiftly paced.

And to his great credit, Kellogg delivers one of the best busses (sudden shock scenes) of the period, when Ann opens that kitchen door. In the long shot, we glimpse the shrew inside the kitchen before it leaps forth in the close-up. The 1959 audiences bounced a foot off their seats.

The Killer Shrews is marked by an intelligent attitude toward its limitations; Kellogg rarely tries for effects he cannot bring off. This film is to the point, modest and effective. In marked contrast, of course, to its cofeature, *The Giant Gila Monster*, which continually tries for big-scale special effects, and just can't do them.

However, the film is still low-class. There's that terrible Jay Simms dialogue, for one thing. None of his films amounted to much, but all were especially dismal regarding dialogue: this, *The Giant Gila Monster*, *Panic in Year Zero!*, *Creation of the Humanoids*.

In one scene, Ingrid Goude runs through a virtual catalog of clichés (perhaps intended to be cut into individual shots): "I love an open fire, don't you? The wind has a lonesome sound, doesn't it? You're a strange man, Thorne. I've never met anyone like you." These lines run consecutively without a cut.

Goude herself, however, may have been slightly above this. Later, she quizzes Thorne. "Don't you wonder about the unusual things around here? The guns? The fence? The chattered windows? My accent? Anything?" The crack about her accent can probably be attributed to Goude (rhymes with "mood") herself; though no actress, she showed a sharp wit in her season on "The Bob Cummings Show"; she may have realized that the audience would be wondering why Craigis has a daughter with a heavy Swedish accent.

Simms gives us not just clichés but especially tired ones: the laconic adventurer (though, as mentioned earlier, Best gives him added dimensions), the eccentric scientist, his beautiful daughter, the cowardly scientist, the dedicated researcher, even – and most unattractively – the "nigger" sidekick of the hero. The patronizing, unconscious racism in the treatment of the Rook character may be mild, but it is distasteful.

The production is cheap and shoddy. The interior sets are overlit and extremely drab; the bare walls have a slight marbled look common to low-budget films, and there's no character at all to the interior of the house or the furnishings.

Cinematographer Wilfrid M. Cline was a long-established pro, working primarily in lower-berth As. He started at Warner Bros. in the early 1940s, but seems to have had war service after that; the next film for which I have a credit for Cline is One Sunday Afternoon (1948). He photographed several of Doris Day's musicals for Warners, including the underrated Calamity Jane (1953). After his departure from the studio in 1954, Cline worked primarily on medium-budget Westerns, such as The First Texan, The Last Wagon (both 1956) and Face of a Fugitive (1959).

His work on The Killer Shrews is strictly businesslike, nothing more. There are few close-ups, as usual with swiftly-made films, and a preponderance of long and medium shots. The film stock itself seems to be of inferior quality, and being in Texas, far from the professional Hollywood crews he was used to, Cline doesn't seem to be able to light his sets in any way except too much or too little. Several of the scenes involving just the shrews are well done, but most of the dialogue scenes are drab.

Although the music is attributed to Harry Bluestone and Emil Cadkin, it is primarily standard library music, often heard in low-budget films, making it sound vaguely like a cut-down serial. Furthermore, as usual with such cheap pictures, there's far too much music. Several scenes are scored so peculiarly as to verge on parody; when Best simply goes to a bathroom to wash his face, the music that accompanies this action is so ominous as to make you expect murderers behind each door.

Overall, the acting is above average for a regional film. Both James Best and Ken Curtis had been working for at least eight years in Hollywood, primarily in supporting roles in Westerns, but in enough variety of roles to give their performances in Shrews a professional gloss, though Curtis shows little variety. Best known for playing "Festus" on "Gunsmoke," Curtis also produced the film. He was the star of a series of low-budget Westerns for Columbia in the 1940s; he was a singing cowboy, and had begun his show business career as a straight singer.

Among his Hollywood films were a great number for John Ford: Rio Grande (1950), The Quiet Man (1952), Mr. Roberts (1955), The Searchers (1956, in a role that should have been cut), The Last Hurrah (1958), The Horse Soldiers (1959), Two Rode Together (1961) and Cheyenne Autumn (1964). His voice was heard in the Disney animated film Robin Hood (1973).

In The Killer Shrews, Curtis has a thankless role: a cowardly scientist, all too willing to sacrifice anyone and later talk himself into believing it was the right thing to do; Farrell is a distasteful character.

James Best is an amusing hero, shrewd in a native, red-neck fashion, hardly a typical romantic lead, but believable in that area, too. He's rangy and tough, appropriately weather-beaten. Best began his Hollywood career in 1949, playing supporting parts in many films, including *Francis Goes to West Point* (1952), *The Caine Mutiny* (1954), *Forbidden Planet*, Sam Fuller's amusing *Shock Corridor* (1963; Best is particularly good in this), and *Shenandoah* (1965). After an absence from the screen, he returned in *Sounder* (1972), then tried to retire to Florida, only to be brought back from time to time by his pal Burt Reynolds: *Nickelodeon* (1976), *The End* and *Hooper* (both 1978). He became a regular on the TV series "The Dukes of Hazzard."

Baruch Lumet makes a believable old scientist, although the difference in accents between his and Goude's puts a lie to their relationship. Lumet is the father of director Sidney Lumet, and made his screen debut in *One Third of a Nation* (1939). His next film appears to be *The Killer Shrews* itself, but he appeared in several more in the 1960s, including *The Interns* (1962), Sidney's *The Pawnbroker* (1965) and *The Group* (1966), as well as Woody Allen's *Everything You Always Wanted to Know About Sex but Were Afraid to Ask* (1972).

Dr. Radford Baines, the obsessed scientist, is played by Gordon McLendon, the head of a chain of radio stations and motion picture theatres in Texas, and the financial backer of *The Killer Shrews* and *The Giant Gila Monster*. McLendon is an astonishing character: he invented Top 40 Radio, wrote eight books, produced a record album, and is one of those fabulously wealthy Texas millionaires who are beloved in stereotype and cliché: only he's *real*. He produced only these two films at the time, but in 1982, backed a flop (but McLendon made a profit), John Huston's *Victory*. In the *Los Angeles Times* Calendar section for 18 March, 1984, there appeared an article on McLendon, which included the announcement that he had recently decided to get back into movies, and was busily raising $80 million for six or seven films. He also amiably chatted with reporter Dennis McDougal about *The Killer Shrews* (which made a million dollars). "I had a minor, almost insignificant role in which I was on the screen maybe six or seven minutes," McLendon said. "As I look back and view the picture now, I wasn't very good, but then again I didn't much give a damn. I just thought it'd be a kick to do it." McLendon *isn't* very good; his performance is amateurish, but forgivable: he seems to be having a very good time.

Kellogg presumably did the scant special effects himself. The shrews are played in long shots by dogs with shaggy fur coats, long ratlike tails, and fangy masks. (Shrews generally have short tails, and are not rodents.) For close-ups, as when they are peeking into the house, or reaching under the edges of the upended tubs, the shrews are depicted by means of large, wild-looking hand puppets. The masks are elaborately sculpted, but have preposterously long and vicious fangs. They also have a generally canine look, to match the real dogs used elsewhere.

Variety's "Bark" was reasonably impressed. "As a 'horror' film it's quite good under the economics involved.... The production is better than the script.... Assets include excellent direction by Ray Kellogg, fine lighting and photography in the numerous outdoor shots. Special effects by Kellogg, especially in the closeups of the 'huge' shrews are firstrate."

The *Monthly Film Bulletin* gave the film a II, and said, "shot in a fortnight at a patently low budget, this ... suffers from a weak script and acting. Nevertheless, the action builds up from a shaky start to a suitably horrific climax, and Ray Kellogg's direction and special effects ... are well calculated."

More recent commentators have found little of interest in the film. Don

Willis (I) dismisses it as "not too good," while *Psychotronic* found it a laff riot. "Ken Curtis ... produces and stars in a homemade horror (in both senses of the word) from Texas. He creates and is later gobbled up by a couple of dogs with phoney fangs. James Best is the hero who loves Ingrid Goode [*sic*] (Miss Universe of '57) [she was in fact Miss Sweden that year]. Watch the cast members escape while hiding in barrels! The best thing about this little disaster was the poster showing a giant shrew tail (nothing like the furry tails actually used) [the tails in the film are bare, like the one in the superlative ad] knocking over a high-heeled shoe. The same people made *The Giant Gila Monster* to complete a dynamite double bill."

In his intelligent but pompous *Dark Dreams*, Charles Derry used *The Killer Shrews* as an example of that kind of "amateurish horror film [which] constantly surprises us by tying into [common] fears so effortlessly." (Derry mistakenly believes shrews are small rats.) He decries the special effects, but says, "Nevertheless, these creatures take on a rather adult, existential meaning. Almost the entire film takes place in the house of the scientist as it is constantly besieged at night by the killer shrews. And this is only right, for it is in the night that we are the most susceptible to our fears. There are some very powerful scenes of people running crazily to get back in the house while the fanged shrews frenziedly chase them. Some of the scenes work powerfully despite their amateurish execution because they tie into a kind of universal childhood fear: the recurring dream of so many children of being chased by a vicious and gigantic dog.... Even in such a crude film, the water [that saves the hero and friends] works symbolically as a kind of river of life that simultaneously re-baptizes the characters in a more natural faith, and repudiates the modern faithless science that created the shrews." Of course, one of the survivors is the man who created the shrews...

The Killer Shrews is a cheap little picture made by some amateurs and professionals in exotic Texas. The props and other technical aspects betray its low budget, and the trite script is populated by stereotypes. Nonetheless, it is intelligent and consistently logical; the director manages several good scares, and some of the cast is above average. *The Killer Shrews* recapitulates the science fiction movies of the 1950s in miniature: partly stupid, partly inspired.

The Man Who Could Cheat Death

Although it has never been confirmed by research I've done, nor is it asserted in the various books on the subject, I've always presumed that there were two kinds of remakes undertaken by Hammer: those that they instigated themselves, such as *Curse of Frankenstein* and *Horror of Dracula*, new versions of classic horror tales in the public domain, and those made in partnership with American studios from properties that those studios owned. This includes Hammer's version of *The Mummy* (1959) and this remake of *The Man in Half Moon Street* (1944), redubbed more sensationally *The Man Who Could Cheat Death*. Both these films were released by the companies that made the originals, respectively, Universal and Paramount.

I don't otherwise know why Hammer would redo the Paramount film which wasn't a horror movie at all, but a serious, romantic film about longevity, from a play by Barré Lyndon. Paramount was presumably anxious to jump onto the horror movie bandwagon, and probably searched their copyright holdings for a property that could be easily made on the budget Hammer had; this let out such costly items as a new version of *Island of Lost Souls*, but did allow the mild *Man Who Could Cheat Death*.

Unfortunately, Lyndon's play simply is not the material of horror movies. The original film was a mystery with romantic and philosophical overtones, and was released in a period heavily influenced by the adult-oriented Val Lewton movies. The picture seems to try to bridge the gap between those movies and the psychological thrillers of the period, such as *Gaslight*, *The Lodger* (both 1944) and *Hangover Square* (1945).

The Hammer version tries to be both a murder thriller and a horror movie, but comes up short in the latter department. Perhaps because of budgetary cutbacks, perhaps because Peter Cushing, originally set to star, was not available, *The Man Who Could Cheat Death* is peculiarly reticent in terms of horror. The official synopsis as well as the novelization describe the protagonist exhibiting a glowing green head from time to time, the bones shining through the flesh. But this simply does not happen on screen; when I first saw the film, having read the book, I squinted hard, trying to imagine that Anton Diffring's glacially handsome face resembled a skull, but I soon realized I was fooling myself. He only had some bags under his eyes, and a tortured, pop-eyed expression. No glow, no skull, nuthin'.

Diffring plays sculptor and doctor Georges Bonner in the Paris of 1890 (the first movie was contemporary). The film opens with the anonymous murder of an innocent passerby, but it's clear that Bonner has committed the crime. After Georges shows his latest bust of model Margo (Delphi Lawrence) to his friends, Dr. Pierre Gérard (Christopher Lee) and Janine Dubois (Hazel Court), they leave and Georges starts to drink a glowing green potion. He's surprised by Margo, also his lover, and when she screams, he claps his hand across her face. His hand *burns* her. (Why? This is never explained nor does it happen again; it's just a horror touch that Hammer apparently felt compelled to include.) She collapses, and Georges desperately takes the potion.

Soon, Professor Ludwig Weisz (Arnold Marle), an old friend of Georges, arrives in Paris to perform an operation on Bonner. Although he appears to be around 35, Georges is actually 104. Years before, as fellow researchers, he and Weisz had discovered a gland transplant that, performed in conjunction with taking a certain fluid, would create perpetual youth and immunity to all disease. Providing that the gland keeps being replaced with a new one.

As Weisz is now too old and palsied to operate on Georges, the sculptor asks Pierre to perform the operation. He's reluctant to replace what he presumes is a healthy gland with another one, but Georges assures him he's doomed to die if the operation isn't performed.

Margo has now disappeared, and a police inspector (Francis De Wolff) questions both doctors about this.

Weisz's arrival has been postponed several times, and Georges keeps getting fresh glands as the old ones spoil, or something. Weisz learns that Georges has committed murder to get the glands he needs, so he refuses to participate and tries to destroy Georges' supply of the green fluid. The bottle smashes, and Georges kills his oldest friend.

When Pierre learns that Weisz has "returned to Vienna" unexpectedly, he at first refuses to perform the operation. Later, the inspector tells Pierre that there were several unsolved murders over a period of thirty years that have attracted his attention. In each case—in Berne, San Francisco and London—the victim was a woman who had just posed for an artist-doctor, who then disappeared. (Why a French police inspector would even become aware of murders spread out over 30 years in widely separated cities is an interesting question.)

Pierre warns Janine against Georges, but she has been posing for his newest sculpture and has fallen in love with him. She pooh-poohs Pierre's fears, but she should have listened. Georges takes her across town to a cellar where he has some other busts stored. As she realizes from the dates on the busts—he *would* add the dates, of course—that Georges must be a great deal older than he looks, he sneaks out and locks her in.

He then tells Pierre that if he does not perform the operation, he, Georges, will kill Janine. So Pierre goes ahead with it.

Meanwhile, back in the cellar, Janine is horrified to find that there's a second prisoner: the scarred Margo, now insane.

Pierre flees from Georges and gets the police inspector. Georges heads back to the cellar to make preparations to perform the longevity operation on Janine: he's gotten lonely all these years. Pierre and the inspector figure out where Georges' secret cellar must be, and Pierre reveals that while he made the incision in Georges, he did not transplant the new gland.

Back in the cellar, Georges suddenly feels strange. All of his accumulated aging *and* disease are starting to catch up with him. Earlier in the story, he had described the effect we now see: "I shall become the inheritor of all my 104 years. Of all the sickness I never had. Of every pain, blemish, disease, a lifetime of illness in one moment." He turns gray and wrinkled, and staggers toward Janine just as Pierre arrives. Margo cackles and tosses a lantern at Georges, setting him ablaze; the whole cellar goes up in flames as Pierre and Janine beat a hasty retreat.

The science fictional aspects of the film probably have their origin in various theories in the early 20th century that glandular secretions were responsible for all of mankind's ills and, if they could be handled properly, would solve all of mankind's health problems. There was much discussion of "monkey glands" in the 1920s, and several films featured such operations as part of their plots.

However, in *The Man Who Could Cheat Death*, this emphasis on glandular activity doesn't seem to make much sense. A gland is replaced in Georges' body and he doesn't age. But why not? The gland is taken from a normal person around Georges' age—surely that gland had aged normally. But no matter, it's just another gimmick, like the glowing green fluid. It's merely a more rational way of explaining what's going on, without resorting to black magic. It also gives a sense of urgency to the story and makes Georges a murderer.

As Georges, Anton Diffring is a mixed bag. The role certainly brought him to the attention of fantasy film fans the world over; I suspect whatever career he's had since owes a great deal to his stepping in for Peter Cushing in this movie. He's an elegant actor, and his striking features and arresting pale eyes have led to him playing several different varieties of villains over the years. He is one of the most frequent portrayers of Nazi military figures since the death of Peter Van Eyck. However, his sculpted face and icy eyes also keep him from being very good at expressing more gentle emotions. Here, he gets Georges' mania very well; it's quite an intense performance. But the loneliness and the passion elude him; he certainly doesn't seem to be in love with Janine. His efforts to turn her into a long-lived creature like himself seem to stem more from selfishness than love. Diffring has a very self-involved air that makes

Georges' murders quite credible, and even his being a fine sculptor is convincing. But in the older film, Nils Asther made us feel the sadness of the death-cheater; Diffring gives us only his wickedness. Still, it's a strong performance and well above average for this kind of film.

The rest of the cast is unmemorable. Christopher Lee plays The Hero; the role was written with no shadings, and Lee plays the character blandly. At this point in his career, he hadn't yet developed the sometimes riveting assurance he was able to bring to a variety of roles in later years. However, even if he had been able to tap his skills more effectively, there's not much he could have done with his role.

The two actresses are just heroine number one and heroine number two. At least Delphi Lawrence has the melodramatic advantage of turning up ugly and spectacularly mad at the end; Hazel Court is attractive but, as with Lee, there's no depth to her part.

Arnold Marle overplays the part of old Weisz; he struggles hard to be a charming old man, but never succeeds in being anything more than mildly irritating. There's no feeling of loss (only of betrayal) when Georges throttles him.

Jimmy Sangster's screenplay becomes logically muddled again and again, although the overall thrust of the story is clean and precise. Bonner lies to the inspector about having done a sculpture of Margo, which is reasonable only if he knew the inspector was interested in sculptor-doctors. Why does Pierre cover for Georges' lie? Both actors are so cold in their parts that there's no hint of friendship, nor does the film hint in this direction, either.

The reason for Georges' murders for gland "donors" is obvious, but why does he murder his model-lovers after he finishes the busts? There's no explanation, unless he's just perversely destroying the thing he loves, time and time again.

The idea of eternal youth is intriguing, of course, and has fascinated various writers for years. Indeed, in his review of *The Man Who Could Cheat Death*, Jack Moffitt began by saying, "Tales of immortality have been popular around Paris ever since Cagliostro, in the 18th century, claimed he had lived forever"; he also refers to Simone de Beauvoir. The one sticking point for immortality, according to writers, has always been that the immortal person is not immune to normal human emotional involvement, and having to leave loved ones behind again and again as they age and he (or rarely, she) does not is usually a major crisis, early or late, in the tale of the immortal one. Sangster here more or less sweeps the idea under the rug, although it was important in *The Man in Half Moon Street*. It does pop up near the climax, but isn't credible because of Diffring's chilliness.

Still, it's an unusual Hammer film in that it is more talk than action, and the character of the central figure is more important. Though a verbose film, it is a careful and serious one, intended for grown-ups. However, the horror elements tossed in from time to time—the murders, the disfigurements—probably made the film unappealing for grown-ups at the time.

The usual sumptuous Hammer set design hadn't palled yet, and a somewhat unusual score by Richard Bennett adds to the appeal of the film. But the labored script and Terence Fisher's pedestrian direction make the film ponderous. Fisher was far better at his horror-adventure and suspense films made around the same time; this set-bound and gabby film doesn't seem to have engaged much of his attention.

Reviews of the time were typical for a Hammer film. In the *Motion Picture*

Herald, Allen M. Widem said it was "a surprisingly effective, even literate treatment on the oft-used premise of a man prolonging life through scientific research and accumulated formulas.... *The Man Who Could Cheat Death* reflects top production values, and the acting is far from slipshod. This can be recommended for use on adult programming, for it is far above the rank-and-file science-horror releases of the modern day."

However, "Powe" in *Variety* thought the film indicated "that horror films are nearing the end of their current cycle.... It is well-acted and intelligently conceived. But invention and embellishment in this field appear to have been exhausted.... As ever-greater horror is required, there is less and less that is horrible enough.... Hammer is still the only production unit concentrating on class horror films. Like its past successes, *The Man Who Could Cheat Death* has nothing foolish about it. Sangster's intelligent screenplay is directed seriously and straight by Terence Fisher. The cast responds with alacrity. The trouble is as a straight story it does not have enough about it to keep it consistently or intermittently interesting. And there's not enough horror to compensate."

The British *Monthly Film Bulletin* was always much harsher on Hammer films than almost any American reviewer, and they gave *The Man Who Could Cheat Death* their lowest rating, usually reserved for films of the like of *Frankenstein's Daughter.* The *MFB's* attitude toward Hammer has always seemed infused with a kind of reverse nationalistic pride; their point of view seems to be that Britons just can't do this kind of thing well. The unnamed reviewer said the film "offers little in the way of entertainment beyond bizarre Paris backdrops ... and Doctor Bonner, who supplies the horror by periodically turning a hangover green. Otherwise, the film crawls from one ingenious absurdity to the next until it reaches its inevitable and portentous close – the usual sadistic set-piece, with the monster burned alive as the heroine is rescued."

More recently, Bhob Stewart in *Castle of Frankenstein* had some words of praise: "Eschewing heavy sentiment and romance element of [the original film], Hammer's remake is in moodier Victorian period ... but this one's livelier, sensational under topnotch Hammer treatment with characteristic fine performances, particularly Anton Diffring as lead." British Alan Frank (*Horror*) found it a "surprisingly lacklustre Hammer effort, more talk than terror."

Over the years, many have found that the Hammer films do not wear well. (I disagree.) They looked splendid when they were new, especially inasmuch as they came along in a period when American fantastic films were running out of steam. Certainly compared to other films of the same year, such as *Return of the Fly, Monster of Piedras Blancas* and *The Cosmic Man, The Man Who Could Cheat Death* looks opulent and adult. While it still has some virtues to offer, today the film looks somewhat dead and dreary.

The Man Without a Body

Have I got a film for you. If you, like me, occasionally enjoy outrageously bad films which have ludicrous premises, you're bound to find *The Man Without a Body* of interest. But please don't spread it around; it's almost worthy of being lumped in with such now-notorious films as *Plan 9 from Outer Space, Attack of the 50 Foot Woman* and *Cat-Women of the Moon,* but let's keep this one just for us, and prevent it from being appropriated by the trend-followers and the pseudohip. It is astonishing, however, and has continuity by the one and only Splinters Deason. Unfortunately, it's very slow going.

This little-known film is set in London. American industrialist Karl Brussard (George Coulouris at his most monomaniacal) is quickly established as vulgar (we see him first in his pajamas), envious (he rips out a phone on hearing of another's success), tyrannical (curt to underlings) and egotistical (gazing at an X ray of his own skull, he sighs rapturously, "Beautiful, the brain of Karl Brussard!"). However, this tycoon has problems. He's afflicted with double vision and a ringing in his ears (answers three silent phones in increasingly angry succession: "Hello?" slam "Hello?!" slam "Hello!" slam). To his great horror and dismay, Brussard learns he has an incurable, fatal brain tumor.

He approaches American scientist and expert on disorders of the brain, Dr. Phil Merritt (Robert Hutton, playing the entire film with raised eyebrows, as well he might). He wants to brain-scan Brussard, to read his brain waves. Merritt's been experimenting with brains, decapitating monkeys and keeping their little heads alive sitting on tables, staring wildly around the room with a sense of loss.

And some room it is, too. It's a lab with lots of bubbling noises, a beautiful female assistant, Jean (Julia Arnall), a handsome male assistant, Lew (Sheldon Lawrence), one of those disembodied monkey heads on a table, organs in jars, and, mounted on a wall disc, an eyeball which gazes balefully at Brussard when he enters.

Brussard learns that Phil has not only been reviving the heads of dead monkeys, but that sometimes these monkeys have been dead for months, even years. Brussard is at first incredulous. "Restored a dead monkey's head [to life] after six years?"

"Revitalized the tissues," Phil explains less than illuminatingly.

Brussard becomes obsessed with finding a new brain to replace his own diseased one. What's that you say?

Here's where the most peculiar aspect of this peculiar film comes into play. Apparently William Grote, who wrote the film, believes either that personality resides elsewhere than in the brain, or that it can be imposed quickly from without, making the new person exactly the same as the old—and that there would be a continuity of consciousness. Wow. Brussard hopes to persuade some new brain that *it* is Karl Brussard, so when it is transplanted into his body, everything will go on as before. Perhaps Grote is wiser than I suspect, and all this is to indicate that Brussard has bats in his belfry, that his mad scheme could never work. But the film doesn't play that way. This is the most cockamamie view of the mind, consciousness and personality that I have ever seen in a movie. It compares quite well with the views on thoughts expressed in *Fiend Without a Face*.

Brussard, whose mistress Odette (Nadja Regin, very hammy), is out cheating on him all the time, decides to shop for a new brain. Phil tells him that brains can be made to function even after centuries (Grote also seems to have odd ideas about the shelf life of soft tissues), and that even a brilliant brain could be made to change its way of thinking, its personality. He says the body of a strong, alert circus monkey with the transplanted brain of an ordinary monkey would at once do the tricks that monkey's body had learned. Sure.

Brussard prowls through Madame Tussaud's Wax Museum, and eventually comes upon the historical character he thinks is best suited to his needs: the Sphinx of France, as the guide says among a long string of descriptions, Michel de Notre-Dame, Nostradamus.

Nostradamus (1503–1566) was a French physician, astrologer and clairvoyant of the 16th century still famous for his many mysterious predictions, published in his lifetime, which he wrote in the form of quatrains. Interpreting them liberally and imaginatively, some of his "predictions" seem to be accurate, but most regard this as a coincidence. It's something of a mystery why the makers of *The Man Without a Body* decided upon Nostradamus as Brussard's ideal choice, as little is made in the film of Nostradamus' powers as a seer, the only reason he's remembered today. Perhaps someone associated with the film recalled the short subjects made by MGM from 1938 to 1953, in which the prophecies were dramatized.

Brussard hires former scientist Dr. Brandon (Tony Quinn) and has him go to France to steal Nostradamus' head from its crypt. He delivers the shriveled, bearded head to Phil, who is singularly incurious about its origin. Brussard says the "donor" is unknown, unmourned, so Phil goes to work reviving it, testily telling the impatient Brussard that "this is a scientific laboratory, and we don't work on a timetable."

After a lot of fussing around with the head, and some illicit hanky-panky between Lew (Phil's assistant) and Odette, the head revives. "It's alive!" cries the ecstatic Brussard. "My brain! It's alive!"

The head comes to, speaking English. Phil and Jean sit around telling the head, which is perched on a table like one of those monkey heads, about the wonders of modern technology. Eventually Nostradamus tells Phil who it is, or was, or something, but no one does much about this astonishing revelation for some time.

In the meanwhile, Brussard closets himself with the head and argues. "Your name is Karl Brussard!" the tycoon growls.

"I am Nostradamus," claims the head, and back and forth they wrangle, Brussard trying fruitlessly to convince another man that he is not actually who he believes he is, but is instead the very person who is doing the arguing. Is that clear? The scientists pay little attention to this.

Lured on by Odette, Lew tries to kill Nostradamus, but the French prophet talks him out of it, saying that he, Nostradamus, will take care of Brussard in his own way. And he does. Believing in Nostradamus' powers of prophecy, Brussard makes major investments based on what the head tells him, but since Nostradamus was lying, Brussard is ruined. When he realizes that Odette has been working against him (inexplicably, all things considered), Brussard strangles her with her own jewels. He then chases Lew through foggy London streets and shoots him. Lew's body is delivered to Phil, who sagely notes that the "cranial nerves have been severed."

In the meantime, Brussard sneaks in and vengefully shoots Nostradamus right in the equipment, and sneaks out again. Presented with the dilemma of Lew dying for want of a head, and the head of Nostradamus dying for want of a body, Phil makes the obvious decision, and transplants the prophet's head onto Lew's body.

The result—referred to in the pressbook as the Monster—is a bizarre-looking creation, with the face of Nostradamus completely surrounded by plastered bandages, in a tall, cylindrical shape. One source described it as looking like a man with a wastebasket on his head.

The Frankenstein–like Monster shambles out of the lab. It has gone mad, and has neither Nostradamus' nor Lew's mind (nor Brussard's, for all his arguing). Brussard chases the Monster through London streets and up stairs in an old tower. They struggle, and Brussard falls to his death. The Monster topples too—but the freshly-transplanted head is caught in a handy noose, and is jerked off Lew's body, which crashes to the floor near Jean and Phil. The last thing we see is the head, still in its shell of plaster, twisting slowly in the rope.

If this film was something other than ponderous and boring, it would be a true delight, and one for the collector's shelf, but it drags itself from scene to scene, and except for those with patience and a taste for the bizarre, it borders on the unwatchable. The murky photography by Brandon Stafford is uninteresting and highly variable, Harry White's sets are drab (except for that inexplicable eye in the disc), and other production credits the same. The film isn't even second-rate.

Except, of course, for its admirably outlandish storyline. A mad industrialist tries to convince a 400-year-old living head that *it* is *him*. It's too bad the film is so grim, because if directors W. Lee Wilder and Charles Saunders had showed anything like a sense of humor, the film could have been a minor screwball classic. But it's just a glum aberration, though fascinating on a certain level.

Neither of the codirectors have had impressive careers. Wilder (Billy's brother) also made *Killers from Space*, *Phantom from Space* and *The Snow Creature*, all in the SF genre (covered in Volume 1). His other films, including *The Great Flammarion* (1944), *Manfish* (1956) and *Bluebeard's Ten Honeymoons* (1960), are also "low-budget oddities," as Leslie Halliwell puts it. Unlike the sardonic wit of brother Billy, W. Lee has shown only a few signs of a thick, leaden humor, and never in his genre films.

Charles Saunders began his career as an editor as early as 1930, and began directing in 1944 with *The Tawny Pipit* (codirected with Bernard Miles). As with Wilder, few of his films are memorable, tending toward minor crime titles: *Dark Interval* (1950), *The Black Orchid* (1953), *The Scarlet Web* (1954), *Danger by My Side* (1962). His only other genre film I know is *Womaneater*, also included in this volume.

I have no idea how (or even if) Wilder and Saunders divided up the directorial chores. I suspect, but have no proof, that either one began the picture and the other finished it, or one directed interiors and the other exteriors. It's also possible that Wilder directed the whole film, but that British union or other regulations required a British director to be given co-credit. This is only speculation, however. In any event, the films of Wilder on his own seem slightly better-paced than *Man Without a Body*, while *Womaneater* has the same thick, gummy pace.

The acting is neither nonexistent or terrible or, in the case of Coulouris, so far over the top as to make it hard to imagine that the actor (who got his start in *Citizen Kane*) took the proceedings seriously. Hutton and Arnall wander through the film without any sense of involvement. He in particular seems distant from all that happens, perhaps feeling contempt for the picture. If so, he seems to have done little to disguise this attitude. Nadja Regin is almost the equal of Coulouris in her hammy outrageousness, but in her case, it seems due to a lack of ability. Her part is so pointless and empty that she can go without much notice, even at her scenery-chewing peak.

As Nostradamus, Michael Golden has little to do except poke his head through a hole in the table, and talk. He's so heavily made up that the actor's own features are not visible. Golden has turned up, walking and beardless, in other films, such as *Murder, She Said* (1961). He probably completed all his work as Nostradamus in three or four days, as many of the shots of the prophet's head are of a dummy cranium, obviously not Golden.

The film strains so for horrifying effect, and is so preposterous in the first place, that it begins to take on an almost surrealistic feel. This is heightened by the fact that only Brussard and Odette seem to have any interest in what's going on; the rest of the characters seem like zombies, giving the film a dreamlike mood which certainly must have been unintentional.

Reviews of the film are scarce. The *Monthly Film Bulletin* had a low opinion of it. "This remarkable shocker piles its horrors up with such extravagant bathos that it finally achieves an almost surrealist quality of absurdity. Script, direction and playing are banal and amateurish; while a new foreign actress, Nadja Regin gives a performance of joyous inadequacy, quite in keeping with the general atmosphere."

Don Willis (I) felt that "fancy directorial touches" were "wasted on a story which reaches awesome heights of ludicrousness." I didn't spot any fancy directorial touches myself, but it is certainly ludicrous. In *A Heritage of Horror*, David Pirie also found the film "a particularly ludicrous piece."

The Man Without a Body is rarely shown today. No wonder.

The Monster of Piedras Blancas

On the California coast somewhere between Morro Bay and Big Sur lies Piedras Blancas (white stones), a flat, uninteresting area that's also desolate and eerie. It would make an admirable locale for a ghost story, and the ghosts would be interesting—nearby is San Simeon, the celebrity-haunted castle of William Randolph Hearst. Yes, Piedras Blancas is an ideal locale for a tale of terror. *The Monster of Piedras Blancas* was filmed at Point Conception, not Piedras Blancas, probably because the lighthouse wasn't right, and there's no nearby town. *The Monster of Point Conception* conjures up images altogether too outré for a little film like this.

The film opens with establishing shots of the "Piedras Blancas" area, and we see an enameled pan snatched from view by clawed hands. Nearby, lighthouse keeper Sturges (John Harmon) warns away some trespassing fishermen; Sturges is clearly aware of what lurks down there in those rocks.

When a couple of decapitated fishermen are found in a boat after a storm, townspeople suspect that Sturges knows more about the deaths than he lets on. Constable George Matson (Forrest Lewis) assists in putting the bodies in cold storage in the general store managed by gossipy Kochek (Frank Arvidson), who mentions the local legend of a monster living near the lighthouse.

Back at the store, Doc Jorgenson (Les Tremayne) is amazed to find that the dead men have been decapitated by something as sleek and sharp as a guillotine blade. (This odd detail doesn't jibe with the appearance of the monster's hands.) Once again, Kochek brings up the legend of the Monster of Piedras Blancas.

Sturges' daughter Lucy (Jeanne Carmen) has been dating biologist Fred (Don Sullivan), and she tells of her father's hatred for the world. Years earlier, Sturges' wife died when he was forced to tend the light, and a doctor refused to come to the lighthouse in a storm.

After a midnight swim, during which she's watched by the (as yet) unseen monster, Lucy tells her father she overheard heavy breathing, which alarms him.

Back in town, the monster raids Kochek's store, killing him. He is found the

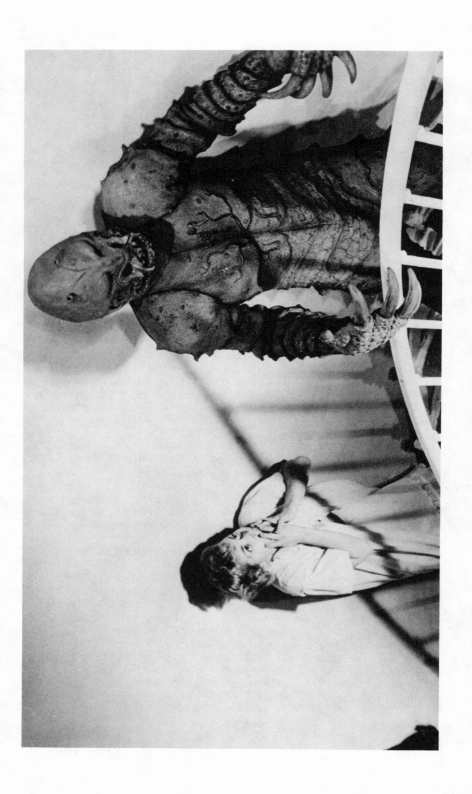

next morning by crippled little Jimmy (Wayne Berwick, son of the director); a claw (or something) of the monster is also found. Later, a little girl is killed, and a man (Eddie Dunn) left to guard Kochek's corpse is beheaded. (It is unclear as to just what the monster wants with the heads; perhaps he regards them like big nuts, hard to crack but with good stuff inside.)

Finally, Matson sees the monster, and it's traced to a cave, where the guard's head is found. The monster attacks, and kills one man while injuring another. Jorgenson and Fred want to capture the monster alive for a zoo or something, while Matson wants to kill it.

Back at the lighthouse, Sturges, who's been injured in a fall, reveals to Lucy that not long after his wife's death, he encountered the monster in the caves below the lighthouse, and began leaving it scraps of food. (Why the monster begins attacking when it does is unexplained; it starts before Sturges is injured.)

The monster turns up at the lighthouse, smashes into Lucy's room, and carries her off. From the top of the lighthouse, Sturges bangs it on the head with an oil can, and it roars up the stairs after him. They have a confrontation at the top of the lighthouse, and the monster hurls Sturges to his death.

By this time, Fred has arrived, and while he is backing around the circular top of the lighthouse, waving a gun at the monster, he tells Lucy to turn on the main beacon. The light blinds the monster, and when Fred clubs it with the gun, it falls off the lighthouse tower to its death.

Jack Kevan had been one of the major figures in the makeup department at Universal-International for many years, but was rarely credited for his work because of studio policies. But since his apprenticeship at MGM, where he'd worked on the extensive makeups for *The Wizard of Oz* (1939), Kevan was involved with many significant and famous makeups and costumes. Along with Millicent Patrick and a few others, Kevan was responsible for most of Universal's best-known monsters of the 1950s, including the Creature from the Black Lagoon, the Zenomorphs from *It Came from Outer Space*, the Mutant from *This Island Earth* (the head of which was based on a rejected Xenomorph design), Eddie Parker's Hyde face in *Abbot and Costello Meet Dr. Jekyll and Mr. Hyde*, James Cagney's various makeups in *Man of a Thousand Faces* (1957), the ape-man in *Monster on the Campus*, and so forth.

At this point, it is very difficult for outsiders to determine precisely who was responsible for the actual design of these memorable beasties. Over the years, I've heard different names mentioned, most frequently Patrick and Kevan. It's probable that Patrick worked on the designs in both sketch and sculpting, and that Kevan took over the actual creation of the masks and makeups.

Certainly the design of the Monster of Piedras Blancas isn't as interesting or as logical as those for the 1950s Universal monsters, although it is well-constructed. (Indicating Kevan's long suit was not design, but long suits.) The Monster, Fred speculates, is in the "diplovertubron" family, and was "created at the bottom of the sea." An amphibious "mutation of the reptilian family," he deserves comparison with the Creature from the Black Lagoon, the Gill-Man. And on the basis of reasonableness, the Monster doesn't measure up to the Gill-Man. The Creature, of course, is unlikely, but has an overall logic: to protect against water, the eyes are shielded and glassy; it has a mouth like a

Opposite: At the climax of The Monster of Piedras Blancas (1959), the title beastie (Eddie Dunn) heads up the stairs of a lighthouse, followed by a scared Jeanne Carmen. Notice that the Monster has an unlikely head and the hands of a Mole Person.

frog, and no nose at all; there are highly visible gills; the hands and feet are webbed. While it plays hob with any known ideas of adaptability to water, it has its own logic, and is such a plausible design that creators of amphibious monsters, whether for comic books, films or TV, have to work hard to make their monsters *not* look like the Gill-Man. It's that persuasive and compelling and logical.

On the other hand, the Monster of Piedras Blancas seems to be designed solely to be *scary*. It follows no obvious logic, and while individually its various characteristics may seem plausible, and though it's well-designed in that all its body parts seem to hang together (though it has the Mutant's feet and the hands of the Mole People), it completely misses on the basis of amphibious monster logic.

The Mole People hands are large and clawed, fine for digging through the ground, but lack dexterity and are ill-suited for swimming; the Mutant feet are even worse, just being large pinchers. The head is preposterous. It has inexplicable stubby little horns, huge flared nostrils (in a sea creature?), and a mouth which, though full of sharp teeth and inclined to drool, seems to be incapable of being opened: there are two extrusions from the upper lip which are fastened to the lower. It's a monster, all right, and certainly ugly—but it does not make sense. And when that happens, a monster is likely to be greeted with laughter rather than shrieks, or even bemused acceptance—and it will never be rated as a classic. Eddie Dunn enthusiastically plays the monster *and* a victim.

The film itself is even less successful. The plot line rests on a major absurdity: that this lighthouse, so easily accessible and picturesque, is not overrun with sightseers. If it had been, the monster would surely have been frequently seen, not to mention caught and put in a zoo. The Gill-Man, of course, was found in the Black Lagoon, way up the Amazon, isolated from civilization. He was given a past as well as a present, and hard to find. To place a monster, with no adequate explanation as to origin, on the busy coast of California, is ludicrous. The Gill-Man is a primordial mystery; the Monster of Piedras Blancas is a plot contrivance.

Jack Kevan and Universal-International dialogue coach Irvin Berwick formed a partnership under the company name VanWick Productions. *The Monster of Piedras Blancas* was intended to be the first of five films for VanWick; I have been unable to determine if they ever made any more under that company name. Working from a script by himself and Kevan, Berwick produced and directed *The 7th Commandment* (1961); he and Kevan wrote the original story for *The Street Is My Beat* (1966), and Berwick again directed. He also directed *Strange Compulsion* (1964), but Kevan's name does not appear in the credits. By 1967, Berwick was back working as dialogue coach at Universal.

Scenarist Haile Chace acted in a few films in the 50s and 60s, and wrote and directed *V.D.* (1961). He, too, was a dialogue coach on several films in the 1960s.

Even if well-directed by Berwick, which it is not, *Monster of Piedras Blancas* would still be dreary, because it is so perfunctory and unimaginative. The storyline seems peculiarly clumsy; the lighthouse keeper feeds the monster, but lacks any real motivation. He's also afraid of the monster, so he sends his daughter away. Except as a "legend," no one knows about the monster, which suddenly decides to start ripping heads off. Can't this thing fish? Or even raid the icebox? When it finally grabs the heroine, rather than lunch, it seems to regard her as a girlfriend (though like the Gill-Man, it clearly lacks the right equipment for rape).

For such a decent actor, Les Tremayne finds himself at times in the most hopeless films; his SF work ranges from a high of *War of the Worlds*, in which he was sharp and efficient as the general, to a low of *Creature of Destruction* (1967), the remake of *The She-Creature* (1956) which is, if possible, even more turgid than the original. Tremayne was also in *The Monolith Monsters*, *Angry Red Planet* and *The Slime People* (1963); he was everything the part required in each of these films (and perhaps a bit more than was necessary in *The Slime People*). Tremayne is also frequently used in animated cartoons as a voice. He's so expert at what he does that it's too bad he's never risen above the status of a little-known character actor. He's even good in *Monster of Piedras Blancas*, with a dispensable role.

In fact, *Piedras Blancas* is generally well-cast. John Harmon, the lighthouse keeper, was in films at least from 1938 through 1968. He's a dedicated, professional actor, giving his all every time up. He's a familiar face without a name attached, the fate suffered by so many good Hollywood character actors. Among Harmon's other films are *Union Pacific* (1939), *Brute Force*, *Monsieur Verdoux* (both 1947), *Run for the Hills* (1953) and *Funny Girl* (1968).

Like Tremayne, Forrest Lewis had an active radio career. He plays a policeman in *Piedras Blancas*, a role Lewis often had, and he was perfectly suited for his cop roles. He also appeared in *Francis Covers the Big Town* (1953), *The Sheepman* (1958), *The Shaggy Dog* (1959), *Red Line 7000* (1965) and *Skin Game* (1971).

Juvenile lead Don Sullivan was briefly in something resembling demand during this period. He also starred in *Teenage Zombies* and *The Giant Gila Monster*, in which he was allowed to sing several songs. Oddly enough, and very unusual for horror-movie male ingenues, Sullivan was not at all a bad actor. However, he vanished after 1962.

Reviews were not favorable. Fred W. Fox in the Los Angeles *Mirror-News* considered it a "slow-moving and unwieldy melodrama (except for its opening scenes) [which] points up again how difficult it is to make a good screen thriller."

Charles Stinson of the *Los Angeles Times*, thought that "C. Haile Chace's script is fairly free from gross verbal clichés and from gross inaccuracies, but it is turgid with conversation.... Berwick's direction [is] too slow to maintain suspense."

Don Willis (I) dismissed it with a terse "not much," and Joe Dante in *Castle of Frankenstein* #19 showed a certain kind of sardonic enthusiasm: "One of those 'so awful that it's good'; C-budgeters.... Funniest scene [is one in which] the hero throws a rock from the lighthouse and hits the monster (who's a mile down the beach) right on the head." (Not the hero, not a rock, but otherwise accurate.)

Monster of Piedras Blancas has a surprisingly detailed but unsophisticated monster suit, several decent performances and some moderately interesting location photography. But the plot is muddled, erratic and silly, and the pace is slow and talky.

However, it sometimes seems as though every monster movie has its adherents, and *The Monster of Piedras Blancas* isn't alone. To begin with, it was apparently awarded "The Shock Award" by Forrest J Ackerman's *Famous Monsters of Filmland* magazine. I presume that the distributor of the film paid *Famous Monsters* publisher James Warren* something for the right to use the

---

*No, repeat no relation to me. His real name is Hymie Taubman.

name of the magazine in advertising. However, inasmuch as the name of the magazine is wrong on the posters, it's doubtful that this did either the movie or the magazine any good. (In fact, Ackerman received a few outraged letters from fans who went to the movie on what seemed to be his recommendation.)

The greatest praise the film received was in *The Monster Times* #18 (31 December 1972). After a sarcastic, insulting lead by the editors, writer David Stidworthy tried his best to demonstrate his affection for the film. "This Monster and his sleeper vehicle left an indelible inner terror on me comparable to the world's first look at the face of Lon Chaney's Phantom of the Opera, acclaimed for years as the single most horrifying scene in the long history of horror," Stidworthy said. He praised director Berwick for introducing the monster gradually, rather than "letting the Kevan monster parade all over every scene; ...first a claw, then an arm, followed by its silhouette gliding across ... walls— saving for last the Monster's face, salivating and horrendous, at the door of Lucy's room."

Stidworthy concluded his love letter to *The Monster of Piedras Blancas* with what I find to be a touching and charming example of childhood affections carried over into later years. (I *should* find such thoughts appealing; this book is founded on mine.) "All in all, the movie is a beautifully crafted 'cult' picture although my personal admiration for this showcase for Kevan's Krowning Kreature is largely psychological.... *The Monster of Piedras Blancas* is always the [movie] I think of when my mind sifts through the hundreds of horror movies I have seen and the question is raised to me 'What's the scariest one you ever saw?'"

The Mouse That Roared

The science fiction elements of this film are slight but they're there. There's a fearful bomb, the Q-bomb, the focus of much of the action, and of course it is political science fiction in that it deals with a war which the United States loses. The victorious nation is the tiny (and fictional) Duchy of Grand Fenwick, which sends a task force of 20 longbowmen clad in chain mail to attack the United States. To their surprise, they win.

How this came about: Since 1430, the Duchy of Grand Fenwick has existed in the middle of Europe (in Leonard Wibberly's mind). It was founded by an Englishman, and still has English as its mother tongue. Its one major source of revenue lies in profits from the export to the United States of its wine, Pinot Grand Fenwick, but now profits have been almost wiped out by sales of a California imitation, Pinot Grand Enwick.

Prime Minister Count Mountjoy (Peter Sellers) calls a council meeting and, for once working with Benter (Leo McKern), leader of the opposition, persuades Grand Duchess Gloriana (Peter Sellers) to declare war on the United States. They don't expect to win, of course; in fact, they count on losing. Mountjoy points out that "There is no more profitable undertaking for any country than to declare war on the United States—and to be defeated." After all, the Americans are almost guiltily generous to defeated countries: "They pour money into the country of their former enemies and do anything to save the people they've beaten."

Grand Fenwick hasn't been to war in several centuries; the army consists of a group of volunteer bowmen, led by Hereditary Field Marshal and Grand Constable Tully Bascombe (Peter Sellers), who would really rather be a forester. However, despite a load of physical infirmities, Tully agrees to cross the Atlantic in a seagoing tug with the longbowmen and invade New York City—finding someone to surrender to as soon as possible. Gloriana sets the stage by sending a polite declaration of war, but it's regarded as a joke by the U.S. State Department—they've never heard of Grand Fenwick.

Tully and his men sail into Manhattan, and march up Wall Street, looking for someone to surrender to. However, there's no one around—everyone is underground for an air raid drill. Tully misreads a map and winds up at the laboratory of Professor Kokintz (David Kossoff), a great scientist who has just perfected the Q-Bomb, capable of wiping out an area of 2,000,000 square miles. Tully is ecstatic, Grand Fenwick will have not just a bomb, but the bomb of all bombs—and heads back to the tugboat with his men, Kokintz's attractive daughter Helen (Jean Seberg), Kokintz and the Q-Bomb. Along the way, several New York policemen mistake the bowmen for Martians, so Tully and his men round up the cops as well as General Snippet (MacDonald Parke), the stiff-necked officer in charge of the air raid drill.

Back in Grand Fenwick, Mountjoy is furious at Tully. By now, the United States has learned that Fenwick has the Q-Bomb, and has surrendered. Tully was not supposed to win the blasted war, he was supposed to lose it. Now, representatives of all the world's powers are knocking at Grand Fenwick's gates, anxious to make a deal.

Mountjoy and Benter are determined to snatch defeat from the jaws of victory, and offer to help Helen, the cops and the general escape with the bomb. However, Tully has fallen in love with Helen, and Mountjoy has forgotten to help Kokintz himself escape, so Helen refuses to go—but Mountjoy runs off with her.

Tully, still seeing his country as a great victor and wanting Helen, chases after them, and there's a silly scene of Tully running around a field with the football-shaped bomb.

Eventually, Mountjoy concedes victory. Tully ends up with the bomb and the Americans agree to withdraw Pinot Grand Enwick from the market. But Grand Fenwick refuses to return the Q-Bomb; instead, they set up a United Nations of *small* countries to maintain stewardship of the bomb. After all, it's the small countries who have the least to gain in starting a war and the most to lose if the giant nations start batting atomically at one another.

After all this has been settled, Tully and Helen notice the jolted bomb making strange noises, indicating it's about to detonate, but the bomb is a dud. Later, a little white mouse that has made a nest in the bomb crawls out unseen.

To everyone's surprise, The Mouse That Roared did very well in the United States, earning over two million dollars on its first release, prompting a sequel, even more science fictional in nature, The Mouse on the Moon (1963), but it wasn't as interesting. In Britain, on the other hand, the film was not at all successful; despite the presence of Peter Sellers, then building a major following, and despite being loaded with what Americans thought of as typical British humor, Britons tended to regard the film as too provincially Yankee and more than a little silly. It was, after all, based on a story by an Irishman long living in the United States, and was produced and directed, as well as financed, by Americans. It was British only in the cast.

The film was based on the novel of the same name by Leonard Wibberly.

By the time he died in 1983, Wibberly had written at least 100 novels, several of which dealt with Grand Fenwick. The idea for *The Mouse That Roared* originated in an editorial Wibberly wrote for the *Los Angeles Times* when he was a staff writer. The novel was serialized as *The Wrath of Grapes* in *The Saturday Evening Post*. It remains by far Wibberly's most famous book.

The oddest aspect of the production was the choice of a director. Bypassing various Britons who would have seemed ideal for the material, or even Americans who had worked in British comedy, producer Walter Shenson chose, of all people, Jack Arnold. The same Jack Arnold who'd become famous for his science fiction films in the 1950s, *Creature from the Black Lagoon*, *Tarantula*, *The Incredible Shrinking Man*, and so forth. As it turned out, Arnold did a satisfactory job on *Mouse*, playing some of the comedy scenes far too broadly, but maintaining a decent pace and keeping things lively. The major success of the film resulted in an abrupt change in Arnold's career. With the semiexception of *The Lady Takes a Flyer* (1958), Arnold had never directed a comedy before — but his next several films were all comedies, *Bachelor in Paradise* (1961), *A Global Affair*, *The Lively Set* (both 1964) and *Hello Down There* (1969). And he became the resident director of the slapstick TV series, "Gilligan's Island." He appeared as an actor in John Landis' *Into the Night* (1985), sort of a comedy itself.

Almost everyone connected with *The Mouse That Roared* did better work elsewhere. Though it's a bright, sunny picture and the scenes of the bowmen in New York are funny, mostly Arnold is not up to the material, which is slight in the first place, and has no ending. Peter Sellers here seems uneasy playing multiple roles, and impressed few with his performances; Duchess Gloriana is a caricature, Tully is a standard schlemiel-hero, but there's more life to Mountjoy: Sellers really seems to enjoy playing such a nasty type. Jean Seberg is pretty and pert but shallow as Helen. David Kossoff and Leo McKern probably fare the best of the leads (most of whom are Peter Sellers, after all).

Sellers was better in his other three films released in 1959: *Man in a Cocked Hat*, *The Battle of the Sexes* and *I'm All Right, Jack*. He had two more years of yeoman leads before *Lolita* and *Dr. Strangelove* made him a major star.

Reviews of *Mouse* were mixed, but mostly favorable. Americans were amused by the satire directed at American generosity/obliviousness (how many other countries could lose a war and not notice for a while?). Also, political satire, even if broad and comic, was very rare in the 1950s, so the film came as something of a surprise. Americans have always been magnanimous when it comes to affectionate satire of their country; it's when the satire gets critical that Americans wince angrily.

Time was more or less charmed, noting the film avoided "the narrative trap" of the ending, "but in the process its tail end is somewhat mangled. Up to that point, though, the Roger MacDougall–Stanley Mann script is a fairly witty example of a rare film form: political burlesque. It keeps the show bouncing along despite a director ... and a star ... who have not mastered the light-fantastic style that suits and supports this sort of flimsy British whimsy."

Newsweek mostly concurred. "This charming movie is the sort a group of very talented friends might make on weekends, an easygoing fairy tale that succeeds by not pushing too hard."

Jack Moffitt thought the film might not succeed because of its satirical intent, and seems to have been slightly sour on its subject himself, pointing out that "the audience" at the preview laughed a lot. He himself thought that "in a comic strip sort of way, the picture is pretty good."

John McCarted in the *New Yorker* felt that "Mr. Sellers is competent in each of [his] assignments, but the picture, after a fairly amusing start, runs down badly."

Saturday Review regarded things a little more seriously: "Funny though the film may be – and some of its sequences are downright hilarious – there is no doubt that its makers are kidding in earnest…. Topical comedy is too rare upon the screen today for us to demand of this one a fully practicable answer to questions beyond the grasp of even our most astute politicians. It is enough that *The Mouse* restores to comedy its tonic purpose of puncturing political and militaristic shibboleths, and exposing to healthy laughter some of the more ridiculous aspects of these over-cautious times."

Wibberly's former newspaper's reviewer heartily disliked the film, in a minority opinion. Geoffrey Warren said that the film "laid an egg." While the idea "offers a most wonderful opportunity for satire," the film failed to respond to the opportunity. "There is a desperate, frantic struggle made by all concerned to put across as many knee-slapper laughs as possible…. As it is, one is inclined not to laugh at all…. The direction, by Jack Arnold, is heavy handed, but no more so than the other elements of the production."

Americans responded to the film's good-natured ribbing, and mostly didn't mind that it ran down in the second half. Pauline Kael spoke for most: "The film abandons its small, amusing idea and goes off on a wearying tangent about a scientist with a big bomb and an ingenue-daughter, but it was hugely and inexplicably popular." Its success really wasn't so inexplicable: it was a moderately funny, modest little picture about something very unusual. That it didn't answer the questions it raised is of little importance. It was a surprise.

The Mysterians

Although fantasies had long been popular in Japan, it wasn't until the late 1950s and the aftermath of *Godzilla* and his ilk that science fiction films in the American mold began to emerge from Toho and other Japanese studios. The first to be released in the United States that did not center around a city-smashing monster was *The Mysterians*, a lively, colorful epic which is a bit incoherent and, to Western eyes, more than a little silly.

In Japan, the title was *Chikyo Boeigun*, which translates as "Earth Defense Forces," about as good a title as any, but not gaudy enough for American purposes. The film was acquired by RKO for American release, but the U.S. distribution arm of that company folded before the film could be released. Various studios took over the already-purchased RKO films, including Universal, Warner Bros., Allied Artists and others. MGM, apparently hoping for something like a follow-up to *Forbidden Planet*, took over *The Mysterians*, ad campaign and all. (In England, it was still listed as being presented by RKO, though Rank distributed it there.)

The ads for *The Mysterians* were very cartoonish and seem to have come from art prepared for the Japanese release. The appeal was not, to say the least, to the sophisticated, so the simple cartoons probably didn't turn anyone away who might enjoy this ripsnorting, disaster-laden opus.

The film is difficult to synopsize adequately, because so much happens, but a synopsis is also almost beside the point, because very little of what

happens really matters. In this film, the message is the spectacle, and the plot is the battle.

In a Japanese village during a harvest festival, astronomer Ryoichi (Akihiko Hirata) seems troubled, perhaps because he doesn't really have a reason to be there. A fire starts in a forest near the village, a strange blaze in which the flames rise from the bases of the trees. Ryoichi tries to stop the villagers from extinguishing the flames.

Elsewhere, scientist Dr. Adachi (Takashi Shimura) is explaining to an audience about the Mysterioids, a "group of small stars between Mars and Saturn." A chart shows us that he's actually referring to the asteroid belt. He says that the small chunks of rock were once a planet.* Reporter Atsumi (Kenji Sahara) is prominent in the group listening to the lecture.

When reports of a massive earthquake come in from the village where the forest fire took place, the scientists and reporters rush out there, staring in amazement at the devastation. "It's as though everything was put in a big washing machine and whirled around," someone says, gazing at the ruined miniature landscape. Although they note many dead fish and much radioactivity, no one seems concerned.

Then a hillside splits open and a giant, pot-bellied, pointy-nosed robot strolls out, emitting bursts of aquamarine radiation from its huge glassy eyes. The big robot, a hundred feet high or so, has spines down its back and a tail like Godzilla, and was probably played by Haruo Nakajima, who played Godzilla in almost all films featuring the big bruiser.

The robot stomps around for a while, destroying the village, wreaking havoc here and there. As it crosses a bridge, authorities blow up the structure; the robot falls into a valley and is destroyed.

Later, at the Diet Building, everyone seems very surprised to learn that it was a robot, although it hardly looked like anything else, despite its dinosaurian shape.

By this time, Ryoichi the astronomer has disappeared.

Dr. Adachi points out that something has been hiding behind the Moon, and what may be spaceships have been spotted headed towards Earth. They are traced to a lake in Japan not far from Fujiyama, and when Dr. Adachi arrives, a whirling dome arises from the ground near the lake. A voice calls out, "Attention Earth people..."

It turns out that the alien visitors are Mysterians, who originally inhabited that vanished fifth planet mentioned before. As a result of nuclear war, it was destroyed 100,000 years ago, and the surviving Mysterians emigrated to Mars. It's unclear why they waited 100,000 years to move on to Earth, but now they are here, wanting only a few acres of ground and a few dozen Earth women to mate with. Their intentions, they say, are peaceful.

Of course, that doesn't take into account the giant robot, which was anything but peaceful, but inasmuch as the whole episode of the robot seems strangely detached from the rest of the storyline, maybe the Mysterians don't know anything about it. Perhaps it was all a big mistake. In any event, perhaps

Opposite: The giant birdlike robot featured (without much explanation) at the beginning of The Mysterians (U.S. release, 1959) prepares to stomp on some of Toho's typically well-made miniatures, here spectacularly aflame.

*This was long a popular theory, but recently it has been supplanted by a new theory, that the asteroids congealed just as they are at the same time that the planets formed.

out of fear of causing the Mysterians undue embarrassment, no one mentions it again in the film.

The entire Earth is outraged at the idea of sending our young women to be the mates of aliens (which, although they all wear capes and helmets, otherwise seem human), and preparations are made to battle the "invaders." Ryoichi appears on television, clad as a Mysterian, but without the helmet, and urges his sister Etsuko (Yumi Shirakawa) to cooperate and to bed down with a Mysterian. I myself know several young women to whom such an idea would be appealing, but Etsuko is having none of it.

Battle breaks out, very colorfully too. The Mysterians shoot rays out from their dome, which melt the advancing tanks. Airplanes dive-bomb the glowing white dome, but it seems impervious to attack. While this noisy brouhaha is going on, Mysterians descend from small scout-ships, floating downward as if in invisible elevators, and abduct Etsuko and her friend Hiroko (Momoko Kochi), taking them back to the underground chamber the Mysterians have excavated beneath their dome.

Eventually, thanks to the United States, the Earth Defense Forces have developed a ray machine of their own which they call, for no apparent reason, a Markalight. These resemble huge radar dishes mounted on tank treads. They drop from the skies on all sides of the dome, advancing on it while shooting out their own variety of crackling rays.

Meanwhile, inside the Mysterians' hideout, reporter Atsumi sneaks in to rescue the heroines, and Ryoichi has finally wised up, so he too helps the young women to escape. As they flee and while the Markalights bombard the dome with rays, Ryoichi uses one of the Mysterians' ray guns to blast an important piece of equipment inside the dome, and the whole thing blows sky-high. (Around this time we see the Mysterians' faces for the first time—gaudy radioactive burns, which in 100,000 years, one might have expected to fade.)

A few Mysterians escape in their little glowing spaceships. There's an implication that the constant threat of a new invasion by the aliens will keep Earth's nations united.

The script for *The Mysterians* was adapted from Jojiro Okami's story by Shigeru Kayama; the final script was by Takeshi Kimura. In all this writing and rewriting, it seems that the scope of the picture might have been enlarged. Although the last third is a colorful display of pyrotechnics and pretty little toy-like miniatures, it all takes place on the same few acres of ground. It doesn't seem as though the Mysterians present a threat to the whole world, or even to very much of Japan. They simply sit next to a lake in their glowing dome and demand women. The fuss that follows seems way out of proportion to their apparent menace.

I suspect that when the script was first completed, there was no giant robot at all, and that it was added later to make the film more appealing to audiences which, Toho may have surmised, were expecting some kind of giant menace. As it is, the robot is interesting and spectacular, but it looks more than a little silly to Western eyes—like Godzilla in samurai armor—and has no clear plot purpose. Nor do the mysterious fires, earthquakes and dead fish. They all seem as if they were intended to be eerie harbingers of doom, or examples of what the Mysterians might do if they don't get their order of women, but there is no clear connection between them and the Mysterians.

The art direction by Teruaki Aba shows some intelligence. Although the film is as gaudy as costume jewelry throughout, there seems to be some kind of hierarchy in the Mysterians based on the color of their capes—there are blue

Mysterians and orange Mysterians. The capes are said to be necessary because of the temperature and pressure differences between the dome and Earth, but I call that a likely story. I think the capes are just decoration.

There's a credit for "special technique art direction," which probably refers to the elaborate miniatures. Inside the dome and the Mysterians' underground enclave, the complicated miniatures are designed to resemble the world of the Krell from *Forbidden Planet*. The various war machines of Earth and the Mysterians' all-purpose dome are not convincing, but are involved in action so fast and colorful that the lack of realism is of little importance; more on this later. The whole film has such an air of big kids playing with toys that the unconvincing miniatures don't harm it much.

The special effects by Eiji Tsuburaya and his staff are typical of Japanese films: brightly-colored, extravagant and showy. Many American fans of fantastic films deplore the Japanese effects, claiming that they are totally unrealistic, but that seems to be like complaining about broad acting in silent films: beside the point and missing the point as well.

The intent in every Japanese fantasy film that I have seen is *not* to duplicate reality, but instead to present attractive, exciting imagery, sometimes bordering on the poetic and evocative, but not really to make it look as though it is really and truly happening, the goal of *all* American special effects in SF films, and in most fantasy films. In Japanese films as varied as *The Lost World of Sinbad* (1964), *Son of Godzilla* (1968) and *Demon Pond* (1980), the special effects are colorful, extravagant and detailed—but not realistic in the American sense, even when they could be.

Some American effects technicians were hired for a very expensive Japanese SF film called *Virus* (1980), an attempt at creating a truly international product. (The cast includes Glenn Ford and Chuck Connors.) To the surprise of the Americans, most of their painfully-wrought realistic effects were cut from the film—because the Americans did not understand what the Japanese wanted, and the Japanese did not understand what they would get when they hired Americans.

In almost no Japanese visual art is there an attempt to be "realistic" in Western terms. It is simply not a concern, and to complain about a lack of realism in Japanese art is inappropriate. American effects-laden films are popular in Japan because the effects are attractive not because they are *convincing*, which is what Americans have been "taught" is the primary goal of special effects. What American fantastic film fans are stumbling over is a convention in *American* art that is not present in Japanese: realism. Although *The Mysterians* is a hell of a long way from being art, this still applies: you must appreciate it as a *Japanese* science fiction extravaganza, or you must let it alone. To complain that it does not meet American standards of realism is being culturally jingoistic. My associate Bill Thomas suggests that it's like complaining about people suddenly bursting into song and dance in a musical: it goes with the territory. I am making no defense of the movie's quality, only trying to suggest an explanation as to why Japanese fantasy films always look so peculiar to some Americans.

As far as the film itself goes, it's entertaining enough. The story is mostly an excuse for miniatures shooting off rockets and rays at each other. There's a slight attempt at something like maturity in the handling of the Mysterians, with the air of atomic tragedy that hangs over them, but this is compromised by the big robot and the actions of the turncoat Earth scientist.

In the face of all the razzle-dazzle of rays, tanks, planes, Markalights and spaceships, acting and direction matter little. Takashi Shimura is the face best-known to American audiences. There are those who remember him as the dour, kindly scientist of *Godzilla* and similar films, and there are those who recognize him from his frequent appearances in Akira Kurosawa's films, such as *Ikiru* (1952) and *The Seven Samurai* (1954): he had the lead role in both. Those of us who know him from both worlds are always a little bemused by the wide disparity in the films in which he appeared. He was under contract to Toho, and appeared in whatever role he was appropriate for. He died in 1982.

Director Inoshiro Honda, who was Toho's specialist in science fiction and monster films, does try a few interesting ideas here and there. A woman spots the giant robot while she's bathing in her room; she sees its head over the top of some nearby trees. This has both a comic and a surprisingly creepy effect, the gigantic Unknown intent on its own business parading along behind the leafy Known. But for the most part, Honda primarily just keeps things moving, at which he was very good.

Reviews were mixed. The *Monthly Film Bulletin* rightly pointed out that "the film's main weaknesses are a slight and confused plot, underdeveloped characterisation and artless acting; its strength lies in its imaginative art direction and spectacular staging, in which respect it is possibly the most dazzling display of pyrotechnics in the *genre* to date."

Gene Gleason in the *Herald-Tribune* was patronizing but pleased. "Followers of science fiction and interplanetary stories should have a very enjoyable time.... The process shots in the battle action are executed with great skill, and the sky shots of missiles, saucers and jets have a strange, fatal kind of beauty."

On the other hand, Howard Thompson in the *New York Times* viewed *The Mysterians* with a disgruntled and grumpy eye, referring to its "routine footage of death rays and scrambling civilians, not one of whom can act," and regarded the whole picture as a "mess."

Jack Moffitt was much more favorable, as he often was to space and monster extravaganzas. "The early sequences have a stunning shock impact the later footage unfortunately is unable to top." The film is taken over by "the hokey clichés of Buck Rogers comic strips," he felt, and by the end is "getting the wrong kind of laughs." But found an odd area to praise: "Whoever supplied the English voice of the space leader attained a vocal masterpiece in propaganda-smugness and hypocrisy."

In the *Los Angeles Times*, Charles Stinson, who genuinely liked SF movies, considered *The Mysterians* "science fiction in the grand manner."

Castle of Frankenstein #19 said it featured "way above average [special effects] in [a] shallow Japanese space opera [and] spectacular production [that is] poorly dubbed." Alan Frank (*SF*) found it "short on plot and continuity and high on special effects and spectacle with Eiji Tsuburaya's model work a distinct plus." *Psychotronic* said, "[L]ots of massive destruction and good special effects make this an all-time favorite."

The film proved reasonably popular worldwide, and so Toho immediately produced *Battle in Outer Space* with much the same crew. However, for those who came first to *The Mysterians*, as I did, it will probably remain the ultimate example of flashy Japanese science fiction.

On the Beach

When it was released, *On the Beach* was treated as if it were something approaching the most important event in (at least) film history. Linus Pauling was quoted, "It may be that some years from now we can look back and say that *On the Beach* is the movie that saved the world." It generated peculiar but mostly favorable reviews and much controversy. There were those who considered its nuclear-war-is-bad message as being defeatist and anti–American; others carefully pointed out, while missing the point, that if fought with the weapons available in 1959, nuclear war would not in fact destroy all life on Earth, as it does in the film.

Seen today, after the fanfare has long since quieted, the film has turned in its profits, and the actors and filmmakers have done other, more significant films (in some cases), *On the Beach* looks much like any other Hollywood movie of its time, somewhat better acted than most, certainly much better photographed than anything else released in 1959, but just another Hollywood movie. It has some telling moments, but the major thrust of the story seems to be to answer the question of whether Gregory Peck will finally wise up and hop into bed with Ava Gardner before everyone croaks of radiation poisoning.

The movie is pompous and trivial at the same time, overwritten and insufficiently tense. It isn't half the film *Dr. Strangelove* is; though that's a comedy, it's more powerful in its effect than *On the Beach*. And small, intimate *Testament* (1983) is more personal; *The Day After* and *Special Bulletin* (both 1983) are more immediate. Even *The World the Flesh and the Devil*, also out in 1959, is more haunting in its opening scenes than anything in *On the Beach*.

The tag "science fiction" wasn't just avoided for *On the Beach*, few at the time even thought it might be SF. I mean, here was an expensive movie, shot on location in far-off Australia, starring Anthony Perkins, Ava Gardner, Fred Astaire and Gregory (my god) Peck, how on Earth *could* it be science fiction? Of contemporary reviewers, only Jack Moffitt recognized that it was indeed a science fiction tale, and even he quickly dodged past the idea. (He was much more concerned with the fact that people in the film hadn't achieved the placid acceptance that they were all going to Heaven.)

Today, *On the Beach* is usually not just regarded as SF, but rather *tame* SF. Nonetheless, as can be seen from the number of atomic cataclysm films released or in the planning stages as I write (June, 1984), the message of *On the Beach* is as timely today as it was in 1959, when it seemed urgent. (A remake was announced but by fall 1985, none of these planned films had materialized.)

Nevil Shute's above-average novel, *On the Beach*, was published in 1957 and became an immediate worldwide success. It seems highly likely that the great success and fame of the novel, more than its message, led to its being filmed. Not that filmmaker Stanley Kramer wasn't taking a chance; he had, in a loose sense, built a career on taking chances.

In terms of a discussion of his career, Kramer's a hard man to get a grip on. He seems almost a joke today, but it's unquestionable that he was a daring producer early in his career; he made, mostly, serious dramas on timely topics, and made them work as films. He was of course aided by good directors, actors, and writers, but films like *Champion*, *Home of the Brave* (both 1949), *The Men* (1950), *Death of a Salesman* (1951) and other early works, seem more clearly the work of Stanley Kramer than of the other creative people involved.

These films were successful enough that he signed a contract with Columbia Pictures in the early 50s, and then, on all but two of his Columbia films, proceeded to lose money. (The two exceptions: *The Caine Mutiny* and *The Wild One*.) Now, some of those films are cult favorites, such as *The 5,000 Fingers of Dr. T*, but they were box-office poison at the time, and he and Columbia parted ways in 1954.

In 1955, Kramer turned an abrupt corner, apparently but not definitely out of financial need. Not only did he begin directing his films, but many were based on popular novels or plays, and generally were not as hard-hitting or topical as the earlier Kramer films: *Not As a Stranger* (1955), *The Pride and the Passion* (1957), *Inherit the Wind* (1959), *Ship of Fools* (1965) and, of course, *On the Beach*. The films that weren't based on popular novels were based on popular *themes*; instead of pioneering in treatment of ideas, Kramer found ideas that were current and filmed them. *The Defiant Ones* (1958) brought up The Race Question just as American culture was beginning to be concerned about it; *Judgment at Nuremberg* (1961) dealt with the question of the Holocaust; *Guess Who's Coming to Dinner?* (1967), Kramer's last really successful film, suggested that perhaps if a black man and a white woman were to get married, the world would not crumble. It was considered daring that the film was a comedy.

But since 1960, most of Kramer's films have been tepid comedies, romances or thrillers. He tried to tackle campus unrest in *R.P.M.* * (*Revolutions Per Minute*) (1970), but didn't have a clear perspective; casting Ann-Margret as a campus protester, when she was still in her kitten-with-a-whip phase, indicates a certain concession to the box office. *Bless the Beasts and Children* (1971) and *The Runner Stumbles* (1979) are hackneyed treatments of artificial themes.

Kramer retired to Seattle, puzzled and introspective. The world had shifted position around him, and he was now in the rear guard, not the leader. To his credit, he seems to be aware of his many shortcomings. He's an intelligent man who probably got caught up in Hollywood's gears; he cannot be counted out.

It's perhaps ironic that of all his films, the one most frequently shown on television is the elephantine, bloated *It's a Mad, Mad, Mad, Mad World* (1963), an unpleasant epic and unfunny comedy shot in Cinerama. His best film as director, *Inherit the Wind*, good because of fine acting and the fact that it's irresistible theatre, isn't shown half as often.

The marketing strategy for *On the Beach*, orchestrated by Kramer and distributors United Artists, in retrospect seems blatant and manipulative. The company and the producer-director were clearly worried that the film might be considered downbeat, too serious, even scary, so it was turned into An Event— the one film you *must* see, literally how it was sold. The ad copy read, "If you never see another motion picture, you must see *On the Beach*." In advertising for the United States, the atomic-disaster theme was soft-pedalled; it wasn't even sold as a big-cast film, but instead by the use of that line, UA and Kramer tried, as *Variety* put it, "to create the impression that *On the Beach* is the single most fashionable picture to see." There isn't a clear indication that they tried to tell the public that the picture was so important you had to see it, just that to be up-to-date, you needed to see it. This seems to have worked. It made $5,000,000 in the United States alone.

The same *Variety* article (21 October 1959) said UA planned to sell the film differently overseas. "UA's foreign representatives stressed that it would be a mistake to try to circumvent the theme in appealing to foreign audiences who are more attuned to so-called 'thinking entertainment' and who seem to be more concerned about atomic warfare than Americans."

To drum up favorable word-of-mouth, the film was screened for "opinion makers" around the world. In the Los Angeles *Mirror-News*, Dick Williams expressed his annoyance about UA's thinking that Americans were unconcerned about atomic war, "but I am inclined to think these movie boys know what they are doing." He reported that among the "opinion makers" the film had been screened for in the Los Angeles area included "leaders of the Democratic and Republican Parties, clerics, members of the county medical association, business agents and secretaries of labor unions, community leaders in the field of human welfare, legislators on the federal, state and county level. At one showing, a group of high ranking Air Force officers [was] combined with members of the Los Angeles and Hollywood SANE Committee against nuclear explosions.... In all, showings for some 25 groups—from PTA leaders to Nobel Prize winners are being held in the Southern California area.... [This approach] has been tried on a limited scale with other films, but never so extensively before."

As the grandest gesture of Importance, the film was premiered on 17 December 1959 in major cities around the world, including Amsterdam, Berlin, Caracas, Chicago, Johannesberg, Lima, London, Los Angeles, Madrid, Melbourne, New York, Paris, Rome, Stockholm, Tokyo, Toronto, Washington and Zurich. This list (from trade papers) omits one world city in which the film was also premiered: Moscow. Because the film doesn't lay blame on any nation for the end of the world, it was ideologically safe and apparently well-received in the Soviet capital.

If you were anywhere in the world in 1959 and didn't hear of *On the Beach*, it was not the fault of United Artists and Stanley Kramer.

The film was in black and white, of course; color wasn't serious. Set in 1964, it begins after a nuclear accident or war (never specified) has sent a cloud of radioactive fallout slowly covering the globe. So far Australia has not been affected, but soon will be; there is simply no hope. It's all up, not just for mankind, but for all life on Earth.

American nuclear submarine *The Sawfish*, commanded by Dwight Towers (Gregory Peck), arrives in Melbourne; they escaped death by being submerged when whatever happened, happened.

In Melbourne, we also meet Peter Holmes (Anthony Perkins), an Australian naval officer whose young wife Mary (Donna Anderson) has recently had a baby. Towers and Holmes meet at a party, where bitter scientist Julian Osborn (Fred Astaire) talks about the war or whatever it was. It was due, he says, to "a handful of vacuum tubes and transistors." Julian, whose hobby is racing powerful cars, is especially bitter because he helped develop the Bomb.

At a beach party given for him by Holmes and his wife, Towers meets attractive, hard-living Moira (Ava Gardner); they are strongly attracted to one another, but Towers still clings to the forlorn hope that his wife and family might be alive in Mystic, Connecticut.

The government has been issuing suicide pills for those who wish to avoid the lingering, painful death by radiation poisoning that will otherwise be their fate. Holmes acquires some for his wife and baby, but she's horrified, and accuses him of wanting to murder the child.

Scientists suspect that by now rains may have washed the atmosphere in the Northern Hemisphere clean and that life may be possible there. In fact, they are picking up indecipherable radio signals from San Diego, perhaps an indication of life. *The Sawfish* is sent north to investigate, and Holmes and Julian go along.

They begin in Seattle and head south, but nowhere is there any sign of life. When the sub passes under a deserted Golden Gate Bridge (did the cars disintegrate?), Yeoman Rob Swain (John Meillon) becomes distressed, as Frisco is his hometown. He leaves the sub via the emergency escape hatch, and swims ashore.

But everyone is dead, and he will be soon. He's floating alone in the harbor, fishing fruitlessly from a little rowboat. The sub's periscope abruptly surfaces beside him, and he talks to Towers via radio. (This scene is unexpectedly funny, although it's unclear if that was the intent.) Swain wishes to die where he lived, and bids his shipmates farewell.

The sub heads for San Diego. One man goes ashore in a radiation suit to investigate the radio signals, and finds a Coke bottle caught in a window shade; the bottle is resting on a telegraph key—the power is still on—and the wind bounces it up and down, accounting for the signal. That's it friend, it's all over.

Aboard the sub, Julian says the war was really begun by Einstein, but adds that "the wars started when people accepted the idiotic principle that peace could be maintained by arranging to defend themselves with weapons they couldn't possibly use without committing suicide." Amen, brother, amen.

The Sawfish returns to Melbourne. While on vacation with Moira, Towers finally decides to allow himself to love her in the time they have left. Moira and Julian are former lovers, and she and Towers go to see Julian and other drivers in a fierce, no-holds-barred auto race, in which no one cares if they live or die. Julian wins, then returns home; in his garage, he sits in his car, revs up the motor, and dies from carbon monoxide poisoning.

Finally, even Brisbane in northern Australia is dead, and it's merely a matter of days for Melbourne. Holmes convinces his wife to take the pills with him, and to give one to their baby; they die in their bed at home. His crewmen wish to return to the United States to die at home, so Towers bids farewell to Moira, and departs in the sub. She stands on the shore watching it leave.

Final scenes are of deserted streets in Melbourne; a sign seen frequently in the film, "There Is Still Time ... Brother" (presumably meaning there is still time to find God) flaps loosely in the wind, an ironic comment on the death of mankind and a Krameresque message to All Of Us.

Directorially, *On the Beach* is simple and straightforward. It's also flat and unimaginative. The only attempts to go beyond simple reportage are melodramatic errors. When the ship surfaces in San Francisco to peer through the periscope at the convincingly dead city (great care was taken in the selection of shots), each seaman aboard first peers through the scope then slaps the handles upward in a gesture of angry resignation, the clanging sound of the handles forming a rhythmic punctuation. But all it *is* is punctuation; there's no conceivable reason for all of the men to do exactly the same thing. It becomes comic instead of dramatic.

When Towers finally abandons his hopeless hope that his family may still be alive and decides to enjoy his relationship with Moira, they are in a hotel. Behind them drunken revelers sing "Waltzing Matilda" as Peck and Gardner embrace; the camera circles around them in a 360° shot. The singers suddenly become a full-bodied professional chorus on the ghostly last verse of the song. This is intended to mirror the reactions of Peck and Gardner: they become enveloped in romance. But the effect is corny and, with that bravura circular shot, the entire scene sinks into melodramatic bathos.

In fact, the entire film seems on the verge of teetering into melodrama or even self-parody. Throughout the film, everyone is so stiff-upper-lipped and resigned that it becomes frustrating. Aren't there any rioting young people, outraged because the adults wiped out their future? Isn't there anyone, stubborn, obstinate and foolish, who refuses to accept the inevitable? Aren't there small fleets of ships headed for Antarctica? Must everyone be so ready to bravely accept doom? This aura of sad resignation overwhelms the film at times, and constantly edges toward the comic.

There are some very effective scenes scattered through the film, but few involve the main characters, other than Astaire's suicide scene, and that's most affecting because we see him as suave Fred, not as the character he is playing; seeing light-footed Fred kill himself is disquieting. Australia is now cut off from the dead world and all its fuel, so the streets of Melbourne have a few cars, but more horses and buggies and bicycles. This is heavily emphasized, detracting somewhat from its reasonableness.

Two elderly clubmen find themselves among the very last to visit daily their fine old clubroom, realizing with vexation that there's gallons of wine they won't have time to sample. We see them occasionally through the film, bickering over the wine and keeping a porter busy fetching it for them. Near the end of the film, the two old men are gone, presumably dead, and only the porter is left, sipping the wine and playing pool alone. The lights go out.

Also through the film, we see Admiral Birdie (John Tate) and his aide, pretty young Lieutenant Hosgood (Lola Brooks); cornily, it's clear to us (and no doubt to them) that they have been in love for many years, but neither dares say anything about it, due to military protocol and personal shyness. They choose to take their final leave, via the government's suicide pills, in each other's company. As corny as the setup is, this is far more poignant than the deaths of Holmes and his family.

As the film progresses and more suicide pills are used—discreetly offscreen for the most part—it becomes less populated. People are dying constantly.

The scenes aboard the submarine have a realistic, documentarylike feel, and are the most believable in the film. The sequence of the exploration of the dead San Diego is spooky and almost depressing, but it's a foregone conclusion that no one will be found alive. The only mystery lies in what was making the signals.

There should have been more scenes like the crash-studded auto race. There is an attempt at a similar scene, a fishing stream lined with dozens of exuberant anglers all trying to have a last good time before the end. We see almost every reaction to impending doom except panic and fury; where are they? This reticence gives the film a dying fall, not to make a play on words; it could hardly be else, but I don't think everyone had to be so damned brave and calm.

We never see anyone die of radiation; the one person who falls ill from it exhibits no symptoms other than a fever. I am not saying that Kramer and company should have shown us suppurating wounds, hair falling out, bleeding gums, all which accompany death by radiation. But in On the Beach when people die, they must evaporate. There are no dead bodies anywhere. By the end of the film, the streets should have been lined with corpses. It is simply too tidy and too clean for its own good. Granted, the true horror of the result of atomic catastrophe isn't that everyone will die horribly, but simply that everyone will die. But Kramer makes the end of the world antiseptic.

The script for the film is by John Paxton (Michael Hayes says that James Lee

Barrett cowrote the film), a writer of minor but occasionally solid talents. His good films include *Murder, My Sweet* (1944), *Crossfire* (1947), *The Wild One* (1954) and, sort of, *How to Murder a Rich Uncle* (1957). His not-so-good pictures include *Rope of Sand* (1949), *The Cobweb* (1955) and *Kotch* (1971).

He can't avoid clichés. For *On the Beach*, Paxton actually includes a trite thanks-I-needed-that scene, in which Astaire first tells Perkins he envies him, and then to buck up and stop blubbering. And he overuses ideas: later, after the futile trip to North America, both Perkins *and* Peck enter their respective reunion scenes before the women in question are aware they're back.

The characters are uninteresting and do not develop. What we learn about them in their first scene is all we ever know. Towers has a stiff upper lip, crying on the inside but brave and military. Moira has lived a hard, fast life, but has a heart of gold, and will come through in a pinch. Julian is a bitter, failed romantic. Holmes is just Dedicated Young Love, and his wife is Refusal to Face the Obvious.

Kramer does little to help, and actors who seem to need the most help from directors in the first place, Peck and Perkins (both of whom can be excellent) come off the worst. They seem to be hollow shells of familiar mannerisms, never connecting with what reality the story has. On the other hand, Gardner, usually good, is outstanding here; she makes her clichéd part alive and real, by employing her own pantherish personality. She understands Moira, and her understanding illuminates her scenes.

This was the first of Fred Astaire's few dramatic roles, and he's very good. His part is weakly conceived, but like Gardner, Astaire fills out the empty spaces with his own talent and stylish personality. Their performances alone are almost reason to see the film.

Ernest Gold's score is not good. It's too melodramatic, too self-consciously important, and outrageously overuses "Waltzing Matilda," apparently trying to generate a popular song out of a long-standing regional favorite. It almost worked but, speaking as one who loves that song, by the end of the movie you're thoroughly sick of that jolly swagman, the jumbuck and the billabong.

But despite the many flaws of the film, it has a certain undeniable power from the subject matter alone. Despite the doubts of some, atomic extinction is an entirely real possibility. We cannot rely forever on the goodwill and good sense of those with their fingers on the button. The film does establish a sense that the world is ending, not with a bang but with a whimper (as in "The Hollow Men," the poem by T.S. Eliot that gives the film its title). The melodrama gets in the way of this repeatedly, but the film returns to that idea: everyone is going to die. The star casting heavily compromises this—we know at once that Gregory Peck, Fred Astaire and Ava Gardner can't *die*, for crying out loud, they'll be back soon. (Anthony Perkins, on the other hand, looks mortal.) The intent of the film—the ostensible intent—would have been better served if the leads had been played by unknowns or character actors.

But since the real purpose was to make money off nuclear paranoia, it wouldn't have been a success. Or so, undoubtedly, the thinking must have gone. The film seemed a chancy proposition, so it was a good commercial idea to load it with stars in an effort to get their fans out to the theatres.

When *On the Beach* was released, reviewers acted strangely. Clearly some of the critics who don't quite say so weren't really all that taken with the film. It's as if by criticizing it, you would be in favor of atomic annihilation. And of course, to a certain degree that reaction is just what Kramer and United Artists were counting on.

Furthermore, the film is not a bad example of Hollywood moviemaking circa 1959, at least on a technical level. It is photographed by the great Giuseppe Rotunno, the Italian master of cinematography (who later worked often with Fellini and occasionally in the United States, as in *Carnal Knowlege*). The photography is imaginative and intelligent, especially in the faintly grainy scenes ashore in San Diego: it's as if the radiation has affected the very film we're watching.

But the movie was not the masterpiece many were hoping for. Jack Moffitt was impressed but slightly hedged his praise. "Stanley Kramer's brilliantly executed and thought-provoking film ... is worthy of the studious consideration of every member of the public.... Both Shute, in his book, and Kramer, in his film, avoid the fantasies and extravagances usually associated with science fiction [and] avoid any head-on and melodramatic statements of the theme.... The actors are so good it's impossible to choose among them.... A review of this film would not be complete if it failed to recognize Kramer's ability to interject moments of frolicsome humor into his somber subject.... *On the Beach* maintains that the fateful decision of the 20th century is the choice between life and death.... [Isn't] the choice we are faced with the choice between eternal life and slavery? Yet none of the principal characters of Shute's book or of Kramer's film shows the slightest interest in religion or life after death." (The film does indeed avoid almost all religious overtones, probably to avoid embarrassing anyone.)

"Powe" in *Variety* described it as a "gripping, grim meller.... [A] solid theatrical film of considerable emotional, as well as cerebral, content.... The final impact of *On the Beach* is as heavy as a leaden shroud.... The real point of [the] emphasis on self-destruction [involving the use of the suicide pills] is that the conditioning that leads to its acceptance is the same fatal lassitude that allowed men the use of such dangerous weapons as the H-Bomb without aggressive opposition. Man, the story says, was doomed before he pushed the button."

Bosley Crowther wrote several pieces on the film, beginning with his review in the *New York Times*, which concluded, "The great merit of this picture, aside from its entertaining qualities, is the fact that it carries a passionate conviction that man is worth saving, after all." A month later, he commented on the "reservations" that had arisen about the film. "The acerbity with which some authorities have lashed out at this film is ... uncommonly surprising and hard to understand.... [The] curious objection [of Lt. Gen. Clarence R. Huebner, director of New York State Civil Defense] was that it fails to advise the public reassuringly that it is possible to defend against radioactive fallout— as if that were sufficient to obviate the peril.

"The next day, an editorial in the *New York Daily News* charged the film with being 'defeatist' and said it 'plays right up the alley of (a) the Kremlin and (b) the Western defeatists and/or traitors who yelp for the scrapping of the H-Bomb.'

"Senator Wallace F. Bennett of Utah proclaimed that the premise is 'dangerously misleading' because, as he said, it has been 'clearly demonstrated' that there would be many survivors even in a country subject to heavy nuclear attack!

"They serve to point up the implication of the film, which is that mankind, by haggling and wishful thinking about the new bombs, can sadly and almost assuredly stumble down the path to nuclear war."

In *The Saturday Evening Post* (23 July 1960), Stewart Alsop wrote an incredible editorial in which he claimed that "it is simply not true that a nuclear war would mean 'everybody killed in the world and nothing left at all, like in *On the Beach'* [certainly not] a technically accurate presentation of the radio-active side effects of nuclear warfare." At length, he tried to demonstrate that the film was wrong about the effects of fallout—ignoring the basic message of the film which is that nuclear war, everyone dead or not, is the ultimate disaster. He did somewhat cheerfully add, "Mind you, radiation is not a pretty thing, and if nuclear war comes, it will be no picnic."

"R.V." in the *Monthly Film Bulletin* said that "the gulf between honest intentions and commercial realisation manages to seem wider than in any of Kramer's preceding films.... The picture, in short, lacks depth, shading, above all a thoughtful and intelligent viewpoint.... The characters remain little more than spokesmen for tired ideas and Salvation Army slogans, their emotions hired from a Hollywood prop-room; which is all pretty disturbing in a film about nothing less than the end of the world.... The questions *On the Beach* raises remain unanswered; and others, as pertinent, not even asked."

While *Newsweek* called it "an extraordinary movie" and summed it up as "the year's most devastating picture, and one of the best," *Time* jauntily dismissed it as "a Hollywood vision of the end of the world ... a sentimental sort of radiation romance, in which the customers are considerably spared any scenes of realistic horror.... Aside from its sentimentality, the worst of the film's offenses is its unreality.... The picture actually manages for most of its length to make the most dangerous conceivable situation in human history seem rather silly and science-fictional.... What could any actors make of a script that imagines the world's end as a scene in which Ava Gardner stands and wistfully waves goodbye as Gregory Peck sails sadly into the contaminated dawn?"

There are still those who champion the film, although usually with reservations. In *Science Fiction Movies*, Philip Strick described it as "achingly sincere yet curiously resistible; it has an air of immaculate calm, as though nothing unusual were happening, and although one could argue that this would be precisely the effect of global catastrophe, the ugly explosions of anarchy that have been described by [some writers] read more plausibly."

In *Future Tense*, John Brosnan says, "Despite its flaws of mawkish senti-mentality and pretentiousness it remains a chillingly realistic portrayal of doom and despair in the face of an implacable force." Similarly, in *Science Fiction in the Cinema*, John Baxter said, "Like all Kramer's films, *On the Beach* is variable in style, its script sometimes over-written and marred by a tendency to reduce important issues to choices between black and white, but as an exercise in science fiction, its worth is undoubted. There is no better film on the mood and feel of atomic destruction, no fable so relevant to our own time. Technically brilliant, this film is one of science fiction's legitimate masterpieces ... a brilliant film and a moving document." *Psychotronic* said, "[M]any of us preferred to watch *The Tingler* and *The Wasp Woman*."

On the Beach is, unfortunately, a major theme in the hands of a resolutely uninspired director; at times, it has great impact, but that isn't due to Kramer, but to the basic story material. Perhaps this film *should* be remade, by someone with insight and talent in the areas of death and bleakness, but should the remake materialize, in the way of such things, it probably won't be up to the best things in *On the Beach*: the strange mood toward the end, Fred Astaire, Ava Gardner and Rotunno's majestic photography.

Return of the Fly

Apparently the magnitude of the success of *The Fly* in 1958 caught 20th Century–Fox by surprise, if not shock. The studio seemed faintly embarrassed by the picture, for many years didn't make anything remotely like it. But they were also astute enough to realize that a follow-up would turn a profit. So they farmed out sequel rights to their subsidiary, Associated Producers, though Fox allowed the film to be shot on the studio main lot.

Stuck with an extremely dead protagonist—parts of him crushed with a press, parts smashed with a rock—writer-director Edward L. Bernds had to have a different fly-headed man for the central character, despite the title *Return of the Fly*.

Peculiarly enough, Bernds seems to have ignored much of the first film; undoubtedly he saw it, but it seems unlikely that he read the original short story by Georges Langelaan. Bernds gets oddball little details wrong, and doesn't seem quite to have grasped the idea of matter transmission, which would seem to be as elementary a science fiction concept as there is: sending matter through space by electronic transmission, just like TV pictures.

A different crew was hired for *Return of the Fly*, which was made on what must have been a considerably lower budget than that of the first film. In black and white (although CinemaScope was retained), *Return of the Fly* looks shopworn and cheap, where *The Fly* looked bright and shiny. The sole returning cast member was Vincent Price, who had only recently become Hollywood's horror king.

Quoted in *Vincent Price Unmasked* by James Robert Parish and Steven Whitney, the actor said that initially the film sounded good. "The script was one of those rare cases where the sequel proved to be better than the original. When I first read it, I was very excited about the possibilities. Then the producers, in obvious bad judgment, proceeded to put in a lot of gimmicks in the belief that films needed gimmicks to be popular. In the end, they lessened and very nearly ruined the dramatic effect that could have made a truly superior picture."

In *Fantastic Films* #38, Bernds told interviewer Tom Weaver, "Vincent Price liked my script for *Return of the Fly*. He wouldn't sign to do the film until he read a script, so as soon as I had a first draft I sent it to him.... Some time later a problem came up—what Vincent read was a first draft and like many first drafts it was a little overlong, and some cuts were made to trim it down and some changes were made to bring about budget economies. Vincent liked some of the scenes we had cut, and he objected. If I recall correctly; they were mostly scenes with Danielle De Metz—scenes of warmth and charm—but, when you're pressed for footage, not truly essential to the progression of the story [you have to cut]."

Judging from the finished film, it's hard to imagine what possibilities might have excited Price. It's doubtful that his own role was all that fascinating, as it is even smaller here than it was in the first film. As it stands, *Return of the Fly* is a confused, junky picture with a few interesting sequences, and some truly grotesque horror scenes. It's fueled by coincidences and improbabilities, and although it's not unimpressive on the big screen, being very well photographed by Brydon Baker, on television it looks little different from the other cheap SF-horror movies of the period.

The improbabilities start early. Said to be set 15 years after the action in *The Fly*, the film looks like it is taking place the same year. *The Fly* itself was clearly contemporary; the producers assumed (undoubtedly correctly) that the audience for this film wouldn't care or notice that the lapse of 15 years made no changes in dress, automobiles, or anything else. It would have to be set in 1973, but that's overlooked.

The film opens with the rainy funeral of Hélène, widow of André Delambre, the Fly, and father of Philippe (Brett Halsey, who actually does resemble David Hedison, André in the first film). After the funeral, Philippe and his uncle François (Price) visit André's long-closed laboratory (another inconsistency: in the original film, the lab was in the house, but here is in the family foundry), where he portentously relates the story of *The Fly* to the shocked young man, with emphasis on the breakdown of the "molecular" structure of matter (rather than atomic, as in the first film). François has made a big mistake, however: instead of turning Philippe away from researching matter transmission, this results in his becoming obsessed with it.

In short order, we meet Philippe's fiancée Cecile (Danielle De Metz), and his British assistant Alan Hinds (David Frankham), who has been working with him for some time. Because of the ghastly fate that befell his father (which he tells no one of), Philippe acquires a shuddering fear of flies. This fear is overemphasized and seems to develop immediately. But it has a plot point to play.

After the conventional setbacks, the disintegrator-reintegrator apparatus, much less convincing than in the first film, is developed, despite the suspicions of elderly Gaston (Michael Mark). Alan says he will lure Gaston away, clearly a setup for a later murder of the old man, but we never see this, though we also don't see Gaston again.

François learns what Philippe is up to, in some time-consuming plot developments—they lead nowhere, and add nothing to the storyline. Philippe scares François off from shutting down the experiments by threatening to sell his interest in Delambre Frères, the family company.

Alan meets with sinister undertaker Max Berthold (Dan Seymour), and we learn that Alan is actually Ronald Holmes, a murderer the British are seeking. He offers to sell the secret of the matter transmitter to Big International Cartels, and Max will act as intermediary. Bernds as writer apparently assumed that this made sense; it doesn't. The money that Alan/Ronald could make from his share in the matter transmitter would be far greater than he'd get as a thief. But no matter. At one point, Philippe happens to meet Alan in front of Max's mortuary, another coincidence that exists to solve later plot problems.

Finally, Philippe and Alan successfully test the matter transmitter, and are excited enough to immediately transmit a guinea pig, but the focus is off and they end up with a huge one. They try again, and transmit and "hold" the guinea pig, intending to reintegrate it in the morning. (This is patently absurd. Where is the guinea pig's atomic structure, now in the form of electronic waves, being stored? It's details like this that nag at me. They are simply wrong in terms of what we know about the machine, and exist solely for later horror effects.)

As Alan is alone in the lab and preparing to steal interesting stuff, a British detective we've seen hanging around appears to take Alan back to England, where he's wanted for a hanging offense. The two fight, and Alan kills the detective.

Knowing Philippe will hear the commotion—the lab has been moved back into the house—Alan quickly transmits the dead body and puts it on "hold" too.

After Philippe has been mollified and leaves, Alan reintegrates the corpse, and gets a dead man with the "hands" and feet of a guinea pig, which looks pretty silly. He also gets a guinea pig with human hands (and presumably feet), which he immediately drops something heavy on. There's a horror close-up of tiny human hands protruding from beneath the heavy object as the dying guinea pig shrieks. (In one shot the rodent clearly has its own little feet.)

Alan disposes of the mixed-up bodies and returns to the lab, only to discover Philippe waiting; he's heard too much. Once again, Alan overpowers his opponent — he's a swell fighter — and tosses Philippe into the matter transmitter. (Why?) Then, out of sheer diabolical nastiness, he puts a highly coincidental fly in with him, having remembered Philippe's earlier fear of such insects. (However, he doesn't seem to know what might happen.) Just as Alan begins the transmission cycle, Philippe awakes, and realizes to his horror there's a fly in with him just before he vanishes.

Alan makes his getaway, shooting and wounding François as he does. François and Cecile come downstairs slowly, and reintegrate Philippe. Sure enough, just like daddy, Philippe emerges with the head and arm of a fly, and the foot as well. This time, instead of the fly head being in proportion to its human body, so it could have been hidden under a scarf as in the first film, the fly head is in correct proportion to a *fly's* body, and is anatomically correct (although the legs are still wrong). It's a gigantic, flattened, hairy thing, extending beyond Philippe's shoulders on either side. It looks like a Mardi gras mask.

In a highly confusing and contrived sequence, the Fly immediately escapes just as the police arrive. He runs around the nearby woods for a while, then flees.

After this absurd, almost surrealistic scene of the fly-man in the forest, he vanishes, and police lieutenant MacLish (Barry Bernard) says his men have orders to shoot Philippe on sight. Why? Was something left out of the script? At this point, he has done nothing illegal whatsoever, except not to halt when the police told him to.

Everyone marvels at Philippe's ability to get around town unobserved — he is, after all, noticeable — but he does anyway, without any explanation.

He goes to Max's mortuary and kills him. Being part fly must have made him psychic.

In the meantime, the wounded François is returned to the mansion from a hospital, having told Inspector Beacham (John Sutton) the whole sad tale of the fly-men, father and son. At the mansion, Beacham sees evidence the story is true: the (highly unconvincing) man-headed fly. He imprisons it, and in a humanitarian gesture, gives it something to eat.

Meanwhile, back at the mortuary (the time scale seems hopelessly confused), Alan arrives and is promptly strangled by fly-headed Philippe who, for no good reason, stuffs him into a coffin. Well, there's one good reason: a watchman comes in and sees Alan weakly trying to open the coffin before he dies. I suspect the coffin-lid–raising scene was included for use in the previews.

Back at the mansion, François darkly muses, "What if Philippe does not have the mind of a human, but the murderous brain of a fly?" Overlooking the confusion between mind and brain and the cosmic absurdity of the line, one can still question what makes François think flies have *murderous* brains? The insects are scavengers, after all; if Philippe did have the mind of a fly, he might be expected to be found crawling around on a pile of shit somewhere.

Instead, he appears at Cecile's bedside, and collapses from unmentioned injuries. He's escorted downstairs, placed in the transmission booth with the carefully-kept fly, and retransmitted. This time, he comes out okay. The last shot shows that the fly also is okay, in case anyone was worried. No one mentions that Philippe will probably be charged with murdering Max and Alan.

The sets are used strangely. As the film opens, we see an elaborate recreation of the laboratory from the first film (the blackboard inconsistently still reads "I love you"), but the new film's activities are set in a new lab. Why?

The editing is reasonably tight, but there are several zoom shots done in postproduction on an optical printer. This is probably because Bernds shot the film with little camera movement or any visual tricks.

The major defect in the film is the trite, unimaginative, illogical script. It merely recapitulates the ideas from the first film, cumbersomely and uncreatively. The story leans heavily on coincidence throughout, and simply avoids things that would be hard to explain—how long was Philippe a fly-man? How did he get across town *and back* without anyone seeing him? Why did he collapse at the end?

When one considers the incredible range of story ideas that spring from matter transmission treated imaginatively, the woeful thinking that went into *Return of the Fly* becomes painfully obvious. This is merely a remake of the first film, with crooks added. The new material doesn't connect in any interesting way with the basic story ideas, and seems cheap and conventional.

I suppose the idea of giving the new Fly a head in proportion with a fly's body was dictated by two ideas, simple (and I do mean simple) logic, and the idea that bigger is scarier. In the first film, there was the unmasking scene which powerfully affected audiences, producing an effect of numbing horror and lots of screams. Here, after the first "ugh" reaction, the big fly-head simply seems silly, and instead of screams, drew laughter. It's overdone, and has a vaguely comical air. The makeup is credited to Hal Lierley. The fly monster after the transformation is played by big Ed Wolff, the Colossus of New York.

The acting in the film is generally uninteresting. Price seems bored with the proceedings; his role is quite thankless and could have been dispensed with altogether. He had no opportunities for his entertainingly showy acting style to be used, and even his horror-laden speech at the beginning falls flat because of poor writing and mediocre direction. He's just telling a story.

Brett Halsey was in films as early as 1953, when he appeared in Jack Arnold's 3-D film *The Glass Web*. He had leads in some low-budget films, such as *Hot Rod Rumble* (1957), *Speed Crazy* (1958) and *Submarine Seahawk* (1959), and played small roles in big-budget films, including *To Hell and Back* (1955), *The Best of Everything* (1959) and others. In the 1960s, he went to Italy and starred in a number of swashbucklers, spy thrillers and Westerns, including *Avenger of Venice* (1963) and *Spy in Your Eye* (1965). Among his other genre films are *Revenge of the Creature*, *The Atomic Submarine* and *Twice-Told Tales* (1963). He's a handsome utility leading man, still often on TV, of no great talent or memorable qualities, and his performance in *Return of the Fly* is routine.

David Frankham is a little better as the villainous Alan, but his career never reached even Halsey's level of success. He also appeared in *Master of the World*, *Tales of Terror* (1962), *Hands of the Ripper* (1971) and even *King Rat* (1965) before apparently retiring. His oddest credit is as one of the voices in Disney's *One Hundred and One Dalmatians* (1961).

The photography by Brydon Baker is the best thing about *Return of the Fly*. For what was a low-budget film, he achieves some good, atmospheric effects, although the lab scenes have a flat, overlit look. Bernds and Baker seem more comfortable with the Gothic scenes in the forest and the mortuary.

Apparently someone thought a fly head that was in the same proportion to a human body as it is to a fly's body would be scarier, or make more sense, or something, because the eerie little head of the first film was abandoned in favor of this Mardi Gras extravaganza in Return of the Fly (1959). Ed Wolff stunt-doubling for Brett Halsey.

The Fly had a kind of personal horror; there was an attempt at making the leads characters you could care about. The monster stuff didn't start up right away, and by the time it did, you knew who these people were. In *Return of the Fly*, we are given no reasons to care about any of the good guys; we actually see about as much of Alan as we do anyone else. Unlike the grotesque but carefully developed *The Fly*, *Return of the Fly* is just another science fiction–horror movie, with only the grotesquery remaining.

Nonetheless, it isn't terrible. It's relatively fast-paced, and only 78 minutes long. The horror scenes may be contrived, but for 1959, they delivered the goods. The scenes of the fly monster stalking those who've victimized him are eerie and tense. But the film is basically routine.

Reviews generally reflected this. Although *Films in Review* thought it "a better sequel than you'd expect," and *Parents Magazine* considered it "good of kind," adding that it came off "rather well," many reviews were downbeat. "Glen" in weekly *Variety* thought it was "inept" and cautioned that "word-of-mouth will injure the film's chances ... because, with justice, it will be unfavorably compared with the first." Glen thought the film had an "amateurishly contrived plot" and that it was typical of the script that François' retelling of André's fate "should be made to seem almost banal for a lack of imaginative dialog and absense of appropriate tempo in the scene." Glen noticed plot holes and absurdities, and concluded that "without the reputation of The Fly to trade on, this one would be a dud."

As if in confirmation of this, Fred W. Fox in the Los Angeles Mirror-News was nonplussed. He had not seen the first film, and had some difficulty with the new one. "If this is what the public wants, it's easy to understand why producers of intelligent entertainment are often baffled and discouraged." (In fairness, it should be pointed out that Fox expressed hostility to science fiction in general.)

Some liked it, with reservations. Jack Moffitt thought that the film stressed "plot gimmicks at the expense of honest human values," but did conclude that "though not a classic, it is considerably better than the run-of-the-mine [sic] B horror picture." Film Daily concurred: "the sequel does quite well in the horror department [although] it lacks its predecessor's carefully and logically built up suspense and philosophical undertones."

It isn't likely that Return of the Fly was a major hit for Fox. They treated it like a second cousin, double-billing it with The Alligator People, which received equal prominence in advertising. It's almost as if the studio felt they were required to make a sequel, and then gave it as little attention as possible. The outlandish Curse of the Fly (1964) was the third and final in the series, but came several years later and bore little resemblance to the first two.

Teenagers from Outer Space

One night in 1959, I sat glassy-eyed in the Port Theatre in North Bend, Oregon, watching Teenagers from Outer Space amid a mob of howling, contemptuous teenagers from Earth. Usually, when I saw a science fiction or horror film being greeted with noisy derision, I seethed with anger, even if the film was truly terrible. I felt that the producers had probably tried to do a good job, and the noise was getting in the way of my enjoying the film to whatever extent possible. But Teenagers from Outer Space was something different; I simply didn't know a film could be that bad, and I was dumbfounded. This time the laughter seemed not only justified, but apart from leaving the theatre alto-gether, just about the only rational response.

For many years, I was convinced that this was the worst movie ever made. And then I saw it again for this book. To my surprise, not only is it not anywhere near the worst movie ever made, although it is quite bad, it has many points of interest and even some promising features. It made me curious as to what happened to Tom Graeff, the busy young man who wrote, produced, photographed, edited, did the sound and special effects for this film, and starred in it (apparently as David Love, who's billed over the title).

The script for the film is loaded with stilted dialogue, and is so peculiarly plotted that it feels like some plot elements were invented simply to make sure others came out right. Of various directorial contributions, the most visible, the acting, is uniformly weak to terrible. But there's some intelligence in the direc-tion; more camera angles are used than in most low-budget films; the camera setups and blocking of the actors show imagination; the editing is conventional but competent (except for a few surrealistic cutaways to literally nothing at all: a white blur).

Overall, as a director Graeff was no worse than many and better than some working at this budget level, and clearly a person of fierce, burning ambition. So what happened to him? Research at the Motion Picture Academy indicates he made one film prior to this, an unreleased story of fraternity life called *Toast to Our Brothers*, and nothing at all afterward.

Graeff popped up again in 1968, in Joyce Haber's column in the *Los Angeles Times*. Graeff had placed a *Variety* ad which caught the columnist's eye; it offered for sale (at $500,000) a script described as "remarkable, tensely exciting, superbly written, a spell-binding masterpiece, hilarious and chilling at once." Curious about this paragon of cinematic excellence, Haber called Graeff, and he told her the 173-page script, called "Orf," would cost $3 million to shoot, and be 2½ hours when finished, and was to be shot in Graeff's own process, Cinemagraph. Graeff claimed that (in today's terminology) Robert Wise was to executive produce this film, and that Carl Reiner was the star.

Haber contacted Wise, who denied even reading the script; Reiner admitted that he read it (and said that the plot dealt with "a man's head that's kept alive on a machine and goes to court"), and even said he might have agreed to star. But nothing more was reported on Tom Graeff and "Orf."

As far as I know, none of the people who make it a point of looking up such filmmakers as Graeff have ever located him. It's not that I miss having a body of Graeffian cinema to study, it's that it would seem that anyone with the ambition to make the film, and the sheer gall required to sell such an unfortunate project, would at least have made another one or two. But apparently such is not the case here. Maybe he went back to outer space.

The film opens in an observatory, as one astronomer, who's just seen a screw-shaped object in the sky, is gloomily observing to another, the Earth is "hanging in space like a speck of food, floating in the ocean, sooner or later to be swallowed up by some creature floating by."

That drill-shaped craft, actually quite pretty, augers itself into the ground, the hatch pops open, and a helmeted figure fires a ray gun at a passing dog, reducing it at once to a neatly-wired skeleton. (The dog is dubbed by a human being, who yells "brah! brah!")

A spaceship captain (Robert King Moody) and some militaristic, uniformed young men emerge from the ship and report on conditions. "42 saturation degrees in 96 volumes," snaps Thor (Bryan Grant). Mohr (?) adds, "Diagonal adjustment reading resisting structural forms by two point eight point zero vernums." All this seems to be what the captain wants, who orders the Gargon specimen brought from the ship.

But first, Derek (David Love) tries to talk them into not planting herds of Gargon on the Earth; he's found a dog tag among the bones, which leads him to conclude the planet has a high civilization. The others scoff; what do they care of "foreign beings"? Derek pulls a gun, complaining that he's tired of the regimented life. "We live like parts of a machine—we don't know our fathers or mothers. We're raised in cubicles. The sick and the old are put to death." (He got all this from reading a book he has with him that "escaped the flames of the annihilators.")

This is not news to the others, who overpower him, then bring the Gargon out. It is a dispirited lobster in a glass jar, but we're told that in one day, "by the elements alone" the Gargons will grow to "millions of times their original size."

Tom Graeff (right), acting under the name of David Love, is seen as the hero of Teen-agers from Outer Space (1959) as he confronts the Leader (actor unidentified) of his home planet in the sentimental climax of the film. (For one thing, the hero has just learned the evil Leader is his own father.) The beard on the Leader looks no more realistic in the film; here you can admire the keen cap pistol the teenage villain used to blast the flesh off humans. I wish I still had mine.

Gargon herds apparently provide the main source of food for these aliens.
   Someplace in here, they forget to tie Derek's hands, and he flees. The captain has just learned surprising news: Derek is the son of their Leader, who is proud of the boy, so the captain stops envious Thor from blasting Derek;

Thor is ordered to get Derek and bring him back unharmed. Meanwhile, the captain leaves to bring back the lobster fleet.

By means of the dog tag, Derek locates the late animal's owners (he can speak but not read English, but can read numbers), Betty (Dawn Anderson), a young woman his own age, and her folksy Gramps (Harvey B. Dunn), who immediately (a) invite Derek to live in their spare room rent free, (b) give him some of a departed, married son's clothes, and (c) invite him to go swimming.

Meanwhile, Thor has hitched a ride into town, belligerently forcing a driving lesson from the car's owner, whom he soon converts into a skeleton with his ray gun. He does the same to a garage attendant who had earlier spoken to Derek. Just after Derek and Betty leave to go swimming, Thor arrives and finds out from helpful Gramps where they've gone.

At the home of wealthy Alice (Sonia Torgeson), Betty learns the awful truth about her dog Sparky, and they leave to see the skeleton. Thor arrives and when Alice gives him some lip, turns her into a skeleton, too (the bones collapse into a dry ice–befogged pool).

By now, whew, Derek and Betty have checked back in with Gramps, and have headed for the university to talk to Professor Simpson. So Gramps sends Thor after them, and he gets to Simpson before they do, leaving him as another neatly wired skeleton (or probably the same one; we never see two skeletons together).

By now, Derek is convinced that Thor is after him, so Betty alerts the police, who believe her story of a ray gun–wielding maniac. Several plainclothesmen with guns (which emit scratches-on-emulsion gunfire) hide around city hall and have a dull gunfight with Thor, who turns two into skeletons before he's wounded, and hides someplace. It happens to be a car, and from there, he gets the drop on Betty and Derek. "You will take me to a man of surgery," he orders stiltedly, "to remove the metal pellets from my flesh."

Meanwhile, Betty's erstwhile boyfriend, reporter Joe (Tom Lockyear), decides to drive with a surviving cop to the abandoned mine (Bronson Caverns) where Derek correctly believes the Gargon has been incarcerated. Offscreen, where it remains most of the time, it has now grown, and eats up the cop (which makes it get even bigger), but Joe escapes in his car. Somehow, the town is alerted to the presence of a monster (never described in the newspaper we see, or by the TV newscaster) which is eating people up. Later, it eats several members of a posse.

Back at the doctor's office, Derek, the doctor and Betty escape from Thor, who passes out. However, he recovers soon and forces the doctor's nurse to drive him to the mine (I don't know why). He passes Joe, then taking over the car, chases him (I don't know why he does that, either), but goes off a hill. Thor is taken to a hospital.

Derek realizes that only Thor's ray gun, "the focusing disintegrator ray" which "projects an isolated beam which separates the molecules of living material in chain reaction" can stop the Gargon. He and Betty look for the gun after dark, finding it only when Derek picks up a rock to throw at the stealthily-arriving Gargon. (The gun was under the rock.) They flee.

At Gramps' house, Derek discovers the gun needs power; they go back to the hills, where Derek hooks the gun to some power lines, while a frantic Betty convinces a power station operator to feed all the available power into those lines. Just as the enormous lobster (played by a stiff-looking, too-dark crawfish) looms over him, Derek gets the gun to work. But he knows it is too late.

Donning his teenager-from-outer-space uniform, he gets Thor out of the hospital, forces a disappointed Betty to drive him back to the cave, where he leaves her, Gramps and Joe behind as he and Thor meet the arriving auger ship, which this time bears the Leader (in a phony beard). Confirming that the Leader's death will lead to a democratic revolution back home, Derek pretends cooperation and locks himself in the ship, directing the oncoming fleet of lobster transports to smash into the Earth, with himself, the Leader, Thor and the others at ground zero.

Betty sadly recalls that Derek did live up to his promise: "I shall make the Earth my home, and I shall never, never leave it." A phantom image of martyred Derek is seen against the cloudy sky.

Teenagers from Outer Space was filmed as "The Boy from Another World," and was also called "Invasion of the Gargon" before release. In England it was *The Gargon Terror*, but no name change could have helped the dreary little picture. The most unusual aspect of the film, apart from the title, was that it was distributed by Warner Bros., one of the most prestigious studios in Hollywood. It went out as a companion with *Gigantis the Fire Monster*.

Films like this are something of a mystery. It's clearly an amateur effort, yet just as clearly was intended for commercial release. But it is so badly made that it's hard to imagine on what basis Graeff was able to sell it.

The strange idea of using an animal as familiar as a lobster as an *alien* menace, as well as giving it a name so similar to "gorgon" indicates that Graeff was either very naive himself (he's clearly not truly stupid), or thought his audiences would be. I presume Warners was merely looking for an already-made film to send out as a double-bill monster-movie package, but then chose to exploit the teenage aspect of the film rather than use a giant lobster as a come-on. This was probably a wise decision.

Graeff's dialogue is hopeless; it's banal for the human beings—"Somehow I feel that I've always known you," Betty says to Derek—and stilted, pompous and ponderous for the aliens, except for Derek. Most of it is perfunctory and exists only to further the busy but aimless plot.

One of Graeff's strangest conceits is that all of this, from the landing of Derek's ship to the (offscreen) destruction of the lobster transports, takes place in *one day*. Even the captain's ship leaves Earth, picks up the Leader (who is clearly established as having been on the home planet) and returns to Earth, all within a 24-hour period. With ships as fast as that, you'd think they would have conquered the galaxy long ago.

Apparently for commercial considerations, Graeff includes trite elements such as a guy on the lookout for the Gargon who's seen swigging gin and reading a science fiction book. The romantic developments border on the mystical, which is not a bad idea—as it takes place in one day, something has to happen to speed things up. But in all cases, the characterizations are stereotypes; Joe the reporter keeps his Tyrolean hat clapped on the back of his head, carries a big camera bag, but looks more like Jimmy Olsen than Clark Kent.

He shows considerable imagination as a cinematographer; there's a nicely-staged and inventively-shot scene in which Thor returns to Gramps' house with gun drawn; the camera moves with confidence and intelligence. Later, as Derek faces down the Gargon, the final camera setup is designed for maximum scary impact, diminished considerably by the fact that the monster is (a) altogether too dark, and (b) a lobster anyway.

One aspect of *Teenagers from Outer Space* impressed me without reservations: the spaceship the teenagers arrive in is unique. I don't know of any other movie in which the spaceship screws itself into the ground like an auger.

Graeff's props are, well, obvious. The dreaded focusing disintegrator ray is played by a large shiny cap pistol popular in the 1950s (I had one), which says "Buck Rogers" on the side. The proud name is visible in 35mm prints of the film.

Only Harvey B. Dunn seems to have been a professional actor at this time, and *he's* little more than competent. When I spend more time noticing that a performer has a missing finger than I do in watching what he's doing, then I can assume his performance isn't involving. Dunn also appeared in *Bride of the Monster*, *Sabrina* (1954), *It's a Dog's Life* (1955), *Desire Under the Elms* (1958) and *The Remarkable Mr. Pennypacker* (1959), among other films. Though *Teenagers from Outer Space* isn't the pinnacle of Dunn's career (one hopes), he does have his largest film role here.

The only actor in *Teenagers from Outer Space* who began here and went on to other films seems to be Robert King Moody, the spaceship captain. Among other films, he appeared in *The Rotten Apple*, (1963), *The Glass Cage* (1964), *Any Wednesday* (1966), *The Destructors* (1968) and *The Strawberry Statement* (1970).

"Ron" in *Variety* found positive elements in the picture: "While Graeff may not have made a good picture, he has made an interesting one that every now and again smacks of brilliance. Several scenes—e.g., a sequence of youngsters peering wide-eyed at their first spaceman—are composed of an artistry that marks Graeff as a filmmaker to be heard from."

On the other hand, Jack Moffitt said, "Technically, there haven't been many films of this sort since the days of the nickelodeon. The acting ranges from bad to no acting at all.... Tom Graeff's production constantly struggles to overcome the disadvantage of his own bad direction which, in turn, is gravely handicapped by a script written by himself.... Now that monkeys have been trained to successfully execute space flight, it is to be hoped that they can be induced to collaborate on an improved science-fiction."

Charles Stinson in the *Los Angeles Times* was bemused. "What a really curious little film this is. Its plot is rambling; its extreme low budget insures a thoroughly sleazy quality of photography, costume and prop. And though the direction is all right, ninety per cent of the script is either stereotyped 'action talk' or portentous, badly stilted attempts at motivation or romance."

Teenagers from Outer Space was greeted with gales of laughter from the teenagers it was intended for; the poignancy of Derek's sad but brave fate was lost on the crowd, and well it should be. The film indeed has almost nothing to recommend it. It is silly, ponderous and trite, but occasionally there are glimmerings of an intelligence real enough that I'm still curious as to why Tom Graeff seems never to have made another film.

Terror Is a Man

Despite an intriguing title, this lesser film is primarily notable for being the first Philippine–made horror film to be released in the United States. Although somewhat slow, it is surprisingly well-done, and is probably the best such film from that area. It's derived without acknowledgment from H.G. Wells' *The Island of Dr. Moreau*; the number of beasts-turned-into-men has been reduced from a jungleful to just one; nonetheless, the origin of the story is obvious.

Wells' novel had been filmed twice before, once in France during the silent era (see the entry on *Mysterious Island*), and once, with great success, as *The Island of Lost Souls* (1933). It was filmed yet again in 1977, under the title of the novel; the latter version had a stellar cast (Burt Lancaster, Michael York), color, and expensive makeup, but was nowhere near as good as *Island of Lost Souls*. In fact, it wasn't even as good as *Terror Is a Man*.

A boat drifts slowly ashore on a small Philippine isle known as Blood Island; it bears the only survivor of an explosion at sea, American Fitzgerald (Richard Derr). The dazed man is found by Dr. Girard (Francis Lederer) and his assistant Walter (Oscar Keesee), and they take him back to Girard's lavish home.

Fitzgerald is nursed back to health by Girard's lonely wife Frances (Greta Thyssen) and two servants, young houseboy Tiago (Peyton Keesee) and his older sister Selene (Lilia Duran). As he recovers, Fitzgerald learns that Girard gave up a lucrative medical practice in New York to isolate himself on Blood Island; this has led to estrangement between Frances and Girard. She and Fitzgerald fall in love.

We see a strange, bandaged form kill a few natives; then all the natives (lots of them) rush to canoes and paddle away en masse.

Fitzgerald discovers the abandoned native village on the island, as well as a number of fresh graves nearby. He becomes uneasy, and curious as to Girard's activities. This curiosity is aroused further when he sees Girard and Walter laying traps for some large animal.

Frances tells Fitzgerald that Girard is attempting to recapture a large panther* which has escaped from his laboratory. The scientist has been conducting surgical experiments on the animal; even though Frances is a nurse herself, she has become sickened by the beast's screams of agony. So far, there have been over fifty operations on the big cat, and more are planned. (The fresh graves are villagers killed by the beast in its occasional escapes.)

Frances begs Fitzgerald to help her escape from Girard, and to return to civilization. He agrees.

After the animal is recaptured, Girard encounters Fitzgerald poking through papers in the doctor's study, and being arrogantly proud of what he is trying to do, tells him the end goal of the experiments. The operations, so painful to the animal, are designed to surgically transform it into a human being. Girard is delighted with his progress; already the man-beast (Flory Carlos) has begun to walk upright, and soon will be able to speak. Girard invites Fitzgerald to observe the next operation, one of the less painful. The creature is at all times wrapped like a mummy.

While Frances is alone in the laboratory with the man-beast strapped to the surgical table, the constantly-complaining Walter enters and attacks her. The man-beast tries to free itself to help her, as she's one of the few to show it any kindness, but the straps prevent this.

Fitzgerald and Girard argue the next day about the wrongness of the scien-

---

*Actually, "panther" is a general, nonscientific name for any of several large cats, usually when they are in a melanic, or all-black phase, like the one in the film. Black leopards, jaguars and (rarely) cougars (pumas) have all been called panthers at one time or another. Since it seems unlikely that the writer of Terror Is a Man knew this, and assumed that "panther" referred to a specific big cat, it's impossible to determine just what kind of big cat the subject of the experiments is. However, a leopard seems most likely, considering the story's locale. The photo seen of the cat "before" is no help. The genus Panthera refers to all big roaming cats. Pedantry lives.

tist's experiments, and the usual phrases are bandied about: playing God, unwritten rules, etc. Girard is basically unruffled; when Fitzgerald declares that the operations won't succeed anyway, Girard shows him that the creature can say one word: "man."

Walter returns to the lab, and the man-beast breaks loose and attacks him, but Walter sets the beast's bandages afire and all three men recapture it.

Frances tells Girard that she's in love with Fitzgerald and is leaving the island. While she's alone upstairs with Fitzgerald, the man-beast breaks loose again, kills Walter, and flees into the jungle.

It tears the bandages off its hands and face at this point; the hands still have claws, and the remarkably good facial makeup is very catlike. (There seem to be two different makeups, one with huge fangs, one without.)

Fitzgerald and Girard head into the jungle to search for the creature, but it ducks back to the house, kills Selene and captures Frances, carrying her off. Fitzgerald and Girard pursue the monster to a conveniently high cliff, where it gently puts Frances down, then attacks Girard, throwing him off the cliff to his death.

Fitzgerald shoots the creature several times. Tiago, who lost both mother and sister to the animal, takes the wounded, staggering thing to a small boat. The animal-man is presumably carried away by the currents, one of the most unusual endings for a monster film of the period. (But, like the rest of the film, not original in concept: it comes from the novel *Frankenstein*.)

Francis Lederer, who played Girard, was born in Czechoslovakia in 1906, and by the late 1920s, was a matinee idol in Berlin. He appeared in G.W. Pabst's *Pandora's Box* (1929), and in 1932 came to the United States. Because of his sensuous good looks and elegant accent, Lederer soon became popular as a romantic lead and/or continental seducer. His range was broader than that, though, as he ably showed in *Midnight* (1939), but by the early 40s, his popularity, never great, had begun to wane. He continued to make films, though they were of less importance; among his later films were *The Bridge of San Luis Rey* (1944), *Captain Carey, U.S.A.* (1949) and *Lisbon* (1956). In 1958, he played the most notorious continental seducer of all, Count Dracula, in the pretty good *Return of Dracula* (also known as *Curse of Dracula*). *Terror Is a Man* was his last film. He has continued to be active in Los Angeles civic affairs, and was involved with one of the several Hollywood Museum projects. (He doesn't seem to be connected with the one that finally resulted.) He's remained wealthy from extensive real-estate investments.

His part here seems to be a typical mad scientist; Girard is arrogant, self-involved, brilliant and ruthless. However, these characteristics are softened, made less sinister, because of Lederer's personal charm, and he really *isn't* a mad scientist. He's an above-average actor, and reads his lines with more conviction than most; the obsession of Girard seems both real and possessed of a kind of rationality. His goal of turning an animal into a man seems singularly pointless, but Girard clearly believes in it.

In other films, Fitzgerald's origin would make him seem shady, but the shipwreck is merely a device of getting him onto the island with no immediate way off again. His poking and prying are dictated by exigencies of the script, rather than arising out of his personality. Fitzgerald is merely the hero, our spokesman. He doesn't even really play a part in the action of the story; things would have happened about as they do even if he'd never arrived. It's Walter's attack on Frances that triggers the climax; Fitzgerald is just a bystander, and someone for Frances to turn to.

Richard Derr has been active in Hollywood since the early 1940s. He's slender and mildly handsome, but lacks a strong screen personality; as a result, despite being a decent enough actor, he rarely plays leading roles. Among his few are his three genre films, *Terror Is a Man*, *Invisible Avenger* and *When Worlds Collide*. He's still active today, appearing on television and from time to time in a feature film; for instance, he was in *The Drowning Pool* (1975) and *American Gigolo* (1979).

Greta Thyssen was a utility leading lady in minor films at this time, unquestionably beautiful, she's also somewhat stiff and inexpressive, and in recent years has disappeared from films. She also appeared in *Bus Stop* (1956), *Shadows* (1959), *The Double-Barrelled Detective Story* (1965), a semi-experimental film based on a Mark Twain story, and *Cottonpickin' Chickenpluckers* (1967), not an experimental film. Her other genre movie was *Journey to the 7th Planet*, in which she was a figment of John Agar's imagination.

Director Gerry de Leon, more frequently billed as Gerardo de Leon, is fairly busy in the Philippines. He's directed several types of films, but specializes in overheated, lurid monster tales, such as *Blood Drinkers* (1966), *Brides of Blood* (1968), its sequel *Mad Doctor of Blood Island* (1969), and *Curse of the Vampires* (1970). Although none of these films could be called good, they do have some flashes of eccentric imagination and a certain understanding of what's really scary. (However, the vicious butterfly in *Brides of Blood* was probably a mistake.) Nonetheless, each film is steamy, outrageous and silly.

In *Terror Is a Man*, working from Harry Harber's script, de Leon manages to generate an eerie atmosphere; perhaps working in black and white kept him from employing the kind of bizarre visuals that turn up in his later pictures. In any event, *Terror* is relatively restrained and imaginative; if anything, it is too reticent for some. (Don Willis (I) called it "silly and slow.") Most of the horror comes in the last reel.

A gimmick was used in promoting the film: a bell was sounded at certain presumably scary points in the film, allowing those of nervous disposition to hide their eyes. Though the storyline allowed gruesome sights, they are infrequent in the picture. In prints on TV, there's only one such shot, a throat incision.

The reviews were mildly favorable. The genuinely pleased Saul Ostrone in the *Motion Picture Herald* considered it "a solid attempt ... both exciting and technically creditable [despite occasional] gory footage.... Harry Paul Harber's screenplay is reasonable and provocative." (The only other credit for Harber I've located is another Philippine–made film, 1964's *The Kidnappers*.)

Film Daily also liked it. "A mood of evil broods over [the film] and the fans will be easily pleased. There are some novel story turns that flare with excitement though the story is a bit slow in unfolding."

Howard Thompson, the jumpiest reviewer in motion picture history, was even more impressed. In the *New York Times*, he said, "[W]ith a fairly familiar plot, this ... is quiet, sensibly restrained and quite terrifying.... The well-photographed little picture is chillingly suggestive until a climax that almost made one reviewer tear off a chair arm."

The film had several different working titles, including "Beast from Blood Island," "Creature from Blood Island," "The Gory Creatures" and perhaps others. The title finally used is evocative, vague and poetic, elements certainly absent from the titles of most low-budget SF-horror movies. It's a shame that it was retitled *Blood Creature* when reissued in 1965 by Hemisphere, in an effort to tie it to the *Brides of Blood/Mad Dr. of Blood Island/Beast of Blood* trio. Although all four take place on Blood Island, there's no story link between them.

Though *Terror Is a Man* is low-budget, derivative and slow, it is also moody, creepy and even imaginative at times. It is more deserving of TV revival than many others of its period.

The 30-Foot Bride of Candy Rock

Almost lost in time now is this limp SF spoof, sunk by mediocre direction and an overly-gimmicked script. But it has one claim to a place in film history: it was the last film of Lou Costello, his only feature without Bud Abbott. It was released several months after Lou died.

The last Universal film of the team was *Abbott and Costello Meet the Mummy* (1955); unlike their other films for the company, it was released as a B movie — a cofeature for *This Island Earth* — rather than the top of the bill. Their vaudevillian antics had no place in the then-current Universal-International program, which concentrated on glossy melodramas, Westerns, science fiction and a different kind of cornball humor — Ma & Pa Kettle, Francis the Talking Mule — than the pratfalls, puns and wisecracks of Bud and Lou.

The various books on the team ascribe their breakup to many different factors, including Bud's alcoholism and Lou's eagerness to prove himself as an actor. Whatever other causes there might have been, Lou, who initiated the breakup, felt that time had run out for the team. They were simply tired of one another, which showed in their acts. In 1956, they made one last film together, *Dance with Me, Henry*, but it was unfunny and cheap, and received little distribution.

Lou appeared without Bud several times on "The Steve Allen Show" in early 1957, and soon thereafter, announced that the team had broken up. He did a couple of dramatic shows on TV, a "G.E. Theatre" episode, and a "Wagon Train," but though Lou was good, the scripts were maudlin and contrived. He was never a good manager of his business affairs or career, and seems to have taken the role in *30-Foot Bride* (then called "Lou Costello and His 30-Foot Bride") mostly for the money, but it was also clearly an effort to establish himself as a solo comedian.

The film was shot quickly in late 1958. According to Chris Costello in her loving memorial to her father, *Lou's on First*, Lou "was much less boisterous on the set than he had been in the Abbott & Costello pictures. He wasn't part of a team now — just another actor in a picture. This time he went off alone between takes, finding himself a quiet corner so he could study lines. It was the first time in his movie career that he actually studied dialogue for a film. There was now something about the man that seemed almost melancholy."

Lou had good reason to be melancholy; the split with Bud had depressed him, even though he thought it was a good idea; 21 years together formed habits, if nothing else. His wife drank heavily, and he was still in financial trouble, though his highly-publicized bouts with the IRS were in the past.

Lewis Rachmil, who produced *The 30-Foot Bride of Candy Rock*, told Chris Costello, "Lou appeared at first as if he might be just a bit overwhelmed in not having Abbott as his foil.... We were filming by a process [apparently a matte] method and Lou was working in front of a blank screen. Lou would ask, 'Well, how high is she? Where is she supposed to be?' As a result, Lou became increasingly nervous." He'd never acted alone before, but here was working in effects shots without Dorothy Provine, who played the 30-foot woman. Her scenes were filmed separately—which, according to Chris Costello, was better for both of them. Allegedly, Provine was having an attack of the I'm-a-star syndrome.

Lou occasionally forgot his hard-learned lines, and was in a general state of depression during the brief filming of the movie.

Instead of being funny, the plot line of The 30-Foot Bride of Candy Rock is merely silly. Sources differ as to what actually happens in the film, but a great deal does go on. (For instance, an undated clip from a Portland, Oregon newspaper, presumably 1958, gives a plot that varies from the one in Filmfacts.) Having seen it once in 1959, my memory is not at all clear, although I recall that Lou was doing his best. He just didn't have the right things to do.

Lou is Arnie Pinsetter, a garbage man in the desert town of Candy Rock, who has invented a kind of computer–time machine which he calls Max, and which talks. Arnie's in love with Emmy Lou Raven (Provine), the blonde niece of harrumphing local big shot Raven Rossiter (Gale Gordon), opposed to his niece marrying the town eccentric, Arnie.

One day, Emmy Lou is exposed to strange radiation in "Dinosaur Springs" or, another source says, becomes entangled with one of Arnie's inventions. Whatever happens, she grows to a height of 30 feet. Arnie tells Rossiter that Emmy Lou has gotten, er, big, and Rossiter assumes the worst. He arranges for Arnie and Emmy Lou to marry at once.

In the meantime, the Army is on local maneuvers, and officers become convinced that Emmy Lou the giant is a creature from outer space. They launch a guided missile attack on her, and Arnie uses Max to save her by fouling the guidance systems of the missiles, which spell out "I love you" in the sky with their contrails. This befuddles the generals.

The generals then send troops after her, but Lou—who somehow can now fly—uses Max to turn the soldiers into Civil War infantrymen, Revolutionary troops, Napoleon's forces, and finally into cavemen throwing rocks. This does drain off the attack. Lou sails in circles around Emmy Lou.

They are married, and Max tries to return Emmy Lou to normal, but instead shrinks her to two inches. The machine tries again, but restores her to 30 feet. She takes up residence in a barn, and Arnie goes broke trying to feed her with truckloads of bread, milk and butter.

She finally declares that she wants a divorce, and begins crying, which almost drowns poor, long-suffering Arnie. Max finally comes to the rescue, and restores Emmy Lou to her normal size.

At least, I think that's what happens. The film is almost impossible to see now, rarely on television; it's available from several different 16mm rental companies, but for good reasons, it's never shown at science fiction conventions.

It received mostly lukewarm to negative reviews. Parents called it "fair," and "Glen" in Variety thought that while "the film is technically slick [it is only] mildly amusing."

Jack Moffitt had a bit more to say, but didn't like it any better; he found it only "an attempt at slapstick burlesque of science fiction.... Truthful reporting compels the admission that this reviewer got about a dozen laughs out of the proceedings.... The remainder of the preview audience scarcely laughed at all. The sad facts are that the people associated with Costello in this last enterprise seem to have known practically nothing about making a slapstick talkie.... The result is sophomorically dreary."

Don Willis (I) felt it had "lots of gimmicks, a few of them amusing." Psycho-

tronic considered it "a very light counterpart to *Attack of the 50 Foot Woman*."

Even Lou's own family was disappointed. Chris Costello says, "[I]t was a bomb.... I don't think he could've handled having his first movie without Bud Abbott be a failure.... After [seeing it], Mom said, 'This would've killed Lou if he'd seen it.'"

On the other hand, the *New York Times* enjoyed it. "Lou Costello's last legacy to his fans is something to leave them laughing.... He signs off in high spirits as a man on the threshold of a blissful hereafter."

The film was based on an original idea by those omnipresent effects men, Jack Rabin and Irving Block, who had many good ideas and some bad ones, too, such as this film. But perhaps it was the story by Lawrence L. Goldman that brought the film down, or the script by Rowland Barber and Arthur Ross. Barber cowrote the book *Somebody Up There Likes Me* with Rocky Graziano, and the work on which *The Night They Raided Minsky's* (1968) was based; presumably he was a hired hand on *Candy Rock*.

It's unlikely that the frenetic, let's-try-everything attitude displayed by *Candy Rock* is due to Arthur Ross, but it's possible. He seems to have tried everything in his own career. Among his screenwriting credits: *The Creature from the Black Lagoon*, *Star Spangled Rhythm* (1942), *The Stand at Apache River* (1953), *Port of New York* (1949), *The Three Worlds of Gulliver* (1960), *Harold Lloyd's World of Comedy* (1962), *The Great Race* (1965) and *Brubaker* (1980). I can't spot any trends.

The script mixes many ideas, but would have been better to stick to fewer. Concentrating just on Lou and his big bride probably would have produced more laughs than all the gags centering around Max, or dragging in peculiarly Sinclair Lewis–like spoofs of small-town boosterism; surely the lame, obvious and familiar Army jokes were unnecessary.

Furthermore, there are too many SF gimmicks. The idea of the regression of the troops should have been discarded, and to burden Lou with a giant wife *and* a talking computer is overkill.

The best films of Abbott and Costello still provide laughs, and are constantly shown on television all over the world. At their funniest, when the films were paced to their rapid-fire comedy routines and the slapstick was lively, Bud and Lou are among the screen's great comedy teams. If Lou had lived longer (he was only 53 when he died), it seems not impossible that they would have gotten back together. Bud hung on for many sad years, and surely *The 30-Foot Bride of Candy Rock* would have given Lou Costello second thoughts about a solo career.

The Tingler

In this William Castle film, it's hard to say what's more outrageous, the plot itself, or "Percepto," the gimmick that was conceived for the movie and used in some of the larger theatres. The idea that fear generates a living creature in your body which grows along your spine and threatens to crush it unless you scream, is pretty imaginative. It is also ludicrous, brazen and unique. "Percepto" I'll discuss later.

William Castle labored in the Hollywood vineyards for years. He was a director of lesser films, frequently for Columbia, for most of his career. He began in 1943 with *The Chance of a Lifetime*, and received good notices the next year for *When Strangers Marry*, released by Monogram. He went back to Columbia, and directed minor crime films, including several in the studio's "Whistler" and "Crime Doctor" series. In 1948–51, he was at Universal-International, turning out films like *Texas, Brooklyn and Heaven* (1948), *Undertow* (1949), *Cave of Outlaws* and *The Fat Man* (both 1951). He went back to Columbia in 1956, still on crime films, Westerns and adventure films, including *Serpent of the Nile*, *Fort Ti* (in 3-D), *Slaves of Babylon* (all in 1953), *The Saracen Blade*, *Jesse James vs. the Daltons*, *The Law vs. Billy the Kid* (all in 1954) and so forth. If he had continued in this vein, he probably would have shifted over to television and spent the rest of his career in that medium.

But he didn't. In 1958, he realized that horror movies were becoming popular again, and had himself been electrified by Henri-Georges Clouzot's *Diabolique* (1955). He acquired the rights to a peculiar novel called *The Marble Forest* (written under a joint pseudonym by 13 well-known mystery writers in a round robin), and tried to persuade Columbia to allow him to produce as well as direct the film. But they refused, and Castle raised the $90,000 budget on his own. He had some difficulty in selling the completed film, even with the title *Macabre* and a truly fine gimmick: you were insured by Lloyds of London against death by fright during the watching of the film. (Castle never had to pay off, although as Joe Dante points out, he was heard more than once wistfully musing, "Of course, it would have been *terrible* if anyone actually died while watching, but...") Allied Artists finally released *Macabre*, which made as much as $5,000,000 (Castle's figure; *Variety* said it grossed $1,200,000; I suspect Castle is correct), against all odds, as it is a dull, claustrophobic film.

But its success financed *House on Haunted Hill* (1959), which Castle again produced and directed, and which was also written by Robb White, who scripted *Macabre* and was to write *The Tingler*. *Haunted Hill* involved strange goings-on in an old house, and did actually have several scary scenes, but they were improbable and disconnected from the action. Furthermore, all the characters were unpleasant and bitchy (Robb White trademarks), and it seemed endlessly talky.

But Castle came up with another gimmick for *Haunted Hill*. Near the end, Carol Ohmart is frightened by a skeleton that floats up from an acid pit (plausibility was not Robb White's long suit) and chases her around a room. At this point, a box next to the screen popped open and a large luminous skeleton drifted on wires out over the audience, balefully eyed those in the front row of the balcony, then shot back into its box for the next screening. This limited gimmick was called "Emergo" (Castle had a knack for naming his gimmicks). It was confined to *House on Haunted Hill* and used only in the big theatres in the largest cities. Nonetheless, the film outgrossed *Macabre*, establishing Castle as America's leading horror director though his films were generally only competent, and rarely frightening. It also established Vincent Price as America's leading horror star.

With the success of *House on Haunted Hill*, Columbia lured Castle back. He was expected to come up with something to top the previous two chillers. Robb White devised the plot of *The Tingler*, and if Castle's breezy, simple-minded and uninformative autobiography, *Step Right Up! I'm Gonna Scare the Pants Off America* is to be believed, Castle himself came up with "Percepto." Since he doesn't even describe his own gimmick correctly, we might be permitted some doubt.

Castle bought hundreds of small war surplus motors, which were fastened to several hundred seats in the larger theatres. The control boxes were in the projection booth. At a certain point in the film, the projectionist pushed a switch and the little motors buzzed and vibrated against the bottom of the seat. Also, the house lights were doused, and Vincent Price's voice was heard coming from the back of the theatre, exhorting the audience to "Scream! Scream for your very lives! The Tingler is loose in this theatre!" On screen, the Tingler was seen to be loose in a movie theatre before the film blanked out altogether.

Castle says that in one theatre, the Percepto buzzers were installed ahead of time. During a screening of *The Nun's Story*, a bored projectionist tried out the buzzers on an audience of little old ladies, and caused pandemonium.

Several authoritative sources, including Castle's book, claim that Percepto involved small electric shocks administered to unsuspecting rears, but since that can be fatal to people who are extremely susceptible to electricity, and so possibly could have gone wrong quite spectacularly, I tend to doubt that. No report on the gimmick at the time the film was released said it involved electrical shocks, and those I know who actually experienced Percepto claim there were no shocks. An article in weekly *Variety* (5 August 1959), headed "Goosepimple Saga With Seats to Suit," began, "About 30% of the viewers seeing William Castle's latest chiller-diller, *The Tingler*, will experience a tingling sensation in their seats ... accomplished via the installation of special motors on the bottom of every tenth seat in each theatre in which the picture is shown.... Castle is seen on the screen before the start of the film [explaining] that only certain people are capable of experiencing the tingling sensation."

The article also explained the installation of the Percepto motors, which took about four hours to hook up under the supervision of Milton Rice and D. Hollaway. The negative cost of *The Tingler* was $400,000, and the Percepto gimmick represented an outlay of $250,000. With the usual ad campaign costs, the total budget for the film was around $1,000,000. It seems to have been quite profitable.

Even theatres not equipped with the seat buzzers were announced as featuring Percepto, such as the Egyptian in Coos Bay, Oregon, where I first saw *The Tingler*. I'm not sure how Percepto was feigned in drive-ins; probably merely ignored. Some suggested that every tenth car had a burly worker stationed behind it, who would shake the car during the Percepto scenes, but that's a joke.

The film opens as silent-movie theatre owner Ollie Higgins (Philip Coolidge) comes to watch research doctor William Chapin (Price) do an autopsy on Ollie's executed brother-in-law. Chapin points out the dead man's broken vertebrae, which he has seen many times in people who died in the extremeties of fear. He's very curious as to what this force is; "Something real and powerful broke those bones," he says, noting that it "ties in with my experimental work in fear."

Ollie suggests that "maybe it's the force that makes your spine tingle when you're scared," which leads Chapin to call this as-yet unknown force The Tingler. Need I point out that these shattered spines are a fantasy created by Robb White? (The film was initially called "The Chiller," a more amusing title, but Castle probably couldn't come up with a gimmick to tie into that name.)

Chapin goes with Ollie to the apartment over the silent movie theatre Ollie shares with his miserly wife, Martha (Judith Evelyn). She actually owns the theatre, and seems to live in terror that someone is going to steal her money. Appropriately enough for the owner of a theatre specializing in silent movies,

Martha is a deaf-mute. She also has more than a normal set of phobias: she's terrified of blood and is extremely germ-conscious. During Chapin's visit, something terrifies her and, clutching her spine, she collapses. Chapin points out that she can't scream to release tension vocally. When she wakes up, she immediately checks her safe.

Back at his home, we see Chapin's marriage isn't any happier than Ollie's. Robb White seems to think that husband-wife tensions make good material for horror movies. He uses them in both *House on Haunted Hill* and *The Tingler*. Chapin spars verbally with his bitchy, unfaithful wife Isabel (Patricia Cutts), who's tired of being married to a stick-in-the-lab dullard. Isabel is a social gadabout who is nasty to everyone around her, including her younger sister and ward Lucy (Pamela Lincoln), who is engaged to Chapin's assistant David (Darryl Hickman).

Isabel, who apparently murdered her father, is opposed to Lucy's planned marriage for no apparent reason other than spite. "The only way Dave Morris will marry my sister," she declares, "is over my dead body." "Unconventional," purrs Chapin, "but not impossible." In a typical Robb White "twist," it turns out Chapin married Isabel for her money.

In the lab, Chapin tells Dave his theory about The Tingler. "It may only exist for a fraction of a second, but for that fraction of a second there's something inside every frightened person that's as solid as steel." He wants to try to generate a Tingler and remove it from the body. "The Tingler," he says, "is stronger and denser than bone"; fear causes The Tingler to spread along a spinal column, and to bend it. The Tingler is made of "sinews of some very powerful material."

Chapin hints that perhaps if Dave would be willing to be frightened to death, they might get a real, live Tingler, but Dave understandably demurs. "If that's your attitude, Dave," says Chapin, smiling, "we'll just have to wait for someone who's willing to die for science"—he suddenly frowns—"and eventually we will."

Alone in his lab, Chapin takes a drug (LSD, in fact) in an effort to frighten himself. It works, all right; as Lucy and Dave watch through a transom, Chapin staggers around the lab in growing terror, opens a window while thinking he can't open it, blunders into a skeleton, and screams "the waaaaaalls!" Typical for Castle, he utterly fails to exploit this sequence. In efforts to frighten, Castle always relied on the most obvious gimmicks—hand-on-the-shoulder shots, "busses," and horror faces. If he had tried to show us what Price is supposedly reacting to, this sequence might have been frightening. As it is, it's somewhat embarrassing and more than a little comic. At one point, a ripple effect is added to make the walls look like they're moving, but it's not enough.

Later, X-rays reveal the dark outline of The Tingler on Chapin's spine shrinking back to microscopic size. Viewed in reverse, they show how the critter grows, clutching the spine with its little feet. The evolutionary purpose of such a thing is impossible to guess.

There are now extremely strong hints that Chapin plans to frighten the deaf-mute Martha to death so he can get his very own Tingler to fool around with.

At the theatre apartment, Martha wakes up alone to find a man in her room. She runs out and locks the door. The lights blink, and a hairy hand throws a hatchet at her. She flees into the bathroom and slams the door.

In the film's most arresting scene, and one that must have been difficult to accomplish, the bathtub is seen to be filled with bright red blood. It's a black-

and-white bathroom with a bathtub filled with thick, red blood. A hand, also red with blood, reaches up out of the bloodbath, and Martha turns to the basin, whose black-and-white faucets also run with bright red gore. The medicine cabinet opens to reveal her death certificate, and she does indeed drop dead, clutching her spine.

Ollie rushes her body to Chapin (no reason for this is given), where the corpse reflexively sits up. Chapin does remove a living Tingler from Martha's body. We first see the thing in silhouette, and hear a heartbeatlike thumping whenever it's around. When we see The Tingler itself, it looks like a cross between a lobster, a cockroach and a centipede. It is positively onychophoran-like. It appears to be made of rubber. It briefly clutches Chapin in a vicelike grip before he can manage to get it into a Tingler-sized steel box he happens to have lying around.

"It's a little late to call a funeral parlor," Chapin politely tells Ollie, "so perhaps you'd like to take your wife's body home."

Ollie does so, alone, and we learn that he and not Chapin scared Martha to death with an array of gimmicks (on the face of them, impossible for one man to do). We also learn he committed the murder his brother-in-law was executed for.

Elated, Chapin suggests to Isabel that they share a toast, for now he will be a more concerned husband. "Let's celebrate finding The Tingler," he says, "and me." But Isabel has her own ideas, and dopes Chapin's drink. He falls asleep on the couch. Isabel brings the Tingler box in and opens it near him. Why she thinks The Tingler would kill Chapin, instead of scuttling off to hide in a dark corner, is no bigger a mystery than anything else in the film.

In footage that looks like it was filmed in reverse, The Tingler crawls out of the box and slithers up on the sleeping Chapin. It clutches at his throat and is on the verge of killing him when Lucy comes in and screams, causing The Tingler to fall off. (But not to shrink, in violation of what we've been told about this fabulous creature.) Isabel flees, never to be seen again.

Chapin now feels that The Tingler is too dangerous to mess around with. He fears it can't be destroyed, so he decides not to reveal what he's learned (instead of finding a way to innoculate people against Tinglers), and to restore it to Martha's body, so it will shrink and maybe die. The Tingler is ugly, says Chapin philosophically, "because fear is ugly, and dangerous because a frightened man is dangerous." There's something wrong with that logic.

He takes The Tingler to Ollie's apartment, where Ollie surprisingly claims his wife tried to kill *him*, so he acted first. The Tingler forces its box open, unseen by the men, and creeps into the theatre below. Realizing it's gone, Chapin and Ollie rush down and try to warn the people that there's a horrible creature crawling around. It's creeping along under the theatre seats, occasionally grabbing someone by the ankle until they scream, then the frustrated Tingler drops off and inches away in search of another ankle to clutch.

Needless to say, this is the point at which Percepto went into operation. The screen went black, Price's voice was heard from the back of the theatre, and the little seat motors buzzed the butts of lucky patrons. (When Castle tried it out on a visitor to his office, *The Saturday Evening Post* reported, the man leaped up, pale, and glared at Castle. "Don't ever do that to me again!" he growled.)

Finally The Tingler is seen silhouetted on the now-white screen as it crawls across the projection window. (The movie on screen is *Tol'able David*, 1921, undoubtedly in public domain.) Chapin corners the monster in the projection booth and puts it in a 35mm film can. After restoring it to Martha's body, Chapin, who knows Ollie killed his wife, tells him that the jig is up.

Chapin doesn't know the half of it. After he leaves, the doors slam and the window closes, and Martha's body sits up. We hear Tingler throbs and she slowly advances on Ollie, who can't scream. The End.

Despite Castle's ponderous, pedestrian direction, in which everything is spelled out 1–2–3, *The Tingler* overall is one of his most entertaining films. It's silly, sure, but that's part of its charm. No one else has ever made a story like this, and the chutzpah of its premise is almost breathtaking. It's similar to the more bizarre Japanese films, such as *The H-Man*: we're told as if they were long-standing facts things that are patently impossible. And the plot proceeds from these impossibilities.

Furthermore, some of the acting is very entertaining. Price doesn't have quite as slick an opponent in Patricia Cutts as he did in Carol Ohmart in *House on Haunted Hill*, but they deliver the waspish Robb White dialogue with infectious glee. Price is clearly enjoying himself in these catty exchanges. He's best as a comic actor, with his exaggerated eyebrows and fruity voice, and is his most pleasing in satires or as sarcastic types. In more conventional roles, in more conventional films, he can seem tired and uninterested, as in both *Fly* movies; but when he can be broad, menacing, and either mad or cynical (or, best, both), he's really a delight. In the next decade Price would reach his peak with the Roger Corman Poe films, which were as broad and theatrical as Price is. His best horror role of all, that of the mad actor in *Theatre of Blood* (1973) was precisely and intelligently tailored to his real if special gifts. He was truly magnificent in that film.

Philip Coolidge is required to be mousy and henpecked, while still having a shade of possible menace, which he accomplishes quite well. Judith Evelyn is good in her mime performance as the ill-fated Martha; her angular, coarse features and popping eyes express her terror well. The people at Chapin's home are uninteresting, with little to do.

There are virtually no special effects. There's only The Tingler itself, a molded rubber creation that is always unconvincing, even when it is on its little excursion in the theatre. When it moves, it always looks as if it is being pulled along by strings. The most menacing "effect" shot of the creature is the series of X-rays, as we see it grow to its full size.

White's screenplay is lumpy and really has no plot at all. Price wants a Tingler; Coolidge wants his wife dead. Both get what they want. The film is a horror movie with SF elements, but structured as a 1940s-type murder melodrama. The attempt on Price's life by his wife seems like an effort to add running time.

White clumsily tries to hint that Price is Evelyn's murderer, but inasmuch as the nasty person in the film (his wife) hates Price, and the two nice young lovers like him, by the unwritten laws of melodrama he can't be guilty. It's just a thick, obvious attempt to divert suspicion from the only other character in the film.

The bizarre tag, in which the doors and windows slam shut and Martha's walking corpse attacks Ollie, is just a trick. It has nothing to do with the story, just a last-minute chill. It also pushes the film toward fantasy rather than science fiction, but I doubt that such distinctions were of any importance to Castle and White.

Castle rarely took his films seriously, and White seems to have been cynical, unable to regard this kind of thriller material as other than a joke. In addition to the sub–Noel Coward bickering between Price and Cutts, there are several spoofy lines in the "straight" scenes, such as Price's suggesting that Coolidge take his wife's body home. The film isn't quite a send-up of the thriller genre, it's more of a snide comment on it. This "kidding-on-the-square" approach is extremely difficult to accomplish. Alfred Hitchcock, James Whale and the few others who brought it off also didn't spoof the thriller material, but took it seriously enough for it to work on audiences as intended, acknowledging but not emphasizing the absurdities. *The Tingler* and the other Castle-White films *generate* the absurdities (the last was *Homicidal* in 1961); instead of taking a thriller situation and finding the humor in it, they create such situations *to* find the humor. Castle was too conventional and unimaginative a director to make this approach consistently, and White had no affection for his material. As a result, the films seem naive and too sophisticated at once.

Nonetheless, it was this combination of straight horror and laughs at its expense that appealed to some reviewers, such as Jack Moffitt, who thought *The Tingler* was "a lot of fun," and that it followed "the highly individual recipe of Castle's humor, which lays down a persuasive and realistic pattern for horror and then starts kidding it outrageously at precisely the right time.... Castle manages to bring about uproarious confusion of identity between the spectators on the screen [watching the silent movie] and the audience he is playing to."

The *Monthly Film Bulletin*, giving the film an average rating, was amused. "The sheer effrontery of this piece of hokum is enjoyable in itself, while the script and direction follow Castle's usual format of laying down a persuasive horrific exposition and then, at the right moment, parodying it outrageously." The *Monthly Film Bulletin*'s reviewer must have read the *Hollywood Reporter*.

"Ron" in *Daily Variety* also liked it: "*The Tingler*, right down to its bright red corpuscles, indelibly stamps producer William Castle as an imaginative, often ingenious, showman. The film abounds in hokum, camouflaged in science, and it has been successfully gimmicked to insure maximum exploitation.... Almost staggeringly effective is a hairraising sequence in which a bathtub full of blood blares out in all its rich sanguinary color amid the remaining blacks and whites."

Other reviews were much less favorable. Howard Thompson in the *New York Times* said that "William Castle has been serving some of the worst, dullest little horror entries ever to snake into movie houses," and thought that *The Tingler* was just another one. "It failed to arouse the customer seated in front of this viewer yesterday — a fearless lad who was sound asleep, snoring. Just keep us awake, Mr. Castle."

On the other hand, Alan Frank (*Horror*) thought it "immensely enjoyable horror hokum with a ripe performance from Price and a bizarre monster," and *Psychotronic* described it as "a brilliant legendary gimmick film." Don Willis (I) thought it merely an "ineffective shocker."

While *The Tingler* is no great shakes as a film, it is better than the Castle films which preceded and immediately followed it; *Macabre* and *13 Ghosts* (1960) border on the unwatchable, while *House on Haunted Hill* is endurable only for Price, Carol Ohmart and a few shock scenes. *The Tingler* is at least novel, and its preposterous premise carries the viewer to the end.

William Castle was never a particularly good director; he was just another competent studio hack until he shrewdly entered the horror market. When it faded, he had no recourses, and flailed around with bigger budgets in a variety of genres.

His next few films after *The Tingler*, *13 Ghosts*, *Homicidal* and *Mr.*

Sardonicus (1962) featured minor gimmicks, built into the film and which could thereby be used at any theatre. Except for a few plastic coins for *Zotz!* (1962), he gave up gimmicks thereafter. His next were *13 Frightened Girls* and *The Old Dark House* (both 1963), pedestrian ventures filmed in Europe. He bounced back, however, with *Strait-Jacket* (1964), a reasonably diverting thriller written by Robert Bloch and starring Joan Crawford, again battling her way to stardom. Castle moved over to Universal with *The Night Walker* (1965), also by Bloch, which many regard as Castle's best film. (I think it's *Homicidal*.) *I Saw What You Did* (1965) was also a pretty decent thriller, but Castle's comedies, *Let's Kill Uncle* (1966, the last in his Universal contract), *The Busy Body* and *The Spirit Is Willing* (both 1967) were moderately disastrous. He then switched from directing-producing to just producing, and made the finest film he was ever associated with, Roman Polanski's *Rosemary's Baby* (1968).

Castle tried to retire from directing, although one film, *Project X*, remained to be released in 1968, long after it was made (it was awful). He produced a conventional prison film, *Riot* (1969), then was inactive for five years. He didn't want to direct *Shanks* (1974), but his star, none other than Marcel Marceau, requested that Castle helm the film. It was barely released. The next year, Castle produced *Bug*, a bizarre little film based on a decent novel, *The Hephaestus Plague*, about fire-breathing cockroaches from the center of the Earth. It was the last film Castle was associated with behind the cameras.

He appeared in cameos in a few films, including *Day of the Locust* and *Shampoo* (both 1975), and always hinted that he was on the verge of producing another film. His autobiography, published in 1976, was trivial and self-serving, and ignored many of his films. It was a major disappointment to those who had followed his career with interest and amused affection (for the man, rarely for his pedestrian films). William Castle died unexpectedly in 1977. As a director, he's scarcely missed, but as a grinning, brassy presence, there's never been anyone like him. He was obnoxious, more than a little foolish; but he had a kind of all-American bravado and enterprise that made him unique in films. The King of the Gimmicks reigned only a short while, but he left his mark. And boy, do I miss him.

The Wasp Woman

Clearly made in imitation of *The Fly*, this Roger Corman quickie seems to have been made without anyone involved actually having seen *The Fly*, for it misses that film's major selling point: a careful mystery with a horror payoff. It gives us an insect-headed person and little else. *The Wasp Woman* was the first production made for Corman's own company, Filmgroup; it was shot in five or six days and, as even Corman admits, looks it. He believes it had a budget of $50,000, but it may have been lower, as it is seedy, as well as jumbled and unpleasant. Somewhat redeemed by Susan Cabot's intelligent performance, it is nonetheless lesser Corman.

Eric Zinthrop (Michael Mark) has for years been supplying honey to a company that sends a representative out to check on Zinthrop. The elderly beekeeper is excited about his work with "queen wasps" and their royal jelly; he claims to have slowed the process of aging using the jelly, and seeks even to reverse it. He shows his visitor a full-grown Doberman and a Dobie puppy, saying they are the same age. The visitor is not impressed, and informs Zinthrop that funding for his experiments is cut off.

Cosmetics firm owner Janice Starlin (Cabot) complains to her board of advisors about a decline in sales. Bill Lane (Fred, later Anthony, Eisley) points out that when Janice stopped using her own picture in ads, sales fell off. But Arthur Cooper (William Roerick), a longtime employee, tells Janice that her fears were correct: the sales fell off *before* she ceased using her photos to promote the cosmetics. Janice is getting older (she might even be, gasp, 40), and people don't want to buy cosmetics from an aging woman.

Zinthrop arrives at the cosmetics firm, hoping to sell Janice on royal jelly. (There was widespread belief around this time that royal jelly from honeybees could slow aging, or provide some other kind of benefit; the stuff really does work just as promised — on bees.) Arthur tries to tell Janice that everyone reacts differently to royal jelly, adding that female wasps kill their mates by paralyzing, then slowly devouring, them. (No one seems to point out that it's royal jelly from bees that's the hot stuff; I don't know if wasps even have it.)

But Zinthrop persists, and tells Janice that he can give her ten, maybe 15 more years of relative youth. He injects a guinea pig and it turns into a white rat. What this is supposed to demonstrate is unclear, but it certainly impresses Janice. He doubts (all of a sudden) that the formula will work on human beings, but she insists that he continue his research under her sponsorship, then try out the formula on her.

Zinthrop busies himself in the lab for some time, and later tries out the formula on a cat which (offstage) turns into a kitten. He then tries a first injection on Janice, but it has no obvious effect.

Elsewhere, Bill and Janice's loyal secretary Mary (Barboura Morris), in love with Bill, try to find out from Cooper what Janice is up to, but they do not believe his truthful story.

Janice goes to the lab for more enzyme in Zinthrop's absence, and gets the superwasp jelly Zinthrop had previously recommended only as an emollient. As Janice leaves the lab, there's a close-up of a bedraggled cat; apparently the kitten reverted to its true age.

Finally, the stuff has an effect on Janice: she shows up at work one morning looking much younger. Bill is impressed, and she's mildly interested in him, but the main focus of the romance is on Bill and Mary, not Bill and Janice, slightly unusual in films of this nature.

In his lab, Zinthrop is suddenly attacked by the cat, which has something odd about its back, perhaps a pair of wasp wings, but we never see this clearly enough. He manages to kill it, but the event temporarily unhinges his mind, and he wanders blankly out into the street where he's hit by a truck and taken to a hospital. He had no identification, and no one at Janice's company saw him leave. This is called expedient plotting; what would movies do without providential trucks?

While Zinthrop remains in a coma, Janice, apparently getting older again, returns to the lab and looks frantically for Zinthrop's formula. Cooper enters too, curious about Zinthrop's absence and determined to prove the scientist a charlatan. Suddenly there's a buzzing sound and Janice, now the Wasp Woman of the title, rushes out of hiding, claws Cooper and drinks his blood.

At the staff meeting the next day, she seems remorseful and still wants the big new ad campaign for the wasp jelly. In a plot element that smacks of rewriting, Zinthrop is back, but is still in bed and cannot remember what he wanted to tell Janice.

That night, a night watchman (Bruno Ve Sota) is attacked by Janice in her Wasp Woman form and apparently killed. Janice goes later to see Zinthrop, but he cannot remember his important message. Off camera, she turns into the monster and kills the nurse attending the old scientist.

Mary stops in to visit Zinthrop, who tells her Janice is in danger. Mary rushes heedlessly down to the lab. Zinthrop tells Bill that "Miss Starlin is not a human being any longer. She'll kill Mary, as any wasp will kill its enemy, and devour the remains." Bill helps Zinthrop down to the lab where, sure enough, Janice as the Wasp Woman has grabbed Mary. Zinthrop hits Janice with a bottle of acid, and Bill shoves her out the window of the skyscraper. Zinthrop dies.

There's some, but not enough, amusing dialogue in Leo Gordon's script for *The Wasp Woman*. Two secretaries chat about the movie *Dr. Cyclops* for some reason, and the dialogue characterizes these minor figures rather well. The scenes in the cosmetics company board meetings have a certain degree of realism, but mostly it's the same old thing.

This kind of plot, wherein a new discovery is made and immediately misused, is common in low-budget monster movies, even in some relatively expensive ones: the same basic storyline recurs in recent films like *Altered States* and *Brainstorm*. Usually it's the discoverer himself who gets into trouble, but having a relatively innocent bystander, like Janice, the victim of the SF trouble, is also standard.

The monster that Janice becomes is pretty silly and, as a result, the film goes out the window before she does. The first time I saw it, I was frustrated because there didn't seem to be any clear shots of the Wasp Woman. More recently, however, I discovered that there is at least one very clear shot of the mask—but it still looks out of focus. The mask was constructed as hastily as the rest of the film, and is simply big, bulbous eyes, small antennae and perhaps some mandibles. The rest is black hair. As the Wasp Woman, Cabot also wears black fuzzy mittens. The rest of her remains human; she even keeps on her high heels.

I never expected science fiction movie advertising art to accurately reflect the film—after all, advertising for all other kinds of movies was equally misleading—but the ads for *The Wasp Woman* were especially outrageous. They showed a wasp the size of an automobile, clutching a screaming man (apparently from art for some other ad) in its forelegs. The wasp has Susan Cabot's face. Of course, not many people would have been interested in the film if that silly wasp mask had been used in the advertising, but this ad was a flat-out lie, although it's an exceptional poster.

Susan Cabot is surprisingly good, especially considering the film's short shooting schedule. To look old, Cabot wore a severe hairstyle and high collars; the makeup was scant and simple. When her youth is restored by the wasp jelly, Cabot actually seems youthful, and her joy seems genuine. Cabot was around 32 at the time the film was made, but is convincingly several years older and younger than that in the course of the movie. She's intelligent and driven, believable qualities in an executive.

Cabot began in films as early as *On the Isle of Samoa* in 1950, and later had a brief contract with Universal-International, where she made mostly Westerns and adventures like *The Prince Who Was a Thief* (1951), *Battle at Apache Pass* (on loan to Fox, 1952) and *Gunsmoke* (1953). From 1954 to 1957, she may not have made any films, but returned in the latter year in two films for Roger Corman, *Sorority Girl* and *Carnival Rock*. For Corman, she also appeared in 1958 in *War* of the *Satellites*, *Machine Gun Kelly* and *The Saga of the Viking Women and Their Voyage to the Waters of the Great Sea Serpent*. I have been unable to locate any films for her after 1959; *The Wasp Woman* may have been her last movie. Perhaps the hectic pace of Roger's films soured her on acting.

If so, it's too bad for us. Susan Cabot was distinguished from the other dark-eyed, dark-haired starlets of the 1950s: she could act. But then, whatever qualities Corman films of this period (by far his busiest) might have had, they generally featured reliable performers, such as Cabot. (She married a nobleman and retired; recently, she's been trying to get back into films.)

Visually, the film is flat and uninteresting. It was made in such a great hurry that there's little that could be done to make it look better; Corman was probably fearful of wasting his *own* money this time. The music by Fred Katz tries to add interest in the boring opening scenes with Michael Mark, but isn't good enough. Later, when the Wasp Woman is buzzing around, Katz's music becomes busy and full of xylophones; when we see pudgy Bruno Ve Sota as the night watchman, the score becomes Funny Music to accompany this Funny Guy.

Gordon's script is cluttered with characters. There's no time to develop a romance between Mary and Bill, much less to raise the faint possibility of a romantic triangle, but it's sketched in, as if the film required one as much as it did a monster. And yet other scenes that only consume time and add nothing occur again and again. The suspense is reduced to scenes of people wandering in and out of the laboratory; the door gets a heavy workout. As Janice is the central character, it's hard to lose track of her, and so her sudden entrances as the Wasp Woman are anything but unexpected.

Furthermore, the tone of the film is more that of a drawing-room melodrama than of a horror film. There's nothing of a horrifying nature in the early slow portions of the picture, and no buildup to the first appearance of the Wasp Woman, so her suddenly dashing in and grabbing Cooper seems comically intrusive. The Wasp Woman is a speedy little devil, which makes all her attacks seem comic, in fact.

There's also the problem of the bodies. Before she's done, the Wasp Woman kills three people. Zinthrop says she'll "devour the remains," but it's hard to imagine how a woman the size of Susan Cabot could eat three whole raw people and not look the least bit bulgy around the middle. The peculiar plot also requires Janice to know about the killings, yet feel no evident remorse, and still try to solve the problem of the wasp jelly. She may not, as Janice, know what she's done, as the Wasp Woman, but this issue is never touched on.

Still, as John Brunas said in *Trumpet* 4, it is "a few steps above the trite trash of this period." Even in his worst films, and this is one of them, Roger Corman's intelligence (if not his taste) shows through in places. It's a silly, bad movie, but it is not a stupid movie, just foolishly conceived. And it does have Susan Cabot's interesting performance.

"Glen" in *Variety* thought it was an "unexciting but exploitable horror film [with] interesting points ... but it's pretty slow and not very frightening.... Gordon's screenplay does provide [the actors] with a gentle, believable humanity, which is a pleasant relief."

Charles Stinson in the *Los Angeles Times* thought it was not "nearly as bad as we had expected.... Just a little more effort to co-ordinate script and 'monster' would have resulted in a pair of superior low-budget science-fiction pictures." (He saw it with its standard cofeature, *Beast from Haunted Cave*.)

Stinson thought *The Wasp Woman* had a "fairly sophisticated story.... Leo Gordon's script is smoothly urbane with nice surprising little touches here and there. Slim, intense, brunet Susan Cabot, who always impresses, does excellently nuanced work as the neurotic lady with the worries and the wasps."

The *Monthly Film Bulletin*, on the other hand, gave the film its lowest rating. "The earlier, more realistic scenes of this modest shocker ... are pretty unlikely, while the later bouts of fantasy are ludicrous rather than terrifying. Routine stuff, in fact, for determined enthusiasts only."

Fortunately for Roger Corman, there were many determined enthusiasts.

The Wild Women of Wongo

I consider all films about prehistoric life to be science fiction, which is how this limp little epic qualifies for the book. It's silly, dull claptrap, an uneasy, erratic blend of comedy and melodrama, but it is about life 10,000 years ago, no matter how unconvincing it might be.

This film is virtually unknown, and no wonder. It was not widely distributed, stars total unknowns, and is shot in ugly color on boring locations. I'll bet that no matter how unappetizing I try to make it sound, there will be those of you reading this who'll become almost desperate to see it. Such is life, such are film fans. I know *I* was anxious to see it—until I did.

The film begins with disconnected shots of tropical animals and birds, crashing seas, beaches, palm trees, and so forth. "I am Mother Nature," a voice says, "designer of all the things you see and all the things you are. For millions of years, Father Time and I have worked hand in hand to make the world a better place to live in." I didn't know all this was planned so carefully.

We learn of two tribes living on the same tropical island; they do not seem to know of each other. (The only previously-published synopses of this film incorrectly had the tribes living on adjacent islands. We must be accurate.) The tribe of Wongo lives far to the south of the tribe of Goona. We first meet the Wongese tribe, which has beautiful women and ugly men, or so we're told. The men looked perfectly ordinary to me, although the women have styled hair, lipstick, eye shadow, and like that, and are reasonably attractive by 1958 standards. Once we are told this ugly/beautiful dichotomy, we know that symmetry will demand the Goonese people be the reverse, and we know where the plot will wearily go.

A high priestess and a young man consult the Dragon God (a lethargic alligator; gators are a Theme in the film). Something is going to change, the oracle says. At the Wongese tribal village of thatched huts, we are treated to little homey scenes of children playing and women engaged in housewifely activities, pounding food, scraping hides, unconvincingly starting fires. The men of Wongo are lazy bums who sleep through all this.

Then a stranger, Engor (Johnny Walsh), arrives in a canoe, bringing words from his father, the King of Goona. Engor tells the King of Wongo that his father fears a tribe of strangers is coming from the sea in big canoes, and that the Wongese and Goonese should combine forces.

When Engor spies Wongese princess Omoo (Jean Hawkshaw), they immediately fall in love, which doesn't go unnoticed by the resentful Wongo men.

The tribal leaders confer, but suspect a trap. They decide to kill Engor so the women will not look on him so fondly. This is emphasized when Omoo tells her father the King that she wants to marry Engor; he declares this treason, and makes a deal with tribesman Ocko. He will give Omoo in marriage to Ocko, and Ocko will kill Engor the next day. (I hope you are following all this.)

This is overheard by Omoo, who goes to Engor in the night (an alligator wanders by), and they kiss. In the morning, the emblem of the Dragon God, a stuffed alligator on a stick, is knocked over when all the Wongese women jump on Ocko to prevent him from killing cute Engor, who flees.

This, the men declare, is sacrilege. The women of Wongo are sent away in canoes to make amends.

Engor reaches Goona and tells his tribesmen (who actually don't look notably better than the Wongese men) about the beautiful women of Wongo. They gather in a football huddle for this, and all shout Wahoo.

The Goona women are indeed much less attractive than the wild women of Wongo—they're tall, short, fat, thin, and all are scornful of this information about the Wongese women.

Who, elsewhere, arrive at their Dragon Temple, a kind of castle made of pink coral. The priestess sits down on her throne, turns into someone else, and performs a dance. This is a shade more interesting than most such dances, which seem to be a requirement of all films with exotic and/or primitive locales. There's lots of hair-tossing, foot-pounding and arm-waving, with an occasional ballet move.

The Wongese girls then go for a swim, giving occasion for some very pretty underwater scenes. Another alligator swims by, and Omoo fights it, but the battle, which is very long, consists mostly of writhing around while she holds the gator's mouth shut.

The Wongese women, the oracle/dance informed them, are to go one by one each night and wait for one of them to be eaten by an alligator, which will propitiate the gods and make things all better. The rules seem to allow the potential victim to try to escape.

Mona is not eaten on her night. Ahtee says, "Perhaps the god is more particular than you think."

"I'm sure he's particular," Mona bitchily responds. "You've awaited the god twice and he has not come to seek you any more than a man has."

Suddenly the women are attacked by two men, called ape-men but who don't look it. An alligator gets one of them, while the other is dispatched by the women with the most fatal of all wounds in such films: a spear between his side and his elbow.

Apparently assuming the Dragon God has been satisfied, the Wongese women return to their village only to discover it has been wiped out by the ape-men (who are never mentioned again). Deciding that they do not want "to live and grow old and die without men," they leave, heading for Goona. The surviving Wongese men return, and also head south for Goona.

Meanwhile, in an amazing coincidence no doubt of interest to anthropologists, the young men of Goona are sent out into the jungle to live for one moon (which the writers seem to think means a couple of days) without weapons and without speaking to women. When they return, they are to be married, which they regard as a horrible fate.

Surprise, surprise. The Goona men meet, one by one, the wild women of Wongo, and they appropriately fall in love. But first, to show they are indeed wild, when the women learn the Goona men are defenseless, in a lengthy sequence, they capture them. They take the men back to Wongo and the Dragon God temple (why haven't these tribes met before?), where they are soon met by the Wongo *men* and the Goona *women* who, against all logic, find each other attractive. I guess it's kismet. They are all married. Each of the Goona men winks at the camera in turns.

This leaden piece of tripe was directed by James L. Wolcott and written by Cedric Rutherford (which sounds like a pseudonym). It's hard to say just what was intended. Even if all the comedy worked, there isn't very much of it, and even if all the melodrama was thrilling and exciting, there isn't enough of that, either.

A macaw is seen sitting on the same branch, no matter where the master scene is taking place, and occasionally comments on the action, mostly asking "What?" which is more appropriate than the filmmakers guessed. There are also occasional cutaways to other birds.

There's far too much music, and it's rarely good.

In fact, there is nothing to recommend about *The Wild Women of Wongo*, except that it is an oddity. The only thing that keeps me from declaring that it is one of the worst I've seen is that it is harmless, good-natured and occasionally has some pretty photography. It's just not vivid enough in any way to get angry about.

Engor is played by Johnny Walsh, who may or may not be the juvenile actor who appeared in *Boys Town* (1938), *Adventures of Huckleberry Finn* (1939) and *Mildred Pierce* (1945), among others. He is definitely an atrocious actor. The Adrienne *Bourbeau* in the cast is not the same person as Adrienne *Barbeau*, the current television and movie actress. Bourbeau still works occasionally in a production capacity on films made in Florida, where *Wild Women of Wongo* was shot.

Ed Fury appears as Gahbo, but has almost nothing to do, which is not a complaint. He was a muscleman who appeared in a few Hollywood films, including *Female on the Beach* and *I Died a Thousand Times* (both 1955) before heading east to Italy. He starred in several Italian muscleman epics in the early 1960s, including *Colossus and the Amazon Queen*, *Samson Against the Sheik* (both 1960), *Mighty Ursus*, *Ursus in the Valley of the Lions*, *The Seven Revenges* (all 1961) and *Son of Hercules in the Land of Fire* (1963). Fury could flex a bicep with the best of them, but was a bad actor.

I have been able to discover nothing about the crew. They probably were Florida businessmen who decided they could make a low-budget film and simply did so. There seem to have been no other sets than the thatched cottages. The Dragon God temple was the "Coral Castle of Florida," also used in *Nude on the Moon*. Other locations, duly credited, included Tahiti Beach, Parrot Jungle, Fairchild Tropical Garden and Silver Springs.

The only contemporary review of this film I have seen was in the *Monthly Film Bulletin*, which gave it their lowest rating: "The crudity of this extravaganza has to be seen to be believed, though up to a point its unintended comedy is quite entertaining. The underwater Pathé Colour photography is pleasant enough. The dialogue is a knockout."

The Wild Women of Wongo is indeed very entertaining if seen in the right frame of mind; it's a silly, trivial little picture full of scantily-clad young men and women doing silly, trivial things. It was one of the last gasps of the truly low-budget, regional exploitation film.

Womaneater

In one of the triumphs of mismatched double bills, this dreary British film was released with the lively, colorful Japanese movie, *The H-Man*. While no one could ever claim that *The H-Man* is an outstanding picture, its science fiction thrills and fast pace made *Womaneater* seem even more leaden and ponderous than it actually is, which is saying a great deal. *Womaneater* is one of those throwbacks to the 1940s that turned up occasionally in the 50s, when horror thrillers were sometimes made by people who didn't understand or care that the market had changed.

The film opens in the Explorers Club, with a discussion of the remnants of a tribe of Incas in South America who have *juju* (magic) that can bring the dead back to life. This catches the attention of Dr. James Moran (George Coulouris), a scientist with more than a hint of insanity in his background. An onlooker says that Moran suffers from his "family trait—several of them have been sent away."

Moran heads off into the Amazon jungles with Lewis Carling (Robert MacKenzie) in search of this life-restoring secret. We see some stock footage of jungles, and studio shots of the two actors hacking their way through nondescript shrubbery.

They finally find the lost tribe of Incas, who look distinctly African, and who chant an African chant as they dance around a strange, shaggy tree, the Womaneater of the title.

The tree has some thick, snaky tentacles, clearly the covered arms of people hidden inside it. Carling is killed as he prepares to rush heroically ahead and rescue the young woman about to be fed to the tree. Later, Moran turns up in civilization with jungle fever.

Then it is England, five years later. Tanga (Jimmy Vaughan), the "Inca" we saw beating drums before the tree in South America, is doing the same here in a vault beneath Moran's ancestral home. Moran, who keeps a skull on his desk, supervises the throwing of a young white woman to the tree, which eats her. The exposition in the film is rather stark: "She'll become part of the plant," says Moran, "and from it I'll get the serum to bring the dead back to life. She won't have died in vain." He must be saying this to us, as Tanga knows that.

Tanga assists in bringing a heart (which looks more like some kind of vegetable) back to life; the heart dies again, then revives to self-important, melodramatic music (by Edwin Astley).

At a nearby funfair (carnival), Sally Norton (Vera Day) is dancing in a grass skirt, distracting a guy at a shooting gallery so that he *hits* targets. When the barker talks rough to Sally, Jack Venner (Peter Wayn) punches him. The next day, Sally comes to the garage where Jack works, saying she's quit the funfair and is looking for a job. Jack suggests she work for Moran.

Sally is a very accommodating potential victim: she walks up to the monster's lair and rings the bell. Moran gives her the job, but doesn't otherwise seem interested in her. He'd earlier told a bobby that "as a scientist, I'm more interested in things with six legs than two." However, Margaret (Joyce Gregg), his housekeeper and sometime lover, is furiously jealous, resenting Sally.

Cops arrive at Moran's to search for the most recent missing girl, but leave without getting any further information.

Downstairs, Tanga tells Moran about the serum the womaneater ap-

The carnivorous plant that's the title menace in Womaneater (U.S. release 1959) gobbles up another young woman (Sara Leighton) in the basement dungeon of very mad scientist George Coulouris. No performers are identified for the plant's grabby arms.

parently exudes: "With this our people make live the dead, Master." Tanga wants to sacrifice Sally right away, but instead Moran goes into London at night, prowling around Piccadilly looking for a suitable victim. He finds one, and gives her doped cigarettes.

Back home, Margaret acts jealous again, but Moran firmly tells her that "all that's over between us," ever since he returned, adding, "my dear Margaret, I've never trusted you or any other woman with anything I didn't want anyone else to know." Down in the vault laboratory, he muses, "What are a few worthless lives compared with what I'm giving to the world? It's turning death into life."

Sally and Jack are seeing each other, and after he admires her breasts, he proposes.

Back at the house, Moran is making plans to get rid of Margaret and hire Sally full time. (Feeding *Margaret* to the tree doesn't occur to him; probably the family taint acting up again.) Margaret tries to kill him, and he inadvertently strangles her.

In a completely unprepared-for twist, though hardly surprising, Moran is lustfully drawn to Sally. Matching this new development, Sally is terrified of him, without any cause.

Meanwhile, the police are ploddingly drawn toward Moran's house.

Down in the vault, Tanga thinks Moran is going to feed Sally to the tree, which delights the cheerfully bloodthirsty native, but actually, Moran is just showing off his carnivorous pet. He injects Margaret's corpse with serum from the tree, and she sits up.

Alas for Moran, she has no mind. "Only the body, not the mind!" gasps Moran. Tanga is delighted. "The brain for us only," says Tanga, "our secret not for you." Tanga's motives are, to say the least, foggy.

Making strange clutching motions, Margaret advances on Sally, then collapses. While Moran is standing around in an agony of despair, Tanga goes to throw Sally to the tree, but Moran recovers and jumps him. Jack enters, and Moran shouts at him (rather nobly, all things considered) to get Sally out of there, which he does. To Tanga he shouts, "You cheated me, now I'll destroy your idol as you have destroyed me." He sets fire to the tree, but Tanga stabs him, then kneels before the tree, presumably going up in flames with it.

Charles Saunders' ponderous direction makes a slow story painfully halting, in a point-by-point plodding technique of showing all actions. It makes *Womaneater* one of the dullest science fiction–horror thrillers ever made, almost unbearable to sit through. It isn't even campy.

There's one reasonably interesting scene in Piccadilly Circus, when Moran is on the prowl for another victim. The scenes were actually shot at night, and seem to have been filmed from concealment, with Coulouris and the young woman playing his prey moving through real crowds. But apart from that, there's nothing of any visual interest in the film; even the womaneater tree is dull.

This is one of the most misogynist movies I've seen. Beginning with the premise (it is clearly not a *man*-eating tree), right until the end, when Sally can't even leave the vault without the help of a man, almost everything in the film indicates if not a hatred of women, at least a totally uncaring attitude. Women are beauty objects or things to be used and discarded, such as Margaret and the victims of the tree.

The plot is obscure. There isn't the slightest hint as to how Moran got the tree out of Brazil, why Tanga came with him, or why Tanga now serves him. And for the "Inca" to stay there, helping to throw women to the tree, assisting Moran in everything, but *still* withholding the vital secret about reviving minds with bodies, seems perverse beyond any possible rationale.

George Coulouris gives a physically vigorous performance, almost as if he knew the slow direction of Saunders needed to be enlivened. He virtually dashes everywhere he goes, and seems almost electrified by his nervousness. It's not an especially hammy performance, but Coulouris is jumpy.

Vera Day is pretty as Sally, but doesn't have much to do (she's been acceptable in other films), and Jimmy Vaughan is wildly miscast as the drum-thumping Tanga. Joyce Gregg is a bore as Margaret.

No one seems to have liked the film. Even the usually very lenient *Motion Picture Herald* thought it "is hardly the type of horror film that will have audiences screaming in the aisles." The *Hollywood Reporter* called it "a slow-paced entry that attempts ineffectually to generate more than moderate suspense," and noted that the direction by Saunders was "slow and ponderous." "Whit" in *Variety* felt that "for American audiences, it's unable to overcome an old-hat plot carelessly put together."

The *Monthly Film Bulletin* gave it their lowest rating, noting that "the production is poor and the acting, if anything, worse; not even George Coulouris can do much with his stereotyped role, though he understandably emerges from the ordeal the least scathed." Alan Frank (*Horror*) described it as "The British B picture at its most threadbare, with poor production values and acting to match."

Womaneater resembles those plodding Bela Lugosi pictures of the mid-40s, which he made for PRC and Monogram. It's an old-fashioned, uninteresting disaster, barely even a footnote in film history.

The World the Flesh and the Devil

This serious end-of-the-world film, with an excellent first half, is gravely compromised by what follows, and unfortunately, finally is destroyed by a foolish ending. It's also damaged by a refusal to take seriously the scientific underpinnings of the premise. Many reviewers compared the film favorably to science fiction, adopting blatantly that annoying theory, "if it's science fiction, it can't be good." The makers of the film seem to have agreed, deciding that (a) the film was definitely not science fiction, but rather an allegory, and therefore (b) didn't have to be logical.

But it *is* science fiction and today, it's hard to take the film seriously, particularly because of its patronizing, naive view of the racial question, which in 1959 was just beginning to heat up nationally. Harry Belafonte, who helped get the film made as well as starring in it, was one of the leaders of the civil rights movement within show business over the next decade, making the peculiar, cautious attitude of the film toward race even more puzzling.

The film had its genesis in the most famous book of the relatively obscure M.P. (Matthew Phipps) Shiel, *The Purple Cloud*, which first appeared in 1901. (Shiel did a revision in 1929.) According to the *Science Fiction Encyclopedia*, it is a "novel depicting a world disaster, the sole survivor of which expiates his fears of loneliness through a lifelong orgy of destruction." The same reference source contradicts itself elsewhere, saying that in the novel, "a mysterious gas kills all but a handful of men and women." Whether the gas killed all but a handul, or all but one, little of the book other than the very general premise of worldwide death is left in the film.

Shiel's novel was popular both in Britain, Shiel's home, and the United States. It was first optioned for filming in 1927 and, one source claims, over the years there had been at least a dozen screenplays prepared. By 1958, the possibility of world catastrophe had become more real, and science fiction had begun to attract the attention of the larger studios. I presume that Metro-

Goldwyn-Mayer gave the go-ahead for the film because it could be exploited in several ways, whichever seemed the most likely to be profitable: as science fiction, as a nuclear warning, as a romance, as a melodrama on racial tensions. As it turned out, the ads emphasized the end-of-the-world aspect in most areas, while others were so general it was impossible to tell what the film might be about.

The film opens with Ralph Burton (Harry Belafonte), a young coal miner below ground somewhere in Pennsylvania. There's a cave-in, and Ralph is trapped alone. He isn't especially worried; there are lights, air, and plenty of food in other miners' lunch buckets, and he can hear the rescue squads digging closer. But after a few days, the digging ceases, and Ralph comes to the frightening realization that if he's going to survive, he has to dig his way out himself. This involves some danger and much struggling, but he finally makes it, only to discover the coal field deserted. In a shed, he discovers newspaper headlines: the world has come to an end, everyone else is dead.

He wanders shocked through the nearby small town; there's a sense of the aftermath of panic, with abandoned cars, newspapers blown around, and so forth. (There are no bodies visible, an omission that bothers almost every viewer of the film.) He gets a Geiger counter from Civil Defense headquarters, and takes a new car from a showroom. He heads for Manhattan, filling up at gas stations on the way. But he can't drive into Manhattan; the George Washington Bridge and the Lincoln Tunnel are clogged with abandoned cars.

He crosses the Hudson in a small skiff to Manhattan. The film's most powerful and eerie scenes show Belafonte wandering through the vacant streets of downtown Manhattan (including Wall Street), running in apprehension; he finally pulls a little wagon of supplies behind him, occasionally stopping to shout, and sometimes firing a pistol. The buildings look just the same as always, and he angrily cries out that everyone is hiding, that they're still there. All he hears are echoes of his own, lone voice. Frightened and oppressed by the empty city, he builds a fire in the middle of a street; his fear of going into the buildings that were so recently filled with people is obvious and does not need to be spoken. (He carefully disposes of his trash in a waste-basket.)

In a radio station, he finds the emergency power still on, and a tape of a last broadcast still cued up. He listens to the story of what happened: after a walk-out from the U.N., an unidentified force sowed the air with radioactive sodium, blanketing the Earth. In 53 hours it's clear what will happen: the poison, which is deadly for five days, will wipe out all life on Earth. One by one, the voices on the tape fade out, leaving only one person talking sadly before he, too, falls silent. Tears run down Ralph's cheeks. This is one of the most powerful scenes in the film, and all of it consists of voices on a tape and one man's silent face. (Belafonte is generally excellent.)

Ralph sets up housekeeping in one of the high-rise luxury apartments on Fifth Avenue. He finds plenty of canned foods, laboriously wires the building and sets up a generator. He even has a little electric train run through the apartment, and follows it, singing "Gotta Travel On." (Some resented that an opportunity was found for Belafonte to sing three times in the film.)

He has added a couple of department store manikins for company, but eventually becomes depressed by the unending grin of the male dummy, and tosses it out a window. As it crashes to the street several floors below, he hears a scream, and is amazed to see a woman on the street. (We've seen her several times, watching Ralph from concealment.)

Ralph catches up with her. He's jabbering with joy; it's been several months, and he's nearly mad with loneliness. She's Sarah Crandall (Inger Stevens), who escaped the disaster with some others by hiding in a decompression chamber, but her companions left too early, and died. She's been furtively watching, fearful of approaching Ralph. She screamed when she saw the dummy fall because she thought it was Ralph himself.

Under the circumstances, there's little they can do except become friends; it's very obvious that Sarah wants to move in with Ralph as his lover, but Ralph's racial pride (or something), surely misplaced now, prevents him from "taking advantage" of her. The question isn't just one of race, to Ralph; he's disturbed that in the world that was, the social gulf between them would have prevented them from even meeting. He hooks up power to her apartment, rather than allow her to move into even the same building with him, and ingeniously strings a telephone line between them.

At one point, Sarah bitterly (and unconsciously) says that she's her own person, "free, white and 21"—which hurts Ralph deeply. She continues to suggest that other arrangements are possible, and even seems to be in love with him. Ralph is on the verge of giving in when, during one of his daily radio broadcasts, he picks up voices in French. There are other survivors—doubtlessly white. He saves this revelation for an elaborate birthday party for Sarah at a rewired nightclub; she hopes the occasion will mark a change in his feelings and behavior, but he still won't touch her.

Another survivor turns up, right there in Manhattan. Ben Thacker (Mel Ferrer) arrives in a boat, ill and injured. He's nursed back to health, and explains he's traveled all the way from South America by himself. (No explanation is offered as to how he survived the worldwide devastation.)

With Ben's arrival, the film goes more rapidly downhill. Several things become clear to Ben at once: Sarah is in love with Ralph, who is steering clear of her, almost forcing her into Ben's arms, and that race is a factor. Though not at all a racist, Ben does want Sarah himself, so decides to claim her for his own. Things go from bad to worse as Ben insists on a confrontation, so finally, armed with rifles, the men begin stalking each other through Manhattan.

But Ralph sees the inscription across from the U.N. building, about beating swords into plowshares, and cannot continue in the manhunt; it's really World War IV. He drops his rifle and confronts Ben, who cannot kill Ralph. Ben walks away angrily, and, indicating they can become lovers, Ralph takes Sarah's hand. Then they catch up with Ben, and walk off into the sunrise, hand in hand, as a cloud of pigeons flies by.

Originally, the film had a different ending. During its production (under the title "End of the World"), news stories were released about squabbles with MGM's management over the ending of the picture; reviews allude to this controversy. The originally-filmed ending seems to have been without the reconciliation with Ben, but presumably fears of racists objecting to a black man bedding down with a white woman, even under these circumstances, resulted in the compromised ending the film has.

Of course, as many reviewers noted, Belafonte himself is relatively light-skinned, and Ferrer is of Cuban ancestry; they look nearly the same shade on the black-and-white screen, and Belafonte is more handsome and more personable, so the racial issue almost literally fades into meaninglessness. Both white people in the film make it clear that it's of no great concern to them. But to come up at all seems so out of place as to have largely destroyed the film for many viewers; it is rarely shown today, probably because of this.

When you have what are possibly the only two people left in the world, certainly the only two for thousands of miles, even in 1959, the issue of race seemed no issue at all. In terms of different skin color, race became meaningless when compared to the survival of humanity itself. Even if there are other people alive elsewhere (which seems likely fairly early on), children will still be necessary, and their race won't matter.

Furthermore, you might presume that the immensely overwhelming pressure of loneliness would soon force these two into bed, but they do not even hold hands until the end.

The entire issue of race and sex is clearly a problem to writer-director Ranald McDougall, so he tries to make it more understandable and less touchy by making the reluctant one of the pair the black man, not the white woman. But this brought in a painful note of patronizing. Ralph is so good, so decent, that he will not take advantage of the white woman even under these, to say the least, extreme circumstances. Also, he's a paragon of humanity himself, making the possibility of their being lovers less distasteful. (The idea was handled in much the same way in *Guess Who's Coming to Dinner*.) If the film were made today, audiences would have no problem with them tearing off their clothes and screwing in the street the minute they met, but in 1959, Belafonte wasn't allowed even to *kiss* Stevens.

I suspect the makers of the film weren't quite aware of how appealing Harry Belafonte is, both in and for himself, and as Ralph Burton. But MacDougall and, presumably, Belafonte were so anxious to avoid questions of miscegenation, they run screaming away from it, down those empty Manhattan streets. Even the ending doesn't answer anything: yes, Belafonte and Stevens join hands, but then they walk off with Ferrer, hand in hand in hand. What are we to make of this? Are the two men going to share the woman? Will she be able to choose which is to be the father of their children? The ending, with a huge "The Beginning," is a question-dodging cop-out.

The scenes in deserted Manhattan were difficult to shoot. The production company was so proud of their results that a handbook of information and questions-and-answers about the movie was released to the press; the following information comes from that publication.

"No process shots were used in the film, no trick shots, no double exposures, no fake backdrops," the publication says proudly. There were two exceptions, both "MGM trade secrets." One is clearly the long shot of the bridge stuffed with abandoned cars. The "two exceptions" were, therefore, probably matte paintings; there are several other shots that may be mattes, including the scene in which Ralph turns on the lights, and a shot of the church. There's also a shot of distant lightning which is clearly an effects shot.

The shot in Times Square was carefully planned in Los Angeles before the crew went to New York to shoot it. A crew of 35 and two cameras were required; platforms were constructed to get the right angle for the shot, and various prop trucks were stationed to litter, then un-litter, the streets with debris left by evacuating New Yorkers.

MGM's research indicated that Friday morning, rather than Sunday, was the most deserted time in Times Square. All traffic entering the Square was stopped six times, three minutes each, and all the traffic lights and advertising signs were briefly shut down. Because of overcast skies on the day of shooting, the shot could not be made at the planned 6:45 a.m. time, but had to be delayed almost an hour. An unexpected water truck went through, wetting down one side of the Square; so worried filmmakers had it *come back*, wetting down the entire visible street. This was explained by references in the film to a rainstorm. (But the sidewalks remained dry.) This shot, plus one with Inger Stevens, runs less than a minute on the screen. It's one of 37 similar setups in Manhattan. The other street scenes were filmed in Culver City.

The question-and-answer portion of the fact sheet admitted that several birds are visible (before the pigeon-filled ending) if "you look very closely indeed." It added, "In order not to fool the eyes of the viewer, but to force him or her to look for signs of life, there is always something moving in each shot besides the central characters. Newspapers are seen blowing along the street, a baby carriage is pushed by the wind, even a beach ball is seen in one shot rolling up Fifth Avenue. All were used deliberately to make the viewer hunt for signs of life as the central character is doing. The [birds] got in by mistake, however."

Anticipating objections, but failing to understand them, the fact sheet also asks "Where are all the bodies?" The answer: "In one scene, if one looks very carefully, there is a man lying dead on the sidewalk. Otherwise, there are none shown. Originally, there were four bodies seen in the picture. For reasons not easily explainable, not seeing *any* was more powerful in its effect.... The city is just as the people left it. Where they went and precisely how they died is left to the imagination, where it belongs." Unfortunately, this is a classic case of begging the question, and the film provides no answer at all. If there had been a line about how the radioactive sodium dissolved bodies, it might have been specious but at least it would have been an answer.

Answering their self-asked question about where the pigeons come from at the end, the fact sheet responds that they are there "deliberately and for a specific reason.... There have been many signs of life returning to the city—trees are beginning to grow again, blossoms are found, voices are heard on the shortwave radio—life is coming back. The pigeons ... are one more sign of life at a time when two of the characters are ... trying to destroy each other." Of course, another question is avoided: Where were the pigeons when the sodium killed everything? In eggs? In a decompression chamber? With Mel Ferrer?

Many years later, *The Omega Man* (1971) tried to duplicate the atmosphere of the opening scenes of *The World the Flesh and the Devil*, copying some ideas almost exactly, including taking a car from a showroom and using the window dummies as company. However, the filmmakers weren't anywhere near as careful about their backgrounds as Ranald MacDougall and his crew, and very often cars, people and other signs of human life are highly visible. (But that's okay; the film is very bad.)

In a movie that has only three characters (the makers thought this the smallest cast of all time, forgetting at least *The Four Poster*, with two), the actors become even more important than in films with a conventional cast. Under the circumstances, there are few people more pleasant to be alone with than Harry Belafonte. He'd only made three films as an actor before this, *Bright Road* (1953), *Carmen Jones* (1955) and *Island in the Sun* (1957); *Odds Against Tomorrow* was also released in 1959. Belafonte was highly dissatisfied with his performances—though he needn't have been—and didn't return as an actor until 1970, in *The Angel Levine*. He also appeared in *Buck and the Preacher* (1972) and *Uptown Saturday Night* (1974) with his friend Sidney Poitier; he was especially good as the rascally Preacher, but seems to have given up acting.

Belafonte's popularity during the 1950s cannot be overestimated: his initial album of calypso songs was for many years the largest-selling of all long-playing records. His rich, husky voice has a broad range, and he can sing almost any kind of material. He was a media star before his initial appearance in a mixed-race film, *Island in the Sun*, but hardly needed the career boost.

In *The World the Flesh and the Devil*, Ralph is a quiet, charming man, from a blue-collar class but intelligent and adept—but the most important aspect is that he's the *only* person we see for much of the film, and for all of its best scenes. Belafonte's performance is varied and detailed; he convinces us he's alone, anguished and afraid, and that he eventually makes a resigned adjustment to a lifetime of loneliness. He believably comes to feel he was spared in order that he might rescue and preserve humanity's culture, and begins collecting paintings, sculptures and books. He's never cynical or, after a while, bitter, but reaches an almost serene acceptance, tempered with underlying unhappiness. He's anything but a stereotyped Decent Negro; he truly is Everyman, the representative of *all* humanity, and is easily accepted as such. The performance is not only rich with Belafonte's own immense personal charm, but the character himself, by his actions and monologues, has his own style and personality. Though occasionally slightly amateurish, Belafonte is believable and winning.

Inger Stevens fares less well; her character isn't as well drawn, nor as appealing. She seems less of an individual and more of an allegorical figure, and Stevens doesn't rise above the script. Still, she's acceptable, and more appealing than other actresses might be under the circumstances. It isn't her fault that after her relationship with Belafonte is established, the film stalls until the final member of the conventional romantic triangle turns up. In fact, after the birthday party scene, the movie becomes boringly talky.

Stevens seems to have been unhappy. She rose from burlesque to a chorus girl, then to Broadway and films. She made her movie debut with *Man on Fire* in 1957, and had an unhappy romance with Bing Crosby before his second marriage, and one with another actor. She attempted suicide in 1959, and didn't make another film until 1964. During the 60s, she was relatively busy, having a hit TV series, "The Farmer's Daughter." However, personal satisfaction must have eluded her, for she committed suicide in 1970. An interesting, ironic sidelight on the racial issues in *The World the Flesh and the Devil* is that after her death, it was revealed that she'd been married for nine years to black musician Isaac Jones, according to Katz's *The Film Encyclopedia*.

As the third corner of the triangle, Mel Ferrer has a handicap going in: he's a cold, distant actor, making Ben a suspicious character from the beginning. We just can't like Ferrer, a curse that has plagued his mixed career.

In a highly unusual development, Ferrer was a movie director before he was a movie actor; his first film as director was in 1945, and his acting debut was in 1949. Ferrer played a black man in his first movie, *Lost Boundaries*. He became a star at MGM in the early 50s, appearing in a wide range of films, including *The Brave Bulls* (1951), Fritz Lang's *Rancho Notorious*, and *Knights of the Round Table* (1954, as King Arthur). His most famous role was that of the crippled puppeteer in *Lili* (1953), where for once he used his coldness to advantage. His best role, however, was as the arrogant villain in the wonderful *Scaramouche* of 1952.

He was in Europe from the mid-50s on, working in such films as *War and Peace*, Jean Renoir's *Elena et les Hommes* (both 1956) and *The Longest Day* (1962). *The World the Flesh and the Devil* was his only U.S.–filmed movie of this period.

Ferrer produced two horror films in the early 60s, *Blood and Roses* (1960) and *Hands of Orlac* (1961), acting in both. His career began to decline. A late attempt at directing, Green Mansions (1959), was poorly received, despite the presence of his then-wife Audrey Hepburn in the leading role. He later produced a number of unusual films, including the hit Wait Until Dark (1967), The Night Visitor (1971) and W (1974). He was off the screen as an actor from 1964 to 1972, and since that time has appeared in a series of low-quality films: Eaten Alive (1977), The Norseman (1978), Guyana—Cult of the Damned (1979) and several Italian imitations of Night of the Living Dead. He had a brief comeback as a star of TV's "Falcon Crest," but was quickly written out of the series.

In the late 40s and early 50s, Ranald MacDougall was one of the head writers at Warner Bros., turning out several Joan Crawford vehicles of that period; Mildred Pierce (1945) and Possessed (1947). He also wrote Objective, Burma! (1945), The Hasty Heart (1949) and Bright Leaf (1950). Among his other films as writer: The Naked Jungle (1954, for George Pal), Secret of the Incas (1954) and We're No Angels (1955). He began as director with Queen Bee (1955), which he also wrote; he wrote and directed Man on Fire (1957) and Go Naked in the World (1961), and was one of several writers who struggled with the script of Cleopatra (1963). Later, he turned to producing movies for television, including Jigsaw (1968, also released to theatres) and The Cockeyed Cowboys of Calico County (1970). MacDougall died in 1973.

As a director, he shows considerable power in the first half of The World the Flesh and the Devil; it's dramatic and atmospheric, self-consciously arty at times—one sequence of a series of stone lions "roused" by the sound of a church bell is effective, but was "inspired" by such a scene in Potemkin (1925)—but on the whole, interesting and engrossing. But as a writer, MacDougall lets the director down. Instead of treating the material at hand with the approach it deserved—it was the first major studio film ever on the end of the world—he felt it necessary to dress it up with another trendy concern, race relations, and so compromised his film that it became embarrassing. It's as if the end of the world alone were not important enough.

He claimed that the film was primarily an allegory, and he may have been telling the truth. It doesn't function as scientific speculation: there's little validity in the idea of radioactive sodium which is deadly only five days. If it were merely radioactive, people and animals could linger for weeks before dying. His intent was merely to clear out the world and set up the situation, but unfortunately, the setting—a depopulated world—is more compelling and interesting than whether or not Harry Belafonte will ever go to bed with Inger Stevens.

Still, the film does have that undeniable, eerie power at the beginning. Belafonte wandering stunned through Manhattan provides great images, immensely enhanced by Harold J. Marzorati's fine photography. Miklos Rozsa's music is excellent, though occasionally overdramatic.

Virtually all reviewers were disappointed in the film, but it received exceptionally wide coverage, primarily because of the end-of-the-world theme. "Powr" in Variety considered it "a provocative tour de force.... A thoughtful, adult film [that] is also a superior exploitation picture.... [The early] 'Robinson Crusoe' approach, in the heart of Manhattan, is dramatically fruitful and often amusing.... Although, overall, the film is engrossing, it gets curiously less effective as additional survivors turn up. When Belafonte is entirely alone on the screen ... the semi-documentary style keeps the film crisp and credible."

Bosley Crowther wrote, for him, an unusually interesting review for the New York Times: "They have stretched their imagination a great deal further than they have stretched their intellects" in the film, he said. Up to the point before Belafonte meets Stevens, "the drama is graphic and interesting, presenting a science-fiction idea in good, vivid cinematic style.... Mr. MacDougall has presented this awesome phenomenon [of deserted Manhattan] with pictorial force and clarity.... All of this part of the picture has been done dramatically, with the shots of New York, the actual city, filmed in the dawn light, particularly superb.... [The happy ending] is such an obvious contrivance and so cozily theatrical that you wouldn't be surprised to see the windows of the buildings suddenly crowded with reintegrated people, cheering happily and flinging ticker tape.... A good idea, good direction and good performances [by Belafonte and Stevens] have been sacrificed here to the Hollywood caution of treating the question of race with continuing evasion of more delicate issues and in polite, beaming generalities."

Time called it "a passionately sincere, pictorially brilliant, monumentally silly example of how people who are obsessed with the race question tend to see everything in Black and White.... [With Stevens' appearance,] all at once the grand drama of humanity's survival collapses into an irrelevant wrangle about racial discrimination that has no more real significance, under the circumstances of the story, than a hotfoot in hell.... Which boy will get the girl? In this instance, the answer is intended to answer the race question.... Black boy gets white girl—or seems to. But then in the confusing finish (which was reshot after a big front-office foofaraw), all three wander off together hand in hand—with the girl in the middle."

"R.V." in the *Monthly Film Bulletin* found it "more notable for its pretensions than its convictions." Again praising the opening scenes, R.V. said they "are beautifully developed in a semi-documentary style by expressive camerawork, some good editing and an imaginative use of sound, all of which distracts attention from Belafonte's overplaying and an excessive reliance on gimmicks and shock effects." The ending gave R.V. problems, too. "The absolutely banal and schematic handling of the 'racial' problem is typical of the whole project: it is impossible to accept Belafonte's idealised, handsome portrayal of the Negro as a valid characterisation, any more than the muddleheaded and obscure denouement, which appears to suggest that only friendship and/or polyandry can avert world catastrophe."

More recent writers have also commented on the sharp division in the film, such as Don Willis (I), who said "the awful and the striking are indiscriminately mixed. Good one minute; bad the next."

Alan Frank (*SF*) was less equivocal. "A dreadful movie that reduces postholocaust life to a tedious reworking of that old faithful, the eternal triangle, complete with racial tensions and a totally unbelievable happy ending. Only the settings impress."

As some other writers did, John Brosnan noted the similarity to *Five*. "Compared to Oboler's talkative and dreary film, MacDougall's post-atomic war vision is superior in both script and direction."

In *Nuclear War Films*, Frank W. Oglesbee concluded his sour analysis of the film, "The only credible moments in *The World, the Flesh and the Devil* result from Harold Marzorati's serene cinematography, and the cast's valiant attempts to overcome the material. The foreboding landscapes ... serve as a memorable apocalyptic sermon. Cinematically, the aftermath of the bomb, as presented in WFD, is an artistic achievement. But overall, WFD is a disappointing, unimaginative and unreasonable view of the problems of race and nuclear war."

The film attempts a great deal, and it is difficult to question MacDougall's sincerity, but his taste and judgment seem to have fled him partway through. What is the ultimate message of the film? Few will be offered the opportunity to answer, as the movie is rarely shown today.

The Amazing Transparent Man

Believers in Edgar G. Ulmer's ability to transcend the B-movie strictures will have their faith sorely tried by this painful entry. One of a pair of films (the other was *Beyond the Time Barrier*) made by Ulmer in Texas in the late 1950s, this is a useless amalgam of the gangster and science fiction movie genres. Apart from a moderately interesting performance by James Griffith as a would-be world dictator, the film has nothing to recommend it. I have heard it said that the film was mostly not directed by Ulmer, and that he was instead concentrating his energies on *Beyond the Time Barrier*, which wasn't made back-to-back with *Transparent Man*, but *simultaneously* with it. Neither film is much good, but *Time Barrier* is less rotten than *Transparent Man*, which has few if any directorial touches of any value.

According to John Baxter in *Science Fiction in the Cinema*, Ulmer shot both of them "on location at the Texas State Showground, commuting from one production to another across the arena until he ran out of money, whereupon the star brought both films in with his own money." Typically of someone who doesn't understand how films are made, Baxter says of 1950s SF films, "The cheapness of the films combined with the juvenile simplicity of the plots made it alarmingly easy to embark on an SF film, though problems of sets and effects generally arose halfway through. The two Ulmer films solved this ingeniously by using ace designer Ernst Fegté, an old associate of the director's, who created a system of triangular module panels from which sets could be created, then easily broken down later."

Very few producers, no matter how low-budget or inexperienced, charged into a film unaware of possible problems with sets and effects. Baxter also says "the star" financed both films, but there's no star in common to the films. Robert Clarke did finance *Time Barrier* from the start, while *Transparent Man* is likely to have been made on money saved from the budget for the other film, but it's unlikely they "ran out of money." Fegté's triangular module sets are used in *Time Barrier*, but not in *Transparent Man*. Take that, John Baxter.

It's doubtful that *The Amazing Transparent Man* had a shooting schedule any longer than a week. Aside from the laboratory scenes, which are visually more interesting than the rest of the film, and which look more like Ulmer's work, most of the film takes place outdoors and in the living room of what seems to be an actual farmhouse. These scenes are pedestrian to the point of boredom, unimaginatively filmed and thoroughly clichéd. If indeed Ulmer only directed parts of the picture, these location shots could very well be the portions directed by someone else.

The story opens as thief Joey Faust (Douglas Kennedy) breaks out of prison—the titles are picked out by searchlights—and is picked up by Laura Matson (Marguerite Chapman), an attractive blonde Faust has never met. She's working for Krenner (James Griffith), who needs Faust's safecracking abilities. The two far too easily pass through a police roadblock and arrive at an interesting old house out on the Texas plains.

Krenner proves to be a megalomaniac, a professional soldier who goes by the self-given rank of major; he's served in "several" armies. Krenner alludes to Faust's never-seen daughter, which angers the safecracker. "If you ever mention my daughter's name again..." he growls threateningly, though Krenner *didn't* mention her name.

Faust is over a barrel because of the implied threat, and has to cooperate with Krenner. Faust is taken upstairs to the laboratory where Dr. Peter Ulof (Ivan Triesault) is found bending over a microscope. Ulof has devised a machine that works on the principle of an X-ray but "goes farther" and can render things "transparent." (The word "invisible" is avoided at all times.)

Faust is imprisoned in a room below, but manages to escape, knocking out Julian (Red Morgan), a thug who works for Krenner. But instead of fleeing, Faust goes back up to the laboratory where he learns that Krenner keeps Ulof's daughter prisoner in another room. As Faust himself has that nameless daughter, he feels a kinship with Ulof. The scientist tells the safecracker that he was forced to kill his own wife in concentration camp experiments, and that "spies like Krenner" knew he was a scientist. Also, he's dying, with only a few more months to live.

Faust decides not to leave, finding time to fall in love with Laura and to woo her away from Krenner. It isn't hard; she's lonely, depressed and frightened; when she drinks heavily, as she often does, Krenner sometimes slaps her around. (Shades of *Key Largo*.)

Finally, Faust is made invisible—er, transparent—by Ulof's machine, in one of the few interesting shots in the picture. As his head and hands turn into negative images before vanishing, followed by his clothing, Faust screams in pain.

Now invisible, Faust goes to a nuclear power plant and simply opens the vault, as if he knew the combination. He takes the radioactive material back to Krenner, who needs it to power a lot of Ulof's machines; his goal is to create an invisible army and conquer the world.

Faust's own goals are more immediate. With Laura's help, he renders himself transparent again and goes into town to rob a bank. Unfortunately, during the robbery, he reappears, disappears, and reappears again, before shooting his way out, to vanish once again. (In a plot element that may have had more relevance in an earlier draft, it's carefully established that the same security firm guarded both the atomic power plant and the bank.)

Back at the ranch house, we learn that Krenner also forced Julian's cooperation by playing on an absent child; he'd falsely told Julian that his son was alive in prison in Europe. (One wonders if Krenner also obtained Laura's cooperation by threatening a child; writer Jack Lewis found one surefire area of human vulnerability, and leans heavily on it.)

Ulof urges Faust to sacrifice himself to prevent Krenner from overrunning the United States with an invisible army. Although as seen so far, Faust would be more likely to tell Ulof to get some other patsy, he weakens. The clincher comes when Ulof tells him that the invisibility ray treatments have given Joey only one month to live. (This might make recruiting an invisible army difficult.) So the safecracker turns hero. Ulof describes him: "There is a man who has unlocked every door except the one to his own soul and now he has the key." No one could ever accuse Jack Lewis of being flatly realistic in his writing.

Krenner kills Laura, which doesn't improve Faust's opinion of the would-be dictator. The two battle it out in the lab, and in the struggle, radioactive material is struck by the invisibility rays. This causes an atomic explosion which blows up half the county.

Elsewhere, Ulof, who escaped, talks to policemen about what should be done with the invisibility ray; he then addresses the camera directly, speaking to us, the audience: "What would *you* do?"

This enigmatic ending was enthusiastically pounced on by the initial distributors, Miller Consolidated Pictures (MCP). They staged a contest on the theme of what should be done with the invisibility ray, with the prize a scholarship. I was in high school then and really got behind this contest, pushing it to my fellow students and announcing it prominently in the school paper. I never heard a damned thing from MCP, nor from American International, which shortly took over distribution. If anyone knows who got the Amazing Transparent Man scholarship, I'd like to find out.

The other imaginative aspect of the campaign, which featured simple but arresting artwork, was the following "WARNING!" which appeared on posters: "Joey Faust, escaped convict, *The Amazing Transparent Man*, has vowed to 'appear' invisible IN PERSON at every performance of this picture in this theatre. *Police* officers are expected to be present in force, but the management will not be responsible for any unusual or mysterious happenings while Faust is in the theatre." He didn't turn up at the Pacific Theatre in Reedsport.

The Amazing Transparent Man is clumsy and contrived, from the outrageous and meaningless name of its criminal hero, to all those children Krenner uses to gain his advantages.

Producers of low-budget films are ill-advised to attempt something as ambitious as an invisible-man movie, which, to be successful, requires careful, intelligent use of traveling mattes, subtle work with wires, and a kind of overall special effects sleight of hand. The effects in *Transparent Man* are credited to the Hollywood–based Howard A. Anderson Company, and while they are imaginative in concept, there're actually only two or three optical effects in the film: when Faust disappears in the lab, and when he later reappears in the bank. In the latter scene, at first only his head and hands appear (symmetrically with the disappearing scene, where his head and hands vanish first), which is an interesting if comic effect. The other invisible-man stunts involve bags of money, cannisters of atomic material, etc., being moved by wires, which are occasionally highly visible.

Apart from these brief effects, the film is just a crime thriller, with an escaped con hero, a criminal mastermind, and a romantic triangle involving a girl who's been around, as they used to say. The story has a SF resolution — good bad guy and bad bad guy are blown up with an atomic bomb — but the plot and character interactions are strictly B-movie crime formula.

The only interesting set is that of the lab, which has a corrugated tin ceiling, implying it is just under the roof; the sound in the lab, perhaps as a result, is always flat. The decorations in the lab, however, are a bit silly: at one point, Ulof moves two metal globes on a rod closer together and puts some kind of electrical zapper between them. This is to look Scientific. There are also some snapping and sparking electrical devices which resemble (and may be) those invented by Kenneth Strickfaden. The lighting in these scenes is more interesting than in the rest of the film, with harsh contrasts playing over the faces. Ivan Triesault's performance is better here, too; his weariness in explaining the machine to Faust is an imaginative idea. This poor old geezer dislikes the use to which his remarkable invention is to be put; he's just worn out and his caring is running down.

Mostly, however, the film is very dully directed; it consists primarily of long shots in boring rooms, with few close-ups and little intercutting, generally indications of a very low budget. About the only clever touch in the directing, and it's *too* clever, is when Faust is breaking out of his room: he tosses a blanket over the camera for a cut.

The dialogue is pseudo–tough guy, and Faust is established as the toughest guy around quickly: he plucks a shrapnel fragment out of the air as Krenner tosses it to him. Later, there's a line as to how a bullet will "rip out your spine and roll it up like a ball of string," which makes one wonder what part of the anatomy the gun would be aimed at.

The leads in the film were all experienced actors. Douglas Kennedy died in 1973, but had long been around Hollywood, usually playing bad guys in second-feature Westerns. He was not an accomplished actor, but was a reliable one. You wanted a tough, slightly laconic guy who resembled Fred MacMurray, you got Doug Kennedy. I had a fondness for him while I was a child, because he seemed somehow to be better than his material, and to have an out-of-character warmth that came through even at his toughest. Other films of Douglas Kennedy include *The Ghost Breakers* (1940), *Possessed*, *Dark Passage* (both 1947), *The Adventures of Don Juan* (1948), *The Next Voice You Hear* (1950), *Invaders from Mars*, and a whole posse of Westerns in the 1950s. He was also in the SF films *The Alligator People* and *The Destructors* (1968).

Pop-eyed, soft-voiced James Griffith usually borders on the sniveling-weasel type; his megalomaniac Krenner here is just one of those weasels with more ambition than most. Like Douglas Kennedy, his range is not broad, but that isn't important; he was hired to be a certain type, and brought that off well. He works in a variety of films, because his type, that slightly unctuous person who could be treacherous or loyal as the role demanded, turns up in many movies. Among his other films are *The Breaking Point* (1950), *Dragnet* (1954), *Son of Sinbad* (1955), *The Vampire*, *North to Alaska* (1960), *Spartacus* (1960) and *Heaven with a Gun* (1969).

This seems to have been the last film of Marguerite Chapman. She was a reliable, intelligent actress who never rose above leads in B movies, though she was more than acceptable in those parts. It's just that there were always better or more famous or more attractive actresses ahead of her in line. She's not given much to do in *The Amazing Transparent Man*, beyond working the vein that Claire Trevor mined so effectively in several films. Among Chapman's other films were *Charlie Chan at the Wax Museum* (1940), the fine serial *Spy Smasher* (1942), *The Body Disappears* (1941), *The Gallant Blade* (1948), *Flight to Mars* (1951) and *The Seven Year Itch* (1955).

Ivan Triesault rarely had a role of more prominence than the third little old man on the left. He was never a character lead, but was not bad in the wise-old-man roles he often played. Among his films were *Mission to Moscow* (1943), *The Mummy's Ghost*, *Cry of the Werewolf* (both 1944), *Notorious* (1946), *Journey to the Center of the Earth* and *Batman* (1966).

Reviews of *The Amazing Transparent Man* were no better than it deserved. It doesn't seem to have been covered by the movie trade publications, which is a little unusual. The *Monthly Film Bulletin* gave it its lowest rating. "Gimcrack SF-cum-crime melodrama, lacking in personality and invention. The film resembles nothing so much as those tatty little mad-scientist thrillers Bela Lugosi was making ... twenty years ago, with the exception that their saving grace of unconscious humor is here totally absent. Acting, staging and script are all consistently abysmal."

Alan Frank (*SF*) described it as "tedious and too long for its feeble narrative and execution," but I disagree. In fact, apart from the slightly interesting laboratory scenes and the reliable if two-bit performances by the leads, the only saving grace of *The Amazing Transparent Man* is its relatively fast pace, for such a shoddily-conceived film with dull scenes, and its brevity. But it is a waste of anyone's hour.

The Atomic Submarine

Although I doubt that anyone would ever call this little movie a good film, it has a certain odd likability that makes it a more watchable film than it has any right to be. Despite a shortage of action, and especially lame direction by veteran Spencer Gordon Bennet, the film is relatively brisk, and the acting by a crew of old (and young) pros is considerably above average for a low-budget film, although the script by Orville H. Hampton is so full of clunker lines and wildly wrong character reactions as to be frequently hilarious.

The film was shot in probably just over a week, with not much more time spent on the inadequate but exuberant special effects by Jack Rabin, Irving Block and Louis DeWitt. There are plenty of stock shots, and the movie generates its *own* stock footage as well. One shot, used at least five times, shows a sub passing what are supposed to be underwater cliffs, but which look like foil-wrapped lumps of coal. Another shot of the underwater flying saucer winking its light at us from within a cave turns up at least four times.

The film's basic premise is okay: aliens that live underwater are checking out Earth for a possible home, and knocking off submarines (*cargo* and *passenger* subs!) that come too close to the North Pole. However, as is usual with Hampton, the film raises more questions than it answers. For instance, much is made of the fact that the saucer always destroys craft 100 "nautical miles" from the North Pole, but there's no clue as to why it insists on such a precise boundary. Nor, for that matter, why it's destroying the subs at all; such actions would seem only to call attention to the saucer—which, of course, is what happens.

After several subs are destroyed by electrical charges near the North Pole, Admiral Terhune (Selmer Jackson) calls a meeting in Washington, D.C., where he reveals that seven atomic submarines and several surface vessels have been destroyed or disappeared. He assigns Captain Wendover (Dick Foran), skipper of the *Tiger Shark*, to investigate, and to take with him scientists Dr. Clifford Kent (Victor Varconi) and Sir Ian Hunt (Tom Conway).

Wendover sends for Commander "Reef" Holloway (Arthur Franz), interrupting his romantic dalliance with Julie (Joi Lansing). Reef and his buddy Lt. Dave Milburn (Paul Dubov) report for duty at Bremerton in the state of Washington, along with the other crew members. Reef is annoyed that the maneuverable diving bell aboard ship is under the direction of Dr. Carl Nielson (Brett Halsey). Carl is the son of an old friend of Reef's, but is also an ardent pacifist, which royally pisses off career officer Reef. They have a few clashes.

The atomic submarine takes a very curious route from Bremerton to the North Pole—going *around* the Aleutians for instance—but no sooner has it neared Nome than it is attacked by the mysterious undersea force.

There follows a great deal of time-wasting, dull footage (interspersed with animated chart lines) as they gradually figure out what is going on. This is one of those films in which every idle speculation is confirmed by events as fact.

Eventually, the *Tiger Shark* and the spaceship—dubbed "Cyclops" because of a lighthouselike turret at its top—square off. The sub launches a couple of torpedoes, but the first is deflected and the second becomes embedded in what one cast member describes as a mass of jelly extruded from the flying saucer. (On screen, the "jelly" looks like a blur.) So Wendover rams the sub into the Cyclops, but the sub becomes stuck.

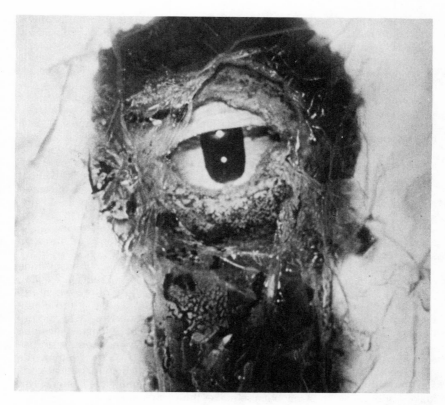

The cyclopean octopoidal alien at the end of The Atomic Submarine (1960) makes its appearance. No, it is not peeking through a hole in the ice; this is what it looks like in the film. Below this, it has some tentacles. Inside, it is Irving Block's arm.

Locked together, the two craft sink to the sea bottom. Reef is surprised when Carl shows backbone by insisting on guiding the submersible to the eye of Cyclops, and breaking into the flying saucer that way. Along for the ride are Reef, Carl, Dave and two frogmen.

They enter the flying saucer through the "eye," which has a two-lobed iris, and find themselves in a black chamber with good air. Carl remains aboard the submersible, while the two frogmen try to cut the bow of the sub loose from the flying saucer.

Everyone seems astonished that the flying saucer has *any* atmosphere inside and that there is anything alive aboard it. There are several lines by characters about how they thought they "killed" Cyclops; we later learn that the spaceship actually *is* alive, but that's hardly what anyone might have suspected.

Reef but not Dave hears a strange voice calling, and wanders off with Dave to find a huge sphere at the center of the spaceship. Inside the sphere is a cyclopean alien (interesting how things work out), which has stiff, waving tentacles. It tells Reef telepathically that it has been checking out several planets for colonization, and has decided on Earth.

Meanwhile, one of the two frogmen is sort of melted by a bright light and while fleeing, the other is crushed by the closing iris. (This is not what happens in the shooting script; I suspect the filmmakers decided that since they paid for that iris, they might as well get some use out of it.)

Dave comes up to see what Reef is talking to, which annoys the alien. It kills Dave, hardly seeming to bother Reef, who shoots it in the eye with that all-purpose science fiction weapon, a Very pistol.

The alien shrieks and waves its arms around, and Reef runs back to the submersible, almost getting caught in that damned iris. Carl asks what happened to the others, and Reef tersely tells him "fortunes of war." Now that's one tough cookie.

Back aboard the *Tiger Shark*, they realize that the spaceship is going to leave soon. Fortunately, it has to go back to the North Pole for magnetic "refueling" (established earlier), so our heroes have time to fix a missile to shoot down the spaceship. It is totally opaque as to why it is such a problem to reset a guided missile designed to blow up a city into one that will blow up a flying saucer, but this is presented as a truly big deal.

The saucer takes off, flying in the air now, and the missile is launched. It blows up the saucer. Aren't you surprised? Back at Bremerton, Carl and Reef show every sign of being pals.

The special effects in *The Atomic Submarine* are not so much inept as done on a budget far too low for the concepts. In one of the earliest shots in the film, a sub glides by in extreme close-up, and the rough texture of the miniature, plus clumsy lettering, make it look like nothing so much as one of those little baking powder–powered subs you used to find in cereal boxes. According to the effects crew, the models were three feet and 1½ feet in length, but none looks as though it could have been any bigger than six inches. There's a strange shot in which to avoid the Cyclops, the *Tiger Shark* rests on the bottom. We can't see the tail end of the sub, but the actions of the camera in following the sub's movements make it very clear that the ship is fastened to the camera. This makes for excellent tracking, but also makes things look unreal.

In the fine article on Rabin and Block in *Fantascene 2*, Rabin told interviewers Robert and Dennis Skotak (now effects men themselves) about *The Atomic Submarine*. "It was a horrible picture," he said. "I never saw it completed, though I built a submarine that cost a fortune. It worked. What I did to duplicate water: in the back room, I made a whole channel of crazy-looking rocks and took the miniature submarine ... along a fine wire on a track above. I put little pieces of aluminum foil atop the water in a large tank, and shone a light on it so that when we jiggled the water, it reflected rays like underwater currents." The sub was shot dry, with the tank of water above the miniature set.

The saucer itself was another problem. The interiors, the Skotaks said, "consisted entirely of a darkened sound stage, a thin, flat walkway and an iris-like hatchway. The rest was effects work, such as the inhabitant of the ship. This was a one-eyed creature dwelling within a huge metallic-looking sphere. The creature itself was built around [Irving] Block's arm which was inserted up into a hollow sphere lined with foil. The base of the monster (in actuality Block's elbow) was encircled by a row of rubber tentacles which he manipulated with wires. The walkway to the sphere was surrounded by a machine with crystal-like components. This was a matted-in miniature construction."

Amazingly, the alien almost works. It is certainly better than most such creatures in cheap films, and doesn't look much like any other space invader, except perhaps the Xenomorphs in *It Came from Outer Space*. It's black and hairy, with a thick, white base with suckers and also long, stiff tentacles or tendrils. The eye of the monster is a mistake; it's oversized, and looks like glass. When the eye is shot out, a lot of goo oozes forth; this is run in reverse later when the alien heals itself. The alien is at once inspired and silly, with a kind of crazy integrity.

Producer Alex Gordon was not happy with the alien. In *Fangoria* 1, he told interviewer John Hoxley that "sometimes the studio insisted on inserting effects that drove me crazy." For *Atomic Submarine*, said Gordon, "we were given $135,000 and six days to do an invasion epic. [Allied Artists] stuck us with this monster that we really didn't want to use. It was puppet-sized and looked awfully cheap and awfully phony. But the head of Allied Artists insisted we have the monster in the finale. So we showed this 'eyeball' puppet, which has since gone on to certain 'cult' joke status in SF circles. I thought it looked dreadful."

It *does* look dreadful, but it is also unusual and imaginative, and in some senses is the best thing about the film, giving it a peculiar air of alienness just when it needs it the most. (His *Underwater City* looked better, and had no aliens, but is less fun than *The Atomic Submarine*.)

The storyline of *Atomic Submarine* is trite, and tritely developed. For the most part, the film resembles a low-budget, stereotyped military film more than a science fiction picture. The title doesn't suggest anything futuristic; when the film was made, atomic-powered submarines had been reality for some time.

The characters are standard types: the military-minded hero is opposed by the traditional pacifist. It's a little different in that the pacifist comes around to the military way of thinking without the military man learning anything himself, but that's probably compression of story, not a point of view by Hampton. The two scientists are just more of the same: eggheads with one or two character traits each. The film is cut from well-worn cloth.

However, some of the dialogue and situations are so absurd as to make the film fun to watch. When Dave tries to tell Reef that maybe Carl has his own side (i.e., point of view), Reef snaps that Carl is "all front but no back. How could he have any sides?" The solemn narration heard throughout the film (to give it a documentary flavor) has its own share of howlers. "The *Tiger Shark* left her dock at Bremerton at 0335 hours, the morning of May 11, on what was to prove the strangest, most fearful voyage ever made by a submarine, atomic or otherwise." Orville Hampton describing telepathy: "You do not 'hear' me," the alien tells Reef. "Our individual brain frequencies are now attuned, and we exchange wave-thoughts."

Hampton tries to make Reef no-nonsense, but makes him sound incredibly callous, not only in the "fortunes of war" line quoted earlier, but upon Dave's death, to which Arthur Franz has no visible reaction. The alien doesn't kill Reef, and he asks, "What am I, the closing act?" Levity at that time makes Reef not only sound like he has balls of steel, but a head to match.

The narrator comes in near the end with the kind of line best avoided. Talking about the efforts to turn the missile into something that will shoot down Cyclops, the narrator tells us breathlessly, "It was foolish, it was insane, it was fantastic!" describing the film as well.

Hampton's ideas about science are even foggier and more in error than his view of correct military attitudes. One of the scientists suggests that Cyclops is magnetically powered, not atomically (although it is spotted by its radiation), and so must go to the North Pole to replenish itself in Earth's magnetic field. But as every schoolchild is taught, the Earth's magnetic pole and the true North Pole are hundreds of miles apart.

Of course, the film let *Hampton* down, too. He carefully describes in the script the chart that Sir Ian uses to point out the relationship between the attacks on the ships and the North Pole itself. The attack locations were to describe a nearly perfect circle around the Pole, but the locations we see marked simply do not form a circle. However, there is *another* circle drawn on the map, pointed out by a hand in an insert shot—but what that has to do with the story is a mystery.

Furthermore, the little animated line tracing the path of the *Tiger Shark* itself becomes a joke. Not only does the sub not follow anything remotely resembling a normal route from Bremerton to the Pole, but the dizzy course the ship follows in vainly trying to catch up with Cyclops describes a loopy flower around the Pole, making the captain seem demented.

The veteran cast does the best they can with the material. They were probably chosen by movie-fan Alex Gordon. Dick Foran had been in films since 1934, and was a reliable lead in second-string A films and many B movies, including many Westerns and a few serials. He appeared in the first two in Universal's revived Mummy series, *The Mummy's Hand* (1940) and *The Mummy's Tomb* (1942), as well as *Horror Island* (1941). Foran was always pleasant and likable, and remains so here. He died in 1979.

Tom Conway was the brother of George Sanders, and took over the role of "The Falcon" in that film series from his brother in 1942. Conway was always smooth and suave, with a superlative speaking voice. Because of his elegance and urbane charm, he worked frequently until his death in 1967. Unfortunately, in *The Atomic Submarine*, he seems out of touch with the film; in many reaction shots, he smiles and gestures but says nothing, as if he forgot his lines. Conway appeared in several fantasy films through the years, including *Tarzan's Secret Treasure* (1941), *Tarzan and the She-Devil* (1953), *Voodoo Woman* , *She Creature* (both 1957), and *12 to the Moon*. His best-liked genre films are the trio he made for Val Lewton in the 1940s: *Cat People, I Walked with a Zombie* and *The Seventh Victim*. He narrated Disney's *Peter Pan* (1953).

As the tough CPO, Bob Steele presents authority and capability, which he always showed in his hundreds of films and television shows. An actor since 1920, Steele appeared in many Westerns in the 30s and 40s, and occasionally showed himself as an above-average actor in other types of films as well, including *Of Mice and Men* (1940). He was also in *Revenge of the Zombies* (1943), but primarily has appeared in character roles in big-budget Westerns, often as the chief henchman of the villain.

The film was directed none too well by Spencer Gordon Bennet who, in his very long career, helmed almost no SF or fantasy features apart from *The Atomic Submarine* and a few 1950s Jungle Jim movies. Bennet began in films in 1912 as a stunt man, and as early as the 1920s, began in the field for which he is best known: serials. These are usually fast-paced and full of stunts, whereas *The Atomic Submarine* consists almost entirely of people standing in rooms talking. Bennet directed over 30 serials, from some very early ones (1925) to the last serial ever made, 1956's *Perils of the Wilderness*. Some of his serials are outstanding, such as *The Secret Code* (1942), *The Purple Monster Strikes* (1945), *Batman and Robin* (1949) and *Atom Man vs. Superman* (1950). Others he directed (or, often, codirected) are not thought of so highly: *Mysterious Island* (1961), *Captain Video* (1951), *Blackhawk* (1952). He was primarily efficient in getting things done quickly and in setting a fast pace. However, there just wasn't anything *to* move fast in *Atomic Submarine*. His last film was released in 1965, and he retired—as well he might. He was 72.

Of the other credits, cinematographer Gilbert Warrenton does all he can with the limited sets, and composer Alexander Laszlo provides a surprisingly good score.

"Glen" in Variety didn't care for it. "The exploitation value of the title is about all this one has to recommend it, though it's based on a fairly good science-fiction monster story idea. The directing is sluggish, special photography loses effectiveness by repetition of scenes and the screenplay wanders aimlessly.... Some of the special effects are good ... the monster ... is quite satisfactory. The importance to the film of the monster and the untidy deaths it inflicts on some mariners would indicate the film's title isn't apt."

The Monthly Film Bulletin gave the movie its lowest rating. "A moderately ingenious idea, ruined by indifferent acting, poor special effects, and a lumbering script which tries to take in a few shopworn thoughts about pacifism and war-mongering in a good cause. The interstellar mastermind is unimpressively conceived as a large eye in a woolly wig waving a tentacle or two."

Some more recent writers also disliked it. Alan Frank (SF) thought that "poor acting, poor special effects and too much would-be philosophical chat [what??] render this one unseaworthy."

However, Parish and Pitts had another opinion. "Of all the features made in the 50s and 60s by producer Alex Gordon, this entertaining B thriller is probably the best. The film boasts solid direction ... a literate script [what??], good art direction (done in part by future director Daniel Haller), and a cast chock full of veterans.... The early scenes of the private lives of the ship's crew being interrupted for the voyage are amusing. Once aboard the craft, the experienced cast more than holds the script together, making it a most enjoyable double-bill entry."

If viewed in the right, nonjudgmental frame of mind, The Atomic Submarine is enjoyable, but probably not as the makers intended.

Attack of the Giant Leeches

Gene and Roger Corman produced this minor thriller unconvincingly set in the Florida swamps. Unlike most of the films Roger Corman was connected with in this period, there's very little about it that is distinctive. The character relationships are standard, the exploitation of the monster material is unimaginative, and the film has a hangdog air about it. There's a good but brief performance from Yvette Vickers, and Bruno Ve Sota has some good moments, but overall, Attack of the Giant Leeches is not only undistinguished, it's downright bad.

There's no real explanation offered for the monsters, they aren't a great deviation from reality—leeches the size of a man are very unlikely, but not impossible—and they even aren't all that dangerous. For instance, they would be less dangerous than alligators, although their blood-sucking makes leeches somewhat more disgusting to most people than alligators. (Then again, alligators often drag their prey off to lairs like those the leeches have in the film, where they allow the body to rot until it can be easily eaten. That's pretty disgusting itself.)

The story opens in a swamp not far from Cape Canaveral, as Lem (George Cisar) fires at a weird shape he sees in the swamp water; bubbles (from dry ice) rise in the water as the credits roll. At the nearby hangout for local good ol' boys, Lem has a hard time convincing anyone that he saw what he saw, some awful thing with sucker-covered arms.

Homely, pudgy Dave Walker (Bruno Ve Sota) is married to much younger and sluttish Liz (Yvette Vickers), who delights in tormenting her husband by parading around in leopard-skin panties and a black bra, while refusing to allow him to touch her. He's just spoken kinda mean to her in front of the guys, and she's peeved. She slinks out.

Not long later, while game warden Steve Benton (Ken Clark) and his girl-friend Nan (Jan Shepard) are out dismantling illegal trap lines, Liz screams: she's encountered Lem, who is dying from wounds similar to those (allegedly) made by an octopus' suckers. Steve can't convince lethargic local sheriff Kovis (Gene Roth) to do anything about the strange death.

Later, Liz slinks out again, this time for a tryst with local lothario Cal Moulton (Michael Emmet). They're necking on a swamp bank, while she tells him the reason she hooked up with Dave was because he was the first guy who was nice to her after her divorce from her bum of a first husband. Unluckily for her, her second husband is alert: he catches Liz and Cal together, and forces them back into the swamp with his shotgun.

Liz and Cal start squabbling over whose fault this is. Cal whines, "If it wasn't for you, I wouldn't be in this fix and my old friend Dave wouldn't be doin' this thing to me." Only intent on putting the fear of God into them, Dave starts to let them out of the swamp—they're in the water up to their waists—but the giant leeches grab them and haul them away.

Later, Dave despondently tells the sheriff he loved good-for-nothing Liz, but the sheriff doesn't believe Dave's tale of monsters attacking the hapless lovers, and tosses Dave into the clink. Later, still in jail, Dave hangs himself.

After a talky, pointless scene, two good ol' boys begin poking around gator holes, but the leeches, which make a grumbling, bubbly sound, grab them too, and take them to a gator cave under the bank of the swamp. Cal and Liz are there, too, as blood supplies, and the leeches add their new victims to the larder. They slither over all four in turn, sucking blood from their necks.

Steve organizes a fruitless (and boring) search of the swamp, and announces his intention to find the monsters, which he believes in. He refuses to allow any use of dynamite by Doc Greyson (Tyler McVey), Nan's father, because it might destroy other wildlife than the monsters. (The fact that it has been pointed out several times that almost all the wildlife is gone, supposedly scared off by the monsters, goes unrecalled at this point.) However, Doc does throw in the dynamite, which explodes and brings up the bodies of the three men the leeches had captured. They are dead; all the blood in their bodies is gone, through suction wounds on their throats.

Doc and Steve recall that caves and caverns were carved out of the area by the ocean years ago. Liz Walker might still be down there, they think, and the film cuts to a shot of Liz Walker, still down there.

Steve is now convinced that something needs to be done, and with another diver, he begins to plant dynamite in the area; Steve is chased by a giant leech, but gets away.

While the divers are bubbling around beneath the water, much to the annoyance of the sheriff, who feels his official territory is being trampled, Doc discusses the origin of the giant leeches. "Maybe the proximity of Cape Canaveral's got something to do with it," he opines. "They use atomic energy in the first stages of launching. Not all of them have been successful."

Liz finally succumbs to loss of blood, falls into the pool in the cave, and drifts to the surface outside. Steve battles a giant leech underwater, but gets away just before the dynamite goes off. The explosion brings some of the big leeches to the surface, and everyone thinks the menace is ended. But just before "The End" appears on the screen, we hear the leeches' sounds again. The horror continues.

In all advertising and trailers, *Attack of the Giant Leeches* was called more simply *The Giant Leeches*. Perhaps there had been too many SF movies with "attack" in the title recently, two the year before. In any event, despite what the posters and ad art say, the title on screen is definitely *Attack of the Giant Leeches*. In England, the film was *Demons of the Swamp*, but by any title it's a second-rate offering despite some bright spots.

The movie was written by character actor Leo Gordon (who sometimes bills himself as a writer as Leo V. Gordon), a better actor than a writer. He's been in films as an actor for 30 years, usually as a villain or a hot-tempered heavyweight; he appeared in several John Wayne pictures, including *Hondo* (1953), *The Conqueror* (1956) and, most famously, *McLintock!* (1963). In that entertaining Western, Gordon is the big bruiser to whom Wayne says, while struggling to keep his temper, "I haven't lost my temper in 40 years. But, pilgrim, someone ought to belt you in the mouth. But I won't. I won't. The *hell* I won't!" Socko.

I suspect Gordon turns up in muscular fare like this, right up to the present, because he's a large, solid-looking man, with beetling brows and a scowl that won't stop. Wayne and other big men could slug him without looking like bullies.

Gordon has had an association with Roger and Gene Corman since the late 1950s, mostly as a writer. In addition to *Attack of the Giant Leeches*, Gordon also wrote *The Wasp Woman*, *Valley of the Redwoods* (1960), *The Cat Burglar* (1961), *Tower of London* (1962), *The Terror* (1963), *The Bounty Killer* (1965) and *Tobruk* (1967). All of these but *The Bounty Killer* were for one or the other of the Corman brothers, and none is much good. *The Terror* has some fame for its brief and complicated production, but there's little else of interest to the film.

Attack of the Giant Leeches obviously resulted from a search to find one more ugly bug to enlarge and make a menace to mankind. However, leeches are a singularly uninteresting idea. Their size is the only odd thing about them here; otherwise, they behave much like leeches really do, although real leeches don't have arms. The creatures live in the water and seem to be confined to it (unlike real leeches). They don't exhibit much intelligence, aren't more dangerous than any other carnivore of similar size; all in all, they're a tame menace. The fact that they suck blood, which is made much of in the film, is the only thing that distinguishes them from any other large aquatic predator.

Gordon does keep things to the point, however: all of the action in the film revolves around the presence of the leeches; there's no extraneous material.

The leech suits have a shiny plastic look, and are voluminously folded and creased. Actually, when we see someone heroically swimming along underwater, encumbered in a leech suit, the resemblance to a real leech is moderately accurate; leeches do have a soft, flabby appearance. However, they don't have gigantic, fanged, lampreylike mouths and rows of suckers down their sides.

As Tom Reamy said in *Trumpet* #1, "We see the giant leeches for the first time [in the cave], and it's much too soon. They look like men in black plastic pup tents. Occasionally, the outline of an arm or leg can be seen.... One of them carries a body exactly as a man would—in his arms through the leech suit. He also can hardly walk in all the drapery." However, complaining about the quality of monster suits in a picture like this is certainly pointless and probably ungenerous.

Director Bernard L. Kowalski at least makes the most of the leech suits in the ghastly scene in the cave, in which the leeches squidgily slither over their screaming victims, slurping blood from their pulsing throats; as Reamy said, here "the picture manages one scene of genuine horror."

The cave looks like what it is: a small corner of a sound stage equipped with a shallow pool and draped in Spanish moss or its equivalent. It's large and well-lit for a cave under the banks of a swamp, and seems geologically incompatible with swamps. It also seems unlikely that someone could fall into the water in the cave, sink down to the bottom and slide out the entrace, to surface again in the lagoons in the swamp. They had to get those bodies out into the open somehow.

The only explanation for the leeches is that line about Cape Canaveral. As a glance at a map of Florida will show, the most extensive swamps (the Everglades) are many miles from Cape Canaveral. But that's okay, as the swamp in the film is actually the Los Angeles County Arboretum, which has always been heavily used as a location for films. But if atomic-powered rockets lost in the swamp made the leeches big, why not alligators, crane flies or manatees?

Kowalski eventually went on to bigger if not better things. He'd already directed *Hot Car Girl* and *Night of the Blood Beast* in 1958, and did *Blood and Steel* for Fox in 1959, but his next credit as a feature director was *Stiletto* in 1969. He also directed *Krakatoa, East of Java* (1969), *Macho Callahan* (1970) and *Sssssss* (1973). He's helmed several films for television, including *Terror in the Sky*, *Black Noon* (both 1971), *The Woman Hunter* (1972), *Flight to Holocaust* (1977), and *The Nativity* (1978). Kowalski is a director without any visible personality, and as his most pleasing touches can be found in those films that are in the fantastic genre, particularly *Blood Beast*. Perhaps he actually has talent in those directions, but it's hard to see much style in his other films. He's not one of Roger Corman's significant discoveries.

However uninteresting *Giant Leeches* is in general, the love triangle of Dave, Liz and Cal does have some pleasing aspects. Leo Gordon's dialogue is generally better than his plots, and so it is here, too. Although the little segment seems to be made of equal parts of *Tobacco Road* and *The Postman Always Rings Twice*, the actors are in there trying. Bruno Ve Sota and Yvette Vickers are especially professional. (For more on Vickers, see the entry on *Attack of the 50 Foot Woman*.)

Bruno Ve Sota has what is probably his best screen part in *Attack of the Giant Leeches*, although that isn't saying much for the actor. He'd been appearing in small parts for years, as early as 1954 in *The Wild One*. His sloping eyebrows and round face gave him a slight resemblance to Orson Welles, of which Ve Sota was proud, according to his friend, the late Barry Brown. Ve Sota did not have a broad range as an actor, partly because he was short, fat and too distinctive. Among his other films as an actor were *Jupiter's Darling* (1955), *The Last Time I Saw Paris* (1954), *Kismet* (1955), *The Choppers*, *20,000 Eyes* (both 1961), *The Case of Patty Smith* (1962), *Hell's Angels on Wheels* (1967) and *Single Room Furnished* (1968). He was in several films from the Corman factory, including *The Undead* (1957), *War of the Satellites*, *A Bucket of Blood* (1959), *The Wasp Woman* and *Night Tide* (1963). He also appeared in the American scenes for

Creature of the Walking Dead (1960/1965), and was in the truly terrible *The Wild World of Batwoman* (1966).

Eventually, Ve Sota was noticed by fans of SF and horror films, and as a result, eventually got work in some unexpected places. My friend Ted Zaske was, may God have mercy on his soul, briefly the casting director on the TV series "My Mother the Car," and saw to it that Ve Sota worked frequently on the series. When Ve Sota died in 1976, Barry Brown arranged an old-fashioned actor's wake for him.

Ve Sota never rose above the ranks of minor character actors, but within his field, he delivered good work. (As an actor; he was a bad director; see comments on *The Brain Eaters*.) He usually played greasy villains, unsympathetic preachers and Southern-fried red-necks. Here, he's greasy again, but sympathetic. He's dominated by his sluttish wife, but is also genuinely in love with her; he's given an opportunity to murder her under circumstances in which few would consider him actually wrong, but is prepared to let her go anyway. Ve Sota gives his all to the part, and actually comes close to being touching; considering the circumstances, that is a genuine accomplishment.

Liz's paramour, played by Michael Emmet, is also good in his few scenes. Emmet also appeared in *Night of the Blood Beast* for Kowalski, and was in *The Human Jungle* (1954) and *The Great Impostor* (1961) in small roles.

The rest of the cast is less distinctive. The hero, Ken Clark, is standard as such characters go. He's rather expressionless, and it's not surprising that he appeared almost entirely in small roles in major films, with a few leads in exploitation and B movies. Among his other films were *The Last Wagon*, *The Proud Ones*, *Love Me Tender* (all 1956), *South Pacific* (1958) and *12 to the Moon*. He later went to Europe and appeared in a few spear-and-sandal epics, some spaghetti Westerns and imitation James Bond films, including *Defeat of the Barbarians* (1962), *None but the Lonely Spy* (1964), *Mission Bloody Mary*, *Savage Gringo* and *The Road to Fort Alamo* (all 1965).

Heroine Jan Shepard made very few films; considering her nonexistent appeal in *Giant Leeches*, it's not surprising. She was also in *King Creole* (1958), *Third of a Man* (1962) and *Paradise—Hawaiian Style* (1966).

Gene Roth is good as the lazy sheriff, who gripes when the game warden usurps his authority because the sheriff won't exercise it. Roth appeared in dozens of films and serials during his career, first under his original name, Eugene Stutenroth and later, interchangeably, as Gene Roth and Eugene Roth. He was in many serials, including *Captain Video* (1951) and *The Lost Planet*. Among his features were *Where There's Life* (1947), *Red Planet Mars*, *Prince Valiant* (1954), *Seven Brides for Seven Brothers* (1954), *Jupiter's Darling* (1955), *Earth vs. the Spider*, *Tormented* (1960), *Atlantis the Lost Continent*, *The Three Stooges Meet Hercules*, *Twice Told Tales* (1963) and *Rosie!* (1967). Roth was always delighted to visit with youngsters who recalled him from his films while he worked in a drugstore on Hollywood Boulevard. Tragically, he was hit and killed by a truck near the drugstore in 1976. For more commentary on Roth, see the entry on *She Demons*.

Tyler McVey, the heroine's father, was an active character actor all through the 50s and 60s, appearing in dozens of films, usually in roles not unlike the one he has here. He was an accomplished if invisible character actor.

There were almost no reviews of *Attack of the Giant Leeches* when it first appeared; even for low-budget films of its nature, this was unusual. It has received scant mention since then. Don Willis (I) comes comes to praise (for him) for the film: "A few crude *Beast from Haunted Cave*–like thrills and enough plot for 65 minutes." *Psychotronic* called it a "fun cheapie," but Alan Frank (*Horror*) thought it "tedious" and undeveloped; he also quoted the Cinematograph Exhibitors' Association of Great Britain and Ireland's *Film Report*: "A routine production [which has] effective underwater scenes which provide a gruesome touch."

On the other hand, the *Monthly Film Bulletin* gave the film its lowest rating, saying it was "a feeble addition to the cycle. As in the same company's *Night of the Blood Beast*, the 'creatures' are poor things and the staging meagre."

This is not inaccurate. But for those who are looking for a few moments of quality among hours of dreck—and you are probably one of those, otherwise why are you reading this?—there are some admirable elements in *Attack of the Giant Leeches*; it's a bad film, but not entirely devoid of interest.

Battle in Outer Space

Some have described this colorful, childish spectacle as being a sequel to *The Mysterians*. Although both are Japanese, made by Toho, there's no story connection. I suspect they were, in fact, made as a contrasting pair; in *The Mysterians*, the aliens come here and we have a big battle on the ground. In *Battle in Outer Space*, we go to the Moon (and find the aliens there), and the final clash takes place in the skies over Japan.

I have not seen *Battle in Outer Space* in many years, but my memory tells me I thought it better than *The Mysterians* at the time; it had a cleaner (even empty) storyline, and more spectacle. In general, however, Japanese space movies are inferior to Japanese monster movies: the space films are too easily compared unfavorably to similar American and British products, while the monster movies occupy their own branch of SF moviemaking.

In *Battle in Outer Space*, disasters sweep over the Earth, and scientists in Tokyo begin to suspect that these occurrences (shown primarily in drawings) are the work of aliens bent on conquering the Earth. In the meantime, the first Earth expedition to the Moon has been launched.

When the lunar explorers arrive on the "dark side" of the Moon, they are shocked to discover a base populated by aliens, who immediately attack. One of the two Earth ships is destroyed, but the other makes it back to Earth.

The aliens' flying saucers begin attacking the Earth openly now, striking at major cities—Tokyo, Paris, New York, Moscow. The people of the Earth unite and manage to turn out a fleet of fighter spacecraft in time to engage the enemy. After a fierce series of dogfights, during which Tokyo is severely damaged by an alien mother ship, the aliens are finally routed and Earth wins the battle in outer space.

One of the more interesting touches in the film is the aliens. Generally in Japanese films, aliens are either almost comically nonhuman (though almost always humanoid), or simply people in colorful cloaks, as in *The Mysterians*. In *Battle in Outer Space*, we never really get a look at an alien, although we often see them (in their space suits). They are the size of human children, with a big pointy nose; they have four fingers and walk in a crouch. In other words, they are slightly but not extremely alien, an interestingly restrained approach for a Japanese film.

The big space battle at the end (actually fought in blue skies) becomes wearisome before it finally ends, with several shots being repeated, and an overall sameness to the conflict anyway. The film seems to have run short of money: some of the big attacks on Earth cities are represented by drawings, while others are full-scale miniature havoc. As usual for Toho in this period, Eiji Tsuburaya was in charge of the special effects; his scenes are bright and colorful, fun to watch. In a peculiar (and ultimately comic) decision, the attacking flying saucers always fire their beams downward, while the quickly-built Earth rockets always fire their atomic heat rays upward.

There's a slight romantic interest, but it's kept in the background and is of little importance to the overall story, otherwise an orgy of special effects, with zaps, pows, bangs and booms on the busy soundtrack. As in *The Mysterians*, an Earthman comes under the control of the aliens but heroically overcomes this. The film somewhat resembles a serial, improbably made in color and in Japan, cut down to feature length. There's lots of pointless but fast and repetitious action. If you turn your mind off, the film can be quite entertaining, but start thinking about what you're seeing, and the film disintegrates into episodic battle scenes.

Reviewers overall were not thrilled with *Battle in Outer Space*, but the U.S. movie trade publications liked it. "Gilb" in *Variety* thought it was a "rousing exploitation entry for the youngsters as well as adults who dig sci-fi pix.... [There's] lotsa action and suspense [but it] has a number of flaws including some stereotyped performances and a dubbing job that isn't always synchronized with the players' voices.... Direction of Inoshiro Honda draws ample tension from the action scenes."

Howard Thompson of the *New York Times* had a good time, in a sense. He said *Battle in Outer Space* "is the least painful to watch of several such Japanese imports in recent years.... Far and away the most attractive thing about this Toho Production is the decor—the clean, bright color and a fetching assortment of obvious, but effective, miniature settings and backgrounds. Some of the art work is downright nifty.... The Japanese have opened a most amusing and beguiling bag of technical tricks."

The *Monthly Film Bulletin*, on the other hand, was not amused. "Aimless, witless war-of-the-worlds story ... partially redeemed by one or two elaborate trick thrills ... and special effects. The dubbed dialogue is as dated as a Flash Gordon serial, the ludicrous overacting of the Westernised Oriental cast says little for Inoshiro Honda's direction, and the attempt at futurism is ruined by scenery which has a distinct cardboard look about it."

Unlike American films, sometimes cursed by a desire to be topical, important or responsible, Japanese science fiction films of this period were out to entertain and occasionally to suggest that international cooperation in a good cause was the right thing to do. In Japan, comic books have always been for adults as well as for children, so to suggest that films like *Battle in Outer Space* were designed to appeal to children alone is probably incorrect. However, it was made for the naive and uncritical, and if it can be watched from that perspective, it is still reasonably enjoyable.

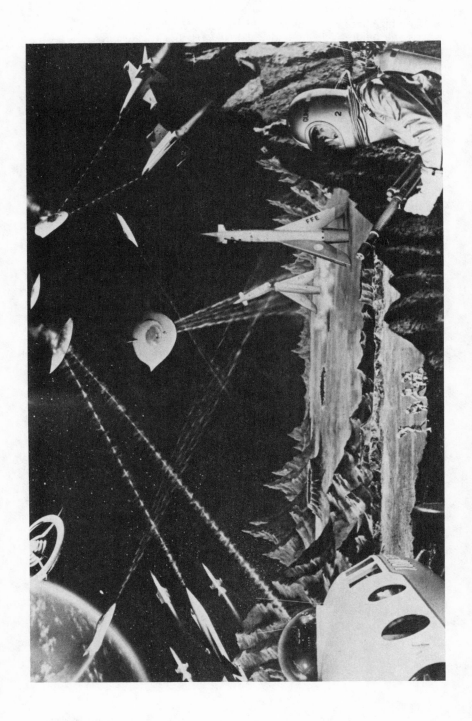

Beyond the Time Barrier

Although this reunited Robert Clarke and Edgar G. Ulmer, the star and director of *The Man from Planet X*, and although it seems to have had a relatively higher budget, *Beyond the Time Barrier* is far less interesting and imaginative than the earlier film. It is a drab, stale imitation of H.G. Wells' *The Time Machine*, and has virtually no plot. Our hero goes to the future, is told how it got so bad, and returns to tell us about it. Arthur C. Pierce, who wrote the film, has only one view of the future—it will be worse than now, and it will be ruled by inimical dictators—and he gives it at least twice, in this film and in *Cyborg 2087* (1966). Pierce was a hack writer who knew slightly more about science fiction than his contemporaries, which made his pictures a shade more credible than theirs. But his clichéd dialogue, cardboard characters and insistence on a good-guy–bad-guy plot mean that his pictures rarely rise above the routine.

This film was shot in Texas by Miller Consolidated Pictures under the title "The Last Barrier," and was initially intended to be released as a double bill with *The Amazing Transparent Man*, but like that film, was soon being released by American International Pictures. The direction of both films is credited to Ulmer, and *Time Barrier* probably was directed by him. See the entry on *The Amazing Transparent Man* for more speculation on this topic.

Beyond the Time Barrier begins with the first part of a frame story: a test rocket plane crashes and the pilot (whose face we do not see) is rushed to a hospital. There's a great deal of fuss about something mysterious that happened to him which makes a nurse scream when she sees him.

The man is test pilot Maj. Bill Allison (Robert Clarke), who that morning had taken up the X-80, and has now returned strangely altered. He also has a strange story to tell, which we see in flashback.

After the plane headed upward almost to the beginning of space (Pierce isn't content with just a time-travel story), Bill started the test run, but something happened. He can't get a response from the ground control, and has to land at the base on his own.

To his shock, the base is in decrepit ruins. It's clear to us that not only has some great catastrophe befallen the world, but that much time has passed. Throughout the story, however, Bill is never quite convinced of this. He's a hardheaded, pragmatic realist, and something of a dolt.

He sees a drawing of a futuristic city in the distance, and begins walking that way, but doesn't make it. He's been watched by the Supreme (Vladimir Sokoloff) and the Captain (Red Morgan) on electronic gadgetry, from some underground location. Bill is zapped by them and carried by silent soldiers into this underground city. (We never learn what that city in the distance was.)

He wakes up in one of those standard science fiction devices, a transparent cylinder resembling a giant toothbrush tube, but can't gain the attention of the silent people watching him, not even beautiful Trirene (Darlene Tompkins), who shows signs of sympathy.

Opposite: A typical action-packed paste-up for Toho's Battle in Outer Space (U.S. release 1960) virtually tells the story of the film in one shot. There's the Earth off to the left, the surface of the Moon below, disclike alien ships blasting Earth lunar rockets, and X-15–like Earth ships destroying the alien craft. Whew. The film is a lot like this.

When he recovers, he's brought before the Supreme and the Captain, who assume he's a spy and interrogate him. The Supreme is, of course, Trirene's grandfather; in lost-race stories, of which this is a variation, the hero never falls in love with a mere commoner. The Supreme tells the surprised Bill that, except for himself and the Captain, all inhabitants of this underground civilization, called the Citadel, are deaf-mutes, though some have telepathic powers. We later learn that all are also sterile, except Trirene.

Oddly enough, the Supreme does not recognize Bill's insignia. We eventually learn this is only 62 years in Bill's future, and the Supreme is clearly older than 62. Yet he's never seen an American flag. How quickly we human beings forget, how transitory is fame. How silly are some writers.

Bill keeps his mouth shut, and the Captain eagerly (but pointlessly) suggests torture to get some truth or other out of him. We soon learn their main enemy is a band of mutants, and Bill is obviously not a mutant. Even though we soon learn there are other accidental time travelers imprisoned in the Citadel, no one thinks to ask him what year he is from. This withholding of vital information is a cheap ploy, especially when you consider that the title itself reveals that the movie is about time travel. The main result of this vapid trickery on Pierce's part is to make everyone in the story seem amazingly stupid.

Bill is tossed into a room with a pit in it, and in the pit are stock-footage uglies from *Journey to the Lost City** and two or three bald mutants made up quickly and shoddily by Jack P. Pierce. The mutants mutter something about "scapes" like Bill, and also mention a plague. This clumsy semiexposition is interrupted by guards who take Bill back to the Supreme. It seems Trirene has become attached to Bill.

He meets with her, and she mimes a sad story (with unconvincing eloquence). The plague and the mutants that resulted killed her parents and forced her people, led by the Supreme, to take refuge in the Citadel. She can't transmit thoughts, just read them, so Bill is still frustratedly short on information. He seems to think he is still in the present.

The mutants had mentioned Karl Kruse, and after Bill asks about him, Trirene takes him to Kruse and two other "scapes," Markova (Adrienne Arden) and Dr. Bourman (John Van Dreelen). Kruse (Stephen Bekassy) is a little cautious about Bill, who isn't sure how long he's been in the Citadel. "Time has little meaning here in the catalisosphere," says Kruse enigmatically.

Bill tells them what he still thinks is the date, March 5th, 1960. Even now he doesn't tumble to the fact that he's in the future, and no one tells him. He's shocked when Kruse finally reveals it is 2024.

At least Pierce's explanation for how the world got the way it is in the story is slightly novel, and he's more forward-looking than most SF movie writers. Bill is told that in 1971, there was a bombardment of cosmic radiation, which caused a "plague" (although that would seem to be a misuse of the term). This mutating bombardment was due to the many atomic tests which sent "tons of radioactive dust" up into the "ionosphere," thereby "destroying the protective screen that has filtered deadly cosmic rays from space since time began."

Pierce says that after the first Moon landing, the nations of the Earth banded together and, by 1970, colonies had been established on Mars and Venus. When the radiation started in 1971, those who were uncontaminated fled Earth for the planetary colonies, making them the "scapes."

**Itself made of two European-produced films directed by Fritz Lang, released overseas in 1959; the combined, shortened version was released in the U.S. in 1960.*

Half the population of Earth was destroyed, and most of the rest were mutated; the remainder live in these underground cities, in the first stage of mutation themselves. If they are becoming mutated anyway, why is there a battle going on between the underground people and the mutants? If Trirene is the sole fertile woman, what good would having her bear children by Bill do? (For such is the Supreme's plan.) What's wrong with the fertility of Kruse, Bourman and Markova?

Markova (note her suspiciously Slavic name) convinces thickheaded Bill that if he can get back to his own time, he might be able to prevent this blighted future. We later learn all she wants is the plane, so why she even brings this up is a mystery.

Bourman and Kruse explain how Bill broke the time barrier. In the late 1960s, Bourman himself found a way to travel faster than the speed of light, which occasionally sent craft crashing through the time barrier. Markova herself broke through in 1973, and Kruse and Bourman traveled forward from 1994.

Bourman explains how Bill did it. He points out (with blackboard illustrations) that the Earth is rotating at 1,000 miles per hour, and traveling around the sun at 66,000 mph. The Solar System is moving at over 6,000,000 mph. "You had a velocity approaching the speed of light before you ever left the ground," says Kruse. Yes. He was only short by 664,548,200 mph. Well, never mind. If you don't know the answer, dazzle them with numbers.

Bill finally shows some signs of intelligence. He decides that if he follows the exact same flight plan, although in reverse, he will arrive back in his own time. Never mind that this would *subtract* the speed of his plane from all those other velocities, making him go relatively *slower*; this film works by symmetry, not logic.

Trirene helps Bill get plans to the tunnels that lead to the air base where the plane is. All this time the Captain and the Supreme have been watching what's going on, and for no conceivable reason, try to talk Bill out of the plan. Markova knifes a guard and sets the imprisoned mutants free, who immediately begin slaughtering everyone they encounter. Bill is shocked by this, but mollified by Markova's cogent explanation: "It's part of the plan."

Bill dons his flight suit and joins Markova. He wants to take Trirene with him, but Markova pulls a gun on him and announces that the two of them are going back to her time of 1973. This doesn't seem to make a great deal of sense, but it doesn't matter as she is immediately killed by Kruse.

The four of them run down the corridors while mayhem erupts around them, and find the right exit for the air base. Bourman then kills Kruse. Bourman wants to return to *his* time. Bill is understandably surprised, as it was Bourman who talked him into making the return flight. Trirene jumps between Bourman and Bill and takes the shot meant for the pilot.

Bill kills Bourman, then takes the body of Trirene back to the Supreme, instead of immediately getting in his plane. Impressed by this show of idiot self-sacrifice, the Supreme decides their only hope is for Bill to return to his own time, and so Bill takes off in the plane.

The frame story picks up where it left off. At first, no one is willing to believe Bill's story, but offscreen Kruse and Bourman turn out to be real students in Europe. We finally see Bill's face: he is an old, old man (wrinkly makeup by Jack Pierce), and he has Trirene's ring with him, as if the ring is more of a clincher than his aging 40 years in one day.

Every now and then, someone will make a film that is well-intentioned, trying to make an argument against some horrible ongoing evil—the If This Goes On premise. Generally, these movies lack the talent, the insight and/or the courage to make their message meaningful. Arthur C. Pierce doesn't seem committed to the idea of ending nuclear tests, however. It's just a cheap gimmick used in SF films before, a premise that can lead him to the ends he wants: a desolated (i.e. cheap) future world that can be saved by our hero. In a way, these half-smart movies are worse than the dumb ones: they give us reason to think they might have been better, that there is something behind them. There really isn't; they are no more altruistically conceived than *Teenage Zombies*.

Ernst Fegté was an interesting art director who made his reputation at Paramount with films including *Anything Goes* (1936) and *The Miracle of Morgan's Creek* (1944). He later became independent, and among other films, designed *Specter of the Rose* (1946), *Destination Moon* and *Actors and Sin* (1952). He seems to have worked well with Ulmer, or perhaps was a personal friend, as he designed both *Beyond the Time Barrier* and *The Amazing Transparent Man*. The latter film required little from Fegté, being almost entirely shot on real locations, but *Time Barrier* is, if anything, overdesigned.

The inhabitants of the Citadel seem to be in love with triangles. The tunnels are triangular, the walls are made of triangular panels—even optical "wipes" used to change scenes are triangular. There's no particular reason for this, other than that triangular panels are easy to reshape into new sets, and that it makes the whole movie look odd, maybe even "futuristic." However, the futuristic look is compromised by the presence of common gadgetry in several scenes.

We see Fegté's sets often enough—Clarke walks down the same corridor three times. Ulmer and Fegté make full use of the largest set, stairs where several corridors intersect, but being shot in the standard, flat, drab black and white, this set soon becomes boring. (The film is notably short on true blacks.)

Ulmer even frequently uses triangular compositions, carrying out this motif. Some of these compositions are quite interesting, but they also seem artificial. At times, he uses contrasts between light and dark scenes, light objects and dark backgrounds, and human being–triangle contrasts, but this seems gimmicky.

But at least there is something resembling a visual scheme for the film, very rare in American science fiction films. No matter how pointless, some inventiveness has been used for the design.

Not for the story, however, which is just another variation on *The Time Machine*. The Morlocks are the mutants, and the Eloi are the inhabitants of the Citadel. Coincidentally, David Duncan's script for the movie of *The Time Machine*, released the same year, came up with a similar idea for the origins of the Eloi and the Morlocks.

However, in that film, there's a good reason for the interdependence of the Eloi and the Morlocks: the Morlocks care for the Eloi because they eat them. Here, the mutants just seem murderous, although there are some hints that the Citadel has food and won't share it. But as with most of Pierce's ideas, that's tossed away.

As usual for a film with some ambitions, the low budget harms it. The drawing of the unexplained futuristic city is so bad as to be completely unconvincing on any level. Even the city on the poster looks more lifelike. The sound throughout the film is very poor, tinny and indistinct. There are only two or three mutants visible at any time, and the mass attack by the freed mutants at the climax becomes comic: it's hard to stage a mass attack with three extras. The special effects are trivial; there's one shot of the plane "splitting" as it crosses the time barrier, which is standard low-budget effects, so poor that it almost seems as if it isn't supposed to be convincing. It's as if the effort passes for the result: we're supposed to believe because we have always believed.

Robert Clarke, who once gave signs of being an acceptable leading man, is quite bad here, and he produced the film. He's harmed by playing a character who is a hero only because that's the position he holds in the story. Bill the pilot seems little better than a cretin, and the role requires Clarke to spend most of his time looking perplexed. For more on Clarke see the entries on *The Hideous Sun Demon* and *The Astounding She-Monster*.

The other professional actors in the cast acquit themselves about as well as possible, under the circumstances. Vladimir Sokoloff, Stephen Bekassy and John Van Dreelen are acceptable, but not much more. Red Morgan doesn't seem to be an actor at all, and is about as convincing as that drawing of the city. (He's also in *The Amazing Transparent Man*.) As Trirene, Darlene Tompkins is at least spared dialogue, and hence isn't too unbelievable, although a woman of the year 2024 wearing a ponytail does give one pause.

One of the most peculiar aspects of the film is the oddly tragic ending. Now, in lost-race, time travel and similar films, where the hero falls in love with a woman of that time or place, the rules of melodrama usually dictate that the woman must not, under any circumstances, be allowed to return to the hero's time/country.* So it's not surprising that poor, mute Trirene is shot dead at the end of the picture. What is surprising (and hard to justify in any way) is the fact that the hero winds up in a bad way, too; he's aged prematurely by his fooling around with time.

I suppose that this ending is supposed to be unexpected, poignant and the big clincher for those in Bill's own time. Because the downbeat ending is so out of character, however, it merely seems cheap and strained. We don't care about this guy, so dooming him to early old age seems affectless sadism.

Reviews of *Beyond the Time Barrier* were mostly unfavorable. "The only ingredient," said "Tube" in *Daily Variety*, "that distinguishes this effort from its many predecessors is the presence of a timely moral message.... This preach-peace aspect is put over with some impact via the absence of the expected happy ending, but is preceded by too much quasi-scientific mumbo-jumbo and melodramatic absurdity to register with a desirable degree of conviction."

James Powers at the *Hollywood Reporter* thought the film was "not well made," and while it does bring in "some interesting premises [it] does nothing to explain or develop them." He added that "Edgar G. Ulmer directs with what excitement he can, although with no clear conflicts laid out."

The *Monthly Film Bulletin* gave the film its lowest rating, saying "Uninspired science-fiction melodrama with a crudely expressed political message. Director Edgar G. Ulmer is happy enough, in a routine way, when the action is set in 1960, but his conception of 2024 behavior is pretty absurd.... The film is notable for its return to the technique of early silent serials, cutting in and out of scenes by means of triangular wipes; unfortunately, this tends to make the whole thing seem even more dated than it is." (The latter comment was repeated from the *Hollywood Reporter* review.)

---

*One of the very few films in which the heroine escapes being killed and/or left behind is Time After Time (1979), in which H.G. Wells himself unexpectedly returns to his own time with the heroine.

Alan Frank (*SF*) called it "undistinguished in all departments ... notable only for being directed by Edgar G. Ulmer, whose cult status takes yet another battering."

Although it does deserve some respect for its efforts at being slightly unusual, *Beyond the Time Barrier* is a depressingly uninteresting film, and I'm quite astonished that I found this much to say about it.

Caltiki, the Immortal Monster

Movies in which the monster is an amorphous blob occasionally turned up in the late 1950s — *The Creeping Unknown* (sort of), *X the Unknown*, *The H-Man*, *Enemy from Space* and, of course, *The Blob* — and their minor but real popularity makes it a little surprising that in recent years someone hasn't tried to make the definitive blob movie.*Italy gave the world *Caltiki, the Immortal Monster*, a vaguely Quatermassian tale of an unexplained slimy glob of doom (said the ads) that though it presents a few problems, is quite easily vanquished.

Somewhat overplotted, *Caltiki* was also cut for American release, so perhaps we've been spared the worst excesses the film had to offer. There's a reel change indicated five minutes into the American print, so whatever was cut probably didn't involve the immortal monster itself.

In Mexico, archaeologist John (John Merivale) leads an expedition to an ancient Mayan temple, peculiarly checking for radiation as they enter a cave beneath the temple. One member of their expedition has already vanished, but Bob (Daniel Pitani) still dives into an underground lake beneath the temple to look for remains of sacrifices.

He finds the remains all right — skeletons in gold pre–Columbian jewelry — but he encounters what the victims were sacrificed to. Now just a skeleton covered with goo, Bob's body pops out of the water, and Caltiki itself suddenly and impressively erupts from the pool and sits quivering at the edge. (At this point, Caltiki looks like a huge heap of wet leather.)

The monster seizes expedition member Max (Gerard Herter) by the hand, but heroic John pulls him free. They flee the cave, hotly pursued by the shape-less monster. John leaps into a truck and smashes it into the monster, which emits a peculiar wail before it dies.

A fragment of Caltiki has adhered to Max's hand, and John peels it off; the flesh of the hand comes with it, leaving bones; it looks more than satisfactorily ghoulish. Max goes slightly out of his head.

Back in Mexico City, John peers through a microscope at a chunk of the creature (and we unilluminatingly see what he sees). He concludes that the monster was one big cell, and when he uses an atom-powered "electric brain" to check the specimen's age, he discovers it is 20 million years old, which generates newspaper headlines.

An inscription from the temple sounds ominous: "Caltiki is one, the only immortal god. When her mate appears in the sky, the power of Caltiki will destroy the world."

*As possible source material for a high-tech blob movie, I recommend adapting either The Clone by Theodore L. Thomas and Kate Wilhelm or Phantoms by Dean R. Koontz. The Stuff (1985) isn't really a blob movie, although it tries.

Here, Caltiki, the Immortal Monster (U.S. release, 1960) resembles a huge heap of wet canvas and, in fact, may be a huge heap of wet canvas; in other scenes, it looks like entrails. Gerard Herter (back to camera) and John Merivale confront the bloblike creature in a Mayan temple. The atmospheric photography suggests the fine Italian hand of Mario Bava, who directed much of the film.

John assumes the monster has been eating human beings to keep itself alive, which, as the temple was sealed, means it was very hungry for a century or more.

Elsewhere, Max has gone crazy; who could blame him, with his hand eaten off by an immortal monster. Scars disfigure his face, and as if it could be saved, his hand is bandaged. He's in a hospital now. Max's adventures are intercut with John's through the rest of the film.

John realizes that Caltiki is something like an amoeba, perhaps activated by radiation, but probably doesn't get dangerous until subjected to "electronic bombardment." (At this point, the small chunks of monster look like little bags of mud.)

Meanwhile, back at the hospital, Caltiki poison in his bloodstream has driven Max totally psychotic. He viciously clubs a nurse to death and heads in search of Ellen (Didi Perego), John's wife, whom Max now hates. In American prints, his hatred is unmotivated, but in original prints, he apparently made a pass at Ellen back at the expedition camp. I referred to this film as being over-plotted, because much footage is wasted on the search for Max.

John learns that the ancients feared the Arsinoe comet, which has a period of 1,352 years; they thought it was evil because of the "amount of radioactive damage" it seemed to cause. This comet must be the "mate" of Caltiki referred to in the ancient inscription, for both at the lab and at John's house, the fragments of Caltiki begin to grow. On his way to warn Ellen, another scientist drives off a cliff.

Max's busy flight brings him to Ellen's house, where this fragment of Caltiki is beginning to get out of hand. (At this point, Caltiki somewhat resembles a man in a slime suit.) Max kills one woman and heads for Ellen and her child, then hears a noise in the kitchen. "Come out, John," he calls, "are you afraid?" Caltiki bursts out of the kitchen and devours Max—his head vanishes into thick folds, then emerges as a skull—making this one of the few blob movies in which the monster saves the heroine.

Meanwhile, Ellen and the child have run upstairs, which would seem to be an unwise move. And sure enough, here comes Caltiki, getting bigger all the time (now looking like piles of tripe), slithering up the stairs.

Racing to the rescue of his family, John escapes a police roadblock. He saves Ellen and the child, but the house is now pretty well engulfed by Caltiki. Troops arrive with tanks and fire flames at the blob monster, killing it. (Caltiki is one of the most vulnerable of all monsters.)

After a gabby opening, *Caltiki* becomes reasonably exciting after the comet shows up. Mario Bava's moody photography impresses throughout; the entire film seems to be taking place at night, but we never lose track of the action. Bava, later an acclaimed director of horror films himself, was also responsible for the special effects, which at the end are outstanding, especially for a low-budget Italian picture. The major problems with the film are the trite and cluttered plot, the truly awful dubbing, and a vaguely hangdog air about the proceedings, as if the movie slightly embarrassed everyone involved.

The film's credits list the director as "Robert Hamton," though most sources logically credit "Robert Hampton." Actually, Hamton/Hampton is a pseudonym sometimes used on English-dubbed prints of his films by Italian cult favorite Riccardo Freda. Although not in the same league with Mario Bava as a director, Freda is an above-average director of spectacles and horror films. His movies generally are more impressive than the similar-in-content films made by other Italian directors during the same period.

Freda was born in 1909 in Alexandra, Egypt, and after university studies, became an art critic for a daily newspaper. He began working in films in 1937, primarily as a writer. In 1942, he started his career as a director with *Don Cesare di Bazan*. Over the next 15 years, Freda directed about 20 films, primarily action-adventure epics. Among these were a version of *Les Misérables* in 1947, *The Black Eagle* (1946) and its sequel, *La Vendetta di Aquila Nero* (1951), *Il Figlio di d'Artagnan* (1949), *Sins of Rome* (1952, about Spartacus), *Theodora Slave Empress* (1953), and his first horror film, *I Vampiri* (1956), released in the United States as *The Devil's Commandment*.

After *Caltiki*, Freda made mostly spear-and-sandal cheapies, sometimes being called in as an expert to direct only a fight sequence or two. He also made two stylish horror films, *The Horrible Dr. Hichcock* in 1962, and its sequel *The Ghost* in the same year. Among his other 1960s films were *The Giants of Thessaly* (1960), *Samson and the Seven Miracles of the World* (1961), *The Witch's Curse* (1962), and, shifting gears to spy thrillers, *The Exterminators* (1965); his most recent film I know of is *Superhuman* (1979). He seems to have retired.

Although not an expensive film, *Caltiki* had an adequate budget. Atmospheric and handsome most of the time, it is somewhat slowly paced at the beginning; it should not be considered the usual hackwork. It can't be called a good movie, but is above average for monster thrillers of this period in the departments that really count for such things: design, photography and special effects. Although Caltiki never seems to threaten the world as promised in the ads, the film climaxes on a note of satisfactory suspense.

Unfortunately, the terrible dubbed dialogue makes the film hard to follow at times, and comic at others. Oddly, even John Merivale is dubbed, and he's British. Among the worst of the dialogue: "The first thing I think about this is, as soon as that reaches a point, the radioaction [sic] will appear, and then it will show life." And this: "When the explosion ceases, it's just as you know it. It's absolutely still. *But* because the Betatron rays did not destroy it, it can also multiply itself."

Its peculiar premise also does not help the film. Rationalizing why an amorphous, carnivorous blob would live for 20 million years and then be found and tamed or something by Mayans presents many difficulties, to say the least. Presumably the Mayans knew the comet would activate Caltiki by simple observations, but how did they know the next time the comet returned, it would make Caltiki big enough to destroy the world? And what happened 1,352 years *before* Caltiki's last activation?

Having Max go mad seems cheap. Perhaps Riccardo Freda and his writer, Filippo Sanjust, didn't trust the strength of their monster-movie premise, and felt that for grown-ups in the audience, a berserk psychotic killer would provide more familiar and acceptable thrills. Max's madness seems arbitrary and cruel; in the European prints, it was more like retribution for his having made a pass at Ellen.

None of the actors gets much of a chance to do anything, and the characters are there just to keep the plot going. The film was clearly made for an international market. British John Merivale, the star, made relatively few films; among them, *A Night to Remember* (1958), *Circus of Horrors* (1960), *King Rat* (1965) and *Arabesque* (1966). Busy supporting player Gerard Herter usually appeared as villains through the 1960s, often in multinational "spaghetti" Westerns; his films include *The Great War* (1959), *Any Gun Can Play* (1967), *The Big Gundown* (1968), *Fraulein Doktor* (1969), *Morire Gratis* (1968) and *Adios Sabata* (1971), among many others. He also appeared in Freda's *The White Warrior* (1959). Of the two leading actors, Herter is by far the more interesting, but then, actors are rarely dull when playing homicidal lunatics.

The two leading actresses were also busy through the 60s; Didi Perego (here billed as Didi Sullivan), Ellen, appeared in *Kapo* (1960), *La Visita* (1963), Philippe De Broca's *Give Her the Moon*, Sidney Lumet's ill-fated *The Appointment* (both 1970), and Ettore Scola's fascinating *La Nuit de Varennes* (1983). Perego has since moved to character parts. On the other hand, Daniele Rocca as Linda, whose part was presumably larger in the original cut, starred in the popular *Divorce—Italian Style* (1961) as the homely wife Marcello Mastroianni tries to rid himself of. The great international success of that film resulted in her appearing in other would-be international films, including *Behold a Pale Horse* (1964), *Conquered City* (1962) and *The Sucker* (1965). Although in her later films, Rocca showed talent as a comedian, in *Caltiki* she's just part of the furniture.

The script of *Caltiki* was credited to one "Dr. Philip Just." To promote the picture, the American distributor, Allied Artists, referred to "Just" as a science writer, researcher and medical doctor. It's possible that the writer of the film is indeed all those things, but I doubt it. His real name is Filippo Sanjust, and in the 1960s, he primarily cowrote swashbuckling adventures, such as *Morgan the*

Pirate (1960), *The Thief of Bagdad* (1961), *Seven Seas to Calais* and *The Golden Arrow* (both 1962). The American Film Institute Catalog for the 1960s credits Sanjust with the *costumes* for Freda's *The White Warrior*, which seems unlikely.

Judging the writing in a script so ineptly translated presents difficulties, but there are some touches of novelty apparent. Having the hero and heroine married when the film opens makes the movie a bit different from American pictures of this type; the pseudo–Mexican settings are also unusual, but the effort to make Caltiki an ancient Terrestrial menace triggered by something from space, while odd, is invention of the wrong sort.

At the climax, when Caltiki is dominating John's house, the miniatures are extremely good, among the best ever done in a film of this nature. Only the fact that miniaturizing flames is impossible gives away the fact that the house is not full-sized. The real secret in filming miniature sets lies in control of the lighting, and Bava shows himself to be a master of that skill here.

The sets for the Mayan temple resemble redressed sets for some other kind of film, but are interestingly photographed. The film was presumably made entirely in Italy, although officially an Italian–U.S. coproduction; sources occasionally claim the film was made on location in Mexico, but this is hardly the case. *Psychotronic* said it was shot in Spain.

In Parish & Pitts, Mario Bava claimed that he, not Riccardo Freda, actually directed most of *Caltiki*. Parish & Pitts quote *Photon* (probably incorrectly cited), where Bava said that the film was a "take-off" on *The Creeping Unknown*. "Riccardo Freda ... left soon after production had begun. The slime monster was just a ton of cow's entrails with a man hidden inside to make it move. It was summertime, so the big problem was to keep the flies away from it."

Reviews were scant; neither the *Hollywood Reporter* nor *Variety* seem to have covered the film. Allen M. Widem in the *Motion Picture Herald* thought it was moderately well done, and pointed out that it occasionally got too gruesome for "the smallest tykes inevitably lured to this type of film." The movie "has ... been designed with skill and a certain sagacity. It has a few obvious contrivances while neatly knitting up the loose ends at the climax ... but beyond this irritating flaw, the Just story holds up well."

The *Monthly Film Bulletin* gave the movie (known in England more compactly as *The Immortal Monster*) a II rating. "Phony sets, bad acting and the limitations of a small budget seriously hamper the first half of this co-produced SF film, but once the monster asserts itself, things begin to liven up. Looking at first like a soggy old rag, it develops into a kind of jam pudding and then reproduces itself as mountainous coils of animated mud. The spectacle of the half-clothed heroine being pursued around her house by this mud/jam-pudding has a certain bizarre splendour, and the pyrotechnic finale allows for the total destruction of everything in sight."

Don Willis (I) found it "rather tame after an eerie beginning," while Parish & Pitts considered it "respectable." *Castle of Frankenstein* #8 thought it was "trite but fairly engaging."

The Cape Canaveral Monsters

Little things mean a lot. In *The Cape Canaveral Monsters*, which brought director Phil Tucker back to Bronson Caverns, the site of his earlier triumph, *Robot Monster*, litmus paper, wallet inserts and pig Latin are used in a successful effort to defeat alien invaders. The film itself is a stilted, limited disaster, although Tucker seems to be sincere in his efforts to make it a good low-budget film. The effort, though, is too much for him, and because the script is so dreadful, the effort was doomed anyway.

Aliens, represented by small circles of unexposed areas of film, arrive on Earth to sabotage our space efforts. Supposedly set in Florida near the space base of the title, the film was actually shot in Southern California, and looks it.

The two aliens, male and female (apparently), take over the bodies of two human beings after killing them, and thereafter Hauron is played by Jason Johnson and Nadja by Katherine Victor. The bodies seem to be slightly decomposing throughout the film, and the auto accident the aliens caused tore off the man's arm and scarred the woman's face. Hauron acquires another arm, only to lose it again in a guard dog attack.

Dauntlessly, the aliens set up camp in Bronson Caverns and begin sabotaging U.S. missiles. (Why don't these anti–space-test aliens ever attack the Soviet Union? Could it be they are Commies from space?) A couple of stock footage missiles explode before our hero, Tom (Scott Peters), a bright science student, begins to suspect that aliens are responsible. He cannot convince the General (with a perpetual cigar) that he's right.

Back at Bronson Caverns, Hauron and Nadja confer. "Did you reset the beam?" she asks. He nods; "and the line core."

Tom and his girlfriend Sally (Linda Connell) pick up interference from the alien ray shooting down the missiles and try to trace it. At the cave, Hauron and Nadja are accepting by radio the congratulations of their leaders; they are Earth Expedition #2. (In some details, the plot is absurdly reminiscent of *Plan 9 from Outer Space*.) "The council," says the radio, "has voted both of you full membership for this effort" at stopping the Earth's space plans. The radio voice says that "we need more Earthlings for our experiments. Especially females."

Despite the scars, missing arms, etc., the aliens have settled quite nicely into their Earth bodies, and seem to enjoy an active sex life, probably a first in invading aliens. Although they constantly quarrel, Hauron and Nadja find time to make up in bed: "Let's get some rest," Hauron suggests, lifting her chin with a finger.

Acting on those orders for more Earthlings for their experiments, Hauron and Nadja capture Bob (Gary Travis) and Shirley (Thelaine Williams), pals of Tom and Sally. After Bob and Shirley are caught by the aliens, there's a moment of desperation as Tom and Sally search for them to get the car keys.

But poor Bob and Shirley are doomed. Hauron and Nadja disrobe Shirley, then wrap her in metallic cloth and put her upright in a clear tube which becomes opaque. The purpose of this, unguessable. Hauron removes one of Bob's arms and, later, his chin (another first). "He had a nice chin, except for that tiny scar." Chinless and armless, Bob is somehow sent with Shirley to the other planet.

Meanwhile, Tom and Sally, still seeking those car keys, blunder into Bronson Caverns and trip a light device which signals the aliens. "Turn on the statsis [sic] beam!" cries one of the aliens. Tom and Sally are paralyzed, but later Tom talks with Hauron. "You're breathing our oxygen mixture," says the amazed science student, "and the odds against that are fantastic." (Of course, Tom doesn't react to the fact that the aliens look exactly like human beings, less likely than their breathing oxygen.)

We learn the real reason the aliens don't want Earthlings puttering around in spaceships: they think they own the Solar System, presumably because they are from around here themselves. Selfish things.

In further discussions, we learn that the aliens' power source is an "element that would correspond to your hydrogen." Tom perks up. "Same atomic weight?" he asks. Hauron replies loftily, "much higher." (Which means that it does *not* "correspond" to hydrogen at all, but Tucker is blithely confident that the little science he knows is still a good deal more than that known by the average member of the audience; he was probably correct.)

Meanwhile, outside in the real world, the absence of Tom and Sally has been noted, and most of the rest of the cast is converging on the cave.

Tom realizes that the aliens' element Drazanon "corresponds" to radium, so he uses the radium in his wristwatch dial to escape momentarily. He lies to Hauron about important rocketry matters, and when Sally seems about to object, Tom cries out, "Ixnay! Oneyphay opeday!" Then explains to Hauron that that was "just my way of telling her I love her."

Because Tom lied, Hauron's latest effort at wrecking a missile is wasted, and the launch is successful. The group searching for the lost pair shows up, and Hauron uses a ray on them. They are all brought into the ship, buried in the mountain. The aliens turn back into little spots of light and immerse themselves in a liquid for the trip back to their home planet. The professor who was captured happens to have litmus paper with him, and tests the liquid. After some discussion of chemical reactions of salt, polyethylene and hydrogen, Tom uses his scientific ingenuity to find a way out of their dilemma. Using polyethylene from those transparent inserts found in wallets, Tom blows up the tank of liquid, and everyone flees the spaceship as there's another explosion.

After congratulations all around, everyone climbs into a car to return to Cape Canaveral. But after the auto disappears from view, we hear an explosion and a scream. The aliens are victorious—offscreen.

Phil Tucker has been excoriated by writers who seem more intent on proving their own cleverness than in being informative, balanced and fair. Tucker is not a good movie director, and he's a terrible writer, but that doesn't make *him* a joke, though his films can be; it just shows he lacks talent. There are worse things than being untalented in a field you love, such as being viciously sarcastic about people who cannot defend themselves.

At least Tucker does show a little inventiveness here and there, and while *Cape Canaveral Monsters* is unquestionably a stinker, in fact it shows improvement over *Robot Monster*, technically and conceptually. Instead of a gorilla in a space helmet, the monsters are little discs of light; disappointing, but at least it isn't surrealistically ludicrous. Tucker has a print of the film in which he has carefully hand-colored the discs. He has some pride in his work.

The title shows exploitative cleverness. When it was made, it was timely as all get-out. However, indications are that the film may not have been released theatrically, though it was made available to theatres. Unfortunately, by the time it was generally shown on television, Cape Canaveral had been Cape Kennedy for several years, and the timeliness had not only vanished, the title had become outmoded.

In *Scream Queens,* Barry Brown says in his piece on Katherine Victor that the movie never had a theatrical release. Brown was himself an actor with an intermittently promising career cut short by his untimely and bitterly tragic death in 1978. His article is full of the powerful affection Barry felt for actors and actresses who did good work in the worst possible films, leading him to write a lengthy piece on Victor, who was surprised and flattered by Barry's attentions.

In the article, Barry provided the only information ever printed on the production of *Cape Canaveral Monsters.* "'I had great hopes for that picture because everybody was so enthused,' [Katherine Victor] said. [Phil] Tucker knew what he wanted and didn't hesitate to fulfill his responsibilities as a director. This, plus a two-week shooting schedule, enough money to enable him to shoot several takes per shot if something went wrong, and the added attraction of color, all made the project seem promising. The color was the first thing to go. Last-minute budget cuts restricted it to black and white. Then, as the filming days went by, the cost of necessary special effects ate away at the money reserve and made it necessary to take shortcuts in the acting department. Scenes were shortened, changed or compromised. When the film was finally screened, it proved a disappointment for everyone involved.... A year went by before the actors received their salaries."

The budget of *Cape Canaveral Monsters* must have been miniscule to begin with, so cuts were probably even more limiting than they would have been on a more expensive film. The film does look cheap indeed.

As a director, Tucker has few ideas, and handles virtually everything in the most unimaginative manner possible, even given the limiting circumstances. Acting is either dull or too broad, when there's acting at all.

As a writer, Tucker is much worse. He has a few good concepts, such as the amusingly grotesque idea of the aliens in their scarred, battered and rotting bodies sneaking off for some quick sex. But his science is hopeless and his dialogue worse. "You mean we must not kill our little Earth friends?" asks a disappointed alien, near the climax. At other times, Tucker seems to be trying for wordless eloquence, as at the beginning of the picture. His leaden ear for dialogue and his total failure to understand the effect some of his ideas (e.g., the pig Latin) might have on audiences doom the picture. He occasionally cuts away to nothing at all—rocks, landscape shots—apparently as punctuation, and still shows us full takes of the ray machine's cover being raised.

The acting in the film is on four levels: competent (Jason Johnson), marginal (Scott Peters), hammy (Katherine Victor) and nonexistent (everyone else). Although not helped by the director, Johnson, a very ordinary-looking man, has an unusual alien mastermind. There's no room in the dialogue for a real performance, but at least Johnson seems to know his way around a movie set. He also appeared in *A Hatful of Rain, The Three Faces of Eve* (both 1957), *Seven Ways from Sundown* (1960), *Strange Compulsion* (1964), *If He Hollers Let Him Go* (1968) and *The Andromeda Strain* (1971), among other films.

Scott Peters was just another handsome male ingenue, although he did appear in a wide variety of films, including *The FBI Story* (1959), *The Canadians* (1961), *Panic in Year Zero!,* and *Madmen of Madoras* (1963), which, in a different cut, is also known as *They Saved Hitler's Brain.* He had a small role in *Marooned* (1969), and rather surprisingly appeared in the mild sexploitation film, *The Soul Snatcher* (1965). Peters was a regular on the short-lived TV series, "Get Christie Love."

The main claim to fame of heroine Linda Connell is that she is the daughter of cinematographer (W.) Merle Connell.

In *The Golden Turkey Awards*, the reprehensible Harry and Michael Medved, who consistently display a repulsively arrogant attitude toward the efforts of haplessly untalented but comparatively more sincere people, get the plot of *Cape Canveral Monsters* entirely wrong: "a plot concerning starfish-zombies who do battle with a pack of ferocious dogs." However, the Medveds are to be thanked (and cursed simultaneously) for bringing to light another Phil Tucker film, *Space Jockey*, which he made just before *Robot Monster*. "My other films are okay," the Medveds quote Tucker as saying, "but this *Space Jockey* — now that was a real piece of shit. In fact, I'd say it's probably the worst film ever made." Considering Tucker's other accomplishments, that's an awesome claim. Tucker also said that no prints of *Space Jockey* are known to survive, which is a shame; I for one would very much like to see it.

The Medveds claim that Tucker's worst features are his "bizarre artistic pretensions" and "strained seriousness," quoting some of the more alarming lines from *Robot Monster* in an effort to make their point. But however bad *Dance Hall Racket* (1954, with Lenny Bruce) and *Cape Canaveral Monsters* might be, they don't have *Robot Monster's* overweening pretension. They're simple and direct, and more imaginative. Tucker is indeed a very bad director, but unlike his detractors the Medveds, he is not smug, merciless and belittling.

Cape Canaveral Monsters does qualify for any list of the 50 worst films of all time, and probably is one of the 15 or so worst science fiction movies. But that's not a sin against mankind, it's only bad moviemaking.

Dinosaurus!

After the interesting promise of *The Blob* and *4D Man*, I eagerly anticipated *Dinosaurus!*, the first Jack H. Harris–produced and Irvin S. Yeaworth, Jr.–directed film to have a reasonable budget, but despite some bright moments, the picture is disappointing. Howard S. Thompson of the *New York Times* was even appalled: "Motion picture art hit rock bottom [with the release] of *Dinosaurus*," he said. "If ever there was a tired, synthetic, plodding sample of movie junk, it's this 'epic.'" It's actually not all *that* bad, but is tepid and un-imaginative, especially in its centerpiece — the dinosaur scenes.

Dinosaurus! is a peculiar blend of melodrama and comedy, unusual enough for some people to regard the film as a spoof. It's nothing of the sort, overall, though there are spoofy scenes. The dinosaurs are played straight, and while the caveman stuff is funny, it's not a lampoon of anything, just jokes. As a resurrected Neanderthal, actor Gregg Martell makes those jokes the best part of the picture.

The film was aimed almost entirely at children, with a few mild "grown-up" jokes tossed in for those adults who happened to see it. A little boy is a central figure, the pivot around which the plot revolves. In keeping with the juvenile aim of the film, the characterization is strictly good guy–bad guy in form. For kids, the movie worked well; for those over about 14, the movie presented problems. Today, *Dinosaurus!* looks plodding and cheap; the stop-motion animation of the dinosaurs is among the worst ever done in an American sound film, further injuring the already crippled movie.

It's set on a Caribbean island, where an American crew, headed by Bart (Ward Ramsey) and Chuck (Paul Lukather), is dredging out an improved harbor. An explosion knocks pretty Betty (Kristina Hanson), Bart's girlfriend, out of her skiff, and when he dives in to rescue her, he sees a Tyrannosaurus rex at the bottom of the bay.

Cables are hooked to the two dinosaurs—a brontosaurus* was also found—and they are hauled ashore. "Two huge ugly dinosaurs," says Bart, "perfectly preserved at the bottom of the channel, frozen solid." Giving the film its stab at scientific rationalization, he says the dynamite used in the dredging operations "must have blasted through the rock that entombed them. Some compressed gas must have caused the freezing, I guess." I guess so.

We are introduced to "lovable" island boy Julio (Alan Roberts), the ward of scurvy scoundrel Mike Hacker (Fred Engelberg), the "island manager." Hacker's erratic and pointless enforcement of the rules has already brought him into conflict with Bart and Chuck, who have befriended Julio. "I wouldn't trust [Hacker] as far as I could throw a dinosaur," one of them says, but they entrust him with a telegram to the head office informing them of the discovery of the dinosaurs.

On his own, Hacker and his henchmen make a discovery of their own: along with the dinosaurs is a mud-covered, frozen Neanderthal man (Martell); figuring on making some money off this find, Hacker and his men hide the Neanderthal in some bushes. He later burns the telegram.

Hacker smashes Julio's toy dinosaurs, surely causing most little boys watching the film to wince in sympathy. Later, Chuck starts to get in a barroom fight with Hacker over his mistreatment of Chica (Luci Blain), and the bearded villain smashes a bottle on his bar. However, he only cuts his hand—the first time I ever saw that gag.

Meanwhile, back at the beach, lightning strikes the frozen forms of the dinosaurs and the caveman. They smoke for a moment, then begin twitching. The old Irish drunk (James Logan) assigned to watch the creatures has a "never again" scene—seeing the monsters, he assumes they are alcoholic hallucinations, and decides never to drink again. The tyrannosaur gets him, and there's an explosion. The three prehistoric survivors wander off as everyone rushes down to the beach. Someone points out ironically that the dinosaurs didn't just walk away, at which point (of course) there's a deafening "screeoowww" from offscreen.

The tyrannosaur stomps on a full bus, killing the people inside, then eats them (offscreen). The brontosaurus eats bushes.

Elsewhere, the curious Neanderthal happens upon a house, encountering first glass, then a woman in a mudpack with hair in her curlers. The glass baffles him, and the woman terrifies him as much as he scares her. She flees, and he wanders into the house.

Elsewhere yet, young Julio happens upon the friendly brontosaurus, browsing in the jungle. (The brontosaurus always goes boom-boom-boom when it walks, as if the jungle floor is a giant kettledrum.) Julio knows the brontosaurus won't hurt him. In the usual movie notion, a herbivore is viewed as good and a carnivore as evil.

Back at that house, the caveman is trying to puzzle out modern living, 1960-style. He finds a fine axe in a workroom, and when a ham radio crackles at him, smashes it with the axe. He bites curiously into some wax fruit, then

*I am aware that the correct term for the dinosaur formerly referred to as a brontosaurus is "Apatosaurus," but when this film was made, even paleontologists used the word "brontosaurus," and that's the term used in the film, so I'll use it too. Sorry, Don.

The villainous tyrannosaur ferociously attacks the kindly, heroic brontosaur in this miniature shot from Jack H. Harris' disappointing Dinosaurus! (1960). The quickly-built models were by Marcel Delgado, probably his least satisfactory; the animation was by divers hands, including those of Tim Baar, Wah Chang and Gene Warren.

discards it. He pulls a book off a shelf, takes a tentative bite, then plucks out a page and bites that. He disappears from our view down a hallway; there's a crash, a thud, and a pause. Suddenly there's the sound of a toilet flushing and the caveman rushes out in panic. Granted, that's not exactly sophisticated, but the timing is good and the sound of a toilet flushing was very unexpected.

Martell makes almost all this innocent-at-large stuff work. He creates a believable and sympathetic character with no dialogue. He is not playing the caveman as a child or a fool, but as an inexperienced adult, who is always pleased when he figures something out. After smashing one mirror, he realizes it's his reflection. In the jungle, he takes charge.

Julio, fleeing Hacker (and having left behind the brontosaurus) arrives at the house, and mistakes the caveman for a somewhat uncouth houseguest. It's Betty's house, and Julio is familiar with it. The boy and the caveman are beginning to hit it off when Hacker arrives.

The villain and his henchmen are clearly up to no good; this is clear even to the caveman who, feeling around for a weapon, picks up a pie and hits Hacker in the face with it. As I said, the humor is not sophisticated; however, despite this slapstick comedy bit, the music remains dead serious in a reasonably amusing contrast.

The caveman and Julio flee, and encounter the brontosaurus; the caveman immediately climbs aboard, taking the boy with him. The Neanderthal seems familiar with the creature, but no one claims they were contemporaries.

Alone in the jungle, Betty is captured by the tyrannosaur; the caveman sinks his axe into the tyrannosaur's foot, causing it to drop her. He catches her and flees with her and Julio into a nearby cave.

There's a strange scene, almost funny, in which Betty tries to interest the caveman in anything other than sex, which he obviously has on his mind.

Outside, the tyrannosaur and the brontosaurus are having a singularly unexciting, poorly-staged fight. The tyrannosaur downs his opponent, then tries to claw open the cave. Its tail lashes, its tongue waggles, and it issues shrieks.

Hacker sees what's happening, and manages to enter the cave, hoping still to capture the dinosaur and the caveman for exhibition purposes. Bart and Chuck also arrive, and battle the tyrannosaur, tossing a Molotov cocktail into its mouth.

Hacker shoots the caveman, but a cave-in kills Hacker. The caveman holds up the ceiling of the old mine (or whatever) while Bart rescues Julio and Betty; the cavern collapses, killing the caveman.

Meanwhile, Chuck and the leadenly uncomic Dumpy (Wayne C. Tredway) have been building defenses around the old fort to which the island's inhabitants have been evacuated. They've dug a moat and filled it with gasoline, as if the tyrannosaur is some unstoppable force of nature, instead of merely a large carnivore.

Bart, Betty and Julio arrive at the fort before the dinosaur, and the gasoline is ignited. Painfully like a fiend from hell, the dinosaur roars at them through the flames.

Bart leaps into a "steam" shovel nearby, and battles with the tyrannosaur at the edge of the sea cliff, finally knocking it into the ocean, where it immediately sinks to the bottom.

As had become traditional with a Jack H. Harris film, the words "The End" are followed by "?"

The aspirations of *Dinosaurus!* are simple enough that in a real sense the picture can't be considered a failure; if you're only aiming at the Moon, people shouldn't complain if you don't hit Mars. But even on this limited level, the film is weak.

The dinosaur models were designed and built by Marcel Delgado, the master craftsman who had built the creatures for *King Kong* and *Mighty Joe Young*. However, this time he was rushed and the technique used was inadequate. The sculpting is dull and simplistic, and the armatures within the models (now owned by Forrest J Ackerman) were hastily built, using wire in many places where stable joints were required. The two dinosaurs are not typical of Delgado's generally fine work and are, in fact, embarrassing.

The stop-motion animation is among the poorest ever done for a feature film. Producer Harris was very much in favor of using animation to bring the creatures to life, but no one seemed to want to turn to the few men in Hollywood who actually had done extensive model animation previously. The animation was under the direction of Tim Baar, Wah Chang and Gene Warren; I do not know who manipulated the models.

The company owned by these men, Project: Unlimited *was* limited—by money and by time. While the company was capable of doing good work, this time the budget was so low, the models were so unstable (they are very light for animation models), and the work had to be done so fast that there's little even a master animator could do, and the animators of *Dinosaurus!* were not masters.

The film is not only plagued with the "strobing" problem almost all stop-motion features have faced, the models don't hold their positions well from frame to frame, resulting in a true jerkiness, a fluttering of motion. The cumbersome models never seem real, and the complete lack of flexing in the body of the brontosaurus makes it look like a big toy being pulled along by a string.

The direction of the animation scenes is also poor. The tyrannosaur shrieks constantly, eventually sounding comic. Its tongue wabbles up and down much of the time, and the sculpted-in expression of furious rage makes the tongue-waggling seem even sillier.

The two "set piece" fights are highly unimaginative, even boring. The clash between the dinosaurs is staged in long shots blended with confusing quick cuts; we never get the impression of two animals battling. The fight between the tyrannosaur and the power shovel is no more interesting. For one thing, this time there's a live-action participant to compare with the actions of the animated model, and the comparison makes the mismatches obvious. The concept of the fight is excellent—dinosaur versus machine—and has yet to be used effectively; it is badly developed here.

Furthermore, the separate large models of the heads of the dinosaurs don't match the animation models well. These heads are live-action, manipulated from below by wires and levers, used in some of the close-up action scenes. But as they differ so much from the animation models, I doubt that even children were fooled.

The models were retired, but the brontosaurus appeared in an episode of "Twilight Zone" called "The Odyssey of Flight 33." Perhaps because the action of the model was so limited (it glanced up at a passing jet plane from the miniature jungle set built for *Dinosaurus!*), perhaps because more time was available to the animator, the model looked more believable on "Twilight Zone" than in the film for which it was constructed.

The script for *Dinosaurus!*, by Jean Yeaworth and Dan E. Weisburd, varies from amusing to thick-witted, and the virtues and flaws stem from the same impulses and intentions: to keep the film light. The ideas pay off in the sequence of Gregg Martell prowling around the house: ideas and actor come together for an obvious but funny sequence. Some of the touches involving Hacker also work: he's an overbearing bully, but also a coward and at least once a funny klutz.

But there are also all those scenes that don't work. There's Dumpy the unfunny bulldozer operator, and the clichéd Irish drunk (he even says "seints presarv us"). The writers may have intended these to be lighter, satiric versions of the same types found in other movies, but neither the director nor the actors make this intent clear.

Yeaworth did reasonably well directing *The Blob*, and even better with *4D Man*; the actors he has been given here, unlike in the earlier films, are just the usual sort of thing. Ward Ramsey, Kristina Hanson, Paul Lukather and Fred Engelberg are cast for their visual appeal, like for a television show.

Whereas *The Blob* and *4D Man* seemed as if they were made by people who had only *heard* of low-budget SF-horror movies, *Dinosaurus!* is obviously aping the usual thing. The more intelligent aspects of the earlier pictures have been shunted off to comedy, and not very successful comedy at that. The conventional aspects of the film (and Ward Ramsey, for one, never has any scenes with comedy) are *very* conventional, even ordinary.

There is, however, the caveman. Gregg Martell is even better than the role calls for. His wide-eyed innocence never seems like stupidity, and no matter how clownish he gets, his quick action and physical strength keep him from becoming a clown. He remains an intelligent, primitive presence. His death at the end, however, is not poignant, it's cruelty to the kids in the audience who admired the character, and afterward the film seems anticlimactic. When Martell leaves the film, much of the energy as well as interest departs; his performance is both clever and energetic, and good enough that it's too bad his career never rose above supporting roles, except for this unforgettable caveman. Although he's not "realistic," he's the most appealing primitive survivor in U.S. films, until John Lone's excellent performance in a rather similar role in *Iceman* (1984).

Martell appeared in many films until the late 1960s, usually as virile henchmen to bad guys, or the fourth soldier on the left. Among his other movies: *Kiss of Death* (1947), *Undertow* (1949), *Gunfight at the O.K. Corral* (1957), *Tonka* (1958), *Seven Ways from Sundown* (1960), *How the West Was Won* (1963) and *The Singing Nun* (1966). In none of these films are his roles of any importance. He appeared in other films included in this book, *Space Master X-7*, *Return of the Fly*, *Valley of the Dragons* (as a caveman) and *The Three Stooges Meet Hercules*.

Especially in contrast to Martell, the rest of the cast is colorless. Ward Ramsey was a Universal contract player, apparently assigned to Harris and Yeaworth as a result of their contract with the studio; *Dinosaurus!* seems to be his first film. He's harmless and forgettable as an actor; the role is perfunctory, and he's physically just another George Nader type—handsome, square-faced—so he makes little impact. Like Martell, he appeared in *Seven Ways from Sundown*, as well as *The Great Impostor* (1961), *Cape Fear* (1962) and *Moment to Moment* (1966) among other Universal films. After his contract with the studio expired, he appeared in much smaller parts in *Speedway* (1968), *Maryjane* (1968) and *The Comic* (1969) before apparently retiring as an actor.

Paul Lukather is slightly more interesting; handsome but a touch sinister, he could have played John Saxon–type sleek baddies, but worked very little. He's also in *Hands of a Stranger*, as well as *Drango* (1957), *Alvarez Kelly* (1966) and *The Way West* (1967), among other films. He seems to have vanished from the screen until *Hot Lead and Cold Feet* (1978).

Alan Roberts was a mildly obnoxious, mostly untalented child actor; he appeared in *Ice Palace* (1960) and *Two Loves* (1961) before outgrowing his slight charm. Julio is a trite, conventional role, similar to monster-loving kids in many another film.

I have been unable to locate any other credits for Kristina Hanson. She's just another pretty ingenue, although she does reasonably well in the scene in which she fends off the caveman's advances. Engelberg, who's also in *The Lost Missile*, isn't bad as the ethnically-odd Hacker, but not especially interesting, either.

The location exteriors are so pretty and sunny that they make the studio interiors look especially heavy and artificial. Unlike the previous Harris productions, the music is standard Hollywood stuff. All in all, whatever the minor but unusual virtues the Harris films derived from being shot in Pennsylvania have mostly been lost by the move to bigger budgets and more studio control.

Paul V. Beckley in the New York *Herald-Tribune* considered the film "for the most part pretty low voltage monster stuff.... Gregg Martell as the Neaderthal provides a few innocent chuckles.... However, such occasional evidence of humor only suggests how amusing the film might have been and cannot overcome the general crudity of workmanship or dialogue."

"Tube" in *Daily Variety* thought that the film was "above all, a comedy," but also wondered "whether [Yeaworth's] tongue was consistently in cheek." He also thought that "much of the comedy may be crude, but its charm ranges from [slapstick] to sophisticated satire."

More recently, Parish & Pitts thought that the film was "an amusing romp filmed in Scandinavia" (!?) which featured "excellent animation (!!)." *Psychotronic* had little to say other than that the animation "is pretty lousy."

A Dog, a Mouse and a Sputnik

This little-known French Farce was primarily a vehicle for comedian Noël-Noël, who at this point in his career had begun specializing in petit-bourgeois characters, the sort of placid, complacent, middle-class gentleman often the subject of satire in French films. Noël-Noël had a long screen career, but relatively few of his movies saw release in the United States, perhaps because of their provincial nature.

Such seems to be the case for *A Dog, a Mouse and a Sputnik* as well; if it hadn't been for its SF elements, it probably would not have been released here at all. As it was, the film was released in France in 1958, but not in the United States until 1960, when it played a few art theatres in the larger cities, then vanished. Rarely on television (when it is called *Sputnik*), it seems fairly typical. Originally called *À Pied, à Cheval et en Spoutnik* (By Foot, by Horse and by Sputnik), it was called with a bizarre disregard for grammar, *Hold Tight for the Satellite* in Great Britain and Australia. Furthermore, Don Willis (I) cites *Rocketflight with Hindrance* as yet another title, but fails to give the origin.

Noël-Noël plays gentle, elderly Frenchman Léon Martin, who because of an automobile accident, cannot recall anything more recent than World War I. Recovering quietly in the country with his wife Marguerite (Denise Gray), one day Martin finds a dog and a mouse, and mistaking the dog for a long-dead pet of his own, he takes both animals home. He's unaware that they are from a Soviet sputnik, come to Earth nearby.

Eventually, French and Soviet officials discover that M. Martin has the animals, and begin trying to persuade him to give them up. According to reviews, at this point there's a fair amount of okay satire of minor French officialdom (apparently even more fussy and officious than such types elsewhere), featuring appearances by two other comedians, Noël Roquevort as a local mayor, and Darry Cowl as a deputy attaché of the Foreign Office. Soviet officials also get into the act, and the irreplaceable Mischa Auer appears as Professor Popov.

M. Martin resists all attempts to get the animals away from him, and holes up in a barn, threatening to take on all comers. However, he is eventually persuaded to allow the animals to go to Moscow for scientific tests; he and his wife accompany them there.

At a space research institute, Martin and Popov investigate a supposedly deactivated man-carrying satellite, but it's accidentally launched, going into orbit around the Moon. On its way back to Earth, Popov, who has been controlling the sputnik, becomes ill and M. Martin is forced to take over. His inexperience at spaceflight results in wild orbits of the Earth, but he manages to make a successful landing.

Although acclaimed by all Moscow as a great hero, M. Martin prefers to return quietly with his wife, dog and mouse to his French country home.

The film received mostly mildly favorable reviews. In *Variety*, Gene Moskowitz reported that "science fiction and French bourgeois situation comedy are fairly well mixed in this spoof. Some good comic invention goes astray when the amnesiac middle-aged hero gets mixed up in a trip in a man-carrying Russian sputnik.... Noël-Noël's clever acting gets the most laughs in this easygoing pic.... So-so special effects detract from the final episodes. Russian scenes are well done and the kidding hits home at times, especially in the scenes where the absent-minded Frenchman keeps asking about the Czar, etc."

Film Daily's "M.H." said, "The film churns up a lot of action and comedy, some of it very funny indeed, other parts a bit on the corny side. In general, it has enough qualifications to easily make it satisfactory for the art houses."

Paul V. Beckley in the New York *Herald-Tribune* said, "*A Dog, a Mouse and a Sputnik* is a droll comment, a bit wistful perhaps, on French and Russian manners. Unfortunately, once it has seized on a delicious situation, it lets go as though realizing too late the whole thing is a bit too hot to handle."

Giving the film a II rating, the *Monthly Film Bulletin* considered it "a curious and somewhat ambiguous comedy. Beginning with some good-natured satire directed at French officialdom, it then tries to do the same for the Russian scene, only to hover uneasily between 'funny foreigner' slapstick and a seemingly serious appraisal of Russian scientific achievements. Neither the script nor [Jean] Dréville's rather ham-fisted direction can make much of these situations. The film's main assets are Noël-Noël's gently perplexed hero, a few characteristic moments from Darry Cowl as an agitated French attaché, and Mischa Auer's Russian scientist, played almost straight."

It would be especially interesting to see *A Dog, a Mouse and a Sputnik* today; the satire of bureaucrats and mild little men would be about the same as in contemporary films, but the observations of Soviet science and the mild spoofs on *Soviet* bureaucracy make it sound quite appetizing. It was rare for a movie of the time to engage in satire (as opposed to spoofery) mixed with science fiction. This may not be an especially good film, but sounds more than usually promising on some levels.

The Electronic Monster

Some science fiction ideas are ideal for movies but producers rarely treat them in an imaginative, intelligent fashion. One of these is presented in *The Electronic Monster*; it turned up in a somewhat different form in *Brainstorm* (1983): the recording and playback of the experiences of another person. *The Electronic Monster* (British title: *Escapement*) avoids how these experiences are recorded and, in fact, the only ones we see being played back are staged dreams. Unfortunately, this interesting premise is maltreated by being dropped into a conventional cloak-and-dagger plot dealing with megalomaniacal ex–Nazis, bent on controlling people for power and wealth.

Driving a Mediterranean highway, movie star Clark Denver suddenly screams, clutching his head; the car crashes, Denver is killed. When insurance investigator Jeff Keenan (Rod Cameron) is given the assignment, he is told that

Somers (Larry Gross), Denver's publicity agent, has already done some investigating, and found that another man died after going to the Clinique Privée d'Ameriçon, the same Riviera psychiatric clinic Denver had been visiting.

Jeff goes to the Riviera to investigate the clinic, and by an outrageous coincidence, encounters Ruth (Mary Murphy), his former fiancée and a movie star herself, now engaged to Paul Zakon (Peter Illing), the owner of the clinic. She denies any connection between the clinic and Denver's death.

Dr. Maxwell (Meredith Edwards), inventor of the process that makes the clinic unique, demonstrates his dream machine. An electrode on a skullcap of tubes and blinking lights transmits taped emotions directly into the minds of patients. We see Kallini (Carlo Borelli) used as a demonstration: placed in a transparent coffinlike cubicle in a room resembling a crypt, and transmitted oddball, almost surrealistic but soothing dreams. Presumably, after several weeks of this, the patients (or "unfortunate sick people," as Maxwell says) are well on their way to recovery.

The dream machine is, says Maxwell, "a more perfect kind of escape," as compared to books, television, theatre, cinema, daydreams. Jeff informs him that Denver died *before* his car smashed, of cerebral thrombosis. After Jeff leaves, Maxwell, a decent man, goes to see Zakon about possible problems with the dream machine. Zakon scoffs at Maxwell's worries, and demands to see evidence that the treatment might be fatal.

Back in the city, Jeff goes to visit Somers—to whom Zakon has just made a cryptic reference—and finds him dead, hanging from a fixture in his room.

Maxwell's wife (Kay Callard) tells him there was a connection between the two dead patients, and refers to another patient (never seen) who also died after treatment by a special tape ordered by Zakon.

In the clinic, Zakon confers with his assistants, Blore (Carl Deuring), a thug, and Hoff (Carl Jaffe), who has a thick German accent and smokes a cigarette in a holder. Zakon wears a monocle. This Nazi iconography is neither subtle nor misleading. "May I remind you, Dr. Hoff," says Zakon threateningly, "that you are no longer in charge of experimental surgery at that concentration camp?"

Zakon and Hoff take over Kallini's treatment, changing the tapes and turning all relevant dials up to high. Now the dream Kallini is being fed begins with a big, papier-mâché head of Zakon, and features a dancing woman with a whip, dungeon, and black torturer. Most of the figures in the dream wear the same skullcap as Kallini. At the end of the dream, a masked figure representing Zakon restores order and tranquility.

Zakon says that all the patients will now be subject to the same indoctrination: "the unscientific term is, I believe, brainwashing." All tapes will feature nightmarish images followed by peaceful ecstasy in which Zakon's image predominates as a symbol of benevolence and mercy. He will then gain their trust and their money, controlling their lives.

Appalled at this horrendous misuse of his wonderful machine, Maxwell threatens to tell the authorities. Zakon reminds him that he, Maxwell, is not actually a doctor and that his practice of medicine would be frowned on; as an added inducement to cooperate, he threatens to harm Maxwell's wife. But she herself goes to Zakon and tells him off, and Blore grabs her.

Suspicious of the clinic, under a pretext Jeff manages to visit one of the sound stages where the "dreams" are being filmed, and sees a man in a Zakon mask. Ruth now suspects that something is amiss, and after being told that Mrs. Maxwell hadn't visited the clinic, she discovers a charm dropped by Mrs. Maxwell.

When Mrs. Maxwell's body is found, Jeff and Maxwell team up to defeat Zakon, and in the general melée that follows, Hoff shoots Blore and Jeff grapples with Hoff. Maxwell forces Zakon to don the electronic skullcap, then turns the power up all the way, electrocuting the villain. Maxwell smashes the equipment and a fire breaks out; Maxwell presumably dies in the conflagration.

Although this is one of the very few mentally-oriented SF films, the SF element is so minimized as to make the movie more of a postwar Nazis–still–scheme thriller than anything else. The unimaginative script by Charles Eric Maine was adapted from his 1956 novel *Escapement* (*The Man Who Couldn't Sleep* in the U.S.), but it isn't even a good adaptation.

As an author, Maine has always had a propensity for finding an interesting premise and then working it out in a conventional, even hackneyed fashion, as here. Maine doesn't seem to be able to devise a means of recording the dreams, so he avoids the question. That isn't too important, but his misuse and failure to explore the idea is. Why only dreams? What is the advantage of showing people these pompously choreographed dances? Are the images varied for different patients? Out of all possible plotlines involving this idea, why does he use clichéd ex–Nazis as the villains?

The answers to all these are the same: at heart, Maine is conventional, so that even good films based on his stories would be conventional at their core; *The Electronic Monster* is a long way from being a good film.

Montgomery Tully, who directed, was a plodding, minor filmmaker, working almost entirely in low-budget crime thrillers. He staged scenes unimaginatively and conventionally; each seems to have too much footage at the beginning and end, making a slow picture even slower, despite its fast wrap-up. Tully also directed *The Diamond Wizard*, *The Terrornauts* (1967) and *Battle Beneath the Earth* (1968), his only other SF films; they are also heavy going.

Rod Cameron walks through his part as the investigator, as he sometimes did, although a caring Cameron performance resembles an uncaring one more than slightly. Stalwart, moderately good-looking, Cameron is basically an uninteresting actor, but had enough star presence to play leads in dozens of films from the early 1940s, including two serials, *G-Men vs. the Black Dragon* and *Secret Service in Darkest Africa* (both 1943). He also appeared in *The Monster and the Girl* (1941), *The Jungle* and *Psychic Killer* (1975). Most of the large number of B movies that Cameron made from around 1943 to the late 50s were Westerns. But the 6'3" Cameron looked right in the parts, he had an excellent speaking voice, and he could ride and shoot convincingly. Few would ever think he was a good actor, but he was competent enough for most films. He looks lost in *The Electronic Monster*, however, with an undefined and vague role.

Mary Murphy fares much better as the heroine, but her presence in the story is so preposterous and convenient that she's uninteresting. Her character exists solely to give Cameron someone to talk to from time to time. Murphy worked frequently from the early 50s, sometimes in leads even in important films, but usually in supporting roles. She was out of her depth in *The Wild One* (1954) — she was the one who asked Brando what he was rebelling against — but was probably not given much help by the director. She appeared in *When Worlds Collide*, *Houdini* (1953), *The Mad Magician* (1954), *The Desperate Hours* (1955), one of the two 1965 films called *Harlow*, *Junior Bonner*, *Airport '77* (both 1977) and even Woody Allen's *Manhattan* (1979). *The Electronic Monster* probably seemed like a good way to visit Europe and be paid for it.

The self-consciously weird dream sequences in *The Electronic Monster* were directed by David Paltenghi, apparently beyond the capabilities of Montgomery Tully, but even he might have done as well as Paltenghi. Full of sadomasochistic symbolism, stark sets—spider webs, organ pipes—the "dreams" are still tame, boring and silly. They have a slightly sensual aura, but it's more like a burlesque show taking itself seriously than anything else. The dreams also don't seem to have any psychological application. Even the dreams designed to depict Zakon as a benevolent god are wrong: they make him seem monstrously deformed, and no help at all. The reaction one would expect from someone meeting the real Zakon after being exposed to these dreams would be to run screaming.

One further note: the dream machine itself has one of my very least favorite design aspects, often found in low-budget SF films and serials: the dials, knobs, etc., on the front of the machine make it look like a face.

The *Monthly Film Bulletin* gave the film a II, almost entirely because "the theme gives this science fiction melodrama a certain originality."

"Tube" in *Variety* thought the film was "passable" and that it had been produced with "cinematic skill" but remained "strictly routine." Len Simpson, in the short-lived trade magazine *Limelight* was unimpressed; this British film, he thought, was "one of the finest arguments for American movies ever to hit the American screens."

More recently, reaction varies. Alan Frank (*SF*) found it "zestful hokum with risible fantasy sequences," *Psychotronic* thought it was "interesting," and Joe Dante in *Castle of Frankenstein* #9 said that though the "good premise isn't taken far enough," the resulting film was "interesting."

The electronic music by "Soundrama" that permeates the film seems as unimaginative as the rest of it. The peculiar location of the story, the French Riviera, doesn't lead to anything, and the film wastes its premise. *The Electronic Monster* is just a programmer.

The Incredible Petrified World

This god-awful film was released on a double bill with *Teenage Zombies*, producing an evening in the theatre of mind-numbing awfulness matched only by the pairing of *Invasion of the Star Creatures* and *The Brain That Could Not Die*. Both *Petrified World* and *Teenage Zombies* were produced and directed by Jerry Warren, thoroughly discussed elsewhere in this book and Volume 1. Suffice it to say that he is working at or even below his usual worthless level. Unlike *Teenage Zombies*, *The Incredible Petrified World* has a great deal of stock and industrial film footage; however, there doesn't seem to have been a specific Mexican film raided for its pictorial glories.

Robert Clarke stars; between him and costar John Carradine, they have appeared in more bad science fiction films than perhaps any other two actors you could name. After pictures like this and *The Astounding She-Monster*, it's no wonder Clarke felt he could do no worse and probably better, in producing his own film. (He was almost wrong.)

Even though it is still depressingly cheap, this seems to have been almost an "A" production for Warren; it has several actors who have appeared elsewhere, including Clarke, Carradine, Phyllis Coates, George Skaff and even

Lloyd Nelson (often in Warren films). There are even minimal special effects (some borrowed, some original) to add to the appeal of this appalling film.

The film may have taken an entire week to shoot, and Carradine probably did all his work in one day. The film may be terrible, but if someone would add to my list of film credits — especially in a starring role — requiring me to work only one day, no matter how rotten the film, I'd probably do it. One assumes Carradine was also paid reasonably well. He undoubtedly (correctly) felt that it would neither help nor harm his career. The major productions which used him as a character actor would still do so, and the minor films would still seek him out as a star.

Of course, Carradine made the error of filming just too many of these things, and gradually slid from being an interesting eccentric into something of a joke; he was rescued from this, oddly enough, by having been in the very films that made him a joke. Young directors who grew up seeing all those cheap films began to hire him to be in *their* science fiction and horror films, and Carradine turned from a joke into an institution. Apparently this is not a role he finds comfortable, but like it or not, he is the greatest trouper in the history of horror movies, and literally goes around the world to appear in them.

The Incredible Petrified World may be the worst film of Carradine's career, but it isn't really so much worse than indecipherable dreck like *Blood of Ghastly Horror* (1971) and *The Astro-Zombies* (1969).

Carradine plays Dr. Wyman, an oceanographer who has developed a new type of diving bell. From a ship in the Caribbean, the bell lowers to the sea bottom, with diving expert Craig Randall (Robert Clarke), reporter Dale Marshall (Phyllis Coates), scientist Paul Whitmore (Allen Windsor), and college student Lauri Talbot (Sheila Noonan) aboard. However, something goes wrong and the bell breaks loose, plummeting to the ocean floor.

There, they discover some caverns which have an air supply, and they take refuge. As Charles Stinson said in the *Los Angeles Times*, they have "to cope with the following: (1) a shaggy old man with a vaguely Balkan accent and only too clear designs on the girls; (2) an active volcano which, however, not only supplies them with lava but with the air they breathe, and (3) an avalanche which terminates the drama."

Before the avalanche, however, we are treated to interminable scenes not only of our little band of survivors pottering about the cave and speculating on the old man (George Skaff, perhaps), but scenes of Carradine fulminating about the delivery of another bell to rescue those trapped below.

Just as the old man has worked up the courage to attack one of the women, separated from the others, the volcano acts up and starts that landslide which, according to Allen M. Widem in the *Motion Picture Herald*, kills Whitmore. However, the second bell arrives in time to rescue the survivors, and they are hauled to the surface.

The film is just as uneventful as the synopsis sounds; it has enough story-line for perhaps a bad half-hour television show, certainly not enough for a 70-minute film. Don Willis (I) called it "one of the dullest movies ever, with lots of padding to make it to feature length." It's not without justice that writers often turn the title back on the film, so that it's referred to as "The Incredible Petrified Movie."

In fact, nothing *is* incredible about it, and it only barely qualifies as science fiction (it's those air-filled caves that do it). There's nothing in the film that fulfills the promise of the ad line: "A Nightmare of Terror in the Center of the Earth With Forgotten Men, Monsters, Earthquakes and Boiling Volcanos [*sic*]!"

Though there is a forgotten man, an earthquake and a volcano (only one though), there are no monsters to be seen, and the film doesn't take place in the center of the Earth.

The film is so uneventful that it's puzzling as to why it was even made. Terrible as they are, Jerry Warren's other films have a bit more to offer; there is at least one Zombie in *Teenage Zombies*. In an interview with Tom Weaver (who thinks this is Warren's best film), it was revealed that Warren had a monster suit built, but a comedy of errors kept it from being used. It ended up looking too bad even for Warren. And the movie really *is* petrified.

Charles Stinson summed the film up well: although "the cast does its level best ... the picture's incredible petrified script wins clichés down. It starts out with some pretense at oceanological science but, within five minutes, it settles right to the silty bottom where hunks of bad dialogue and old stereotypes drift eternally."

Thomas Reddy in the Los Angeles *Examiner* called the film "petrifyingly dull.... In a picture of this sort, you'd expect a monster or two. But, no; not one teensy-weensy monster. The closest thing to it is a bearded bum found living in the cavern, and he looks less frightening than a character out of 'The Beggars' Opera'.... It's incredible that for more than an hour nothing the least bit exciting happens."

Giving it their lowest rating, the *Monthly Film Bulletin* said, "Altogether crude in conception and execution, this underwater thriller offers nothing but its own unabashed naiveté to relieve the tedium."

Don Willis had a more personal reason than mere boredom for disliking the film: "Jerry Warren's greatest sin this time is wasting Sheila Carol, who was an actress as well as a presence in *Beast from Haunted Cave*." (Willis apparently recognized Sheila Noonan as Sheila Carol.) In *Castle of Frankenstein* #11, Joe Dante rightly called it "startlingly unimaginative, stupefying tedium."

The Incredible Petrified World is a meaningless film; it has no possible reason for existence; it offers no undersea thrills, no monsters, and no excitement. I hope I have not made it sound appetizing.

Last Woman on Earth

Despite the steamy promise of the title, *Last Woman on Earth* is a lesser Roger Corman picture involving a conventional romantic triangle; there's no sexual hijinks, just a lot of talk. The slow, stilted film has a hangdog air, and the third lead, billed as Edward Wain, is clearly no actor. He's actually screenwriter Robert Towne, and this is his first film as writer; the very *film noir*–type relationships between the three main characters indicates the clear understanding of the genre that reached its fruition in Towne's later script for the superb *Chinatown* (1974), which won him an Academy Award.

Towne was not originally scheduled to act in this film, but because he's a slow writer, was pushed into the job by Corman. The director told interviewer Ed Naha, "This was an interesting movie because we never actually had a finished script to work with." Corman always liked to make the most out of location shooting. "We were going to Puerto Rico to shoot this back to back with *Battle of Blood Island*. [Towne] didn't have the script finished in time, though. Our budget was so low I couldn't afford to bring him along as a writer so I decided to make him an actor. I made him the juvenile lead because I *did* have it in the budget to take my actors along. [That's good.] He wrote the script as we filmed. Essentially, there never was a script. We just got pages day by day. We never knew one day what we were going to do the next. We still managed to shoot it in two weeks." Which, incidentally, still left Corman with money in the budget for a third film; for that story, see the entry on *Creature from the Haunted Sea*, in which Towne also played third lead to Antony Carbone and Besty Jones-Moreland.

In Puerto Rico, wealthy Harold (Carbone) and his wife Evelyn (Jones-Moreland) are seeing the sights with their self-loathing lawyer Martin Joyce (Towne). Harold is a shady figure, a gambler. He's not altogether the typical gangster type, however; he's intelligent and shrewd, but as obsessed with personal power and his hold over other people as most gangsters in movies are. He takes Evelyn and Martin to a cockfight, depicted more graphically than actually seems necessary.

"I fail to see the point of two animals clawing each other to death in a ring," one says. This is called foreshadowing.

They later go spearfishing in a rented boat. Just to provide a touch of suspense, underwater someone shoots at Martin with a speargun; it's Evelyn, aiming at a ray beyond him. When the three come out, the air seems funny so they put their scuba gear back on. The boat won't work, and the radio is playing only one tune, over and over.

Returning to Puerto Rico, they find some bodies here and there. (No animal bodies are seen.) Something in the air smothers life, Martin suggests. The oxygen went away, he says – but it comes back. Not in time, however, for anyone other than people who were already carrying their own oxygen. Martin assumes everyone else in the world is dead, forgetting about submarines, airplanes, and sealed environments of other kinds, as well as other scuba divers.

What happened? they wonder. Maybe it was a bomb, Martin suggests. "A bigger and better bomb, an act of God. What's the difference? The result's the same." To signify that things have changed for good, he smashes his watch, a surprisingly eloquent touch.

Harold wants to go to northern Canada to avoid disease from the rotting bodies and the insects that will feed on them. He figures, rationally, they can't be the only people left, there must be birds and chickens.

The three spend most of the rest of the film squabbling among themselves, as Evelyn gradually comes to prefer Martin to the cold-blooded Harold. "You are the thinkingest man," she says admiringly to Martin. They make love on the beach, and afterwards, she tosses the sand they lay on into the air.

Harold in beginning to turn really ugly, especially as Martin has started to exhibit a bit more spine. Finally, Evelyn and Martin try to run off, but are pursued by Harold. When he catches up with them, there is an "epic" fistfight on a dock, in the water, on a reef, in El Morro, the old Spanish fort, and finally in a church.

Unexpectedly, after symbolically going blind, it is Martin who dies. The man who thought there was no use in trying, who egocentrically stopped time by smashing his own watch, has died, and the pragmatic, rational thug survives.

"I killed him," Harold says. "Will we never learn?"

"He didn't think so," replies Evelyn.

"Let's go home."

"Where's that?"

"Help me find out," says Harold.

Like most of the Filmgroup productions, *Last Woman on Earth* has an unusually intelligent script (despite that pretentious closing dialogue), with an attempt at creating strong characters who come into believable conflict. The characters are standard for romantic triangles, but are well worked out, and Martin especially is complex. He takes the end of the world as a personal affront, and refuses to consider that the phenomenon might not have been so globally fatal as he perversely wants it to be. His view of the world was bleak and fatalistic from the beginning; he was a walking dead man when the film began, and he wants the whole world to suffer his fate. In his relationship to the others, he's a standard leech type, working for a cruel, rich but vital man. He hates himself for his enslavement, but his spinelessness and love of luxury keep him tied to Harold. Martin takes refuge in wisecracks and a feeling of superiority to the more uncouth Harold. When he gets drunk, he quotes Lewis Carroll's "Jabberwocky" to Evelyn, assuming that neither she nor Harold have ever heard it before.

Evelyn and Harold are not as richly developed as Martin; although he does exhibit unexpected tenderness for Evelyn from time to time, and he's not really a vulgarian, Harold is still just a gambler. Evelyn, too, is fairly standard; she's not a floozy, but she's no better than she should be. She's somewhat tired of Harold, though she actually cares about him, and when there are only two men left to choose from, being a romantic herself, she is drawn to the more philosophical, doomed Martin. Her key scene is the odd one in which she tosses the sand on which she has just had sex.

This set of characters is not at all what we would ordinarily expect in an end-of-the-world melodrama. Corman had previously destroyed the world in *The Day the World Ended* (and did again, more or less, in *Gas-s-s-s*), and there the characters were neatly labeled. There was a very clear Hero, and a very clear Villain. In *Last Woman on Earth*, things are much more sophisticated (though the film is inferior): Martin, at first, seems to be the hero because he's younger and more intelligent than Harold, and because that corner of the triangle usually is the hero. But as the story progresses, Martin becomes weakened by events while Harold draws strength from them; Martin becomes more assertive because he now has nothing to lose, but he really wants to curl into a ball and die. Harold wants to keep living. Towne votes for crude vitality over sensitive apathy.

Unfortunately, overall the film is not one of Roger Corman's prouder moments. Though there are signs of greater care than he sometimes took (a scene on a boat features two or three angles and more than one lens, where Corman would have usually shot the whole thing in one setup), the film itself is pretentious and boring. Although the characters are more complex than the norm for Corman, they are also singularly uninteresting. Towne's thesis required him to feature a boor and an effete snob as antagonists, but those really aren't people we want to spend a long time with. In an effort to make this end-of-the-world film approach actual drama, he drained it of the vitality of melodrama. In most respects, *The Day the World Ended* is a cruder film, but it's also livelier and, oddly enough, in some ways less dated.

Towne also leans too heavily on symbolism: the battling roosters prefigure the battling men at the climax, and Martin's going blind overburdens a slight film. Furthermore, his means of ending the world is not credible. The oxygen-deprivation phenomenon only lasts a couple of hours, and it's hard to imagine an atmospheric phenomenon of such short duration that would blanket the world. Towne really wasn't interested in the mechanism of how the world came to an end, he just wanted to wipe people out and get on with the story. Unfortunately, this lack of care on his part results in a lack of belief in the audience, fatal to fantasy films. We must believe what we're seeing, even if only temporarily; anything in the script which interferes with belief is harmful to the film overall.

Roger Corman is not a director of actors, so he relies on the same performers again and again. He's generally able to spot good actors—the level of acting in his films is quite high—and the "Roger Corman repertory company" contains many able performers. But if the actor is green, Corman apparently lacks the ability to bring out quality. In a much later film, *Drive, He Said* (1971), Towne gave a good performance under the direction of Jack Nicholson.

Towne was not unhappy with his association with Roger Corman. As he told interviewers for *The Movie World of Roger Corman*, he understood Corman. "Roger had no patience, and that was his great strength. He has the intelligence and originality of a Fellini or a Truffaut, but let's say you're shooting *Lawrence of Arabia* and you have in your mind that you want this figure to emerge out of the desert as just a shadow, as just a mirage—you may have to wait three weeks to get that shot. If you don't have the patience to do that, then there's no point in having the discussion. And if Roger can't do that, it's not because of a lack of raw talent or intelligence—it's because it's either a character flaw or a virtue, depending on how you look at it. He's someone who just doesn't have the patience—he's gotta do it fast. I really love the man. He's an extraordinary person."

So is Robert Towne. He wrote a later script for Corman, *Tomb of Ligeia* (1965), Corman's final film in his Edgar Allan Poe series, the most complex and polished of all (although the ending gives evidence that, once again, Towne was turning in pages as fast as they were being shot). In addition to scripts that appeared under his name, including *Villa Rides* (1968), *The Last Detail* (1973) and *The Yakuza* (1975), Towne was often called in to rewrite or polish scripts by other writers, always without credit. Among these rewrites (which were really what established his reputation in Hollywood) were *Bonnie and Clyde* (1967) and *The Godfather* (1972). He also wrote a couple of scripts for Corman that were rewritten by other and much inferior writers, *A Time for Killing* (1967) and *Captain Nemo and the Underwater City* (1969). Neither were made by Corman.

In more recent times, in addition to continuing his script-doctoring (as on *Reds*), Towne has turned to directing as well, and made a superlative debut in that job in *Personal Best* (1982). He worked several years on a script of the definitive Tarzan movie, but when the film finally went into production, Towne did not direct it, and the script was largely rewritten by another; *Greystoke, the Legend of Tarzan, Lord of the Apes* (1984) was credited to the rewriter and Towne's pseudonym.

Antony Carbone (*not* Anthony) was a Los Angeles stage actor and acting teacher who occasionally appeared in movies, sometimes for Roger Corman. He was also in *Creature from the Haunted Sea, Pit and the Pendulum* (1961), *A Bucket of Blood, Arson for Hire* (1959), *Newman's Law* (1974) and *Skateboard* (1978) among other films. His somewhat Bogart–like features meant he's generally been cast as shady characters; he's a decent enough actor, but similar to better-known players.

Betsy Jones-Moreland began her film career as a Columbia contract actress, and appeared in several films for that company in 1956 and 1957, including *Full of Life* and *Operation Mad Ball*. She appeared in a few films for Corman, including *The Saga of the Viking Women and Their Voyage to the Waters of the Great Sea Serpent* (1957), *Creature from the Haunted Sea* and *The St. Valentine's Day Massacre* (1967). After 1960, she appeared in relatively few films, doing bit parts in *The Hindenburg* (1975), *Gable and Lombard* and *The Last Tycoon* (both 1976); she died in the mid-70s. Jones-Moreland was one of the best minor actresses Corman worked with; she was very good as a floozy, straight or comic, and was capable of surprising sensitivity. She was clearly overqualified for most of the parts she played, and it's a shame that her career was never given the push it deserved.

Reviews of *Last Woman on Earth* were probably a little worse than it deserved. Giving the film a III, the *Monthly Film Bulletin* said, "The Theme of survivors in a world catastrophe is anything but new, and this present variation is frankly dull, burdened with pretentious dialogue." "Tube" in *Daily Variety* considered it an "unappealing picture" and "a weak supporting attraction." He thought none of the actors were convincing, "nor do they have a chance to be under the circumstances.... Corman's direction is generally lacklustre."

In *Science Fiction Movies*, Philip Strick said that the film had "a complex, introverted story.... There is a superb high-angle shot as they wander down a sun-baked street littered with corpses, but the spectacular aspects of the situation are on the whole ignored; as can be detected from the final confrontation in a church, Corman had other things on his mind (it was one of those years when he made six films)."

There wasn't very much daring about *Last Woman on Earth*; the title lured people in, the grainy color photography of Puerto Rico may have made them stay. But there was little reason for anyone who saw it in 1960 to recall the film with any fondness. Despite a careful working-out of some of the aspects of characterization, Robert Towne's debut as a screenwriter was inauspicious, and gave little hint of the ability he would show over the next 25 years. It is also little more than a footnote in Roger Corman's career.

The Leech Woman

When the horror film revival sprang into full flower in the late 1950s, Universal-International, long a major purveyor of such fare, began releasing imported films, generally those made by Hammer in England, and found the need to have backup features to fill out a double bill. These lesser, quickly-made films had less-than-stellar casts, low budgets, mediocre production values and oddball or tired fantasy elements. Among these titles: the strange combination of Western and horror movie, *Curse of the Undead*, released with *The Mummy*; the tale of a mesmerizing head, *The Thing That Couldn't Die*, the cofeature for *Horror of Dracula*, and *The Leech Woman*, made as a cofeature for *Brides of Dracula*.

Perhaps the female-gender noun in each title was what linked the latter pair, but the lively, colorful Hammer film, one of their best, made *The Leech Woman* look drab and old-fashioned. Which it is, although the estimable Vivian C. Sobchack suggests an alternative and intelligent "reading" of the film that uncovers merit in *The Leech Woman*. I'll quote from the article later.

Dr. Paul Talbot (Phillip Terry), an endocrinologist in his 50s, specializes in the rejuvenation of elderly women. It's never stated explicitly, but there's a suggestion his "research" is primarily designed to soak money from rich old women. His own wife, the slightly alcoholic June (Coleen Gray), though still attractive in her mid-50s, holds little interest for Paul, and when she tells him she's decided to get a divorce, he does nothing to dissuade her. He's having an affair with his nurse Sally (Gloria Talbott), some 25 years his junior.

However, an ancient black woman, Malla (Estelle Hemsley), comes into Paul's office on the day June announces the divorce. Despite Sally's protestations, Malla firmly insists on seeing Paul. While Sally and Paul are carrying on in a randy fashion elsewhere in the office suite, Malla momentarily encounters June, and recognizes her as someone she's seen in her nightmares.

After June has gone, Paul does meet with Malla; she convinces him that she is 152 years old, and that the almost-depleted powder she has with her, which she calls nipé, has enabled her to age very slowly over the years since she was captured by a slaver. She tells Paul that there is yet another substance, unknown to her, that when mixed with nipé, will actually make a person young again. The other substance is known only to her tribe, somewhere deep in Africa.

June is at home talking with her lawyer Neil Foster (Grant Williams), who has known her since he was a child. There's no romance between them, but they are good friends. Paul suddenly rushes in to tell June that he's changed his mind about the divorce, and that they are going to Africa together.

June is excited and happy at this news, even though there are clearly ulterior motives to Paul's sudden change of heart. He tells them he's found "the most powerful concentrate of the juvenile hormone known to science." This hormone, he explains, is a substance found in some insects which retards aging; this find is the first that works on human beings. It would be worth untold millions. But first they have to go to Africa on the trail of Malla (who leaves before them) to find the plant that produces the juvenile hormone. He does not tell June or Neil about Malla's other claim—that there is a method of actual rejuvenation.

So off June and Paul go to back-lot, stock-footage and sound-stage Africa. Despite objections from guide Garvay (John Van Dreelen) that June is too old for the trip, Paul insists she come along. June does hold the party back, and they can't catch up with Malla's group—even though, we learn, Paul financed the old woman's trip. Paul rebuffs June's attempts at rekindling their romance, which puzzles her, because he'd said they would "get acquainted" again on the trip.

And then she learns the hideous truth: Paul has brought her along only as an experimental subject, to discover if there really is any truth to Malla's story of a rejuvenation substance. June refuses. "Why not?" Paul asks rhetorically. "You're my wife. I have to make sure I'm getting the right product."

June complains to the mildly sympathetic Garvay who says that, in view of everything, maybe the risk of taking the stuff is worth it from June's own point of view. "I'm beginning to hate all men," June says bitterly.

Eventually, June, Garvay and Paul are captured by Malla's tribe, the Nandos, and taken to their village. After the three newcomers are imprisoned, Malla sardonically shows them an orchid which grows only in that section of Africa; its pollen is nipé. Paul at once offers anything the Nandos could want for the orchid, but she says he should wait until the actual rejuvenation ceremony. (Garvay sourly observes that secrets are shown only to outsiders about to be killed.)

After a rather dull ceremony, Malla makes a speech, worth quoting in full. "For a man, old age has rewards. If he is wise, his gray hairs bring dignity and he is treated with honor and respect. But for the aged woman, there is nothing. At best, she's pitied. More often, her lot is contempt and neglect. What woman lives who having passed the prime of life would not give her remaining years to reclaim even a few hours of youth and beauty, to know again the worship of men? For the end of life should be its moment of triumph. So it is with the aged women of the Nandos—a last flowering of love and beauty before death." (Neither Paul nor June note the clearly-expressed idea that the rejuvenation is momentary, followed soon by death.)

A drugged young man is brought forth, and the witch doctor dons a ring with a long, curved blade on it, and plunges it into the back of the young victim's neck; when he withdraws it, a fluid clings to the blade. Paul realizes that the ring has "lanced the pineal gland deep in the cerebellum."

The fluid is mixed with *nipé*, and Malla drinks the compound. And lo and behold, she becomes younger (Kim Hamilton). She tells Paul that they shall live as long as she, so he says Malla should make his wife young again, too. June objects—it would mean the life of a man. But Paul insists, so June finally agrees—and chooses Paul as the "donor." "An excellent choice," says Malla. "He hates old women. This should make him happy at last."

So the ceremony proceeds, while Garvay does everything in his power to ingratiate himself with June. After Paul's death and June's rejuvenation, there's a celebration, during which Garvay grabs the skull containing the *nipé* and the ring, then sets dynamite in a hut. While Malla suggests June enjoy this night— her youth won't last long—Garvay ignites the dynamite. During the confusion, he and June escape.

June and Garvay become lovers as they flee toward civilization. After two weeks pass, June awakes to discover that she has become older than she was before rejuvenation. The horrified Garvay declares the old woman a monster and murderer, and not June. He tries to flee, but falls into a bog; June dons the ring, declaring, "Because I'm old, you'd have left me to die! From now on, I'll hate all men!" She stabs him in the neck with the ring, and rejuvenates herself. We learn that just as each reversion leaves June older than she was before, each rejuvenation leaves her more sexually enticing and beautiful.

June returns to Los Angeles, passing herself off to Neil and Sally as Rachel Hart, June's niece from New York. She is immediately attracted to Neil and catty with Sally, then learns that the two are engaged. They drive her home, and while Sally waits in the car, June tries to seduce Neil. "I'm quite brazen," she tells him brazenly, "quite without shame. Once I was otherwise, but men didn't like me that way. They wanted me to change to please them. So I did change. And now I've come to like it myself. It's wonderful to be young!"

But just as they embrace, old age again begins to overtake June, and she shoves Neil out the door. She is now an ancient crone. She goes to Neil's office, heavily veiled, as herself and retrieves jewelry she'd left with him before the trip. He's shocked at her increased age, but she passes it off as rigors of the trip, and says Rachel wants to see him again.

Seeking another source of pineal fluid, June goes to a seedy area of town, and after a couple of strikeouts, attracts nasty young Jerry (Arthur Batanides), who spots the jewelry. He drives her to a secluded spot, ascertains that she's all alone in the world, and starts to strangle her—but she plugs him with the ring.

Angry with Neil because of his sudden infatuation with Rachel, when she learns he's to meet Rachel again, Sally goes to June's home first, with a gun. She orders "Rachel" to leave, because she knows June had no niece. After a struggle for the gun, June kills Sally with the dagger ring, muttering about saving the pineal fluid until later.

Neil soon arrives, and after he and June neck a little, he begs her to marry him, but she refuses. At this point, the police arrive looking for June for the murder of Jerry; they found her calling card in his pocket. The cops say there was another murder in which the cerebellum was punctured, a week before. Neil is relieved, he says, because Mrs. Talbot was in New York then. "So," the cop says, "was the murder."

They discover Sally's body, and June tries to flee upstairs — but begins to age again, and Neil realizes Rachel and June are the same person. She's aging rapidly, and flees into a locked room, where she mixes Sally's pineal fluid with the *nipé*, and quickly swallows it. But it has no effect — only male pineal glands will do — and as the police burst in, she falls from a window. Downstairs, they find her body turning to dust.

David Duncan's script has a slightly more original conclusion. She turns to dust without falling out the window, and cries out that she'll be back. "The wind increases with a moaning sound and June's body begins to turn to dust and blow away through the open French door." Neil and the policeman look out the window. "Moving away through the dark shrubbery is a dusty shadow, darker than the rest, suggestive of a hobbling woman."

Other than its perfunctory just-get-it-over-with air, the major problem with *The Leech Woman* is its structure. More than half the film is spent in simply setting up the rejuvenation gimmick; June's life as a leech woman occupies a very small part of the film.

The movie is almost more of a jungle adventure than a science fiction–horror thriller; if it weren't for Coleen Gray's vigorous, involved performance — like she's going for an Oscar — dramatically the film would be a complete bore.

It's just a variation on the vampire theme, but Duncan has taken some care to give June justification for her actions, and all the victims we see certainly deserve their fates, in a melodramatic sense. Even Sally is a two-timing greedy bitch. We're supposed to feel some sympathy for June, judging from the screenplay and Coleen Gray's performance, but not from the lackluster direction by Edward Dein. He merely gets everything over and done with in the least involving manner.

Dein had been a screenwriter at Universal since the early 1940s, when he wrote or cowrote minor films including *Calling Dr. Death* (1943), *Jungle Woman* (1944) and *The Cat Creeps* (1946). For other studios, he wrote *Soul of a Monster* (1944) and *The Gallant Blade* (1948). He did additional dialogue on Val Lewton's *Leopard Man* (1943). He directed and cowrote *Curse of the Undead*. The *American Film Institute Catalog* makes a bizarre error in claiming that Edward Dein and Italian Ubaldo Ragona are the same person; Ragona was an Italian director, who helmed *Sweet Smell of Love* (1966), and the Italian scenes of *The Last Man on Earth* (1964). It's impossible to tell from the AFI catalog whether Ragona or Dein directed *The Psychic Lover* (1969).

The Leech Woman was produced by Joseph Gershenson, long a fixture at the Universal lot. In the 1940s, he was executive producer of a handful of films, including *The Climax* (1944), *House of Frankenstein*, *House of Dracula* (both 1945) and *The Time of Their Lives* (1946), but from 1950 to 1968 was "music supervisor" on virtually every film the studio produced. In the late 50s, he returned again to producing, apparently taking up the slack left by the departure of William Alland. Most of his films as producer were low-budget exploitation movies.

The Leech Woman was shot on existing sets at Universal, using a combination of players who'd been around a while, like Coleen Gray and Gloria Talbott, and hapless contract players like Grant Williams, who had no choice about appearing in certain films. It's little wonder his performance seems uninvolved. (He died in 1985.)

But Coleen Gray's performance is surprising. She'd rarely had a starring role before, and her few leads were mostly of the colorless hand-wringing "Oh-Jed-don't-go" type, or cheap molls, or the heroine's girlfriend. She'd been in films since 1947, and in addition to starring in minor As and some Bs, such as *The Sleeping City* (1950), *The Fake* (1953), *Twinkle in God's Eye* (1955) and *The Black Whip* (1956), she also appeared in *Kiss of Death* (1947), *Red River* (1948) and *The Killing* (1956). Her other genre films include *The Vampire* and *Phantom Planet*; she's uninteresting in both. She made only a few more movies after *The Leech Woman*.

Perhaps the strange, quasi-sympathetic role of June Talbot liberated or energized her; it's one of the few really memorable performances of her career, and the greatest strength of the film.

Like the film, reviews were perfunctory. "Tube" (who had an apparent antipathy to horror and science fiction) called *The Leech Woman* quite correctly a "lower-berth item" with "a tendency to meander into lengthy, irrelevant passages.... Edward Dein's direction," said "Tube" in *Variety*, "adds no novel flair or approach to horror, but is mechanically sound."

The *Monthly Film Bulletin* gave the film its lowest rating, calling it "a dull horror picture.... The acting and overall presentation are proficient, but Edward Dein's direction is mechanical, revealing neither novelty nor any flair for the macabre." There's an echo in here.

Vivian C. Sobchack, author of the recommended *The Limits of Infinity*, found defensible virtues to the film in an article called "The Leech Woman's Revenge, or A Case for Equal Misrepresentation" (*Journal of Popular Film*, vol. 4, no. 3, 1975). That issue of the magazine dealt with "Women in Film," a topic title that Sobchack quite reasonably found vague.

Near the end of her piece, she restates her guiding principle: "The major problem with feminist film criticism has been that it is so deeply concerned with the relationship and responsibility of films to women outside the theater, it, unfortunately, has been frequently negligent and unconcerned about the relationship and responsibility of feminist criticism to the films inside the theater—and to their existence as aesthetic, *whole* works and *ambiguous* visions.... Feminist criticism as a historical and descriptive approach to cinema is of the greatest value to film scholarship. But feminist film criticism as an act of sexual politics can be accused of the same distortion, stereotype and misrepresentation it finds in the Hollywood film."

As part of her corrective to the narrowness of this approach (which can be equally applied to almost any school of film criticism), she discusses *The Leech Woman*.

Although the main character, says Sobchack, can be seen "negatively as a predator, as violent, as stupidly desirous of all the wrong things, as weak or as vampirish," she claims the film can also "be seen as a feminist indictment of the premium men put on female youth and beauty, of men's greed, fickleness, stupidity, and callousness.... The only unjustifiable murder June commits is Sally's [of course, Sally *was* trying to kill June...] ... which is seen unsympathetically by the camera.... It is, finally, poetic justice that Sally's hormones don't work. If the film sends any messages, one of them is 'Don't kill your sister. There's nothing to gain by doing in your own kind.'"

After quoting Malla's speech just before her rejuvenation, Sobchack says, "The complexity of cinema is such that *The Leech Woman* or any other movie can be read in numerous ways and evidence can be found to support such readings at various levels of the text. But no film should be read from an isolated element (the plot, the dialogue, the lighting, the editing, etc.); rather it should be read as the sum of these elements in a constant interaction which may be complementary or contradictory or both. *The Leech Woman* is neither 'just another movie' nor 'a feminist parable.' It lies satisfyingly somewhere between the two as a multi-leveled movie, the sum of the "superimposition of texts.'"

While I respect this point of view, and this reading of the film is justified by the movie, *The Leech Woman is* just another movie. It has a more interesting justification for the activities of its "monster" than most such films, there's an attempt to make June the victim of masculine callousness, and David Duncan seems to be trying to make a point. But Sobchack is more or less doing here what she warns against: she is reading the film "from an isolated element," the plot. Nonetheless, I think this approach to movies is highly useful and needed.

I realize that my goals and Sobchack's are different: the overall quality of the movie as a movie is not what she's talking about, but her enthusiasm for the plot could mislead some into thinking that it is a *good* and not merely an *interesting* movie.

Except for Coleen Gray's performance, there's little to recommend. The aging makeups on Gray are the standard latex wrinkles so often used at that time to simulate aging; they're elaborate but not convincing. *The Leech Woman* is worth watching for its odd plot and for Gray, but it cannot be recommended.

The Lost World

Though gaudy, this travesty insults its marvelous source, Conan Doyle's original novel, filmed in 1924 by First National pictures in a production far more entertaining than this garish remake. The silent film has a verve and spirit totally lacking in Irwin Allen's lugubrious vulgarization; Wallace Beery made a lively, colorful and funny Professor Challenger, while in the remake, Claude Rains provided one of his very few poor performances as Challenger.

The initial publicity for Irwin Allen's *Lost World* was varied. Stout claims were made that all the animals in the film were real (true) and that they looked exactly like the dinosaurs they were impersonating (emphatically false). The poodle in the film, one of the more repulsive ideas added by Allen, was supposedly provided by the daughter of Edgar Rice Burroughs, widely announced as an effort to gain quality by association. Willis O'Brien, who had done the primitive but exciting stop-motion animation in the silent version, was hired by Fox as "technical advisor" for the new version, but his advice—to use stop-motion models—was not followed (perhaps for budgetary reasons). The pinnacle of hype: a 45 rpm record of Fernando Lamas singing a song from the film was issued.

All this publicity must have had favorable results; despite general critical disfavor, and despite the usually negative reactions of the audience, *The Lost World* was successful enough that Irwin Allen was given the go-ahead for another relatively expensive science fiction adventure, *Voyage to the Bottom of the Sea*, also covered in this volume. Further notes on Mr. Allen's depressingly successful career may be found in that entry.

Irascible Professor Challenger (Rains) returns to London after an expedition into the inner reaches of the Amazon Basin in South America, to announce to a skeptical world that he has found a plateau full of dinosaurs and other prehistoric life. No one pays much attention until he also adds that the place is full of diamonds. At once, several people are anxious to accompany him, including aging Lord Roxton (Michael Rennie), a playboy and big-game hunter fond of Jennifer Holmes (Jill St. John), daughter of the publishing magnate willing to finance Challenger's expedition. Reporter Ed Malone (David Hedison), Jennifer's brother David (Ray Stricklyn), doubting scientist Professor Summerlee (Richard Haydn) and Jennifer herself also join the expedition.

When they arrive at a trading post up the Amazon River, they are joined by guitar-strumming helicopter pilot Gomez (Fernando Lamas), and scuzzy native guide Costa (Jay Novello). Gomez hates Roxton, blaming him for the earlier death of the pilot's brother.

The helicopter carrying the expedition lands atop the plateau, where a "brontosaurus" promptly smashes it flat. Throughout the adventures that follow, Roxton battles occasionally with Gomez, while Jennifer's heart is gradually won by dashing Ed Malone.

They find a diary of Burton White, an earlier explorer who sought The Lost World. The group battles man-eating plants and big green spiders that do no worse than dangle in front of them, before they are captured by a band of cannibalistic natives. A Native Girl (Vitina Marcus, never identified by any other role name) helps them escape as she has fallen in love with David.

She leads them into a series of dangerous caves—the only way off the plateau—where they find a big lizard unaccountably living in bubbling lava, as well as diamonds and elderly Burton White (Ian Wolfe) himself. Gomez dies helping them escape, but makes his peace with Roxton before doing so. The survivors reach safety, taking with them a baby "Tyrannosaurus rex."

The characters are drawn in the crudest terms, and played that way as well; it is hardly a landmark in the career of anyone involved. Rather than exuberant, Claude Rains is boringly hammy as Challenger, overacting for one of the few times in his career; perhaps he thought his pink wig and beard needed to be overcome, but more likely he was encouraged by director Irwin Allen to "have fun" with the material. Instead, he insults it.

By contrast, Michael Rennie underplays his part, resulting in his seeming stiff, generally expressionless. It doesn't much matter what Jill St. John does; she's there to fill out a pair of coral-colored slacks, and to scream at appropriate moments. Likewise, David Hedison (who found himself battling stock footage monsters from *The Lost World* several times in the TV series "Voyage to the Bottom of the Sea"); he's the male equivalent of St. John, around to look pretty and to be someone for Jennifer to fall for. Fernando Lamas leans heavily on C*H*A*R*M; he's tiresome almost as soon as he appears.

But, as I'm sure Irwin Allen believed, why even talk about the cast? They don't matter in a Special Effects Extravaganza; Allen's thinking is that you just load up your film with known performers who appeal to a broad spectrum of tastes, have them play clichéd characters just to keep the plot going, and give the audience what it "really" came for, lots of color and excitement in the form of plenty of special effects. Certainly this formula served Allen well in his later series of big-budget Disaster films.

Unfortunately, the special effects here are obvious, inept and wildly inaccurate. The set design by Duncan Cramer and Walter M. Simonds is ugly and garish; things are painted in bright, even fluorescent colors, highly unnatural.

But the big calling card of the film was the dinosaurs, advertised as being the most lifelike ever filmed. (Ads in some newspapers showed crudely-rendered but technically accurate dinosaurs, truly false advertising.) Leading amateur paleontologist and monster movie buff Don Glut summed it up well in his entertaining *Dinosaur Scrapbook*. "Perhaps if the reptiles had gone unidentified ... the picture might not have been so ludicrous. But no one, not even the youngest dinosaur buff in the audience, could rightfully accept it when Professor Challenger ... declares that a monitor lizard with a rubbery ceratopsian frill attached to its neck was really a *Brontosaurus*. The horned and fin-backed lizard that rises from a steaming pool of lava might have been more believable had Challenger not officially identified it as *Tyrannosaurus rex*. Other animals in the picture, including an iguana with a horn over each eye and another fin-backed alligator, this one also sporting horns on its head and spikes along its back, resembled nothing found in paleontology and went unnamed, though I wonder what Challenger might have dubbed them had he the opportunity."

The Lost World was released at a time when there was a minor boom in dinosaurial stuff for kids. Model kits, plastic dolls and books were plentiful; as a result, even ordinary children knew a brontosaurus when they saw one, and the sight of a live, ordinary lizard identified as a brontosaurus brought gales of laughter from even the youngest audiences.

Still, the picture might have survived poor, stereotyped characters, hackneyed plot elements and stupidly inaccurate dinosaurs if it weren't also so boring and badly written. This big-budget film was far inferior to much less expensive movies, such as *Gorgo* and *The Giant Behemoth*. Even the roughly comparable *Lost Continent* didn't make such demands on the patience of the audience.

Allen tried to ride over the deficiencies of his film by adopting a smirking attitude, but that only succeeded in making his contempt for his material more obvious. Those who tended to share this contempt for science fiction and monster films were entertained by *The Lost World*; they couldn't take *anything* like this remotely seriously, so a Hollywood–type bad film with what seemed to be a sophisticated (i.e. mocking) attitude was preferable to a good low-budget film with an imaginative premise, but a respectful, serious treatment of the material.

There's precedent for treating the story lightly; Harry Hoyt's silent film had much humor. Even Conan Doyle's original novel had its own jokes; for example, it was initially published as if it were a true story, with drawings by "expedition members" and a photograph of the expedition as the frontispiece. (In this photo, the glowering, bearded Challenger is Conan Doyle himself.)

But Sir Arthur and Harry played fair with their audiences; the humor grew out of the characters and wasn't imposed on the situations. The characters were exaggerated but not lampoons; in Allen's *Lost World*, Richard Haydn (for example) is encouraged to act even prissier than usual, a painful thing to see.

Instead of an intrepid rescue expedition, the group in Allen's *Lost World* are mostly greedy treasure hunters. Perhaps Allen felt that audiences in 1960

wouldn't accept humanistic impulses as motives for an expedition; it had to be money. Then to add Human Interest (or something), he felt it necessary to load the plot down with (a) *two* women, (b) *two* romances and (c) hatred between two members of the group. The adventure of finding a prehistoric plateau isn't enough; Allen had to add all this stupid melodramatic baggage.

Almost everything wrong with *The Lost World* can be ascribed to Irwin Allen; he produced, directed and cowrote the film. But he initially had more promising plans for it, at least in terms of the special effects. In June, 1959, he visited New York as part of his promotion tour for his previous film, *The Big Circus*, and told an interviewer for the *New York Times* that he'd purchased the rights to the Conan Doyle novel for $100,000 and was planning the film as "a $3,000,000 production in either the Todd-AO or Technirama wide screen process." He intended to film it on location in England and Brazil, as well as in Hollywood. At that point, the film was expected to be an Allied Artists release like *The Big Circus*, but apparently the success of *Journey to the Center of the Earth* brought the project and Allen to 20th Century–Fox. *Journey* was released in December, 1959, so if Allen and *The Lost World* came to Fox *after* that, the production was extremely rushed. It was still shooting as late as April; an article in the Los Angeles *Examiner* in that month was about a visit to the set.

The stars originally announced were intended to be Gilbert Roland (whom Allen claimed was also in the silent version), Victor Mature and either Trevor Howard or Peter Ustinov. The article in the *New York Times* said, "Willis O'Brien has been engaged to create mechanical counterparts of some of the prehistoric giant monsters such as dinosaurs, pterodactyls and brontosauruses."

Stop-motion scenes of the extent that the script probably required would have taken at the very least six months to complete satisfactorily, so perhaps all these years, Irwin Allen has been unjustly blamed for their absence from the film. Maybe he, too, was disappointed in not being able to use OBie's talents again (he'd hired O'Brien for *Animal World* some years before).

However, even if O'Brien had been hired, and been allowed to do the effects exactly as he wanted, they would have been superlative effects in a movie with bad script and direction.

Charles Bennett is credited as cowriter of the film, and probably wrote to Allen's specifications. He was associated with SF as early as 1934, when he cowrote *Secret of the Loch*, but most of his best films were for Alfred Hitchcock. See the entry for *Voyage to the Bottom of the Sea* for more on Bennett.

The trade reviews of *The Lost World* are interesting in how they dance around the idea that it is actually a very bad movie. It was Fox's major summer release, and neither *Variety* nor the *Hollywood Reporter* could afford to alienate Fox. You can usually tell when a trade critic dislikes a film but can't afford to admit that: he will sing the praises of the production values and/or say "audiences will like it."

Here, for instance, is *Variety*'s "Tube": "Although basically as plodding and cumbersome as its dinosaurs, [*The Lost World*] contains enough exploitable spectacle and innocent fun to generate a respectable boxoffice response.... The picture's chief attraction is its production gusto. Emphasis on physical and

Opposite: This production drawing by an unidentified 20th Century–Fox storyboard artist clearly shows that the use of real lizards instead of stop-motion models was a decision made relatively early in production, rather than a last-minute decision as apologists for Irwin Allen have suggested (The Lost World, 1960).

pictorial values make up, to some extent, for its lack of finesse in the literary and thespic departments.... A choppy, topheavy, deliberately paced screenplay ... labors too long with exposition and leaves several loose ends dangling [and is] loaded with romantic platitudes and ludicrous situations.... Allen's direction is not only sluggish but has somehow gotten more personality into his dinosaurs than into his people.... With the exception of one or two mighty ineffectual spiders and a general absence of genuine shocks or tension, the production is something to behold." Some translations: "innocent" means "brainless"; "gusto" means "vulgarity"; "finesse" means "quality"; and so forth.

Paul V. Beckley, writing in the New York *Herald-Tribune* seems to have actually enjoyed the film. "Pleasingly chipper.... Has much in common with the recent *Journey to the Center of the Earth* in that it refuses to take itself too seriously and maintains a consistent tone of easy good nature.... Today's children are peculiarly sophisticated in matters of paleontology as well as rocketry and will no doubt see through the make-believe of live lizards with spinal plates or horns pasted on.... But such young sophisticates will appreciate the mobility and flexibility of these living creatures, which is a great improvement on the mechanial fumblings of old-style movie reptiles." Actually, Mr. Beckley's "young sophisticates" gave the phony dinosaurs the horselaugh. Live lizards with horns pasted on are simply *fakes*, and not what anyone wants to see when they come to a movie about dinosaurs. No matter how lifelike, they are more annoying in a way than metal-jointed, rubber-covered models moved a frame at a time. At least the latter have a kind of dynamism and reality of form totally lacking in sleepy lizards being prodded around miniature sets.

The most scathing (and to my mind, accurate) review was in the *Monthly Film Bulletin*, which gave *The Lost World* its lowest rating. "This infuriating travesty of Conan Doyle's story, of the marvelous silent version ... and of many of the pleasures of *Journey to the Centre of the Earth*, which it is only too obviously trying to emulate, resembles nothing so much as a ride on a rundown fairground Ghost Train [spooky ride].... The film [is] as joyless, plodding and out-of-date as its dinosaurs.... The unintentional humour is substandard, the characters quite without personality, and it is left to the heroine's poodle, surprised by a diplodocus, to make a stand and yap with apposite scorn."

In *Future Tense*, John Brosnan adequately described both Allen and *The Lost World*: "Allen's approach is appallingly juvenile: he ignores logic, scientific facts, characterization and story construction.... His attitude toward the genre was obvious from the start in this lifeless, mechanical and clumsy version of Conan Doyle's story."

Alan Frank (*SF*) was also on target: "Childish vulgarization of Conan Doyle's novel, with vulgar art direction, uninteresting monsters and indifferent special effects. The modernization of the story merely serves to underline the general tattiness of the production and the actors enter into the spirit of things with over-the-top performances. It is a tragedy to see Willis O'Brien, working on his last genre movie, associated with the picture."

This was only the first of several Irwin Allen SF movies and even more TV shows; it is, sadly, typical of the man's attitude toward SF. I don't think any filmmaker has ever really accomplished good things by making films they wouldn't go see. Irwin Allen made a film for which his contempt is obvious; it's almost impossible not to return that contempt. *The Lost World* is a lumbering, synthetic bore, big-budget Hollywood SF filmmaking at its dreary worst.

Nude on the Moon

This film seems to have the distinction of being the first feature-length SF-oriented nudie; for more on that subgenre of films see the entries on *Magic Spectacles* and *Paradisio*. Until Hollywood poster dealer Ron Borst loaned me a pressbook from this film, all I knew about it was that it probably existed. Both Walt Lee, in his *Reference Guide to Fantastic Films*, and Don Willis (I) cite the same source, the extinct French genre magazine, *Midi-Minuit Fantastique* (#8, p. 31). There the title was given variously as "Nature Girls on the Moon," "Nudes on the Moon" and "Girls on the Moon." The pressbook calls the film *Nude on the Moon*, although as was common for nudies, an alternate title, complete with ads, was offered for theatres in towns where merely the word "nude" was frowned on by those determined to keep others from knowing people sometimes took their clothes off. The alternate title was *Moon Dolls*.

As given in the pressbook, the plotline is one of those unfortunate "do-they-or-don't-they" stories, the kind of film that only some filmmakers seem to think are of interest. Certainly people who go to movies don't seem to like them; such movies are usually regarded sourly by all. But there are several movies in film history that at first seem to involve a fantastic element, which later proves to be all a plot or a big mistake. Inasmuch as these films are designed to appeal to those who like fantasy, this aha-we-fooled-you type of ending is the equivalent of pulling the rug out from under that audience. I recall my anger at the ending of *Curucu, Beast of the Amazon* (1956): it wasn't much of a film in the first place, but when the parrotlike monster was revealed as just an Indian in quilted long johns, I felt cheated. I assume the only reason anyone produces a film in which the monster/ghost/alien/whatever turns out to be a human villain or prankster is for the simple novelty of the "surprise ending." But such endings are never surprises, only disappointments, and almost always are used on films that aren't good in the first place. (*Mark of the Vampire* is a notable exception.)

At least *Nude on the Moon* seems to have novelty on its side, even with the maybe-we-imagined-it ending. At least, I don't recall any other movie in which lunar explorers discover a nudist camp on the Moon, though *Cat-Women of the Moon* isn't far off.

Quoting the pressbook, here's the plot of *Nude on the Moon*: "Jeff Huntley, a scientist, inherits three million dollars. He uses this money to build a space ship with which to go to the Moon, and persuades his associate, Prof. Bill Nichols, to go along.

"After seven months of intensive research and study, Jeff and the Professor begin their journey. They reach their destination and believe the planet on which they have landed is the Moon.

"Jeff and the Professor, excited and bewildered, take pictures and make notes. Suddenly, they are confronted by a huge stone wall.

"They are amazed to see, behind the wall, a panoramic view of a nudist camp.

"Jeff and the Professor are discovered and taken prisoner, but released when the Queen is convinced that these Earthmen are their friends.

"Jeff is attracted to the Queen and tries to speak to her. She seems to understand what he is saying but does not answer him.

"Jeff and the Professor continue to take pictures and make notes.

"After several hours the Professor seeks out Jeff who is again trying to speak to the Queen. He tells Jeff that their oxygen is running out and they must return to Earth. Jeff will not leave, he is in love. The Queen touches him with her wand and Jeff becomes unconscious. The Professor thanks her and takes Jeff back to the ship.

"In the ship, Jeff is angry with the Professor. Suddenly they both realize they do not have their camera or notes. This means they have no proof they were on the Moon.

"Jeff is in his laboratory when the Professor calls and is advised that the government have looked over the space ship and do not believe it ever got off the ground.

"Jeff is miserable as he hangs up the phone. Cathy, his secretary, walks in. Jeff cannot believe his eyes for Cathy looks exactly like the Queen. He smiles and says, 'I did not lose you after all.'"

Inasmuch as the sole reason for the existence of *Nude on the Moon* is to show unclad women, it would seem meaningless to point out flaws in this fascinating plot. Such as Jeff and the Professor never wondering what it is that these completely (even emphatically) human women are breathing. Or Jeff not realizing that the Queen looks like his secretary back home, rather than the other way around. Or just what Jeff and the Professor actually do, if they don't go to the Moon.

The stills in the pressbook show men *and* women in the lunar nudist camp —although, presumably for the still camera, they are all wearing trunks. For those like me who like to keep track of such things, *Nude on the Moon* was shot at Coral Castle, Florida, where many scenes for *Wild Women of Wongo* were also filmed. Both prominently feature a big coral throne.

The costumes for Jeff and the Professor are simply a breastplate over black tights, with dime-store space helmets. They look considerably sillier than naked people draped over coral.

The advertising text for the film ranged from the blatant—"Man Discovers a NUDIST CAMP on the MOON!"—to the inappropriately poetic—"And The Heavens Brought Forth The Wonder Of Woman!" (I think the distributors realized that mentioning there were also nude men on the Moon would be unwise.)

The people who made *Nude on the Moon* continued to work in this field. Coproducer Doris Wishman also worked on *Nature Camp Confidential* (1961), *Blaze Starr Goes Nudist* (1962), *Gentlemen Prefer Nature Girls* (1963), *Behind the Nudist Curtain* (1964), *The Prince and the Nature Girl* and *The Sex Perils of Paulette* (both 1965), among others. Cinematographer Phelan shot others, and William Mayer appeared in other nudies.

Not surprisingly, I have been unable to find any reviews of *Nude on the Moon*. These nudies were usually ignored by everyone, not so much in hopes that they would go away, but because reviewing would simply call attention to them, and they would have to be dealt with somehow. So reviewers and Hollywood turned their backs on these movies. As a result, for film historians they are extremely hard to research. In the massive *American Film Institute Catalog* for the 1960s, many of the early 1960s nudies and sex films have very short entries, because even those indefatigable researchers were unable to turn up any information on them apart from their mere existence. Many probably slipped through the net, because there is no documentation on them at all.

These extremely low-budget films were aimed primarily at the lowest common denominator in audiences, the men who wanted to see naked women and cared little about anything else. Many of these films were simply shot at nudist camps with an improvised plot, and wouldn't even be called soft-core pornography today. Nothing very sexy happened, unless you consider nude volleyball games or scenes of naked women doing housework to be stimulating. Toward the end of the 60s, as true pornography began being released in theatres devoted to it, the producers of the nudies moved into another market for cheap films: Saturday matinee movies for kids, and very low-quality films based on classic fairy tales were made by the same people who earlier had been concentrating on bare, jiggling breasts.

Rocket Attack U.S.A.

Barry Mahon's plea for eternal vigilance and preparedness is also an earnest cry against space satellites. It is also a boring and jingoistic potboiler coming from a subterranean world of moviemaking that rarely deals with science fiction material. These films lie in the darkness beneath even the trashiest of SF and horror films, beneath even what most moviegoers think of as exploitation films—the women-in-bondage and kung fu cheapies.

Barry Mahon was one of the busiest makers of these true exploitation films during the 1960s and early 70s. His budgets were among the lowest ever for theatrical films, and the results reflected this, as well as the haste and lack of care that went into the films' making. But he *was* busy, and this partial list of his films from the 1960s AFI catalog will give an indication of the audiences he was seeking. (Note: Mahon was producer and director on most of these, and also photographed some.) *Pagan Island, The Dead One* (both 1961), *1,000 Shapes of a Female* (1963), *The Adventures of Busty Brown* (1964), *The Beast That Killed Women* (1965, a nudie), *Nudes on Tiger Reef* (1965), *P.P.S. (Prostitutes' Protective Society)* (1966), *Fanny Hill Meets Dr. Erotico, Fanny Hill Meets Lady Chatterly* (both 1967), *Fanny Hill Meets the Red Baron* (1968), and in a change in direction but not budget, *The Wonderful Land of Oz* (1969), *Thumbelina* (1970) and a music documentary, *Weekend Rebellion* (1970). This is only a portion of Mahon's output for the period.

These were generally the sexy sort of films found in this rather sleazy area of moviemaking; as the three Fanny Hill titles indicate, Mahon occasionally jumped onto what seemed like a trendy topic. Albert Zugsmith had made a version of the famous erotic novel, *Fanny Hill,* but the name itself was in public domain. Mahon, nothing loath, grabbed the name and ran with it, even dragging in the Red Baron, fixed in the popular mind by Charles Shulz's "Peanuts." Joe Dante adds that one of Mahon's cheekier ploys was the production of a compilation film purportedly composed of "sizzling outtakes," but made up entirely of new footage especially shot to conform to then-current standards of explicitness, thus ensuring maximum playdates and no censorship problems. (For more on this kind of filmmaking, see the entries on *Magic Spectacles, Nude on the Moon* and *Paradisio.*)

Mahon also made *Rocket Attack U.S.A.,* a grab at topicality. Although the film shows a certain burst of creativity at the very end, most of it is simply dreadful, so dull and plodding that it will never be among those bad films that have developed into well-liked objects of fun. The photography is grainy, the plot is preposterous, the acting is nonexistent, there's no structure and nothing much to look at, just people in rooms talking, and a lot of stock footage. However, it is one of the few films that ends with the onset of what will probably be World War III. The ultimate message seems to be that nuclear war is inevitable, survivable, winnable and desirable.

Note: as usual with Mahon, there is no credited screenwriter for *Rocket Attack U.S.A.*; Michael Hayes suggests that Mahon outlined the film, and his casts improvised the dialogue.

The heavily-narrated film begins by telling us the Soviet Union changed the concept of modern warfare by putting up a satellite, and adds that the story to follow would be "inevitable" if the wrong people gained control of the Soviet government. That slight hint that the wrong people are *not* in control is among the very few expressions of that idea in popular entertainment from the 1940s through the 1960s, although I suspect that Mahon was gingerly hedging his bets.

The Central Intelligence Group wonders what, if anything, the Soviet satellite is doing. They deduce that it's up there "to find out if (1) the density in air in outer space, (2) effect of radioactivity, and (3) do other planets exert enough gravitational pull to affect missiles." This is a direct quote.

American spy Johnny Marston (John McKay) is sent to the Soviet Union to make contact with an agent already there, and to get information on satellites. He enters the country in a disarmingly simple manner: he simply flies a small plane and lands in a pasture. He then walks to Moscow "inconspicuously" dressed in a trench coat. He does not speak Russian.

After seeing a dance in a nightclub that seems to go on forever, Johnny meets his contact, Tanya (Monica Davis), who seems about as Russian as Doris Day, but even good movies make that kind of mistake. Tanya was once married to an American airman (to explain her English) and now, conveniently, is the mistress of the minister of defense, one Josef. He'll be easy to get information from; "when the pig gets drunk," says Tanya, "he talks."

She tells Johnny that the satellite is gathering information on how best to launch missiles at the United States, a true fear-mongering concept. Josef is coming over that very night, and she suggests Johnny should leave her apartment, as he wouldn't like what he hears. "If you can stand it," he says gallantly (and voyeuristically), "I can."

The film veers abruptly into a minidocumentary on rocket construction, including comments on automation. This is all stock footage.

Johnny hides in Tanya's closet when Josef arrives, and uneasily listens to yelps and whoops from the room. After Josef departs, Tanya tells Johnny that the military wants to strike at the United States as soon as the Soviet missile is ready.

Josef comes over again and Johnny hides in the closet again. By this time of course, Johnny and Tanya have fallen in love.

Back in the U.S., a general has a long talk on the telephone with his wife, and we are shown stock footage of a satellite, and a rocket exploding.

Back in the U.S.S.R., Marston meets Steele from British Intelligence, and they go to Leningrad, played by a broken brick wall. This scene exists to add running time.

Tanya and Johnny Marston go to the missile site to demolish the rocket, as it is to be launched at New York that very night. However, after wandering through the woods for some time, Tanya is fatally shot. "Johnny," she says before expiring, "go on. Don't worry about me." He does, and she shoots a soldier before dying herself.

Johnny arrives at the missile base, and we can see the base of the killer rocket (the prop was constructed for this film, surprising when you think about it). After a great deal of Russianesque dialogue, Johnny's bomb is removed from the missile, and it is launched. Johnny is killed.

Suddenly the film becomes slightly imaginative. We see several married couples in the New York area, parting in the morning, the husbands going off to work in the city. (Comedian Art Metrano plays a truck driver in this sequence.) There are some quick cuts of scenes in New York, showing people who do not expect the attack, and then the bomb goes off, apparently destroying Manhattan. "We cannot let this be – The End," concludes the film.

The film exhibits simpleminded thinking throughout, from the silly scenes of Johnny's arrival in the Soviet Union by private plane, to the total lack of any hint as to why the Soviets would launch a single-missile attack. The idea seems to be that they are berserk madmen who are likely to do something of that nature at any moment. There is also the usual fatheaded, jingoistic idea that U.S. missiles are good and will kill only bad, militaristic wrong-thinkers, while U.S.S.R. missiles are evil and will kill happy married couples.

I assume the few special effect scenes were made for other movies, perhaps for military use or those dreadfully dull classroom films students in the 50s had to sit through. There is a poor effects shot of a sputnik at the beginning, and mediocre animation of the Soviet rocket heading for New York at the end. (The rocket does not match the prop we saw Johnny failing to sabotage.)

Of the two leads, Monica Davis appeared in Mahon's *1,000 Shapes of a Female*, and also in *The Pill* (1967) and *The Road Hustlers* (1968). Both she and John McKay, Johnny, were in Mahon's *The Dead One*. In *Rocket Attack U.S.A.*, neither seem to be actors at all, but at least Davis is reasonably sexy, which I presume is what was wanted.

Mahon's direction seems to have consisted of simply turning the camera on and off; the film is made of long, one-angle (and seemingly one-take) scenes; it's also lethargically edited, so that with these interminable scenes, the picture is excruciatingly slow.

During a period in which the *Motion Picture Herald* seemed reluctant to give any film a negative review, even *Rocket Attack U.S.A.* was described by Allen M. Widem as having been "filmed modestly," and was rated as "fair." *Boxoffice*, also eager to kowtow to studios in this period, seemed almost ecstatic: "The 66 minutes running time is the only thing running against its complete success, in that the just over an hour's span doesn't permit a full dimensioned story treatment, although, conceivably [sic] the audience for which the vehicle is obviously destined won't quibble." The unnamed reviewer even liked the stars. "The two, certainly, emerge as an engaging starring couple."

Joe Dante gave a more reasonable response to the film in *Castle of Frankenstein* #24. "Sexploitation king Barry Mahon ... turns his heavy hand to Big Themes with defeatist spy-fi mini-budget melodramatics.... Lacks the verve of your cousin's bar mitzvah movies and isn't as well acted." *Psychotronic*, always willing to have fun with cheapies, called it "an amazing low-budget feature with tacky sets, great stock footage and a romantic subplot."

Rocket Attack U.S.A. is possibly the cheapest film in this book, and looks it. The slow pace, vapid content and wretched production values make it almost unwatchable today.

Sex Kittens Go to College

Reputedly, this film stinks, and I see no reason to doubt that, inasmuch as it was both produced *and* directed by the one and only Albert Zugsmith, the man who gives sleaze a bad name. The science fiction element is minor, but it's present enough so that the film is called *Beauty and the Robot* on television.

The plot, in brief: a robot called Thinko, located at Collins College, chooses Dr. Mathilda West (Mamie Van Doren) to head the science department. Dr. West is a blonde woman with enormous breasts. She makes the football star, Woo Woo Grabowski (Woo Woo Grabowski), faint whenever she is near, which upsets his girlfriend Jody (Tuesday Weld, who must really regret this).

Thinko the robot also bets on the horses, which causes gangsters Boomie (Mickey Shaughnessy) and Legs (Allan Drake) to descend on the campus looking for one Sam Thinko, whose accurate predictions are causing the Big Boss to become very upset.

George Barton (Martin Milner) is attracted to Dr. West. Other professors, including two played by John Carradine and Irwin Berke, are interested in her, too. Legs is interested in French foreign exchange student Suzanne (Mijanou Bardot), researching how American men make love. Texas oil millionaire Wildcat MacPherson (Jackie Coogan), Thinko's builder Dr. Zorch (Louis Nye), envious Dr. Myrtle Carter (Pamela Mason) and Conway Twitty (Conway Twitty) are also involved. Vampira plays Etta Toodie.

Legs and Boomie recognize Dr. West as stripper Tassels Monclair, which outrages the campus, and she is forced to resign. (It's not clear from material available for research whether she really did have the 13 PhDs she claimed.) She marries Barton. Wildcat marries Dr. Carter. Jody and Woo Woo end up with each other. Thinko gives up gambling. Boomie and Legs leave town.

I doubt that this is riotously funny.

Zugsmith has not always (or ever) been a producer of great taste and insight—just recall that he is the man who made *The Private Lives of Adam and Eve* (1960), *The Incredible Sex Revolution* (1965) and *Movie Star American Style or LSD I Hate You* (1966). (See comments on Zugsmith in the sections on *Invasion U.S.A.* and *The Incredible Shrinking Man* in Volume 1.)

In the *Motion Picture Herald* which, after all, was intended for theatre owners, Allen M. Widem described the film as being "very good." He said, "An all-fun picture is, in the parlance of the customer, difficult to come by. So it is that release of this Albert Zugsmith ... attraction with no less than an even dozen marquee-commanding names should be greeted with more than passing enthusiasm by exhibitor and customer alike. Robert Hill's screenplay practically screams with joy, leaps with brisk, good humor, providing, straight down the runway, as much clean-cut comical action as has been seen in many a moon.... The story line is such that the broad humorous strokes aren't obliterated in a storm of supplementary plotting developments." (Which, in Widemese, means the film has no plot.) Widem adds, "Zugsmith's direction is studied, subtle and sometimes satirically sharp."

James Powers in the *Hollywood Reporter* found it a "harmless little farce [which] will do reasonably well on double-billing for mass bookings on a hit-and-run basis." (Which sounds like assault.) "As might be expected, it is a vulgar and often double-meaning film, but not offensively so.... There isn't really any plot, just [a] series of blackout gags and situations."

Newspapers, not constrained by fears of upsetting distributor Allied Artists, were more severe. In the *Los Angeles Times*, Charles Stinson said, "Mr. Chips, if he could see *Sex Kittens Go to College*, would be very grateful to have said good-by to the world of education when he did."

And in the *New York Herald-Tribune*, Paul V. Beckley said, "Puerile and precious, *Sex Kittens Go to College* has the distinction of making Mamie Van Doren, Tuesday Weld and Mijanou Bardot (Brigitte's sister) seem dull. Such a mawkish script and directionless direction make even Mickey Shaughnessy, Jackie Coogan and John Carradine seem like amateurs.... It is a very sorry venture into slapstick that never manages to get within halooing distance of merit." Even *Psychotronic* called it an "all-star mess."

Don Willis (I) helpfully informs us that *Sex Kittens Go to College* is "not half as funny as *Invasion of the Star Creatures*" which, he adds under that title, is "more than twice as funny as" *Sex Kittens Go to College*. That clever ol' Don.

I suspect the title was a lot more daring than the film, because it now plays on television in what seems to be exactly the form in which it was first released to theatres, with only the title being different.

Teenage Zombies

This dreadful, leaden and depressingly cheap film does have one unusual (though not unique) aspect: it was actually made by Jerry Warren in its entirety. Most of Warren's films are composed primarily of footage from previously shot films, often Mexican in origin. That *Teenage Zombies* is an, ah, original film isn't really a virtue, merely a distinction. Except for an amusingly hammy though stiff performance by Katherine Victor, it is as bad as Warren's cobbled-together films.

A group of carefree teenagers is out for a bit of waterskiing, when Skip (Paul Pepper) suggests a visit to an island nearby. Regg (Don Sullivan), Julie (Mitzi Albertson), Pam (Bri Murphy) and Skip go to the island, where Morrie (Jay Hawk) and Dot (Nan Green) are to join them later. On the island, the quartet finds people slouching around like zombies, and later happens upon a strange old house hidden in trees.

Inside the mansion, they find exotic mad scientist Dr. Myra (Katherine Victor) who, as Charles Stinson of the *Los Angeles Times* said, resembles Vampira after a muscle-building course. Sultry and slinky, Dr. Myra is working for an Unnamed Foreign Power in devising a drug which will transform people into obedient zombielike slaves. With the help of the U.F.P., she plans to drop this stuff into reservoirs all over the United States.

With the help of her goonlike servant Ivan (Chuck Niles) and her pet gorilla (Evan Hayworth), she imprisons the four teenagers with the intention of using them as subjects of further experiments.

Meanwhile, Dot and Morrie have been unable to find Regg, Skip, Pam and Julie, so they turn to the local sheriff (Mike Concannon) for help. He takes them directly to Dr. Myra's laboratory, for he is (gasp) a traitor in league with her, and has been bringing people to be turned into zombies. Other representatives of the U.F.P. have shown up by now, so we know things will end soon.

Regg manages to overpower everyone, the sheriff is shot, Ivan turns on Dr. Myra and, as the six teenagers escape, blows everything sky-high. There is also a confusing fight between Ivan and the gorilla before things fly to flinders.

Barry Brown's article on Katherine Victor in *Scream Queens* has some interesting commentary on Jerry Warren and a touching tribute to Victor.

"I can think of only four positive aspects of Warren's entire output," said Brown. "(1) the laughs provided by his editing and dubbing work, (2) the few glimpses of Mexican horror-film art direction and lighting, (3) the money Warren made for himself at the expense of the audience and the actors who labored for him for a song, and (4) the discovery and use of Katherine Victor."

Miss Victor, said Brown, "is painfully aware of the dubious distinction of being a 'star' creation of Warren's, but the fact is that her reputation was made from *Teenage Zombies*, *Creature of the Walking Dead*, *Curse of the Stone Hand* and *The Cape Canaveral Monsters*, three of which are Warren releases."

In mid-57, Warren and Victor met by chance just as he was preparing *Teenage Zombies*. "It so happened that the house he was using for Dr. Myra's dwelling belonged to an old friend of Jack Hearn's," said Brown, "and the old friend mentioned to Hearn that Warren had not yet cast his leading lady ... even though the film was scheduled to begin in less than a week." Hearn got an introduction to Warren for Victor, and she got the part without reading for it. Warren was probably glad to get anyone. As Brown said, "If Tor Johnson [had] walked in that day, Jerry would have put a wig on him and cast him as Dr. Myra."

Victor was surprised that Warren gave her such scant directorial help. She told Brown that Warren's instructions were only, "Keep it simple." Brown praised her ripe but awkward performance. "An actress more cynical about the Warren operation and less intensely serious about her career and the part she was playing would have been a distinct liability to so tenuous a project. If the actress had been one of those naturalistic stammerers, afraid of the broad stroke and the overdone action, the movie would have been as disjointed in concept as its editing was in reality. What Katherine brought to the role was a flair for the melodramatic that raised the film from general dullness to a level where it could actually be enjoyed."

Describing her performance, Brown said, "Dr. Myra, as Katherine plays her, is one of those imperious, ice-palace bitches, the kind described in movie publicity releases as beautiful but deadly.... Every minute you expect her to give one of those irritating, self-satisfied smiles and say, oh so quietly, 'Let them eat cake.' When she isn't dressed in her white laboratory coat with its high-necked Mandarin collar, she flaunts her sex appeal in a sophisticated, form-fitting evening gown with two straps in front forming a seductive V at her neckline." (Victor provided her own costumes.)

Evan Hayworth, then working as Mitch Evans, played the gorilla in a cheap rented costume. Near the end of the film, there was supposed to be a fierce battle between the gorilla and Ivan the Zombie but, according to Hayworth, Chuck Niles was unavailable on the day the scene was to be shot, so Hayworth played both the gorilla *and* the zombie, making for something of a disjointed fight. (Niles is now an announcer on Los Angeles jazz radio station KKGO.)

Jerry Warren had only elementary ideas of direction (as indicated above) and his concept of editing is even more primitive. Scenes sometimes begin with close-ups, without establishing shots. Close-ups are generally scant, however; most of the film is in long, boring takes of people, filmed in medium shot, talking a great deal on dull sets.

The ads promised "Young Pawns Thrust Into Pulsating Cages of Horror in a Sadistic Experiment," but it's doubtful anyone expected much more than the dreck they got. By this time the audience for these films had grown cynical and bored. A film as bad and false as this one could be released only because exhibitors and distributors were even more cynical than audiences. They knew no matter how poor the film might be, there were still diehards who expected something good, as well as a certain small kernel of the filmgoing public who simply went to see everything of this nature, without any thought as to potential quality. *They* were the teenage zombies, shuffling into and out of the theatres and drive-ins, expecting nothing more than the same thing they'd seen and laughed at before. (Warren returned to filmmaking in the early 1980s with *Frankenstein Island*, a loose remake of *Teenage Zombies*. I am assured he has not lost his touch.)

But eventually, the loyalties of the audience, worn out by garbage like *Teenage Zombies*, swung toward the beach party films and the colorful, sexy and gory Hammer movies from England. The bloom was off the rose as far as low-budget SF movies went. But there were still a gullible, declining few.

The few reviews *Teenage Zombies* received were no more than it deserved. A weary and sarcastic Charles Stinson, who bravely sat through both halves of the *Incredible Petrified World*/*Teenage Zombies* double bill, found both of them worthless. In his *Los Angeles Times* review, he referred to *Zombies* as a "shoestring saga" with "a carelessly-done script—also cleverly uncredited."

The *Monthly Film Bulletin* gave it the lowest rating, saying, "Juvenile in every sense, this is a crude horror comic, amusing only in the closing scenes, which are reminiscent in style of pre-war serials."

Even Barry Brown found little to recommend about the film other than Katherine Victor, though he thought that it "was not the worst of [the teenage monster] genre." He did say that "Jerry Warren's films are notorious for their slipshod production values: uneven sound and atrociously expeditious editing that makes *Dragnet* look like [an Ingmar] Bergman film.... Everything was done in one take, usually a master shot. Only rarely was a closeup included. Still, a few positive tones crept in quite accidentally—snatches here and there of a solitary, elegaic ambiance uncommon to horror films of any budget—yet this was quite by chance."

In *Photon* #20, Ron Borst termed *Teenage Zombies* "incredibly inept," feeling that the film "epitomized the worst of the fifties." Borst claims the film was released in 1958; no other source indicates this, and I have chosen to side with the majority in the matter of date. Don Willis (I) had only slightly more to say about the film, but thought no better of it: "Half the film is riotous dialogue ('The army will be very grateful to you kids'); the other half is just monotonous walking around and bad acting. The whole film is a bad joke."

Of course, a movie called *Teenage Zombies* could hardly hope to be anything else; it is one of the crassest titles of the period, and the film reflects the thinking behind the name: it is not just bad, but terrible.

The Time Machine

Except for *The Wonderful World of the Brothers Grimm*, George Pal never got the budget his SF or fantasy films required; one of the main defects of *The Time Machine* is that its ambitions outstrip its abilities. The special effects showing the time machine making its headlong journey through the centuries are generally effective—a cheat is used when the Time Traveler is entombed and can't see what's happening around him—but overall, the effects are imaginative. On the other hand, the atomic destruction of London in 1966 (didn't you notice?) is done on the level of a cheap Italian movie, with depressingly unconvincing miniatures and oatmeal lava.

The script by David Duncan was unwisely "updated," although to have followed H.G. Wells' own intent would have been just as anachronistic. Wells' novel, his first, was a socialistic polemic, or so he thought; his outstanding skills as a novelist—he's still *the* best science fiction writer—overrode his intent as a pamphleteer and his earlier SF novels are superlative.

In Wells' 1895 novel (he invented the concept of time machines), the two races of the far distant future that the Time Traveler finally reaches, called the Morlocks and the Eloi, were derived from workers and the elite. Even the names are a hint as to that concept. Wells speculated that the great division between the lower and upper classes might eventually divide mankind into two actual races, loathing one another, yet interdependent. The Morlocks made clothing and food for the apparently carefree Eloi, but exacted a stringent price: they also *ate* the Eloi. The Morlocks dwelled in caves beneath the exotic but worn and aging cities of the Eloi, who frolicked happily in the daytime, playing and making love continually. At night, the Morlocks emerged and caught their prey. (The question of Morlock and Eloi children is only lightly touched on in the novel, and totally ignored in the film.) Wells' unnamed Time Traveler feels mostly a sense of despair; he observes what is going on, and is moved by it, but seems to realize there is nothing he can do to change the conditions of this future world.

Duncan's script kept the basic outline of the novel, until the Morlock-Eloi sequence; he changed the reason for the division of mankind into happy, useless adult children, and dank, clammy cannibals. In the film, the Time Traveler encounters a fierce atomic war in 1966; he flees farther into the future, halting in the year 802,701. The Morlocks of the film catch the Eloi with sirens; the transfixed victims march into a sphinx. When enough have entered, the door slams shut. The reason they march in is a main difference between the book and film: after the sirens shut off, the Eloi return to normal and tell the Time Traveler it is "all clear," the same phrase he heard in earlier stops.

That concept ties the film much too firmly to its own time, as well as being inherently preposterous: surely such ideas would change after eight thousand centuries? This topical irony is supposed to make us believe several unlikely things, such as that a war has raged for 800,000 years, even though the Time Traveler sees peaceful cities being built as he rushes through time, that after a war using atomic satellites the *concept* of all clear would still exist, and, most importantly, that somehow those who sought shelter beneath the ground (becoming Morlocks as time passed) would become cannibals on those who lived above. Also, there's no thematic or sociological reason for those who remained above to become elfin lotus-eaters. Wells' ideas were naive and he didn't yet seem to be aware of the increasing importance of the middle class (into which he was born), but at least the worker-elite split was metaphorically mirrored with some relevance in the Morlock-Eloi division. Duncan's thesis that atomic war would generate both troglodytes and the indolent doesn't grow out of *any* kind of logic. It's anachronistic *and* dated; merely two-bit irony, seriously damaging the film. Even when the film was made, the term "all clear" was outmoded.

The film is also compromised by the blood-and-thunder climax, involving leaping Morlocks, whips, explosions and fistfights; the peculiarly delicate mood of the earlier parts of the film is shattered into something vaguely resembling a Polynesian thriller: cannibals versus the happy smiling natives, freed by a white man. There's also the direct statement (in the narration) that "the underground world of the Morlocks was destroyed" forever, overlooking questions as to what the world is like in 802,701 elsewhere than what had been London.

But in a limited sense, none of this matters much: the inadequate budget, the botched philosophizing, the abrupt switch to horror adventure, don't affect the overall impact of the film. Although I do not think it is George Pal's best film (despite flaws, *The War of the Worlds* and *tom thumb* are superior), it is his most beguiling. The general mood is very odd, and seems to have been achieved almost accidentally: wistful nostalgia for the future. There's some warm romanticism to the film in its best scenes that makes it appealing; it was apparently Pal's biggest box office success. It's Pal's most romantic film, as well as his most traditionally good-looking (except for *Brothers Grimm*, actually a studio project). Despite a lack of attention to period behavior by the actors, it may also be his best-acted film.

And its popularity continues. A few years ago, I encountered Rod Taylor, star of the film. A big, friendly man (he immediately insisted that Cathy Hill and I call him Rod), he seemed a bit nonplussed when I suggested I could tell him the name of the film that he is asked about the most. When I said it was *The Time Machine*, he blinked and smiled, then said I was definitely right.

A few days into 1900, David Filby (Alan Young), Dr. Hillyer (Sebastian Cabot), Anthony Bridewell (Tom Helmore) and Walter Kemp (Whit Bissell) meet in the home of their friend George for dinner, although he's not there.

As the guests prepare to dine, housekeeper Mrs. Watchett (Doris Lloyd) screams as a disheveled, exhausted figure bursts into the room. It is George (Taylor), who's clearly been through a lot since his friends last saw him on New Year's Eve. After he catches his breath, he tells of his adventures, and we see them in flashbacks.

The group had gathered in George's clock-filled home on December 31, 1899, for drinks and cigars before each went his separate way to celebrate New Year's Eve. George is proud of his new invention, something to do with time; he keeps it hidden like a magician in a small ebony box. It's not a timepiece, he says, it is a time *machine*, for traveling through the fourth dimension—time itself. His friends are disbelieving, even when he shows them the tiny, exquisite machine itself. He finally agrees to demonstrate it, but also admits that the demonstration will work only once. He borrows a cigar from principal scoffer Hillyer and seats it in the tiny chair that's the "saddle" of the Time Machine. Using Hillyer's finger, he advances the level on the little machine's controls, and the vertical disc behind the chair begins to revolve. With a humming that shakes the dishes and a final boooweeep, the machine vanishes.

The friends are still skeptical, especially when George says that the machine is not traveling through space—in fact, it is still in the same spot it was—but only through time, and by now is many years in the future, going literally forever.

His friends suggest that George devote his efforts as an inventor to the then-raging Boer War, but he says that he has other plans. Everyone leaves but Filby, George's best friend and the only one of the group near his own age. He's been worried about George for some time, fearing his friend has changed. George says he doesn't much care for the time he was born into, and is heading into the future in his full-sized time machine, which he offers to show Filby. Filby indignantly refuses, and begs George to destroy the time machine before it destroys him. George promises Filby he won't walk out the door that night, and Filby leaves him alone.

George keeps his promise; in his workshop, a former greenhouse, he makes the final adjustments on the time machine, and immediately heads into the future.

He watches the sun swing by overhead, trees bloom and bear fruit, and clothes on a manikin in Filby's shop change with changing styles. He halts on September 13, 1917. His house has become dusty and cobwebby, and the clocks have (of course) all stopped. In the street outside, he sees a young soldier going into Filby's shop and learns to his unhappiness that this is Filby's son James (also Alan Young); Filby himself died the year before. James tells George that the house (George's own) was kept by his father for years in the expectation that its owner might return. James also says there's a war on.

Shocked by David's death and disillusioned by the war, George presses on into the years, halting briefly on June 19, 1940, when he is buffeted by explosions. He wearily realizes a new war has begun, and goes farther into the future.

He stops again on August 18, 1966, comfortably in the future from 1959, when the film was made. He again meets James, a very old man now, who tells him to get into a shelter as an atomic satellite is coming. (James recognizes him.) The orbiting bomb explodes, and George barely makes it to his time machine. Unpersuasively, the ground splits and lava oozes forth, filling the streets and carrying cars along.

The time machine rushes forward into the future as lava covers it and immediately solidifies. He has little choice now but to rush on through the centuries; stopping the machine while it is in the mountain would cause unguessable but undoubtedly calamitous consequences.

The mountain eventually wears away around him, and the Earth seems green and lush again. Busy machines erect a city in the distance, but after it exists in splendor for a few centuries (George's seconds), it falls into some ruin. Curious, George brings the machine to an abrupt halt on October 12, in the year 802,701.

The machine spins around and falls over. It begins to rain. Taking note of a sneering statue nearby (he refers to it as a sphinx), he heads off toward the buildings. At first he thinks he's found paradise: lush vegetation, fruit everywhere, a pleasant climate. But then he fears it may lack people altogether. But he hears laughter and splashing sounds, and happens upon a group of small, slender blonde people, clad in Greek–style pastel tunics. Now George is convinced that mankind has reached its pleasant afternoon. "So this is man's future," says George's narration, "to bask in the sunlight, bathe in the clear streams and eat the fruits of Earth with all knowledge of work and hardship forgotten."

But then one of the small people, a pretty girl, swims out too far and is caught in a current. Two men on a rock glance casually at her but do nothing to save her (this is a pointless idea: they should have wondered how to save her but been unable to arrive at a means). Angry and perplexed, George doffs his velvet smoking jacket, leaps into the stream and rescues her. She leads him back to the crumbling dome where her people live.

From the girl, whose name is Weena (Yvette Mimieux), George learns her people are the Eloi. In the dome, where the Eloi are laughing and eating fruit

This set shot from The Time Machine (1960) shows the time-traveling device itself, a splendid design, within the sphinx, where Rod Taylor finds it near the end of the film.

and vegetables, one of the young men—and everyone seems to be in their early 20s—tells George there's no government, no laws, but has a hard time recalling the word "book." The light dawns, and he shows George some books, now crumbling into powder. Bitterly, George realizes that the state of the books tells him everything about the Eloi he wants to know.

"What have you done?" he shouts to the startled Eloi. "Thousands of years of building and rebuilding, creating and recreating, so that you can let it crumble to dust. A million yesterdays of sensitive men dying for their dreams. For what? So you can swim and dance and play." (What *else* might it have been for?)

He storms out of the dome, intent on returning to his own time "so that I can die among *men*." But the time machine is gone, dragged into the sphinx; metal doors are shut, George cannot open them. As he's pounding, Weena unexpectedly turns up: she's come to warn him about the Morlocks. No one goes out at night, she says, because of the Morlocks; when they call, the Eloi must "go below." George realizes this future is more complicated than he thought, another Dark Age, which needs someone to light the way out. Somewhat vainly, he thinks he might be the one to do that, and feels obliged to stay.

The next day, Weena takes George to a museum, showing him talking rings (Duncan's brightest idea, a science fiction innovation): when spun on a glass-topped table, a light appears beneath them and a voice (Paul Frees) is heard. George learns that many centuries before, the war between the East and West finally ended. Part of the population elected to go below, to huge caves, while the others remained above. (As this is after the war, this decision seems inexplicable.)

Weena shows him also a small barren meadow with several walled holes dotting it, like miniature craters. From one of these well-like openings, descending into darkness, George hears the throbbing of machinery. Despite Weena's objections, he decides to go below and see what he can learn about the Morlocks. As he begins his descent, Weena impulsively gives him a flower.

But then George hears sirenlike sounds, and Weena disappears from the well opening. He clambers back up and finds dozens of Eloi wandering in a trancelike state toward the sphinx, which now has screaming metal cones rising from its base. Eloi walk blankly through the open door in the sphinx. George arrives just as Weena, along with a dozen or so others, disappears within and the doors slam. He asks one of the nearby Eloi what's wrong, and is told that nothing is, it is now all clear. (Again, if the division between Morlocks and Eloi took place *after* the war, why would this response remain?)

George rushes off for the well opening again, followed by a few curious Eloi, attracted by his vigor and intensity. He descends into the underground world of the Morlocks.

He soon discovers the Morlocks are eating the Eloi. From concealment, he watches the hairy green Morlocks use whips to drive the Eloi down a ramp. But George battles them, using fists and a grabbed Morlock whip. He discovers that struck matches momentarily blind the Morlocks (whose eyes glow impressively), but they get the upper hand. As George goes down beneath a Morlock who is throttling him, one of the Eloi slowly makes a fist, then slugs the Morlock. George takes over the battle, leading the Eloi to the well. As they climb up, he tosses a torch back into the Morlock's den, then, with Weena, makes his own getaway.

Fire spouts out of the various well openings, explosions are heard and as George and the Eloi flee, the barren meadow collapses.

The most unnecessary scene in the film follows. George and Weena sit by the stream and aimlessly chat, as she tries to arrange her hair in a style like the women of his time. George sees that the sphinx is open, and the time machine is there. He jumps into it and is about to get it going when some dazed, injured Morlocks appear. The sphinx door slams shut. There's a brief fight, and George manages to get the machine going, and returns to his own time.

Naturally, his friends are dubious about the tale. George accepts their disbelief, and shows them out. Filby returns. He and Mrs. Watchett hear a strange sound and dash into the laboratory, but the time machine and George are gone. Filby notices the machine had been moved again so it would appear outside the sphinx. Mrs. Watchett says that he took three books with him, but doesn't know which three. "Do you think he will ever return?" she asks. "One cannot choose but wonder," Filby responds with a glow, "you see, he has all the time in the world."

When I first saw *The Time Machine*, I was simultaneously enchanted and disappointed. My appreciation of the handsome design of the film, of Rod Taylor's strong, masculine performance, of the wonderful time machine itself, and of Yvette Mimieux's delicate but sensuous beauty (among other virtues) was offset by dislike of the sometimes tacky future sets, the poor miniature work, the grotesquely overdone makeup of the Morlocks, and a generalized feeling of awkwardness. The film would have been better if it had tried to be less topical, less contrived (three stops, three wars) and more polished.

The association of Wells' novel with movies, oddly enough, goes back almost as far as its publication. In 1895, inventor Robert W. Paul was so taken by the just-published novel that he approached Wells, and together they drew up a patent for an ingenious if cumbersome device-cum–viewing room for representing time travel to interested spectators. In addition to slides, Paul wanted to use Edison's Kinetoscope (movies) to help make the illusion of traveling through time more convincing. Nothing came of this attempt, however, although Paul made a patent application in October, 1895. This remarkable story is told in Terry Ramsaye's pioneering book on films, *A Thousand and One Nights* (Simon and Schuster, 1926).

On January 25, 1949, the BBC telecast a dramatization of the Wells novel, with Russell Napier as the Time Traveler and Mary Donn as Weena.

In 1953, the estate of H.G. Wells was impressed enough by *The War of the Worlds* to offer George Pal an option on any of Wells' other SF novels; he chose *The Time Machine*. Unfortunately, Paramount, Pal's distributor, was interested only in space movies; they thought that was the limit for colorful science fiction adventures.

At that time, Pal had David Duncan write the screenplay. Duncan remained associated with the production from then until it was filmed, and seems to have been the only writer involved (although a few pages of the final draft are apparently the work of another writer). Duncan was a competent, intelligent writer working in several genres. He's one of a small handful of writers of science fiction who had also written SF movies, although none are similar to his novels, which were well-written and unusual. His first was *The Shade of Time* (1946), about "atomic displacement," according to the *Science Fiction Encyclopedia*. Later, Duncan wrote *Dark Dominion* (1954), about an element that changes atomic weight in relation to the star Sirius; *Beyond Eden* (1955) involves water-making, huge crystals and human fulfillment; *Occam's Razor* (1957) concerns travel between alternate worlds with the key being "surface tension on a soap film." Duncan also wrote the script for *The Black Scorpion*, which seems like a rush job; according to Richard Matheson, Duncan's *Fantastic Voyage* (1966) script was quite good, but heavily rewritten by inferior writers. Those for *The Thing That Couldn't Die* (1958), *Monster on the Campus* and *The Leech Woman* were written to studio specifications; I doubt that Duncan brought much of his own type of creativity to them.

According to Gail Morgan Hickman's useful *The Films of George Pal*, the producer was afraid that what he and Duncan were working on would leak out and the market would be flooded with time-travel movies before Pal finished his, as had happened (on a small scale) with *Destination Moon* and *Rocketship XM* in 1950. He needn't have feared; other movie men are just as cautious as those at Paramount. A time-travel film, *World Without End* did precede *The Time Machine*, but although it was an unabashed imitation of Wells' novel, the time travel in the film was heavily under-emphasized (the heroes might as well have been going to another planet), both in the story and the advertising. *Beyond the Time Barrier*, still another variation on the novel, was finished before *The Time Machine* but followed it to theatres, probably in an effort to capitalize on the success of the bigger-budgeted Pal film.

Despite continued efforts to film *The Time Machine*, Pal was unsuccessful. In 1958, when he was in England making *tom thumb*, Pal impressed Matthew Raymond, then head of the British division of MGM. He had Pal draw up a script for his favorite unfilmed project, so Pal chose *The Time Machine*; already having a script, he prepared a budget of $800,000, and approached Paul Scofield to star.

Back in the United States, Pal's economical budget for *The Time Machine* and his bringing in *tom thumb* for less than the studio expected convinced studio head Sol Siegel to give Pal the go-ahead on *The Time Machine*. It was filmed at the studio lot in Culver City (which must embarrass Parker Tyler, who in the belief that the film was British, included it in his *Classics of the Foreign Film*) and came in slightly under budget. Unfortunately, it tends to look as cheap as it was.

The decision was wisely made to keep the film's opening and closing scenes close to the period of the novel. In program notes for a screening of the film at the University of Texas at Austin, Mike Grossberg suggests some reasons why this was useful: "The quaint atmosphere of the past works to heighten the contrast with the fantastic world of the future.... Indeed, the Victorian decor of the Time Traveler's house is at least as important to the overall theme of the film as its visual beauty is in highlighting the futuristic sets. The reason is that the theme of *The Time Machine* is the ambivalence of man's emotions towards time. The Time Travler simultaneously feels a wondrous anticipation of man's future along with a sense of nostalgia for his own past." Moving the date of the beginning of the story to New Year's Eve, 1899, was an evocative idea: the turn of any year brings thoughts about time and its passage, and the turn of a century makes these thoughts even more powerful.

Pal and Duncan kept the period setting because they wanted to show the Time Traveler passing through the years we know that lie between his and our times, to increase the sense of reality of the film. They erred by putting an atomic war so soon in their future, but perhaps chose 1966 to allow the reintro-duction of Filby's son. Furthermore, the sets could still reasonably resemble the period the Time Traveler left, allowing a considerable saving in budget.

I suspect it was Pal himself who chose to show the passage through time partly by the clothing styles of women. Unfortunately, this is painfully trivial, and slightly patronizing: it seems to be in the picture more for the sake of a cheap laugh at the quaint clothing styles of the recent past than for its ostensible purpose. Duncan does manage to instill a sense of wistful longing (a mood that recurs again and again) in the Time Traveler: in a world changing with the swiftness of thought, only he and the manikin in the window don't change.

Duncan also plays with some of our favorite clichés about time. Helmore asks Bissell what time it is, in a room full of clocks (the man who never knows what time it is); kept waiting for George, Bissell complains about a "waste of time"; Young refers more than once to Taylor having "all the time in the world." And in a little nod to Wells, Duncan has Taylor wonder if man can change "the shape of things to come."

I suspect the strange blend of horror movie and action thriller in the Morlock scenes was altered from the original concept. In the copy of the script I have, all pages other than those are dated April 16, 1959; only the Morlock scenes were written in June of that year, and give some indication that the pages may not have been written by Duncan. (For instance, elsewhere the Time Traveler is referred to by that term; on those pages alone, which have a different level of diction, he's abbreviated as T.T.)

This change in tone from nostalgia for the past set in the future, a strange but affecting emotion, to blood-and-thunder action, may have been a result of Pal's last-minute attempts to placate the MGM studio brass. In the Hickman book, Pal said, "The executives complained that I didn't make enough 'cover' shots.... Everyone seeing the rushes was worried about what [I] was doing.... When the fight scenes with the Morlocks came, we had to overshoot; suddenly they said I shot too much film." Pal convinced Siegel to allow him to present a completed sequence from the picture, and he and editor George Tomasini worked all weekend swiftly cutting together the Morlock battle scenes. They showed this to the executives, who were impressed and allowed Pal to have his own way thereafter.

Art directors George W. Davis and William Ferrari, working with set decorators Henry Grace and Keogh Gleason, created an attractive home for George, the Time Traveler. The house is small and crowded with books, but not cluttered. It's warm, familiar and comfortable, very much the home of a young, intellectual Victorian gentleman of independent but not lavish means.

Before the credits we see a series of floating timepieces, each a more modern refinement of keeping time. And George's house is full of clocks; their soft ticking (and occasional exuberant chiming) fills all the scenes at the beginning and end; the sound is dampened but always present, so that when George walks through the house in 1917, the silence of the stopped clocks makes it seem as if the house itself had died.

And of course, there is the wonderful set piece of the film, the time machine itself. It's doubtful that the film would have had quite the charm it does if another design had been used. In Wells' novel, the machine is never quite described; he alludes to crystal bars, gleaming shapes and so forth, but there's no actual description. Even in David Duncan's script the machine is not described, and in the comic book adaptation of the movie that came out when the film was released, the machine is a huge, hideous boxy affair totally unlike what we see in the film.

It looks something like a rococo Victorian sleigh. Built around an antique barber chair, which looks suitably overstuffed and overdecorated, the time machine is actually simple. There's an oval brass hoop at the base, parallel with the floor, the sleigh-shape of the brass "runners" which swoop up to the controls in front of the chair, complicated and glowing doodads behind the chair, and a tall, concave disc vertically mounted at the back of the machine which spins as it travels through time. The most commented-on feature of the machine is a brass plate between the day and date indicators (which use archaic printing): it reads "Manufactured by H. George Wells," a not-very-in-joke that may also have been intended to suggest that the Time Traveler is H.G. Wells, as in Time After Time.

One of the most enchanting and fairy-tale-like aspects of a film which constantly verges on being a fairy tale is the tiny model of the time machine which George loses forever when he demonstrates it to his friends. Exquisitely crafted and immensely appealing, it was lost in a fire at George Pal's home some years later. Among others, model-builder Harvey Mayo has painstakingly recreated the lovely little time machine. The full-sized prop itself, now owned by Bob Burns, can be spotted in *Gremlins*.

The biggest problem confronting the makers of the film was how to depict travel through time. On the short scale, it was no problem: time-lapse photography, "which," said Mike Grossberg, "had long been a beautiful but conceptually useless technique" was used to show flowers blooming, candles swiftly melting, etc. More complicated or harder-to-depict "fast action" was accomplished by stop-motion animation, as with the snail rocketing around the floor, or with a series of oil paintings depicting apples bursting forth where apple blossoms had been. (According to animation expert Mark Kausler, animated oil paintings have not been used in any other feature film.) To show years swiftly passing, the somewhat vulgar device of the clothing manikin was used. To show centuries—well, they fudged, and buried the Time Traveler in an opaque mountain.

For the short scale time travel, inventive cinematographer Paul Vogel found ways of manipulating lights. The machine was in George's laboratory, a former greenhouse. Vogel used huge circular filters mounted in front of each of the largest lamps used to illuminate the scene. The seven-foot discs were divided into four sections, indicating the different times of day. One segment, for daylight, was clear; another used a pink gelatin for sunrise, a third an amber for sunset, and the fourth, a blue gel for night. Furthermore, Vogel had a seesaw arrangement under the lights to raise and lower them as the sun rose higher and sank lower. Coordinating the turning of the discs and the tilting of the seesaw device was difficult.

When the lava envelops the time machine, Project Unlimited provided a rear-screen image of large rocks forming on the inside of the mountain. Smaller rocks were used on the set around the machine itself. As the rocks on the rear screen vanished in course of time, stop-motion was used to remove them, but the rocks on the live set had to be whisked out of the way by means of wires.

The Time Machine makes extensive use of matte paintings. There were paintings for the exterior of George's house, the city and landscape around him, the upper portions of the ruined dome, and so forth. While to contemporary eyes these paintings may seem obvious, in 1960 they were convincing enough to allow a willing suspension of disbelief.

On the other hand, the unfortunate atomic war scene almost destroys belief. After the "atomic satellite" detonates, the city is engulfed in unrealistic "lava," oatmeal dyed red. Obvious model cars float in the steaming mass, and what look like burning sugar cubes dot the surface.

The use of oatmeal caused unexpected problems. According to Harold Schechter and David Everitt in *Film Tricks*, at the end of a week, Gene Warren and Wah Chang had a huge vat of oatmeal cooked and set aside. Unfortunately, the weekend was hot and the oatmeal fermented, making it not only smell terrible but have the wrong viscosity, so it poured out like noxious water rather than like thick lava. After this problem was solved and the oatmeal filmed as intended, it was washed down into drains under the Project Unlimited stage. And there it stayed, again fermenting, filling the stage with a powerful stench.

Despite the inadequacies of the special effects, *The Time Machine* won the Oscar in that category.

The Morlocks present another problem. Working from detailed drawings by George Pal, William Tuttle's crew designed the overemphatically ugly

Morlock faces. With their gigantic, thick and downturned lips, protruding teeth and sagging upper faces, the Morlocks look too cartoony for belief. They're like a caricature of stupid evil, and although we rarely see their too-rubbery faces clearly, even that bit is too much. Furthermore, their fingers and toes have grown together into grotesque clumps: three digits on the hand, two on the feet. It's hard to imagine these guys running the machines we see in their caves. Wouldn't evolution have pushed them in the direction of greater dexterity, rather than less?

Even the hair growth on their arms and legs seems wrong: thick, white hair of uniform length down the backs of the arms and the fronts of the legs. And nowhere else on their bodies, which are dark green. Cave dwellers usually turn pale over the years and develop huge eyes, but not William Tuttle's Morlocks.

On the other hand, the tiny lights in the Morlock's eyes are marvelous, and startled audiences. In at least one Morlock, the little lights don't come on simultaneously; maybe he was winking, as Bill Thomas suggests.

Bill also notes that "the Morlocks seem strangely fragile in the battle in the Sphinx, and earlier, when the Eloi literally punches that Morlock's lights out. Another, set afire, runs off-camera and actually explodes. They're built like sumo wrestlers, but take a punch like wimps. Lois Thomas suggests that it's their poor eating habits."

One of the most vivid scenes in the film, not in the script, comes at the end of the brief fight in the sphinx over the time machine. George knocks one Morlock aside just as he shoots forward into the future momentarily. The dead Morlock suddenly ages into a crumbling corpse in one of the most unusual uses of stop-motion in any film. The skin shrivels, the eyes pop out and dry, the flesh withers into black flakes and falls off the skull, which itself collapses. This was the work of David Pal, George's son, and is one of the peaks of inventive gruesomeness of the 1950s. The term "jaw-dropping" really applies here.

Many of the problems with *The Time Machine* are linked to its budget. The highly variable special effects, the inadequate exterior set of the meadow of wells, the sometimes mediocre acting (the Eloi) — these are hard to avoid. So is the highly unlikely survival of English as a language (among the Eloi; the Morlocks growl) in the year 802,701. Wells didn't pretend the language would be the same, but his novel was being narrated by its protagonist throughout. Although Taylor does provide some narration, to have eschewed English as the language of the Eloi would have required too much narration. I cannot see a realistic way around this problem, but it does require mentioning.

David Duncan's script dated 16 April 1959 is almost exactly the film as it was shot, but even at that point, the much too-small budget caused problems. In the 1966 sequence, the Time Traveler was to enter Filby's store for his last confrontation with James, but this sequence was dropped. A brief scene of the dome under construction was added.

Duncan's script makes occasional logical hiccups: the Eloi know what government and laws are, but have a harder time with books — which are right there in their dome. Furthermore, the idea that the Eloi don't mind that one of their group drowns before their eyes is just too blatant a presentation of their spiritual lassitude. If they don't *care*, what's to prevent the Morlocks from strolling among them and simply walking off with the tastiest Eloi?

The Eloi change from apathetic to violent with far too much ease and speed; George is a lively example of strength, all right, but the problems presented in the film would seem to be harder to solve than just by the example of one man who does care.

The main theme of the film is self-sacrifice, expressed in many ways. Filby wants to give up his own New Year celebration to help his friend George; we later learn that Filby left George's house vacant rather than selling it; the first thing George does when he meets the Eloi is to save Weena; Weena herself leaves the safety of the dome to warn George about the Morlocks, and one almost gets away with her then and there. George acknowledges in her attempt the most explicit statement of the self-sacrifice theme: "The one characteristic which distinguished man from the animal kingdom was the spirit of self-sacrifice." And of course, the entire climax of the picture, George's descent into Morlock Hell, is because he's willing to risk himself to save Weena. Finally, the coda: George returns to the future with those unnamed three books to help the Eloi rebuild.

This theme is common in Hollywood movies, and does not really occur in Wells' novel, primarily concerned with social commentary. However, it's not alien to him; at the end of the novel, the friend of the Time Traveler who has been relating his story to us, the reader, says that he has kept the flowers the Time Traveler brought from the future, which Weena gave to him. "And I have by me for my comfort, two strange white flowers—shriveled now, and brown and flat and brittle—to witness that even when mind and strength had gone, gratitude and a mutual tenderness still lived on in the heart of Man." (This is, in fact, the last line in the novel.) Generally in Wells, however, the leading characters in his SF novels are motivated by self-interest and/or greed.

Duncan's most noticeable innovation, the talking rings, may be impractical, but are fanciful and intelligent. However, what the rings have to say is simpleminded. There's not the slightest hint as to how the Morlocks came to be the devourers of the Eloi, which would seem to be useful information.

As a director, George Pal is pedestrian and unimaginative, with only a few good ideas. Virtually all scenes are handled in the same fashion: master shot, two-shots, close-ups as punctuation. There's a good shot of Taylor at tabletop level, head resting on laced fingers, smiling at his tiny time machine with pride and joy. But Pal also includes the scene in which George says he wants to kindle a spark in the remnants of humanity, and the camera pans down to a fire. Pal is probably primarily responsible for the gentle, even sweet tone of the film, because he was a gentle and sweet man himself. Movies don't always reflect the personalities of their directors, but *The Time Machine* does.

The mood of the film is extremely elusive, very hard to describe, but it is real, and is in all the film except the overdone sequences with the Morlocks. *The Time Machine* is almost haunting, and I suspect this quality was partly accidental. It almost echoes the evocative lines from the novel quoted above.

Yvette Mimieux made her evocative debut in the film. Only 17 at the time, her own lack of sophistication aided the characterization of Weena; at the time, several reviewers noted it was hard to tell if Mimieux were giving a performance or merely being herself. In light of her later roles, in some of which she has been very good, it seems that she actually was acting in *The Time Machine*. It's not a polished performance, to say the least, but her gentle, strangely sensual opacity is exactly right for the character. The film made her a star, if not quite of major magnitude. In *Starlog* #36, she told interviewer Samuel J. Maronie that she was dazzled by the film's production. "I suppose the whole crazy production made me more lost than I already was at the time. I'd never acted before, let alone appeared in a film—which is in itself a very technical event.... I was never really quite sure where the camera was.... I was too embarrassed to show my ignorance by asking questions."

Mimieux also appeared in Pal's *The Wonderful World of the Brothers Grimm*. Her other genre films include the TV movies *Black Noon* (1971), *Snowbeast* (1977) and *Devil Dog the Hound of Hell* (1978); her theatrical films include the unfortunate ventures *The Neptune Factor* (1973) and *The Black Hole* (1978). Hard to cast but versatile, she's appeared in a wide variety of films, including *Light in the Piazza* (1962), *Toys in the Attic* (1963), *Dark of the Sun* (1968, with Rod Taylor), *The Delta Factor* (1970), *Jackson County Jail* (1976), and many others. She wrote as well as starred in the TV movie *Hit Lady* (1974). She has also written poetry and music.

Rod Taylor was born in Australia. After appearing in some stage productions and two films there, he emigrated to the United States. He so successfully lost his Australian accent that when he appeared in the entertaining Australian film *The Picture Show Man* in 1977, he played an American. He seemed headed for major stardom in the late 50s and early 60s, but though he's a better actor than most of his physical type, he never quite made it to the upper ranks. But he's never had to accept demeaning assignments, and is almost constantly working, almost always in starring roles.

He had a nonexclusive contract with MGM, and for that company appeared in several major productions, including among others, *The V.I.P.s* (1963), *Young Cassidy* (1965), *The Liquidator* (1966, a good J. Bond imitation), Antonioni's *Zabriskie Point* (1970), and finally the almost worthless *Trader Horn* (1973). For other studios, he appeared in *The Birds* (1963), *Fate Is the Hunter* (1964), *Hotel* (1967), *Darker Than Amber*, *The Man Who Had Power over Women* (both 1970) and others. He starred in the TV series "Hong Kong," "Bearcats," "The Oregon Trail" and "Masquerade." Coincidentally, he appeared in the first U.S. feature about time travel, *World Without End*.

Taylor is hardly a Victorian type, and seems far too ruggedly masculine to embody the scientific tinkerer of the novel. But as George, he's surprisingly sensitive to his fellow players. We can imagine his being devoted to Alan Young far more easily than we can Young's being devoted to him. Although the film is not quite a love story—Taylor's interest in Mimieux seems rather avuncular—romanticism as an approach to life is evident in Taylor's playing. Perhaps passionate love was intended, but it isn't really there in the film—and the movie is the better for it. Taylor doesn't sweep Mimieux off her feet; he's just more *alive* than anyone else around. She's drawn to his caring the way a cat is drawn to a spot of sunlight: there's more warmth there. And despite what seems almost like an effort on Taylor's part in other films at times to suppress it, his biggest strength as an actor is precisely this warmth. Taylor is likable, friendly and open; these qualities make his Time Traveler a memorable character. George is not just a Victorian visiting the future, he is Everyman, and perhaps more period feeling would have lessened this. His performance is literally time-less.

The other actors have little to do. Helmore and Bissell seem appropriately Victorian (though Bissell seems American as well), and Cabot is unpleasantly blustering as the Doubting Thomas of the group. Alan Young unsuccessfully plays the first Filby with a Scottish accent and aggressive gestures. I suspect this was more due to Pal's direction than to Young's acting abilities, but the character is quite tiresome, whoever is to blame.

Pal was quite taken with the picture; it was probably his own favorite film. He often discussed doing a sequel, and had at least one script prepared, although the first storyline I heard doesn't match the one Pal talked about later, shortly before his death.

In the first-announced sequel script, the Time Traveler was to go on into the future even farther, as in the novel; Pal prepared moody sketches of this unimaginably distant time, with the prescribed crabs and the huge, dim sun on the horizon. But he also included giant insects, and human beings who hide from them in huge honeycombs. The Time Traveler was to do for these people what he wanted to do for the Eloi.

Actually, according to an interview with Pal in *Starlog* #10, in another draft, this Time Traveler was supposed to be the son of Weena and George. The film was scheduled to open with their deaths in the London Blitz of 1943 – the time machine's tendency to stop in wars brought disaster. "Suddenly," Pal told interviewer Ed Naha, "we hear a baby cry. Then we pan over to the time machine, and next to it, is a [modern] version of the machine. A brand new one. A young man stands there who looks like both the Time Traveler and Weena. He has just witnessed the death of his parents and his own birth."*

Pal here demonstrated a more sophisticated concept of time travel than that which seems to have been used in the original film. After the Morlocks have been destroyed, George says he's almost "late" to get back to London – as if he couldn't return to any time at all. The time he spends in 802,701 seems to be exactly the same length of time he is missing from 1900; a week then is a week now. Odd.

Although Pal never got around to filming his sequel, other time travel films continue to be made, but the idea of time travel remains badly used in movies; most show little imagination. Among those with actual travel through time explained scientifically are *Cyborg 2087, Dimension 5* (both 1966), *Beyond the Time Barrier, The Time Travelers* (1964), *Journey to the Center of Time* (1967), *Je T'Aime, Je T'Aime, Planet of the Apes* (both 1968), *Escape from the Planet of the Apes* (1971), *Time After Time* (1979), *Timerider* (1982), *The Terminator, The Philadelphia Experiment* (both 1984) and *Traneers* (1985). Several episodes of the TV series "The Twilight Zone" centered on time travel, as did "Timetrain," "It's About Time" and "The Time Tunnel." The latter featured Whit Bissell, a supporting player in the Pal film. There was also a pilot film, aired as a movie, made by Irwin Allen, called *Time Travelers*; he made that and "The Time Tunnel" center largely on travel into the past because props and sets representing past eras are commonly available at movie studios.

There was also a TV movie based on H.G. Wells' novel, also called *The Time Machine* (1978). It was amazingly bad (and Whit Bissell appeared again). Wallace Bennett's teleplay was supposedly taken from the "Classics Illustrated" comic book version, but that interesting graphic story adaptation was not the source; nor, for most of the film, was Wells' novel used. Instead, we were shown a modern-day scientist (John Beck) who spends most of the story visiting known historical periods of the past (cheaper to do) and very little time in the future world of the Morlocks and the Eloi. Weena was played by Priscilla Barnes, but she lacked the winsome charm of Yvette Mimieux. The movie itself

---

In 1981, Dell Books published the novel Time Machine II *by George Pal and Joe Morheim. This was a novelization of the son-of-the-Time-Traveler script, and deals with the efforts of the son to discover his origins and destiny; he heads into the future to try to prevent the deaths of Weena and his father. There's another sequel to Wells' novel,* Die Reise mit der Zeitmaschine *(1946) by Egon Friedell. It was published in English translation by DAW Books in 1972. It's very boring, and those who want to know the plot will have to be more tolerant and curious than I.*

is nothing less than one of the worst TV movies ever made, ponderous, silly and insulting.

The amusing *Time After Time* may have its faults, but it also has a clever premise: H.G. Wells himself is shown as the inventor of the time machine, and uses it to pursue Jack the Ripper into the present.

The Time Machine was released in August, 1960, catching the tail end of school vacation; it was a fine way to end the summer. Reviews were generally very favorable, and the film was more widely reviewed than most other obviously science fiction films of the period. It was a solid financial success for MGM and Pal, making the later cut-price approach to *Atlantis the Lost Continent* disappointing and inexplicable.

"Tube" in *Variety* thought it a "delightful experience.... An enchanting adaptation and materialization."

Edward Lipton in *Film Daily* was impatient at first. "Apparently, there is an unwritten law that all science-fiction pictures, particularly the ones based on classics, must have a scene at the beginning in which the main characters sit around stuffily discussing grade school science in terms oh so clear, reading their lines as if they are staring at a teleprompter, in an atmosphere that might charitably be described as dull." However, he felt the film then turned into "a surprisingly warm and tender [love story] ... not just a vehicle for bug-eyed monsters.... This is a surprisingly tender, beautiful and haunting love story that is, in a way, dedicated to the human race." (Lipton is one of the few who responded to the film's wistful romanticism, and even then he saw it as more of a love story than it seems to be.)

Joe Morgenstern in the *Herald-Tribune* considered the film "lots of fun [that] degenerates into a conventional horror story.... Until the nasty Morlocks come along, *The Time Machine* is an engrossing piece of science fiction."

The *Monthly Film Bulletin* felt that though the movie simplified Wells, it "has a bizarre quality of its own.... Pal's visual flair and genuine feeling for his fantasy world help to maintain an entertaining surface for most of the time."

Even sarcastic *Time* liked it. "*The Time Machine* deserves a place on the very short list of good science fiction films.... Its human characters are compounded ... of flesh, blood and imagination."

Among the voices of dissent was the *New Yorker* which almost always deemed it necessary to protect novels from the onslaught of Hollywood. The film "converts [Wells'] good simple-minded material into bad simple-minded material [by] unwaveringly obeying two queer and venerable West Coast laws—that all films set either in the past or the future shall not be acted by their participants, but shall be walked, hunched, grimaced, gesticulated, wrestled and lurched through, and that all such productions, even though largely aimed at ... ten-year-olds, shall be enhanced with Love Interest.... The Eloi are lumpy bleached blonds; the Morlocks are big, fat and floury; the greenery has a rubbery cast; and the models used for sets in the cataclysmic sequences don't touch the lowest-priced Lionel train."

Later commentators include Parker Tyler who, though he thought the movie was British, discusses it in his *Classics of the Foreign Film* in perhaps the most prestigious company *The Time Machine* has ever joined: *The Passion of Joan of Arc, M, Rules of the Game, Day of Wrath, Rashomon, La Strada* and other great classics. Happily, Tyler announces he will ignore the fact that the film is based on Wells' novel. "I place most of my faith in film classics on what is visible, literally rather than figuratively.... Many worldly, and very timely, things are implicated in this banally worked-out movie, so much like filmed science fiction. Yet what is so 'classical' as present dreams bearing some necessary resemblance both to present and future? The human race is at stake. One, more specifically classical, dilemma is the concept that man divides himself into angels and demons. Here, in this life-sized gadget shaped like a sleigh and brilliant in Metrocolor, the angelic imagination is pitted against the demonic.... This film, corny in a few obvious ways, holds enough charm, pathos and wonder to be classified as an enduring fantasy."

In *Science Fiction Studies in Film*, the woefully wrong-headed book by Frederik Pohl IV and his father, the well-known SF writer Frederik Pohl, uses a curious and highly arguable premise: films are inherently inferior to fiction. They considered the movie "good" and a "pleasure to watch," but added that "what is wrong with it is that it does not say to the audience what Wells wrote it to say." Which, of course, is beside the point; the filmmakers were adapting the story, not the philosophy. It would have been naive to emphasize the worker-elite split that's at the core of the novel; Wells was simply incorrect. Even those who read the novel today read it for its splendid story, not its message, and even the Pohls concede the story is preserved pretty much intact. Perhaps *The Time Machine* doesn't reflect Wells' socialism — but it's naive to ask it to.

More to the point, John Baxter in *Science Fiction in the Cinema* says that the script "suggests nothing of Wells's polemic and abandons the specific social allegory of the original in favor of some thin moralising about initiative and independence." Baxter then takes the film to task more for the *way* it deviates from Wells than for the fact that it does. Though I disagree, this makes more sense than the Pohls' approach.

In general, the film is still well thought-of. It has dated less severely than other Pal films, including *The War of the Worlds*. It has only a few fleeting scenes set in a roughly contemporary time; everything else, future and past, still has no immediate contact with our present. The film exists in its own time.

Except for *The Wonderful World of the Brothers Grimm* (1962), none of Pal's later films were successful, and he often went through long periods of relative inactivity. After *Brothers Grimm*, there were only three more Pal movies: *7 Faces of Dr. Lao* (1964), *The Power* (1968) and *Doc Savage, the Man of Bronze* (1975). Pal claimed to the end that he was about to make "The Disappearance," or "Lost Eden," or "Odd John," or "Voyage of the Berg," or "Return of the Time Traveler." But he seemed an anachronism in Hollywood; despite his good track record, studios were not willing to make deals with him. The public probably would have appreciated his films, and he was well-remembered; at a Filmex showing of a program of Pal's classic Puppetoons, the startled and deeply moved Pal received a standing ovation, leaving him in grateful tears and almost speechless. Despite his failings as a producer and director, George Pal was a decent, lovely man, who tried more than any other producer during his lifetime to make decent, respectable science fiction films. He didn't always succeed, but he always tried.

When he died in 1980, he was ignored by Hollywood and mostly forgotten by the moviegoing public. But though we've outgrown his films to a certain extent, and are aware of his occasional naivité and vulgarity, his concessions to the box office and the general underfinanced look of his movies, there are those of us who do remember George Pal. We eagerly anticipated each of his new films, and we were saddened by his death. Because of his career-long devotion to fantasy and science fiction, he is unique among producers, and deserves more fame than he now has. Science fiction has become a staple of

Hollywood; it's too bad Pal, who was highly regarded by filmmakers such as John Landis, isn't around to see how the seeds he sowed have grown.

12 to the Moon

This eight-day quickie, shot on a budget of $150,000, is a dismal, tedious and scientifically outrageous story of the first expedition to the Moon. It adds nothing but silliness to previous tales of lunar exploration; the special effects are minimal, the actors uninteresting and the "message" hackneyed. I have not seen it in some years, and am relying on the script for some of my commentary; the final film may have varied from the script in some particulars, but I'll stand by my judgment of the film's quality.

An international expedition of twelve scientists is launched in a rocket to the Moon; at the beginning, each is introduced by the Director of International Space Order (Francis X. Bushman). They are the captain, John Anderson (Ken Clark), an American; Hideko Murata (Michi Kobi), a Japanese of Chinese ancestry; Feodor Orloff (Tom Conway), an obstreperous Russian; Luis Vargas (Tony Dexter), from Brazil; Erik Heinrich (John Wengraf), a German with a dark past; Sigrid Bromark (Anna-Lisa), a romantic Swede; Sir William Rochester (Phillip Baird), a Briton who comes to a sad end; Etienne Martel (Roger Til), a snotty Frenchman; Asmara Makonnen (Cory Devlin), from Nigeria; Selim Hamid (Tema Bey), a romantic, fatalistic Turk; David Ruskin (Richard Weber), a peculiarly-named Pole, now a citizen of Israel; and Roddy Murdock (Bob Montgomery, Jr.), a teenaged mathematics genius discovered on a TV quiz show.

In producer Fred Gebhardt's story, scripted by the usually much better DeWitt Bodeen, each person acts in accordance with national stereotypes, and has virtually no other characterization.

On the way to the Moon, everyone spends a good deal of time in petty squabbling. We learn that Ruskin and Heinrich are pals, but Ruskin doesn't know that Heinrich is the son of the Nazi scientist responsible for the deaths of Ruskin's family. Everyone except Martel likes Roddy, and even he comes around when the boy finds a way to shield the fillings in Martel's teeth from being painfully affected by "magnetic eddy currents."

People occasionally look out the windows and have little conversations about how poetic it is or just it is that space is black instead of blue. Vargas says "it's more real, more clearly defined. Illusion is gone. We see the Universe as it is, through the naked eye of its Creator." Despite the skill of the crew, every few minutes someone expresses a doubt about their safe return. They dodge meteors. The women take showers and fix the food.

They finally land safely on the Moon and begin exploring. There's a strange concept that the Moon is continually under bombardment by showers of meteors, like hail. Several magnets are deployed to keep the meteors from hitting our intrepid dozen.

Lovers Sigrid and Hamid enter a cave alone and find a wondrous space flower, water and atmosphere. She begins acting strangely and leads him into a cloud of mist at the back of the cave. They are never seen again; when the others enter the cave, the wall of mist has become impenetrable ice.

Heinrich, Makonnen and Orloff become very excited about finding a strange, new kind of mineral. Others become jubilant over the discovery of plenty of gold here and there. This idea, that other planets will be rich in gems and precious metals turns up occasionally, even in Fritz Lang's *Frau im Mond*, but is impractical. The value of whatever is discovered on the Moon is not likely to lie in such luxury items, due to transportation costs.

A small atomic explosion causes a river of silver to run down a crater wall, and greedy Orloff tries to pick up the molten metal. Of course, this immediately burns holes in his space gloves, and after he's saved from asphyxiation, he's sent back to the ship like a naughty child.

Poor Sir William stumbles into a vast pit of powdered Moon dust, and is *sucked* out of sight to his death—even though several people try to pull him out. Anderson almost gets sucked in, but quick-thinking Roddy (who continues to be useful in crises while everyone else dithers) pulls him out with an unanchored meteor-deflecting magnet.

When the air starts to run out, the nine left return to the ship. They can't reach Earth by radio, but a magnetic tape begins exhibiting *printed* symbols that none but Hideko recognize. It is an ancient Chinese "dialect," and Hideko translates the symbols instantly and fluently. It's a message from beings who live inside the Moon, and tells them to "return to your Earth at once. You have done enough damage. You have been bombarding us for years, incessantly. Our equilibrium has been shaken. Leave us in peace." At some length, the Grand Coordinator of the Moon tells the desperate nine that Hamid and Sigrid have found a home in the underground Moon city. The Lunarians are interested in the strange emotion they show, which the two Earth people say is love. However, everyone else has to leave at once. "We could not allow you to stay among us, for you would only contaminate our perfect form of harmony."

The ship takes off for Earth (the return trip seems faster). Henrich, the oldest member, collapses and begins talking deliriously—in English—and his good friend Ruskin learns Heinrich is the son of that family-destroying Nazi pig.

As the ship approaches the Earth, the passengers observe the daily life of North America, but are puzzled to see everything halt, like a freeze-frame in a movie. The Grand Coordinator contacts them again, and reveals that all of North America has been frozen solid as another sign that we are to leave the Moon the hell alone.

There's North America, frozen solid, and there's only one thing to do: drop an atomic bomb in Mount Popocatapetl in Mexico, which will somehow reverse the freezing process. Lots are drawn, and by a remarkable coincidence, Heinrich and Ruskin are selected to pilot a little space taxi (which has no other function in the film) over the volcano and drop the bomb.

Roddy is especially worried. He was "calculating in the field of cryogenics" and discovered that "with such intense cold, the law of Earth's gravity is affected." The ship can't land. The idea that gravity is dependent on temperature is preposterous, just as is the thought that when the freezing is reversed, everyone in North America will come back to life, instead of being thawed out dead.

Martel prepares the bomb, then while Orloff is standing there, sabotages it. Martel is actually a dedicated Communist who thinks leaving North America frozen solid is a dandy idea. He's upset by Orloff's horrified reaction, and exclaims, "You are not *one of us*?" Orloff replies, "I am a scientist. I am a human being. I am not an insane murderer." They grapple, the others rush in, overcome Martel, and Ruskin and Heinrich make up then rush off to drop the bomb in the volcano, which instantly erupts, killing the two heroes.

All looks well as North America begins to thaw out (of course, it's possible that Mexico City was obliterated, but win a few, lose a few). But wait! The spaceship itself becomes all frosty! It freezes in space! Everyone becomes immobile! It's all up for the last of our explorers. But then the Moon people have a change of heart and so thaw the ship out, having been impressed by sacrifice and love. The Grand Coordinator invites everyone to come back to the Moon.

I suppose 12 to the Moon must have had plenty of special effects, but I have only a foggy memory of seeing the Earth covered with ice. Mark McGee says the effects were cheap and primitive, which is in keeping with the film's low budget. The space suits are those same military surplus high altitude suits occasionally turning up in cheap SF films. They are dramatic, but don't look like they'd work in space conditions.

In addition to numerous other scientific blunders, the Big Freeze at the climax is off in the realm of fantasy, like science in a serial or a 1950s kiddie SF TV series; it's even sillier than Flash Gordon. Freezing an entire continent—and only one—is black magic, not science. Gebhardt probably wanted a bang-up ending to distinguish his Moon movie from other Moon movies, and introduced the Freeze at this point because all other Moon movies had their crises on the satellite, not on the way back to Earth.

12 to the Moon was directed by David Bradley and written by DeWitt Bodeen. Bradley is an intelligent, interesting film history teacher (at UCLA) and collector of old films. He knows his material intimately, and is an excellent judge of the good and bad in films made by others. He made a promising beginning as a director in the 1940s, with several feature-length amateur films. He produced, photographed, directed, wrote and acted in a version of Peer Gynt (1941), did the same for an adaptation of Julius Caesar (1949, which had some commercial release in 1952), and also directed Oliver Twist in 1940. Charlton Heston's first screen appearances were in Peer Gynt and Julius Caesar. The latter film demonstrates Bradley's vivid imagination and some good ideas; it's also self-consciously "arty," and the very bad acting by some of the principals makes the film unintentionally hilarious. Nonetheless, upon seeing it, most would judge Bradley a "promising" director.

The promise was not fulfilled in his later professional films. I know nothing about Talk About a Stranger* (1952), and very little about Dragstrip Riot (1958). However, 12 to the Moon is poor in all departments. Bradley makes an effort to give the movie a slightly Gothic look, but it is still ponderous, badly acted and very heavy going. The script is hopeless, and overall, Bradley does nothing right. His later film, Madmen of Mandoras (1963), was later recut and is shown on television as They Saved Hitler's Brain. With some justice, it has become notorious as one of the worst films of all time. What survives of Bradley's footage in the film is distinctly more professional in appearance (photographed as it was by Stanley Cortez) than the rest of the film, featuring amateurish cinematography, but it is shoddily conceived, and Bradley exercises a heavy hand to no good end.

DeWitt Bodeen is also an expert on film history, and has written several books and many magazine articles on it. He is best known as a screenwriter for the films he wrote for RKO in the 1940s, including three for Val Lewton: Cat People (1942), The Seventh Victim (1943) and The Curse of the Cat People

*Joe Dante says this is "an offbeat semi-horror film with moments of true grade-B brilliance, offset by a ruinous MGM–style happy ending. His best film."

(1944). However, his movie that was most popular with average filmgoers must have been his cowritten adaptation of *I Remember Mama* (1948). Bodeen was credited with cowriting *Billy Budd* (1962), but some have disputed his claim, saying that Bodeen's credit was due to arbitration with the Writers' Guild. Among other films Bodeen wrote or cowrote were *The Enchanted Cottage* (1945), *Mrs. Mike* (1950) and *The Girl in the Kremlin* (1957). With the possible exception of *Kremlin*, *12 to the Moon* is by very far the worst film Bodeen was associated with. In general, his films show a poetic, sensitive touch, with haunted romanticism lurking around the edges. He seems to have written *12 to the Moon* according to Gebhardt's specifications.

Of the actors, only Tom Conway and John Wengraf have extensive professional credits. Conway, George Sanders' brother, was in very Sanders–like roles all through the 40s and 50s (even taking over Sanders' own character, The Falcon, in a 40s series), but eventually underwent a career decline.

Hero Ken Clark has little to do except be stalwart. Usually, someone is pulling his fat out of the fire, but he is still the hero. He appeared in *Love Me Tender* (1956) and was okay as the star of *Attack of the Giant Leeches*. See that title for more information on him.

Anthony Dexter and Francis X. Bushman both turned up in *The Phantom Planet*, and there is more information on them there. Dexter appeared in a variety of minor films after his ill-fated debut in the wildly inaccurate *Valentino*, usually in swashbuckling roles, but he soon declined to films like *Fire Maidens of Outer Space* and *Saturday Night Bath in Apple Valley* (1965). Although he was an especially stiff and inexpressive performer early in his career, he occasionally showed real promise in his worst films.

Reviews varied; most were negative. In *Motion Picture Daily*, Saul Ostrove called it "a science fiction picture unusual only in its political ramifications." "Tube" in *Variety* thought it "timely, but crude and cliché-ridden.... Its characters ... are straight out of the funnybook pages.... Under [Bradley's] guidance, the emoting is extremely stiff and postured."

The reviewer in England's *Kinematograph Weekly* thought it was a classic: "Extravagant and intriguing science-fiction melodrama.... Fascinating subject, sound acting, resourceful technical presentation."

On the other hand, the *Monthly Film Bulletin* gave *12 to the Moon* its lowest rating, dismissing it tersely: "Apart from some naive and sentimental philosophy, this juvenile piece of hokum has only its special effects and weird lunar landscape to recommend it."

As a matter of fact, the lunar landscape constructed for the film is elaborate, but resembles a rocky beach. Most of the budget must have been expended on this set, which seems to fill a large portion of a sound stage.

More recently, the film has received little notice. Leonard Maltin's *TV Movies* calls it a "bomb" and "aimless." Don Willis (I) thought it was "just plain dumb," and *Psychotronic* felt that "most of the movie is devoted to examining the astronauts and their petty, boring personal problems."

For one of the first space films to be made in the wake of real manned flights beyond the stratosphere, *12 to the Moon* is remarkably inaccurate, scientifically; as a drama, it is childish, boring and trivial, best forgotten.

Opposite: The film 12 to the Moon (1960) is no more exciting than this dull shot suggests, but at least the producers did spend money on a reasonably extensive lunar landscape.

Village of the Damned

Although hampered by a low budget, infrequent but not well-handled sentimentality, and too much ambiguity, *Village of the Damned* is very nearly a classic science fiction film. It is an original, verging on the unforgettable because of the impact and implications of its central idea. The hidden theme in the film is common to SF movies of this period — too much intelligence will make you not only a soulless robot but dangerous to others — but the presentation is so intelligent and politely low-key and the basic idea so compelling, that this well-made film is one of the most *respectable* science fiction films.

It is based reasonably closely on the novel *The Midwich Cuckoos** by John Wyndham (pseudonym of the very fully-named John Wyndham Parkes Lucas Beynon Harris), and was shot in England for around $225,000. After being temporarily shelved — MGM thought the film had no commercial possibilities — it was released in 1960 to critical acclaim and good box office. It was, in fact, so successful that *Children of the Damned* (1963) followed; not a sequel, and in fact the children in the new story were benign, it reused some of Wyndham's story ideas. *These Are the Damned* (1961) is an unconnected film for which advertising was devised to resemble that for *Village of the Damned*, hoping to fool potential audiences. (What they saw was something different but almost as good, but that's another story.) A remake of the Wyndham film has been announced several times.

The story of *Village* is simple. Wyndham's post–WWII novels were SF in the H.G. Wells vein: introduce one major fantasy element and develop its impact and implications carefully.

The small British town of Midwich is suddenly affected by a blackout. Around 11 a.m. one quiet morning, every living thing in the town abruptly falls asleep. Among those affected is Gordon Zellaby (George Sanders), a middle-aged scientist living in a mansion with his much younger wife, Anthea (Barbara Shelley). Gordon is in the middle of a phone call to his brother-in-law Maj. Alan Bernard (Michael Gwynn) when he falls asleep. Alan, worried, can't raise anyone else in Midwich, and heads for the town to investigate.

Just outside Midwich, he sees a bus at the side of the road, with no one moving. On his way to investigate the lack of communication with Midwich, a bobby falls with his bicycle as he nears the bus.

Alan contacts the military on maneuvers in the region, and a perimeter is set up around the town. A spotting plane is directed by Alan to fly quite low; the pilot falls asleep too, and crashes to his death.

Just as suddenly as they fell asleep, everyone in Midwich wakes up again, seemingly none the worse for their experience. No one can find explanations for what occurred: the field of "sleep" was static, odorless, invisible, didn't register on radar, wasn't metallic and left no residual radiation.

Despite intense official curiosity about the event, things soon return to normal in Midwich. Zellaby notes that a plant seems to have been affected by the blackout (an odd idea dropped at once), but the people who were affected are the women in the village. Every woman in Midwich capable of childbirth,

---

*So called because in Europe, cuckoos, like North American cowbirds, lay their eggs in the nests of other birds, forcing the parents to raise the cuckoos/cowbirds, which usually means the death of the other birds' offspring.

including Anthea, is pregnant. (The film avoids the use of that word.)

Gordon is overjoyed; he and Anthea had vainly hoped, until now, to have children. Others locally are not so happy. Mr. Harrington (Richard Warner) is furious that both his wife and teenage daughter are pregnant; James Pawle (Thomas Heathcote) has been away for a year, and suspects his brother Edward (actor not identified) has made James' wife Janet (Charlotte Mitchell) pregnant, although this disagreement is only hinted at. Milly (Pamela Buck) is especially upset by her condition, for she is a virgin. (Another word awkwardly avoided in the reticent script.)

Zellaby and local Dr. Willers (Laurence Naismith) realize that the pregnancies all date precisely from the blackout. When they realize this, the women are quite naturally terrified, for they have been well and truly violated.

Time passes quickly. Three months later, and the women are being examined by a mobile clinic set up for the purpose. Five months later, the embryos have the development of those of seven months. The babies are all born on the same night; each of the twelve children (it was 60 in the novel, where budget is not a consideration) weighs around ten pounds at birth, all have pale blonde hair, "strange" eyes, fingernails that cover less than normal of the finger, and hair which is a **D** in cross section.

Four months after the children are born, they show the development of 18-month-old children. And they show other things, too. As Gordon is talking with a visitor, they are interrupted by a scream, and rush upstairs to find Anthea blindly thrusting her hand into boiling water. Her quiet son David sits in his crib placidly watching. His bottle was too warm for his pleasure, and so he reacted.

When the children are a year old (but looking like three-year-olds), Gordon demonstrates a remarkable discovery to Alan. He shows David how to manipulate the secret slides on a Chinese puzzle box to open a small drawer where Gordon has hidden a piece of candy, which David pops into his mouth. Gordon leads Alan to the Harrington house, where there are two of the "blackout" children. He hands the box to the first, a little girl; without being shown its solution, she promptly opens it and takes out the candy. What one child knows, Gordon says, they all know; they have only one brilliant mind among them: one mind with twelve bodies.

He hands the box to the other blackout child, who begins operating the box's slides, but it is snatched by a normal Harrington child. The eyes of both the strange children begin glowing, and the normal boy is forced against his will to return the box to the second blackout child.

Four years later, the Children look around nine years old. They dress alike. Walking smoothly and unhesitatingly, more like adults than children, they move around the village in little groups. By now, Anthea's son David (Martin Stephens) has become the spokesperson of the group; despite their group mind, he does occasionally have to stop one of the Children from showing individual initiative (a script error, made for good reasons). A normal kid bounces a ball off one of the Children, and David dissuades the offended one from retaliating. (We later learn that a normal child who taunted the Children inexplicably drowned in the local pond.)

The villagers have become distrustful of the blackout children, but don't know how to deal with them. (Note: the plot seems a little unclear at this point; the Children visit a local shop to buy supplies, but what they are buying and why, as they still live with their mothers, is unanswered.)

The Children decide it would be best for their purposes if they all moved to

a house on the edge of Midwich, where Gordon can continue instructing them, as he has for several years now. He's fascinated by their intellects; Alan fears that the Children are evil, but Gordon believes they can readily be taught morals and ethics precisely because of their great intelligence.

Earlier, in one of several conferences we see with other military and scientific leaders, we learned that there were several other instances of blackouts in widely separated areas of the world. In northern Australia, something went wrong and all the children died. In an Eskimo community in northern Canada, again none of the children survived and the implication is that the fathers— upset by the birth of blonde children to Eskimo mothers—killed the infants. That definitely happened in Irkutsk in Mongolia—the children *and* their mothers were murdered by the outraged men. In the Soviet Union, all the children survived and are being trained by the State.

Several ideas concerning the children are bandied about, but no one (*ever*) decides what really happened. Another scientist suggests that as the mutation theory doesn't explain the blackouts, that perhaps some kind of radiation from another planet, a combined pregnancy-blackout ray, may have been used. Gordon tells the conference that he, too, thinks that's the most likely theory, but it's never confirmed.

A military leader wants to destroy the children at once—their power is increasing, and they clearly have no feelings for human beings; they do not care who or what they hurt. But Gordon successfully convinces them to allow him one year more to see if he can convince the children to aid their adopted world.

Gordon later is told by the children that they can read minds, but as yet not deeply, though their power is growing. They have been nervous before when planes flew over, but are not now: their power extends that far. He also asks them if they are aware of life on another planet, and they all lower their eyes in unison. (This is what is known as a cop-out.)

As David prepares to move into the house, walking solemnly along with his concerned but wary mother, some other Children come out of an alley near them, and are almost struck by a passing car driven by Edward Pawle. He apologizes profusely, but the Children give him their glowing stare; he climbs into the car again and drives head-on into a brick wall. The car explodes. (And David very faintly smiles.)

At the inquest, Anthea is telepathically prevented from revealing her conviction that the Children forced the "accident." As she walks home with Gordon and Alan, James Pawle passes them, carrying a shotgun, prepared to kill the Children. But Gordon and the others dissuade him—more from concern for what the Children might do to him than for what he might do to them—and he reluctantly starts home. But the Children see him. One freezes Gordon, Alan and Anthea with a look, while the others turn their full power on hapless James. He hesitatingly lowers the shotgun, places the barrels under his chin, and pulls the trigger.

At home, Gordon begins to despair of reaching the children; it's as though, he muses, their minds were surrounded by—he glances over the fireplace—a

Opposite: The alien-fathered children from the well-done Village of the Damned (1960) try to stare us down. Martin Stephens, foreground, is the spokesperson for the cold-blooded little bastards. One explanation for their disquieting appearance is that the children were actually dark-complected; the fair hair makes them seem slightly out of the ordinary.

brick wall. The conference reports that the village of children in the Soviet Union is no more. The Children there developed faster and had taken over the town completely; an army squad sent in merely to rescue the normal inhabitants was forced to kill each other. A long-range cannon "test-fired" an atomic shell and the Soviet village of blackout children, as well as all its normal inhabitants, was "accidentally" destroyed.

Led by Harrington, the villagers pay a torch-carrying visit to the Children's isolated home. David confronts the frightened, belligerent men. He forces Harrington to drop his torch, which (in an unconvincing scene) ignites his clothing. Again smiling very faintly, David turns his back on the blazing man, and returns to the house. Alan, who was passing and saw all this, confronts the children, but they surround him, chanting "leave us alone" and Alan's eyes go all pearly.

Later, Dr. Willers says that although Alan is now returning to normal, it was the worst case of shock he had ever seen. (There's no good plot reason why the children didn't kill Alan.)

David returns to the Zellaby house for a final visit, and Gordon has a conversation with his strangely adult "son." David says they are going to spread out and disperse; they will soon reach the stage when they can form new colonies (i.e. be capable of reproduction). The Children more or less trust Gordon, as he has seemed to worship intelligence, and David blithely assumes that Gordon will assist them in sneaking out of Midwich. He directs Zellaby to report to them on Friday.

Friday comes, and Gordon sends Anthea and Alan off to London. He prepares a time bomb set for 8:30, placing it in his briefcase. Knowing he will have to have some way to avoid the Children's telepathic probings, he fastens on that brick wall image again, trying to keep that in the forefront of his mind. He arrives at the isolated house and begins at once some meaningless school lesson. The Children insist on knowing what arrangements he has made for spiriting them out of the village. They try to read his mind but can get only an image of a brick wall. They try to force their way past this literal mind block (and we see it literally crumble); they succeed in doing so just as the clock reaches 8:30. The Children turn as one to the briefcase, but it's too late: the bomb goes off, killing the Children and Zellaby.

Anthea and Alan, who turned back to Midwich moments before, see the explosion from a distance.

In an interview with Tony Crawley in *Starburst* #4, mostly on the subject of Stirling Silliphant's planned production of Stirling Lanier's novel *Hiero's Journey*,* the screenwriter talked about his involvement with *Village of the Damned*, originally to have been produced by Milo Frank. Silliphant said that Wyndham's novel was bought by MGM in an unusually direct and immediate fashion: "I remember they had microfilm made of each page as he finished typing the manuscript. This was then flown over to us in Hollywood, typed up and given to us to work from.... The change came when turning the finished script over. It wasn't to the people who had gone to all this microfilming trouble, but another bunch of people appalled to find they had bought what they termed an 'anti–Catholic' film." Silliphant told Crawley that the studio personnel felt the impregnation of the village women "parallelled the

---

*Oddly, Starburst assumed that Stirling Lanier was a pen name for Stirling Silliphant. They are two different men, despite the coincidence of their first names. Hiero's Journey was never filmed, incidentally.

Immaculate Conception." As a result, the studio "junked the script. Put it on the shelf. I got so mad I broke my contract with MGM and went into television." When the film was finally made, Silliphant's name was on the script, "and the best reviews I've ever had in my twenty years of writing came on that film." Silliphant was writing the film as a vehicle for Ronald Colman, who died before it was made.

After worrying about the script for a couple of years, MGM apparently decided to try to recoup their losses in all that microfilming, air freight and options, and hired Wolf Rilla, a then-promising director, to film the movie for MGM's British branch in a great rush. Rilla told interviewer Al Taylor in *Fangoria* #5 that six weeks after he was contacted, he was filming the movie.

Because of Silliphant's unfamiliarity with English village life, Rilla and his producer Ronald Kinnoch realized the script needed to be rewritten — in a great hurry. They divided the script up between them and did a rewrite over a weekend (Kinnoch is credited as "George Barclay"). The first draft had to be rewritten again, however, and some characters were removed, such as Zellaby's adult daughter, mother of one of the Children; Anthea was made the blackout mother (in the novel, her child is normal), and Alan is made Gordon's brother-in-law rather than his son-in-law. Events were compressed, and the film was quickly shot. Locations used were found swiftly: Letchmore Heath, near Borehamwood Studios where interiors were shot, was used as Midwich, primarily because of its proximity to the studio.

Rilla told Taylor that he insisted on a documentary-style approach. "It made, I think, the weird happenings even stranger. I remember having some arguments with the studio heads about the approach to the film.... It seemed to me the horrors were so much more horrible because they were so much more normal. I wanted the children to look nice, to be apparently very pleasant." Rilla is quoted further in *Science Fiction Studies in Film* that the studio suggested "that all the children should be harelipped or hunchbacked or something," but Rilla, who says he's read most of Wyndham's work, insisted on maintaining the look of the Children as described in the novel: ordinary, even attractive children, with unusual eyes and gleaming, golden hair.

Rilla's direction of the children was ingenious. He wanted them not to behave like ordinary kids at all. He told Al Taylor, "I've got to confess I've been complimented over the years for my direction of the children. And who am I to scoff at compliments? In fact, there was no particular art to directing these children. The trick was entirely in the concept.

"The only principle from which I started was that the normal behavior of children is very restless.... I made these children keep very still at all times, move very deliberately, in a very unchildlike way.... They sat upright and very still; they stood very still.... That is what made them rather frightening."

They chose ordinary children, matching them for size and unusually dark eyes (like Stephens, the others were probably brunettes) — Rilla thought the contrast between the dark eyes and the pale hair would be striking. Their wigs were designed to give their heads a domed appearance. The studio still wanted something they could use heavily in the advertising, some visual device, and effects man Tom Howard came up with the gimmick that, to this day, MGM remains convinced is what sold the film. (Typical thickheaded studio thinking.)

Howard used two small matte inserts of just the iris of the children's eyes, and reversed them, positive for negative. The result is those startling, glowing eyes that some people remember so well from the film. The first time it is used it is arresting indeed, but primarily because the children with the glowing eyes are so young. The device is heavily overused and so becomes comic — audiences sometimes howled with laughter. There are some scenes of the Children giving their whammy in which the glowing-eye mattes were not employed, and the dark, deep eyes seem much creepier than the whited-out pupils. (Some Americans believe that the glowing eyes were not used in the British prints, but that seems to be incorrect.)

These glowing eyes are virtually the only special effect in the film. The crumbling wall that Zellaby tries to keep in his mind at the climax is another, but it's minor and not unusual. The miniature of the children's house is poor; it would have sufficed if flames weren't necessary, but the impossibility of "miniaturizing" flames calls attention to the small size of the house model.

One final effect in the film is nothing less than a terrible idea, so damaging to the film that, despite its momentary use, it ruined it for some people. To this day, some despise the film as claptrap because of that wildly ill-considered last shot. Over the burning wreckage of the house, the Children's eyes (without heads) appear again, glowing against the fire, they go flitting off into the sky like matched pairs of fireflies. Not only comic, it heavily damaged the suggestion of the film, that the children are the offspring of aliens; this shot makes it seem that somehow the eyes possessed the children, by magic, and have gone in search of other children to possess. It was probably intended to be metaphorical, to suggest that the aliens can do all this again, but film is a *literal* medium: you show this, and it is real, not metaphorical.

On the level of production, the film is a model of low-budget filmmaking. The photography by Geoffrey Faithfull is very simple, clear and clean. For the most part, Rilla and Faithfull resist stylistic touches. Several scenes end with the camera panning off to some significant object, and there are several crane shots. But the camera is not restless; most scenes involve some movement, but it is not emphasized. Although, as Rilla told Taylor, he had to trick his way out of shooting a particular close-up of George Sanders, the film does have many close-ups as it is: as befitting one of the central images, eyes are often emphasized. Composition and staging are notably good, with the still, fair children in the dark, heavy overcoats often placed in scenes with adults and almost never with other children. There's one overhead shot, as the children crowd around Gwynn. In the final sequence, in which Zellaby concentrates on that wall, there's some elegant, swift camera movement, which, used with imaginative superimpositions, good choice of angles and speedy editing, makes the scene alive with swiftly-built tension.

The editing throughout is notably good. Like the overall style of the film, it's not flashy, but editor Gordon Hales can rise to the appropriate occasion, as in the shocking scene of the car smashing into the (other) brick wall, the only on-screen violence in the film.

One major virtue of the film not often remarked on is the excellent use of sound and sound effects, credited to A.W. Watkins — but I presume the dramatic use of sound is the responsibility of the director. The credits have no music behind them at all, just the sound of the village clock tolling 11. After the small plane crashes, the shocked onlookers are silent. The night the Children are born, the village men gather in the pub, but all are silent except for ordering their pints. Sounds that are used are sometimes sharper and louder than natural, usually intruding on a quiet scene, as when Anthea screams while plunging her hand into the boiling water.

Rilla is clearly trying for naturalism whenever he can. As Gordon demonstrates the Chinese box to Alan, there's an almost successful attempt at naturalistic muttering ("that's right," "now push there," etc.), quite unusual in films of the day. In one memorable scene, sound and camera movement are used together naturalistically to convey the sense of eerie quiet in Midwich just after the blackout begins: the camera cranes slowly over the village street, with people scattered here and there, and rises slowly as we hear a wind-up phonograph slowly run down, the repeating music becoming slower and slower.

However, there are several flaws in the presentation. We never see enough of the daily life of Midwich to believe in it as a small town; it steadfastly remains a collection of character actors we see only when necessary for the story. Every scene makes its point, but there are no scenes of normal village life to compare with the weird changes that follow the blackout. There's a silly bit with Gordon's dog Bruno growling at the newborn David, another idea which pushes the film in the direction of a supernatural explanation. From their simple, stark presentation, the reactions to the pregnancies verge on the comic.

Though sparse, the music is standard creepy-crawly stuff of little distinction. Composer Ron Goodwin also scored another John Wyndham film, *Day of the Triffids*, as well as *Children of the Damned*. He improved as the 60s wore on, and proved himself most adept at jaunty, bouncy scores, such as the title theme for Margaret Rutherford's Miss Marple films, and the extravagant score for *Those Magnificent Men in Their Flying Machines*. (Which condemned Goodwin to scoring *Those Fantastic Flying Fools* and *Those Daring Young Men in Their Jaunty Jalopies*.) His scores for adventure films, like those for his few SF and horror films, were conventional; there's little to remember about his scores for *633 Squadron*, *Operation Crossbow* or *Where Eagles Dare*.

The acting is generally excellent. Some have criticized George Sanders for walking through the role of Gordon Zellaby (something he sometimes did when he didn't give a damn), but that's a puzzling reaction, based on a recent viewing of the film. Sanders is clearly involved with his role; he may have been intrigued by the film's premise, or liked working with Rilla. It was a starring role, something that didn't often come his way during this period. Sanders was always an underplayer, in a traditionally cool British manner, lacing his performances with sardonic wit. He's doing that here, too—it fits Zellaby's own controlled manner. The only time Sanders looks uncomfortable is when he's required to react in a highly clichéd manner upon learning his wife is pregnant: he's awkward and unconvincing. At other times, such as in the eerie scenes with the Children, he's in control and on target. In fact, a great deal of the strength of the film comes from Sanders' fine performance.

The unexpected popularity of the film seems to have helped somewhat in reviving his career — he hadn't appeared in a successful film in some time—and he turned up in some relatively major films in the next couple of years, including *In Search of the Castaways* (1962) and *A Shot in the Dark* (1964). However, in the late 60s, his career again declined, and he was clearly once again walking through his roles. After appearing in *The Body Stealers* (1969), *The Kremlin Letter* (1970), *Doomwatch* and *Psychomania* (1972), Sanders wrote a note saying he found life too boring to continue, and killed himself.

Barbara Shelley is an attractive, talented actress who seems to have been trapped by her frequent appearances in horror and science fiction films. In addition to *Village of the Damned*, Shelley appeared in *The Cat Girl* (1957), *Blood of the Vampire*, *Bobbikins* (1959), *Shadow of the Cat* (1961), *The Gorgon* (1964), *Rasputin the Mad Monk*, *Dracula Prince of Darkness* (both 1965), *Five Million Years to Earth* (1967) and *Ghost Story* (1974). She's also worked occasionally in the genres on television.

In *Village of the Damned*, she's required only to be attractive and feminine and to impersonate a good wife and mother; however, within the restrictions of the role, she's intelligent and believable. It's hard to imagine a lonely middle-aged man *not* falling in love with her. Shelley does her best to fill out the details of Anthea—note her almost instantaneous hesitation on entering David's room—but the script hems her in, just as being typed in horror films hemmed in Shelley's career.

Michael Gwynn plays Alan as a decent, understanding chap, actually one of the two pivots of the film. He's required at one point to say the Children are evil, but it's clear he doesn't really believe it. Like Shelley's, Gwynn's role does not require detailed acting or a strong characterization, but he is more than acceptable. For more on Gwynn, see the entry on *Revenge of Frankenstein,* in which he played the Monster.

Apart from Sanders, the one actor people remember most clearly from *Village of the Damned* is Martin Stephens as David. Ten when the film was made, Stephens was a beautiful child, with delicate, angelic features, slightly pouty lips, and wide-set, dark brown eyes. Almost any British child, especially a well-behaved, polite one, seems a little odd to most Americans, but there never was one like this. Icy, distant, controlled, anything but a fiend, Stephens' David is one of the eeriest children in film history. The script gives him adult dialogue, and his controlled, specific movements make him seem like a miniature grown-up rather than a child. There's no gaiety to him, no spontaneity—David is a little iceberg. And he's at once both amusing—*such* a serious child!—and scary as hell. A child who has no fear at all of adult power is unnerving, even if he or she has no powers. There's also something faintly androgynous about David, as if gender is of little importance now, and will never be greatly important. But we also know his ruthlessness and beauty will enable him to get any woman he wants. He's blown up not a minute too soon. This is one of the most remarkable performances by a child in any science fiction or fantasy film, and I'd very much like to know what instructions Rilla gave him; it is a powerful performance even by adult standards.

Not long thereafter, Stephens was back with an even better performance in one of the great horror films, *The Innocents* (1961). He was precocious there, too (and had his own dark hair), but to Miles, the character he played, his precocity was merely a game he played, though he also had aristocratic imperiousness. It was again a strong, compelling performance. However, it was essentially Stephens' swan song.

He'd been in films as early as 1958's *Another Time, Another Place,* and in the next few years appeared in, among others, *Harry Black and the Tiger* (1958), *Count Your Blessings, The Witness* (both 1959) and *A Touch of Larceny* (1960). By 1961, he had become the leading male child star in England, but was eclipsed internationally by Hayley Mills, just as talented, but with the added advantage of having an adorableness Stephens lacked. His roles after 1961 were few: *The Hellfire Club* (1961, in a brief scene), *The Battle of the Villa Fiorita* (1965) and, finally, *The Devil's Own* (1966), in which he is almost unrecognizable and demonstrates little of his earlier ability. According to his *Innocents* costar Pamela Franklin, Stephens lost all interest in acting as he grew older, and at last report, was working as an architect in London. Some consider it almost a crime when an actor as talented as Martin Stephens was gives up the profession, but his first duty is to himself. Franklin added that Stephens was very happy working as an architect; that's more important than doing good work in a profession you dislike.

Wolf Rilla apparently worked primarily in minor films before *Village of the Damned*; titles include *Noose for a Lady* (1953), *The Blue Peter* (1955), *Pacific Destiny* (1956) and *The Scamp* (1957); only *Bachelor of Hearts* (1958) seems to have gained him any recognition before *Village*. He also directed *Piccadilly Third Stop* (1960), *Cairo* (also with Sanders), *The World Ten Times Over* (both 1963), *Secrets of a Door-to-Door Salesman* (1973), *Bedtime with Rose* (1974) and *Naughty Wives* (1976). He also wrote a book on filmmaking, *A–Z of Making Movies*. He is the son of well-known character actor Walter Rilla.

None of Rilla's other films gained him even a small percentage of the acclaim he justly received for *Village of the Damned*. It seems the studios just did not believe that the quality and success of the film was due to him — even though he directed and cowrote it. He told Taylor in *Fangoria* that he was personally fond of science fiction, but though he made a successful science fiction film, he's never been hired to direct another. MGM seems to have assumed it was those damned glowing eyes that sold it, not the skill with which it was made.

The film's story has certain flaws, principally its ambiguity. In the novel, there was no doubt whatever that the children's fathers were from outer space: something like a spacecraft was seen on the ground in Midwich by an aerial spotter during the blackout. In the film, there's a suggestion that the women were impregnated by long-range radiation. But that raises another question: what was the purpose of the blackout? If you can zap a woman into pregnancy from millions of miles away, why do you have to put everyone around her to sleep first, including dogs and farm animals? In the novel, the blackout was necessary because the aliens were walking around Midwich in person, and the impregnation was accomplished physically (though, one hopes, not in the normal fashion, which raises unpleasant images of extraterrestrial necrophilia).

Rilla and his writers, perhaps under the direction of MGM, backed away from explicit explanations of the phenomenon, so far that some viewers have assumed the children were some kind of natural mutation (the explanation used in *Children of the Damned*), while others believed they were the work of evil spirits. Ambiguity is sometimes useful to a film; not all questions that are raised need to be answered. But in this case, it seems like overcaution, a fear of being lumped in with the cheaper SF films. *Village* raises questions and then withdraws from the answers.

The powers of the Children are greater than those they exhibit in the novel; the sixty children have two group minds, one male and one female, and look so much alike that even Zellaby cannot always tell them apart. Other than reducing the number of children to 12, a necessity, the changes were practical and intelligent.

It's almost ironic that one of the words most often used, even by me, to describe *Village of the Damned* is "intelligent," for in some ways, the film is an attack on that quality. At the core of the story is that hoary cliché of science fiction films: too much intelligence isn't good for you. In that sense, the Children aren't much different from the Brain from Planet Arous; they are so smart they are soulless, and are here to take over. We've seen this again and again in the films I've discussed: when you get too smart, you lose your humanity. This seems to indicate a kind of worship of the status quo; we, the current human race, may be imperfect, but we are better than anything else out there (or in here). We love, we laugh, we care — while all those overbrainy aliens, whether they be flying brains or glowing-eyed children, lack our virtues. They've sacrificed emotion for the amplification of intellect. This attitude is so prevalent in these films that the few of the period that go against the grain can be counted on the fingers of one hand. (Four: *The Day the Earth Stood Still*, *Stranger from Venus*, *The Cosmic Man* and *The 27th Day*.)

Still, one of the worst reasons not to tell a good story is because some elements have been told by inferiors before; Wyndham's novel was certainly worth filming. And in the novel, Wyndham isn't so clearly condemning advanced intelligence as merely working out a particularly eerie and, so far as I can recall, unique method of alien invasion.*

The film has such great power because this central idea is so disturbing, striking both men and women in areas that are among their most vulnerable. One common belief among fathers at one point or another is that perhaps his child isn't really his; and sometimes women resent that creature growing within them during pregnancy. Wyndham's simple, brilliant idea trades on those fears and others as well; it may be one of the most basic, primal ideas ever created in science fiction.

But there's more too it, too. The relationship between adults and children is always complicated and at times disturbing. There are aphorisms, wisecracks and even entire stories about how children really aren't little human beings, but alien creatures, fairies, sprites, nasty little things here to take over the world. (And in a metaphorical sense, that's exactly true.) Children don't think like adults; that is part of their charm, of course, but it can also be more than a little unnerving. These children don't just act weird, they really *are* from outer space.

Furthermore, children represent innocence, coming into the world trailing Wordsworth's clouds of glory. We are bombarded with the idea that childhood is our great time of innocent joy (although children usually have altogether different opinions on that point), and we want children to bounce about harmlessly, with laughing abandon. To see solemn, black-clad children walking in a tight little cluster, passing ordinary kids playing, is an image that is at once frightening and amusing. In each child is the implicit adult, and the adults these children will become are people we don't want as neighbors.

Finally, the idea of destroying the children raises feelings of ambivalence in most audiences. (Most *adult* audiences, that is; kids were longing to blow up the cold little bastards from the moment they saw them.) Children are our hope for the future, and in the story Zellaby is the spokesperson for this viewpoint. Longer than it would seem possible, based on a bare reading of the plot, it seems reasonable to let them go on living. It isn't, in fact, until David coolly tells Zellaby that soon they will be able to form new colonies, that the deaths of the Children seem mandatory. As long as they are beautiful (if dangerous) children, that's one thing—but they will all too soon be beautiful and dangerous teenagers, bent on impregnating or being impregnated by every Earthling they encounter. Alien children are eerily disturbing; alien teenagers are a force too monstrous to reckon with. (That's not really a cheap joke; in the film it isn't the "teenage" mythos that's scary, but rather their intention of forming colonies.)

When the film was completed, Rilla told Taylor in *Fangoria*, "the dis-

---

A later novel, Shepherd Mead's The Carefully Considered Rape of the World (1965), had invading spacemen with ray guns which impregnated women, but the offspring resembled baboons. Jack Williamson's The Moon Children (1972) turn out to be asexual alien envoys. The movie The Godsend (1980) has another cuckoo child that kills its "siblings," but the mother in question seems to be an unusual human being.

tributors felt so uncertain about [it] that they actually left it on their shelves for quite a few months. MGM believed they had a dud on their hands—they showed a print to British theatre circuits and none of them would take it. It lay molding away for some time; it only came out by accident. One of the British cinemas owned by MGM in London happened to have a gap between pictures, so they ran *Village of the Damned*." It was an immediate financial success.

The first review of the film was anything but favorable; "Rich" in *Variety* panned it: "George Sanders' name is not enough to sell this rather tired and sick film which starts off promisingly but soon nosedives into bathos. It is merely a moderate filler for undiscriminating audiences.... If there had happened to be any hint of why this remarkable business should have occurred the film would have been slightly more plausible.... Should moppets be used in such unpleasant pix?" (Actually, the children probably had fun.)

Later reviews were more favorable. The *Monthly Film Bulletin* gave the movie its highest rating. It was very unusual for that magazine to praise a British work in this genre. The reviewer called it an excellent adaptation of the novel, capturing Wyndham's "ruthless ingenuity; the story is original as things go and has grip, the village background is pleasing, and Wolf Rilla's direction (except for some irksome glimpses of George Sanders' marital bliss) both sharp and discreet. Altogether, in fact, with chillingly effective performances from the children to add to the tension, this is probably the neatest science fiction film yet to have come out of a British studio."

John L. Scott in the *Los Angeles Times* liked the film with some reservations: "As a Wyndham fan, I found the cinema version less effective than the book." (At the time, Wyndham was one of the extremely few SF writers ordinary people felt comfortable in admitting they liked.) He felt the "fatalistic, conventional ending solves nothing," even though it was Wyndham's own. "The cast performs competently. Sanders seems a bit puzzled by the strange assignment, which is a definite change of pace from his usually suave villain roles, but offers a reasonably good characterization."

Reporting on it in the *Los Angeles Mirror*, Margaret Harford disliked the film. "A clever, macabre science fiction idea gets stalled in a flood of incredible melodrama and *Village of the Damned* turns out to be as jerrybuilt as its countless predecessors.... The ending is a letdown because it solves nothing.... The kids are totally unsympathetic [!] and blond wigs give them the look of trick-or-treaters on Halloween." Did she want them to be *sympathetic*? Yipe. And no, the ending doesn't prevent the aliens from doing the same thing over again. So what?

Howard Thompson didn't flinch in this one. In the *New York Times*, he allowed that while it "doesn't rank with the horror classics of the screen, not by a mile-long werewolf's whisker, [nonetheless] as a quietly civilized exercise on the fear and power of the unknown this picture is one of the trimmest, most original and serenely unnerving little chillers in a long time.... The fadeout is blunt, abrupt, and about as logical as could be expected. The picture will get you, we guarantee, and anyone coming upon it cold will exit colder. Under Mr. Rilla's smooth guidance ... the incidents unfold with eerie placidity and awful conviction."

Time liked it. "*Village* is one of the neatest little horror pictures produced since Peter Lorre went straight." So did *Parents*: "this is science fiction at its low budget best."

Although not often shown today, for the most part *Village* has maintained its early reputation. Don Willis (I) is about the most dissatisfied viewer: "*Village* has imaginative stretches and powerful bursts of violence, but 'human interest' angles in the plot and typical dull s-f film dialogue weaken the film."

Psychotronic called it "excellent British science fiction," and Alan Frank (*SF*) considered it "a superior adapatation of Wyndham's science fiction classic with near unbearable tension and a stunning opening sequence. Direction, script (apart from some tedious excursions into domestic conflict), and performances are all excellent and the movie stands out as a near classic of the genre."

John Baxter, who perversely preferred the interesting but inferior "sequel," considered *Village* "a routine reading of Wyndham, deriving little atmosphere from the story.... George Sanders as the investigator of this phenomenon has the right air of icy detachment ... but the story is told with a slowness and lack of involvement almost worthy of silent cinema.... Unfortunately the entire film lacks a coherent style." (*Science Fiction in the Cinema*.)

The follow-up, *Children of the Damned*, tried an about-face: there are only six children (with normal hair) born around the world, but though they are superintelligent and mutually telepathic (and emotionless), they are not villainous, nor do they have alien fathers. They are, in fact, more or less the Second Coming en masse, but the conclusion leaves us with six Christs and no Resurrection. It was an interesting attempt to make a legitimate *variation* on Wyndham's themes, instead of just aping the first film, but it was mostly a device to sell those glowing eyes again. Scenes of the children forcing their will on others didn't jibe with their benign intent. It was a nice try, but it didn't have anything like the impact, commercially or artistically, of *Village of the Damned*.

The idea of doing a remake is probably going to remain that. In the intervening years there have been many movies about evil children (mostly supernatural), and the story idea has been robbed of some of its uniqueness.

Village of the Damned is rarely shown these days, which is curious. Although it has its share of mistakes and occasionally is comical when it should be eerie, it is still a powerful, even haunting little chiller.

Visit to a Small Planet

As science fiction became more profitable (if not more respectable), it began to turn up in major studio films. Jerry Lewis, not long shed of Dean Martin, took the plunge with *Visit to a Small Planet*, very loosely based on Gore Vidal's television and Broadway play of the same name.

However, the film is more fantasy than science fiction. The basic idea is that aliens will (a) look just like us, (b) be curious about our strange emotion of love, and (c) work magic, being from outer space. Vidal wasn't required to make his alien anything other than a dark angel, or a full-sized elf; the science fiction trappings were only to make it more topical. Kreton, the alien, might just as well have strolled in from fairyland as from another planet.

Vidal is a sharp, observant satirist, and his play was primarily a satirical look at mankind's activities, seen as futile and silly, even puny (hence "small planet" in the title). Kreton was a lofty, arrogant and altogether superior sort, sarcastic and cynical. At the climax, it is revealed that Kreton is an alien *child*, despite his appearance; it was very Vidalesque to make this superior, threatening sophisticate a spoiled child, but one still superior to Earthlings.

Jerry Lewis and his flying saucer arrive on Earth for a Visit to a Small Planet (1960); he's carrying a carpetbag because he thinks the United States is still involved in the Civil War. The film isn't bad for a Lewis vehicle, but it is not what the author intended.

The play was first presented on "TV Playhouse," 5 August 1955, with Cyril Ritchard as the alien. (Supporting America's undying suspicion that the British are our social superiors.) Vidal rewrote the work, and it was successfully staged for Broadway; Ritchard repeated as Kreton.

The play must have been popular and well-known, or it would not have been purchased for filming. Paramount then altered it drastically to fit Jerry Lewis' antic, slapstick screen persona. *This* Kreton really is a cretin – Lewis' character "That Kid" as a stranger from another world, acting about the same, but gifted with wacky powers.

The film opens somewhere in outer space, at a kind of school for young spacemen. As Jack Moffitt said, "Since they all live eternally, there is no need for sex among them, and they find it hard to understand love, which is such an important element in the affairs of the small planet Earth." Kreton, whose hobby is studying Earth, defies the orders of his teacher Delton (John Williams), and takes off in his flying saucer to study our planet firsthand.

Believing it's still the period of the Civil War, he arrives in Virginia dressed as a Confederate general. He saunters into the home of Roger Putnam Spelding (Fred Clark), a colossally misinformed broadcaster, a fanatic right-winger (though political considerations are assiduously soft-pedaled), who has just been telling everyone there is no life in outer space.

Because a masquerade is going on, at first no one pays attention to Kreton, but the next day, he demonstrates his powers. By using what he calls "the 14," he can make anyone's secret thoughts audible, proving embarrassing to

Spelding and his family. This convinces them that Kreton is indeed from outer space. He levitates Spelding's toupee, and reveals that he is surrounded by an invisible force field, like a glass wall, which prevents anyone from touching him.

Hoping to prevent his antispaceman broadcast from making him look ridiculous when Kreton reveals himself to the world, Spelding insists that the slaphappy alien remain in seclusion as his houseguest. Inasmuch as Kreton has begun falling in love with the broadcaster's daughter Ellen (Joan Blackman), he is only too happy to do so. This does not sit well with Conrad (Earl Holliman), Ellen's fiancé, but he puts up with things for a while.

Delton meets Kreton in the nearby woods, and sternly warns him not to become further involved in Earthly affairs, but although Kreton agrees, he continues his meddling. George Abercrombie (Jerome Cowan), a clichéd Madison Avenue advertising man, threatens to fire Spelding from his broadcasting job, but Kreton uses his spaceman powers to blackmail Abercrombie into allowing Spelding to continue.

Furthermore, Kreton can talk with animals, and he causes the Spelding's pets, a cat (Rhubarb) and dog, to end their longtime antagonism. The cat even becomes friendly with a mouse.

He begins to have trouble with local civil defense warden Mayberry (Gale Gordon), who vainly seeks to photograph Kreton to prove his existence. He can't *tell* anyone about the visitor; whenever he tries, Kreton's magic makes Mayberry recite "Mary Had a Little Lamb."

Kreton has some encounters in town, visiting a local beatnik hangout and being chased by cops. He and Ellen get away, however, when Kreton uses his powers to make the cops' pants fall down, and Ellen's car to fly. (It's hard to envision Cyril Ritchard doing this sort of thing.)

Kreton becomes frustrated when he can't kiss Ellen—that force field prevents it—and so, to teach him a lesson, Delton turns Kreton into a human being, and he loses his powers. (I told you it was magic.)

By now, Conrad has eloped with Ellen. When Kreton realizes this, he tries to tell pleasant lies about his feelings concerning Ellen, but Delton uses "the 14" on him, and Kreton blurts out the truth. Conrad punches him. Kreton tries to flee in his flying saucer, but it's gone.

There's a big chase climax, with Mayberry and other civil defense workers arriving en masse with the state militia, who use lots of water and tear gas. At the last moment, Delton restores Kreton's powers and his flying saucer, and he zooms back into space, dangling by his fingertips.

Perhaps the differences between the play and the movie are best exemplified by the ways the two Kretons demonstrate their powers. Kreton/Ritchard blows up a globe of the Earth to show that he can do the same to the real planet; Kreton/Lewis makes cops' pants fall down. Satire is turned into slapstick, and although the movie is slightly more cerebral than most Jerry Lewis films, it's still a vehicle for him.

After Lewis' split with Martin, the quality and budgets of his films underwent a sharp decline for a while, although things improved for him by 1960. (This was filmed in 1959, and was the last Lewis film produced by Hal Wallis.) But the revenues from the films, according to Arthur Marx's book on the team, were never as high as Lewis likes to pretend. They turned a profit, but were almost never blockbusters. He seems to have had a contract with Paramount that was unusual in that it was more restrictive on the studio than on Lewis.

Still, things couldn't have been as bad as some writers have claimed—*Small*

Planet was one of three Jerry Lewis films released in 1960. His next, *The Bellboy*, was his first as director. He made 15 further films as a star until 1970; *Which Way to the Front?* was the last in a series of increasingly less profitable Lewis films.

However, he bounced back in a big way in 1979 with *Hardly Working*. Since then, he's made several films, but only Martin Scorsese's excellent *The King of Comedy* (1983) had significant distribution. The other Lewis films made during this period, including the science fictional *Slapstick of Another Kind* (1984, finally) are either the work of relative amateurs or are made by Lewis himself. (One was made in France.)

Lewis can be a good comedian and, as *King of Comedy* showed, an outstanding dramatic actor as well. Unfortunately, Lewis is a tireless egocentric who insists on being involved in all phases of a production, even those he seems basically unqualified for, such as direction. He tried again at a TV series in 1984, but it was stupefyingly bad and demonstrated again his colossal ego. (Of his 13 or so films as a director, none are consistent works; some have several brilliant sequences, while others, such as *The Family Jewels*, are ghastly.*)

Here, it's pretty much Lewis business as usual. He mugs, shouts, bugs out his eyes, rushes around with his knees close together, and screams a good deal. And he's sometimes very funny. However, like virtually all Jerry Lewis films, including most of those with Martin, the film is infrequently shown.

Reviews were typical for Lewis. Jack Moffitt who, judging from his reviews, was politically conservative, thought the film a general improvement on the play. Unlike the original, Moffitt noted "the screenplay ... contains no political propaganda for disarmament.... Left-wing critics may gripe about what has been left out. But the general movie public probably will prefer the Wallis version to the original.... Unlike Kreton in the stage version, there is no malice in the Lewis concept of the character and he is as apt to get himself into jams as he is to foul up the Earthlings.... Neither Jerry nor Clark do their usual wild mugging. Both Lewis and [director Norman] Taurog have made better integrated comedies than this one but the total result is a lot of fun."

"Ron" in *Variety* demurred, considering it "a watered-down film version of the Broadway romp.... Whoever dictated the changes gave neither the screenplay nor the star a fair shake. Vidal's original had a good deal of thoughtful commentary on the stupidity of war, hidden adeptly behind a facade of farce. The picture tries, with only moderate success, to replace that commentary and, indeed, the core of the play with a poor stab at romance."

Joe Pihodna in the *Herald-Tribune* felt that "somewhere in the Paramount studios, much of the fun and all of the satire of the original play were lost." Howard Thompson in the *New York Times* concurred, feeling the result wasn't a particularly good film. The picture, Thompson said, "is meandering, slowly-paced ... with long pauses for all the old laughs and about as subtle as a meat cleaver. Once or twice it almost gets off the ground.... Joan Blackman and Earl Holliman, as two eagerly amorous youngsters, are considerably more appealing than Sarah Marshall and Conrad Janis were on the stage.... Only one new and overdone sequence is really funny — when Mr. Lewis clears out a

---

*I should admit that one of the motion pictures I want most to see is Lewis' unreleased *The Day the Clown Cried*, but not because I think it will be good. On the contrary, it seems likely to embody all of Lewis' vices. I'm curious to see how far he will go. It is not a comedy.

dingy den of beatniks, with his tearful reaction to a gibberish ballad and a wild, slick dance with Barbara Lawson."

The *Monthly Film Bulletin* gave the film a rating of II. "Gore Vidal's play is shorn of its propaganda for disarmament and its satire on American manners and institutions to make a vehicle for the grimaces and zany chatter of Jerry Lewis. What is left of Vidal becomes a mixture of domestic farce and unsubtle mockery of conventional Aunt Sallies like television commentators.... All in all, an inoffensive entertainment for those who like Lewis' slapstick."

Ruth Waterbury of the Los Angeles *Herald-Examiner* couldn't have praised the film more if she'd been paid by Paramount, but surely they would have paid for better writing: "You take the crazy idea of the first space man arriving on your small Earth, and you give it to a clever comedian like Jerry Lewis to play, and what do you get? Craziness! The absolute craziest craziness.... Sparked by the wonderful comedy direction of that most reliable comedy director, Norman Taurog, this is the usual Jerry Lewis type of romp, full of sight gags, almost no plot, a couple of spots of double meaning that would annoy only the most blue nose, and a beatnik ballet is hilarious.... Broad fun, this, broad as a prairie, but what's the matter with that, huh? Who wants *Medea* every night?"

Keep Watching   1961   *the Skies!*

The Absent Minded Professor

Strangely enough, one of the major virtues of this film is that it is good science fiction. That is, the scientific premise is still fantasy, but everything in it works logically from the premise. Within the bounds of the story, the scientific jabber by Fred MacMurray sounds logical, realistic and accurate. I don't recall having heard the film praised for this, but it pleased me when I saw it.

It's also a fairly funny if conventional comedy, having a good performance by MacMurray, some excellent special effects, and some amusing comedy situations. However, it's broad. The characters are stereotypes, and it takes place in one of those typical Disney small towns. The film clearly imitates *The Shaggy Dog*, the Disney fantasy of the year before which was a stunning surprise to the studio: an inexpensive, black-and-white comedy that far out-grossed their big-deal animated feature, *Sleeping Beauty*.

Fred MacMurray plays Ned Brainard, a small-town college science instructor known as Neddy the Nut to student Biff Hawk (Tommy Kirk). He's worn thin the patience of his fiancée Betsy Carlisle (Nancy Olson); Ned has twice been so engrossed in his scientific experimentation that he forgot to attend their wedding. It's scheduled again, and he's determined not to forget.

But Ned becomes so involved in his experiments that the wedding again slips his mind, and his experiment blows up in his face, knocking him unconscious. Over at the wedding, his fiancée fumes, consoled by poetry-quoting Shelby Ashton (Elliott Reid), who also wants to marry her. He's a professor at Rutland, rival of meek Medfield College, where Ned teaches.

In the morning, which Ned thinks is the night before, he awakes in the ruins of his lab and surveys the wreckage, when he hears queer bubbling noises; his experimental kettle slowly rises to the ceiling. Ned's jaw drops. He may be absent-minded, but he's not a fool, immediately realizing the many implications of what he's found. A substance that can generate its own energy is of great potential use: the stuff gives off slightly more energy than it receives, and responds in the opposite direction from the original impetus.

Ned makes a ball out of the goop, and bounces it. The ball goes *higher* with each succeeding bounce. He immediately makes several more balls and starts them flying around the room, in one of the movie's most remarkable, funny scenes, somewhat spoiled by frequent cutaways to Ned's little dog Charlie watching the balls fly by. The balls soon rocket around the room; we hear little crashes and other sounds of destruction offscreen as the balls zip back and forth. (The movie has great and plentiful sound effects throughout, perhaps too many.)

Holding a big wad of the goo in his hands, Ned proudly proclaims it "flubber" for "flying rubber." He mounts a small fragment of radioactive isotope in a shielded cylinder equipped with a shutter controlled by a dial. He places this under the kettle of flubber so the gamma rays strike the flubber, and finds he can make the kettle rise off the ground, no matter how much weight he attaches.

When his housekeeper tells the astounded Ned he missed his third try at a wedding, he dashes off to the office of Medfield College President Rufus Daggett (Leon Ames), for whom Betsy works. But she still fumes, and won't listen to Ned's excited but technical explanation as to why he's late, and what flubber might mean.

Nasty local businessman Alonzo Hawk (Keenan Wynn) strides in. Ned flunked his basketball star son Biff and he can't play in that night's big game with Rutland. Furthermore, Hawk, president of the Auld Lang Syne Loan Company, intends to call in his loan to Medfield, ruining the college. The Hawks depart. We learn later he hopes to tear the campus down and put up apartments; Biff, something of a jerk but true to his school, feebly protests.

Ned realizes that flubber could save the college financially, and goes home to prepare a suitably spectacular demonstration. He mounts the kettle of flubber in place of the engine of a Model T Ford he's been restoring; around this he rigs a series of isotope-containing cylinders, so he can bombard the flubber from any angle, thereby not only lifting the car, but controlling its actions. He hooks the cylinders to the standard controls of the car, and even installs a noisemaker which sounds like a conventional Model T engine. In a shot that is truly full of wonder, he flies away over the quiet town.

Ned larks about for a while, scaring cows and doing a loop-the-loop, finally landing with hopes of demonstrating his wonderful car to Betsy. However, she refuses to listen to him, and goes to the Medfield-Rutland basketball game with Shelby. Ned follows, still hoping to prove himself.

Since few knew Biff, the best player on Medfield's team, would be sitting the game out, Alonzo bet heavily on the rival team. It looks at first as though it's going to pay off, for by halftime, the taller, more agile Rutland players kept Medfield almost scoreless, while racking up a high score themselves.

But Ned gets a bright idea, and swipes a bunch of sneakers from the Medfield locker room. He irons flubber onto their heels and returns them to the team. Unaware of their now flubberized feet, the Medfield players are astonished to discover they can easily jump over the Rutland team, and go on to win the game.

These scenes were done by means of wires, and apparently were well-received in sneak previews, as we see so many variations on bouncing basketball players that it's clear nothing was cut. The joke stays funny for a while, but soon wears thin as the game seems to go on forever.

Ned can't convince Betsy that he was responsible for the victory, and Shelby derides him for trying to hog the glory of the team. After Shelby lets Betsy out, Ned follows him in the Model T. Looking past Elliott Reid, we see the Model T behind his car, then it slowly lifts into the air. This shot is almost exactly like one in *Close Encounters of the Third Kind*, in which Richard Dreyfuss tries to wave a "car" past his stopped truck and it flies overhead instead. Spielberg is a Disney fan.

In a scene played rather remarkably without any music, Ned fiendishly bounces his flying car off Shelby's roof, while tootling his aaooogah horn. Shelby can't see what is doing all this, and it sends him into a shrieking panic; he drives madly and recklessly through town.

I find it interesting that we are supposed to admire Ned, though we've seen him cheat to win a basketball game, and seriously endanger the life of a man who's never really done him any wrong. Yet Fred MacMurray remains charming enough that we never take Ned as anything but the likable hero.

Officer Hanson (James Westerfield, in the same role he had in *The Shaggy Dog*), is furious when Shelby runs head-on into Hanson's police car. Ned drives up (on the ground) as Shelby in extreme panic tries to explain that some strange, flying, aaoogahing thing battered his car from above.

As Ned flies cheerfully home, the fuming Alonzo Hawk — he'd lost all that money on the game — catches sight of the Model T floating over the rooftops.

He sees possibilities. Hawk confronts Ned the next day to attempt to browbeat him into forming a partnership for the exploitation of flubber, but patriotic Ned plans to make the stuff available to the government.

However, when he calls Washington, D.C., he gets the royal runaround, being sent from one department to another. He ends up trying to convince the Secretary of Defense (Edward Andrews) that he really does have an antigravity substance. The Chiefs of Staff pretend to agree with the pompous Secretary's patronizing put-down of the professor, but each secretly heads for Medfield.

Meanwhile, Ned has gone to a big dance, still hoping to win Betsy back. He flubberizes his own shoes, and puts on a wild demonstration of leaping and bouncing during the dance, impressing everyone.

But outside, Alonzo and Biff swap Ned's car for a nonflying Model T, so that when the Chiefs of Staff show up and get in the car for a demonstration, it sits firmly on the ground.

Again a laughingstock, Ned is consoled by Betsy, who now believes him. He realizes the car was switched, and that Alonzo must be responsible. The next day, they visit the greedy capitalist, pretending to deal with him, and add flubber to his shoes too, pointing out that more people buy shoes than cars, hence flubber on shoes will be profitable.

When Ned leaps out the window to demonstrate the bounciness of flubber-soled shoes, the impressed Alonzo follows suit. He has a great time bouncing higher and higher—until he wants to stop. Ned refuses to tell him how, unless Alonzo reveals where the flying flivver is hidden. Hawk reveals it's in his warehouse, so, with Alonzo still bouncing, Ned and Betsy leave to retrieve it.

The neighbors and fire department arrive (led by Keenan Wynn's father Ed, briefly reprising his famous 1930s radio role as the Fire Chief), but no one can stop Alonzo from heading higher and higher with each bounce. Biff summons the football team (in uniform), who, as Alonzo hits the ground, pounce on him, thus rescuing him.

Meanwhile, Ned and Betsy enter Alonzo's warehouse, and despite opposition from Alonzo's hired thugs, manage to make off with the flying car. Alonzo arrives, and begins chasing the Model T in another (ground-bound) car, while firing a pistol wildly. The bad guys also run head-on into Officer Hanson's car, and Ned and Betsy wave goodbye as they head for Washington, D.C.

The Model T is mistaken for an enemy craft, and jets scramble to investigate, missiles are readied for launch, but things soon calm down. Ned lands on the White House lawn, finally proclaimed a hero. He and Betsy marry at last, and fly off in the car for a honeymoon.

Though generally entertaining, the major problem with *The Absent Minded Professor* is that the plot is thin. The film proceeds from one "flubbergasting" event to another: the discovery of the goo that flew (so called in the ads), the flying car, the basketball game, bouncing Ned, bouncing Alonzo, and the scenes over the Capitol. Ned's rivalry with Shelby, the crisis over Alonzo's foreclosing on his loan, both seem artificial; they don't tie in well with the flubber elements, seeming more a means of providing something to watch while we wait for the next flubberized spectacle.

Furthermore, Robert Stevenson directs films dully, by and large. Given an interesting, colorful story, he can do competent work, as with the later *Mary Poppins*, but generally he shows no style and little creativity. He overuses close-ups, though not as depressingly here as in this film's sequel, *Son of Flubber*. Fortunately, *Professor* is short on dialogue scenes, and usually the close-ups are of Fred MacMurray and Keenan Wynn, who know what to do with them. But during the climax, an actor I believe is Alan Hewitt heavily overplays his role as the general in charge of aerial defense of Washington, and Stevenson compounds the actor's smug hamminess by the most overemphatic close-ups of the film. Elliott Reid lacks close-ups, but performs in the wrong style; his blind weak-kneed panic following Ned's aerial assault on his car disturbs rather than amuses.

But for most audiences the virtues of the film obviously outweighed its defects, as it grossed over $11 million on its first release, making it one of Disney's most successful films. Understanding the reason for this great success is easy: the film is pleasant, lightweight entertainment, but also about something odd: a flying car and rebounding goo. The gimmick is simple, easily understood, and all the situations are imaginative even if the comedy is obvious. (Unlike *Son of Flubber*; the comedy is more obvious, the situations less imaginative, and the scientific aspects confusing. But it did well too.)

The special effects in *Professor* are outstanding, adding to the acceptability of the concept. The dialogue is not broadly comic *or* witty; in fact, the dialogue lacks jokes almost completely. It's straightforward and not too juvenile; no one acts silly (until the climax), although they are all comic characters. It is truly a *family* film.

One of the best reasons to watch the film today is the performance of Fred MacMurray. Although he began as early as 1934 in a wide variety of films, he soon settled into comedy. Highly adept at it, sometimes almost brilliant, MacMurray works in a quiet, understated manner. His friendly, squinty little eyes, his quizzical brows and long chin make him average-looking in a harmless, handsome manner. Sometimes dynamic, sometimes relaxed, always believable and professional, even in the least promising situations, MacMurray delivers the goods. He made seven films for the Disney studios, this being by far the best.

MacMurray's personable likability and his transformation of this tissue-thin character keep Ned the true hero of the piece. Unlike many actors, MacMurray is a great *reactor*; he responds to events and dialogue as if encountering them for the first time; there's never any trace of overrehearsal in his performances. This freshness keeps *The Absent Minded Professor* buoyant almost all the time.

The believability of the scientific talk MacMurray spouts aids the believability of his comedy performance. "The application of an external force," he hypothesizes, "triggers a molecular change liberating energy of a type previously unknown." Later, he enthuses in nonstop chatter to Betsy about flubber: "This change in molecular configuration liberates enormous quantities of energy but they act only in a direction opposite to the force which triggered the molecular change.... The total effect is transient and upon the shutting-off of the externally-applied energy the elemental particles return to a state of pseudo-equilibrium." Whoever was the technical advisor earned his money.

However, nothing much could help the very lame climax in the Washington D.C. skies, and the reasonableness of Ned's previous behavior evaporates as he behaves like a dunderhead.

In the 40s, MacMurray was one of Hollywood's biggest stars, appearing in more successes than most people realize. He had his most famous role, luckless Walter Neff, in Billy Wilder's *Double Indemnity* (1944), but MacMurray also shone in Wilder's *The Apartment* (1960) as a no-good dirty rat of an oversexed boss. (He received some criticism for this, as he'd become recognized as a

Disney Star.) His career declined in the 50s, with a few high points such as *The Caine Mutiny* (1954), in which he nicely played a manipulative weakling. He'd been relegated to lesser A Westerns, with forgettable titles like *Gun for a Coward* (1957), *Day of the Bad Man* (1958), *Face of a Fugitive* (1959). The Disney films and *The Apartment* revitalized his career, and with the success of his long-running TV series, "My Three Sons," made him a star again. MacMurray is one of the wealthiest men in Hollywood, and I don't begrudge him a penny.

Some of the lesser actors are unfortunate, but others are excellent. Keenan Wynn in particular delights as Alonzo Hawk (a role he reprised as late as 1972's *Herbie Rides Again*). This film came in the middle of Wynn's best period as an actor, when he turned up in film after film during outstanding work, usually as a fulminating tyrant, as here, but sometimes as a thick-witted jerk, as in *Dr. Strangelove*. For a while, Wynn almost seemed like insurance: producers seemed to believe a film would do better if he appeared in it somewhere.

The many scenes of the flying Model T were accomplished in several ways. Peter Ellenshaw supervised the miniature car for scenes of it flying in and out of clouds, looping around a church steeple, and so forth. These are moderately effective, working better on television than on the big screen. He also did some conventional matte shots, presumably using the Disney sodium–light matte; these show MacMurray and his various passengers against aerial backdrops of Washington, D.C. and the area of the San Fernando Valley standing in for Medfield. As was usual for Disney, these are far superior to matte work at other studios during this period, and are almost acceptable by today's standards.

By far the most impressive flying-car scenes are those involving a light-weight but full-sized Model T raised off the ground by invisible wires fastened to what must have been a colossal crane. The car at times flies at least 50 feet in the air. Furthermore, under the direction of Robert A. Mattey, the control in these scenes, smooth and convincing, approaches elegance. They have exactly the right magical lift. The car never trembles or wavers, always making smooth and graceful turns and banks. When the car flies by a smokestack and casts its shadow on it, the illusion is complete. Neither in the theatre nor on television could I spot wires. These are among the most successful "flying" scenes ever.

The film received generally favorable reviews, catching some critics off-guard. They didn't expect a film this inventive from the Disney studios. In *Limelight*, Jack Moffitt expressed great approval, describing it as being "even funnier than the recent smash boxoffice success, *The Shaggy Dog*.... In its worst moments the film is merely hilarious. At its best, it's uproarious.... MacMurray, without mugging or takeums, achieves the comedy masterpiece of a serious man trying earnestly to carry on as normal in a fantastically mad world. Though he has yet to be recognized as such, he's probably one of the alltime greats among screen funny men."

"Tube" in *Variety* found something deeper in the "comedy-fantasy of infectious absurdity.... Beneath the preposterous veneer lurks a comment on our time, a reflection of the plight of the average man haplessly confronted with the complexities of a jet age civilization burdened with fear, red-tape, official mumbo-jumbo and ambitious anxiety. Deeply rooted within associate producer Bill Walsh's screenplay, is a subtle protest against the detached, impersonal machinery of modern progress. It is an underlying theme with which an audience today can identify. It is the basic reason why this film is going to be an enormously popular attraction.... This picture is a winner in every department. It is profoundly easy to enjoy, and there is more in it to enjoy than meets the casual eye."

Even *Time* was pleased, describing the film in painful Timese as "the season's kookiest science-fiction farce.... A very funny piece of hyperbolic humor in the grand American tradition of Paul Bunyan."

As usual with nonserious films, the *New York Times'* Bosley Crowther patronized, as if he was patting the movie on the head. "It is really a modest little picture ... casually cornball and screwloose.... Some of these magical machinations ... may amuse the more sophisticated, too.... Fred MacMurray does a fair enough job for an actor not equipped with the talent and the physical grotesquery of one of the old-time silent comedians who were deft at this sort of sport.... Robert Stevenson's direction, we must add, is something less than inspired. The style and movement have no distinction. They are those of conventional farce. Even so ... it is remarkably bouncy entertainment. What is more, it is absolutely clean."

As a footnote to their review, *Time* helpfully provided allegedly the Disney special effects department's recipe for flubber: "To 1 lb. saltwater taffy add 1 heaping tbs. polyurethane foam, 1 cake crumbled yeast. Mix till smooth, allow to rise. Then pour into saucepan over 1 cup cracked rice mixed with 1 cup water. Add topping of molasses. Boil until it lifts lid and says 'Qurlp.'"

Technically, *The Absent Minded Professor* can't be faulted. The special effects are outstanding, the photography is excellent, even the music, often overdone in Disney comedies, is modest and to the point. The science fiction aspect is impeccable, MacMurray is fine. All in all, it is about as good a film as one could expect from the Disney studio in this period.

Assignment Outer Space

Dull but colorful, this Italian film at least has the advantage of a slightly unusual plotline, which is similar to stories that appeared in the "Mystery in Space" and "Strange Adventures" comic books. It's one of the few films of the period, furthermore, to be set in a future in which spaceflight is commonplace. The basic premise of a reporter in space is novel, although his journalistic activities play little part in the story.

In *Trumpet* # 10, Tom Reamy wrote the only full-length review-synopsis of the film I have seen, and it is worth quoting in full:

"This is a very strange one. Its purpose is the best in the world because it accepts science fiction on its own terms and proceeds from there. Technically, it is very uneven. The spaceship interiors are superb but most of the exterior miniatures look just like that. The station on Venus is particularly bad.

"The Dialogue ranges from banal to excellent with an emphasis on the former. The actors are speaking English, but, as is the custom in continental studios, everything is dubbed anyway. This makes the lip synchronization a little better but doesn't help the pathetically stilted voices of the dubbing actors.

"Ray Peterson [Rik von Nutter] is a reporter for Interplanetary News of New York. He is assigned to write a story (no one thinks to mention on what) which requires his presence at the space station. There he is given a number: IZ41 or "India-Zulu-Four-One" if you wish to use it in conversation. All members of the space service are addressed by number and are regarded with about the same concern as any other inventoried item.

"Peterson is regarded as a fifth wheel on the space station and the commander is not noted for his tact. Interplanetary News of New York, however, has a great deal of influence with the "High Command" and Peterson gets just about everything he wants much to the Commander's increasing ire. We never get to know a great deal about the civilization of the 21st Century but there are lines tossed off occasionally which give clues. But the clues are contradictory. Apparently there is a world government and, from the way the space station is run, you would think it a little like 1984. Though from Peterson's actions he would seem to have all the freedom anyone could want. (A later film, *Battle of the Worlds*, takes place against the same sociological background.) Perhaps something was lost in the dubbing as occasionally the lip synch is completely off—as if we are hearing other than what was intended. American International is one of the worst meddlers with foreign films in the world. [With apologies to the shade of Tom Reamy, the American company responsible for the dubbing was Four Crown, not AIP, which merely distributed the film.—B.W.]

"Peterson saves the life of Y13 (Yankee-One-Three), an action resulting in the loss of 500 gallons of fuel. The Commander feels the fuel to be far less expendable than Y13 and tells [Peterson] so. Y13 turns out to be [Lucy (Gaby Farinon)], a pretty young girl who immediately falls in love with Peterson and vice-versa, though Peterson seems to feel that it is his due.

"Now an emergency arrives. Alpha Two has re-entered the Solar System and is out of control. No one bothers to inform the audience just exactly what Alpha Two is, but whatever, it is radiating enough heat to destroy the Earth. They try to shoot it down but the tremendous heat prematurely detonates all missiles 5000 miles away. However, one missile gets within 2000 miles before it explodes. This seems to prove that Alpha Two's two photon generators (that's what they said) are creating not one spherical field around the ship but two, with a channel between them. I don't know; would heat be that directional?

"Anyway, Peterson, hero to the bitter end, makes the trip down the channel in a two-man work-craft, throwing things from the repair kit to either side. The point at which they vaporize indicates the edge of the heat-field. He enters Alpha Two but, being a hero by profession and not an engineer, doesn't know how to turn off the photon generators. He decides to cut the cables; a fine idea but he doesn't know which cables are which. So, he cuts them all. It shuts off the photon generator all right but gets the airlock too. Now he can't get out. Never fear, the others cut him out before the ship is vaporized in the Earth's atmosphere.

"For some reason, all the shots in space are black and white. It's a striking effect but hardly accurate. The ship (Bravo-Zulu-Eight-Eight) is well designed and photographed but the stupid thing lands flat on its exhausts! I don't know from spaceships but, according to Woody Woodpecker in *Destination Moon*, they work on the same principle as a gun. Jam the muzzle of a gun into the ground getting it clogged and it will be more likely to explode than fire. But BZ88 keeps doing it.

"There's a lot to like in the film and a lot to dislike. Your overall opinion will depend on which predominates."

Overall, I disliked it.

The film's script is far more imaginative than most such low-budget foreign films. It presents an attempt at a coherent future and, as Reamy said, genuine science fiction. The interior sets are excellent, and the costumes are fine. The art director, whose name I have been unable to discover, shows intelligence and imagination.

However, the film is simply too erratic in conception. The imaginativeness of the script is offset by flat, leaden direction; the design and good photography are compromised by bad, ignorant special effects. The dubbing itself is harmless, but the lines that are dubbed in are occasionally hilarious. The audience I saw it with was reduced to hysteria by the Brave Commander's shouted "I'm comin' in!" at a crisis point.

The special effects are credited to "Caesar Peace," sounding like an Anglicized Italian name, but the original has proved illusive. Peace seems to have been impressed by George Pal's Conquest of Space, as the space suits and some of the smaller spacecraft resemble such items from that film. The main spaceship is from a plastic model kit based on a design from the Walt Disney TV show. That Disney ship was a three-stage rocket, with clearly visible stages: an enormous launching stage, a small intermediate stage, and the final, small winged stage, designed to bring the spacemen back to Earth. Peace didn't know or care that the Disney ship was supposed to separate as each stage was exhausted, because BZ88 flies about the solar system as one gigantic, ungainly craft. And of course, the final stage still has useless wings.

While the ships are in space, they look okay visually, although the shots are in black and white, there are few stars, and the rockets all make roaring sounds. When they land on various asteroids and planets, the ships wobble and the terrain looks awful: a tabletop set.

The film was directed by the prolific but unimpressive Antonio Margheriti (incredibly credited "Anthony Daisies" on U.S. prints), most of whose films are slow and boring. He apparently specializes in fantasy films, and has made some in almost every subgenre. Space: this, Battle of the Worlds (1961), Wild Wild Planet, War Between the Planets, War of the Planets and Snow Devils (all 1965); spear-and-sandal fantasies: The Golden Arrow (1961), Hercules, Prisoner of Evil (1967); Mario Bava–like horror/mystery thrillers: Horror Castle, Castle of Blood (both 1963), Long Hair of Death (1964), Web of the Spider (1971, a remake of Castle of Blood), and the Dario Argento–inspired Seven Dead in the Cat's Eye (1972). He has also made others, including James Bond–styled films like The Killers Are Challenged (1965) and Lightning Bolt (1966), an imitation Disney comedy, Mr. Superinvisible (1970) and at least one Jaws imitation, Killer Fish (1979). I doubt that this list is complete.

Margheriti's films are usually credited in the United States to "Anthony Dawson" (though there's no connection to the British actor of that name), but under any name, he's a lame, derivative director who doesn't seem to have been handed a script of any originality since Assignment Outer Space, and even that was like a comic book. He's busy but unimaginative, showing no signs of interest in his films apart from perhaps a couple of the early horror thrillers. He uses little creativity in staging, favoring medium shots and close-ups; under his direction, actors usually give either hammy or lifeless performances: that is, they are on their own.

Handsome American Rik von Nutter, star of Assignment Outer Space, infrequently appears in European films, being mostly a pretty boy with little discernible talent. He popped up in Thunderball (1965) as James Bond's pal Felix Leiter. Von Nutter was married for a while to Anita Ekberg, his main claim to fame.

Archie Savage, playing Al, whose name sounds so phonily Anglicized, is actually a black American actor and dancer who was working under that name as early as 1942, when he appeared in Tales of Manhattan. He had small or supporting roles in a number of American films of the 50s, including Carmen Jones

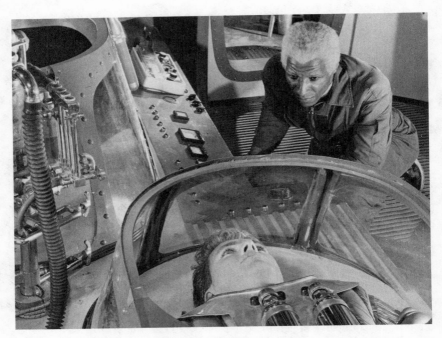

Rik von Nutter (in transparent cabinet) and American dancer Archie Savage in an interesting still from the trivial Assignment Outer Space (U.S. release, 1961). The interior sets for this film were far superior to the lousy miniatures.

His Majesty O'Keefe (both 1954), *The Ten Commandments* and *South Pacific* (1958). In the late 50s he went to Italy, where the novelty of a black American actor locally available resulted in his being cast in large roles in minor films, and occasionally showy parts in notable movies, including *La Dolce Vita* (1960). He's primarily decorative in *Assignment Outer Space*, being quite striking with his very dark skin and (here) snow-white hair.

In many situations, *Assignment Outer Space* was booked with *Phantom Planet*, and was the better of the two films. Though slow and a little boring, being in color and having a somewhat novel plot lifted it a bit above its drab cofeature.

Assignment Outer Space received few reviews. *Boxoffice* thought it had "a trimly functioning story framework" and felt that "the kiddies will love this." They probably did, for half an hour.

Atlantis, the Lost Continent

This sorry mess is the worst film George Pal ever produced. Some consider *Conquest of Space* or *Doc Savage, Man of Bronze* worse, but those films have some virtues raising them above the level of *Atlantis*, which not only has a mediocre script, bad performances and little imagination, but even the special effects don't pay off for the most part.

Although many writers have claimed a historical basis for the sunken continent of Atlantis, it seems to have originated in Plato's "Dialogues." He used Atlantis as an example of a perfect society, which unfortunately sank beneath the waves. Plato was cagey about the actual location of the sunken continent, but writers generally place it somewhere west of the Strait of Gibraltar. (The name of the Atlantic Ocean derives from the same Greek root as that of Atlantis.) True Believers say that the Canary Islands are the mountain peaks of the drowned continent, still peeking above the waves.

Many books, to put it mildly, have been written on the subject of Atlantis, mostly stemming from Ignatius Donnelly's *Atlantis: The Antediluvian World*, first published in 1882. Dozens of other factual books have sought to prove or disprove the existence of Atlantis, and probably as many (if not more) science fiction and fantasy novels used the sunken continent as a locale. Some comic books also lean heavily on Atlantis for story material, notably in the Marvel series about Prince Namor, the Submariner, and the DC series about Aquaman.

But as material for films, Atlantis remains relatively uncommon. Only one other film that I am aware of, released here as *Hercules and the Captive Women* (1961), features the sinking of the continent. Part of it briefly *rises* in the serial *Undersea Kingdom*, but of course that's not quite the same thing.

As a locale, Atlantis turns up in the various films based on the novel *L'Atlantide* by Pierre Benoit, including a French version in 1921, *Die Herrin von Atlantis* (German, 1932), *Siren of Atlantis* (1947) and *Journey Beneath the Desert* (French-Italian, 1961). The ancestors of the inhabitants of the moon of Jupiter visited in *Fire Maidens of Outer Space* originally came from Atlantis. Reversing that, in *Warlords of Atlantis* (1978), the inhabitants of the sunken city originally came from Mars. In *Toto Sceicco* (1950), the famous Italian comedian meets the Queen of Atlantis, and two Mexican wrestlers battle Nazis in Atlantis in *Santo contra Blue Demon en la Atlántida* (ca. 1968). There's scant connection with the lost continent in *Beyond Atlantis* (1973), which peculiarly sets Atlantis in the Pacific. The classic Atlantis movie remains to be made.

George Pal first became interested in filming a story about Atlantis in the mid-50s, when he encountered a published version of *Atalanta, a Story of Atlantis*, a 1949 play by Sir Gerald P. Hargreaves. Paramount turned down the film, however, and Pal went on to other projects. As a follow-up to *The Time Machine*, Pal's new studio MGM wanted another science fiction spectacle, but insisted on a low budget.

Pal commissioned a script from Daniel Mainwaring, a generally mediocre writer; the two were in the midst of the script when MGM abruptly gave word to begin actual production. Pal later told the depressing Jeff Rovin that *Atlantis* suffered by comparison with his other films because of "the writing. We weren't ready to go with the picture because we had a poor script. But it was scheduled to shoot [when] a writer's strike broke out, and we couldn't get anyone to rewrite it. We had a very pedestrian script, but the studio told me not to worry. 'You'll pull it out with the special effects,' they said, which we did. But the story and dialogue were horrible." (*The Fabulous Fantasy Films*, A.S. Barnes, 1977.)

Pal told Gail Morgan Hickman, "The MGM executives realized while we were shooting that the script wasn't good enough, and they tried to doctor it. But you can't doctor this type of film during production. They came in with suggested pages that were worse than what we had." (*The Films of George Pal*, A.S. Barnes, 1977.)

Pal's anxiety to avoid responsibility for the failure of *Atlantis* is clear, but unfortunately, he's more to blame than anyone else. He commissioned the script from Mainwaring in the first place, and added some of the worst ideas to the script (such as the "animal men"). Furthermore, Pal not only produced *Atlantis*, he directed it, and he was simply not a good director of live actors. Finally, although he may have believed, as he told Rovin, that he "pulled it out" with the special effects, the budget was too low for the extravagance of the elaborate effects required in the sinking of a continent; for the most part, those scenes are quite poor.

The movie opens with an intriguing prologue pointing out that pyramids, concepts of witches and calendars and (apparently) even elephants were known on both sides of the Atlantic. However, the film does nothing with this idea until literally in its last minute of running time. By then, of course, it's far too late.

In the Mediterranean near Greece, fisherman Demetrios (Anthony Hall) and his father (Wolfe Barzell) find a raft with an unconscious girl on it. She's Princess Antillia (Joyce Taylor) of Atlantis, an island kingdom she says lies to the west of the Pillars of Hercules (Gibraltar). She's a shipwreck victim and drifted on the raft for a month. This means she drifted across part of the Atlantic and almost all the Mediterranean without any food or water. Atlanteans were made of stern stuff.

Demetrios doubts her, and will not return her to her home, so she steals his fishing boat, heading out on her own. Demetrios catches up and agrees to search for Atlantis for one month before turning back. They head west. At one point, Poseidon (a.k.a. Neptune, here) rises from the depths of the sea and waves his trident at them, but seems to be a dream, or hallucination, or wishful thinking.

Eventually a sea monster rushes at the small craft, and Demetrios flings his spear at it. The spear goes "clang" harmlessly, for the monster is actually a semi-submarine from Atlantis, built in the shape of a great fish. (It never seems quite to submerge; it is entirely enclosed, and cruises along with its back awash, por-poising through the waves.)

Zaren (John Dall) commands the craft, being one of the ten warlords of Atlantis and the film's painfully epicene villain. He promises Antillia that he'll tend to Demetrios—of course, the two young people are falling in love—because her father is King Kronas (Edgar Stehli) of Atlantis.

But Zaren is the power behind the throne these days, and tosses Demetrios into the slave pens where, like all foreigners in Atlantis, cruel overseers use him to quarry minerals from the mines. If the prisoners act up, they are taken to "the House of Fear" where an evil surgeon (Berry Kroeger) turns them into part-animal creatures.

Clearly a steal from *The Island of Dr. Moreau*, which features a "House of Pain," this idea is merely tossed into the film; Pal does nothing with it, although it does give the film its creepiest scenes and funniest line. "Repeat after me," the surgeon says to one of his subjects, "'In every day, in every way, I'm getting to be more and more like a bull.'" Bull is right.

The mines are for excavating crystals used to capture energy from the sun. Zaren desperately wants to unearth an especially huge crystal which he intends to use in conquering the world.

One day on his way back from the mine, Antillia passes Demetrios, and he throws mud at her, a crime for which he is sent to the House of Fear.

Antillia tries to get Demetrios sprung, but in this her father is powerless. Taking a chance of escape through the Ordeal of Fire and Water saves

Demetrios from being turned into a pig-man. Zaren wants to get Antillia on his side, so he allows this, but he also feels confident that the Greek will be killed in the process.

The Ordeal is a battle waged in a pit of burning coals, with small rocky platforms scattered about; Demetrios' opponent: a 7 foot, 350 pound gladiator (Buck Maffei). They grapple for a while over the burning coals (Fire) and later water (Water) pours in. Demetrios defeats his opponent.

Freed, he later meets high priest Azor (Edward Platt, the Chief on TV's "Get Smart"), who pretends to worship the multitude of Atlantean gods, but secretly worships the One True God. (Hence, he's a good guy.) He impresses Demetrios, who agrees to help Azor in a plan to stop Zaren. Azor points out that the giant crystal's destructive ray will indeed allow Zaren to conquer the world.

Demetrios pretends to come over to Zaren's side. On the day of the dedication of the giant, globular crystal, mounted on a swivel base on a wooden platform, Demetrios frees the slaves.

As usual in films dealing with island civilizations that need wiping out, at this moment the smouldering volcano erupts. Also, Zaren begins firing his destructive ray hither and yon, bringing down Atlantis' main city and wiping out fleeing people. Pandemonium reigns.

Along with freed slaves, Demetrios and Antillia manage to reach some ships and they set out to sea as the crystal really goes wild, swinging this way and that. It destroys Azor and Zaren who are fighting, and still blasts away as Atlantis unimpressively sinks beneath the waves.

The little knot of ships of slaves has a brief palaver, then all set off to the four corners of the world, answering the questions asked in the opening prologue.

Atlantis, the Lost Continent depresses on all levels, except for some moments of fleeting splendor. The "sea monster" ship is the most impressive prop in the film, both in concept and design, although it slightly resembles Disney's "Nautilus" from *20,000 Leagues*. Unfortunately, the film uses it only at the beginning. The big crystal is also a good prop, and used well at the climax. But most of the other fanciful props in the film come from other movies. A statue built for *The Prodigal* (1955) glowers at worshippers in Azor's temple, and in a laboratory can be seen several items left over from *Forbidden Planet*.

With such an interesting, unusual premise, setting a film on Atlantis before it sinks, it's a pity that Pal and Mainwaring couldn't come up with something more novel and interesting than this hackneyed storyline. The commoner hero who loves a princess while opposing a power-mad despot is the basis for *most* of the tawdry spear-and-sandal films that poured out of Hollywood between the mid-40s and the mid-50s. Other than the big crystal, we see almost nothing of the superscientific aspects of Atlantis; turning people into semianimals is used strictly for its horror impact, with nothing to do with the storyline, dropped in like a fragment of another film.

Originally, Pal featured some men who flew by means of Leonardo da Vinci–inspired harnesses, but the special effects for these sequences were so poor that all glimpses of the flying men were removed after the first previews.

The sinking of the continent fails to impress. Miniature buildings topple and crumble, and the city actually lowers into a huge tank, but there's no sense of an *entire continent* disappearing beneath the waves.

Everything looks colorful, with a sense of panic and doom, but plentiful stock footage—fires, lava flows, crowds from *Quo Vadis*—severely reduces the overall impact. Furthermore, this was not the best period for art direction by MGM; things tended toward the gaudy.

Joyce Taylor also appeared in *Ring of Fire* (1961), *Beauty and the Beast*, *13 Frightened Girls* and *Twice Told Tales* (all 1963), and sometimes isn't bad as an actress, but her performance here is wooden and uninteresting. She's pretty enough, but Pal failed to bring any fire or color out of her.

Anthony Hall is hopeless; handsome, but only as expressive as a department-store manikin, unbelievable at all times. He sounds and looks 20th century. Fortunately, Mr. Hall realized his limitations; this is apparently his only film.

The late John Dall plays the prissy, mincing villain. Unfortunately, he's usually one of the least convincing actors I have seen, generally theatrical and affected. In his debut, *The Corn Is Green* (1945) opposite Bette Davis, he was only fair. His most highly regarded films are Hitchcock's *Rope* (1948) and Joseph H. Lewis' *Gun Crazy/Deadly Is the Female* (1949); the latter features his best performance, so good as to make his usual inadequacy more mysterious. He was off the screen between 1950 and 1960, when he returned in *Spartacus*, but his only film after that is this one. He died in 1971.

The only other really interesting actor in the film is Berry Kroeger as that fiendish surgeon. Kroeger is one of the great slimy creeps of movie villainy, with his piggy face, stooped posture and hissing voice making him instantly recognizable and memorable. Though failing to get a good part in a major film, he's been in there plugging since 1944. He was Alexandre Dumas in *Black Magic* (1949) and has crept through *Blood Alley* (1955), *Chamber of Horrors* (1966), *Nightmare in Wax* (1969, a bad movie in which Kroeger is great), *The Incredible 2-Headed Transplant* (1970, a rare sympathetic role), *The Mephisto Waltz* (1971) and *Demon Seed* (1977). He's the kind of performer you half expect to see leaving a slimy trail behind him.

Reviews were mixed, but plentiful. Critics still gave George Pal high marks for special effects, almost by rote; recalling *The Time Machine* and earlier films with fondness, they allowed Pal one bad movie. In *Limelight*, Jack Moffitt showed that he was one of the few who knew much about Atlantis: "The people of the lost continent, Atlantis, vanished into the depths of the Atlantic Ocean some 9,000 years before the time of [Plato's] writing. If they get word of the movie Metro has made about them, they'll never come back up.... Of the five thousand scholarly works dealing with the Atlantis legend, [Hargreave's] must come pretty close to being the worst.... It is to be hoped that this [film] will satisfy an undiscriminating audience that will fall for a pedestrian type of science-fiction. But the suspense, novelty and suspension-of-disbelief which producer George Pal so successfully brought to *The War of the Worlds* and *The Time Machine* is sadly lacking in this film. So is the charming humor which spiced so much of *tom thumb*."

"Tube" in *Variety* found it a "lesser fantasy effort by George Pal.... The film as a whole is strictly lower-grade Pal [who ignores] the more compelling possibilities of the [opening] hypothesis in favor of erecting a tired, shopworn melodrama.... The picture closely parallels in style and structure of content the sort of escapist screen entertainment being fashioned in great abundance by Italian filmmakers over the past few years."

On the other hand, James Powers at the *Hollywood Reporter* sounded like a press release from MGM: "A class science fantasy film, [this] is one picture that can back up a sensational exploitation campaign. Particularly outstanding ... are the special effects, done with a realism and conviction rare and valuable."

Bosley Crowther showed contempt for science fiction in general, seeming to think it all trash, and so *Atlantis* lived down to his expectation: "It does have enough trick stuff in it," he said in the *New York Times*, "to amuse mildly any adult who has to sit there and watch it with a bug-eyed kid…. Youngsters may find the wooden acting of Joyce Taylor and Anthony Hall … highly inflammable, and they may very well be stimulated by the only stalwart members of the cast. This film, as should be fairly obvious, is primarily for primary-school kids. But an adult may find some wry amusement in spotting a couple of noticeable little things such as the fact that Greeks and Atlantans [sic] all speak English and use underarm deodorants." Was it in Smell-O-Vision in New York?

Kay Proctor in the *Los Angeles Examiner* reported that the preteen neighbor she took to the film thought it was "real neat" with "lots of gore and lots of action," but Proctor herself didn't care for it: "the plotted conjecture as to the fate of a 'lost continent' … here is made so ludicrous as to discourage even those who want to believe the unbelievable. The entire continent of Atlantis is made to disappear almost in a flash, for instance, because of divine intervention." (Indeed, the good-guy priest does pray to the One True God not long before the end.)

Time was oddly impressed: "In the process [of recreating Atlantis, Pal] has admirably fulfilled his ambition to supply escapist entertainment 'with an element of wonder, stressing man's suppressed desire to travel away from himself.' … It is no wonder that Producer Pal 'feels sort of like God sometimes,' but he must also feel like the Devil sometimes, too."

More recently, *Psychotronic* called it a "silly adventure film" and felt the animal-headed slaves were "the film's highlight." Don Willis (I) said, "the effects almost save the rest, which is quite a feat," and Alan Frank (SF) found it a "comic strip fantasy, a disappointment from Pal."

Disappointment was the major reaction I had to the film when I first saw it in Portland, Oregon, where I had gone with some friends to see the Kingston Trio. (We were supposed to be there on behalf of the Russian class, but, well…) I virtually dragged Ron Hale to see *Atlantis*, promising him something as good as *War of the Worlds* or *The Time Machine*, and could scarcely meet his eye when we came out. I tried my best to find something good to say about the film, but in so doing, I felt like a hypocrite.

Atlantis, the Lost Continent is a bad movie and a blot on George Pal's record. But in a way, he can't be blamed. He didn't have the time to find a script he wanted; Metro forced him to proceed before he was ready and with a shamefully low budget. Also, Pal never really understood the demands of his audiences, often playing to the lowest common denominators. But he was a decent man who, within his limits, tried to do respectable work. With *Atlantis*, the limits were too much for him.

Beast of Yucca Flats

This low-budget independent production is not only hard to see, it's hard to watch. Surely one of the cheapest feature films ever to see release, *Beast of Yucca Flats* also shows no talent, inventiveness or interesting ideas, which sometimes make cheap films endurable. Its sole virtue is enormous Tor Johnson, whose career as a horror film "star" confined itself almost entirely to the cheapest productions. As a movie monster, Tor remained something of a joke, but being one provided him with virtually the only fame he had outside the wrestling ring, though he'd been in films since at least the early 1930s.

After the credits, a narrator tells us the story of the film. He speaks in a world-weary, portentous voice throughout. We're told about Joseph Jaworsky (Tor), a defecting Soviet scientist.

The film lacks synchronized sound, nor was sound recorded while filming. Occasionally someone will be heard speaking with his or her back to the camera, or will shout after carefully cupping hands around mouth, so we cannot see the lips move (or not). We're dispirited because of the cheapness, but it does provide some entertainment in allowing us to watch for inventive ways of hiding out-of-sync lip movements.

The film opens with what seems to be a flash-forward: to the accompaniment of loud ticking, a woman alone in a room dries herself off after a shower. A huge male figure (presumably Tor, but it is another actor) enters the room, strangles her and begins to rape her. Despite suggesting events to come, this scene does not recur, nor is there any reasonable point the scene could take place.

Jaworsky is bringing secret data on Russian Moon tests to the United States, but two of the Kremlin's most ruthless agents are after Jaworsky's briefcase, and they chase the fugitive genius into the desert. (The narrator informs us that the Soviets have already landed on the Moon. Hah.) The fleeing cars pass a crudely painted sign reading "Yucca Flats." The U.S. scientist (or agent) with Jaworsky runs out of bullets, so Jaworsky leaves him behind, proceeding on foot, though where he's going is unclear.

He strips off his jacket and tie, and then, represented by brightness and stock footage, an A-bomb detonates. The explosion destroys Jaworsky's briefcase and kills the agents chasing him, but it turns the big Russian into (ta daaa) the Beast of Yucca Flats. His face supposedly has been burned, but looks more like bubble gum has been smeared on it. Otherwise, he's the same old Tor.

A man working on his car in the desert; supposedly eerie desolation. I feel ungenerous in asking how this guy got so near the atomic test site himself. 370 pounds of Jaworsky creeps up on the guy and kills him, unseen by the woman in the car. Jaworsky really surprises when he reaches out of the *back seat* and grabs her, suddenly there through the miracle of editing.

Jaworsky wanders off, and a traveler finds the dead man. He rushes off to encounter at a café young Joe Dobson, highway patrolman. At the car, Joe examines the body. "Joe Dobson," the narrator says, "caught in the wheels of progress." Expanding on his theme of machinery, the narrator says "Touch a button—things happen. A scientist becomes a beast."

We see a chesty girl get out of a bed, then get back in. This scene has nothing to do with the rest of the film, being perhaps the most gratuitous insert of cheesecake I have ever encountered.

Back in the desert, Jaworsky takes the girl from the car to a cave, bends over her, and begins chewing on her hair. "Joseph Jaworsky," says the omniscient narrator, "respected scientist. Now fiend. Kill just to be killing." The girl, however, still lives. We hear dialogue but never see them talking. Joe finds her, but she dies.

A headline appears: "Beast Kills Man and Wife." This is impressive journalism, as the paper has been printed and delivered before Joe returns from discovering the dead woman.

We next meet the Radcliffes, Art and Randy and their two sons. The narrator obscurely tells us "Nothing bothers some people, not even flying saucers." (There are no flying saucers in *Beast of Yucca Flats*.) The boys climb around on rocks for no clear reason, and Jaworsky hides as they pass.

Jim, a friend of Joe's, parachutes onto a plateau to "kill the killer." He operates on a shoot-first, ask-questions-later policy, firing at almost everything he sees. However, he never runs out of bullets. Later, we see him firing at Art Radcliffe from a plane, in a clear homage (if that's the right word) to *North by Northwest*. Director Coleman Francis even tries a joke at this point: we see a "Slow" sign and Art runs fast by it. He leaves his wife and drives away without an explanation.

Meanwhile, back in the desert, the two boys still aimlessly wander around, as does Jaworsky. "Always on the prowl, looking for somebody, anybody to kill, to quench the killer's thirst," says the narrator, doing the actor's job for him.

Jim's derring-do in parachuting to Jaworsky's plateau puzzles, as Joe simply *drives* to the same place. "Kill or be killed," goes on the narrator, on his major theme, "Man's inhumanity to Man." (If my paragraphs seem disjointed, this only reflects the film with accuracy.)

The boys happen upon Jaworsky, who goes "yahhhh" and waves a stick at them. They flee. "The Beast, finding his victims gone, unleashes his fury." Jaworsky throws a rock. The boys haplessly hide in Jaworsky's own cave, but later sneak out. He walks up, throws another rock, then chases the boys. Joe or Jim fires at the Beast, and one shot brings him down.

But, aha, he jumps up, tosses the troopers around, and almost strangles one of them in a wrestling-like hold, but shot again, he collapses. "Come on," says an offscreen trooper, "let's go." And they do, leaving the body in the desert.

Jaworsky still lives. A little bunny hops up to him and licks his face. Jaworsky gently grasps the rabbit, and dies. This attempt at poignancy is about as effective as anything else.

In a way, *Beast of Yucca Flats* dazzles. I find it difficult to imagine a film as thoroughly inept as this one; absolutely nothing whatsoever works. It may very well be the worst nonporno science fiction movie ever made. The photography varies from murky to overexposed; some scenes are apparently supposed to be day-for-night, but look like day. At best, the editing confuses and verges on surrealism at worst. The film reaches new heights of incoherence.

At the beginning, we cannot tell who the Russkies are shooting at, nor can we discern relative distances between the characters. The geographical continuity is flabbergasting, as in the business with the parachute and car; everything seems to be happening at once, in the same place, in some strange soundless void.

Psychotronic pegged the film: "The narrator repeats absurd philosophical lines over and over ... and informs us of things after they've happened on the screen. The actors stare blankly waiting for direction.... A senseless nonmovie, worse than anything Tor did for Ed Wood, Jr."

Except for Tor, the acting does not exist. People walk about doing the major physical action the scenes call for—move from here to there, stop, look at the mountain—but without any characterization at all. Tor as a defecting Soviet scientist was an attempt at having a character, but his nationality has nothing to do with the story; he might as well have been a plumber. Or a wrestler, or an aging, overweight actor.

"Dale Steele" in *Modern Monsters* 4 talked to writer-director Coleman Francis, a bit player in several films, including *This Island Earth*, *Cimarron* (1960) and *Beyond the Valley of the Dolls* (1970). Francis told the interviewer Tor was too heavy to climb a hill in the Mojave Desert, where the film was shot, and had to be dragged to the top by a pulley. He mentioned few other incidents, hardly surprising, as the film took only a few days to shoot.

As amazingly bad as *Yucca Flats* is, Coleman Francis did direct other films, including *The Skydivers* (1963) and *Night Train to Mundo Fine* (1966), in which star John Carradine sings the title song. Francis is one of those types often found in Hollywood, hanging around the edges of the industry, occasionally surfacing as a bit player in major films, or a character actor in films made by directors like Russ Meyer. I hope he has enjoyed himself through the years; to spend the vast sum of $34,000 on *Beast of Yucca Flats* is a sign of some kind of commitment.

Oddly enough, the film received almost favorable reviews from the movie trade papers. James Powers in the *Hollywood Reporter* considered the film "equal or superior [to] at least 30% of the program pictures picked up abroad," and thought Francis' incoherent script "well planned." Powers does, however, point out that the film was shot without sound, and said the "characters do not have much individuality because [Francis] has neglected the establishing shot and closeup." At least.

At *Variety*, "Tube" was more critical, finding the film an "earnest but uncertain effort to tell a taut and different screen-story-with-a-message on discouragingly limited means," he thought it "crude even by lower berth program standards, which are, realistically, all it can aspire to." He also said that "dialog is held to a bare minimum in favor of narration which is frequently too stilted, superfluous and condescending to be of much aid in advancing the story or developing interest.... [The film] displays a jarring lack of geomorphic perspective.... Credulity, in short, is strained throughout.... The actors actually benefit from the absence of much dialog, relying on visual projection to get their feelings across, capably in most cases."

I suspect that Coleman Francis himself invited "Tube" and Powers to the screening, and that they were straining to be fair to him and his film. It's otherwise hard to account for their reactions to this virtually unbelievable film. Just having someone turn into a monster because of an atomic bomb is hardly criticism of nuclear weaponry, but at least it's a faint perspective. But *Beast of Yucca Flats* has nothing else; Tor Johnson is earnest, like the picture, but strained seriousness and awesome ineptitude sink it.

Creature from the Haunted Sea

The advertising for *Creature from the Haunted Sea* looks as if it were prepared by someone who knew only the title, who desperately struggled to come up with a salable image. Aside from the usual stuff, the text on the ad screams "What was the unspeakable secret of the SEA OF LOST SHIPS?" Near the bottom of the ad was a cautionary if confusing note: "Please do not give away the answer to the secret." The art showed a yacht sinking in the background on the right, and a man on the left clinging to an overturned rowboat. Prominent in the foreground is a gigantic, scaled, clawed hand rising from the sea, with a woman in a pink nightgown straddling the big green thumb and looking more startled than frightened. The thumb seems like some colossal penis.

Those lured in by this, to say the least, sensationalistic ad were undoubtedly nonplussed and perhaps angry. Whe could blame them? Only Roger Corman, producer-director of the film, who's quoted in *The Movie World of Roger Corman* as somewhat plaintively complaining about lack of business. "The film had a mild success. I couldn't believe you could do such insane stuff on film and get a little tiny profit.... It should have been a big success or a big failure."

It might have been one or the other if it had been legitimately promoted, but the advertising promised a giant monster. The film itself was a dizzily aimless comedy about gangsters, fleeing Batista Cubans and a man-eating sea creature resembling the Cookie Monster. When people have been led to expect an all-out thriller and get instead a loopy spoof, they have reason to be annoyed. No wonder the film didn't bring in money up to Corman's expectations. At least with *A Bucket of Blood* and *Little Shop of Horrors*, his previous comedy-horror films, the advertising clearly promised comedies.

Quoted in the same book, Beach Dickerson said, "Chuck Griffith got conned into writing a rewrite of *Beast from Haunted Cave*, which was a rewrite of *Naked Paradise/Thunder over Hawaii*. This was the third time he'd written the same script." Even the title harks back to *Beast from Haunted Cave*. This time, using the same plot, Griffith gave Corman a comedy.

Corman and company had gone to Puerto Rico, as related in the entry on *Last Woman on Earth*, and found themselves with enough time and money to do another film beyond the two they had already prepared. In this period, Corman was eager to see how fast he could make films; he felt that *Creature from the Haunted Sea* could be done in a short time.

Again quoting from *The Movie World of Roger Corman*, "From Puerto Rico," Corman told the interviewer, "I called Chuck Griffith and said I wanted a comedy-horror film to be shot in Puerto Rico in six days. I told him a rough story line and pointed out how many and what actors I had there, and I said, 'It's got to be written for these same actors—I'm not flying anybody in—and I've got to have the script in a week.'" Griffith convinced Corman to play one of the roles in the film, as he had done on a couple of other pictures. "When [Griffith] woke up in the morning, he read his notes, decided I hadn't offered him enough money, but took the assignment anyway. But in order to get me, he made my part the most complex role it was possible for an actor to play—laughing hysterically in one scene, sobbing in another scene, trying to kill somebody in the next scene, even a victim of the killer in the next scene, and so on. It would have taxed the abilities of the finest actor in the world. I was supposed to direct, and he had increased the size of my role."

A high school actor named Robert Bean had, on Corman's okay, paid his own way to Puerto Rico and arrived in time to be the boom man on the picture made prior to *Creature*. Corman got cold feet at the thought of playing the complicated role (Jack) and directing at the same time, so he gave the part to Bean. "He may have been the only person in the history of motion pictures to have gone from boom man to a starring role within the span of a week," Corman told Ed Naha (*The Films of Roger Corman*). Corman didn't appear in *Haunted Sea* at all, although some sources claim he did.

Corman received Griffith's script on Thursday, rewrote parts of it between takes on Friday, had it duplicated that afternoon, gave it to the cast and rehearsed on Friday, Saturday and Sunday, and started shooting on Monday. Despite many virtues, the film certainly looks rushed, underrehearsed and improvised.

To the basic plot of conniving gangsters versus good guys, Corman added material based on his own experiences in Cuba. He had gone to the island country with the Woolner brothers to talk with a Cuban film company about doing movies there. One night, he heard what he thought was a car backfiring, but soon realized it was machine-gun fire. In the morning, he learned that Fidel Castro's troops had fled after killing the police chief and some other people. When Corman and the Woolners saw that Batista's men also had machine guns, they left Cuba.

Creature from the Haunted Sea's mock-hip narration is spoken by Sparks Moran (Edward Wain, i.e., Robert Towne) who, though posing as a notorious gum machine burglar for Renzo Capeto (Antony Carbone), is in reality American spy XK-150. "Survivors of the old regime" in Cuba (most sources suggest that the name of the island is not specified, but it is) have approached gangster Capeto, "the most trustworthy man ever to be deported from Sicily," to take them and the Cuban treasury to safety.

Capeto is a crook of many aliases, including Capo Rezetto, Ratto Pezetti, Zeppo Stacatto and Shirley LaTour. His moll, Mary-Belle Monahan (Betsy Jones-Moreland), also known as Belle Mary Monahan, Monahan Mary Belle, etc., is just as cheap and greedy as he is, making her immensely attractive to Moon-struck Sparks.

Among Capeto's crew is Peter Peterson, Jr. (Beach Dickerson), a bird mimic who blew his brain out of whack while imitating a whooping crane at the Elk's Convention Picnic in 1942. He's a dim-witted, good-natured assassin who constantly makes animal noises.

After Colonel Tostada (Edmundo Rivero Alvarez) and his men come aboard with all that appetizing money, Capeto hatches a scheme to get the loot for himself. He's heard of a Cuban fisherman named Hemingway who hooked a monster some time ago, so Capeto and his crew make plans to fake monster attacks, kill the Cubans, and get the loot. There's no clear reason why they don't just toss all the Cubans over the side.

He uses a plunger to make sucker-cup-like marks on the deck, and kills one of the Cubans with garden forks. The Cubans, however, don't seem especially distressed by this news, and continue dancing. After we see another Cuban killed, in the morning *two* are missing. Sparks' narration tells us the monster "had already been invented by somebody else—by a couple of other monsters, I guess." The monster itself unintentionally helps Capeto's scheme proceed, which baffles the gangster, who knows nothing of the monster.

A patrol boat happens by, and Mary-Belle sings a song to distract them while Pete kills them all. (When Pete gets a plan right, Capeto gives him a lollipop.) Mary-Belle keeps singing.

Finally, Capeto deliberately runs the boat aground near La Isla de Borracho; the strongbox is tossed into a skiff which immediately sinks. The monster grabs a couple of guys who go in after it, but still no one knows the monster is real.

On the island, Pete meets Rosina Perez, who also does animal noises, and they do a kind of courting dance. Sparks meets Carmelita Rodriquez, who had been living "in a sort of sorority house down by the docks."

The Cubans and Capeto's men jump into the bay to look for the strongbox. A Cuban swims by the camera; Renzo follows with a garden fork, and Jack (ex-boom man Robert Bean) follows with a plunger. Renzo and the monster separately kill more Cubans, whose supply seems nearly inexhaustible.

Pete and Jack decide to kill everyone else, take the money, and settle down on the island with the various women they've encountered. Jack has fallen for sweet little Mango Perez (Sonya Noemi), who thinks everyone on the boat looks like "bottom row prizes in a shooting gallery."

When Capeto goes for the strongbox himself, the monster spots him but kills Mango instead. Jack blames Capeto, but nothing comes of this. During another dive, more Cubans, including Tostada, are killed, and later the monster kills Jack, too.

Sparks falls for Carmelita, abandoning his great love for the unresponsive Mary-Belle, still crazy for Capeto. In fact, she tells the gangster "I'll love you until the day I die" just as the monster kills her. The monster then kills almost everyone else. Capeto tries to escape in a little boat, but the monster gets him, too. Sparks and Carmelita are the only people left alive. "So I got the girl," he says, "and guess who got the gold?" The final shot is of the monster sitting on the strongbox at the bottom of the bay, surrounded by bones, picking his teeth with Capeto's garden fork.

Corman did say that he wanted to make a movie in which the monster won.

Obviously, *Creature from the Haunted Sea* overflows with running gags, spoofy lines, and almost surreal touches. Sparks constantly romances Mary-Belle, who thinks he's a jerk, which he is. He tries to tell her that she's too good for her life with Capeto, but she actually enjoys being a criminal. She cannot discourage him, and he again and again leans over her, breathing heavily, talking like a hero. To no avail.

In addition to the bizarre if pointless touch of Pete's bird and animal sounds, there's an odd scene in which Jack makes a call from a pay phone attached to the side of a rock. He's watched by a grinning man (not Roger Corman), and another man in a suit wanders by. Pete always wears vertical stripes, and Jack wears horizontal stripes.

The constant narration is overdone but gives a shape and direction to the aimless movie. And occasionally it hits the right note: we will see, Sparks tells us, "the most astounding adventure to be inflicted upon man."

There's a fresh feeling to the acting, as if good if underused players were having fun with the material. It shows in Antony Carbone's performance, which may be his best. He's finally given free reign to play with his facial resemblance to Humphrey Bogart, and he makes the most of it without doing an impression. He plays Renzo with a straight face and straight acting, which helps make the crazy lines and material more funny than overtly comic playing would.

Betsy Jones-Moreland is also fine and funny as the happily rotten Mary-Belle. She lolls around the deck, aloof to lovesick Sparks, and passionate to aloof Capeto. Somewhat more than Carbone, she lets us know she's in on the joke, but that doesn't harm things much.

Beach Dickerson is more amusing than you might expect as the guy who sings like birdies and talks like Katnip the Cat. The more grandiose emoting required of Robert Bean seems to have been toned down, and he's not memorable as Happy Jack Monahan (who's never happy).

Robert Towne is better here than he is in *Last Woman on Earth*, but that's only by comparison. He's still more of a writer than an actor, although he does try to play the part in the required straight-faced tone.

The film opens with amusing, wacky animation of the monster ambling back and forth, being pursued by (or pursuing, it's hard to tell) carloads of rebels and military types.

Corman gave Beach Dickerson $150 and told him to make a monster suit that could be used on land or in the water. After some argument, Dickerson and Bean did it. "It was a funny monster," said Dickerson. "We stole Army helmets and stacked them to form its face. We draped its body in oilcloth, to give it a sleazy look, and we gave it fangs—we cut out holes and pasted in the teeth. We got two tennis balls and a ping-pong ball and cut them in two—that was the monster's eyes. Then we draped it in steel wool. That monster was seven and a half feet tall—we spent a fortune on steel wool. Those were the good old days." (Quoted in *The Movie World of Roger Corman*.) The monster also had swim fins and a skirt made of seaweed. Anything but convincing or even really serviceable, its Muppetlike appearance was appropriate to this film.

The film was released at 60 minutes, but is usually shown on TV in a 72-minute print which, Joe Dante says, was "padded with numerous underwater shots and extra narration. Unfortunately, TV stations usually *include* the padding, and often cut the scene in which the heroine sings the title song during a gun battle."

Corman's six-day wonder wasn't released until 1961, and received few reviews, but they were favorable. *Boxoffice* considered it "a most engaging spoof on the horror element," and felt it contained "some engaging thespians who cavort with spiritedness" in this "unanticipated entertainment.... If there exists a 'New Wave' in the U.S.–based film industry, it must be Corman, who ranks as chief of state."

Allen M. Widem of the *Motion Picture Herald* enjoyed Antony Carbone in the film, and thought it good, displaying Corman's "distinctive, decisive flair."

Corman was nearing the end of his most prolific period as a filmmaker, and his career was undergoing a change of direction. By the time *Creature from the Haunted Sea* came out, Corman's *House of Usher* (1960) had already been released, and *Pit and the Pendulum* was in production. Corman had been found by intellectuals as well as audiences, and his increasing fame brought increasing responsibilities. He felt the time for seeing how fast he could make movies was over, and while still working with limited budgets, he began to broaden his horizons. As a director, he made only two more black-and-white pictures, and virtually all of his subsequent pictures of any size had name stars. With films like *Creature from the Haunted Sea*, he had more freedom yet more constraints than he would have in the decade ahead. The picture reflects this, in its half-good, half-terrible quality.

It's the least of the three comedies Corman made from Griffith scripts. The poor, badly processed photography and truly terrible, tasteless score, forcing every gag, continually sounding Funny, seriously harm the picture. It wanders, seems enervated and lame. But there's liveliness in the performances, a sense of fun in the making, and a kind of impish spoofing of conventions of storytelling and moviemaking that would vanish from even the best of Corman's films in the years to come. *Creature from the Haunted Sea* is far from being Corman's best film, but in some ways, it's among the most representative: talented, intelligent people swiftly rushing through sleazy material, with a different viewpoint and a kind of camaraderie that extends to the audience.

The Day the Sky Exploded

Don't get your hopes up. Despite its exciting title, this little movie proves to be a cheap European coproduction relying almost entirely on stock footage for its spectacle. Most of the scenes of the actors take place on only a few sets, underlit in a peculiarly overatmospheric style, like a gothic horror movie. Probably because of the low budget and lack of original spectacle footage, the film concentrates on how the story affects the main characters. This can be done to good effect, as in *The Day the Earth Caught Fire*, but here the characters are dull, and so is the talky, claustrophobic film.

The rocket scientists of all the world's nations join forces to launch an atomic-powered rocket with scientist John McLaren (Paul Hubschmid) aboard. However, just as it's leaving the atmosphere, the rocket malfunctions and McLaren is forced to jettison his capsule. Along with the other scientists, he watches with worry as the rocket later crashes into the sun, causing enormous explosions on the sun's surface.

Among the effects of the solar explosions are tidal waves, typhoons and heat waves, which cause further disasters, including enormous fires. Animals leave their natural haunts and begin migrating across the land. Although the solar explosions cause some problems on Earth, they really stir things up in outer space, sending a cluster of asteroids on a collision course with Earth.

When the population of the world learns of the impending disaster, chaos ensues as desperate thousands seek refuge in tunnels, caverns and mines.

Meanwhile, the scientists have their own problems. McLaren has been estranged from his wife (Fiorella Mari), but they patch up their differences and prepare to face the end together. Another scientist, according to *Boxoffice*, "displays a hitherto unexpected sense of responsibility and self-sacrifice; a third goes mad."

As the disasters batter the Earth and the asteroids approach, McLaren realizes there is but one hope left for mankind: the team of scientists persuades all world governments to sacrifice their atomic missiles in an effort to blast the asteroids into dust. At a given time, they launch missiles all over the world at the oncoming asteroids. Their attempt is successful and they save the world.

The most significant historical aspect of *The Day the Sky Exploded* is that it was photographed by Mario Bava, cinematographer and special effects director, who soon became a director of note. See the entry on *Caltiki the Immortal Monster* for more on Bava.

The film was an Italian-French coproduction, released in Europe in 1958. The Italian title was *La Morte Viene dallo Spazio* (Death Comes from Space), and the French title was *Le Danger Vient de l'Espace* (Danger Comes from Space). The film was released in England in 1961 as *Death Comes from Outer Space*. (I don't know if *The Day the Sky Exploded* ever played on a double bill with *The Night the World Exploded*, but it should have.)

There's little of interest to the film. Lead Paul Hubschmid had a brief career in the United States in the early 1950s under the name Paul Christian, appearing under that name in *Beast from 20,000 Fathoms*. He returned to Europe and resumed his original name, making few significant U.S.–released films, although he did appear in *Funeral in Berlin* (1966) and *Skullduggery* (1970). As a leading man, Hubschmid was generally colorless and stiff, but as he moved into middle age, he became a character actor of some distinction.

The extensive and ingenious use of stock footage received the most praise. This activity sometimes impresses viewers (see comments on *The Lost Missile*), but just as often annoys them. While the film overall is third-rate, it does look more exciting by this use of stock footage. However, ingenuity at hiding a low budget may be interesting or amusing, but hardly seems reason to praise a film's quality.

Nonetheless, the *Monthly Film Bulletin* (giving the film a rating of II) seems to have considered this raiding of film archives almost a kind of art. "Faced with a small budget and an extremely elaborate subject, the producers of this ... film have turned to stock footage to such an extent that this might well be termed the stock-shot film *par excellence*. This aspect gives an otherwise routine, tamely directed programme picture a certain bizarre interest: some of the disaster footage is perilously old and grainy and the spectacular finale includes every rocket shot one has ever seen and many more. In fairness, it should be added that this disparate material has been quite ingeniously assembled."

Allen M. Widem in the *Motion Picture Herald* called the film "good," saying that "it's geared, from blastoff to reasonably happy ending, to the timely, topical premise of what can happen to us mere Earthlings once appraised [sic] of an oncoming shower of asteroids from Outer Space. The special effects department is to be congratulated for its ingenuity."

More recently, Joe Dante in the *Castle of Frankenstein 1967 Annual* disparaged the film for its "excess of stock footage and ludicrous dubbing (including tape-looped background voice saying 'Oh, my baby' amid screams every 10 seconds through most of pic)." After describing the action-packed plot, *Psychotronic* dryly noted that the movie was "not as exciting as it sounds." Don Willis (I) was not impressed: "Hard-to-follow, or rather, hard-to-want-to-follow dubbed mess."

Along with a great low-budget and/or imported science fiction films of the 1950s and 60s, *The Day the Sky Exploded* has apparently vanished from American television. It is not a great loss.

Dr. Blood's Coffin

This peculiar throwback to horror films of the 1940s is at least notable for its confident exuberance. Director Sidney J. Furie handles it as if no one had ever made a picture like this before. Unfortunately, that wasn't the case; the plot was not only preposterous but hackneyed, and despite some good per-formances and a resolutely adult approach, *Dr. Blood's Coffin* remains minor, though distinctly better than its companion feature, *The Snake Woman*.

There are few other films with a title more redolent of mad scientists and ghoulishness; the title may have preceded the plot. Mad scientists, if any exist in reality, would of course be more likely to be called Dr. Smith than Dr. Blood. Having a scientist of that name in your film somewhat forces the issue; he has only the choice of being a mad scientist or turning pirate (as another Dr. Peter Blood did in *Captain Blood*).

Dr. Peter Blood (Kieron Moore) of this film is a modern-day medical researcher, expelled from his studies for unorthodox theories and, worse, practices. Peter's experiments in Vienna involved restoring life to dead animals by transplanting into the corpse a living heart taken from another animal paralyzed with curare. When Peter began showing interest in expanding his experiments to include people, he was drummed out of the research field.

Peter's convinced himself that he's working for the betterment of mankind. He wants to restore life to worthy dead people by using the hearts of unworthy living ones. He returns to the small village in Cornwall where his father, Dr. Robert Blood (Ian Hunter), is a general practitioner.

His father offers to make Peter a partner in his practice, but Peter is not interested in anything so mundane. His father's receptionist Linda (Hazel Court), however, does catch Peter's interest. Widowed a year, Linda has begun to become more interested in the outside world again, and Peter attracts her.

Several villagers disappear soon after Peter's arrival, and although he does help in a search of nearby abandoned tin mines, we know what's going on, don't we?

Linda falls in love with Peter, and things are proceeding swimmingly until one night she finds him cutting up the living body of one of his victims in the undertaker's shop. This somewhat sours Linda on viewing Peter as a potential husband. They quarrel.

Peter feels vengeful, so he prepares a nasty surprise for Linda in his secret laboratory in a tin mine that *wasn't* searched. He kidnaps Linda and takes her there, to show her his handiwork: the resurrected body of her husband Steve (Paul Stockman), who's been given the heart of a murdered hobo.

Steve comes back to life muttering "Linda, Linda," and immediately advances on her, apparently intending to resume his marital pleasures, but is somewhat the worse for wear, having been dead and buried a year. He is falling apart. Linda is not happy.

Furious, she calls Steve a "creature from Hell," which hurts his feelings. He realizes Peter is the author of his misery, and attacks the screwy biochemist. As the two kill each other, Linda escapes from the mine.

To say that the science in this film is unlikely is a major understatement. The science in this film is outlandish, almost lunatic. The film might almost be considered a fantasy rather than science fiction, if not for the approach. The major stupidity must be the idea that just sticking a functioning heart back in a body restores life. Even a body a year dead, in which the veins, arteries and, in fact, all tissues have begun to decay. A new heart would just spray blood around. No wonder Peter Blood was kicked out of Vienna—he's a fruitcake.

The script is credited to Jerry Juran, for whom I can find no further credits as writer. Harris M. Lentz's book of credits for SF & horror films indicates a Jerry Juran also directed many episodes of TV series produced by Irwin Allen, and others have told me that Jerry Juran is the same person as Nathan Juran, the director of several SF films (see *Brain from Planet Arous* in this volume). This seems not unlikely, as Nathan Juran also directed several episodes of the same Irwin Allen series. Whether or not Nathan Juran, director, and Jerry Juran, director, are the same person, I do not know if Jerry Juran, writer, is the same as Jerry Juran, director.

Whoever Juran the writer is, he has some original and alarming ideas about appropriate science. Almost any other method of corpse-revival would seem more plausible. Whoever wrote this film seems to have concluded that means are justified by the end: you want a walking corpse, so you do any old thing to get one.

Kieron Moore does fairly well with the character of Peter Blood. He's handsome in a slightly eccentric fashion; being young makes him an odd choice for a mad medico, but his lean intensity makes him seem a true fanatic.

The script soon defeats him, requiring Blood to do truly foolish things—killing people in town, then cutting them up in a local shop—but Moore makes the most of his material.

He seems to have retired from acting in 1967; at least I can find no film credits for him after that. He came on strong early in his career, which began in 1944 after Irish stage experience. He showed both wit and intensity as an actor, and was notable in *A Man About the House* (1946), *Mine Own Executioner* (1947) and the American film *Ten Tall Men* (1951). He was Vronsky in the 1947 *Anna Karenina*, and a good Uriah in *David and Bathsheba* (1952). However, by the mid-50s his career had gone into something of a decline. While he continued to play mostly leading roles, the quality of the films slipped, and in major films, he began to appear only in character and support roles. He was in *Satellite in the Sky*, *The Key* (1958), *League of Gentlemen* (1960), and *I Thank a Fool* (1962). He was the lighthouse keeper in the added scenes in *The Day of the Triffids* (1963) and the heroic scientist in *Crack in the World* (1965). Americans are most likely to remember him as the Arab in *Arabesque* (1966) and as the rascally village lout in *Darby O'Gill and the Little People* (1959).

Hazel Court is a big, attractive redhead with a sense of humor, better served by villainous roles than ones in which she has to be the menaced maiden. She always looks like she could clobber whatever it is that's out to get her, but also as if she could easily fall victim to her own schemes. She's good but wasted in *Dr. Blood's Coffin*. After appearing in *The Curse of Frankenstein*, she became typed in horror films, turning up again in *The Man Who Could Cheat Death*. She came to the United States, where she was in three of Roger Corman's Poe films, *The Premature Burial* (1962), *The Raven* (1963; she was a lot of fun), and *The Masque of the Red Death* (1964), her last film to date. She married American director Don Taylor, himself a former actor, and retired from the screen. One source claims she was in *The Final Conflict*, but this is not confirmed by credit lists.

Of Canadian origin, Sidney J. Furie began making films in his own country, including *A Cool Sound from Hell* (1958), then emigrated to England where his flashy visual style swiftly developed over just three years. During that time, he directed not only *Dr. Blood's Coffin* and its cofeature *The Snake Woman*, but *Night of Passion*, *Three on a Spree*, *Wonderful to Be Young* (all 1961) and *Swinger's Paradise* (1964). In particular, *The Boys* (1961) and *The Leather Boys* (1964) developed a good reputation for Furie, and he filmed *The Ipcress File* (1965) in a highly decorated, overwrought visual style that impressed most viewers (certainly including me). He came to the United States to make the peculiar Marlon Brando film, *The Appaloosa* (1966), and continued to helm major pictures, including *The Lawyer* (1967, his best film after *The Ipcress File*), *Little Fauss and Big Halsey* (1970), *Lady Sings the Blues* (1972), *Sheila Levine Is Dead and Living in New York* (1975) and *Gable and Lombard* (1976). Others of his films have been of lesser interest, including *Hit!* (1973), *The Boys in Company C* (1978) and *Night of the Juggler* (1979).

In general, while Furie does have a vivid surface style, he rarely goes beneath that to anything resembling content; he's one of several directors who seem to feel that the look of a film *is* the content. His career is especially notable for having risen from inexpensive horror movies to major films; he's one of the few from this period to have done so.

Reviews were peculiarly mixed for *Dr. Blood's Coffin*. The *Monthly Film Bulletin* gave the picture a contemptuous III. "The mad doctor theme is hoary and improbable enough without the abundance of extra improbabilities which this ill-constructed story imposes on it, not least a high-speed, one-man, heart-grafting operation in a tin mine. The result, though rich in curare, flashing scalpels, decayed flesh and Cornish landscape, lacks style, suspense and imagination and will scarcely satisfy even the most naive necrophiliac."

On the other hand, Jack Moffitt in *Limelight* was especially pleased. "The more discriminating horror fans ... may find merit in this intelligently directed and well written British recapitulation of the Frankenstein formula [which is] well acted [and which has] an interesting background of Cornwall and its ancient tin mines.... The buildup is much better than that of a penny dreadful.... Producer George Fowler can take a medium-sized bow for this one. Color photography by Stephen Dade (some of it hand-held) increases the credibility. The music composed by Buxton Orr and conducted by Philip Martell has lyrical passages for the lovely Cornish coastal shots and is satisfactorily eerie for the monster theme."

Charles Stinson in the *Los Angeles Times* thought it "a rather mild tincture of the old mercurochrome [with a] routine and stereotyped script [which was] directed unimaginatively." On the other hand, Stinson thought Moore and Court turned in "solid" performances.

Variety's "Tube" seemed appalled *and* impressed. "Repulsive is about the most congenial word for *Dr. Blood's Coffin*, yet its very repellent nature figures to be its staunchest ally in luring the customers.... To compound the decidedly Rh-negative circulatory aspects of the sanguinary United Artists release, the picture does not even benefit from sound story construction. As the responsible British themselves might say, it's a bloody shame."

Dr. Blood's Coffin is mostly just a footnote in Sidney J. Furie's career; its peculiar attempt to blend science fiction and horror resulted in a primitively plotted, erratic film. Perhaps United Artists lost faith in it; by the time I saw it in North Bend, Oregon, the color print of *Dr. Blood's Coffin* had been replaced by one in black and white.

The Fabulous World of Jules Verne

This is the best film covered in this book.

Karel Zeman's masterpiece is so charming, so witty and so sophisticated, while remaining faithful to the spirit of Jules Verne, that it's breathtaking. Yet upon its initial release in the United States in 1961 (three years after its debut in its native Czechoslovakia), many of the young people attracted to it by the title were disgusted. They found the special effects "fakey" and the storyline familiar and trivial. Even today, there are those who fail to recognize the film for what it is: the best movie ever adapted from a work of Verne's. (And of course, there are those who simply disagree.)

One of the central problems in the acceptance of films such as this is that Americans have trained Hollywood to give them films with lots of special effects, and Hollywood has responded with films in the mode of stylization called "realism." That is, effects that always are *supposed* to look as if they were happening in reality. Actually, that's not quite what it is: Hollywood gives us heightened, interpreted "reality": spaceships that roar in the airless vacuum of space and bank like fighter planes against the resistance of air that isn't there; floods that tower above buildings like waves instead of welling up around them; waves at sea that are higher than ships; dinosaurs that behave like crabby lizards.

Nonetheless, effects generally do not depart much from our observable, day-to-day reality, and are judged by how well they duplicate it. Moviegoers watch for wires, matte lines and the heightened clarity of action (strobing) that results from the use of stop-motion animation. (This demand for "realism" extends to acting, so that broad strokes and grand gestures are interpreted these days as "hamminess.") I have more to say on this subject in the section on *The Mysterians*.

What Karel Zeman did in *The Fabulous World of Jules Verne* was simple, yet rejected by many moviegoers: he tried to bring to life on screen the style of illustrations that accompanied the first editions of Verne's works. These were generally done in woodcuts (some sources say steel engravings, but the original illustrations were wood-engraving or line block reproductions), and as a result, there were many horizontal lines in the finished picture. The lines were shading, because with this kind of printing, grays were not possible. However, in our perception today, the horizontal lines seem quaint, and are an integral part of the drawing.

As a result, the black-and-white film lies far from our notions of "realism," and so the rejection by some U.S. moviegoers. It couldn't have been very profitable.

Others, who appreciated the film's deliberate quaintness, raised almost to the level of art, failed to understand that the film is more than just the old drawings brought however inventively to life. It is at once an affectionate spoof of Verne and the 19th-century attitudes toward science, a tribute to both Verne and these attitudes, and a reinterpretation of them in pacifist terms. Furthermore, it is a richly conceived, superbly structured and even wistful period science fiction tale.

The tone of the film is complex yet sustained: wistful, ironic, witty, satiric, and altogether haunting. The term "poetic," which I generally avoid as being nebulous, has some application here. The film is both childlike and sophisticated—yet not aloof from its material. Zeman embraces Verne for his virtues, while being aware that, while predictive, the author's works are dated and charming because of that.

There's also an elusive, hard-to-describe tone found in slightly satiric films from Slavic countries and France, but rarely anywhere else. It's perhaps typified best in *Fabulous World* in the little scene in which the heroine irons her clothing on the back of a cannon, using the heated head of the ramrod as her iron. There's a very faintly mocking tone to the scene, presented absolutely straight, but the mocking is affectionate. It's not quite whimsical, though the film does have its share of whimsy. This unnamed tone of sweet, detached irony is common in comic period pieces which try to maintain a true mood of the period, still filtering it through modern sensibilities. *The Fabulous World of Jules Verne* virtually defines this tone, and Zeman may have been the one to establish it. If only he would have named it. Perhaps Zemanesque will do.

The storyline of the film is derived in part from Verne's novel *Face au Drapeau* of 1896 (published in English as *Face the Flag*), although Zeman says he was inspired by other Verne novels, without naming them. The film follows Verne's plot for about half its length, then switches to a variation on *20,000 Leagues Under the Sea*.

Though the plot is familiar, much of what is splendid about the film lies within the plot, so some detailing of it is necessary.

Simon Hart (Lubor Tokos*) returns to his native land from a trip, noting the wonders of his age: steamships, balloons pedaled through the sky like bicycles, submarines, an airplane, a steam automobile, a train, even the *Albatross* from *Robur the Conqueror*. Hart fills with joy; the world is being tamed by Man in a rational and lucid manner, with the betterment of all as the goal. Hart, who narrates throughout the film (there is little actual dialogue), assists noted scientist Professor Roche (Arnost Navratil), researching into the nature of "pure matter" in an effort to find an explosive.

On the way back to Roche's mansion by the sea, Hart takes time to watch a little newsreel (moving pictures!) on the train. We see skating camels, and a report that the submarine Hart had seen from his ship has been lost at sea with all hands.

Hart arrives at Roche's palatial home, and joins the scientist in his study. While they work, we see a boatload of piratical sailors arrive through the pounding surf at the rocks beneath Roche's home. Hart and Roche spill some papers, and while they are picking them up, observed from floor level by the camera, we get a glimpse of a pirate in a curtained doorway beyond them.

After the two men retire, they are awakened by noises. There's a quick, funny scene in a bedroom; in the manner of some 19th century illustrators, the bed and candelabra are somewhat exaggerated in size, making the men look childlike. Both Roche and Hart are kidnapped by daring men, and taken to a waiting ship. A helper discovers them gone and reports this to alarmed authorities, who mount a fruitless search.

Hart awakens to find Roche being treated with great respect by their captor, whom we later learn is Count Artigas (Miloslav Holub). The giant *Nautilus*–like submarine which was reported lost is towing the sailing ship they are on. Aboard the sub, we are treated to views of lots and lots of fish through the gigantic undersea viewing port.

Artigas is wealthy, gaining his riches by plundering treasures of sunken ships. He wants to use Roche's invention of the explosive to conquer the world; Roche is blithely unaware of this, though Hart realizes the nobleman's nefarious scheme.

Artigas commands the submarine to wreck a passing merchantman. We see the pirates aboard the sub in a little waiting room, facing each other in two rows, whetting their swords in unison; this is visually linked to the big engines of the sub, pounding away in the same rhythm. When the sharp nose of the submarine penetrates the ship, Zeman cuts to a shot of the ship's figurehead, in the form of a woman, to suggest rape.

He quickly runs through a little anthology of disaster scenes as the ship sinks, including a remarkably complex shot in which the nose of the sub is withdrawn and real water gushes into a wood-engraving room. Unaware of the cause of the disaster, pretty and serene Jana (Jana Zatloukalova) frees some caged birds as the ship sinks beneath her. We see a brief scene in the salon of the tilted sub as a chair slides by the big window.

The pirates don (too modern) diving gear, and emerge (as stop-motion puppets) from the submarine. Some ride bicyclelike undersea craft, one of which has a bicycle bell. Some (live action) divers find treasure in the wreck, and briefly cross swords over it before Artigas stops them. A shark briefly

*The names of all performers and most crew members were Anglicized for publicity connected with this film, though they remained in the Czech original in the credits included in the film. I have used the Czech names throughout.

menaces another diver. A conveyor belt ferries loot to the sub, which heads on toward its destination. But, of course, they rescue the girl first.

They arrive at Artigas' volcanic island, issuing huge clouds of smoke so that casual passersby will think the volcano is active. However, as with Captain Nemo's base, the volcano is actually hollow, with a lagoon which has an underground water passage to the sea.

Artigas, the "last and most diabolical of the buccaneers," takes his guests to his castle within the volcano, where he has an elaborate factory chugging away, generating the smoke. While Roche delights in the opportunity to try to produce what sounds from the narration like heavy water, Hart is stuck for months in an isolated shack across the lagoon.

Artigas tries to win Hart's cooperation by showing him a flying contraption, but Hart goes back to his shack, which has been turned in his absence into a laboratory.

In a shot which spoofs Zeman's own approach, we see Roche's sketch of his planned giant electromagnet dissolve into a "real" scene – which, of course, is only a more elaborate drawing. Doing this tosses off so many jokes in different directions – conventions of movies, the idea that the recreated "living" drawings that make up the film are "reality," etc. – that it's delightful.

Hart uses the equipment Artigas gave him to make a balloon and send it out of the volcano with a message to the world revealing Roche's location. "How ironic," Hart muses on using Artigas' devices against him, as he watches the balloon rise upward through birds, smoke and sunlight.

The balloon reaches civilization, and eager hands pass the message on and on to a telegrapher, who informs the world leaders. (The balloon, its work done, drifts away over stately buildings.)

Back at the volcanic island, Jana, blithely oblivious to the warmongering activities around her, grows flowers in an abandoned helmet. Hart gives her a note for Roche, and she happily takes it to the inventor, but a gust of steam blows it away.

Hart goes to Serke (Vaclav Kyzlink), Artigas' chief engineer – daintily handed a cigar by a gigantic crane – and offers to work underwater in the lagoon to fix a broken cable. While Hart is undersea with two other men in diving suits, they are attacked by a giant squid (done in what seems to be three-dimensional paper sculpture stop-motion), which kills the other two. Hart wounds it, and the squid sends out dense clouds of ink before it swims off.

A search is mounted for Hart, but he hides and is presumed drowned. He begins making his way slowly toward the seaward entrance to the tunnel, but his air runs out and he collapses in a faint on the seabed. He has a strange little fantasy as he lies there: two fish swim toward each other in profile, vanishing from nose to tail as they meet. This leaves only their two tails to form a butterfly, which flies away.

An adorable little submarine enters the tunnel, attracting the attention of some playful sea lions. The narration tells us the sub was sent to the island by the fleet of ships from all nations come in search of Roche and Hart. The sub has an animal-like appearance, with four little leglike fins, which beat against the water like flippers. It also has a fishlike tail and two windows where eyes would be. However, Zeman doesn't overdo this, and the sub looks like the sea-

Opposite: The charming fishlike submarine from Karel Zeman's superlative Fabulous World of Jules Verne (U.S. release, 1961); the look of wood-block engravings obvious here is used throughout the film.

going equivalent of one of those early flying machines that tried to fly like birds by looking like a bird. It scurries along through the water, and its captain (there are only two men in it) spots Hart on the seafloor. The sub backs up, a ladder comes down, and Hart is rescued.

Alas, his freedom is short-lived. Artigas' submarine passes through the tunnel and spots the rescue sub. It gives chase, and finally rams the brave little sub. Only Hart survives.

He swims ashore in the lagoon and climbs to Jana's window in the castle. As she is not yet dressed, she insists he remain outside while she finishes; he calmly dangles by his fingertips until she tells him he can come in.

She's surprised that Artigas sunk the ship she was on, but as she at once has fallen in love with Hart, she believes and agrees to help him. They secretly observe Artigas and his men conferring in an enormous rococo room, and later escape, disguised as two guards. They get aboard Artigas' observation balloon.

Meanwhile, on the cliff overlooking the sea, an enormous cannon is prepared. Roche's terrible explosive has been perfected, and Artigas' first step in conquering the world will be to obliterate the fleet bearing down on his island.

Roche is horrified to learn that what he considered an exploration into pure science (and perhaps of benefit to construction) is going to be used as a weapon of war. Artigas dismisses him airily, then spots Hart in the balloon. He fires at it with a clockwork pistol which expels bullets like a machine gun, but Hart and Jana cut their tether and soar free.

Roche is left alone with the bomb which is about to be loaded into the cannon. He pulls it free, and it tumbles down an incline. Artigas and his gang see it, but it's too late—boom, the bomb goes off in an atomic explosion. Artigas' hat floats on the breeze as the hero and heroine sail away in their balloon.

Georges Sadoul's *Dictionary of Films* quotes Karel Zeman: "I used ideas from different novels by Jules Verne.... My film reaches the imagination through the engravings of Bennett and Riou who illustrated the novels during his lifetime. In some scenes cartoons and puppets are used alongside live actors. I have stylized the smallest details."

Zeman carries out the woodcut look even on the actors themselves: the shading lines are everywhere but on their faces. One sailor even has white patches in the lines, places where the "ink" didn't "print." For live-action stock footage, as of the sea, birds, seals, and so forth, a lined filter is used in printing, to make those scenes—which often have etched matted-in skies—look like woodcuts as well.

Throughout the film there are inventions galore. There's the little catalog of inventions that opens the film; those which had been perfected by Verne's time are rendered as they really were, like steamships and locomotives. Those which were still in the realm of the imagination are taken directly from illustrations for Verne's novels.

Thus, the film is not only set in the period, it is as if it were *made* in the period: prediction remains just that, no hindsight is used in "correcting" the various machines into the forms they had when finally made. This isn't just drollery (though it is droll), it's a rigid discipline that shapes everything about the film. The only "modernity" allowed is in the approach and tone: considering these Victorians as quaint in their social relations which, even by standards of their own time, they were. To have poor Hart dangle by his fingers while Jana finishes dressing would have amused people of the 1890s, but they still would have felt it the only acceptable behavior for a gentleman under those circumstances.

Other than Jules Verne, another source of inspiration for Zeman was almost surely the often-enchanting little trick films of Georges Méliès, which often drew imagery from Verne (who may have seen some of them). The daffy humor of these films turns up sometimes in *Jules Verne*, but the primary inspiration must have been in the way the films were made for, like Méliès, Zeman uses virtually every form of special effect available to him.

There is animation of every form: cartoon, cutout, silhouette, stop-motion with figures, stop-motion with paper sculptures. There are matte shots, split screens, rear screen shots, what may even be front screen projections: it's all one to Zeman, one of the most eclectic special effects experts in the world. What matters to him is the image on screen, and he seems to have no biases as to how to get that image. In his approach—broad and perfectionist—he is inspirational.

Zeman was born in 1910 in Czechoslovakia. He was a poster designer (Czech posters have a long tradition of excellence), a window dresser and director of publicity films before turning to other kinds of films after WWII. According to Sadoul's *Dictionary of Filmmakers*, "Since his first postwar film, *A Christmas Dream*, which combined puppets and live action, he has never stopped experimenting with new techniques and exploring new genres. The didactic film series that he made in the late Forties, which centered on his famous wooden puppet character 'Mr. Prokouk,' was created in a simple, functional style, as was his first medium-length feature, *King Lavra*. For *Inspiration* [also called *Imagination*], he had accepted a bet: to animate glass figurines." This little film features figurines gliding around like skaters. Zeman animated them by heating their joints until the glass became flexible, then allowed them to cool in their new position before shooting a frame of film. This could only have been as laborious and time-consuming as it sounds, but the results are enchanting.

Zeman turned to features in 1952, although he made a few more Prokouk shorts later. His first feature was *Poklad Ptachio Ostrova* (The Treasure of Bird Island), which combined several animation techniques. His next was released in Czechoslovakia in 1955, under the title *Cesta do Pravěku*. It seems to have been shown in its original form on U.S. television in the form of a serial some time in the late 1950s, but was released theatrically in the United States in 1966 as *Journey to the Beginning of Time*. This may be Zeman's least effects-laden film but, typically, he used whatever style of effects necessary to achieve his desired goal.

Some American scenes, similar to the Czech original, were added for the 1966 release. A few boys tour the Museum of Natural History in New York, fascinated by prehistoric life. Later, they go for a row on a lake in Central Park, and discover a stream that is a passage into the past. They drift along the river, seeing progressively more ancient forms of life: early mammals, dinosaurs, etc. Finally, they awaken back in the museum. The film has design partly by the great illustrator of prehistoric life, Zdenek Burian. It seems to be Zeman's only film in full color.

In Czechoslovakia, *The Fabulous World of Jules Verne* had a more rational title, *Vynález Zkázy* (An Invention of Destruction); some sources indicate it was released there in 1957, but the usually-reliable American Film Institute Catalog places the release date as June, 1958.

The imagination shown in the film, and doubtless its pacifist, antibomb message, led to it being chosen to represent Czechoslovakia at the 1958 Brussels Film Festival held in conjunction with the world's fair. The film won the Grand Prix.

Zeman's next film was the handsome *Baron Prašil* (1961), shown in the United States under the familiar title *The Fabulous Baron Munchausen*. This film is also excellent, done in the same mode as *Jules Verne*, only this time the illustrations are drawn from those for Rudolf Raspe's tales of the famous liar, Baron Munchausen. The illustrations are also colored in a style reminiscent of the hand-tinting used on Méliès' films, and is as splendidly imaginative, if not more so, than *Jules Verne*. It features an astronaut (or cosmonaut) meeting Munchausen and Cyrano de Bergerac on the Moon; he accompanies the wonderful Baron on some of his adventures. The film ends with a moving tribute to the spirit of man.

Technically, and in terms of aspiration, it is even better than *Jules Verne*, but it is also very slow going in some places. Zeman seems to have become too fond of the beauty of his own scenes, and dwells on them too long.

This was even more true of *Bláznova Kronika* (also known as *A Jester's Tale*), which followed in 1964. The tendency toward a poky tempo which surfaced in *Baron Munchausen* sets in solidly in *A Jester's Tale*, so slow as to be nearly immobile. Alas, trick work is reduced to a minimum and satire is uppermost. Rarely shown in the United States, it is now available on videotape.

Zeman returned closer to his earlier form with his next film, *Ukradena Vzducholod*, released in 1966, which had some U.S. showings as *A Stolen Airship*. Zeman returned to Verne for inspiration, and the adventure film combined, to good effect, elements of Verne's *Two Years' Vacation* with *Mysterious Island*; even Captain Nemo turned up. The film was still slow, but much faster than the glacial pace of *A Jester's Tale*.

I have not seen Zeman's most recent (and perhaps last) Jules Verne film, *Na Komete*, also known as *Archa Pana Servadaca*. (Sadoul has these as two separate films, but this is unlikely as the alternate titles of the film are actually alternate titles of the Verne novel from which the film is adapted. I saw this and it did live up to my rather great expectations.) Released in 1970, it is adapted from the novel by Verne that was published in English as *Off on a Comet*. It is one of Verne's most fabulous flights of fancy, a story which would seem to provide Zeman with plenty of opportunities for both his skill and his approach. The novel was also the basis of the American film *Valley of the Dragons*, covered in this volume. (Outstanding; available on videotape as *On the Comet*.)

I have been unable to discover anything about Zeman's films after *Na Komete*, other than the barest details; *Pohádky Tisíce a Jedné Noci* (A Thousand and One Nights, 1974), *Carodějuv Učen* (1977) and *Pohádka o Honzíkovi a Mařence* (The Tale of John and Mary, 1980), were done in "paper cut animations." These, and *Krabat* (1977), have good reputations.

In *The Fabulous World*, by using Verne's story and keeping the look of the film firmly in period, peppering it with real and imaginary inventions of the period, Zeman not only recreates the attitude toward the perfectibility of inventions, but comments on it as well. Usually, atomic power is tossed into films of Verne stories to make the author seem even more accurately predictive than he actually was. Here, the purpose seems somewhat different; Zeman has already shown us some of Verne's wonderful machines that simply never came to pass, so to include atomic energy as the source for the bomb isn't a comment on Verne or an effort to bring him up to date.

Furthermore, Zeman does not seem to be sounding a particularly cautionary note about the bomb in our day; the menace we are confronted with is not a titled pirate out to rule the world, but rather those who already *do* rule it. (The very people shown riding to the rescue in *Jules Verne*.)

Instead, by including atomic energy as the power source in the period setting, Zeman is telling us that the source of our troubles with atomic energy and any other form of science gone wrong lies back in this 19th-century isn't-science-wonderful attitude. We encouraged scientists in pure research, regardless of the consequences; as long as this research bettered our own lot, things were wonderful. Interestingly, the film does not suggest that the scientist *not* do his research, but rather that he be more careful for whom he is doing it. The primary note in a tone of wistful regret is that this delight in technology almost necessarily leads to dire consequences. We can be delighted, but the machines may be misused; the wonderful submarine everyone cheers at the beginning is used to kill before the film is over.

Unlike Zeman's later films, *The Fabulous World of Jules Verne* is sprightly, swift-paced and consistently amusing. He doesn't dwell on any of his wonders, for they are too busily zipping around on their own errands to pose.

The satire is directed as much at the Victorians as at technology, such as the fingertip-dangling scene. There are also tiny jokes, flashing by in scenes devoted to something else. The occasional exaggerations of scale never seem forced, but rather like the result of grandiose dreams of the Victorian builders: they can, so they do, build giant beds, oversized candelabras, immense ornate rooms for small meetings.

The acting reflects the tone of the film: no one stands out, everyone plays their part with grace, small gestures and intelligence. The style and approach of Zeman are the stars, not the actors.

This is perhaps the only film which climaxes with an atomic explosion, but then fades out on a sweet scene of aerial romance as the hero and heroine sail off to safety,* and Artigas' hat vanishes on the wind. It's a lovely, graceful conclusion to a film of marvels and wit.

The film was critically well-received. Gene Moskowitz reviewed the film from the Brussels Film Festival for *Variety*. He found it a "possible Yank item for arty houses or specialized theatres. It definitely has moppet appeal and will divert older crowds familiar with the works of Verne.... Trick footage is exemplary while characters have the right attitude to fit in with this cheery adventure tale. Pic is laced with fine visuals, humor and outstanding special effects."

The film was reviewed again by *Variety* under its U.S. title; the critic this time was "Tube," who considered it a "fascinating motion picture.... Certainly the oddest and essentially the most artistically authentic translation of Verne's works to the screen.... Novel in style, offbeat in technique and remarkably durable in story content, it conveys the image and flavor of Verne to an astonishing degree.... Happily, it is a black-and-white picture, in keeping with the period. A great variety of shading has been accomplished in those basic tones. The acting is suitable and secondary. Post-dubbing hardly interferes."

Paul V. Beckley in the New York *Herald-Tribune* seemed puzzled. "The picture could appeal to the very young, scarcely to the sophisticated—but one can't help wondering if children of the space age can respond with any suitable awe to forecasts long since surpassed by reality. The picture does boast a novel

Bill Thomas suggests This Island Earth, *but I think the explosion and following scene are very different in intent.*

process of blending animated drawings with photographed actors acting—rather stiffly."

Howard Thompson in the *New York Times* was bowled over. "Fresh, funny and highly imaginative…. This delightfully wrought screen curio … is something pretty special, [unreeling] in a devastating blend of live-action, animation and panoramic sets…. Expect and get a marvelous eyeful of trick effects, in a flowing succession of Verne backgrounds…. The picture is worth seeing for its technical wizardry alone…. Better still, for such a formidable text, all this is fun to watch, shot through with droll touches at the most crucial moments."

Joe Dante, in *Castle of Frankenstein* #9, considered the film a "very clever Czech combination of live-action and animation patterned after original steel engravings [sic] of 1870 first edition of *20,000 Leagues Under the Sea*. Enjoyable action film, slight story … with charming atmosphere."

The Los Angeles *Examiner* was enthusiastic. "It's a real fun picture…. Unsophisticated, uncomplicated fantasy kind of fun (with a sly touch of spoof) that makes for happy and relaxed viewing…. It also proves there IS something new under the sun."

In *Cinema, the Magic Vehicle*, by Garbicz and Klinowski, the commentator said that the story was not important. "It was not at all that the stunning imagination of [Jules Verne] would provide locomotion for any such project…. The revelation rests elsewhere—in the fact that Zeman with remarkable intuition expressed on the screen the moods dominant at the time when the novel was written. This was his only concern and he resisted the temptation to wink his eye at the audience or to modernize the story or its message."

One of the best summations of Zeman and his films is provided by Robert Skotak's article on the filmmaker in *Fantascene* #3: "Zeman is not a polished effects 'realist' in the tradition of a Ray Harryhausen or Jim Danforth. Nor is he seeking to be. His work is complete unto itself and 'realistic' consistent with his personal intent…. [He] is one of the world's foremost cinema wizards—a conjuror of visions and ideas rarely equalled in their richness, variety, and sense of wonder. Creating images like a painter working on a celluloid canvas, Zeman opens the viewer's eyes and feelings to the dreams of less cynical times, to the exhilaration of youth-filled imagination."

Karel Zeman is one of cinema's true geniuses. And *The Fabulous World of Jules Verne* is one of those extremely rare films that provides each viewer with a sense of personal discovery—and a rediscovery of the joy and wonder we found in films as children.

Gorgo

"Like nothing you've seen before!" the advertising for *Gorgo* proudly claimed. And it was true—if you hadn't seen the silent *Lost World*, *King Kong*, *Beast from 20,000 Fathoms*, *The Black Scorpion*, *The Giant Behemoth*, or a growing number of Japanese films, because though it didn't start out that way, *Gorgo* is another movie about a giant monster attacking a city. It's a good example of such a movie, however, and one of the best-made in the giant-monster subgenre.

Frank, Maurice and Hyman King, independent Hollywood producers who initially made their fortune dealing in slot machines, profitably distributed

Rodan in the United States. They felt there were more bucks to be made out of trouncing another city, so approached Eugene Lourié, who directed both *Beast from 20,000 Fathoms* and *The Giant Behemoth*. At first reluctant, feeling there wasn't much more to be said on the topic, Lourié finally agreed to make the film, partly because he conceived an unusual idea: the monsters would *win*.

In an interesting interview conducted by Paul Mandell in *Fantastic Films* #16, Lourié talked about *Gorgo*. After his daughter cried at the end of *Beast from 20,000 Fathoms* when the monster died, Lourié told Mandell, "I knew that someday I would have to write a story in which the creature does not die — it just goes away!" His initial conception was somewhat different from what finally resulted. "The problem with *Gorgo* was my producers," Lourié told Mandell. "The story as originally conceived was far more poetic. But the King Brothers butchered the idea entirely."

Most of the financing for *Gorgo* was initially scheduled to come from Japan, so with his friend and collaborator Daniel Hyatt, Lourié embarked on a screen story then called "Kuru Island." Mandell said that the story was set on "a fictitious atoll in the South Pacific where cultured pearls were the main export. After a tremendous storm and an underwater eruption, the baby creature surfaces and adheres [sic] to the island.... The beast was to have been captured and brought to a Tokyo zoo for observation when the mother beast surfaces to rescue it."

Lourié suspected that it was the novel element of mother love (not common in reptiles, to say the least) that appealed to the King brothers. "I believe they had a bit of a mother complex," the director told Mandell.

One other novel element of the storyline that did *not* appeal to the Kings, and which was gradually altered as the story took shape over the next year or so, was something that Lourié was especially fond of: *no* scenes of mass destruction. "I wanted the creature to confront human beings," Lourié told Mandell, "but there were no scenes of the military shooting at it and not being able to destroy it. That concept is really ridiculous.... The creature was not supposed to destroy the town, and there were no stock shots planned of military intervention.... I recently acquired an old print of *Gorgo* ... and made a 35-minute version by taking out all those unnecessary scenes. Everything was so much better."

The Japanese financing fell through and the King Brothers began a search for a new locale. At one point in 1959, they had definitely decided on Paris, as no big monster had trounced that city (nor has one yet). They talked with a bemused Art Buchwald about the project in his column for 18 May, 1959. Maurice King was quoted as saying the monster "looks like a giant lizard. But it's not a mean-looking lizard. It's a friendly-looking lizard." Frank added, "The eyes are very sad. You immediately have sympathy for it." The Kings told Buchwald they almost made *Gorgo* in Australia, "but there are no monuments in Australia, and besides, who cares if a monster destroys Australia?"

"We're going to destroy Paris like it's never been destroyed before," Maury said; "Frank's dying to because of the prices. But Paris has something. Tokyo's already been destroyed [onscreen and in real life], and so has Berlin. And King Kong wrecked New York." Frank had a guidebook of destruction. "In trying to find her baby, [the mother monster] wrecks the Eiffel Tower, the Arc de Triomphe, the Louvre, the Opera, the Grand Palais and two bridges on the Seine." That sounds at least colorful, but one suspects outraged Parisians would have found some way to keep Gorgo's mommy from creaming the City of Lights, even if it was just for a movie.

The finished film opens with a highly unlikely underwater volcanic eruption in the Irish Sea, tossing around the ship owned by Joe Ryan (Bill Travers) and Sam Slade (William Sylvester). Strange, prehistoric-like sea animals are found floating on the surface. Mysterious Nara Island is nearby, once inhabited by Vikings, now the home for Irish fishermen. A diver from the island dies of fright, and we see Gorgo underwater for the first time. That night, the monster, somewhat resembling a therapod dinosaur, with large forearms, a huge jaw and strange fan-shaped fins over the ear region, comes stomping and roaring ashore. The 65-foot Gorgo is driven back into the sea by villagers flinging torches at him.

Joe and Sam meet fatherless young Sean (Vincent Winter), the ward of a mercenary archaeologist living on the island, who has been squirreling away Viking artifacts for his own gain.

Joe and Sam suddenly see in Gorgo a way to make a bundle of money—salvage pays poorly—and begin trolling for him, with Joe in a diving bell. Gorgo tries to eat the diving bell. The dinosaur is snared in nets from the ship, and hauled aboard. Sean has stowed away aboard the ship, and begins communing with the captive monster he calls Ogra. To prevent him from drying out, seawater is pumped over him, washing off into the sea. The water glows.

Irish paleontologists try to convince Joe and Sam to allow them to claim the monster for study, pointing out the dangers of disease-bearing parasites and the value of the creature for scientific study. But Joe and Sam have visions of wealth and ignore the scientists' wishes.

Instead, they make a deal with Dorkin (Martin Benson), an entrepreneur who builds an enclosure for the monster in Battersea Park, an amusement park in London. The shrouded, chained Gorgo is driven through London to Battersea, while interested spectators watch the sight on television (but not in person; more on that later).

An announcer refers to the monster: "Gorgo, as he is called—we don't know why." Dorkin later says that the name comes from the mythological monster Gorgon. (Most sources say the name comes from gorgosaurus, a real therapod dinosaur 35 feet long and strongly resembling a Tyrannosaurus rex,[*] but this connection is not mentioned in the film. It is, however, referred to in the preposterously sexy novelization.)

Despite some setbacks, Gorgo is successfully penned. The exhibit opens to brisk business, with gawking onlookers amused by the forlorn dinosaur.

Sam has begun to regret it all; he has, according to Joe, "been listening to our new partner [Sean] too much." When drunk, Sam even tries to free Gorgo. The two partners are contacted again by paleontologists who have some disturbing news (an understatement). Gorgo, it turns out, is not full grown at all, but an infant. The parent would be 250 feet tall.

We return to Nara Island in time for the arrival of Big Momma. She demolishes the place, stepping on the unpleasant archaeologist. Planes and ships try to attack Momma as she follows Gorgo's trail toward London (remember the glowing water?). She sinks a battleship. Cannons, depth charges, bangs, booms, and explosions—nothing is effective, and she heads up the Thames. The city is in a snit, but so is Momma.

---

[*]As occasionally happens in paleontology, gorgosaurus has proven to be the same as albertosaurus, and as albertosaurus was an earlier name, gorgosaurus has been dropped as a designation. However, if this were known before the production of Gorgo, it's not likely the movie monster would have been called Alberto.

At the climax of the very well-produced Gorgo (1961), the title creature's mother rips down one of the towers of London's famous Tower Bridge. In this behind-the-scenes shot, you can see the pant leg of the stunt man protruding from the leg of the monster suit, between the two girders at the lower left. The monster feet tended to fill with water, making walking difficult.

The Thames is flooded with flaming gasoline; this doesn't stop her, but does fricassee some foolhardy onlookers. Londoners flee, and soldiers shoot at Momma, wading *down* the Thames. She demolishes Tower Bridge, smashes the Tower of London, Big Ben, Parliament and eventually Piccadilly Circus. She finally arrives at Battersea Park, wading through a roller coaster, and flattens the fences around little Gorgo. Momma gives Gorgo a come-on wave, and the two head off toward the rising sun, down the Thames.

Despite lifts from previous monster movies—the diving bell, threat of germs and roller coaster are from Lourié's own *Beast from 20,000 Fathoms*—*Gorgo* is one of the best of the genre. Even including the most maligned of all techniques for the creation of monsters.

The special effects by Tom Howard for *Gorgo* are erratic, ranging from outstanding to terrible, sometimes in the same sequence. But they are generally daring, even when they don't work, and the picture is surprisingly effective in this area, especially on the budget it had (well under a million dollars).

The worst effects scene in the film, unfortunately, is the opening sequence, as a volcanic island rises from the Irish Sea. Later, apparently fearing that the effects weren't working, many scenes have a very thick fog added optically in postproduction, only calling attention to the phoniness of the fog itself.

The miniatures of Nara Island are especially good, and those of London are far above average. The stills from the movie don't do it justice, because they are lit differently than the film. This crucial aspect of miniatures—accurate lighting—is generally dealt with successfully in *Gorgo*. The masonry crumbles believably, and the overcranked camera gives weight and power to Momma as well as dramatic scale to the miniatures as they crumble. But the lighting makes it look real.

According to Mandell's article, up to 80 blue-screen matte shots were used in *Gorgo*, many split screens as well. Tom Howard developed a moving split screen for *tom thumb*, and it was employed effectively here. In addition to the usual vertical splits, to put the monsters and full-sized props and actors into the same scene, horizontal splits were employed in the scenes of mass destruction. While Momma was banging away at miniature props of the tops of buildings, real crowds were streaming past the actual locales on the lower portion of the screen. This is generally used effectively, becoming apparent only when the miniature masonry vanishes at the split line. Even then, Howard occasionally uses his moving split screen (called "Automotion") to bring the masonry tumbling right to the bottom of the screen.

In a brief piece in *Daily Variety* (26 May 1960) announcing the acquisition of *Gorgo* by MGM, reference is made to the name of the process used to bring the monsters to life: "Sutomotion." Surely this was a joke? Could they have meant "Suitomotion" or "Pseudomotion"? Or was it a typo of "Automotion"? In any event, although stop-motion animation was used to bring the monsters to life in Lourié's two previous films of monsters on the loose, this time he reverted to the most disparaged and generally misused of all techniques for bringing monsters to life: a man in a rubber suit. (Or, as special effects expert Tom Scherman calls such creatures, "Maninsuitasaurus.")

However, *Gorgo* almost validates this much-aligned technique. The monster suits are almost state-of-the-art for such things, and their lack of realism is betrayed only by a rubbery look around the joints, and unconvincingly hinging for the jaws. (Also, the roars don't seem properly "lip"-synched.)

Again turning to Mandell's thorough article (recommended): Lourié again came into conflict with the King Brothers over the design and construction of the Gorgo suit. (Only one design was used for both Gorgo and Momma.) In the United States, Lourié sculpted a large model of Gorgo, and turned to Russian special effects expert Nicolai Wilke. He wanted Wilke to do something different, to build a lightweight suit with electronic controls for eyes, jaws, tail, etc. But when Lourié reached England, he discovered that the Kings had hired a crew of effects engineers to build a more conventional rubber suit with hydraulic controls. "Each meeting added some heavy hydraulic equipment on the head, shoulders and back of the poor man inside the rubber skin. The movements of the eyes, ears and tail were all activated by independent hydraulic systems. A helmetlike contraption was strapped onto the man's head, and the studio blacksmiths were manufacturing these supports that looked like armor of a medieval knight."

The resulting suit, made of rubber, was so heavy that it exhausted one man after only a short time, so four stunt men played Gorgo and Momma in shifts. (Presumably, these were David Wilding, Michael Dillon, Peter Brace and Peter Perkins.) The heavy suit made wading in water difficult, so one of the three standby skins was cut off below the knees. "It was a strange sight to see a dragon like Gorgo wading through the water in white socks and tennis shoes," Lourié told Mandell.

One drawback of the monster suits, well-engineered and imaginatively photographed though they are, is their lack of expression. The actor within can wave his arms frantically, or droop dejectedly, but there's not much else room for expression. The script presents few opportunities for characterization of the creatures, but surely inasmuch as Sean is already drawn to Gorgo, we could have seen Gorgo reciprocate these emotions a little. As it is, both Momma and Gorgo are like natural disasters, not characters, like the big ants in *Them!*, rather than in the personality-monster field, like King Kong.

Overall, except for that damned flapping jaw and the overall human shape of the monsters (although the stunt men do valiantly walk with bent knees), the monster suits for *Gorgo* are probably the best such ever done.

A full-sized partial Gorgo was also built for the scenes in which he's tied down. The head, paws, and tail were cast from plastic, and a tarp covered the rest of the body, a plywood framework. The eyes blinked and glowed, the fingers and ear-flaps twitched and all in all, it was an acceptable stand-in.

For the scenes in which Gorgo travels across London chained to a truck, Lourié suggested that the Kings hire a few hundred extras, feeling that a crowd of paid onlookers would attract unpaid ones. However, in order to save money, the Kings didn't do this; they assumed their monster caravan would attract lots of completely free rubberneckers. But in order to comply with police regulations, the truck had to pass through London on a Sunday morning—when it was cold and foggy. Virtually no one turned out to watch; Gorgo passes through streets eerily devoid of onlookers.

Satisfactory effects and props will not make a film good, however. Script, acting and direction do that. The script for *Gorgo* is especially good for one of these things, even though it seems to have been assembled like a Frankenstein Monster out of bits and pieces of previous giant-monster epics; even a money-hungry entrepreneur somewhat like *King Kong*'s Carl Denham turns up, although Martin Benson is good as Dorkin.

One of the more sophisticated touches is the archaeologist on Nara Island, a greedy son of a bitch, finding ancient artifacts to use for his own profit. He's a foreshadowing of what Joe and Sam are in danger of becoming. However, unlike the archaeologist, Joe and Sam survive the film; their salvation lies in being kind to young Sean, whereas the archaeologist is cruel to the boy. At the climax, as Momma is bringing London down around everyone's ears, Joe and Sam risk their lives to find Sean.

Gorgo may be the only giant-monster movie which has absolutely no romantic interest whatsoever—except for The Giant Behemoth, which, of course, was also made by Eugene Lourié. But more than that film, Gorgo was made for children. The character of Sean was added to appeal to kids, but was unnecessary and perhaps even a mistake. Sean's mooning over Gorgo is of little interest to children; what they want is the monster, and probably Joe and Sam are more appealing as characters. Nonetheless, to eschew romantic folderol altogether (and there's a pair of young lovers in Behemoth, however briefly) probably was an act of courage for all concerned. After all, such "identification" was generally felt to be necessary in almost every other film ever released of any nature whatsoever.

The film is simply and intelligently structured, almost classical. It follows the old King Kong format to a degree (island, capture, smash city), but with that novel kicker of having two monsters, both of which survive. Bringing in Momma, the Colossus of the Irish Sea, is a stroke of ingenuity. (It was copied later in a Japanese film shown on U.S. TV as Monster from a Prehistoric Planet.) It gives the film two stages, and provides the city-smasher some real motivation: as unlikely as dinosaur mother love might be, it's still a solid reason for Momma to knock London to pieces. (Like all good city-destroyers, she has an affinity for recognizable landmarks.)

Eugene Lourié really isn't a director of actors, so it's a good thing he has appealing leads in William Sylvester and Bill Travers. Sylvester later played Heywood G. Floyd in 2001, of course, but also appeared in Devil Doll (1964), Devils of Darkness (1965) and The Beast of Morocco (1966). A Canadian, he returned to North America in the early 1970s, appearing in the TV movie Don't Be Afraid of the Dark (1973); he had a small part in Heaven Can Wait (1978). On television, he had a regular role in the mediocre invisible man series, "Gemini Man." Never a star, Sylvester is a comforting, avuncular fellow, well-suited to play the doubting partner in Gorgo.

On the other hand, Bill Travers was at this time near the height of his two periods of stardom. He'd received good reviews for Wee Geordie (1955) and was reasonably well-received in The Barretts of Wimpole Street (1957) and The Bridal Path (1959). After Gorgo, he was charming in Invasion Quartet (1961) and okay in Duel at Diablo (1966). Except for the latter film and a couple of minor pictures, he seems to have made few films between 1961 and 1966, when he appeared in the biggest hit of his career, a film which seems to have strongly affected both his public and private life: Born Free. This worldwide hit apparently created in both Travers and his costar/wife Virginia McKenna an interest in the welfare of animals. After Born Free, Travers appeared in Ring of Bright Water (1969), An Elephant Called Slowly (1970), which he coproduced and cowrote, The Belstone Fox (1973) and Christian the Lion (1976), which he co-did almost everything on. He's returned to other kinds of films recently, and he and McKenna were exuberant as the parents of an Australian track star in the fine TV movie The First Olympics—Athens 1896 (1984). Travers is not taxed in Gorgo; his role is simplistic, but Travers' personal warmth and conviction make Joe believable.

Vincent Winter previously received a special Oscar for his role in The Little Kidnappers (1954), but by 1960 had outgrown most of his charm. In his defense, the role he has in Gorgo would be difficult for anyone to play. Sean is one of those children's roles written by people who do not understand children, who seem to feel that because kids are young, they are more in touch with nature, or with animals. Sean is wise because he is young, which is condescending, and children spotted the condescension. Sean is unreal. Winter made a few more films in England, including Disney's *Almost Angels* (1962) and *The Three Lives of Thomasina* (1963). According to Ephraim Katz's *The Film Encyclopedia*, Winter went to Australia, where he is still active on the stage.

Angelo Francesco Lavagnino's score, especially the title theme, is impressively moody and evocative, a notable accomplishment for such a madly prolific composer. Among his other scores: *The Colossus of Rhodes*, *Nude Odyssey*, *Goliath and the Vampires* (all 1961), *The Wonders of Aladdin*, *Damon and Pythias*, *The Son of Captain Blood* (all 1962), *Samson and the Slave Queen*, *Dark Purpose* (both 1964), *The Tramplers*, *Wild, Wild Planet* and Orson Welles' *Falstaff* (all 1966). This list is only representative. *Gorgo* is one of his best scores.

There's nothing particularly notable about Lourié's direction until the city-in-panic scenes at the climax, among the best such sequences in movies, primarily for the details chosen to illustrate the terror. The onlookers who crowd down onto the riverside steps to watch the flaming gasoline on the Thames, and are killed themselves; in a crowd of fleeing Londoners, a little girl drops a doll and others tromp on it as they pass in panic; hoping for safety, a crowd runs downstairs into an underground station, which collapses on them; "Repent! The End Is Nigh!" says the sign on a sandwich-board man, but he's trampled to death—the end *was* nigh, for him.

There are too many scenes of tanks and other military vehicles roaring around; although this adds to the sense of general confusion, there doesn't seem to be any method to Momma's wandering through the city. Instead of making a beeline for Battersea, her path is confusing; she comes up the Thames from the sea, but then goes back *down* it for the city-smashing business. There's one nice shot of her arriving at Battersea, an "aerial" perspective, inventive and imaginative, even though the props look more like models than usual.

Freddie Young's cinematography is especially outstanding for a film of this nature, but is in keeping with the quality of his usual work. Later, he became associated with David Lean, and filmed such movies as *Lawrence of Arabia*, *Dr. Zhivago* and *Ryan's Daughter*. Young has a sense of epic sweep few photographers exhibit. He's let down from time to time by that phony fog, and by atmospheric but excessively dark processing of the night scenes. There's only one howler of a shot, and was probably handled by the effects crew: when a ship's captain watches Momma through binoculars, we can see the water tank behind the monster.

Scale is muddled throughout the film. When he grasps the diving bell, Gorgo seems much larger than he did ashore on Nara Island, although from then on, he seems about right—but not the announced 65'. The ratio of size between Momma and Gorgo (played by a marionette in their scenes together, when it isn't actually the same suit optically appearing twice) doesn't seem correct, either. But then again, few scenes of Momma or Gorgo are clearly visible on TV, because of that dark printing.

There's also a foolish attempt to add "depth" or something to the film by having an announcer describe most of the later events while standing onscreen with a microphone. Not only is the narration itself dully pretentious and redundant, the effects placing the announcer onscreen are poor; he's transparent much of the time.

Gorgo received generally very favorable reviews, and continues to be well-regarded. The *Film Bulletin* thought MGM had "a sock exploitation attraction" in the "exciting" film. *Limelight* thought it "better than many in this category."

The *Monthly Film Bulletin*, usually hardly sympathetic to British thrillers, thought it was "really rather splendid ... the film has a touch of grandeur ... though the script could perhaps have worked harder exploiting the potential element of fear and horror.... But *Gorgo* remains a gripping, sympathetic variation on an overworked theme, with a moral no less valid and timely for all that it is trite." The *Bulletin* gave *Gorgo* its highest rating.

Gorgo could be called original only in its absence of a romance and in letting the monsters get away at the end, but the film still showed that even in the most tired and hackneyed formulas, there was room for a well-done thriller. Better than any of the (serious) Japanese films, *Gorgo* is almost a model for medium-budget monster thrillers. Though not up to the level of *King Kong* or even *Them!*, *Gorgo* is nonetheless an entertaining, even exciting movie.

The Head

Although in terms of production, the science fiction/horror boom was at first largely confined to the United States, Britain and, to a lesser degree, Japan, eventually other regions began to be heard from. Occasionally these films were released in the United States. *The Head* is the American retitling of the West German film *Die Nackte und der Satan* (The Naked One and the Satan), released in that country in 1959. The major plot elements are similar to American films (though harking back to the 1940s), but the approach is certainly different; according to those who have seen it, the atmosphere is dark, disturbing and eccentric.

Aging Professor Abel (Michel Simon) has devised a fluid he calls Serum Z, which he uses to keep alive the severed heads of dogs. He meets Dr. Ood* (Horst Frank), who becomes obsessed with the idea of using Serum Z on human subjects, but Abel objects. Later, Ood agrees to help Abel's assistant Dr. Burke (Kurt Mueller-Graf) in a heart-transplant operation on Abel. However, after Abel has been anesthetized, the donor dies; Burke wishes to terminate the procedure, but Ood disagrees. They have a fight, Burke is killed, so Ood proceeds with his own idea of "saving" Abel.

He decapitates the old man, and making some improvements of his own in Serum Z, keeps Abel's head alive. According to Charles Stinson, "The jugulars, the other arteries and veins, are all delicately connected with plastic tubes which regularly pump in nice clear Serum Z instead of messy old blood. Strange, Medusa–like wires are also attached to the crown of the skull— probably for aesthetic effects. Our German friends think of everything."

Not unexpectedly, this turn of events upsets Abel. He had expected to wake up with a fresh new heart, but instead has no heart at all—nor anything else below the neck. He can still talk, however, and gloomily asks Ood to kill him, but Ood refuses. Storing Abel's ungrateful head in one corner of the laboratory, he begins other ventures. (And Abel ceases having much to do with the plot.)

*It's explained in the film that the mad scientist was an orphan, and his name was taken from that of the ship on which his parents were wrecked and drowned. However, as the Los Angeles Times reviewer said, "that monicker alone should have put everybody on guard."

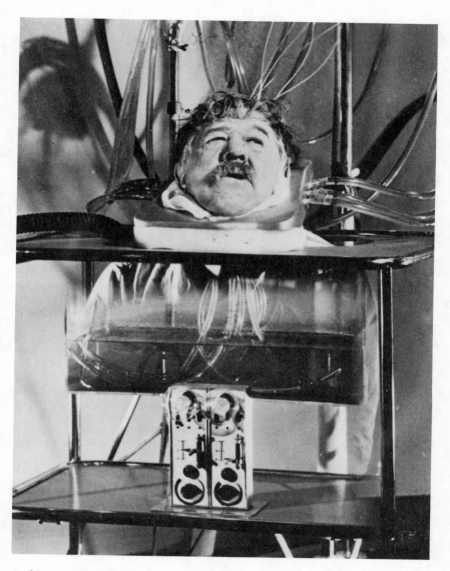

In this scene from **The Head** (U.S. release, 1961), famed actor Michel Simon plays the part of a disembodied head – none too convincingly, as his shoulders are clearly visible.

Ood has been attracted to Abel's beautiful but deformed nurse, Irene (Karin Kernke). She is a hunchback; Ood falls in love with her mind. And face. (None of the reviews indicate if Irene is curious about the disappearance of Dr. Burke and the transforming of Abel into a talking disembodied head.) Ood decides to help Irene achieve bodily beauty to match her face, and renews his acquaintance with Lilly (Christiane Maybach), a stripper. Ood gets Lilly drunk and returns with her to the laboratory, where he removes her head and replaces it with Irene's. I suppose he throws everything else away.

Upon awakening, Irene thinks only that she has been cured of her deformity, and is immensely grateful. Ood becomes devoted to her (listening occasionally to Abel's pleas for death), but Irene is strangely drawn back to the nightclub where the unfortunate Lilly worked. There she meets Paul (Dieter Eppler), Lilly's boyfriend, and they fall in love.

Later, Paul becomes suspicious when he sees Irene carrying Lilly's purse. At least that's what the *American Film Institute Catalog* says; I wonder if in the original German version there were clues Paul uncovered by other means, so to speak.

Meanwhile, the police have become suspicious themselves for some reason, and discover Dr. Burke's body in the woods under some leaves.

Paul and Irene return to the laboratory, where Ood discovers and tries to kill them. The police arrive in time to save them. Ood sets the laboratory afire and as he is trying to escape, he falls to his death. (Some sources say Ood kills himself.) I presume Abel goes up in flames too, but at least Irene ends up with a fancy new body.

The Head was written and directed by Victor Trivas, whose career in films is unusual and a little sad. Born in Russia, he came to Germany and by the late 1920s, was an occasional art director for G.W. Pabst. He also wrote or cowrote some scripts in the 1929–33 period. He directed and wrote *Niemandsland* in 1931 (U.S. title: *Hell on Earth*), a plea for peace, but all prints of it were destroyed when the Nazis came to power.

As did so many in this period, Trivas came to the United States by way of France. He cowrote the story for *Song of Russia* (1943) and for Orson Welles' *The Stranger* (1946), which got Trivas an Oscar nomination. He also wrote the original story for the Mexican film *A Modern Bluebeard* (1947), which starred Buster Keaton. He adapted the stories of *Where the Sidewalk Ends* (1950) and *The Secret of Convict Lake* (1951), but unless he worked in unbilled capacities on other films (highly likely), those seem to be all his American credits.

His script for *The Head* has a European outlook in its emphasis on passion (rather than love) as a motivation, and a certain American quality in the plotline.

Even without my having seen it, *The Head* seems to me to be awkwardly structured. The decapitation of Professor Abel seems at first to be the main thrust of the storyline; certainly the American title implies this, but Abel is literally put aside as Ood turns his attention to the improvement of Irene. Thereafter, Abel only bitches from the sidelines and has no effect on the plot. The entire business of the preservation of Abel's head, then, is apparently in the story for no reason other than sheer sensationalism, even though the story *without* the living head is pretty sensationalistic.

Living-head films are an unfortunate subgenre of science fiction films; I've never heard of a good one. In addition to *The Head*, there's *The Man Without a Body*, *The Brain That Wouldn't Die*, *Madmen of Mandoras* (1964) and *The Frozen Dead* (1967); all include scenes in which the head begs to be killed. The few other living-head films are either fantasies, like *The Thing That Wouldn't Die* (1958) and *The Living Head* (Mexican; 1961) itself, or the head is a minor element in the plot. It's not an honored tradition.

The most unexpected element of *The Head* is the actor who plays Professor Abel. Beginning in the silent era, Michel Simon became one of the most honored actors in French films. He often played common men with tortured souls who came to no good end, with occasional comedy roles, often as a crude buffoon. But always, Simon gave performances of great detail, energy and even subtlety, even when his character was a lively vulgarian. His thick, peasant features belied a great expressiveness.

He appeared in many major, classic films of the 1930s and 40s, including Jean Renoir's *La Chienne* (1931) and *Boudou Saved from Drowning* (1932, as Boudou), Jean Vigo's *L'Atlante* (1934), Marcel Carné's *Bizarre Bizarre* (1937) and *Port of Shadows* (1938), Julian Duvivier's *La Fin du Jour* (1939) and *Panic* (1947), and René Clair's wonderful *Beauty and the Devil* (1950), in which Simon was both Faust and Mephistopheles by turns. For someone who looked like Margaret Rutherford in a fright wig and mustache, Simon was an astonishingly touching actor at times, and when he was loud and brash, he was the only thing you watched.

Simon's career in the 1950s declined severely—no doubt explaining his appearance in *The Head*—and in 1957, he used a makeup dye that paralyzed part of his body and face. However, in the 1960s, Simon made a comeback, first as an elderly but brave engineer in the American film *The Train* (1964), and later as a humane old farmer who happened to be almost reflexively anti–Semitic, in *The Two of Us* (1967). When Simon died in 1975, much of his former reputation was restored, both by the revival of his great films of the 1930s and by the more recent films he'd made. Simon was married only briefly; he lived most of his life on a country estate with four apes and a parrot. His son François is also an actor.*

Horst Frank, the ambitious Dr. Ood, continued to appear in mostly low-brow German films, with an occasional foray into international coproductions. Among his other films are *The Pirates of the Mississippi* (1963), *The Corpse of Beverly Hills* (1964), *Vengeance of Fu Manchu* (1967), *Cat O'Nine Tails* (1971), and the variously-titled *Night of the Askari/Albino/Whispering Death* (multinational, 1971), in which Horst plays a black Albino African who rapes and murders white women.

The Head was launched in the United States with an enthusiastic and sardonic ad campaign, which included such lines as "Professor Abel has developed a detached point of view" and "It just won't lie down and stay dead"; it even cautioned potential audiences for *The Head*, "Be careful! Don't drop it!"

Unusually enough for a film from relatively minor distributor Trans-Lux (specializing in American releases of European exploitation films, with a few "art" films tossed in), *The Head* was quite widely reviewed, and not always unfavorably.

Allen M. Widem in *Motion Picture Herald* considered it "good" and said that "it accomplishes its objectives with a flare [sic] that spells out dramatic dash of unprecedented lure." "R.S." in *Film Daily* thought that Horst Frank was "outstanding" and that the music was "unusual and effective"; overall, R.S. said, the film has "solid box office appeal." On the other hand, "Tube" in *Variety* thought it "a tedious and tasteless horror film.... Trivas' direction is heavy, choppy and disjointed, but there are one or two passages endowed with a desirably eerie quality via the art, music and photography department contributions."

Charles Stinson, cited earlier, wasn't impressed, feeling that *The Head* "must roll down towards the foot of the class.... The script by director Victor Trivas is thoroughly trite. The English dialogue is flat and awkward in spots and

---

Most of this information comes from Ephraim Katz's infuriating, opinionated and absolutely indispensable The Film Encyclopedia.

the performances are quite undistinguished. This, after all, was old hat 30 years ago."

Lowell E. Redelings in the *Hollywood Citizen News* took a dim view of the film. "It is doubtful that other than people with time to kill, and a curiosity about a foreign picture, will patronize this tedious and monotonous picture.... The photography isn't half bad, and the score suggests the proper mood for a horror thriller—except this one doesn't thrill."

The Head seemingly vanished. It apparently is not available for television, and I do not think it is available in 16mm. Of more recent writers, only Joe Dante (in *Castle of Frankenstein* #10) seems to know anything about it, and that isn't good: "Grotesque German horror film.... Ghastly, grisly stuff with uncomfortably strange atmosphere. Terrible English dubbing."

The Head seems to have been cut off and thrown away.

House of Fright

Hiding behind this meaningless title is Hammer's second version of Robert Louis Stevenson's *The Strange Case of Dr. Jekyll and Mr. Hyde*. (Their first was *The Ugly Duckling*, a modern-day comedy never released in the United States.) It was originally scheduled to be released by Columbia in the United States under its British title, *The Two Faces of Dr. Jekyll*, the title it has now on television. American International obtained the film, first releasing it in Detroit and Cincinnati as *Jekyll's Inferno*, but apparently deciding that it was best to keep hidden the fact that it was based on Stevenson's often-filmed story.

This was in the period when Hammer was redoing all the classic horror stories—Frankenstein, Dracula, the Mummy, Phantom of the Opera, zombies, etc. The studio seems to have regarded the tale of Jekyll and Hyde as something befitting a more intellectual treatment than they had been according their new versions so far. Wolf Mankowitz rather than Jimmy Sangster wrote the script, and although it was entrusted to Terence Fisher to direct, it was a little more expensive and prestigious than usual for Hammer.

The approach taken by the film is eccentric—older, plain Jekyll becomes young, handsome Hyde—but Mankowitz said at the time he felt evil was attractive, and should look so. In the original novel, Hyde isn't so much ugly as disquieting: "He is not easy to describe," said Enfield in Stevenson's novella; "There is something wrong with his appearance; something displeasing, something downright detestable. I never saw a man I so disliked, and yet I scarce know why. He must be deformed somewhere; he gives a strong feeling of deformity, although I couldn't specify the point. He's an extraordinary looking man, and yet I really can name nothing out of the way.... I can't describe him. And it's not want of memory; for I declare I can see him this moment." Later, Stevenson describes Hyde briefly as "pale and dwarfish" with "a displeasing smile."

Jekyll's original purpose was trying to find a drug to separate the "just" from the "unjust," but upon unleashing Hyde—"less robust and developed than the good"—Jekyll found that he was the embodiment of "the evil side of my nature," not merely the unjust: "Edward Hyde, alone in the ranks of mankind, was pure evil." And not attractive, but highly repellent.

It may have been that Hammer was a shade cautious about bringing forth a monstrous Hyde (in their later *Dr. Jekyll and Sister Hyde*, Hyde is downright gorgeous), as (a) that had been done before, and therefore (b) might be intruding on copyright. This is merely speculation.

When Jekyll turns to Hyde in *House of Fright*, he not only becomes young and handsome, he loses his beard in the process. Conceptually, this was an interesting idea, but visually it's a dud. People seem to have little trouble imagining someone magically becoming a hairy werewolf, or in using chemicals to become hideous, but for a normal-looking bearded man to turn into a normal-looking clean-shaven man—and back again—was more than most reviewers could handle. They were accustomed to beards, how long it takes to get one, and what's left when they are removed. The business with the beard was commented on in virtually every review.

The makeup on Paul Massie as *Jekyll* was quite elaborate; a handsome young man was made to look middle-aged and plain, but the work was unconvincing.

Mankowitz not only altered both Stevenson's original intent and the traditional movie concepts in treating the story, but completely jettisoned Stevenson's plot. The film seems as if he never read the original work at all; not only is the plotline totally different, but no characters except Jekyll/Hyde from the original story occur in *House of Fright*, essentially an original work.

In some ways, Mankowitz's new story is one of the most sophisticated Jekyll/Hyde tales, resembling in some respects Oscar Wilde's story of Dorian Gray more than the usual Jekyll/Hyde murder business. Mankowitz (rather conventionally) said he wanted to disclose the corruption that lay behind the staid facade of Victoriana. Indeed, that seems to be the general thrust of the film, with opium dens, cancan dancers and other telltale signs of decadence and depravity.

In Victorian London, dedicated, austere Dr. Henry Jekyll (Paul Massie) is warned by his friend Litauer (David Kossoff) that his researches into the nature of good and evil may be leading him into dangerous territory. Jekyll's much younger wife Kitty (Dawn Addams) is bored with hanging around the house, and has secretly embarked on an affair with her husband's friend, devil-may-care playboy Paul Allen (Christopher Lee), who has been borrowing money from Jekyll for gambling and romancing Kitty.

Partly because of annoyance with Kitty's uncaring behavior, Jekyll finally does inject himself with his drug, which transforms him into young, handsome Edward Hyde (also Massie). At a nightclub, the Sphinx, Hyde sees Kitty and Paul together and realizes for the first time that they are lovers.

Hyde is self-assured, witty and attractive, but also cold and vicious, perfect material for a Victorian rake. Hyde dances with Kitty, but Jekyll begins to emerge, and he flees.

Against his better judgment, Jekyll again transforms himself into Hyde and returns to the Sphinx, where Paul takes him under his wing. A cad himself, Paul is astonished that though a beginner, Hyde is far more depraved than he is himself. With Jekyll's money, Paul gambles and loses heavily, while upstairs Hyde makes love to Maria (Norma Marla), the snake charmer. He later signs promissory notes for Paul (in Jekyll's name), ironically wondering aloud how Jekyll would feel if he knew he were financing his own cuckolding. Paul laughs nervously.

Hyde tries to persuade Kitty to be his mistress, but she rejects him, preferring Paul. Once again he begins to return to Jekyll in Kitty's presence—she brings out the best in him?—and has to flee.

Litauer discovers the secret of Dr. Jekyll and Mr. Hyde, and urges his friend to end his dual existence, but Jekyll is too caught up in his life as Hyde to agree. And he has a plan for revenge on Paul.

When Paul again loses heavily at the tables, Hyde agrees to help him only if he will procure Kitty for him; Paul agrees. Hyde uses Paul's notes in an effort to "buy" Kitty later, but she throws him out.

Hyde is beaten and wakes up in a gutter as Jekyll, who decides to end the double life. For the first time as Jekyll, he discovers Kitty and Paul together, and his rage transforms him back into Hyde without the use of drugs. (They don't see this.) Kitty's indifference to her husband, plus his increased desire for revenge, leads Jekyll to decide to become Hyde permanently.

At the Sphinx, Hyde locks Paul in a room with Maria's python, then rapes Kitty. The snake kills Paul. (It's unclear how; the official synopsis says it crushes him, but the film implies that this is one of those common-in-movies but never-found-in-real-life poisonous pythons.) In terror, Kitty tumbles over a balcony and spectacularly falls to her death through a pretty leaded-glass window.

Hyde later strangles Maria, then turns back into Jekyll. In a mirror at his laboratory, Jekyll sees only Hyde, as evil has now taken over both Dr. Jekyll and Mr. Hyde. He transforms himself into Hyde again, kills a stable boy and, placing the body in it, sets the laboratory afire.

Hyde tells the police that Jekyll committed suicide. During the coroner's court hearings, Hyde maintains his cool, but afterward, in talking with Litauer, Jekyll slowly takes over again. Exhausted and aged, Jekyll has conquered Hyde at last, but has destroyed himself in the process.

The usual approach to Jekyll and Hyde is to treat their story as either a conventional monster tale or something of a variation on drug addiction: Jekyll turns into a monstrous Hyde because he's hooked on it. About half the time, Hyde is just a monster; the other films treat the story as an examination of the duality of Man. The best version, with Fredric March, has Hyde as an amoral primitive; in the best-known versions, with Spencer Tracy and Jack Palance, Hyde is an *im*moral, fiendish libertine. Not uncivilized, but brutal.

Whatever the virtues or defects of Mankowitz's script, it is not a traditional Jekyll/Hyde story. Here, Hyde isn't just the evil side of Jekyll, as in the March version, he's the *repressed* side (but at that, not a primitive), the Jekyll that perhaps Kitty thought she was marrying. In fact, Paul Allen is similar to Edward Hyde—except that Hyde's charm is at once more ruthless and more obvious. Allen still has some of the restrictions of society; he has a certain degree of kindness and other tender emotions, and although he's almost as immoral and self-centered as Hyde, is fond of Kitty. Paul lies somewhere between Jekyll and Hyde, but is still a relatively humane being.

Maria presumably plays the typical Bad Woman to Kitty's Good Woman, but things aren't that simple. After all, Kitty is cheating on her husband. The main purpose of Maria in the plot seems to be to give Hyde someone to fool around with and later murder, and to give Hyde a means of murdering Paul. Maria does not seem as conceptually essential to Mankowitz's thesis as the other characters.

Paul Massie looks right for this Hyde: slightly heavy lips such as traditionally indicate depravity, and his relatively low brow gives a hint of bestiality. For Jekyll, makeup artist Roy Ashton moved Massie's hairline back, built up the bridge of his nose, gave him different eyebrows, added bags under the eyes and, of course, that beard which annoyed people so much. This is the only Jekyll/Hyde film I know of where the actor's natural, unadorned face was used for Hyde, while he's heavily made up as Jekyll.

To his credit, Mankowitz tried to develop the story in ways that made the handsome Hyde–ugly Jekyll idea more than a gimmick. His target wasn't the duality of Man, but the corruption of society behind an attractive facade. To have a handsome Hyde mirrored his idea that respectable Victorian society hid vices. Terence Fisher, however, was not really the man to emphasize that. He was a competent enough director of horror movies, occasionally better than that, but this is a horror movie laced with drama, and the best Fisher can manage is a depravity parade.

Some of the depravity, incidentally, was missing from American prints. According to an unidentified trade paper article dated 9 May 1961, Maria's snake dance was removed from *House of Fright* because of complaints by the Production Code Administration and the Catholic Legion of Decency. The film ran 88 minutes in England and 80 in the United States, so more than a snake dance went. In England, sex was okay, but violence had to be trimmed; here, the situation was reversed, said the paper. (Probably *Daily Variety*.)

For several years, Christopher Lee maintained that Paul Allen was his favorite role, and that the film contained his best acting. This claim seems somewhat peculiar, for although Lee is perfectly okay in the part, he shows none of the fire he displayed as Dracula, none of the sadness of the Mummy, and since 1961, has turned in far better performances from time to time. (His best is probably in the TV miniseries, *The Far Pavilions*.) Perhaps Lee was proud that Mankowitz wrote the role for him. In *The Films of Christopher Lee*, published in 1983, he still said "I think it was one of the best performances I've given." He also added that "it was a good picture, with beautiful clothes and wonderful to look at, but in my opinion the premise was wrong."

That may be true, but any writer assigned to script a version of Jekyll and Hyde should be forgiven for trying something new. It didn't really work, but that was probably due more to Terence Fisher and Paul Massie. He looked right, but his talent was limited, and Fisher wasn't the director to bring out what ability Massie had. He was better in other films of the period, *Orders to Kill* (1958), *Libel* and *Sapphire* (both 1959), though still not notable. A Canadian, he seems to have retired from the screen not long after making *House of Fright*.

Reviews were bemused. As occasionally happened when films were re-titled for distribution in the United States, *House of Fright* was reviewed twice in *Variety*, without any indication the writer of the second review knew it had another title. As *Two Faces of Dr. Jekyll*, it was reviewed first 11 October 1960 from London by "Rich," who said "this one has all the earmarks of being a b.o. winner, if shrewdly handled. Mankowitz has palpably distorted ... Stevenson's original story and the affair becomes mostly a straightforward horror meller, but with the benefit of some good opportunities for characterization and a useful climax. However, there are some blatantly inserted spots of sadism.... As a psychological study in scientific research, this pic is well down the lists; but as a full-bodied frolic of sadism, murder, lust and nightclub capers, it's well done."

On the other hand, when "Pit" reviewed it 17 May 1961 as *House of Fright*, he called it "an uninspired ... meller sans much shock and with only fair b.o. outlook.... Unfortunately, the effort has been lavished on form but not enough on content in this film.... There is little to horrify audiences, of whatever age. There is, however, abundant flouting of the moral code—adultery, two rapes and the standard shocker genre violence—that make this anything but a kiddie's matinee film.... The Wolf Mankowitz screenplay is superficial and surprisingly uninspired.... There are also moments of unintended comedy that don't help."

"P.H." in the *Monthly Film Bulletin* thought that the film "may be forgiven for tampering with a classic, but not for doing so with such a depressing lack of either wit or competence.... Silliness, in fact, has got the better of the film.... One looks back affectionately to the Fredric March version, which allowed itself a little humour, as well as giving some dignity to the conflict within the mind of poor Dr. Jekyll."

James Morgenstern in the New York *Herald-Tribune* considered it "a colorful, ingenious remake of the Stevenson story. Wolf Mankowitz' literate and slightly satiric screenplay conjures up a Mr. Hyde whose monstrosity resides not in his fangs, for he is quite fangless, but in his suave handsome features and his thorough-going hedonism." (For more on Mankowitz, see the entry on *The Day the Earth Caught Fire*.)

In *Classic Movie Monsters,* Don Glut felt that the film "was not one of Hammer's more successful enterprises, partially due to a bland script and the audience's unwillingness to accept a handsome Hyde."

In an article on Terence Fisher in *Cinefantastique* (vol. 4, no. 3), writer Harry Ringel said, "Under Fisher's direction, *everything* reverses. Mrs. Jekyll dressed 'good,' so she is good; the exotic dancer moves with a suggestive suppleness, so we label her bad. As Fisher wishes. But then Desire levels them both, and the entire madonna/prostitute moral system Fisher had evoked in us collapses. Mrs. Jekyll dies most gracefully, falling through a lightscape [*sic*] to her death. The exotic dancer dies on her back, in bed, and Fisher has seen to it that she dies dressed in Mrs. Jekyll's nightgown."

Fisher himself, interviewed in the same issue of *Cinefantastique,* had some commentary on the film. "There was not one redeeming character in [it]," he told interviewer Ringel. "Only one person had any semblance of good in him, and that was Jekyll's friend [Litauer].... And he didn't do very much stopping.... Jekyll, who allowed himself to become shoddy. Chris Lee, who was shoddy. A wife who was no good anyway. God—raped by her reconstructed husband! It was an exercise, rightly or wrongly, badly done or well done, in evil. You didn't have a single character in that story who was worth tuppence ha'penny. I liked the script. I think Wolf Mankowitz wrote it partly from the point of view that Victorian England was corrupt. But it wasn't fundamentally a very deep script, was it? Its strength, I think was that Wolf Mankowitz realized that evil wasn't a horrible thing crawling around the street. It's very charming and attractive and seductive. Temptation! That was the only strength of the script and the only interesting thing, too."

Don Willis (II) had some interesting commentary: "Hammer's first serious Jekyll–Hyde film is a not-wholly-unworthy addition to the ranks. It's fairly inventive at devising ways to confront Jekyll with Hyde and vice versa—e.g., Jekyll seeing himself as Hyde in a mirror; Hyde alarmed at signs of the encroaching Jekyll; Jekyll awaking to find one of Hyde's victims beneath him; Jekyll's voice conducting a duologue with Hyde's (with Jekyll as 'host'). Unfortunately, the dramatic ball is bounced back and forth between them so often and so regularly that this begins to seem like a game: Dr. Ping and Mr. Pong. The movie threatens to become a comedy in spite of itself.... And Paul Massie is one-dimensional as either Jekyll *or* Hyde."

The film was not a box-office success. Although it did receive more critical attention than most of the films American International was releasing in this period, it was merely tossed out and allowed to sink of its own weight. It went unseen again in the United States for many years, until it resurfaced on television under the original British title, then promptly vanished again. The Jekyll and Hyde story is one that may not deserve retelling as often as it has been retold,* but at least this time, someone was trying something different. It doesn't succeed, but it is an intelligent variation on a theme.

Journey to the Seventh Planet

The ads for this American film made in Denmark show a bizarre buglike thing half the size of a spaceship, clutching the body of a rocket with one claw while it reaches for an armed spaceman with the other. Nothing remotely like this turns up in the clumsily-produced film, which though it has some imagination in its concept, is so poorly written and acted that it fizzles out soon after it begins.

The basic gimmick: spacemen are menaced by a creature that conjures up their own fears and desire as weapons against them. This was used in other films, such as *Forbidden Planet* and *Solaris*, and in countless SF short stories and comic book scripts. Ray Bradbury's "Mars Is Heaven" is one of the eeriest and most effective uses of this idea. Sidney Pink devised the story of *Journey to the Seventh Planet*; he directed and produced, neither very well. Ib Melchior wrote the script, but it was drastically altered; Pink rewrote much of Melchior's dialogue, as well as the action.

Melchior's script isn't very good, and the characters are strictly clichés — wisecracking, womanizing pilot, stalwart leader, Irishman and two blanks — but it has more vitality in the dialogue and more interesting material for actors than the flat, badly acted film. You know you are in trouble when John Agar is the best actor in the film.

It seems likely that American International, which released the film, also cofinanced it with Sid Pink and perhaps a Danish production company. Completed longer before its release than is customary with such low-budget films, the movie's special effects turned out to be so bad that even American International couldn't bring themselves to release the film in its original form.

In the year 2001 (a coincidence that some idiots have made much of), a spaceship containing five astronauts heads for the planet Uranus. "There are no limits to the imagination," says the narrator of a film which later shows great limits to its own imagination. "Man's ability to make reality out of his vision is his greatest strength." The United Nations spaceship, *Explorer 12*, is to check out Uranus for signs of life.

It's established early on that Don (Agar) has a pinup of actress Greta Thyssen in his locker, and that the others of the crew, except for commander Eric (Carl Ottosen) are all your typically horny young men.

The interior of the spaceship is slightly more imaginative than most, "inspired" by the control room of the *C-57D* from *Forbidden Planet*, just as the central idea of this film is derived from the same movie. The room has two levels, and little one-man elevators connecting the two. However, it is also overlit and badly photographed, sabotaging the art director's work.

After an uneventful journey to the seventh planet, the ship goes into orbit around Uranus just as crewman Barry (Ove Sprogøe, a Dane with a dubbed

---

*In fact, both Christopher Lee and Oliver Reed (who has a small role) later appeared in Jekyll/Hyde films of their own; Lee was in I, Monster (1971), based closely on Stevenson with the names changed, and Reed was in Dr. Heckyl and Mr. Hype (1980), a spoof.

American voice playing an Irishman) begins to eat an apple. Suddenly a bright golden lens distortion appears over the scene and everyone freezes. We hear a strange voice: "Come! Come! ... that I may learn and judge. I shall drain your minds and then you will be put to the test, and I shall possess you" – and more to that effect, in similar stilted diction.

When things return to normal, no one notices what happened – but the apple is shriveled and rotten: obviously several days have passed. However, no-nonsense Eric does not let a little thing like a few missing days dissuade him. "We'll figure that out later," he snaps, and lands the ship.

Before the view port is open, we see the frozen landscape of Uranus around the ship. Suddenly, in quick cuts, trees and grass appear, the rocks become brown instead of white, and it all takes on an earthly appearance. (This is one of the very few Danish–made special effects in the film that has any value at all; it looks exactly like a tabletop miniature, but the rippling landscape changes are visually interesting.)

To say the least, the men are not prepared for the sight of a lush evergreen forest (stock footage) surrounding their ship. But they adjust to it quickly – no one ever seems very surprised or disturbed by anything that happens in the film – and, discovering the atmosphere is Earth–normal, go for a walk in the forest.

One of the men, Svend (Louis Miehe Renard), is slightly surprised that the landscape exactly duplicates an area on Earth he is familiar with. The men proceed on their way, without radioing Earth for instructions and/or advice. Soon, they discover that the plants have no roots. They're simply stuck in the ground. An apple tree turns up that wasn't there a moment before. (All this is filmed on a tiny sound stage.)

They discover that they are in an enclosed area: a force field, visible as a dark gray wall, surrounds them. It can easily be penetrated with a stick, but when a man pokes an arm through, his hand is almost frozen off. Beyond the wall is the true atmosphere of Uranus: methane 200° below zero.

Around a fire that night, as Eric describes his boyhood home – a mill, two birches, etc. – the others are astonished to see it take form behind him. Though one of the eeriest touches in the film, it doesn't make any sense. The thing on the planet can obviously read their minds, so why does it wait until Eric verbally describes the location to manifest it?

Going to the instant farm, the men discover it's an *exact* duplicate of Eric's small Danish farm, complete with his fantasy girlfriend Ingrid (Ann Smyrner). Eventually, the other guys find their perfect women, too, including Don, who meets a duplicate of Greta Thyssen (Greta Thyssen). Though she's apparently an American actress – she was in some Three Stooges shorts – she's also dubbed. She's quite awful, like a parody of the Gabor sisters, already parodies themselves.

The men don space suits and head out to explore the real Uranus, stepping easily through the force field, represented this time by a split screen with nothing on the right side of the split. They find a landscape of twisted, sharp crystals, lots of rocks, and piles of what looks like styrofoam "snow." Don almost sinks out of sight in a pit of this, ammonia frozen so hard and dry that it acts like frictionless sand. He's pulled free by Eric – the same shot of their gloves almost touching is used twice – and they continue on.

In a pit, they see what looks like a distant glob of green bubble gum, which reacts when they shoot at it with guns whose beams are represented by scratches on the film. They all freeze for a moment while the Voice is heard

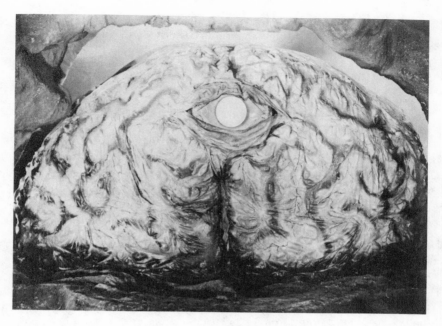

The silly giant alien brain that's the cause of all the problems in Journey to the Seventh Planet (1961); we never get this good of a look at it in the film itself, and that's no loss.

again: "You have come to me, feeble stupid men, armed only with courage and foolish weapons ... but my weapons are more powerful than yours. Your own fears created the means of your destruction."

The unseen monster quickly conjures up a strange lizardlike, rat-faced cyclopean thing which menaces them for a few minutes until it is shot in the eye.

In an interview with Robert Dyke and Robert Skotak in *Fantascene #2*, Jim Danforth told how this scene came to be. The original Danish special effects, perhaps of the cyclopean snake described in Melchior's script, were inadequate, possibly even comic. "When [AIP was] trying to upgrade the film for U.S. release," Danforth told *Fantascene*, "they wanted new creature shots. Project Unlimited originally did them, I believe, with a kinkajou they had obtained from an animal man. They'd built a little cave, then tried to get him to do the various things they wanted. They squirted him in the eye with freon and so forth. I guess nobody bought it.... It didn't [work], because the next thing I knew we were building ... the thing [we dubbed] the 'furry uni-optic' because it had one eye. We took the armature from the Harpy that was made for *Jack the Giant Killer*. I took the wing armatures home and built hands over them, brought it back and then Wah Chang covered it with fur. They shot the whole thing once in this 'furry' version and AIP didn't like it. They thought it looked too cute. But ... it was one of those things where they'd seen the model and everybody said, 'fine, go ahead and shoot it,' [but] when they finally saw it on the screen it wasn't what they wanted.... We stripped all the fur off and Wah Chang made up some latex skin with scaled, reptile texture on it, covered it over and did it again. It was actually much ado about nothing."

That seems a fair assessment. The resulting stop-motion creature is mostly out of focus, and does little other than lurch back and forth across a small cave. There are a couple of shots of what looks like the head of the puppet being manipulated by an offscreen hand, shot in real time, so it can drool. Over most shots of the thing are spirals and circles in constant motion. This puzzled me until I read Melchior's script: the thing is supposedly hypnotic, though there's no evidence on screen of this.

After they've returned to the farm, Ingrid tells Eric and the others that the power behind everything is "a lone being on this planet [that] can use its brain at nearly full capacity." (As it is entirely a brain, that may be quite something.) It took over their minds in the ship because they were momentarily weightless—their minds were "free and light."

Karl (Peter Monch) earlier revealed that the creature in the cave came from him. "I have always had an abnormal fear of rats. That's why I couldn't stand up to that rat thing." I was surprised to learn that it was supposed to look like a rat. It more resembles a cross between a kangaroo and a dragon, not a rat.

"Of course," Eric says. "Our deepest, gravest fears are being dug up from our subconscious ... and pitted against us." Barry points out that the presence of the women also indicates the being uses their "greatest desires" (which seem pretty banal) against them as well.

They realize the green goo they saw must have something to do with what's going on, and head into its cave to confront it. They find themselves facing a painfully unimaginative monster: a great big brain with an eyeball in the middle of it. Monsters from outer space often resemble brains to indicate they are very smart. (Agar had previously battled *The Brain from Planet Arous*.)

It conjures up what Melchior's script enthusiastically described as a "mole grub," a monstrous insect of some sort. The Danes delivered what, on the basis of one photo, may be the phoniest monster in screen history, a big head with some teeth, eyes on stalks, and a large pincher. It looks like a second-rate parade float from a small-town festival.

Once again, American effects substituted for the original Danish shots, although as in the earlier monster scene, a couple of shots remain of the spacemen being grabbed by the Danish original. This time, no *new* effects scenes were filmed. Instead, footage from *Earth vs. the Spider* was tinted blue and used as stock. They fire at some rocks above the monster, which fall and squash it most disgustingly: its guts ooze out in huge volumes. (This must be from the Danish footage.)

Back at the farm, Eric and the others build a giant acetylene torch to try to kill the big brain. In one of the film's few good touches, they build the torch in the brain's own conjured-up blacksmith shop. However, the alien checkmates them by having one of the girls replace the torch with one it has imagined into reality.

Don has a little conversation with Greta, who tells him that "the Earth is going to be the new home of this being you find so alien." With great naiveté, Don asks her how she knows that. "Who do you think is telling you?" she asks in a scene intended to be a shock, but because of bad direction and acting, comes across as silly.

The Earthmen return to the brain's cave, and prepare to burn it with their giant acetylene torch when, surprise, it vanishes. Karl, who was holding it, rushes at the alien brain. Suddenly, we see footage from *Angry Red Planet*, of Jack Kruschen being devoured by the giant amoeba. This replaced an extraordinarily silly Danish shot of Karl's death. The brain oozed something that dissolved his legs from the knee down, leaving bones. There's a common still of the dead man, lying on his back with skeletal legs and feet sticking out of his space suit.

Eric suddenly realizes that the cave they are in is slightly warmer than the rest of Uranus—the being uses the volcanic heat of the planet. So they spray the brain with the liquid oxygen intended to fuel the acetylene torch, freezing it. They are able to blow chunks of frozen brain matter away. Things begin acting up, and they get back to the ship at once.

Just before the ship takes off, we see another shot of that miniature terrain, turning from lush and green back into frozen wasteland (the mill is visible, and vanishes). Ingrid boards the ship with Eric, but soon vanishes in what was intended to be a wistful ending.

Over the end credits we hear an insipid song by Jerry Capehart and Mitchell Tableporter (?), sung by Otto Brandenburg. "Journey to the seventh planet, come to me, let your dreams become reality. I wait for you, somewhere on the seventh planet out in space, you and I will find a magic place like lovers do" and so on and so forth.

Ib Melchior told Robert Skotak and Bob Scott (*Fantascene* #1) that Sidney Pink "unfortunately re-wrote the scripts [of *Seventh Planet* and *Reptilicus*] and also directed the films himself with no prior experience. The original Sid Pink story [for *Seventh Planet*]—more of an undeveloped idea—had little to do with the script I wrote." When the effects, credited to Bent Barfod's company, proved unsatisfactory, Melchior supervised fixing up the films in the United States, as described earlier.

Melchior's reputation has been overinflated in recent years. He has a certain talent, not in story construction, characterization or dialogue. He is reasonably capable of adapting the ideas of other people to new situations: not at all plagiarism, but reinterpretation, a respectable endeavor. The humans-go-home message of *Angry Red Planet* was not new to that film, but the parade of strange monsters arrayed against our heroes was unusual. *Reptilicus* is the same old monster-on-the-loose stuff, though the monster is more than usually unstoppable. *The Time Travelers*' story is similar to much other time-travel fiction (but few films), though its bleak, unusual ending is out of the ordinary. The tremendously overrated *Robinson Crusoe on Mars* begins as clever and inventive, but the coincidences and wildly inaccurate science soon sink the film. *Planet of the Vampires* mixes living-dead stuff and a we'll-name-it-Earth ending to good effect (helped immensely by director Mario Bava's hyper-atmospheric visuals). *Death Race 2000*, from a story by Melchior, is a different if-this-goes-on story, a kind of SF rarely done in films.

In *Journey to the Seventh Planet*, Melchior brings in an array of interesting ideas—the rootless plants, duplicated landscapes, a few story tricks (creating a device to destroy the monster by using tools *it* created) but he doesn't hook them together in a useful way. (This kind of material remains rare in feature films, but often turns up on television, especially in "The Twilight Zone.") Melchior's script is better than the finished film, but even had it been made by a talented director with an adequate budget for effects and actors, the result would still have been trashy. The characters reek of cliché, the situations are malformed and unimaginative (surely someone could have had a secret desire other than a pinup girl?), and the monster battles are trite. There is a nice touch in that the giant snake that Melchior originally described has the same eye as the malevolent brain, but that's just cute, not profound. It's also contradictory. If the brain can conjure up perfectly accurate women, why not a snake?

Someone once said that if a few performances in a film are good, you can credit the actors, while if *all* the performances are good, you can credit the director. But whom do you blame when virtually all the performances are rotten and empty? In this film, no one shows any surprise, fear, curiosity or anger; nor do they seem like by-the-book military martinets. They're just acurious, unreactive blobs.

Apart from Ann Smyrner, who's attractive and seems to be giving a fairly good performance, the other actors are inadequate at best, and dreadful at worst. Even John Agar is usually better than this; when he has to be jauntily youthful, as here, he's out of his depth, and director Pink didn't help him. Technically, Agar does everything correctly, but his voice carries no conviction, and he is inexpressive.

Agar had more than Pink's unhelpful direction to contend with. The actor told Mark McGee that Greta Thyssen kept trying to steal scenes. "They'd play a two shot," McGee said, "and she would back up so that he would keep turning [with his back to the camera]. At one point, he just backed her into the set so that she couldn't go further, to play the shot 50–50."

Pink seems to feel that camera movement is needed, but has no idea what it is for. In one scene, the camera slowly moves in on Agar—*after* he has finished speaking.

The art direction of the film has something to recommend it, but it's vastly underfinanced, like all the movie; there's no specific credit for that, unless it's Scenemaster Herbi Gartner. The design is both professional and naive, as if the designer(s) had never worked on a film before, but had done plays. There are colored lights playing on set walls, objects are built in peculiar perspectives; it resembles a kiddy playland more than a movie.

Reviews were not favorable. "Tube" in *Variety* called it "mediocre" and "routine," but conceded it was "more resourcefully mounted than written," and that it had "sufficient thrust and a light enough payload to make the customary swift single boxoffice orbit around the saturation loop."

The *New York Times*' Howard Thompson, who often enjoyed low-budget SF movies, found this one not to his liking. "A chap named Sidney Pink," said Thompson, "rates the ripest raspberry of the season for ... this terrible little film."

The *Monthly Film Bulletin* gave *Seventh Planet* their lowest rating, but their commentary was not insightful.

More recently, comments have been unsympathetic. In *Castle of Frankenstein* #11, Joe Dante called it a "poorly done Danish–made SF adventure with [an] interesting idea buried in cliché-ridden, woodenly-acted foolishness.... Visually colorful, with rubbery special effects." Alan Frank (*SF*) considered it "uninspired space opera with moderate special effects and brisk execution."

Journey to the Seventh Planet is awkward and confusing. We never know where the Brain came from, why it is doing all this, why it seems to have no control over its creations at some times and total control at others. Its powers come and go at the script's whim, not with any sense of logic. The space suits are moderately interesting, and there are a few ideas buried in it, but aside from that—and aside from its being the only cinematic visit to Uranus—*Journey to the Seventh Planet* is a boring trifle.

Konga

I've always heard rumors that this film was originally called "I Was a Teenage Gorilla"; absurd as that sounds, it may be the truth, as the plot is basically that of *I Was a Teenage Werewolf* with Michael Gough in the Whit Bissell part, a gorilla standing in for Michael Landon, and a bunch of extraneous material cluttering up the story.

Konga is a boring, talky film with the shakiest of premises; the entire picture is nothing more than an excuse for the last fifteen minutes or so, when we finally get the giant gorilla promised on the exciting posters. The film is overacted, lumpily plotted and silly; it's hard to choose the worst Herman Cohen film, as there are so many contenders, but *Konga* is a leading candidate. As Don Willis (I) says, it's "about as good as you would expect a Herman Cohen version of *King Kong* to be." (Cohen recapitulated the classic 1930s monsters— werewolf, vampire, Frankenstein, Jekyll–Hyde and, here, King Kong—without bothering to secure rights. How did he miss a mummy?)

Not only does the title show brassy nerve in, er, aping that of *King Kong*, but the ads actually read "Not since 'KING KONG' has the screen exploded with such fury." In the ads, an ape twice as tall as the tower of Big Ben, clutching a woman who is about half the size of the tower, is shown wading through London, an expression of insane rage distorting his face. People stare in amazement or flee in terror. To make sure we know it is London, St. Paul's and one of the towers of Parliament are also visible, as well as a London double-decker bus and one man in a bowler carrying an umbrella. In the film, we get a brief scene of the ape standing in front of Big Ben. Even for American International, this ad is awesomely outrageous.

Especially in its vapid climax, the film shows none of this spectacle. The story shouldn't have been tried on the obviously deficient budget; there's no way the special effects could have been anything other than disappointing. Herman Cohen says that *Konga* was his last film for American International because of difficulties he had in dealing with James H. Nicholson, then cohead of the distribution company; even AIP had their limits, and perhaps the pathetically low quality of *Konga* caused a rift. (The real conflict was probably over money, however.)

Botanist Charles Decker (Michael Gough) returns to London a year after he crashed in the Ugandan jungles; he brings with him Konga, a baby chimpanzee who led him to a village. In an interview with the press, Decker tells them of his amazing findings, unusual carnivorous plants "with animal properties." He says that they need more than air, sun and water (as if other plants don't); "I discovered species of animal growth I had never seen before," he tells the press, listening with curiosity. (And who wouldn't be, upon hearing of "species of animal growth.") Decker is seeking a link between animals and plants, using Konga as an experimental subject, which seems ungrateful.

Back home, Decker is reunited with Margaret (Margo Johns), who has been many things to Decker—secretary, assistant, housekeeper, confidante and—ahem—good friend. She is clearly madly in love with the aloof, arrogant Decker, who doesn't give a damn about her. There's "very little room for sentiment in the life of a scientist," he tells the disappointed Margaret.

Konga, he says, is "first in the line of kings of the Earth," and together, they will "dominate a corner of the Earth and blaze a new trail in science." He goes out to his greenhouse, where he rips out Margaret's lovingly-tended flowers, and refuses to send them to hospitals "to help brighten the lives of the sick." Instead, he will use them as mulch for his carnivorous plants, which soon fill the greenhouse.

Decker gabs on and on about a plant-animal combination (which would seem to be pointless at best and which we never see anyway). Conveniently, the seeds of the carnivorous plants provide a serum which enables him to control minds. He gazes proudly over his greenhouse full of phony-looking, writhing carnivorous plants (vaguely based on real plants of this nature, such as Venus flytraps and pitcher plants).

Decker injects Konga with his all-purpose serum, which not only allows him to dominate Konga's mind, but also causes the young ape to become an adult at once. Decker keeps claiming that he can inject the essence of plant cells into people, changing their shape (but never demonstrates this—could a giant gorilla have been an *afterthought*?).

He has a conflict with Dean Foster (Austin Trevor) of the college where Decker is employed; Foster does not approve of Decker's wild comments to the press. "As long as I'm dean of this college," Foster says very unwisely, "you'll do as I say."

"Please leave," Decker says angrily. "I want to be alone with Konga." After he gives Konga another injection, there's a rippling effect to hide lap dissolves as the chimpanzee turns into a gorilla. Decker gazes at the ape with rapt fondness. "We know each other so much better than the world suspects," says Decker, leading to speculation that perhaps he had been in the jungle too long. This is not a healthy relationship.

Many have wondered why, when given this injection, Konga turns into a gorilla rather than an even bigger chimpanzee. Jack Moffitt, in *Limelight*, had perhaps the most reasonable suggestion: "perhaps ... there were no mansized chimpanzee suits in the London studios where the film was shot—but, more likely, because a chimp face, even when magnified, would remain too grinningly good-natured." The gorilla suit that was used was built and owned by George Barrows (who wore it, except for the head, in *Robot Monster*); he rented it to Herman Cohen for the film. According to Don Glut, when Barrows got his suit back, it was in sorry condition.

Another possible (probable) explanation is that Cohen and the crew needed a giant gorilla; the ads promised one, so they had to deliver one. Logic is of no concern in situations like this. In any event, Konga does become a blue-eyed gorilla, a man in a suit that does not resemble the real ape.

Back to the story. Decker hypnotizes Konga (showing us that Konga understands English), and sends him out to kill Dean Foster, which he does, by ripping off his head. The police know it was an animal, but never suspect Decker, even though Foster and all subsequent victims are linked to Decker.

Margaret figures things out, though. "You went beyond rabbits and guinea pigs," she complains, and Decker responds that he had to test Konga's obedience. Decker calms her down. Margaret insists on marriage, and he seems to agree. She kisses him on the cheek and leaves; when she's gone, he wipes the kiss off. The cad.

Rival botanist Professor Tagore (George Pastell) confronts Decker and is promptly killed by Konga. The character was introduced solely to be killed, not the most inventive type of plotting.

Decker meets with very American–type students (the film was probably written to be filmed in the United States), and is immediately attracted to pretty

Sandra (Claire Gordon). He lectures them on plants, plucking a fern and saying less about it than a dictionary would. This impresses the hell out of Sandra, however, who may have never read a dictionary entry on ferns. Sandra's breasts impress Decker.

Bob (Jess Conrad), Sandra's boyfriend, has a fight with Decker, but briefly. Bob is soon killed by Konga, sending his pointlessly-introduced family into mourning. "Oh, what good is this," moans Bob's mother, with great accuracy.

Margaret is now very angry with Decker. Not only is he killing people right and left, using obedient Konga as his weapon, but he's now got a younger, prettier girl hanging around, so Margaret responds to lame sarcasm at breakfast. "What are you having with your poached eggs," she sneers. "Murder?"

Decker is as frosty as ever. "If there's one thing I can't abide, it's hysteria, especially in the morning." Once again he mollifies her with the same preposterous proposition that these murders are just to check Konga's obedience, although Margaret still has her doubts.

While Decker is demonstrating his setup to Sandra, Margaret overhears him out in the greenhouse telling Sandra that Margaret is outmoded, so she heads for Konga's cage in the basement.

Meanwhile, Decker begins madly pawing Sandra in a fairly revolting scene of what director John Lemont apparently considered unbridled lust. In the basement, Margaret hypnotizes Konga and gives him mysteriously inaudible instructions. She also injects Konga with that stuff, and he begins growing even more, rocking back and forth from one foot to the other (I suspect this was so the feet won't look like they are sliding across the floor as Konga enlarges). He bursts through the roof, killing foolhardy Margaret and starting a fire.

Meanwhile, out in the greenhouse Decker and Sandra are still locked in that clumsy embrace — you'd think one or the other would have been strong enough to bring about a conclusion — when Konga suddenly reaches down and picks up Decker. I guess he remembers just how much *better* they knew each other. Meanwhile, Sandra is grabbed by a carnivorous plant and gobbled up offscreen. The perils of not knowing enough about ferns.

The police, alerted by reports of a 100-foot gorilla bursting out of a house, have arrived. Konga wanders off into London, apparently confused by his new height. He's a little destructive here and there, but nothing major. He passes Big Ben (*de rigeur* for monsters at large in London), while in his hand, Decker struggles and screams, frequently saying, "Put me down, Konga, put me *down* you fool!" I don't know about you, but if a giant gorilla that understands English had *me* in his hand, I would not be inclined to call him a fool.

Eventually, Konga stops strolling about, apparently to give the police time to draw a bead on him, which they do. Shot full of holes, he suddenly throws Decker — maybe that "fool" finally got to him — and collapses. Decker, of course, is killed, and Konga shrinks back to a baby chimpanzee.

Herman Cohen told *Newsweek* "I always think of the title first." *Konga* certainly gives every evidence of having been planned that way; "Konga" implies a giant ape, and the film gives us a giant ape. But only after giving us lots of things we're not interested in, including an especially hammy performance by Michael Gough (who, in "straight" films can be a subtle, effective actor), carnivorous plants and a homicidal regular-sized gorilla. In fact, until the last ten minutes or so, *Konga* more resembles a film like *Gorilla at Large* than it does *King Kong*. The title, the gimmick — they lure the kids into the theatres; after that, irresponsible hacks like Herman Cohen think they can get away with almost anything.

Konga is unconscionably padded throughout: long, meaningless dialogue scenes that simply repeat what we've heard before, as well as extraneous murders that exist solely to *keep* from showing us a giant gorilla by using up time. We didn't pay our two bucks or so to see a man in a seedy gorilla suit strangle George Pastell, but that's what Herman Cohen gives us. In terms of the plot, there's no reason for Decker to kill anyone at all; he isn't even depicted as much of a megalomaniac. He does seem to be in *love* with Konga, and there are those outré hints of a Meaningful Relationship between him and the baby chimpanzee, but those are just hints. The script, by Cohen and his frequent collaborator Aben Kandel, must have been devised simply to get a gorilla and Michael Gough together, finishing up with a giant-ape-on-the-loose sequence. The film has a patched-together feel, and a complete lack of conviction.

There's a strange undercurrent of misogyny to the Cohen–Kandel scripts. Phyllis Coates in *I Was a Teenage Frankenstein* is fed to the alligators, and in both *Konga* and *Horrors of the Black Museum*, a beautiful and innocent girl is killed simply for thrills. Sandra's death in *Konga* is particularly distasteful. In *Photon* #26, Herman Cohen told Mark McGee that he'd paid for those elaborate carnivorous plants, and felt the need to actually use them, so there went Sandra. He added an unconsciously telling comment: "I wanted to use my carnivorous plants. [The actress] was a very pretty girl, and very sexy, and I thought the audience would get a [bigger] kick out of seeing her killed ... than Margo Johns or Michael Gough." It doesn't seem to have occurred to Cohen that audiences would want to see villains like Gough killed rather than an innocent bystander like Claire Gordon. To him, she's just meat for his plants, and a way of giving an audience a "kick"—a completely gratuitous death.

Sometimes a script as cynically shoddy as that for *Konga* can be supported by good acting or fine special effects, or perhaps an overall sense of humor. But *Konga* lacks any of these qualities. The uncredited special effects are cheap and unconvincing; the only sequence that works at all is when Konga bursts out of the house and reaches for the policemen, in "SpectaMation." The model of the house isn't bad, the perspective holds well, and there doesn't seem to be a matte line at all. But the rest of the scenes involving the giant Konga are not done well: whenever the real Michael Gough is clutched unconvincingly in Konga's hand, the black ape appears brown; at other times, an unacceptable doll of Gough is used. Konga strolls through London with badly matted-in crowds running in front of him. The few monuments he passes are always isolated in blackness, with no other buildings around them. And of course, Konga himself does damned little other than stand there looking confused.

As mediocre as the special effects in *Konga* are, Cohen is proud of them. He told interviewer David Everitt in *Fangoria* #18 how they were done. "We were experimenting with a lot of effects at the Rank labs," said Cohen, "and I supervised it myself. I stayed over in England, for Chrissakes, for almost one year just working on the effects to get them the way I wanted them to be." If the effects in the film are indeed the way Cohen wanted them, he must be perverse. "*Konga* cost around $500,000, which at the time was a lot of money," Cohen told Everitt, "but with all the effects we had, people thought it cost around three or four million." Well, maybe *some* people did.

Konga was filmed in "SpectaMation," seemingly a name for the new matte process then being developed, which uses yellow sodium light rather than the then–more conventional blue-lit mattes. Everitt discusses this further in his recommended article.

Michael Gough is way over the top in his role as Decker. Presumably encouraged by Cohen, he clearly is playing down to the part, hammily trying for cheap laughs at the expense of the believability of the picture. Mark McGee asked Cohen a pointed question: "[Gough] is completely corrupt, unlikable, arrogant and void of humanity. Don't you think this would tend to alienate an audience from identifying with him and therefore cancel any real participation?"

Cohen responded, "Not at all.... The audiences won't take a character like that serious. [sic] They're having fun with the picture. Even if you play it straight, they're sitting in their seats with tongue in cheek. They know exactly what's going to happen. The only thing I can hope to do with my audience is to let them have a good time and make them scream now and then. When they're laughing at Michael Gough, throw them off-balance and make them scream." This sounds like a tacit admission of an inability to make a horror film that works on a serious level.

I have been unable to locate any other credits for Margo Johns, and Claire Gordon seems to have made very few other films. Jess Conrad was relatively busy through the 1960s, appearing in a variety of pictures. Director John Lemont may have made only one other film, *The Frightened City* (1961), although this is unlikely. His direction of *Konga* is lethargic and cramped; when people aren't sitting still, they are in close-up. The big attack-on-the-city scenes are ponderous, unimaginative and unexciting.

Konga received basically unfavorable reviews. "Tube" in *Variety* thought it was "burdened with verbose, repetitive scientific gobbledegook" but also thought it was "diverting" from time to time, thanks to Lemont, "who has managed to keep his actors disciplined and concerned, [to] cameraman Desmond Dickinson [later a director] whose Eastman–tinted views of plant, animal and human monstrosities are often intriguing; and [to] art director Wilfred Arnold, who has designed some admirable ornate and employable sets and objects for the occasion."

On the other hand, the unidentified *Boxoffice* reviewer typically went gaga over the movie, declaring it "downright superior" and praising it for "its spectacle, tempo and its abundant capacity to deliver bumper crops of chills and thrills to spectators of all ages."

Jack Moffitt in *Limelight* declared the film "America's first propaganda victory since the start of the Cold War" because it was not "defeatist" in ascribing the creation of the monster to radioactive fallout; he described the film in tongue-in-cheek terms, saying that the script "should appeal to all audiences willing to play 'let's pretend.'"

The *Monthly Film Bulletin* gave *Konga* its lowest rating, and although admitting it had "undeniable exuberance," complained about its direction and acting, and "slow development and ludicrously inadequate dialogue.... [The climax] is unimpressive and the trick work is deplorable. Though good for a laugh, the film is in every other respect a wasted opportunity."

More recently, *Castle of Frankenstein* #12 felt it was "quite poor" with "tastelessly lurid sub-plots" and "outrageously hammy acting ... a slow, dull British failure." Don Willis (I) felt it was "crude" and "simple-minded," while Leonard Maltin's *TV Movies* dismisses it as "silly sci-fi."

The movie is a rip-off of *King Kong* with no imagination and little talent expended on it. The lurid romantic angles of the plot didn't appeal to children, and the crudeness of the rest of the production probably alienated what few adults saw it. Its smug, smarty-pants spoofery alienated people looking for a good monster movie. I suspect the film performed well below expectations, which may have had much to do with Cohen's departure from AIP. None of the rest of his films involved special effects or giant monsters; Cohen proved with *Konga* that not only could he not make a decent second-string *King Kong*, he couldn't even beat Bert I. Gordon at his own game.

The Little Shop of Horrors

More than any other film, this confirmed Roger Corman as America's most inventive director of mainstream, low-budget films, although by the time it came along, those of us who saw most of what he did—damned few could have been busy enough to see *all* his films—had begun to recognize him as the best director of the least promising films.

Corman told Ed Naha (*The Films of Roger Corman*), "This movie had no budget to speak of, yet it has made me more fans and friends than some of my bigger pictures. People come up to me on the street who have memorized parts of the dialogue."

The film has been popular so long, turning up frequently on late-night television and capturing a new group of fans every time, that in 1982 it was turned into an off–Broadway musical which, though clever, distorted where it did not miss altogether the shrewdly conceived tone of the film. The play itself has now been filmed.

There's a name missing from discussions of the picture. Carolyn Perkins wrote notes for the University of Texas Cinema Department about *Corman's* use of dialogue, references, Jewish humor, etc. When the play opened, Corman's name was prominently displayed—rights had been secured from him.

Missing altogether from these discussions—and from the play's initial credits—was the name of Charles B. Griffith, who had to make legal noises to get his name added to the credits. All Griffith had done was *write* the movie.

There's an old joke in Hollywood about the starlet who was so stupid that to get ahead, she screwed the writer. *The Little Shop of Horrors* is known as one of Roger Corman's best films—and it is—but the things that people like most about it, even the voice of the talking carnivorous plant, are the work of Charles B. Griffith. He's largely a mystery figure in film reference sources, none of which have any information on him. So I asked Griffith.

He revealed that his grandmother and mother (Myrtle Vail and Donna Damerel) were radio's famous "Myrt and Marge," for five years the top radio stars of their network. He came to Los Angeles in 1949 at the age of 19, hoping to break into show business as a lyricist, and was taken on by his grandmother's agent. He wrote some TV scripts and made an unsold pilot film starring Franklin Pangborn.

His agent sent Griffith to meet Mel Welles, then a hopeful producer himself, and he also met Dick Miller and other people in the "Roger Corman Repertory Company." With Jonathan Haze, Griffith took seven scripts to Corman who, at the time, had a one-room office with a love seat usually occupied by Miller and Haze. Corman was scheduled to make a film in Portugal and signed Griffith to write a script for him, to be called "A Thief in Heaven," but the film was not made. Nonetheless, Corman was impressed with Griffith's ability and *very* impressed with his speed.

Corman's next assignment for Griffith was a Western, "Girls of Hangtown Mesa," which Griffith ambitiously based on *Rashomon*. But Corman regarded it as too expensive, and instead took Griffith to see the Western *Three Hours to Kill* (1954). Corman told Griffith to rewrite it for him with a woman in the lead role, and *Gunslinger* (1956) resulted.

For Corman, Griffith wrote or cowrote the following films: *Gunslinger, It Conquered the World, Attack of the Crab Monsters, Not of This Earth, The Undead, Rock All Night, Thunder over Hawaii* (all 1956!), *Teenage Doll* (1957), *Bucket of Blood* (1959), *Creature from the Haunted Sea, Beast from Haunted Cave, Ski Troop Attack, Atlas* (all 1960), *The Little Shop of Horrors* (1961), *The Wild Angels, Devil's Angels* (both 1967) and *Death Race 2000* (1975). He was assistant director for Corman on *Young Racers* (1963) and *The Secret Invasion* (1964); he directed *Up from the Depths* (1975, the worst film he was ever associated with), wrote and directed *Eat My Dust* (1976) and *Smokey Bites the Dust* (1980). And this is just his activity for Roger Corman.

While working for Corman, Griffith was approached by a man living in the same apartment house who wanted to be a producer. They tried to raise money around town, and finally approached a lawyer for Columbia, landing a deal with that studio. Griffith was to produce, write and direct five films, but only two resulted: *Forbidden Island* (1959) and *Ghost of the China Sea* (1958), which Fred F. Sears directed.

When summoned by Corman, Griffith went to Europe, and wrote *Atlas* while on a ship to Israel, but the film was relocated to Athens, and when Griffith arrived there, he did rewrites and was scheduled to play the heavy for $200. Judging from conversations with both Corman and Griffith, the making of *Atlas* would be a fit subject for a movie.

Griffith returned to Israel, where he eked out a living for a few months around the fringes of the movie industry—he was David Niven's stand-in on *Best of Enemies*, for instance—before and while working in more prestigious capacities. In Israel, he directed *Ha Tsankhanim* (The Paratroopers), following it with *Gvoul* (Frontier) in 1962, about a romance between a Jewish girl and an Arab boy, shot at a kibbutz run by Argentines. This film won awards at film festivals in the Ivory Coast and in Helsinki.

Corman called again, and Griffith worked as assistant director on Corman's European–shot *Young Racers* and *Secret Invasion*. During this period, he also directed dubbing adaptations in Rome. He wrote *The She Beast* for director Michael Reeves to film in 1965, although the script is credited to Michael Byron; Griffith was also second-unit director on the film. He did rewrites on *Barbarella* (1968), but received no credit.

Then Griffith returned to the United States and wrote *The Wild Angels*. (Peter Bogdanovich claims he extensively rewrote Griffith's script.) In preparation for *The Trip*, Griffith and Corman went to Monterrey and took LSD, then returned to Los Angeles, where Griffith spent ten months writing the film as a rock opera. Ultimately, however, Jack Nicholson wrote the shooting script. Since that time, Griffith has worked primarily with or for Corman, though occasionally he makes films for others, such as *Dr. Heckyl and Mr. Hype* (1980), a failed attempt at the kind of horror comedy Griffith did so well for Corman.

As can be seen from the list of films Griffith wrote for Corman, several are among Corman's best-regarded low-budget films, and one—*The Wild Angels*—generated an entire subgenre of movies, the motorcycle-gang picture.

Charles B. Griffith is not a great writer; he never creates memorable characters, only manipulates existing stereotypes, usually because of the genres in which he works. He is a writer of superficial cleverness—but at that, he is actually brilliant, if someone can be superficially brilliant, or brilliantly superficial. His films are hard to analyze because they were all written to specific formulas; it's hard to find a (Chuck) Griffithian theme, unless it is The Schnook Who Makes Good.

Griffith is especially good at dialogue, though he can occasionally go overboard; he's also good at setting up shock situations with a small kicker of humor in them, and in the three Corman comedies, shows that he knows how to create spoofs that still play fair by the rules of their genres. What he did, in fact, was simply to write the kind of film he ordinarily wrote—and extend everything.

Like some almost bohemian talents, Griffith seems to produce better work when he's under pressure. His incredible slew of scripts in 1956 contains some of his best and a little of his worst writing, and his most inventive ideas: the space vampire and matter transmission in Not of This Earth, the oddball relationship between Lee Van Cleef and Beverly Garland in It Conquered the World, the highly imaginative gimmicks in Attack of the Crab Monsters, and the occasionally interesting The Undead—which Griffith wrote in blank verse.

He's not as good when trying to match his earlier triumphs, to recreate inspiration instead of being inspired. In Dr. Heckyl and Mr. Hype, for instance, Griffith isn't content to do a hit-and-run with gags, as in the Corman comedies; he leans on everything, and seems almost to have forgotten what he knew about subtlety. Yet his script for Death Race 2000 has many fine moments. Perhaps it was the Golan-Globus Curse that sank Dr. Heckyl. (No one seems to be able to make good films for Golan-Globus, except Michael Winner [The Wicked Lady], who generally makes bad films for everyone, including Golan-Globus.)

There are several stories as to how The Little Shop of Horrors came into being; Corman and Griffith offer slight variations. According to Griffith, Corman was offered the use of standing sets (left over from Diary of a High School Bride) for a week or so. He contacted Griffith, showed him the sets, and asked him to write a script around them.

Griffith did, and gave Corman A Bucket of Blood. Corman was surprised—he'd never directed a comedy, and wasn't sure how to proceed. Griffith and others suggested that Corman direct in his usual fashion, allowing comedy to come out of the material. After the first take wrapped, the cast and crew applauded; this had never happened to Corman before, and he was delighted. He instructed Griffith to write the same film again—there were other standing sets available—and Griffith wrote The Little Shop of Horrors, which does have a plot similar to Bucket of Blood. (Which has no science fiction elements.)

Corman's story differs slightly. There was a gap between Bucket of Blood and Little Shop, according to this scenario; when Corman was offered the use of the second sets, he and Griffith "went back to the coffeehouse on Sunset Strip for an evening and worked out a new storyline which had a little similarity to Bucket of Blood. [Griffith] wrote the script in a week and shifted the scene to a florist's shop." (Quoted in The Movie World of Roger Corman.)

This was in a period in which Corman was excited to see just how fast and cheap he could make a film. Bucket of Blood was shot in five days, and he was determined to beat that with Little Shop which, after all, had only five interior sets. According to Hollywood legend, Corman shot the film in only two days and one night, probably the record for a feature film. He was helped in his high-speed endeavor by shooting the film with two cameras simultaneously, one of the few times he did this, if not the only time. Corman doesn't like to reveal the budget, but it was probably no more than $100,000. ($225,000 was reported in the trades, undoubtedly a gross exaggeration.)

Chuck Griffith says that he, rather than Corman, did most of the night shooting in the film, on locations around Los Angeles, but even that took only two or three nights on a budget of $1,100. By whatever reckoning, the film was in the can in less than five days.

Griffith worked with cinematographer Vilis Lapenieks for the night shooting, but Corman wouldn't give them any long lenses. Griffith also did the location shots of Jonathan Haze and Mel Welles in downtown Los Angeles. Most of the bums seen in the film are *real* bums, who were paid 10¢ for their appearance; when the cameras started rolling, the bums started emoting, apparently thinking a real performance would get them more money. In one nighttime scene, an unexplained mob of children boils up out of a sidewalk underpass and chases everyone down a street. The kids had been hanging around the location, getting in the way, and Griffith paid them each a nickel to be *in* the film, which kept them out of his hair.

The story of *Little Shop* is simple, even stark. Gravis Mushnick (Mel Welles) runs a florist shop in, of all places, Los Angeles' Skid Row. His assistant is pretty, dopey Audrey Fulquard (Jackie Joseph), who seems to have learned English (but not accent) from Leo Gorcey. Mushnick's general factotum is Seymour Krelboined (Jonathan Haze), an inept schlemiel in the Jerry Lewis mold, a shy, enthusiastic idiot, clumsy and maladroit.

As the film opens, Mushnick fires Seymour, but flower-eating Burson Fouch (Dick Miller) — as opposed to the later man-eating flower — suggests that if Seymour has the unusual plant he's just told Mushnick about, it would be a money-earning proposition for the shop.

Seymour brings in the plant, a lumpy egg-shaped thing which opens like a clam, a strange hybrid he has raised at home in a coffee can. Because of his unspoken crush on her, he has named it Audrey Jr., which delights Audrey (Sr.). The plant is indeed odd, and Mushnick agrees to give Seymour and Junior a week's extension.

The plant looks droopy, however, and Seymour's job is again in danger, so that night he sits up with Junior. At sunset (the same shot is used three times in the film, perhaps as an in-joke on low budgets), the plant opens up. Seymour accidentally cuts his finger; the blood falls into the plant, which smacks its "lips" enthusiastically. This dismays Seymour, but he now has a way of feeding Junior.

When he comes in the next day, all his fingertips are bandaged — ten bees, he explains — and the plant is larger and healthy-looking. Mushnick is delighted, calling Seymour "son" and having visions of opening a huge florist shop in Beverly Hills, with a sign "Gravis Mushnick — in French." But all affection vanishes when constantly mourning customer Mrs. Shiva (Leola Wendorff) points out that Junior is again dangerously droopy.

That night, having no more blood to give, Seymour is wandering disconsolately by the railroad yard, where he accidentally beans a drunk (a railroad cop, we later learn), chopped up by a passing train. Seymour unsuccessfully tries to dispose of the remains, and he desperately returns to the florist shop where the plant — which has begun talking, saying mostly "Feed me!" — refers to the contents of the seeping gunnysack as "food." Dismayed again, but willing to try anything, Seymour begins feeding the chopped-up body to the plant.

Junior, of course, is delighted. But Mushnick isn't. He glimpsed the disappearance of the corpse into the happy plant, and plans to go to the cops. But the next day, there's such a crowd in the shop—the plant has grown—and the cash register is jingling so loudly that, when Seymour says he thinks the plant won't grow anymore, Gravis decides to forsake justice for commerce.

Seymour has developed a toothache, and visits Dr. Phoebus Farb (John Shaner), a wildly sadistic Skid Row dentist, who greatly enjoys inflicting pain on his poverty-stricken patients. Seymour rebels against Farb, they duel with dental instruments; Seymour accidentally kills Dr. Farb.

Another patient, Wilbur Force (Jack Nicholson), enters and, Seymour, after hiding Farb's body, tends to him. Force is just as masochistic as Farb was sadistic, and enjoys himself as Seymour removes, without anaesthetic, every other one of Force's teeth. It's a shame that Force and Farb never met.

Seymour feeds the dentist's body to the plant which, sure enough, is even larger the next day. A society woman (Lynn Storey) wants to present Seymour with an award, and intends to come back later when the buds now present around the gigantic, wrinkled body of Junior, have opened.

A pair of Dragnet-styled cops, Joe Fink (Wally Campo) and Frank Stoolie (Jack Warford), quiz Mushnick about the missing dentist, and he's nervous, knowing where Farb must have gone. That night, he insists on sitting up with Junior himself, to make sure that Seymour doesn't feed more Skid Row denizens to the plant.

Seymour takes Audrey to dinner with his hyperhypochondriacal mother (Myrtle Vail, Griffith's grandmother). But a would-be holdup man (Charles B. Griffith himself) draws a gun on Mushnick and demands to be given all the money he knows the shop has been pulling in. Up against the wall, Mushnick tells the crook the money is in Junior—"just knock" to get it to open, he says—and, of course, Junior gobbles the bandit up. (But spits out his gun.)

By the next evening, Seymour is under a lot of pressure. His mother doesn't like Audrey, Mushnick wants Junior removed, and those people are coming with the award. He even has a falling-out with Audrey, who mistakes the plant's shouts for "chow" as Seymour's own—he desperately tells her he's a ventriloquist. Audrey leaves, and Junior hypnotizes Seymour, rather easily done: "Close your eyes. Go to sleep. Now open your eyes," says Junior. "Yes, master," says Seymour.

Seymour encounters enterprising prostitute Leonora Clyde (Meri Welles, then wife of Mel), who practically begs to be taken home. Still under Junior's spell, Seymour tosses a rock in lieu of a coin, and it comes down heads—Leonora's head. Seymour dutifully feeds her to Junior.

The next night, all concerned enter the florist shop to see the buds open. Four of them do—adorned with pictures of the four people who were food for Audrey. The cops and, oddly, Mushnick pursue Seymour through the streets, and through piles of tires and toilets, before giving up the chase. Seymour returns to the florist shop and climbs into Junior with a knife. When everyone comes back, there's one unopened bloom: it blossoms to reveal Seymour's face (a lousy likeness), while we hear his often-repeated phrase, "I didn't mean it!"

There are no straight characters in Little Shop of Horrors; the most normal person is Fouch, a commentator throughout, and he eats flowers. Not all of this idea pays off, and after a while the film seems to be taking place in some mad dreamworld. But there's one overriding virtue to The Little Shop of Horrors: it is that very rare horror spoof that is actually funny. (The only other ones I can think of are Abbott and Costello Meet Frankenstein, Schlock, Young Frankenstein and Corman's The Raven.)

In his only notable movie role, Mel Welles is outstanding as the greedy, pompous Gravis Mushnick. In the script, Mushnick is described as "Turkish," but he's clearly and very Jewish in the film. No fun is being made of him for being a Jew — even his greed comes from being a florist on Skid Row rather than out of stereotyped Jewish avarice — but a great deal of fun comes from his immigrant's mangling of the English language. This is Jewish humor as even Jews often perform it, and Welles is very funny.

He stays in character and with the dialect throughout. He wants to open "a new flower saloon in Beverly 'Ills." "I'll be beck in a flesh with the kesh," he tells Audrey. Not only do I have a talking plant, he says aloud to Junior, but "we got one dot makes with smott crecks."

He also mangles delivery: "To my throat I would be giving a cut rate," he tells Mrs. Shiva when she asks for a volume discount on cemetery flowers. "Look on this boy," he exults about Seymour. "My flowers got something the others isn't," he brags to two high school girls looking for flowers for a Rose Parade float. And there's some specifically Jewish stuff, too. When he's mad at Seymour at one point, Mushnick tells him that great sign in the sky (he's fond of this idea) will say "Seymour Krelboined — Rest in Peace. In *Arabic*!" And he occasionally says "fency-shmency," too.

Even his shop signs are in dialect. "40% Off From Everything." "We don't letting you speed so much." "Lots Plants Cheap." "Look on the Phantastik New Plant Audrey Jr. Right from the jungle in Africa," and so forth.

None of this would work, however, and might seem distasteful if it weren't for Welles' breezy confidence as Mushnick. Nothing stops him — except Junior — and he has the pleasant arrogance of someone who believes he speaks English as well as, say, the Chief Justice of the Supreme Court. It's a general stereotype of immigrants, but it's affectionate and even charming.

Mrs. Shiva is also a Jewish joke. Her name is actually Siddie Shiva ("sitting shiva" is mourning), and she's living up to her name: she's constantly buying flowers for the funerals of relatives in far-flung parts of the country — Tenafly, New Jersey, for instance. And she has relatives near at hand. Fouch tells about a florist who outfitted his shop with poison ivy and scratched himself to death in an insane asylum. "Oi!" cries Mrs. Shiva, "That was my cousin Harry!"

Audrey (Sr.) talks in full-blown but not overwhelming malapropisms. She wants Mushnick to give Seymour a chance "to resurrect himself." Seymour is "the most magnanimous [intelligent] person in the whole world," Audrey declares. She admires Junior: "isn't it empirical?" She identifies a salad as "caesarian." And Junior finally becomes "monstrositous."

But as with Mushnick, the humor doesn't lie so much in the script as in Jackie Joseph's winsome, daffy charm. She has a vividly distinctive but nearly indescribable voice — it's both foggy and squeaky — and a unique delivery. (When she turns up in Joe Dante's *Gremlins*, as Dick Miller's wife, many in the audience immediately recognize her voice, even when failing to recognize her face.) Audrey is, thanks to Joseph herself, one of the sweetest characters in any Corman film, usually short on such types.

Jonathan Haze, who popped up in many Corman films both in front of and behind the camera, is amusing as Seymour, but there's also something forced about his performance. You're usually aware that this is a bright guy acting dumb. However, for the most part, that doesn't get in the way. Seymour is undeveloped in the script — just a device to keep the plot going — and his repeated "I didn't mean it!" doesn't have the clearly intended mark of a signature refrain. Haze added a certain klutziness to Seymour, but most of his best scenes come from playing things blankly. Seymour's funnier when he's obsessed than when worrying about feeding corpses to his plant, because he's required to *think*.

Something about this quick, two-day schedule seems to have brought out the best in everyone. Not only are Mel Welles and Jackie Joseph better in this than anything else I've seen them in (though neither had such showy roles elsewhere), but almost the entire supporting cast is nearly perfect. Dick Miller changes Fouch from the script's one-joke character to an affable wise guy who is so memorable that some remember Miller raising Audrey. As Farb the dentist, John Shaner is so manic and creepy that he becomes an embodiment of all our fears about dentists. Even Wally Campo as Fink and Jack Warford as his partner turn a quick "Dragnet" parody into a little gem.

But the one brief role that people remember the best from *Little Shop of Horrors* is Jack Nicholson as giggling masochist Wilbur Force, and this isn't merely because he later proved himself to be an accomplished actor, turning up in a freakish role. Force is memorable because Nicholson was *then* an accomplished actor. Along with Dick Miller, Nicholson adds to the character as delineated in the script. The dialogue is the same, but Nicholson's delivery makes Force not only funny but unforgettable. He walks with his head cocked forward, a mad grin fixed to his face. He's constantly chuckling to himself, occasionally bursting into laughter, and right from the first glimpse we have of him, we know that this guy is an authentic loony. While conversing with Seymour, he stabs himself with a dental instrument, giggles, and keeps talking.

His single funniest take is after Seymour reluctantly begins drilling; Wilbur screams in pain and laughs in joy simultaneously, and when Seymour hesitates for a moment, sits bolt upright to shout frantically, "Oh, my God, don't stop *now*!" He seems like someone whose orgasm was interrupted. (Years later, when asked about *Little Shop* and his performance, Nicholson was pleased that it was so well remembered. It is, in fact, better-remembered by most moviegoers than any of his early *starring* roles.)

The cast also makes use not only of throwaway lines, but throwaway dialogue exchanges: "I'm not worth it," Seymour says; "Who says you're not?" Audrey asks; "Everybody," Seymour says; "Yeah, I know," Audrey replies. A moment later: "You're gonna be another Luther Glendale," Audrey says; "Pasadena," Seymour responds absently, "Burbank," Audrey finishes. All this done quickly but not rapid-fire, and not emphasized.

Nor are similar exchanges with Mushnick overdone. In the midst of congratulating Seymour on his wonderful plant, Mushnick quickly asks, "What happened to your fingers?" "Bee stings. How come I'm all of a sudden so wonderful?" says Seymour. "Five bees, one from each finger?" asks Mushnick. "Ten bees," says Seymour, holding up the other bandaged hand, "do you say I got a ten dollar raise?" "You sure did, my very excellent Seymour Krelboined. Ten bees," muses Mushnick, dropping the subject. The center of action in the scene takes the focus off the talk about fingers, so that it remains an odd subtext.

At its best, *The Little Shop of Horrors* plays like a polished performance of a well-rehearsed script, written and rewritten until every line and nuance was right. Even Audrey Junior's lines are excellent. The plant is certainly single-minded, never talking about anything but food. (In the ill-conceived ending to the play, the plant is out to conquer the world.) "Feed me," says the plant. Varying this: "I'm hungry." "I want foooood." "FeeEEEd me. Feed meeeee!" "I'm starved." "Give me to eat." "I'm dying from hunger." "I want chow." "Food for an empty stomach!" When Mushnick asks rhetorically, "Who would you like to have tonight?" Junior mutters, "You look fat enough," and, when Mushnick refuses to feed the plant, growls, "you'll get yours."

The plant wants only one thing, but knows many ways to ask for it. But, as with the other actors, though the script is bright and inventive, it's the delivery that makes these lines so funny. The voice is Griffith's, and it gets deeper as the plant gets larger, always a greedy, self-centered growl. It is, in fact, one of the funniest offscreen performances. (As the burglar, Griffith also exhibits good timing, but it's not a comic performance.)

There's an odd little scene not in the script, the encounter the hypnotized Seymour has with Leonora Clyde. She, in fact, delivers the single weirdest line in a movie full of them: she's tried to catch Seymour's attention several times by dropping her handkerchief which he ignores. (She keeps reappearing ahead of him, like a character in an animated cartoon.) She finally drops a banana peel which he promptly slips on. Bending over him, Leonora breathes, "Hi, I'm Leonora Clyde. How's the rain on the rhubarb?" (Griffith believes he lifted the line from Phil Silvers.)

Not everything works. Seymour's mother is an outrageous hypochondriac, but this is an isolated joke, having nothing to do with the carnivorous plant story. (There is one funny joke: she listens to a radio show called "Sickroom Serenade.") It might have worked if it were funny enough, but it isn't, although Griffith works almost every possible change on the idea within the limits of the production.

Fred Katz's score is unfortunate. It seems arranged for xylophone, bass and tympani, and emphasizes the funniness going on in a ham-fisted manner, as if we might mistake the film for Serious Stuff, or miss a joke; this flaw is common to all of Corman's comedies, so the fault probably lies with the director. Things would have worked better if the music had been played dead straight. The score was lifted from *Bucket of Blood*; it actually worked better there, as that film was less of a comedy, and a comic score played well against some of the horror scenes.

The photography by Archie Dalzell (and Vilis Lapenieks) is as accurate a parody as the basic premise of the script. Nighttime exteriors are shot in a hard-edged, shadowy *film noir* style, with pools of light playing over brick walls, long shadows preceding the actors down streets, and so forth.

The film is hard for some to take. It's clearly incredibly cheap, and looks much like other incredibly cheap films. The pacing is a bit slow throughout, and there's no comic rhythm to most of the scenes. As a work of moviemaking, it looks rather trashy, but the actors, dialogue and story make it a classic low-budget film.

The film received little notice when it was released. I saw it on a double bill with *Black Sunday*, a memorable afternoon to say the least—and both films took me aback in different ways—but it wandered around the country with a variety of other cofeatures. A cheap, short film with unknowns didn't usually get reviewed much, but there's been a fair amount of commentary on it since.

Allen M. Widem at the *Motion Picture Herald* seemed unsure as to the film's intent, although he did call it "horrorifically funny." He said, "If Charles Griffith intended tongue-in-cheek story treatment, he's admirably succeeded. The deft production-directorial touches of the resourceful, redoubtable Roger Corman are very much present.... Exploitation tieups are seemingly endless."

Years later, in *Castle of Frankenstein*, Joe Dante said, "very inventive, resourceful and darn funny self-parodying spoof about a man-eating plant in a

Brooklyn [sic] flower shop. Kinky, full of in-jokes, good lines, keen fun. This is the legendary Corman effort filmed in 2½ days, and astonishingly smooth-looking! See it." (Years later, Corman gave Dante his first chance as a director; when *Newsweek* reviewed Dante's *Gremlins*, the review was headed "Little Toyshop of Horrors.")

Psychotronic said it is "crowded with great gags and characters.... A wonder with the ultimate hypochondriac mother, a junkyard chase, and the world's most famous talking plant. Every time it's on television, school kids go around yelling 'Feed me! I'm hungry!' the next day. Not to be missed."

Reviewing the commercial videotape of the film in *Fangoria* #28, "Dr. Cyclops" said, "You can't exactly call the picture a sophisticated satire, but it still holds up as ... [an] unique and endearing adventure in shoestring film-making."

In the University of Texas film notes referred to earlier, Cynthia Perkins said, "The whole film is a sort of colossal in-joke for Corman, cast, and crew, and if the joke seems occasionally overlong and the ethnic humor sometimes labored, the film is still an enjoyable surprise.... Filmically the movie is pretty crude in some spots; heads are obscured by other heads or barriers, the edited match-action often doesn't quite match.... On an aesthetic continuum, *Little Shop of Horrors* hardly reaches the status of a masterpiece, but it is a refreshing poke at the foibles of its own genre."

In his first volume, Don Willis seems to have liked it slightly more than he did in his second (funny how films change): "Funniest three-day movie ever. Joseph, Miller and Nicholson ... have some memorable comic moments. And the plant doesn't get all the good lines." In volume 2, he said, "Funny (if one-note) characters in a very strange situation comedy. Alternately awful and inspired. Each actor has his or her shining moments, but only the plant seems to have *all* shining moments. (It's its delivery.)"

The film's fame has increased since its release; it could hardly be otherwise. In 1973, the soft-core sex comedy *Please Don't Eat My Mother* was released; the plot was so similar to that of *The Little Shop of Horrors* that it went beyond mere flattery and approached plagiarism, but apparently nothing was done about this. Dick Miller and Jackie Joseph were reunited in Allan Arkush's underrated *Get Crazy* (1983) and Joe Dante's dazzling *Gremlins* (1984), and the musical is being filmed by director Frank Oz starring Rick Morams.

The other actors have been less visible than Miller, who pops up everywhere these days. Mel Welles had been a supporting player in a variety of films before becoming one of Corman's repertory company. He had small roles in *Appointment in Honduras* (1953), *Abbott and Costello Meet the Mummy, The Silver Chalice* (both 1955), *The Brothers Karamazov* (1958) and other films. He's occasionally directed minor films over the years; he directed *Code of Silence* in 1958, and in Europe, where he worked through most of the 1960s, he directed *Island of the Doomed* (1966) and *Lady Frankenstein* (1971). He also found time for acting while overseas, and appeared in *The She Beast, The Red Sheik, The Reluctant Saint* (both 1962) and *The Christine Keeler Affair* (1964). He returned to the United States in the 1970s, and appeared in Griffith's *Dr. Heckyl and Mr. Hype*. He did an offstage voice for *Wolfen* (1981).

By 1962, Jonathan Haze apparently gave up acting to work behind the camera. He wrote *Invasion of the Star Creatures*, and worked on a variety of films, including *Blood Bath* (1966), *Born Losers* (1967) and *Medium Cool* (1969).

Jackie Joseph, who was in *Ma and Pa Kettle in Waikiki* (1955) and *King Creole* (1958), became a local Los Angeles television personality and an animal rights activist. She later returned to acting, with small roles in *A Guide for the Married Man*, *Who's Minding the Mint* (both 1967), *The Split*, *With Six You Get Eggroll* (both 1968) and *The Cheyenne Social Club* (1970, as one of the whores).

Dick Miller, of course, is still around, and seems like he always will be, as long as there are directors and producers who remember his sharp, funny performances in any number of Corman films. He went through some slightly lean years between the time Corman himself stopped directing and the time when those who had grown up on Corman films started making movies themselves, but he now works steadily. He's been virtually canonized by *Fangoria*, and is still one of the actors whose work I admire so much that I get nervous talking to him.

Although the film passed without notice when it was made, *The Little Shop of Horrors* has perhaps been the most influential and popular two-day movie in film history. Twenty-five years after it was made, it is still delighting surprised viewers, and has developed its own cult following. Some have called the film an accident, but it isn't that at all; it's an example of what can happen when talented people allow their imaginations free reign, while still working within a restrictive format. If the movie had more money and more time, it wouldn't have been the little wonder it is.

Magic Spectacles

Although the word "magic" in the title implies this is fantasy rather than science fiction, the plot as given in the *American Film Institute Catalog* indicates it is SF, and as I would much rather err on the side of inclusion rather than exclusion, here it is.

Magic Spectacles, rereleased in 1964 as *Tickled Pink*, is what was known in a more innocent era as a "nudie." At the time, true pornography was mostly confined to grainy 8mm showings; scenes of people actually Doing It were just not shown in regular theatres where you could buy a ticket and go in and sit down and watch like a regular person. The closest ordinary commercial films got to porn were these naive, unsophisticated nudies, in which the entire "pornographic" element consisted of (usually) attractive young women with nothing on. Their breasts, usually large and well-shaped, were prominently on display, but pubic areas were always demurely hidden. The topless women often carried large purses, potted plants, or some other bulky object, or were seen from the side with their legs crossed. They were always smiling, but it was unclear just what was so pleasant; unless they were chatting with another pretty naked woman, they were alone. Certainly no men so much as touched them. These movies were anything but smutty; they had an almost sweet ingenuousness, certainly by the standards of our more bawdy times.

Oh well, of course they were sexist—what else could they be? They were worshipful of women, rather than disrespectful (not necessarily an improvement, of course); men were onlookers, and the women moved in a kind of golden glow, like distant goddesses. While I don't mean to sound sentimental over movies designed to give lonely men momentary arousal, these films were no closer to true pornography than was *The Police Gazette*. Men came to and left these films rather furtively—unless they were of college age, in which case they went in large, noisy and embarrassed groups—and I doubt that the films did much harm. They promoted a kind of *Playboy*-like view of women as icons of perfection, but that was only one step away from the entire Hollywood treatment of men *and* women (and pets, and children, etc.) anyway.

As for *Magic Spectacles* itself, it's the usual wish-fulfillment fantasy. Usually a nebbish of some sort found himself in a position to observe naked young women engaged in some healthy outdoorsy sport. We'd see the women bouncing around; there'd be a cut to the actor playing the voyeur (often a burlesque comic), grinning sheepishly in the bushes or up a tree. And then back to the women. It was all done from a distance. In this film, our nebbish finds a pair of glasses which make clothing invisible; this breathtakingly simple idea was repeated the next year in *Paradisio*, and in that, the nude scenes were also in 3-D.

In the 17th century, Dr. Paul Ner De Nude (Tommy Holden), a scientist in Paris, discovers an ancient Chinese formula for improving the vision of the elderly, and uses it to produce a pair of lenses. However when the *young* wear the glasses, clothing becomes invisible. Hubba hubba.

The glasses are lost in the passage of time. One day in Los Angeles, nebbishy Angus L. Farnsworth (Holden again) breaks his glasses, and fearing the wrath of his fat, domineering wife Myra, buys another pair at a second-hand store. Guess what? Why, they are Dr. Ner De Nude's glasses. Angus is amazed and delighted at what he now sees; even his secretary at the advertising agency where he works suddenly appears unclad before Angus' popping eyes.

Myra is constantly berating poor Angus for trivial things. She exercises furiously, then eats boxes of candy, wondering why she can't lose weight. With his new glasses, Angus isn't eager to go home; he's seen his wife naked and it wasn't that big a thrill.

In his 1927 Flint automobile, Angus runs off with his secretary to a plush seaside resort, cavorting with the pretty girls he meets there. Then he blissfully drives across the countryside. In an unusual plot development for a nudie (usually in nudies, there's no plot to develop), the glasses not only give Angus literally a new outlook on life, they do so figuratively as well. He gains more self-confidence and a new attitude of freedom.

After some adventures, including a visit to a ghost town, a few art students recognize Angus from his picture in the paper—his wife has reported him missing—and they tell Myra where he is. However, all ends happily, for now Myra is a devoted and kind wife. Angus, nonetheless, is still a little wistful about his now-lost glasses.

Unlike most nudies, *Magic Spectacles* received some reviews. Judging from the *Hollywood Citizen-News*, it was also quite profitable for its initial distributor and producer, Fred W. Krueger, who had owned a theatre chain. "N.M.E." in the *Citizen-News* was puzzled by the appeal of such films. "I'm constantly amazed at the uninhibited daring of so many independent producers who flaunt [*sic*] the production seal and come up with varied concepts of nudity in their film releases. I'm even more amazed that enough people frequent this type of film to substantiate its being made and released to the public in the first place.... Beyond the bevy of nude beauties parading before the color lenses, there is scarcely anything else to go on—certainly no legitimate entertainment."

Boxoffice's unidentified but flowery reviewer, who covered the film on its 1964 rerelease, was apparently pleased with it. "Likeable Tommy Holden, with demeanor not unlike the 'little' people of the world so wonderfully personified by Chaplin, Lloyd, Keaton and others of their ilk, may well have generated a humdinger of a series project in this Arch Hall effort." (Arch Hall [Sr.] rereleased the film on a states' rights basis.)

Bob Wehling, who directed *Magic Spectacles*, later wrote *Eegah*, which Arch Hall, Sr. did almost everything else on. Wehling continued his association with Hall, Sr. in *What's Up Front* (1964), which Wehling directed and cowrote.

Vilis Lapenieks, who photographed *Magic Spectacles*, soon rose from very minor films like this to more important projects, although he never reached quite the heights of other cameramen with funny names, like Vilmos Zsigmond. Lapenieks filmed *Eegah*, but also *Night Tide* (1963) and *Queen of Blood* (1966) for Curtis Harrington, who is concerned with the visual qualities of his films. Lapenieks also shot parts of *Little Shop of Horrors*, and all of *Deathwatch*, *Mother Goose A-Go-Go* (both 1966), *Hot Rod Action*, *If It's Tuesday, This Must Be Belgium* (both 1969), *Cisco Pike* (1971) and *Capone* (1975).

It's interesting to realize that a film like *Magic Spectacles*, which seemed so naughty in 1961, would possibly receive only a PG rating today.

Man in the Moon

Talented people working somewhat below their abilities made this typically amiable British movie, *Man in the Moon*. A spoof of both science fiction and space research, it features the usual sort of smirks at bureaucracy common in intelligent British comedies of this period. However, the film is too crazy in some scenes, and not nearly weird enough in others; to mangle metaphors, in attempting to beat a middle path, it falls between two stools. Still, it's moderately amusing, and star Kenneth More is his usual cheerful, pleasant self.

Here he plays William Blood (no relation to Peter of *Dr. Blood's Coffin* fame, one hopes), a phenomenally healthy Briton who makes his living renting out as a test subject for medical research. However, he is so very healthy that he cannot catch a cold even after spending the night in a brass bed planted in the middle of a meadow. He meets attractive stripper Polly (Shirley Anne Field) as she strolls by in an evening dress, but his failure to catch even the sniffles loses him his job.

Blood ascribes his good health to a total lack of matrimony, which doesn't please Polly as they become more involved, but his robustness seems promising to the Atomic Research Center. Head scientist Professor Davidson (Michael Hordern) is looking for a perfect physical specimen with no family ties to use as the first British astronaut—to be, in fact, the first man on the Moon.

Davidson offers Blood a tidy sum to undergo extensive testing, but wisely doesn't tell him the end goal of the tests. Blood breezes through everything the research facility has to offer—rocket sleds, centrifuges, hot rooms, etc., even a foggy, rainy, windy chamber labeled "Simulated English Summer." He emerges unscathed, but arouses the professional jealousy of Leo (Charles Gray), who had hoped to gain the prize money to the first man to reach the Moon.

However, scientists spot this developing friction, and quickly brainwash Leo into becoming very fond of Blood. Almost too fond, in fact, as Leo complains that he's not French and therefore can't kiss Blood on his cheeks. This brainwashing is briefly debated in Parliament, until someone points out that the very purpose of Parliament is to brainwash its members.

Finally, however, Blood learns that he's destined for a lunar landing, and tries to back out. The prize money is increased, however, and he agrees to the tests. He is, however, no longer immune to disease—he's fallen in love with Polly, putting an end to his great good health.

Still, he's the only trained astronaut Britain has, and is shipped off to the launching area in Australia. The Moon rocket takes off. After he arrives at his destination, the scientists are delighted to receive Blood's reports on the eerie lunar terrain—until he reports an inhabitant of the Moon is a kangaroo. The rocket has landed in the Outback, rather than on the Moon.

Williams returns to his base to tell the scientists, "Sorry, chaps. I guess it's back to the old drawing board." He returns to London and marries Polly.

The film is only barely science fiction, but it's a pleasant enough comedy. It bounces lightly through the same kind of testing treated with grim seriousness in earlier films such as *Riders to the Stars*. It never quite catches fire as satire, but is agreeable enough. Films don't have to succeed at all their goals to be worthwhile.

Most of the satire in the film is aimed at petty bureaucrats and scientific testing; very little is expended on wondering if space travel really is such a fine idea. To a degree, that's inherent in the material, but not really what writers Michael Relph and Bryan Forbes are kidding. The satire is essentially subordinate to the comedy, and the whole thing is too good-natured to offend anyone.

Cowriter Bryan Forbes was an actor for several years, appearing in (among many others) *Satellite in the Sky* and *Enemy from Space*; he began writing such films as *Cockleshell Heroes* (1955), *The Captain's Table* (1959) and *Of Human Bondage* (1962). He overlapped careers for a while, but when he later turned director, he ceased acting. He often writes or cowrites the films he directs. His career as a director has been mixed, but there are some notable high points, including *Whistle Down the Wind* (1961), *Séance on a Wet Afternoon* (1964), *King Rat* (1965), *The Wrong Box* (1966) and *The Whisperers* (1967). His later films are much inferior to the earlier ones; despite some good scenes, his science fiction–horror thriller *The Stepford Wives* (1975) is much less than a success.

Basil Dearden, who directed, had a long-time partnership with producer Michael Relph (occasionally they codirected a film). While never a director of the first rank, Dearden was usually above average and occasionally his films were important and interesting, such as an early treatment of homosexuality, *Victim* (1961), another, *Sapphire* (1959), touching on race relations, and a failed but interesting attempt to probe psychological testing of human beings, *The Mind Benders* (1963). His films got bigger and brawnier in the 1960s, with *Khartoum* (1966) being a highlight. Despite some serious faults, *Masquerade* (1965) and *The Assassination Bureau* (1969) have much to recommend them. Dearden died in a car accident in 1971.

Kenneth More appeared occasionally in films in the 1930s and 40s, but didn't gain stardom until the 1950s. Though an accomplished dramatic actor who had the useful ability to enable the audience to feel his sorrow, he fit more easily into light comedies, where he was almost always breezy, cheerful and attractive in a nonthreatening way. He was outstanding in many films, including *Genevieve* (1953), the international hit about a race between old cars, *Doctor in the House* (1954) and other comedies. He was also impressive in dramatic roles, such as *The Deep Blue Sea* (1955), *Reach for the Sky* (1956), *A Night to Remember* (1958) and *Sink the Bismarck!* (1960).

Almost inexplicably, his career entered a slump in the 1960s. He was still charming and talented, but good roles became harder for him to find. He was excellent in a minor role in *Oh! What a Lovely War* (1969), and a superlative Ghost of Christmas Present in *Scrooge* (1970). The script of *The Spaceman and King Arthur/Unidentified Flying Oddball* (1979) did not serve More's King Arthur well, and some of the films he made after 1965 received little or no theatrical release in the United States. He went to Spain to star in a dull and lackluster remake of *Journey to the Center of the Earth*, which had scant release as *Where Time Began*. He was more visible on TV in adaptations of *The Forsyte Saga* and G.K. Chesterton's "Father Brown" stories; this series of too-few episodes was being shown on American television when More died in 1983. He wrote two installments of his autobiography, *Happy Go Lucky* (1959) and *More or Less* (1978), but they do not make up for his loss. Kenneth More was one of those actors we don't even recognize as being irreplaceable until it's too late to praise them for that. He added to every film he ever appeared in, with easy but skilled professionalism and a true British charm and carefree air. He wasn't in the top rank of actors, but was one of the most pleasant screen presences of the 1950s.

Typically, *Man in the Moon* was more appreciated on this side of the Atlantic than in Britain. The *Monthly Film Bulletin* grudgingly gave it a II, saying "Kenneth More agreeably if mechanically pursues this outrageous story to its foregone conclusion. [The] script is an unattractive mixture of macabre savagery (in its brainwashing and training sequences) and tepid satire on bureaucracy, medicine and science."

"Rich," who reviewed the film for *Variety* from London, thought it an "amusing but disappointing ... spoof of science fiction [that is] rarely as funny as its original idea promises.... There are quite a number of yocks but the film is a tame return for More to the type of comedy that he can handle so well.... Basil Dearden's direction is uneven as, indeed, is the script. The whole affair has the air of a serious film into which comedy has been rather desperately dumped."

Newsweek, however, thought it "a timely British comedy spoofing the space age.... [More] adroitly plays the healthy bachelor.... As the girl who changes More's mind—and his health—Shirley Anne Field proves she is a looker who can act."

Paul V. Beckley in the New York *Herald-Tribune* found *Man in the Moon* "decidedly pleasant," and it did well on its American release. The film, incidentally, had its American premiere at Cape Canaveral.

Master of the World

Though watchable, *Master of the World* seems plentifully compromised. Instead of using the plots of either of the two Jules Verne novels that are ostensibly its basis, it's really an aerial remake of *20,000 Leagues Under the Sea*, Disney version, on a budget too low for its ambitions. Still, it has one of Vincent Price's best performances in an American International picture, and Charles Bronson's hero is solid and believable, though Bronson is cast against type. Furthermore, the flying ship the *Albatross* that's the centerpiece of the film is a delight. As *Time* described it, "Made entirely of impregnated paper, it checks out at 200 m.p.h. and looks like a cross between a blimp, a helicopter, a giant bat and a 19th century resort hotel. It even has a side porch."

In the early 1960s, American International apparently was beginning to hunger for respectability, but had become locked so firmly into cheapness of production and sleaziness of approach that they were having a hard time finding their way out. They never actually did. (See Mark McGee's book on the studio, *Fast and Furious*.) The Roger Corman–Edgar Allan Poe films were something of a beginning, but even there compromises were made. In *House of Usher*, Price is required to whisper lines about the house being alive. AIP insisted on having some sort of monster, and director Roger Corman and scenarist Richard Matheson had to imply that the house *itself* was a monster in order to placate AIP (i.e., James H. Nicholson and Samuel Z. Arkoff).

There are no monsters at all in *Master of the World*, but there is that exploitable airship and Vincent Price as star. (Bronson was not yet a star.) To do *Master of the World* properly, an amount approximating that spent by Disney on *20,000 Leagues* was necessary, but AIP couldn't or wouldn't raise that kind of money. There was apparently something of a struggle between James H. Nicholson, the slightly more aesthetic-minded of the two studio heads, and Samuel Z. Arkoff, the more profit-oriented one. *Master of the World*, completely unlike anything AIP had previously done, was Nicholson's personal production. I don't mean to imply that Nicholson was altruistic, but rather that he felt that better-made films, aimed at wider audiences, would improve the financial standing of AIP. Arkoff seems to have been content to let things go the way they always had. In his book on AIP, Mark McGee seems far more cynical about Nicholson than I am, but then McGee is far more cynical in general.

In any event, Nicholson backed *Master of the World*, and it was made. The film does not seem to have been a financial success, however, and nothing similar from AIP followed it. Nonetheless, from the early 60s on AIP began including a few more respectable films among their usual output (often picking up already-completed features). This reached something of a climax with *Wuthering Heights* in 1970.

Richard Matheson's script for *Master of the World* allegedly was based on *Robur le Conquérant* (1896), translated as *Clipper of the Clouds*, and its sequel, *Maître du Monde* (1904). However, except for the initial action, the film is a transposition of Disney's film, itself already at variance with the plotline of that Verne novel.

From Verne's first Robur novel, Matheson took the characters of Prudence (called Uncle Prudent in the novel) and Philip. Robur presents himself to the Weldon Institute in Philadelphia, where inventors are wrangling over where to put the propellers on an "aerostat" (lighter-than-air craft); the imperious Robur says that "aeronefs" (heavier-than-air craft) are the wave of the future, but he's scoffed at. Prudent and Phil and their black valet Frycollin are captured by Robur and taken aboard his ship *Albatross*, not unlike the craft in the film. Apparently just to demonstrate the superiority of his craft, Robur keeps them prisoner and flies about the world, doing good deeds and playing a few pranks here and there. Later, the captives plant dynamite aboard the *Albatross* and escape as it explodes, presumably killing Robur. But he turns up at the end of the novel, in his rebuilt *Albatross*. He literally flies rings around the Weldon Institute's balloon, clearly demonstrating the superiority of his craft. He destroys the balloon but rescues Prudent and Phil, then flies away.

In *Clipper of the Clouds*, Robur was clearly intended to be an allegorical figure. "Who is this Robur?" the novel concludes. "Shall we ever know? ... Robur is the science of the future, perhaps that of tomorrow. He is the forerunner of what is to come."

However, when Robur returns in Verne's sequel, called *Master of the*

World in English, he is quite another figure. First there are mysterious reports from all over the United States: an incredibly swift automobile plunges into Lake Michigan; a submarinelike craft later appears off the New England coast; a mysterious amphibian craft is seen in Kansas; strange noises are heard from the Great Eyrie in Pennsylvania. (Matheson used this in the film.) Investigating, John Strock comes to believe these are all the work of the same man. And sure enough, he's captured by Robur and taken aboard Robur's new craft, the *Terror*, which is at once a boat, an auto and an airplane. Robur has become furious with humanity, and plans to make himself Master of the World. But his amphibious craft is destroyed in a lightning storm, and Strock alone escapes to tell the tale.

The film begins as at the Great Eyrie, a buttelike cratered mountain near Morgantown, Pennsylvania, in the year 1868, a loud voice (Price's) shouts warnings from scripture down to the people below. The voice is so amplified that the ground itself shakes.

The Weldon Balloon Society wrangles over where to install the propeller on a powered balloon, and eventually all agree to use both front and rear props. (As in the novel.) Agent Strock (Bronson) from the Department of the Interior arrives at the Society to find someone to fly a balloon over the Eyrie to investigate the source of the sounds.

Soon, the balloon of Prudence (Henry Hull), with Strock, Prudence's daughter Dorothy (Mary Webster) and her fiancé Philip (David Frankham), is putting along over the Eyrie. They just begin to see something below when a rocket strikes the balloon and brings it to the ground inside the Eyrie, where it is found by Robur (Price) and his minions. All aboard the balloon are unconscious.

When Strock awakes, he tries to pick the lock of his room with a knife made in Prudence's munitions factories. The other three also awake, and all are greeted pleasantly by Robur, who explains that the shiplike conveyance they are all in is actually a gigantic airship, capable of cruising at 150 miles per hour, and of circling the globe in ten days.

The *Albatross* resembles a dirigible with fluted sides; like a dirigible, it has a gondola beneath it, but rather than being supported by gas, is borne aloft by a multitude of propellers mounted on top. It is not a lighter-than-air craft, but is relatively lightweight nonetheless, made of paper, "dextrin and clay," squeezed in a hydraulic press. There's an exterior catwalk around part of the ship, with a net beneath for safety. The big tail rudder is scalloped like an umbrella, and a large sun emblem is painted on the side. There's a large propeller at the front, and a bomb bay beneath the gondola. The ship is powered, Robur tells them, by the actions of a "mass of metal cutting through ... magnetic force lines," creating electricity.

When Robur learns Prudence is an arms manufacturer, he declares this to be "the father of all irony" for, like Disney's Nemo, AIP's Robur is determined to wipe out all warfare. He will bombard Earth's wars from the air, without regard to any territorial or political distinctions. Strock and his friends arrived on board the *Albatross* just as Robur has decided to begin his war against war. As an opening volley, Robur blows up a warship, then sends word to all nations to disarm or perish.

Strock thinks Robur's goal is laudable, but his means evil. For his part, Philip thinks Strock is a coward; there's not much justification for this in the script, other than merely to provide conflict. Matheson intended to imply that Philip was motivated more by jealousy of Dorothy's growing fondness for

Strock, but this isn't brought out in performances or direction, and Philip merely seems obscurely petulant.

Tired of their wrangling, Robur dangles both men from the *Albatross* by ropes, and they have something of a fight. However, a storm comes up and Strock saves Philip from falling when there is some trouble with the flying machine.

Eventually, Robur flies over London, and we see aerial views of the city, lifted from the prologue to Olivier's *Henry V*, showing an early 17th-century view rather than the required late 19th-century view. AIP presumably had only that view available for stock (and in color), and probably correctly felt most audiences wouldn't notice the great differences.

Newspaper front pages whirling up at the camera, an old movie device, tell us that Robur also attacks Paris and Madrid. He heads on to North Africa, where we see some (black-and-white) footage of warring tribesmen, and the footage is manipulated to give us the idea that bedouins are battling fuzzy-wuzzies (in the wrong area). Robur bombs the warring tribesmen, but gets too low and his own explosions damage the *Albatross*.

He flies into some mountains through a narrow pass, with the crew on the side porches using long poles to ward the ship away from rocks. Strock uses this time to plant a bomb aboard the wonderful flying machine. In a cheesy melodramatic turn, he's attacked by Philip as the fuse burns. Strock knocks Philip out but rescues him, Dorothy and Prudence—frozen by horror from seeing what his munitions actually do to people.

After Strock's party bails out, the bomb goes off and the *Albatross* spins out to sea, with Robur staring fatalistically out the front windows. The crew gallantly reports that they prefer to stay with him rather than to save themselves, and, burning and exploding, the *Albatross* plunges into the sea.

Although AIP was probably ill-advised to take on as ambitious a project as *Master of the World*, much of the film is surprisingly effective. The weaknesses lie in the direction and the rather tired storyline.

In all William Witney's long directorial career, this is the only science fiction film I am aware of. His *Darktown Strutters* (1975) has some fantasy elements. He did do some fantasy serials, a form at which he was above average, including *Drums of Fu Manchu, Mysterious Dr. Satan* (both 1940) and *Adventures of Captain Marvel* (1941). Except for three years during WWII, in which Witney served in the Marines, he was very busy from 1937 to 1967. All his first 40 or so films were Westerns, many of which starred Roy Rogers. When the films were set outdoors, Witney managed to pack in the action; when things moved indoors, it was almost as if the film were taken over by another director—it stopped dead.

When B-Westerns declined in appeal in the mid-50s, their function having been usurped by television, Witney began making other kinds of films, still interspersing them with Westerns. *Stranger at My Door, Strange Adventure* (both 1956) and *Juvenile Jungle* (1958) were among the films Witney made before he did several for AIP, including *The Cool and the Crazy* (a cult favorite for its ludicrous view of marijuana use), *The Bonnie Parker Story, Young and Wild* (all 1958) and *Paratroop Command* (1959). He did several for 20th Century–Fox in the early 60s, then worked for several other studios. All the films were low-budget exploitation pictures, with titles like *The Girls on the Beach, Arizona Raiders* (both 1965) and *I Escaped from Devil's Island* (1973).

Witney is another of those basically styleless hacks who churned out the lower-half-of-the-bill Hollywood fodder for years. Sometimes, he was able to rise above the material and deliver fast, exciting action scenes, but when he was confined to sets and dialogue scenes, he was notably dull. Unfortunately, *Master of the World* has virtually no action scenes and, except for a few shots in what seems to be the Bronson Caverns area, almost no exteriors at all. By its very nature a set-bound film, what excitement it has comes almost entirely from the special effects, in which Witney presumably was not involved.

The film is respectable but plodding, and the slowness stems mostly from Witney's staging—people tend to plant themselves in one spot and deliver their dialogue—and the lethargic editing. The sameness of the sets (they must have got a good buy on blue paint) is also dull, and the completely misfired comedy scenes involving Vito Scotti as a cook aboard the *Albatross*, heavily underscored by the music, make the film even more labored.

Clumsy comedy intrudes at other times as well. There seems to have been the idea, not uncommon in movies, that the past is automatically quaint and amusing. Presumably, we have only to see people dressed in period costumes talking about what we know to be unworkable ideas on transportation, science, manners, etc. for us to burst into knowing laughter. This arrogance and condescension can work sometimes, but only when mixed with affection. There's not much of that in *Master of the World*.

The interior sets seem cramped, and as many shots are in that most boring of angles, medium close, the film has a claustrophobic atmosphere. The exterior views of the miniature *Albatross*, though inexplicably blurry, seem expansive and refreshing: at least we are seeing something from a distance.

The effects are mixed. They're confident and plentiful, but the budget is so low that they never look like anything but effects. Still, the design of the *Albatross* is splendid, and its charm makes up for a great deal lost in the area of realism.

Matte paintings of the Great Eyrie were created by Butler–Glouner, Inc., and they did the unsatisfactory shot of the clockwork mechanism in the engine room of the ship, as well as a few explosions.

Most of the effects were by the group that would soon be called Project Unlimited, Tim Baar, Wah Chang and Gene Warren. The effects were submitted for Academy Award consideration; in the official form for that purpose, the miniatures and other effects were described as follows: "*Miniatures: The Albatross*, Jules Verne's airship, as the star of the film had to be shown in its entirety and functioning in all aspects. To have built a practical life-size model 200 feet long, would have been a physical as well as a financial impossibility. A scale model was constructed which was complete in all respects, 39 practical [rotating] propellers, mechanized trap doors, rocket devices, controls, etc. The only life-size portion built was the rear deck. [I presume this means the side porch.] In the miniature, puppet figures duplicated the live figures on deck for long shots. The balloon was handled the same way as the *Albatross* and for the same reasons. *Optical Effects* Intriguing color effects of oil and fog—and revising quality of period black and white shots. Made several colorful inserts for special effects."

The exterior views of the *Albatross* are the most pleasing scenes in the film; other effects don't come off as well. Robur's engine room is rendered by matting in shots of big clock gears, which looks phony and almost surrealistic. The shot is so poorly done that it calls attention to itself, and should have been avoided altogether.

The various scenes in which people dangle from the *Albatross*, or it passes by dangerous rocks, were managed in a fairly obvious manner: the people and aircraft were stationary while the landscape, presumably mounted on wheels, moved by *them*.

Vincent Price has one of his best roles as Robur the Conqueror. Although clearly the intent was to create a Nemoesque figure, Price's Robur is at once more lofty and more congenial than Nemo. He's in love with the *Albatross*, and delighted to share this love with others; Nemo was jealous of the *Nautilus*. Price seems more controlled here than in his other AIP films of the time, although his best performances for them would be in the two Corman–Poe films made in England, *Masque of the Red Death* and *Tomb of Ligeia*. Price has a strong tendency to go over the top, but keeps it in check here, and his Robur is more than adequate, though not as vivid as James Mason's Nemo.

In their *Vincent Price Unmasked*, Steven Whitney and James Robert Parish said, "If anything [Price] was even better as Robur than he had been as the Poe protagonists. Perhaps that was because he liked the character so much. As he later revealed, 'I loved *Master of the World* because I thought it had a marvelous moralizing philosophy. I adored it. It was of a man who saw evil and wanted to destroy it. And if that meant the whole world, then it had to go.'"

The other most interesting performance is that of Charles Bronson as Strock. Bronson had begun to be known to audiences; he'd started to have starring roles in low- and medium-budget films a few years before, such as *Gang War*, *Showdown at Boot Hill* and, notably, *Machine Gun Kelly* (all 1958). His TV series "Man with a Camera" was telecast in the 1959–60 season, and he was getting big character parts in major films like *The Magnificent Seven*. True stardom was still almost ten years off, but the best elements of his later performances, including some good features he unfortunately shed, are present in *Master of the World*, except for the air of violence that permeates many of his most famous parts of the 1970s.

Bronson is, in fact, excellent as the atypical hero. The part was written as a standard apparent-coward-but-true-hero, often seen in war films, prison pictures, and the like, but Bronson plays Strock in a manner effectively at odds with Matheson's rather shallow characterization. Bronson is relaxed, controlled and confident at all times; despite his homeliness, it's easy to understand why the heroine is so swiftly attracted to him. Strock is the man in charge; he's clearly holding himself in check. In fact, Philip's opposition to Strock seems even more childish and pointless than written. In this period, Bronson was nonchalantly expressive; in later years, his acting became more and more minimal, almost disappearing at times. But his decency and humor had begun to be used effectively, both by directors and by Bronson himself, in the late-50s–early-60s period. By the late 70s, he was coasting, but in *Master of the World*, he's near the peak of his abilities. It's the best performance in the film; Bronson has tremendous personal magnetism, and it was most noticeable in pictures of this nature. It is good, but not one of his best performances, because the film and character are too conventional, but when Bronson's on-screen, you don't watch anyone else, not even Price.

As the ingenue, Mary Webster is actually quite good; the part is thankless, as are all the roles except Robur and Strock, but Webster is well above average for a young leading lady. She had relatively few roles in films, however; she was in *The Delicate Delinquent*, *18 and Anxious* and *The Tin Star* (all 1957), turned up again in *The Clown and the Kid* (1961) and vanished. Even more than young leading men, the Hollywoods are full of young leading ladies; I suppose Webster found the competition not worth locking horns with, and returned to "real life."

David Frankham is also given a conventional role, one the film could easily have done without. The conflicts between him and Strock seem especially contrived, and Frankham plays the hapless Philip as such an unpleasant schnook that it's hard to accept Strock's saving him at the end. We wish only that he had never come aboard the *Albatross*. It's not entirely Frankham's fault, but he's deserving of some blame. For other notes on Frankham, see the entry on *Return of the Fly*.

Henry Hull, now best-known for having been *The WereWolf of London*, was a mainstay character actor in Hollywood for decades, having made his first film in 1916. He worked steadily for the next 40 years in a broad range of films; Hull often played a canny, folksy old gent, the elderly friend of the hero, bumped off partway through the movie. Among his better-known films are *Great Expectations* (1934, in which he was star-billed as Magwich), *Jesse James* (1939), *High Sierra* (1941), Hitchcock's *Lifeboat* (1944), *Mourning Becomes Electra* (1947) and *The Buccaneer* (1958). He seems to have made only two more films after *Master of the World*, *The Fool Killer* (1965) and *The Chase* (1966). Hull died in 1977 at the age of 86.

As with the rest of the roles, Matheson kept Prudence simple, and even a character actor as shrewd as Hull can bring little to the part, which begins as a quaint inventor and ends as a sorrowful little man who's learned he's a merchant of death.

Throughout *Master of the World*, Matheson seems to have been instructed to play to the lowest common denominator; not only is Robur altered from his peculiar characterization in Verne's novels, but all other characters are in the simplest and most basic of colors. I don't hold Matheson to blame for this; I suspect that he was told what he had to do by Nicholson and others. Matheson has shown in his many other fantasy teleplays and screenplays, his novels and short stories, that he is capable of much richer characterizations than he gives in *Master of the World*. Clearly, simplicity was the order of the day.

Despite Witney's flat direction, the thin characterizations and the familiar plot, *Master of the World* remains a reasonably entertaining film. It looks good, it's about something moderately unusual, and Price and Bronson are fine. Except when he's giving us Funny Music, the score by Les Baxter is one of his best; there's a popular sound-track album available. It's low-budget epic music, but still decent.

Eugene Archer in the *New York Times* was moderately pleased by the film, thinking it had "pleasantly nostalgic qualities.... The hero, quietly acted by Charles Bronson, is a likeable type, homely, modest and altogether noble [behaving] with consistent calm sensibility." Price, Archer felt, was "surprisingly restrained," and overall Archer considered it "devoid of artistic pretentions, but a lot more sufferable" than he clearly expected.

Paul V. Beckley, however, wasn't impressed, and said as much in the New York *Herald-Tribune*. "It's not so much the inevitable grotesquerie of the picture's mechanical marvels but the drabness of the characterization and dialogue that keeps it well below the level of interest adult moviegoers would expect. One can't help wondering if a younger generation that takes for granted the likely invasion of the Moon will be suitably impressed by the mechanical ingenuity or amused by the archaic decor."

S.A. Desick in the *Los Angeles Herald-Examiner*, mistaking Matheson's interpolations for Verne's ideas (as usual in film versions of his novels), praised the story for foreseeing "some of our technological feats." (I haven't noticed any spindle-shaped, paper helicopters with dozens of tall skinny propellers going by lately.) "This is technical accomplishment of a high order," Desick concluded.

Daily Variety's "Tube" didn't much care for it, considering it "watered-down Jules Verne, diluted by modern dramatic agents foreign to the nature of the author's original fantasy," and called special attention to the dialogue, rightly pointing out that it had the "distracting ring of mid-20th century idiom and expression." Tube added, "also, there is a certain element of monotony and repetition about the long ride in the air, a suspended lethargy that director William Witney has not been able to disturb too frequently."

The *Monthly Film Bulletin* gave the film a II, calling it "watered down Jules Verne, in which generally unexciting acting and lethargic direction take second place to the astute special effects and art direction," but also added that it had "a certain lively vulgarity."

Joe Dante's comments in *Castle of Frankenstein* #17 are apposite. "Bigger budget certainly would've helped this ambitious but very weak Verne adaptation. William Witney's flat ... direction doesn't bring out needed charm inherent in tale of inventor dedicated to stamping out war in his amazing airship. Occasionally interesting."

Because AIP didn't know at what crowd to aim the film, it didn't attract the attention of teenagers or adults. It's not witty enough for adults, nor does it have enough action for kids. It was James H. Nicholson's favorite of all his AIP films, but he should have been more daring, less conventional. It's not a bad film, but there's much that's wanting in *Master of the World*.

Most Dangerous Man Alive

Made in 1958 but not released until 1961, *Most Dangerous Man Alive* has several unusual features, but none are connected with the film itself, a contrived but not unintelligent gangster–revenge thriller crossed with science fiction.

Ron Randell, from Australia, plays gangster Eddie Candell, framed on a murder charge, who escapes from police custody on his way to prison. He wanders into an atomic test area, where Dr. Meeker (Tudor Owen) is conducting an experiment in "Cobalt Mutation." From the blockhouse, Meeker sees Candell on his monitor, but is unable to prevent the explosion, which has a high yield of radiation but low blast effects. To Dr. Meeker's surprise, Candell survives the explosion and flees.

While Candell is hiding in a shack, Meeker points out to Los Angeles Police detectives Captain Davis (Morris Ankrum) and Sergeant Fisher (Gregg Palmer), that the test was designed to induce mutations. A watermelon at the site has shrunk to the size of an apple, while a carrot has grown to five feet in length. Another watermelon has absorbed steel from a tower, and Meeker fears this may have happened to Candell. (In *Trumpet* 4, Tom Reamy points out that "The conclusion that Candell will react like the second watermelon and not the first or the carrot seems a little presumptuous of Dr. Meeker, but that's what happens." Anyway, we'd already had a shrinking and a growing man.)

In that shack, Candell awakes. He discovers that the handcuffs on his wrist have vanished, while their connecting chain remains, now anchored to his wrists as though growing from them. He jerks his hands apart in horror, and the chain breaks; Eddie watches in numb shock as his wrists absorb the steel of the chain. He steals a dynamite truck and flees.

He has become a man literally of steel, with superhuman strength and the ability to absorb metal (like bullets). This wouldn't seem to be entirely undesirable in some ways, but it upsets Eddie.

A great deal of plotting and counterplotting follows, involving Andy Damon (Anthony Caruso), the gangster who framed Eddie, and Eddie's former lover Linda (Debra Paget), who helped Damon do it. They try to set a trap, but Eddie kills a gang member and flees with Linda, absorbing bullets as he goes.

Eddie goes to the home of Carla (Elaine Stewart), a nice ordinary girl unaware of the extent of Eddie's criminal activities; she believes he's the victim of police persecution. Eddie confesses that he's worried that his atomic transformation has left him, ahem, less than a man.

The police have traced Eddie to Carla's, but he escapes with Linda, hiding out elsewhere. With great dint of effort (hoping to save her life), she seduces him. But at the gang's offices, Damon and his men are waiting. He kills two more of the gang, tossing them out a window, and flees.

Dr. Meeker explains to Carla that the change in Eddie's body is progressive – he will not only become increasingly steellike, but will eventually begin giving off powerful atomic radiation, endangering everyone. However, Carla doesn't believe this, and refuses to cooperate.

Damon and his gang try to kidnap Carla, but fail; she becomes convinced that Meeker is his only hope, and takes the scientist to Eddie, who is becoming deranged. He only hates, he says, and has lost feeling, which he demonstrates by holding burning coals in his hand. Before the doctor can try to treat him, Damon and his inexhaustible supply of henchmen kidnap Meeker.

He forces Meeker to contact Eddie, who goes to Damon's brewery hideout to confront him. He has set an electrical trap for Eddie, but it doesn't work, though Eddie kills a few more gang members. He captures Damon and flees the arriving police, taking Damon and the two women and heading into the hills (some sources say the film was shot entirely in Mexico, but the hills resemble the Bronson Canyon area).

By now, the police have called in the National Guard. Meanwhile, Damon kills Linda and Eddie kills Damon, tossing him off a cliff to the police. He begins to get delusions of murderous grandeur, threatening cops and the world. Suddenly, he lurches and his face changes from shadowed-looking to normal. Eddie is then wounded by the police. As "Tube" said in *Variety*, the "funniest line in recent screen annals occurs when the unfortunate fellow's bullet-proof epidermis suddenly and unaccountably begins to revert to normal flesh as he is sprayed by gunfire. His beloved cries happily, 'Eddie, you're bleeding!' "

The police and others resort to flamethrowers to combat Eddie, and apparently are ready to unleash the fire with Carla standing next to him. Eddie pushes her away, and is sprayed with flame. His body turns to powder and blows away on the breeze.

Peter Bogdanovich did a book on the director of the film, Allan Dwan; the book was *Allan Dwan, the Last Pioneer* (1971). In his interview with Bogdanovich, Dwan said of *Most Dangerous Man Alive*, that it "was a synthetic thing. In the first place, there was a deception about it. Even I got hooked. [Producer Benedict] Bogeaus said that it was to be a pilot for a television series – in two episodes – and employed everybody on that basis. But when he presented the two parts to the syndicates in Mexico, they said, 'This is a [feature] script that's been cut in half. It's a continuous story.... You must take a full crew and do it at feature rates....' Pretty soon the actors got on to that and then the whole roof fell in on him."

Most Dangerous Man Alive looks cheap and is; shot mostly on real locations, it has more the feel of a low-budget crime picture than a science fiction film, which isn't surprising. The milieu of the film is like one of those minor crime films that filled the bottoms of double bills during the 50s: bleak landscapes, cheap hoods and molls, tough cops, and a doomed man on the run. There is a certain creativity in linking the SF and crime genres. They have a down-and-dirty vitality that's quite similar. Crime pictures are rougher—the violence is stronger, there's plenty of sex; the ending is more foredoomed and inevitable than tragic, but the stories of SF and crime films often describe the same kind of trajectory.

The SF element in *Most Dangerous Man Alive* is not much more than a gimmick designed to allow the protagonist to carry out his revenge. But it works in the context—rather than recruiting a new gang to conquer the old, Randell is a one-man gang, killing only those who try to kill him, but doing it all by himself. Traditionally in American crime movies, the bad gang leader is always expecting retribution, and the cops always worry about some sharp crook going really bad. Here the worst happens—and it's a heck of a lot worse than the gang leader or cops were expecting. Instead of tucked away in prison, Eddie is absolutely unstoppable for most of the picture. The crooks try everything they can to bring him down, and so do the cops, but he just keeps coming.

Writers James Leicester and Phillip Rock intelligently make the power that enables Eddie to get his revenge also a curse. The stronger he gets, the less human he becomes, and the longer he stays this way, the more crazy he grows. Early in the film, it's established that Eddie is quite a stud, but because of the mutation, he has difficulty being seduced by Linda. He's turning to steel.

Though this melding of the crime and SF traditions has novelty, it's also contrived. Instead of Eddie's gang activities leading somehow to his gaining his steely strength, which might have been interesting, he simply blunders into an atomic test area. Even Bert Gordon had a better explanation for The Amazing Colossal Man than the writers here can devise for The Most Dangerous Man Alive. They also run out of ideas by the end, and simply have Eddie's power wear off.

The late Tom Reamy had some excellent commentary on the film in *Trumpet* 4 (April, 1966). "There have been numerous films of a man who, exposed to various and sundry radiations, has [turned monstrous.] The major failure of these films ... is a lack of motivation.... Eddie Candell, the man who turns to steel, has ample motivations. The machinations of the script to get him into his lamentable position are contrived and utterly unconvincing; but after that, the film has a certain charm....

"The performances of Randell and Stewart are the film's greatest assets. Randell has done the almost impossible. He has—at least partially—convinced me that he has turned to steel, though he never quite convinces me that he is a gangster; he is simply too likeable and moral....

"There is one silly thing that happens. Candell's shirt is almost blasted off during the explosion but his tie is still around his neck. During the seduction scene Miss Paget removes it. After the fadeout, it's back around his neck. It seems unlikely that he would ever put it on again himself so the scriptgirl must have goofed. (It seems unlikely, actually, that he would have kept it on at all.)

"The production values are slight and the low budget is quite evident but the film is fast paced and avoids the lethargy usually found in these things. I liked it."

Others were not as fond of the film. "Tube," in *Variety*, called it a "grade B melodrama ... shopworn, absurd and tasteless," thinking it had little chance even on a double bill; "even in that subsidiary capacity, the [film] will be a burden for major theatrical product aimed at enlightened 1961 audiences.... Allan Dwan's direction is sluggish and repetitious, Carl Carvahal's photography is dark and shadowy, Carlos Lodato's editing far from skillful, Joe Kavignan's soundtrack frequently noisy. Louis Forbes' score is unobtrusive." The title theme is oddly romantic.

The unnamed *Limelight* reviewer (probably Jack Moffitt) thought the story "had the glimmerings of a good idea when [the writers] decided to cross-breed science fiction with gangster melodrama. But it turned out to be a sterile union.... Directed by Allan Dwan, the film has pace enough to keep the second half of a double bill from sagging."

The reviewer in *Castle of Frankenstein* #19 indicated he knew a bit of film history. "A potentially interesting routine SF–horror quickly degenerates to boring pin-headed action.... Director Allan Dwan is a cult figure in France—but not for this one!"

Perhaps taking Dwan's longevity for evidence of brilliance, in *Science Fiction in the Cinema*, John Baxter intelligently if extravagantly overpraises the film, claiming it "remains a classic of its kind. Squarely in the tradition of Tourneur and a prime example of the annihilating melodrama, Dwan's story of a gangster turned to steel by an atomic explosion was shot with a cold ferocity and icy lack of feeling entirely appropriate to the subject.... Accepting the elements of SF film, Dwan ... has cleverly utilised them to record a brutal allegory." I suspect that instead of a lack of feeling, Dwan made the film with a lack of involvement, not the same thing.

More than any other director represented in this book, Allan Dwan deserves to be called a movie institution. His early career was the jumping-off point of the plot of Bogdanovich's movie, *Nickelodeon*. Dwan was born in 1885, and in 1911, while working for the American Film Company, was sent to Hollywood to find out about the progress of movies being made there. The director was drunk and the film was shut down, so Dwan himself was made the director. Between 1911 and late 1913, he directed more than 250 one-reel movies, and continued to be busy until the 1930s. The peak of his career was his association with Douglas Fairbanks; he directed 11 of Doug's films, including *Robin Hood* (1922) and *The Iron Mask* (1929). During the 1920s, Dwan directed many prestigious films for Paramount and Fox; among the stars whose films he directed were Mary Pickford, Lillian and Dorothy Gish and Gloria Swanson.

When talkies began, his career fell on hard times, perhaps because he was in England when they got going. He did several B movies for Fox, then sprang back to prominence with *Rebecca of Sunnybrook Farm* and *Suez* (both 1938). In 1939, he did a couple of Ritz Brothers comedies, *The Three Musketeers* and *The Gorilla,* and directed a well-regarded Western, *Frontier Marshal.*

Dwan began the 1940s with several comedies based on classic farces: *Up in Mabel's Room* (1944), *Brewster's Millions* and *Getting Gertie's Garter* (both 1945). Most of his films after that were lower-berth A films or more important Bs, including *Sands of Iwo Jima* (1949), *Woman They Almost Lynched* (1953), *Cattle Queen of Montana* (1954) and *The River's Edge* (1957).

Through his long career—and *Most Dangerous Man Alive* was his last film— Dwan frequently produced and wrote or cowrote his films. He had a long career for a director—47 years—and may well have directed more than 200 features. He's a puzzle to various film theorists. Far too important and talented to be lumped in with hacks like William Beaudine and Edward L. Cahn, Dwan lies in a middle range between the kind of director who can do just about anything, however mediocre, like Richard Fleischer, and true artists-within-the-system like Howard Hawks. Even Andrew Sarris, in his *The American Cinema*, who seems so anxious to pigeonhole every director, essentially gives up when it comes to classifying Dwan, who ends up in Sarris' "Expressive Esoterica" category. Sarris said, "Dwan's career is still being mined for a possibly higher assay of gold to dross.... It is too early to establish any coherent pattern to Dwan's career as a whole, but it may very well be that Dwan will turn out to be the last of the old masters.... There may be much more to be said about Dwan."

In the book mentioned earlier, Peter Bogdanovich allowed Dwan himself to have a lengthy if not last word, in the fascinating book-length interview. For film historians like Bogdanovich, to have been able to interview Dwan, who actually traded ideas with D.W. Griffith during their most active years, is akin to a military historian interviewing someone who advised Napoleon.

It's amusing that no one has been able to classify Dwan, just to list his films; he probably would have chuckled at the idea. Even reviews of *Most Dangerous Man Alive* reflect this inability to get a grip on Dwan; some cite his speedy direction, while others complain of the film's sluggishness. The truth, of course, lies between: the film is fast when the script allows it, and slows down in dramatic dialogue scenes, never Dwan's forte.

In one sense, Dwan *was* Hollywood; he originated in the East, found strength and vitality in California, and turned out the kind of movies audiences wanted to see. Even in this, his last film, he was dealing in popular genres. This seems to be his only science fiction film, unless there's one buried among the dozens of movies he made before 1920.

Ron Randell had an unusual career as an actor. As a teenager, he appeared on stage and radio in Australia, and made at least one film there, but by 1947, was in the United States. He starred in some minor movies, including attempts at reviving the Bulldog Drummond and Lone Wolf series (*Bulldog Drummond at Bay*, *The Lone Wolf and His Lady*), and had supporting parts in some more important films, including *Lorna Doone* (1951), *The Mississippi Gambler* and *Kiss Me Kate* (1953; in the latter, he played Cole Porter). He bounced back and forth from England to the United States in the 50s, mostly in lesser films, but turned up in *King of Kings* (1961, as Lucius) and *The Longest Day* (1962). A decent enough actor, Randell is probably too much like other better-known actors to get major roles. Handsome and sensitive, he has never been less than good—but also rarely noticeable.

Elaine Stewart retired from films not long after *Most Dangerous Man*. An attractive, talented redhead, she probably suffered like Randell from being too easily replaced by better-known (but not necessarily more talented) performers. Actors with talent but little personal style usually become character actors, if they have the right kind of face—but Stewart was at once not distinctive enough and too pretty for this. She later worked on TV game shows produced by her husband. Among her other films: *Take the High Ground* (1953), *The Adventures of Hajji Baba* (1954), *Young Bess* (1953, as Anne Boleyn) and *Night Passage* (1957). Although she made a couple of films after it, *Most Dangerous Man* is apparently her last-released film.

Debra Paget was a sultry, exotic presence at 20th Century–Fox in the early 1950s, where she was under contract, and occasionally played the loveliest

Indian women in films, as in *Broken Arrow* (1950). Her unusual but gorgeous features served her well for a time, in movies such as *Les Misérables* (1952), *Demetrius and the Gladiators*, *Prince Valiant* (both 1954) and *Love Me Tender* (1956), in which her acting ability — or lack of it — was unimportant. When her Fox contract ran out, her career underwent a change. She was still a star, but the films were of less interest, although she did make a pair of bizarre adventures in Europe for Fritz Lang in the late 50s, which were combined into one movie and released in the United States as *Journey to the Lost City*. She also appeared in *From the Earth to the Moon*, *Tales of Terror* (1962) and *The Haunted Palace* (1964), her last film to date.

Benedict Bogeaus, who produced the film, was an independent producer of long standing in Hollywood, some of whose films are notable, including *The Shanghai Gesture* (1941), *Bridge of San Luis Rey* (1944), Jean Renoir's *Diary of a Chambermaid* (1946) and *Captain Kidd* (1945). In the 1950s, he formed a partnership with Allan Dwan, and as a producer-director team, made at least nine films, including *Most Dangerous Man Alive*, Bogeaus' last film. He died in 1968.

The film is basically just another low-budget SF film, with somewhat more to recommend it than many. But it has sort of resonated down through the years since it was released, and ostensibly turned up in an odd context in Wim Wenders' *The State of Things* (1982). Wenders had a bad experience making his first Hollywood film, *Hammett*, and *The State of Things* is a response to what befell him during the production of that movie. The story centers around a group of filmmakers who are, according to the story, doing a remake of *Most Dangerous Man Alive*, of all things, and many scenes from the film-within-a-film are included. However, they give the impression that Wenders knows Dwan's film from its title alone, as his movie's story has nothing to do with the older film. Called "The Survivors," it seems to deal with a post–nuclear holocaust world, and not a steel gangster. Indeed, each "Survivors" sequence we are shown appears to be a vague restaging of scenes from Joseph Losey's *The Damned* (1961), right down to locations and costumes.

As this book was being prepared, a new film called *Most Dangerous Man Alive* was in production, but it, too, has nothing at all to do with Allan Dwan's interesting if hackneyed film.

Mysterious Island

Despite the usual problems associated with the Ray Harryhausen films produced by Charles Schneer — underfinancing, pandering to the "appropriate" audience, a slightly cheesy air — *Mysterious Island* is one of Harryhausen's most entertaining pictures, holding up well today. It was one of the best Jules Verne films released in the United States in the 1960s, and there were three others in 1961 alone.* Only *The Fabulous World of Jules Verne* in this period is better than this adaptation of Verne's sequel to *20,000 Leagues Under the Sea.*

*1961: The Fabulous World of Jules Verne, Master of the World, Valley of the Dragons; 1962: Five Weeks in a Balloon, In Search of the Castaways; 1963: The Three Stooges Go Around the World in a Daze; 1965: Up to His Ears; 1967: Those Fantastic Flying Fools; 1969: The Southern Star, Strange Holiday.

Ever since the birth of movies, Jules Verne has been one of the most popular authors for adaptation; because of *Around the World in 80 Days* and *20,000 Leagues Under the Sea*, he was an especially popular source in the late 1950s.

The most frequently-filmed Verne books have been *20,000 Leagues* (six films since 1905), *The Children of Captain Grant* (five since 1901), *Michael Strogoff* (13 separate versions, including one sequel, making this one of the most-filmed of books), and, oddly *Mysterious Island* itself, with at least nine versions and variations. Why there should be more films of the sequel to *Leagues* than versions of that story itself is a puzzle akin to wondering why there are so many more horses' asses than horses. The reason is that *Mysterious Island*, in its original form, is (a) a mystery, and (b) cheaper to film than most Verne stories of sufficient fame.

According to the excellent Verne filmography printed in the French magazine *L'Ecran Fantastique*, the first film version of *Mysterious Island* was the 1921 German film *Die Insel der Verschollenen* (Island of the Vanished), combining themes from *The Island of Dr. Moreau* by H.G. Wells, *Docteur Lern* by Maurice Renard, and Verne's novel. "Two friends, castaways on an apparently-deserted island, attempt to survive, then discover that it is inhabited by a mad scientist who practices monstrous experiments on animals. They save a woman from the clutches of the doctor and succeed in escaping." (Translations by Jean-Marc Lofficier.)

Next was the incredible MGM production that was filmed by a variety of directors and casts from 1926 to 1929. This time, the Mysterious Island was a fortress of peace guarded by its ruler, Prince Dakkar (Nemo's rarely-used real name), played by Lionel Barrymore. In his submarine, he encounters some tiny undersea people resembling Donald Duck in diving suits, as well as a sea dragon and a sort of squiddy undersea monster. This film was partly in color and sound. It's rare, and baffling to watch.

In 1941, the Soviet Union filmed a faithful version of the novel, though some propaganda found its way into the story, as might be expected. *L'Ecran* said that it was "filmed in the Odessa studios and on the shore of the Black Sea.... [It's] a hymn to collectivism and technical progress, and a condemnation of Yankee slavery and British colonialism."

Ten years later, the alarming Columbia Pictures serial of the novel, starring Richard Crane, was released. It kept the right period—the Civil War—and, amazingly enough, kept surprisingly closely to the plot of the novel. It did add a few details. Like ray guns and a princess from the planet Mercury, in search of a radioactive metal. It followed the usual serial format of escapes and rescues. Captain Nemo helps defeat the invaders.

There were French TV versions in 1963 and 1969 with, respectively, René Arrieu and Pierre Dux as Nemo. Another TV version was a coproduction between France, Spain and Italy, and was shown in a six-part serial form. Omar Sharif was Nemo. When it was edited into feature length for release in the United States as *The Mysterious Island of Captain Nemo* (1972), it received poor reviews and did little business.

Karel Zeman's *The Stolen Airship* (1967) borrowed some details, including Captain Nemo (Josef Vetrovec) from Verne's *Mysterious Island*, but also based it on Verne's *Two Years' Vacation*. Though slow-moving and not Zeman's best work, the film is delightful.

In January, 1955, Bryan Foy signed Crane Wilbur to script *Mysterious Island*, intending it to follow the Disney film of *20,000 Leagues*. Wilbur helped

Stop-motion animation maestro Ray Harryhausen with some of his production drawings for Mysterious Island (1961); the drawing at the lower left depicts a carnivorous plant scene that was never filmed.

secure the film rights to the novel for Foy, acting as a go-between to the producer and Verne's great-great grandniece, then living in Virginia. Foy later announced his intention of signing James Mason to reprise his Nemo role. By September, novelist James Whitfield Ellison was signed to do the script for Foy.

However, it was Crane Wilbur's script, with a Daniel B. Ullman rewrite, which was passed on to Schneer and Harryhausen when they signed to do the film with and for Columbia. Harryhausen told me in a letter, "I do remember well that Columbia owned the story and a version of the shooting script which was never produced." Harryhausen, Schneer and their director, Cy Endfield, seem to have jointly chosen John Prebble to do a final draft of the script. (Prebble also wrote Endfield's later and good film Zulu.)

The storyline took some juggling to make it appropriate for a Harryhausen special-effects film. "If I remember correctly," he said, "the script went through a number of changes, one of which involved prehistoric animals and the sunken Atlantis. However, the final script dropped many of these ideas, including the 'green man sequence.' Part of the Atlantis idea was left in the underwater sequence."

The "green man sequence" has resulted in strange errors down through the years. Excellent British character actor Nigel Green was hired to play the novel's Thomas Ayerton, living on the island for years. One of the Dynamation sequences planned for the film involved a giant carnivorous plant, with poison tipped tentacles, that grabbed at its prey. Ayerton had discovered that eating certain mushrooms made him distasteful to the plant, but had the side effect of dying his skin green. (This was in the final draft of the script.)

According to Harryhausen, "although Nigel Green was in mind for the casting of the 'green man' role (no relation to his name), the sequence was never photographed. It was cut out of the script on location just before it was scheduled to be shot, because of several reasons, including an over-long script. The man-eating plant was also dropped for the same reasons." However, Columbia's official synopsis and pressbook include both Tom Ayerton and the man-eating plant, which may have resulted in some embarrassment for "P.P.," who reviewed the film for the Hollywood Citizen-News; the review included a discussion of the green man and man-eating plant scenes.

Virtually every reference book on films includes Nigel Green in the cast of Mysterious Island, but in fact Tom Ayerton appears in the film only as a skeleton; Nigel Green is not in the film and never was.

As does the novel, the film opens during the siege of Richmond in 1865. Union Captain Cyrus Harding (Michael Craig), soldiers Herbert Brown (Michael Callan) and Neb (Dan Jackson, who is black), plan to escape from war prison along with painfully cynical Northern journalist Gideon Spilett (Gary Merrill). On a stormy night they make their attempt, leaping into a nearby observation balloon. Just as it takes off, Rebel soldier Sergeant Pencroft (Percy Herbert) scrambles into the balloon in an effort to stop them.

The untethered balloon is captured by the gale and swept westward across the United States and Mexico, out over the Pacific. Somewhere near New Zealand (!), the gale subsides and the balloon springs a leak. Harding falls off, and the others wash ashore on an island dominated by a smoking volcano.

Herbert and Neb are depressed by Harding's disappearance, but they soon find him, also safely ashore and far from the surf. When he awakes, Harding takes charge, and they search the island, discovering it isn't large, but does feature geysers. And other things.

As they walk along the beach, it suddenly stands up under them, and they battle a giant crab which had buried itself in the sand. The crab is one of Harryhausen's most realistic creations, although it does clatter its claws too much. It's about 15 feet wide, and Harryhausen took a cast from the shell of a real crab for his animation model. It never behaves like anything but a real crab: it scuttles sideways, and is much more anxious to escape than to attack.

Our heroes upend it into a hot spring, and it is cooked in no time. Spilett is puzzled by the crab, but the others are pragmatic, and simply eat it. There's a weird and unwelcome scene of high spirits, as they all burst into a chorus of "ahhhhh!" (To indicate they are now a group.)

Soon, they discover a high cliff with a cave way up on it, and a suddenly-appearing vine dangling from the cave entrance. They climb up, and discover it has been used as the home of a man whose skeleton they find; he had been abandoned by pirates, and killed himself out of loneliness.

Soon, the castaways find several things washed ashore, just what they need: a sealed chest packed with tools, weapons, etc., and a useful book: *Robinson Crusoe*. Also a boat washes ashore with more desirable items: two women, Lady Mary Fairchild (Joan Greenwood) and her niece Elena (Beth Rogan).

Based on what's found in the chest, Spilett suspects Captain Nemo may have been involved. He tells the others the story of Nemo and his fantastic submarine, lost in the vicinity eight years before.

Some time later, Spilett is pursued back to the recently built compound and corral by a giant bird, which leaps over the fence in a dramatic-comic entrance.

Like the crab, the flightless bird is another fine Harryhausen creation, one of his few that is both comic and exciting. The droll seriousness inherent to birds is offset by this one's huge claws and wicked beak, but it also has tiny little wings it vainly flaps from time to time. It menaces the women and Spilett, and Herbert heroically leaps onto its back with a knife. The bird suddenly falls dead.

Harryhausen seems to have been especially pleased with the bird, as well he might. It's genuinely funny, has its own almost endearing personality— momentarily tragic when it is killed—unlike most of the monsters he's created.

In keeping with the initial concept of the story, Harryhausen said in his *Film Fantasy Scrapbook* that the bird was a prehistoric Phorohacos. "Originally, the bird was supposed to have an antediluvian background, but owing to some script deletions, its origin was discarded. Most reviewers assumed it to be an overgrown chicken. Its awkward movements turned it into a 'comedian.' However, a good laugh in the story was a pleasant relief from all of the melodramatic thrills of the rest of the film." Harryhausen's films could in general have used more of this comic-action material; usually, when comedy scenes turn up, they're lame. However, the giant bird here is in exactly the right tone.

When the bird is roasted, a bullet is found in its flesh. The mysterious benefactor of the castaways shot the bird while Herbert was riding it. (And indeed, a shot can be heard on the sound track.)

While Herbert and Elena are exploring the island, they discover vast quantities of honey dripping down a rock. They enter a cave to discover giant honeycombs and, arriving shortly, bees the size of Volkswagens. The two young people take refuge in one of the open honeycombs. Failing to reach them, the bee philosophically walls them up. (The editing is askew in this scene.)

The bees are excellent, although their wings look wrong because stop-motion animation does not allow for realistic blurring unless very careful precautions are taken. Harryhausen seems to have tried this, but it doesn't always work. Like all the giant animals Harryhausen has done, the bees act like what they are—bees.

Unfortunately, Harryhausen has a tendency to try to allow people to think that the monsters they are watching in his films are real, living creatures. I don't think that any but the very naive ever believe that they're seeing reality, so his slavish and painstaking copies of real animals are probably futile. He should have reached more for the fantastic, to include (as he does in some of his fantasies) creatures that no one has ever seen before.

He probably included real animals among the fantasy creations to make them both look more real, but unfortunately the reaction of most audiences is the opposite. The inherent irreality of stop-motion animation makes those "real" animals, which we know from life and nature films, look less like living things and more like models—making the imaginary beasts look less real as well. Harryhausen's work was always more effective in fantasy films than science fiction. (The bees, for instance; as fantasy creations, they make sense; as science fiction creations, we wonder what they live on. Giant roses?)

Meanwhile, back in that honeycomb, Elena and Herbert have been sealed up altogether. He strikes a fire and melts the back of the comb (made from Fibreglas), and they tumble into a new cave, which opens on the sea. A lagoon stretches before them. And in the lagoon is a submarine.

Outside, the others are being menaced by a pirate ship sailing unexpectedly into the bay. It's apparently come back for Ayerton, but no sooner do the pirates realize there are people on the Mysterious Island than their ship explodes.

Exploring the sub, Herbert and Elena discover it is the *Nautilus*. As they rejoin the others, a man clad in black, carrying a trident, emerges from the sea. His helmet and backpack underwater breathing device are giant seashells. He removes the helmet to reveal a stern, aristocratic face, with blonde hair and beard. Spilett recognizes him: Captain Nemo (Herbert Lom).

Nemo invites everyone aboard the *Nautilus*, and explains that he'd come there after his supposed death to try to combat war by conquering the reasons for war: starvation and want. He's been trying to enlarge food animals to provide plenty to eat for the increasing population of the world: hence the giant crab, bee and bird.

Throughout the film, the island's volcano occasionally rumbles, and Nemo tells the others it will soon erupt, destroying the island. He proposes to help them raise the pirate ship, which he sunk, so that they might escape. Nemo's initial plan seems wrong to the others, who suggest using the balloon as a means to raise it, by patching the hole in the ship, putting the balloon in the hold, and inflating it by means of the *Nautilus*' pumps. They follow this plan.

As they walk along the bottom of the bay using Nemo's diving apparatus, our heroes are surprised (and well they might be) to see the ruins of a Greek-styled city, which goes without explanation. Air soon begins pumping into the balloon.

All this activity disturbs a red-eyed giant chambered nautilus—some have described it as a squid in a snail shell—which briefly grapples with our heroes. Unfortunately, this is a seriously unexciting sequence. Because it takes place underwater, the movements of everyone concerned, including the tentacled monster, are slowed down. This, plus Bernard Herrmann's very labored theme for the sequence, makes all action ponderous and dull. It's spectacular in concept, but the execution makes this the least exciting and most enervating animation sequence in the film, especially unfortunate as it is the climax.

The creature is eventually dispatched, and the ship raised. The volcano begins to erupt, and everyone but Nemo heads for the ship. He's trapped in the *Nautilus* by falling rocks. Everyone else reaches the ship safely, but Nemo goes down with the island.

The clichéd volcanic destruction in the film, plus the ponderous fight with the giant nautilus, occurring as they do at the finish, tend to make audiences disappointed in the film—they're the last things they see, after all—but the film that precedes these scenes is well above average for Harryhausen and Schneer.

As usual, the faults with the film lie elsewhere than with Harryhausen's effects. The characters are uninteresting, and for the most part are played by dull performers. Michael Craig's American accent is acceptable, but although he's built like a hero, he doesn't give a heroic feel to his performance. He's a reasonably good actor in other than adventure films, and while never a major star, has appeared with distinction in a variety of movies: *Svengali* (1954), *The Angry Silence* (1960, which he cowrote), *Stolen Hours* (1963), *Vault of Horror* (1973) and *The Irishman* (1978). Here, Craig isn't helped by the thin script. Harding has no characteristics other than Hero of the Piece. He's only strong, firm and brave.

Michael Callan, added to appeal to the Youth Market, is pretty good in light films, comedies, and frivolous adventures; he's appropriately cast in *Cat Ballou* (1965) and *The Cat and the Canary* (1978), but is out of his depth in more serious films, such as *The Interns* (1962) and *The Victors* (1963). He brings much enthusiasm to the part of Herbert, and is lively throughout, but he's never once believable as a Civil War soldier.

Gary Merrill is best when more typically cast as a grim second lead. In lighter parts, where he's required to deliver comedy lines, he seems awkward. The role of Spilett is poorly conceived—the Voice of Cynical Reason—and Merrill is tiresome. Most of his best roles were earlier in his career, in pictures like *All About Eve* (1950) and *Phone Call from a Stranger* (1952). After 1961, he appeared in lower-class pictures, as well as several genre films: *Around the World Under the Sea*, *Destination Inner Space* (both 1966) and *The Power* (1968). His best later role was in the underrated *The Incident* (1967), where his occasional apparent uneasiness before the camera was made part of his characterization.

Percy Herbert is outrageous as the Rebel soldier. He does a broad, thick accent—it's not British, but not remotely Southern. Herbert usually turns up as lower-class military figures, rarely higher in rank than sergeant and usually lower, often playing comic roles. He's usually on for only a few brief but memorable scenes, and has been in a number of first-class productions: *Bridge on the River Kwai* (1957), *Tunes of Glory* (1961), *Becket* (1964), *Casino Royale* (1967), *Valentino* (1977), and many others. But mixed in are a bunch of exploitation thrillers, with the occasional crude comedy: *Curse of the Demon* (his part was cut from the initial U.S. prints), *Enemy from Space* (both 1957), *Carry on Venus* (1964), Harryhausen's *One Million Years B.C.* (1966), *Captain Apache* (1971) and *Sweet Suzy* (1973). I suspect Herbert ran away with the role of Pencroft, and the director assumed that was better than an underplayed part.

Because of his strength as an actor, his unusual face and general fame, Herbert Lom has become a common fixture in horror and SF films, though not quite a star of them. He's been in an amazing variety of films, displaying talent as almost everything but a shy romantic. Typically, he's cast in glowering, crafty parts, whether as criminals or as here, dedicated geniuses. He's effectively played Napoleon more than once, and has also been such villains as Simon Legree, Herod and Attila. However, Lom is also a fine comic actor, as his wonderful series of performances in the Pink Panther films indicated. His other genre films are generally not distinguished, but it is hardly the fault of Herbert Lom, who is always more than up to the demands of the part. Among his other

SF and horror films: *Phantom of the Opera* (1961, fine in a lesser production), *Journey to the Far Side of the Sun* (1969), *Count Dracula, Dorian Gray, Mark of the Devil, Vampyr* (all 1970), *Murders in the Rue Morgue* (1971), *Dark Places, Asylum* (both 1972), *And Now the Screaming Starts* (1973), and *The Dead Zone* (1983).

Joan Greenwood is certainly an odd actress to find in a science fiction film with giant bees. Her distinctive voice and delivery make her much more suitable to witty ladies of the type found in Oscar Wilde films, but she enters into the spirit of things in *Mysterious Island*. She was more at home in *The Man in the White Suit*; later, she received an Academy Award nomination for her wonderful Lady Bellaston in *Tom Jones* (1963).

Neither Beth Rogan nor Dan Jackson makes much of an impression; they are merely the Screaming Ingenue and the Noble Black Man.

Director Cy Endfield was born in South Africa, but first made his reputation as a movie director in the United States, with several good crime pictures, including *The Underworld Story* (1950) and *Try and Get Me* (1951), but after *Tarzan's Savage Fury* (1952), he was identified as a Communist in the House Un-American Activities Committee witch-hunt in Hollywood, and like others, fled to England where he directed several films anonymously or under pseudonyms. By 1956, however, he had begun using his own name again.

In the 1960s, in partnership with actor Stanley Baker, Endfield made two adventure films, the outstanding *Zulu* and the lesser but still interesting *Sands of the Kalahari* (both 1964). After that, however, Endfield seems rarely to have completed a project; he was one of several directors on the ill-fated *De Sade* (1969), but did complete *Universal Soldier* (1971); he cowrote the prequel to *Zulu*, *Zulu Dawn*. According to *The Film Encyclopedia*, "in 1978, Endfield invented a computerized pocket-sized typewriter."

The effects other than the animation in *Mysterious Island* are also under Harryhausen's direction. Graphically, they are generally excellent, but also look like effects. The several matte paintings are handsome, and have a pleasingly *King Kong*–like aura, but don't convince us they are reality. Realism isn't as important as a sense of awe and wonder, and intermittently, *Mysterious Island* gives us that.

The film doesn't have the puzzling sense of mystery of Verne's original novel, although Nemo's activities do go unexplained for most of the picture. It isn't much like Verne in mood, but I suspect it's a kind of picture the French author himself would have liked. *Mysterious Island* is pleasant, escapist fare.

Bernard Herrmann scored several films for Harryhausen/Schneer. None were as good as his greatest scores, those for *Citizen Kane* (1941), *North by Northwest* (1959), *Psycho* (1960) and *Taxi Driver* (1976), but they were still superlative. Herrmann was quite possibly the greatest film composer of all time. His scores, even lesser ones, are rich, evocative and distinctive. Only rarely does one Herrmann score sound much like another, and even more rarely like music by anyone else. His score for *Mysterious Island* features an excellent title theme, and that for the deserted island is also excellent. Though the themes for the crab and bird are fine, those for the bees and the nautilus are disappointing. Nonetheless, Herrmann's score gives the film a vitality and feeling of opulence that music by almost any other composer would have failed to provide. The other scores Herrmann did for Schneer and Harryhausen: *The 7th Voyage of Sinbad* (1958), *The Three Worlds of Gulliver* (1960) and *Jason and the Argonauts* (1963).

Mysterious Island was Columbia's 1961 Christmas family movie, and was generally reviewed favorably. *Parents'* called it "entertaining.... [It] has enough tricks, surprises and mystery for a dozen plots."

Monthly Film Bulletin gave the movie its highest rating, and thought that while the film "is cheerful, [it is] dramatically uneven ... [and Harryhausen's monsters are] ineffectual." But also said, "On the whole, however, the distinguished cast ... dispatch the nonsense with spirit, and the trick work is quite inventive, notably in the way that it matches the incongruous elements on the screen with a reasonable degree of conviction. Bernard Herrmann's characteristically full-bodied score adds to the excitement; Cy Endfield's direction is clean and vigorous."

Castle of Frankenstein thought it was "fun," though Don Willis (I) considered it "lesser Harryhausen." Alan Frank (*SF*) said, "Briskly scripted, well acted and directed and with some excellent Ray Harryhausen creations, the movie is a first-rate Dynamation fantasy-adventure." John Brosnan, in *Future Tense*, felt it had "good, tight direction ... and a better than average script."

Mysterious Island was apparently quite successful. The next film from Schneer and Harryhausen, *Jason and the Argonauts*, though not much more expensive, was given a class-act publicity campaign by Columbia, and treated as a major production. However, it wasn't as good as *Mysterious Island*, and became lost in the cloud of spear-and-sandal epics emerging from Italy at the time.

The Phantom Planet

This well-intentioned, earnest (boy is it ever) but utterly deadly movie goes wrong so thoroughly that its failure achieves epic ineptitude. Technically, it's better than some others: the camerawork is competent, the special effects, though obvious, are okay; all in all, the film has an air of being moderately expensive for a low-budget SF film. I suspect it may have been made in color—color stills exist—but that the film was not good enough to justify the extra expense of releasing it in color.*

The direction by William Marshall (not the distinguished actor) is so leaden and the script by William Telaak, Fred De Gorter and producer Fred Gebhardt is both so overplotted and full of such a miasma of scientific gobbledegook that the film is difficult to sit through. It even has scant camp value: there's some funny dialogue, but there's also so *much* dialogue that the laughter soon freezes and you become restless with boredom. The film is also strangely uneventful, and fails to exploit one of its central gimmicks. A great deal of it consists of people talking endlessly in medium shot, interspersed with shots of others, also in medium shot, listening. Nonetheless, the film deserves more attention than the usual quickie, because it really seems to be trying for something beyond that.

In the 1960s, especially, color films were occasionally released in the United States in black and white, only to turn up later on TV in color, confusing everyone. Among these: The Underwater City, The Vulture, The Old Dark House, The Vengeance of Fu Manchu. Even more confusingly, Dr. Blood's Coffin, Devils of Darkness and Terror of the Tongs played in some areas in color, and others in black and white. The Phantom Planet has, to my knowledge, never been shown in color; it may have been shot monochromatically.

The story is actually one of those ever-popular lost-race tales, in which a hero from Our World happens upon a city of peculiar aspect, populated by a group cut off from the outside for a heck of a long time. Sometimes, as here, it ends with the hero returning to Our World, knowing no one will ever believe him — but he still has a trinket to prove that It All Really Happened.

It seems clear those who made *The Phantom Planet* were trying to create a decent SF movie, but were unaware of their own shortcomings. It doesn't seem exploitative, it's not violent, it tries at times to deal with real human feelings. Four Crown Productions tried hard to do a decent job. But they botched it.

What are you to make of a film which includes lines like "We managed, just in time, to control your landing by releasing the pressure in our space warp"? They just aren't in the same world as the rest of us. The crew of writers — and there's an Additional Dialog credit for director Marshall — seem to have felt that using known sci-fi terms like "space warp" would make the movie authentic science fiction, but they don't know what it meant.

The film opens as a couple of space pilots find themselves being inexorably pulled down to a crash landing on an asteroid that suddenly appears in front of them. (It's March 16, 1980, and although the Moon is colonized, the other planets don't seem to have been explored, and there's no mention of a space platform, so where all this spaceship traffic is going is a mystery.) After the crash, we see the titles.

This is the second such crash in a few days; there seems to be an unknown, invisible planet out there. "It's against all theories of space," says the Moon base commander's aide. Captain Frank Chapman (Dean Fredericks) is sent with co-pilot Ray Makonnen (Richard Weber) to look for this Phantom Planet. In space, after discussing beauty for a while, Frank says that it's quiet. "It's almost *too* quiet," he adds. Did he expect brass bands in airless space? A cracking twig? Owls?

After a great deal of nonsense involving various navigational hoohah, Frank adds, "You could go nuts out here waiting for something to happen." By this time, the audience has begun to feel the same way. But there comes a standard feature of space movies: meteors.

More long boring scenes in the cramped cabin follow, then *both* Frank and Ray go outside the ship to repair something. As Ray rescues Frank from a mishap, tucking him back into the ship, little whistling streaks zip by. One knocks Ray away; he floats off to his death, saying the Lord's Prayer.

When Frank revives, he's unhappy to discover Ray gone. He's also upset to find that the ship is being drawn toward an uneven little asteroid by a highly visible ray. Once the ship has set gently down, Frank emerges and inexplicably collapses. He gets up again, and sees a group of tiny people (without helmets) watching him curiously from behind some rocks. He collapses again, and in the one imaginative shot in the film, the tiny people peer into his faceplate.

He opens the faceplate and suddenly shrinks. The space suit collapses quite believably, but the shot of Frank's face disappearing down into it is unacceptable.

He's captured by the tiny people and brought before the ruler of the asteroid, one Sesom (Francis X. Bushman). You'll note that "Sesom" is "Moses" spelled backward, but apart from Bushman's built-in patriarchal air, there's no apparent reason for the name.

Frank is amazed that they speak English. Sesom smiles indulgently. "We do not *speak* it. But here on Rehton ... we are able to translate all languages through *tone* waves." (?)

Frank is swiftly tried by a jury of women, and found guilty of attacking someone. He is sentenced to be "a free subject of Rehton." I doubt that there are many cultures where, if you're found guilty of a crime, you are *condemned* to be a free member of that culture.

Frank is led away by Liara (Coleen Gray), a pretty young woman related to Sesom whose immediate interest in Frank does not go unnoticed by Sesom's right-hand man, Herron (Tony Dexter). Frank, however, is more interested in Zetha (Dolores Faith), a beautiful brunette who's been mute since an attack by the Solarites, enemies of Rehton, some years before.

Frank asks Liara about their relative sizes. "Our atmosphere," she explains, "together with some acceleration from our gravitational control, has reduced you to normal ... for us." Size, she adds, varies according to the size of the world of origin of any species. While this may prove to be generally true, it does not seem likely that, as she claims, "Oxygen in your atmosphere would restore you immediately to your regular size." What are *they* breathing?

Frank and the Rehtonites being six inches tall has no function in the story-line whatsoever. It doesn't matter whether they are six feet or six microns tall. There are no giant menaces after them, there's no scene in which Frank has to find his way around his full-sized spaceship. For all the effect on the plot, Frank might as well not have shrunk at all.

Sesom tells Frank he can't leave Rehton, because he wants the Earthman's assistance in keeping spaceships from running into the highly mobile little planet. This, too, is puzzling: the planet's mobility is demonstrated spectacularly; why can't it dodge the ships? At the end of the film, this problem is not solved, nor is it mentioned again.

After raising jealousy as an issue, the script brings in social criticism. Frank has noted that the Rehtonites live "primitively," in rock-walled caves, which would seem to be a result of living inside a planetoid. Sesom tells him that once upon a time an overreliance on machines led to disaster for the Rehtonites, and so they learned better. Frank remarks that Earth is heading in the direction of too much leisure time.

Later, Liara tells Frank he is eating the "equivalent of your breadfruit. We make it chemically since nothing grows on this planet.... Our bodies are so constructed that we need very little food, because of the air we breathe." Though that seems unlikely, I can buy it, but if nothing grows on Rehton, where did the Rehtonists come from? And why do they bother generating pseudobread fruit when *pseudobread* would probably be a better idea?

We return to the Moon base, where a rescue operation is launched to find Frank and Ray. We are shown in long, explicit detail the overtaking of Frank's ship (which Sesom had sent away from Rehton), including someone arriving on it, getting it, playing Frank's often-heard recorded last message, etc.

When we finally get back to Rehton, a long time seems to have passed, for Frank is now a busy member of Rehton's society. He is shown the marvelous machine that controls Rehton's gravity: it looks like a small collection of broken goblets, over which Sesom waves his hands. On the screen, we see a planetoid jumping about; as it is not only not clear we are looking at Rehton (where are we looking *from*?), it is opaque as to what is being demonstrated.

Then Sesom explains that Rehton has a high density but is getting smaller (the first we've heard of this presumably serious problem), and adds that "the planet is slowly using up the energy that holds the atomic particles together." (Which would seem to cause it to expand while becoming more tenuous.)

Frank finally has to tell the pushy Liara that he's not interested in her, but

instead is drawn to silent Zetha. Herron overhears this and tells Sesom that Frank's attitude is an insult to Liara and, obscurely, to Herron himself. He challenges Frank to the dreaded Duel of Rehton.

Holding each end of an H-shaped bar, Herron and Frank attempt to push the other onto a plate set into the floor. The plates have extremely high gravity which, according to the film, makes things like rocks fade away. But stalwart, fair Frank refrains from killing Herron, pulling him back at the last moment.

Liara is thrilled, but Frank tells her off. That night, Herron awakens Frank by holding a knife to his throat, and offers to help him leave Rehton. This seems to indicate they are friends.

We are told about the Rehtonians' enemies, the Solarites who, Herron says, come from a "sun satellite, and are after Rehton's fabulous gravity controls.

Liara, apparently forgiving, shows Frank a Solarite prisoner (Richard Kiel), a tall, spindly creature with a doglike face, large, dimly-glowing eyes, shoulders like small volcanoes, tubular fingers, and eyebrow ridges like lumps of cauliflower. It looks anything but dangerous, just ugly, and a little like Goofy. It is, however, nasty and very strong, continually breaking off chunks of rock and flinging them at the hazy "gravity barrier" that keeps it prisoner. Now, children, we've been shown a monster in a prison; how many here think that monster is going to *stay* in that prison the rest of the movie?

Rehton is under attack by Solarite ships, resembling small blazing coals whizzing through space. Occasionally they join up into strings, making the battle look like a big rock under attack by shish kebabs. Sesom suavely dodges the Solarite ships. (We see a Solarite in his ship, looking up close like a blazing orange crate; he is roaring, apparently with good reason.)

Although Herron and Sesom manage to outwit, dodge and destroy the Solarite fleet, a Solarite missile disables the gravity screen imprisoning the Solarite, and he wanders off. In a long, peculiar scene which involves much switching on and off lights, he happens upon Zetha, then scoops her up in the time-honored stance of monsters, and meanders off to the now-deserted control room.

There is a very funny scene in which the Solarite dabbles at the controls, which emit bleeps, causing the Solarite to turn to the camera blankly, not unlike the masked apes of Ernie Kovacs' Nairobi Trio. In search of Zetha, Frank strolls into the control room; she recovers her voice just in time to scream and save Frank from being grabbed by the Solarite. Herron and Frank manage to force the monster back toward one of the gravity plates. It is an accommodating foe; as he misses stepping on the plate, he glances back, sees it, and plants himself squarely in the middle. He wails, raises his hands over his head, and slowly fades from view.

During his escape, the Solarite wounded Sesom, but Frank is assured the old gentleman will be all right. "The aura is with him," Herron says. (I hope never to discover if George Lucas saw this film.)

Now that she can speak, Zetha has the traditional *Phantom Planet* long boring conversation with Frank, this time about love and stuff like that. She gives him a rock on a string so he will always remember her. Herron then ushers Frank out to his space suit, still lying undisturbed on the planet's

Opposite: The dog-faced alien is played by Richard Kiel; the Earthman hero at the right is Dean Fredericks, and at the left, Tony Dexter is seen from a less-than-flattering angle. They're trying to get the evil alien to jump onto the plates on the floor, in this scene from the climax of the ambitious The Phantom Planet (1961).

bombarded surface. Frank climbs in, the footage from the shrinking sequence is run in reverse, returning him to full size just as two other astronauts walk up.

As he is returning to the Moon base, Frank has time to ponder friendship, love, truth, beauty, reality, etc. After all, though Zetha is now no bigger than his hand, he still has the rock on a string—which grew with him—and all his wonderful memories.

As the ship flies off, the narrator asks, not only rhetorically but without reference, "What then will the future reveal if this story is only the beginning ... only the beginning ... only the beginning." As the voice fades away, instead of THE END, we see, surprise, THE BEGINNING. (In this context, this is baffling.)

The labyrinthine, stilted and earnest dialogue of the film was forecast in the opening narration which talks about mankind's "God-given genius of science," but does go on to wonder, "is [man] a mere unimportant piece of driftwood floating in the vast ocean of the universe?" The opening narrator, Marvin Miller, continues to read the most unnecessary prologue in the history of films. "Is it not possible that atmospheric conditions of relative environments control their shapes and forms?" (Whose shapes and forms?) "If so, would they be giants? Or [in a drawing-closer tone] could perhaps the opposite be true?" At this point—before the titles—anyone who grabbed their hat and headed for the nearest exit could hardly be blamed.

The faults of The Phantom Planet are manifold, the film is hopeless. It isn't the Cat-Women of the Moon of Volume 2, because it's so dull and lethargic, but in small doses, it does have a certain inept charm. It might hold the tolerant, experienced viewer aghast, but such a viewer might also stick with the film to see if it could sustain its strange, gabby level of inaction. The Phantom Planet may be the most talky American science fiction film—and almost none of the talk is any good.

It has plenty of ideas—invisible planets, teensy tiny aliens, gravity control, a lost race—but fails to find any way to link them. They just occur again and again, like nuts in a stale bun.

William Marshall's direction isn't flaccid; it's not limber enough to be flaccid. It's set in concrete. People enter, stop, give endless speeches (or watch them), and go out; the camera rarely moves, and close-ups are used almost exclusively as punctuation. This kind of direction isn't merely unimaginative, it's antiimaginative. Other SF films on this budget level often have a kind of tacky liveliness, but The Phantom Planet is played at a dead stop.

The actors are all stiff. They seem to have been told to keep physical movement to a minimum, to play the film not only straight but glumly. This comes naturally to Dean Fredericks who, though having a good speaking voice, has one of the least expressive faces and most immobile bodies I've seen. Fredericks had played Milton Caniff's hero in the "Steve Canyon" TV series 1958–59, but he and the show were roasted by critics. He later appeared in Wild Harvest (1961) and Savage Sam (1963), but wisely retired from acting. He probably would have been fine on radio.

Dolores Faith was a lovely but limited actress; she was supposedly introduced in The Phantom Planet, but had already appeared in V.D. (1961). She also starred in Wild Harvest with Fredericks, and later appeared in Hugo Grimaldi's The Human Duplicators and Mutiny in Outer Space, again as a mute who regains her speech. Her last film seems to have been That Tennessee Beat in 1966.

Coleen Gray, whose career is discussed in the entry on The Leech Woman, is trapped in a trite role here: the woman who wants the first stranger she sees.

Gray struggles to invest the role with more meaning than the script supplies, but this was beyond either her ability or interest.

Anthony Dexter, billed here as Tony Dexter, was a big discovery in and as *Valentino* (1951), but though he was handsome, his acting was stilted and inexpressive. Oddly, he's actually better in *The Phantom Planet* than almost anything else he did. He also appeared in *Fire Maidens of Outer Space* and *12 to the Moon*; *Thoroughly Modern Millie* (1967) is apparently his last film to date.

Francis X. Bushman was one of the great stars of the early silent screen. A strong, handsome man with a classic Romanesque profile, he began his career in 1911, and by 1915 was one of the greatest successes of the period, earning as much as a million dollars a year. He came by it legitimately: in 1914, he starred in no fewer than 22 movies. However, by 1918, he had already begun to fade in popularity, and the role for which most remember him, Messala in *Ben Hur* (1926), was actually a major comeback for Bushman.

It didn't take. He appeared in a few more films before the end of the 20s, but his fortune was wiped out in the stock market crash, and he never regained any cinematic popularity. He often worked on radio and occasionally appeared in a peculiarly wide variety of films, including the serial *Dick Tracy* (1937), *Wilson* (1944), *Sabrina* (1954) and *The Ghost in the Invisible Bikini* (1966). He narrated and appeared briefly in *12 to the Moon* and played Sesom's reverse namesake in the execrable *Story of Mankind* (1957). Bushman died in 1966.

As Sesom, Bushman is dignified, managing to read the pedantic, meaningless dialogue as if it were his normal mode of address. But he was also a tired, elderly man, often seeming to be reading offscreen cue cards. He was trying to wrap himself in a kind of dignity, but the film didn't allow him this.

I do not know of any other movies directed by William Marshall (no wonder), but assistant producer Hugo Grimaldi was busy for several years. He distributed some foreign films, including *Assignment Outer Space*, *First Spaceship on Venus* and *Hercules and the Captive Women*. He produced *The Human Duplicators* and *Mutiny in Outer Space* in 1965, but by 1969 had slid back to the position of editor on several films, including *Chastity*, *Two Roses and a Golden-Rod* (both 1969), and *Bigfoot* (1971).

There was a major effort made in promoting *The Phantom Planet*; there was even a comic book based on the film, a practice generally reserved for major releases. But the promotion efforts probably were to no avail. The material is just too shoddy; it doesn't really insult the audience, though; its failings are not those of cynical opportunism, but of ineptitude.

Reviews were not favorable. The *Monthly Film Bulletin* gave it a III rating, referring to it as "a corny slice of SF hokum." More recently, *Castle of Frankenstein* #22 (probably Bhob Stewart) called it an "atrocious space opera.... As deadly and illiterate a pic as you've ever seen."

The special effects by Charles A. Duncan and Louis DeWitt are extravagantly conceived, with attacking armadas of Solarite craft, several different Earth spaceships, the maneuverable asteroid, a Moon base, and so on. However, for the most part, the effects are not well executed, though above average for the budget. But the budget wasn't large enough. The miniatures look like nothing else, the spaceships are often transparent, and only the swiftly-moving asteroid has any visual appeal.

There's a kind of unfortunate arrogance about *The Phantom Planet*. In other low-budget SF films a kind of distasteful cynicism operates: it doesn't matter if the film is good, it just has to have the right kind of stuff. In the case of *The Phantom Planet*, there was an effort to do good work, but the writers were inept, the scientific aspects scream for good technical advice, and the direction is impossibly stodgy. The story is different, but not all that is different is worth doing.

The Secret of the Telegian

Understandably, this film is sometimes confused with *The Human Vapor*. Both were made by Toho, produced by Tomoyuki Tanaka with special effects by Eiji Tsuburaya, were released in 1960 in Japan, and concern the vengeful criminal activities of a young man who has gained a fantastic power. The original title of *The Secret of the Telegian* was *Denso Ningen*, and that of *The Human Vapor* was *Gasu Ningen Daiichigo*. The problem is compounded in that while *The Human Vapor* was released in the United States in 1964 (and hence is not included in this volume), it is unclear as to whether *The Secret of the Telegian* had general U.S. theatrical release at all.

While the American Film Institute catalog for the 1960s does not generally include films released only in theatres catering to ethnic groups, it does list many Japanese films shown in the United States in Japanese–language theatres only, though they do omit Chinese-language films shown in the U.S. in subtitled versions.

This presents a problem. I've tried to avoid listing such ethnic-audience releases, as well as those not shown theatrically (though I have made some exceptions in the latter case). *Secret of the Telegian* was scheduled for U.S. distribution in a dubbed print by Herts-Lion International in 1964 in a 75-minute print (ten minutes shorter than the original version), but was not then released, according to information given me by Japanese SF film expert Greg Shoemaker. Toho released it to U.S. television in 1963, Shoemaker says. But it was available to American audiences in the correct period, and was occasionally reviewed in mainstream U.S. newspapers, so I have included it. I explain my problem at this length to explain some of the difficulties encountered in trying to limit yourself to standards that at first seem very clear, but which cloud up on closer examination.

A body is found in an amusement park, the victim having been slain by a single thrust of a bayonet. Science reporter Kirioka (Koji Tsurata) of the *Toho News*, finds a small metal coil near the dead man. A famous scientist tells him that it is an advanced device called the "Clariotron" which will soon replace the transistor.

A second murder takes place, when Kirioka and his detective friend Kobayashi (Akihiko Hirata) are nearby. They chase the murderer, Nakamoto (Tadao Nakamaru), to a deserted warehouse but there's a tremendous explosion. Kirioka and Kobayashi discover only the ruins of a freezing apparatus in the burnt-out warehouse.

They learn that the two dead men were given death warnings accompanied by identification tags worn by soldiers of the defunct Imperial Japanese Army. A third warning is sent to a man named Taki, who seeks police protection, and tells them the story that links him and the two dead men.

Near the end of World War II, Taki, Onishi (Seizaburo Kawazu) and the two murdered men were ordered to hide eminent scientist Dr. Niki, along with his research material. However, young Corporal Sudo (now using the name

Nakamoto) discovered that instead of research materials, the four were attempting to steal gold. Taki and his companions decided to murder Niki and Sudo by blowing up a cave where they are trapped.

Years later, the four returned to retrieve the gold, but the gold as well as the bodies of Niki and Sudo were missing. Taki knows that it is Sudo who is trying to kill him. Though Taki is protected by a cordon of police, Sudo does murder him, and makes another mysterious getaway.

We learn that unknown to Niki, Sudo has been using the great scientist's new device to carry out the murders. It is a matter transmitter, similar to that in *The Fly,* but instead of a receiving booth, Sudo has been transmitting himself to Clariotrons, which he has hidden in a cold area near each victim. (The device works only at a "state of 4.2 degrees below zero," according to the Toho synopsis.)

Onishi now receives the death threat, and despite all efforts of police to halt Sudo, he kills the last of the four men who betrayed and attempted to murder him and Niki.

However, when Sudo tries to make his final getaway, the transmitting machine malfunctions, and he and the device are destroyed.

According to Greg Shoemaker in his article "The Toho Legacy," serialized in several issues of Shoemaker's *The Japanese Fantasy Film Journal, Secret of the Telegian* was a below-par effort from Toho. "Handled matter-of-factly throughout the movie, the teleportation device is clumsily portrayed by a telephone booth-like [prop] ... and features a rather disappointing disappearing act from [Eiji] Tsuburaya's usual extravagant imagination.... Jun Fukuda's leaden direction appears starved for Tsuburaya's garnishes."

Arnold Babbin in the *Beverly Hills Citizen* (24 July 1961), on the other hand, found Fukuda's direction praiseworthy. "While there is little in the way of originality in the basic situations of the film, director Fukuda moves the action suspensefully and effectively toward its conclusion."

When American films deal with new inventions, they generally feature the scientist who devised the gadget as the central character. Often, the motivation for the crimes (if any) is passion, or attempts at restoring himself to normal, sometimes a psychotic rage. In Japanese SF films, professional crooks sometimes get their hands on the miracle machine, or become otherwise involved in the goings-on. Usually, the protagonist is someone *removed* from the activities centering around the invention—a police inspector, a reporter, on the track of the mysterious happenings. And the person using the gadget, or who has turned into whatever, is usually bent on revenge or monetary gain, or both. (Revenge is a powerful motivation in Japanese films of all types.)

I doubt that this indicates a great difference in our cultures, but rather that Japanese movie fans like crime films more, and also that these crime-oriented SF films are what the Japanese filmmakers think of as American–type movies. They're imitations of an older model than 50s SF films. In the 1930s and 40s, American SF and horror films were often mysteries, as *Dr. X* (1932), in which the central character was a policeman or reporter on the trail of mysterious events. I suspect it's this mode that the Japanese are imitating in films like *The Secret of the Telegian,* rather than the later typical 1950s SF film with the independent scientist or military man as hero. (If present at all, military figures are almost invariably peripheral in Japanese SF films, and with some exceptions, the scientists are associated with institutions.)

Rather than trying to compare and analyze these differences in approach to SF on the part of American and Japanese filmmakers, I offer it as material for further research.

The Snake Woman

Like *Voodoo Woman* in Volume 1, *The Snake Woman* hovers somewhere between science fiction and fantasy, probably because writer Orville H. Hampton presumed there was no real difference between the genres. He seems like the kids in my home town, who thought it was all rotten because "it's impossible and can't happen," so Hampton paid no attention as to whether the material was properly SF or properly fantasy.

For instance, the creation of the snake woman is detailed in scientific terms—but she's destroyed by something akin to voodoo. Granted, it's really *all* fantasy, but to be logically believable, a story should follow its established premises. If Atheris the Snake Woman is created by scientific means, she should be dispatched that way.

Fantasy, especially science fiction, follows certain laws. To work within these laws is the discipline of the writer. For instance, a major flaw of *Superman II* is that both Superman and the villains from Krypton develop new superpowers, never exhibited in the comic books, whenever they need them. If this is possible, there's no dramatic tension—Superman can't be a hero, no one can stand against him, if he can do literally anything.

Furthermore, in *The Snake Woman*, if a supernatural solution to a science fiction problem could be found all along, why does it take 20 years to be implemented? The solution finally found—the snake woman is simply shot—would seem to have been available at any time. Even on its own mixed terms, *The Snake Woman* doesn't make any sense. It's also about as slight a story as has been filmed by anything approaching competent filmmakers, and fully deserves the almost total obscurity into which it has fallen. It certainly is not one of the proudest moments of director Sidney J. Furie, who later directed, among others, *The Ipcress File*, *Lady Sings the Blues* and *Gable and Lombard*. (For more on Furie, see the entry on *Dr. Blood's Coffin*. Joe Dante informs us that "Furie himself once lamented that this [*Snake Woman*], his first directorial effort, must surely rank as 'the worst film ever made.'" It actually isn't quite *that* terrible.)

There's something classic about a woman who can turn herself into a snake. It's a common legend in many parts of the world, and occasionally turns up in movies, although these films aren't usually very distinguished, to put it mildly. There's some of this in Maria Montez's *Cobra Woman* (1944); Faith Domergue became a cobra in *Cult of the Cobra* (1955); another were-cobra woman was in *Night of the Cobra Woman* (1972). (Cobras seem to be the favored snake for woman-into-reptile transformations, probably because they are the most infamous and among the most beautiful of poisonous snakes.) Treacherous women are often described in terms linking them to reptiles, specifically snakes. There's something sensuous about snakes; they're sleek, slender, even beautiful. Despite the obvious resemblances, snakes are not one of the more popular phallic symbols; despite their shape, they seem more feminine than masculine, as in *The Reptile* (1966). Man-into-snake transformations do turn up, as in *Conan the Barbarian* (1982), but generally they are treated as science fiction, as in *Sssssss* (1973), with its reluctant, tragic serpent man.

The Snake Woman begins in the late 1890s, although the period setting has nothing to do with the story, and has no effect on any events. In a hut on the Northumberland moors, Dr. Adderson (John Cazabon) conducts his research surrounded by cages and boxes of snakes. He's a herpetologist, perhaps driven to this profession by his name. His pregnant wife is in agony, and against her wishes, he gives her another injection of snake venom, which he has used to cure her insanity.

As the child begins to be born, local Dr. Murton (Arnold Marle) and mid-wife Aggie (Elsie Wagstaff) arrive. Adderson's wife dies during delivery and Aggie, horrified that the baby is icy cold and has permanently open eyes, declares it to be an evil child with the evil eye, then dashes off into the night.

Adderson gives the baby into Murton's care, and the doctor flees as a bunch of guys from the local pub show up with torches and a constable. The policeman is powerless to prevent them from killing Adderson and setting his house ablaze. Some of the snakes escape.

Murton turns the baby over to a shepherd (Stevenson Lang), forever playing his flute in the neighborhood, then departs at once for Africa. Ten years later, from the back we see a little girl in a flock of sheep, swaying to the tune of the shepherd's flute. She sinks down out of sight; later, two sheep are found dead of snake bite.

Ten years more pass, Murton returns, and the shepherd tells him that some time ago, the girl, whom he named Atheris (Susan Travers), disappeared. We learn that she lives in the ruins of her father's laboratory.

A man bitten by a snake staggers into the local pub, and seeks help from Colonel Wynborn (Geoffrey Danton), a retired Army medical officer, back from India. He recognizes the man's wound as being due to cobra bite, and writes to an old friend at Scotland Yard.

Young Charles Prentice (John McCarthy) is sent from the Yard to investi-gate, and learns to his surprise that for the past twenty years, the village has averaged more than one death per year from poisonous reptile bite, something of a record for Great Britain as it has no deadly reptiles at all, though this isn't noted. (Hampton probably didn't know it.)

Prentice is told the story of the "curse of the serpent child," and goes off to interview Aggie while tootling on a fakir's flute he found in Wynborn's home. Atheris appears, attracted by the flute. This is as close to a romantic scene as the film has, and consists of them sitting on a stump, chatting. (Travers' patrician, well-educated accent was noted by several reviewers.) Atheris becomes upset when Prentice shoots at a snake. Writer Hampton apparently felt that she was being weird and inhuman to so object, but inasmuch as the snake was harmless, today she sounds humane.

Prentice arrives at Aggie's hut; she has tea waiting, as she clairvoyantly knew he was coming. At once she convinces him to fire three bullets into an effigy of Atheris. Unlike most such charms, this doesn't have its effect right away, but Aggie assures him that he will soon fire three bullets into the snake woman.

Not much happens for most of the rest of the film. A boy is killed by a snake, which turns out to be a fer-de-lance, not a cobra. The boy's father hunts down the snake and kills it, but Atheris, who has appointed herself guardian of all local snakes—a most unreptilian attitude—kills the father.

Murton realizes what's going on, and seeks out Atheris, but she ungrate-fully kills him, too. Prentice finds Atheris' shed skin, realizes the Awful Truth, and heads off into the moors with his little flute while another mob of villagers with torches is organizing. He confronts Atheris, she turns into a cobra, he shoots her the predicted three times, and she dies. Scotland Yard decides to hush the case up.

In a film with a script as sketchy and trivial as this, most probably wouldn't bother to point out certain errors, but I will. First of all the central gimmick of the flute is impossible, as snakes are deaf. In India, they are attracted by the rhythmic swaying of the fakir, not by the sounds of his flute, yet in *The Snake Woman*, not only Atheris but several real snakes react to the flute as if they hear it. (The idea of a snake woman constantly going, "Hey? What was that?" would not be an improvement.)

Furthermore, Hampton seems to have confused the misleading term "cold-blooded" with actually chilly. A cold-blooded animal takes on the temperature of its surroundings, so the newborn child wouldn't have felt cold, but rather especially warm, having just been taken from the blood-temperature womb of its mother.

But in a film that is at heart so stupid, it's pointless to complain about lack of logic. Nonetheless, an important point is illustrated; as Jack Kruschen said in *War of the Worlds*, don't mess around with something when you don't know what it is. Hampton seems to have known nothing about England or snakes, apparently getting all his information on both from movies. The town in the movie is a thudding stereotype, with pink-cheeked barmaids, constables on bikes, a witchy midwife, a harrumphing pukka sahib, and warm beer. The characterizations aren't drawn in broad strokes, they are simply shorthand means of reminding us of similar characters we've seen in other films with this setting.

The *Monthly Film Bulletin* justly gave the film a rating of III. "A lurid shocker, set in a North country village in the 1890s [actually most takes place in 1910 or later]. Direction, acting and script are all so painfully inept and primitive that the film might well date from the same period."

"Tube" in *Variety* thought it a "second-rate supporting number for a horror package ... equally unsound in dramatic structure ... and horror content.... [Director Furie] succeeds in instilling an eerie mood, but meets with little success in attempting to deal credibly with Hampton's flimsy fiction. At times the interpretation hovers about a step away from lapsing into a parody of itself, which might have been a more sensible concept to begin with."

Raymond Durgnat, a somewhat surprising critic to be found reviewing the likes of *The Snake Woman*, said in *Films and Filming*, "There are scripts that we ordinary mortals are powerless against, and on reading this one Sidney Furie must have muttered 'It's the curse' and resigned himself, perhaps with a faint hope of creating a real collector's piece. The most rhetorical dialogue is delivered 'realistically' in close-up, to hilarious effect. The snake-girl ... speaks in purest charm-school.... The script is full of clumsy re-tellings of the story, and the trickwork is dismal. The photography is competent, and there are some nice shots of snakes, the real ones being more impressive than the rubber ones, but even these are overdone by the end of the first scene. All in all the producer's best hope is to offer £10,000 to the first spectator to die laughing."

Valley of the Dragons

Perhaps too often, the major source of satisfaction for directors of low-budget films lay not in the quality of the finished work, but in bringing in anything under difficult conditions, on or under budget. In *Fantastic Films* #38, director Edward Bernds told interviewer Tom Weaver about his pleasure in finishing *Valley of the Dragons*: "I had the satisfaction of thwarting the Columbia brass, who were waiting for us to go over budget."

I'm pleased that Mr. Bernds was happy in completing the film on budget. However, the film isn't any good at all, so his own satisfaction is about the only pleasure he's given anyone with this picture, which he also wrote. It uses the premise of Jules Verne's *Hector Servadac*, but is primarily constructed from very extensive stock footage from *One Million B.C.* (1940), a film already heavily mined by previous cut-rate filmmakers.

According to the Bernds interview in *Fantastic Films*, Donald, son of producer Al Zimbalist, found the 1877 Verne book in a British shop. Bernds was convinced the book had never been published in the United States, but it saw print here as *Off on a Comet*, the title by which it is best known. It was published in England under two titles, the original French (the name of the leading character), and *The Career of a Comet*. It also seems to be known as *Mr. Servandac's Arc*.

Under any title, it's one of Verne's oddest books. A comet brushes against the Earth in North Africa, and sweeps away Hector Servadac, who finds a strange mixture of life on the comet. There are dinosaurs, other prehistoric animals and human beings, indicating the various times the comet had previously grazed the Earth.

Bernds did accurately remark on one aspect of the novel fortunately omitted from the film (under the circumstances, it's hard to imagine how it could have been fitted in, even if anyone wanted to). Like many other Frenchmen of his time, Verne seems to have been virulently anti–Semitic; he usually kept this trait in check, but apparently indulged himself in *Hector Servadac*.

Although all he had done was find the book, Donald Zimbalist asked for story credit on the film, and proud daddy gave it to him. Zimbalist was enthusiastic about the project, apparently pleased at finding a Verne novel before someone beat him to it. (And apparently also unaware of the many other, highly filmable, Verne novels which even yet await being made into movies.) He told Murray Shumach of the *New York Times* News Service (in an undated clipping in my old scrapbook) that "Jules Verne is as big a name as Marlon Brando. Maybe bigger. Verne has never had a flop. And there is no limit to how much money you can make with Verne.... Verne is for any size budget. If you want to spend millions like Mike Todd [on *Around the World in 80 Days*], you can spend. If you want to spend less than half a million, like me [Zimbalist's actual budget: .125 of a million], that's okay, too. With Verne you don't have to have Marilyn Monroe." (Shumach himself said that "one advantage shared equally by high and low budget producers is that Verne is in public domain.")

Zimbalist went on. "Verne is the purest kind of escapism, and at the same time he is timely. His books have imagination, adventure, danger, even terrible beasts. You don't have to go in for violence with Verne. You can even try for a little comedy here and there." Of course, Zimbalist said, there was a drawback. "One thing about Verne, whatever you say about his imagination and genius, he just did not have a good storyline." Not enough sex no doubt.

The storyline of *Valley of the Dragons* is that of *One Million B.C.*, with dialogue, two duelists from Earth and fake Morlocks added, taking place on Verne's comet. Bernds seems to have little opportunity at varying the story, as he used so very much of the old film. The names of the Rock and Shell people are changed to the Cave and River people, but the same conflicts recur. It is basically a remake.

In 1881, Capt. Hector Servadac (Cesare Danova) and Michael Denning (Sean McClory) prepare to fight a duel in Algeria, but a strange light in the sky, followed by a tremendous wind and what seems to be an earthquake, break up their fight. When the men recover their equilibrium, they find their seconds have vanished, and the nearby desert has been replaced by a lush valley full of mastodons and giant armadillos.

A big lizard chases them into a cave, then fights with another big lizard with a fin on its back. They are also attacked by a giant spider left over from *World Without End* (also directed by Bernds). After the big arachnid is killed, the two men agree to forget their duel, and work together to survive in this strange world.

After seeing the Earth in the sky, they deduce they are somewhere else. In fact, true to Verne, they are off on a comet which bumped into the Earth at Algeria and swept away the portion they happened to be standing on at the time.

They encounter some Cave People, who flee. Servadac and Denning dress themselves in fur garments they steal from the Cave People's cave, but then a mammoth knocks Servadac off a cliff, and Denning thinks he is dead.

However, Servadac is found by Deena (Joan Staley), a beautiful member of the River People tribe, and she takes him home to meet the family, who accept him.

In the meantime, Denning saves Patoo (I. Stanford Jolley) of the Cave People from a musk ox, and Patoo takes Denning home to meet his daughter, Nateeta (Daniele de Metz, who was in Bernds' *Return of the Fly*). Denning impresses Nateeta when he defeats Anoka (Mike Lane, the monster of *Frankenstein 1970*) in a fight.

Meanwhile back at the River People, Deena and Servadac fall in love; he wins her respect when he saves a little girl from a prehistoric monster. This also impresses her tribe. Servadac finds the ingredients to make gunpowder, and he and Deena are poking around a cave when they are attacked by what the Columbia synopsis calls a "teranodon." The two are separated, and she's almost killed by a group of albino troglodytes in awful makeup modeled after the Morlocks in *The Time Machine*. Give Bernds and Zimbalist a break, though; apart from the opening, this stuff in the cave is about the only part of the storyline not dictated by *One Million B.C.*

Deena flees the caverns and is captured by the Cave People, surprising Denning when she speaks English. This indicates that Servadac is alive somewhere. (Although why Servadac would not teach Deena *French* is a good question.)

The River People and Cave People start to fight, a volcano explodes, Deena and Denning meet Servadac while separated from the River People. Using homemade dynamite, Servadac saves the Cave People from some big lizards, also with the help of the River People. Both tribes become friends.

Servadac and Denning know the comet will return in seven years (astronomically as preposterous as everything else), at which time they can step across, or something. Until then they have Nateeta and Deena to console them over the loss of their home planet.

Aside from the business of the comet swiping parts of Earth, there's no real connection with Verne's whimsical, imaginative story. The book features a tour of the solar system, and though the basic idea is outrageous, Verne tried to tell a good story.

But the film was a business deal, not a creative enterprise, a way to make a

Verne movie without spending much money. Bernds told Weaver he already knew both Zimbalist and his partner Byron Roberts, and was hired to put together the Verne story and the *One Million B.C.* stock footage. Using as little creativity in handling stock footage as I have ever seen, Bernds assembled— correct term—*Valley of the Dragons*. He told Weaver, "I used the Jules Verne premise of the comet scooping up the men and taking them into outer space.... I wrote about a ten-page outline and Al Zimbalist took it to Columbia in New York ... and sold the deal.... The Columbia executives in Hollywood were not pleased at all; Al had gone over their heads to make the deal." They were prepared to take any over-the-budget costs out of the money going to Zimbalist and Roberts, but Bernds brought the film in on budget. As Weaver correctly points out, "Whatever ... flaws the film may have had, for Bernds it remains a personal triumph."

But, of course, the film *is* an abortion. The use of stock footage fooled almost no one; first, it simply *looked* like stock footage, with the costuming in the style of the early 1940s. But more importantly, and disastrously for audience acceptance of the film, much of it had been seen again and again already. In *Tarzan's Desert Mystery* (1943), *The Adventures of Superman* (1948), *Jungle Manhunt*, *Untamed Women*, *Robot Monster*, *King Dinosaur*, *Two Lost Worlds*, *Teenage Caveman* and many TV shows. Furthermore, the original film was by that time being shown widely on television. *Valley of the Dragons* looked painfully familiar.

Instead of Bronson Caverns, Bernds used a big mountainside set left over from *Devil at Four O'Clock* (not all that much better than *Valley of the Dragons*) for all his cave and rocky-area scenery. The film was made entirely in the studio, and looks it.

None of this borrowing of stock footage would have mattered overly much if Bernds and Zimbalist had been an exciting, well-paced film, but *Valley of the Dragons* is a lethargic, uninteresting mess. Cesare Danova is a dull hero; Sean McClory, generally amusing, is much better, and would have been even more entertaining if he'd been allowed to be a little shifty, something at which he excels.

The trade reviewers recognized the film for the patchwork piece it is, and reviewed it accordingly. James Powers in *Hollywood Reporter* thought it would "have some success as an exploitation feature." Allen M. Widem of the *Motion Picture Herald* called the film "improbable improvisations of a kind and situation best welcomed by the not too discriminating audience."

Parents didn't like it. "For the first time a movie has not done right by author Jules Verne! ... This is a slipshod sex and horror film with a few scientific theories mouthed by the actors.... Poor."

"Tube," in *Variety*, called it for what it was, "a corny caveman spectacle that is shopworn even by 20-year-old cinema standards.... Even the story here related is astonishingly similar to that fossiliferous fricassee of two decades ago.... Bernds' direction is mechanically capable, considering the patchwork aspect of his chore."

There was a cheap Australian cartoon version of the novel, shown on U.S. TV. Also, in 1970, the great Czechoslovakian fantasy filmmaker Karel Zeman filmed his own version of *Hector Servadac*, called *Na Komete*, which has had few or no showings in the United States. Now available on videotape, perhaps it will help obliterate the fading memory of *Valley of the Dragons*. Although ingenious, it was no one's finest hour.

Voyage to the Bottom of the Sea

Despite a fast pace, good special effects and a lively, amused performance by Walter Pidgeon, *Voyage to the Bottom of the Sea* is so amazingly stupid in terms of both science and fiction that it's almost a total failure; dramatically, it sucks rocks. Nonetheless, it was profitable, and generated the long-running (1964–68) TV series of the same name.

The basic premise of the film is so preposterous that it's hard to imagine how anyone even considered presenting the idea. The Van Allen Radiation Belts (discovered by *Explorer I* three years earlier) are two belts of radioactively charged particles circulating along Earth's magnetic field. These belts exist outside the Earth's atmosphere, and yet in the film, the Van Allen Radiation Belts *catch on fire*. Not only is there not enough oxygen at that height to sustain combustion, there's about as much chance of belts of radiation catching fire as there is of a beam of sunlight bursting into flames.

Furthermore, when at the beginning of the film, the Belts ignite, this somehow sinks icebergs. Now, the only way icebergs could sink would be if they were suddenly to become more dense than water. While I don't expect moviemakers to realize that (a) the ocean is saltwater, more dense than fresh, and (b) icebergs are freshwater, less dense than the ocean they float in, I would at least expect them to realize, simply from glancing at their own gin and tonics, that *ice floats*. Yet at the beginning, the big submarine that's the central and best feature of the movie is almost crushed by a subsea rain of icebergs. There must be a causal connection between the fire in the sky and the sinking icebergs, but it's not mentioned.

Theodore Sturgeon, a fine writer, was hired to write the novel based on the film. While he was a "soft" science fiction writer rather than one dealing in "hard" science, Sturgeon still had enough scientific knowledge to try, in a rather embarrassed fashion, to explain just how a radiation belt could burst into flames, and how icebergs might sink.

If the film had attempted to make such explanations, it would still be a mediocrity. There's nothing but trite characterizations, coincidental "crises" and rotten dialogue from beginning to end. If this turkey could sing like a canary and have all its science be precisely correct, if speculative, it would still be a turkey.

The source of the baseness of the film is the producer referred to by John Brosnan (in *Future Tense*) as "the dread Irwin Allen." More about Mr. Allen later.

The film opens aboard the *Seaview*, a sleek, attractive submarine with a flared bow and windows in the front. Although it is neither in the U.S. Navy nor the U.S. Merchant Marine, it seems to have a connection with the American government; everyone wears uniforms, and naval titles and discipline are used throughout. I suppose this is because Fox (or Allen) thought audiences would not accept a nonmilitary submarine.

The *Seaview* was designed by Admiral Harriman Nelson (Walter Pidgeon), aboard with some visiting dignitaries, including psychiatrist Dr. Susan Hiller (Joan Fontaine), studying the effects of prolonged confinement on human behavior. Inasmuch as Dr. Hiller later turns out to be the secret saboteur plaguing the ship, it would seem to be a notable case of physician-heal-thyself.

The *Seaview* is under the North Polar Cap on its shakedown cruise when those suddenly-heavy icebergs come raining down around her. The ship surfaces, and Nelson and the *Seaview*'s captain, Lee Crane (Robert Sterling), come out onto deck to see the entire sky aflame from horizon to horizon. Meteor activity has set afire the Van Allen Belt of Radiation (as they're called in the film), and it's obvious that soon the Earth will be destroyed by the heat. As Nelson says later, "This planet is impaled on a roasting spit."

The *Seaview* heads back to the United States at once, while Nelson and his old friend Commodore Lucius Emery (Peter Lorre) struggle to find a solution to the problem of a fire in the sky. In a nod to tradition or something, they use slide rules rather than the sub's elaborate onboard computer to work out their calculations. Television aboard the ship shows (in stock footage) the Ural Mountains, the Black Forest and French timberlands all ablaze. (Of course, if the air had become so hot as to cause pine needles to spontaneously burst into flame, as implied, it would have been all over for animal life long before.)

Finally, the two have things figured out. "It clicks on the nose," Nelson says in a peculiarly mixed metaphor. "It has to be the 29th." We are forced to accept that Nelson is the smartest scientist in the whole world; why is he the only one to have come up with the answer? It's too bad the film didn't allow the possibility that he might be wrong; that would have increased the realism of the characterizations and added real suspense.

In New York, Nelson speaks before the highly skeptical United Nations assembly. His chief rival (Henry Daniell) is Dr. Zucco (!), a suavely arrogant genius who feels there is no need to take direct action against the fiery belt, for it will burn itself out at 173° (Fahrenheit, one fervently hopes). On the other hand, Nelson feels that the belt must be snuffed out with a Polaris missile launched at precisely the right spot and precisely the right moment on the 29th; we'll lose our angle of trajectory otherwise, he explains. If the bomb is not set off, he says, the heat from the burning belt will continue to rise; when it reaches 175° all human life will die (as if a 2° rise would make that much difference—but of course, all this is utterly ridiculous, and in the story only to give a time-and-space limit to actions for purpose of suspense—a ticking clock).

Nelson wants to go set off the bomb, which will increase the belt's radiation and thereby (?) fling it away from the Earth. The U.N. sees this as being something potentially catastrophic and which therefore must be prevented. There's no reason to think that this measly bomb would be anywhere near as dangerous as the burning radiation belt, but Nelson is told to cease and desist in his plans.

But because he's the greatest scientific mind in the world, as well as a pig-headed old military man, he knows he must persevere. Pursued by authorities, he and his crew flee back to the *Seaview* and make their getaway.

Also on board are traditional types: there's Cathy Connors (Barbara Eden), Nelson's gorgeous secretary sort of going with Captain Crane; boyish, enthusiastic ensign Chip Romano (Frankie Avalon); and a recently-rescued religious fanatic, Miguel Alvarez (Michael Ansara), who wanders around holding a puppy dog, and who is against any attempts to snuff out the burning radiation. "Man must accept what is ordained," he says.

As they head for the Marianas in the Pacific, the Right Spot, the crew of the *Seaview* learns that the Panama Canal is impassable—as if they could somehow sneak through, eluding authorities on their trail—so they will have to go around the Cape of Good Hope. This involves tapping the transatlantic telephone cable to get certain information. Miguel, Chip and the apparently-expendable Captain Crane go out in colorful neoprene suits to try to find the cable (you'd think the great pressure would present some problems). This is done, but a giant squid grabs Crane and almost kills him before he's rescued by Miguel. Asked why he did that, in apparent violation of God's commandments (after all, the giant squid is presumably as much one of God's creatures as Crane, perhaps more so), Miguel says that his "hand was guided by the Lord."

The sub makes its way through a bunch of mines left over from World War II; a minisub is launched to cut the mine cables with crewmen Smith and Gleason aboard. Since none of the high-paid actors are on the little submarine, we know it is going to buy it, which it does, kaboom. Some water from unspecified sources briefly pours into the Seaview (apparently self-sealing, like a tubeless tire), causing colorful, sparkling explosions which do no harm. In the meantime, there have been some acts of sabotage, but Lieutenant Hodges kills himself, leaving behind a note taking blame for the problems.

Suddenly—and much in this film happens suddenly—a derelict yacht is spotted. Apparently everyone on board died of heatstroke or something. Around this time, there have been subdued mutters of mutiny from some of the more disloyal members of the Seaview crew, so Nelson and Crane allow those who don't trust the admiral's plan to go aboard the yacht (to die of heatstroke?). Quite a few do. Miguel stays behind, and in the only intelligent line in the film says, shrugging, "Stay or go, what's the difference? What will be, will be." (Lucius snarls, "That guy gets on my nerves." Mine too.)

Based on little other than uneasiness, by this time Crane himself (but never the audience) has begun to doubt the wisdom of Nelson's plan, and announces that he's going to put the admiral in custody. "Not arrest, sir," he explains apologetically but firmly, "I'm placing you on a sick list." As Nelson has behaved just the same all the way through the film, this seems arbitrary and just what it is: a plot device.

But just at this moment (coincidentally as usual), some submarines ordered to sink the Seaview before it can launch the missile turn up. Instead of continuing with his arrest of Nelson and surrendering peacefully, Crane gets his dander up and they decide to flee from the subs which are by now firing torpedoes. The supersub dives deep into the Marianas Trench and, by another swell coincidence, is grabbed by a titanic octopus. In the meantime, the pressure of the great depths crushes one pursuing sub and disables the other. An electrical current shot through the outer hull of the Seaview discourages the octopus.

The Seaview surfaces and as it's just about time to fire the missile, Dr. Hiller shows her true colors and reveals that she's the saboteur. (Her motivations go unexplained.) However, she's exposed herself to a fatal amount of radiation and, oops, falls over the dangerously low catwalk around Lucius' shark tank. I hope the sharks didn't die of radiation.

Okay, so now the missile can be launched, right? Nope. Miguel has finally decided that God needs some help—like most religious fanatics, it doesn't occur to him that his opponent might be following God's will—and threatens to explode a grenade, as if that would stop anything. "God's will is written across the heavens," he says.

However, he is overcome, the missile is launched. And, of course, as we knew from the beginning, it does the trick and the burning radiation belt is blown out like a big candle.

The screenplay for Voyage to the Bottom of the Sea is by Charles Bennett and Irwin Allen, although I suspect Allen was more responsible for it than Bennett. Then again, after 1954, Bennett rarely produced anything worthwhile; before that, however, his credits are impressive. He wrote or cowrote several films for Alfred Hitchcock, including *Blackmail* (1929), *The Man Who Knew Too Much* (1934), *The Thirty-Nine Steps* (1935), *Secret Agent, Sabotage, A Woman Alone* (all 1936), *Young and Innocent* (1937) and, in the United States, *Foreign Correspondent* (1940). After that, according to Donald Spoto in *The Dark Side of Genius*, Hitchcock severed almost all professional and social connections with Bennett, apparently choosing to make his movies as American as possible.

While this wasn't a bad decision for Hitchcock in the long run—few would disagree that most of his greatest films were made after 1940—it must have been a severe blow to Bennett, whose scripts for Hitchcock had been extremely good. It may serve to explain why (according to Spoto), years later Bennett told Hitchcock that *Psycho* was the work of "a sadistic son of a bitch." The same year that *Psycho* was released, Irwin Allen's *The Lost World*, co-written with Bennett, came out. *The Lost World* may not have been the work of a sadistic son of a bitch, but it was a hell of a lot worse than *Psycho*.

Bennett also wrote other notable films, including *King Solomon's Mines* (1937) and *Kind Lady* (1951). In the 40s, he worked for the only major producer to top Irwin Allen in vulgarity, Cecil B. DeMille, and worked on *Reap the Wild Wind* (1942, also featuring a giant squid), *The Story of Dr. Wassell* (1944) and *Unconquered* (1947). Perhaps Bennett felt he needed to collaborate with a strong producer or director. In DeMille he found one who occasionally made a good movie; in Irwin Allen, he found one who seems almost incapable of doing so.

Missing from the films he wrote for Allen, which include *The Story of Mankind* (1957), *The Big Circus* (1959) and *Five Weeks in a Balloon* (1962), as well as *The Lost World* and *Voyage to the Bottom of the Sea*, are wit, intelligence and structure. It's difficult to believe that a writer who could have created the dialogue in the Hitchcock films could have come up with the lame language found in the Irwin Allen pictures.

The film opens with naked exposition (the same idea was later used in *The Concorde Airport '79*): a TV announcer simply *tells* us all about Admiral Nelson, his *Seaview* and an airplane bringing a congressman to the sub. We are also carefully told that Nelson is a visionary: Crane says, "You taught us at Annapolis [that] the wild dreams of today are the practical reality of tomorrow." (That's the general apologia for science fiction by people who are not comfortable with it.)

This is the same Nelson who explains that the ballast system aboard the sub works like an elevator, it takes us up and lets us down. So do rockets and yo-yos. Marveling at the roomy, glossy interior of the *Seaview*, equipped with thousands of blinking lights, turning reels and switches, someone says, "Not even Jules Verne dreamed of anything like this." (The title was intended to remind us of Verne, of course.) I suspect Verne would not have written an open-topped aquarium into any story he set aboard a moving craft, and his plots were usually much better than this one.

The special effects, under the direction of L.B. Abbott, are bright and colorful but unconvincing. They are expensive enough that things look as though we *should* find them convincing, so they at least pass muster on a certain level remote from criticism. There are several good underwater shots of the *Seaview* gliding by (every one of these shots turned up again and again in the TV series), and other miniature work is elaborately detailed. The burning radiation belt is at least awesome, although it seems unlikely that a belt of fire around the equator could be seen from the North Pole.

The film's giant squid is second-rate; we see only its head and arms; the stunt double for Sterling is quite obviously wrapping himself in the unyielding tentacles. The octopus, a real one, is much more successful, but there's a poverty of imagination shown in having as menaces two cephalopods recognizable to most audiences.

The effects in general are as usual, matte shots, matte paintings and miniatures. There's little originality in terms of design or execution, but it's good medium-budget major-studio stuff for the period, and the effects are plentiful.

Walter Pidgeon is clearly having a great time; it doesn't seem to matter to him that the dialogue is terrible. Nelson is a big, showy role he can sink his acting teeth into, and he surely does. Loud, firm and domineering, Pidgeon, by far the liveliest performer, steals the show from everyone; occasionally, he's fun to watch. It's no surprise that, according to rumors, he detests *Forbidden Planet* and loves *Voyage to the Bottom of the Sea*. This stereotyped military genius was obviously more accessible to Pidgeon as an actor, and he shows none of the peculiar (but naturalistic and pleasing) hesitation that marked his performance in the earlier film.

Peter Lorre is helplessly lost, as he was from the early 50s on. He rarely appeared in a major film, and even the halfway decent films he made for Roger Corman in the 1960s probably embarrassed him. Lorre was quite literally one of the greatest actors ever to appear in movies, and, like all truly great actors, he was unique and irreplaceable. He should have been cast with great and loving care, but people used him for his screen image, not his ability; his unusualness probably stymied even imaginative casting directors.

In *Voyage to the Bottom of the Sea*, he has almost nothing to do, unless you consider walking around in a shallow tank with a rubber shark something like a performance. Although the script insists on it, due to the direction and the dialogue, there is no feeling of friendship between Lucius and Nelson. They're just in the same film together. And about all the dialogue allows for Lorre are little meaningless asides: "Harry, take it easy" is a highlight. As Stephen Youngkin, James Bigwood and Raymond G. Cabana, Jr. said in their estimable *Films of Peter Lorre*, "It is truly depressing to watch Peter Lorre and Joan Fontaine, twenty years after their charming and subtle performances in *The Constant Nymph*, trapped in the unrelenting mediocrity of *Voyage to the Bottom of the Sea*. The ludicrous script is hackneyed, unimaginative and obvious, peopled with characters that do not even qualify as cardboard. They are paper cutouts, too flimsy to stand up without help ... not provided by the script, the direction or even the special effects."

Joan Fontaine, Robert Sterling, Frankie Avalon and Barbara Eden have little to do in terms of acting; each role is a broad generalization, even less real than a stereotype: Confused Psychiatrist, Brave Captain, Spunky Youth and Girlfriend of Brave Captain. All of them have been acceptable, even good at other times, but in this picture, they could have been replaced by inflated dolls.

Michael Ansara is a little more colorful, but he's just another generalization: Religious Fanatic. However, by the very nature of religious fanatics, even inconsistent ones, he's got more to do. Henry Daniell makes the most of his Doubting-Thomas smug scientist; his slimy suaveness helped every film he was ever in.

The film was produced and directed by Irwin Allen, one of the great mediocrities of our time. Born in 1916, Allen began as a magazine editor, and later was the producer and director of a Hollywood radio show. It should come as no surprise to those familiar with Allen's busily self-promoted career that he owned an advertising agency before he began working in films in the early 50s.

His first significant effort was *The Sea Around Us* (1953), taking its title but little else from Rachel Carson's well-known book. The film was composed primarily of stock shots, with little (if any) new material. Still, it was a modest box-office success and led to his next project, *The Animal World* (1956). Like *The Sea Around Us*, most of *The Animal World* was made of previously-filmed footage of animal life, but he did commission some gaudy, underfinanced stop-motion footage of dinosaurs animated by Willis O'Brien and Ray Harryhausen, in a period when most producers were ignoring O'Brien.

Allen turned up the next year with *The Story of Mankind*, an astonishing aberration notable solely for its bizarre cast, which included Vincent Price as the Devil. It certainly owed nothing to the Hendrik van Loon book from which it took its title. It was the last film for actors as varied as Ronald Colman and Harpo Marx. (Harpo played Sir Isaac Newton, which may give you a rough idea of the level of seriousness of this movie calamity.)

Fortunately, Allen didn't direct his next production, *The Big Circus*, which makes it among his most watchable films.

But unfortunately for followers of science fiction, Allen arrived at 20th Century–Fox just as that studio seems to have made the decision to move up from medium-budget SF films like *The Fly* to somewhat bigger-budgeted ones for "the entire family," prompted by the success of *Journey to the Center of the Earth*. (See notes on that film for the resemblances between it and Allen's films for Fox.) *The Lost World* and *Bottom of the Sea* were apparently quite successful, *Five Weeks in a Balloon* much less so.

Allen then moved into television, producing the TV series of "Voyage to the Bottom of the Sea." The only actor retained from the movie was Del(bert) Monroe, who played "Kowski" in the film and "Kowalksy" in the series. Richard Basehart was Nelson, David Hedison was Crane, and Robert Dowdell was Chip Morton. Other actors in the series included Henry Kulky, Terry Becker, Allan Hunt, Paul Trinka and Richard Bull.

The same sets and often much of the same footage were reused for the series, which overall was slightly better than the movie. But Allen's pernicious influence couldn't be shaken, and the series eventually fell into a series of ruts (it changed its format occasionally). There was the imitation James Bond formula; there was the magnified sea-creature format, with men in funny-looking suits tossing around the giant miniature of the *Seaview*; there was the what-got-aboard-*this*-time, with crewmen battling fairies, leprechauns, magicians, and so forth; and there was the "I-know-you-say-you're-Admiral-Nelson-but-who-are-you-*really*?" format, in which alien beings or other malign beings took over or duplicated crew members. The series finally sank without outcries from fans, although, except for the earliest, black-and-white episodes, it is still in syndication.

Allen produced other SF series for Fox, including "Lost in Space" (1965–68), "Time Tunnel" (1966–67) and "Land of the Giants" (1968–70), but none of them developed the following of "Voyage to the Bottom of the Sea." Except for a brief comeback with the typically childish, obvious and bad "Swiss Family Robinson" series in the mid-70s, Allen has not been directly involved with series TV. And why should he? In 1972, he produced *The Poseidon Adventure*, one of the biggest commercial successes in the history of movies.

Allen is certainly no fool when it comes to promoting, but he does make other kinds of mistakes. Having launched (or rather rediscovered) the disaster genre, he promptly drove it into the ground by simply remaking the same film again and again, with a new all-star cast and a new kind of disaster, but this had such diminishing returns (especially in terms of quality) that by the time his last such film was released, great care was taken in the advertising to hide the fact that it was, indeed, a disaster film. He burned up a big building in *The Towering Inferno* (1974), unleashed a flock of killer bees in *The Swarm* (1978, his worst film), found that ship again in *Beyond the Poseidon Adventure* (1979), and set off a volcano on a Pacific island in *When Time Ran Out...* (1980). He also did several disaster films for television, but a couple of those were so bad that they, too, were held back and given slightly misleading titles when finally shown. He also did a few SF movies for TV, hoping they would generate series: *The City Beneath the Sea* (1970), *The Time Travelers* (1976) and *The Return of Captain Nemo* (1978).

In the last few years, little has been heard from Irwin Allen; he's almost unnecessary, now that we have been inflicted with Glen A. Larson, virtually Irwin Allen, Jr. in his efforts at making a shambles of science fiction.

I think that Irwin Allen may have been (however undeliberately) one of the worst things that ever happened to filmed science fiction; he may have been a primary cause in preventing the field from developing on television in a more dignified manner than it did. Those who came to think of Irwin Allen and science fiction as being firmly linked probably hated the genre (in two different seasons, he had three SF TV series on the air). He did the same with the disaster movie subgenre.

There are some producers who have gotten a bad name who didn't really deserve it, but Irwin Allen has never made any science fiction (TV, series, feature) that could be called good. All of his TV series, all of his SF movies, are not only bad, but notoriously so. He's not a villain out to destroy SF, merely a commercially-minded man who has latched onto what seemed to be a good thing. Judging from his work, I presume that he just doesn't have the foggiest idea of what good science fiction is. He was probably puzzled by the success of *Star Wars*, *2001* and *Close Encounters*: they didn't have any of the elements Allen seems to think must be included in SF. (Although he was probably comforted by the presence of the funny robots in the *Star Wars* series.)

Reviews of *Voyage* weren't all unfavorable because, for one thing, critics seemed not only to expect but hope for the worst from science fiction films; by 1962, they could hardly be blamed.

Howard Thompson in the *New York Times* liked the trappings of *Voyage to the Bottom of the Sea*. "Good color, handsome photographic effects and a submarine to end them all make [the film] a mildly diverting but far from memorable screen plunge.... Lubricated with a little wit and human perception, the result could have been a sleekly fetching thriller [but it becomes] increasingly absurd and not a little dull. The same applies to the starchy dialogue, the slackening pace and the triumphant fadeout, with the cast barely glancing overhead."

"Tube" in *Variety* reviewed the film, appropriately enough, as a commodity, describing it as a "fast-paced if dramatically unsound sci-fi adventure." Arthur Knight in the *Saturday Review* was unaccountably impressed, saying it "is the kind of stirring adventure tale artfully designed to take one's mind off the heat and international tensions."

Paul V. Beckley in the New York *Herald-Tribune* found the film to have unsavory ideology. "*Voyage* follows the rather common practice of introducing little bits of everything that might appeal in passing to any conceivable hobby of any conceivable audience and yet, in the final analysis, is essentially a children's picture.... The picture seems to be dedicated to the proposition that an eminent man with a theory ought to be allowed to try it out even though it may be at the risk of the world.... The very fact that the film is so obviously intended for children made me uneasy about its unquestioning obedience to a strong man's will."

Giving the film its lowest rating, the *Monthly Film Bulletin* fairly bristled. "This is a vapid piece of science fiction, hysterical and jingoistic of tone. The action jerks from one unrelated crisis to the next, stumbling over each superfluous, inconsistent and generally incongruous character in its path to arrive at a foregone, stagy conclusion. The dialogue is fatuous rather than funny."

More recently, some have expressed a certain admiration for it. Even the usually discerning *Psychotronic* considers it "Irwin Allen's best film," which really may not be that much praise. (It does helpfully note that the underwater photography is by John Lamb, who did the same for *Mermaids of Tiburon*.)

Don Willis (I) is nearer the mark: "Fairly good special effects don't quite atone for a plot full of amazing coincidences, dull incidents, incredible theories and ridiculous speeches."

Quite a bit of money was expended on this lackluster film, while better scripts received less money than they needed. If it's made for children, it ignores many of the things they like in favor of simple visual flash and flare; if adults are to be attracted, they'd be repelled by the stupidity of the whole venture. Yet obviously I was in the minority in disliking the film when it was first released, and even I liked it better then than I do now. The movie was successful. You sometimes can get rich by playing to the lowest common denominator of the audience.

The Brain That Wouldn't Die

As my associate Bill Thomas has noted in an uncompleted article, this cheap, ugly film "has an insidious anti-transplant tone and a pervading deep cynicism and tone of disappointment, dissatisfaction, despair, depravity, deprivation and deceit." The six deadly Ds?* The cynicism lies more in the existence of the film, as the makers assumed that almost any garbage would be salable. They were almost wrong. They filmed *The Brain That Wouldn't Die* in 1959 as "The Black Door," later calling it "The Head That Wouldn't Die" before finally unleashing it on an "appalled public," as *Psychotronic* put it.

But the gloomy, tawdry movie does conclude on a note of despair. In *The Frankenstein Legend*, Don Glut reveals that a sequel was planned, an idea almost too depressing to even consider.

Almost everything is unforgivably bad in *The Brain That Wouldn't Die*; even the sets look cheap and cramped. The interior of a mansion consists of one basement lab and one entranceway, nothing else. Apartments are couches against walls. The camerawork is dull and pedestrian; the sound makes everyone's voices seem like they were recorded in a soundproof room. (Which they probably were.) The direction is almost nonexistent, with the only "stylistic" flourish being a series of road signs the leading character passes as he rushes on toward doom: STOP, CURVE, WINDING ROAD. But we see the car placidly tooling along a straight, flat road.

Plastic surgeon Dr. Cortner (Bruce Brighton) still works as a regular surgeon at times, and gives up on a patient under the knife. Despite Dr. Cortner's assertion that the "human body is not a jigsaw puzzle to experiment on," his surgeon son Bill (Herb Evers) is given permission to try some radical techniques on the patient, and he applies electrical stimulus to the brain while massaging the heart; this hardly seems radical, but it does revive the patient.

Dr. Cortner is impressed but not grateful. "Don't try to play God," he says; "there are things you shouldn't do." Doesn't anyone who writes these cheap pictures recall that such lines are heavily overused? Probably—but they also probably don't care.

Bill wants to do transplants, but is told it just isn't possible. "The line between scientific genius and obsessive fanaticism is a thin one," Dr. Cortner warns his son. We learn that Bill has been stealing amputated limbs from the hospital for some ungodly purpose (we later learn what it is). Bill and his assistant Kurt (Leslie Daniel) have been taking the limbs to Dr. Cortner's "mountain home," which the older man no longer visits. He says the place gives him the creeps.

Kurt phones Bill about an emergency at the secret lab, so Bill hops into her car with his fiancée Jan (Virginia Leith), and they go roaring out into the country. Bill's reckless driving causes a disaster: the car plunges off the road and Bill is thrown clear. He rushes over to the burning car and wraps something in his coat, then dashes off to the "mountain home," conveniently near. The something, we soon learn, is Jan's head. I'm not sure what Bill expected the police to think when they found Jan's body in the wrecked car sans her head; this question never comes up.

In the lab, Bill and Kurt quickly place the head in a photo-developing tray,

*Bill was especially important in preparing the comments on this film.

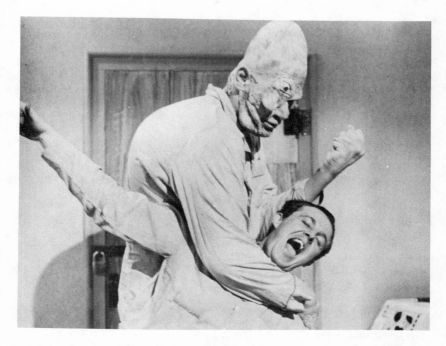

Leslie Daniel (presumably) meets his end at the very large hands of monster Eddie Carmel in the climax of The Brain That Wouldn't Die (1962); the makeup is credited, if that's the word, to George Fiala. There's a question about this picture: the victim doesn't really look much like either lab assistant Daniel or mad scientist Jason Evers. Does anyone know what's what?

hook it up to appropriate tubes and wires, and keep it alive. Bill figures it can survive for maybe 50 hours without his getting a new body for Jan.

Kurt wonders if the severed head can really be called Jan. Bill declares that "there's a pattern to all that lives. She had a heart and a brain and her spirit was in both, not one or the other." Warming to his theme of patterns: "Life has a pattern. The whole pattern of my life is shaping itself to save her now."

Before Bill returns to town to look for a fresh body, we learn he'd earlier grafted a new left arm on Kurt, but it didn't work right; the arm is withered and useless. Bill departs in search of bodies.

In a closet in the lab, Bill and Kurt have a gurgling, grunting monster confined. Kurt got antsy over its latest mad rages in confinement, and it was his call over this that led to the fatal car crash.

In town, Bill meets an old girlfriend and tries to pick her up as a replacement body for Jan, but another woman arrives and they briefly fight. The camera cuts to a painting of cats, and we hear meowing on the sound track, another instance of the sheer raw style of writer-director Joseph Green.

Meanwhile, back at the lab, Jan has bitterly begun telepathic communication with the thing in the closet, which answers her with yes-no thumps. Kurt creeps downstairs as the head converses with the monster, and looks puzzled. We don't really know at any time if Kurt hears what the head says, even though in due course Kurt and Jan have their own conversation.

In town, Bill and the two women go to a beauty contest; he contemplates each contestant as a potential new body for Jan. (He seems to be paying more attention to his *own* needs for a woman's body than to Jan's; you'd think that he would have grabbed the first available body. Better life in a dumpy, homely body than in a developing tray, but Bill clearly has his own goals. He's looking for that body he longs to touch.)

Back at the lab, as she bitterly talks to the monster in the closet, we learn that Jan thinks Bill should have let her die. "Do you know what it's like?" she asks the monster, which replies with an affirmative thump. "My brain's still untouched," Jan says (and so is her makeup). "It's keeping me alive, it's giving me a power he didn't count on. Together we're both more than things—we're a power as hideous as our deformities. Together we'll wreak our revenge. I shall create power. And you will enforce it. You, the thing inside, me, the thing out here."

The scene cuts between Jan's gabby head and the worried assistant during the above monologue, but she soon turns her attention to Kurt. "What's behind that door?" she asks, as if she didn't know.

"Horror," Kurt replies unhelpfully. "Something no normal mind can imagine, something even more terrible than you."

"No, my deformed friend," Jan replies condescendingly. "Like all quantities, horror has its ultimate, and I am that." (There's a credit for additional dialogue; I hope it wasn't this.)

"No," Kurt politely disagrees, "there is a horror beyond yours, and it is in there." This dialogue, like something from a 1910 thriller, occurs in chunks throughout the film.

"Paths of experimentation twist and turn," Kurt goes on, "through mountains of miscalculation and often lose themselves in error and darkness. Behind that door is the sum total of Dr. Cortner's mistakes." He explains how the stolen limbs and other organs were stitched together and brought to life with the serum that is keeping Jan alive.

"It's impossible!" declares the living decapitated head.

Bill returns and joins the conversation, explaining his determination to keep Jan alive. "The alcoholic has his bottle, the dope addict has his needle. I have my research." (Which seems to be saying his research is a disastrous weakness.) And he goes out again, to Doris Powell (Adele Lamont), a pretty model whose face was injured in an accident, leaving her with a hatred of men.

He meets her at her studio apartment, still modeling in a swimsuit for a slavering group of paying "photographers." Alone, Bill overcomes Doris' cynicism with disarming candor: "I want to cut off your head" and use your body. She takes this for humor, and as his father is a noted plastic surgeon, agrees to go with him to the country lab, in the belief that he will eliminate her hideous facial deformities. (She has a small scar on her chin.)

Meanwhile back at the lab, Kurt is having trouble with Jan and the horror in the closet. Unwisely, he approaches the closet door, and through the door's window the monster seizes him by his good arm, ripping it off. He staggers up the stairs, smearing the wall with blood from his shoulder, lurches around the entranceway to the house, and returns to the lab where he collapses and dies.

Bill and Doris arrive; he promptly drugs her and prepares for decapitation. Jan, still gabby, protests this, and Bill tapes her mouth shut. But Jan telepathically urges the monster to burst out of its closet, and we see it for the first time in all its hideous glory.

The monster stands about seven feet high, clad in white shirt and pants; its head comes to a point, its mouth is distorted, and its eyes are askew. The skin seems lumpy and pale. All in all, a makeup worthy of the film it appears in.

The monster immediately grabs Bill, bites a chunk out of his neck, then removes the fragment from its mouth for the benefit of the camera. During the struggle, some flammable liquid spills, and bursts into flames. The monster grabs Doris and heads for the great outdoors, perhaps to live happily ever after. As the flames leap higher and Bill dies, Jan exults, "I told you to let me die!" This is probably not how Bill planned to spend the weekend.

The Brain That Wouldn't Die as a film lacks the ghoulish grandeur of its title, although the climax is pretty lively and extremely gory for the period.

Rex Carlton produced the film and cowrote the original story. During the 1960s and on into the 70s, he was associated with several other SF and horror films, most of which were on the same level as this one, although one he wrote, *The Unearthly Stranger* (1964) can be recommended. Among the others: he coproduced and cowrote *The Devil's Hand* (1961), about as boring a film as I've ever seen; he coproduced and wrote the truly dreadful yet unusual *Blood of Dracula's Castle* (1969); he was coexecutive producer and writer of the vigorous, sleazy *Nightmare in Wax* (1969), and was coexecutive producer of *Hell's Bloody Devils* (1970).

Herb Evers, the lead, soon changed his name to Jason Evers and came to Hollywood. (*The Brain That Wouldn't Die* was filmed in New York.) He was the star of a short-lived summer TV series in 1960, "The Wrangler," and the costar of "Channing" (1963–64); he occasionally appeared as Walter Brennan's son in "The Guns of Will Sonnett" (1967–69). He also began playing supporting roles in movies, including *House of Women* (1962), *The Green Berets*, *The Illustrated Man* (both 1968), *Escape from the Planet of the Apes* (1971), *A Piece of the Action*, *Claws* (both 1977) and *Barracuda* (1978), both the latter two being *Jaws* imitations. He was also in the TV movies *Shadow of Fear* (1970) and *Fer-De-Lance* (1974).

His part in *The Brain That Wouldn't Die* is so confused and confusing that Evers, generally an okay actor, can make nothing of it. He seems to be a standard mad-scientist type, with his experiments, dedication, and monster in the closet, but the role isn't played that way. Evers plays Bill as if no one told him this guy were written not as the hero but as the *villain*.

None of the other actors makes any impression, and few have appeared elsewhere. But then again, in a film with no sympathetic characters, and a movie that's so badly made, it's hard for anyone to make any impression at all. Bill's father presumably represents the voice of reason, but sounds more like a grouchy old curmudgeon. Kurt is a whining loser; Jan goes crazy from being a living head; Doris is an unpleasant, bitter woman, and Adele Lamont, who plays her, is amateurish in her overly-careful diction and stiff performance. The closest thing to a sympathetic character must be that pseudo–Frankenstein monster in the closet, and he spends most of his time out of the closet savaging Kurt and Bill who, after all, really haven't yet killed anyone.

The film received very few reviews, being an especially minor picture almost tossed out the door by American International. With its gleeful appetite for the sleazy, *Psychotronic* considered it a "great, absurd movie" and, in a way, it's hard not to have some affection for a film so crudely deformed yet forthright in its intent. Don Willis (I) considered it "remarkably bad." Don Glut hoped that it "surely was not three years in the making, since it ranks [with] *Frankenstein's Daughter*."

However, *The Brain That Wouldn't Die* actually plays somewhat more entertainingly than *Frankenstein's Daughter*; despite its crudity, shapeless, thin plot and smutty atmosphere, *Brain* possesses a kind of ripe ludicrousness that makes it almost watchable. But not quite.

The Creation of the Humanoids

Andy Warhol thought this film was great, but you know old Andy, he's a real kidder. The movie's story is reasonably sophisticated, involving several different types of robots and a strange master plan for the salvation of the human race, but plays almost indescribably stagily and tediously, with remarkably flat acting and direction. Still, it makes an attempt to be *about* something; that, plus its flat visuals and lack of action mean no one can blame *Creation of the Humanoids* for going for the sensationalistic. It's too bad that the people involved in writing and directing it had no talent, because it has the germ of a good film.

Some have claimed that the movie was derived from the famous novel by Jack Williamson, *The Humanoids* (1949), but apart from the use of the term "humanoid" to describe a humanlike robot, and one line of dialogue ("Can't you see [the robots are] killing us with consideration?") there's no resemblance between the two works. However, Jay Simms, who wrote the script, also wrote the story for *Panic in Year Zero!*, similar to two published science fiction stories. Perhaps the best judgment would be that Mr. Simms was acquainted with written science fiction. Far be it from me to accuse anyone of plagiarism.

The Creation of the Humanoids opens with a montage of atomic explosions while a narrator tells us that during the long-feared nuclear war, which lasted 48 hours, 92 percent of humanity died. It is now many years after that time, and while there still aren't very many people, robots have been developed to help them. We see a series of robots, the R-1, the R-2, etc. (but no R2-D2). One is played by the space suit from *Earth vs. the Flying Saucers*, another by the robot from *Bowery Boys Meet the Monsters*. Eventually, the robots become humanoid in appearance with R-21, and variations on that model, presumably up into the R-80s, are now the main servants of mankind, doing all of Man's unsavory tasks. The robots are called the Clickers, and are played by bald men in suits borrowed from *Forbidden Planet*. They have metallic eyes, and always stare straight ahead while talking.

Captain Kenneth Cragis (Don Megowan), sometimes called *The* Cragis, is one of the high members of the Order of Flesh and Blood, in favor of human beings and opposed to Clickers. The organization would be called "racist" if the oppressed group were human.

Cragis learns of the existence of the R-96 robot series, only four points off from being human. (Apparently Simms forgot that the numbers following the R were the *series* of robots, like the X-series of test planes, and came to think that 100 indicated full humanity.) We overhear two Clickers talking about the R-96s; "to become an R-96," one says, "is a real sacrifice" because the new R-96 experiences all the emotions of a human being. The other Clicker points out that "by the first of next month, we will outnumber the humans."

Elsewhere, Dr. Raven (Don Doolittle), a human being, assists the Clickers in some sort of secret plan, doing it for money. He's making R-96 duplicates of dead human beings, and installing in the new R-96 all the memories of the real person; they look and act just like the person they replace, except that they have green blood. ("The copper tubing turns it green," explains Dr. Raven.) The R-96s even think they *are* the person they've replaced, except between 4 and 5 a.m., when they must return to Raven's lab to get recharged. Not all R-96s are grateful, it seems, or perhaps they're a little crazy; the most recent revival immediately throttles Dr. Raven.

At a big meeting of the Order of Flesh and Blood, Cragis makes his worries known, and tells the audience (and us) everything we have seen in the film so far, except those few facts Cragis doesn't yet know. We do learn one new fact: the robots from R-21 to R-70 now number about a billion. The human beings fear a rebellion of the robots, but the human beings can easily destroy the Clickers. After all, Cragis says, "the only crime that can be committed against a robot is vandalism." He fears the development of the R-100s because such a robot "would be one of us, a perfect man."

Cragis learns his own sister (Frances McCann) is "in rapport" with a Clicker; that is, she has married an R-94 called Pax (David Cross). She left her previous husband, one Stafford Miles, because he was "a filthy, stinking, drunken, insensitive beast."

"Miles had his [pause] eccentricities," Cragis says in defense of his absent brother-in-law. (Throughout the film, robots are shown to be the superior race.)

Cragis meets Maxine Megan (Erica Elliott); they immediately feel a mutual attraction. "Cragis," his sister says chidingly, "your eyes are sticking out like a snail's."

We learn that Cragis is sterile from playing in radioactive ruins as a child. But that doesn't matter; it's pretty clear to the audience (though not yet to the characters) that Cragis himself is an R-96, unaware that he's now a machine. But then again, so is Maxine an R-96, likewise unaware of her mechanical nature. In an interesting touch, it is made clear that they fell in love *because* they are robots.

Dr. Raven revives as an R-96, a younger version of himself. We learn that 17 people so far have been duplicated as R-96s, and that the people who died did so accidentally, with the exception of Raven. The Clickers are not out to destroy humanity, but to save it. Cragis is appalled to learn of the duplications, and doesn't cheer up when a robot stabs him and Cragis himself bleeds green. He tries to prove his own humanity by recalling growing up, and declares that "I can hate. I can kill."

He is told that *he* killed the real Maxine (during a blackout), whereupon the Clickers revived her. They kindly brought her back thinner; Raven says, "you had a tendency to be plump." "Thank you," Maxine says absently.

The Clickers explain to Cragis that "Rule 1 of the manual" says that robots have to work in humanity's best interests, a clear borrowing from Isaac Asimov's "Three Laws of Robotics." Therefore, as the human race is dying off, it's up to the Clickers to do their best to make sure it somehow continues. So they have developed the R-96s; as each live human being dies, he or she will be replaced by a robot duplicate, all memories intact.

"Are we machines?" Maxine worriedly asks Cragis. "Yes," he says reassuringly, "but you're a beautiful machine." Cragis realizes he didn't lose his soul in this change from flesh to metal (or whatever), but Maxine is unhappy that she can now never bear a child.

But Dr. Raven says he can make them self-procreating, then turns to the camera. "Of course the operation was a success," he tells us smugly, "or you wouldn't be here." Thus making this one of the few movies to put its *audience* in the future.

The Creation of the Humanoids is boring, making it more difficult to sit through than other films made with the same level of skill, such as *Cat-Women of the Moon* or *Robot Monster*, which have far stupider scripts. The performances are stiff and awkward; actors enter rooms, stand in one spot, and declaim their lines. It's a very stagey picture, with even the air of having been written for live theatre. There are no exteriors, and no action scenes. The special effects are limited to the slightly lavender makeup and steely eyes of the Clickers, and one shot of a disembodied arm on a table clenching its fist. The sets are roomy but unattractive, having the appearance of being built for some other film.

Wesley E. Barry's direction is ponderous and unimaginative; having robots like the Clickers stop and deliver their lines while staring straight ahead is one thing, but all the *people* do it too. (Eventually, however, the only human being left is Cragis' sister.) Every scene begins with an entrance and seems to conclude with an exit; almost everything is filmed in long takes, and with the slow pace of the dialogue delivery and the lack of excitement, *Creation of the Humanoids* either hypnotizes audiences into a state of torpor, or sends them out of the theatre before it ends. It's a notably dull film.

Yet there are some rewards, not all intentional. Jay Simms' dialogue is stupefying; not lame, but overworked, overstressed—he tries too hard. Someone is dismissed: "Why don't you beat it while you still have a beat to beat." Defense of finding memory in a dead brain: "Memory consists of facts. Facts can't be destroyed. They can only cease to be used." Pax explains why people are dying off: "Each dynasty devises its own end. The animal develops a brain, and the brain destroys the animal." Cragis to Maxine: "You must be right. You're too beautiful to be wrong." An R-96 to Dr. Raven: "How do you apologize to someone for killing them?"

Simms' notions of drama are equally eccentric. He shows us Clickers talking where people could overhear them, and they tell each other many important secrets. That may work in Shakespeare, but it doesn't in a story which is supposed to be "reality." Later, Cragis repeats everything we need to know, just in case we didn't see it or hear what the Clickers said. Perhaps Simms merely has original ideas about exposition.

At least the storyline isn't hackneyed. There aren't many SF films dealing with robots in this fashion, not only part of everyday life, but as important as people. The odd business at the end, in which *we* are transformed into an audience of R-96s (or R-100s?) by Raven's last words is certainly unique.

Years later, George Lucas would borrow from many different sources to create *Star Wars*, but the result is vital and, in its imaginative synthesis, original. *Creation of the Humanoids* has an unusual story for movies, but it is highly derivative of written science fiction; perhaps Simms doesn't borrow from any specific stories, but there's little that's fresh in the storyline. It's not hackneyed, but it's not new.

This may be the only full feature directed by Wesley E. Barry. He directed the added scenes for *Invaders from Mars*, but was primarily an assistant director on minor films. Judging from his work on *Creation of the Humanoids*, we should be grateful he didn't continue as director. The direction is as bad as the writing: leaden, lengthy, unimaginative, flaccid, immobile. The film was probably shot in a very short time and clearly had a tiny budget, but surely the director could have breathed some life into it. Maybe Barry did try, but most could have been better than this. He didn't set out to make a bad film, but his skills are so limited that he didn't make just a bad film, but a classic turkey.

Born in 1906, Barry was a minor star of silent films, often billed as Wesley "Freckles" Barry, playing teenaged roles until he grew too old for them. Later, in addition to working as an assistant director, he occasionally played bit parts in films of the 1940s. According to David Ragan's *Who's Who in Hollywood 1900–1976*, Barry was discovered by director Marshall Nielan, who later came to regard the young actor as his son. Barry was an actor from the 1910s, and appeared in *Go and Get It*, *Dinty* (both 1920), *Bits of Life* (1921), *Penrod* (1922), *In Old Kentucky* (1927), *The Life of Vergie Winters* (1934), *Night Life of the Gods* (1935) and others. Perhaps it's only appropriate that after his retirement from films, which came soon after *Humanoids*, Barry became a successful turkey rancher in southern California.

Producer Edward J. Kay was primarily a music supervisor and composer for low-budget films, such as *Black Gold* (1947), *Kidnapped* (1948) and *Arctic Flight* (1952). I suspect he got all there was to get out of *Humanoid*'s budget, and I'd be surprised to learn that the film failed to make a profit. But it's also no surprise that, as far as I have been able to discover, Kay produced no further films.

Resembling Rod Cameron, big, burly Don Megowan was a supporting player from 1951 on. His perpetual scowl and thick features made him suitable to heavy roles, and he often appeared in Westerns and adventure films. He's a limited actor, but carries some conviction. He comes off a little better than others in *Humanoids*, probably because he was more familiar with movie technique. Among his other films are *Prince Valiant* (1954), *Davy Crockett, King of the Wild Frontier* (1955), *To Catch a Thief* (1955), *The Creature Walks Among Us* (title role), *The Great Locomotive Chase* (1956), *The Werewolf* (as the sheriff), *The Buccaneer* (1958), *Tarzan and the Valley of Gold* (1965), *Scream of the Wolf* (TV), and *Blazing Saddles* (both 1974). Megowan died in 1981.

Most of the rest of the cast appeared in very few other films; Erica Elliott was also in *The Spiral Road* (1962), Don Doolittle was in *Hawaii* (1966), and Dudley Manlove was in *Plan 9 from Outer Space*. The cast mostly is talentless amateurs or minor professionals, and looks it.

Sometimes what seem to be sad stories are told by movie credits, such as those for *Creation of the Humanoids*. Cinematographer Hal Mohr had been one of the great cameramen of Hollywood from the mid-1920s to the mid-40s, when he began working primarily in independent films of less and less value. He shot Lon Chaney's *The Monster* (1925), *The Jazz Singer* (1927), *The Last Warning* (1929), *King of Jazz*, *The Cat Creeps*, *Outward Bound* (all 1930), *The Front Page* (1931), *A Midsummer Night's Dream* (1935, for which he received the Oscar), *Green Pastures* (1936), *Destry Rides Again* (1939), *Phantom of the Opera* (1943; another Oscar, shared this time), *Member of the Wedding* (1952), *The Wild One* (1954), *The Last Voyage* (1960) and *The Bamboo Saucer* (1968). His last credit was as photographic consultant on Hitchcock's *Topaz* (1969). From the 1950s, says Ephraim Katz's *Film Encyclopedia*, Mohr worked primarily in television. The reason for his decline from the heights of the 1930s and early 40s to the likes of *The Creation of the Humanoids* and *The Bamboo Saucer* is unknown to me.

Jack P. Pierce did the makeup. In this same period, on approximately equal budgets, however, even Harry Thomas was doing more imaginative work than Pierce. I understand his eyesight was failing which probably contributed to the decline of his abilities; he also had small budgets and no doubt small minds to contend with. His work on *Humanoids* is minor, and reflects nothing of the glories of the past. He and Mohr frequently worked on the same films in the 40s; I hoped they weren't embarrassed at finding themselves working together on such an inconsequential project. See *Teenage Monster* for more on Pierce.

Oddly enough, for a film that is notorious for being bad, among the very few reviews I discovered for *Creation of the Humanoids* were two favorable. George H. Jackson in the Los Angeles *Herald-Examiner* considered it "fanciful and imaginative," and while allowing "there is a stilted quality to much of the dialogue," the film showed "enough imagination ... to overcome this." He considered it, in fact, "a good picture" of its type.

Boxoffice, which fairly drooled over almost every released film at this time, thought it "a most enterprising effort in the highly marketable science-fiction field," and that the distributors "have a package of considerable impact, one certain to lure the sizable quantities known to clamor for science-fiction." Barry directed "with a fine, imaginative touch," *Boxoffice* thought.

In fact, because of its strange, spare sets and peculiarly stilted style, as well as its storyline, *The Creation of the Humanoids* has adherents in addition to Andy Warhol. But despite these virtues, it's a dreary, boring little film; a genuine curiosity, perhaps, but it takes more than being peculiar to make a film good.

The Day the Earth Caught Fire

The reasons films fall into obscurity vary, of course; usually they're ordinary productions with nothing special to recommend them and no reason to remember them. But there are a few whose obscurity is a mystery; one is *The Day the Earth Caught Fire*, an engrossing, intelligent and very successful film about the end of the world.

It may be Val Guest's best film as a director, featuring an uncommonly adult script by Guest and Wolf Mankowitz, a strong masculine performance by Edward Judd and a pert but mature performance by Janet Munro. Leo McKern as a troubled science reporter is fine as always. There is much to recommend about the film, so much that it verges on being a genuine science fiction classic. But it's almost never shown on television, very rarely revived at science fiction conventions, and despite a theme of great topicality, even today, the film is almost completely forgotten. I suspect this is because it was in black and white and amazingly unsensational. The other best-remembered SF films of its period are either in color or more sensational in content. *The Day the Earth Caught Fire* is a strong adult drama—which could be the real reason it's so rarely spoken of.

Some feel the film is talky and that there's little of visual appeal, both of which are technically true. But the talk is almost all good, and one of the main virtues of the film—its viewpoint is limited to that of the main characters—results in its being necessarily unspectacular in effects and art direction.

In brief, the story of the film deals with the accidental simultaneous detonation of two huge nuclear bombs, not only tilting the Earth 11° off its axis, but sending it falling slowly toward the sun. There are many ways this tale could have been told, and Guest and Mankowitz, both former journalists, imaginatively chose to tell it from the perspective of a large London newspaper, personified by two of its reporters.

We see a few newsreel scenes of worldwide disasters (stock footage), but these are limited; the story sticks with the main characters and their inter-relationships. The science fiction aspect of the story is not subordinated to the human elements; each is told *through* the other.

Time and again, people say they want science fiction that depicts strong characters, stories in which the human element is uppermost. Science fiction, that is, with the perspective of solid popular fiction or even good literature. Often, the pretentious, pompous *Charly* (1968) is pointed to as just such a film, but *The Day the Earth Caught Fire* is more successful in all ways. Greeted with rave reviews when it opened, it was a financial success. Val Guest told John Brosnan (in *Future Tense*) that both he and Mankowitz "made an enormous amount of money on it.... The money is still coming in."

Perhaps the reason that *The Day the Earth Caught Fire* has not been acknowledged as the near-classic it is, lies in the fact that it was made for adults, not children — and those who were children in the 1950s and early 60s are those who now determine which films do have classic status. Many movies in all genres that were hits and/or critically acclaimed when released (in all periods) are now virtually forgotten.

In its original release, the opening and closing reels of the film were tinted a bright yellow (some sources say sepia-toned, but that is incorrect) to emphasize the extreme heat, but this tinting is absent from television and 16mm prints. Guest's direction and the performances of the actors in these scenes, however, certainly give plenty of indication that it's too damned hot, and while the vivid yellow did help, the film successfully indicates heat without it.

The Day the Earth Caught Fire opens with a still, dusty scene of London; the Thames is dried up, and almost no cars or people are moving. It's 10:41 a.m., "nineteen minutes before countdown," a loudspeaker truck says. Drenched in sweat, Peter Stenning (Edward Judd) walks through the deserted streets. The town looks trashed — not by bombs, but by riots. In the newspaper office, he starts to roll a sheet of paper into his blistering hot typewriter, but discovers the platen has melted into black goo. He insists on doing his story nonetheless, so begins dictating it over the phone 30 minutes "after the corrective bombs were detonated."

He begins, "The final fire was kindled. The Earth that was to live forever was blasted by a great wind towards oblivion." As he says everything started "barely 90 days ago," we flash back to that period, and the slightly overexposed yellow scenes are replaced by normal black and white.

Pete is a reporter; we gradually learn that he was once one of the top writers, but has (in traditional, even clichéd fashion) begun to drink too much. He found his wife in bed with another man; she was resentful of the time he spent on his job and simply fell in love with someone else. Pete is devoted to his small son, however, and bitter over the unexpected direction of his life.

It's raining, and the *Daily Express* offices are active and chattery. As Pete wanders through the City Room we overhear, almost in the background, important information: a big bomb was detonated by the United States in the Antarctic ten days before, and since then there have been reports of increased sunspot activity, plenty of static on radio and television, and earth tremors. There's also been some odd compass trouble.

Pete is now working as a leg man for Bill Maguire (Leo McKern), the science editor, who has assigned him to dig up what he can from the meteorogical bureau (the Met Centre), which doesn't please him. Pete quarrels with an operator there over the phone, one Jeannie Craig (Janet Munro), and when he later meets her when he visits the Met Centre, she slaps him. However, he's able to learn only that there's something mysterious going on, and that the officials are not anxious for the news media to get wind of the real problems, whatever they are.

Bill realizes that the seismograph readings for the U.S. bomb indicated a far stronger explosion than was reported; he investigates further and learns that the U.S.S.R. also set off a huge nuclear explosion (in the Northern Hemisphere) by chance at exactly the same time. It's the "biggest jolt the Earth's taken since the Ice Age started," Bill says, but the newspaper's editor (Arthur Christiansen) thinks all this is mostly good for science-oriented articles, but not much else.

Pete and Bill spend much of their off hours in a nearby bar frequented by newsmen, and the action returns there from time to time. The other newsmen also don't know what to make of the Soviet bomb. Pete is more concerned with the fact that his son is being brought up to be a "right bowler-hatted-who's-for-tennis gent," and not *his* son at all. Maguire toasts the lad. "Well, here's to him. May he turn out to be a hard-drinking, hard-fighting son of a—"

"—bitch," finishes Pete. "Well, that part of his parentage is for sure."

The next day, while Pete watches an antibomb demonstration in Trafalgar Square, a banner-waving probomb group appears, and the two groups clash. Stenning is jostled about by the fighting when the sky suddenly darkens. It's an eclipse—ten days before it was due. Pete grabs a tourist's camera and shoots the unexpected phenomenon.

The editor at the *Daily Express* (never named) immediately recognizes the unusual aspects of the story, and assigns a somewhat disgruntled Bill Maguire to find out about it, to interview Sir John Kelly, a government official with the Met Centre. Maguire says that Pete saw Kelly, and Pete adds, "he wouldn't even say good night in case it was taken as an official comment on the future of mankind." On TV, Sir John tries bluffing his way through an eclipse that just shouldn't have happened when it did.

As time passes, more disasters befall the world. Headlines in the *Express* announce that the Nile has flooded the Sahara, and that there have been floods in a line down the world from Great Britain to Australia. "Brighton at 95°!" shouts another headline. "Phew! 80! 88! 90!—and it's going to be hotter."

Battersea Park crowds take advantage of the summery weather; Pete Stenning goes with his son on a Ghost Train (spookhouse) ride, much to the consternation of the boy's nanny. After the child leaves, Pete again meets Jeannie near the park, and they hit it off much better. Suddenly, a soupy, thick fog sweeps up the Thames, snarling traffic and bringing the holiday mood to an end.

Pete and Jeannie head home on a double-decker bus, looking out over the blanket of fog until their bus hits a car. It's *dark* down at ground level. The fog eventually reaches four stories in depth. The streets are almost impassable, and the underground stops running when the tunnels fill with fog, so Pete walks Jeannie home. They have some amusing, realistic banter as they look out over the fogbound city from her apartment. He's surprised to learn she knows he drinks too much. "It's in the Met Centre facts of life file," she says; "dogs bark, cats meow and Stenning drinks."

Back at the newspaper office, Maguire and others talk about the inexplicable fog, blanketing much of the world. "The question is," says the foreign editor, "how do we get home tonight?" "Yes, I know," Bill smiles, "isn't it wonderful?"

Finally convinced the weather changes are big news, the editor assigns stories right and left. "I want a recap on the rain, the heat wave and the eclipse. I want a comparison on the statistics and weather charts going right back to the first meteorological reports in 1854. You can go back as far as Galileo if you like. I want to know if anything like these conditions ever happened in recorded history.... Let's have an aerial panorama of London above the fog"—and so on. These scenes were generally praised by reviewers as being among the most realistic newsroom scenes in movie history; not, in fact, until the TV series "Lou Grant" was newspaper activity again shown so believably.

Bill suggests that the fog, actually a heat mist, could be the result of a huge mass of cold water entering warmer currents, possibly the results of unusual amounts of melting ice at both poles. Which would also explain the massive flooding some areas of the world have been suffering. "Supposing the combined thrust to the explosions tilted the Earth?" Bill muses. "That would alter the climactic regions. Cause a complete change in the world's weather. A new ice age for some, new tropics, a new equator."

The fog hangs on, and Pete returns to visit Jeannie. There are (for 1961) some very sexy scenes of Janet Munro greeting him in a towel, and a surprising shot of him glancing at her underpants on the bed. He can't go home that night—the fog is too thick—and he prepares to spend the night on her bathroom floor. But they spend the night in the same bed, as lovers.

Outside, the fog hangs on until a tornado strikes. (It's called a "cyclone" in the film, a common error.) The fog is swept away, trees are toppled and cars upended as the tornado passes over London.

Later, Jeannie meets Pete secretly at Battersea; she's frightened about what she's learned at the Met Centre, and tries to get him to promise not to tell anyone what she's telling him. But he's a reporter and the news she gives him is so sensational that as a good journalist, he cannot keep it to himself.

He reveals to Bill that the nutation* of the Earth has changed: there has been an 11° variation in the axis rotation. Bill realizes his guess was right, and the paper carries the story. As a result, Jeannie not only loses her job, she's sent to jail.

The world suffers from the blunders of mankind: snowstorms, floods, droughts, and other disasters are seen in quick cuts.

The prime minister tries to assure the British populace that the axis tilt "is not a catastrophe nor is it the millennium." It's all routine, he says, though things will be different. "But I have the utmost confidence the world's scientists can produce solutions for any of the climatic problems we are likely to meet. Many of you are blaming the combined effects of the nuclear tests for this disturbance of the Earth. Let me tell you the majority of the world's scientists deny this is the cause."

This speech is heard over scenes of blizzards, wrecked houses, smashed water mains, floods, riots and other examples of weather and human disturbances.

Water rationing becomes necessary, and many leave London. (Autos begin wearing strange, unexplained "hats" of gridded metal, presumably air conditioners or water recyclers.) While waiting in a water queue, Peter encounters his ex-wife and her present husband on their way to the country; their problems seem petty now, and Pete feels more sadness and regret than anger.

*"A small periodic motion of the celestial pole of the Earth with respect to the pole of the ecliptic"—American Heritage Dictionary.

Riots continue to tear London, and reservoirs near the danger point as Jeannie is released from prison (this also seen in headlines), but hers is only one small story in scenes of dying animals, fires and other disasters. Bill helps get Jeannie a job at the *Express*; still angry with Pete, she's worried she might encounter him.

It becomes clear that the government knows things are going to get worse before they get better: community washing compounds are being built, which means no more private ownership of water. The editor informs his reporters that he's learned even worse news: the Soviets, he said, "held an international press conference. Had their top scientists present. They say those two bangs did more than alter the tilt. There's been an 11° shift in our orbit and we are moving towards the sun." Maguire estimates four months before the Earth becomes too hot for life.

Bill helps Pete and Jeannie make up. Later, in Bill's car, Pete tries to reach her apartment, encountering police roadblocks and riots—but these are a new kind of riot. Stunned, giddy young people roam through London, playing music, dancing, and splashing and spilling gallons of precious water. We're all done for, so why not have a good time? Cynical despair drives them to waste the most precious substance: water itself. This may be the highlight of the film, and a sharp insight from Guest and Mankowitz: this *is* how it would be.

Pete battles his way into Jeannie's apartment, where beatnikky youths are dunking her in a bathtub, splashing water around. It isn't until one of them falls to his death down the elevator shaft that they calm down and leave.

The film returns to the point it began, and again turns yellow. We learn four nuclear bombs, the largest ever devised, will be detonated simultaneously one hundred miles apart in the wastes of Siberia. No one is certain this will have any effect, but without the bombs, the world is certainly doomed.

Pete sits in the office, concluding his flowery news story. "So man has sown the wind and reaped the whirlwind. Perhaps in the next few hours there will be no remembrance of the past and no hope for the future that might have been. All the works of Man will be consumed in the great fire out of which he was created. Yet perhaps at the heart of the burning light into which he has thrust his world, there is a heart that cares more for him than he has ever cared for himself. And if there is a future for Man, as insensitive as he is, proud and defiant in his pursuit of power, let him resolve to live it lovingly, for he knows well how to do so. Then he may say once more, 'Truly the light is sweet, and what a pleasant thing it is for the eyes to see the sun.'"

As Pete speaks, we see two newspaper headlines prepared (as in *Citizen Kane*): "World Saved" and "World Doomed." Some claim the film ends on an entirely ambiguous note, but the very last scenes convey some hope: as Pete concludes, the camera pulls away from the dome of St. Paul's, and bells chime out. Surely the correct headline will be "World Saved."

Val Guest told John Brosnan in *Future Tense* that the film had been entirely his own idea, springing from the nonsensical claims of others that atomic tests had changed the world's weather. He began to wonder what things would be like if that were *true*. He found great difficulty in getting the movie financed; he had a treatment prepared for some seven years before producer Steven Pallos took interest in it. Everyone else had turned Guest down, and perhaps this was for the best, because he had just made *Expresso Bongo* (1959) from a script cowritten with Wolf Mankowitz, whom he approached to cowrite *The Day the Earth Caught Fire*. Guest told Brosnan that he was basically responsible for the plot, while Mankowitz provided the dialogue and newspaper milieu.

Much of the film was shot in the real *Daily Express* offices. Arthur Christiansen, who played the unnamed editor in the film, had been that paper's editor for many years. So as Guest told Brosnan, Christiansen was probably simply playing himself. Christiansen helped Guest obtain permission from Lord Beaverbrook, the paper's owner, to shoot in the paper's offices.

Filming in the streets of London was not so readily accomplished, yet for the look of the film, Guest considered it necessary, and judging from the results, he was correct. *The Day the Earth Caught Fire* seems more realistic in setting and less studio-bound than any other SF film of its period, even considering that these have often been virtues of British SF movies. Scenes of devastation in what are clearly real London streets, the riot in Trafalgar Square and the foggy scenes near Battersea Park create a powerful sense of reality. The studio built sets are few—Jeannie's rooms, the pub, perhaps the offices at the Met Centre—and even they are realistic. The general approach of the story plus this realism generate a sense of real life and immediacy rare in any films of the period; that it's also a SF film about doomsday made it frighteningly realistic to many viewers of the time.

Guest told Brosnan that he "had to show Fleet Street completely deserted and desolate with windows boarded up, overturned buses and cars and an enormous layer of dust over everything." After much arguing with Scotland Yard, the Home Office and even the prime minister's office, the film crew was granted limited access to the street. They were allowed to shoot for three minutes at a time, providing traffic wasn't much delayed. The set dressers rushed in the fuller's earth, demolished cars and the like, and set up the shots. The crew shot for the brief time allowed, and let the traffic back through for a while.

Les Bowie, the greatest talent in low-budget special effects in England (probably the best on any level) had charge of the effects for the film. He was involved with the film from its beginnings, he told John Brosnan in *Movie Magic*, when it was only a brief outline by Val Guest.

Considering their cost, some of Bowie's effects in the film have great impact. But he was dissatisfied with the matte shots of the fog sweeping up the Thames, as there was considerable matte fringing (darker lines around the matted-in portion of the scene), which led to some complaints from reviewers. On the other hand, some reviewers were impressed by Bowie's work, especially the later scenes of the fog blanketing London. The high-angle shots from the perspective of Jeannie's window are especially interesting, despite the apparent models. Light streams out of windows and makes bright squares on the fog, and as the "cyclone" begins, lightning in the skies casts dark, sudden shadows over the billowing fog.

The matte painting of the dried-up Thames is important and big in concept; the camera dwells on it several times, as if defying us to consider it less than believable. This cheeky attitude sometimes works well: everyone in the film acts more like real people than usual, and the settings are real. Paradoxically, this pulls the effects toward realism, rather than pushing them farther away. They are more believable in a realistic context than they would be in a more movielike milieu, which doesn't often happen in films. Furthermore, the film itself is good enough that we're willing to forgive the occasional obviousness of the special effects.

Leo McKern later became one of Britain's best-liked character actors, especially with his "Rumpole of the Bailey" TV appearances, but at this time, he was moving away from being a lesser-known supporting player. As Bill Maguire, he's as believable as the newsroom and Trafalgar Square; the character is less stereotyped than the others. Rarely seen in a suit and tie, Bill is always rumpled and tired-looking; you get the impression that he has something in his past that forced him to the science desk at the paper. His career is ebbing, and while he's not happy about it, feels content to allow things to drift—until this crisis. His reporter's instincts work with his scientific insight to make believable leaps in imagination; he's hesitant about them, and yet you can see that Maguire believes his fears are real. He's real to us, so his fears are communicated.

Maguire has some of the better lines in the wisecrack-laden script, and makes the most of them. For a potato-faced actor of great gifts, McKern is one of the least hammy of performers, although he can rise to the occasion, as in *Help!* (1965). Bill Maguire was McKern's biggest film role to that time, and while he more than delivered the goods as an actor, he didn't try to run away with the picture. His is primarily a supporting role to Edward Judd's lead, and McKern knew it. He's a generous actor, and although he probably could, never tries to take a scene from his costar.

McKern's career seems to have been helped by *The Day the Earth Caught Fire*. He'd previously appeared in *Murder in the Cathedral* (1952), and was notable in *X the Unknown*. After *Caught Fire*, his roles became larger, and he occasionally played leads. He starred in *They All Died Laughing* (1964, aka *A Jolly Bad Fellow*), and also appeared in *A Man for All Seasons* (1966, as Cromwell), *Shoes of the Fisherman* (1968), *Ryan's Daughter* (1970), *The Adventure of Sherlock Holmes' Smarter Brother* (1975, as Moriarty), *The Omen* (1976), *Candleshoe* (1977) and *The Blue Lagoon* (1980). Patrick McGoohan cast McKern three times as "Number 2" on the TV cult favorite "The Prisoner."

Edward Judd had his first starring role in *The Day the Earth Caught Fire*; although Pete is something of a cliché, Judd's performance is distinctive enough that this isn't readily apparent. He keeps moving both physically and as an actor; his heavy features and large frame make him masculine and brooding, and yet he's sensitive and witty when necessary. Judd is just fine in the role; too bad his career as a leading man petered out so fast. He's worked often in science fiction and horror films, perhaps because of his memorable work here, but rarely had leads in major pictures after the early 60s. He played opposite Susan Hayward in *Stolen Hours* (1963), and was as unpleasant as required as the nominal hero in *First Men IN the Moon* (1964). Judd also appeared in *The Long Ships* (1964), *Invasion* (1966), *Island of Terror* (1966, in which he and Peter Cushing made an entertaining team), *The Vengeance of She* (1968), *O Lucky Man*, *The Vault of Horror* (both 1973), *The Incredible Sarah* (1976) and *Hound of the Baskervilles* (1983). He was a regular in the British SF TV series, "1990."

Janet Munro starred in several Disney films, including *Darby O'Gill and the Little People* (1959), *Third Man on the Mountain* (1959) and *The Swiss Family Robinson* (1960). Her roguish face and delightful smile made her appropriate for such roles. She was also in *The Crawling Eye*, *They All Died Laughing* and *Sebastian* (1968). More talented than most British actresses of her exceptional generation, she had something of a fan following. However, her life wasn't satisfactory to Janet Munro, and in 1972, at the age of 38, she killed herself.

Originally a show-business journalist, Val Guest worked for a time in Hollywood. He began in films as a writer, working on pieces like *Alf's Button Afloat* (1938) and the often-filmed *Ghost Train* (1941). He began as a director in 1943 and occasionally, later frequently, cowrote his films. For the most part, Guest's films are mediocre with occasional flashes of real talent; it almost seems that

Guest as writer is holding Guest as director back. He seems occasionally to go for the cheap effect, the tawdry idea, but then directs them with verve and skill. *The Day the Earth Caught Fire* is the kind of film Guest has always done best: terse, low-budget, confined to a small cast and dealing with one central idea. The more fanciful he gets, the weaker his films become, down to a low of *Killer Force* (1975), a well-cast but meandering, unpleasant tale of dirty deeds for diamonds.

Over the years, Guest occasionally returns to science fiction topics, and has often been good at them. Even *Mr. Drake's Duck* is in the genre; his two Quatermass films, *The Creeping Unknown* and *Enemy from Space* are as good as *The Day the Earth Caught Fire*, though as the plots demand, more sensationalistic. *The Abominable Snowman of the Himalayas*, also from a Nigel Kneale original, is set-bound and somewhat slow, but intelligent and respectable. (Kneale himself is not fond of Guest's treatment of the writer's material.)

After *Earth Caught Fire*, Guest turned away from science fiction, to both the genre's and his own loss. His following films, including *Jigsaw* (1962), *80,000 Suspects* (1963) and *The Beauty Jungle* (1964) saw little if any distribution in the United States. *Where the Spies Are* (1966) was more successful, but still the David Niven–starring film was pretty clearly imitation James Bond, and didn't show anyone at their best. In 1969, he directed *When Dinosaurs Ruled the Earth*, an underbudgeted spectacle with fine Jim Danforth special effects, but hurt by a silly story and cheap sets. His rock-musical–SF-comedy, *Too-morrow* (1970), was never released theatrically in the United States at all, and wasn't even sold to television until late in the decade. Guest was one of many who worked on the script and direction of the appalling/fascinating *Casino Royale* (1967). He eventually turned to cheerful sleaze with *Confessions of a Window Cleaner* (1973), so successful that it kicked off a series of "Confessions of" films, greeted with indifference by critics. He's been relatively inactive in films since 1975.

According to Keith Parkinson in *Dead of Night* #2, "It was [Wolf] Mankowitz who was responsible for the 'mordant and laconic wit' [in *Earth Caught Fire*] mentioned by one critic whilst Guest took care of the story's exposition." This seems likely (and is confirmed by Guest), as the only other Val Guest films to show wit are *Expresso Bongo* (1959) and *Where the Spies Are*, on both of which Mankowitz also worked as a writer.

Mankowitz first came to prominence in the early 1950s, when he wrote the script for the movie of his own novel, *A Kid for Two Farthings* (1955), an ambitious, heady stew of romantic realism and comedy, filmed rather unexpectedly in vivid color. His next film was *Expresso Bongo*, a show-business satire, a success everywhere it played. His Jekyll/Hyde film, *House of Fright*, is also discussed in this volume. For the most part, Mankowitz's films after 1961 have been uneven; *The 25th Hour* (1967), *Black Beauty*, *The Hero* (both 1971) and *Treasure Island* (1972), the latter cowritten with Orson Welles, were at best mediocre and at worst bad. Although the directors didn't help, many of the faults of the films were in Mankowitz's scripts. On the other hand, *The Long and the Short and the Tall* (aka *Jungle Fighters*, 1961), *Waltz of the Toreadors* (1962) and *The Hireling* (1973) are above-average films with good dialogue. Mankowitz also worked on *Casino Royale* and *The Assassination Bureau* (1969), but his contributions are unclear. Like Guest, Mankowitz started as a journalist, no doubt helping the realism of the newsroom scenes in *Earth Caught Fire*. He also wrote books on pottery and porcelain.

The Day the Earth Caught Fire was greeted with almost unanimously favorable reviews, both in the United States and Great Britain.

Hollis Alpert in *Saturday Review* felt that the film's premise was "so close to prevalent and widespread fears and worries that it is not so much science fiction as it is a dramatic and imaginative extension of the news," as if science fiction couldn't encompass that. It "is a model of expert moviemaking," Alpert said, "continually and excruciatingly suspenseful, with even a love story that is not too hard to take amid the apocalyptic events.... It is crisply written and acted, always absorbing, and makes no bones about what it has to say."

Stanley Kauffmann in *The New Republic* considered the love affair trite, but still thought the film was "genuinely and viscerally scary, far superior to the usual science-fiction horror. The newspaper-office view of the approaching doom as geared to the headlines makes the holocaust convincing.... [It] is not intrinsically serious, but its catastrophe is seriously credible."

"J.G." in the *Monthly Film Bulletin* was slightly puzzled; "one is never quite sure how seriously one is expected to take this examination of newspaper ethics in time of crisis; the shot of the two headlines is certainly ironic, but the final narration is so noble and portentous that its effect is dissipated." He was also not impressed by the characterization and the jokes. "Here is a film touching on the major issue of our time, which apparently asks to be taken seriously. Yet instead of presenting a point of view and a defined attitude towards their theme, the authors have tricked it out with all manner of exploitable devices and cheap Shaftesbury Avenue giggles. As in *On the Beach*, good intentions are not enough."

Time's unnamed reviewer regarded the film, as that magazine always regards SF, from a lofty, snobbish perspective: "This arrant piece of fiction is always sensational and sometimes silly, but it reminds the viewer, perhaps salutarily, that with a little nuclear encouragement this really could be a cock-eyed world."

Newsweek, generally more fair to fantastic films than *Time*, was pleased. "Bless the British anyway. They have succeeded in making the first witty movie about the end of the world. They have managed, further, to do it with taste.... The story is spiced with some funny secondary characters, and laced with satire on the hypocrisies of governments.... The documentary footage and special effects are beauts.... Edward Judd and Janet Munro turn in truly original performances: they are persuasively gay, frightened, and nervous all at once, but never melodramatically grim."

In recent years, when it is mentioned at all, *The Day the Earth Caught Fire* doesn't fare as well. Don Willis (I) said "The plot gets lost in sub-plots, and vice versa. Then again, the plots are such that they should get lost." Fredrik Pohl and Fredrik Pohl IV, in *Science Fiction Studies in Film*, missed the point: "Guest's direction moves it right along, and almost takes your mind off the fact that most of what happens on the screen takes place in an office, with the dramatic events being told to the audience as much as shown." *Psychotronic* said "excellent end-of-the-world drama ... mostly concerned with personal reactions to the disaster, and there's more talk than action, but the cast is always convincing." Alan Frank (*SF*) called it an "efficient documentary-style science fiction chiller with an anti-bomb message [which is] given some verisimilitude by good use of locations."

In addition to the realistic background of the film, the scientific aspects are plausible enough to make the whole thing seem real, not just the newsroom and street scenes. Although I'm told by those more knowledgeable in science that the possibility of this happening is extremely remote; any impact or explosion large enough to move the poles and knock the Earth into an orbit heading for the sun would be so big that it would destroy the planet in the first place. But that's not important; what is, is that the film makes it seem real. It is not the responsibility of science fiction or any fiction to be accurate in terms of prediction or possibility; it has to be *convincing*, that's all, not the same thing as .real. *The Day the Earth Caught Fire* is immensely plausible.

The attitude of the characters is reasonable at all times. Pete behaves in a logical, consistent way. We believe in him because, though he's a stereotype, he still seems real.

The general approach of the film, of allowing us to see and experience only what the leading characters do, and selecting characters likely to see and experience somewhat more than the average person, is the major triumph of the film. Usually in films of this nature, the main characters are scientists who were in on the whole thing from the beginning; this was done originally to put us close to the center of action, a laudable goal, but it does also make the rest of the world seem remote and unimportant. If such a disaster happened, we would see it only in bits and pieces, the same way the characters here learn things. However, to have had the main characters not be journalists but, say, bankers, would have put the events even *more* remote than would be useful. Reporters *must* find out what is going on, and must tell others; we are led into the events by their activities.

This is even made a part of the human plot, when Pete uses the information Jeannie gives him; he's still a newspaperman, and the story she gives him, as important as it is, means more than their relationship: the world must know. The film comes down hard on this right to know, and on the responsibility of good journalists to satisfy that right.

Some have complained about the human-interest plot, but it is done with care and taste. Pete is randy already; he's unhappy about his divorce, and on the make simply to find something to do. Jeannie not only rejects him, she slaps his face; to a degree, this is a standard Hollywood–type "meet-cute," but then they don't meet again for some weeks. By that time, the strange weather events have become obvious; Pete is beginning his rehabilitation, and when he again encounters Jeannie, he's not quite the same person as he was before. Bill's wisecrack near the end of the film, "it's a beautiful thing to watch a woman reform a man—it only needed for the Earth to catch fire," is both apt and slightly wrong. It wasn't the woman who reformed the man, it was the Earth catching fire. His involvement with Jeannie is not the cause of his reform, it's the result.

The script is a careful design of interlocked themes: with each new bit of information about the fate of the world and what caused it, we also advance a bit with the relationship between Pete and Jeannie, and one influences the other. If the reform of Pete was due to Jeannie, he wouldn't have turned in the information she gave him; it's his reporter's instincts and the threat to the world that is the impetus to all that Pete does. Jeannie is an extra reward.

The wisecracks in the film are plentiful, but they aren't the polished, Noel Coward–type drolleries or the "Front Page"–style rapid-fire smarty-pants lines usual in newspaper films. Instead, they're the kind of low-level, slightly funny lines people say in real life.

The film is not only amusing, it's fast-paced. The opening newspaper scenes are filled with overlapping and even some *simultaneous* dialogue; Guest relies on the delivery and on the audience's judgment to pick out the important elements. These breezy, busy scenes fascinate, pull us at once into the film, and set the structure for the rest of the picture: the quick pace, the obliquely-provided information, the newsroom milieu. It's an excellent opening, and the rest of the film, though it stalls partway through (before we learn what really happened) maintains this fast pace.

The film even gets sexy in some scenes with Munro. Her clean, bright sex appeal keeps these scenes from being tawdry or smouldering; though she's not voluptuous, she is very attractive. These scenes are surprisingly good, holding up very well today.

The big "beatnik" riots near the end of the film are impressive in concept and visual qualities, but trite in characterization. Monty Norman's music for these scenes is driving and unsettling, and by this time, the fact of water shortages has become almost palpable; we in the audience are disturbed by the water wantonly wasted here. I suspect theatres sold a lot of soft drinks during the latter part of this film.

The ending is too cagey for its own good, and a weakness. The irony of having two headlines is interesting, but is offset by the following shot in which the sound of the church bells and the swelling music make it obvious which headline will be used. It's not at all a lady-or-the-tiger ending, but the film-makers do manage to avoid making the whole endeavor seem specious by having the happy ending presented even more obliquely than the bad news at the beginning.

Throughout, the production is attractive and beautifully planned. Guest told Brosnan the film cost only £300,000, which was around $1 million at the time. The film was shot in a wide-screen process and in black and white, making it seem more "real" than color films, while still having an impressive sweep.

Those who feel *The Day the Earth Caught Fire* lacks spectacle miss the point. That wasn't what the film was getting at (nor is it really a ban-the-bomb message movie). Guest was trying to make a fantastic situation plausible, and to do that, he wanted to keep everything on a level where he could control the realism, to show how relatively ordinary people would view and react to such a crisis. The sharp pace of the film, the head of suspense it develops, and the realism make it memorable and effective. Despite its sensationalistic title, it is a fine, unsensational film. It is one of the best SF films of the period covered in this volume, and certainly deserves to be rediscovered by audiences today. Things have swung around again, and the bomb-protesters shown in the film could be the same crowds in the same place today protesting cruise missiles. *The Day the Earth Caught Fire* is as timely today as it was over 20 years ago.

Eegah!

Arch Hall, Jr.'s squidgy, pushed-in face with its startling but glowering blue eyes and shock of blond hair made him perfectly suited to play the Charles Starkweather–inspired maniac in *The Sadist* (1963), but he seemed out of place as the hero of *Eegah!* (sometimes subtitled "The Name Written in Blood!").

Of course, the film itself seemed out of place, resembling as it does a home movie with a storyline. Few films seem so cheap and shoddy: the processing is grainy, the color muddy, the lighting variable, and the acting uniformly terrible.

Arch Hall, *Sr.*, who produced, directed and cowrote the film (as Nicholas Merriwether) told interviewers for *The 50 Worst Films of All Time* that despite production snafus (loss of sound, hot locations and so forth), "we actually had a lot of fun." I hope so; they probably had more fun than any audiences did who saw the film. *Eegah!* might have been a camp classic if it weren't so boring and disjointed, but it is somehow memorable and does manage to provide a few laughs. But there's nothing in the film as wild as the ad line from the poster: "The Crazed Love of a Prehistoric Giant for a Ravishing Teenage Girl!"

While driving near Palm Springs, teenage girl Roxy Miller (Marilyn Manning, who is pretty but not ravishing) sees a "giant" in her path (7'2" Richard Kiel), who terrifies her. She escapes and tells her boyfriend Tom (Arch Hall, Jr.) and father (William Watters—actually, Arch Hall, Sr.) about this, and the father investigates, wandering around the desert until the giant clubs him.

Tom and Roxy return to the desert to look for her father, and soon enough, the giant kidnaps Roxy and takes her to his cave. Mr. Miller is there, and tells her that "it must be the sulfur in the walls of his cave that has kept this creature alive for all these years." (Hence the film's inclusion in this book; if Eegah were just a bearded, albeit large, imbecile wandering around the desert, I wouldn't find it necessary to mention him, but he's a genuine, authentic, millions-of-years-old prehistoric giant. We won't bother to wonder why no one has noticed him until now, even though he lives within walking distance of Palm Springs.)

Eventually, Roxy and Mr. Miller conclude the giant's name is, in fact, Eegah, and they give him a shave. He seems very young. Roxy induces Eegah to take her outside where somehow the lurking Tom manages to knock the giant down. The three then escape, while Eegah wails sadly behind them.

Later, while Tom and his friends are singing some lousy rock songs at a pool party, Eegah shambles into Palm Springs, disrupting the patrons of a restaurant. Soon enough, he spots Roxy by the pool, but as he approaches her, some policemen shoot him and, dying, the giant falls into the pool for the big finish, not without a touch of heavy-handed poignancy.

As noted in the comments on *Phantom Planet*, Kiel went on to better things, and became even bigger (if not taller) himself. He was 22 when the film was made, and despite being so tall, looks somewhat spindly; over the years, he has, to say the least, fleshed out. For such a huge man, his proportions are very normal, and upon meeting him, I was surprised that he didn't look enormous—until I shook hands, and saw my own (not small) hand vanish within his like a child's in mine. Because of his unusual physical structure, Kiel generally plays the kind of oddball roles available to actors who are 7'2". So far, despite being a decent enough actor, he's rarely had a chance to prove it; only in *The Longest Yard* (1974), *Force Ten from Navarone* (1978) and *So Fine* (1981) has he had the opportunity to play more or less normal—if large—people. Despite his craggy features, distorted by the glandular disorder which gives him his height, Kiel can easily project a tragic air, leading him to occasionally play sympathetic roles. He's probably best known as the steel-toothed "Jaws" in *The Spy Who Loved Me* (1977) and *Moonraker* (1979); he also had metal teeth in *Silver Streak* (1976). Among his other films: *The Magic Sword* (1962), *House of the Damned* (1963), *The Human Duplicators* (1964), *Two on a Guillotine* (1965), *A Man Called Dagger* (1967), *The Phoenix* (retitled *War of the Wizards*), *The Humanoid* (both 1979) and *Hysterical* (1982). Unique among performers of his size, Kiel can actually be counted as a movie star, a position he has worked long and hard for. *Eegah!*, according to some sources, is his first film, though *Phantom Planet* was released first.

Arch Hall, Jr., on the other hand, appeared in only a few more movies after *The Sadist*, including *Deadwood '76* and *The Nasty Rabbit*; according to *50 Worst Films*, he is now a pilot for a small airline.

Eegah! is peculiar; it's so bad that it becomes almost minimalist: desert, four actors, phony cave, scant plot, not much action, nothing to recommend. Hall (Sr.) told *50 Worst Films* that he quickly concocted the story upon meeting Kiel, then a bouncer. The film was shot on a very low budget ($15,000 or less) in a week or less. It recouped its cost in its first week in Omaha. Hall sent Arch Jr. and Kiel on tours to promote the film, eventually bubbling along on its own; they didn't bring their road show to Eugene, Oregon, where I was fortunate enough to catch *Eegah!*

The galumphing giant of the film is matched by the galumphing film itself. Despite being thoroughly rotten—and one of the six movies actually worthy of being included in the *50 Worst Films* book—it is somehow endearing. Its attempt at sentimentality is obvious and heavy-handed, and its unrelenting cheapness is irksome—but somehow it becomes memorable. I remember many scenes from *Eegah!*, and I haven't seen it since 1962, while I have forgotten the film I saw it with. That's a triumph of a kind: make a movie so bad that it becomes crudely lovable, like a scabby old dog, and you will gain a kind of immortality.

The Final War

This obscure and now little-seen Japanese film, released in its home country in 1960, is often confused with the similar *The Last War* (1961), also Japanese. *The Final War* is a Toei production released theatrically in the United States by Sam Lake Enterprises in 1962; it had few bookings. According to the *American Film Institute Catalog*, *The Last War* had no theatrical bookings in the United States at all, not even in Japanese-language theatres; though shown on U.S. television fairly often, it is omitted from this book.

The Final War is given a detailed plot synopsis in the *AFI Catalog*. An American Air Force plane accidentally detonates a nuclear bomb over Korea, which causes great international tensions, especially between North and South Korea. Tensions mount and the U.S. 7th fleet mobilizes at a Japanese port.

The scenes of international conflict are intercut with the story of newspaperman Shigero, involved in reporting on the incidents. His girlfriend, a nurse, prepares to tend to casualties.

Eventually, negotiations between the West and the Communist countries break down and the nuclear war that results destroys most of the world. Shigero realizes that his girlfriend was killed during the destruction of Tokyo, and he dies of radiation poisoning.

I have been unable to discover any reviews or other material on the film; all information is from the *AFI Catalog*.

The two Japanese nuclear-disaster films are easily distinguished. This is in black and white, *The Last War* is in color; their storylines, however, are similar. In *The Last War*, Franky (or Frankie) Sakai plays a Japanese husband and father who returns after a long absence. He has a reconciliation with his wife, and grudgingly approves the marriage of his daughter to a naval officer. The international tensions in *The Last War* build in a fashion similar to scenes in *The*

Final War, and include a scene in which some missiles are almost launched accidentally from an American base in the Arctic.

The destruction of the world is shown in quick scenes of models of landmarks being blown to bits. Tokyo's demise is treated in more detail, with lava swallowing up the city. The last sequence is aboard the fiancé's ship, as we hear children's voices singing the Disney song, "It's a Small World."

Both films are bleak and despairing, but are essentially trivial because they reach for sensation rather than drama. However, neither should be completely disregarded. Neither are even alluded to in the book *Nuclear War Films*, a serious omission.

First Spaceship on Venus

One of the very few Communist–bloc films to receive general theatrical release in the United States, this earnest, gaudy movie was cut by some 52 minutes for its release in English–speaking countries. Presumably what was cut were scenes of character development and interaction, because most of what seems to be the main story remains. I have not read the novel by Stanislaw Lem on which the film is based, but presumably that wouldn't do me any good anyway, as Philip Strick in *Science Fiction Movies* says the film was "disliked by Lem himself."

I suspect almost all the scenes aboard the spaceship and on Venus itself are left intact; in those sentences, the film is reasonably tight and feels complete. I doubt that much that would be of real interest to American audiences was removed, even though the missing scenes total almost an hour.

First Spaceship on Venus was an East German–Polish coproduction; it was known as *Der Schweigende Stern* (The Silent Star) in East Germany, and *Milczaca Gwiazda* (Planet of the Dead) in Poland; it was released in 1960 in Europe, and in the United States in 1962. The English dubbing is poor and distracting, although the dialogue we hear isn't any worse than that in American films of the same ilk.

The movie is actually an anti–nuclear war film masquerading as a space-exploration story; what is found on Venus is primarily a warning not to fool around with nuclear attacks. It's easy to see the film as a political allegory, with Venus standing in for an aggressor nation that threatens a nuclear war.

In the film, Venus is a devastated planet, with no life of any sort left. In terms of plot the film it most resembles is *Rocketship XM*, which found Mars to have been similarly destroyed by nuclear war. Both films deal with the first expedition to another planet, both have elements of romance, both have meteor encounters, both discover a destroyed civilization, and in both, some members of the expedition die on the alien planet. The two films were trading on public interest in space exploration and on public fears of nuclear holocaust.

In 1985, a strange rock is found while the Gobi Desert is being irrigated. The rock contains a spool, "extraterrestrial in origin and not of human manufacture," the constant narrator tells us. It turns out that the spool came from the Siberian "meteor" (probably a comet) of 1908, really a spaceship that exploded. The spool was ejected from the ship before the explosion.

Several scientists make an effort at translating the sounds on the spool, including Professor Sikarna (Kurt Rackelmann), who looks like Nehru, and Dr. Tchen Yu (Tang-Hua-Ta). Although they learn that the spool originally came from Venus, it cannot as yet be translated.

A multinational expedition to Venus is swiftly mounted. The *Cosmostrator I*, the spaceship of the title, is tested and soon ready to go. Among the crew are American pilot Robert Brinkman (Guenther Simon) and medical doctor Sumiko Ogimura (Yoko Tani); they had once been in love, but now she's mourning the death of her husband, killed in a recent accident at a Moon base. (There's some slight indication that the death of Sumiko's husband may have been in the original cut.)

Talua (Juliusz Ongewe) is black, a concession to racial equality that couldn't have been found in an American film of this type during the same period. Furthermore, Brinkman is treated as a hero; it's hard to imagine a Soviet character in an American film being anything other than a villain.

After the launching of the ship, there's some of the usual free-fall-means-things-fall-up business, and they deal with the usual meteor shower more realistically than in American films, mostly avoiding the danger. A meteor fragment slightly damages the ship, which lurches, throwing everyone into a heap. French robotics expert Durand (Michal Postnikow) goes out in a spidery little ship and makes the repairs.

As the ship nears Venus, Sikarna and Tchen Yu finally manage to translate the mysterious spool, and all are horrified as they hear the message. "We will initially subject the planet to a very intense bombardment of radiation. Conquest and occupation of the Earth will then present no difficulty. When the ionization intensity has fallen by one-half, the final extermination phase can start." In 1908, Venus has been about to conquer the Earth when the spaceship exploded.

The crew have lost radio contact with Earth, but decide anyway not to let the folks back home know that Venusians are not likely to be friendly.

Brinkman makes a one-man landing in a small spacecraft, taking with him small robot Omega, traveling about on tanklike treads. He finds no life; everywhere the landscape is black and shiny, with metallic-looking trees, drifting wisps of color and bright lights here and there (clearly filmed on an interior set). He falls into a pit and is immediately surrounded by bouncing, chirping bird-like thingies, later proving to be recording devices.

When the spaceship lands, they discover that the "vitrified forest" nearby is actually a gigantic weapon, presumably the device designed to bombard Earth with radiation. Clearly, some major catastrophe has befallen the planet, but Sikarna can't deduce what it is. A huge sphere like an immense golf ball is found nearby, and power cables still run through the ground.

A small group begins exploring in a vehicle. They find distorted structures like partly-melted buildings; within one is a giant model of the solar system, still functioning. Beneath the surface is the "nerve center" of Venus, apparently a still-functioning computer, a la *Forbidden Planet* (which I suspect the makers of this film had seen).

One of the expedition members accidentally knocks a rock into some sinister goop, which begins chasing them up a spiral ramp, in the film's most impressive and memorable sequence. It's like a lake of living mud, black with red highlights, and it seems intent on eating them, or something. One fires a radiation burst at the lavalike flow; it suddenly reverses and backs away.

The giant golf ball begins glowing red, the nerve center acts up, and Venus shows signs of doing something awful. Aboard the ship, Sikarna realizes that the "vitrified forest" is building up an immense charge which will soon shoot the ship back into space by some kind of repelling force. The ship has to be held in place by constantly firing its retro-rockets.

As they head for the ship, it becomes clear to Sumiko and the others what happened. As the Venusians were preparing to launch an attack on Earth, their own nuclear weapons backfired and wiped out the planet. The only traces of the inhabitants are their shadows (as in Ray Bradbury's "There Will Come Soft Rains," and at Hiroshima), burned into the walls of the buildings. The writhing, agonized shadows are humanoid, but subtly unlike human beings.

Things start happening fast, but the dubbing and apparent cuts make it unclear as to what's going on. It has something to do with energy turning into mass and vice versa, but it's hard to tell what everyone is so excited about. All we need to know is that disaster looms. Tchen Yu and Talua return to the melted city to make a direct attack on the planet's nerve center. When it's clear they won't make it back, Brinkman tries to rescue them in the small ship, but is flung into space by the Venusian force field, and lost. Tchen Yu's space suit is torn, and he dies; Talua watches helplessly as the ship, unable to wait any longer, leaves without him.

In the last reel, as the survivors are cheered on their return, there's some moralizing about the dangers of nuclear accidents, and the three who died are saluted.

In some ways, *First Spaceship on Venus* is a difficult film to evaluate. First, it's been cut almost by half by American distributors Crown International, rendering its plot a bit foggy around the edges. The English dubbing isn't good, and at times borders on the dadaesque: the little robot that has a Greek letter Omega on it is called by several names during the film. Mostly, the robot's name is pronounced to rhyme with "foamy saw." Though not a major matter, it does indicate that the film was treated rather sloppily.

Most Communist bloc science fiction films are of this nature: big, splashy productions with lots of special effects, international spaceship crews and a humanistic plea. In general, inhabitants of those countries have a more positive image of Americans than we do of them; in fact, in their films, as in this one, Americans are often heroes.

The tone and mood of these European SF films are alienating for Western audiences; seriousness becomes pomposity, deliberation becomes slowness, and eloquence becomes sententiousness, viewed through American eyes. The films don't change, it's the needs of the audiences that differ. *Solaris* (1972), also based on a Stanislaw Lem novel, is a case in point; some have found it a superb science fiction drama, remarkably dealing in human terms with issues it raises; others have been bored by *Solaris* to the point of screaming; still others find it both fascinating *and* boring. (I'm in the last group.)

First Spaceship on Venus is peculiar. Although an hour has been removed, the pacing of each individual scene is still that of a middle–European movie. People take their time, but then there's a quick cut, and they are now taking their time to do something else. This makes the film jumbled and confusing, even when it really isn't; when it becomes *actually* jumbled and confusing, as at the climax, you might as well give up. No amount of intense concentration will reveal what these slow-moving people are up to, so just relax and watch the pretty pictures.

That's mostly what *First Spaceship* has to offer: pretty pictures. The film is hampered by a particularly ugly color process (Agfacolor), making everything simultaneously pastel and too intense. The process loves oranges and blues, and other colors almost don't exist. But aside from the color, the film is not cheap, and has some intriguing design elements. For instance, the computer room seen near the beginning is a huge, pastel cavern with gigantic machines along the distant wall. Because the scale is so vast, it almost looks like one of those oversized sets designed to make people look tiny.

Cosmostrator I, the spaceship itself, is an unusual construction, unlikely but sleek and beautiful. The center portion is the usual 1950s spindle shape, more slender than most and golden rather than silver, but it also has three rocket nacelles like outriggers, connected to the center portion of the ship by graceful curved buttresses. These three nacelles are almost as big as the passenger portion of the ship, and are the same shape. The whole thing looks like some bizarre martial arts weapon. It also looks as though it would shake itself into flinders five minutes after takeoff.

The production of the film is more easily dealt with than the approach. The interior of the ship is spacious and open, with comfortable chairs and open grillwork. It looks rather advanced for the first interplanetary ship. The spacesuits look Russian, but are less bulky and more attractive than the real thing.

The scenes on Venus contain an astonishing fantasmagoria of effects, many, like the drifting washes of color, added postproduction. There's a better physical match between miniatures and full-sized sets than in most science fiction films, but the miniatures are shot at normal speed, making the model car look like a toy.

The crusty black soil, with little solidified heaps of what looks like lava, makes the surface look desolate indeed, but in terms of perspective, sets are badly designed. It always looks as if there's a wall about 20 feet behind the actors. The big golf ball shape is standard, but the partly melted city is intriguing in concept and design: a partly destroyed city not built by human beings. The art director had an unusual task. The most interesting touch, of course, is those haunting shadows, arms upraised in agony as they were caught in a nuclear glare, photographed onto the walls by heat.

There's one attractive shot of the spaceship with a searchlight panning around from its nose, making the ship look like a lighthouse designed by Richard Powers.

In general, although the scenes set on Venus look all too much like they were filmed on a sound stage, at least there's an attempt to show us things we've never seen before. The attempt must be applauded even if the result is wanting.

Though colorful and phantastical, the effects are relatively scanty. There's not even one shot of the *Cosmostrator I* whizzing through space, nor do we see a long shot of Brinkman's little ship as it lands on Venus. When the *Cosmostrator* passes the Moon, there's a bizarre shot of a lunar landscape with very faulty perspective: it seems as though they are flying over a big balloon painted to resemble the Moon. The best effect is the living mud, which chases Yoko Tani and others up the spiral ramp, and that was easily done by filming the sequence in reverse. (I don't imagine that setting up that shot was easy, however.)

There's a couple shots of the ship taking off and landing, but those are not complicated. There are a few matte paintings and one odd shot of a miniature of the ship outside the windows of the rocket test chamber. In general, however, either the effects scenes were removed from the film before it was shown here, or (more likely) they were never there at all.

There's some obnoxious comedy relief, unlike that in U.S. films, in the person of Omega the robot, programmed to play chess. It beats everyone, causing ill will and general depression, until Durand reprograms Omega to lose occasionally.

It's difficult to judge performances when a film has been dubbed. Kurt Rackelmann shows a tendency to overact, but everyone else seems adequate, even Yoko Tani, generally not a good actress.

Philosophically, the message seems mainly to be don't blow people up unnecessarily. International understanding is implicit in the makeup of the spaceship's crew. The most interesting aspect of the film, in one sense, is the idea that the famous Siberian meteor was an exploding spaceship.

When compared to the average American SF film of the period, *First Spaceship on Venus* is clearly more ambitious and expensive, but the poor dubbing and removal of so much of the footage make it primarily a curiosity. It's neither good nor bad, but exists in some kind of limbo where criticism is pointless.

It didn't receive many reviews. The *Monthly Film Bulletin*, giving it a III, really seemed to hate it. "A comic-strip science fiction essay with an erratic and confused script, and wooden acting rendered even more inanimate by dubbing. Its only virtue lies in the design and special effects, which are above average, particularly in the Dali-esque and quite imaginatively contrived Venusian landscapes."

"Tube" in *Variety* had seen it all before. "Colorful, but shopworn sci-fi meller.... All the familiar crises of the cinematic journey into space are crammed into [this film]. Appreciation is restricted to buffs of the sci-fi melodrama who are content to wade through an 80-minute barrage of post-dubbed, pseudo-scientific gobbledegook to enjoy the splashy special photographic effects."

Castle of Frankenstein #9 regarded the film as "spectacular but routine," which seems a fair summation.

Hand of Death

By 1962, the straining for effect in SF movies had developed into occasional wildness—in an effort to make a monster different, the filmmakers sometimes made them silly. The bizarre makeup on John Agar in this film surely was unusual, but also reduced audiences to gales of laughter. Other than his odd face, the film is a routine minor melodrama, whose only other point of interest is being the first film directed by Gene Nelson, formerly a fine dancer.

John Agar plays Alex Marsh, a researcher working with his assistant Carlos (John Alonzo) in an isolated desert laboratory in Southern California. Quoting Tom Reamy from *Trumpet* #1: Marsh "has perfected a nerve gas which paralyzes without unconsciousness or other ill effects. Now he is trying to combine it with scopolamine so that an army can paralyze a populace, move in, and, when the paralysis wears off, occupy without effort as everyone will be in a hypnotic state."

Alex feels this will be dandy for the military, as it will mean they won't have to blow everyone up to take over a country. In short, a way of preventing atomic war by making conquest a breeze. (However, to deal with a zombie-ized population would present its own problems.) His fiancée Carol (Paula

Raymond) wants Alex to give up this kind of research, as it might be dangerous. Quoting Reamy again: "She uses as an example another scientist who is paralyzed from the waist down because he experimented with live viruses in an attempt to find a polio cure."

Alex, however, persists. Carol's direst fears are realized. Wearing protective gloves and a mask, Alex is stirring up his latest batch of nerve gas. He takes off the mask and gloves and immediately spills the stuff, in liquid form. He grabs a rag and starts mopping it up—he's careless because of overwork—and suddenly begins writhing in pain, located in his hands. He passes out.

When he comes to the next day, his skin has darkened, like a suntan, and he's still in pain. He happens to grab Carlos' arm, and the assistant turns black, shrivels up, and dies. Alex realizes although he has a certain immunity to the gas, it has given him a *HAND OF DEATH!* He leaves the lab, soon accidentally causing the deaths of a hitchhiker and a gas station attendant.

Alex rushes to his former colleague, Dr. Ramsey (Roy Gordon), who can't do a thing for the agonized scientist, whose skin continues to darken. In fact, it finally turns black altogether, and instead of shriveling, he becomes bloated and swollen. A monster.

When Dr. Ramsey suggests that Alex go to the police, he becomes angry, touching the old man, killing him. By now, however, the police and Carol are on his trail. Donning a trench coat and hat, Alex flees, pursued by the police. Trapped on the beach, he refuses when Carol pleads with him to give himself up so, having little choice, the police shoot him dead.

In an interview for *Photon*, John Agar told Mark McGee that it was he himself and not a stunt man sweating under the thick rubber of the monster mask and gloves. (He even wore padding under his pant legs.) When the police shot him at the end, Agar fell backwards into the surf, and the mask immediately filled with water, both frightening and a relief—he might drown, but at least he wasn't steamy hot any longer.

Bob Mark is credited with makeup on the film, and while he used some admirable imagination—the monster doesn't look like any other movie creation—he also doesn't seem to have realized that some would find it ludicrous. In fact, Agar looks like a cross between the grossest possible caricature of a black man, and Marvel Comics' "The Thing" of the Fantastic Four. Agar's nose, lips and throat are swollen and cracked (but his ears look normal). I suppose director Nelson's having Agar plunk a hat on his head before he rushes off to the beach was an attempt at pathos—does he really think this will disguise him, with a face three times normal size?—but instead, it is pathetic, and caused many in the audience to collapse in laughter.

I suspect that those responsible for the mask may have studied photos of people whose faces actually were swollen from injury, allergies or illness, as the mask has an authentic look: the lips are puckered and enlarged, which happens in some histamine reactions. The texture, like dry cracked mud, is interesting, but having him turn black was truly a blunder.

Hand of Death begins reasonably well, and is about something a little different—the last "touch of death" movie like this seems to have been *The Invisible Ray* (1936)*—so there was some promise. Agar is more believable than usual. But when the direction of the plot becomes clear, with Agar

---

*The Astounding She Monster killed with a touch, but that was a side issue; the 4D Man walked through people to kill them, death by a nontouch; Man-Made Monster shocked people by electricity he contained.

At the end of Hand of Death (1962), it isn't enough that poor John Agar has the unwanted ability to kill people with a touch, but he swells up and turns black as well. And yes, that is Agar in the mask.

simply killing a bunch of people before he is shot himself, most audiences lost interest. They'd seen it before, and the early promise was betrayed.

Gene Nelson danced gracefully in films of the late 40s and early 50s, appearing in several light but entertaining Warner Bros. musicals in that period. His genial, relaxed personality was reflected in his dancing style, unlike that of most other hoofers of the period (only Dan Dailey was similar). He was never one of the great movie dancers, but was always pleasant. His musical career climaxed with Oklahoma! (1955), and he turned to dramatic acting thereafter. I've heard from a forgotten source that Nelson was injured, and thereby was forced to retire from dancing, but that seems unlikely inasmuch as he did dance in some 1970s Broadway musicals, including *Follies*.

His last film as an actor was 1963's *Thunder Island*. By that time, he'd turned to directing. Most of his movies have some music connection, including *Hootenanny Hoot* (1963), *Your Cheatin' Heart — The Hank Williams Story* (1964), and two poor Elvis Presley vehicles, *Kissin' Cousins* (1964) and *Harum Scarum* (1965). His last theatrical film to date as director was *The Cool Ones* (1967). All of his features were second-rate at best, so it's not surprising that Nelson switched to television, where he directed episodes of dramatic series, and at least two made-for-TV movies, *Wake Me When the War Is Over* (1969) and *The Letters* (1973).

The *Monthly Film Bulletin* gave *Hand of Death* its lowest rating. "The intriguing opening shots promise something different in the line of pseudo science fiction; this promise, maintained for a while despite unconvincing acting, collapses when the distressed scientist is transformed (too quickly) into a conventional monster figure. Later developments, as well as the climax, are completely routine and unenterprising."

Even *Boxoffice* found the film rather humdrum, calling it "program filler," noting somewhat curiously that the touch-of-death business had "been put forth with far greater dramatic credibility in past years." Observing technique a little more closely than usual for *Boxoffice*, probably because of Gene Nelson's fame as a dancer, the reviewer said, "Inevitable, certainly, is movement; in the laboratory, in the street, in the country, conveying a feeling, minimum effect though it may be, of tremendous urgency, of a once-dedicated scientist spurred on to finish a project." The reviewer remarked that while kids and the "science-fiction crowds" might enjoy it, "the far more discriminating ... will squirm with disgust."

Robert Salmaggi was also aware of Nelson as a dancer. In the New York *Herald-Tribune*, Salmaggi said "Mr. Nelson's directing, unlike his dancing, is lethargic, and the camera work is static."

Twentieth Century–Fox picked up and distributed *Hand of Death* as a double bill with *The Cabinet of Caligari*; both films seem to have dropped into obscurity today, but they certainly affected audiences strongly in 1962. Not necessarily the same way.

Hands of a Stranger

This film is usually identified as another movie based on *Les Mains d'Orlac*, the 1920 novel by Maurice Renard, France's most illustrious science fiction writer in the three decades following the death of Jules Verne. Renard's novel was filmed in 1924 in Germany as *Orlacs Haende* (U.S. title, *The Hands of Orlac*), in 1935 as *Mad Love* with Peter Lorre and Colin Clive, and in 1959 as *The Hands of Orlac* with Mel Ferrer and Christopher Lee. (The latter version wasn't released in the United States until 1964, making it ineligible for this book.)

These films tell essentially the same story: a gifted musician loses his hands in an accident, and a surgeon replaces them with the hands of a murderer. The musician then finds that the hands are making him feel impelled to murder (against scientific logic but with a kind of poetic validity).

There is no credit on *Hands of a Stranger* for Maurice Renard, and the hands in question, while powerful, are not those of a murderer, but rather of a murder victim. Unlike the novel and the previous film versions, the central character does become a murderer himself, not because the hands compel him to, but because his frustration over losing his musical abilities (as he believes) drives him mad.

Some writers assume that *Hands of a Stranger* was based directly on the novel, others have felt it was merely a plagiarism; either (or both) of these ideas may be true, but there may be another answer. It's not impossible the film is similar to the novel by simple happenstance. The idea of hand transplants lends itself naturally to a story about a man whose hands are overwhelmingly important to him; one of the most obvious for that is a concert pianist. I feel no need to try to convict writer-director Newton Arnold of plagiarism when stealing the material and accidentally duplicating it are both possible.

The hands of pianist Vernon Paris (James Stapleton) are horribly mutilated in a taxicab accident. Dr. Gil Harding (Paul Lukather) decides to transplant the powerful hands of a murdered man to the pianist's wrists in a daring operation. Dina (Joan Harvey), Paris' sister, and his manager Britton (Michael Rye) concede that it is the only hope for Vernon ever to play again.

The operation is a success, and the hands seem to work fine, but Vernon is disturbed by the scars and the differences between these hands and those he was born with. Morose, he visits his fiancée Eileen (Elaine Martone), but the scars repel her, and she backs away in horror. She knocks over a candle which sets fire to her dress, but Vernon is psychologically paralyzed, and watches her burn to death.

Feeling the taxi driver (George Sawaya) was responsible for his sorry condition, Vernon visits his home, but he's not there. He meets the cabby's son Skeet (Barry Gordon), and to his surprise, discovers the boy himself is an accomplished pianist. Skeet demonstrates his talents and Vernon tries unsuccessfully to follow suit, becoming convinced he can't make the new hands do what he wants. He accidentally kills Skeet.

Paris becomes more and more unbalanced, and takes out his revenge on Dr. Ken Fry (Michael du Pont), who assisted at the transplant operation; he kills both Fry and his fiancée (Sally Kellerman).

Unaware that the police have begun to suspect him, Vernon goes to a deserted concert hall, maniacally trying to regain his piano-playing prowess. He's followed by Dr. Harding and Dina, who have fallen in love. Vernon attacks Harding, but police arrive and kill him before he kills the doctor.

Hands of a Stranger cost $168,000, putting it in the upper range of low-budget films of the period. For a film of its background, the production was unusually well-documented, undoubtedly because one of the producers was Michael du Pont, a scion of the Du Pont chemicals family. (His father was Felix du Pont, Jr.) Michael himself owned a restaurant and nightclub in the San Francisco area in 1960, when the film was made. The money for producing the picture was raised partly because of the heavyweight nature of his name.

Michael told Thomas McDonald of the *New York Times* (30 October 1960) that his first love was acting, and after college theatre, he acted for a while at the Neighborhood Playhouse in New York. "Nobody else has any money in my ventures," he added to McDonald; "I wouldn't even let my father invest in [the restaurant, nightclub and movie]. I know they're a gamble, but I'm not doing them gratuitously. I think I'll make money on them." Du Pont has a role in *Stranger*, but does not seem to have acted in films again.

He produced *Hands of a Stranger* (filmed under the title "The Answer!") with Newton Arnold, who had made films while a student at the UCLA film school. After graduation, Arnold was hired by producer Hall Bartlett, for whom he worked for six years. He wrote and directed *Hands of a Stranger*, apparently his only film as a director. He became an assistant director (usually a second-assistant), and worked on many major productions—usually ones involving location shooting—from the mid-sixties on. Among his films: *In the Heat of the Night* (1967), *The Green Berets* (1968), *The Sterile Cuckoo* (1969), *Skullduggery* (1970), *The Godfather Part II* (1973), *The Towering Inferno* (1975) and *Sorcerer* (1977). He played a bit part in *I Wanna Hold Your Hand* (1978). He continues to work as an assistant director.

Arnold was determined that the picture look like a finished studio production. (The film was made on the sound stages of Desilu Studios.) "We wanted maximum control over the picture," Arnold told McDonald. "The quality we want is available only in a studio. Too many people go out in the hills with a camera and come back with nothing worth showing in a theater."

Whatever Arnold's sterling qualities as an assistant director, as a director he shows many deficiencies. *Hands of a Stranger* is glum, ponderous and over-stylized, in deadly earnest, but slow and conventional. Of all the variations on the *Hands of Orlac* plot, this is the least interesting by far.

Lead James Stapleton seems to have made no other films. Nominal lead Paul Lukather appeared in several others, including *Dinosaurus!*; there's a brief discussion of his career there.

The most notable actors in *Hands of a Stranger* have lesser roles. Irish McCalla made few films, but became famous for her television role as "Sheena, Queen of the Jungle"; she's also in *She Demons*, covered in this book. Sally Kellerman, who has the small role of the murdered doctor's girlfriend, became famous in Robert Altman's film of *M*A*S*H* (1969); though her career never seemed to quite catch fire, she's still a star, and has a career as a singer as well.

Barry Gordon, the murdered young pianist, almost made a career as a child actor in the 1960s, but he seems to have been managed by an idiot, or perhaps his interests lay elsewhere. He made a notable appearance in *A Thousand Clowns* (1965), but most of his other films are insignificant. He seems to have made few or none between 1969 (*Out of It*) and 1979 (*Love at First Bite*).

Hands of a Stranger was completed in 1960, but wasn't released until late 1962. Reviews were basically unfavorable; it played only as a supporting feature, and was shuffled off to TV quickly.

"Whit" in *Variety* thought it stirred up "enough mild suspense to rate as an okay entry for the program market. Its theme is sufficiently novel to attract less discriminating audiences, but much of the unfoldment is sloppy, which militates against what might have been a fairly strong melodrama.... Paul Lukather handles himself well but James Stapleton is frequently over-directed."

The *Monthly Film Bulletin* was unimpressed, giving the film its lowest rating. "The treatment is prosaic in every department, not even succeeding on a melodramatic level, and is topped by lashings of treacly music. The weakest story point is that the beauty-loving Vernon, though taking the news of the transplantation hard (naturally so), shows complete lack of patience and fortitude, and goes berserk after a very desultory attempt to play the piano."

The Horror Chamber of Dr. Faustus

Now better known as *Eyes Without a Face*, the translation of the original French title, *Les Yeux Sans Visage*, this evocative, poetic but strangely chilly film was first released in this country under the two-bit title above, double-billed with the poor *The Manster*, and promoted as a schlocky horror film. A horror film it is, with a science-fictional basis, but so poetic, moody and "foreign" that American audiences, mostly teenagers, thought the film was a pile of crap. From their point of view, that was probably a fair, balanced assessment. They just weren't the crowd it was made for. It's hardly surprising that they reacted as did the audience Pauline Kael described in *I Lost It at the Movies*: "It was Saturday night and the theater, which holds 2646, was so crowded I had trouble finding a seat.... [The audience was] so noisy the dialogue was inaudible; they talked until the screen gave promise of bloody ghastliness. Then the chatter subsided to rise again in noisy approval of the gory scenes. When a girl in the film seemed about to be mutilated, a young man behind me jumped up and down and shouted encouragement. 'Somebody's going to *get* it," he sang out gleefully. The audience, which was, I'd judge, predominantly between fifteen and twenty-five, and at least a third feminine, was pleased and excited by the most revolting, obsessive images as that older, mostly male audience is when the nudes appear in [nudie films]. They'd gotten what they came for: they hadn't been cheated. But nobody seemed to care what the movie was about or be interested in the logic of the plot—the reasons for the gore."

It's depressingly true that a large section of the film-going audience doesn't care at all about story logic; they want thrills. These are the people who think John Carpenter's incredibly overrated *Halloween* (1978) is a "masterpiece" because it effectively delivers a few shocks. The facts that the story makes no sense and the killer lacks motivation are beside the point to these film fans. There are even those who lionize Herschell Gordon Lewis, whose films give new meaning to the word "repugnant." Lewis receives praise as a kind of genius for merely pandering to the lowest possible common denominator in his audience, and dishing up pile upon heap of intestines, blood and lopped-off limbs. *This* group not only doesn't care that these films are illogical—they don't even care that Lewis' films are among the worst ever made anywhere in the world. They want only that bucket of gore, and he gives it to them.

This sensation-loving section of the audience flocked to *Horror Chamber of Dr. Faustus* but was put off by the story, characterization, mood and style, then embraced the several scenes of truly alarming gore. It apparently never occurred to any of them that these same gore scenes would have been less effective in a film that was itself less effective—that was beside the point. The American distributors aimed this film at precisely the right crowd, and probably made a bundle. Word-of-mouth was bad on the film, good on the gore.

On the other hand, I have never quite understood the objection some people have to those who make exploitation films: these critics seem annoyed that the filmmakers make films of a type they would not wish to see themselves. But that's the nature of pulp fiction—it's made by shrewd people for a thick-eared audience. So what? Is it wrong to play to an audience? I am not fond of explicit gore, but have no quarrel with those who want it. I think they should be more attuned to the context, however.

This film, which is very nearly a work of art, was often treated as if it were just another horror thriller. That's different from just making an exploitation film, and undoubtedly more reprehensible.

According to several sources, *Horror Chamber of Dr. Faustus* was deplored upon its release in England. Raymond Durgnat, commenting on it in his book on the film's director, Georges Franju, said that when the film "was presented in the Film Festival at Edinburgh ... seven people fainted, and public and press were outraged. Franju didn't improve matters by saying that now he knew why Scotsmen wore skirts. In England, [it] was greeted with a unanimously shocked, or contemptuous press. Critics were already disturbed by the Hammer horrors; and here was a horror film which really hurt.... The critics disagreed as to whether it was actually too horrible to bear, or whether it incompetently failed to horrify, or whether it incompetently failed in every respect except horrifying."

To the sound-track melody of an eerie waltz by Maurice Jarre, the film opens as Louise (Alida Valli), clad in a black raincoat, drives through the night down a lane of whitened trees; she pulls a body out of the back seat of the car, and dumps it in a hole. We soon learn what's going on: respected plastic surgeon Professor Génessier (Pierre Brasseur), who earlier restored the face of his assistant Louise, was responsible for an automobile accident in which his daughter Christiane (Edith Scob) was badly mutilated. The delicate, graceful Christiane now lives in a white room, her ruined features covered by a white mask.

Génessier is determined to restore Christiane's face, not so much out of guilt or love for his daughter, but because it is a surgical problem that needs to be solved. His mansion, near the hospital where he works, contains cages of doves and large hounds, upon which he has been experimenting.

Louise is devoted to Christiane and to the doctor (though there doesn't seem to be a sexual liaison), and assists him in obtaining young women for use in his experiments. She kidnaps a young woman who resembles Christiane, and Génessier removes the victim's face surgically, but the operation fails and the victim dies. It was her body we saw Louise disposing of in the opening sequence.

When this body is found by the police, Génessier identifies it as that of Christiane. However, Christiane phones her fiancé Jacques (François Guérin) several times, each time saying only his name; he eventually recognizes her voice as that of his supposedly-dead Christiane.

Louise kidnaps another young woman, Edna (Juliette Mayniel); this time we see the face-removing operation in detail. The doctor slices around the perimeters of the face with a scalpel and lifts it away. Even today, after all the excesses of the *Halloween* and *Night of the Living Dead* (1968) imitators, this loses none of its power, as it is presented so coolly and clinically.

Edna, too, is reduced to eyes without a face: her head is swathed in surgical bandages, only her eyes are visible. She later attempts to escape and is killed in the process (or commits suicide; memory fails, sources disagree).

By now, Jacques has convinced Inspector Parot (Alexandre Rignault) that Christiane is still alive, and that Génessier has something to do with the disappearances. The police place Paulette (Béatrice Altariba), another young woman who resembles Christiane, in the hospital as a patient, and sure enough, Génessier takes her to his home. Paulette is on the operating table, the lines for guiding the surgery actually drawn on her face, when Parot summons Génessier back to the hospital.

Christiane approaches Paulette with a scalpel, but to the impending victim's relief, the masked woman merely cuts the straps holding Paulette down. As Paulette escapes, Louise intervenes, and Christiane stabs her in the throat. Génessier returns, and Christiane frees the experimental hounds, which attack him, tearing away his face before he dies. Now apparently quite mad, Christiane wanders off into the night, surrounded by fluttering doves.

The plot is of no great importance here. There have been many films with similar storylines; the obsessive scientist trying to restore the beauty (or other aspect) of the woman he loves. The plotline is conventional and, as Joe Dante points out, the "plot" scenes, such as those involving the police, are handled by Franju with little imagination or apparent interest; he wasn't interested in plot mechanics. It isn't the story that counts in *Horror Chamber of Dr. Faustus*, it's the approach, unlike that of any other film in this subgenre.

Franju made his initial reputation with the short *Le Sang des Bêtes* (1949), an antivivisection documentary. He continued to make short subjects until 1958, when he made what has been described as an impressive feature debut with *La Tête contre les Murs*.

For the most part, Franju's later films have not been released extensively in the United States. His *Judex* (1963) is a slow but handsome, witty homage to the silent serials about that hero, far superior to the rival *Fantomas* (1964), featuring the villain from the *Judex* serials acting on his own. Franju's *Shadowman* (1974) is a similar film, also slow, but haunting and evocative. Franju's poetry is not romantic, but sardonic and darkly witty.

In Sadoul's *Dictionary of Filmmakers*, Franju is quoted: "I am a realist through the necessity of things. An image on the screen has an immediate presence. It is perceived as if it were actual. Whatever one does, a film is always in the present tense. Past time is spontaneously made actual by the spectator. That is why what is artificial ages badly and quickly. Dream, poetry, the unknown must all emerge out of reality itself. The whole of cinema is documentary, even the most poetic. What pleases is what is terrible, gentle, and poetic." Those words admirably describe *Horror Chamber of Dr. Faustus*, one of the most real, yet most poetic, of horror films.

Durgnat quotes Franju: "When I shot *Les Yeux Sans Visage*, I was told 'No sacrilege because of the Spanish market, no nudes because of the Italian market, no blood because of the French market and no martyrized animals because of the English market.' And I was supposed to be making a horror film!" He seems to have overcome some of those restrictions, however—the film lacks sacrilege, nudes and martyrized animals, but it does have some blood. It is not, however, a frightening horror film, though occasionally tense, and the operating scenes are immensely powerful—they disturb, they do not frighten.

Franju, quoted by Durgnat, thought it really wasn't a horror film after all: "It's an anguish film," Franju said. "It's a quieter mood than horror, something more subjacent, more internal, more penetrating. It's horror in homeopathic doses."

The film is carefully made; as Durgnat points out in his intelligent if over-interpretive article on the film, Franju is careful to counterpoint clothing, textures and other physical details. Almost every image is echoed or contrasted by another somewhere in the film.

Some of the imagery is derived from other films. Valli's raincoat, for example, is similar to those worn by the representatives of Death in Cocteau's *Orpheus*. (Franju later adapted one of Cocteau's works for the screen.) The film evokes Cocteau in other ways, but doesn't take the breathtaking and dangerous leaps of imagination and spirit that Cocteau sometimes did in his own films. It's more conventional by far.

This is not to say the film lacks powerful imagery of its own. Edith Scob's immobile mask alone makes the film haunting, and Scob's evocative, touching performance illuminates the movie throughout. We only once see her with a "normal" face in a series of photos (like, weirdly enough, in *The Neanderthal Man*), in which the new skin breaks down and rots away. We see her ruined face only once, briefly, in a shot from the point of view of one of the face "donors." Scob has to make do with that frozen, white mask, and she's brilliant. (With her own face in *Judex*, she was again excellent.)

Brasseur is icy, controlled and remote; he's almost eyes without a face himself, he's so still. It's a superlative performance, however; we are always aware that it is the scientist and not the actor who seems almost inexpressive. Brasseur was long one of the great stars of French films, and as *The Film Encyclopedia* says, he was "an imposing performer, superb at expressing irony and wit; he appeared in a great variety of roles in more than 80 films.... He was also a poet and wrote several plays and an autobiography." His most famous role was the actor in *Children of Paradise* (1945), and he is known to Rasputin fans for having played the mad monk in *Raspoutine* (1935). He played General Geranium in the insufferably fey *King of Hearts* (1966). His son Claude, a well-known actor on his own, also appears in *Horror Chamber of Dr. Faustus*. Pierre Brasseur died in 1972.

Alida Valli was briefly a Hollywood star, billed as Valli; she's a weak spot in the film, both in conception and acting. She's something of a link between father and daughter, and may even be homosexually in love with Christiane, but apart from her echoes of Cocteau's characters, the role isn't adequately developed. At the end, when Scob stabs her, she manages to gasp out "why?" before expiring. Some believed that the raucous audience laughter that greeted this was because of the impossibility of speaking with a scalpel stuck in your throat, but it was probably because the image was silly — surely you'd find something more serious to say than to whimper "why?" when stabbed. Also, neither the weapon nor the wound seemed severe enough to kill her.

The film was greeted more seriously in the United States than in England by those few reviewers who bothered to see it. In more recent years, however, it has been thoroughly discussed.

Peter John Dyer, writing in the *Monthly Film Bulletin*, was among those English critics moderately appalled by it: "When a director as distinguished as Georges Franju makes a horror film as fundamentally trite as [this one], one cannot but feel tempted to search for symbols, an allegory, layers of interpretation. Unhappily, there is practically nothing in this inept work to offer any encouragement for doing so.... [After an evocative opening], the film degenerates into the gratuitous shock effects of the face-grafting procedure, and mismanages its several comedy touches so badly that it is impossible to tell whether or not they are intentional.... But the many errors of timing, taste and judgment are Franju's alone, and in the context of [his previous work], it is difficult indeed to forgive them."

Pauline Kael found it "austere and elegant.... It's a symbolist attack on science and the ethics of medicine, and though I thought this attack as simple-minded in its way as the usual young poet's denunciation of war or commerce, it is in some peculiar way a classic of horror.... It's both bizarrely sophisticated ... and absurdly naive.... Although I dislike the mixture of austerity and mysticism with blood and gore, it produced its effect—a vague, floating, almost lyric sense of horror, an almost abstract atmosphere, impersonal and humorless."

Durgnat, of course, took the intellectual pretensions very seriously indeed. After a long discussion, he concludes that the character we identify with the most is Christiane, which seems rather obvious. "Franju's style itself constitutes a unity, linking the everyday, the atrocious, the pessimistic, the demented, the beautiful. It's no accident that our first identification ... leads to an identification with a victim of mystification [Christiane], whose one violent act [killing Louise] springs from a reflex of compassion." I thought she was just fed up.

Psychotronic calls it "a classic, poetic horror film with a much-copied plot.... Even now, over 20 years later, modern gore makeup effects haven't duplicated that unsettling closeup" (of the doctor peeling away the victim's face).

In *Castle of Frankenstein* #10, Joe Dante described the film as an "artistic French rendition of [a] venerable old B-movie theme.... Scenes of horrendous grue alternate with moments of quiet beauty. Quite a fine job all around." On the other hand, Don Willis (I) was annoyed by the dubbing: "Some stray breathtaking images, but the dubbing pretty much ruins the English[-language] version."

In his pompous *The Horror Film*, Ivan Butler found much to praise in *Horror Chamber of Dr. Faustus*. "Despite the fact that it contains three of the most horrid scenes yet filmed ... the main impression left by the film is strangely one of austere beauty.... Franju's purpose is not altogether clear—the film could be regarded as an attack on the *hubris* of medical scientists, or even as a melodramatic tract against vivisection. What it certainly is not, is just another 'mad doctor movie.' ... On the framework of a gruesome Boileau-Narcejac [the writing team responsible for, among other things, the original stories of *Diabolique* and *Vertigo*] mystery thriller ... Franju has constructed a work which transcends its horrific content and leaves the spectator haunted, thoughtful and disturbed, even if not quite knowing why he should be."

Although I agree with much of what Butler has to say here, particularly in his conclusion, he's wrong in one thing: in a very real sense, it *is* "just another 'mad doctor movie.'" In France, genres are not automatically frowned upon as being unfit for artists to dabble in. Franju chose to make a movie with a traditional mad-doctor plot, to find what values he could within that framework. He doesn't seem to feel "above" the material, but instead immerses himself in it.

Of various writers on the film—and I have only scratched the surface—I find I agree most with Garbicz and Klinowski in *Cinema, the Magic Vehicle*: "Franju has ... treated the story mainly as an exercise in style, without worrying much about philosophical or social implications.... [It] should not be treated as more than a film of atmosphere—and as such it works very well right from the first."

The film has been subject to a wide variety of interpretations. It seems to be an attack on science—but only incidentally. The "attack" is inherent in the material, the storyline, and is not what Franju is trying to get at. He seems to be attempting (mostly successfully) to elevate horror movies and their imagery to the level of art. He has altered the various emotional tones and responses of the characters, but that's for the tone of the film, not as a commentary; the plotline remains standard. The fact that the movie deals with a scientist doing murderous experiments simply goes with the territory.

It is not clear at all whether Franju saw a dispassionate stance as necessary to the film, or if it were an accidental result of the tone. Or perhaps he just couldn't come any closer to reaching our emotions. Surely, the last few minutes of the film, with Christiane releasing the animals, is meant to evoke some response beyond "my, isn't that beautiful"—but what that response was meant to be is unclear. Franju was attempting to enrich horror films, and certainly he did that—even clods in the audience I saw it with at the Egyptian Theatre in Coos Bay contradictorily thought it was a "good movie" even if they personally found it a pile of crap—but what lay beyond that attempt at enrichment is illusive. *The Horror Chamber of Dr. Faustus* is a fascinating film, and truly beautiful and horrifying—but it is also cold and distant.

Invasion of the Animal People

For a confused, mediocre movie, this is not without interest. It has a much above-average monster, some satisfactory special effects, and occasionally good photography. But thanks to Jerry Warren, who prepared it for American release, it also has some of the most impenetrable gobbledygook for narration, and among the most static and meaningless scenes ever.

Swedish producer Gustaf Unger opened an office in Hollywood and formed a partnership with American director Virgil W. Vogel to make a Swedish-American coproduction. The U.S. title was to be "Terror in the Midnight Sun," and the Swedish title was *Rymdinvasion i Lappland* (Space Invasion of Lappland). Arthur C. Pierce, who later turned out a number of slightly interesting, mediocre, low-budget SF films in the 1960s, wrote the script, which may have been his first to be filmed.

The movie as shot did not receive any U.S. distribution. Based on Virgil Vogel's two SF films for Universal-International, *The Mole People* and *The Land Unknown*, I presume that "Terror in the Midnight Sun" was flat, plodding and almost austere. I've read Arthur C. Pierce's original script, filmed much as written, except for the destruction of the monster, and it is certainly better (if not good) than the released film. "Producer" Jerry Warren would have done much better if he had edited the original film for length, tightening scenes and speeding up the action, instead of altering the plot and adding his own amazingly awful, preposterously boring footage.

Warren's restructuring gave the film surrealistic geography. Although the actors' lips tell us "Sweden," the sound track tells us "Switzerland"—even though all references to Lappland stay the same. (Warren may have thought Switzerland was somehow more acceptable to Americans than Sweden.) Light planes fly back and forth from Switzerland to Lappland quite easily. To compound the confusion, in one of the Warren–added scenes, a group comments on what we've already seen; they are following the action on a map of *Greenland*.

Jerry Warren is one of the most uncaring movie "producers" in the history of the medium. He generally finds foreign films, sometimes ones with striking visual qualities, and dubs them into English, cutting out large swatches of exposition and character development, while shooting a few scenes of new footage in this country. Invariably, his new footage features either people standing around a room talking, or a narrator standing in one place and talking.

The narrator has occasionally been John Carradine, as in *Invasion of the Animal People.*

Warren recut films from Brazil (*The Violent and the Damned*), Mexico (*A Bullet for Billy the Kid, Attack of the Mayan Mummy, Face of the Screaming Werewolf, Creature of the Walking Dead*), and at least one international co-production (*No Time to Kill*). The imported films were occasionally (though rarely) made by people with some talent, so Warren's new scenes looked even worse by comparison.

His few apparently (mostly) original films, which he produced, directed and wrote himself, were, if anything, worse than his imports. These include *Teenage Zombies, The Incredible Petrified World, The Wild World of Batwoman* (1966) and perhaps *Terror of the Bloodhunters* (1962); they were static, unimaginatively and excruciatingly dull. Nothing much happens in *The Incredible Petrified World*, and what does happen in *Batwoman* (also known as *She Was a Hippy Vampire*) is so ludicrous and vapid that it plumbs new depths of pointless incoherence.

The Warren–filmed scenes of John Carradine here show him sitting in a lablike room equipped with a globe and blueprints on the wall. Carradine maunders on about the difficulty of the comprehension of time and space. "Comprehension and Control," he tells us, are the main functions of science. "Micrometeors and radiation that originate from the stars and distant galaxies" seem to be of great importance. "Our quest for comprehension is perhaps most complicated by the failure to discover reality in ourselves." Although Carradine reads these incomprehensible lines with great conviction, we sit there in dull stupefaction and with a dawning sense of having been fooled again. If this is the opening, what follows must be worse, and we begin looking hastily for the exits. As it happens, what follows has nothing to do with what Carradine is talking about. (Carradine is given no role name or designation; maybe he's just supposed to be John Carradine himself.) If you saw this much, you'd already bought your ticket, and Jerry Warren didn't care if you could make sense of the movie; he certainly wasn't out to entertain anyone, just to take the money and run.

Warren adds completely meaningless and boring scenes of several people discussing the encounters of three women with flying saucers, which somehow leads to a long discussion of *ears*. This goes on and on and on and on, until you are ready to scream. I believe I did. Oddly, for all of his added scenes, Warren's film is only 55 minutes long. It seems a great deal wider.

The plot that remains gives signs that the original film had its flaws. Scenes of skiing and skating seem to have been added to pad the picture (Warren, of course, retains these).

Our heroine Diane (Barbara Wilson) suddenly sits up screaming, then flees in terror. She seems to have some link with a mysterious object in the sky, but this is never made clear. In the original script, Diane (there called Judy) had *no* such connection. Warren tried to invent it out of the footage he was given. He adds a scene of Diane's parents worriedly discussing what happened to her the night before; they argue over whether Diane should go to Switzerland to train for the Olympics.

Recovered, Diane arrives in Switzerland, but the sky object is seen again. And how. It crashes to Earth in Lappland, skidding along under the snow, glowing like a fireball, and fetches spang up against a mountain. Lapplanders stare in astonishment at this spectacle.

Dr. Frederick Wilson (Robert Burton), coincidentally Diane's uncle, flies up to look at the meteor, still embedded in the mountain. When he returns to a small village, he encounters Diane, to his (understandable) surprise. She also meets Erik Engstrom (Stan Gester), Dr. Wilson's assistant, and they go skiing so a romance can develop.

Dead animals are found in the vicinity, and Diane sees some tracks of something that "has to be at least 20 feet tall." Looking at photos of the "meteor" crash, Wilson and Erik realize that it skidded along a valley before striking the mountain. The small crater and the horizontal flight path of the object indicate it was making a landing rather than simply falling to Earth.

They fly back to the meteor site; Diane stows away on the plane. They all gaze at the spaceship, a dark sphere with a pattern of small white hexagons. For the first time, we see one of the alien occupants of the ship, watching our heroes on a television screen.

Meanwhile, back at the plane, a young soldier fires at a huge advancing *something* (seen from the point of view of the *something*), which kills him and causes an avalanche which buries the plane. Big footprints are found leading away from the wreck. (More Jerry Warren footage here, of a group standing around a radio discussing Greenland.)

Erik and Diane ski back toward a nearby Lapp village to try to get help. (More Warren footage here.) Back at the ship, one of the party begins to climb down the icy wall of the trench plowed out by the landing spaceship, but the alien within, watching, somehow contrives to make him fall to his death.

Erik and Diane take refuge in a rescue cabin as, unknown to them, the monster approaches. Indeed about 20 feet tall, it's covered in long, shaggy fur, with a bestial face, heavy brow ridges, a nose like a New World monkey, deep-set eyes and huge tusks. It seems to have, rather charmingly, big furry ears.

The monster walks by, causing an avalanche, which smashes the cabin. Eric is rescued, but Diane is lost in the storm. The monster, wandering around at loose ends, is attracted by her screams, and carries her off. There's an electronic beeping sound, to which the monster seems to respond. It puts her down, and she is found by the aliens. They are dressed in monklike garments, have slender, expressionless, hairless faces and high-domed heads, but otherwise look perfectly human.

The big shaggy monster approaches a Lapp village, throws a wall at a plane, causes a fire, smashes a building and wreaks minor havoc while growling and snarling. Torch-carrying villagers on skis pursue Big Shaggy, who returns to Diane (the aliens are gone) and picks her up. Erik tries to stop the villagers from throwing torches at the monster, fearing they will injure Diane. But, Kong–like, it puts her down before the villagers' torches catch its fur afire, and it topples off a cliff in a blaze.

The spaceship takes off (the landing footage run in reverse), and one of the characters muses, "I wonder if they found out what they wanted to know." We return to narrator Carradine, who obscurely informs us that "without a future, there would be no present." The numbed, baffled audience files silently out.

The original script, pretty clearly a blend of *It Came from Outer Space* and *King Kong*, begins with the landing of the ship, leads to Wilson being sent to investigate it, and then basically follows the same story as told above. The monster saves Diane from a bear, and there are scenes of dead animals. Someone offers an explanation for the monster—completely lacking in the released film—suggesting that it was a test animal which escaped from the crashed ship, and that the aliens were just trying to get it back. In the film as it is, there isn't any clear connection between the aliens and the monster; they just arrive at thte same time, although it may be reacting to that beeping. In Pierce's script, the monster is white and is friendlier, although it does wreck the village; it's killed by jets.

The scene of the landing of the spacecraft has a frosty beauty; I've never seen anything else quite like it. It skids along under the snow, glowing through the snow. It's one of the most attractive spaceship landings in movies.

The monster itself is not unsuccessful; the suit is not especially imaginative, but it is well-made, and the face is quite good. The photography to make it look huge is unusually successful; Vogel even contrives several times to have the monster and human beings in the same shots (by forced perspective), which work well. The miniature buildings are especially good. All in all, the special effects are very much above average for American films of the same budget level; the film cost only $40,000.

But monsters, no matter how good, rarely raise the quality of the movies they're in, and we don't see enough of Big Shaggy. The romantic interest, more prevalent in Pierce's original, is neither better nor worse than most such stuff. Erik is shown to be a womanizer reformed by meeting his true love, but that's about all there is to it. None of the actors has much to do, and although they aren't terrible, they also aren't very interesting.

Some sources say that Robert Burton appears only in the footage shot by Jerry Warren, but this is definitely not the case. He actually went to Sweden to make the picture, and appears throughout. Burton was a good character actor, physically resembling Jean Hersholt, but didn't have Hersholt's range. Burton usually played weak-willed doctors, minor politicians and the like. He appeared frequently for ten years in a wide range of films. He could rise to the occasion when required, or be virtually invisible at other times. He was solid and reliable; while he rarely made a major contribution to the films he was in, he was above average and a welcome sight. Among his other films: *Above and Beyond* (1952), *The Big Heat* (1953), *I Was a Teenage Frankenstein*, *Compulsion* (1959) and *The Manchurian Candidate*. What seems to have been his last film, *The Slime People* (1963), was released the year after Burton died.

Barbara Wilson is very attractive, but rarely had a leading role. It's quite impossible to tell from *Animal People* if she was a good actress; one suspects she was hired either because she could ski, or because there was a Swedish skiing double available who resembled her. She was also in *The Best Things in Life Are Free* (1956) and *The Man Who Turned to Stone*. The Barbara Wilson who appeared in *The Murder Clinic* (1969) was probably not the same actress.

Virgil W. Vogel began as an editor of Universal-International films, including *Son of Ali Baba* (1951) and *This Island Earth* (1954). He directed *The Land Unknown* and *The Mole People*; the latter is quite bad. He moved into television, and became much better as a director; he has helmed several notable television movies. Understandably, Vogel was not at all happy with what Jerry Warren did to "Terror in the Midnight Sun." According to *Fantastic Films* #24, Vogel was "deliberately trying to create a 'Bergmanesque' feel and [Warren] felt the film was too 'arty' for a 'monster movie.'"

Arthur C. Pierce was never a good writer of dialogue or characters, but had a knack for coming up with a medium-good storyline for low-budget SF films. His movies center around a basic gimmick, being slightly more reasonable than similar films from other writers. He's not notable or important, but clearly strove for some quality. He rarely achieved it, but there are details in some of his films that show he was a man of some taste.

The Cosmic Man was an insignificant imitation of *The Day the Earth Stood*

Still, but some of Pierce's 60s films were better. Among other films, *The Human Duplicators* (1965) featured a giant alien, played by Richard Kiel, that is sad and lonely; *Mutiny in Outer Space* (1965), with a tyrannical, Queeg–like space station commander; the time-traveling cyborg played by Michael Rennie in *Cyborg 2087* is desperately trying to engineer events which will result in his own destruction; *Destination Inner Space*, a lively little picture with a good monster and a slightly off-kilter romance; *Dimension 5*, a spy thriller with a twist, a belt which enables the wearer to move a short "distance" through time. Some of Pierce's other films, such as *Women of the Prehistoric Planet* and *Las Vegas Hillbillys* [sic] (all 1966) have little, if anything, to recommend them. In *Invasion of the Animal People*, the distant cool aliens, who never really make any significant contact with Earthlings, are somewhat unusual and deserve mention. But it's not otherwise even one of Pierce's better pictures.

A strangely inaccurate plot for this film found its way into otherwise reliable sources, such as the *American Film Institute Catalog*. "In an effort to save [Diane, captured by space monsters], Dr. Wilson and Erik start an avalanche. Frightened, the monsters release her and take off in the spaceship, narrowly escaping the avalanche." It's not the only film which the AFI got wrong (their plot for *Homicidal* is askew), but as they were usually so careful, I wonder how they arrived at this particular error. The AFI also says that Carradine plays Dr. Wilson and Burton his assistant; of course, this is wrong as well, as is their assertion that Burton's scenes were added by Jerry Warren. (Warren's added scenes were shot in color but printed in black and white.)

Films distributed by minor companies, in this case A.D.P. Productions, are notoriously hard to find reviews on. The only contemporary review I've been able to locate was in the *Monthly Film Bulletin*, which gave the movie a rating of II, generous enough. "An uncommonly distinguished monster, Lapp actors and finely photographed natural backgrounds are not enough to compensate for a woefully contrived story.... Nor can the totally enigmatic ending be excused in the light of the film's flimsy and unconvincing preliminaries. Even so, addicts will find the novelty of this American-Swedish item useful."

In *Castle of Frankenstein* #11, Joe Dante described it: "Revised, badly cut and senseless Americanized version of Swedish SF–fantasy.... Pointless story with no continuity due to indiscriminate hacking." Don Willis (II) thought it an "endearingly inept SF–mystery, with so few elements to its mystery-plot that the script has to dispense them very carefully."

Invasion of the Animal People is a mishmash of good and bad scenes, good and bad ideas, with some really bright moments. It's as incoherent as most Jerry Warren productions,* but the source material is better than usual. Also, it is fortunately very short.

Invasion of the Star Creatures

The title of this film is promising, and the attractive advertising art showed beautiful women imprisoned in giant toothpaste tubes. However, the movie itself is an astonishingly bad attempt to repeat the modest success of the little parodies like *Bucket of Blood* perpetrated by Roger Corman and Charles B.

*I am eager to point out again that I am not related to Jerry Warren.

Griffith. Instead of modeling the film on those, the moviemakers instead chose to emulate possibly the worst available original: the Bowery Boys.

On top of that, the director was Bruno Ve Sota, who shows no subtleties as a director; even his melodramas are overdone yet inadequate, and this was probably more hastily made than even the quickest of those. The result is a film so haplessly bad that it's almost unwatchable. It consists mostly of the least funny comedy team in the history of movies running around on cheap cave sets, battling men in cloth suits with enormous stuffed heads (the Vegemen) and trying to win the love of two gorgeous women from outer space. I'm tempted to call the film loathsome, but that implies it has a certain power, and it lacks power, interest, humor, intelligence, talent, imagination, etc. It's a motion picture cipher.

The credits say "R.I. Diculous Presents an Impossible Picture," perhaps the best joke in the film. A pompous narrator tells us that "This is a true story. Only the facts have been completely distorted." We meet Army rookies Philbrick (Robert Ball) and Penn (Frankie Ray), and they immediately begin comedy team–type slapstick involving squirting one another with a garden hose.

We are treated, if that's the word, to lots of jokes and wisecracks, very few of which are remotely funny: "I wanted to go to the Moon," Philbrick (the silly one, like Huntz Hall) says; "Yeah, and I wanted to send ya there," Penn (the Leo Gorceyoid) replies. Later: "You're the backside of the Army, and don't you forget it." These are the jokes, folks.

Their platoon is sent by their tough sergeant into the woods to do some exploration with a Geiger counter. While doing a conga they happen upon Bronson Caverns. Entering, they discover that it is made of "indigenous rock" (a serious line). Inside, they find something they describe as being seven feet tall, woody and humanoid. Actually, it's a stunt man dressed in a body stocking with a large head, with various vegetables tied to it. This and other Vegemen grab the platoon.

Philbrick and Penn wake up in a spaceship from the planet Kallar of the Belfar Star System, commanded by Professor Tanga (Gloria Victor) and Dr. Puna (Dolores Reed). (Other sources list them as Dr. Tanga and Professor Puna; not that it could possibly matter, but I have them correct here.) They use brain-reading devices on the men which makes Puna talk like a hepcat; Penn's brain is blank.

When Philbrick's brain is tapped, he is envisioning himself as a superhero, "Senior Flight Leader Philbrick of Commander Connors' Secret Space Patrol," and sees himself catching a car and stopping it by sheer strength. (In a Hitch-cockian cameo, director Ve Sota is the thug in the car.) Philbrick then thinks of Puna and blows out the machine.

After a brief struggle with the Vegemen ("that's the first time a salad ever tossed me"), Philbrick and Penn escape from the ship, and there's more wandering through the caves. They discover the origin of the Vegemen—they're grown in pots, like a geranium. A hand grows out of one, a foot out of another.

The rookies are recaptured and imprisoned in a force field. Penn tries to communicate with the Vegemen to get out: "Look 'em right in the eye," he says, "the one next to the carrot." He describes this as "Operation T'ink." While he is t'inking, he starts talking like Bela Lugosi. This affects Philbrick, who somehow frees himself.

They find the rest of the platoon paralyzed, then reencounter Tanga and Puna, and find a ray which makes the Vegemen vanish. After a strange cut which looks as though they simply ran out of film, Tanga and Puna are strongly attracted to our heroes. Philbrick tells Puna about love and kisses her, making an electrical crackle.

Tanga and Puna converse in their own language, and decide maybe to side with Philbrick and Penn. The Vegemen give chase, and Philbrick and Penn roll phony-looking rocks down at the plant monsters, who toss the rocks back. The Vegemen are called back to the cave.

Philbrick and Penn cannot convince Col. Thomas Awol that any of this (whatever it is) has happened, until Awol learns that Philbrick is a fellow member of Commander Connors' Secret Squadron.

A group of Indians (why not?) rides by, and when they hear the name "Custer" at first are about to go to war, but they, too, are fans of Commander Connors' TV series, and decide to help our heroes. There is a long diversion with the Indians which goes nowhere, as if there were anywhere to go.

Eventually, everyone arrives back at the cave. The spaceship takes off, presumably loaded only with Vegemen; Tanga and Puna decided to stay with Philbrick and Penn, now sergeants. All march out of the cave whistling "The Colonel Bogey March" from Bridge on the River Kwai.

Invasion of the Star Creatures looks like it were made without a script. It has no focus, no plotline, no structure at all, just a bunch of pointless wanderings about a cave set, with the leads being captured and recaptured aimlessly. Perhaps the exteriors and interiors were shot at widely separated times, and the script was lost between. Probably not, though.

Jonathan Haze, who was okay as the schlemiel hero of Little Shop of Horrors, wrote the script for Star Creatures, originally calling it "Monsters from Nicholson Mesa" in tribute to his friend Jack Nicholson. (There's a mention of the earlier title in the credits.)

Probably the filmmakers knew they could sell whatever they made to American International at a profit; perhaps the two stars, Robert Ball and Frankie Ray, really did have hopes of being a movie comedy team. It was an easy way to make a few bucks.

Robert Ball, the pseudo–Huntz Hall, makes no impression at all. He's not quite a hole in the screen, but there's little about him that's worth mentioning. This seems to be the only film, other than The Brain Eaters (also directed by Ve Sota) in which he has a substantial role. He appeared in small roles in several other films, including Mother Goose A-Go-Go (1966), Who's Minding the Mint (1967), Madigan (1968), Easy Rider (1969) and Bunny O'Hare (1971).

Frankie Ray has a showier part as the Brooklyn–accented Gorcey type. The film is something of a showcase for his, er, talents, as he frequently breaks into mediocre impressions, including James Cagney, Bela Lugosi and Edward G. Robinson. Aside from the obvious fact that those actors are among the most frequently imitated by impressionists, showing a low level of creativity, sometimes they are only barely recognizable.

As a team, Ball and Ray show no rapport, just two guys hired to go through the motions of a comedy team, and even those motions are tired and repetitious. There's no originality, no lunacy, no meshing, and their characterizations are borrowed.

The film is painfully shoddy. The set representing the interior of the Army base is merely a corner, and the cave interiors are apparently left over from some other film. There's one long shot of Tanga and Puna talking in which the edge of the set is clearly visible, even on television. The sound is tinny, the lighting poor, with "hot spots" plentiful. The spaceship interiors, in which wrinkled paper backdrops are used, wouldn't pass muster on a children's TV show in the 1950s in, say, Cody, Wyoming. Then there's the Vegemen costumes. There's a slight attempt to make their very sleaziness something of a joke, but they're even too bad for that.

Tanga and Puna are supposed to be very tall, but the actresses are standing on boxes when they talk to Ball and Ray. When Ball kisses Puna, he visibly steps up.

The script is disorganized; once Our Heroes arrive at Bronson Caverns, they spend time wandering about the cheap studio interiors until a sufficient amount of film is exposed. (It looks as though every take were used.) Indians, dream sequences and conga lines are tossed in to make the film seem like a madcap comedy, but it merely seems chaotic.

The funny stuff is bleak; there's lots of lamebrained comedy that doesn't work, and the "satire" of TV kiddy spaceshows misfires because, for all their faults, they were much better than this movie. If you're going to spoof something, you have to do it in a slightly more sophisticated context than the target.

The two items in the film that come the closest to being funny (the line about being tossed by a salad, and the potted Vegemen), are lost in the rest of the low-class, crass humor. The most cited element from the film is the names of the two spacewomen, always referred to in the order I have used, when they're mentioned as a pair. Never, of course, as Puna and Tanga; that's called subtlety. For those unfamiliar with American slang, "poontang" is Army talk for female genitalia. I suppose Haze and Ve Sota felt pretty smug about slipping that one past everyone. Their smugness is misplaced; getting a mildly smutty joke onscreen is a waste of time if the overall joke is on you. Who's going to notice or care about salacious sniggering if the film is a stinker? (Well, I did, but then again no one has ever written this much about this movie, nor is it likely anyone else ever will.)

The film went virtually unreviewed as it crawled across the country in the modified states' rights method of distribution American International employed at this time. (Appallingly, it was generally the cofeature with *The Brain That Wouldn't Die*.) For instance, it was officially released in 1962, but as late as 1964, an exhibitor commented on playing it at his theatre. The exhibitor, A. Madril of Antonio, Colorado, population 1,255, had it at his La Plaza Theatre. "Whàt a lot of baloney!" he wrote to *Boxoffice*. "Such a waste of time, film and effort. The title was good, but was it a spooky film? Nope! A comedy!! Closed the first night."

Understandably, *Invasion of the Star Creatures* has received little notice since 1962. In *Castle of Frankenstein* #11, Joe Dante said, "wacky but extremely poor attempt to follow up Roger Corman's low-budget movie parodies, devoid of the slightest wit or charm.... A few funny moments are due only to ludicrous budget restrictions; mostly bottom-of-the-barrel and just awful." *Psychotronic* called it a "stupid science-fiction comedy."

Invasion of the Star Creatures is not a charmingly inept freak show, like *Cat-Women of the Moon* or *Devil Girl from Mars*; it's a disaster: boring, unfunny, trite and seemingly endless. It has absolutely nothing in it worth watching.

It's Hot in Paradise

Later recut and rereleased under the lurid but more accurate title, *Horrors of Spider Island*, this doesn't seem to have been any good under any title; reviewers disliked it, except for *Boxoffice*, which loved it under both titles—but under the *Spider Island* title, categorically if paradoxically stated, "This is not a new picture nor a reissue."

Finding information on the picture is difficult; it doesn't seem to be available for rental, I've never heard of it turning up on television, and even the seemingly insatiable maw of videotape rentals has yet to gobble it up. I have not seen the film; on the other hand, based on the best evidence available, I have no great desire to see it.

Released in 1960 in West Germany under the title *Ein Toter Hing Im Netz* (A Body in the Net), the film was first shown in the United States by Pacemaker Pictures in 1962 on a states' rights basis. They later recut it from 86 minutes (longer than the German version), to 75 minutes for the *Spider Island* reissue. Pacemaker may also have distributed the film as *The Spider's Web* and/or *Girls of Spider Island*. Pacemaker had an irritating habit of continually reissuing their films under new titles.

Hollywood talent agent Gary (Alex D'Arcy) heads for Singapore with seven showgirls, but their plane develops engine trouble, wanders off course, and crashes into the sea, killing the crew. Gary and the girls make it to a nearby island on a rubber raft.

They hear a strange humming sound, tracing it to a hut in a jungle clearing. Inside, they find a dead man caught in a gigantic spider's web (hence the German title). They discover he was a research scientist.

They cut the corpse free from the web, then go in search of food. A big spider sneaks up on the one girl left behind, and, unseen, almost gets her, but the others return, and the spider departs.

That night, Gary unwisely goes for a walk in the woods. You'd think that he would consider the possibility that a giant spiderweb might mean the presence of a giant spider or two, but I guess when you gotta walk in the woods, you gotta walk in the woods. There's quite a bit of woods-walking in this film.

The giant spider—rather small, actually, about the size of a cat—jumps on Gary and bites him. He kills it, but the poison has a strange effect: he falls to the ground, then grows fangs and hair like a werewolf. (Why he was thus affected, and not the dead man in the net, is a question of great importance.)

One of the girls wanders off by herself while the others are searching for Gary. Seated by a pool, she sees a strange reflection, which turns out to be Gary, of course. He kills her.

Understandably, the girls are upset, and fall to quarreling among themselves. Gary tries to attack them, but gives up and goes back into the forest. (Apparently the girls are not aware the monster is Gary.)

Meanwhile, two other men, Robby and Joe, arrive on the island separately. Joe is almost killed by one of the girls, but they all go back to the hut together. Once again, against all good sense, someone goes wandering. This time, it's Robby. His dead body is found later.

Gary chases Gladys through the forest and up a rocky peak. Joe starts to shoot Gary, but finds the rifle has no shells; he sends Georgia back to the hut for ammunition, but Gary kills Gladys before Georgia gets back. Joe rushes back to the hut, and encounters Gary. They fight, Gary is getting the best of his opponent when, on an inspiration, Georgia grabs a torch and thrusts it in Gary's face. He recoils. The surviving girls and Joe arm themselves with torches, forcing the monstrous Gary into a quicksand pit, where he sinks from sight.

Now, if you had bought a ticket to a film called *It's Hot in Paradise*, seemingly promising brown-skinned maidens, tropic moons and some sex, and instead saw a movie with the above plot, don't you think you might feel at least a little disconcerted, if not cheated? At least those who later went to see *Horrors of Spider Island* would merely have the quality of the film to complain about.

The stills show a giant spider that is preposterously unreal. It quite literally looks like a spider from an animated cartoon, with large, glaring eyes, a sculpted scowl, and rubbery legs. The body resembles a coconut.

Aside from the fact that this isn't the sort of film one expects from Germans — their horror films of this period tended toward old dark house type mysteries or glum crime films derived from Edgar Wallace — the most unexpected aspect of the picture is Alex D'Arcy.

D'Arcy was an urbane, sophisticated, but not very talented actor, somewhat resembling Billy De Wolfe. He bounced around the world making films almost everywhere but his native Egypt. Born in 1908, he seems to have made his first film in 1928. He was in some very important movies, including *A Nous la Liberté* (1931), *Carnival in Flanders* (1935), *The Prisoner of Zenda, The Awful Truth* (both 1937); some fairly obscure ones, such as *Fifth Avenue Girl* (1939) and *City of Chance* (1950). After *How to Marry a Millionaire* in 1953, he returned again to Europe and appeared in a bizarre variety of pictures, including *Soldier of Fortune* (1955) and *Fanny Hill, Memoirs of a Woman of Pleasure* (1964). Back in the United States yet again, he was in Jerry Lewis' unfunny *Way ... Way Out* (1966), Roger Corman's *The St. Valentine's Day Massacre* (1967) and Russ Meyer's *The Seven Minutes* (1971). He was a dispirited Count Dracula in *Blood of Dracula's Castle* (1969), and, in Europe, appeared in one of Sam Fuller's worst films, *Dead Pigeon on Beethoven Street* (1972). D'Arcy may be the only actor in film history to have been directed by René Clair, Elia Kazan, Roger Corman, Sam Fuller and Russ Meyer. When D'Arcy, who usually plays slick gigolo types, played his only monster role, he was 52. (It seems highly unlikely that D'Arcy played Gary after his transformation.)

Boxoffice's reviewer seemed almost satirical, but is actually just inept: "Very much in the mold and manner of sensationalized themes that have gone on to resoundingly profitable engagements, particularly in the larger, metropolitan centers, this Gaston Hakim production, teaming the personable talents of Alex D'Arcy, whose raw, sensual virility [!] will appeal to the distaff side of the audience, and a new-comer Barbara Valentine, as cuddlesome and fetching as any 'fresh' face on the international screen scene." [*Sic* — it's not a sentence.] The unnamed reviewer felt the cast of *It's Hot in Paradise* presented "an esprit de corps refreshing and commendable indeed to behold," adding, "The more impressionable minds — and the junior set shouldn't be urged to plunk down the coin of the realm for admittance! — are the viewers to which the basic story plays best. The discriminating and intelligentsia no doubt would find man-sized holes in the plotting pattern." I wish *I* could write like that, gosh.

In less baroque language, the film was again reviewed by *Boxoffice* as *Horrors of Spider Island*, but the reviewer (someone else, apparently) still liked it. "In a trim hour and 15 minutes, [the director] spins out a most spirited yarn very much within sphere-and-scope of like-mannered entertainment that has appeared for lo! these many years." (Perhaps it *was* the same reviewer.) "D'Arcy seems to be ... forceful, infusing his role with much more than bold, broad movement calculated to frighten his beholders," said the dazzled *Boxoffice*.

In the *Los Angeles Times*, reviewing the film as *Horrors of Spider Island* in 1967, Kevin Thomas expressed a dissenting opinion. "The real 'Horrors of Spider Island,'" Thomas said, "are its uniformly dreadful script, direction, acting, dubbing, photography and projection."

The reviewer in *Castle of Frankenstein* #8 found some enjoyment in the picture: "Astoundingly bad German horror.... Island infested with spiders resembling overgrown watermelon rinds. Ridiculous action, dialog, acting—stands with *Plan 9 from Outer Space* as grade-Z rock-bottom filmmaking. Much, much funnier than most comedies!" In a like mood, *Psychotronic* called it an "outrageous oddity."

Perhaps it was because of the quality of this film that we saw no further monster movies of this type emanating from Germany. For lo! these many years.

The Manchurian Candidate

This is without a doubt the best film John Frankenheimer directed; it contains a good performance by Frank Sinatra, one of the few good ones by Laurence Harvey, and a superlative one by Angela Lansbury. It is stunningly photographed, inventively designed and edited, and altogether one of the funniest, most suspenseful political satires masquerading as melodrama ever made in Hollywood. It is a delight from beginning to end, and unlike any other movie. (Only *Dr. Strangelove* is at all similar, and it's far more overtly comic.)

If you haven't seen it by now, you may never.

Frank Sinatra's company coproduced the film, which was very popular and engendered much controversy. According to Hollywood gossip, the reason it is currently withheld from showings is this: the film deals with political assassination, and Sinatra was friends with both John and Robert Kennedy. He had the deeply troubling feeling that perhaps, somehow, *The Manchurian Candidate* may have contributed to the atmosphere in this country that led to the political assassinations and similar murders that have plagued us since 1963. The full rights to the film reverted to Sinatra in the early 1970s, and along with his earlier film about an attempted presidential assassination, *Suddenly* (1954), Sinatra withdrew *The Manchurian Candidate* from all forms of distribution. So says Hollywood gossip.

However, at a rare screening of the film in 1984, it was revealed that it is being held back because of Sinatra's anger at claims by United Artists, who distributed it, that it had no profits. According to secondhand reports by his attorney, Sinatra intends on someday reissuing the film. (*Suddenly* is now widely available on videotape, being in the public domain.)

The Manchurian Candidate is based on the 1959 novel of the same name by Richard Condon, and is an accurate reproduction of the book. Condon is an erratic but often thrillingly inventive satirist. He worked in advertising for years before turning to novels, and has occasionally produced stunning, devastating and dazzling works unlike those by anyone else. In *Whisper of the Axe*, he postulates all too believably that the economy of the entire world is based on heroin, and there are indissoluble links between the Mafia, terrorists, the U.S. government and the Communist world—all hinging on heroin. In *Prizzi's Honor*, Condon eviscerates the *Godfather*esque concept of honor among gangsters. Perhaps his most outrageous novel was *Winter Kills*, successfully filmed, which more or less says that John F. Kennedy was killed by his own family.

One of the great virtues of Condon is his wildly inventive yet compelling dialogue and description. He never seems to be taking anything seriously, yet virtually defies the reader not to—while still being funny. Evidence of Condon's playfulness can be found in the names of the platoon members in *The Manchurian Candidate*; except for Marco and Shaw, the names he uses are those of the actors who played Sergeant Bilko's platoon in "The Phil Silvers Show/You'll Never Get Rich," plus the names of the show's creator and star: Melvin, Gossfield, Lembeck, Mavole, Freeman, Hiken and Silvers.

Condon is a heady diet for any reader, and can fail spectacularly—*The Vertical Smile* is appalling—but he's breathtaking even in his worst books.

Relatively few of his novels have been filmed, for a writer with a general popular success, because almost no filmmakers are willing to go as far as required to make Condon come to life. Only William Reichert, in *Winter Kills*, and John Frankenheimer and George Axelrod in *Candidate* have met the crazy challenge of filming Condon, with daring, bravura films. Frankenheimer's is the most successful. (*The Happy Thieves* [1961] was lesser Condon and an unimpressive movie; *A Talent for Loving* was not released theatrically, but intermittently caught the Condon flavor. *Prizzi's Honor* was released in 1985.)

Quoting an interview with the director in *The Films of John Frankenheimer*: "This is the film I did exactly as I wanted it to be; we had a lot of difficulties, George Axelrod and I, as it was not a subject that most studios wanted to make. But it meant a great deal to me.... Fortunately, all our difficulties disappeared because George was friendly with Frank Sinatra ... and told him he [Axelrod] owned *The Manchurian Candidate* and Sinatra said, 'God, I always wanted to do that.' As soon as Sinatra said he wanted to do it, we could have shot it at any studio in town. After that there were no problems."

The film was made relatively swiftly—39 shooting days—almost entirely in Hollywood, with a few days of shooting at Madison Square Garden in New York, and at Olympic Stadium in Los Angeles.

The science fictional aspects of the film are subdued but not minor. The type of brainwashing depicted is still impossible: Raymond Shaw is hypnotized and drugged, with his brain not only washed but "dry-cleaned," as the cheery villain puts it, so that even years later he can be turned into a puppet at will by his controller, a puppet who will do whatever he is told, then completely forget whatever it was he did. Furthermore, the plot hinges on an attempt by the Communist world to take over the United States, pushing the film into the realm of political science fiction—a real subgenre, but one not often recognized as such.

Some found the film's eccentric but controlled narrative structure to be unbearably confusing, but it is really merely sophisticated. There are numerous flashbacks and even occasional nightmares, but the story is, though full of incident, relatively straightforward.

In Korea, antagonistic, aristocratic Sgt. Raymond Shaw (Laurence Harvey) rouses his platoon from off-duty relaxation, and leads them on a patrol guided by Chunjin (Henry Silva), near enemy lines. But they are overwhelmed by enemy soldiers; Chunjin is a double agent.

All but two of the patrol are apparently rescued by Shaw and return to the United States; through the intercession of his dim-witted and hated stepfather, Senator Johnny Iselin (James Gregory), Shaw is awarded the Congressional Medal of Honor. His domineering mother (Angela Lansbury), who completely guides the career of rabid right-wing, Red-baiting Iselin, again attempts to assume control of Raymond's life.

Ben Marco (Sinatra), also from the platoon, is now a major in Army intelligence; he begins having nightmares about his experiences in Korea over the next several years. In his dreams, he sees himself and the other members of the platoon sitting bored to distraction on a stage in a small hotel in New Jersey, waiting for a storm to end and listening to some old ladies talk about gardening. But occasionally the scene shifts, and (though still in the hotel), Marco sees the old ladies as a group of Communists, Russians and Chinese, talking about brainwashing the patrol, especially Shaw.

These dream sequences are, to say the least, bravura. Frankenheimer shot the entire sequence three times, once with the old ladies in the garden room of the hotel (and with old *black* ladies for the dream of the black corporal), once with the Communist scientists and military men in the hotel, and once with the Communists in the real interrogation chamber. The 360° pans (cinematographer: Lionel Lindon) and brilliant editing by Frankenheimer and Ferris Webster blend these sequences in a fascinating manner. I've never seen anything else like them.

In one shot, we'll see an old lady talking about gardening; the camera slowly revolves, observing the other little old ladies listening attentively, and returns to the lectern. The old lady has been replaced by chuckling, witty Yen Lo (Khigh Dhiegh, who is terrific as this homespun Fu Manchu), who tells about the brainwashing. But we sometimes see the scientists in the garden room, and sometimes even the old ladies in the conference room. There's more subtle and exotic blending, as an old lady, seen as both black and white at different times, talks about the brainwashing. Another old lady hands up a scarf (for throttling) past the camera, and Yen Lo, on the interrogation set, takes it in the next cut. The scene is obviously difficult to describe, but both clever and sinister, as well as funny, it's quite the most brilliant thing Frankenheimer has ever done.

In the nightmarish flashback, we learn that the platoon was brainwashed into believing the cover story about Shaw's bravery. But for unlovable Raymond Shaw, something more sinister has been prepared. He's been thoroughly brainwashed into being a controlled puppet (with a triggering mechanism; we—and Marco—see Raymond's hands make odd motions). At Yen Lo's direction, he uses that scarf to strangle another patrol member. Later, in another nightmare, Yen Lo asks Raymond which member of the platoon he likes best, and after being turned away from Marco, chooses smiling, open-faced youngster Bobby. Yen Lo then directs Raymond to shoot Bobby in the head, and he does, spraying blood and brains over a photo of Stalin.

Understandably, these nightmares result in Marco's waking up screaming.

Marco tells his superior officer about the nightmares, and furiously tries to remember what Raymond is doing with his hands in the dreams. When the colonel (Douglas Henderson) asks Marco what he thinks of Raymond, he responds that "Raymond Shaw is the kindest, bravest, most wonderful human being I have ever met in my entire life."

In New York, Raymond has a job with grandfatherly publisher Holborn Gaines (Lloyd Corrigan), a position he obtained through his own initiative and not through his mother's connections. Unaware of what really happened in Korea, when Chunjin shows up in New York, Raymond hires him as a houseboy.

Corporal Alan Melvin (James Edwards) is also having nightmares about the brainwashing, and his wife urges him to write to Raymond. After all, she says, you liked Sergeant Shaw, didn't you? "Raymond Shaw is the kindest, warmest, bravest, most wonderful human being I have ever met in my entire life," says Melvin.

Shaw receives the odd letter from Melvin, but disdains it—Shaw really *is* a creep—and then gets a call which suggests he pass the time by playing a little game of solitaire. Glassy-eyed, he complies at once (and that's what he was doing with his hands). He pauses with a blink when he turns up the queen of diamonds. The phone rings again, and the voice tells Raymond to go at once to a certain address, which he does. It's reported to the paper that Raymond was injured in an automobile accident, and is spending time at a convalescent hospital.

Yen Lo turns up, intending to ascertain if all the linkages carefully built into Raymond's mind while he was in Manchuria are still in operation. He playfully suggests that the perfect victim might be dedicated, humorless Zilkov (Albert Paulsen), the Communist spy whose front organization is the rest home where Raymond is being kept after his "accident." (Raymond sits quietly in traction through all this dialogue, his face blandly expressionless.) This suggestion shocks Zilkov, but Yen Lo chuckles. "Always with a little humor, comrade," he says, "always with a little humor." Instead, they select Holborn Gaines as the victim, and Raymond walks zombielike into the kindly old man's bedroom and smothers him.

In Washington, Ben Marco has been moved to the public relations corps, and is running a meeting when Iselin begins shouting (for the benefit of TV cameras) about a number of Communists in the state department. Ben trips him up on the number, and later Iselin begs Raymond's mother to choose a number, just any one number, he can be sure to remember next time. He's pounding on a bottle of Heinz ketchup at the time; in the next scene, he specifies 57 known Communists.

After Holborn's death, we return to Washington to find Marco deteriorating; the nightmares are wrecking him. To the colonel, he repeats the refrain about Shaw, but adds that Shaw isn't difficult to like, "he's *impossible* to like." The colonel sends Ben on sick leave.

On the train to New York, he meets Rosie (Janet Leigh), who immediately falls for him. Taken largely from the novel, Axelrod's dialogue crackles and sizzles in this scene, another highlight of the film.

Marco visits Shaw, and Chunjin opens the door. Ben immediately attacks him, and they have a devastatingly violent and spectacular fight, one of the most exciting in films. They rage around the apartment, smashing everything in sight. It was the first major demonstration of Oriental martial arts in an American film, and is still stunning. It ends with Marco kicking Chunjin in the throat, screaming, "What was Raymond doing with his hands?!" and karate-chopping the cops who try to pull him off.

Rosie bails him out of jail, and they realize they are in love. Ben meets with Raymond, who tells him about the odd letter from Corporal Melvin. Ben realizes that Melvin's nightmares sound like his own, and so immediately returns to Washington, where from slides he identifies several of the people who were in his nightmare. The powers-that-be now know that Raymond is part of some unknown Communist scheme, and Ben is placed in charge of the group that is going to watch Raymond to see what happens.

Ben befriends the friendless Raymond, and one drunken Christmas Eve, Raymond tells Ben about the only time in his life that he was lovable. He met Jocie (Leslie Parrish), the daughter of Senator Thomas Jordan (John McGiver), the liberal enemy of Iselin—meaning, of course, Raymond's mother, who loses no time in breaking up the romance. But Shaw is still pathetically in love with Jocie, whom he hasn't seen in years.

In the normal course of events, Raymond arrives at a bar where he's to meet Ben, and coincidentally (the film has a few), the bartender is telling some friends a story, which includes the phrase "play a little solitaire," which Raymond does at once. He sits like a dummy waiting for the next command. Ben enters just as the bartender says, "so I told him, 'why don't you hop in a taxi, go down to Central Park and jump in the lake?'" Followed by a baffled Ben, Raymond does just that. But he now has a clue as to how Raymond is controlled.

Time passes while Ben and his crew try to find out just what it is that Raymond has been programmed to do. Eventually, Raymond's mother has a lavish costume ball; the nominating convention is coming up, and she wants Jordan to back the Iselin ticket. Raymond goes with his mother to an isolated room, and she suggests he pass the time by playing a little solitaire, then returns to Jordan. (I was thunderstruck, and tried to figure out ways that his mother *couldn't* be the longtime American Communist agent who is Raymond's operative, but I underestimated Condon.)

Jordan, however, refuses to back Iselin and "Iselinism," and, in fact, vows to do everything in his power to stop Iselin from getting any place on the ticket.

In the meantime, Jocie Jordan has found Raymond, still sitting placidly, waiting for his new command. Jocie comes into the room and Raymond flinches: she's costumed as the Queen of Diamonds.

His mother hurries back to the room, hoping to prevent Raymond from seeing Jocie, but it's too late. Raymond and Jocie have eloped. Momma hadn't known about the costume, which Jocie happened upon.

Ben considers ordering Raymond back by using the solitaire trick, but Jocie begs him to allow Raymond some happiness, and he lets them stay together, to give unhappy Raymond a little joy. This, of course, is a Big Mistake.

Raymond's mother is furious at Jordan for not siding with Iselin, and knows he can make good his threat at stopping Iselin's plans to become the vice-presidential nominee. So using the solitaire technique, she sends Raymond out to kill Jordan. He does this. Jocie suddenly rushes in, and, acting according to his programming, sure-shot Raymond kills her, too. (Audiences were stunned.)

Marco manages to meet Raymond, devastated by the Jordans' murders, in a hotel room, and deliberately begins the programming technique: play a little game of solitaire. But this time, Marco is using what might be called a forced deck: 52 queens of diamonds. Raymond is visibly jolted with each queen, and with each queen Marco struggles to erase the programming so carefully planted by the Red Chinese. During the process, Raymond realizes who killed Holborn Gaines and Jocie and her father.

His American operative calls Raymond, and Marco is jolted to learn it's his famously right-wing mother. Thinking the delicate linkages have all been wiped out, Ben allows Raymond to leave.

Raymond's mother has a wonderful speech. A dedicated Communist all her life, she's now furious at her superiors in Moscow and Peking. All along, her plan has been to get Iselin named the vice-presidential candidate, then have the presidential candidate murdered, resulting in Iselin's being elected on a sympathy vote. She was then to turn the country toward Communism. To do this, she insisted on a controllable robot killer, and, thinking to bind her closer to them, they gave it to her in the form of her son. She considers this a major insult and a gross underestimation of her power. Her intention now is to proceed with the plans up to Iselin's election, but then to take over the country with "powers that will make martial law seem like anarchy!" And to make it her *own* country. She plans to pull her masters down and grind them into the dirt.

Raymond eludes Marco and his men, and dressed as a priest and carrying an attaché case, Raymond later enters Madison Square Garden, the site of the nominating rally that night, at which both the presidential nominee and Johnny are scheduled to speak.

Ben and the colonel arrive as the ceremonies begin, and look around frantically for Raymond. Marco spots a light booth high overhead where Raymond has hidden and is assembling his high-powered rifle. Ben runs off, climbing ladders and stairs, heading for the booth.

The suspense by this point is so powerful that most people don't notice that Raymond loads his rifle with *three* cartridges. As the nominee begins his speech, Marco races for the rafters. Raymond takes sight at the nominee's head, but just before Marco reaches the room, quickly shifts the barrel to Johnny Iselin and shoots him dead. Before anyone can react, he kills his mother, too.

Marco bursts into the room, and Raymond whirls on him with the gun, then says sorrowfully that there was really no other way to stop his mother and her puppet Iselin. And then Raymond shoots himself.

The sound of the gunshot mingles with that of a thunderclap, and Rosie listens sympathetically as Marco painfully reads the proper inscription for Raymond's once-undeserved Congressional Medal of Honor: "Made to commit acts too unspeakable to be cited here by an enemy who had captured his mind and his soul.... He freed himself at last and, in the end, heroically and unhesitatingly gave his life to save his country. Raymond Shaw."

I've described the plot in detail because it is such a wonderful tower of cards. Some people found the complexity too much for them. *Playboy*'s reviewer (Stanley Kauffmann?) said Frankenheimer "directed it all into almost complete confusion." But that point of view was definitely in the minority.

The film's juggling act is carefully balanced: the incredible, even outrageous plot is developed through a visual scheme that emphasizes reality to the point that some rather stupefyingly called it "semidocumentary." In fact, it's anything but; reality is carefully controlled and shaped, and every tool of live-action filmmaking is employed, at times extravagantly. In some ways, the film had almost as much influence as *Citizen Kane*, but its great influence has rarely been noted.

In the congressional hearing, for instance, Frankenheimer employed a deep-focus camera and a video monitor to show us Iselin, his puppet master (Raymond's mother) and the opposing senator (on the TV screen) all at once. This setup is anything but natural, but the controlled "confusion" of the scene makes it seem spontaneous. Frankenheimer's control is firm enough that we never lose track of any of the dialogue or action.

He compresses and expands time to suit his needs. When Raymond is accidentally programmed to go jump in the lake, things happen far more swiftly than they could in real life—it's a necessary but throwaway scene, after all. When Marco is racing to try to stop Raymond's assassination attempt, even though Sinatra is moving at top speed, time is stretched.

Deep-focus is used throughout the film, but rarely obtrusively. On the train, we get a big, sweating close-up of Sinatra with Leigh in the background, cool, relaxed but attentive. Raymond's discovery of Jocie in the card outfit uses deep-focus, and is given greater impact by sharp editing techniques. When Raymond-the-robot is about to shoot Jordan, his gun hangs down near the camera, while the senator is at a refrigerator in the distance.

There rarely has been a more sardonic view of American politics. Only in *Winter Kills* has a damn-you-all viewpoint been expressed more vividly. In fact, *Manchurian Candidate* caused great confusion among both American right- and left-wing groups. The former thought it was nothing less than Communist propaganda, while the latter thought it was a vicious attack on Communism.

Among the right-wing responses: *Variety* for 24 October 1962 reported that the extremely conservative Catholic film critic William H. Mooring was afraid that the film would "tend to create confusion and distrust among those who do not yet comprehend the nature of Marxism and the sinister aims and tricks of the pro–Communists in the country." *Variety* added that he considered the film a "brutal morally mish-mash [sic] version of Richard Condon's novel.... Its melo-dramatic excesses may warn the alert," said Mooring. "Its effect upon politically supine [sic?] citizens is liable to be mischievous. The picture inferentially exonerates extreme, left-wing activities in this country, while insinuating that corresponding right-wing organizations ... are instrumental of dissention and disloyalty, forged by the Russo-Chinese Communists themselves.... This is anti-anti–Communism gone crazy, like a fox. Like a red fox."

The 23 November 1962 Los Angeles *Herald-Examiner* reported that the 23rd District of the American Legion was up in arms about the film, feeling that it was showing a new wave of Communist infiltration of the movie industry. The article said that the Legion urged a new congressional probe into Communist activities. Part of the resolution calling for the probe declared that "Communist infiltration in motion pictures has been accelerated since the last investigation ten years ago." Remarking on the film itself, the resolution said it featured a "vicious and impossible portrayal of a U.S. senator."

Inasmuch as the basis for the novel in the first place was the frequent remarks of his period that Senator Joe McCarthy couldn't have done any more harm to the United States than if he'd been an active agent of the Communists, for the American Legion to declare the senator in the film as being impossible is impossibly naive.

Reporting on the same American Legion resolution, *Variety* quoted more of it in a November 28 article. The Legion seems to have found a sinister motive in the film's gleeful satire, feeling that it depicted the conservative senator as it did "in a successful attempt to create a hostile image of patriotism in the minds of the audience. In one scene, another Senator [Jordan] makes an impassioned plea against so-called witch hunting, gloating over his victory in a law suit [and saying] that he turned the money over to the American Civil Liberties Union," which the Legion found to be a "blatant Communist technique." The Legion also found the film's apparent anti–Communist stance just another clever left-wing trick as they tried to demonstrate "the extent to which Soviet brain-washing can go, thus giving the writers and producers an excuse that this picture is really anti–Communistic."

On the other hand, real Communists felt wounded by the film, too. In a 21 December 1962 article, *Film Daily* reported that *The People's World*, a West

Coast Communist paper, attacked *The Manchurian Candidate* as "the most vicious attempt yet made by the industry to cash in on Soviet-American tensions." A small clipping in the 25 February 1963 *Los Angeles Times* reported that the movie was "banned in Finland because it is considered anti–Communist propaganda." And right-wing columnist Victor Riesel reported in the *Citizen-News* for 28 May 1963 that there was a Communist–backed attempt to ban the film at its premiere in Georgetown, British Guiana.

Several sources reported that Frankenheimer was delighted with this confused response, and there's little doubt–judging from his subsequent books–that Richard Condon was. Actually, the film takes no stance on Communism versus the West as philosophies; it's against plotting and excess. Iselin isn't an idiot because he's a Communist tool, nor even because he's a right-wing lunatic (or so it seems); he's an idiot because he's an idiot. Jordan isn't presented as a decent man because of his political views, but a decent man who holds those views–and yet, when Raymond shoots him through a milk carton, the milk (of human kindness) pours forth.

The film really has no political viewpoint–Condon, Frankenheimer and Axelrod are standing off to the side someplace, seeing all the fuss attendant on political activity as absurd.

The Manchurian Candidate baffled some critics, because they weren't prepared for an *original* film; by and large, originality troubles critics in all fields; they can't get their bearings. *Playboy*'s critic thought "Angela Lansbury is wasted in the whacked-up part of the mother. Harvey looks most expressive when in a hypnotic trance. Janet Leigh ... seems welded of chromium. And there's obviously a standard clause in all Sinatra's movie contracts that he must (a) have a punch-up with a bigger man whom he beats [and] (b) have a girl who flips and flops for him on sight. John Frankenheimer, bedeviled by memories of early Hitchcock and middle Capra, has directed it all into almost complete confusion." Except for plot itself, the film bears little resemblance in technique or viewpoint to either Hitchcock or Capra.

Time also missed the point and the boat: "the story is notable chiefly for a systematic error it makes. It tries so hard to be different that it fails to be itself." Very few movies are more "themselves" than *The Manchurian Candidate*; despite imitations, it still looks and sounds as original as when it was first released, although in today's fast-paced film world, it no longer seems quite as swift as it once did.

In his review of the film in the *New York Times*, Bosley Crowther reported that it deals with "a rash supposition that could serve to scare some viewers half to death–that is, if they should be dupes enough to believe it." He felt the approach should have been more serious, apparently failing to recognize the picture as a satire; he wanted the portrayal of the red-baiting senator to be more realistic, so the guy wouldn't look like "a dunce, a joke."

Still, Crowther allowed that "the film is so artfully contrived, the plot so interestingly stated, the dialogue so racy and sharp and John Frankenheimer's direction is so exciting in the style of Orson Welles when he was making *Citizen Kane* and other pictures that the fascination of it is strong." Indeed, visually the film does resemble Welles' earlier movies, and the sardonic viewpoint is similar. Crowther betrays his naiveté, however, when he says he feels that the incredible plot makes one "suspicious of the author's sincerity." One should never be suspicious of Richard Condon's sincerity; one should not entertain it as a possibility.

Later, however, Crowther thought further about the film and began to consider it dangerous. In a further article on it (4 November 1962), he thought that "it's as though the fellows who made it said to heck with truth and credibility, all that's important is a picture that tickles its audiences' ribs and makes their hair stand on end. But when the matter is serious and even tragic, as it certainly is here, it's not right — it's not honest or moral — to treat it as a great big gruesome joke." If Condon, who has a strong moral viewpoint, really, has a recurring theme in his writing, it's that everything is a great big gruesome joke; it's all the same to him, which is what can make his fiction so devastating: nothing is taken seriously.

In the same article, Crowther concluded that "the possible explosion of satire simply does not come off because the elements are not well equated and the melodrama takes control. What we're left with is a demonic Communist plot that has just enough intimation of reality to make it uncomfortable.

"It is peculiar that truth has been distorted and angled to get wild effects in several films of Mr. Sinatra. This is almost as bad as the 'big lie' [of Communism]. The actor should look to his productions. This does not do credit to American films."

However, to their credit, there were those who saw through the apparent "realism" of the film's surface. Cue said that "although much of it is medically, politically and dramatically absurd, novelist Condon and scenarist George Axelrod are such old hands at whipping up audience interest and maintaining it, that you're likely to be fascinated as all get-out until you find yourself out in the fresh air again — wondering what the picture was all about."

In Saturday Review, Arthur Knight gave evidence that he was heading down the Crowther path, until he suddenly caught on. He was thinking about the sardonic mastermind Yen Lo: "This was not Yen Lo, the Red superman, but our old childhood friend, the insidious Dr. Fu Manchu.... Oddly enough, this identification, far from breeding contempt, made [the film] a good deal more enjoyable for me.... John Frankenheimer, working from George Axelrod's taut script, fills every restless shot with an unrelenting tension, alternates the subtleties of psychological warfare with flare-ups of frightful violence, and at the same time maintains a tone that is seemingly as detached and objective as a newsreel.... Without question, it is the best-told story of the year. Without question, it is also the most irresponsible." Oh, pooh.

Paul V. Beckley, in the New York Herald-Tribune, seemed the most on-target: "The characterizations have a razor edge, the dialogue is pertinently impudent, the story is tense as well as funny.... Early in [the film, the] shots of a night patrol ambushed in Korea are so dry and good they get you set for a nervous but naturalistic story. When it dawns on you that you're deep in Fu Manchu territory you may put up some resistance. Don't. Just settle back and let yourself be treated to one of the brightest fantasy thrillers in a long while."

In her collection 5001 Nights at the Movies, Pauline Kael described the film with her usual terse accuracy: "A daring, funny, and far-out thriller.... John Frankenheimer came to life as a director. This picture plays some wonderful, crazy games about the Right and the Left; although it's a thriller, it may be the most sophisticated political satire ever made in Hollywood."

Don Willis (I) found it "offbeat, sometimes brilliant political s-f [which] becomes a little too strange when it tries ... to make the unlovable Raymond human. Powerful, spectacular violence is somehow mixed with misanthropic humor, somehow to the advantage of both."

In Science Fiction Films, Philip Strick described it as "intelligent, funny, superbly written, beautifully played and brilliantly directed."

This was not Frankenheimer's first film. That was *The Young Stranger* (1957), a remake of one of his many television dramas. (Frankenheimer was one of several young directors who moved from TV to films with varying success during this period.) *The Young Savages* (1961) followed after a period in which he returned to television; it received good notices for its strong (even overdone) visual style. In 1962 alone, in fact, *Candidate* was the *third* Frankenheimer film to be released. *All Fall Down*, early in the year, earned him good notices; *Birdman of Alcatraz*, out in the summer, was a smash hit—but nothing prepared audiences for *The Manchurian Candidate* which (despite United Artists' bookkeeping) was also immensely popular.

Frankenheimer was so dazzling in this film, seemed to show such great and firm command of story and technique that he seemed like the young god of films. I was absolutely blown away by the picture, and eagerly anticipated his next, *Seven Days in May* (1964). But though it dealt with similar material, it was glum rather than impish, with a story notably lacking in action and infected by extraneous characters. Though not a bad film, it was a distinct disappointment.

It was followed the same year by *The Train*, which though it did have plenty of action, was severely compromised by the presence of Burt Lancaster, Frankenheimer's most-often-used star (five films), as a French railroad worker. It was too long and too epic.

The general decline of Frankenheimer was considerably offset by *Seconds* (1966), an almost-brilliant, deeply disturbing science fiction story about remaking one's life; an uncomfortably uncompromising film, not well structured, but extremely affecting at times. But instead of presaging a return to greatness, it was, alas, Frankenheimer's last outstanding film (to date).

A few of his later films have been above average, such as *The French Connection II* (1975) and *Black Sunday* (1977), an almost-bravura thriller somewhat in the *Candidate* style, but again compromised and damaged by a weak structure and tendency toward epic-itis. At least three of his films, *The Extraordinary Seaman* (1967), *Impossible Object* (1973) and *99 and 44/100% Dead* (1974) received little if any release in the United States. Although he occasionally shows he can rise to the occasion, most of his pictures are indifferent, such as *The Gypsy Moths* (1969), *I Walk the Line* (1970, though it has its moments), and *The Horsemen* (1971). His one utter disaster was *Prophecy* (1979), blatantly subtitled "The Monster Movie," a ghastly, silly science fiction–horror thriller about mutated bears. It failed at the box office.

Perhaps the most quirky Frankenheimer film was the bizarre *Grand Prix* (1966), which had all the most banal racing stories—and yet also delivered incredible excitement in the racing scenes, involving excellent use of multiple images (then very much in vogue), fast cutting and great technical effects. And all in Cinerama, too. *Grand Prix* represents at once the worst and best of Frankenheimer.

The cast of *The Manchurian Candidate* is uniformly good, even Laurence Harvey, who died in 1973. He began well, working his way up through a series of films of increasing importance, showing himself adept at many types of roles. He became a star with the releases of *Room at the Top* (1958) and *Expresso Bongo*, but suddenly seemed frozen in style, as if once arrived at stardom, he didn't need to exert himself any longer. He soon became known as the most prominent bad actor in films, a stiff, cold presence in movie after movie. (It was reported in 1962 that the only way Frankenheimer could get Harvey to flinch at seeing the queen of diamonds was literally to shoot off a cannon behind him. And even then, he gave only a slight start.)

Harvey was almost laughed off the screen in *The Outrage* and *Of Human Bondage* (both 1964), showed a little more vitality in *Darling* (1965) and *The Spy with the Cold Nose* (1966), but then vanished into multinational pictures, few of which were released in the United States. His last film, *Welcome to Arrow Beach*, which he also directed, went unreleased for some time. It was retitled *Tender Flesh* (1974) and was released after Harvey's death with a horror-movie campaign.

The Manchurian Candidate features what is probably Harvey's best movie performance; he is perfectly cast as the icy, unlovable Raymond Shaw, the kindest, warmest, most wonderful human being I've ever known in my life.

James Gregory is so funny and creepy as loudmouthed, confused Johnny Iselin that he became typed as a blowhard, even playing one in his recurring role on TV's "Barney Miller." He's excellent as this type, though eventually his continual presence in that role became boring.

Probably only because of his unusual appearance, Khigh Dhiegh did not become a star as a result of his performance here. He's a delight as the amused psychological genius from Manchuria. He's never had another role in films remotely as good as this and, in fact, is seldom in films at all. (He is, or was, an instructor at Los Angeles City College.) His only other notable part was in the TV movie/pilot film *Judge Dee and the Monastery Murders* (1974). Americans know him best as Wo Fat, the continuing (and unlikely) villain on TV's "Hawaii Five-O," a role clearly modeled on his part in *The Manchurian Candidate*.

Sinatra and Leigh are fine, but they often are, and Henry Silva makes an admirable Korean baddie, but apart from Dhiegh, the most memorable player in the film is Angela Lansbury, completely convincing as Harvey's mother — although she was only three years older. She's simply wonderful, perfect, even; it may be the role of her career, though she's never less than good. She gave "bitchy" a new meaning with this part, and is riveting and hilarious in almost all her scenes. Not only is she convincing as the slightly bubbleheaded but fiendishly ambitious right-wing fanatic she seems to be for most of the story, but when she's unveiled as a brilliant espionage agent, the earlier impersonation suddenly seems to have been just that all along. More recently, of course, Lansbury has become a major star on stage with a series of starring roles in Broadway musicals. Her TV series, "Murder She Wrote" is popular primarily for her.

Individualistic, quirky and vastly entertaining, *The Manchurian Candidate* is a high-water mark in the careers of everyone involved. It is not an irresponsible film — it is a masterwork of entertainment.*

The Manster

This incredibly-titled film is a bizarre, atmospheric but stupid story about the world's first two-headed monster. (And except for cartoons, it seems to be just that.) This seems to have been the inspiration for the entire picture: a desire to get there first with a double-dome drama. Nothing else about the picture makes much sense and it is, overall, very bad; there are a couple of

---

*It was inspirational, even. In *The Psycho Lover* (1970), a character uses a brainwashing technique which he says he models on that in *The Manchurian Candidate*. At the climax of *Phantom of the Paradise* (1974), there's an attempted assassination modeled directly on that in *Candidate*.

very interesting shots, and one that has a nightmarish impact. But since all logic and coherence (and most quality) was sacrificed to the dubious idea of having a two-headed horror, the film is only a curiosity and a footnote in the peculiar career of George Breakston.

The story of the production of The Manster would almost certainly be more interesting than the film itself. Almost everyone involved has credits in more respectable pictures; to find out how British stars, an American but globe-trotting producer and an American editor ended up working on this partly-Japanese film fascinates me.

In Tokyo, American reporter Larry Stanford (Peter Dyneley) is sent to a lab at the edge of a volcano to interview wealthy but eccentric scientist Dr. Suzuki (Satoshi Nakamura). Unknown to Stanford, Suzuki is a madman who has already turned his brother and his wife into distorted horrors; the wife has long, slender claws, a broadened face and misplaced eyes. The brother looks like a furry white ape, and is shot down in the opening scenes.

Suzuki sees in Stanford an ideal subject for further experimentation in evolution and with the help of his attractive assistant (Terry Zimmern), Suzuki manages to feed Stanford his serum. Stanford soon begins acting sulky and angry, alienating his wife Linda (Jane Hylton) and his friends. He has a love affair with Suzuki's assistant.

Stanford worries about this, and also experiences pain on his shoulder. He takes off his shirt and looks into the mirror, and in one of the most surrealistically horrifying moments in any cheap monster picture, discovers an eye on top of his shoulder, gazing placidly at the ceiling.

Soon, things get much worse. Stanford's hands grow hairier, he develops fangs and, even worse, another head. He is now not responsible for his actions; presumably, the extra head is. He scares his wife, commits various murders around Tokyo, and attracts the attention of the police.

Although both heads are now monstrous, Stanford still retains enough of his own mind and memory to know that it was Suzuki who did this to him. He (or they?) returns to Suzuki's lab, where he kills the scientist.

The two-headed monster and the assistant end up at the brink of a volcano. The serum hasn't finished its work, for now, in agony, Stanford splits entirely in two (the British title of the film was, in fact, The Split), leaving a good Stanford and a hairy, apelike monster which immediately starts to run off with the assistant, and throws her into the volcano. Stanford, his mind restored, battles the creature that was recently a part of him and tosses it into the volcano.

Judging from the music and the embrace between Stanford and his wife, we are to take this as a happy ending, but he still has to answer to those police on his trail. I think his explanation might understandably be met with skepticism.

George P. Breakston produced the film and codirected it with Kenneth G. Crane, who also edited. The script by Walter J. Sheldon was adapted from Breakston's original screen story, "Nightmare." The film was made in Japan as a coproduction between United Artists of Japan (their subsidiary Lopert released it in the United States) and George Breakston Enterprises. It was shot in English on a low budget, and uses no major Japanese actors.

Breakston had a strange, perhaps unique, career. Born in Paris in 1920, by the age of 6 he was in the United States. He soon became a well-known child actor, appearing on radio, in the theatre and films. His most prominent role in the early 1930s was as the boy Pip in Great Expectations (1934), although he also

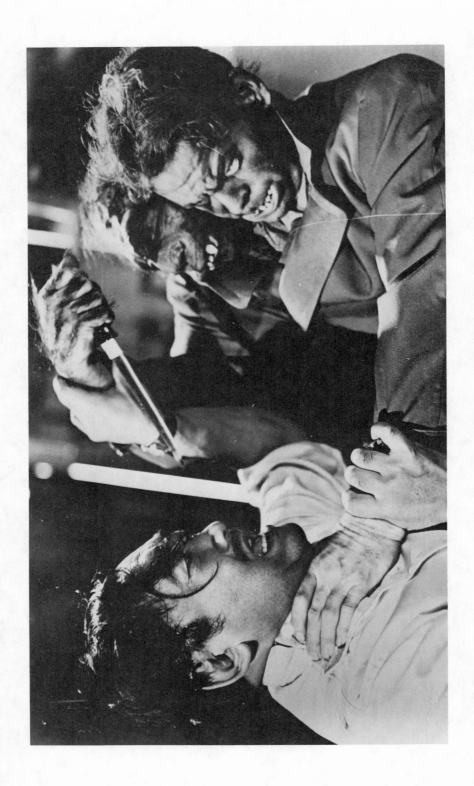

appeared in *It Happened One Night* (1934) and *The Return of Peter Grimm* (1935). He was a busy actor both as a child and as a teenager; he was a regular in the Andy Hardy series as Andy's pal "Breezy." By the late 1940s, however, Breakston seems to have wearied of Hollywood, and left for Africa. There he began producing and directing pictures, sometimes also writing and starring in them. Among these films were *Urubu* (1948) and *Golden Ivory* (1955).

In the late 1950s, Breakston started wandering again; he made *The Manster* in Japan, *Shadow of Treason* (1963) and *Blood River* (1968) in other parts of the world, and *The Boy Cried Murder* (1966) in Montenegro. He finally returned full circle, and died in Paris in 1973. Although it does not appear that any of Breakston's films as a director were notable, his career as a filmmaker is certainly unusual and perhaps worthy of a book in itself.

Star Peter Dyneley, the two-headed man, was a British actor of no great fame, who worked busily for many years. He was handsome enough, somewhat resembling Dennis O'Keefe, and had some of O'Keefe's breezy charm; it's not surprising that he here plays an American. Among Dyneley's other films were *Beau Brummel* (1954), *The Roman Spring of Mrs. Stone* (1961), *Call Me Bwana* (1963) and *Chato's Land* (1972). He died in 1973.

Kenneth Crane, who codirected *The Manster*, was otherwise an editor of insignificant films; low- and medium-budget Westerns and minor action films seem to have been his forte. Among the other films that Crane edited were *The Flight That Disappeared* and *Gun Street* (both 1961), *Devil's Angels* and *Thunder Alley* (both 1967). He is credited as director of the U.S. scenes in *Half Human*, and directed all of *Monster from Green Hell*.

The rest of the cast and crew seems to have been assembled from Americans in Japan who spoke Japanese, and Japanese who spoke English, with little other qualifications necessary. The evil Dr. Suzuki was played by Satoshi Nakamura, the dialogue coach on Frank Sinatra's dreadful *None but the Brave* (1965); Jerry Ito, a police superintendent, was in the strangely-titled *Wall-Eyed Nippon* (1963); scenarist Walter J. Sheldon directed the Japanese sequences of the "exposé" *Mondo Teeno* (1967).

The Manster might have been entertaining if the absurdity of its story had been emphasized, with imagination; the eye-on-the-shoulder is a genuinely haunting shot, and the film could have used more of that kind of thing. But no one seems to have been very concerned with making something good, only something exploitable. The silly little apish head that sits on Dyneley's shoulder bounces when he walks, and except for one memorable shot, looks like nothing more than a grapefruit-sized, lifeless toy. But there is one shot of raincoat-clad Dyneley advancing at the camera: he's snarling, and so is that other head. Now that's a bit unnerving.

Sometimes pioneers just aren't appreciated. But although two-headed monsters were a novelty and still are uncommon, they are basically silly. There was a two-headed monster in *Jack the Giant Killer* (1962) and, of course, *The Incredible 2-Headed Transplant* (1971) and *The Thing with Two Heads* (1972) (but not in *The Man with Two Heads* [1972] or in *The Two-Headed Spy* [1958]). There's a two-headed Cyclops in *The Three Stooges Meet Hercules*, but like most two-headed creations, he's played for (scant) laughs. *The Manster* is the first serious two-headed monster movie; it isn't good, but these little advances should perhaps be applauded.

Opposite: Peter Dyneley (right) gets the upper hand on mad scientist Satoshi Nakamura in this scene from the decidedly peculiar The Manster (U.S. release, 1962); this still has more ferocity and dynamism than anything in the film.

Breakston's original story was called "Nightmare," and no wonder; there are few other science fiction–horror films with plots that seem more like they sprang from someone's bad dreams than *The Manster*. It's too bad the film itself is poor, because it's the nightmarish plots that sometimes click with audiences, such as *The Fly* or *Gremlins*.

The film was released with *Horror Chamber of Dr. Faustus*, which makes it one of the most inappropriate "official" double bills of all time. Not only is there a vast chasm between the films in terms of quality, but their intentions are so divergent that audiences were (at the least) nonplussed. I saw the double bill at the Egyptian Theatre in Coos Bay, and *The Manster* was the kind of film the noisy audience had come to see; it had a monster, several in fact, a wild plot and some action. It was clearly a monster movie, and even though it stunk, it satisfied the desires of the audience. On the other hand, the evocative and poetic *Horror Chamber of Dr. Faustus* wasn't a monster movie, it was an *art film*, for god's sake. It's doubtful that anyone there except me preferred *Dr. Faustus* to *The Manster*.

The film received few reviews. *Boxoffice*, whose reviewer at this time had only the foggiest idea about clear prose, thought it "on a par with similarly projected attractions, the roles enacted with a minimum of histrionic ability and the special effects assuming dominant position through anticipated exploitation activity."

The *Monthly Film Bulletin*, giving the film a III, was more to the point: "The incredible far-fetched rehash of all the ingredients of the conventional SF–Horror film is in every way a thorough waste of effort. The idea of a two-headed man may have seemed ambitious but it has turned out abysmally silly.... All in all a pathetic pot-boiler, occasionally risible and never frightening."

In fairness, *The Manster* does have one or two eerie scenes, but the general hangdog air of production, the very poor makeup and special effects, and the inept direction make the outlandish plot even sillier than it was standing alone.

Moon Pilot

Despite the kind of flaws you'd expect from a Disney film in this period, *Moon Pilot* is entertaining and surprisingly satiric. Of perhaps more interest to readers of this book is that it is one of the few American films until *Close Encounters* to even suggest that aliens want Earth people to start space travel. Even friendly aliens usually tell us to stay the hell home.

Movie critics were taken aback to find amusing satire in a Disney film, especially because of the targets of the satire. As *Time* put it, bludgeoning a metaphor, "Sacred cows, if skillfully milked, produce tuns of fun; but Hollywood usually avoids them because they often kick back. The more reason to be pleasantly surprised that Walt Disney, not specifically known for sociopolitical daring, should have herded three of these pampered critters – the FBI, the Air Force and the astronaut program – into the same plot."

Charlie (played by a chimpanzee named Cheeta) returns from a rocket flight somewhat shaken up, and is placed in the care of astronaut Capt. Richmond Talbot (Tom Tryon), a nice guy not quite as bright as Charlie. The chimp has successfully orbited the Moon, and NASA decides that it's time for a man to do the same. At a dinner, this is put forth to the astronauts. To quote *Time* again, " 'Gentlemen,' brffsks the general, 'we are sending a man around the Moon—this week! I'm asking for volunteers.' The astronaughts turn pale, drop their eyes, examine their nails, twiddle their fingers, fiddle with buttons, brush their sleeves, blow their noses." Charlie stabs Talbot with a fork. Talbot yelps and leaps to his feet, and so is chosen to be the first man to fly around the Moon. He is not happy about this.

He gets permission to fly back to California to see his mother (one last time, it's implied), and because Charlie has grown fond of him, Talbot takes the chimp along.

On the plane, a gorgeous girl who introduces herself as Lyrae (Dany Saval) becomes very chummy with Talbot, and alarms him by revealing she knows all about his mission. She also seems to be able to read his mind. All this, plus her foreign accent, leads him to fear she's a Soviet spy, so he dodges her when the plane lands. He reports her to Major General John Vanneman (Brian Keith, in a funny if hammy spoof of Gen. Curtis LeMay), who promptly orders Talbot locked up in a hotel room.

But Lyrae appears there too, and convinces Talbot—now falling in love with her—that she's not a spy, but an alien from Beta Lyrae, another planet. The Beta Lyraeans are anxious to help us get into space, and have sent Lyrae with a formula for a necessary protective coating for the Moon rocket.

Lyrae and Talbot dodge security precautions and see a little of the town, not only sending everyone into a tizzy, but causing Vanneman to clash head-on with McClosky (Edmond O'Brien), an agent of the "FSA" (i.e., FBI/CIA). They spend more time quarreling over jurisdictions than looking for Talbot.

Eventually, Talbot contacts them and agrees to come back only if the protective coating—guarding against "proton" rays—is applied to his spaceship. This done, he blasts off. No sooner is he on a lunar trajectory than Lyrae appears in his capsule, to the great consternation of ground control. Lyrae teaches Talbot a song about her home planet, and they decide to get married, taking a detour to Beta Lyrae before continuing around the Moon. The film concludes as they sail off happily, singing to each other, while on Earth Vanneman keeps bellowing "What's going *on* up there?!"

The film was adapted from a novel of the same title by Robert Buckner, serialized in *The Saturday Evening Post* in 1960. The pleasant quality of the film is due in part to following the novel closely, for the plot isn't the sort that the Disney studio would be likely to have come up with on their own. (In general, the studio has had much happier results with adaptations than original material.) The spoofing is broad and sometimes clumsy, but it's a kind of lampoon that was unusual for anyone in this period.

The oddest area of satire for Disney were the jokes aimed at the space program. Throughout the 1950s, Walt Disney had promoted space travel on his television program, making it seem more and more real to millions of Americans. I suspect that he may have had a major influence in changing the minds of his audience about the possibility of space travel, and thus had an impact on changing our national goals. On these excellent shows, space travel was treated with seriousness but not solemnity, and was shown to be a very good idea. He was so matter-of-fact about the coming space age, that he turned the silly jokes and lack of belief in it, prevalent at the time, into archaic mistakes.

On the other hand, Disney feature films have almost never dealt with space travel. The few SF comedies, like *The Absent Minded Professor* and *The Misadventures of Merlin Jones* (1964), were strictly Earthbound. After Disney's death, a few more SF comedies were produced, but even though some of these dealt with aliens (*Escape to Witch Mountain*, *The Cat from Outer Space*), they were still set entirely on Earth. Only *The Black Hole* (1979) was set in space, and that one was pretty bad.

This strange difference between the television shows and the movies must have been a corporate decision at the highest level which, in this period, meant Walt Disney himself. Perhaps he wanted to avoid being tarred with the monster movie brush. Certainly by the late 50s the genre had been polluted by quick-buck artists and wasn't respectable, causing most studios to shy away from solid SF concepts. In one sense, Disney had led the way with *20,000 Leagues Under the Sea*, but the financial disappointment of that film meant he wasn't inclined to follow it up with more SF material.

The positive approach to technology adopted in the Disney space travel TV shows simply is not echoed in his films. Based on watching the shows, and the serious approach taken at Tomorrowland in Disneyland (the park), you'd have expected a Walt Disney *Destination Moon*-like film somewhere along the line (and it's a great shame that George Pal and Disney never formed a partnership). In the 50s, Disney made several films that, while not entirely adult, were not laden with what most people think are the usual Disney cutesy-poo elements. Certainly, somewhere in there a serious SF film was possible. (I heard persistent rumors for years that the company was considering a dead-serious animated version of *War of the Worlds*.)

Animation expert Mark Kausler tells me that although there exists an excellent script for a proposed Mickey Mouse feature (dating from 1938) that dealt with space travel, *none* of the short Disney cartoons dabble in that area, making them unique among American short cartoons, which sooner or later sent their main characters rocketing off in one direction or another.

Of the features made by his company in Disney's lifetime, only *Moon Pilot* deals with space travel, and *it* spoofs the subject, the astronaut program (the right stiffs?) and aliens.

Nonetheless, it's above average for Disney comedies which, in this period, tended to be either pretty good (*The Absent Minded Professor*), mixed (*The Parent Trap*) or dismal (*Bon Voyage*). *Moon Pilot* is better than the others, though not quite as good as *Professor*.

Writer Maurice Tombragel also wrote *Monkeys Go Home* (1967) for Disney, but lacking good source material, that was pretty lame. The other films James Neilson directed for the studio, including *Summer Magic* (1963) and *The Adventures of Bullwhip Griffin* (1967), were inferior to *Moon Pilot*, though not bad; those he made after leaving the studio, including *Where Angels Go Trouble Follows* (1968) and *Flareup* (1969) were poor.

Part of the quality of the film is due to the cast. Tom Tryon was an appealing, handsome leading man, with reasonably good comedy timing, an ideal choice for the role of the slightly dopey astronaut. He has the clean-cut, all-American look the part required, and a slightly blank face. Disney was trying to build Tryon into a star, with this movie and the "Texas John Slaughter" segments of the Disney TV show. Tryon's career before *Moon Pilot* had been mixed, and the films he starred in were standard Hollywood fare. After *Moon Pilot*, he was lost in the all-star cast of *The Longest Day* (1962), but then had the great misfortune to be given the leading role in the trashy *The Cardinal* (1963) by producer-director Otto Preminger. Tryon acted in only three more films.

However, there's a happy ending, of sorts, to the Tom Tryon story. He retired from acting and soon became a best-selling novelist; *The Other*, *Harvest Home* and part of *Crowned Heads* were filmed. Perhaps it's all for the best; although his timing was good in *Moon Pilot*, he was still somewhat stiff, and while that was made part of the joke in the film, it has nothing to base a career on.

As Lyrae, Dany Saval charmed millions of American boys. She was at once cute and All Woman, attractive yet approachable. She was also a good comedienne, and all of us were aching to see her in something else. (We even forgave the movie for passing off her obviously French accent as that of an alien.) But she went straight back to France; the only other American film she's appeared in that I know of is the pathetic *Boeing Boeing* (1965), which failed to use her well. A marriage to composer Maurice Jarre interrupted her career, and very few of her French films were released in the United States anyway. In a way, it's just good luck she made *Moon Pilot* at all.

Most of the spoofiness of *Moon Pilot* is carried by veteran actors Brian Keith and Edmond O'Brien. Both tend to shout while their bull necks swell and their faces turn red, and they occasionally become more than you want to watch, but both are good comic actors.

The film slackens in the middle, with scenes of the astronaut and the space-woman out on the town, but picks up again at the end. Even during the romantic scenes, most people were still marveling at the idea of a Disney comedy with a point of view so that they didn't notice the film's lagging pace.

Reviews were favorable if bemused. "Tube" in *Variety* generally praised the film, adding that it was an "amusing, frequently uproarious comedy-fantasy," and then philosophized about it, as he sometimes did on the most unlikely movies. "At first gulp, [it] is a marvelous mixture of absolute nonsense, a thoroughly intoxicating, high-spirited and full-bodied blend of moonshine and monkeyshine. A careful analysis of the ingredients, however, uncovers a more significant reason for its potent kick. For within the frivolous surface merriment of its story lurks a most disarmingly irreverent spoof of the current morbid [!] preoccupation with reaching various heavenly bodies."

Also noting flaws, the *Monthly Film Bulletin* still gave the film its highest rating. "It starts promisingly with satirical punch ... and the tone is regarded later in some richly irreverent moments involving the bombastic, hot-tempered Major-General, [the] exasperated blundering security chief, and the comic rivalry between their two departments.... It is a pity that the attack should have given way in the middle passages to characteristic Disney gimmickry.... A healthy, iconoclastic film for the most part, though, and one that goes as far as one can reasonably expect its producers to go."

The *Bulletin* also correctly pointed out that the production values were not geared to the material. *Moon Pilot* looks like any other Disney film: polished, clean, even antiseptic, with every hair in place, all the colors bright and geaming, and with a view of America as wholesome as a Hallmark greeting card. It should have come down to Earth a bit, which would have made it more watchable today. It is rarely revived, which in a way is a shame. Although the spoofing is light, not to be taken seriously, it's really there; with the revival of interest in this period occasioned by the fame (though, sadly, not the success) of the outstanding *The Right Stuff* (1984), perhaps it should be given a second look.

Mothra

This Japanese epic is a fairy tale with science fiction overtones, intended as a family film; there are plenty of elements intended for kids—heroic little boy, giant moth, lots of destruction—and other elements for adults—satire on the United States, pretty girls, hints of nudity. In some ways, *Mothra* is the most sophisticated of all the Toho Studios giant-monster films. It is in fact, the only one (until, unlikely as it may seem, *Godzilla vs. the Smog Monster*), to show *any* sophistication. There seems to have been less effort to direct the film at an international market—the villain is, after all, a thinly-disguised American—and perhaps the movie overall is the stronger for it. *Mothra* has more striking visuals in the miniature scenes (photographed by Sadamasa Arikawa) and shows a wider range of setups and lighting than almost any other Japanese monster picture; it's one of the best in this regard, and although the whole thing is a shade silly to Americans, deserves to be more appreciated than it now is.

Films such as *Mothra* are easily dismissed; it is, to say the least, hard to take seriously. A giant caterpillar-god comes from an atomic test island to rescue tiny twin girls who were its priestesses; the caterpillar turns into a gigantic moth, rescues the girls, and flies off into the sunset with them. As I suggested in my comments on *The Mysterians*, one of the problems Americans have with such films is that they seem superficially like western movies in the same vein, but there are so many hard-to-swallow elements that the films seem ludicrous. However, this is due more to cultural differences between Japanese and Occidental tastes. If you can watch pictures such as *Mothra* with at least an effort toward being acultural, the films are far more rewarding on every level. As I said elsewhere, the special effects are not intended to look "realistic" by western standards, but to be attractive and dramatic; so, too, are the films themselves. And few Japanese monster pictures are as physically attractive as *Mothra*.

A ship hits a reef during a typhoon, and the survivors are rescued from Beiru Island by a helicopter. The island was one used in a series of atomic tests by the Rolisican government (i.e. the United States).* The men were not hurt by radiation, claiming that natives there fed them juice which protected them.

Everyone goes into a tizzy at this; natives on an atomic test island? Meiji (Hiroshi Koizumi), a pretty newspaper photographer, and pudgy reporter "Bulldog" (Franky Sakai), who have sneaked into the debriefing of the shipwreck survivors, are excited by this and go to get an interview with eccentric Dr. Chujo (Ken Uehara?), an ethnologist and linguist who hates to have his picture taken. However, he's charmed by Meiji and Bulldog, and amused when the pet mouse belonging to Chujo's young brother runs up Bulldog's pant leg and the compassionate reporter rescues the animal un-harmed. He agrees to help them.

An expedition to Beiru Island is mounted by Clark Nelson (Kyoko Kagawa), a shady Rolisican businessman, who screens carefully all scientists coming on the expedition. Chujo is chosen and Bulldog has to pretend to be a steward to get aboard, but he's found out and allowed to stay as a guard.

*In other published materials, the island is called "Infant Island" and the government is called "Rosilican." In the film, the island and government are called as I have them above; the errors apparently originated in the pressbook prepared by Columbia Pictures.

Even behind-the-scenes shots in Japanese films are sometimes very attractive; the biggest model from Mothra (U.S. release, 1962) here hovers in front of what seems to be a blue-screen for matte shots.

The island is found to have a big, forested valley in its center. Wandering off on his own, Chujo finds giant mutated molds, and is grabbed by a tentacled, man-eating plant. He sees what he thinks at first is a hallucination—twin girls (Yumi and Emi Ito) about a foot high, dressed as Polynesians (but clearly Japanese). He faints, and is rescued by Bulldog and others.

When the twins are found again, Nelson grabs them and pulls a gun on the others, but normal-sized natives show up, threateningly banging on rocks, and Nelson frees the girls. The expedition returns to Japan, where Bulldog tells Chujo and Meiji that Nelson made his fortune by robbing tombs.

Nelson returns secretly to Beiru Island and captures the twins, killing a few natives as he escapes. A wounded old native crawls to an altarlike structure, cries "Mothra!" and dies. Rocks above the altar tumble down to reveal a colossal egg.

Back in Tokyo, Nelson opens his "The Secret Fairies Show," featuring the twins as star performers. They sing a song about their home island (featuring the chorus "Mosura-yah") to a tune we heard on the island. What no one knows is that somehow the song reaches back to Beiru Island, where a hell of a lot of natives dance around beneath the huge egg, singing the same song.

Chujo and Bulldog try to get Nelson to release the twins, but he refuses, although he does allow them a few minutes alone with the girls. The twins begin speaking to our heroes, although they assure the startled men they are actually conversing telepathically. The girls generally speak in unison as they warn that Mothra will soon rescue them. "All you good ones are sure to be hurt," they say regretfully.

Back on the island, all the singing and dancing have their effect: the big egg cracks, and a huge, rather indistinct head pokes out. Not long after, ticker tapes report on a big object in the sea, swimming toward Japan.

Even when the oncoming Mothra smashes a ship, Nelson denies any responsibility. Convinced the twins were telling the truth, Bulldog and Chujo battle their way past Nelson's guards and talk again with the girls, who admit they are powerless to stop Mothra. Nelson allows Chujo to place translucent amber sheets around the girls' cage in an effort to block their thoughts from Mothra.

The Rolisican government backs Nelson in his refusal to free the girls, and planes bomb and strafe the swimming giant caterpillar. There's little visible effect, but Mothra seems to vanish. Later, however, Bulldog and Chujo rush to a huge dam where there have been reports of major disturbances, convinced they are the work of Mothra. As water is about to pour over the dam, Bulldog rescues a baby in the nick of time.

Chujo's kid brother now tries to rescue the girls (momentarily seen apparently naked through the translucent shielding). There's a lot of running around involving the kid brother, but he's found safely, though Nelson and his men have fled with the girls.

Mothra crawls along through the Japanese countryside, implacably ignoring bombs and obstacles alike; she smashes a Birelys ad, a Mobil station and other buildings as she homes in on Tokyo. Unusually for a color monster film from Japan, some of these sequences take place at night.

After smashing a path through Tokyo, Mothra topples the Tokyo Tower and rapidly begins weaving a cocoon about herself. The silk (which, in the interest of decency, perhaps, she squirts out of her mouth) at one point snares a helicopter.

While Mothra busily seals herself up, much to the puzzlement of onlookers, Nelson beats a hasty retreat to Rolisica. Trying to make amends for earlier stupid decisions, Rolisica sends giant atomic heat ray cannons (once again in the shape of big radar dishes) to Tokyo to help in the effort at destroying Mothra. The guns blaze away at Mothra's completed cocoon, and all the loose silk is burned spectacularly away, though the cocoon itself isn't harmed, and the heat of the rays speeds up the metamorphosis of Mothra.

In Rolisica, Nelson takes refuge on his ultramodern ranch (we hear cattle mooing in the background), and he and his cohorts laugh at their narrow escape from the giant insect. But back in Tokyo, Mothra's cocoon begins glowing blue, then cracks open. Now a titanic moth, what else, Mothra emerges and flies off toward Rolisica. The wind from her immense wings tosses cars around and smashes roofs.

Nelson is not happy to hear about this.

Chujo and Bulldog also fly to Rolisica, more conventionally in a jet, and land in "Newkirk City," apparently the major city of Rolisica. It's a little like New York, San Francisco and Los Angeles, the American cities the average Japanese movie patron was most likely to be familiar with. (Interestingly, and perhaps a first for a Japanese film, there are a few scenes actually shot in Los Angeles.)

Nelson tries to flee the oncoming Mothra, but is recognized and his car is at once surrounded by an angry crowd (making him briefly recall the Beiru Islanders in flashback). He tries to make a getaway on foot, but is shot by police just as Bulldog and Chujo arrive on the scene.

Mothra is circling around the downtown area, blowing cars around, when Chujo catches sight of the sun picturesquely behind a cross on a church steeple, making him recall an emblem he saw on Beiru Island. Having little else to go on, as the giant moth is invulnerable, the government cooperates with Chujo: the same symbol is quickly painted on an airport runway by street-washing trucks whose tanks are filled with white paint. At exactly 3 p.m., all the church bells in the city ring and the twins are brought to the airport runway. Meanwhile, Mothra's wing-wind is swamping ships, knocking down buildings and a big bridge, but she does land at the airport. This vast creature flies away with the tiny girls.

(But Mothra returns in *Godzilla vs. the Thing*, *Godzilla vs. the Sea Monster* and *Destroy All Monsters*.)

When I was younger, I saved clippings on science fiction and horror movies from various publications, and didn't know about proper citations. I have an undated clipping on *Mothra* from a Portland, Oregon newspaper. An AP news service article by Bob Thomas is probably the first mention in America not only of *Mothra* but of Eiji Tsuburaya, the principal figure in Japanese special effects.

The film was in preparation when Thomas visited the Toho studios. Then intended to be called "Dai Kai Ju" (Great Strange Beast), *Mothra* was, said Thomas, "the costliest movie ever made in Japan, $700,000 worth ... 10 times what the average Japanese feature costs." Thomas met with Tsuburaya, "Japan's master of special effects."

Thomas said, "Tsuburaya was sitting in the Toho commissary, which was just like those in Hollywood.... The filmmaker is a quiet unassuming man who wears glasses and slouch hat.... He had started in Japanese films 40 years [before], first as scenario writer and later as cameraman and director.

"'The change in my life came [said Tsuburaya] when I saw *King Kong*.... That inspired me. At that time, Japanese trick photography was very backward. I started working in that field and by 1937 I began to accomplish some of the things I wanted to do.'"

After the war, Tsuburaya got his major opportunities and made the most of them. "Tsuburaya put Japan into the horror market with the successful *Godzilla*," Thomas said. "In *Three Treasures* he managed to create a serpent with eight heads. *Storm over the Pacific* depicted the great naval battles of World War II, all recreated in miniature on movie stages. The film was a success in Japan even though it depicted American victories. The explanation was that the Japanese are now so pacifist-minded that they welcomed any subject that showed the folly of war."

Most of the earlier Japanese science fiction epics also dealt with the dangers of war, especially imperialistic warmongers. When the alien or hidden races were in the right, they were threatened by imperialistic or exploitative forces, as in *Mothra*. The Beiru Islanders just want to be left alone; when this proves to be impossible, they unleash their ultimate weapon. Even then, this weapon proves to be less warlike than simply unstoppable; Mothra isn't out to destroy cities, she's just trying to rescue the tiny twins. All destruction is a side effect of this goal. It's passive aggression, aggression in a good, or at least under-standable, cause.

The only villain is Clark Nelson, the Rolisican entrepreneur who sees big bucks to be made from exhibiting the girls. He's more of a monster than Mothra, greedily exploiting the girls and letting nothing stand in his way. Although played by a Japanese actor with no attempt made to make him look Occidental, Nelson is obviously an Ugly American. Perhaps it was unusual for Americans to see themselves depicted so unflatteringly, but Nelson isn't any worse than similar characters in American films. Nonetheless, the satirical

thrust is at Americans; the Rolisican government's atomic tests, Nelson's greedily kidnapping the girls, and the government's at first siding with him. All this results in Tokyo and Newkirk City being damaged and, presumably, hundreds of lives being lost.

For most viewers, *Mothra* is pretty much the same old stuff — monster destroys Tokyo — but in books like this, we become concerned with variations on a familiar theme. After all, the majority of films in this book fall into narrow categories, and are largely much like the other films in those categories. All genre criticism faces this problem.

Mothra rings some charges on the Tokyo–smashing theme, still getting started by 1962. It scores high marks in originality of monster, for one thing. Yes, Mothra is a giant bug, but she's totally unlike other giant bugs. For one thing, no one had been quite so ingenuous as to use a moth as a monster — what's it going to do, eat sheep? — but the Japanese are habitually ingenuous in this area, and so simply made a giant moth movie.* But also, Mothra is a giant bug with a *mission*, not to eat people, but to rescue the tiny twins. The only motivation other giant bugs have is to either (a) escape or (b) eat as many people as possible.

Then there's the truly odd aspect of the tiny girls from Beiru Island. Yumi and Emi Ito (also transliterated as Itoh) were entertainers known in Japan as The Peanuts. According to *Psychotronic*, "One of their albums ... was released on London International in America. They do selections by Gene Pitney, Paul Anka and Tchaikovsky." They're quite lovely, and have attractive singing voices. I suspect that the idea of miniature twins may have been developed rather late in Shinichi Sekizawa's script for *Mothra*. The captive could have been a tall man for all the difference it makes to the story itself. I presume The Peanuts were used because of their fame, but they are a benefit to the picture; they lend an air of fairy-tale quaintness to the proceedings, and the idea of this tremendous creature causing destruction to rescue tiny twins is almost piquant.

There are many pleasing touches, such as The Peanuts' serene acceptance that Mothra will rescue them, and their mild regret that even nice people will come to grief when Mothra arrives. This is disconcerting: even our heroes are just minor troubles to be brushed aside by Mothra.

When Mothra is weaving her cocoon, the sound track is silent except for the unexpected but appropriate sound of what seems to be every dog in Tokyo barking at once. I suspect that someone who survived an earthquake recalled what the stillness when everything stopped moving was filled with, and used that sound here.

The idea that not only do humankind's weapons have no destructive effect on Mothra but actually serve to speed up her change from one form to another is alarming and amusing. I don't recall this being used in a film before *Mothra*, but the Japanese used the idea again in a couple of later films, when energy beams just make a monster friskier.

The most imaginative scene in *Mothra* is almost haunting; it shows an

Opposite: The crane supporting the model of Mothra is visible at the left in this interesting behind-the-scenes shot. The cityscape represents the San Francisco–like American–like city to which the villains flee at the end of the film.

There was another oversized moth in The Vampire-Beast Craves Blood *(1968), but that was quite another matter.*

understanding of screen storytelling, as well as a good use of imagery; I would be interested in learning who originated the idea. In Nelson's Tokyo nightclub, he's arranged for the twins to glide on wires over the heads of the audience in a little gilded coach. We see them from below as the little golden coach, sharply in relief against a deep blue ceiling with tiny winking "stars," rolls along the wires. There's a slow matching dissolve to Mothra (caterpillar) swimming along at sea; the horizon of the sea is carefully matched to the same line as the stage, so that we see the girls in the tiny coach against the night sky, while below and behind them, Mothra swims through the sea. Mothra seems to be pursuing the coach itself. It's only a brief scene and doesn't make the film any better overall, but this kind of scene almost never turns up in monster movies. It should be appreciated when it does. Maybe director Inoshiro Honda had a repressed flair for the poetic.

Most of the special effects in *Mothra* are well above average for a Japanese monster movie. There are a few matte shots that work almost as well as in American films, such as when Nelson grabs the fleeing twins, or when he opens their tiny carriage door so they can sing the Mothra theme song.

There was clearly more money expended on *Mothra*'s effects than on any similar previous picture. There are very large landscapes for the caterpillar to crawl over, with painstakingly detailed miniature fields, roads and buildings. The cityscapes are vast (but lit wrong, as usual for miniatures everywhere) and varied—Tokyo and Newkirk City don't look alike. Not all of these effects work, but it's still on a grand scale, and in general they are good. They require a willing suspension of disbelief, but it's not hard to grant.

There's an especially effective twilight scene of Mothra crawling into Tokyo, raising clouds of dust as she flattens buildings. This is seen from a moving aerial perspective, rare in color Toho monster movies. Even though the big caterpillar puppet looks unreal, in this scene it comes the closest to seeming awesomely gigantic and alive.

The scene of Mothra cocooning herself is also good, and there's a nice shot in which we see Mothra *within* the cocoon, outlined against the dark blue sky, as she busily encases herself in silk. Even the finished cocoon has a kind of bizarre splendor, as it lies entangled in the ruins of Tokyo Tower. More care seems to have been taken with imagery and design in *Mothra* than in any other Japanese monster movie.

I do not mean to be making claims for *Mothra* as a classic. Most of it is flatly directed; the actors are clumsy and the efforts at poignancy centering around the pudgy little brother are awkward and distasteful. Franky (sometimes Frankie) Sakai is a very Japanese comedian, and most Americans find him peculiarly unfunny; although he has been a star in Japan for well over 20 years, and is occasionally a good dramatic actor, he has almost no appeal as a comedian outside Japan. Howard Thompson in the *New York Times* seems to have been taken aback by Sakai: "the hero is a jazzy newspaper reporter who looks and behaves like Porky Pig."

The dialogue in American translation (by Robert Myerson) is thuddingly literal and pedestrian. A ghastly choice in voices was made, and the dubbing actors all speak in embarrassing Japanese accents. And dubbing, even when well done (it's badly done here) makes a film seem more awkward than it is.

Variety's "Tube," who generally disliked science fiction and loathed monster movies (unless he could find some kind of moral), despised *Mothra*. "A ludicrously written, haphazardly executed monster picture ... too awkward in dramatic construction and crude in histrionic style.... Neither the spectacular visual effects nor the adept miniature work makes up sufficiently for what otherwise is a pretty embarrassing effort on the part of the Toho people to duplicate a western screen staple."

On the other hand, Howard Thompson in the *New York Times* was pleased with the film, calling it a "Japanese fantasy-shocker in really excellent color and so-so dubbed English [featuring] an overpowering blend of scenic effects, ranging from obvious to striking. [*Mothra*] is different, if not exactly superior.... The direction, acting and dialogue are clumsy and absurd.... [But it has] as touchingly bizarre a climax as we've seen in years ... [and] some genuinely penetrating moments.... Several of the special effects shots are brilliant."

Psychotronic thought it (as I do) "one of the best Japanese monster movies." It's inventive, with its three-stage monster and the tiny twins, it has colorful settings and flashes of pleasing imagination, and it's swiftly paced and never boring. It's also silly, stereotyped and, ultimately, trivial. But for what it is, it's very good of kind.

Nude in His Pocket

This obscure French comedy was one of the most difficult films in this book to research. I was unable to find a file on it at the library of the Academy of Motion Pictures, it does not seem to have been reviewed in the *Monthly Film Bulletin* under any of its various titles, and except for Lee and Willis, is not mentioned in SF film reference books. But it does exist, is occasionally shown on television, and is reportedly not too bad. Furthermore, it stars Jean Marais who, when this film was made (1957), was one of the most popular leading men in France. It also has a relatively amusing and unique idea, which is breathtakingly sexist.

Improbably, the film was based on the short story "The Diminishing Draft" by Waldemar Kaempfert, published in *Argosy*, 9 February 1918. (The *AFI Catalog* says the story was published in *Astounding Science Fiction* for that date, but *Astounding* didn't begin until 1930.) One wonders how writer France Roche happened across it.

In the film, Jean Marais plays professor Jérome, who has been researching suspending animation. His stuffy fiancée Edith (Geneviève Page) wants him to give it up and go into the soft drink business, and he reluctantly agrees. On the last day in the lab, however, his pretty assistant Monette (Agnès Laurent) accidentally spills some experimental formula. A pet dog laps up the spilled solution, and immediately shrinks to a 3" statue. Jérome and Monette are baffled, but find a way to restore the dog; they dip it in saltwater, a common solution (so to speak) to science fictional problems, at least in movies.

Jérome and Monette have fallen in love by this time, trying to keep in a secret from Edith. Edith pounds on the lab door, demanding to be let in, so Monette drinks some of the solution herself, turning into a tiny nude figurine, which Jérome puts in his pocket.

The next day, Jérome goes to the beach, and immerses the little statuette in the sea. Presto, Monette is restored to normal. They become lovers, but eventually Edith learns what's going on. While Monette is in her figurine form, Edith places her aboard an ocean liner bound for the United States. Jérome chases after in a motorboat and rescues her in time.

According to "Jecko Wright" (Forrest J Ackerman) and Eric Hoffman in *Famous Monsters of Filmland* #27, the original short story "had a nitemarish downbeat ending when, in her doll-like form, [the doctor's lover] was smashed to smithereens." The original story seems to have influenced at least one story in the classic E.C. comics, Al Feldstein's "Something Missing!" in *Weird Science* #7.

Nude in His Pocket was directed by Pierre Kast, a film critic known primarily for a series of short subjects he made in the 1950s. He is well-known in France, but despite a good critical reputation, almost unknown elsewhere. In his *Dictionary of Film Makers*, Georges Sadoul said Kast's "features—ingenious, intelligent, intellectual, introspective and intimate—are sometimes irritating but never lacking in feeling or sincerity. He has said of his approach, 'Handled in the right way, anything, even very personal things, can be communicated to others, even though some details might not be directly understood.'"

Nude in His Pocket was Kast's first film. It was undoubtedly chosen with an eye to its commercial possibilities; it has that weird, titillating storyline, and also gorgeously handsome Jean Marais.

The actor began in films in the 1930s, but although he was very good-looking, his acting abilities were limited, and it wasn't until Jean Cocteau befriended Marais and starred him in many of his most famous films (including as the Beast in *Beauty and the Beast* and as Orpheus in *Orphée*) that Marais began to be regarded as a star. His acting improved through this period, and in the 1950s, he began appearing in commercially-successful films, often in swash-bucklers (D'Artagnan, at least once) or light spoofy adventures (he was *Fantomas* in the revival).

Nude in His Pocket is not typical of Pierre Kast's films, few of which have been released in the United States. He moves back and forth from films to television, still occasionally making short subjects, a much more frequent route to directing features in France than in Hollywood.

The only review of the film I have been able to discover is Gene Moskowitz's lukewarm commentary in *Variety*. He said, "This is an attempt at a situation comedy with a scientific background. Meandering direction, telegraphed proceedings, sans the needed snap, lilt and sympathetic characterization, [mean] this does not quite come off.... Agnès Laurent shapes well in her first big role, but has a long way to go as an actress. Jean Marais is adequate as the scientist while Geneviève Page is the proper cold fish as the fiancée. Production and technical values are average."

Panic in Year Zero!

This simple, grim movie was directed by its star, Ray Milland. (The title is not, as some have it, "Panic in the Year Zero." Announced as "Survival," it was rereleased as *End of the World*.) The film is without frills and is played seriously, but also dodges many of the issues implied by the subject matter, and ends on a highly inappropriate optimistic note. The budget, as so often, is too low for the premise, and it occasionally veers into sensationalism, but perhaps some of that was unavoidable. The first half is considerably better than the second, which has a falling instead of rising action; the climax takes place well before the film ends. And the philosophical considerations are muddled and simplistic.

But as end-of-the-world melodramas go, *Panic in Year Zero!* is above average; as films in general go, it's about average. It isn't as flossily produced as *On the Beach*, and overall it's not as good a movie, but it deals with some of the questions of the aftermath of a nuclear war in a more effective manner, and one more easily grasped by the man in the street. After all, the central characters *are* Just Folks.

The Baldwin family is preparing to leave their suburban Los Angeles home for a two-week fishing vacation in the Sierras. Father Harry (Ray Milland), mother Ann (Jean Hagen), 17-year-old Karen (Mary Mitchell) and 19-year-old Rick (Frankie Avalon) are a typical family, with the two youngsters bickering in an ordinary sibling fashion.

In their station wagon and pulling a small house trailer, they are driving into the mountains when they see several brilliant flashes of light back over Los Angeles. Pulling off the road, to their horror they see a gigantic mushroom cloud rising over the Los Angeles basin. The radio tells them that bombs have fallen on San Diego, Long Beach, San Francisco and Los Angeles. At first, they head back toward L.A., but when hordes of panicked motorists rush up the highway at them, they decide to turn back to the mountains. One passing motorist tells them, "I heard L.A. being torn apart and watched it being tossed into the air."

After an unpleasant encounter at a gas station, Harry decides their best temporary solution is to go on to their fishing spot, secluded and little known, and wait there until they see what's going to happen in this new post–Bomb world.

They stop at a roadside cafe, but the atmosphere is tense and the cafe owner's greedy decision to raise prices astronomically leads Harry to realize things are going to be very bad for some time. He decides to act on a me-first policy; grimly, he tells his family, "When civilization gets civilized again, I'll rejoin."

They stop in an out-of-the-way store, presuming the owner may not have heard of the bombs yet (which seems unlikely), and begin buying provisions. At a hardware store, they buy more equipment, but come up short of cash, so Harry pulls a gun on the owner (Richard Garland) and signs an I.O.U. for the rest.

They continue to head into the mountains, and hear on the radio that a retaliatory attack has been launched. We're never told who the enemy was, but context makes it clear it was the Soviet Union and Red China. In addition to those on the West Coast, the "free world" cities that were bombed were New York, Chicago, Philadelphia, London, Paris, Rome and parts of Canada. (But not Washington, D.C., a peculiar oversight by either the Communists or the scriptwriters.)

The family encounters a roadblock around a small town; looting has already become widespread, and the townspeople aren't taking any chances. But Harry crashes through the roadblock and passes through the town without further incident.

When car difficulties force them to stop, they encounter three jive-talking hoodlums, Carl (Richard Bakalyan), Mickey (Rex Holman) and Andy (Neil Nephew). It's clear these guys are up to no good; "We're the new Highway Patrol," one says menacingly. "Somebody dropped a bomb, dad," another says. "Crazy kick, eh?" When it's clear the hoods are going to try something, Rick shoots Carl in the arm and the family makes a getaway. As they leave, Harry sternly tells Rick that violence may sometimes be necessary, but he's not to learn to like it.

As Jack G. Shaheen points out in his interesting article on the film in *Nuclear War Films*, some Biblical parallels begin to manifest themselves, sometimes quite explicitly. Harry sees the mammoth automobile herd as the new Exodus, and when they have to cross the highway against the flow of traffic, Harry spills and ignites gasoline, parting the sea of cars like Moses with his staff parted the Red Sea.

They arrive in a secluded mountain area, and begin setting up housekeeping. "This whole thing is a bore," says Karen, "it's such a *drag*." But Harry insists they maintain the amenities of civilization, although for no conceivable reason he ditches the potentially-useful trailer. After they bury several bundles of supplies in various spots against future troubles, they hear on the radio that the United Nations has met and declared this to be "Year Zero." The world was so devastated by the brief nuclear exchange that the calendars are being set back to the beginning, so civilization can start anew.

They encounter Johnson, the owner of the hardware store, but he bears them no ill will, and just wants to hide out with his wife. Harry, however, is not anxious to make friends.

Later, while deer hunting, Rick hears shots and discovers Johnson and his wife dead; she is lying in an attitude suggesting rape. Elsewhere, Ann and Karen are doing laundry in a stream; a garment drifts downstream and is found by Andy and Mickey; this is now a very small world.

They come back upstream and encounter Karen. Although she's been decrying Harry's increasing violence, when Ann sees the hoodlums menacing her daughter, she shoots at them, but they get away. It's unclear as to whether or not Karen was raped; she stammers, "They tried to—" but later there are indications she was raped.

Harry and Rick trace the two bad guys to a cabin and kill them both in cold blood. In a back room, they discover young Marilyn (Joan Freeman), looking ill-used; she doesn't want Rick to touch her. Harry's not happy about any of this; "I looked for the worst in others," he says, "and found it in myself." Of course, this pang of guilt comes after he has killed the hoodlums, giving his words a sanctimonious air. It's okay to bitch and moan about being a bad guy if the advantages to be gained by being a bad guy have already been achieved.

Marilyn eventually gets over her fear of Rick, and a romance seems to be in the offing. But while they're alone in the woods, Carl, the third hood, gets the drop on them. Marilyn and Rick each claim to have killed Carl's friends, and Rick throws an axe while Marilyn grabs Rick's rifle and kills Carl. However, Carl gets a shot off first, seriously wounding Rick.

Harry realizes he'll have to return to civilization to have Rick's wound tended (didn't this possibility occur to him before?), and on the way into town they hear that the enemy has requested an immediate cessation of hostilities.

The small town they enter looks the worse for wear; there's some damage to buildings, cars on their sides, etc. A cynical, tired doctor (Willis Bouchey) checks Harry's arm before he lets them in. "Dope addicts have been running wild," he says. As the doctor works on Rick, Harry tells him the war's over and "we won."

"Well, ding ding for us," the doctor says.

After Rick is seen to, they hear that the fallout danger is over in Los Angeles (!), so they decide to return home. They pass through a roadblock operated by the Army. As they leave, the two soldiers on guard pronounce the film's moral, or something: "That's five more," the private says. "Five more what?" asks the sergeant. "Five more that are o.k. They came from the hills. No radiation sickness." The sergeant says, "Yep, five more good ones." Instead of "The End," the film concludes self-importantly with this big bold message: "There must be no End, only a new Beginning."

As Shaheen points out in his perceptive article, cited earlier, *Panic in Year Zero!* is very much an artifact of its time. The family unit is assumed to be the most important single element of civilization, both by Harry Baldwin in the story, and by scripters Jay Simms and John Morton. The family must be preserved at all costs: morality is a function of family survival; anything done to keep the family intact is judged to be moral, or at least expedient.

Harry does eventually come to feel that perhaps he's gone too far, and at the first hint that civilization might be righting itself, he rushes back into its embrace. But the whole first half of the film is virtually a grim textbook on how to get your family through civilization's collapse: be ruthless, brutal, violent— and be those things *first*. Everyone else will be after what you have, so protect it by any means necessary. The idea that people might be brought together by a disaster instead of being made desperate enemies doesn't seem to even be a possibility in the world of *Panic in Year Zero!*

Seen today, the film is a little disconcerting; the family depicted in the film is more like those seen on 1950s situation comedies than real live people, so the film keeps verging on being "The Adventures of Ozzie and Harriet on the Beach."

The film seems quite primitive in its view of men and women. The women are there to be either protected or exploited by men; at the end, Marilyn does manage to kill the last villain, but that's a result of her seeking revenge, not a coolly calculated action of a reasoning being. The mother seems more a burden than anything else, as she refuses to understand Harry's intentions. She's there to cook and clean and do the usual motherly things. However, when her daughter is attacked by thugs, she does respond with violence. As Shaheen points out, although the film would have it that this is the equivalent of Harry's earlier (and later) violence, it actually isn't. Ann is acting in defense of something immediate, forced into a violent position by the exigencies of the moment. Harry emerges in *preemptive* violence, hardly the same thing as Ann's retaliation.

The film seems to be arguing simultaneously for both Harry's and Ann's points of view. When Harry sees that civilization is going to hell in a handbasket, he immediately takes charge of the situation, grabs everything he can and heads for the hills to live in a cave with his little family, prepared to kill anyone who even looks like a threat. However, as soon as the last of the bad guys is out of the way—and the peculiar ending of the film links Carl to the Communist enemy and makes him seem like The Last Looter—the film turns back on itself. Now Harry is *wrong*, because the threat has been removed. He knows it, we know it, and he goes back to civilization (fallout may be no danger, but what about residual radiation?); he's even declared to be one of the "good guys" by soldiers they pass. And this links Harry with the soldiers; they are seen as the harbingers of civilization. The film seems to be declaring that because the Army is now in charge, things will be all right. The Army is violence controlled, directed, channeled, and it's violence we can trust. The soldiers may be carrying guns, but they are the upholders of hearth and home. Carl and his pals are civilization gone rotten; because they talk like hepcats, we are to presume that they hate everything Harry represents. This is *their* time, the panic following the bombs, but they are also burned away by the nuclear fire—represented by Harry.

By completely avoiding certain questions that would seem to arise—radiation sickness, decent folks gone bad, encounters with looting—the film almost makes it seem as though the nuclear war was a *good* thing. It got rid of Carl and his ilk, and at the end, the presumption is made that things will soon return to normal, with improvements. The war was just a hitch in civilization's gitalong, nothing really to concern ourselves with.

The film was clearly not intended to be so philosophically specious, but the undeveloped script and uninflected direction by Milland make things seem less threatening, less serious, than they were intended to appear. At the time, Milland seemed concerned about nuclear war, and considered this film to be something of his own statement on it. But it's a confused, compromised statement. Perhaps American International, who financed and distributed the film, feared going so far as to actually offend anyone with the idea that war might change civilization irrevocably. But whatever anyone else might say about the possibility of any large segment of the population surviving an atomic war, things will *not* be the same afterward. And yet, that's exactly the message of *Panic in Year Zero!* By not even bringing up the idea that the return to normalcy, even under the conditions depicted here, would be a very long, hard struggle, the film does suggest that the war was not really that much of a disaster.

The low budget makes some of the scenes slight and ineffective. If you're paying attention, you soon notice that all those cars roaring by the Baldwins are the *same* cars, over and over. The budget didn't allow the rental of enough cars.

There's only one special effects shot in the picture (a matte of a bomb cloud). And perhaps the total avoidance of the question of radiation and its effects may be due to a lack of money to depict such effects.

Apparently, while shooting Milland didn't film enough close-ups, because several are done in postproduction on an optical printer, and there's even one optical printer zoom shot.

Perhaps the biggest budgetary-enforced lack is that there just aren't enough people. Los Angeles is a very large city, and the thousands who would be fleeing an atomic attack should be swarming all over the small towns we see, but there's no one around. This may also explain why the Baldwin family twice encounters the same two sets of people.

The origins of the film are a little clouded. In 1953 and 1954, American SF/fantasy writer Ward Moore published two novellas, "Lot" and "Lot's Daughter." According to Peter Nicholls' invaluable *Science Fiction Encyclopedia*, they feature "a great motorized exodus from a doomed Los Angeles, seen through Biblical parallelism as the city of Sodom. The hero jettisons his irredeemably suburban wife and his sons, continuing to make a new and incestuous life with his daughter in the mountains. The ironies are savage and the latter-day Lot suffers from toothache."

When I first saw *Panic in Year Zero!*, I assumed that the film was based on Moore's stories, with obvious alterations made in attempts to make the film more acceptable to audiences. The basic storylines were very similar, and although *Panic in Year Zero!* ends on a far more optimistic note than Moore's stories, I thought there was simply no question that they were the basis for the film.

But Moore's name is not in the credits. Over the years, I've heard persistent rumors that the filmmakers became involved in a plagiarism suit over the Moore stories. Moore himself is now dead, and his widow had only a faint recollection of an out-of-court settlement involving "a film directed by Ray Milland." This, of course, is not enough to accuse anyone involved in the making of *Panic in Year Zero!* with plagiarism, but I should point out that the *Science Fiction Encyclopedia* simply cites Moore's stories as the basis of the film.

The credits of the film list Jay Simms as the author of the original screen story; he also wrote *Creation of the Humanoids*, *The Killer Shrews* and *The Giant Gila Monster*. I have no idea how much Simms' story was changed for filming as *Panic in Year Zero!*

Born in Wales in 1905, Ray Milland had become a useful actor in supporting roles by the mid-30s, but soon his charm, debonair manner and good looks brought him leading roles, mostly light comedies, mystery thrillers and other melodramas. He was one of Paramount's major stars of the early 40s, climaxing with his Oscar–winning, highly effective lead in *The Lost Weekend* (1945). But despite proving himself in such a difficult part, most of the rest of his starring roles tended toward lightweight fluff. This may explain why Milland was no longer a major star by the mid-50s, though his polish and suave elegance— so easily turned to villainy or heroism—would seem to have been highly salable commodities. (Since the late 60s, however, he has worked steadily in features around the world, and is frequently in television movies.)

His first film as a director was, surprisingly for a Welshman, a Western, *A Man Alone* (1955), routine but not bad, which describes all his later films as a director as well: *Lisbon* (1957), *The Safecracker* (1958), *Panic in Year Zero!* and *Hostile Witness* (1967).

He was absent from the screen for several years after *The Safecracker* (but present on television), returning with *Panic in Year Zero!* and Roger Corman's *Premature Burial* the same year. After Corman's underfinanced *X the Man with X-Ray Eyes* in 1963, Milland was again absent from American screens for several years, though he did make a few movies in Europe and some TV movies. He returned with *Love Story* (1970), for the first time appearing without the toupee he'd been wearing since the mid-40s, but returned quickly to horror films, international coproductions, and TV movies, where he is virtually a staple.

While he's rarely identified as a horror movie actor, Milland has appeared in enough genre films to be classified as one. Among his SF and fantasy films: *Menace* (1934), *The Uninvited* (1944), *It Happens Every Spring*, *Alias Nick Beal* (both 1949), *Panic in Year Zero!*, *Premature Burial*, *X the Man with X-Ray Eyes*, *Frogs* (1971), *The Thing with Two Heads*, *The Night of the Laughing Dead*, *Terror in the Wax Museum* (all 1972), *Escape to Witch Mountain* (1975), *The Uncanny* (1977), *Battlestar Galactica* (1978) and *The Attic* (1980). And he's been in plenty of TV horror movies, too: *Daughter of the Mind* (1969), *Black Noon* (1971), *The Dead Don't Die* (1975), *Look What's Happened to Rosemary's Baby* (1976), *Cruise into Terror* (1978) and *The Darker Side of Terror* (1979), among others. He's a busy man.

As an actor in *Panic in Year Zero!*, Milland is grim, tight-lipped and believably American. There's relatively little shading to his part, and for an actor so adept at comedy, it's too bad that Milland didn't allow any of that side of him to come out here. Harry is bleak and depressing from one end of the film to the other. Granted, the circumstances are trying; still, the characterization is limited. When he finally admits he's "found the worst in himself," it's hard to believe Harry really means it. He's too serious, too selfish.

As a director, Milland is a bit better, but flat. The film adopts a matter-of-fact tone, trying to make the events seem believable by being realistic. There are opportunities for sensationalism, but Milland avoids most of them. The film keeps an even keel in terms of tone, and this is probably its greatest strength. Even the rapes and murders of the latter half are underplayed and treated seriously; most of the deficiencies lie in the undeveloped, trivial script.

Frankie Avalon is not bad as the Son Who Grows Up; he's clearly in the picture to appeal to the teenage element, and his Italian good looks are so at odds with Milland's British blandness that it's impossible to believe they are related, but that's not their fault. Avalon is here struggling to prove himself as an actor, and any problems a viewer might have with him are probably because of his Beach Party associations and his lightweight songs.

Jean Hagen has little to do, which unfortunately describes much of her screen and TV parts. She was an outstanding actress, as her role in *The Asphalt Jungle* (1950) shows; her priceless, hilarious Lina Lamont in *Singin' in the Rain* (1952) is one of the gems of the best musical I've ever seen. But Hagen was under contract to MGM, and they weren't interested in building her as a star just as the studio system was collapsing. She was so versatile that, paradoxically, she became hard to cast. She was fine in the overheated *The Big Knife* (1955), but her remaining films were few. She was the mommy in *The Shaggy Dog* (1959), had a supporting part in *Sunrise at Campobello* (1960) and in *Dead Ringer* (1964), her last film. She died in 1977 at the age of 54, an actress of great ability who was rarely given a chance to demonstrate it.

Her role in *Panic in Year Zero!* is virtually a microcosm of her Hollywood roles: supporting, minor and thankless. She does her best with it, but the virtually misogynistic viewpoint of the picture, and a script that gives her little to do than look worried, makes Hagen almost invisible. And this from a woman who had more talent than Lana Turner put together.

Almost all the other roles are subordinate to Milland and Avalon. The daughter is a cipher, whining until she's attacked, more or less silent thereafter. Joan Freeman is somewhat better as Marilyn; her haunted eyes make the scene in the cabin powerful, but her regeneration is too swift and easy. Writers Simms and Morton don't seem to know how to deal with woman characters, though their viewpoint of men is almost as simplistic.

A major deficiency is Les Baxter's music; here he has adopted a highly inappropriate score, apparently what he thought of as rock 'n' roll or perhaps jazz. It's shrill, brassy and strident, unpleasant and distancing, and now very dated.

Boxoffice found the film "well produced on a modest budget" and felt that "Avalon [turned] in his best screen performance to date." David Bongard in the Los Angeles *Herald-Examiner* was impressed, warning that the film "will scare the daylights out of you." He felt that Milland "directs economically and pointedly.... This very unhappy and demoralizing picture is told with all the stops out. It wasn't too expensive to make, but the story is a blockbuster."

James Powers in the *Hollywood Reporter* thought it a "good, sound melodrama," and that Milland directed it with "some dignity and intelligence." Powers found the script "generally superior to its class, with some of the dialogue very sharp. The story itself tends to run down in the closing minutes of the film ... but the approach to a ticklish subject is generally good."

Joe Dante in *Castle of Frankenstein* #22 thought that the "Script is best when stealing shamelessly from John Christopher's *No Blade of Grass*, and goes awry only when it starts inventing stock AIP–type situations of its own. First half is pretty good, but lowly budget, fast schedule and relentless sensationalism win out."

Panic in Year Zero! is earnest, but the weaknesses of the script are emphasized by the earnestness; it attempts to be straightforward and free from sensationalism, but the material is sensationalistic. It has a confused moral viewpoint, a TV-oriented view of the family, a deplorable treatment of women, and a bizarrely upbeat ending. But it's still a film that can be taken seriously.

Paradisio

This was the first real sex film I ever saw, and inasmuch as I grew up in the repressed 1950s, the very sight of a bare female breast was very arousing. I sat through most of this film with my coat over my lap. All the scenes of nudity were filmed in muddy 3-D which looked yellow, but was in the red-green anaglyph process, and was the main reason I went to see it. It isn't a *good* movie, of course, but quality didn't matter to me. For the first time, I was seeing pretty women totally unclad (with the pubic region discreetly covered). I don't think I was prepared for the experience.

Oddly enough, the film was actually shot all over Europe—Paris, Vienna, Berlin, Florence, London, Venice, Munich and the Riviera—but the travelogue aspect is minor. It's the bare skin that counts.

The science fiction element is exactly the same as and is introduced for the same purpose as that in *Magic Spectacles*: eyeglasses that enable the viewer to see people stark naked. Mostly, of course, the people are women, as this type of film has always been aimed at men.

Professor Sims (Arthur Howard) arrives in Austria just as the lab of a scientist is blown up by Soviet spy Lisa Hinkle (Eva Waegner). Sims receives a package from the exploded scientist containing a pair of sunglasses with a note which asks him to deliver them to a physicist in Munich. When Sims dons the glasses (and people in the audience put on their red-and-green viewers), he is astonished to see people stark naked: the glasses make their clothing invisible. These scenes are in unimaginative 3-D; people just pass by.

In Munich, Sims finds the physicist dead; followed secretly by Lisa, Sims goes on to Paris, where yet another contact is found dead. Another note leads Sims on to Venice, where he does manage to turn the glasses over to the contact there, who is promptly murdered. Sims retrieves the glasses and finds that they can decode a secret message which leads him to Florence and another murder.

Lisa contacts him, posing as a friend of the first murdered scientist, and lures him to West Berlin where she tries to trick him into entering the Eastern sector. But Sims escapes on a motor scooter and drives onto a cargo plane as it is taking off, eluding the pursuing Russians. He heads for the beaches of the Riviera, to watch the bikini-clad beauties through the sunglasses.

Paradisio is a drab, unfunny comedy, with an unpleasant emphasis on death and a trivial plot. Though it's not badly produced, it's just a pretext for the nudity. In 1962, that alone was enough to make a film popular; the added 3-D element was to set the movie off from similar nudies. Today these films would look about as sexy as an anatomy book, but in its day, *Paradisio* was hot stuff. It is also, quite incidentally, science fiction.

Reptilicus

This is an atrocity, perhaps the worst giant-monster-on-the-loose film ever made, a category with several contenders for that position. Furthermore, *Reptilicus* has the dubious distinction of being a movie so bad that American International almost refused to distribute it; unfortunately, compromises were made, and when the film came out, audiences collapsed in laughter.

The story was by Sid Pink, who either directed or codirected (sources differ), and the script was by Ib Melchior. Inasmuch as it was just another giant monster movie, not much could be expected of the film. If it had been made to represent the script more accurately—with a decent budget, good special effects and acting, etc.—the film would, even with the same script, be regarded as an average monster film with a slightly unusual gimmick. That's if everything had gone *right*. Unfortunately, Pink made the film entirely in Denmark, displaying such an astonishing ineptitude in all departments as to make the film one of the classic stinkers. It is, however, also ponderous and boring, so it doesn't even deserve to be shown as an entertaining turkey.

The film begins with an original touch: the lettering of the main title is made of chunks of meat. Except for the strange development of the monster, it is a clumsy crossbreeding of elements from *The Thing from Another World*, *Godzilla* and *Rodan*, adding nothing to any of the swiped ideas; the *Rodan*esque scenes were removed from American prints anyway.

In Denmark, an oil well drill unexpectedly brings up blood and scraps of flesh. Excavation uncovers a frozen, buried section of tail of a prehistoric monster; this idea was derived from the finding of frozen mammoths in tundra in Siberia. The tail is taken to a laboratory in Copenhagen, where to general astonishment, the drill-hole soon heals. The scientists realize that the monster, which a reporter dubs Reptilicus, might regenerate from the tail alone.

In Melchior's script, Professor Martens says "advanced regeneration goes even farther than [a lizard growing a new tail]. A starfish will regrow an entire new organism from each one of its severed arms, and a flatworm can be cut into numerous pieces, and each separate piece will regenerate itself into a complete animal." Reptilicus' tail is growing itself a new body. So far, so good; it's preposterous, but acceptable.

Soon, thanks to a lightning bolt, the monster completely regenerates, and bursts out of its tank. It rampages around the country, killing people, battling the military, and so forth. Not only does it eat people (unconvincingly), but Reptilicus occasionally barfs green on Copenhagen. The monster spews forth some kind of green poison in a clumsy optical effect. I presume this was to match Godzilla's radioactive breath, but dragonfire is a potentially awesome idea; a monster vomiting poison is at best disgusting and, at worst (as here), ludicrous. (This idea is not in Melchior's script.)

Fighter planes bombard the monster in the sea and blow off one of its fore-limbs, which sinks to the ocean bottom. Everyone presumes that Reptilicus will die, but it turns up again, healed and ready for action.

Reptilicus barfs on a beach, then enters a city and wreaks more havoc there. The American general in charge of operations is prepared to blow Reptilicus to smithereens, but fortunately cooler heads prevail. If Reptilicus' tail could grow a whole new Reptilicus, so could each smithereen—and the world would be threatened by hundreds of Reptilici.

The means of destroying the beast is finally found: a poison-filled shell is shot into the creature's mouth, and it dies. A squad disassembles the monster, pulling the scales off its back and destroying each fragment totally. But off in the sea, that blown-off forelimb twitches along the seafloor, growing a new body.

The film has the usual other elements: scientist, beautiful girl, stalwart leading man, comedy relief and tragic sacrifice. They're business as usual, and have no interest.

What is remarkable is how extremely inept the special effects are. This may have the most unconvincing monster in the history of motion pictures, including *The Giant Claw* and *Creature of Destruction*. Reptilicus is impersonated by a marionette, with the strings often highly visible. But it isn't even a *good* marionette; the head looks crudely carved, the neck is too long and inflexible, the forelimbs are comically diminutive and immobile, and we rarely get a look at whatever might lie below them. The jointing is awkward, so that Reptilicus constantly flops around, moving too quickly and loosely. There are virtually no scenes involving the monster and live actors: we cut from scenes of Danish military might massing in the city streets, to a marionette moving among totally unconvincing miniatures. They don't even seem to belong in the same universe, much less the same movie. The tabletop sets have no depth—we can see the backdrop immediately behind the unconvincing cardboard buildings.

This is much worse than dismal; these special effects, uncredited in any source available to me, are insulting. It's difficult to imagine how even the crassest, most commercially motivated producer could have thought anyone, anywhere, would accept these scenes without storming out of the theatre to demand a refund.

Things, however, could have been worse. In European prints of the film, Reptilicus flew. The few stills of this look faintly better than the rest of the effects, but they must have been even worse, for they were cut from the picture altogether for its American release. This means that Reptilicus gets around quickly at times, turning up unexpectedly far from the sea, but that's one of the least of the film's flaws.

The acting is also dreadful, and not helped by terrible American dubbing. (Ib Melchior told Mark McGee that he himself had to dub at least six different performers.) Carl Ottosen, the Danish actor playing the American general, is stiff, thick-featured and wooden, anything but a hero.

There are numerous almost impressive scenes of what looks like literally thousands of Danes fleeing in terror from the onslaught of Reptilicus—a scene of a mob trying to escape over an opening drawbridge is especially spectacular —but someone failed to convince the extras not to smile and laugh. Thousands of happy Danes swarming down a street don't look like a panic-stricken mob, and when the scene then cuts to a marionette on a table as the big menace, reality doesn't go out the window, it never comes into the room.

The film was completed in 1960, and seems to have been delivered to American International, which cofinanced it, late that year or early in 1961. In that form, the film was even too awful for AIP to release, and they actually sued Sid Pink. According to an article in the 29 June 1961 *Film Daily*, AIP filed suit "seeking declaratory relief and clarification by the court.... Cited as basis of the suit is a contract assertedly entered into March 7, 1960, and an amendment dated Feb. 1, 1961. In an extensive presentation of the AIP claim, which also asks general and punitive damages in several amounts on a number of

individual complaints, it is set forth that defendants [Sidney Pink, Bernard Greenbaum, and Cinemagic, Inc.] agreed to produce and deliver a picture of the stated title [*Reptilicus*], conforming to several physical requirements, at a given date, now past, and did not perform the contracted production activities agreed upon."

Two months later, Sid Pink sued American International and Monarch Books. He alleged "unauthorized use of his name in publication of the book, *Reptilicus*. Complaint alleged that in book written by Dean Owen, Pink was identified as author of the original story on which picture of the same title was based, and from which book was adapted, without Pink's consent. As a result ... Pink was held up to 'public contempt and ridicule.' Book ... contained passages of 'such lewd, lascivious and wanton desire as to inflame unsavory and lascivious desires in the reader.'"

Now, speaking as someone who read that novelization, I can testify it certainly did inflame lascivious desires in me. Along with Monarch novelizations of *Konga, Stranglers of Bombay* (1959), *Brides of Dracula* (1960) and *Gorgo*, it was the closest thing to over-the-counter pornography as you could find in the early 1960s. Owen (whose real name was Dudley Dean McGaughy) added sizzling, overwrought sex scenes to these very tame movies; *Gorgo* doesn't even have a female lead, except in the novel. A friend of mine was so taken with this steamy ribaldry, especially by a scene in which the hero takes the heroine "with the savage lance of his manhood," that he had his mother embroider several hankerchiefs "Lance Savage." The friend (Dick Plov) often referred to Dean Owen as his favorite science fiction writer.

However, we never thought that Sid Pink had anything to do with this smutty stuff; we knew damned well that those scenes were just to sell the books, which they did. And as far as public ridicule and contempt go, nothing could have brought more of both than the film *Reptilicus* itself. Nonetheless, Pink's nuisance suit seemed to have the desired effect. It stirred up AIP, who had Pink's suit dismissed almost immediately. Their own $1,530,000 suit must eventually have been resolved satisfactorily to all parties. The movie, like Pink's *Journey to the 7th Planet*, was "fixed up" — presumably by dubbing and the removal of the flying scenes — and released the next year, confirming the uncaring nature of American International.

Because of the various lawsuits, the film's release was delayed; the novelization came out long before the movie did. So did the grotesquely bad comic book based on this grotesquely bad film. The comic book was released in the summer of 1961, and appeared for two issues under the title "Reptilicus." According to Don Glut's essential *Dinosaur Scrapbook*, with the third issue, the title was changed to "Reptisaurus the Terrible," and the monster turned from green to red. It continued to look just like Reptilicus, however, until the seventh issue when perhaps another lawsuit compelled Charlton, the publisher, to alter the design of the monster. (Charlton also produced comics based on *Gorgo* and *Konga*.)

Sid Pink stayed in Europe at least through the end of the 1960s, producing and sometimes directing low-budget films distributed by lesser U.S. companies

Opposite: Every book of this nature should have a still that is notable for its ludicrousness, and I suppose this shot from Reptilicus (1962) fills the bill here. The bad miniatures are placed all too obviously in front of a depthless background, and the awkward model of the monster has permanent, built-in drool. We can also note with appreciation the tiny, stiff forelimbs and the curve of the wings at the left. The flying scenes were removed from U.S. prints.

when they were released here at all. For example, neither *Sweet Sound of Death* nor *Operation Atlantis* (both 1965) got any U.S. theatrical release. Pink tended to produce Westerns and adventure thrillers, with the occasional odd-ball film such as *Madigan's Millions* (1968), Dustin Hoffman's first movie. Pink often cast American actors who'd fallen on hard times, including Rory Calhoun, Cameron Mitchell, Tab Hunter, Jeffrey Hunter and Broderick Crawford; he occasionally used more successful actors apparently between assignments, such as Barry Sullivan, Martha Hyer, Tom Bosley and Anne Baxter. None of Pink's films are in any way notable; the titles include *The Christmas Kid*, *A Witch Without a Broom* (both 1966), *Pyro* (1964—which AIP released), *Flame Over Vietnam*, *The Fickle Finger of Fate* (both 1967), and *The Bang Bang Kid* (1968). I have no further information on Pink after *The Man from O.R.G.Y.* (1970).

AIP tossed *Reptilicus* out onto the exploitation circuit, and it received few reviews. However, Nadine M. Edwards in the *Hollywood Citizen News* wrote a long review, but didn't like it: "I suppose it would be supercilious to say *Reptilicus* is ridiculous. But in critical essence, it ranks far below most films of this nature, failing even in the technical department to register any appreciable degree of surprise or 'horrifying' suspense."

The *Monthly Film Bulletin*, giving the movie its lowest rating, understated matters: "A disappointing addition to the abnormal zoology cycle. The lame and plodding narrative is made worse by singularly bad acting.... The thin story is padded out by superfluous material, including a contribution by a cabaret singer, and some travelogue views of Copenhagen. The trick photography and model work are below par, though the monster itself is a little unusual in design."

Reptilicus is not recommended.

The Road to Hong Kong

The seventh and last of the Bob Hope–Bing Crosby "Road" pictures qualifies for the book because of the ending, which finds the boys in a space-ship landing on the planet "Plutonius." Otherwise, it's the same sort of Road thingy as before: sight gags and wisecracks, songs and dances, complications, clichés, spoofs of each other and the movie itself. Oddly, it was filmed in black and white rather than the expected color (the previous "Road" picture was the only one in color), which may have limited its success. Nonetheless, the film did all right, and some years later Hope and Crosby had scheduled another Road film—variously referred to as "The Road to Retirement" and "The Road to the Fountain of Youth"—when Crosby collapsed on a golf course and died in 1977.

Crosby was a star when he and Hope began traveling those roads in 1940 with *Road to Singapore*. That film was originally set to feature other Paramount stars, Fred MacMurray, Jack Oakie and George Burns, and was to be slightly more serious than the film that resulted. *Singapore* was a big hit for Paramount, and established Hope and Crosby as a comedy team. They went on to other roads, to *Zanzibar* (1941), *Morocco* (1942, the best of the series), *Utopia* (1946), *Rio* (1947) and *Bali* (1952).

After *Singapore*, the plot mixture was much the same: the boys are seedy entertainers moonlighting as con men, though Crosby's favorite target is always Hope. The two compete over Dorothy Lamour (in all the films), are almost killed by the bad guys, and end up poorer but wiser. Crosby always got the girl, even in *Utopia*, where this doesn't seem to be the case at first. (See the film.)

The best element of the series was the relationship between Hope and Crosby, which not only traded on their established screen images, but allowed those images to mesh as a comedy team. Crosby is always insouciant, glib, carefree, and irresistible to women; Hope is always clumsy, venal, cowardly and lecherous. At some point in the film, Crosby finds it airily expedient to throw Hope to the wolves, but later finds it even more necessary to become chums again. (Chuck Jones used this same formula brilliantly in a few cartoons with Bugs Bunny standing in for Crosby and Daffy Duck for Hope—a wonderful transposition.) This combination of slick and slicker con man turned up in some of Abbott and Costello's films too, but it reached its greatest fruition in the Road films.

Quoting Pauline Kael: "Maybe you have to have seen the Bob Hope–Bing Crosby road movies ... when they came out to understand the affection people felt for them, and to appreciate how casually sophisticated the style seemed at the time. The pictures haven't weathered as well as 30s comedies, because they were satirizing melodramas that are already forgotten. The series spoofed the fancy backgrounds of adventure movies; Hope and Crosby ambled through exotic, nonsensical light-hearted situations with no pretense to believability. They took the thud out of the dumb gags and topical jokes by their amiable comic intimacy. And the rare good jokes shone in the unpretentious atmosphere. Hope and Crosby's rapport has great charm, and every once in a while Hope does something—a gesture or a dance movement—that is prodigiously funny. Dorothy Lamour is their joint inamorata and the foil of the series; inimitably out of it, she was taken over from the pictures being satirized, and she played in the same coy, eager-to-please manner." (From *5001 Nights at the Movies*, Holt, Rinehart & Winston, 1982.)

Audiences today often sit in stony silence through the *Road* films, sometimes unaware that the gags are even supposed to be gags. The nature of comedy has changed so greatly since the 1940s that the idea of a comedy team floating like a bubble on their plots, always showing us they are aware of the artificial nature of movies, is both alien and too familiar to today's moviegoers, drenched in Monty Python (actually similar, in many ways). The gags strike the new audiences as corny; the effortless professionalism of Hope and Crosby seems slight and uninteresting.

Maybe their time will come around again; the idea of actors turning to the audience and making wisecracks about the movie and their offscreen lives was new in the 40s. At times the boys would be scurrying down an alley somewhere, realize their doom was sealed, then call for "special effects" to get them out of it, and the movie complied. (They did this four times in *The Road to Hong Kong*, three times too many.) Reality isn't just unsteady in the Road films, it comes and goes at the will of the leading men—but not always. They are sometimes trapped by their own coyness; occasionally a thug will have seen a Road movie already, and their patty-cake routine (ending with a sock to the jaw) doesn't work.

The Road to Hong Kong was the creation of Norman Panama and Melvin Frank, quite a team themselves. They wrote the script, Panama directed and Frank produced. They'd been partners since the early 30s, when they met at the University of Chicago. By 1938, they were in Hollywood, writing comedy for radio shows, and eventually moved into films. As writers, and later as a writing-directing-producing team (sharing all three credits), they were bright and sassy, producing good comedies that miss being classics but are still funny. Among their films are *Mr. Blandings Builds His Dream House*, *A Southern Yankee* (both 1948), *Callaway Went Thataway* (1951), *Knock on Wood* (1954), *That Certain Feeling* (1956) and *The Facts of Life* (1960). They also turned their hit Broadway musical *Li'l Abner* into an inferior movie, and some of their other films are less than outstanding: *The Return of October* (1948), *The Trap* (1959) and *Not with My Wife You Don't* (1965), their last collaboration.

They created some of Bob Hope's funnier films, including *My Favorite Blonde* (1942) and *Monsieur Beaucaire* (1946). They also wrote the wildest of the Road films, *Road to Utopia*, and a couple of minor pictures for Crosby. Their place in screen history, however, would be assured with just one picture, the best film Danny Kaye ever made, one of the best comedies of the 1950s: *The Court Jester* (1956).

As both a Road picture and as a Panama-Frank collaboration, *The Road to Hong Kong* is disappointing. The routines look silly instead of funny, and much of the comedy is lame. The movie is both overproduced and shoddy, and although Hope and Crosby are clearly having a grand time, they don't communicate enough of the fun to the audience. Nonetheless, most audiences found the movie reasonably funny.

Plots in Road movies are of little importance, but we might as well get it over with—the attitude the film adopts. This time, Hope and Crosby are Chester Babcock and Harry Turner, song-and-dance men touring Ceylon, as unlikely as that may seem. While trying to sell the natives their phony Fly-It-Yourself Kit, Chester is knocked unconscious and awakes with his memory gone. Knowing Chester is his meal ticket, Harry takes him first to an Indian doctor (Peter Sellers, in a standout, unbilled bit), then to a Tibetan lamasery, where not only is Chester's amnesia cured, but he is given a photographic memory.

At the airport, Chester encounters Diane (Joan Collins), a beautiful spy for the Third Echelon, an organization of mad scientists hoping to conquer the world before the U.S. and the U.S.S.R. blow it up. She mistakes him for a photographer she was assigned to meet, which somehow results in Chester seeing the secret rocket fuel formula, which he memorizes at a glance.

The Third Echelon, headed by the Leader (Robert Morley), captures Chester and Harry, both of whom fall for Diane. They try to escape, but the two jokers end up substituting for a pair of apes in a test rocket flight around the Moon, during which they are force-fed bananas from a feeding machine that goes haywire.

After their return from orbit, they escape the harem they're offered and flee through Hong Kong. (The Third Echelon's headquarters are underwater near Hong Kong.) They're helped out of a bad situation by Dorothy Lamour, appearing in a local nightclub, but eventually through further complications, Harry, Chester and Diane end up in another rocket, which deposits them safely on the Earthlike planet "Plutonius." It looks like the boys will have to share Diane, but Frank Sinatra and Dean Martin drop in and win her away.

The finished film met with a mixed response, mostly downbeat. "Rich" in *Variety* was probably closest to the mark; the laughs, he said, "come thick and fast in this genial piece of nonsense. Perhaps the old formula creaks occasionally, but not enough to cause any disappointment, and the zany situations and razor-edge wisecracks keep the whole affair bubbling happily.... The result is an amiable comedy which should please nostalgic customers and entice those who haven't seen any of the previous Road pix."

Bosley Crowther in the *New York Times* also liked the movie. "The old boys still come through nicely," he said, adding that "practically every moment spent with Bing and Bob is good for consecutive chuckles and frequent belly-deep guffaws."

On the other hand, there were those like Hazel Flynn in the Beverly Hills *Citizen-News*. She said that "after seeing it, I vote that the 'Road' should be destroyed forever.... One reason is because the camera has been terribly unkind to Bing. Hope fares better before the lenses but somebody should shoot their gagwriters. They have been mean to both.... Please, boys, BURY this series."

Newsweek's unnamed reviewer was also disappointed. "It is good to see Bob Hope and Bing Crosby side by side again, but it is not good for very long. In fact, two hours of the old troupers induce a kind of instant nostalgia: by the movie's end, many people will be yearning for the good times at its beginning.... Where the old Road pictures were breezy and informal, this one is often just sloppy."

More recently, in *Castle of Frankenstein* #24, Joe Dante seemed to speak for his generation of film fans. "Last entry in the series has a few good gags, but the huffing and puffing [are] a lot more obvious." More recently, for this book, Dante noted that "one of the most off-putting aspects to this film is its stodgy British 'international hit' quality. Even though it's drab, the picture is over-produced, it's just too big for its own good."

The movie opens with a very good song, "Teamwork," by Sammy Cahn and Jimmy Van Heusen, one of the best duets by Hope and Crosby from any of their films. The rest of the songs are second-rate, as is the film itself. Hope and Crosby could have risen to whatever levels were called for; they were still fine performers. However, for both of them, this was nearly the last movie that was any good at all (but Hope still has a chance). Hope still had the pretty good *Critic's Choice* (1963) in his future, but from *Call Me Bwana* (also 1963) onward, it was downhill for Bob; his last starring film to date, *Cancel My Reservation* (1972), is one of the worst of his career. Except for brief guest spots in *The Muppet Movie* (1979) and the Road-like *Spies Like Us* (1985), he made no other theatrical films. Crosby made two more theatrical films, *Robin and the 7 Hoods* (1964) and *Stagecoach* (1966), and one TV movie, *Dr. Cook's Garden* (1971).

Neither man needed to work, of course; they were among the wealthiest in show business, having parlayed their great talents (often underestimated) into great wealth. And *The Road to Hong Kong* is not a complete waste, not by a long shot; it's drab, though, and especially disappointing in retrospect. It's too bad that Panama and Frank couldn't have dug a bit deeper into their own talents, and too bad that one more Road couldn't have been found for Bob and Bing to saunter down.

Siege of Syracuse

A book needs to be written on the dozens of Italian miniepics of the late 1950s and early 60s. These spear-and-sandal movies began by imitating the big-budget American spectacles like *Ben-Hur*, but soon started pulling in their own ideas, including heroic musclemen like Hercules. These copycat productions were eventually replaced by, first, spy thrillers in the James Bond mode, and later by the spaghetti Westerns. Usually the same people made all these films.

Various means were tried in hopes of making these films palatable to Americans, usually by casting an American actor in the lead, but sometimes by using a homegrown star known to Americans. (When neither type was available, the names of Italian actors were sometimes Anglicized, occasionally with bizarre results. Gian Carlo Giannini became John Charles Johnny, and Olga Solbelli became, equally literally, Olga Sunbeauty.)

Another way of increasing the apparent importance of the film was to include historical figures whether or not they fit the story accurately. In *Siege of Syracuse*, the hero is mathematician and scientist Archimedes. He's played by Rossano Brazzi, deprived of his fine, distinctive voice, replaced by a dubbed American voice, described by the *New York Times* as being Brooklynate.

The film has momentary but real science fiction elements, stemming from a famous but almost certainly apocryphal story about Archimedes.

In nebulous "ancient times," Syracuse, a large city in Sicily, is beset by both the Romans and the Carthaginians, and Archimedes is in charge of defense preparations. While he's testing his latest invention, a huge "burning glass," he accidentally sets fire to the clothing of Diana (Tina Louise), bathing nude in a nearby stream. Naturally, after this "meet-cute" they can only fall in love. Eventually, she becomes pregnant, but her evil stepbrother Gorgia (Enrico Maria Salerno) turns Diana over to some Roman soldiers, conveniently causing her to lose her memory. She bears Archimedes' son.

Time passes, and she marries Roman consul Marcello, while back in Sicily, Archimedes marries Clio (Sylva Koscina). Archimedes goes to Rome in hopes of establishing an alliance. He meets Diana, whose memory returns, but they agree to part and not to inform their son of his true parentage.

Archimedes fails to establish the alliance, and returns to Syracuse. The Roman fleet finally attacks, and he uses giant versions of his burning glass to set fire to their fleet and save Syracuse. During the battle, both Gorgio and Marcello are killed; Clio has already died, so Archimedes and Diana are reunited.

The science fiction element is, of course, the burning glasses. Not having seen the film, I cannot state whether they are giant magnifying glasses or, as the poster art seems to indicate, parabolic reflectors; the legends about Archimedes are also unclear on this, although they do maintain he did set fire to a fleet this way. According to Isaac Asimov's *Guide to Science*, Archimedes himself was, like some other Greek inventors, more interested in gaining fame as a mathematician than an engineer, so he never bothered to record his practical inventions, only his discoveries in pure mathematics. (He did become famous for having discovered the principle bearing his name.)

His defense of Syracuse, according to *The People's Almanac*, not only involved the burning glasses, but huge devices that lifted Roman ships out of the water and then dropped them back with enough force that they sank.

When Syracuse was finally taken, Archimedes was murdered by an impatient soldier against the orders of Roman general Marcellus; his wonderful defense only held off the fleet for a while.

Archimedes actually was born in Sicily, but gained his fame in Greece; the film's accuracy is only incidental.

The American press did not greet it with favor. "Haphazardly trimmed and edited and erratically post-dubbed," said "Tube" in *Variety*, "with the result that performances emerge ludicrous and story emerges senseless, [this] has merit only as a means for emotional escape on the part of customers who seek nothing beyond that."

James Powers in the *Hollywood Reporter* was even less impressed. "Judging by [this film], the Italian epics have run their course and are now retreading the original paths. The Paramount release is ineptly made, even allowing for the difficulties of dubbing and re-editing, and is not even a very plausible item for double-billing."

The vogue for such pictures has long since passed, and *Siege of Syracuse* is rarely shown today.

This Is Not a Test

This is an intelligent but limited and very low-budget film about events before a nuclear war, shown in tensions among a group of people trapped on an isolated California side road during dawn of the morning of the day they did it.

Elderly Jake (Thayer Roberts) and his granddaughter Juney (Aubrey Martin) are stopped by Deputy Sheriff Dan Colter (Seamon Glass); he's clearly tense and upset about something, behaving in a terse and officious manner not designed to put anyone at their ease. He orders them to get out of their pickup when Cheryl (Mary Morlas) and Joe (Mike Green) also arrive at the roadblock in a convertible; they're arguing with each other.

Next, a big truck from "Discount World" arrives, driven by Al Weston (Alan Austin); he has an enigmatic young blond guy (Ron Starr) with him, a hitch-hiker he picked up in Reno. (The story is apparently taking place in the Sierra Nevadas north of Yosemite.) Another car arrives; this contains Mr. and Mrs. Barnes and their little dog, arriving from Tahoe.

Colter is brusque and unpleasant, refusing to answer any questions of the growing crowd. The implication is clearly that he *has* no answers, and is uncertain as to why he's been instructed to set up the roadblock. His radio occasionally gives out little bursts of phrases, but they're not helpful either, being jargon and code.

Suddenly, the hitchhiker runs away, and others try to stop him. He drops a knife, but makes his getaway into a nearby stand of trees. Joe, who talks in hip slang, says the hitchhiker was undoubtedly a wanted criminal who killed a girl and probably others.

The cop's radio begins chattering again, with phrases like "Operation Eager" and "yellow alert," and then says something everyone recognizes: "This is not a test, this is a state of emergency." The others try to use the radios in their cars to pick up commercial stations, but because there are "too many minerals" in the surrounding mountains, this isn't possible.

Colton fires off his shotgun, and everyone gathers around him. Warnings are continuing to issue from the radio, climaxing with an announcement that it is now condition red, situation red. Martial law has been declared. "Crazy, man," says Joe. Realizing they are near a city, as well as western air defense headquarters and a missile fuel refinery, Al reveals they are near ground zero. This does nothing to cheer anyone up.

Joe belligerently says that if he and his chick want to see the world end, it's none of the cop's business. As he starts to leave, Colton handcuffs him to his car. Acting on the martial law ruling, Colton orders the others to begin unloading Al's truck.

June gets hysterical and runs off into the woods, where she encounters the hitchhiker sitting on a rock, calmly watching her. "Hello," he says politely, "how are you?" She soon learns that even though he does seem to be slightly cracked, he's not the killer, but just an ordinary guy named Clint. She cries that they are all going to die, but Clint assures her that though "*they* are," she's not.

Newcomer Peter (Don Spruance) arrives on a motor scooter and helps the others unload the truck. It's near Christmas, and the truck is loaded with luxury items, including mink coats, caviar, and a diamond tiara, as well as Christmas ornaments.

Frank and Karen have been quarreling, and Al, who was eager to get to Sacramento to meet a certain redhead, flirtatiously gives Karen the diamond tiara and caviar.

The cop smashes bottles of booze. "I said there'd be no drinking here," he says sternly, "and I meant it." There is also some food in the truck; it is promptly confiscated by Colton. When Clint steals some canned food, the others chase him, and Colton issues angry orders: "If you see him, shoot him." The police radio confirms this policy: the police have orders to shoot all looters. Jake privately tells Colton that they both know there's no chance to survive.

Karen wanders off the road and encounters Al; they grab each other and begin making love. Al's shotgun slides away, stopping at Frank's feet. The two don't see him, and he goes back to Colton, lying that he didn't see his wife anywhere.

Eventually Karen and Al come back, and although Frank momentarily considers killing them, he changes his mind, and all help the cop move the truck and the police car. Clint runs out after they leave and grabs a suitcase; he tries to start a car, but there are no keys.

Down the road, the cop pulls the truck over and pours out some water to make mud to cover the truck's air vent. In the meantime, the police radio announces incoming missiles. By now, it's daylight. Fearing the worst, some people run off, and while the others climb into the truck, Frank kills himself.

Outside, Jake sends Peter and June to a mine where he thinks they will be safe, while he makes plans to climb to the top of a hill to see things happen.

Inside the truck, things become tense: the cop hates the dog, and Joe makes a fan out of money. Cheryl freaks out, Colton slugs some people, then realizes that as things haven't gone boom yet, perhaps they can open the truck.

They discover it is surrounded by looters who fled San Francisco. The gang jumps Colton and takes Karen, then flee in the police car.

Al, Joe, Cheryl and Clint, out of the woods, climb into the truck and slam it shut. Colton comes to and realizes he's locked out. As he bangs on the truck door, begging to be let in, the camera slowly pulls back. There's the sound of an explosion, and the film turns from positive to negative: the bombs have gone off.

Unlike with some low-budget films, the makers of This Is Not a Test did not try to do more than their budget allowed. The entire story takes place on and around a short stretch of highway; there are no special effects, no mob scenes; it must have taken only a week to shoot. Despite all this, and to an extent because of it, in some ways the film is surprisingly effective. By limiting the viewpoint to such a narrow focus, the film manages to realistically suggest the horror of oncoming devastation. As with The Day the Earth Caught Fire and atomic-devastation films, we are made more aware of the errors of destruction by this focus on a small group of people and a brief span of time. The story, in fact, takes place in the time it takes to watch it, about 80 minutes. It's a modest film with modest goals, but some of those are attained.

The acting is variable. Some of the performers are professional, others are not. This is not as much of a drawback as it might be, because the varying level of ability suggests a wider range of personalities.

Seamon Glass isn't bad as the frightened, tyrannical cop, and continually makes us aware that Colton is not as bright as he should be, that he's ill-informed and acting more out of bureaucratic bullheadedness than courage or a desire to protect the lives of the others. Glass is a supporting actor and bit player in other films, appearing in a wide variety in the 1960s and 70s, including *Spartacus* (1960), *Confessions of an Opium Eater* (1962), *Deliverance* (1972), *The Apple Dumpling Gang* (1975) and *Damnation Alley* (1977).

The only other lead actor who has had much screen exposure is Thayer Roberts who plays the stereotyped old codger, Jake. He was also in *Miracle of the Bells* (1948), *King Richard and the Crusaders* (1954), *Lady Godiva* (1955) and *The Buccaneer* (1958), among others. His character in *This Is Not a Test* is conventional, and Roberts plays him that way.

The script by Peter Abenheim, Betty Laskey and director Fredric Gadette is limited, and some of the dialogue is trite and/or silly; hipster Joe is especially exasperating. But it keeps the characters in focus, has a good structure, and doesn't waste too much time over extraneous details, although the little instant romance between Al and Karen is unnecessary and seems forced.

Director Gadette is probably the weakest element; he rarely uses close-ups (perhaps a budgetary consideration), the staging is awkward, and there's no flow to the picture. It's told in little set pieces and the continuity sort of lurches. I presume it was his first and only film; I have been unable to uncover any other credits of any nature for him.

The film may have been an outgrowth of a little theatre project: the way the characters are introduced and the ironic, bitter ending are similar to the kind of ensemble pieces often done at little theatres all over the country. Because of its grimness and lack of melodramatic material, it doesn't seem like a TV show. All this is speculation, but it's worth wondering about, because *This Is Not a Test* is a film that seems to have come from nowhere. It's an attempt at a serious drama about impending nuclear war, showing its effect on a microcosm of America. It's not really successful, because the talent involved is limited, but for such a very low-budget film, it does have some virtues and deserves to be better known.

The Three Stooges Meet Hercules

This film established the Three Stooges as feature film stars, but their rise to that status didn't last very long; their films pooped out before the decade was over, but served to reestablish them in the public mind. This and the immediate (same year) follow-up, *The Three Stooges in Orbit*, were surprisingly funny. There's less of the violent, repetitious slapstick of the shorts, more emphasis on comedy situations and, in this film, a surprisingly sturdy plot. Its focused flow is interrupted by a side trip to Rhodes, but inasmuch as no one could have expected Three Stooges movies to have plots at all, that's a minor failing. (*In Orbit* offset this by having a plot that's a real mess.)

The Stooges are clerks in a pharmacy in Ithaca, New York. After the usual slapstick hijinks—Moe gets bopped on the head by flying chemical bottles (Curley Joe is making some tranquilizers he calls "calmdown pills"); he retaliates, more slapstick—we're introduced to their scientist friend, Schuyler Davis (Quinn Redeker), who has a lab next door. He's working on a "time-space conveyor" for a science contest, but mostly just creates vibrations which knock bottles off the shelves in the pharmacy.

We also meet Ralph Dimsal (George N. Neise), the nasty owner of the pharmacy, who constantly bullies Schuyler, upsetting not only the Stooges but Schuyler's pretty girlfriend Diane (Vicki Trickett), on whom Dimsal has designs. Dimsal hopes to foul up Schuyler's invention, and so draws a tangle of extra circuitry onto the plans when they temporarily fall into his hands.

The Stooges try to help Schuyler, and rebuild the time machine from the altered plans. It looks mostly silly, with a lot of wires, levers and lights. However, when Schuyler and Diane walk in while the machine has begun throwing sparks, setting off fireworks, etc. it begins to work properly. Fed some of Curley Joe's inexhaustible supply of calmdown pills, it promptly whisks the Stooges and their friends back in time to Ithaca, Greece.

The arrival of the time machine causes the tide of a battle to swing in favor of the bad guy, Odius (George N. Neise again), and, regarding the Stooges, Schuyler and Diane as gods, he takes them back to Ithaca, Greece with him. Outfitted in Greek clothing, the newcomers are treated to a meal, but when they see Odius mistreat his captive Ulysses (John Cliff), they know Odius is odious indeed.

After an attempt at escape, they are recaptured by Odius' henchman Hercules (Samson Burke), and are made galley slaves while Odius drools over captive Diane.

They row around the Aegean for a while, Schuyler developing muscles (and a beard) from the exertion, while the Stooges just develop beards (shaved off later). They use the calmdown pills to dope their captors and take over the ship, but it sinks, and they wind up in Greece, where they get genuinely funny directions from a shepherd (Emil Sitka, in many Stooges shorts).

Recaptured, they wind up back on a galley, where Schuyler continues to become stronger. (A body double is used for the close-ups of Redeker, who actually does look fairly muscular.) This time the ship is that of the obnoxious, silly, sissy King of Rhodes (Hal Smith). When he mistakes Schuyler—now rowing the ship alone—for Hercules, Moe encourages his belief. The King agrees to give them their freedom if they can conquer the Siamese Cyclops of Rhodes, who has (or have) been terrorizing Rhodes.

The Siamese Cyclops is a silly creation: one body, four legs, two arms, two heads, and a total of two eyes. It is also a giant (played by Mike and Marlin McKeever), and menaces the Stooges for a while, as the often-nervous Schuyler passes out in terror, before Curley Joe can manage to use those pills again. The Cyclops swoons, and the Stooges convince Schuyler he was responsible for its defeat, which gives him self-confidence.

Passing off Schuyler as Hercules, they soon make a great reputation. (In fact, writers Elwood Ullman and Norman Maurer cleverly give many of the 12 Labors of Hercules to Schuyler.) Curley Joe always dopes the opponents, usually animals. A great number of stuffed cats fly through the air in this sequence. After some setbacks involving gangsters, the four return to Ithaca.

Hercules is by now furious at the impostor he's heard so much about. In a peculiar turn, probably due to budget limitations, the Stooges and Schuyler simply turn up at Odius' palace, where they are soon captured and sentenced to die in the arena. However, Schuyler defeats Hercules, and forces him to live up to his legendary self. "I've built up your reputation as a great man," Schuyler says while holding Herc in a headlock, "now live up to it ."

Hercules promises to do so, and is as good as his word. He helps defeat Odius' forces and, grabbing Diane, Schuyler and the Stooges jump in a pie wagon (guess what's coming) and head for the time machine, pursued by Odius. The villain gets a faceful of pies, and ends up in a mudhole. However, he arrives just as the time machine is taking off, and clutches it desperately as it whirls back toward the future, passing through a great deal of stock footage of historical events. Odius himself falls off in the Old West, where he is promptly pursued by howling Indians.

Back in Ithaca, the now-confident Schuyler settles things with Dimsal, who zips off on a time trip and rapidly returns in Puritan garb and in stocks.

The Three Stooges Meet Hercules is clearly no classic comedy, but it has its moments. There's none of the sticky sentimentality that seriously marred *Snow White and the Three Stooges* the previous year; even the love story between the ingenues is minimized: it merely drives part of the plot, and takes up little screen time. The film is briskly and efficiently plotted.

The film originated in the then-current popularity of the spear-and-sandal epics from Italy. Distributor Joseph E. Levine managed to parlay *Hercules*, a blah cheap epic starring American Steve Reeves, into a worldwide hit. He quickly followed it with *Hercules Unchained* (both films were several years old by the time of their U.S. releases) and other distributors jumped into the togaed hero field, grabbing even more of these usually poor films. (As always, there were exceptions: *Hercules in the Haunted World*, directed by Mario Bava, and *Hercules and the Captive Women*, both 1961, directed by Vittorio Cottafavi, have much to recommend them.) Norman Maurer, the Stooges' new business manager (and Moe's son-in-law) saw rightly that the films were ripe for satire. *The Three Stooges Meet Hercules* was quickly shot in the summer of 1961 at a budget of $450,000, and grossed at least $2 million on its early-1962 release.

According to the interesting *The Three Stooges Scrapbook* (by Jeff and Greg Lenburg and Joan Howard Maurer), during production, Joe De Rita fell off a moving chariot onto Larry Fine, knocking Fine unconscious. At the hospital, he discovered he had diabetes, a disease which plagued him the rest of his life. Director Edward Bernds told the Lenburg brothers and Mrs. Maurer that Samson Burke, the muscle-builder who played Hercules, was nervous about his performance. "He was a thorough amateur," Bernds said, and certainly Burke's awkward performance in the film confirms this. Bernds added that "Samson was a bit on the timid side.... Moe was braver in doing all the physical stuff than this mighty mass of muscle."

The supporting performances in *Meet Hercules* are variable. Vicki Trickett was a minor starlet of the period, who appeared in relatively few films, including *Pepe* (1960), *Gidget Goes Hawaiian* (1961) and *The Cabinet of Caligari* (1962). She's decorative here, and little more. On the other hand, as the villains, George Neise is quite splendid. His performances are precisely in the right tone for a slapstick villain: self-obsessed, greedy, quick-tempered, lecherous, mean and cranky. Everything is a touch broad, pleasantly reaffirming that we are indeed watching a comedy. Neise had been around since the mid-40s, but rarely had large roles. Among many other films, he was also in

Experiment Perilous (1944), No Time for Sergeants (1958), Two on a Guillotine (1965) and On a Clear Day You Can See Forever (1970). He was wasted as one of the Martian spies in The Three Stooges in Orbit.

Quinn Redeker is a surprise, not for what he does here, but for his later career. He's spirited in Meet Hercules, taking pratfalls and bouncing around with an appearance of having fun, but the role is ill-defined (what do you expect?), and Redeker sometimes seems stiff and uncertain. But still, for the kind of film it is, he's not bad. Redeker has been busy since in a variety of films, sometimes in larger roles in minor films, and in supporting roles in major films. Among his other acting assignments were Spider Baby or, the Maddest Story Ever Told (1965), Airport, The Christine Jorgensen Story (both 1970), The Andromeda Strain (1971), Rollercoaster (1977) and The Electric Horseman (1979). He was a regular on the TV soap opera "Days of Our Lives" for some time. But his most surprising film credit is that he cowrote The Deer Hunter (1978), a heck of a long way from The Three Stooges Meet Hercules.

The jokes start as soon as the film does: the animated credits feature several gags, including the Stooges, as pillars holding up a statue of Hercules, dropping and breaking it. The film is announced as being in "glorious black and white," and it actually is fairly glorious. Cinematographer Charles S. Welborn makes the most of the inexpensive sets, and gives the film a handsome look, though the extra investment required for color might have been worth it.

The movie is often described as a spoof, but it really isn't—there's almost no satirical content. It's simply a comedy version of a time travel movie crossed with a Hercules adventure. The same idea was used in the Italian film Hercules in the Vale of Woe (1962), and that film is actually a bit more of a spoof than Meet Hercules, though it's not as funny.

About the only real spoofing the film does is of its own low budget: late in the film, as the fake Hercules, Schuyler announces he is going to fight the Hydra. He leaves the set; we hear some offscreen cheers, and he bounds back to announce, "Well, that takes care of the Hydra."

The low budget doesn't usually show; even more expensive films of this type often have stock footage. But there's an underpopulated look to the "crowd" scenes. And sometimes the cuts don't match, as in the slapstick scene in the pharmacy.

Reviews were not unkind. Variety's "Tube" called it with some inaccuracy "typical Three Stooges slapstick.... The sustained force of the slapstick is bound to be diffused over the feature length course, and this inevitably puts a strain on comic invention and limits appeal and response.... The screenplay provides ample excuse for the patented messy pratfalls of the starring trio."

Howard Thompson of the New York Times seemed delighted, saying the "complications are as corny as they are funny, but anybody who doesn't chuckle at some of the bedlam should consult a Delphic Oracle.... [It's] about as subtle as a bulldozer. But credit Moe, Larry and Curley Joe with stepping on the gas and knowing what to step on for fun, if not art. Hurry back boys, and don't forget the pies."

There were dissenting voices, of course. The Three Stooges are resolutely lowbrow in all departments, and some simply don't like that kind of thing. Like Paul V. Beckley in the New York Herald-Tribune: "In a mild way, a very mild way, [it] is something of a satire on the Italian historical films ... the only trouble is that the originals are themselves such parodies that anyone accepting them on their face value conceivably might take this film seriously.... It is probable the nursery set will find this reasonably amusing."

The *Monthly Film Bulletin* gave the film its lowest rating. "Lamentable slapstick rubbish, which stout-hearted fans might just conceivably find amusing. The script has one or two glimmerings of ideas for parody, but the production is tawdry, the comedy very tired indeed."

The film is not as lively as it might be, and doesn't try for as many laughs as expected. Moe Howard carries the brunt of the comedy, which he had to do after the deaths of his brothers Jerry and Shemp. But Moe is essentially a straight man, which makes the comedy often thin. Larry Fine is reactive, with no personality except for a kind of earnest stupidity. Curley Joe De Rita is almost a hole in the screen, certainly by far the least of the four "third stooges." (The others were Jerry "Curly" Howard, Shemp Howard and Joe Besser.)

But the film pleased its fans, and it has not dated. The Stooges exist in a timeless limbo; their humor is so very basic that it dates less than far superior comedy teams, including Abbott and Costello, Martin and Lewis and even, at times Laurel and Hardy. Small children who happen upon the movie probably don't have any idea it was made more than 20 years ago. And wouldn't care.

Note: although it is incorrect alphabetically, overriding logic compels me to list *In Orbit* after, rather than before, this entry.

The Three Stooges in Orbit

Hard on the heels of *The Three Stooges Meet Hercules*, another low-budget, more-competent-than-you'd-expect slapstick Stooges comedy came gallumphing to the screen. *The Three Stooges in Orbit* is purer science fiction than the earlier film (although "purer" is perhaps not the term called for). It sticks to fanciful inventions and invading Martians, and churns this stuff up with the Stooges. To be sure, there's a haunted castle at the beginning, but it's just window dressing.

As in *Hercules*, the Stooges are more subdued here than in their incredibly long string of two-reel shorts; not only were they now getting to be rather elderly, but there had been complaints from parents' groups and the like that too much violence was not good for children. (None of these protesters ever seem to realize that they themselves grew up with the Three Stooges shorts, animated cartoons and the like, and were presumably not harmed by them.)

The Three Stooges in Orbit is a silly, trivial little picture, but then again, that's what you'd expect, isn't it? The main appeal of the Stooges was always to children and the childish, and still is. Back when Curly Howard was in the group, his wild improvisations, plus genuinely weird vocal tricks, made the shorts more unusual than they later became, but by the early 60s, Curly was long gone.

In *Orbit*, the Stooges play themselves, Moe Howard, Larry Fine and Joe De Rita, TV comics. Ousted by their landlord, they move to Lompoc, California (apparently because that was the setting of W.C. Fields' *The Bank Dick*) and take rooms in the gloomy, castlelike mansion of eccentric inventor Professor Danforth (Emil Sitka). The professor is clearly a screwball—demented grin, frizzy hair and thick glasses—but he's also a pleasant old coot. His butler Williams (Norman Leavitt) is more sinister.

Danforth happily shows the Stooges his newest invention, a vehicle that can travel on water, land or in orbit: it looks like a submarine with tank treads and a helicopter propeller. (The writers seem to have only the foggiest idea of what the term "orbit" means; they seem to think it is synonymous with "outer space.")

The Stooges aren't impressed and go off to bed. That night, a clawed thing in a hood carries Larry off. It's actually Williams the butler, a Martian spy disguised as a human being. (Larry comes to no harm, and never really knows what happened.) He converses with other Martians back on Mars by television. Although the Martians talk their own language (in which "Mars" means Mars), they are helpfully subtitled throughout.

The Chairman of Mars (Nestor Paiva) fears that the professor's new invention will give Earthlings the power to crush the proposed Martian invasion, though the Martians have rockets and Ray Harryhausen's flying saucers from *Earth vs. the Flying Saucers* (via stock footage). The Chairman isn't happy with Williams' progress, and so sends two more Martian spies, Ogg (George Neise) and Zogg (Rayford Barnes) to help out. They don't adopt Earth guises.

The Martians look rather like exaggerated versions of the Karloff Frankenstein Monster, with huge square heads and wrinkled brows. The makeup, by Frank McCoy, is amusingly grotesque and has a comforting air of familiarity.

The next day at their TV station, the Stooges learn their show is being canceled. Their sponsor, N'Yuk N'Yuks, the Breakfast of Stooges, wants a cartoon show, and the Three Stooges cartoon that has been prepared is too terrible to air. The Stooges are challenged to come up with a better cartoon idea, and the professor promises to help.

In the meantime, Ogg and Zogg arrive in their spindle-shaped spaceship, and Williams goes back to Mars.

Back at the professor's mansion lab, his pretty daughter Carol (Carol Christensen) arrives just as handsome Capt. Tom Andrews (Edson Stroll) shows up to evaluate the professor's machine for the military, and of course they fall in love.

Danforth's first experiment with the cartoon-making machine isn't a success, but the grateful Stooges still offer to help him demonstrate his all-terrain vehicle. There's a strange little scene involving a miniature prototype of the machine, which crawls about the lab in search of water, then flies madly about, pursued by everyone, until it settles on the professor's arm like a pet parrot.

Elsewhere, Ogg and Zogg report to the Chairman on various earthly pleasures, including the Twist. They show him some silent movie footage, which convinces him the Earth must be destroyed.

Lurching back to the Stooges, the film next shows the demonstration for military brass of the professor's machine, described at one point as a "seagoing helitank, or landgoing helisub, or airborne whatinhell." But with the Stooges in charge of the demonstration it is, of course, a fiasco, effectively ruining the professor's chances of selling the thing.

The machine flies erratically out to the desert with the Stooges aboard, and lands at some atomic proving grounds next to an "atomic depth charge," which will detonate when it is dropped into water. Curley puts it in the sub, thinking it's the carburetor and, with this new power, the machine suddenly becomes very effective indeed. It even flies briefly into outer space, but the Stooges aren't quite aware of this.

Eventually, Ogg and Zogg get control of the machine, and with the Stooges clinging to the outside, fly around over Los Angeles. The Stooges unhook the conning tower, which has the helicopter blades; seeking water, the machine flies to the ocean and plunges in, setting off the atomic depth charge. Ogg and Zogg are destroyed.

The Stooges fall into the television station, and Professor Danforth turns up, having perfected his cartoon-making machine. The Stooges are outfitted in costumes and makeups of exaggerated, contrasting black and white, and photographed. This results in an awkward, stilted "cartoon," but everyone seems impressed. Carol gets Tom, and the Stooges save their job.

Edward Bernds gave the film the kind of direction called for: loud, fast and simple. There's something going on most of the time, and many of the sight gags actually work. Being aimed at children as it is, there's no need for subtlety, nor does Bernds provide any.

There is another romance here, but it's no more obtrusive than that in *Meet Hercules*. Still, with Paul V. Beckley in the *Herald-Tribune*, I find it "endlessly perplexing ... how anyone could suppose children of an age responsive to Stooge humor would care for romantic interludes that ... cheat them out of what they came to see." After all, it's not too likely that many adults went to see the film on their own, and those that did probably wanted more to see eye-gouging, head-slamming and pie-flinging than they did scenes of Edson Stroll and Carol Christensen mooning at each other. (In fact, I question the entire concept of "love interest," but that's not a topic for discussion here.)

In their shorts, the Stooges never had to have personalities. They just had to be stupid little guys constantly hitting each other or having endless accidents. Here, as in their other features, they are required to be lovable as well, not a good idea, and the Stooges aren't really up to it. But for that reason, too, there's less of their traditional slapstick violence.

In one sense, the most distasteful thing about *The Three Stooges in Orbit* is the subplot about doing animation electronically. Cartoon animation is an art, and it's possible to create that art by using computers—but that's not what's being done here. What actually is, seems to be what was attempted in *Angry Red Planet*, coproduced by Norman Maurer, producer of *In Orbit*. Allegedly, the strange Cinemagic scenes in *Angry Red Planet* were intended to look as if they were drawn; the actors wore flat white makeup and, as with the Stooges at the end of this film, their costumes were also done in high contrast. However, it didn't come anywhere near succeeding in that film.

But at the end of *In Orbit*, the goal seems to have been achieved, for the cavorting chalk-white Stooges are turned directly into bogus "drawings" resembling animated cartoons. Not only does this circumvent the cartoonist's abilities, it promulgates the reprehensible theory that cartoons *in and of themselves* are what children want to see. It doesn't matter how the cartoons were created, how good they are, or that no imagination or creativity went into their production—drawn figures in motion are the end goal. It is an antiart, anticreativity idea; it may be technically ingenious, but it is little else. And technical ingenuity without creativity is in limbo: the tool has become an end in itself.

As if emphasizing the connection between these two films, slightly revised production drawings from *Angry Red Planet* are used as the backgrounds behind the animated titles of *In Orbit*.

In 1960, Maurer and the Stooges made a TV pilot film in color called "The Three Stooges Scrapbook," on a $30,000 investment. But it didn't sell. Maurer showed the film to Columbia execs, and received the go-ahead to build *In Orbit* around this footage. Quoting from the book also called *The Three Stooges Scrapbook*, the footage from the TV pilot that turned up in the feature included "apartment eviction for home cooking; searching for a new residence;

retiring for the night in Danforth's mansion; then meeting ... the Butler; and a montage of the Stooges, in pajamas, thumbing a ride, traveling in a boat, taking off in a helicopter, and parachuting into the studio in time for their TV show."

"Tube" in *Variety* considered *In Orbit* superior to *Meet Hercules*, and felt that "the wild Stooge approach manages to extract the last ounce of visual fun from creaky ideas for the young and easy-going audience."

The *Monthly Film Bulletin* gave the film a II rating, and said of the Martians, "their grotesque makeup ... is a good deal better than that gracing many a horror film. Although the knockabout remains crude, it is considerably better and more restrained than the old hitting, bashing, pulling and poking style, and there are at least two quite funny sequences."

The Three Stooges in Orbit is undemanding, trivial fun for kids and the childlike; it's not badly made, it delivers the goods for its intended audience, and even provides some laughs for adults.

The Underwater City

Alex Gordon is a man of great personal charm and cheeriness; a bouncy little guy with a nearly-permanent smile and a great love for movies, he's instantly likable. He's clearly fond of SF and horror movies, and is devoted enough to movies in general to try to cast the actors he loved as a child in his various films. Gordon is, in fact, such a thoroughly nice person that it's more than a little sad that his films are generally so mediocre, when they aren't actually awful. Gordon is not a cynic, but finds himself in a cynical business and, artistically, in over his head. He's not really torn between art and commerce, he's torn between being a movie fan and a quickie producer; aside from any question of whether he has the ability to make good films, he just doesn't seem to be able to bring together all the necessary elements to make them.

The Underwater City seemed more promising than most of his genre projects. It was one of the earliest films to deal with the possibility of founding long-term colonies on the ocean floor, a prospect not yet realized on the scale depicted in the film. It is a sober film, remarkably lacking in villains and melodrama. It is realistic enough, in fact, that Gordon has always (misleadingly) described it as "science fact" rather than science fiction. (A science fact film is a documentary.) While *The Underwater City* is cautious, it's prediction on a scientific basis, with a fictional storyline. Science fiction.

The intention was to make it calm, respectable and reasonable, but the result is ponderous boredom, clotted by talk; a struggle to do underwater scenes on a dry stage results in unreality. *The Underwater City* is considerably better than some other films produced by Gordon, such as *The She Creature* and *Voodoo Woman*, but remains pedestrian and unthrilling. Even less promising movies Gordon was associated with, such as *The Day the World Ended*, produce more excitement.

Gordon is not to blame for an almost outrageous marketing mistake committed by Columbia Pictures. He had been given what was for him a respectable budget (not reported in the press), and although he had only six days to shoot the live action, he had 22 days for effects, and was filming in Eastman Color. The movie was scheduled for a major release in the summer of 1962, but for unexplained reasons, Columbia decided to toss it out onto the market earlier in the year, and released it on the bottom half of double bills in black and white. (It's on TV in color.)

According to various interviews with him, Gordon wasn't informed that this was going to be done, and says he learned of it only when the film unexpectedly opened in Los Angeles. He brought a $500,000 breach of contract suit against Columbia over the matter, claiming that the black-and-white, early release "destroyed [the] commercial value of [the] film and [damaged] Gordon's reputation as a producer." (*Variety*, 18 December, 1963.) I do not know the outcome of the lawsuit, but perhaps it explains why the film is shown on television in color.

Engineer Bob Gage (William Lundigan) has his heart set on working on a space station, but instead is hired to supervise the construction of the city of the title, designed by Dr. Halstead (Carl Benton Reid) of the Institute of Oceanography, who tries to enlist Gage's enthusiasm. Gage is skeptical of the subsea city and its reported ability to be a haven in the event of atomic war.

However, once he's been shown around the preliminary structures he's won over. Especially when he finds himself falling in love with Halstead's niece, Dr. Monica Powers (Julie Adams).

A geologist who started the necessary survey of the region is killed by a giant eel, and his report goes uncompleted; nonetheless, no follow-up report is prepared, and the construction of the city—at the edge of a vast marine abyss—goes ahead under Gage's direction.

The various sections of the city are constructed on the surface, towed to the appropriate place, and sunk. They are then anchored, hooked to previous sections, and filled with air.

Finally, named "Amphibia City," it is ready for an inspection by government officials, but then Gage realizes that the chasm near the city is gradually undermining it, soon leading to disaster. He orders the immediate evacuation of the city, but an undersea earthquake brings the catastrophe: several of the cells of the city fall into the canyon, killing Dr. Halstead and others. One of the cells survives the cataclysm and Gage, now converted to the undersea way of life, makes plans for a new Amphibia City.

In his regular column in *Fangoria*, Alex Gordon sometimes chats about his films, and covered *The Underwater City* in issue #20. His wife Ruth found an article in the November 1958 issue of *American Weekly* called "Your Future Home Under the Sea," and she wrote a story treatment based on ideas in the article. Most aspects of the various theories concerning the practicality and use of such a city were covered. "They would harvest the sea," Gordon said, "fish, plant life and other edibles—like farming or ranching, to provide food for the world's ever-increasing hungry people."

Writing as Owen Harris, Orville H. Hampton, a bad writer, did the final screenplay for the picture, shot at Columbia studios in Hollywood.

In his article, Gordon says that he originally wanted Richard Denning and Audrey Dalton for the leads and Basil Rathbone for the part of Dr. Halstead. However, Columbia turned him down on Denning; "Columbia executive Irving Briskin, self-styled 'Keeper of the B's,' insisted on William Lundigan, who gave us nothing but trouble, and Audrey Dalton was too expensive." Basil Rathbone couldn't be in it because of a lecture tour, and replacement Raymond Massey was delayed in New York.

"Since almost the entire story took place on the bottom of the ocean," Gordon continued, "new camera techniques, new devices, new directorial aids, all had to be conceived, devised and tested. The combined shooting methods which enabled this project to be filmed were designated ... 'Depthovision.'"

There was one hitch. As Gordon said in an earlier *Fangoria* interview (#1), "The problem was that our budget didn't allow us to shoot any *real* underwater scenes. We had to shoot the entire sea adventure *dry* on a sound stage." (Note: when the film was released, it was said to be shot in "FantaScope" rather than "Depthovision.")

A narrow tank filled with water, which also had ripple glass and an agitator, was placed between the camera and the set. A series of huge foil-covered reflectors were mounted above the set; lights bounced off these gave illusion of sunlight filtering down through water. With the actors moving in slow motion, the illusion that they were actually underwater seemed satisfactory—except there were no air bubbles issuing from their tanks.

The special effects were under the supervision of Howard Lydecker, Howard A. Anderson, Jr. and Richard Albain, and the solution they devised was ingenious (if, after a few moments watching the film, obvious): the prop air tanks were filled with a plastic liquid; a telephonelike dial released a small amount of plastic at a time, inflated by helium being piped to each actor's back. The resulting tiny bubbles rose realistically out of sight.

"So," said Gordon in *Fangoria* #1, "we now had all these bubbles rising up in the air. That was fine. The only problem was that they also floated back down onto the stage, bouncing around on camera. This caused us a great deal of grief in that it looked tremendously fake. We finally decided to have grips lying flat ... in the rafters above the stage with air machines to chase the bubbles off to the side." However, in the finished film, frequently bubbles can be seen slowly cascading down behind the actors, some distance away.

Most of the 22 weeks of effects work was occupied in building and photographing the elaborate but obvious miniatures of the underwater city itself.

One of the difficulties with the film was hiring Frank McDonald as director. McDonald had a long career in B movies, so Gordon may have been partly motivated by his often-apparent nostalgia. But there were other available directors who probably would have brought more of a sense of liveliness to the film, already set-bound and talky. McDonald was quick, but he wasn't what the film called for.

He was a director from 1935 to 1965, and never made a distinctive or really memorable film. Among his titles: *Murder by an Aristocrat* (1936, a year McDonald made eight films), *Jeepers Creepers* (1939), *Barnyard Follies* (1940), *Hoosier Holiday* (1943), *Bells of Rosarita* (1945, probably his most famous film), *My Pal Trigger* (1946, probably his best), *13 Lead Soldiers* (1948), *Son of Belle Starr* (1953) and *Mara of the Wilderness* (1965).

As Owen Harris, Orville H. Hampton wrote *The Flight That Disappeared* (1961), *Secret of Deep Harbor* (1961) and *Deadly Duo* (1962), among others. Under his own name, he wrote genre films *The Alligator People*, *The Snake Woman*, *The Atomic Submarine*, *Jack the Giant Killer*, *Beauty and the Beast*, *The Four Skulls of Jonathan Drake*, and did additional dialogue on *Rocketship XM*. For more on Hampton, see the entries on *The Alligator People* and *The Snake Woman*.

William Lundigan was probably chosen for the lead for his popularity with SF-minded children after the TV series, "Men Into Space"; adults knew him for "Climax" on TV. This was his first film since *The White Orchid* in 1955, and he seems to have made only two later, *The Way West* (1967) and *Where Angels*

Go... Trouble Follows! (1968). He was a mild, competent actor, mostly a serviceable pretty boy who played leads in minor As and major Bs. Lundigan began in films in 1937; among his better-known titles were *The Old Maid* (1939), *Pinky* (1949), *I'd Climb the Highest Mountain* (1951) and *Inferno* (1953). His only other genre film is *Riders to the Stars* (1954).

Julie Adams, of course, was the leading lady in *Creature from the Black Lagoon.* After her Universal contract ran out in 1958, good roles came farther between for Adams, rather a pity, because her good acting, amused sexiness and no-nonsense, teacherlike qualities made her well suited for a broad range of roles. She still turns up on television, but seems not to have had the right agent, or something. Perhaps she's content to work only occasionally.

The Underwater City received negative to tepid reviews. Bosley Crowther, undoubtedly the wrong man to review it, walked out: "You will have to judge *The Underwater City* for yourself," he wrote in the *New York Times*. "After a few minutes of total immersion in it, we had to come up for air."

In the *Herald Tribune*, Robert Salmaggi termed it a "soggy melodrama.... The boring narration, to begin with, eliminates the need for sound nearly half the time.... The basic premise ... could have been interesting, but the way it's all mounted leaves one seasick."

James Powers in the *Hollywood Reporter* noted that it was "extremely episodic [and] static," but complimented Ronald Stein's music. The *Monthly Film Bulletin* gave it a rating of II, and called it "an enjoyable enough piece of hokum, and a welcome change from science-fiction. [*sic*]."

The most telling review was that of "Tube" in *Daily Variety*. While later in the review noting that the film "drags along" and that "most customers may find themselves nearly asleep in the deep until the turbulent conclusion," he began by commenting on the switch from color to black and white. "Although filmed in Eastman Color and apparently designed for somewhat more ambitious commercial purposes, [it] has been re-ticketed by Columbia for domestic release in black-and-white, a marketing revision apt to alter its programming status and resultant boxoffice destiny. Being an underwater melodrama, there is no question but that disregard of tint represents a significant loss of pictorial value. However, color alone does not make an attraction of 'A' quality out of a product in which more attention has been devoted to exploitability than to dramatic flow and substance. Chances are *The Underwater City* has found a home in its natural element—the bottom half of a double bill."

This proved to be accurate prophecy, and a fair judgment of the film.

Varan the Unbelievable

Even among Americans who are fond of Japanese monster films, such as myself, the name of *Varan the Unbelievable* carries little weight. The film was severely cut in the United States, and new scenes were shot here. It ran 87 minutes when it was released in Japan in 1958 (as *Daikaiju Baran*); the U.S. print was only 70 minutes, including the new scenes. Probably as much as half an hour was removed from the running time. For instance, all scenes of Varan flying were removed. In the photos I've seen, he doesn't look any too convincing a flyer anyway, but as flight was the only thing that distinguished Varan from Godzilla in the first place, they probably should have let Varan

In the extensively-reconstructed U.S. prints of Varan the Unbelievable (U.S. release 1962), the monster never gets off the ground; in fact, he hardly gets out of the lake where he's first found. But in Japanese prints, the monster had glider-wings and flew. For all frustrated U.S. Varan fans, here is a shot of the big guy in all his flying glory.

spread his "wings" in the United States as well. (He had glider-vanes from fore-legs to hind legs, like a flying squirrel.)

The two versions have similar plots with major differences. Quoting the official synopsis from Toho (headed "Knocked for a Ghoul by *Daikaiju Baran*"): "A schoolboy captures an 'unearthly' butterfly while vacationing in northern Japan. Scientific party sets out to investigate and find an eerie lake not listed on their maps. Out of the dark depths suddenly erupts 'Varan'—a prehistoric creature that had been assumed extinct for tens of million of years. The stunned scientists are wiped out. The terrifying news reaches an agonized nation. All-out efforts are made by Japan's self-defense forces to hunt down and kill the elusive reptile which flies off into the Pacific Ocean after causing havoc among its attacks. Conventional weapons, however, fail to penetrate the tough hide of the monster. Then the murderous creature starts to smash its way toward Tokyo. It is decided to use the powerful new type explosive as a last resort. Realizing that the most effective way would be to destroy it from within, cans of the explosives are sent up into the sky tied to balloons in the hope that the creature will gobble them up. As it swallows them one after another, deafening explosions occur and the reptile sinks into the slick waters of Tokyo Bay."

In the American print, the central character is Commander James Bradley (Myron Healey), who arrives on a small Japanese island with his Japanese wife Anna (Tsuruko Kobayashi). He's been sent there by a joint U.S.-Japanese commission which is seeking to find a way to desalinate seawater. The island has a large saltwater lake intended to be used for the experiments.

Anna learns that there is a legend of a monstrous beast living in the water, but Bradley scoffs and proceeds with his experiments. Varan pops out of the water roaring and thrashing about, raising a commotion without leaving the lake. Eventually, of course, he does come out—like most four-legged Japanese dinosaurs, he walks on his knees—and begins wreaking havoc. He sinks a ship, smashes a plane, and heads for Tokyo. He does little more than bellow and scream on an airfield near the bay.

Bradley, still hanging around (though not very visibly), gets a bright idea: if the desalinization chemicals roused Varan, perhaps more will kill him. The chemicals are blasted into Varan's soft underbelly, and this does the trick. (Sources and my memory are unclear as to whether the balloon gambit was used in the American prints.)

The very existence of *Varan* is a mild puzzle. The film was produced by the same studio and filmmaking team that made *Godzilla*. Were they trying to generate a new series with Varan, or what? This was apparently the next to be made after *Rodan* in 1956, and the lead monster has features of both Godzilla and Rodan. (The next Toho giant-monster film appeared in the early 60s.)

Whatever the goal of making the film was, it's a lame attempt. The effects aren't as interesting as in the previous three giant-monster films, and the monster itself is undistinguished. Varan looks simply like a large lizard with gliding vanes; he has a spiky head with hard-to-discern features, and no personality whatsoever. It's understandable that Varan didn't end up starring in his own series. He did come back very briefly as a sideline spectator in *Destroy All Monsters* (1968), but he did little more than kind of bounce up and down, as the monster suit was worn out.

If the monster Varan is a puzzle, the American-shot scenes are even more peculiar. It's somewhat stupefying that Dallas Films (the company that did the reshooting) would think that Myron Healey was more of an attraction than an all-Japanese cast. Granted, he'd been around since the early 40s, but was confined mostly to supporting roles. He occasionally had the lead or second lead in minor Bs and serials, but couldn't have been considered a star.

Among Healey's other credits: *I Dood It* (1943), *Crime Doctor's Manhunt*, *The Time of Their Lives* (both 1946), *Panther Girl of the Kongo* (a serial), *African Manhunt* (both 1955), *The Unearthly* (1957), *The Incredible Melting Man* (1977), and hundreds of television shows.

Healey's not a bad actor, but he's also not capable of carrying a picture—

he's limited. But here he is, replacing the Japanese leads. Surely dull scenes of Healey arguing with his Japanese wife couldn't have been as entertaining as shots of Varan flying through the skies, but someone must have thought so.

Variety's "Tube" said that it "adds nothing to the genre [of giant monsters]. It is hackneyed, uninspired carbon copy, serviceable only as a supporting filler.... Photography is too dark, editing is jagged."

The *Monthly Film Bulletin* gave it a III, and concurred (suspiciously closely) with "Tube": "Hackneyed and repetitious carbon copy of *Godzilla*, substantially made over by an American company in such a way that its arrogantly patronizing American hero and his simpering Japanese wife are almost entirely divorced from the film's climactic action scenes. The monster itself ... has the usual prodigious immunity to army bombardment. Photography (irritatingly dark) and cutting are ragged – hardly surprising under the circumstances."

Varan the Unbelievable is frequently shown on television, but there's no reason for rejoicing. Despite occasionally good special effects work by Eiji Tsuburaya and his hardworking crew, *Varan* is a very minor entry in Toho's monster parade. The most entertaining (and outrageous) Japanese monster movies still lay in the future.

One final note: although I don't imagine the Japanese version of the film was substantially better, I still would like to see Varan fly, and I have a curiosity about that "unearthly" butterfly.

The Wacky World of Dr. Morgus

In the southeastern part of the United States, the area generally called "the South," states' rights film distributors still flourish. Films made by small production companies are leased to distributors which operate only in a given area, usually a single state. The films are played off by that distributor in the assigned area. This was once a very common way of distributing films, but as transportation and communications systems improved, it became possible for even a small distributor to handle larger areas.

Occasionally, films would be released on a modified states' rights basis; American International often operated that way, raising money for their films from small distributors who then had the right to a larger share of the profits for their region (although the films were still advertised as being distributed solely by AIP).

States' rights distributors still operate in the South, and perhaps because of that, some films are made in that area and are distributed only there, rarely if ever surfacing in other parts of the country, even on television. At the home of Forrest J Ackerman many years ago, I met a young man who claimed to know literally dozens of titles of SF and horror movies made and shown only in the South. It's entirely possible that this person (whose name I have forgotten) was prevaricating, but he did give Don Willis and me a list of amazing titles, including *There Dwelt on Earth an Alien*, *The Mad Vampire*, *Robots from Mars*, *The Witch of Endor*, and *Sam, the Friendly Vampire*. We've never encountered any independent confirmation of these titles (and he named others, now lost in the mists of memory); if anyone out there in readerland knows anything about these pictures, I would be interested in the information.

This young man also pointed out that occasionally, films from that area do surface, being sold for whatever reason to "outside" distributors; these titles include *Night of Bloody Horror* (1969), *Shock Waves* (1977), *The Alien Dead* (1980), and *The Wacky World of Dr. Morgus*. (And of course, there's Earl Owensby, virtually a one-man film industry, who's made many films, including several in 3-D, shown almost exclusively in the South.)

According to the *American Film Institute Catalog*, an actor named Sid Noel was in a 1950 film called *A Modern Marriage*; whether or not he is the same Sid Noel who appears in *The Wacky World of Dr. Morgus* is unknown to me, although the AFI assumes they're the same. In any event, Sid Noel became locally famous (or notorious) in New Orleans because he was one of that strange category of performer known as Horror Movie Hosts.

While this isn't the place to go into an exhaustive discussion of this peculiar phenomenon, some salient features may be noted. Vampira (Maila Nurmi) seems to have been the first one, modeling herself on Charles Addams' slinky ghoul, who appeared in many of his *New Yorker* cartoons. (See the entry on *Plan 9 from Outer Space* for more on Vampira.) Vampira more or less set the form, and virtually all female horror movie hosts imitated her, including Tarantula Ghoul, who hosted films out of Portland, Oregon, and Elvira (Cassandra Peterson), who even as this book is prepared, is unfortunately still doing the same in Los Angeles, in syndication and on videotape.

Male horror hosts were more common; the most famous was Zacherley (John Zacherle), who hosted a series in New York, and who still occasionally pops up. In New Orleans, Sid Noel became Dr. Morgus.

The big boom in Horror Movie Hosts came in the late 1950s, when the Screen Gems "Shock" package of old Universal and Columbia films was initially released to television. Never shown there before, they were instantly successful, and were very much responsible for the revival of that kind of film in movie theatres.

It doesn't seem to have occurred to anyone at a TV station (certainly not in the late 50s) that these films should be treated with respect, and were in fact almost always harshly judged by critics at the time. (Until recently, Philip K. Scheuer's book of TV movie ratings said that *Bride of Frankenstein* was "way above average for this kind of trash.") So instead of having a relatively serious host, who might have emphasized the positive qualities of the film, these actors made outrageous fun of the films, and filled intermissions with terrible puns and what were then called "sick jokes."

Interestingly enough, when a TV station in Los Angeles tried this again with "Seymour" (Larry Vincent) in the mid-70s, they found that he could get away with kidding only movies that were generally regarded as being bad. When he tried this "ain't-this-awful-folks" approach with *Bride of Frankenstein*, among others, the station received outraged complaints. Nonetheless, Elvira gets away with vilifying films as good as *Peeping Tom* (1960) and *Village of the Damned*.

Sid Noel's Dr. Morgus must have been popular in New Orleans, because he's the only Horror Movie Host (so far) to have had a film built around him. His skills must have been in his presentation, because Dr. Morgus looks singularly unfunny: a standard fright wig, big snaggledy teeth, warts, and a dirty doctor's smock. Not one of your great clown outfits.

Apparently, on his show Morgus invented an "instant people" machine: a wacky (what else?) gadget that could turn people into sand. Later, when water was added or the machine was run in reverse (sources differ on this important question), the people would return to normal. This may have been the most popular aspect of Dr. Morgus' TV show, because it's the basis of the film.

In his New Orleans French Quarter laboratory, the highly eccentric Dr. Alexander Morgus has invented his Instant People machine. Even though a group of scientists in New York is interested in Morgus' machine, reporter Pencils McCabe (Dana Barton) cannot convince his editor that there's a story in the machine.

But Bruno (David Kleiberger), either a representative of Microvania or the ruler of that obviously Iron Curtain country (sources differ) does believe in the machine. He sees great possibilities for the machine in the field of espionage: merely reduce to sand your spies, even an entire army, take them into the country you're trying to spy on or conquer, restore them to normal, and voilà, an instant fifth-column force, as big as you want to make it.

Bruno has spy queen Mona Speekla (Jeanne Teslof) vamp Morgus to get the secret for Microvania. This works so well that Morgus himself goes with the machine to Microvania and dehydrates an invading force of 300 Microvanians.

However, when Bruno and Morgus return to New Orleans with the spies in the form of sand, a shipping crate breaks open, and the sand falls out, where it is swept up and loaded on a dump truck. In Morgus' 1920 hearse, Bruno and Morgus chase the truck across New Orleans, but it gets away from them. When they finally catch up, they discover that the sand has been mixed with concrete and is being poured "as a final link to Peoples Avenue" (says the pressbook). This hard end for a band of loyal Microvanians is the big comic finish.

Another synopsis says that Mona falls in love with Pencils, and they work together to overcome the menace of the Instant People machine.

Because of the elusive nature of these Southern-made films, it's very difficult to get information on them. The *American Film Institute Catalog* tells us that Sid Noel is known also as Noel Rideau. Of the other members of the cast and crew, Corelli Jacobs also did the music for *The Sin of Mona Kent* (1961), Dana Barton appeared in *The Debauchers* (1970; could be a different Dana Barton—it's a male role in *The Wacky World of Dr. Morgus* and a female role in *The Debauchers*), and Roul Haig also directed *Okefenokee* (1960). And that's about it. No reviews.

The Weird Ones

This very obscure little film was unknown to me until it turned up as a short entry in the *American Film Institute Catalog* for the 1960s. *Psychotronic* adds that it has some credits in common with *No Man's Land* and *Dungeon of Harrow* (both 1964), also filmed in San Antonio, but even Michael Weldon has never seen it.

No wonder. According to comic book artist Pat Boyette, who produced the film, some years ago fire destroyed everything connected with his film projects: "I lost it all," he said in a letter, "equipment, prints, paperwork, etc.... The problem was that for the most part it was uninsured."

The press sheet on the film describes it this way: "A strange visitor from Outer Space, probably an 'ASTRONIK,' is on the Earth, bent upon murder and other equally diabolical crimes, all of which involve the fair maidens of our own planet. It seems possible that if the love bug would bite the brute he might simmer down and submit to capture and so a pair of intrepid press agents enlist a gorgeous Cosmos-Cutie as the lure for a trap in which they hope to enmesh It, Him, or What Have You. Will they succeed with only sex for bait?"

The pressbook adds that how it turns out is "really unimportant, since the screen is treated to a brace of most intriguing and dedicated dolls, seen via the most exciting new film treatment since 3-D, 'PEEP-O-VISION,' probably the one 'gimmick' impossible to follow and one that will provide your patrons with a series of thrills comparable only to a roller coaster ride on an empty stomach. They don't need glasses but they do get, hold your sides now, a 'magic' keyhole viewer which becomes both a souvenir and an ad!"

The ad art is unilluminating, featuring a drawing of a strange, dog-headed thing peering at a girl in a bikini, and lines such as "Lastnite—Elvis! Tonite—Ye Gads the MONSTER!" and "You can see it but you won't believe it" and "By the way, if you think this is nonsense, where are you living?"

I'm very curious about *The Weird Ones*, but if Boyette's sad tale tells of the complete finish of all prints, my curiosity will remain unsatisfied.

Addenda

Or even Jove nods. The following are a few films that were omitted from Volume 1, their proper location, because of either ignorance (as in the case of *Spoilers of the Plains*) or second thoughts (as with *Kiss Me Deadly*). I have included them here simply to be as thorough as possible.

Fury of the Congo (1951)

A confusing entry in the minor Jungle Jim series, this does have stronger SF elements than many of the others. This time, the story opens as an airplane crashes in a jungle lake and the pilot, Cameron (William Henry), is rescued by stouthearted and thickset Jungle Jim (Johnny Weissmuller). Cameron claims to be a police inspector trying to find Professor Dunham, a biochemist who vanished in the jungle while trying to find a rare animal called the Okongo.

A tribe of natives also called the Okongo worships the ponylike animal (played by ponies), so Jim and Cameron go to the Okongo village, but find that all the men have been taken away by a band of white men who want to use them in tracking down and capturing a herd of Okongo ponies. The women have banded together in an Amazon–like group led by Leta (Sherry Moreland).

It turns out that Cameron himself is the leader of the villains, a gang of drug smugglers who have somehow learned that the Okongo (the ponies, not the natives) feed on a certain jungle plant, and that as a result, a gland in the Okongo produces a very highly addictive narcotic. Professor Dunham knows how to extract the fluid, and so has been captured.

Still unaware of Cameron's involvement, when the Professor falls down a cliff and lands at Jim's feet, he turns the unconscious man over to Cameron, and dashes off in search of the Professor's erstwhile captors. When the Professor revives, Leta learns the true relationship between Cameron and Dunham, and she runs off in search of her tribe.

There follows a great deal more running around in the jungle and elsewhere, interspersed with much stock footage. According to Don Willis (I), who found the film "incredibly bad," Jim encounters a man-eating plant, not mentioned by other reviewers. However, several do mention a giant spider which Jim battles in a desert he has to cross. My memory of this film is, I hope understandably, quite hazy, as I saw it only once, over 30 years ago. But the giant spider remains etched in my mind's eye: it approaches Jim from the left, clearly fastened to a long board extending out of camera range. It's about the size of a small car, and very hairy. Jim battles and soon dispatches it.

Note: even though in replaying the scene in my head, I realize that the big prop was mounted on a long board, at the time, eight-year-old me was convinced that it was an absolutely *real* giant spider, and I spent some time browsing among books on invertebrates trying to find proof that great big spiders did live in the African desert.

At the end of the picture, the Okongo (the natives, not the ponies) are fleeing from the bad guys; Jungle Jim is chasing Cameron, having learned that he's a bad guy; the native women are chasing the native men; the stampeding Okongo (the ponies, not the natives) are chasing everyone *and* running from everyone. There is also a sandstorm. At least the climax sounds like it had adequate action. As "Brog" said in *Daily Variety*, the "final fifteen minutes of footage finds the entire cast ... running furiously and aimlessly about the screen."

Brog considered the film "mediocre filler fare at best," and said "film's over-length doesn't help, either"—this of a film that's only 69 minutes long.

The unnamed *Hollywood Reporter* reviewer was more favorable, saying that the film "packs enough excitement and color to please the juvenile and action fans.... The direction of William Berke is geared to lure as many thrills as possible from the fumbling amateurish script."

Fury of the Congo is just another Jungle Jim adventure, much like the others, with a touch of animal action and a giant spider.

Jungle Boy (1955)

This is a little-seen and obscure film starring Sabu; even Ephraim Katz in his usually well-researched *Film Encyclopedia* errs in identifying it as an Italian film with the original title of *Il Tesoro de Bengala*. Known under the above title in England and the United States, it is also called *Jungle Hell*, but by any title doesn't seem to be a lost classic.

While Walt Lee's *Reference Guide to Fantastic Films* was being prepared, film fan Larry Richardson contacted Lee to tell him of seeing this film on television. Until recently, that was the sole authority for even the existence of the film. However, upon examining *Monthly Film Bulletin*, I found it listed in the 1956 volume as *Jungle Boy*. (Richardson had given the title as *Jungle Hell*.)

The plotline given in the *Monthly Film Bulletin* review omits the most striking feature cited by Richardson: "Working in an Indian village, Dr. Paul Morrison [David Bruce] treats two cases of burns caused by radiation from a certain kind of rock. He cables a colleague in London who sends his assistant, Dr. Pam Ames [K.T. Stevens]. The plane in which she is traveling crashes, and she is the only survivor. She is rescued by Sabu [Sabu], an elephant boy, who works with Paul. Once Paul has recovered from the shock of discovering his visitor has not only survived the crash but is a woman, he falls in love with her and asks her to marry him. They plan to do research on the mysterious rock and to destroy the power of the local witch-doctor."

That radioactive rock would qualify the film for this book (or for Volume 1, had I but known) anyway, but Richardson's report included a wild ending: a passing flying saucer blows up the radioactive rock with a ray, then departs. Richardson was always accurate in the information he provided Walt Lee, so I see no reason to doubt him in this case.

The *Monthly Film Bulletin* gave the film a rating of III. "The story is slight and unintelligibly disjointed, and it is tediously padded out with a large number of [stock shots], mainly of trumpeting elephants engaged in teak-logging, etc. This extraneous material is made all the more conspicuous by its poor photographic quality. All in all, a dispirited production."

According to Joe Dante, this cheap film was made of episodes of an unsold TV series called "Jungle Boy," put together with added stock shots and released as a feature.

Kiss Me Deadly (1955)

I intended to include this in Volume 1, but thought later that the science fiction element was so slight it should be excluded. Then I thought a third time, and decided that despite the slenderness of the sci-fi, it's still there in the film. And so I've included it. Give me a break.

Kiss Me Deadly has been discussed extensively in several other books; I do not intend to examine it thoroughly as an example of *film noir*, partly because doing so lies outside the parameters of this book in one sense, and partly because *film noir* is difficult to define.

Kiss Me Deadly is a swift-paced, exciting but pretentious detective story starring Ralph Meeker as Mickey Spillane's Mike Hammer, the crudest, most violent of fictional private eyes. The climax of the novel *Kiss Me Deadly* essentially has Hammer beating up the Mafia; Spillane seems to assume that no matter how powerful an organization is, Hammer is tough enough to call their bluff and reduce them to jelly. Spillane sure can write, as said in *Marty* (1955), but Hammer himself is somewhat repellent. Far from the knights in trench coats of Raymond Chandler, Ross McDonald and Robert B. Parker, Hammer is a savage; as Ian Jarvie said in *Film Culture* (Summer, 1961), "In a society he despises, Hammer feels at liberty to be as ruthless as he wishes in achieving his ends." Hammer never bothers to justify his actions—he never questions them, so no justification is necessary.

When producer-director Robert Aldrich and writer A.I. Bezzerides adapted the novel, they made a basic change, but one that's implicit in Spillane's novels about Hammer. Mike Hammer's world always seems to be on the verge of apocalypse, but he's not fighting it; he's part of it. Only his secretary-lover Velda keeps him from plunging into the abyss of terminal violence and the seething hatred he expresses toward everything. (When Velda vanishes in a later novel, Hammer completely collapses and only pulls himself back together in order to [a] get revenge and [b] find Velda, whom he learns may yet be alive.)

This feeling that everything is about to collapse into bones and slime is made more explicit in the film, and the plot device expressing this gives it its science fiction elements. The novel and film have similar storylines, except that what everyone wants in the novel is information; in the film, it's a nuclear device in a suitcase, something highly radioactive being sought by foreign agents. At the end, this box is opened by a greedy Pandora, and she is turned into a tower of screaming flame by the brilliant atomic light from within. Then the box explodes for no clear reason, and the ending is ambiguous as to whether Hammer and Velda survive. (According to Carrie Rechey in the *Village*

Voice, Aldrich told François Truffaut that he "made the ending ambiguous to avoid police interference." Of course, Truffaut asked if the ending signified the actual end of the world...)

The linking of *film noir*–type concerns of ambiguity (no private eye is *less* ambiguous than Mike Hammer, however), guilt, corrupt romance and other dark thoughts and deeds with the nuclear tragedy facing the entire world was more than clever. It actually expresses something: men of good will can keep us from disaster when the seeds of the disaster lie within ourselves, with our greed and passions. But nuclear disaster is beyond all humanity, and to stop it will take more than simple bravery. Hammer's world is bleaker, more violent and nastier than that of any other private eye, so it's only right that he confront the spectre of atomic power – and lose.

The plot of *Kiss Me Deadly* is almost impossibly convoluted, and most reviewers have either expressed an inability to figure things out, or declared that figuring out exactly what happens is beside the point. They're probably right.

Mike Hammer (Ralph Meeker) picks up a bonde (Cloris Leachman) in a raincoat; she's Christina, and seems to be an escapee from a mental institution. Hammer and Christina are almost immediately waylaid by thugs, who knock out Hammer and begin torturing Christina. Hammer is semiconscious during this, and sees her die. They're pushed off a cliff in Mike's car; he's thrown clear and wakes up in a hospital badly battered and with a thirst for revenge.

The complicated story involves a conspiracy to kill a scientist, a local gangster named Carl Evello (Paul Stewart), Evello's sister who tries to seduce Mike, and other assorted good and bad guys. Evello tries to buy Hammer off with a sports car, but there are two bombs in it which, at Hammer's direction, his mechanic friend Nick (Nick Dennis) finds.

Christina's roommate Lily (Gaby Rogers) moves in with Mike for protection, but Nick is killed and Mike is abducted by Evello's men. At the gangster's hideout, he recognizes Dr. Soberin (Albert Dekker) as the villain who tortured Christina. Mike escapes and finds Velda missing. He recalls Christina's last words to him, and finds a clue in a poem by Christina Rossetti.

From the dead woman's effects at the morgue Mike gets a key to a locker containing what Velda had earlier termed "the great whatsit," the thing everyone is after. He leaves the box in the locker and finds that Lily is missing.

FBI agent Pat (Wesley Addy) tells Hammer that the box contains radioactive material sought by spies, but Hammer refuses to divulge the location of the box. Which then vanishes from the locker. So Hammer gets the address of Soberlin's beach house, and goes there to find Velda captive and Soberlin murdered by the real villain, Lily.

She shoots Hammer, who staggers away to rescue Velda and try to make a getaway, while insatiably curious Lily opens the box. A brilliant light pours out, she screams and bursts into flames, and the beach house blows up in an atomic explosion.

Jack Moffitt said, "I never did figure out who the bomb belonged to, what the doctor wanted it for, what the gangsters had to do with it, or why [Christina] was in the asylum." Nor did I. Scripter Bezzerides may have lost track of some of the story in adapting the novel; he retains many of the elements of the original story and discards others, so he may have forgotten to tie everything together.

It really doesn't matter. The film is fast, violent and entertaining; it's not illogical, just confused. Aldrich finds Los Angeles locales that are right for the story—unpleasantly seedy—and sees to it that all performances are edgy, terse and filled with underlying tensions. It's one of his very best films, precisely because it's so nasty; Aldrich always had a rather unpleasant view of the world, and in his best films, such as *The Big Knife* (1955), *What Ever Happened to Baby Jane?* (1962), *The Dirty Dozen* (1967) and *The Longest Yard* (1974), his outlook found expression in sour, sardonic stories. His best films are violent, cynical and witty; his worst, such as *The Grissom Gang* (1971) and *Hustle* (1975), become either overheated melodramas in which not only everyone is unpleasant but downright disgusting, or pseudointellectual horseshit. Sometimes both at once. Aldrich was not a deep thinker, but he knew how to present grim, suspenseful material, and despite an air of poverty hanging over the film, in *Kiss Me Deadly*, he's at the top of his form.

Ralph Meeker never had a better part in films than Mike Hammer. Always at his best playing cocky but not intellectual thugs with a strong violent streak, and as that is nearly a definition of Mike Hammer, Meeker was superbly well cast in this film. But more than that, Meeker seems to understand Hammer, if not necessarily approve, and more than in any other Mike Hammer movie, at least until Armand Assante in the second *I, The Jury*, Hammer never seemed so real as in *Kiss Me Deadly*. Meeker is still the champ Hammer.

Meeker has always been hard to cast; he's an especially good actor, but his fast speech and square, scowling face make him suitable primarily for villains, unpleasant military types and private eyes. Of genre films, he also appeared in *The Food of the Gods* (1976), *The Mind Snatchers* (1972, in which he was especially good), *The Alpha Incident* (1976) and *Without Warning* (1980).

For more on *Kiss Me Deadly*, I recommend Alain Silver's somewhat overwritten but insightful commentary in *Film Noir* (Overlook Press, 1979), which he coedited with Elizabeth Ward.

Lost Planet Airmen (1951)

Althought it may not have yet become obvious, by 1949, the bloom was off the rose for serials. After that date, not only were there no great serials produced, most were mediocre at best and/or reused stock footage from earlier serials shamelessly. It was especially shameless because, in many parts of the country, many of those older serials were still in circulation, so in a matter of months, kids would see the same stunts, the same escapes, the same special effects. Usually, this didn't bother kids; they were there on Saturdays for their 15-minute fix; the serial chapter was only part of a program that included cartoons and generally a Western with a currently-popular star.

By general consensus and in fact, Republic was the studio that turned out the best "chapterplays" (as magazines like *Variety* often termed them); except for a few with John Wayne, their feature films were generally of little interest. But their serials were often terrific, with fast action and suspenseful cliffhangers. The plots were no more interesting than those of serials made by other studios, but plots (and acting) weren't what lured kids to the serials anyway, and aren't what make them watchable today. Although even the best serials are boring when seen in one sitting, when seen a chapter at a time, instead of all at once, taken on their own terms, serials can still be loads of fun.

By 1949, the popularity of what we now call superheroes seemed to have been clearly established (although shortly they would fall into disfavor for almost a decade), and there were a few serials about heroes from the comics. Republic wanted one they could call their own, and instead of a specific hero, developed a specific costume that turned up in three serials and a semiserial, although in three out of the four outings, a different hero wore the costume. Republic knew it was the Rocket Man suit that kids loved rather than whatever colorless actor inhabited it. And they certainly didn't want to get locked into one actor playing Rocket Man; they'd had enough trouble with Roy Rogers and John Wayne already.

The first Rocket Man serial was *King of the Rocket Men*, released in 1949; it was turned into an incredibly swift-paced—and confusing—feature released as *Lost Planet Airmen* in 1951.

The costume was simple: a bullet-shaped helmet, that wonderfully simple control panel, and a leather jacket; on the back were the classy-looking rocket tubes that always looked to me like they should ignite Rocket Man's ass. The Rocket Man suit is discussed elsewhere in this book in the entry on *Satan's Satellites*.

The Rocket Man suit returned in *Radar Men from the Moon* (1952), with George Wallace (not the politician, of course) playing Commando Cody, Sky Marshal of the Universe. Judd Holdren played the more drably-named Larry Martin in *Zombies of the Stratosphere*, which became *Satan's Satellites*. The Rocket Man suit returned for the last time in the odd *Commando Cody, Sky Marshal of the Universe*; to the confusion of kids following Rocket Man from film to film, he was again played by Judd Holdren, but he was called Commando Cody, who looked like George Wallace last time. (That outing was peculiar because it was made as a TV series, but shown serial-fashion in theatres as well.)

Rocket Man dashed at the camera, bounced off a hidden springboard, and shot over the camera rather smoothly; this stunt was done by the master leaper of stunt men, small Dave Sharpe. Others who did the stunts for Rocket Man included Tom Steele and Dale Van Sickel; that helmet effectively hid the face of whoever wore it.

The very good special effects of the flying scenes were done by Howard and Theodore Lydecker, and were generally quite simple: an almost full-sized dummy, dressed as Rocket Man, zipped along nicely-invisible wires, followed by the camera from almost every position except right overhead. These flying scenes were highly satisfactory, especially for the kids for whom the serial was made.

The plot of *King of the Rocket Men/Lost Planet Airmen* was the sort of thing often found in serials. A group of scientists is being killed one by one by a mysterious fiend calling himself Dr. Vulcan (seen only as a shadow on a wall); he is actually one of the group himself (Professor Bryant, as it turns out), and is seeking to get the fabulous inventions of the group. He wants to conquer the world, a not-uncommon goal for serial megalomaniacs.

Vulcan/Bryant (I. Stanford Jolley) thinks he's killed Professor Millard (James Craven, usually a fiend himself), but he's actually been rescued by hero Jeff King (Tristram Coffin) and spirited away to a cave. Millard gives King his great invention, the Rocket Man suit, and wearing it, King zooms about for 12 chapters, putting a stop to the activities of the thugs working for Vulcan.

In the serial, by using a swell new weapon called a Decimeter, Vulcan is able to raise an earthquake and resulting tidal wave to smash New York flat. This is accomplished by Ned Mann's ambitious if obvious special effects taken from *Deluge* (1933), previously used in serials and other features. In the feature *Lost Planet Airmen*, however, the catastrophe is depicted as merely being one of Dr. Vulcan's (literal) dreams.

In any event, both serial and movie end in a whirlwind of action as Air Corps planes are about to bomb Vulcan's island hideout while Rocket Man battles to destroy the Decimeter and escape those oncoming bombs. Of course, he did in the nick of time, and the villain was blown to smithereens.

The title was another example of Republic's opportunistically naming heroes "King" so they will have a colorful title for the serial. They did this with *King of the Royal Mounted* (1940), *King of the Texas Rangers* (1941), *King of the Forest Rangers* (1946) and *King of the Carnival* (1955).

The title of the feature version is peculiarly misleading: the only planet in the film, lost or otherwise, was good old Earth. Republic was merely overemphasizing the science fiction aspect of the serial, which didn't really need it. I presume they felt that the word Rocket Man wasn't sci-fi enough for the sophisticated audiences of 1951.

Tristram Coffin, who played the hero, was a slender, mild actor, active in films since at least 1939. He appeared frequently in serials, including *Dick Tracy's G-Men* (1939), *The Mysterious Dr. Satan*, *The Green Hornet Strikes Again* (both 1940), *Spy Smasher*, *The Perils of Nyoka* (both 1942), *Brick Bradford* (1948) and *Radar Patrol vs. Spy King* (1949).

He was also in *The Corpse Vanishes* (1942), *Radar Secret Service* (1949), *Rhubarb* (1951), *Flight to Mars*, *Creature with the Atomic Brain*, *Night the World Exploded* and *The Crawling Hand* (1963). Coffin (apparently named after a politician—there are *several* people named Tristram Coffin) was also in small roles in bigger films, such as *They Met in Bombay* (1941), *Destroyer* (1943), *The Gallant Blade*, *Romance on the High Seas* (both 1948) and *A Star Is Born* (1954), among others.

His leading lady in *Lost Planet Airmen* was Mae Clarke. In the late 1920s and early 30s, she seemed to be a sought-after independent actress; although she's certainly most famous for being Dr. Frankenstein's fiancée in *Frankenstein* (1931), she was also in *The Front Page* and *Public Enemy* in the same year; in the latter film, she was the woman Jimmy Cagney smacked in the face with a grapefruit. However, by 1936, her days of playing leads or major support in MGM, Fox, Universal and Columbia films were over; from that date on, whenever she turned up in major studio films, she played very minor roles, but she was busy. She had several leads in Republic movies through the late 30s and all the way through the 1940s. Among the major films she was in were *The Great Caruso*, *Royal Wedding* (both 1951), *Pat and Mike*, *Singin' in the Rain* (both 1952), *Not as a Stranger* (1955) and others. She was still appearing in films as late as 1967's *Thoroughly Modern Millie*. The only reason for her abrupt and permanent decline seems to have been that she simply wasn't a good actress. She may have been well liked, however, judging from the large number of films she appeared in.

As Jim Harmon and Don Glut said in their book *The Great Serial Heroes*, *King of the Rocket Men* "showed the downward trend of the late 1940s Republic serials, with stock footage serving most of the cliffhangers requiring miniatures." That being said, it is still above average for serials, with lots of fast action, a leading man a shade more interesting than most (with his mustache, Tristram Coffin looked more like a villain than a hero, but did lots of heroic stuff), and that wonderful Rocket Man suit.

Being only 65 minutes long yet featuring a large percentage of the thrills from the serial, at the expense of almost all narrative coherency, *Lost Planet Airmen* is one of the most dizzying, frenetic serial featurizations ever pieced together.

Spoilers of the Plains (1951)

I hope I might be especially forgiven for neglecting to include this film in Volume 1. Even though I was one of the biggest fans of Roy Rogers when I was a child, it didn't occur to me that any of his movies might have science fiction elements. But *Spoilers of the Plains* does. (The title is meaningless.)

Roy Rogers has been scorned by people who consider themselves true fans of B Westerns, which usually means they are fans of the B Westerns of the 1930s and early 40s; their nostalgia simply doesn't extend to singing cowboys like Roy, Gene, Rex and the others. Mine, however, most certainly does. Please forgive a very personal digression. I surely loved Roy; I used to read about his children and tried to imagine how it would be to actually be the Son of Roy Rogers. In the mid-70s, Roy made something of a comeback, and issued a new record; along with Bob Greenberg, Jim Harmon, Gerrit Graham, Don Glut and other fans of Roy, I lined up to get his autograph at a record store in North Hollywood. ("Why is it," Glut asked, "that the only people I can impress by telling them I met Roy Rogers are already here?")

But I did get some satisfaction. I called my mother and asked her who, in all the world, would I have most wanted to meet 25 years before. She immediately replied, "Roy Rogers." And at a meeting of the Los Angeles Science Fantasy Society, when I told Professor Ed Buchman that I'd met Roy, he literally threw himself to the ground and kissed my feet. I was not the only one who remembered loving Roy.

There were good reasons why kids like me were starry-eyed about Roy Rogers. In the late 40s and early 50s, most of his films were especially action-packed, with much riding, shooting and fighting. These were often in (rather garish) SuperCineColor, featured Roy's attractive dog Bullet, and the smartest horse in the movies, Trigger, that beautiful golden palomino. The films were, in that mis- and overused phrase, good clean fun, just what children under ten wanted to see.

Rogers' movies were a cut above the other B Westerns turned out in their dying period. They still usually had reasonable production values, and even though the Sons of the Pioneers, the group he helped found, had left Roy's films, Foy Willing and the Riders of the Purple Sage still provided good harmony to Roy's perfectly fine voice. These definitely were singing Westerns, and I didn't mind at all.

Roy Rogers seems to be one of the "realies" — not a phony. The character he played on screen, also usually named Roy Rogers, seems very much like Roy himself: a decent, honest, Christian gentleman, devoted to his family. Although I do not agree with many of his political and social stands, I have never heard of a scandal attached to his name. A little kid could have had far less respectable heroes than Roy Rogers.

In *Spoilers of the Plains*, Gregory Camwell (Grant Withers) is posing as the operator of an oil well, but he's actually a foreign agent trying to get the plans for a long-range weather forecasting device being tested in rockets nearby. (The reason the film is in this book.)

To ingratiate himself with the directors of the project, Camwell offers to supply oil needed in the experiments; however, as he's really not an oil engineer, he has to tap into the oil lines of a company for which Roy Rogers is a superintendent. While searching for the oil thieves, Roy is ambushed, but manages to escape.

Roy's pal Splinters (Gordon Jones) has been hired by rocket base supervisor Jonathan Manning (William Forrest) to track down the rockets once they are fired, and to collect and return them. Roy is friendly with Manning's daughter Frankie (Penny Edwards); she's a mousy type revealed as attractive when she takes off those pesky glasses and puts on a nice dress.

Camwell tricks Splinters into telling him how the rockets are located once they fall, and he and his gang beat Splinters to the next one. They remove the weather-forecaster, replacing it with a time bomb set to go off when the rocket is returned to the base. However, Bullet hears the ticking of the bomb, and Roy removes it in time.

On Trigger, Roy chases down Camwell and his gang; after a big fight, Camwell is brought to justice.

The film is notable for some pretty rough fights, including one Roy loses. The climax is very lively, with stunt men leaping dramatically back and forth between speeding wagons. The movie is a lot of fun.

Notable by their absence from this film are Roy's wife Dale Evans, and either of his frequent sidekicks Andy Devine or Pat Brady. Also, the film was in black-and-white rather than the customary color.

But the trade reviewers were pleased with it. *Hollywood Reporter* said, "Packed with action and thrills in nearly every minute of footage, [this] is a top entry in the Roy Rogers series which should delight the rural and juvenile audiences.... William Witney's direction concentrates on furious action from start to finish."

"Brog" at *Variety* said, "It's one of [Rogers'] better oaters, loaded with fast movement, rough and ready action, and little touches that will go over strong with his juvenile fans."

On the other hand, *Boxoffice* was not impressed; while finding the action "unusually vigorous and original, the story is so lacking in believability that [the action scenes] are considerably discounted." Having seen it, I side with *Variety*.

When viewed today, Roy Rogers' films of this period hold up well as examples of unpretentious entertainment that soon vanished into television (along with Roy Rogers himself).

White Goddess (1952/53)

And at last, the final title—and this one turned up after I received the page proofs for virtually the entire book; I am driving McFarland's Katy Taylor crazy.

But completeness is completeness.

In 1952, one-time movie star Jon Hall appeared in the syndicated TV series "Ramar of the Jungle," as Dr. Tom Reynolds, called Ramar by natives. The stories were the usual sort of jungle adventure, with much stock footage and very white-skinned "natives." Seen today, episodes of "Ramar" look quaint, racist and silly.

But in the early 1950s, many things sold, both on television and in movie theatres. Several TV series were raided to make features: three half-hour shows were edited together to make a feature-length "movie," and were shown in many foreign markets, even those where the series in question was also sold, apparently. For instance, 20th Century–Fox distributed several "movies" made of episodes of the "Adventures of Superman" TV series to foreign markets. These features played in every English–language market except the United States, where apparently the presence of the TV series itself kept them out of theatres. Because they didn't play here, these Superman films are not included in this book, but for the record, they all appeared in 1954, and were *Superman's Peril*, *Superman Flies Again*, *Superman in Exile*, *Superman and Scotland Yard* and *Superman and the Jungle Devil*.

"Ramar of the Jungle" also received this featurization treatment; among the titles so generated were *Eyes of the Jungle*, *Phantom of the Jungle* and the one in question, *White Goddess*, called *Ramar of the Jungle* in England. However, in the apparently sole case of *White Goddess*, it was also shown in the United States, at least according to the *Motion Picture Exhibitor* for May 6, 1953. They ran a synopsis and brief commentary:

"Jon Hall, a doctor, and chemist friend, Ray Montgomery, go to Africa to investigate curative powers of various medicines used by tribal witch doctors. With the assistance of trader Ludwig Stossel, his daughter, M'Liss McClure, and an English guide, James Fairfax, they venture into forbidden territory ruled by white goddess Millicent Patrick, who has remained youthful through the years by using the tribal drugs. She refuses to give them a sample of the medication. They try again, and, at the same time, two escaped convicts, Lucien Prival and Robert Williams, go to Patrick to talk her into splitting the wealth she has amassed. She agrees to escape with them, hoping the blame will fall on Hall and his friends, but the natives track her, and she and the convicts are killed. Hall and Montgomery get their medicinal samples, with a romance in the offing for Montgomery and McClure.

"X Ray: this should wind up on the lower half with a fair story, average action and interest, and standard performances, adequate direction, and production. The screen play is by Sherman L. Lowe and Eric Taylor."

The *Monthly Film Bulletin* mentions that the two escaped convicts kill the white goddess, and the medicinal samples are found in the witch doctor's hut. The *Bulletin* called the film a "thin and unlikely adventure story in which a humourless Jon Hall blunders his way through swamps peopled by crocodiles and cannibals."

The element of eternal youth qualifies the film for this book, of course. I suppose this film exists somewhere, but I can't imagine anyone being eager to sample such synthetic and familiar thrills.

Selected Bibliography
(For Volumes I and II)

In a project as massive as this, many sources are consulted. Those which provided the most interesting or useful material are listed below. Those with * are especially recommended. The Margaret Herrick Library of the Academy of Motion Picture Arts and Sciences was a major resource.

Books

Amelio, Ralph J., ed. *Hal in the Classroom: Science Fiction Films*. New York: Monarch Press, 1976.

Barr, Charles. *Ealing Studios*. London: Cameron & Tayleur, 1977.

*Barsacq, Léon. *Caligari's Cabinet and Other Grand Illusions: A History of Film Design*; revised and edited by Elliott Stein. Boston: New York Graphic Society, 1976. (Revised and expanded edition of Barsacq's 1970 *Le Décor de Film*.)

Bawden, Liz-Anne, ed. *The Oxford Companion to Film*. New York: Oxford University Press, 1976.

Baxter, John. *Science Fiction in the Cinema*. New York: A.S. Barnes, 1970.

Beck, Calvin Thomas. *Heroes of the Horrors*. New York: Macmillan, 1975.

_____. *Scream Queens: Heroines of the Horrors*. New York: Macmillan, 1978.

Bojarski, Richard. *The Films of Bela Lugosi*. Secaucus, NJ: Citadel Press, 1980.

*Brosnan, John. *Future Tense: The Cinema of Science Fiction*. New York: St. Martin's Press, 1978.

_____. *The Horror People*. New York: St. Martin's Press, 1976.

_____. *Movie Magic: The Story of Special Effects in the Cinema*. New York: St. Martin's Press, 1974.

Castle, William. *Step Right Up! I'm Gonna Scare the Pants Off America*. New York: Putnam, 1976.

*Ceplair, Larry and Steven Englund. *The Inquisition in Hollywood: Politics in the Film Community, 1930–1960*. Garden City, NY: Anchor Press/Doubleday, 1980.

*Clarens, Carlos. *An Illustrated History of the Horror Film*. New York: Capricorn Books, 1967.

Costello, Chris. *Lou's on First*. New York: St. Martin's Press, 1981.

Cremer, Robert. *Lugosi: the Man Behind the Cape*. Chicago: Regnery, 1976.

Derry, Charles. *Dark Dreams: A Psychological History of the Modern Horror Film*. South Brunswick, NJ: A.S. Barnes, 1977.

Di Franco, J. Philip, ed. *The Movie World of Roger Corman*. New York: Chelsea House, 1977.

Evans, I.O. *Jules Verne and His Work*. London: Arco, 1965.

Eyles, Allen, Robert Adkinson and Nicholas Fry, eds. *The House of Horror: The Story of Hammer Films*. London: Lorrimer, 1973.

*Flynn, Charles and Todd McCarthy, eds. *Kings of the Bs: Working Within the Hollywood System: An Anthology of Film History and Criticism*. New York: Dutton, 1975. Includes filmographies on many directors mentioned in this book, and articles on Roger Corman, Sam Katzman, Edgar G. Ulmer, Samuel Z. Arkoff, William Castle.

*Frank, Alan (G.). *The Horror Film Handbook*. Totowa, NJ: Barnes & Noble Books, 1982.
_____. *Horror Films*. London: Spring Books, 1977.
_____. *Horror Movies: Tales of Terror in the Cinema*. London: Octopus Books, 1974.
_____. *Monsters and Vampires*. London: Octopus Books, 1976.
*_____. *The Science Fiction and Fantasy Film Handbook*. Totowa, NJ: Barnes & Noble Books, 1982.
Fry, Ron and Pamela Fourzon. *The Saga of Special Effects*. Englewood Cliffs, NJ: Prentice-Hall, 1977.
Garbicz, Adam and Jacek Klinowski. *Cinema, the Magic Vehicle—A Guide to Its Achievement—Journey Two: The Cinema in the Fifties*. Metuchen, NJ: Scarecrow Press, 1979.
Geduld, Harry M., ed. *The Definitive "Dr. Jekyll and Mr. Hyde" Companion*. New York: Garland, 1983.
Gifford, Denis. *Movie Monsters*. London: Studio Vista; New York: E.P. Dutton, 1969.
*_____. *A Pictorial History of Horror Movies*. London: Hamlyn, 1973.
*_____. *Science Fiction Film*. London: Studio Vista; New York: E.P. Dutton, 1971.
*Glut, Donald F. *Classic Movie Monsters*. Metuchen, NJ: Scarecrow Press, 1978.
*_____. *The Frankenstein Legend: A Tribute to Mary Shelley and Boris Karloff*. Metuchen, NJ: Scarecrow Press, 1973.
*Goldner, Orville and George E. Turner. *The Making of King Kong: The Story Behind a Film Classic*. South Brunswick, NJ: A.S. Barnes, 1975.
*Halliwell, Leslie. *The Filmgoer's Companion*; 7th ed. New York: Scribner, 1980.
Harryhausen, Ray. *Film Fantasy Scrapbook*. Cranbury, NJ: A.S. Barnes, 1972.
Hickman, Gail Morgan. *The Films of George Pal*. South Brunswick, NJ: A.S. Barnes, 1977.
Hirschhorn, Clive. *The Films of James Mason*. Secaucus, NJ: Citadel Press, 1975.
Hogan, David J. *Who's Who of the Horrors and Other Fantasy Films: The International Personality Encyclopedia of the Fantastic Film*. San Diego, CA: A.S. Barnes, 1980.
*Jensen, Paul M. *Boris Karloff and His Films*. South Brunswick, NJ: A.S. Barnes, 1974.
Johnson, William, ed. *Focus on the Science Fiction Film*. Englewood Cliffs, NJ: Prentice-Hall, 1972.
*Kael, Pauline. *5001 Nights at the Movies: A Guide from A to Z*. New York: Holt, Rinehart and Winston, 1982.
*Katz, Ephraim. *The Film Encyclopedia*. New York: Crowell, 1979.
*Kneale, Nigel. *The Quatermass Experiment*. London: Arrow Books, 1979.
*_____. *Quatermass II*. London: Arrow Books, 1979.
*Krafsur, Richard P., executive ed. *The American Film Institute Catalog of Motion Pictures: Feature Films 1961–1970*. New York: Bowker, 1976. Two volumes.
*Lee, Walt, comp. *Reference Guide to Fantastic Films: Science Fiction, Fantasy & Horror*. Los Angeles: Chelsea-Lee Books, 1972–1974. Three volumes.
*Lenburg, Jeff, Joan Howard Maurer and Greg Lenburg. *The Three Stooges Scrapbook*. Secaucus, NJ: Citadel Press, 1982.
Lennig, Arthur. *The Count: The Life and Films of Bela "Dracula" Lugosi*. New York: Putnam, 1974.
*Lentz, Harris M., III, comp. *Science Fiction, Horror & Fantasy Film and Television Credits*. Jefferson, NC: McFarland, 1983. Two volumes.
Lyon, Christopher, ed. and Susan Doll, asst. ed. *The International Dictionary of Films and Filmmakers: Volume II—Directors/Filmmakers*. Chicago: St. James Press, 1984.
*Maltin, Leonard. *The Disney Films*. New York: Crown, 1973.
*McGee, Mark. *Fast and Furious: The Story of American International Pictures*. Jefferson, NC: McFarland, 1984.
_____, ed. *TV Movies: 1983–84 Edition*. New York: New American Library, 1982.
Medved, Harry, with Randy Dreyfuss. *The Fifty Worst Films of All Time (and How They Got That Way)*. New York: Popular Library, 1978.
_____ and Michael Medved. *The Golden Turkey Awards: Nominees and Winners, the Worst Achievements in Hollywood History*. New York: Putnam, 1980.
Mulholland, Jim. *The Abbott & Costello Book*. New York: Popular Library, 1975.
Naha, Ed. *The Films of Roger Corman: Brilliance on a Budget*. New York: Arco, 1982.

_____. *Horrors from Screen to Scream: An Encyclopedic Guide to the Greatest Horror and Fantasy Films of All Time*. New York: Avon Books, 1975.

_____. *The Science Fictionary: An A–Z Guide to the World of SF Authors, Films, & TV Shows*. New York: Seaview Books, 1980.

New York Times Film Reviews: 1913–1968. The New York Times and Arno Press, 1970.

*Nicholls, Peter, ed. *The Science Fiction Encyclopedia*. Garden City, NY: Doubleday, 1979. Includes articles on films, written chiefly by John Brosnan.

Parish, James Robert and Michael R. Pitts. *The Great Science Fiction Pictures*. Metuchen, NJ: Scarecrow Press, 1977.

_____ and Steven Whitney. *Vincent Price Unmasked*. New York: Drake, 1974.

*Peary, Danny. *Cult Movies: The Classics, the Sleepers, the Weird and the Wonderful*. New York: Dell, 1981.

Pohl, Frederik and Frederik Pohl IV. *Science Fiction Studies in Film*. New York: Ace Books, 1981.

Pohle, Robert W., Jr. and Douglas C. Hart, with the participation of Christopher Lee. *The Films of Christopher Lee*. Metuchen, NJ: Scarecrow Press, 1983.

Ragan, David. *Who's Who in Hollywood 1900–1976*. New Rochelle, NY: Arlington House, 1976.

Rovin, Jeff. *Movie Special Effects*. South Brunswick, NJ: A.S. Barnes, 1977.

*Sadoul, Georges. *Dictionary of Film Makers*; translated, edited and updated by Peter Morris. Berkeley, CA: University of California Press, 1972.

Saleh, Dennis. *Science Fiction Gold: Film Classics of the 1950s*. New York: McGraw-Hill, 1979.

Sarris, Andrew. *The American Cinema: Directors and Directions, 1929–1968*. New York: E.P. Dutton, 1968.

Schechter, Harold and David Everitt. *Film Tricks: Special Effects in the Movies*. New York: Harlan Quist, 1980.

Shaheen, Jack G., ed. *Nuclear War Films*. Carbondale, IL: Southern Illinois University Press, 1978.

*Silver, Alain and Elizabeth Ward. *Film Noir: An Encyclopedic Reference to the American Style*. Woodstock, NY: Overlook Press, 1979.

*Simon, Randy and Harold Benjamin. *Edward D. Wood, Jr.: A Man and His Films*. Los Angeles: The Edward D. Wood, Jr. Film Appreciation Society, 1981.

*Sobchack, Vivian Carol. *The Limits of Infinity: The American Science Fiction Film 1950–1975*. South Brunswick, NJ: A.S. Barnes, 1980.

Spoto, Donald. *The Dark Side of Genius: The Life of Alfred Hitchcock*. Boston: Little, Brown, 1983.

Steinbrunner, Chris and Burt Goldblatt. *The Cinema of the Fantastic*. New York: Saturday Review Press, 1972.

*Strick, Philip. *Science Fiction Movies*. London: Octopus Books, 1976.

Taylor, Al and Sue Roy. *Making a Monster: The Creation of Screen Characters by the Great Makeup Artists*. New York: Crown, 1980.

Thomas, Bob. *Bud and Lou: The Abbott & Costello Story*. Philadelphia: Lippincott, 1977.

Tyler, Parker. *Classics of the Foreign Film*. New York: Bonanza Books, 1962.

Underwood, Peter. *Karloff: The Life of Boris Karloff*. New York: Drake, 1972.

Ursini, James and Alain Silver. *The Vampire Film*. South Brunswick, NJ: A.S. Barnes, 1975.

*Von Gunden, Kenneth and Stuart H. Stock. *Twenty All-Time Great Science Fiction Films*. New York: Arlington House, 1982.

*Weldon, Michael, with Charles Beesley, Bob Martin and Akira Fitton. *The Psychotronic Encyclopedia of Film*. New York: Ballantine Books, 1983.

Who Wrote the Movie and What Else Did He Write? An Index of Screen Writers and Their Film Works 1936–1969. Los Angeles: Academy of Motion Picture Arts and Sciences & Writers Guild of America, West, 1970.

Will, David and Paul Willemen, eds. *Roger Corman: The Millenic Vision*. Edinburgh: Edinburgh Film Festival, 1970.

Willis, Donald C. *The Films of Howard Hawks*. Metuchen, NJ: Scarecrow Press, 1975.

*_____. *Horror and Science Fiction Films: A Checklist*. Metuchen, NJ: Scarecrow Press, 1972.

*_____. *Horror and Science Fiction Films II*. Metuchen, NJ: Scarecrow Press, 1982.

Wilson, Steven S. *Puppets and People: Dimensional Animation Combined with Live Action in the Cinema*. San Diego: A.S. Barnes, 1980.

Winans, Delbert. *Fantasy Magazine Index*. Baltimore: The Author, 1977. Lists contents of professional and amateur magazines (fanzines) on fantastic films.

*Youngkin, Steve D., James Bigwood and Raymond Cabana, Jr. *The Films of Peter Lorre*. Secaucus, NJ: Citadel Press, 1982.

Periodicals

Castle of Frankenstein. North Bergen, NJ: Gothic Castle Publishing. 1962–75.

CineFan. Los Altos, CA: Fandom Unlimited Enterprises. 1974– .

Cinefantastique [first series]. Elmwood Park, IL: Frederick S. Clarke. 1967.

Cinefantastique. Oak Park, IL: Frederick S. Clarke. 1970– .

L'Ecran Fantastique. Paris: Média Presse Edition. 1977– .

Famous Monsters of Filmland. New York: Warren Publishing. 1958–1983.

Fangoria. New York: O'Quinn Studios. 1979– .

Fantascene. Hollywood: Fantascene Productions. 1975–79.

Fantastic Films. Chicago: Fantastic Films Magazine. 1978–1985.

Fantastic Monsters of the Films. Topanga, CA: Black Shield Publications. 1962–63.

Halls of Horrors. London: Quality Communications. 1976–83. Title varies: *The House of Hammer, Hammer's House of Horror, Hammer's Halls of Horrors*.

Japanese Fantasy Film Journal. Toledo, OH: Greg Shoemaker. 1968– .

Mad Movies. Paris: Jean-Pierre Putters. 1972– .

Midnight Marquee. Baltimore: Gary J. Svehla. 1963– . Title varies: *Gore Creatures* (1963–76).

Modern Monsters. Los Angeles: Prestige Publications. 1966–67.

The Monster Times. New York: Monster Times Publishing. 1972–77.

Starburst. London: Marvel Comics. 1978–1985.

Starlog. New York: O'Quinn Studios. 1976– .

Appendix I

Credits and Casts

I have tried to list all pertinent credits and complete casts for the films included in this book. I include the U.S. release date, as nearly as I can determine it. For most films, my source for dates was the *Film Daily Yearbook*; for the years 1961–62, I have relied on the *American Film Institute Catalog 1961–1970*. Other sources are indicated. I also include, where I can find it, the date of release in their home countries for foreign films. There are some exceptions and problems, which are noted.

These films were often released in pairs, as standard double bills. I have tried to note what the standard cofeature (if a genre film) was in each case, but have probably missed some, and erred on others.

I believe these are the most thorough credits available for each film in question; I was immensely aided by Michael Hayes, Scot Holton, Joe Dante and Tom Weaver in these credit lists.

The Absent Minded Professor. *Director* Robert Stevenson, *Script and Associate producer* Bill Walsh, *Producer* Walt Disney, *Art director* Carroll Clark, *Set decorations* Emile Kuri and Hal Gausman, *Photography* Edward Colman, *Animation effects (flubber balls)* Joshua Meador, *Special effects (miniatures and matte paintings)* Peter Ellenshaw, *Special effects (full-sized mechanicals)* Robert A. Mattey, Danny Lee, Walter Stone, *Optical effects* Eustace Lycett, *Sequence consultant* Don DaGradi, *Optical photography coordinator* Robert Broughton, *Optical printer operator* Art Cruickshank, *Editor* Irvin "Cotton" Warburton, *Sound supervision* Robert O. Cook, *Sound mixer* Dean Thomas, *Special sound effects* William J. Wylie, *Makeup* Pat McNalley, *Costumes* Chuck Keehne and Gertrude Casey, *Hairstyles* Ruth Sandifer, *Music* George Bruns, *Orchestration* Franklyn Marks, *Music editor* Evelyn Kennedy, *Songs* Richard M. and Robert B. Sherman, *2nd unit director* Arthur J. Vitarelli, *Assistant director* Robert G. Shannon.

Cast: *Professor Ned Brainard* Fred MacMurray, *Betsy Carlisle* Nancy Olson, *Alonzo Hawk* Keenan Wynn, *Biff Hawk* Tommy Kirk, *Prof. Shelby Ashton* Elliott Reid, *Pres. Rufus Daggett* Leon Ames, *Defense secretary* Edward Andrews, *General Singer* David Lewis, *General Hotchkiss* Alan Hewitt, *General Poynter* Wendell Holmes, *Admiral Olmstead* Raymond Bailey, *Mrs. Chatsworth (housekeeper)* Belle Montrose, *Reverend Bosworth* Gage Clarke, *Officer Hanson* James Westerfield, *Coach Elkins* Wally Brown, *Sig* Charlie Briggs, *Lenny* Don Ross, *Officer Kelly* Forrest Lewis, *Air Force captain* Jack Mullaney, *TV newsman* Wally Boag, *Man at Dept. of Agriculture* Robert Burton, *1st referee* Alan Carney, *Basketball player (#18)* Leon Tyler, *Youth* Ned Wynn, *Rival basketball coach* Gordon Jones, *Various voices* Paul Frees, *Fire chief* Ed Wynn.

Walt Disney Productions, a Buena Vista release; black and white (converted to color in 1986), 97 minutes. Based on the short story "A Situation of Gravity" by Samuel W. Taylor, published in the May 22, 1943 issue of *Liberty Magazine*. Released March 16, 1961.

The Alligator People. *Director* Roy Del Ruth, *Screenplay* Orville H. Hampton, *Story* Orville H. Hampton and Charles O'Neal, *Producer* Jack Leewood, *Art direction* John Mansbridge and Lyle R. Wheeler, *Set decorations* Walker M. Scott and Joseph Kish, *Photography* Karl Struss, *Special effects* Fred Etcheverry, *Editor* Harry Gerstad, *Music*

Irving Gertz, *Sound* W. Donald Flick, *Sound effects* Arthur J. Cornell, *Makeup* Ben Nye and Dick Smith, *Costume supervision* William McCrary and Ollie Hughes, *Hairstyles* Eve Newing, *Script supervision* Mary Coleman, *Assistant director* H.E. Mendelson.

Cast: *Jane Marvin* Beverly Garland, *Dr. Mark Sinclair* George Macready, *Mannon* Lon Chaney (Jr.), *Paul Webster* Richard Crane, *Mrs. Henry Hawthorne* Frieda Inescort, *Dr. Erik Lorimer* Bruce Bennett, *Dr. Wayne McGregor* Douglas Kennedy, *Toby* Vince Townsend, Jr., *Lou Anne* Ruby Goodwin, *Patient #6* Bill Bradley, *Porter* Dudley Dickerson, *Conductor* Hal K. Dawson, *Sinclair's male nurses* John Merrick, Lee Warren, *Alligator-headed Paul* Boyd Stockman.

An Associated Producers Production for 20th Century–Fox; black and white; Cinema-Scope; 74 minutes. Released July 16, 1959. Double bill with *Return of the Fly.*

The Amazing Transparent Man. *Director* Edgar G. Ulmer, *Script* Jack Lewis, *Producer* Lester D. Guthrie, *Executive producers* John Miller and Robert L. Madden, *Production design* Ernst Fegté, *Set decorations and Set dresser* Louise Caldwell, *Photography* Meredith M. Nicholson, *Camera operator* Jack McCoskey, *Special effects* Roger George, *Photographic effects* Howard A. Anderson, Co., *Editor* Jack Ruggiero, *Music* Darrell Calker, *Sound mixer* Earl Snyder, *Sound editor* Don Olson, *Music editor* Gil Marchant, *Makeup* Jack P. Pierce, *Wardrobe* Jack Masters, *Script supervisor* Shirley Ulmer, *Assistant director* Leonard J. Shapiro, *Property master* Joseph Sullivan, *Head grip* George Fenaja, *Head electrician* Frank Leonetti.

Cast: *Joey Faust* Douglas Kennedy, *Maj. Paul Krenner* James Griffith, *Laura Matson* Marguerite Chapman, *Dr. Peter Ulof* Ivan Triesault, *Julian (guard at ranch)* Red Morgan, *Maria Ulof* Carmel Daniel, *Drake* Edward Erwin, *Smith* Jonathan Ledford, *Woman* Kevin Kelly, *Security guards* Norman Smith and Patrick Cranshaw, *State policemen* Dennis Adams and Stacy Morgan.

A Miller Consolidated Pictures (MCP) production and release; later distributed by American International Pictures; black and white; 60 minutes. Released 1960.

The Angry Red Planet. *Director* Ib Melchior, *Screenplay* Ib Melchior and Sid Pink, *Story* Sid Pink, *Producers* Sid Pink and Norman Maurer, *Associate producer/Assistant director* Lou Perloff, *Production designer* Norman Maurer, *Set construction* Ned Shielle, *Continuity sketches* Alexander Toth, *Photography* Stanley Cortez, *Camera operator* Robert Johannas, *Assistant cameramen* Bert Eason and Mike Walsh, *Special effects supervisor* Herman Townsley, *Special effects crew* Herb Switzer, Howard Weeks and Jack Schwartz, *Editor* Ivan J. Hoffman, *Music* Paul Dunlap, *Sound recording* Glen Glenn Co., *Sound mixer* Vic Appel, *Makeup* David Newell, *Wardrobe* Marjorie Corso, *Hairdresser* Lillian Shore, *Script supervisor* Hazel Hall, *Stills* Roger Mace, *Props* Mel Sternlight and Art Wasson.

Cast: *Dr. Iris Ryan* Nora Hayden, *Col. Tom O'Bannion* Gerald Mohr, *Prof. Theodore Gettell* Les Tremayne, *Sgt. Sam Jacobs* Jack Kruschen, *Prof. Paul Weiner* J. Edward McKinley, *Dr. Frank Gordon* Tom Daly, *General Prescott* Edward Innes, *Maj. Lyman Ross* Gordon Barnes, *Maj.-Gen. George Treeger* Paul Hahn, *Lieutenant Colonel Davis* John Haddock, *Brigadier general* Alan Prescott, *Dr. Muller* Duke Norton, *Dr. Hawley* William Remick, *Martian* Billy Curtis, *First monitor* Richard Baxter, *Nurse Dixon* Joan Fitzpatrick, *Nurse Hayes* Brandy Bryan, *Joan* Arline Hunter, *Joan's friend* Aleane Hamilton, *Air Force news photographers* Fred Ross and David DeHaven, *Newscaster/Narrator/Martian voice* Don LaMond, *Also* William Snyder.

Sino Productions (Cinemagic Productions); briefly released by Sino, then by American International; color and "Cinemagic"; running time as given varies from a low of 83 minutes (*Variety*) to a high of 94 minutes (*Filmfacts*). Working titles: "Journey to Planet Four," "Invasion of Mars." Released September 8, 1960. Joe Dante says the double bill was with *Beyond the Time Barrier*, but this may not have been standard.

Assignment Outer Space. *Director* Anthony Daisies (Antonio Margheriti), *Script* Vassily Petrov, *Photography* Marcello Masciocchi, *Special effects* Caesar Peace (pseudonym), *Music* J.K. Broady. *For English–dubbed prints: Producer and Dubbing director* Hugo Grimaldi, *Music supervision* Gordon Zahler, *Sound effects editor* Josef Von Stroheim.

Cast: *Ray Peterson (IZ41)* Rik von Nutter, *Lucy (Y13)* Gabrielle Farinon, *George* Dave Montresor, *Al* Archie Savage, *The Commander* Alan Dijon, *Also* Frank Fantasia (Franco

Fantasia), Aldo Pini, Joe Pollini, David Maran, José Néstor, Anita Todesco, *Narrator of English–language version* Jack Wallace.

Ultra Film–Titanus S.P.A., dst. American International Pictures; color; 79 minutes; an Italian film. Original Italian title: **Space Men** (in English). U.S. release December 13, 1961; Italian release August 1960. Double bill varied: *Phantom Planet, Journey to the Seventh Planet.*

The Astounding She-Monster. *Producer/Director* Ronnie Ashcroft, *Story and Screenplay* Frank Hall and (uncredited) Ronnie Ashcroft, *Photography* William C. Thompson, *Music* Guenther Kauer, *Sound* Dale Knight, *Makeup* Nicholas Vehr, *Costumes* Maureen, *Wardrobe* Norma (Norna?) McClaskey, *Production manager* John Nelson, *Chief electrician* Lee Cannon, *Properties* Tony Portoghese, *Grip master* Charles Norris.

Cast: *Dick Cutler* Robert Clarke, *Nat Burdell* Kenne Duncan, *Alien* Shirley Kilpatrick, *Margaret Chaffee* Marilyn Harvey, *Esther Malone* Jeanne Tatum, *Brad Conley* Ewing Brown, *Double for Shirley Kilpatrick* Loraine Ashcroft, *Pre-credit narration* Scott Douglas, *Other narration* Al Avalon.

A Hollywood International Production, dst. American International; black and white; 60 minutes. British title: **The Mysterious Invader**. Working titles: "Naked Invader," "The Astounding She Creature." Released April 10, 1958. Double bill with: *The Saga of the Viking Women and Their Voyage to the Waters of the Great Sea Serpent.*

Atlantis, the Lost Continent. *Producer/Director* George Pal, *Screenplay* Daniel Mainwaring, *Art directors* George W. Davis and William Ferrari, *Set decorations* Henry Grace and Dick Peferle, *Photography* Harold E. Wellman, *Special effects* A. Arnold Gillespie and Lee LeBlanc, *Optical effects* Robert R. Hoag, *Matte paintings* Lee LeBlanc and Matthew Yuricich, *Animation effects* Project Unlimited, *Editor* Ben Lewis, *Music* Russell Garcia, *Recording supervisor* Franklin Milton, *Re-recording* William Steinkamp, *Makeup supervisor* William Tuttle, *Hairstyles* Mary Keats, *Color consultant* Charles K. Hagedon, *Assistant director* Ridgeway Callow, *Assistant to the producer* Gae Griffith.

Cast: *Demetrios* Anthony Hall, *Princess Antillia* Joyce Taylor, *Zaren* John Dall, *Azor* Edward Platt, *Xandros* Jay Novello, *Petros* Wolfe Barzell, *Andes* Buck Maffie, *Sonoy* Frank DeKova, *King Kronas* Edgar Stehli, *Captain of the guard* Bill Smith, *Surgeon* Berry Kroeger, *Governor of Rivers* Stanford Jolley, *Governor of the air* Jack Shea, *Governor of animals* Gene Roth, *Governor of agriculture* Hal Torey, *Governor of science* Harry Fleer, *Governor of the mountains* Byron Morrow, *Governor of the seas* Stuart Nedd, *Norseman slave* Allan Callow, *Megalos* Nestor Paiva, *Officers* John Hart, Will J. White, Charles Horvath, *Handsome young man* Anthony Monaco, *Pavlo* Ralph Smiley, *Map makers* Keith Andes, Guy Prescott, *Woman* Ella Ethridge, *Priest* David Dyer, *Girl* Phyllis Douglas, *Norseman* Dennis Durney, *Guard* Roy Jenson, *Slaves* Peter Pal, Bobby Johnson, *King Neptune (i.e. Poseidon)* Charles Morton, *Narrator* Paul Frees.

A Galaxy Productions Inc. Picture for MGM release; color; 90 minutes. Based on the play "Atalanta" by Sir Gerald P. Hargreaves. Released May 3, 1961.

The Atomic Submarine. *Director* Spencer Gordon Bennet, *Screenplay* Orville H. Hampton, *Producer* Alex Gordon, *Coproducer* Henry Schrage, *Associate producers* Jack Rabin, Irving Block and Orville H. Hampton, *Art directors* Don Ament and Daniel Haller, *Set decorator* Harry Reif, *Photography* Gilbert Warrenton, *Special effects designed and created by* Jack Rabin, Irving Block and Louis DeWitt, *Editor* William Austin, *Electro-Sonic Music* Alexander Laszlo, *Sound* Ralph Butler, *Sound editor* Marty Greco, *Music editor* Neil Brunnenkant, *Makeup* Emile LaVigne, *Wardrobe* Roger J. Weinberg and Norah Sharpe, *Dialogue supervisor and Production associate* Jack Cash, *Script supervisor* Judith Hart, *Production manager* Edward Morey, Jr., *Assistant to producer* Ruth Alexander (Gordon), *Assistant director* Clark Paylow, *Props* Max Frankel, *Chief set electrician* George Satterfield.

Cast: *Cmdr. Richard "Reef" Holloway* Arthur Franz, *Carl Neilson* Brett Halsey, *Capt. Dan Wendover* Dick Foran, *Sir Ian Hunt* Tom Conway, *Dave Milburn* Paul Dubov, *Dr. Clifford Kent* Victor Varconi, *CPO "Griff" Griffin* Bob Steele, *Julie* Joi Lansing, *Admiral Terhune* Selmer Jackson, *Secretary of Defense* Justin Murdock Jack Mulhall, *Yeoman Chester Tuttle* Sid Melton, *Helen Milburn* Jean Moorehead, *Seaman 1st class* Don Carney Richard Tyler, *Seaman 1st class Al Powell* Ken Becker, *Narrator* Pat Michaels, *Voice of alien* John Hilliard, *Bit* Frank Walkins.

A Gorham Production for Allied Artists; black and white; 72 minutes. Released February 12, 1960.

Attack of the 50 Foot Woman. *Director* Nathan Hertz (Juran), *Producer* Bernard Woolner, *Screenplay* Mark Hanna, *Executive producer and Photography* Jacques Marquette, *Editor* Edward Mann, *Music* Ronald Stein, *Sound* Philip Mitchell, *Makeup* Carlie Taylor, *Assistant director* Ken Walters, *Props* Richard Rubin.

Cast: *Nancy Fowler Archer* Allison Hayes, *Harry Archer* William Hudson, *Honey Parker* Yvette Vickers, *Jessup (Jess) Stout* Ken Terrell, *Sheriff Dubbitt* George Douglas, *Dr. Cushing* Roy Gordon, *Charlie* Frank Chase, *Dr. Von Loeb* Otto Waldis, *Tony* (and *Space Giant*) Mike Ross, *Nurse* Eileene Stevens, *TV Commentator* Dale Tate, *Prospector* Tom Jackson.

A Woolner Production, an Allied Artists release; black and white; 66 minutes. Working titles: "The Giant Woman," "The Astounding Giant Woman." Released May 19, 1958. Double bill with: *War of the Satellites*.

Note: The Allied Artists TV version, running 75 minutes, includes a long printed crawl at beginning and end, repeated sequences and intermittent hold-frames designed to optically lengthen the running time. Or something—Joe Dante.

Attack of the Giant Leeches. *Director* Bernard L. Kowalski, *Screenplay* Leo Gordon, *Producer* Gene Corman, *Executive producer* Roger Corman, *Art direction* Dan Haller, *Photography* John M. Nickolaus, Jr., *Music* Alexander Laszlo, *Editor* Carlo Lodato, *Associate editor* Tony Magio, *Sound* Al Overton, *Recording* Ryder Sound Services, *Assistant director* John Chulay, *Production manager* Jack Bohrer, *Props* Richard M. Rubin, *Production secretary* Kinta Zertuche, *Underwater equipment* Healthways.

Cast: *Steve Benton* Ken Clark, *Liz Walker* Yvette Vickers, *Nan Greyson* Jan Shepard, *Dave Walker* Bruno Ve Sota, *Doc Greyson* Tyler McVey, *Cal Moulton* Michael Emmet, *Sheriff Kovis* Gene Roth, *Slim Reed* Daniel White, *Lem Sawyer* George Cisar.

A Balboa Production for American International; black and white; 62 minutes. Working title: "Attack of the Blood Leeches." British title: **Demons of the Swamp.** Publicity title: **The Giant Leeches.** Not released until early 1960, but copyrighted October 1, 1959. Double bill with: *A Bucket of Blood*; with *House of Usher* in Los Angeles.

Attack of the Puppet People. *Producer, Director, Story, Special technical effects* Bert I. Gordon, *Screenplay* George Worthing Yates, *Executive producers* James H. Nicholson and Samuel Z. Arkoff, *Assistant producer* Henry Schrage, *Art director* Walter Keller, *Set decorator* Jack Mills, *Photography* Ernest Laszlo, *Assistant technical effects* Flora Gordon, *Special effects* Charles Duncan, *Special design (life-size Jekyll/Hyde puppet)* Paul and Jackie Blaisdell, *Editorial supervision* Ronald Sinclair, *Assistant editor* Paul Wittenberg, *Score* Albert Glasser, *Song ("You're My Living Doll")* Lyrics Henry Schrage, *Music* Albert Glasser and Don Ferris, *Sound* Frank Webster, *Makeup* Philip Scheer, *Script supervisor* Judy Hart, *Assistant director and Production supervisor* Jack R. Berne, *2nd assistant director* Maurice Lindsey, *Production coordinator* Jack Diamond, *Gaffer* Ray Roberts, *Key Grip* Buzz Gibson, *Props* James Harris.

Cast: *Bob Westley* John Agar, *Mr. Franz* John Hoyt, *Sally Reynolds* June Kenny, *Sergeant Patterson* Jack Kosslyn, *Emil* Michael Mark, *Laurie* Marlene Willis, *Stan* Ken Miller, *Georgia Lane* Laurie Mitchell, *Mac (the Marine?)* Scott Peters, *Agnes (little girl)* Susan Gordon, *Brownie leader* June Jocelyn, *Janet Hall* Jean Moorehead, *Doorman* Hank Patterson, *Ernie Larson (mailman)* Hal Bogart, *Elevator operator* Troy Patterson, *Janitor* Bill Giorgio, *Switchboard operator* George Diestel, *Ernie* Jamie Forster, *Salesman* Mark Lowell.

An Alta Vista Production for American International; black and white, 78 minutes. Working title: "The Fantastic Puppet People." British title: **Six Inches Tall.** Released spring 1958 (Los Angeles, August 7, 1958). Double bill with: *War of the Colossal Beast*.

Battle in Outer Space. *Director* Inoshiro Honda, *Screenplay* Shinichi Sekizawa, *Story* Jotaro Okami, *Producer* Tomoyuki Tanaka, *Art director* Teruaki Abe, *Photography* Hajime Koizumi, *Editor* Kazuji Taira, *Music* Akira Ifukube, *Sound* Choshichiro Mikami, *Production manager* Yasuaki Sakamoto, *Assistant director* Koji Kahita, *Lighting* Rokuro Ishikawa. *Special effects crew: Director* Eiji Tsuburaya, *Art director* Akira Watanabe, *Photography* Sadamasa Arikawa, *Lighting* Kuichiro Kishida, *Composition/(Composites?)* Hiroshi Mukoyama, *Optical cinematographer* Kinsaburo Araki.

Cast: *Maj. Ichiro Katsumiya* Ryo Ikebe, *Etsuko Shiraishi* Kyoko Anzai, *Dr. Adachi* Minoru Takada, *Defense commander* Koreya Senda, *Dr. Roger Richardson* Len Stanford, *Dr. Immerman* Harold S. Conway, *Sylvia* Elise Richter, *Koguri* Hisaya Ito, *Iwamura* Yoshio Tsuchiya, *Rocket commander* Kozo Nomura, *Inspector Ariaki of International Police* Fuyuki Murakai, *Also* George Whyman, Nadao Kirino, Ikio Sawamura, Jiryd Kimagawa, Katsumi Tesuka, Mitsuo Isuda, Tadashi Okabe, Yasuhisa Tsutumi, Kisao Hatamochi, Koichi Sato, Tasuo Araki, Rinsaku Ogata, Keisumi Yamada, Osran Yuri, Malcolm (Malcim?) Pearce, Leonard Walsh, Heinz Boimer (Bohmer?), Roma Carlson (Corlson?), Yokikose Kamimera, Yutaka Oka, Snigro Kato, Saburo Kadowaki, Yushihiko Goxoo (?), Shinjiro Hirota.

A Toho Production, released in U.S. by Columbia; color; TohoScope; 90 minutes (93 in Japan). A Japanese picture. Original Japanese title: **Uchu Dai Senso** (War in Space). Released June 10, 1960 in U.S.; December 26, 1959 in Japan. Double bill varied, often *The Electronic Monster*, also *12 to the Moon*.

Beast from Haunted Cave. *Director* Monte Hellman, *Screenplay* Charles (B.) Griffith, *Producer* Gene Corman, *Executive producer (unbilled)* Roger Corman, *Associate producer* Charles Hannawalt, *Photography* Andrew Costikyan, *The Beast created by* Christopher (Chris) Robinson, *Editor* Anthony Carras, *Music* Alexander Laszlo, *Sound* Charles Brown, *Assistant to producer* Kinta Zertuche, *Production coordinator* Beach Dickerson, *Technical advisors* "Birdie" Arnold and Ed Keene, *Key grip* Charles Hannawalt(?).

Cast: *Gill Jackson* Michael Forest, *Gypsy Bollett* Sheila Carol, *Alexander Wood* Frank Wolff, *Marty* Richard Sinatra, *Byron* Wally Campo, *Barmaid (victim of monster)* Linné Ahlstrand, *Also* Kay Jennings; *The Beast* Christopher (Chris) Robinson.

A Filmgroup Production, an Allied Artists release; black and white; length as given varies; the low was given by *Hollywood Reporter*, at 64 minutes, the longest was 75 minutes, reported by the *Motion Picture Herald*. Joe Dante suggests these variations are real, as minor films of this period were often distributed regionally in shorter versions, especially when considered the second half of a double bill. Working title: "Creature from the Cave." *Film Daily* Yearbook says 17 March 1960, but other sources indicate it was in release through Filmgroup in late 1959. Double bill with: *The Wasp Woman*.

Beast of Yucca Flats. *Director-Screenplay* Coleman Francis, *Producer* Anthony Cardoza, *Executive producers* Roland Morin and James Oliphant, *Associate producers* Laurence Aten and Charles Stafford, *Photography* John Cagle, *Camera operator* Lee Strosnider, *Film effects* Ray Mercer, *Editor* Coleman Francis, *Music* Gene Kauer, Irwin Nafshun, Al Remington, *Makeup* Larry Aten, *Production supervisor and Assistant director* Austin McKinney, *Publicity* Ted Charach.

Cast: *Joseph Jaworsky, the Beast of Yucca Flats* Tor Johnson, *Also* Douglas Mellord, Barbara Francis, Bing Stafford, Larry Aten, Linda Bielema, Tony Cardoza, Bob Labansat, Jim Oliphant, John Morrison, Eric Tomlin, Jim Miles, George Principe, Conrad Brooks, *Newsboy* Graham Stafford, *Lost boys* Ronald and Alan Francis.

Cardoza Productions, dst. Crown International; black and white; 57 minutes. TV title: **Atomic Monster – The Beast of Yucca Flats**. Released May 1961. AFI Catalog says it may have been reissued in 1964 as *Girl Madness*.

Beyond the Time Barrier. *Director* Edgar G. Ulmer, *Screenplay* Arthur C. Pierce, *Producer* Robert Clarke, *Executive producers* John Miller and Robert L. Madden, *Production design* Ernst Fegté, *Photography* Meredith M. Nicholson, *Camera operator* Jack McCoskey, *Special effects* Roger George, *Photographic effects* Howard A. Anderson Co., *Editor* Jack Ruggiero, *Music* Darrell Calker, *Sound* Earl Snyder, *Sound editor* Don Olson, *Music editor* Gil Marchant, *Makeup* Jack P. Pierce, *Costumes* Jack Masters, *Hairstyles* Corrine Daniel, *Script supervisor* Shirley Ulmer, *Production supervisor* Lester D. Guthrie, *Location coordinator* W.L. "Pop" Guthrie, *Assistant director* Leonard J. Shapiro, *Props* Joe Sullivan, *Head grip* George Fenaja.

Cast: *Maj. Bill Allison* Robert Clarke, *Trirene* Darlene Tompkins, *The Supreme* Vladimir Sokoloff, *The Captain* Red Morgan, *Markova* Arianne Arden, *Gen. Karl Kruse* Stephen Bekassy, *Professor Bourman* John Van Dreelen, *Air Force Chief of Staff* Neil Fletcher, *Dr. Richman* Jack Herman, *General York* William Shapard(?), *Secretary Patterson* James Altgens, *Colonel Curtis* Russell Marker, *Mutants* Don Flournoy and Tom Rovick, *Colonel Martin* Ken Knox, *General LaMont* John Loughney.

A Miller Consolidated Pictures production, dst. American International; black and white; 75 minutes. Released September 8, 1960. Double-billed in some areas with *Angry Red Planet*.

The Blob. *Director* Irvin S. Yeaworth, Jr., *Screenplay* Theodore Simonson and Kate Phillips, *Idea* Irvine H. Millgate, *Producer* Jack H. Harris, *Art director* Bert Smith, *Photography* Thomas Spalding, *Camera operator* Wayne Tracey, *Special effects* Barton Sloane, *Editor* Alfred Hillmann, *Assistant editor* Floyd Ver Voorn(?), *Music* Ralph Carmichael, *Music supervision* Jean Yeaworth, *Title song* Burt Bacharach and Hal David, *Makeup* Vin Kehoe, *Sound* Gottfried Buss and Robert Clement, *Continuity* Travis Hillmann, *Chief set electrician* Vincent Spangler, *Assistant to the producer* Frank Furth.
   Cast: *Steve Andrews* Steven (Steve) McQueen, *Jane Martin* Aneta (Anita) Corseaut, *Dave (police lieutenant)* Earl Rowe, *Old man* Olin Howlin, *Dr. T. Hallen* Steven Chase, *Burt* John Benson, *George (diner owner)* Vince (Vincent) Barbi, *Mrs. Martin* Audrey Metcalf, *Mrs. Porter* Elinor Hammer, *Danny Martin* Keith (Kieth?) Almoney, *Sally (waitress)* Julie Cousins, *Tony Gressette* Robert Fields, *Mooch Miller* James Bonnet, *Al* Anthony Franke, *Also* George Karas, Elbert Smith, Lee Payton, Hugh Graham, Jasper Deeter, Ralph Roseman, David Metcalf, George Gerbereck, Tom Ogden(?), Pamela Curran, Charlie Overdorf, Josh Randolph, Eugene Sabel, Molly Ann Bourke, Diane Tabben, *Man Fleeing* Jack H. Harris.
   Note: One source says Godfrey Cambridge was an extra in this.
   A Tonylyn Production, dst. Paramount; color; 85 minutes. Some sources say that "The Molten Meteor" was the "foreign" title but it was really the working title. Released September 12, 1958. Double bill with: *I Married a Monster from Outer Space*.

Blood of the Vampire. *Director* Henry Cass, *Screenplay* Jimmy Sangster, *Producers* Robert S. Baker and Monty Berman, *Art direction* John Elphick, *Photography* Geoffrey (sometimes Jeffrey) Seaholme, *Editor* Douglas Myers, *Sound* Bill Bulkley, *Makeup* Jimmy Evans, *Wardrobe* Muriel Dickson, *Hairdresser* Joyce James, *Production manager* Charles Permane, *Assistant director* Luciano Sacripanti, *Production controller* Ronald C. Liles.
   Cast: *Dr. Callistratus* Sir Donald Wolfit, *Madeleine* Barbara Shelley, *Dr. John Pierre* Vincent Ball, *Carl* Victor Maddern, *Kurt Urach* William Devlin, *Chief Guard Wetzler* Andrew Faulds, *Monsieur Auron* Bryan Coleman, *Guards* George Murcell, Julian Strange, Bruce Whiteman, *Tall sneakthief (in cell)* Bernard Bresslaw, *Short sneakthief* Hal Osmond, *Chief justice* John LeMesurier, *Vernhardt Meinster* Henry Vidon, *Madeleine's uncle Philippe* John Stuart, *Drunken doctor (who installs heart)* Cameron Hall, *Serving wench* Yvonne Buckingham, *Housekeeper* Barbara Burke, *Commissioner of prisons* Colin Tapley, *Gravedigger* Otto Diamant, *Gypsy dancer* Muriel Aked, *Warder* Max Brimmel, *Blacksmith* Dennis Sharpe, *Executioner* Milton Reid, *Official* Richard Golding, *Also* Theodore Wilhelm.
   An Artistes Alliance Ltd. (W.N.W.) Production, dst. Universal-International; color; 87 minutes (84 in England). A British film. Released October 7, 1958 in U.S.; August 1958 in Britain. Double bill with: *Monster on the Campus*.

The Brain Eaters. *Director* Bruno Ve Sota, *Screenplay* Gordon Urquhart, *Producer* Edwin (Ed) Nelson, *Associate producer* Stanley Bickman, *Executive producer(?)* Roger Corman, *Art director* Burt Shonberg, *Photography* Larry Raimond, *Editor* Carlo Lodato, *Music* Tom Jonson, *Recording* TV Records, *Sound* James Fullerton, *Makeup* Alan Trumble, *Wardrobe* Charles Smith, *Production manager* Amos Powell, *Assistant director* Mike Murphy, *Gaffer* Gene Peterson, *Props* Tom Hughes, *Title design* Robert Balser.
   Cast: *Dr. Paul Kettering* Edwin (Ed) Nelson, *Glenn* Alan Frost, *Sen. Walter K. Powers* Jack Hill, *Alice Summers* Joanna Lee, *Elaine* Jody Fair, *Dr. Hyler* David Hughes, *Dan Walker* Greigh(?) Phillips, *Cameron* Orville Sherman, *Protector (Prof. Cole)* Leonard Nimoy (billed as "Nemoy"), *Doctor* Doug Banks, *Telegrapher* Henry Randolph, *Also* Saul Bronson.
   Corinthian Productions, dst. American International; black and white; 60 minutes. Taken without credit from *The Puppet Masters* by Robert A. Heinlein. Working titles: "The Keepers," "Keepers of the Earth," "Attack of the Blood-Leeches," "Battle of the Brain Eaters." Released fall, 1958. Double bill in some areas with: *Earth vs. the Spider* or *Terror from the Year 5,000*. Some sources claim John Carradine is in this, but he isn't.

The Brain from Planet Arous. *Director* Nathan Hertz (Juran), *Screenplay* Ray Buffum, *Producer/Photography* Jacques Marquette, *Associate producer* Dale Tate, *Sound effects and Supervising editor* Irving Schoenberg, *Music* Walter Greene, *Makeup* Jack P. Pierce, *Assistant director* Bert Chervin, *Props* Richard M. Rubin, *Technical advisor* J.L. Cassingham.

Cast: *Steve March* John Agar, *Sally Fallon* Joyce Meadows, *John Fallon* Thomas Browne Henry, *Dan* Robert Fuller, *Sheriff Wiley Paine* Tim Graham, *Colonel Frogley* Henry Travis, *General Brown* E. Leslie Thomas, *Colonel in conference room* Kenneth Terrell, *Russian* Bill Giorgio, *Dr. Dale Tate* Dale Tate, *Voices of brains* Dale Tate.

A Marquette Production, dst. Howco International; black and white; 71 minutes. Released December 26, 1957 (FDY), but not generally released until 1958. Double bill with: *Teenage Monster.*

The Brain That Wouldn't Die. *Director/Screenplay* Joseph Green, *Story* Rex Carlton and Joseph Green, *Additional dialogue* Doris Brent, *Producer* Rex Carlton, *Associate producer* Mort Landberg, *Art director* Paul Fanning, *Photography* Stephen Hajnal, *Camera operator* John S. Priestley, *Special effects* Byron Baer, *Editors* Leonard and Marc Anderson, *Music* Abe Baker and Tony Restaino, *Makeup* George Fiala, *Production manager* Alfred H. Lessner, *Assistant director* Tony La Marca, *Assistants to producer* James Gealis, Linda Brent, *Sound* Robert E. Lessner, Emil Kolisch, *Property man* Walter Pluff, Jr., *Gaffer* Vincent Delaney, *Grip* John Haupt, Jr., *Script girl* Eva Blair.

Cast: *Dr. Bill Cortner* Herb (Jason) Evers, *Jan Compton* Virginia Leith, *Kurt* Leslie Daniel, *Monster* Eddie Carmel, *Doris Powell* Adele Lamont, *Dr. Cortner* Bruce Brighton, *Nurse* Doris Brent, *Stripper* Bonnie Shari, *B-girl* Paula Maurice, *Donna Williams* Lola Mason, *Jeannie* Audrey Devereau, *Announcer* Bruce Kerr.

Rex Carlton Prods, dst. American International; black and white; 71 minutes (AFI also cites 81 minutes). Working titles: "The Black Door," "The Head That Wouldn't Die." Released May 1962. Double bill with: *Invasion of the Star Creatures.*

Caltiki, the Immortal Monster. *Director (credited)* Robert Hamton* (Riccardo Freda), *Director (he claimed)* Mario Bava, *Director of "American Version" (i.e. dubbing)* Lee Kressel, *Screenplay* Dr. Philip Just (Filippo Sanjust), *Producer* Bruno Vailati, *Producer of U.S. version (?)* Samuel Schneider, *Photography* John Foam (Mario Bava), *Special effects* Marie Foam (Mario Bava), *Editor* Salvatore Billitteri, *Music* Robert Nicholas (Roman Vlad), *Choreography* P. Gozlino, *Dubbing sound* Maurice Rosenblum.

Cast: *Prof. John Fielding* John Merivale, *Ellen Fielding* Didi Sullivan (Perego), *Max Gunther* Gerard Herter, *Linda* Daniela Rocca, *Bob* Daniele Pitani, *Dancer* Gay Pearl, *Rodriguez* G.R. Stuart (Giacomo Rossi-Stuart), *Lab assistant* Victor Andrée, *Police commissioner* Blake Bernard,* *Nieto* Arthur Dominici (Arturo Dominici).

*Freda's usual pseudonym is Hampton, but prints of Caltiki spell it "Hamton"; the names Victor Andrée and Blake Bernard are probably Americanizations of Italian names.

Galatea Film–Climax Pictures, dst. Allied Artists; black and white; 76 minutes. An Italian (–U.S.?) production. Original Italian title: **Caltiki, il Mostro Immortale.** British title: **The Immortal Monster.** U.S. release September 1960.

The Cape Canaveral Monsters. *Director/Screenplay* Phil Tucker, *Producer/Editor* Richard Greer, *Executive producer* Lionel Dichter, *Production design* Ken Letvin, *Set decorations* Fred Garcia, *Photography* Merle Connell, *Camera operator* Bert Shipman, *Special photographic effects* Modern Film Effects, *Music* Guenther Kauer, *Music conductor* William Hinshaw, *Makeup* Phil Schere (Philip Scheer), *Costumes* Western Costume, *Sound engineers* Dale Knight and Larry Aicholtz, *Lighting design* Jim Woods, *Key grip* Art Manikin, *Production assistant* George Housh, *Set continuity* Cobey Mintz.

Cast: *Tom Wright* Scott Peters, *Sally Markham* Linda Connell, *Hauron* Jason Johnson, *Nadja* Katherine Victor, *Bob Hardin* Gary Travis, *Shirley Carter* Thelaine Williams, *Major-General Hollister* Chuck Howard, *Captain Martin* Bill Vess, *Dr. Meister* Joe Chester, *Dr. Von Hoften* Billy Greene, *Deputy Chief Hoven* Lyle Felisse, *Deputy Moss* Matt Shaw, *Detective Allen* David King, *Woman scientist* Harriet Dichter, *Corporal Wilson* Tom Allen, *Newsboy* Tony Soler, *Elmer Wesson* Brian F. Wood, *Switchboard operator* Flori Jo Johnson.

A CCM release; black and white; 69 minutes. *Boxoffice* said was available in 1960.

The Colossus of New York. *Director* Eugene Lourié, *Screenplay* Thelma Schnee, *Story* Willis Goldbeck, *Producer* William Alland, *Art direction* John Goodman and Hal Pereira, *Set decoration* Sam Comer and Grace Gregory, *Photography* John F. Warren, *Special photographic effects* John P. Fulton, *Process photography* Farciot Edouart, *Designers of Colossus* Charles Gemora and Ralph Jester, *Editor* Floyd Knudtson, *Music* (Nathan) Van Cleave, *Sound* John Wilkinson, *Rerecording* Winston Leverett, *Makeup supervisor* Wally Westmore, *Hairstyles* Nellie Manley, *Production manager* Charles Woolstenhulme, *Assistant director* Ralph Axness.

Cast: *Dr. Henry Spensser* John Baragrey, *Dr. William Spensser* Otto Kruger, *Billy Spensser* Charles Herbert, *Anne Spensser* Mala Powers, *Dr. Jeremy Spensser* Ross Martin, *The Colossus* Ed Wolff, *Prof. John Carrington* Robert Hutton, *Inspector* Roy Engel, *Official* George Douglas, *Chauffeur/Butler* Dick Nelson, *Reporters* Lorence V. Kerr, Foster Phinney, Max Power, Courtland Shepard, Jack Richardson.

Paramount; black and white; 70 minutes. Released June 26, 1958. Intended to be double-billed with *The Space Children*, but they apparently played that way only co-incidentally.

The Cosmic Man. *Director* Herbert Greene, *Story and Screenplay* Arthur C. Pierce, *Producer* Robert A. Terry, *Associate producer* Harry Marsh, *Photography* John F. Warren, *Special effects* Charles Duncan, *Supervising editor* Richard C. Currier, *Film editor* Helene Turner, *Music* Paul Sawtell and Bert Shefter, *Music director* Lou Kosloff, *Sound recorder* Phillip Mitchell, *Production supervisor* Lester D. Guthrie, *Script supervisor* Mary Yerke, *Props* Tony Portoghese.

Cast: *Dr. Karl Sorenson* Bruce Bennett, *The Cosmic Man* John Carradine, *Kathy Grant* Angela Greene, *Colonel Mathews* Paul Langton, *Ken Grant* Scotty Morrow, *Sergeant Gray* Lyn Osborn, *Dr. Richie* Walter Maslow, *General Knowland* Herbert Lytton, *Also* Ken Clayton, Alan Wells, Harry Fleer, Hal Torey, John Erman, Dwight Brooks.

Futura Pictures, Inc., dst. Allied Artists; black and white; 72 minutes. Released February 1959. Double bill (in Los Angeles at least) with *House on Haunted Hill*.

The Cosmic Monster. *Director* Gilbert Gunn, *Screenplay* Paul Ryder and Joe Ambor,* *Producer* George Maynard, *Photography* Joe Ambor, *Art director* Bernard Sarron, *Editor* Francis Briebert, *Music* Robert Sharples.

Cast: *Gil Graham* Forrest Tucker, *Michele Dupont* Gaby Andre, *Smith* Martin Benson, *Dr. Laird* Alec Mango, *Brigadier Cartwright* Wyndham Goldie, *Jimmy Murray* Hugh Latimer, *Gerald Wilson* Geoffrey Chater, *Helen Forsyth* Patricia Sinclair, *Gillian Betts* Catherine Lancaster, *Inspector Burns* Richard Warner, *Mrs. Hale* Hilda Fennemore, *Jane Hale* Susan Redway, *Constable Tidy* Neil Wilson.

*Only the *Monthly Film Bulletin* says cinematographer Ambor cowrote the script, but they aren't often wrong on such things.

An Artistes Alliance Ltd.–WNW Production, U.S. dst. Distributors Corporation of America; black and white; 75 minutes. Based on the novel *The Strange World of Planet X* by René Ray, also adapted as a British television serial. British title: **The Strange World of Planet X**. Publicity title: **Cosmic Monsters**. Reviewed as: **The Crawling Terror**. Released July 7, 1958 in U.S.; February 1958 in Britain. Double bill with: *The Crawling Eye*.

The Crawling Eye. *Director* Quentin Lawrence, *Screenplay* Jimmy Sangster, *Producers* Robert S. Baker and Monty Berman, *Art direction* Duncan Sutherland, *Photography* Monty Berman, *Camera operator* Desmond Davis, *Special effects supervisor* Les Bowie, *Editor* Henry Richardson, *Music* Stanley Black, *Sound recording* Dick Smith,* *Makeup* Eleanor Jones, *Hairdresser* Joy Vigo, *Continuity* Yvonne Richards, *Production supervisor* Ronald C. Lisles, *Production manager* Charles Perhane, *Assistant director* Norman Harrison.

Cast: *Alan Brooks* Forrest Tucker, *Anne Pilgrim* Janet Munro, *Philip Truscott* Laurence Payne, *Professor Crevett* Warren Mitchell, *Sarah Pilgrim* Jennifer Jayne, *Herr Klein* Frederick Schiller, *Dewhurst* Stuart Saunders, *Brett* Andrew Faulds, *Hans* (bartender) Colin Douglas, *Wilde* Derek Sydney, *Little girl* Caroline Glaser, *Pilot* Gerard Green, *Carl* Leslie Heritage, *Fritz* Theodore Wilhelm, *Villagers* Richard Golding, George Herbert, Anne Sharp, *Student climbers* Jeremy Longhurst and Anthony Parker, *Also* Jack Taylor.

*This is neither the U.S. makeup artist nor the U.S. special effects man.

A Tempean Production, dst. Distributors Corporation of America (DCA); black and white; 84 minutes. Based on the BBC-TV serial "The Trollenberg Terror." A British film. British title: **The Trollenberg Terror**. U.S. prerelease titles: "Creatures from Another World," "The Creeping Eye"(?), "The Flying Eye"(?) Released July 7, 1958 in U.S.; October, 1958 in Britain. Double bill with: *The Cosmic Monster*.

The Creation of the Humanoids. *Director* Wesley E. Barry, *Screenplay* Jay Simms, *Producers* Edward J. Kay and Wesley E. Barry, *Art director* Ted Rich, *Set decorator* Morrie Hoffman, *Photography* Hal Mohr, *Editor* Leonard W. Herman, *Sound mixers* Ralph Butler and Charles Cooper, *Makeup* Jack P. Pierce, *Special eye effects* Dr. Louis M. Zabner, *Wardrobe* Oscar Rodriguez, *Set continuity* Eleanor Donahue, *Assistant director* Melville Shyer, *Lighting engineer* Paul Butner, *Producers' assistant* Lynn Waring, *Property master* George Bahr.

Cast: *Capt. Kenneth Cragis* Don Megowan, *Maxine Megan* Erica Elliot, *Esme Cragis Miles* Frances McCann, *Dr. Raven* Don Doolittle, *Pax* David Cross, *Mark* Richard Vath, *Court* Malcolm Smith, *Acto* George Milan, *Logan* Dudley Manlove, *Hart* Reid Hammond, *Orus* Gil Frye, *Moffitt* Pat Bradley, *Ward* William Hunter, *Cop* Paul Sheriff, *Volunteer* Alton Tabor.

Genie Productions, dst. Emerson Film Enterprises; color; 75 minutes. Released July 3, 1962.

Creature from the Haunted Sea. *Producer/Director* Roger Corman, *Screenplay* Charles B. Griffith, *Additional script* Roger Corman, *Associate producer and Key grip* Charles Hannawalt, *Photography* Jacques Marquette, *Monster built by* Beach Dickerson and Robert Bean, *Editor* Angela Scellars, *Music* Fred Katz, *Sound* Roberto Velasquez, *Makeup* Brooke Wilkerson, *Location Manager* Kinta Zertuche, *Production manager/ Assistant director* Jack Bohrer, *Director of pretitle sequence* Monte Hellman.

Cast: *Renzo Capeto* Antony Carbone, *Mary-Belle Monahan* Betsy Jones-Moreland, *Sparks Moran* Edward Wain (Robert Towne), *Colonel Tostada* Edmundo Rivera Alvarez, *Happy Jack Monahan* Robert Bean, *Mango Perez* Sonya Noemi Gonzalez, *Pete Peterson, Jr.* Beach Dickerson, *Also* Elisio Lopez, Bianquita Rome.

Filmgroup, Inc.; black and white; 60 minutes (72 minutes on television). A states' rights release; reviewed Aug. 7, 1961, played Los Angeles in July 1962. No standard double bill, though Filmgroup's *The Devil's Partner* was often paired with it.

Curse of the Faceless Man. *Director* Edward L. Cahn, *Screenplay* Jerome Bixby, *Producer* Robert E. Kent, *Executive producer* Edward Small, *Art director* William Glasgow, *Set decorator* Herman Schoenbrun, *Photography* Kenneth Peach, *Special effects* Ira Anderson, *Effects editor* Robert Carlisle, *Faceless Man suit built by* Charles Gemora, *Editor* Grant Whytock, *Sound* Frank Webster, Sr., *Makeup* Layne Britton, *Hairdresser* Kaye Shea, *Production supervisor* Ben Hersh, *Assistant director* Jack R. Berne, *Wardrobe* Einar Bourman, *Wardrobe woman* Vou Lee Giokaris, *Script supervisor* George Rutter, *Property master* Max Frankel.

Cast: *Dr. Paul Mallon* Richard Anderson, *Tina Enright* Elaine Edwards, *Dr. Maria Fiorello* Adele Mara, *Dr. Fiorello* Luis Van Rooten, *Dr. Enrico Ricci* Gar Moore, *Inspector Rinaldi* Jan Arvan, *Dr. Emanuel* Felix Locher, *Quintillus Aurelius (the Faceless Man)* Bob Bryant, *Narrator* Morris Ankrum(?).

Vogue Pictures, dst. United Artists; black and white; 66 minutes (72 in England). Working title: "Man Without a Face." Released August 14, 1958. Double bill with: *It! The Terror from Beyond Space*.

The Day the Earth Caught Fire. *Producer/Director/Story* Val Guest, *Screenplay* Wolf Mankowitz and Val Guest, *Executive producer (unbilled)* Steven Pallos, *Associate producer* Frank Sherwin Green, *Art director* Tony Masters, *Set decorator* Scott Slimon, *Assistant art director* Geoffrey Tozer, *Draftsmen* Martin Atkinson and Bill Bennison, *Scenic artist* Peter Melrose, *Photography* Harry Waxman, *Camera operator* Moray Grant, *Focus pullers* Wally Byatt and Jimmy Davis, *Camera grip* Tommy Miller, *Special effects* Les Bowie and Brian Johncock (Johnson), *Editor* Bill Lenny, *Assistant editors* Michael Round and Gillian Scott, *Musical direction* Stanley Black, *Beatnik music* Monty Norman, *Sound recorder* Buster Ambler, *Dubbing editor* Chris Greenham, *Sound boom operator*

Peter Dukelow, *Sound camera operator* Jimmy Dooley, *Makeup* Tony Sforzini, *Costumes* Beatrice Dawson, *Hairstyles* Joyce James, *Wardrobe mistress* Dulcie Midwinter, *Continuity* Pamela Carlton, *Assistant directors* Philip Shipway, Terry Lens, Bernard Williams, *Production manager* Clifton Brandon, *Production secretary* Jill Langley, *Chargehand electrician* Bert Owen, *Prop Buyer* Harry Parry, *Chargehand props* Ernie Kell, *Still photographer* John Jay, *Technical adviser* Arthur Christiansen.

Cast: *Peter Stenning* Edward Judd, *Jeannie Craig* Janet Munro, *Bill Maguire* Leo McKern, *Editor* Arthur Christiansen, *Night editor* Michael Goodliffe, *News editor* Bernard Braden, *Harry (publican)* Reginald Beckwith, *May (barmaid)* Gene Anderson, *Angela* Renée Asherson, *Sir John Kelly* Austin Trevor, *2nd subeditor* Peter Butterworth, *Foreign editor* Charles Morgan, *Sanderson* Edward Underdown, *1st subeditor* John Barron, *Pat Holroyd* Geoffrey Cather, *Michael Stenning* Ian Ellis, *Nanny* Jane Aird, *Ronnie* Robin Hawdon, *Also* Michael Caine.

A Melina Productions Ltd. Picture, U.S. dst. Universal-International; black and white (opening and closing reels tinted yellow); 90 minutes in U.S. (99 minutes in Britain); Dyaliscope. Released March 15, 1962 in U.S.; November 1961 in Britain.

The Day the Sky Exploded. *Director* Paolo Heusch, *Screenplay* Marcello Coscia and Alessandro Continenza, *Story* Virgilio Sabel, *Producer* Guido Giambartolomei, *Art director* Beni Montresor, *Photography* Mario Bava, *Editor* Otello Colangeli, *Music* Carlo Rustichelli, *Production manager* Ione Tuzi, *English dubbing* William De Lane Lea.

Cast: *John MacLaren* Paul Hubschmid, *Katy Dandridge* Madeleine Fisher, *Mary MacLaren* Fiorella Mari, *Herbert Weisser* Ivo Garrani, *Pierre Leducq* Dario Michaelis, *Randowsky* Sam Galter, *Sergei Boetnikov* Jan-Jacques Delbo, *General Wandorf* Peter Meersman, *Dennis MacLaren* Massimo Zeppieri, *Also* Giacomo Rossi-Stuart, Anne Berval, Gérard Landry.

Royal Film–Lux Film (Rome)/C.C.F. Lux (Paris), U.S. dst. Excelsior Pictures; black and white; 80 minutes (European length 82 minutes). An Italian-French coproduction. Italian title: **La Morte Viene Dallo Spazio** (Death Comes from Space). French title: **Le Danger Vient de l'Espace** (Death Comes from Space). British title: **Death Comes from Outer Space.** Released Sept. 27, 1961 in U.S.; opened in Italy Sept. 1958, in France, Feb. 1959.

Dinosaurus! *Director/Coproducer* Irvin S. Yeaworth, Jr., *Screenplay* Jean Yeaworth and Dan E. Weisburd, *Idea and Producer* Jack H. Harris, *Development* Alfred Bester, *Story* Algis Budrys, *Art director* Jack Senter, *Set decorator* Herman Schoenbrun, *Photography* Stanley Cortez, *Editor* John A. Bushelman, *Special photographic effects* Tim Baar, Wah Chang, Gene Warren, *Miniature technicians* Marcel Delgado and Don Sahlin, *Music* Ronald Stein, *Sound editors* Jack Cornall and Jack Wheeler, *Sound mixer* Vic Appel, *Makeup* Don Cash, *Wardrobe* Bill Edwards, *Assistant director* Herbert Mendelson, *Director of underwater sequence* Paul Stader, *Assistant to the producer* S. Robert Zanger.

Cast: *Bart Thompson* Ward Ramsey, *Neanderthal man* Gregg Martell, *Mike Hacker* Fred Engelberg, *Julio* Alan Roberts, *Betty Piper* Kristina Hanson, *Chuck* Paul Lukather, *Chica* Luci Blain, *Dumpy* Wayne C. Treadway, *T.G. O'Leary* James Logan, *Jasper* Jack Younger, *Mousey* Howard Dayton, *Islander* William Samuels, *Tourist* Jack H. Harris.

A Fairview Production, released by Universal-International; color; CinemaScope; 85 minutes. Released June 10, 1960.

Dr. Blood's Coffin. *Director* Sidney J. Furie, *Story and Screenplay* Jerry Juran, *Adaptation* James Kelly and Peter Miller, *Producer* George Fowler, *Executive producer* David E. Rose, *Art director* Scott MacGregor, *Photography* Stephen Dade, *Special effects* Les Bowie and Peter Nelson, *Editor* Tony Gibbs, *Music* Buxton Orr, *Music conductor* Philip Martell, *Sound* William Salter, *Production manager* Buddy Booth, *Assistant director* John Comfort.

Cast: *Dr. Peter Blood* Kieron Moore, *Linda Parker* Hazel Court, *Dr. Robert Blood* Ian Hunter, *Mr. Morton* Fred Johnson(?),* *Sergeant Cook* Kenneth J. Warren, *Beale* Andy Alston, *Steve Parker (the corpse)* Paul Stockman, *Hanson* John Romane, *Sweeting* Gerald C. Lawson(?),* *Professor* Paul Hardtmuth, *Tregaye*—??*

*The *Monthly Film Bulletin* lists Fred Johnson in the role of Tregaye, and Gerald C. Lawson as Morton; *Filmfacts* lists Fred Johnson as Morton and Gerald C. Lawson as Sweeting (as we have it here), with no one listed for Tregaye.

A Caralan-Dador Production, U.S. dst. United Artists; color (black and white in some theatres); 92 minutes. A British film. Working title: "Face of Evil." Released April 26, 1961 in the U.S.; January 1961 in Britain. Double bill with: *The Snake Woman*.

A Dog, a Mouse and a Sputnik. *Director* Jean Dréville, *Screenplay* Jean-Jacques Vital, *Adaptation and Dialogue* Robert Rocca, Jacques Grello, Jean-Jacques Vital, Noël-Noël, *Producer* Louis de Masure, *Art director* Serge Pimenoff, *Photography* André Bac, *Editor* Jean Feyte, *Music* Paul Misraki, *Music director* Marc Lanjean, *Sound* Pierre-Henry Goumy.

Cast: *Léon Martin* Noël-Noël, *Marguerite Martin* Denise Grey, *Professor Popov* Mischa Auer, *Deputy attaché* Darry Cowl, *Mayor* Noel Roquevert, *Police superintendent* Robert Rombard, *Dina (interpreter)* Natalie Nerval, *Marie* Pauline Carton, *Chazot* Francis Blanche.

Films J.J. Vital-Regina-Filmsonor, U.S. dst. Films Around the World; black and white; 92 minutes (French length, 94 minutes). A French film. Original title: **A Pied, à Cheval et en Spoutnik** (By Foot, by Horse and by Sputnik). British title: **Hold Tight for the Satellite** [*sic*]. TV title: **Sputnik**. Alternate title?: **Rocketflight with Hindrance**. U.S. release October 31, 1960; reviewed in France in October 1958.

Earth vs. the Spider. *Producer/Director/Special technical effects/Story* Bert I. Gordon, *Screenplay* Laszlo Gorog and George Worthing Yates, *Executive producers* James H. Nicholson and Samuel Z. Arkoff, *Assistant producer* Henry Schrage, *Set designer* Walter Keller, *Set decorator* Bill Calvert, *Photography* Jack Marta, *Assistant technical effects* Flora M. Gordon, *Special devices* Thol Simonson, *Special designs* Paul and Jackie Blaisdell, *Editorial supervision* Ronald Sinclair, *Assistant editor* Paul Wittenberg, *Music* Albert Glasser, *Sound* Ryder Sound Services, *Sound recorder* Al Overton, *Sound effects editor* Bruce Shoengarth, *Makeup* Allen Snyder, *Costumes* Marge Corso, *Hairstyles* Kay Shea, *Script supervisor* Elayne Garnet, *Production supervisor* Marty Moss, *Assistant directors* Marty Moss and John W. Rogers, *Chief set electrician* Cal Maehl, *Property master* Jim Harris, *Key grip* Del Nodine, *Spider handler* Jim Dannaldson.

Cast: *Mr. Kingman* Ed Kemmer, *Carol Flynn* June Kenny, *Mike Simpson* Gene Persson, *Sheriff Cagle* Gene Roth, *Mr. Simpson* Hal Torey, *Helen Kingman* Sally Fraser, *Mrs. Flynn* June Jocelyn, *Mr. Haskel* Mickey Finn, *Joe Troy* Patterson, *Hugo (janitor)* Hank Patterson, *Sam* Skip Young, *Jake* Howard Wright, *Deputy sheriff Sanders* Bill Giorgio, *Mr. Fraser* Jack Kosslyn, *Pest control man* Bob Garnet, *Switchboard operator* Shirley Falls, *Deputy sheriff Dave* Bob Tetrick, *Dancer* Nancy Kilgas, *Man in cavern* George Stanley, *Line foreman* David Tomack, *Mr. Flynn* Merritt Stone.

Santa Rosa Productions for American International; black and white; 72 minutes, 48²/₃ seconds, October, 1958 (Los Angeles opening). Advertising title: **The Spider**. Double billed in various areas with: *The Brain Eaters*, elsewhere with *The Screaming Skull*.

Eegah! *Producer/Director/Story* Nicholas Merriwether (Arch Hall, Sr.), *Screenplay* Bob Wehling, *Photography* Vilis Lapenieks, *Editor* Don Schneider, *Music* Arch Hall, Jr. and the Archers; *Score* Henry Price, *Recording engineer* Sam Kopetzy, *Production manager* H. Duane Weaver

Cast: *Eegah* Richard Kiel, *Tom* Arch Hall, Jr., *Roxy Miller* Marilyn Manning, *Mr. Miller* William Watters (Arch Hall, Sr.), *Also* Ray Dennis Steckler (aka Cash Flagg), Clay Stearns, Addalyn Pollitt, Bob Davis, William Lloyd, Deke Lussier, Ron Shane, Bill Rice.

Fairway International; color; 90 minutes. Advertising title: **Eegah! The Name Written in Blood**. Released June 8, 1962.

The Electronic Monster. *Director* Montgomery Tully, *Screenplay* Charles Eric Maine, *Additional dialogue* J. MacLaren-Ross, *Dream sequences directed by* David Paltenghi, *Producer* Alec C. Snowden, *Associate producer* Jim O'Connolly, *Art director* Wilfred Arnold, *Photography* Bert Mason, *Dream sequence photography* Teddy Catford, *Camera operator* Bernard Lewis, *Editor* Geoffrey Muller, *Electronic music* Soundrama, *Music* Richard Taylor, *Sound recording* Ronald Abbott and Keith Barber, *Sound editor* Derek Holding, *Makeup* Jack Craig, *Wardrobe* Eileen Welch, *Hairdresser* Daphne Vollmer, *Continuity* Marjorie Owens, *Production manager* Bill Shore, *Assistant director* Peter Crowhurst, *Consultant* John Simmons.

Cast: *Jeff Keenan* Rod Cameron, *Ruth Vance* Mary Murphy, *Dr. Maxwell* Meredith Edwards, *Paul Zakon* Peter Illing, *Dr. Erich Hoff* Carl Jaffe, *Laura Maxwell* Kay Callard, *Blore* Carl Duering, *Verna Berteaux* Roberta Huby, *Commissaire* Felix Felton, *Brad Somers* Larry Cross, *Pietro Kallini* Carlo Borelli, *Clark Denver* John McCarthy, *French doctor* Jacques Cey, *French farmer* Armand Guinle(?), *Clinic receptionist* Malou Pantera, *Studio receptionist* Pat Clavin(?), *Wayne (Jeff's boss)* Alan Gifford.

A Nat Cohen and Stuart Levy Presentation of a Merton Park Studios–Anglo-Guild Film, U.S. dst. Columbia Pictures; black and white; 76 minutes (in Britain; possibly 80 minutes in U.S.). Based on the novel *Escapement* by Charles Eric Maine. A British film. British title: **Escapement**. Working titles: "Zez!"; "Zex, the Electronic Fiend." U.S. release May 27, 1960 (British release February 1958). Double bill with: *Battle in Outer Space* in some areas, *13 Ghosts* in others.

Fiend Without a Face. *Director* Arthur Crabtree, *Screenplay* Herbert J. Leder, *Producer* John Croydon, *Executive producer(?)* Richard Gordon, *Set design* John Elphick, *Photography* Lionel Barnes, *Camera operator* Leo Rogers, *2nd unit photography* Martin Curtis, *Animation effects* Florenz von Nordhoff and K.L. Ruppel; *Special effects* Peter Neilson, *Editor* R.Q. MacNaughton, *Music* Buxton Orr, *Music conductor* Frederic Lewis, *Sound* Peter Davies, *Dubbing editor* Terence Poulton, *Makeup* Jim Hydes, *Dress supervisor* Anna Duse, *Hairstyles* Barbara Bernard, *Continuity* Hazel Swift, *Assistant director* Douglas Hickox.

Cast: *Maj. Jeff Cummings* Marshall Thompson, *Barbara Griselle* Kim Parker, *Prof. R.E. Walgate* Kynaston Reeves, *Colonel Butler* Stanley Maxted, *Dr. Bradley* Peter Madden, *Capt. Al Chester* Terence Kilburn, *Dr. Warren* Gil Winfield, *Constable Howard Gibbons* Robert MacKenzie, *Deputy Mayor Melville* Launce Maraschal, *Mayor Hawkins* James Dyrenforth, *Sergeant Kasper* Michael Balfour, *Amelia Adams* Lala Lloyd, *Ben Adams* R. Meadows White, *Nurse* Shane Cordell, *Pete (atomic engineer)* Kerrigan Prescott.

An Amalgamated Production, dst. MGM; black and white; 74 minutes. Based on the short story "The Thought Monster" by Amelia Reynolds Long, published in *Weird Tales* in 1930. A British film. U.S. release June 9, 1958. Double bill with: *The Haunted Strangler*.

The Final War. *Director* Shigeaki Hidaka, *Screenplay* Hisataka Kai, *Photography* Tadashi Arakami.

Cast: Tatsuo Umemiya, Yoshiko Mita, Yayoi Furusato, Nirbumi Fujishima, Yukiko Nikaido, Michiko Hoshi.

New Toei Company, U.S. dst. Sam Lake Enterprises; black and white; ToeiScope; 77 minutes. A Japanese film. Original title: **Dai Sanji Sekai Taisen – Yonju-Ichi Jikan No Kyofu**. Alternate Japanese title: **41 Jikan No Kyofu**. Alternate U.S. title: **World War III Breaks Out**. U.S. release December 3, 1962 (Japanese release October 1960).

First Man into Space. *Director* Robert Day, *Screenplay* John C. Cooper and Lance Z. Hargreaves, *Story* Wyott Ordung, *Producers* John Croydon and Charles Vetter, Jr., *Executive producer (unbilled)* Richard Gordon, *Art direction* Denys Pavitt, *Photography* Geoffrey Faithfull, *Camera operator* Frank Drake, *Editor* Peter Mayhew*, *Music* Buxton Orr, *Electronic effects* Sound Drama (Soundrama), *Sound recorder* Terence Cotter, *Sound editor* Peter Musgrave, *Makeup* Michael Morris, *Wardrobe* Charles Guerin, *Miss Landi's dresses supervised by* Anna Selby-Walker, *Hairstyles* Eileen Warwick, *Continuity* Kay Rawlings, *Production manager* George Mills, *Assistant director* Stanley Goulder, *Location manager* John George.

Cast: *Cmdr. Charles Ernest "Chuck" Prescott* Marshall Thompson, *Tia Francesca* Marla Landi, *Lt. Dan Milton Prescott* Bill Edwards, *Dr. Paul Von Essen* Carl Jaffe, *Chief Wilson* Bill Nagy, *Capt. Ben Richards* Robert Ayres, *Ramon De Guerrera, Mexican consul* Roger Delgado, *Carl Atkins, State Department official* John McLaren, *Witney* Richard Shaw, *Clancy* William R. Nick, *Control room officials* Chuck Keyser, John Fabian and Spencer Teakle, *State trooper* Michael Bell, *Secretary* Helen Forrest, *Truck driver* Rowland Brand, *Mexican farmer* Barry Shawzin, *Doctor* Mark Sheldon, *Nurse* Sheree Winton, *C.P.O.* Franklyn Fox, *Shore patrolman* Laurence Taylor.

*This Peter Mayhew is presumably not the same one who played Chewbacca in the *Star Wars* series.

An Amalgamated Production, dst. MGM; black and white; 77 minutes. A British film. Working title: "Satellite of Blood." Released Feb. 1959 in U.S. (Feb. 1958 in Britain).

First Spaceship on Venus. *European Credits: Director* Kurt Maetzig, *Screenplay* Jan Fethke, Wolfgang Kohlhaase, Guenter Reisch, Guenter Ruecker, Alexander Stenbock-Fermor, Kurt Maetzig and(?) J. Barckhausen, *Art directors* Anatol Radzinowicz and Alfred Hirschmeier, *Photography* Joachim Hasler, *Special photographic effects* Martin Sonnabend, *Special effects* Ernst and Vera Kunstmann, Jan Olejniczak and Helmut Grewald, *Music* Andrzej Markowski, *Editor (possibly a U.S. credit only)* Lena Neumann. *U.S. credits: Executive producers* Newton P. Jacobs, Paul Schreibman, Edmund Goldman, *Executive supervisor (dubbing director?)* Hugo Grimaldi, *Music (selection?)* Gordon Zahler, *Music editor (synchronization?)* Walter Greene, *Music editor (sound editor?)* Josef Von Stroheim.

Cast: *Robert Brinkman* Guenther Simon, *Dr. Sumiko Ogimura* Yoko Tani, *Harringway Oldrick (Oldrich) Lukes, Durand* Michal Postnikow, *Professor Sikarna* Kurt Rackelmann, *Tchen Yu* Tang-Hua-Ta, *Orloff* Ignacy Machowski, *Taljua* Juliusz Ongewe, *Joan Moran* Lucyna Winnicka.
A DEFA/Iluzjon Film Unit–Film Polski–Centrala Productions film, U.S. dst. Crown International; color; Totalvision; 78 minutes in U.S. (109 or 130 minutes in Europe). Based on the 1951 novel *Astronauci* (The Astronauts) by Stanislaw Lem. An East German–Polish co-production. East German title: **Der Schweigende Stern** (The Silent Star). Polish title: **Milczaca Gwiazda** (Planet of the Dead). U.S. prerelease title: "Spaceship to Venus." U.S. release date October 31, 1962 (East German release February 1960; Polish release March 1960). Double bill with: *Varan the Unbelievable.*

The Flame Barrier. *Director* Paul Landres, *Screenplay* Pat Fielder and George Worthing Yates, *Story* George Worthing Yates (and Sam X. Abarbanel?), *Producers* Arthur Gardner and Jules V. Levy (and Arnold Laven), *Art director* James D. Vance, *Set decorations* Rudy Butler, *Photography* Jack MacKenzie, *Optical effects* Westheimer Company, *Editor* Jerry Young, *Music* Gerald Fried, *Sound* William Russell and Frank Moran, *Sound effects editor* Kay Rose, *Makeup* Richard Smith, *Assistant directors* Richard Dixon and Don Schiff, *Casting* Kerwin Coughlin, *Script supervisor* George Rutter.

Cast: *Dave Hollister* Arthur Franz, *Carol Dahlman* Kathleen Crowley, *Matt Hollister* Robert Brown, *Julio* Vincent Padula, *Waumi* Rodd Redwing, *Tispe (Koko?)* Kaz Oran, *Mexican girl* Grace Mathews, *Indian girl* Pilar Del Rey, *Bearer* Larry Duran, *Wounded Indian* Bernie Gozier, *Village Indian* Roberto Contreras.
Gramercy Pictures, Inc., dst. United Artists; black and white; 70 minutes. Publicity title?: **It Fell from the Flame Barrier.** Alternate title?: **Beyond the Flame Barrier.** Reviewed April 1958. Double bill with: *Return of Dracula.*

The Fly. *Director/Producer* Kurt Neumann, *Screenplay* James Clavell, *Art directors* Theobold Holsopple and Lyle R. Wheeler, *Set decorators* Eli Benneche and Walter M. Scott, *Photography* Karl Struss, *Special effects* L.B. Abbott, *Editor* Merrill White, *Music* Paul Sawtell, *Sound* Eugene Grossman and Harry M. Leonard, *Recording supervisor* Carlton W. Faulkner, *Makeup* Ben Nye and Dick Smith, *Costumes* Adele Balkan, *Hairstyles* Helen Turpin, *Executive wardrobe designer* Charles LeMaire, *Assistant director* Jack Gertsman, *Color consultant* Leonard Doss.

Cast: *André Delambre* Al (David) Hedison, *Hélène Delambre* Patricia Owens, *François Delambre* Vincent Price, *Insp. Charas* Herbert Marshall, *Philippe Delambre* Charles Herbert, *Emma* Kathleen Freeman, *Nurse Andersone* Betty Lou Gerson, *Dr. Ejoute* Eugene Borden, *Gaston (nightwatchman* Torben Meyer, *Orderly* Harry Carter, *Doctor* Charles Tannen, *Police doctor* Franz Roehn, *French waiter* Arthur Dulac.
A 20th Century–Fox Production and Release; color; CinemaScope; 94 minutes. Based on the short story "The Fly" by George Langelaan. Released July 11, 1958. Double bill with: *Space Master X-7.*

4D Man. *Director/Coproducer* Irwin Shortess Yeaworth, Jr., *Screenplay* Theodore Simonson and Cy Chermak, *Producer/Original idea* Jack H. Harris, *Art director* William Jersey, *Set decorator* Don W. Schmitt, *Photography* Theodore J. Pahle, *Camera operator* Thomas E. Spaulding, *Special effects* Barton Sloane, *Editor* William B. Murphy, *Music* Ralph Carmichael, *Sound* Carl Auel and Robert Spies, *Makeup* Dean Newman, *Script supervisor* Jean Yeaworth, *Production manager* Jerry Franks, *Continuity* Peggy Sturms, *Studio manager* Frank D. Funa, *Assistant to producer* Al Bennett.

Cast: *Scott Nelson* Robert Lansing, *Linda Davis* Lee Meriwether, *Tony Nelson* James Congdon, *Roy Parker* Robert Strauss, *Dr. Theodore W. Carson* Edgar Stehli, *Marjorie Sutherland (little girl)* Patty Duke, *Fred Guy* Raymond, *B-girl* Chic James, *Captain Rogers* Elbert Smith, *Mr. Welles* Jasper Deeter, *Sergeant Todaman* George Kara, *Dr. Schwartz* Dean Newman, *Man in nightclub* Jack H. Harris.

A Fairview Production, dst. Universal-International; color; 85 minutes. British title: **The Evil Force.** Working title: "The Four Dimensional Man." Common title error: "The 4D Man." Released October 7, 1959. No standard double bill in 1959, but when it was reissued by U.S. Films in 1960 under the title *Master of Terror*, it had a double bill of *Master of Horror*, and later was an occasional double bill with *The Blob*, and on a triple bill with that film and *Dinosaurus!*

Frankenstein 1970. *Director* Howard W. Koch, *Screenplay* Richard Landau and George Worthing Yates, *Story* Aubrey Schenck and Charles A. Moses, *Producer* Aubrey Schenck, *Production design* Jack T. Collis, *Set decorator* Jerry Welch, *Photography* Carl E. Guthrie, *Operative cameraman* William (Wilfred?) T. Cline, *Editor* John A. Bushelman, *Music* Paul A. Dunlap, *Sound* Francis C. Stahl, *Makeup supervisor* Gordon Bau, *Makeup* George Bau, *Script supervisor* Mary Yerke, *Assistant director* George Vieira, *Electrical supervisor* Ralph Owens, *Key grip* Chuck Harris, *Property master* George Sweeney.

Cast: *Baron Victor von Frankenstein* Boris Karloff, *Douglas Row* Donald Barry, *Carolyn Hayes* Jana Lund, *Judy Stevens* Charlotte Austin, *Wilhelm Gottfried* Rudolph Anders, *Mike Shaw* Tom Duggan, *Shuter* Norbert Schiller, *Morgan Haley* John Dennis, *Inspector Raab* Irwin Berke, *Hans and the Monster* Mike Lane, *Assistant cameraman* Jack Kenney, *Cab driver* Franz Roehn, *Station porter* Joe Ploski, *Atomic reactor expert (scenes cut?)* Otto Reichow.

An Allied Artists film; black and white; CinemaScope; 82⅔ minutes. Based on ideas created by Mary W. Shelley. Working titles: "Frankenstein 1960," "Frankenstein 1975." Released November 1958 (Los Angeles opening; probably earlier elsewhere—trade reviewed July 1958). Apparently planned as a double bill with *Queen of Outer Space.*

Frankenstein's Daughter. *Director* Richard E. Cunha, *Screenplay* H.E. Barrie, *Producer* Marc Frederic, *Art direction* Sham Unlimited, *Set decorator* Harry Reif, *Photography* Meredith Nicholson, *Camera operator* Robert Wyckoff, *Special effects* Ira Anderson, *Editor* Everett Dodd, *Sound* Robert Post, *Sound effects editor* Harold E. Wooley, *Makeup* Harry Thomas and Paul Stanhope, *Script supervisor* Diana Loomis, *Production manager* Ralph Brooke, *Assistant director* Leonard J. Shapiro, *Props* Walter Broadfoot, *Electrician* Frank Leonetti, *Grip* Grant Tucker.

Cast: *Oliver Frank(enstein)* Donald Murphy, *Trudy Morton* Sandra Knight, *Carter Morton* Felix Locher, *Elsu Wolfe* Barzell, *Johnny Bruder* John Ashley, *Suzie Lawler* Sally Todd, *Don* Harold Lloyd, Jr., *Lieutenant Boyle* John Zaremba, *Detective Dillon* Robert Dix, *Mr. Rockwell (chemist)* Voltaire Perkins, *Monster* Harry Wilson, *Warehousemen* Bill Coontz and George Barrows, *Also* Charlotte Portney and the Page Cavanaugh Trio.

A Marc Frederic–George Fowley Production, a Layton Film, dst. Astor Pictures; black and white; 85 minutes. Based on ideas created by Mary W. Shelley. 8mm title: **She Monster of the Night.** Released December 15, 1958 (March 4, 1960 in Los Angeles). Double bill with: *Missile to the Moon.*

From the Earth to the Moon. *Director* Byron Haskin, *Screenplay* Robert Blees and James Leicester, *Producer* Benedict Bogeaus, *Production design* Hal Wilson Cox, *Photography* Edwin B. DuPar and Jorge Stahl, Jr., *Special effects/Production coordinator* Lee Zavitz, *Special camera effects* Albert M. Simpson, *Editor* James Leicester, *Music* Louis Forbes, *Sound* Weldon Coe, *Costumes* Gwen Wakeling, *Wardrobe* Georgette, *Assistant director* Nacio Real.

Cast: *Victor Barbicane* Joseph Cotten, *Stuyvesant Nicholls* George Sanders, *Virginia Nicholls* Debra Paget, *Ben Sharpe* Don Dubbins, *Josef Cartier* Patric Knowles, *Morgana* Henry Daniell, *Aldo Von Metz* Ludwig Stossel, *Reporter Bancroft* Melville Cooper, *Jules Verne* Carl Esmond, *Pres. Ulysses S. Grant* Morris Ankrum, *Narrator* Robert Clarke.

A Waverly Production for RKO General, dst. Warner Bros.; color; 100 minutes. Based on the novels *De la Terre a la Lune* (1865) and *Autour de la Lune* (1870) by Jules Verne, first published in English as *From the Earth to the Moon Direct in 97 Hours 20 Minutes, and a Trip Around It* in 1873. In 1902, Georges Méliès produced a short film slightly resembling Verne's stories. A U.S.–Mexican coproduction? Released November 6, 1958.

Fury of the Congo. *Director* William Berke, *Story and Screenplay* Carroll Young, *Producer* Sam Katzman, *Art director* Paul Palmentola, *Set decorator* Sidney Clifford, *Photography* Ira H. Morgan, *Editor* Richard Fantl, *Musical director* Mischa Bakaleinikoff, *Sound engineer* Josh Westmoreland, *Sound supervisor* John P. Liuadary, *Unit manager* Herbert B. Leonard, *Assistant director* Wilbur McGaugh.

   Cast: *Jungle Jim* Johnny Weissmuller, *Leta* Sherry Moreland, *Ronald Cameron* William Henry, *Grant* Lyle Talbot, *Professor Dunham* Joel Friedkin, *Barnes* George Eldridge, *Magruder* Rusty Wescoatt, *Raadi* Paul Marion, *Mahara* Blanca Vischer, *Allen* Pierce Lyden, *Guard* John Hart.

   Essankay Film Company for Columbia; sepia; 69 minutes. Based on the comic strip "Jungle Jim" created by Alex Raymond. Released April 1951.

The Giant Behemoth. *Director* Eugene Lourié, *Screenplay* Eugene Lourié and (uncredited) Daniel Hyatt, *Story* Robert Abel and Allen Adler, *Producer* David Diamond, *Associate producer* Ted Lloyd, *Associate director (union-required credit?)* Douglas Hickox,* *Art director* Harry White, *Photography* Ken Hodges, *Camera operator* Desmond Davis, *Stop motion animation scenes designed and directed by* Willis O'Brien, *Stop-motion animation* Pete Peterson, *Other special effects* Jack Rabin, Irving Block, Louis DeWitt, *Miniature technician* Phil Kellison, *Editor* Lee Doig, *Music* Ted Astley, *Recorder* Sid Wiles, *Sound editor* Richard Marden, *Makeup* Jimmy Evans, *Wardrobe mistress* Freda Gibson, *Hairstyles* Bernie Ibbetson, *Continuity* Jennifer Herrinshaw, *Production manager* Jacques De Lane Lea, *Assistant director* Kim Mills.

   Cast: *Steven Karnes* Gene Evans, *Prof. James Bickford* André Morell, *Dr. Sampson* Jack MacGowran, *Submarine commander* Maurice Kaufman, *Tom MacDougall* Henry Vidon, *Jeanie MacDougall* Leigh Madison, *Ian Duncan* John Turner, *Interrupting scientist* Leonard Sachs, *Announcer* Neal Arden, *Also* Georgina Ward.

   These are inadequate acting credits, but no source seems to have better.

   *Hickox is sometimes listed as director in British sources, but he was working as an assistant director during this period. It is possible he did not have anything to do with directing the film, and that his credit was required by union rules.

   A David Diamond–Artistes Alliance Ltd. Prod., U.S. dst. Allied Artists; black and white; 79 minutes in U.S. (72 minutes in Britain). A U.S.–British coproduction. British title: **Behemoth the Sea Monster.** Working title: "The Behemoth." Released March 3, 1959.

Giant from the Unknown. *Director and Photography* Richard E. Cunha, *Screenplay* Frank Hart Taussig and Ralph Brooke, *Producer* Arthur A. Jacobs, *Associate producer* Marc Frederic, *Camera operator* William Norton, *Special effects and Special prop construction* Harold Banks, *Editor* Screencraft, *Music* Albert Glasser, *Sound mixer* Robert Post, *Makeup* Jack P. Pierce, *Wardrobe* Marge Corso and Grace Kuhn, *Script supervisor* Diana Loomis, *Chief electrician* Lee Dixon, *Property master* Walter Broadfoot.

   Cast: *Wayne Brooks* Edward Kemmer, *Janet Cleveland* Sally Fraser, *Vargas the Giant* Buddy Baer, *Prof. Frederick Cleveland* Morris Ankrum, *Sheriff Parker* Bob Steele, *Ann Brown* Joline Brand, *Townsmen* Oliver Blake, Ned Davenport, Ewing Miles, *Indian Joe* Billy Dix, *Charlie Brown* Gary Crutcher.

   A Screencraft Enterprises production, dst. Astor Pictures; black and white; 77 minutes. Working titles: "Giant from Devil's Crag," "The Diablo Giant," "Giant from Diablo Point." Released March 1958. Double bill with: *She Demons.*

The Giant Gila Monster. *Director/Story/Special effects* Ray Kellogg, *Screenplay* Jay Simms,* *Producer* Ken Curtis, *Executive producer* Gordon McLendon, *Art designer* Louis Caldwell, *Set decorator* Louise Caldwell, *Photography* Wilfrid Cline, *Camera operators* George Gordon Nogle and Henry A. Kokojan, *Camera assistants* William John Ranaldi and Harry I. Ganneschi, *Special photographic effects* Ralph Hammeras and Lee Risser, *Editor* Aaron Snell, *Music* Jack Marshall, *Music associate* Audray Granville(?), *Songs* Don Sullivan, *Sound* Earl Snyder, *Sound effects* Milton Citron and James Richard, *Makeup* Corinne Daniel, *Script supervisor* Audrey Blasdel, *Production manager* Ben Chapman, *Assistant director* Edward Haldeman.

Cast: *Chase Winstead* Don Sullivan, *Sheriff* Fred Graham, *Lisa* Lisa Simone, *Mr. Harris* Shug Fisher, *Wheeler* Bob Thompson, *Missy* Janice Stone, *Steamroller Smith* Ken Knox, *Bob* Jerry Cortwright, *Gay* Beverly Thurman, *Gordy* Don Flournoy, *Chuck* Clarke Brown, *Sherry* Pat Simmons, *Rick* Pat Reeves, *Whila* Ann Sonka, *Compton* Cecil Hunt, *Mrs. Blackwell* Tommie Russel, *Pat Wheeler* Grady Vaughn, *Liz Humphries* Yolanda Salas, *Eb Humphries* Howard Ware, *Agatha Humphries* Stormy Meadows, *Hitchhiker* Desmond Doogh, *Also* Gay and Jan McLendon.

*Text sources credit Ray Kellogg as coscripter, but only Simms is credited onscreen.

A B.B. McLendon and Gordon McLendon Production, dst. McLendon Radio Pictures (screen says Hollywood Pictures Corp.); black and white; 74 minutes. Reviewed July 15, 1959. Double bill with: *The Killer Shrews*.

Gigantis the Fire Monster. *Director* Motoyoshi Oda,* *Screenplay* Takeo Murata and Shigeaki Hidaka,* *Story* Shigeru Kayama,* *Producer* Tomoyuki Tanaka, *Art director* Takeo Kita, *Assistant art director* Teruaki Abe, *Photography* Seiichi Endo, *Music (some or all not used in U.S. prints)* Masaru Sato, *Sound* Masanobu Miyazaki, *Lighting* Masaki Onuma.

Special effects credits: Director Eiji Tsuburaya, *Art director* Akira Watanabe, *Lighting* Masao Shiroda, *Composition(?)* Hiroshi Mukoyama. *U.S.–dubbed version credits: Presented by* Paul Schreibman, *Associate producer* Edmund Goldman, *Director of dubbing and Editor* Hugo Grimaldi, *Sound effects editor* Alvin Sarno, *Music editor* Rex Lipton.

Cast: *Gigantis* Haruo Nakajima, *Shoichi Tsukioka* Hiroshi Koizumi, *Koji Kobayashi* Minoru Chiaki,* *Hidemi Yamaji* Setsuko Wakayama, *Koehi Yamaji (president of the fishery)* Yukio Kasama,* *Yasuko Inouye (radio operator)* Mayuri Mokusho, *Shingo Shibeki (Hokkaido branch manager)* Sonosuke Sawamura, *Dr. Tadokoro (zoologist)* Masao Shimizu, *Osaka municipal police commissioner* Takeo Oikawa, *Captain Terasawa of Osaka defense corps* Seijiro Onda, *Tajima (member of Osaka defense corps)* Yoshio Tsuchiya, *Commander of Osaka defense corps* Minosuke Yamada, *Commander of landing craft* Ren Yamamoto, *Dr. Kyohei Yamane (paleontologist from Tokyo)* Takashi Shimura.

*Various names were mistransliterated in the credits for the U.S. version: Shigeru Kayama was Shigem Kayama, Shigeaki Hidaka was Sigeaki, Yukio Kasama was Yokio Kasama, Minoru Chiaki was Mindru Chiaki, and Motoyoshi Oda was, incredibly, Motoyoshi Qdq.

Toho, U.S. dst. Warner Bros; black and white; 78 minutes in U.S. (82 minutes in Japan). A Japanese film. Japanese title: **Gojira No Gyakushu** (Godzilla's Counterattack). Publicity title (for showings in U.S. Japanese–language theatres): **Godzilla Raids Again**. Planned U.S. title: "The Volcano Monsters." Released June 2, 1959 in U.S. (April 24, 1955 in Japan). Double bill with: *Teenagers from Outer Space*.

Gorgo. *Director* Eugene Lourié, *Screenplay* John Loring and Daniel Hyatt, *Story* Eugene Lourié and Daniel Hyatt, *Producer* Wilfred Eades, *Executive producers* Frank and Maurice King, *Associate producer* James Leicester, *Production administrator* Maurice King, *Art director* Elliott Scott, *Photography* F.A. (Freddie) Young, *Camera operator* Jack Mills, *Additional photography* Douglas Adamson, *Special photographic effects* Tom Howard, *Additional photographic effects* Ray Mercer & Company, *Editor* Eric Boyd-Perkins, *Music* Angelo Francesco Lavagnino, *Music conductor* Muir Mathieson, *Sound editing* Peter Thornton and Archie Ludski, *Recording supervisor* A.W. Watkins, *Sound recordist* John Bramall, *Makeup* Stella Morris, *Wardrobe* Harry Haynes, *Script supervisor* Pamela Davies, *Assistant directors* Douglas Hermes and Joe Marks, *Production secretary* Jean Clarkson, *Production supervisor* George Mills, *Public relations* Herman King, *Assistant to producers* Jack Labow, *Prop buyer* Bryan Siddall.

Cast: *Joe Ryan* Bill Travers, *Sam Slade* William Sylvester, *Sean* Vincent Winter, *Professor Flaherty* Bruce Seton, *Professor Hendricks* Joseph O'Connor, *Dorkin* Martin Benson, *1st mate* Barry Keegan, *Bo'sun* Dervis Ward, *McCartin* Christopher Rhodes, *Admiral Brooks* Basil Dignam, *Radio reporter* Maurice Kaufmann, *1st Naval officer* Tom Duggan, *1st colonel* Howard Lang, *Officer* Nigel Green, *Stunts* Connie Tilton, *Other stunts (Gorgo and Mama?)* David Wilding, Michael Dillon, Peter Brace and Peter Perkins.

King Brothers Prods., Ltd., dst. in U.S. MGM; color; 78 minutes. A U.S.–British coproduction. Working titles: "Kuru Island," "The Night the World Shook." Released February 10, 1961 in U.S.

The H-Man. *Director* Inoshiro Honda, *Screenplay* Takeshi Kimura, *Story* Hideo Kaijo, *Producer* Tomoyuki Tanaka, *Art director* Takeo Kita, *Photography* Hajime Koizumi, *Editor* Ichiji Taira, *Music* Masaru Sato, *Sound recording* Choshichiro Mikami, *Production manager* Teruo Maki, *Assistant directors* Koji Murata and Yoshio Nakamura, *Lighting director* Tsuruzo Nishikawa. *Special effects credits: Director* Eiji Tsuburaya, *Photography* Hidesaburo Araki and Sadamasa Arikawa, *Art director* Akira Watanabe, *Lighting director* Kuichiro Kishida, *Optical printing* Hiroshi Mukoyama.

  Cast: *Chikako Arai* Yumi Shirakawa, *Dr. Masada* Kenji Sahara, *Inspector Tominaga* Akihiko Hirata, *Uchida* Mitsuru (Masaru?) Sato, *Dr. Maki* Koreya Senda, *Detective Taguchi* Yoshio Tsuchiya, *Detective Sakata* Yoshifumi Tajima, *Inspector Miyashita* Eitaro Ozawa, *Emi* Ayumi Sonoda, *Okami* Toshiko Nakano, *Man* Yosuke Natsuki, *Detective Ogawa* Kamayuki Tsubouchi, *Inspector Kusuda* Minosuke Yamada, *Detective Seki* Tadao Nakamaru, *Policeman Wakasugi* Akira Yamada, *Nishiyama* Jun Fujiro, *Horita* Akira Sera, *Yasukichi* Yasuhiro Kasanobu, *Mineko* Naomi Shiraishi, *Shimazaki* Yo Kirino, *Misaki* Hisaya Ito, *Hamano* Shin Ohtomo, *Hanae* Machiko Kitagawa, *Chinese gentleman* Satoshi Nakamura, *An-chan* Yutaka Nakayama, *Oh-chan* Shenkichi Ohmura, *Matsu-chan* Shigeo Kato, *Kishi* Ko Mishima, *Policemen* Kan Hayashi, Mitsuo Tsuda and Akio Kusama.

  Toho, U.S. dst. Columbia Pictures; color; TohoScope; 79 minutes in U.S. (87 minutes in Japan). A Japanese picture. Japanese title: **Bijo To Ekitai-Ningen** (Beauty and the Liquid People). Released June 23, 1959 in U.S. (June 24, 1958 in Japan). Double bill with: *Womaneater.*

Half Human. *Director* Inoshiro Honda, *Screenplay* Takeo Murata, *Story* Shigeru Kayama, *Producer* Tomoyuki Tanaka, *Art director* Tatsuo Kita, *Photography* Tadashi Imura, *Music* Masaru Sato, *Sound* Yoshio Nishikawa, *Lighting* Soichi Yokoi. *Special effects credits: Director* Eiji Tsuburaya, *Optical printing* Hiroshi Mukoyama, *Art director* Akira Watanabe, *Lighting* Masao Shiroda. *U.S. sequences directed by* Kenneth G. Crane.

  Japanese cast: *Takeshi Ijima* Akira Takarada, *Shinsuke Takeno* Kenji Sahara, *Machiko Takeno* Momoko Kochi, *Shigeki Koizumi* Noburo Nakamura, *Chika* Akemi Negishi, *Oba* Yoshio Kosuai, *Old man* Kuninori Kodo, *Kodama* Yasuhisa Tsutsumi, *Norkata* Sachio Sakai, *Shinagawa* Ren Yamamoto, *Kurihara* Koji Suzuki, *Matsui* Akira Sera. **U.S.–filmed scenes:** *Dr. John Rayburn* John Carradine, *Dr. Carl Jordan* Morris Ankrum, *Prof. Phillip Osborne* Russell Thorsen, *Prof. Alan Templeton* Robert Karnes.

  Toho, U.S. dst. Distributors Corporation of America (DCA); black and white; 70 minutes (95 minutes in Japan). A Japanese film. Japanese title: **Jujin Yukotoko** (Monster Snowman?). U.S. release: December 10, 1958 (in Los Angeles; may have seen some U.S. release in 1957; released in Japan in 1955). Double bill with: *Monster from Green Hell.*

Hand of Death. *Director* Gene Nelson, *Producer/Screenplay* Eugene Ling, *Set decorator* Harry Reif, *Photography* Floyd Crosby, *Supervising editor* Jodie Copelan, *Editor* Carl Pierson, *Music* Sonny Burke, *Sound* Vic Appel, *Supervising sound editor* Jack Cornall, *Makeup* Bob Mark, *Wardrobe* John Intlekofer, *Script supervisor* Winifred Gibson, *Production supervisor* Harold E. Knox, *Assistant director* Willard Kirkham, *Property master* Ygnacio Sepulveda.

  Cast: *Alex Marsh* John Agar, *Carol Wilson* Paula Raymond, *Tom Holland* Steve Dunne, *Dr. Ramsey* Roy Gordon, *Carlos* John Alonzo, *Service station attendant* Joe Besser, *Little boy on beach* Butch Patrick, *Also* Jack Younger, Norman Burton, Fred Krone, Kevin Enright, Jack Donner, Chuck Niles, Ruth Terry, Bob Whitney.

  Associated Producers Inc. for 20th Century–Fox; black and white; CinemaScope; 60 minutes. Working title: "Five Fingers of Death." Released March 1962. Double bill with: *Cabinet of Caligari.*

Hands of a Stranger. *Director/Screenplay* Newton Arnold, *Producers* Newton Arnold and Michael du Pont, *Art director* Ted Holsopple, *Set director* John Sturtevant, *Assistant producer* Gerald LeGrand, *Photography* Henry Cronjager, *Camera operator* James Stone, *Editor* Bert Honey, *Assistant film editor* Jack C. May, *Music* Richard LaSalle, *"How's Your Mother"* by John Mosher, *Played by* Red Norvo Quintette, *Sound effects editors* Jack

Cornell and George Eppich, *Music editor* Lee Osborne, *Sound mixer* Vic Appel, *Makeup* Charles Gemora, *Wardrobe* Buddy Clark and Ruth Hancock, *Hairstyles* Lorraine Roberson, *Script supervisor* Diana Loomis, *Gaffer* George Marquenie, *Key grip* Tommy Thompson, *Property master* Richard Brandow, *Technical adviser* Robert Gans, *Executive secretary* Sally Hamilton.

Cast: *Vernon Paris* James Stapleton, *Dr. Gil Harding* Paul Lukather, *Dina Paris* Joan Harvey, *Dr. Ken Fry* Michael du Pont, *Sue* Sally Kellerman, *Skeet* Barry Gordon, *Holly* Irish McCalla, *Dr. Russ Compton* Ted Otis, *George Britton* Michael Rye, *Police lieutenant Syms* Larry Haddon, *Eileen Hunter* Elaine Martone, *Cab driver* George Sawaya, *Carnival barker* David Kramer.

A Glenwood-Neve Production, dst. Allied Artists; black and white; 85½ minutes. Working titles: "The Answer!" "Hands of Terror." Released March 1962? (official form from Allied Artists indicates a release in September 1962).

Note: Many sources list this as an adaptation of *Les Mains d'Orlac*, a novel by Maurice Renard; this question is discussed in the entry on this film in the text.

Have Rocket, Will Travel. *Director* David Lowell Rich, *Story and Screenplay* Raphael Hayes, *Producer* Harry Romm, *Art director* John T. McCormack, *Set decorator* Darrell Silvera, *Photography* Ray Cory, *Editor* Danny B. Landres, *Music conductor* Mischa Bakaleinikoff, *Title song* George Duning and Stanley Styne, *Sound supervisor* John Livadary, *Sound mixer* Harold Lewis, *Supervising sound editor* Joseph Henri, *Makeup* Clay Campbell, *Assistant director* Floyd Joyer.

Cast: *The Three Stooges: Moe* Moe Howard, *Larry* Larry Fine, *Curley Joe* Joe De Rita, *J.P. Morse* Jerome Cowan, *Dr. Ingrid Naarveg* Anna-Lisa, *Dr. Ted Benson* Bob Colbert, *Mrs. Huntingford* Marjorie Bennett, *Newspaperman and Narrator* Don Lamond, *French girl* Nadine Ducas, *Voice of the Thing* Robert J. Stevenson, *Voice of the Unicorn* Dal McKennon.

Columbia; black and white; 76 minutes. Working title: "Race for the Moon." Released July 21, 1959.

The Head *Director/Screenplay* Victor Trivas, *Story* Victor Trivas and Jacques Mage, *Producer* Wolfgang Hartwig, *Associate producers* Otto Reinwald and Kurt Rendel, *Art directors* Hermann Warm and Bruno Monden, *Photography* Georg Krause, *Assistant photography* Andre von Piotrowski and Horst Philipp, *Special effects* Theo Nischwitz, *Editor* Friedl Buckow-Schier, *Assistant film editors* Heidi Rente and Eva Kohlschein, *Music* Willy Mattes and Jacques Lasry, *Music conductor* Erwin Lehn, *Sound structure* Lasry-Baschet, *Sound* Rudolf Kaiser, *Makeup* Karl Hanoszek and Susi Krause, *Production manager* Ludwig Spitaler, *Props* Richard Eglseder.

Cast: *Dr. Ood* Horst Frank, *Professor Abel* Michel Simon, *Irene* Karin Kernke, *Lilly* Christiane Maybach, *Paul* Dieter Eppler, *Dr. Burke* Kurt Mueller-Graf, *Crime commissioner Paul* Dahlke, *Bert* Helmut Schmid, *Mrs. Schneider* Maria Stadler, *Bartender* Otto Storr, *Also* Barbara Valentin, Herb Beschanner.

Rapid Film–Prisma, dst. in U.S. Trans-Lux Distributing Corporation; black and white; 92 minutes in U.S. (97 minutes in West Germany). A West German film. Original title: **Die Nackte und der Satan** (The Naked and the Satan). Prerelease U.S. titles: "A Head for the Devil," "The Screaming Head." Released October 11, 1961 in U.S. (July 1959 in West Germany). Double bill with: *The Black Pit of Dr. M*, on the West Coast, despite the films having different distributors. On the East Coast, *Horror Hotel* (a 1962 U.S. release) was paired with *The Head* for a 1963 release.

The Hideous Sun Demon. *Director/Producer* Robert Clarke, *Screenplay* E.S. Seeley, Jr., and Duane Hoag, *Idea* Robert Clarke and Phil Hiner, *Art director and Creator of monster suit* Gianbiatista (Richard) Cassarino, *Art director* Tom Miller, *Photography* John Morrill, Vilis Lapenieks, Jr., and Stan Follis, *Editor and Codirector* Thomas Boutross, *Assistant editor* Ron Honthaner, *Music* John Seely (Seeley?), *Song "Strange Pursuit"* by Marilyn King, *Sound* Doug Menville, *Makeup* Ben Sarino (Richard Cassarino), *Continuity* Deanie Follis(?), *Production manager and coproducer* Robin C. Kirkman.

Cast: *Dr. Gilbert McKenna* Robert Clarke, *Ann Lansing* Patricia Manning, *Trudy Osborne* Nan Peterson, *Dr. Frederick Buckell* Patrick Whyte, *Police lieutenant* Bill Hampton, *Dr. Jacob Hoffman* Fred La Porta, *Mother* Donna King Conkling, *Susie (little* *girl)* Xandra Conkling, *Radio announcer* Del Courtney, *George* Peter Similuk(?), *Dr. Stern* Robert Garry, *Lady on hospital roof* Pearl Driggs, *Policeman* Richard Cassarino, *Also* Helen Joseph, Bill Currie, Fran Leighton, John Murphy, Chuck Newell, Darryl Westbrook, Bob Hafner, Tony Hilder, David Sloan.

A Clarke-King Enterprises Production, dst. Pacific International; black and white; 74 minutes. British title: **Blood on His Lips**. Working titles: "Saurus," "Strange Pursuit," "The Sun Demon," "Terror from the Sun." Released December 1959.

The Horror Chamber of Dr. Faustus. *Director* Georges Franju, *Screenplay* Jean Redon, *Dialogue* Pierre Cascar, *Adaptation* Georges Franju, Jean Redon, Claude Sautet, Pierre Boileau, Thomas Narcejac, *Producer* Jules Borkon, *Art director* August Capelier, *Photography* Eugen Shuftan, *Special effects* Henri Assola and Georges Klein, *Music* Maurice Jarre, *Editor* Gilbert Natot, *Sound* Antoine Archimbaud, *Production manager* Pierre Laurent, *Presented in U.S. by* William Shelton and Cameo International Pictures.

Cast: *Professor Génessier* Pierre Brasseur, *Louise* Alida Valli, *Christiane Génessier* Edith Scob, *Jacques* François Guérin, *Edna Gruber* Juliette Mayniel, *Paulette* Béatrice Altariba, *Inspector Parot* Alexandre Rignault, *Bereaved father* René Genin, *Also* Claude Brasseur, Michel Etcheverry, Yves Etiévant, Lucien Hubert, Marcel Pérès.

Champs-Elysees Productions–Lux Film, U.S. dst. Lopert Films (United Artists); black and white; 84 minutes (reviewed also at 95 minutes; 88 minutes in Europe). A French-Italian coproduction. French title: **Les Yeux Sans Visage** (Eyes Without a Face). Italian title: **Occhi Senza Volto**. Alternate U.S. title: **Eyes Without a Face**. U.S. release March 28, 1962 (French release March 1960; Italian release July 1960). Double bill with: *The Manster*.

Horrors of the Black Museum. *Director* Herman Crabtree, *Screenplay* Aben Kandel and Herman Cohen, *Presented by* Nat Cohen,* Stuart Levy, James H. Nicholson and Samuel Z. Arkoff, *Art director* Wilfred Arnold, *Photography* Desmond Dickinson, *Camera operator* Harry Gillam, *Editor* Geoffrey Muller, *Music* Gerard Schurmann, *Dance music* Kenneth V. Jones, *Music conductor* Muir Mathieson, *Sound* Sidney Rider and Ronald Abbott, *Sound effects editor* Derek Holding, *Makeup* Jack Craig, *Wardrobe* Maude Churchill, *Hairstyles* Gordon Bond, *Production manager* Jim O'Connolly, *Assistant director* Bill Shore.

Cast: *Edmond Bancroft* Michael Gough, *Rick* Graham Curnow, *Joan Berkley* June Cunningham, *Angela* Shirley Ann Field, *Superintendent Graham* Geoffrey Keen, *Dr. Ballan* Gerald Andersen, *Inspector Lodge* John Warwick, *Aggie* Beatrice Varley, *Commissioner Wayne* Austin Trevor, *Peggy* Malou Pantera, *Tom Rivers* Howard Greene, *Gail* Dorinda Saunders, *Fun Fair barker* Stuart Saunders, *Women in hall* Hilda Barry and Nora Gordon, *Miss Ashton* Vanda Godsell, *Shop manager* Gerald Case, *Sergeant* Geoffrey Den, *Constables* William Abney, Howard Days, *Police surgeon* Frank Hender, *Fingerprint man* Garard Green, *Little girl* Ingrid Cardon. *In "Hypno-Vista" prologue (U.S. prints only)* Emile Franchel.

Monthly Film Bulletin lists Jack Greenwood as producer, an interview suggests Nat Cohen was coproducer. The real producer was undoubtedly Herman Cohen.

Carmel Prods.–Merton Park Prods. for American International release; color; Cinema-Scope; 81 minutes without prologue, 94 with. Filmed in Britain, but perhaps should not be considered a British film, as most financing came from the U.S. U.S. release April 22, 1959. Double bill with: *The Headless Ghost*.

House of Fright. *Director* Terence Fisher, *Screenplay* Wolf Mankowitz, *Producer* Michael Carreras, *Associate producer* Anthony Nelson Keys, *Production designer* Bernard Robinson, *Art director* Don Mingaye, *Photography* Jack Asher, *Camera operator* Len Harris, *Supervising editor* James Needs, *Editor* Eric Boyd-Perkins, *Music and Songs* Monty Norman and David Heneker, *Music conductor* John Hollingsworth, *Sound* Jock May, *Sound editor* Archie Ludski, *Makeup* Roy Ashton, *Costume designer* Mayo, *Wardrobe* Molly Arbuthnot, *Hairstyles* Ivy Emmerton, *Continuity* Tilly Day, *Production manager* Clifford Parkington, *Assistant director* John Peverell.

Cast: *Dr. Henry Jekyll/Edward Hyde* Paul Massie, *Kitty Jekyll* Dawn Addams, *Paul Allen* Christopher Lee, *Ernest Litauer* David Kossoff, *Maria* Norma Marla, *Inspector* Francis De Wolff, *Sphinx girls* Joy Webster and Magda Miller, *Clubman* William Kendall, *Bouncer*

Oliver Reed, *Nannie* Helen Goss, *Girl in gin shop* Pauline Shepherd, *Coroner* Percy Cartwright, *Corinthian* Joe Robinson, *Cabby* Arthur Lovegrove.

Hammer Films, U.S. dst. American International; color; MegaScope; 80 minutes in U.S. (88 minutes in Britain). Based on the novelette "The Strange Case of Dr. Jekyll and Mr. Hyde" by Robert Louis Stevenson. A British film. British and subsequent U.S. title: **The Two Faces of Dr. Jekyll**. Initial U.S. title: **Jekyll's Inferno**. Released May 3, 1961 in U.S. (October 1960 in Britain); originally released as double bill with *Terror in the Haunted House*, but that didn't last long.

How to Make a Monster. *Director* Herbert L. Strock, *Story/Screenplay* Kenneth Langtry (Aben Kandel) and Herman Cohen, *Producer* Herman Cohen, *Executive producers* James H. Nicholson and Samuel Z. Arkoff, *Art director* Leslie Thomas, *Set decorator* Morris Hoffman, *Photography* Maury Gertsman, *Special effects* Charles Duncan, *Editorial supervision* Jerry Young, *Score* Paul Dunlap, *Song "You've Got to Have EE-Ooo" lyrics* Skip Redwine, *Sound recorder* Herman Lewis, *Sound effects editing* Verna Fields, *Music editing* George Brand, *Makeup* Philip Scheer, *Wardrobe* Oscar Rodriguez, *Script supervisor* Mary Gibsone, *Production manager/Assistant director* Herb Mendelson, *Property master* Sam Gordon, *Production secretary* Barbara Lee Strite, *Choreography* Lee Scott, *Masks* Paul Blaisdell.

Cast: *Pete Drummond* Robert H. Harris,* *Rivero* Paul Brinegar, *Tony Mantell* Gary Conway, *Larry Drake* Gary Clarke, *Richards (head guard)* Malcolm Atterbury, *Monahan (other guard)* Dennis Cross, *Captain Hancock* Morris Ankrum, *Detective Thompson* Walter Reed, *Jeff Clayton* Paul Maxwell, *John Nixon* Eddie Marr, *Arlene Dow* Heather Ames, *Gary Droz (Larry's agent)* Robert Shayne, *Lab technician* Rod Dana, *Jane* Jacqueline Ebeier, *Marilyn* Joan Chandler, *Martin Brace (director)* Thomas Browne Henry, *Detective Jones* John Phillips, *Millie (scared maid)* Pauline Myers, *Himself* John Ashley.

*Tom Weaver says "Dumond."

Sunset Prods. for American International; black and white with last reel in color; 73 minutes. Released July 30, 1958. Double bill with: *Teenage Caveman*.

I Married a Monster from Outer Space. *Director/Producer* Gene Fowler, Jr., *Screenplay* Louis Vittes, *Story* Louis Vittes and Gene Fowler, Jr., *Art director* Henry Bumstead, *Set decorators* Sam Comer and Robert Benton, *Photography* Haskell Boggs, *Special effects supervision* John P. Fulton, *Optical photography* Paul K. Lerpae, *Editor* George Tomasini, *Sound* Phil Wisdom and Charles Grenzbach, *Makeup supervision* Wally Westmore, *Monster makeup* Charles Gemora, *Hairstyles* Nellie Manley, *Production manager* Frank Cassey, *Unit production manager* Donald W. Robb, *Assistant director* William Mull.

Cast: *Marge Farrell* Gloria Talbott, *Bill Farrell* Tom Tryon, *Sam Benson* Alan Dexter, *Harry Phillips* Robert Ivers, *Ted* Chuck Wassill, *Francine (prostitute)* Valerie Allen, *Swanson* Peter Baldwin, *Mac Brody* Ty Hungerford, *Dr. Wayne* Ken Lynch, *Chief Collins* John Eldredge, *Weldon* James Anderson, *Helen Rhodes* Jean Carson, *Schultz* Jack Orrison, *Charles Mason* Steve London, *Grady (bartender)* Maxie Rosenbloom, *Mrs. Bradley* Mary Treen, *Minister* Arthur Lovejoy, *2nd girl* Helen May, *Ralph (waiter)* Paul Manza, *Caroline Hanks* Darlene Fields, *Western Union clerk* Tony Di Milo, *1st girl* Scherry Staiger.

A Paramount Picture; black and white; 78 minutes. Working title: "IMAMFOS." Released September 29, 1958. Double bill with: *The Blob*.

The Incredible Petrified World. *Director/Producer* Jerry Warren, *Screenplay* John W. Sterner, *Art director* Marvin Harbert, *Set supervisor* Ray Guth, *Photography* Victor Fisher, *Underwater photography* Mel Fisher, *Editors* James R. Sweeney and Harold V. McKenzie, *Music director* Josef Zimanich, *Wardrobe* Kelpsuit, *Production supervisor* G.B. (Bri) Murphy, *Unit manager* Lloyd Nelson, *Dialogue director* Bri Murphy.

Cast: *Dr. Wyman* John Carradine, *Craig Randall* Robert Clarke, *Dale Marshall* Phyllis Coates, *Paul Whitmore* Allen Windsor, *Lauri Talbot* Sheila Noonan (Carol), *Matheny* George Skaff, *Ingol* Maurice Bernard, *Jim Wyman* Joe Maierhouser, *Captain* Harry Raven, *Radioman* Lloyd Nelson, *Reporter* Jack Haffner, *Man on plane* Jerry Warren, *Also* Milt Collion, Robert Carroll, Lowell Hopkins.

A G.B.M. Production, dst. Governor Films; black and white; 70 minutes. Released April 16, 1960 (filmed in 1958). Double bill with: *Teenage Zombies*.

Invasion of the Animal People. *Director* Virgil W. Vogel, *Screenplay* Arthur C. Pierce, *Executive producer* Gustaf Unger, *Producer* Bertil Jernberg, *Art director* Nils Nilsson, *Photography* Hilding Bladh, *Editor* Ernst Rolf, *Music* Allan Johannson, *Sound recorder* Stig Flodin, *Production manager* David Norberg, *Wardrobe* Nasse Johnson, *Assistant director* Bengt Jarrel, *Script girl* Ulla Ryhge, *Additional scenes written, directed, produced by* Jerry Warren, *Reediting* Jerry Warren, *Additional music* Harry Arnold (Arnald?).

Cast: *Diane Wilson* Barbara Wilson, *Dr. Frederick Wilson* Robert Burton, *Erik Engstrom* Stan Gester, *Col. Robert Bottiger* Bengt Blomgren, *Dr. Henrik* Ake Gronberg, *Singer* Brita Borg, *Also* Jack Haffner, *Narrator (on screen)* John Carradine.

Gustaf Unger Films–Fortuna Film, U.S. dst. A.D.P. Productions; black and white; 55 minutes (original running time 73 minutes). A U.S.–Swedish coproduction. Swedish title: **Rymdinvasion i Lappland** (Space Invasion of Lappland). U.S. Prerelease title: "Terror in the Midnight Sun." U.S. release May 3, 1962 (released in Sweden in 1958).

Invasion of the Star Creatures. *Director* Bruno Ve Sota, *Screenplay* Jonathan Haze, *Producer* Berj Hajkopian, *Art director* Mike McCloskey, *Photography* Basil Bradbury, *Editor* Lew Gunn, *Electronic music* Jack Cookerly and Elliott Fisher, *Sound* James Fullerton, *Makeup* Joseph Kinder, *Wardrobe* Dell Adams, *Production manager* Amos Powell.

Cast: *Philbrick* Robert Ball, *Penn* Frankie Ray, *Dr. Puna* Dolores Reed, *Professor Tanga* Gloria Victor, *Col. Thomas Awol* Mark Ferris, *Thug* Bruno Ve Sota, *Also* Slick Slavin, Mark Thompson, Sid Kane, Mike Del Piano, Lenore Bond, Anton Van Stralen, James Almanzar, Allen Dailey, Joseph Martin, Anton Arnold.

Alta Vista Productions for American International; black and white; copyrighted at 75 minutes. Working title: "Monsters from Nicholson Mesa." Released April 1962. Double bill with: *The Brain That Wouldn't Die*.

Invisible Avenger. *Directors* James Wong Howe and John Sledge,* *Screenplay* George Bellak and Betty Jeffries, *Producers* Eric Sayers and Emanuel Demby, *Set decorators* Sam Leve and Bernard Weist, *Photography* Willis Winford and Joseph Wheeler, *Editor* John Hemel, *Music supervision* Edward Dutreil, *Sound* Dennis Fretwell, *Makeup* Eddie Senz.

Cast: *Lamont Cranston* Richard Derr, *Jogendra* Mark Daniels, *Tara* Helen Westcott, *Felicia Ramirez* Jeanne Neher, *Pablo Ramirez* Dan Mullin, *Tony Alcalde* Steve Dano, *Victor Ramirez* Dan Mullin, *Colonel* Lee Edwards, *Billy* Jack Doner, *Rocco* Leo Bruno, *Charlie* Sam Page.

*The pressbook gives the credits as above, and a length of 60 minutes. The *American Film Institute Catalog* does not list Howe, Sledge, Sayers or Demby, but instead lists Ben Parker as producer-director, and gives a length of 70 minutes. However, a book on Howe includes this among the great cameraman's few directorial credits.

Republic Pictures; black and white; 60 minutes. Based on the character "The Shadow" created by Maxwell Grant. Rerelease title: **Bourbon Street Shadows**. Released December 1958. Further note: The *American Film Institute Catalog* lists this under its rerelease title, and fails to note that it had a release four years earlier than the 1962 date the catalog gives. This is composed of two episodes of an unsold "Shadow" TV series.

Invisible Invaders. *Director* Edward L. Cahn, *Screenplay* Samuel Newman, *Producer* Robert E. Kent, *Art director* William Glasgow, *Set decorator* Morris Hoffman, *Photography* Maury Gertsman, *Special effects* Roger George, *Editor* Grant Whytock, *Sound* Al Overton, *Makeup* Philip Scheer, *Costumes* Einar Bourman and Sabine Manella, *Hairstyles* Kaye Shea, *Production manager* Ben Hersh, *Assistant director* Herbert S. Greene, *Effects editor* Henry Adams, *Property master* Max Frankel, *Chief technician* Buzz Gibson, *Script supervisor* Del Ross.

Cast: *Dr. Adam Penner* Philip Tonge, *Maj. Bruce Jay* John Agar, *Phyllis Penner* Jean Byron, *Dr. John LaMont* Robert Hutton, *Dr. Karol Noymann* John Carradine, *Farmer* Hal Torey, *WAAF secretary* Eden Hartford, *Cab driver* Jack Kenney, *General Stone* Paul Langton, *Pilot* Don Kennedy, *Hockey game announcer* Chuck Niles.

A Premium Picture, dst. United Artists; black and white; 67 minutes. Released May 15, 1959. Double bill with: *The Four Skulls of Jonathan Drake*.

Island of Lost Women. *Director* Frank W. Tuttle, *Screenplay* Ray Buffum, *Story* Prescott Chaplin, *Producer* Albert J. Cohen, *Executive producer (unbilled)* Alan Ladd, *Associate* producer George C. Bertholon, *Art director* Jack Collis, *Set decorator* Frank M. Miller, *Photography* John Seitz, *Editor* Roland Gross, *Music* Raoul Kraushaar, *Sound* Robert B. Lee, *Makeup supervisor* Gordon Bau, *Costumes* Howard Shoup, *Dialogue supervisor* Henry Staudigl, *Assistant director* Russ Saunders.

Cast: *Mark Bradley* Jeff Richards, *Joe Walker* John Smith, *Dr. Paul Lujan* Alan Napier, *Venus Lujan* Venetia Stevenson, *Mercuria Lujan* June Blair, *Urana Lujan* Diane Jergens, *Pilot of passing plane* Bob Stratton, *Copilot* Tom Riley, *Dr. McBain of Australian AEC* Gavin Muir, *Garland* George Brand, *2nd pilot* Stan Sweet, *Copilot* Vern Taylor.

A Jaguar Production (Ladd Enterprises, Inc.) for Warner Bros.; black and white; 66 minutes. Released April 10, 1959.

It! The Terror from Beyond Space. *Director* Edward L. Cahn, *Screenplay* Jerome Bixby, *Producer* Robert E. Kent, *Art director* William Glasgow, *Set decorator* Herman Schoenbrun, *Photography* Kenneth Peach, Sr., *Editor* Grant Whytock, *Music* Paul Sawtell and Bert Shefter, *Sound* Al Overton, *Effects editor* Robert Carlisle, *Makeup* Lane Britton, *Monster suit design* Paul Blaisdell, *Wardrobe* Jack Masters, *Script supervisor* George Rutter, *Production supervisor* Ben Hersh, *Assistant director* Ralph E. Black, *Property master* Arthur Wasson.

Cast: *Col. Ed Carruthers* Marshall Thompson, *Ann Anderson* Shawn Smith, *Col. James Van Heusen* Kim Spalding, *Dr. Mary Royce* Ann Doran, *Dr. Eric Royce* Dabbs Greer, *Lt. James Calder* Paul Langton, *Maj. John Purdue* Robert Bice, *Gino Finelli* Richard Hervey, *Bob Finelli* Richard Benedict, *Joseph Kienholz* Thom Carney, *Martian* Ray "Crash" Corrigan.

Vogue Pictures, dst. United Artists; black and white; 68 minutes. Working titles: "It!"; "It! The Vampire from Outer Space," "It! The Vampire from Beyond Space." Released August 7, 1958. Double bill with: *Curse of the Faceless Man*.

Note: No actor/role names available for military personnel seen at beginning.

It's Hot in Paradise. *Director* Fritz Boettger,* *Producer* Gaston Hakim, *Executive producer* Wolfgang Hartwig, *Photography* Georg Kraus, *Music* Karl Bette and Willy Mattes, *Production manager* Ludwig Spitaler.

Cast: *Gary* Alex D'Arcy, *Also* Barbara Valentin, Harald Maresch, Helga Neuner, Helga Franck, Rainer Brandt, Dorothee Gloecklen, Eva Schauland, Gerry Hammer.

*Under rerelease title, direction of film is credited to Jamie Nolan; this may simply be a pseudonym for Boettger.

Rapid Film GmbH and Intercontinental film, U.S. dst. Pacemaker Pictures; black and white; 86 minutes (82 minutes in Germany). A West German film. Original title: **Ein Toter Hing im Netz** (A Corpse Hung in a Net). Alternate titles?: **The Spider's Web**, **Girls of Spider Island**, **Hot in Paradise**. U.S. release March 1962 (in Germany, 1960).

Note: This was reissued as **Horrors of Spider Island** later in the 1960s, cut to 75 minutes. Its double bill at that time was *The Fiendish Ghouls* (itself a retitling of *Mania*).

Journey to the Center of the Earth. *Director* Henry Levin, *Screenplay* Walter Reisch and Charles Brackett, *Producer* Charles Brackett, *Art directors* Lyle R. Wheeler, Franz Bachelin and Herman A. Blumenthal. *Set decorators* Walter M. Scott and Joseph Kish, *Photography* Leo Tover, *Camera operator* Irving Rosenberg, *Special photographic effects* L.B. Abbott, James B. Gordon and Emil Kosa, Jr., *Editors* Stuart Gilmore and Jack W. Holmes, *Score* Bernard Herrmann, *Song lyrics* Robert Burns and Sammy Cahn, *Music* James Van Heusen, *Music conductor* Lionel Newman, *Sound* Bernard Freericks and Warren B. Delaplain, *Recording supervisor* Carlton W. Faulkner, *Supervising sound editor* Walter Ross, *Makeup supervisor* Ben Nye, *Costumes* David Ffolkes, *Hairstyles* Helen Turpin, *Assistant director* Hal Herman, *Assistant to the producers* Bernard Schwartz, *Technical advisors* Lincoln Barnett and Peter Ronson, *Color consultant* Leonard Doss.

Cast: *Prof. Oliver Lindenbrook* James Mason, *Alec McEwen* Pat Boone, *Carla Goetaborg* Arlene Dahl, *Count Saknussemm* Thayer David, *Hans Bjelker* Peter Ronson, *Jenny* Diane Baker, *Saknussemm's groom(?)* Bob Adler, *Dean* Alan Napier, *Chancellor* Frederick Halliday, *Rector* Alan Caillou, *Prof. Peter Goetaborg* Ivan Triesault, *Groom* John Epper, *Laird of Glendarich* Peter Wright, *Housekeeper Kirstie* Molly Roden, *Shop-keeper* Owen McGivney, *Scot newsman* Kendrick Huxham, *Woman news vendor* Molly

Glessing, *Man and woman in Edinburgh* Thomas F. Martin and Myra Nelson, *English scientists* John Barclay, Peter Fontaine, John Ainsworth, *Proprietress* Edith Evanson, *Professor Bayle* Alex Finlayson, *Paisley* Ben Wright, *Kristy* Mary Brady.

20th Century–Fox; color; CinemaScope; 132 minutes. Based on the 1864 novel *Voyage au Centre de la Terre* by Jules Verne. Released December 17, 1959.

Journey to the Seventh Planet. *Producer/Director/Story* Sidney Pink, *Screenplay* Ib Melchior and (uncredited) Sidney Pink, *Associate producer* J.H. Zalabery, *Set dressing* Helge Hansen, *Architect* Otto Lund, *Scenemaster* Herbi Gartner, *Cameraman* Age Wiltrup, *Special effects camera* Ronny Schoemmel, *Miniatures* Krogh, *Abstracts* Børge Hamberg, *Main titles and Special effects* Bent Barfod Films, *Cutters* Tove Talsbo and Thok Sondergaard, *Music* Ib Glindemann, *Title song* Jerry Capehart and Mitchell Tableporter, *Sound* Paul Nyrup, *Makeup* Calma, *Wardrobe* Hanny Zalabery, *Production supervisor* Eric Moberg, *Assistant director* Szasza Zalabery, *Casting* William Schuller, *Montage director and Postproduction supervisor* Ib Melchior, *Cyclops Monster puppet built by* Jim Danforth and Wah Chang, *Animated by* Jim Danforth, *Other postproduction special effects* Project Unlimited.

Cast: *Capt. Don Graham* John Agar, *Cmdr. Eric Nilsson* Carl Ottosen, *Communications officer Barry O'Neill* Ove Sprogøe, *Chief engineer Svend Viltoft* Louis Miehe Renard, *Astrogator Lt. Cmdr. Karl Heinrich* Peter Monch, *Greta* Greta Thyssen, *Ingrid* Ann Smyrner, *Ursula* Mimi Heinrich, *Ellen* Annie Birgit Garden, *Lisa* Ulla Moritz, *Colleen* Bente Juel, *Title song sung by* Otto Brandenburg.

Cinemagic and Alta Vista for American International; color; 83 minutes. A U.S.–Danish coproduction? Released December 1961. This includes scenes from *The Angry Red Planet* and *Earth vs. the Spider*.

Jungle Boy. *Director/Producer/Screenplay* Norman A. Cerf, *Executive producer* J. Manning Post, *Photography* Gilbert Warrenton, *Music* Nicholas Carras.

Cast: *Sabu* Sabu, *Dr. Pam Ames* K.T. Stevens, *Dr. Paul Morrison* David Bruce, *Mr. Trosk* George E. Stone, *Shan-Kar* Maji, *Kumar* Robert Cabal.

Taj Mahal Productions, TV distributor Medallion; black and white; 85 minutes. Episodes of unsold Sabu TV series edited together as feature. Alternate title: **Jungle Hell.** Released 1955?

The Killer Shrews. *Director/Special effects* Ray Kellogg, *Screenplay* Jay Simms, *Producer* Ken Curtis, *Executive producer* Gordon McLendon, *Art director* Louis Caldwell, *Set decorator* Louise Caldwell, *Photography* Wilfrid M. Cline, *Camera operators* Harry A. Kokojan and George Gordon Nogle, *Camera assistants* William John Renaldi and Harry L. Gianneschi; *Editor* Aarn Stell, *Music* Harry Bluestone and Emil Cadkin, *Music supervisor* Harry Bluestone, *Sound* Earl Snyder, *Sound effects* Milton Citron, *Music editor* Gil Marchant, *Makeup* Corinne Daniel, *Script supervisor* Audrey Blasdell, *Production manager* Ben Chapman, *Assistant director* Edward Haldeman.

Cast: *Thomas Sherman* James Best, *Ann Craigis* Ingrid Goude, *Dr. Milo Craigis* Baruch Lumet, *Jerry Farrell** Ken Curtis, *Dr. Radford Baines* Gordon McLendon, *Mario* Alfred DeSoto, *Rook (Griswold)* J.H. "Judge" DuPree.

*Jerry Lacey in some sources, Jerry Farrell in film.

Hollywood Pictures Corp., dst. McLendon Radio Pictures; black and white; 69 minutes. Released December 18, 1959 (Los Angeles release; perhaps as early as summer 1959 in other areas). Double bill with: *The Giant Gila Monster.*

Kiss Me Deadly. *Director/Producer* Robert Aldrich, *Screenplay* A.I. Bezzerides, *Executive producer* Victor Saville, *Art director* William Glasgow, *Set decorator* Howard Bristol, *Photography* Ernest Laszlo, *Editor* Michael Luciano, *Music* Frank DeVol, *Orchestrations* Albert Harris, *Sound* Jack Solomon, *Makeup* Bob Schiffer, *Production supervisor* Jack R. Berne, *Assistant director* Robert Justman, *Assistant to the producer* Robert Sherman.

Cast: *Mike Hammer* Ralph Meeker, *Lily Carver* Gaby (Gabriele) Rodgers, *Velda* Maxine Cooper, *Dr. Soberin* Albert Dekker, *Christina Bailey (Berga Torn)* Cloris Leachman, *Pat Chambers* Wesley Addy, *Nick* Nick Dennis, *Carl Evello* Paul Stewart, *Eddie Yaeger* Juano Hernandez, *Friday Evello* Marian Carr, *Sugar Smallhouse* Jack Lambert, *Charlie Max* Jack Elam, *Sammy* Jerry Zinneman, *Girl at pool* Leigh Snowden,

Dr. Doug Kennedy Percy Helton, Nightclub singer Madi Comfort, Carmen Trivaco Fortunio Bonanova, Super James McCallian, Old mover Silvio Minciotti, FBI men Robert Cornthwaite and James Seay, Nurse Mara McAfee, Ray Diker Mort Marshall, Mrs. Super Jesslyn Fax, Harvey Wallace (truck driver) Strother Martin, Hood with knife Paul Richards, Radio announcers Ben Morris, Sam Balter and Joe Hernandez, Hotel manager Marjorie Bennett, Kit Kitty White, Bartender Art Loggins, Gas station man Robert Sherman, Athletic club clerk Keith McConnell, Sideman Eddie Real, Title song sung by Nat King Cole and Kitty White.

Parklane Pictures, Inc., dst. United Artists; black and white; 105 minutes. Based on the novel of the same name by Mickey Spillane. Released May 18, 1955.

Konga. Director John Lemont, Screenplay Aben Kandel and Herman Cohen, Executive producer Herman Cohen, Associate producer Jim O'Connolly, Art director Wilfred Arnold, Photography Desmond Dickinson, Camera operator Harry Gillam, Editor Jack Slade, Music Gerard Schurmann, Music director Muir Mathieson, Sound Sidney Rider and Ronald Abbott, Sound effects editor Derek Holding, Makeup Jack Craig, Wardrobe Bridget Sellers, Hairdresser Daphne Vollmer, Continuity Olga Brook, Production manager Bill Shore, Assistant director Buddy Booth.

Cast: Dr. Charles Decker Michael Gough, Margaret Margo Johns, Sandra Banks Claire Gordon, Bob Kenton Jess Conrad, Dean Foster Austin Trevor, Superintendent Brown Jack Watson, Professor Tagore George Pastell, Bob's mother Vanda Godsell, Inspector Lawson Stanley Morgan, Miss Barnesdell Grace Arnold, Bob's father Leonard Sachs, Daniel Nicholson Benton, Mary Kim Tracy, Eric Rupert Osborne, Janet Waveney Lee, Commissioner Garland John Welsh, Konga Sam Sylvano.*

*A note in the AFI catalog implies that Sam Sylvano is the name of the adult chimpanzee playing Konga, but it is probably the stuntman's name.

Herman Cohen–Merton Park Studios for American International; color; 90 minutes. A U.S.–British coproduction. Released March 22, 1961 in U.S. (January 1961 in Britain). Copyright claimed by Alta Vista Productions.

Last Woman on Earth. Director/Producer Roger Corman, Screenplay Robert Towne, Associate producer Charles Hannawalt, Art director Daniel Haller, Photography Jacques Marquette, Editor Anthony Carras, Sound(?) Roberto Velasquez, Sound recording Beach Dickerson, Property master Stanley Watson, Location supervisor Kinta Zertuche, Production manager Jack Bohrer, Boom operator Robert Bean.

Cast: Harold Antony Carbone, Evelyn Betsy Jones-Moreland, Martin Joyce Edward Wain (Robert Towne).

Filmgroup; color; Vistascope; 71 minutes. Released fall, 1960. May have been planned as a double bill with The Little Shop of Horrors.

The Leech Woman. Director Edward Dein, Screenplay David Duncan, Story Ben Pivar and Francis Rosenwald, Producer Joseph Gershenson, Art directors Robert Clatworthy and Alexander Golitzen, Set decorators Clarence Steensen and Russell A. Gausman, Photography Ellis W. Carter, Editor Milton Carruth, Music Irving Gertz and Henry Vars, Music supervision Milton Rosen, Sound Leslie I. Carey and Joe Lapis, Makeup department head Bud Westmore, Costumes Bill Thomas, Hairstyles Larry Germain, Assistant director Joe Kenny.

Cast: June Talbot Coleen Gray, Neil Foster Grant Williams, Dr. Paul Talbot Phillip Terry, Sally Howard Gloria Talbott, Bertram Garvay John Van Dreelen, Malla (old) Estelle Hemsley, Malla (young) Kim Hamilton, Jerry Lando Arthur Batanides, Drunk Murray Alper, Vice officer John Bryant, Superior officer Charles Keane, Detective Harold Goodwin, Head warrior Paul Thompson.

Universal-International; black and white; 77 minutes. Working title: "The Leech." Released May 20, 1960. Double bill with: Brides of Dracula.

The Little Shop of Horrors. Producer/Director Roger Corman, Screenplay Charles B. Griffith, Art director Daniel Haller, Photography Archie Dalzell, Editor Marshall Neilan, Jr., Music Fred Katz, Sound recording Phillip Mitchell, Makeup Harry Thomas, Assistant director Richard Dixon, Property master Carl Brainard.

Cast: Seymour Krelboined Jonathan Haze, Audrey Fulquard Jackie Joseph, Gravis Mushnick* Mel Welles, Burson Fouch Dick Miller, Winifred Krelboined Myrtle Vail,

Siddie Shiva Leola Wendorff, *Wilbur Force* Jack Nicholson, *Dr. Phoebus Farb* John Shaner, *Leonora Clyde* Meri Welles, *Joe Fink* Wally Campo, *Frank Stoolie* Jack Warford, *Mrs. Fishtwanger* Lynn Storey, *Teenage girls* Tammy Windsor and Toby Michaels, *Waitress* Dodie Drake, *Kloy Haddock (holdup man)* Charles B. Griffith, *Drunk at dentist's* Jack Griffith, *Screaming patient* Charles B. Griffith, *Voice of Audrey Junior* Charles B. Griffith.
*It's Mushnick on shop sign, Mushnik in end credits.

Filmgroup; black and white; 70 minutes. Working title: "The Passionate People Eater." Released April 21, 1961, says *Film Daily Yearbook*, but it was in release as early as October 1960. Double bill with: *Black Sunday*; may have been planned as a double bill with *Last Woman on Earth*.

The Lost Missile. *Director/Story* Lester William Berke, *Screenplay* John McPartland and Jerome Bixby, *Producer* Lee Gordon, *Executive producer* William Berke, *Art director* William Ferrari, *Photography* Kenneth Peach, *Editor* Everett Sutherland, *Music* Gerald Fried, *Set decorator* Charles Thompson, *Sound* Jack Solomon, *Sound editor* Anthony Carras, *Music editor* George Brand, *Makeup* Alan Snyder, *Wardrobe* Jerry Bos, *Special photographic effects* Jack R. Glass.

Cast: *Dr. David Loring* Robert Loggia, *Joan Woods* Ellen Parker, *Joe Freed* Phillip Pine, *General Barr* Larry Kerr, *Ella Freed* Marilee Earle, *TV personality* Fred Engleberg, *Ella's mother* Kitty Kelly, *Secretary of State* Selmer Jackson, *Young Joe* Hyams, *Bradley* Bill Bradley, *Narrator* Lawrence Dobkin, *Also* Shirley Shawn, J. Anthony Hughes, Robert Busch, Jack Holland, John McNamara, Mike Steele, Cecil Elliott, Don Pethley, Myron Cook, Mark Dunhill.

William Berke Prods., dst. United Artists; black and white, 71 minutes. A U.S.–Canadian coproduction(?). Released December 10, 1958.

Lost Planet Airmen. *Director* Fred C. Brannon, *Screenplay* Royal Cole, William Livey and Sol Shor, *Producer* Franklin Adreon, *Art director* Fred A. Ritter, *Set decorators* John McCarthy, Jr. and James Redd, *Photography* Ellis W. Carter, *Special effects* Howard and Theodore Lydecker, *Optical effects* Consolidated Film Industries, *Editors* Cliff Bell and Sam Starr, *Music* Stanley Wilson, *Sound* Earl Crain, Sr., *Makeup supervision* Bob Mark, *Unit manager* Roy Wade.

Cast: *Jeff King/Rocket Man* Tristram Coffin, *Glenda Thomas* Mae Clarke, *Professor Bryant/Dr. Vulcan I.* Stanford Jolley, *Professor Millard* James Craven, *Tony Dirken* Don Haggerty, *Burt Winslow* House Peters, Jr., *Chairman* Douglas Evans, *Martin Conway* Ted Adams, *Gunther Von Strum* Stanley Price, *Martin* Dale Van Sickel, *Knox* Tom Steele, *Blears* David Sharpe, *Rowan* Eddie Parker, *Turk* Michael Ferro, *Guard* Frank O'Connor, *Phillips* Buddy Roosevelt, *Clerk* Arvon Dale, *Walter* Jack O'Shea, *Graffner* Marshall Bradford. **Note:** Full serial cast: some actors may not be in feature condensation.

Republic Pictures; black and white; 65 minutes. Released 1951. This is a condensed . feature version of the serial *King of the Rocket Men*, released 1949.

The Lost World. *Director/Producer* Irwin Allen, *Screenplay* Irwin Allen and Charles Bennett, *Art directors* Duncan Cramer and Walter M. Simonds, *Set decorators* Walter M. Scott, Joseph Kish and John Sturtevant, *Production illustrator* Maurice Zuberano, *Photography* Winton Hoch, *Special photographic effects* L.B. Abbott, *Matte artist* Emil Kosa, *Effects cinematographer* James B. Gordon, *Effects technician* Willis O'Brien, *Editor* Hugh S. Fowler, *Music* Bert Shefter and Paul Sawtell, *Orchestrations* Howard Jackson and Sid Cuttner, *Sound mixer* E. Clayton Ward, *Rerecording* Harry M. Leonard, *Sound effects editor* Walter A. Rossi, *Makeup department head* Ben Nye, *Costumes* Paul Zastupnevich, *Hairstyles* Helen Turpin, *Assistant director* Ad Schaumer, *Technical adviser* Henry E. Lester, *Color consultant* Leonard Doss.

Cast: *Prof. George Edward Challenger* Claude Rains, *Lord John Roxton* Michael Rennie, *Ed Malone* David Hedison, *Jennifer Holmes* Jill St. John, *Gomez* Fernando Lamas, *Prof. Walter Summerlee* Richard Haydn, *David Holmes* Ray Stricklyn, *Costa* Jay Novello, *Native girl* Vitina Marcus, *Burton White* Ian Wolfe, *Stuart Holmes* John Graham, *Professor Waldron* Colin Campbell, *Indian chief* Larry Chance, *American TV announcer* Don Forbes, *British members (of Explorers' Club?)* Phyllis Cohlan, Jacqueline Squire, Brian Roper, Ivo Henderson, *French member* Fred Cavens, *Italian member* Ruggero Romar, *German member* Alexander de Naszody, *Other members* Ann Dore and Paul Kremin, *Airline hostess* Jodi Desmond, *Airport attendants* Ross Brown and Peter Fontaine, *Reporters* Gil Stuart, George Pelling, Alex Finlayson, *BBC TV commentator* Ben Wright.

Saratoga Productions, Inc. for 20th Century–Fox; color; CinemaScope; 97 minutes. Based on the novel of the same name by Arthur Conan Doyle. Released July 1, 1960.

Magic Spectacles. *Director* Bob Wehling, *Screenplay/Producer* Arch Hall, Sr., *Photography* Vilis Lapenieks, *Editor* Alex Grasshoff, *Presented by* Fred W. Krueger.

Cast: *Dr. Paul Ner De Nude/Angus L. Farnsworth* Tommy Holden, *Myra Farnsworth* Marilyn Brechtel, *Secretary* Margo Mehling, *The Go Go Go Go Girls* Kay Cramer, Cindy Tyler, Danice Daniels, Jean Cartwright and Carla Olson, *Also* June Parr.*

*AFI says sources disagree in crediting role of Myra; the *Hollywood Citizen-News* says Myra was played by "June Pari."

Dst. Fairway International Films; color; 74 minutes. Released June 23, 1961. Rereleased in 1964 as **Tickled Pink**.

Man in the Moon. *Director* Basil Dearden, *Screenplay* Michael Relph and Bryan Forbes, *Producer* Michael Relph, *Production design* Don Ashton, *Art director* Jack Maxsted, *Set dresser* Peter Murton, *Draughtsman* Elven Webb, *Photography* Harry Waxman, *Camera operator* H.A.R. Thomson, *Focus puller* Steve Claydon, *Camera grip* Ted Underwood, *2nd unit director* Norman Harrison, *Editor* John D. Guthridge, *Assistant film editor* Vera Dover, *Music* Philip Green, *Sound editor* Norman Savage, *Sound recording* C.C. Stevens and Bill Daniels, *Sound camera operators* Roy Charman and Ted Karnon, *Boom operator* Gus Lloyd, *Makeup* William Partleton and John Webber, *Dress design* Anthony Mendleson, *Hairdresser* Pearl Orton, *Continuity* Joan Davis, *Production manager* Jack Swinburne, *Assistant directors* Bert Batt, Denzil Lewis and Ronald Purdie, *Chief floor props* Mark Rowe, *Prop buyer* Jim Baker, *Production secretary* Jean Hall, *Technical adviser* Cmdr. Herbert Ellis, *Still photography* Ian Jeayes, *Chief electrician* Harry Black.

Cast: *William Blood* Kenneth More, *Polly* Shirley Anne Field, *Herbert* Norman Bird, *Dr. Davidson* Michael Hordern, *Dr. Wilmot* John Glyn-Jones, *Professor Stephens* John Phillips, *Leo* Charles Gray, *Rex* Bernard Horsfall, *Roy* Bruce Boa, *Prosecutor* Noel Purcell, *Storekeeper* Ed Devereaux, *Dr. Hollis* Newton Blick, *Doctors* Richard Pearson and Lionel Gamlin, *Woomera director* Russell Waters, *Lorry driver* Danny Green, *Jaguar driver* Jeremy Lloyd.

Excalibur Films for Allied Film Makers, U.S. dst. Trans-Lux Distributing Corporation; black and white; 98 minutes. A British film. U.S. release June 12, 1961 (November 1960, Britain).

The Man Who Could Cheat Death. *Director* Terence Fisher, *Screenplay* Jimmy Sangster, *Producer* Anthony Hinds, *Executive producer* Michael Carreras, *Associate producer* Anthony Nelson Keys, *Production design* Bernard Robinson, *Photography* Jack Asher, *Camera operator* Len Harris, *Supervising editor* James Needs, *Editor* John Dunsford, *Music* Richard Bennet, *Musical supervisor* John Hollingsworth, *Sound recordist* Jock May, *Makeup* Roy Ashton, *Wardrobe* Molly Arbuthnot, *Hairstyles* Henry Montsash, *Production manager* Don Weeks, *Assistant director* John Peverall.

Cast: *Dr. Georges Bonner* Anton Diffring, *Janine Dubois* Hazel Court, *Dr. Pierre Gerard* Christopher Lee, *Prof. Ludwig Weisz* Arnold Marle, *Margo Phillips* Delphi Lawrence, *Inspector Legris* Francis De Wolff, *Street girl* Gerda Larsen.

Hammer Films, U.S. dst. Paramount Pictures; color; 83 minutes. Based on the play "The Man in Half Moon Street" by Barré Lyndon. A British film. Released June 23, 1959 in U.S. (also June in Britain).

The Man Without a Body. *Directors* W. Lee Wilder and Charles Saunders, *Screenplay* William Grote, *Producer* Guido Coen, *Art director* Harry White, *Photography* Brandon Stafford, *Camera operator* Tony Heller, *Editor* Tom Simpson, *Music* Robert Elms, *Sound recordist* Cyrill(?) Collick, *Makeup* Jim Hydes, *Hairstyles* Ivy Emerton, *Continuity* Splinters Deason, *Production manager* John "Pinky" Green, *Assistant director* William Lang.

Cast: *Karl Brussard* George Coulouris, *Dr. Phil Merritt* Robert Hutton, *Nostradamus* Michael Golden, *Jean Kramer* Julia Arnall, *Odette Vernet* Nadja Regin, *Dr. Lew Waldenhouse* Sheldon Lawrence, *Leslie* Peter Copley, *Dr. Alexander* Norman Shelley, *Dr. Charot* William Sherwood, *Dr. Brandon* Tony Quinn, *Guide at Madame Tussaud's*

Stanley van Beers, *Chauffeur* Maurice Kaufman, *Publican* Edwin Ellis, *Stockbroker* Donald Morley, *Detective* Frank Forsyth, *Maid* Kim Parker, *Customs officer* Ernest Bale.

A Filmplays Picture, U.S. dst. Budd Rogers; black and white; 80 minutes. A British film. U.S. release 1959 (British release 1957).

The Manchurian Candidate. *Director* John Frankenheimer, *Screenplay* George Axelrod and John Frankenheimer (latter unbilled), *Producers* George Axelrod and John Frankenheimer, *Executive producer* Howard W. Koch, *Production designer* Richard Sylbert, *Set decorator* George R. Nelson, *Assistant art director* Philip M. Jefferies, *Draftsmen* Lucius O. Croxton, Seymour Klate, John M. Elliott and Joseph S. Toldy, *Photography* Lionel Lindon, *Operative cameraman* John Mehl, *Assistant cameramen* Felix Barlow and Eugene Levitt, *Special effects* Paul Pollard, *Photographic effects* Howard A. Anderson Company, *Editor* Ferris Webster, *Assistant film editor* Carl Mahanian, *Music* David Amram, *Sound mixer* Joe Edmondson, *Sound effects editor* Del Harris, *Music editor* Richard Carruth, *Re-recording* Buddy Myers, *Music recording* Vinton Vernon, *Sound recorder* Paul Wolfe, *Boom operator* William Flannery, *Makeup* Bernard Ponedel, Jack Freeman, Ron Berkeley and Dorothy Parkinson, *Costume designer* Moss Mabry, *Janet Leigh's hairstyles* Gene Shacove, *Hairstyles* Mary Westmoreland, *Men's costumers* Morris Brown and Ronald Talsky, *Women's costumers* Angela Alexander and Rose Veebeck, *Dialogue coach* Thom Conroy, *Script supervisors* Molly Kent, Grace Dubray and Amelia Wade, *Executive production manager* Gilbert Kurland, *Production assistant* Gene Martell, *Property master* Arden Cripe, *Property man* Richard M. Rubin, *Assistant director* Joseph Behn, *2nd assistant directors* David Salven and Read Kilgore, *Still photographer* Bill Creamer, *Gaffer* Robert Campbell, *Key grip* Richard Borland, *Best boy grip* Gaylin Schultz.

Cast: *Bennett Marco* Frank Sinatra, *Raymond Shaw* Laurence Harvey, *Raymond's mother* Angela Lansbury, *Sen. John Dierkes Iselin* James Gregory, *Yen Lo* Khigh Dhiegh, *Eugené Rose Chaney (Rosie)* Janet Leigh, *Jocie Jordan* Leslie Parrish, *Sen. Thomas Jordan* John McGiver, *Chunjin* Henry Silva, *Cpl. Al Melvin* James Edwards, *Colonel* Douglas Henderson, *Zilkov* Albert Paulsen, *Berezovo (lady counterpart)* Madame Spivy, *Berezovo (himself)* Nick Bolin, *Secretary of Defense* Barry Kelly, *Psychiatrist* Joe Adams, *Holborn Gaines* Lloyd Corrigan, *Medical officer* Whit Bissell, *Melvin's wife* Mimi Dillard, *Officer* Anton van Stralen, *Gossfeld* John Laurence, *Silvers* Nicky Blair, *Bobby Lembeck* Tom Lowell, *Ed Mavole* Richard LaPore, *Freeman* Irving Steinberg, *Hiken* John Francis, *Little* William Thourlby, *Nominee* Robert Riordan, *Gomel* Reggie Nalder, *Gomel (lady counterpart)* Bess Flowers, *Miss Gertrude* Miyoshi Jingu, *Korean girl* Anna Shin, *Chairladies* Helen Kleeb and Maye Henderson, *Reporters* Mickey Finn, Richard Norris, Johnny Indrisano, *Manager* Lou Krugg, *FBI men* Mike Masters, Tom Harris, *Soprano* Mariquita Moll, *Convention chairman* Robert Burton, *Secretary* Karen Norris, *Nurse* Jean Vaughn, *Policeman* Ray Spikers, *Jilly* Merritt Bohn, *Photographer* Frank Basso, *General* Harry Holcomb, *Guests at party* Julie Payne, Lana Crawford, Evelyn Byrd, *Page boy* Ray Dailey, *Women in hotel lobby* Estelle Etterre, Mary Benoit, Rita Kenaston, Maggie Hathaway, Joan Douglas, Frances Nealy, Evelyn Byrd, *Men in hotel lobby* Ralph Gambina, Sam "Kid" Hogan, *Chinese gentlemen in hotel lobby* James Yagi, Lee Tung Foo, Raynum Tsukamoto.

M.C. Productions and Essex Productions, dst. United Artists; black and white; 126 minutes. Based on the 1959 novel of the same name by Richard Condon. Released October 24, 1962.

The Manster. *Directors* George P. Breakston and Kenneth G. Crane, *Screenplay* Walter J. Sheldon, *Story/Producer* George P. Breakston, *Associate producers* Robert Perkins and Ryukichi Aimono, *Art director* Nobori Miyakuni, *Photography* David Mason, *Editor* Kenneth G. Crane, *Music* Hirooki Ogawa, *Sound recording* Senri Ohta.

Cast: *Larry Stanford* Peter Dyneley, *Linda Stanford* Jane Hylton, *Dr. Suzuki* Satoshi Nakamura, *Tara* Terri Zimmern, *Emiko* Tohoko Takechi, *Superintendent Aida* Jerry Ito, *Ian Matthews* Norman Van Hawley, *Jennsen* Alan Tarlton.

United Artists of Japan–George P. Breakston Enterprises, U.S. dst. Lopert Pictures (United Artists); black and white; 72 minutes. A Japanese–U.S. coproduction. British title: **The Split**. Working title: "Nightmare." Released March 28, 1962. Double bill with: *The Horror Chamber of Dr. Faustus*.

Note: The *Monthly Film Bulletin* gives a production date of 1959.

Master of the World. *Director* William Witney, *Screenplay* Richard Matheson, *Producer* James H. Nicholson, *Coproducer* Anthony Carras, *Executive producer* Samuel Z. Arkoff, *Associate producers* Bartlett A. Carré and Daniel Haller, *Production designer* Daniel Haller, *Construction coordinator* Ross Hahn, *Set decorator* Harry Reif, *Photography* Gilbert Warrenton, *Aerial photography* Kay Norton, *Photographic effects* Butler-Glouner, Inc. and Ray Mercer and Company, *Special miniature effects* Tim Baar, Wah Chang, Gene Warren and Marcel Delgado, *Special props and Mechanical effects* Pat Dinga, *Editor* Anthony Carras, *Music* Les Baxter, *Music coordinator* Al Simms, *Orchestrations* Albert Harris, *Sound mixer* Karl Zint, *Music recording* Vinton Vernon, *Music editor* Eve Newman, *Rerecording mixer* Jerry Alexander, *Boom operator* Bill Warmarth, *Sound editor* Alfred R. Bird, *Makeup* Fred Phillips, *Wardrobe* Marjorie Corso, *Property master* Dick Rubin, *Special color processes* Modern Film Effects, *Assistant director* Robert Agnew, *Production assistant* Jack Cash.

Cast: *Robur* Vincent Price, *Strock* Charles Bronson, *Prudent* Henry Hull, *Dorothy* Mary Webster, *Philip* David Frankham, *Alistair* Richard Harrison, *Topage (cook)* Vito Scotti, *Turner* Wally Campo, *Weaver* Steve Masino, *Shanks* Ken Terrell, *Wilson* Peter Besbas.

An Alta Vista Production for American International; color; 104 minutes. Based (loosely) on the 1886 novel *Robur le Conquérant* and the 1904 novel *Maître du Monde* by Jules Verne. Released May 31, 1961.

Missile Monsters. *Director* Fred C. Brannon, *Screenplay* Ronald Davidson, *Producer* Franklin Adreon, *Art director* Fred A. Ritter, *Set decorators* John McCarthy, Jr. and James Redd, *Photography* Walter Strenge, *Special effects* Howard and Theodore Lydecker, *Editors* Cliff Bell and Sam Starr, *Music* Stanley Wilson, *Sound* Earl Crain, Sr., *Makeup* Bob Mark, *Costume supervision* Adele Palmer and Robert Ramsey, *Hairstyles* Peggy Gray, *Unit manager* Roy Wade.

Cast: *Kent Fowler* Walter Reed, *Helen Hall* Lois Collier, *Mota* Gregory Gay, *Dr. Bryant* James Craven, *Drake* Harry Lauter, *Ryan* Richard Irving, *Steve* Sandy Sanders, *Trent* Michael Carr, *Watchman* Dale Van Sickel, *Taylor* Tom Steele, *Gateman* George Sherwood, *Grady* Jimmy O'Gatty, *Curtis* John DeSimone, *Crane* Lester Dorr, *Kirk* Dick Cogan. **Note:** The following cast members are confirmed for the full serial only, and may not appear in this feature condensation. *Lewis Ashe* Clayton Moore, *Bill* Dick Crockett, *Boyd* John Daheim, *Cole* Bill Wilkus, *Driver* Chuck Hamilton, *Ed* Saul (Sol) Gorss, *Garrett* Barry Brooks, *Graves* Ken Terrell, *Hagen* Carey Loftin, *Technicians* David Sharpe and Paul Gustine, *Workman* Guy Teague.

Republic; black and white; 74 minutes. Released November 12, 1958. Double bill with: *Satan's Satellites*.

Note: This is a condensed version of the December 1951 serial *Flying Disc Man from Mars*.

Missile to the Moon. *Director* Richard Cunha, *Screenplay* H.E. Barrie and Vincent Fotre, *Producer* Marc Frederic, *Art direction* Sham Unlimited, *Set decorator* Harry Reif, *Photography* Meredith Nicholson, *Camera operator* Robert Wyckoff, *Special effects* Ira Anderson, *Visual effects (Rock Men)* Harold Banks, *Editor* Everett Dodd, *Music* Nicholas Carras, *Sound mixer* Robert Post, *Sound effects* Harold Wooley, *Makeup* Harry Thomas, *Costumes* Marjorie Corso, *Hairstyles* Gail McGarry, *Production manager* Ralph Brooke, *Assistant director* Leonard J. Shapiro, *Key grip* Grant Tucker, *Chief electrician* Frank Leonetti, *Property master* George Bahr, *Script supervisor* Diana Loomis.

Cast: *Steve Dayton** Richard Travis, *Gary Fennell* Tommy Cook, *June Saxton* Cathy Downs, *Lon* Gary Clarke, *The Lido* K.T. Stevens, *Dirk Green* Michael Whalen, *Alpha* Nina Bara, *Zeema* Marjorie Hellen, *Lambda* Laurie Mitchell, *Colonel Wicker (sheriff?)* Henry Hunter, *Sheriff (Colonel Wicker?)* Lee Roberts, *Moon Women (International Beauty Contest Winners) Florida* Sandra Wirth, *New Hampshire* Pat Mowry, *Yugoslavia* Tania Velia, *New York* Sanita Pelkey, *France* Lisa Simone, *Illinois* Marianne Gaba, *Germany* Renata Hoy, *Minnesota* Mary Ford.

*Most sources give this role name as Arnold Dayton, but in the film he is called only Steve Dayton.

A Marc Frederic–George Foley Production for Astor Pictures; black and white; 78 minutes. Remake of *Cat-Women of the Moon* (1953). Released October 1958. Double bill with: *Frankenstein's Daughter*.

The Monster from Green Hell. *Director/Editor* Kenneth G. Crane, *Screenplay* Louis Vittes and Endre Bohen, *Producer* Al Zimbalist, *Executive producers* Jack J. Gross and Philip N. Krasne, *Associate producer* Sol Dolgin, *Production design* Ernst Fegté, *Art director* John Greenwald, *Set decorator* G.W. Gerntsen, *Photography* Ray Flin, *Special photographic effects* Jack Rabin, Louis DeWitt and Irving Block, *Stop-motion animation* Gene Warren, *Special effects* Jess Davison, *Music* Albert Glasser, *Sound (Robert W. Roderick)* Stanley Cooley, *Makeup* Louis Haszillo, *Wardrobe* Joe Dimmitt, *Sound editor* Charles Diltz, *Music editor* Robert Post, *Script supervisor* Doris Moody, *Property master* Robert Benton, *Production manager* Byron Roberts.

Cast: *Quent Brady* Jim Davis, *Dan Morgan* Robert E. Griffin, *Lorna Lorentz* Barbara Turner, *Mahri* Eduardo Ciannelli, *Dr. Lorentz* Vladimir Sokoloff, *Arobi* Joel Fluellen, *Kuana* LaVerne Jones, *Territorial agent* Tim Huntley, *Radar operator* Frederic Potler.

A Gross-Krasne Production, dst. Distributors Corporation of America (DCA); black and white with tinted sequence; 71 minutes. Working titles?: "Creature from Green Hell," "Beast from Green Hell." Released December 12, 1958. Double bill with: *Half Human*.

Note: One source says Paul Blaisdell designed the giant wasps.

The Monster of Piedras Blancas. *Director* Irvin Berwick, *Producer/Builder of monster suit* Jack Kevan, *Screenplay* C. Haile Chace, *Story* Jack Kevan and Irvin Berwick, *Photography* Philip Lathrop, *Editor* George Gittens, *Sound mixer* Joseph Lapis, *Recorder* James V. Swartz, *Script supervisor* Luanna Sherman, *Master of properties* Roy E. Keys, *Production manager* Ben Chapman, *Assistant director* Joseph Cavallier, *Chief electrician* Thomas Ouellette, *Set operations* Walter Woodworth.

Cast: *Sturges* John Harmon, *Doc Jorgenson* Les Tremayne, *Sheriff George Matson* Forrest Lewis, *Lucy Sturges* Jeanne Carmen, *Fred* Don Sullivan, *Storekeeper Kochek* Frank Arvidson, *Jimmy* Wayne Berwick, *Mike* Joseph La Cava, *Eddie/Monster of Piedras Blancas* Pete Dunn.

A VanWick Production, dst. Filmservice Distributing Corporation; black and white; 72 minutes. Floating release, 1958.

Monster on the Campus. *Director* Jack Arnold, *Screenplay* David Duncan, *Producer/ Music supervision* Joseph Gershenson, *Art director* Alexander Golitzen, *Set decorators* Russell A. Gausman and Julia Heron, *Photography* Russell Metty, *Special effects* Clifford Stine, *Editor* Ted Kent, *Sound* Leslie I. Carey and Joe Lapis, *Makeup department head* Bud Westmore, *Makeup design(?)* Millicent Patrick, *Costumes* Bill Thomas, *Assistant directors* Marshall Green and Jimmie Welch.

Cast: *Dr. Donald Blake* Arthur Franz, *Madeline Howard* Joanna Moore, *Lt. Mike Stevens* Judson Pratt, *Molly Riordan* Helen Westcott, *Gilbert Howard* Alexander Lockwood, *Jimmy Flanders* Troy Donahue, *Sylvia Lockwood* Nancy Walters, *Sergeant Powell* Phil Harvey, *Dr. Oliver Cole* Whit Bissell, *Sgt. Eddie Daniels* Ross Elliott, *Tom Edwards* Richard Cutting, *Night watchman* Hank Patterson, *Students* Anne Anderson, Ronnie Rondell, Jr., Louis Cavalier.

Universal-International; black and white. 77 minutes. 16mm title: **Stranger on the Campus.** Working title: "Monster in the Night." Released October 22, 1958 (FDY). Double bill with: *Blood of the Vampire*.

Moon Pilot. *Director* James Neilson, *Screenplay* Maurice Tombragel, *Executive producer /Presenter* Walt Disney, *Coproducer* Bill Anderson, *Associate producer* Ron Miller, *Art directors* Carroll Clark and Marvin Aubrey Davis, *Set decorators* Emile Kuri and William Stevens, *Photography* William Snyder, *Special effects* Eustace Lycett, *Editor* Irvin "Cotton" Warburton, *Music* Paul Smith, *Orchestrations* Joseph Oroop, *Songs* Richard M. Sherman and Robert B. Sherman, *Sound supervisor* Robert O. Cook, *Sound mixer* Harry M. Lindgren, *Music editor* Evelyn Kennedy, *Makeup* Pat McNalley, *Costume design* Bill Thomas, *Costumes* Chuck Keehne and Gertrude Casey, *Hairstyles* Ruth Sandifer, *Assistant director* Joseph L. McEveety.

Cast: *Capt. Richmond Talbot* Tom Tryon, *Lyrae* Dany Saval, *Maj.-Gen. John Vanneman* Brian Keith, *McClosky* Edmond O'Brien, *Walter Talbot* Tommy Kirk, *Senator McGuire* Bob Sweeney, *Secretary of the Air Force* Kent Smith, *Medical officer* Simon Scott, *Agent Brown* Bert Remsen, *Mrs. Celia Talbot* Sarah Selby, *Colonel Briggs* Dick Wittinghill, *Charlie (chimp)* Cheetah, *Nutritionist* Nancy Kulp, *Air Force officer* Bob

Hastings, *Fat woman in lineup* Muriel Landers, *Also* William Hudson, Robert Brubaker.
A Walt Disney Production released by Buena Vista; color; 98 minutes. Based on the magazine serial of the same name by Robert Buckner. Released April 5, 1962.

Most Dangerous Man Alive. *Director* Allan Dwan, *Screenplay* James Leicester and Phillip Rock, *Story* Phillip Rock and Michael Pate, *Producer* Benedict Bogeaus, *Photography* Carl Carvahal, *Editor* Carlos Lodato, *Music* Louis Forbes, *Sound editor* Joe Kavigan, *Wardrobe* Gwen Wakeling, *Production supervisor* Charlence Eurist.

    Cast: *Eddie Candell* Ron Randell, *Carla Angelo* Elaine Stewart, *Linda Marlow* Debra Paget, *Andy Damon* Anthony Caruso, *Lieutenant Fisher* Gregg Palmer, *Captain Davis* Morris Ankrum, *Dr. Meeker* Tudor Owen, *Devola* Steve Mitchell, *Franscetti* Joel Donte.

    Trans-Global Films, dst. Columbia Pictures; black and white; 82 minutes. Released June 28, 1961.

    Note: Some sources say this was based on the story "The Steel Monster" by Phillip Rock and Michael Pate, but that is probably the title of a screen treatment rather than a published story. According to an interview with the director, this seems to have had some Mexican financing, making it a U.S.–Mexican coproduction. Michael Hayes says that this is also indicated by details in the credits.

Mothra. *Director* Inoshiro Honda, *Screenplay* Shinichi Sekizawa, *Story* Shinichiro Nakamura, Takehido Fukunaga, Yoshi Hotta, *Producer(?)* Tomoyuki Tanaka, *Art directors* Takeo Kita and Kimei Abe, *Photography* Hajime Koizumi, *Editor* Echiji Taira, *Music* Yuji Koseki, *Sound recording* Shoichi Fujinawa and Masanobu Miyazaki, *Lighting* Toshio Takashima, *Production manager* Shin Morita, *Assistant director* Masaji Nanagase.

    Special effects crew: Director Eiji Tsuburaya, *Photography* Sadamasa Arikawa, *Art direction* Akira Watanabe, *Optical photography* Yuko Manoda, *Production manager* Nan Marita, *Lighting* Kuchiro Kishida, *Mechanical and explosive effects (? – Usually credited with Composition or Mattes)* Hiroshi Mukouyama.

    Credits for English–dubbed version: Director Lee Krelles, *Screenplay* Robert Myerson, *Producer* David D. Horne.

    Cast: *Tinchan(?) – "Bulldog"* Franky (Frankie) Sakai, *Michi (photographer)* Hiroshi Koizumi, *Dr. Chujo* Ken Uehara(?), *Clark Nelson* Kyoko Kagawa, *The Twins* Yumi and Emi Ito (Itoh), *Editor* Takashi Shimura, *Also* Jelly Ito, Seizaburo Kawazu, Kenji Sahara, Akihiko Harata, Yoshio Kosugi, Yoshibumi Tajima, Yasushi Yamamoto, Haruya Kato, Ko Mishima, Tetsu Natakamura, Shoichi Horose, Koro Sakurai, Hiroshi Takagi, Yasuhisa Tsutsumi, Teruko Mita, Hiroshi Iwamoto, Mitsuo Tsuda, Masamitsu Tayma, Toshio Miura, Tadashi Okabe, Akira Wakamatsu, Yutara Nakayama, Johnny Yuseph, Obel Wyatt, Harold Conway, Robert Dunham, Akira Yamada, Koji Uno, Wataru Ohmae, Toshihiko Furuta, Keisuke Matsuyama, Yoshiyuki Kamimura, Katsumi Tezuka, Takeo Nagashima, Mitsuo Matsumoto, Shinpei Mitsui, Kazuo Higata, Shigeo Kato, Rinsaku Ogata, Yutaka Okada, Arai Hayamizu, Hiroyuki Satake, Kazuo Imai, Yoshio Hattori, Hiroshi Akitsu, Akio Kusama, Haruo Nakajima.

    Toho, U.S. dst. Columbia Pictures; color; TohoScope; 101 minutes (copyrighted at 91 minutes). A Japanese film. Japanese title: **Mosura** (or *Dai Kai Ju* or *Daikaiju Mosura?*). Released May 1962 (Japanese release July 1961).

    Note: Some sources indicate this is based on a story "Shukan Asahi" by Shinichiro Nakamura, while others indicate that was the name of the magazine in which Nakamura's story appeared.

The Mouse That Roared. *Director* Jack Arnold, *Screenplay* Roger MacDoutall and Stanley Mann, *Producer* Walter Shenson, *Associate producer* Jon Pennington, *Presented by (Executive producer?)* Carl Foreman, *Art director* Geoffrey Drake, *Photography* John Wilcox, *Camera operator* Austin Dempster, *Editor* Raymond Poulton, *Music* Edwin Astley, *Sound* Red Law and George Stephenson, *Sound editor* Richard Marden, *Makeup* Stuart Freeborn, *Costume designer* Anthony Mendleson, *Hairdresser* Joyce James, *Continuity* Pamela Davies, *Production supervisor* Leon Becker, *Production manager* James Ware, *Assistant director* Philip Shipway, *2nd unit cameraman* John Wimbolt, *Titles* Maurice Binder.

    Cast: *Tully Bascomb* Peter Sellers, *Count Mountjoy* Peter Sellers, *Grand Duchess Gloriana* Peter Sellers, *Helen Kokintz* Jean Seberg, *Prof. Alfred Kokintz* David Kossoff,

Benter Leo McKern, *Will* William Hartnell, *General Snippet* Macdonald Parke, *U.S. Secretary of Defense* Austin Willis, *Roger* Timothy Bateson, *Cobbley* Monty Landis, *BBC announcer* Colin Gordon, *Pedro* Harold Kasket, *O'Hara* George Margo, *Mulligan* Richard (Robin?) Gatehouse, *Ticket collector* Jacques Cey, *Cunard captain* Stuart Sanders, *Cunard 2nd officer* Ken Stanley, *Army captain* Bill Edwards.

Highroad–Open Road for Columbia; color; 83 minutes (copyrighted at 85 minutes; 90 in Britain). Based on the novel of the same name by Leonard Wibberly. A U.S.–British coproduction(?). U.S. release December 1959 (British release July 1959).

The Mysterians. *Director* Inoshiro Honda, *Screenplay* Takeshi Kimura, *Story* Jojiro Okami, *Adapted by* Shigeru Kayama, *Producer* Tomoyuki Tanaka, *Art director* Terukaii Abe, *Editor* Hiroichi Iwashita, *Music* Akira Ifukube, *Sound recording* Masanobu Miyazaki, *Sound effects* Ichiro Minawa, *Production manager* Yasuaki Sakamoto, *Assistant director* Koji Kajita, *Light effects* Kyuichiro Kishida, *Special techniques* Hidesaburo Araki.

Special effects crew: Director Eiji Tsuburaya, *Photography* Sadamasa Arikawa, *Art director* Akira Watanabe, *Light effects* Masao Shiroda, *Combination(?)* Hiroshi Mukoyama.

English–dubbed version: Supervisor Jay Bonafield, *Also* Peter Riethof and Carlos Montalban.

Cast: *Joji Atsumi* Kenji Sahara, *Etsuko Shiraishi* Yumi Shirakawa, *Hiroko* Momoko Kochi, *Ryoichi Shiraishi* Akihiko Hirata, *Dr. Adachi* Takashi Shimura, *Commander Morita* Susumu Fujita, *Captain Seki* Hisaya Ito, *Commander Sugimoto* Yoshio Kosugi, *Dr. Kawanami* Fuyuki Murakami, *General Hammamoto* Minosuke Yamada, *Also* Yoshio Tsuchiya, Tetsu Nakamura, Hehachiro Okawa, Takeo Ikawa, Haruya Kato, Senkichi Omura, Yutaka Sada, Hideo Mihara, Rikie Sanuo, Soji Oikata, Mitsuo Tsuda, Ken Imaizumi, Shin Otomo, Jiryu Kumagi, Akio Kusuma, Shoichi Hirose, Tadao Nakamaru, Kaneyuki Tsubono, Rinsaku Ogata, Yasuhiro Sigenobu, George Farness, Harold (S.) Conway, Haruo Nakajima, Katsumi Tezuka.

Toho, first set for U.S. release by RKO General (posters prepared), finally dst. by MGM; color; CinemaScope; 87 minutes in U.S. (89 minutes in Japan?). A Japanese film. Japanese title: **Chikyu Boeigun** (Earth Defense Forces). Released May 1959 in U.S. (released in Japan in 1957).

Mysterious Island. *Director* Cy Endfield, *Screenplay* John Prebble, Daniel Ullman and Crane Wilbur, *Producer* Charles H. Schneer, *Art director* Bill Andrews, *Photography* Wilkie Cooper, *Camera operator* Jack Mills, *Underwater photography* Egil Woxholt, *Special effects* Ray Harryhausen, *Traveling matte supervisor* Vic Margutti, *Editor* Frederick Wilson, *Music* Bernard Herrmann, *Sound supervisor* John Cox, *Sound recorders* Peter Handford and Bob Jones, *Continuity* Marjorie Lavelly, *Production supervisor* Raymond Anzarut, *Production manager* Robert Sterne, *Assistant director* René Dupont, *Title design* Bob Gill, *Studio construction manager* Peter Dukelow.

Cast: *Capt. Cyrus Harding* Michael Craig, *Lady Mary Fairchild* Joan Greenwood, *Captain Nemo* Herbert Lom, *Gideon Spilett* Gary Merrill, *Herbert Brown* Michael Callan, *Sergeant Pencroft* Percy Herbert, *Elena* Beth Rogan, *Neb* Dan Jackson.

Ameran Films Ltd. for Columbia Pictures; color; 101 minutes. Based on the 1874 novel *L'Ile Mysterieuse* by Jules Verne. A U.S.–British coproduction. Released December 20, 1961, in U.S. (June 1962 in Britain).

Note: Although listed in virtually every other source, Nigel Green does not appear in this film, and shot no scenes for it at all.

Night of the Blood Beast. *Director* Bernard L. Kowalski, *Screenplay* Martin Varno, *Producer/Story* Gene Corman, *Executive producer* Roger Corman, *Presented by* James H. Nicholson and Samuel Z. Arkoff, *Art director* Dan (Daniel) Haller, *Photography* John Nickolaus, Jr.,* *Editorial supervision* Dick Currier, *Music supervisor* Alexander Laszlo, *Sound recorder* Herman Lewis, *Production coordinator* Jack Bohrer, *Assistant director* Robert White, *Property master* Karl Brainard.

Cast: *Maj. John Corcoran* Michael Emmet, *Dave Randall* Ed Nelson, *Steve Dunlap* John Baer, *Dr. Julie Benson* Angela Greene, *Donna Bixby* Georgianna Carter, *Dr. Alex Wyman* Tyler McVey, *The Alien* Ross Sturlin.

*The studio credits misspell Nickolaus' name as "Nicholaus."

A Balboa Production for American International; black and white; 65 minutes (copyrighted at 63 minutes). Working title: "Creature from Galaxy 27." Released December 5, 1958 (Los Angeles opening). Double bill with: *She-Gods of Shark Reef*.

Nude in His Pocket. *Director* Pierre Kast, *Screenplay* France Roche, *Executive producer* Gilbert de Goldschmidt, *Art directors* Sidney Bettex and Daniel Villerois, *Scenic artist* Jean Alexandre, *Photography* Ghislain Cloquet, *Camera operator* Guy Suzuki, *Assistant camera operator* René Guissard, *Editor* Robert Isnardon, *Music* Cogo Goragher, Georges Delerue and Marc Lanjean, *Chief sound* Jean Bertrand, *Sound recorder* Claude Orbon, *Boom operator* Bernard Souverbie, *Makeup* Alexandre Marcus and Blanche Picot, *Script girl* Claude Levillain, *Production supervisor* René Thévenet, *Technical production supervisor* Jacques Garcia, *Production manager* Pierre Cottance, *Assistant production manager* Maurice Fouhati, *Assistant director* Bernard Toublanc-Michel, *Production secretary* Edwige Jaeger, *Still photography* Jean Schmidt.

Cast: *Professor Jérome* Jean Marais, *Edith* Geneviève Page, *Monette* Agnès Laurent, *Also* Regine Lovi, Amedée, Pasquali, Joelle Janin, Jean-Claude Brialy and Flip.

Madeleine Films–S.N.E. Gaumont-Contact Organisation, U.S. dst. Cosmic Films; black and white; 82 minutes in U.S. (85 minutes in France). Based on the short story "The Diminishing Draft" by Waldemar Kaempfert. A French film. Original title: **Amour de Poche** (Pocket Love). TV title: **Girl in His Pocket.** Released March 1962 in U.S. (November 1957 in France).

Nude on the Moon. *Director* Anthony Brooks, *Screenplay* O.O. Miller, *Idea* Jack Caplan, *Producers* Doris Wishman and Martin Caplan, *Photography* Ray Pheelan, *Editor* Ivan McDowell, *Music* Daniel Hart, *Song "Moon Doll" written by* Judith J. Kushner, *Sound effects editor* Stuart A. Hersh, *Sound* Titra Sound Corporation, *Main title sequence* Tri-Pix, Inc.

Cast: *Queen [probably]* Marietta, *Jeff Huntley [probably]* William Mayer, *Prof. Bill Nichols [probably]* Lester Brown, *Song sung by* Ralph Young, *Also* Pat Reilly, Ira Magee, Lacey Kelly, Shelby Livingston, Robert W. Kyorimee, Joyce M. Geary, Charles Allen, Evelyn Burke, Joyce Brooks, Hugh Brooks, Mary Lassey, Capt. R.C. Lassey, Robert B. Lassey.

A Moon Production Presentation, dst. Jer Pictures, Inc.; color; 71 minutes. Alternate title: **Moon Dolls.** Alternate titles(?): **Nature Girls on the Moon, Nudes on the Moon, Girls on the Moon.** Released 1960 (this date may be wrong; may have been released before 1960, but was definitely in release by 1962).

On the Beach. *Producer/Director* Stanley Kramer, *Screenplay* John Paxton and (?) James Lee Barrett, *Production design* Rudolph Sternad, *Art director* Fernando Carrere, *Photography* Giuseppe Rotunno, *Camera operator* Ross Wood, *Auto race photography* Daniel Fapp, *Special effects* Lee Zavitz, *Special photographic effects* Linwood G. Dunn (Film Effects of Hollywood), *Editor* Frederic Knudtson, *Music* Ernest Gold, *Song "Waltzing Matilda"* by A.B. Paterson (lyrics) and Marie Cowan (music), *Sound engineer* Hans Wetzel, *Sound effects* Walter Elliott, *Music editor* Robert Tracy, *Makeup* John O'Gorman and Frank Prehoda, *Miss Gardner's wardrobe* Fontana Sisters, Rome, *Wardrobe* Joe King, *Hairstyles* Jane Shugrue, *Script supervisor* Sam Freedle, *Production manager* Clem Beauchamp, *Assistant director* Ivan Volkman, *Company grip* Morris Rosen, *Assistant company grip* Martin Kashuk, *Property master* Art Cole, *Chief gaffer* Alan Grice, *Technical adviser* Vice-Admiral Charles A. Lockwood, U.S.N. (Ret.), *Royal Australian Navy Liaison* Lt. Cmdr. A.A. Norris-Smith.

Cast: *Cmdr. Dwight Towers* Gregory Peck, *Moira Davidson* Ava Gardner, *Julian Osborn* Fred Astaire, *Peter Holmes* Anthony Perkins, *Mary Homes* Donna Anderson, *Admiral Bridie* John Tate, *Lieutenant Hosgood* Lola Brooks, *Farrel* Guy Doleman, *Yeoman Rob Swain* John Meillon, *Sundstrom* Harp McGuire, *Benson* Ken Wayne, *Davis* Richard Meikle, *Ackerman* Joe McCormick, *Davidson* Lou Vernon, *Sir Douglas Froude* Basil Buller-Murphy, *Port man* Paddy Moran, *Dr. Forster* Kevin Brennan, *Salvation Army captain* John Casson, *Morgan* Grant Taylor, *Chrysler* Jim Barrett, *Dr. Fletcher* Keith Eden, *Senior officer* John Royle, *Radio officer* Frank Gatcliff, *Dr. King* Kevin Brennan, *Dykers* C. Harding Brown, *Professor Jorgenson* Peter Williams, *Sykes* Harvey Adams, *Jones* Stuart Finch, *Betty* Audine Leith, *Fogarty* Jerry Ian Seals, *Boy* Carey Paul Peck, *Jennifer Holmes* Katherine Hills, *Jorgenson assoc.* Peter O'Shaughnessy, *Stunt driver* Dale Van Sickel.

A Stanley Kramer–Lomitas Production, dst. United Artists; black and white; 134 minutes. Based on the novel of the same name by Nevil Shute. Released December 17, 1959.

Panic in Year Zero! *Director* Ray Milland, *Screenplay* Jay Simms and John Morton, *Story* Jay Simms, *Producers* Arnold Houghland and Lou Rusoff, *Executive producers* James H. Nicholson and Samuel Z. Arkoff, *Art director* Daniel Haller, *Set decorator* Harry Reif, *Photography* Gilbert Warrenton, *Special effects* Pat Dinga and Larry Butler, *Opticals and titles* Ray Mercer, *Editor* William Austin,* *Assistant film editor* Jerry Irvin, *Music* Les Baxter, *Music coordinator* Al Simms, *Sound* Steve Bass, *Sound editor* Al Bird, *Music editor* Eve Newman, *Makeup* Ted Coodley,* *Wardrobe* Marjorie Corso, *Hairstyles* Betty Pedretti, *Production supervisor* Bartlett A. Carré, *Unit manager* Robert Agnew, *Production assistant* Jack Cash, *Assistant director* Jim Engle,* *Property master* Dick Rubin, *Set operator* Harry Reif, *Construction* Ross Hahn, *Still photographer* Ed Jones, *Transportation* Allee B. Reed.

Cast: *Harry Baldwin* Ray Milland, *Ann Baldwin* Jean Hagen, *Rick Baldwin* Frankie Avalon, *Karen Baldwin* Mary Mitchell, *Marilyn Hayes* Joan Freeman, *Carl* Richard Bakalyan, *Mickey* Rex Holman, *Andy* Neil Nephew, *Ed Johnson* Richard Garland, *Dr. Strong* Willis Bouchey, *Hogan* O.Z. Whitehead, *Haenel* Byron Morrow, *Mrs. Johnson* Shary Marshall, *Harkness* Russ Bender, *Becker* Hugh Sanders, *Also* Andrea Lane, Scott Peters, Bud Slater, Kelton Crawford.

*AFI says Anthony Carras was coeditor and Les Gorall was 2nd assistant director, but neither are listed in the film's credits, which spell Ted Coodley's name as "Cooley."

An Alta Vista Production for American International; black and white; scope (type uncredited); 92 minutes. Perhaps based (without credit) on "Lot" and "Lot's Daughter" by Ward Moore. Rerelease title: **The End of the World**. Working title: "Survival." Released July 4, 1962.

Paradisio. *Producer/(Director?)* Jacques Henrici, *Screenplay* Lawrence Zeitlin, Henri Halle and Jacques Henrici, *Presented by* Jack H. Harris, *Music* John Bath, *Played by* Kurt Graunke Orchestra, *Casting* Steve Waen.

Cast: *Prof. Arthur Everett Sims* Arthur Howard, *Lisa Hinkle* Eva Waegner.

A Dramatis Personal Production/Tonylyn Productions, dst. in U.S. Fanfare Films and Evelyn Place Prods. Michael Hayes says that Tonylyn, Harris' company at the time, distributed the film nationally, and that Fanfare and Evelyn Place are subsidiaries); black and white in red/green "Tri-Optique" anaglyph 3-D process. 82 minutes. U.S. release February 23, 1962.

Note: more confusion: European sources, according to Hayes, credit Jack H. Harris as director. The nationality of the film is clouded; the AFI catalog, which says the film may have been made as early as 1956, says it is British in origin, but Hayes says that the British Film Institute denies this. The credits faintly indicate a French–West German–British coproduction.

The Phantom Planet. *Director/Additional dialogue* William Marshall, *Screenplay* William Telaak, Fred De Gorter and Fred Gebhardt, *Producer/Story* Fred Gebhardt, *Executive producer* Leo Handel, *Associate producer/Production design* Robert Kinoshita, *Set dresser* Joe Kish, *Photography* Elwood J. Nicholson, *Camera operator* Ned Davenport, *Director of photographic effects* Louis DeWitt, *Special photographic effects* Studio Film Service, *Special effects* Charles R. Duncan, *Supervising film editor/Assistant producer* Hugo Grimaldi, *Assistant film editor* Don Wolfe, *Music supervisor* Gordon Zahler, *Interplanetary sound* Hayes Pagel and Walter Dick, *Music editor* Ted Roberts, *Sound* Al Overton, *Makeup* Dave Newell, *Costumes* Maria Craig, *Wardrobe* Oscar Rodriguez, *Hairstyles* Mary Westmoreland, *Script supervisor* Hazel Hall, *Dialogue director* Ben Bard, *Production supervisor/Assistant director* Maurice Vaccarino, *2nd assistant director* Lindsley Parsons, Jr., *Gaffer* Frank Leonetti, *Grip* Lou Kusley, *Still photography* Bruce Bailey, *Electronic space equipment* Space Age Rentals.

Cast: *Capt. Frank Chapman* Dean Fredricks, *Zetha* Dolores Faith, *Herron* Tony (Anthony) Dexter, *Liara* Coleen Gray, *Sesom* Francis X. Bushman, *Lt. Ray Makonnen* Richard Weber, *Judge Eden* Al Jarvis, *Col. Lansfield* Dick Haynes, *Pilot Leonard* Earl McDaniel, *Lieutenant White* Michael Marshall, *Captain Beecher* John Herrin, *Lieutenant*

Cutler Mel Curtis, *Navigator Webb* Jimmy Weldon, *Communications officer* Akemi Tani, *Radar officer* Lori Lyons, *Solarites* Richard Kiel, *Also* Susan Cembrowska, Marissa Mathes, Gloria Morelan, Judy Erickson, Marya Carter, Allyson Ames, Marion Thompson, Warrene Ott, *Narrators* Marvin Miller, Leon O. Selznick.

Four Crown Prods., dst. American International; black and white; 82 minutes. Released December 13, 1961. Double bill with (some areas only): *Assignment Outer Space.*

Plan 9 from Outer Space. *Director/Screenplay/Producer/Editor* Edward D. Wood, Jr., *Executive producer* J. Edward Reynolds, *Associate producers* Hugh Thomas, Jr. and Charles Burg, *Set dresser* Harry Reif, *Set construction* Tom Kemp, *Photography* William C. Thompson, *Special effects* Charles Duncan, *Music supervision* Gordon Zahler, *Sound* Dale Knight, *Makeup* Tom Bartholomew, *Wardrobe* Dick Chaney, *Script supervisor* Diana N. Loomis, *Production manager* Kirk Kirkham, *Assistant director* Willard Kirkham, *Production assistant* Donald A. Davis, *Property master* Tony Portoghese, *Grip* Art Manikin, *Electrical effects* Jim Woods, *His narration written by* Criswell.

Cast: *Jeff Trent* Gregory Walcott, *Paula Trent* Mona McKinnon, *Eros* Dudley Manlove, *Col. Tom Edwards* Tom Keene, *Lt. Johnny Harper* Duke Moore, *Inspector Clay* Tor Johnson, *Old man/Ghoul man* Bela Lugosi, *Old woman/Ghoul woman* Vampira (Maila Nurmi), *Tanna* Joanna Lee, *The Ruler* John Breckinridge, *General Roberts* Lyle Talbot, *Patrolman Kelton* Paul Marco, *Patrolman Larry* Carl Anthony, *Danny (copilot)* David DeMering, *Edith (stewardess)* Norma McCarty, *Reverend* Rev. Lynn Lemon, *Girl at the Old Man's funeral* Gloria Dea, *Captain* Bill Ash, *Man at funeral* Ben Frommer, *Patrolman Jamie* Conrad Brooks, *Man who finds Paula* Carl Johnson, *Gravediggers* J. Edward Reynolds and Hugh Thomas, Jr., *Double for Lugosi* Tom Mason, *In Prologue and Narrator* Criswell (Jeron King Criswell).

A Reynolds Pictures, Inc. Production, dst. Distributors Corporation of America (DCA); black and white; 79 minutes. Working title: "Grave Robbers from Outer Space." Released July 1959, although some sources indicate it was released in 1958. It is included in the 1958 *Filmfacts.*

Queen of Outer Space. *Director* Edward Bernds, *Screenplay* Charles Beaumont, *Story* Ben Hecht, *Producer* Ben Schwalb, *Art director* David Milton, *Set construction* James West, *Set dresser* Joe Kish, *Photography* William Whitley, *Camera operator* Val O'Malley, *Assistant cameramen* Walter Blumel and Todd Laclede, *Camera equipment* Mark Armisted, *Special effects* Milt Rice, *Editor* William Austin, *Music* Marlin Skiles, *Sound mixer* Joseph Lapis, *Sound editor* Charles Schelling, *Sound recorder* B.F. Remington, *Music editor* Jerry Irvin, *Boom man* Bill Flannery, *Makeup* Emile LaVigne and John Holden, *Body makeup* Bunny Armstrong, *Wardrobe* Sid Mintz, Irene Caine, Sophia Scott Stutz and Neva Bourne, *Zsa Zsa Gabor's wardrobe designed by* Thomas Pierce, *Hairdressers* Alice Monte and Olga Collings, *Dialogue director* Herman Rosten, *Script supervisor (set continuity)* Richard Caffee, *Production manager* Edward Morey, Jr., *Assistant directors* William Beaudine, Jr. and Harry Sherman, *Props* Sam Gordon and Ted Mossman, *Gaffer* George Satterfield, *Grips* Harry Lewis and Hilton Anderson, *Production secretary* Bette Rehm, *Color technician* Phil Rand, *Stills* Fred Morgan, *Cable man* Al Yaylian, *Best boy* James Peters, *Casting* Joe Rivkin and Mikey Lewis, *Transportation* Frank Duffy, *First aid* John Ward, *Doorman* Charles Holmberg, *Laborer* Art Williams.

Cast: *Talleah* Zsa Zsa Gabor, *Capt. Neil Patterson* Eric Fleming, *Queen Yllana* Laurie Mitchell, *Professor Konrad* Paul Birch, *Lt. Larry Turner* Patrick Waltz, *Lt. Michael Cruze* Dave Willock, *Kaeel* Barbara Darrow, *Motiya* Lisa Davis, *Odeena* Marilyn Buferd, *Colonel Ramsey* Guy Prescott, *Guards* Marjorie Durant, Marya Stevens, Colleen Drake, Mary Ford, Brandy Bryan, *Guard leader* Lynn Cartwright, *Councilors (masked)* Laura Mason, Kathy Marlowe, Tania Velia, *Friendly guard* Gerry Gaylor, *Young woman* Laura Mason, *Officer in anteroom* Ralph Gamble, *Turner's girlfriend* Joi Lansing, *Tattered wretch (being tortured)* John Bleifer, *Amazon in charge of disintegrators* Ruth Lewis, *Amazon leader on Tyrus 4* June McCall.

Allied Artists; color; CinemaScope; 79½ minutes. Working title: "Queen of the Universe." Released September 9, 1958. May have been planned to be double bill with *Frankenstein 1970.*

Reptilicus. *Directors* Sidney Pink and Poul Bang, *Screenplay* Sidney Pink and Ib Melchior, *Producer/Story* Sidney Pink, *Executive producer* J.H. Zalabery, *Danish adaptation* Poul Bang and Bob Ramsing, *Set decorations* Otto Lund, Helge Hansen and Kai Koed, *Photography* Age Wiltrup, *Editors* Svend Mehling and Edith Nisted Nielsen, *Music* Sven Gyldmark, *Sound* Georg Jensen and Poul Nyrup, *Sound effects editor(?)* Kay Rose, *Production supervisor* Erik Larsen.

Cast: *Brig. Gen. Mark Grayson* Carl Ottosen, *Lise Martens* Ann Smyrner, *Karen Martens* Mimi Heinrich, *Prof. Otto Martens* Asbjorn Andersen, *Connie Miller* Marla Behrens, *Svend Viltofft* Bent Majding, *Dr. Peter Dalby* Poul Wildaker (Wøldie), *Dirk Millelsen* Dirk Passer, *Captain Brandt* Ole Wisborg, *Herself* Birthe Wilke, *Police chief* Mogens Brandt, *Olsen* Kjeld Petersen, *Also* Bodil Miller, Alex Suhr, Alfred Wilken, Bent Vejlby, Knud Hallest, Benny Juhlin, Martin Stander, Børge Møller Grimstrup, Hardy Jensen, Poul Thomsen, Svend Johansen, Jørgen Blaksted, Claus Toksvig.

Cinemagic Inc.–Alta Vista Prods. and Saga Film for American International; color; 81 minutes in U.S. (90 minutes in Denmark). A U.S.–Danish coproduction. Released November 1962 in U.S. (February 1961 in Denmark).

Return of the Fly. *Director/Screenplay* Edward L. Bernds, *Producer* Bernard Glasser, *Art directors* John Mansbridge and Lyle R. Wheeler, *Set decorators* Joseph Kish and Walter M. Scott, *Photography* Brydon Baker, *Editor* Richard C. Meyer, *Music* Paul Sawtell and Bert Shefter, *Sound effects* Arthur J. Cornell, *Makeup* Hal Lierley, *Assistant director* Byron Roberts, *Chief set electrician* Robert A. Petzoldt.

Cast: *François Delambre* Vincent Price, *Philippe Delambre* Brett Halsey, *Alan Hinds (Ronald Holmes)* David Frankham, *Cecile Bonnard* Danielle de Metz, *Max Berthold* Dan Seymour, *Inspector Beacham** John Sutton, *Nun* Florence Strom, *Mme. Bonnard* Janine Grandel, *Sergeant Dubois* Richard Flato, *Detective Evans* Pat O'Hara, *Lieutenant Maclish* Barry Bernard, *Granville* Jack Daly, *Gaston* Michael Mark, *Priest* Francisco Villalobas, *Nurse* Joan Cotton, *Fly creature* Ed Wolff, *Policemen* Gregg Martell, Rick Turner, Courtland Shepard.

*Although many sources indicate that Sutton played Inspector Charas, he actually plays Beacham (possibly spelled Beauchamp). If Herbert Marshall had repeated his role from *The Fly*, he would have played Charas, but as he did not, the character was given a different role name.

An Associated Producers Production for 20th Century–Fox; black and white; Cinema-Scope; 78 minutes. Based on characters created by George Langelaan; sequel to *The Fly*. Released July 21, 1959. Double bill with: *The Alligator People*.

The Revenge of Frankenstein. *Director* Terence Fisher, *Screenplay* Jimmy Sangster, *Additional dialogue* Hurford Janes, *Producer* Anthony Hinds, *Executive producer* Michael Carreras, *Associate producer* Anthony Nelson-Keys, *Production design* Bernard Robinson, *Photography* Jack Asher, *Camera operator* Len Harris, *Supervising editor* James Needs, *Editor* Alfred Cox, *Music* Leonard Salzedo, *Music director* Muir Mathieson, *Sound recordist* Jock May, *Makeup* Phil Leakey, *Wardrobe* Rosemary Burrows, *Hairstyles* Henry Montsash, *Continuity* Doreen Dearnaley, *Production manager* Don Weeks, *Assistant director* Robert Lynn.

Cast: *Dr. Victor Frankenstein/Dr. Stein/Dr. Franck* Peter Cushing, *Dr. Hans Kleve* Francis Matthews, *Karl (after operation)* Michael Gwynn, *Margaret Konrad* Eunice Gayson, *Karl (before operation)* Oscar Quitak, *Janitor patient* Richard Wordsworth, *Bergman* John Welsh, *Fritz (first grave robber)* Lionel Jeffries, *Kurt (second grave robber)* Michael Ripper, *President of Medical Council* Charles Lloyd Pack, *Inspector* John Stuart, *Molke* Arnold Diamond, *Countess Barscynska* Margery Gresley, *Vera Barscynska* Anna Walmsley, *Murderous janitor* George Woodbridge, *Gerda* Avril Leslie, *Boy with Gerda* Ivan Whittaker.

Hammer Films, U.S. dst. Columbia Pictures; color; 89 minutes. Based on characters created by Mary W. Shelley; sequel to *The Curse of Frankenstein* (1957). A British film. U.S. release June 18, 1958. Double bill with: *Curse of the Demon*.

The Road to Hong Kong. *Director* Norman Panama, *Screenplay* Norman Panama and Melvin Frank, *Producer* Melvin Frank, *Production design* Roger Furse, *Art directors* Sydney Cain and Bill Hutchinson, *Set dresser* Maurice Fowler, *Assistant art director* Bob

Cartwright, *Sketch artist* Sidney Braham, *Scenic artist* Basil Mannin, *Draughtsmen* Jim Sawyer, Brian Ackland-Snow, Ted Clements, Joel Schiller, *Photography* Jack Hildyard, *Camera operator* Gerry Fisher, *Focus puller* Jimmy Devis, *Camera grip* Frank Howard, *Special effects* Wally Veevers and Ted Samuels, *Animation* Biographic Cartoon Films, Ltd., *Editorial supervisor* Alan Osbiston, *Editor* John Smith, *Assistant editors* Joan Morduch and Ray Thorne, *Music* Robert Farnon, *Musical associates* Douglas Gamley and Bill McGuffie, *Songs* Sammy Cahn and Jimmy Van Heusen, *Sound recordist* A.G. "Buster" Ambler, *Dubbing mixer* Red Law, *Sound editor* Chris Greenham, *Sound boom operator* Peter Dukelow, *Sound camera operator* Jimmy Dooley, *Music editor* Lee Doig, *Makeup* Dave Aylott and Eric Allwright, *Costumes* Antony Mendleson, *Wardrobe* May Walding and Ernie Farrer, *Hairstyles* Joan White and Joyce James, *Continuity* Angela Martelli and Pamela Davies, *Production supervisor* Bill Kirby, *1st assistant director* Bluey Hill, *2nd assistant directors* Gordon Gilbert, Edward Dorian and Ken Softley, *Prop chargehand* Bobby Murrell, *Main title* Maurice Binder, *Musical numbers staged by* Jack Baker and Sheila Myers, *Chargehand electrician* Maurice Gillett, *Production secretary* Inez Easton, *Chinese adviser* Mrs. Fei, *Still photographer* Ted Reed, *Casting* Sally Nicholl, *Production buyer* Terry Parr, *Construction manager* Harry Phipps.

Cast: *Chester Babcock* Bob Hope, *Harry Turner* Bing Crosby, *Diane* Joan Collins, *Herself* Dorothy Lamour, *The Leader* Robert Morley, *Dr. Zorbb* Walter Gotell, *Jhinnah* Roger Delgado, *Grand Lama* Felix Aylmer, *Lama* Peter Madden, *U.S. officials* Alan Gifford, Robert Ayres and Robin Hughes, *Doctor* Julian Sherrier, *Agent* Bill Nagy, *Photographer* Guy Standeven, *Messenger* John McCarthy, *Servant* Simon Levy, *Lady at airport* Jacqueline Jones, *Leader's men* Victor Brooks, Roy Patrick, John Dearth, David Randall and Michael Wynne, *Chinese girl* Mei Ling, *Receptionist* Katya Douglas, *Nubians* Harry Bair and Irvin Allen, *Girls* Yvonne Shima, Camilla Brockman, Lena Margot, Sheree Winton, Edwina Carroll, Diane Valentine, April Ashley, Jacqueline Leigh, Sein Short, Leir Hwang, Michele Mok, Zoe Zephyr, *Indian doctor* Peter Sellers, *Themselves* Frank Sinatra and Dean Martin, *Guest star* Jerry Colonna, *Also?* Zsa Zsa Gabor, Dave King, David Niven.*

*Niven is mentioned in only one review; Michael Hayes is source for Gabor and King.

Melnor Films Ltd., U.S. dst. United Artists; black and white; 91 minutes. A U.S.–British coproduction. Working title: "Road to the Moon." U.S. release May 23, 1962 (British release April 1962).

Rocket Attack, U.S.A. *Director/Producer* Barry Mahon, *Associate producers* Rick Carrier, Steve Brody and Al Baron, *Sets* Al Baron, *Photography* Mike Tabb, *Editor* Alan Smiler, *Music* RFT Music Publishing Company, *Film Processing* Pathé Labs, *Sound* MagnoSound, *Set decorator* Encore.

Cast: *John Marston* John McCay, *Tanya** Monica Davis, *Also* Daniel Kern, Edward Czerniuk, Philip St. George, Richard Downs, Herbert Flato, Ray Brewer, Janice Gilmain, Robert Reeh(?), *Arthur (Art)* Metrano, Jane Ross, Marco Behar, Frank Patrinostrow, Milton Fuchs, William Osborn, Ronnie Cooper, John Horner, Nicolai Grushkow, Sara Amman, Vladovia Lazareff, James Tura, Alan Smile (Smiler?).

*Some sources give this name as Tannah, but it is Tanya in the film.

An Exploit Films Production, dst. Joseph Brenner Associates(?); black and white; 66 minutes (some sources cite 68 minutes). Sources disagree on date of release, some giving March 1961, but it was in release as early as 1960.

Note: No screenplay credit, probably improvised from an outline by Mahon. Michael Hayes suggests Byron Mabe was assistant director, and Clelle Mahon was script supervisor.

Satan's Satellites. *Director* Fred C. Brannon, *Screenplay* Ronald Davidson, *Producer* Franklin Adreon, *Art director* Fred A. Ritter, *Set decorators* John McCarthy, Jr. and James Redd, *Photography* John MacBurnie, *Special effects* Howard and Theodore Lydecker, *Editor* Cliff Bell, *Music* Stanley Wilson, *Sound* Dick Tyler, *Makeup* Bob Mark, *Costume supervision* Adele Palmer, *Hairstyles* Peggy Gray, *Unit manager* Roy Wade.

Cast: *Larry Martin* Judd Holdren, *Sue Davis* Aline Towne, *Bob Wilson* Wilson Wood, *Marex* Lane Bradford, *Dr. Harding* Stanley Waxman, *Roth* John Crawford, *Mr. Steele* Craig Kelly, *Shane* Ray Boyle, *Narab* Leonard Nimoy, *Truck driver* Tom Steele, *Robot* Tom Steele, *Telegraph operator* Dale Van Sickel, *Lawson* Roy Engel,

Kerr Jack Harden, *Fisherman* Paul Stader, *Dick* Gayle Kellogg, *Policeman* Jack Shea, *Elah* Robert Garabedian. **Note:** The following cast members are confirmed for the full serial only, and may not appear in this feature condensation. *Gomez* Jack Mack, *Kettler* Robert Strange, *Pilot* Paul Gustine, *Plane thug* Henry Rowland, *Ross* Clifton Young, *Tarner* Norman Willis, *Train thugs* George Magrill and Frank Alten, *Walker* Tom Steele, *Policemen* Floyd Criswell and Davison Clark, *Bits (and stunts)* John Daheim and Ken Terrell.

Republic Pictures; black and white; 70 minutes. "Rocketman" character created by Royal K. Cole, William Lively and Sol Shor. Released December 1958 (Los Angeles opening). Double bill with: *Missile Monsters.* This is a condensed feature version of the serial *Zombies of the Stratosphere* (released July 16, 1952).

The Secret of the Telegian. *Director* Jun Fukuda, *Screenplay* Shinichi Sekizawa, *Producer* Tomoyuki Tanaka, *Special effects director* Eiji Tsuburaya, *Photography* Kazuo Yamada, *Music* Sei Ikeno.

Cast: Kirioka Koji Tsurata, *Nakamoto (Corporal Sudo), the Telegian* Tadao Nakamura, *Detective Kobayashi* Akihiko Hirata, *Akiko* Yumi Shirakawa, *Onishi* Seizaburo Kawazu, *Also* Yoshio Tsuchiya, Sachio Sakai.

Toho, U.S. distributor unclear, perhaps distributed directly to U.S. television by Toho itself; AFI cites Herts-Lion International Corp., but Japanese film authority Greg Shoemaker says Herts-Lion never distributed the film; color; TohoScope; 85 minutes. Original Japanese title: **Denso Ningen.** Alternate title(?): **The Telegian.** Shown in Los Angeles July 1961 (Japanese release 1960).

Sex Kittens Go to College. *Director/Producer/Story* Albert Zugsmith, *Screenplay* Robert Hill, *Art director* David Milton,* *Set director* John Sturtevant, *Set continuity* Frank Kowalski, *Photography* Ellis W. Carter, *Special effects* Augie Lohman, *Editor* William Austin, *Music* Dean Elliott, *Songs* Conway Twitty, *Sound editor* Charles Schelling, *Recording engineer* Robert Post, *Music editor* Jerry Irvin, *Makeup* Monte Westmore, *Wardrobe* Claire Cramer and Rudy Harrington, *Hairdresser* Elenore Edwards, *Men's Wear* Jim Huffman, *Sportswear designed by* Phil Rose of California, *Dialogue director* Jackie Coogan, *Production manager/Assistant director* Ralph Black, *Props* Richard Rubin.

Cast: *Dr. Mathilda West (Tassels Monclair)* Mamie Van Doren, *George Barton* Marty (Martin) Milner, *Dr. Myrtle Carter* Pamela Mason, *Jody* Tuesday Weld, *Dr. Zorch* Louis Nye, *Professor Watts* John Carradine, *Professor Towers* Irwin Berke, *Wildcat MacPherson* Jackie Coogan, *Suzanne* Mijanou Bardot, *Boomie* Mickey Shaughnessy, *Legs* Raffertino Allan Drake, *Woo Woo Grabowski* Woo Woo (Norman) Grabowski, *Etta* Toodie Vampira (Maila Nurmi), *Miss Cadwallader* Babe London, *Nurse* Arlene Hunter, *Bartender* Jody Fair, *Nightclub hostess* Buni Bacon, *Himself* Conway Twitty, *Fire chief* Charles Chaplin, Jr., *Policeman* Harold Lloyd, Jr., *Woman* Barbara Pepper, *Miss Everleigh* Cheerio Meredith, *Mexican* José Gonzales-Gonzales, *2nd policeman* Jack Carr, *Arab* Noel de Souza, *Shoeshine girl* Beverly Englander, *Midget* Buddy Douglas, *Railroad conductor* Edwin Randolph.

*Inasmuch as it seems to have been contractually required for David Milton's name to appear in this capacity on all Allied Artists films, from Bowery Boys movies to as late as *Cabaret*, it is impossible to determine if he actually did anything on a given film. In this case, it is unlikely that he did.

Photoplay Assocs., Inc., dst. Allied Artists; black and white; 94 minutes. TV title: **Beauty and the Robot.** Working titles: "Teacher Was a Sexpot"; "Sexpot Goes to College." Released late 1960 (December in New York).

She Demons. *Director* Richard E. Cunha, *Screenplay* Richard E. Cunha and H.E. Barrie, *Producer* Arthur A. Jacobs, *Associate producer* Marc Frederic, *Production design* Harold Banks, *Photography* Meredith Nicholson, *Camera operator* Buddy Harris, *Special effects* David Koehler, *Editor* William Shea, *Music* Nicholas Carras, *Sound mixer* Frank Webster, *Makeup* Carlie Taylor, *Costumes* Marj Corso, *Production manager* Ralph Brooke, *Assistant director* Leonard J. Shapiro, *Script supervisor* Judith Hart, *Props* Walter Broadfoot, *Chief electrician* Lee Dixon, *Key grip* Grant Tucker.

Cast: *Jerrie Turner* Irish McCalla, *Fred Maklin* Tod Griffin, *Sammy Ching* Victor Sen Yung, *Col. Karl Osler* Rudolph Anders, *Mona Osler* Leni Tana, *Egore* Gene Roth, *Kris Kamata** Charlie Opuni, *"Storm Troopers"* Bill Coontz, Billy Dix, Larry Gelbman, Michael

Stoycoff, *She Demons* Maureen Janzen, Grace Mathews, *Island Women/She Demons* The Diana Nellis Dancers, *Stunts* George Barrows, *Double for Leni Tana* Kathryn (Mrs. Richard) Cunha, *Also* Whitey Hughes.

*Sources give "Kamara," but it sounds like "Kamata" in the film.

Screencraft Enterprises, dst. Astor Pictures; black and white; 77 minutes. Released March 1958. Double bill with *Giant from the Unknown*.

Siege of Syracuse. *Director* Pietro Francisci, *Screenplay* Pieter Francisci, Giorgio Graziosi and Ennio De Concini, *Producer* Enzo Merolle, *Art director* Ottavio Scotti, *Photography* Carlo Carlini, *Music* Angelo Francesco Lavagnino.

Cast: *Archimedes* Rossano Brazzi, *Diana* Tina Louise, *Clio* Sylva Koscina, *Gorgia* Enrico Maria Salerno, *Gerone* Gino Cervi, *Also* Alberto Farnese, Luciano Marin, Alfredo Varelli.

Glomer Film–Galatea (Italy)/Société Cinématographique Lyre (France), U.S. dst. Paramount Pictures; color; Dyaliscope; 97 minutes (European length 115 minutes). An Italian-French coproduction. Original Italian title: **L'Assedio di Siracusa**. Alternate Italian title: **Archimede**. French title: **La Siège de Syracuse**. U.S. release January 31, 1962 (European release April 1960).

The Snake Woman. *Director* Sidney J. Furie, *Screenplay* Orville H. Hampton, *Producer* George Fowler, *Executive producer* David E. Rose, *Art director* John G. Earl, *Photography* Stephen Dade, *Editor* Anthony Gibbs, *Music* Buxton Orr, *Music conductor* Phillip Martell, *Sound* Bob Winter and H.C. Pearson, *Makeup* Freddie Williamson, *Wardrobe* Dulcie Midwinter, *Hairstyles* Helen Penford, *Production manager* Buddy Booth, *Assistant director* Douglas Hickox.

Cast: *Charles Prentice* John McCarthy, *Atheris* Susan Travers, *Col. Clyde Wynborn* Geoffrey Dainton, *Dr. Murton* Arnold Marle, *Aggie Harker* Elsie Wagstaff, *Dr. Horace Adderson* John Cazabon, *Polly the barmaid* Frances Bennett, *Constable Alfie* Jack Cunningham, *Inspector* Hugh Moxey, *Barkis the publican* Michael Logan, *Martha Adderson* Dorothy Frere, *Shepherd* Stevenson Lang.

A Caralan-Dador Production, dst. United Artists; black and white; 68 minutes. A British film. Working title: "The Lady Is a Snake." Released June 3, 1961 in U.S. (May 1961 in Britain). Double bill with: *Dr. Blood's Coffin*.

The Space Children. *Director* Jack Arnold, *Screenplay* Bernard C. Schoenfeld, *Story* Tom Filer, *Producer* William Alland, *Art directors* Roland Anderson and Hal Pereira, *Set decorators* Sam Comer and Frank McKelvy, *Photography* Ernest Laszlo, *Special photographic effects* John P. Fulton, *Alien built by* Ivyl Burks, *Editor* Terry Morse, *Music* (Nathan) Van Cleave, *Sound* Philip Wisdom and Charles Grenzbach, *Makeup* Wally Westmore, *Hairstyles* Nellie Manley, *Assistant director* Richard Caffey(?), *Process photography* Farciot Edouart.

Cast: *Bud Brewster* Michel Ray, *Dave Brewster* Adam Williams, *Ken Brewster* Johnny Crawford, *Anne Brewster* Peggy Webber, *Hank Johnson* Jackie Coogan, *Eadie Johnson* Sandy Descher, *Lieutenant Colonel Manley* Richard Shannon, *Tim Gamble* John Washbrook, *Joe Gamble* Russell Johnson, *Dr. Wahrman* Raymond Bailey, *Major Thomas* Larry Pennell, *Mr. James* Peter Baldwin, *Sentry* Ty Hungerford (Hardin?), *Saul Wahrman* David Blair, *Phyllis* Eilene Janssen, *Peg* Jean Engstrom, *Frieda Johnson* Vera Marshe, *George* Louis Towers, *Buster* Alan Roberts, *Helen* Gloria Anne Halper, *Wicks* Sid Tomack, *Lloyd* Ray Walker, *Guards* Robert G. Anderson, Burton D. Metcalfe, Arvid Nelson, *Truck driver* Leo Needham, *Doctor* John Morley, *Monitors at loudspeaker* Paul Gary, Allan Ray, *Floor manager* James Ogg, *Communications man* James Douglas, *Radar operator* Howard Joslin, *Radar man* Terry Terrill, *Sentries* James Wilson, John Benson, *Mother* Helen Jay, *Sergeant Cooper* Mike Mahoney.

William Alland Prods. for Paramount Pictures; black and white; 69 minutes. Working title: "The Egg." Released June 23, 1958. Intended as double bill with *The Colossus of New York*, but apparently was not treated as such by Paramount.

Space Master X-7. *Director* Edward Bernds, *Screenplay* George Worthing Yates and Daniel Mainwaring, *Producer* Bernard Glasser, *Production design* Edward Shiells, *Set decorator* Harry Reif, *Photography* Brydon Baker, *Editor* John F. Link, *Music* Josef Zimanich, *Sound* Victor Appel, *Makeup* Robert Littlefield, *Costumes* Clark Ross,

Hairstyles Maudlee McDougall, *Dialogue coach* Henry Staudigl, *Assistant director* Lou Perlof, *Production assistant* Norman Maurer.

Cast: *John Hand* Bill Williams, *Joe Rattigan* Robert Ellis, *Laura Greeling* Lyn Thomas, *Dr. Charles Pommer* Paul Frees, *Miss Meyers* Joan Barry, *Professor West* Thomas Browne Henry, *Morse* Fred Sherman, *Captain* Jesse Kirkpatrick, *Cab driver* Moe Howard, *Miss Archer* Rhoda Williams, *Elaine Frohman* Carol Varga, *Collins* Thomas Wilde, *Engineer Gregg* Martell, *Chief Hendry* Court Shepard, *Passenger* Al Baffert, *Deputy Chief Ryder* Lane Chandler, *Also* Bob Bice, Don Lamond, Judd Holdren, Ellen Shaw, Nesdon Booth, John Ward, Helen Jay, Edward McNally, Joseph Becker.

A Regal Film for 20th Century–Fox; black and white; Regalscope; 71 minutes. Released July 11, 1958. Double bill with: *The Fly*.

Spoilers of the Plains. *Director* William Witney, *Screenplay* Sloan Nibley, *(Associate) producer* Edward J. White, *Executive producer* Herbert J. Yates, *Art director* Frank Arrigo, *Set decorator* John McCarthy, Jr., *Photography* Jack Marta, *Special effects* Howard and Theodore Lydecker, *Editor* Tony Martinelli, *Music* R. Dale Butts, *Songs* Jack Elliott, Aaron Gonzales and Foy Willing, *Sound* Dick Tyler, *Makeup* Bob Mark, *Costume supervision* Adele Palmer and Robert Ramsey, *Hairstyles* Peggy Gray.

Cast: *Roy Rogers* Roy Rogers, *Frankie Manning* Penny Edwards, *Splinters* Gordon Jones, *Gregory Camwell* Grant Withers, *Ben Rix* Don Haggerty, *Brooks* Fred Kohler, Jr., *Scheller* House Peters, Jr., *Scientist* George Meeker, *Guard* Keith Richards, *Jonathan Manning* William Forrest, *Mr. Miller* Lee Shumway, *Beautician* Phyllis Kennedy, *Guard* Rex Lease, *Also* Foy Willing and the Riders of the Purple Sage, Trigger and Bullet.

Republic Pictures; black and white; 67 minutes. Released February 2, 1951.

Teenage Caveman. *Director/Producer* Roger Corman, *Screenplay* R. Wright Campbell, *Executive producers* James H. Nicholson and Samuel Z. Arkoff, *Photography* Floyd Crosby, *Editorial supervision* Irene Morra, *Music* Albert Glasser, *Wardrobe* Marjorie Corso, *Production manager* Maurice Vaccarino, *Assistant director* Jack Bohrer, *Property master* Karl Brainard, *Producer's assistant* Beach Dickerson.

Cast: *The Boy* Robert Vaughn, *The Symbol Maker* Leslie Bradley, *The Maiden* Darrah Marshall, *The Villain* Frank De Kova, *Keeper of the Gifts* Robert Shayne, *Blond(?) clansman* Ed Nelson, *The Fair-Haired boy* Beach Dickerson, *Tom-Tom player* Beach Dickerson, *The man from the burning plains* Beach Dickerson, *Ferocious bear* Beach Dickerson, *Tribe members* Joseph Hamilton, Marshall Bradford, June Jocelyn, Jonathan Haze, Charles P. Thompson.

A Malibu Production for American International; black and white; Superama; 65 minutes. Alternate title: **Prehistoric World**. British title: **Out of the Darkness**. Released September 4, 1958. Double bill with: *How to Make a Monster*.

Note: According to Joe Dante, Corman considered this an adaptation of the novella "By the Waters of Babylon" by Stephen Vincent Benét.

Teenage Monster *Director/Producer* Jacques Marquette, *Screenplay* Ray Buffum, *Story idea* Jacques Marquette and Ray Buffum, *Associate producer* Dale Tate, *Photography* Taylor Byars and Jacques Marquette, *Editor* Irving Schoenberg, *Assistant editor* Morris Feuer, *Music* Walter Greene, *Sound* George Anderson and Phillip Mitchell, *Makeup* Jack P. Pierce, *Wardrobe* Jerry Bos, *Props* Richard M. Rubin, *Assistant director* Ken Walters.

Cast: *Ruth Cannon* Anne Gwynne, *Kathy North* Gloria Castillo, *Sheriff Bob* Stuart Wade, *Charles Cannon* Gilbert (Gil) Perkins, *Charles Cannon (as a boy)* Stephen Parker, *Marv Howell* Charles Courtney, *Deputy Ed* Norman Leavitt, *Jim Cannon* Jim McCullough, *Fred Fox* Gaybe Morradian, *Man with burro* Arthur Berkeley, *Man on street* Frank Davis.

A Marquette Production, dst. Favorite Films; black and white; 65 minutes. TV title: **Meteor Monster**. Working title (according to Willis): "Monster on the Hill." Shown December 1957 in Los Angeles; not released until 1958 elsewhere. Double bill with: *Brain from Planet Arous*.

Teenage Zombies. *Director/Producer* Jerry Warren, *Screenplay* Jacques Lecoutier, *Set decorator* Jack Hoffner, *Set construction* Don Morrison, *Photography* Allen Chandler, *Musical director* Erich Bromberg, *Makeup* Jean Morrison, *Wardrobe* Geraldine Brianne,

Script supervisor Conrad Wolfe, *Production manager* G.B. Murphy, *Assistant director* Ike Jones.

Cast: *Regg* Don Sullivan, *Dr. Myra* Katherine Victor, *Whorf* Steve Conte, *Skip* Paul Pepper, *Pam* Bri Murphy, *Julie* Mitzi Albertson, *Morrie* Jay Hawk, *Dot* Nan Green, *Brandt* J.L.D. (S.L.D.?) Morrison, *Sheriff* Mike Concannon, *Ivan* Chuck Niles, *Major Coleman* Don Neeley, *Gorilla* Mitch Evans (Evan Hayworth).

A G.B.M. Production, dst. Governor Films; black and white; 73 minutes. Released April 16, 1960.* Double bill with: *The Incredible Petrified World.*

*Ron Borst claims it was released in 1958, but it apparently was only produced then; all other sources, including the date of the world premiere in Los Angeles, confirm a 1960 release date.

Teenagers from Outer Space. *Director/Producer/Screenplay/Photography/Sound/Special effects/Editor* Tom Graeff, *Production associates* C.R. Kaltenthaler, Gene Sterling and Bryan G. Pearson (Bryant Grant?).

Cast: *Derek* David Love (Tom Graeff), *Betty Morgan* Dawn Anderson, *Gramps (Grandpa Morgan)* Harvey B. Dunn, *Thor* Bryan Grant, *Joe Rogers* Tom Lockyear, *Spaceship captain* Robert King Moody, *Dr. Brandt* Frederic Welch, *Miss Morse (his nurse)* Helen Sage, *Alice (girl in swimming pool)* Sonia Torgenson, *Also* Carl Dickensen, Billy Bridges, James Conklin, Gene Sterling, Ralph Lowe, Bill DeLand, Ursula Hansen, Bob Williams, Don DeClue, Don Chambers, Jim MacGeorge, Kent Rogers, Sol Resnick, Robert Regas, Horst Ehrhardt.

Topaz Film Corporation, dst. Warner Bros.; black and white; 85 minutes. British title: **The Gargon Terror.** Working titles: "The Boy from Outer Space," "Invasion of the Gargons." Released June 2, 1959. Double bill with: *Gigantis the Fire Monster.*

Terror from the Year 5,000. *Director/Producer/Story/Screenplay* Robert J. Gurney, Jr., *Executive producers(?)* James H. Nicholson and Samuel Z. Arkoff, *Assistant producer* Gene Searchinger, *Art director* Beatrice Gurney, *Scenic designer* William Hoffman, *Photography* Arthur Florman, *Editorial supervision* Dede Allen, *Sound* Robert Hathaway, *Makeup* Rudolph Liszt, *Script clerk* Anita Hathaway, *Production coordinator* Mark Hanna, *Assistant director* Jack Diamond, *Head grip* Jack Wallace, *Gaffer* Richard Gable, *Properties* Henderson "Gus" Brockway. No music credit.

Cast: *Robert Hedges* Ward Costello, *Claire Erling* Joyce Holden, *Victor* John Stratton, *Prof. Howard Erling* Frederic Downs, *Nurse and Future Woman (after)* Salome Jens, *Angelo (handyman)* Fred Herrick, *Miss Blake (Hedges' receptionist)* Beatrice Furdeaux, *Lab technicians* Jack Diamond, Fred Taylor, *Also* Bill Downs, William Cost.

La Jolla Prods., dst. American International; black and white; 74 minutes. Suggested by the story "Bottle Baby" by Henry Slesar. British title: **Cage of Doom.** Working titles: "Girl from 5000 A.D."; "Terror from 5000 A.D." Released October 30, 1958. Double bill with: *The Screaming Skull,* in some areas; in others with *The Brain Eaters.*

Terror Is a Man. *Director* Gerry (Gerardo) de Leon, *Screenplay* Harry Paul Harber, *Producers* Kane Lynn and Eddie Romero, *Art director* Vicente Bonus, *Photography* Emmanuel I. Rojas, *Music* Ariston Auelino, *Makeup* Remedios Amazon, *Special effects* Hilario Santos, *Sound recordist* Pedro Nicolas, *Production coordinator* Artemio B. Tecson.

Cast: *Dr. Girard* Francis Lederer, *Fitzgerald* Richard Derr, *Frances Girard* Greta Thyssen, *Beast-Man* Flory Carlos, *Walter* Oscar Keesee, *Tiago* Peyton Keesee, *Selene* Lilia Duran.

A Lynn-Romero Production, dst. Valiant Films; black and white; 89 minutes. Based without credit on *The Island of Dr. Moreau* by H.G. Wells. A U.S.–Philippine coproduction. Reissue title: **Blood Creature.** Working titles: "Beast from Blood Island," "Creature of Blood Island," "The Gory Creatures." Released December 1959.

The 30 Foot Bride of Candy Rock. *Director* Sidney Miller, *Screenplay* Rowland Barber and Arthur Ross, *Story* Lawrence L. Goldman, *Story idea* Jack Rabin and Irving Block, *Producer* Lewis J. Rachmil, *Executive producer (Costello's agent)* Edward Sherman, *Art director* William Flannery, *Set decorator* James A. Crowe, *Photography* Frank G. Carson, *Special photographic effects* Jack Rabin, Irving Block and Louis DeWitt, *Editor* Al Clark,

Music Raoul Kraushaar, *Sound* George Cooper, *Recording supervisor* John Livadary, *Makeup supervision* Clay Campbell, *Hairstyles* Helen Hunt, *Assistant director* William Dorfman.

Cast: *Arnie Pinsetter* Lou Costello, *Emmy Lou Raven Pinsetter* Dorothy Provine, *Raven Rossitter* Gale Gordon, *Magruder* Jimmy Conlin, *Stanford Bates* Charles Lane, *First general* Robert Burton, *Pentagon general* Will Wright, *Sergeant* Lenny Kent, *Aunt May* Ruth Perrott, *Bill Burton* Peter Leeds, *Bank manager* Robert Nichols, *Jackie Delaney* Veola Vonn, *Pilot* Jack Straw, *Lieutenant* Arthur Walsh, *Military policeman* Michael Hagan, *Announcer* Mark Scott, *Soldier* James Bryce, *Boosters* Russell Trent, Joey Faye, Bobby Barber, Joe Greene, Doodles Weaver, Jack Rice.

A D.R.B. Production for Columbia; black and white; 75 minutes. Working titles: "Lou Costello and His Thirty Foot Bride," "The Secret Bride of Candy Rock." Released August 6, 1959.

This Is Not a Test. *Director* Fredric Gadette, *Screenplay* Peter Abenheim, Betty Laskey and Fredric Gadette, *Producers* Fredric Gadette and Murray De'Atley, *Executive producers* James Grandin and Arthur Schmoyen, *Photography* Brick Marquard, *Editor* Hal Dennis, *Music* Greig McRitchie.

Cast: *Deputy Sheriff Dan Colter* Seamon Glass, *Jacob Elliot Saunders* Thayer Roberts, *Juney Aubrey Martin, Cheryl Hudson* Mary Morlas, *Joe Baragi* Mike Green, *Al Weston* Alan Austin, *Karen Barnes* Carol Kent, *Frank Barnes* Norman Winston, *Clint* Ron Starr, *Peter* Don Spruance, *Looters* Norm Bishop, Ralph Manza, Jay Della, William Flaherty, Phil Donati, Boyle Cooper.

A GPA Production, dst. Modern Films; black and white; approximately 80 minutes. May not have had theatrical release; completed no later than 1962.

The Three Stooges in Orbit. *Director* Edward Bernds, *Screenplay* Elwood Ullman, *Producer/Story* Norman Maurer, *Art director* Don Ament, *Set decorator* Richard Mansfield, *Photography* William F. Whitley, *Camera operator* Emil Oster, Jr., *Assistant camera* Al Bettcher, *Editor* Edwin Bryant, *Music* Paul Dunlap, *Sound supervisor* Charles J. Rice, *Supervising sound editor* Joseph Henri, *Sound mixer* William Bernds, *Recorders* Harry Foy and George Anderson, *Boom operator* Doug Grant, *Makeup supervisor* Ben Lane, *Makeup* Frank McCoy, *Costumes* Ted Tetrick and Pat Page, *Supervising hair stylist* Virginia Jones, *Hairstyles* Peggy McDonald, *Assistant directors* Eddie Saeta and Burt Astor, *Script supervisor* Eylla Jacobus, *Still photography* Homer Van Pelt, *Gaffer* James Field, *Key grip* Les Gaunt, *Property master* Ed Goldstein, *Prop man* Clarence Peet.

Cast: *The Three Stooges: Moe* Moe Howard, *Larry* Larry Fine, *Curley Joe* Joe De Rita, *Carol Danforth* Carol Christensen, *Professor Danforth* Emil Sitka, *Capt. Tom Andrews* Edson Stroll, *Ogg* George Neise, *Zogg* Rayford Barnes, *Williams (Martian spy/butler)* Norman Leavitt, *Chairman of Mars* Nestor Paiva, *General Bixby* Peter Dawson, *Dr. Appleby* Peter Brocco, *Colonel Smithers* Don Lamond, *George Galveston* Thomas Glynn, *Mr. Lansing* Maurice Manson, *WAF sergeant* Jean Charney, *Personnel clerk* Duane Ament, *Colonel Lane* Bill Dyer, *Welby* Roy Engel, *Bathing girl* Jane Wald, *Toothpaste old maid* Cheerio Meredith, *Cook* Rusty Wescoatt, *Mrs. McGinnis* Marjorie Eaton.

Normandy Prods. for Columbia Pictures; black and white; 87 minutes. Released July 11, 1962.

Note: Some of the film was shot in color for a short called "The Three Stooges Scrapbook" that did not see theatrical release in its original form but which was reduced to one reel and released in 1963. For more information on this important topic, see the book also called *The Three Stooges Scrapbook*, by the Lenburgs and Maurer.

The Three Stooges Meet Hercules. *Director* Edward Bernds, *Screenplay* Elwood Ullman, *Producer/Story* Norman Maurer, *Art director* Don Ament, *Set decorator* William Calvert, *Photography* Charles S. Welbourne, *Editor* Edwin Bryant, *Music* Paul Dunlap, *Sound mixer* James Z. Flaster, *Sound supervisor* Charles J. Rice, *Supervising sound editor* Joseph Henri, *Makeup supervision* Ben Lane, *Hairstyles* Virginia Jones, *Assistant director* Herb Wallerstein.

Cast: *The Three Stooges: Moe* Moe Howard, *Larry* Larry Fine, *Curley Joe* Joe De Rita, *Schuyler Davis* Quinn Redeker, *Odius* George N. Neise, *Hercules* Samson Burke, *Diane Quigley* Vicki Trickett, *Ralph Dimsal* George N. Neise, *The Siamese Cyclops** Mike and

Marlin McKeever, *Confused shepherd* Emil Sitka, *Thesus, King of Rhodes* Hal Smith, *Ulysses* John Cliff, *Achilles the Heel* Lewis Charles, *Anita* Barbara Hines, *Hecuba* Terry Huntington, *Helen* Diana Piper, *Simon* Gregg Martell, *Captain* Gene Roth, *Freddie the Fence* Edward Foster, *Matron* Cecil Elliott, *Philo* Rusty Wescoatt, *Refreshment man* Emil Sitka, *Narrator* Don Lamond.

*Some sources give Ajax as Mike McKeever's role name and Argo as that of Marlin McKeever, but they have no name(s) in the film.

A Normandy Production for Columbia Pictures; black and white; 89 minutes. Working title: "Hercules and the Three Stooges." Released January 26, 1962.

The Time Machine. *Director/Producer* George Pal, *Screenplay* David Duncan, *Art directors* George W. Davis and William Ferrari, *Set decorations* Henry Grace and Keogh Gleason, *Production illustrator* Mentor Huebner, *Special photographic effects* Project Unlimited (Gene Warren, Wah Chang, Tim Baar), *Stop-motion animation* David Pal, Don Sahlin, *Matte paintings* Bill Brace, *Editor* George Tomasini, *Music* Russell (Russ) Garcia, *Recording supervisor* Franklin Milton, *Rerecording mixer* William Steinkamp, *Makeup* Charles Schram, Ron Berkeley, *Morlock design* George Pal, *Makeup supervisor* William Tuttle, *Hairstyles* Mary Keats, *Hairstyle supervisor* Sydney Guilaroff, *Assistant director* William Shanks, *Assistant to the producer* Gae Griffith, *Color consultant* Charles K. Hagedon.

Cast: *George, the Time Traveler* Rod Taylor, *Weena* Yvette Mimieux, *David Filby* Alan Young, *James Filby* Alan Young, *Dr. Philip Hillyer* Sebastian Cabot, *Anthony Bridewell* Tom Helmore, *Walter Kemp* Whit Bissell, *Mrs. Watchett* Doris Lloyd, *First Eloi* Rob Barran, *Second Eloi (in white)* James Skelly, *Voice of the Talking Rings* Paul Frees.

A Galaxy Production for MGM; color; 103 minutes. Based on the novel of the same title by H.G. Wells. Released August 4, 1960.

The Tingler. *Director/Producer* William Castle, *Screenplay* Robb White, *Art director* Phil Bennett, *Set decorator* Milton Stumph, *Photography* Wilfrid M. Cline, *Editor* Chester W. Schaeffer, *Music* Von Dexter, *Sound* John Livadary and Harry Mills, *Makeup supervision* Clay Campbell, *Assistant director* Herb Wallerstein, *Associate to the producer* Dona Holloway.

Cast: *Dr. William Chapin* Vincent Price, *Martha Ryerson Higgins* Judith Evelyn, *Ollie Higgins* Philip Coolidge, *David Morris* Darryl Hickman, *Lucy Stevens* Pamela Lincoln, *Isabel Chapin* Patricia Cutts, *Women* Gail Bonney and Amy Fields, *Men* Clarence Straight and Pat Colby, *Projectionist* Dal McKennon, *Prisoner* Bob Gunderson.

A William Castle Production for Columbia; black and white with part-color sequence; 80 minutes. Working title: "The Chiller." Released July 29, 1959.

12 to the Moon. *Director* David Bradley, *Screenplay* DeWitt Bodeen, *Producer/Story* Fred Gebhardt, *Associate producer* Thom E. Fox, *Art director* Rudi Feld, *Set decorator* John Burton, *Special photographic effects* Howard A. Anderson, Co., *Additional special effects* E. (Elwood J.?) Nicholson, *Editor* Edward Mann, *Music* Michael Andersen, *Sound mixer* Herman Lewis, *Production supervisor* Joel Freeman, *Assistant to producer* Ned Roberts, *Assistant director* Gilbert Mandelik, *Technical story adviser* Ronald Grant.

Cast: *Dr. John Anderson* Ken Clark, *Dr. Hideku Murata* Michi Kobi, *Dr. Luis Vargas* Tony (Anthony) Dexter, *Dr. Erik Heinrich* John Wengraf, *Dr. Sigrid Bromark* Anna-Lisa, *Sir Dr. William Rochester* Phillip Baird, *Dr. Etienne Martel* Roger Til, *Dr. Asmara Makonnen* Cory Devlin, *Dr. Selim Hamid* Tema Bey, *Roddy Murdock* Bob Montgomery, Jr., *Dr. David Ruskin* Richard Weber, *Director of International Space Order* Francis X. Bushman.

Luna Productions, dst. Columbia Pictures; black and white; 74 minutes. Released June 24, 1960. Double bill with: *13 Ghosts* or *Battle in Outer Space*.

The Underwater City. *Director* Frank McDonald, *Screenplay* Owen Harris (Orville H. Hampton), *Story* Alex Gordon and Ruth Alexander Gordon, *Producer* Alex Gordon, *Art director* Don Ament, *Photography* Gordon Avil, *Special effects coordinators* Howard Lydecker and Richard Albain, *FantaScope supervisor* Darrel A. Anderson, *FantaScope effects* Howard A. Anderson Co., *Editors* Al Clark and Don Starling, *Music* Ronald Stein, *Sound* George Cooper, *Sound supervision* Charles J. Rice, *Supervising sound editor*

Joseph Henri, *Makeup department head* Ben Lane, *Hairstyles* Virginia Jones, *Production assistant* Jack Cash, *Assistant director* Robert Agnew.

Cast: *Bob Gage* William Lundigan, *Dr. Monica Powers* Julie Adams, *Tim Graham* Roy Roberts, *Dr. Halstead* Carl Benton Reid, *Chuck "Cowboy" Marlow* Chet Douglas, *George Burnett* Paul Dubov, *Phyllis Gatewood* Karen Norris, *Dotty* Kathie Browne, *Lt. Wally Steele* Edward Mallory, *Dr. Carl Wendt* George De Normand, *Meade* Edmund Cobb, *Winchell* Roy Damron, *Civilian* Paul Power, *Also* Frank Lackteen.

A Neptune Production for Columbia Pictures; black and white,* 78 minutes. Released January 10, 1962.

*The film was shot in Eastman Color, and was shown in that process outside of North America and on television.

Valley of the Dragons. *Director/Screenplay* Edward Bernds, *"Story"* Donald Zimbalist,* *Producer* Byron Roberts, *Executive producer* Alfred (Al) Zimbalist, *Art director* Don Ament, *Photography* Brydon Baker, *Special effects* Dick Albain, *Editor* Edwin Bryant, *Music* Ruby Raksin, *Sound supervision* Charles J. Rice, *Sound* Lambert Day, *Makeup supervision* Ben Lane, *Supervising sound editor* Joseph Henri, *Assistant director* George Rhein.

Note: Much of *Valley of the Dragons* consists of stock footage from *One Million B.C.* (1940). In the interest of fairness, here are relevant credits from that film: *Art director* Charles D. Hall, *Costumes* Harry Black, *Special photographic effects* Roy Seawright, *Miniature supervisor* Fred Knoth, *Miniature photography* Frank William Young, *Matte artist* Jack Shaw, *Animal supervisor* Fred Knoth.

Cast: *Capt. Hector Servadac* Cesare Danova, *Michael Denning* Sean McClory, *Deena* Joan Staley, *Nateeta* Danielle de Metz, *Od-Loo* Gregg Martell, *Tarn* Gil Perkins, *Patoo* I. Stanford Jolly, *Anoka* Michael Lane, *Vidal* Roger Til, *Andrews* Mark Dempsey, *LeClerc* Jerry Sunshine, *Doctor* Gil Perkins, *Mara* Dolly Gray.

*Donald Zimbalist is credited with the story, although all he did was to find the novel it was based on in a bookstore.

Z.R.B. (Zimbalist, Roberts, Bernds) Productions for Columbia Pictures; black and white; 79 minutes. Loosely based on the 1877 novel *Hector Servadac* by Jules Verne. Verne's novel is also called *Off on a Comet, The Career of a Comet* and *Mr. Servadac's Arc.* Released October 25, 1961. Double bill with: *Mr. Sardonicus.*

Varan the Unbelievable. *Director* Inoshiro Honda, *Screenplay* Shinichi Sekizawa, *Idea* Takeshi Kuronuma, *Producer* Tomoyuki Tanaka, *Art director* Kiyoshi Shimizu, *Photographer* Hajime Koizumi, *Special effects director* Eiji Tsuburaya, *Music* Akira Ifukube. (Ifukube's music was removed in whole or in part from American prints and replaced with library music, including some from Albert Glasser's score for *The Amazing Colossal Man.*)

Credits for U.S. revised print: Director/Producer Jerry A. Baerwitz, *Screenplay* Sid Harris, *Photography* Jack (Jacques) Marquette, *Special effects* Howard A. Anderson Co., *Supervising film editor* Jack Ruggiero, *Assistant editor* Ralph Cushman, *Music editor* Peter Zinner, *Sound recording* Vic Appel, *Wardrobe* Robert O'Dell, *Makeup* Robert Cowan, *Assistant director* Leonard Kunody.

Starring cast of Japanese prints: *Kenji* Kozo Nomura, *Yuriko Ayumi* Sonoda, *Dr. Sugimoto* Koreya Senda, *Dr. Fujimoto* Akihiko Hirata, *Also* Toshio Tsuchiya. **Starring cast of American scenes:** *Cmdr. James Bradley, U.S.N.* Myron Healey, *Anna Bradley* Tsuruko Kobayashi, *Captain Kishi* Clifford Kawada, *Matsu* Erick Shimatsu. **Others (scenes uncertain):** Hideo Imamura, George Sasaki, Hiroshi Hisamune, Yoneo Iguchi, Michael Sung, Roy Ogata.

Dalls Prods.–Cory Prods. (U.S.); Toho (Japan), dst. Crown International Pictures; black and white; TohoScope/other scope, 70 minutes in U.S. (87 minutes in Japan). Original title: **Daikaiju Baran.** Released December 7, 1962 in U.S. (1958 in Japan). Double bill with: *First Spaceship on Venus.*

Village of the Damned. *Director* Wolf Rilla, *Screenplay* Stirling Silliphant, Wolf Rilla and George Barclay (Ronald Kinnoch), *Producer* Ronald Kinnoch, *Art direction* Ivan King, *Photography* Geoffrey Faithfull, *Photographic effects* Ron Howard, *Camera operator* Frank Drake, *Editor* Gordon Hales, *Music* Ron Goodwin, *Sound supervisor* A.W.

Watkins, *Sound recordist* Cyril Swern, *Dubbing editor* Gordon Daniel, *Dubbing mixer* J.B. Smith, *Makeup* Eric Aylott, *Wardrobe* Eileen Sullivan, *Hairstyles* Joan Johnstone, *Continuity* Lee Turner, *Production manager* Denis Johnson, *Assistant director* David Middlemas, *2nd unit photography* Gerald Moss.

Cast: *Gordon Zellaby* George Sanders, *Anthea Zellaby* Barbara Shelley, *David Zellaby* Martin Stephens, *Alan Bernard* Michael Gwynn, *Mr. Willers* Laurence Naismith, *The Villagers: Harrington* Richard Warner, *Mrs. Harrington* Jenny Laird, *Evelyn Harrington* Sarah Long, *James Pawle* Thomas Heathcote, *Janet Pawle* Charlotte Mitchell, *Milly Hughes* Pamela Buck, *Miss Ogle* Rosamund Greenwood, *Mrs. Plumpton* Susan Richards, *Vicar* Bernard Archard, *Constable Gobby* Peter Vaughan, *Normal children* Brian Smith, Paul Norman, John Bush, Janice Howley, Robert Marks, Billy Lawrence. *Conference members: General Leighton* John Phillips, *Sir Edgar Hargraves* Richard Vernon, *Professor Smith* John Stuart, *Dr. Carlisle* Keith Pyott. *Others: Coroner* Alexander Archdale, *Nurse* Sheila Robins, *Pilot* Tom Bowman, *Lieutenant* Anthony Harrison, *WRAC secretary* Diane Aubrey, *Sapper* Gerald Paris, *Himself (a dog)* Bruno. *The Alien Children*:* June Cowell, John Kelly, Lesley Scoble, Roger Malik, Theresa Scoble, Peter Taylor, Linda Bateson, Carlo Cura, Mark Mileham, Elizabeth Munden, Peter Priedel, Howard Knight.

*Because of the configuration of the Call Bureau Cast Sheet, some researchers have erroneously concluded that all names on the left of the sheet were role names (as is the case generally), and that all names on the right were actor names. This would mean that there were only six alien children, and that (for instance) Roger Malik was played by Elizabeth Munden, and that none of the children (alien or not) had the last names of the village adults. Actually, both lists of children, normal and weirdo, were of the actors *only*; no role names are specified in that list.

MGM; black and white; 78 minutes. Based on the 1957 novel *The Midwich Cuckoos* by John Wyndham. A U.S.–British coproduction (in effect). Released October 28, 1960 (in New York in December).

Visit to a Small Planet. *Director* Norman Taurog, *Screenplay* Edmund Beloin and Henry Garson, *Producer* Hal B. Wallis, *Associate producer* Paul Nathan, *Executive in charge of production (in effect)* Joseph H. Hazen, *Art directors* Hal Pereira and Walter Tyler, *Set decorators* Sam Comer and Arthur Krams, *Photography* Loyal Griggs, *Special photographic effects* John P. Fulton, *Process photography* Farciot Edouart, *Editorial supervision* Warren Low, *Editor* Frank Bracht, *Music* Leigh Harline, *Sound recording* Gene Merritt and Charles Grenzbach, *Sound supervisor* George Dutton, *Makeup supervision* Wally Westmore, *Costumes* Edith Head, *Hairstyle supervision* Nellie Manley, *Dialogue coach* Jack Mintz, *Production manager* Frank Caffey, *Assistant director* D. Michael Moore, *Assistant to the producer* Jack Saper, *Story editor/Talent director* Irene Lee, *Choreography* Miriam Nelson.

Cast: *Kreton* Jerry Lewis, *Ellen Spelding* Joan Blackman, *Maj. Roger Putnam Spelding* Fred Clark, *Delton* John Williams, *George Abercrombie* Jerome Cowan, *Bob Mayberry* Gale Gordon, *Rheba Spelding* Lee Patrick, *Desdemona (beatnik dancer)* Barbara Lawson, *Police commander* Milton Frome, *Mabel Mayberry* Ellen Corby, *Announcer* Richard Lane, *Waiters* John Dennis, Mark Russell, *Melrick* Edward G. Robinson, Jr., *Traffic cop* Michael Ross, *Malcolm* Joseph Turkel, *Policeman* Karl Lukas, *Spinrad* Paul Smith, *General* John Diggs, *Truck driver* Max Power, *Motorcycle policeman* Charles Ward, *Beatniks* Paul Wexler, Gene Collins, Dominic Fidelibus, David Landfield, Beach Dickerson, Hugh Langtry, Louise Glenn, Bob Harvey, Sondra Matesky, Titus Moede.

A Hal B. Wallis–Joseph H. Hazen production for Paramount Pictures; black and white; 85 minutes. Based on the 1955 teleplay and 1957 play of the same title by Gore Vidal. Released February 4, 1960.

Voyage to the Bottom of the Sea. *Director/Producer/Story* Irwin Allen, *Screenplay* Irwin Allen and Charles Bennett, *Art directors* Jack Martin Smith and Herman A. Blumenthal, *Set decorators* Walter M. Scott and John Sturtevant, *Photography* Winton Hoch, *Underwater photography* John Lamb, *Special photographic effects* L.B. Abbott and Davis S. Horsley, *Editor* George Boemler, *Music* Paul Sawtell and Bert Shefter, *Orchestrations* Max Reese, *Title song* Russell Faith, *Sung by* Frankie Avalon, *Sound* Alfred Bruzlin and Warren B. Delaplain, *Sound effects editor* Walter A. Rossi, *Makeup supervision* Ben Nye, *Costume design* Paul Zastupnevich, *Hairstyles* Helen Turpin, *Assistant director* Ad

Schaumer, *Assistant to the producer* Albert Gail, *Technical adviser* Fred Zendar, *Color consultant* Leonard Doss.

Cast: *Adm. Harriman Nelson* Walter Pidgeon, *Capt. Lee Crane* Robert Sterling, *Chip Romano* Frankie Avalon, *Miguel Alvarez* Michael Ansara, *Commodore Lucius Emery* Peter Lorre, *Dr. Susan Hiller* Joan Fontaine, *Cathy Connors* Barbara Eden, *Dr. Jamieson* Regis Toomey, *Dr. Zucco* Henry Daniell, *Congressman Parker* Howard McNear, *Admiral Crawford* John Litel, *Smith* Mark Slade, *Gleason* Charles Tannen, *Kowski* Delbert (Del) Monroe, *Cookie* Anthony Monaco, *Sparks* Robert Easton, *Young* Jonathan Gilmore, *Ned Thompson* David McLean, *Dr. Newmar* Larry Gray, *Lieutenant Hodges* George Diestel, *Italian U.N. delegate* Dr. John Giovanni, *U.N. chairman* Kendrick Huxham, *U.N. commentator* Art Baker, *Crew members* Skip Ward, William Herrin, Richard Adams, Michael Ford, Robert Buckingham, James Murphy.

Windsor Productions for 20th Century–Fox; color; CinemaScope; 105 minutes. Released July 12, 1961.

Note: The first episode of the TV series of the same name as this film was a remake of the movie; the episode was called "Eleven Days to Zero," and used much stock footage from the feature.

The Wacky World of Dr. Morgus. *Director* Roul Haig, *Screenplay* Noel and Roul Haig, *Producers* Eugene T. Calogne and Jules Sevin, *Photography* Irwin Blanche, *Music* Corelli Jacobs.

Cast: *Dr. Alexander Morgus* Sid Noel, *Pencils McCane* Dana Barton, *Mona Speekla* Jeanne Teslof, *Bruno* David Kleinberger, *Chopsley* Thomas George, *Also* Bob Nelson, Marshall Pearce, Chris Owen, Wayne Mack.

Dst. Calogne & Sevin; black and white; 90 minutes. Played New Orleans October 1962.

War of the Colossal Beast. *Director/Producer/Story/Special technical effects* Bert I. Gordon, *Screenplay* George Worthing Yates, *Executive producers* James H. Nicholson and Samuel Z. Arkoff, *Assistant producer* Henry Schrage, *Art director* Walter Keller, *Set decorator* Maury Hoffman, *Photography* Jack Marta, *Assistant technical effects* Flora Gordon, *Editorial supervision* Ronald Sinclair, *Assistant film editor* Paul Wittenberg, *Music* Albert Glasser, *Sound effects editor* Josef von Stroheim, *Sound mixer* Benny Winkler, *Special makeup* Jack H. Young, *Script supervisor* Judy Hart, *Production manager /1st assistant director* H.E. (Herb) Mendelson, *2nd assistant director* John W. Rogers, *Property master* Walter Broadfoot, *Chief set electrician* Babe Stafford.

Cast: *Joyce Manning* Sally Fraser, *Col. Glenn Manning* Dean Parkin, *Major Baird* Roger Pace, *Dr. Carmichael* Russ Bender, *Captain Harris* Charles Stewart, *John Swanson* George Becwar, *Miguel (in truck)* Robert Hernandez, *Sgt. Luis Murillo* Rico Alaniz, *Army officer* George Alexander, *Mexican doctor* George Navarro, *Neurologist* John McNamara, *Pentagon correspondent* Bob Garnet, *Medical corps officer* Howard Wright, *Mayor* Roy Gordon, *General Nelson* George Milan, *Switchboard operator* Warren Frost, *Bus driver* Bill Giorgio, *Joan* Loretta Nicholson, *Mrs. Edwards* June Jocelyn, *Newscaster* Jack Kosslyn, *TV announcer* Stan Chambers, *Also* Raymond Winston, June Burt, Mary Hennesy, Hal Torey, Bob Tetrick, Rod Dana.

Carmel Prods. for American International; black and white with one color scene; 68 minutes. Sequel to *The Amazing Colossal Man* (1957). British title: **The Terror Strikes**. Working title: "Revenge of the Colossal Man." Released July 1958. Double bill with: *Attack of the Puppet People*.

War of the Satellites. *Director/Producer* Roger Corman, *Screenplay* Lawrence Louis Goldman, *Story/Associate producers* Jack Rabin and Irving Block, *Art director* Daniel Haller, *Set decorator* Harry Reif, *Photography* Floyd Crosby, *Special effects* Jack Rabin, Irving Block and Louis DeWitt, *Editor* Irene Morra, *Music* Walter Greene, *Sound* Phil Mitchell, *Production manager* Lionel C. Place, *Assistant director* Jack Bohrer, *Props* Karl Brainard, *Key grip* Chuck Hanawalt.

Cast: *Dave Boyer* Dick Miller, *Sybil Carrington* Susan Cabot, *Dr. Pol Van Ponder* Richard Devon, *Dr. Lazar* Eric Sinclair, *Jason Ibn Akad* Michael Fox, Cole Hodgkiss Robert Shayne, *Monsieur Lemoine* Bruno Ve Sota, *John Campo* Jerry Barclay, *Jay Jay* Sayer, *Mitzi* Mitzi McCall, *Crewmen* John Brinkley and Beach Dickerson, *Ground controller* Roger Corman, *Also* Roy Gordon and James Knight.

Santa Cruz Productions, dst. Allied Artists; black and white; 66 minutes. Released May 16, 1958. Double bill with: *Attack of the 50 Foot Woman*.

The Wasp Woman. *Director/Producer* Roger Corman, *Screenplay* Leo Gordon, *Story* Kinta Zertuche, *Art director* Daniel Haller, *Photography* Harry C. Newman, *Editor* Carlo Lodato, *Sound* Philip N. Mitchell, *Makeup* Grant R. Keats, *Production manager* Jack Bohrer, *Property manager* Karl Brainard, *Music* Fred Katz.

Cast: *Janice Starlin* Susan Cabot, *Bill Lane* Fred (Anthony) Eisley, *Eric Zinthrop* Michael Mark, *Mary Dennison* Barboura Morris, *Arthur Cooper (Coop)* William Roerick, *Les Hellman (private eye)* Frank Gerstle, *Night watchman* Bruno Ve Sota, *Max Thompson* Roy Gordon, *Deliveryman* Frank Wolff, *Jean Carson* Carolyn Hughes, *Maureen Reardon* Lyn Cartwright, *Nurse Warren* Lani Mars, *Emergency doctor* Roger Corman(?), *Also* Philip Barry.

Filmgroup–Santa Clara, dst. Allied Artists; black and white; 73 minutes. Working titles(?): "The Insect Woman," "The Bee Girl." Released March 17, 1960. (May have had some bookings in 1959 through Filmgroup.) Double bill with: *Beast from Haunted Cave*.

The Weird Ones. *Producer* Pat Boyette, *Presented by* Dale Berry and Charles Martinez.

Cast: Mike Braden, Rudy Duran, Phyliss Warren, Lee Morgan.

Dst. Crescent International Pictures and Colonial International Pictures; black and white; 76 minutes. Released February 1962.

Note: It is likely that Boyette also wrote and directed the film.

White Goddess. *Director* Wallace Fox, *Producer* Rudolph Flatow, *Screenplay* Sherman L. Lowe and Eric Taylor.

Cast: *Dr. Tom Reynolds (Ramar of the Jungle)* Jon Hall, *Prof. Howard Ogden* Ray Montgomery, *Trudy* M'Liss McClure, *White Goddess* Millicent Patrick, *Cockey guide* James Fairfax, *The trader* Ludwig Stossel, *Escaped convicts* Lucien Prival, Robert Williams, *Also* Joel Fluellen, Darby Jones.

An Arrow Production; dst. by Lippert in the U.S.; black and white; 77 minutes. May, 1953. British title: *Ramar of the Jungle*.

The Wild Women of Wongo. *Director/Executive producer* James L. Wolcott, *Screenplay* Cedric Rutherford, *Producer* George R. Black, *Photography* Harry Walsh, *Editor* David Cazalet, *Sound* Edward A. Fenton, *Makeup* Rudolph Liszt, *Costumes* Tom McKeehan, *Dialogue director* Owen Phillips, *Production assistants* Richard F. Leavitt, Faith Knobel, Marion Black Vaccaro, *Choreography* Olga Suarez.

Cast: *Omoo* Jean Hawkshaw, *Engor* Johnny Walsh, *Mona* Mary Ann Webb, *Ahtee* Candé Gerrard, *Wana* Adrienne Bourbeau,* *Gahbo* Ed Fury, *Girls of Wongo* Marie Goodhart, Michelle Lamaack, Joyce Nizzari, Val Phillips, Jo Elaine Wagner, *Men of Wongo* Pat Crowley, Ray Rotello, Billy Day, Bart Parker, Robert Serreochia, Whitey Hart, *Girls of Goona* Barbara Lee Babbitt, Bernadette, Elaine Krasker, Lillian Melek, Iris Rawtenberg, Roberta Wagner, *Men of Goona* Roy Murray, Steve Klisanin, Walter Knoch, Ronald Markowski, Gerry Roslund, Varden Spencer, Kenneth Vitulli, *King of Goona* Burt Williams, *King of Wongo* Rex Richards, *Priestess* Zuni Dyer, *Spirit of Priestess* Olga Suarez.

*Despite the coincidence of the names, this is not the same as current actress Adrienne Barbeau. Ms. Bourbeau is still active in production capacities in films made in Florida.

A Jaywall Production (copyright by Tropical Pictures), dst. Wolcott Productions; color; 72 minutes (some sources also cite 52 minutes, but it certainly seems at least 72 minutes). Date is uncertain; some sources indicate 1958; it was definitely in release by 1959.

Womaneater. *Director* Charles Saunders, *Screenplay* Brandon Fleming, *Producer* Guido Coen, *Art director* Herbert Smith, *Photography* Ernest Palmer, *Camera operator* Anthony Heller, *Editor* Seymour Logie, *Music* Edwin Astley, *Sound* Mickey Jay, *Makeup* Terry Terrington, *Hairdresser* Doris Pollard, *Continuity* Vera Pavey, *Production manager* Frank Bevis, *1st assistant director* Douglas Hermes.

Cast: *Dr. James Moran* George Coulouris, *Sally Norton* Vera Day, *Tanga* Jimmy Vaughan, *Margaret Santor* Joyce Gregg, *Jack Venner* Peter Wayn, *Sergeant Bolton*

Edward Higgins, *Detective-Inspector Brownlow* Maxwell Foster, *Judy* Joy Webster, *Detective-Sergeant Freeman* Peter Lewiston, *Lewis Carling* Robert MacKenzie, *Dr. Patterson* Norman Claridge, *Native girl sacrifice* Marpessa Dawn, *Susan Curtis (first victim we see)* Sara Leighton, *Bristow* Harry Ross, *Fair attendant* Alexander Field, *Man in club* David Lawton, *Lascar in club* John Tinn, *Constable* Roger Avon.

Fortress Films, U.S. dst. Columbia Pictures; black and white; 71 minutes. A British film. Publicity title: **The Woman Eater**. U.S. release June 23, 1959 (British release 1957). Double bill with: *The H-Man*.

The World the Flesh and the Devil. *Director/Screenplay* Ranald MacDougall, *Screen story* Ferdinand Reyher, *Producer* George Englund, *Art directors* William A. Horning and Paul Groesse, *Set decorators* Henry Grace and Keogh Gleason, *Photography* Harold J. Marzorati, *Special photographic effects (mattes)* Lee LeBlanc and Matthew Yuricich, *Special mechanical effects* A. Arnold Gillespie, *Editor* Harold F. Kress, *Music* Miklos Rozsa, *Sound supervisor* Franklin Milton, *Rerecording* William Steinkamp, *Makeup supervisor* William Tuttle, *Miss Stevens' wardrobe* Kitty Mager, *Hairstyle supervisor* Sydney Guilaroff, *Assistant director* Al Jennings.

Cast: *Ralph Burton* Harry Belafonte, *Sarah Crandall* Inger Stevens, *Benson Thacker* Mel Ferrer.

A Sol C. Siegel-Harbel Production for MGM; black and white; CinemaScope; 95 minutes. Loosely based on the 1902 novel *The Purple Cloud* by M.P. Shiel. Working title: "End of the World." Released May 1959.

Appendix II

Films in Order of Release

The films covered in this book are here listed in the order they were released in the United States; I do not include those in the Addenda (p. 715), all of which were released before 1958. Most dates were obtained from the *Motion Picture Almanac* which can be, sadly, inaccurate. Other sources include the *Film Daily Yearbook*, which lists films by date of the *Film Daily* review, and the *American Film Institute Catalog*, which lists films by their earliest theatrical opening in the United States.

Some films have only a year available for their release; I have listed all of these at the beginning of the year in question, so it's almost certain they were actually released *after* many of the films they precede. Also, if I have a month and year but not an exact day for the film, I list it under that month, but *before* the films for which I do have exact days. As with the year-only films, this means some of these films will be listed before some they actually followed into theatres.

Finally, the sharp-eyed will notice that some films have a date days or even months separated from those they went out as a double bill with. I really have no idea why this should be, only a few guesses: studio bookkeeping methods, second thoughts, inaccurate reporting, and so forth.

1958

The Brain from Planet Arous (Note: This and its cofeature were released in Los Angeles in December, 1957, but played everywhere else in the U.S. in 1958, so far as I have been able to determine.)
Teenage Monster
She Demons March
Giant from the Unknown March
The Flame Barrier April
The Astounding She-Monster April 10
Attack of the Puppet People Spring
War of the Satellites May 16
Attack of the 50 Foot Woman May 19
Fiend Without a Face June 9
The Revenge of Frankenstein June 18
The Space Children June 23
The Colossus of New York June 26
War of the Colossal Beast July
The Crawling Eye July 7
The Cosmic Monster July 7
The Fly July 11

Space Master X-7 July 11
How to Make a Monster July 30
It! The Terror from Beyond Space August 7
Curse of the Faceless Man August 14
The Brain Eaters Fall
Teenage Caveman September 4
Queen of Outer Space September 9
The Blob September 12
I Married a Monster from Outer Space September 29
Earth vs. the Spider October
Missile to the Moon October
Blood of the Vampire October 7
Monster on the Campus October 22
Terror from the Year 5,000 October 30
Frankenstein 1970 November
From the Earth to the Moon November 6
Missile Monsters November 12
Satan's Satellites December
Invisible Avenger December
Night of the Blood Beast December 5
The Lost Missile December 10
Half Human December 10 (in Los Angeles)
Monster from Green Hell December 12
Frankenstein's Daughter December 15

1959

Beast from Haunted Cave (late 1959)
The Man Without a Body
The Wasp Woman (one source says March 17, 1960, but it was in release in late 1959, according to other sources)
The Wild Women of Wongo
First Man into Space February
The Cosmic Man February
The Giant Behemoth March 3
Island of Lost Women April 10
Horrors of the Black Museum April 22
The World the Flesh and the Devil May
The Mysterians May
Invisible Invaders May 15
Gigantis the Fire Monster June 2
Teenagers from Outer Space June 2
The H-Man June 23
The Man Who Could Cheat Death June 23
Womaneater June 23
Plan 9 from Outer Space July (?? Some sources say 1958)
The Giant Gila Monster July 15
The Killer Shrews (This must have opened as early as summer, 1959, as it was the cofeature with the preceding film, although this one has an official release date of December 18, 1959.)
The Alligator People July 16
Have Rocket, Will Travel July 21
Return of the Fly July 21
The Tingler July 29
The 30-Foot Bride of Candy Rock August 6
4D Man October 7
The Hideous Sun Demon December

The Mouse That Roared December
Terror Is a Man December
Journey to the Center of the Earth December 17
On the Beach December 17

1960

The Amazing Transparent Man
Attack of the Giant Leeches
The Cape Canaveral Monsters
Nude on the Moon
Sex Kittens Go to College (late in the year?)
Rocket Attack U.S.A.
Visit to a Small Planet February 4
The Atomic Submarine February 12
The Incredible Petrified World April 16
Teenage Zombies April 16
The Leech Woman May 20
The Electronic Monster May 27
Battle in Outer Space June 10
Dinosaurus! June 10
12 to the Moon June 24
The Lost World July 1
Assignment Outer Space August
The Time Machine August 4
Last Woman on Earth Fall
Caltiki, the Immortal Monster September
The Angry Red Planet September 8
Beyond the Time Barrier September 8
The Little Shop of Horrors October
Village of the Damned October 28
A Dog, a Mouse and a Sputnik October 31

1961

Gorgo February 10
The Absent Minded Professor March 16
Konga March 22
Dr. Blood's Coffin April 26
Beast of Yucca Flats May
Atlantis, the Lost Continent May 3
House of Fright May 3
Master of the World May 31
The Snake Woman June 3
Man in the Moon June 12
Magic Spectacles June 23
Most Dangerous Man Alive June 28
The Secret of the Telegian July
Voyage to the Bottom of the Sea July 12
Creature from the Haunted Sea August
The Day the Sky Exploded September 27
The Head October 11
Valley of the Dragons October 25
Journey to the Seventh Planet December

Assignment Outer Space December 13
The Phantom Planet December 13
Mysterious Island December 20

1962

This Is Not a Test
The Underwater City January 10
The Three Stooges Meet Hercules January 28
Siege of Syracuse January 31
The Weird Ones February
Paradisio February 23
Hand of Death March
Hands of a Stranger March
It's Hot in Paradise March
Nude in His Pocket March
The Day the Earth Caught Fire March 15
The Horror Chamber of Dr. Faustus March 28
The Manster March 28
Invasion of the Star Creatures April
Moon Pilot April 5
The Brain That Wouldn't Die May
Mothra May
Invasion of the Animal People May 3
The Road to Hong Kong May 23
Eegah! June 8
The Creation of the Humanoids July 3
Panic in Year Zero! July 4
The Three Stooges in Orbit July 11
The Wacky World of Dr. Morgus October
The Manchurian Candidate October 24
First Spaceship on Venus October 31
Reptilicus November
The Final War December 3
Varan the Unbelievable December 7

Appendix III

Announced Titles

... Or promises and threats never kept. As in Volume 1, these are culled mostly from "Scientifilm Marquee," the column by Forrest J Ackerman that appeared usually in *Imaginative Tales*. The following is a selected list of movies announced for production during the period covered by this volume, but which were never made.

Adventure Beneath the Ocean's Floor (announced by Alex Gordon; may be *The Underwater City*)
The Amazing Sea Giant
Atlantis (starring Curt Jurgens)
Atlantis 20,000 B.C. (American International)
Atomic Cannibal
Attack from the Future (screenplay by Charles Beaumont)
Attack of the Jungle Woman
The Beast from Assuan
The Beast from World's End
Beast of Paradise
The Bee-Girl (Alex Gordon)
The Boy Who Saved the World (to feature Robby the Robot)
The Brain Snatchers
The Brother (Martin Varno script)
Chookna—the Beast from World's End
Cobalt Bomb
The Cocoon
Conquest of Infinity
The Cosmonauts (Alex Gordon)
The Country of the Blind (perhaps the TV adaptation of the H.G. Wells story of the same name; the TV show was "The Richest Man in Bogota")
Cowboy from Outer Space
The Crazy Quilt Terror (based on the short story "The Rag Thing" and one of my two favorite unfilmed titles from this list)
Creature from the 4th Dimension
The Day the Adults Died
The Day the Children Vanished
The Day the Sun Grew Cold
Dark Dominion
The Dead Never Die
Debbie and the Demon
The Delicate Balance of Terror (from novel *Two Hours to Doom*)
The Demolished Man (from the novel; to star John Payne)
Descent into the Maelstrom (Alex Gordon from Poe story)
Devil Beast
The Devil from the Deep (Jerome Bixby)
Diamond Monster
Dimension Four (William Alland)

The Disappearance (George Pal)
Dr. Doom the Invisible Monster (Alex Gordon)
Dondi Goes to the Moon
The Doomsday Men
Dragons of Lost World (may be same as *Valley of the Dragons*)
The Dreamers (script by Ray Bradbury)
Earth Around with Satellites
Eighteen Visits to Mars
Envoy Earth
Eve and the Dragon (frequently announced by American International)
The Experiment of Dr. Zahn
The Face of the Deep (by Curt Siodmak)
The Fantastic Little Girl (planned sequel to *The Incredible Shrinking Man*, in which Scott Carey's wife follows him into the world of the infinitely small; a proposed 3rd would have made them giants)
Fiend from Half Moon Bay
The First Day of World War III
Fortress Beneath the Sea
The Frozen Continent
The Giant Sloth
Giganturo
The Girls from Planet 5 (from the novel by Richard Wilson)
Good As Gold
The Green Eye
Hell and High Water (script by Jerome Bixby, not the released, non-SF film of the same title; later called *The Sargasso Monster*)
The Hideous Rock 'n' Roll Creature (this is my second favorite unfilmed title from this list)
Honeymoon in Hell (from the book by Frederic Brown)
House of Monsters (may be *The Unearthly*)
The Humanoids
Hurricane Man
The Id
IGY (presumably standing for International Geophysical Year)
Implosion
In the Year 2889 (AIP announced this repeatedly, sometimes claiming it was to be based on a Jules Verne novel, at other times that it was from H.G. Wells' *When the Sleeper Wakes*, which title they also announced)
Inside the Moon
Invaders from 7000 A.D.
Invisible Sun
The Iron Horror
It Came to Kill (later called *Fiend from the Future*)
It Lived a Million Years (I have this script; you ain't missing anything)
Journey into the Unknown (Ib Melchior)
A Journey to the Moon (Charlie Chaplin)
Journey to Venus
The Jupiter Project
Kidnappers from Space (Forry Ackerman and Louis DeWitt)
Killer Corpse
Killer Smog (Alex Gordon)
King Kong (remake, with Willis O'Brien effects)
King of the Monsters (to star Boris Karloff)
The Kingdom of the Mad
The Kiva Monster
Kra! (William Alland)
Lazarus No. 7
Level 7 (from the novel by Mordecai Roshwald)
The Little Moon
The Man from Beneath the Sea
The Man Who Came from the Other World

The Man Who Could Not Die (Curt Siodmak was to make from Charles Beaumont script)
The Man Who Lived Forever
The Martian Chronicles (scripted by Ray Bradbury for Cinerama production, to star
    Gregory Peck. I have this script too, and you are missing something)
Martian Eye (written by Ted Johnstone, to be directed by Bill Rotsler)
Martian Frankenstein
Metropolis (a remake?)
The Mind Thing (from the novel by Frederic Brown; announced first by John Payne, later
    by Alfred Hitchcock, who instead made the somewhat similar *The Birds*)
Mr. & Mrs. Monster (William Castle)
Monster Assassin
Monster in My Blood
The Multiple Man (Ib Melchior)
Naked Terror (from Richard Matheson's *I Am Legend*; later called *The Night People*;
    finally filmed as *The Last Man on Earth*)
No Time Like the Future
The Nomoglod (by Wyott Ordung)
Once Around the Moon (to star Kirk Douglas and Sophia Loren)
Operation Snowman
Out of the Deeps (from the novel by John Wyndham)
Passage Through the Ocean Floor
The Phantom People
The Planet Men
Project Excelsior
Pygmy Island (from a novel by Edmond Hamilton)
R.U.R.
Rattlesnake
Red Snow
The Rest Must Die (Arch Oboler)
Return from the River Styx
The Return of the Time Traveler (announced repeatedly by George Pal; see the entry on
    The Time Machine)
Rip Van Winkle in the 21st Century
Robotman, USA
The Screaming Head
Screaming Teens
The Screaming Well
The Sea-Man (Alex Gordon)
The Seaweed Creature
The 7th Sense
Shadow Monster
Shadow on the Hearth (by Judith Merril; may have been a TV show)
Silent Sound
Sinvala
Skyport (by Curt Siodmak, who turned the script into a novel of the same name)
The Smashmaster
The Sound of His Horn (from the novel by "Sarban")
Spaceraid 63
Sword in the Sky (may be same as *The Lost Missile*)
Take Me to Your Leader
Take Me to Your President
Takeoff (from a novel by C.M. Kornbluth)
This Time Tomorrow (producer, Sam X. Abarbanel)
A Ticket to Tranai (from a story by Robert Sheckley)
Time of Terror
21st Century Sub
The Two-Headed Monster (*The Manster?*)
The Unseen
Vanishing Island
The Volunteer

The Weapon
Werewolves of Darkness
Wild Talent (from the novel by Wilson Tucker)
The Z-Creature (Alex Gordon)

Index

Important Note: Whenever there is a conflict between the dates of films in the index and in the text, the date in the index should be considered to be correct. The dates of films not included in volumes 1 or 2 of this book are sometimes wrong in the main body of text for reasons too embarrassing to mention. My sources for the dates in this index were usually *The Film Buff's Checklist* and the *American Film Institute Catalog*. I also used *Reference Guide to Fantastic Films* and Leonard Maltin's *TV Movies*. Films without dates are included in Volume 1 or Volume 2 of this book. Subjects are in SMALL CAPS. Page numbers printed in **boldface** indicate a photo.

Blaisdell, Paul 110, 126, 140, 757
Blasdel, Audrey 263
Blast-Off! see *Those Fantastic Flying Fools*
Blaze Starr Goes Nudist (1962) 440
Blazing Saddles (1974) 613
Blees, Robert 97, 101
Bless the Beasts and Children (1971) 332
Blob, The 18–26, 31, 119, 246, 250, 251, 253, 254, 255, 269, 271, 404, 412, 416, 734, 742, 748
"Blob, The" (song) 22
Bloch, Robert 362
Block, Irving 138, 141, 207, 210, 257, 259, 355, 386, **387**, 388
Blonde Crazy (1931) 218
Blondie series 168
Blood Alley (1955) 498
Blood and Roses (1960) 377
Blood and Steel (1959) 394
Blood Bath (1966) 556
Blood Beast Terror, The see *Vampire-Beast Craves Blood, The*
Blood Creature see *Terror Is a Man*
Blood Drinkers (1966) 352
Blood of Dracula's Castle (1969) 107, 609, 651
Blood of Ghastly Horror (1971) 107, 423
Blood of the Iron Maiden (1969) 107
Blood of the Vampire 27–30, **28**, 52, 147, 475, 734, 757
Blood on His Lips see *Hideous Sun Demon, The*
Blood River (1968) 665
Blood Rose, The (1970) 180
Blood Suckers, The see *Island of the Doomed*
Bloodlust (1961) 95
Blue (1968) 227
Blue Angel, The (1930) 151
BLUE DEMON, THE 495
Blue Denim (1959) 298
"Blue Knight, The" (TV series) 131
Blue Lagoon, The (1980) 620
Blue Peter, The (1955) 477
Bluebeard (1944) 107
Bluebeard's Eighth Wife (1938) 298
Bluebeard's Ten Honeymoons (1960) 316
Bluestone, Harry 307
Blumenthal, Herman A. 299
"Bob Cummings Show, The" (TV series) 160, 307
Bobbikins (1959) 244, 475
Bodeen, DeWitt 463, 465, 467
Body Disappears, The (1941) 385
Body Snatcher, The (1945) 279
Body Stealers, The (1969) 475
Boeing Boeing (1965) 669
Bogart, Humphrey 5, 24, 505
Bogdanovich, Peter 549, 569, 571, 572

Bogeaus, Benedict 97, 569, 573
Boggs, Haskell 113
Bohen, Endré 139, 141
Boileau, Pierre 641
BOMBS, NUCLEAR see RADIATION AND RADIOACTIVITY
Bon Voyage (1962) 668
"Bonanza" (TV series) 110
Bonaparte, Napoléon 579
BOND, JAMES (character) 175, 459, 493, 601, 621, 694
Bongard, David 684
Bonnet, James 24
Bonnie and Clyde (1967) 201, 427
Bonnie Parker Story, The (1958) 564
Boogey Man, The (1980) 107
Boomerang (1947) 253
Boone, Pat 295, 299
Bop Girl (1957) 93
Borelli, Carlo 420
Boris Karloff and His Films (book by Jensen) 92
Born Free (1966) 526
Born Losers (1967) 556
Born to Dance (1936) 218
Born to Kill see *Cockfighter*
Borst, Ron viii, 439, 447, 768
Bosley, Tom 690
"Bottle Baby" (story by Slesar) 198
Bottom of the Bottle, The (1956) 239
Bouchey, Willis 680
Boudou Saved from Drowning (1932) 531
Bounty Killer, The (1965) 393
Bourbeau, Adrienne 368
Bourbon Street Shadows see *Invisible Avenger*
Boutross, Tom 278
Bowery Boys Meet the Monsters, The 610
Bowery Boys, The xx, 168, 201, 647
Bowie, Les 53, 619
Boy and the Pirates, The (1960) 64
Boy Cried Murder, The (1966) 665
Boy Who Caught a Crook, The (1961) 57
Boyette, Pat 712, 713
Boys, The (1961) 510
Boys from Brazil, The (1978) 282
Boys in Company C, The (1978) 510
Boys Town (1938) 368
Brace, Peter 525
Brackett, Charles 294, 295, 296, 298, 299, 301
Brackett, Leigh 124
Bradbury, Ray 124, 245, 298, 537, 629, 781, 782
Bradford, Lane 177
Bradley, Bill 220
Bradley, David 465, 467
Bradley, Leslie 190, 194
Brady, Pat 723
Brain Eaters, The 25, 30–3, 395, 648, 734, 739

C

E

H

I

It Takes All Kinds (1969) 251
It! The Terror from Beyond Space 56, 57, 121–8, 132, 243, 737, 750
Ito, Emi 671
Ito, Jerry 665
Ito, Yumi 671
It's a Dog's Life (1955) 206, 349
"It's a Good Life" (story by Bixby) 124
It's a Mad, Mad, Mad, Mad World (1963) 332
"It's About Time" (TV series) 460
It's Alive 2 (1978) 300
It's Hot in Paradise 650–2, 750
Ivers, James D. 245

J

"Jabberwocky" (poem by Carroll) 426
Jack and the Beanstalk (1952) 105
Jack the Giant Killer (1962) 218, 290, 539, 665, 706
JACK THE RIPPER (character) 461
Jack the Ripper (1959) 52
Jackson County Jail (1976) 459
Jackson, Dan 576, 580
Jackson, George H. 614
Jackson, Selmer 386
Jacobs, Arthur A. 104
Jacobs, Corelli 712
Jaffe, Carl 241, 420
Jaguar (prod. co.) 293
Jail Bait (1954) 162
Jalopy 160
JAMES BOND (character) see BOND, JAMES
James Bond Films, The (book by Rubin) 175
Janes, Hurford 174
Janice Meredith (1924) 24
Janie (1944) 290
Janis, Conrad 483
Japanese Fantasy Film Journal, The (magazine) 589
Jarre, Maurice 638, 669
Jason and the Argonauts (1963) 54, 175, 580, 581
Jaws (1975) 493, 609
Jayne, Jennifer 49, 53
Jazz Singer, The (1927) 613
Je T'Aime, Je T'Aime (1968) 460
Jeepers Creepers (1939) 706
Jeffries, Lionel 174
Jekyll's Inferno see House of Fright
Jens, Salome 199, 201
Jensen, Paul M. 92
Jergens, Diane 292
Jesse James (1939) 567

Jesse James Meets Frankenstein's Daughter (1966) 196
Jesse James vs. the Daltons (1954) 356
Jesse James' Women (1954) 91
Jester, Ralph 44
Jester's Tale, A (1964) 518
Jig Saw (1962) 621
Jigsaw (1968) 378
Joe Kidd (1972) 160
Johansson, Ingemar 161
Johnny Trouble (1957) 218
Johns, Margo 543, 546, 547
Johnson, Carl 155
Johnson, Jason 409, 411
Johnson, Russell 182, 185
Johnson, Tor 155, 156, 157, **157**, 160–1, 163, 446, 499–500, 501
Johnstone, Ted 782
Jolley, I. Stanford 594, 720
Jolly Bad Fellow, A see They All Died Laughing
Jolson Sings Again (1949) 300
Jones, Gordon 723
Jones, Isaac 377
Jones-Moreland, Betsy 425, 427, 505
Joseph, Jackie 551, 553, 554, 556–7
Journal of Popular Film, The (magazine) 432
Journey Beneath the Desert (1961) 495
Journey into Fear (1942) 220
Journey into the Beyond, A (1975) 107
Journey to the Beginning of Time (1955/66) 517
Journey to the Center of the Earth (1909) 297, 301
Journey to the Center of the Earth 294–302, 385, 437, 438, 561, 601, 750–1
"Journey to the Center of the Earth" (TV series) 302
Journey to the Center of Time (1967) 460
Journey to the Far Side of the Sun (1969) 580
Journey to the Lost City (1958) 400, 573
Journey to the Seventh Planet 227, 352, 537–42, **539**, 689, 751
Judd, Edward 614, 615, 620, 622
Judex (1963) 639, 640
Judge Dee and the Monastery Murders (1974) 662
Judgment at Nuremberg (1961) 332
Judith (1966) 231
Jujin Yukiotoko see Half Human
Jules Verne's Rocket to the Moon see Those Fantastic Flying Fools
Julius Caesar (1949) 465
Jumping Jacks (1952) 253
Jungle, The 129
Jungle Boy 716–7, 751
Jungle Fighters see Long and the Short and the Tall, The

K

L

S

X

"X-Men, The" (comic book) 246
X the Man with X-Ray Eyes (1963) 683
X the Unknown 54, 404, 620
Xtro (1983) 245

Y

Yakuza, The (1975) 427
Yates, George Worthing 17, 59, 71, 89, 189, 205
Yeaworth, Irvin S., Jr. 18, 21, 22, 246, 252, 253, 412, 417
Yeaworth, Jean 416
Yellowstone Cubs (1963) 278
Yeux Sans Visage, Les see Horror Chamber of Dr. Faustus, The
York, Michael 350
Yorty, Sam 162
"You Bet Your Life" (TV series) 161
You Have to Run Fast (1961) 57
You Never Can Tell (1951) 201
You Only Live Twice (1967) 291
"You'll Never Get Rich" see "Phil Silvers Show, The"
Young, Alan 449, 450, 454, 459
Young and Innocent (1937) 599
Young and Wild (1958) 564
Young Bess (1953) 279, 572
Young Cassidy (1965) 459
Young Frankenstein (1974) 552
Young, Freddie 527

Young, Jack H. 204, 206
Young Racers, The (1963) 193, 549
Young Savage, The (1961) 661
Young Stranger, The (1957) 661
Young, Terence 175
Youngkin, Stephen 600
Your Cheatin' Heart—The Hank Williams Story (1964) 634
You've Got to Be Smart (1967) 197
Yung, Victor Sen see Sen Yung, Victor

Z

Zabriskie Point (1970) 459
Zacherle, John 711
Zacherley see Zacherle, John
Zamba the Gorilla (1949) 129
Zaske, Ted 201, 395
Zatloukalova, Jana 513
Zavitz, Lee 100
Zebra in the Kitchen (1965) 279
Zeman, Karel 511–20, 574, 595
Zimbalist, Al 134, 138, 142, 593, 595
Zimbalist, Donald 593
Zimmern, Terry 663
Zombies of Mora Tau (1957) 12, 57
Zombies of the Stratosphere (1952) 177, 178, 720, 765; see also Satan's Satellites
Zotz! (1962) 362
Zsigmond, Vilmos 559
Zugsmith, Albert 441, 444
Zulu (1964) 576, 580
Zunser, Jesse 85

A Final Word

And now the albatross has dropped from around my neck, and I can go back to thinking about movies made more recently than 1962. But seriously folks, I would be very interested in hearing from readers about this book: queries, complaints (except about length of the entries or opinions on the films), suggestions, and so forth. I am especially interested in hearing from anyone who knows anything about the Deep South–only films such as those discussed on page 710.

This book (or books) is not complete; I thought they were, but then, after the book was completely done I discovered two more: the Austrian film, *April 1, 2000,* contrary to my belief, was released in the United States in the early 1950s. Also, I had disregarded the 1955 Johnny Weissmuller movie *Jungle Moon Men* as I knew that the Moon Men of the title were merely pygmies who worshipped the Moon. Although when I typed Walt Lee's indispensible *Reference Guide to Fantastic Films* when I worked for him, I wrote the note that there was an immortal person in the story, I forgot it when it came time to do my own book. The devil damn me for a cream-faced loon. If any readers know of any other *science fiction* movies released in the United States from January 1, 1950, to December 31, 1962, by all means, let me know.

And finally, a word for Carol Epstein. Research on this book as well as my work for Hollywood Film Archive took me frequently to the splendid Margaret Herrick Library of the Academy of Motion Picture Arts & Sciences. (The library alone justifies any Oscars that you may have disagreed with.) Carol Epstein, who died in late 1985, was unfailingly kind and cooperative; she was the perfect person to work in such a library, a film buff herself who understood our eccentricities (like my passel of strange T-shirts) and catered to our needs like no one else I have ever encountered. And more, she was a friend. That she will never see this book is a source of great sorrow for me; that I can never talk to her again is a tragedy. Goodbye, Carol.